CRIMINAL LAW:
A CONTEMPORARY APPROACH

CRIMINAL LAW:
A CONTEMPORARY
APPROACH
Cases, Statutes, and Problems

Kate E. Bloch
Professor of Law
University of California
Hastings College of the Law

Kevin C. McMunigal
Judge Ben C. Green Professor of Law
Case Western Reserve University
School of Law

ASPEN

PUBLISHERS

111 Eighth Avenue, New York, NY 10011
www.aspenpublishers.com

© 2005 Aspen Publishers, Inc.
A Wolters Kluwer Company
www.aspenpublishers.com

Aspen Publishers
Attn: Permissions Department
111 Eighth Avenue, 7th Floor
New York, NY 10011-5201

Printed in the United States of America.

1 2 3 4 5 6 7 8 9 0

ISBN 0-7355-3965-0

Library of Congress Cataloging-in-Publication Data

Bloch, Kate E., 1961-
   Criminal law : a contemporary approach : cases, statutes, and problems / Kate E. Bloch,
Kevin C. McMunigal.
      p. cm.
   Includes index.
   ISBN 0-7355-3965-0
   1. Criminal law—United States. I. McMunigal, Kevin C., 1950-II. Title.

KF9218.B57 2005
345.73—dc22   2004029176

To Julia, David, and Peter, with love and deep appreciation

&

For J.K. and H.D. Bloch, my loving guides from beginning to end

K.E.B.

To Tara, Moira, Rosemary, and Phillip

K.C.M.

SUMMARY OF CONTENTS

CONTENTS

Chapter 7

CAUSATION

Chapter 10

ATTEMPT AND SOLICITATION

Chapter 11

COMPLICITY

Chapter 12

CONSPIRACY

PREFACE

This book aims to engage students and educators in a vibrant conversation about criminal law. To bring the subject to life, we supplement traditional criminal law materials with real-life examples and problems from the criminal justice system. We underscore the importance of various sources of criminal law, with a particular emphasis on statutes. To address the variety of learning styles teachers are likely to encounter in the classroom, we offer and support multiple teaching methods, including dialogues, role-plays, exercises, and media presentations. We offer materials that graduate in difficulty, allowing students to build confidence before tackling more challenging criminal law problems. We furnish materials to address issues of professionalism at the heart of criminal practice.

To support a community of learners participating in an intellectually dynamic experience, we adopt a set of four guiding principles.

(1) *Highlight a statutory approach to criminal law*

Recognizing the importance of statutes in criminal law and throughout the modern legal world, we balance the traditional use of cases by giving substantial time and attention to statutes. In doing so, we hope to:

- Emphasize statutes as an important source of criminal law
- Develop student skills in statutory analysis and interpretation
- Expose students to the current debate about the proper approach to statutory interpretation

(2) *Present criminal law through a variety of lenses that encourage interactive learning from diverse perspectives*

For example, the materials offer students opportunities to:

- Contrast the punishments of colonial times in America with punishment options today

- Follow the media and legislative response to Maryland cases that authorized manslaughter, rather than murder, convictions for defendants who killed their spouses and argued for mitigation because their spouses had or may have committed adultery
- Watch a prosecutor describe his first contact with a case involving the death of a child and hear why he insisted that it should be treated as murder rather than manslaughter
- Listen to the defense attorney in that case explain his strategy for persuading the jury to reject the second-degree murder charge
- Read an excerpt from Fredrick Douglass's autobiography, explaining why some individuals born in the 1800s may not have known their true ages
- Reconceptualize the provocation theory of homicide, with an excerpt by Professor Victoria Nourse
- Peruse a firsthand account of the fire in the *Welansky* case, and consider the impact on Welansky's liability of a theory about the rapid escalation of the blaze for which witnesses have apparently only recently emerged

We juxtapose material from a variety of sources to engage students and underscore the importance of context in understanding criminal law. In the book itself, we present ideas through traditional media, such as cases, statutes, and scholarly articles, and through newspaper clips, a couple of cartoons, a photograph, and a poster.

To encourage engaged learning, abundant problems populate the pages of the text. They call upon students to analyze and apply their intuition and learning about criminal law to real and fictional situations, often asking students to assume a designated professional role.

A snapshot of engaged learning is commonly one of lively discussion. We hope that these materials will spawn such discussions, by making students not only think, but also feel, reflect, and remember.

The course book recognizes that criminal law is the product of many types of lawmaking, inter alia, statutes, appellate, trial court, and jury decisionmaking, practical and strategic influences, human dynamics, scholarship, and executive function. Our goal is to provide students with an opportunity to consider the characteristics and roles of each source of law. Chapter 3, for example, focuses on making criminal law. It includes not only study of the institution and application of the "common law," but also three divergent perspectives on statutory interpretation, as well as material on executive and jury decisionmaking. The text emphasizes statutes from a wide variety of jurisdictions, as well as the Model Penal Code.

Our text, like a number of others in the field, treats topics that may prove challenging to address for reasons beyond their intellectual complexity. Coverage includes issues that may resonate deeply on a personal level, like sexual assault, domestic violence, racial prejudice, homophobia, and gender bias. Our goal in the text, and especially in the ancillary materials, is to offer a choice of methods, and detailed guidance, if desired, for approaching these topics.

(3) *Furnish and support a variety of teaching methodologies to assist educators in reaching students across the learning spectrum*

Our book is designed to give educators flexibility in presenting the materials. For example, we have tried to adhere to a principle of graduated difficulty within chapters. We start each chapter with basic concepts and then move on to successively more complex material. In this way, students begin their study of topics with a common threshold of knowledge. This furnishes a platform for more advanced work or, for a topic that the educator chooses only to survey, a convenient place to conclude coverage.

We do not present information in the traditional format of "notes" after cases. Instead, we treat critical material as text itself. Additional issues that might have been covered in traditional post-case notes are included in problems or in the ancillary materials. This streamlines the book and, we hope, enhances instructor choice in determining whether to cover such additional material.

Maximizing instructor choice animates our approach to the ancillary materials. These materials supply educators with a range of approaches to convey information. Video (DVD) clips, each of which corresponds to a topic, problem, or case in the text, enable students to hear directly from one or more of the participants. Video suggestions for clips from commercially available movies, such as *The Wizard of Oz*®, offer opportunities to study a topic through a dramatic representation of relevant concepts. Diagrams and other graphics supplement learning, especially for visual learners. Role-plays and exercises enhance opportunities for experiential learners. Writing exercises engage those who learn by putting pen to paper. Educators will find support for reaching students who learn by listening, reading, writing, seeing, collaborating, and experiencing.

(4) *Provide materials to explore professionalism*

Through the text and ancillary materials, we offer opportunities to explore the concept of professionalism. We introduce the idea briefly in Chapter 1. A substantial number of problems designate a role for students to assume in responding to the problem and encourage consideration of professional responsibilities. Appendix D concentrates on a number of vital ethics issues, including prosecutorial charging, confidentiality, perjury, and representing a guilty client. The ancillary materials also supply forums for introducing issues of professionalism.

We hope that our readers will share our philosophy of engagement and find the materials useful as a springboard for robust discussion.

Like most works of scholarship, our text builds on the knowledge and insights of those who have come before. Although we have tried to thank all of those who contributed most directly with explicit recognition in the Acknowledgments Section, we extend our gratitude to all those who have

traveled a similar journey and from whose wisdom and reflection we have
benefited.

Editing Policy: Because this book is designed for classroom use, we
have not adhered to some of the traditional conventions on scholarly citation. In the interests of concision and comprehensibility, we have generally
deleted citations and footnotes without signifying those deletions. Consequently, readers should not rely on the various extracts from cases or other
documents as exact replications of the originals.

We would appreciate any feedback that readers have the time and
inclination to forward to us and would be delighted to address any questions that arise about the materials. We can be reached with the contact
information below:

Kate E. Bloch   Kevin C. McMunigal
University of California   Case Western Reserve University
Hastings College of the Law   School of Law
200 McAllister Street   11075 East Boulevard
San Francisco, California 94102   Cleveland, Ohio 44106
E-mail: blochk@uchastings.edu   E-mail: kcm4@case.edu
Phone: (415) 565-4867   Phone: (216) 368-2735

ACKNOWLEDGMENTS

I would like to give special thanks to Robert Lawry and Gerald Korngold for their friendship, support, and counsel throughout the making of this book. Professor Lawry was kind enough to use various iterations of the manuscript in teaching his criminal law course and provide us with many thoughtful comments and suggestions. Professors Jonathan Adler, Jonathan Entin, Margery Koosed, Peter Henning, Emery Lee, Laurie Levenson, Andy Morriss, and Robert Natelson generously provided suggestions on various aspects of the book. I am also grateful to Professors John Kaplan and Sanford Kadish, who sparked my interest in criminal law and criminal law texts. Alice Hunt gave invaluable help in every aspect of preparing the manuscript. Many students contributed to the making of this book, among them John Gold, Dawn McFadden, Anne Moore, Heather Kern, Bill McCann, Nate Stewart, and Rachel Wyatt. I appreciate their efforts and their interest in the project. Last but not least I would like to acknowledge the many students in my criminal law classes who have helped shape my thinking about teaching criminal law.

K.C.M.

Many kind and wise people contributed to the evolution of this project. Let me begin by thanking all my wonderful colleagues here at Hastings. Quite a few of them were instrumental in helping me decide to embark on this endeavor and in providing advice, ideas, and support during the journey. ("No, Kate, you would not be the first to submit a manuscript later than the date listed in the contract.") These sage folks include George Bisharat, Richard Cunningham, Terry Diggs, David Faigman, David Jung, Mary Kay Kane, Chuck Knapp, David Levine, Steve Lind, Rick Marcus, Leo Martinez, Calvin Massey, Bea Moulton, Melissa Nelken, Roger Park, Steve Schwarz, Gordon Van Kessel, Kelly Weisberg (who, thank goodness, also revised the original book proposal), and Keith Wingate. Thanks go also to Rory Little for help with the Death Penalty Section. Special thanks go to Aaron Rappaport, who furnished invaluable guidance and materials for various portions of the book, especially the Preface, Punishment, and Death Penalty Sections, as well as Appendix E, and who bravely taught from chapters when they were yet in their infancy. The wonderful Margreth Barrett entertained my copyright inquiries without ever a complaint, not to mention inviting my son to join her son, Andrew, on numerous playdates, and thus affording me extra time to work on the book. Thank you to Laurie Zimet (and Paula Lustbader) for working on "Teaching to the Whole Class." Thank you to Geoff Hansen, who generously shared his experiences in federal criminal law regularly with my first-year class. I am deeply grateful to Lois Weithorn for her insightful, generous, and unfailing support throughout the book process and for her extensive contributions to and guidance on the Punishment and Mental Illness Sections, the Preface, and Appendix C.

When I was lucky enough to have Cheryl Hanna as a visiting colleague here at Hastings, she introduced me to some great ideas for enriching the book and tried a number of the exercises that appear in the ancillary materials. Bob Lawry taught from early versions of the manuscript and provided very useful feedback. Thank you. At my first AALS New Teacher's Conference, Marjorie Shultz gave an inspirational talk on the importance as well as methods of addressing issues that can cause controversy or discomfort in the classroom. Her talk (and her co-authored article with Angela Harris) imbued early some of the most essential fundamentals of good teaching. I am grateful to visitors to my class from the bench and Bar, especially Judge Edward Lee, Dale Sanderson, and Phil Pennypacker. Thank you to Dennis Riordan for supplying court papers on the defense of Mr. Rosenthal in a case involving medical marijuana. Thanks go to my colleagues on the Judicial Council Task Force on Jury Instructions, Criminal Subcommittee, for their insights and patience. Thanks go also to Sam Pillsbury, Andy Taslitz, Margareth Etienne, Scott Sundby, and Lynne Henderson. I am also indebted to the many colleagues at conferences who introduced me to materials or approaches, often before I ever seriously contemplated co-authoring a criminal law text, and therefore long before I was sensible enough to keep careful track of their individual influences.

I benefited from reviews by Susan Rutberg, David Steinberg, Steve Friedland, and Evan Lee. Peter J. Henning, as an academic reviewer for Aspen's review process, read each and every chapter, sometimes even multiple revisions of the same chapters. Thank you. Particular thanks go also to Deborah Denno, who undertook a close read of the Rape Chapter. Thank you, too, to Marjorie Koosed for her review of and suggestions for the Death Penalty Section. I extend my appreciation also to those many anonymous reviewers who read chapters during Aspen's review process.

I owe a debt of gratitude to numerous authors whose scholarship has influenced my thinking and writing about criminal law. In particular, I want to thank the casebook and treatise authors from whose books I've taught or which I've assigned as recommended reading. The late Professor John Kaplan introduced me to the formal study of criminal law when I was a first-year law student. As a new teacher, I taught from his text (co-authored at that time with Bob Weisberg). The second book from which I taught was my colleague John Diamond's (in collaboration with Tom Morawetz, Kit Kinports, and Stephen Saltzburg). John has remained a supportive and kind colleague throughout the long process, even as he knew that he was losing an adopter and another criminal law text would be entering the field. Thanks go, too, to Wayne LaFave, whose treatise on criminal law has proven invaluable.

I have kept Joshua Dressler's *Understanding Criminal Law* close at hand since early in my teaching days. The clarity of his approach has strongly influenced my thinking about criminal law. Readers will probably recognize his influence in the text, particularly in the sections on impossibility, mistake, cause-in-fact, and complicity. Thanks to Leo Katz, Michael Moore, and Stephen Morse, among so many of the authors foundational to my thinking and understanding of criminal law. Thank you especially to the casebook, collection, and treatise authors for introducing me to the classic (and not so classic) criminal law cases and to some of the most important and intriguing scholarship in the field.

Several successive classes of my criminal law students helped shape the final product. Their willingness to engage with the unfinished and often unpolished materials was admirable. They shared interesting news items and provided helpful suggestions for changes both substantive and technical, as well as spotting typographical errors. (I think Shiloh Sorbello holds the record for finding the most typographical errors.)

I am indebted to our fabulous Library Staff, and especially to Chuck Marcus and Linda Weir, who managed to locate and make needed sources appear with extraordinary proficiency.

I am grateful to all the support staff here at Hastings, especially the Academic Dean's Office, Faculty Support, Computer Support, and Instructional Media Departments, and particularly Stephen Lothrop, Maria Burgos, Carol Hough, Mercy Osorio, Susan Esveld, and Pat Tashima.

Thank you to all of my research assistants who worked on the book, especially Rob Bader, Joel Buckingham, Scott Dallas, Marisa Diehl, Michael Everett, Christina Helwig, Brandi Redman, and Sarah Zimmerman. Simona Agnolucci and Travis Neal merit special mention for their extraordinary assistance in the final stages of the book. Many, many thanks!

Thank you also to two of my mentors in the field, George Kennedy and Karen Sinunu, from whom I learned much about the pragmatics of criminal law practice.

I would feel remiss if I did not express my deep gratitude to the late Professor Gerald Gunther for his wisdom, guidance, and belief in me from my days as a law student.

My thanks go also to the University of California, Hastings College of the Law for funding support throughout the preparation of the manuscript.

Thank you, too, to Aspen Publishers and the editors who worked on this book for their guidance, patience, and faith in the project.

Myriad others contributed in ways that influenced my thinking about the project. Thank you also to all those who remain unnamed.

Finally, thank you to Peter, my dear, sweet life partner. I know this book would never have reached the ink of print without your loving and unending support.

K.E.B

We would also like to thank the authors, publishers, and copyright holders of the publications listed below for having given their permission to reprint excerpts from their materials.

Ackman, Dan, Goldstein Lawyers Put Mental Healthcare System on Trial, *http://dackman.homestead.com/files/GoldsteinTrial.htm*. Reprinted by permission of the author.

American Bar Association, Commission on Domestic Violence, Statistics, published online at *http://www.abanet.org/domviol/stats.html*. Copyright 2004 The American Bar Association. All Rights reserved. Reprinted by permission.

American Bar Association, Standards for Criminal Justice, Standard 3-3.9 (3d ed. 1992). Copyright 1993 by the American Bar Association. Reprinted by permission.

American College of Trial Lawyers, Proposal: Proposed Codification of Disclosure of Favorable Information Under the Federal Rules of Criminal Procedure 11 and 16, 41 American Criminal Law Review 93, 94-99 (2004). Reprinted with permission of the publisher, American Criminal Law Review © 2004.

American Law Institute, The Model Penal Code, Copyright 1985 by the American Law Institute. Reprinted with permission. All rights reserved.

Antioch College Sexual Offense Policy, Definition of Consent. Reprinted by permission. Courtesy of Antioch College.

Armstrong, Ken & Maurice Possley, Chicago Tribune national investigation on prosecutorial misconduct, collated and reprinted in The Verdict: Dishonor, from articles originally published Jan. 10, 1999-Jan. 14, 1999. Copyrighted 1/10/1999, Chicago Tribune Company. All rights reserved. Used with permission.

Bedau, Hugo Adam & Michael L. Radelet, Miscarriages of Justice in Potentially Capital Cases, 40 Stan. L. Rev. 21 (1987). Reprinted by permission of Stanford Law Review.

Benjamin, Caren, "Strohmeyer confided to friend he killed girl, grand jury told," Las Vegas Review-Journal, Aug. 15, 1997, 1A. Reprinted by permission.

Braithwaite, John, A Future Where Punishment is Marginalized: Realistic or Utopian?, 46 UCLA L. Rev. 1727, 1743 (1999). Reprinted by permission of the author.

Breyer, Stephen, On the Uses of Legislative History in Interpreting Statutes, 65 S.Cal. L. Rev., 845-890 (1992). Reprinted with the permission of the Southern California Law Review.

Brody, Jane E., When Can Killers Claim Sleepwalking as a Legal Defense? New York Times, Jan. 16, 1996, at C1, C5. Copyright ©1996 by The New York Times Co. Reprinted with permission.

Brown, Jeff, "Dealing Away the Defense," The Recorder, Aug. 5, 1991. Reprinted by permission of The Recorder.

Buel, Sarah, Violence Against Women: How to Improve the Legal Services' Response, Nov. 18, 1991 (cited in Defending Our Lives, Study and Resource Guide 13, 19). Reprinted by permission of the author.

Byler, William, Removing Children: The Destruction of American Indian Families, 9 Civil Rights 19 (Summer 1977). Reprinted by permission.

California District Attorneys Association, 13 Uniform Crime Charging Standards 13 (1974). Reproduced with permission from the California District Attorneys Association. Material protected by copyright.

California Jury Instructions—Criminal (CALJIC 6th ed. 1996), ©1996 West Publishing Co. Reprinted with Permission of West, a Thomson business.

C.H., One woman's account. © C.H., Reprinted by permission of the author.

Chamallas, Martha, Consent, Equality, and the Legal Control of Sexual Conduct, 61 S. Cal. L. Rev. 777-859 (1988). Reprinted with the permission of the Southern California Law Review.

Coffee, John C., Jr., Does "Unlawful" Mean "Criminal"? Reflections on the Disappearing Tort/Crime Distinction in American Law, 71 B.U. L. Rev. 193, 201-202, 216-217, 219-221 (1991).

Committee on Model Jury Instructions Within the Ninth Circuit, Manual of Model Criminal Jury Instructions for the District Courts of the Ninth Circuit, Instruction No. 5.6 (2000).

Committee on Pattern Criminal Jury Instructions, First Circuit, Pattern Jury Instructions (Criminal Cases), Instruction Nos. 2.14 and 5.02 (1998).

Coughlin, Anne M., Excusing Women, 82 Cal. L. Rev. 1, 4-6 (1994). Reprinted by permission of the author.

Crump, David & Susan Waite Crump, In Defense of the Felony Murder Doctrine, 8 Harv. J. L. & Pub. Pol'y 359, 362-368, 370-371, 374-375 (Spring 1985). Reprinted by permission of the Harvard Journal of Law & Public Policy.

DeLong, James V., Out of Bounds and Out of Control: Regulatory Enforcement at the EPA, Cato Institute, 2002.

Denno, Deborah W., Crime and Consciousness: Science and Involuntary Acts, 87 Minn. L. Rev. 269, 269-272, 274-275, 361, 369 (2002). Reprinted by permission of the author and the Minnesota Law Review.

DiIulio, John J. Jr., Help Wanted: Economists, Crime and Public Policy, 10 Journal of Economic Perspectives 3-24 (Winter 1996).

DiIulio, John J. Jr., "Prisons Are a Bargain by Any Measure," N.Y. Times, Jan. 16, 1996, A17.

Dolinko, David, Restorative Justice and the Justification of Punishment, 2003 Utah L. Rev. 319, 331. Reprinted by permission of the Utah Law Review.

Dolinko, David, Three Mistakes of Retributivism, originally published in 39 UCLA L. Rev. 1623 (1992).

Dressler, Joshua, When "Heterosexual" Men Kill "Homosexual" Men: Reflections on Provocation Law, Sexual Advances, and the "Reasonable Man" Standard, 85 J. Crim. L. & Criminology 726 (1995). Reprinted with permission of the author.

Dressler, Joshua, Where We Have Been, and Where We Might Be Going: Some Cautionary Reflections on Rape Law Reform, 46 Clev. St. L. Rev. 409 (1998). Reprinted with permission of the author.

Dripps, Donald A., Beyond Rape: An Essay on the Difference Between the Presence of Force and the Absence of Consent, 92 Colum. L. Rev. 1780 (1992). Reprinted by permission.

Edgar, Harold, *Mens Rea*, Encyclopedia of Crime and Justice 1037-1039 (1983). From Encyclopedia of Crime and Justice, by 3 Macmillan, © 1968, Macmillan. Reprinted by permission of the Gale Group.

Erlinder, C. Peter, Paying the Price for Vietnam: Post-Traumatic Stress Disorder and Criminal Behavior, 25 B.C. L. Rev. 305 (1984).

Eskridge, William N. Jr., Dynamic Statutory Interpretation, 135 Univ. Pa. L. Rev. 1479, 1479-1480, 1482-1484, 1496-1497, 1498, 1506-1507 (1987). ©1987 by the University of Pennsylvania Law Review.

Estrich, Susan, Real Rape: How the Legal System Victimizes Women Who Say No, pp. 19-20, 31, 65, 101, Harvard University Press, Cambridge, Mass. Copyright © 1987 by the President and Fellows of Harvard College. Reprinted by permission of the publisher.

Estrich, Susan, Teaching Rape Law, 102 Yale L.J. 509 (1992). Reprinted by permission of the author.

Faigman, David L., The Battered Woman Syndrome and Self-Defense: A Legal and Empirical Dissent, 72 Va. L. Rev. 619, 622, 637 (1986). Copyright 1986 by Virginia Law Review. Reproduced with permission of Virginia Law Review in the format Textbook via Copyright Clearance Center.

Falk, Patricia J., Rape by Fraud and Rape by Coercion, 64 Brook. L. Rev. 39, 120 (1998). Reprinted by permission of the Brooklyn Law Review.

Farley, Melissa & Howard Barkan, Prostitution, Violence, and Post-traumatic Stress Disorder, vol. 27, no. 3 Women & Health 37, 39, 40-42, 44-47 (1998). Copyright 1998 by The Haworth Press, Inc., 10 Alice Street, Binghamton, NY 13904-1580 USA. Reprinted with the permission of The Haworth Press, Inc.

Finnie, Charles, "Accused Prostitutes Want Brothel's Privileged Exposed," San Francisco Daily Journal, Sept. 12, 1991. Copyright 1991 Daily Journal Corp. Reprinted and/or posted with permission.

Fletcher, George P., A Crime of Self-Defense: Bernhard Goetz and the Law on Trial (The Free Press, 1988). Reprinted with permission of the author.

Fletcher, George P., Dogmas of the Model Penal Code, 2 Buff. Crim. L. Rev. 3-5, 6-8 (1998). Reprinted by permission of the Buffalo Criminal Law Review.

Fletcher, George P., Justification, Theory, 3 Encyclopedia of Crime and Justice, 941 (1983). From Encyclopedia of Crime and Justice, by 3 Macmillan, © 1968, Macmillan. Reprinted by permission of the Gale Group.

Friedman, Lawrence M., Crime and Punishment in American History, Basic Books, Inc. (1993). Reprinted with permission of the author.

Gershman, Bennett L., A Moral Standard for the Prosecutor's Exercise of the Charging Discretion, 20 Fordham Urb. L J. 513, 513-516, 517-519, 521-525, 527-529 (1993).

Gledhill, Lynda & Greg Lucas, "Davis Signs Child Assault 'Good Samaritan' Bill," San Francisco Chronicle A3 (Sept. 19, 2000). San Francisco Chronicle. [Staff-Produced Copy Only] by Staff. Copyright 2000 by San Francisco Chronicle. Reproduced with permission of San Francisco Chronicle in the format Textbook via Copyright Clearance Center.

Hanna, Cheryl, No Right to Choose: Mandated Victim Participation in Domestic Violence Prosecutions, 109 Harv. L. Rev. 1849, 1859-1860, 1864 (1996). Reprinted by permission of the author.

Harrington, Matthew P., The Law-Finding Function of the American Jury, 1999 Wis. L. Rev. 377, 377-380. Copyright 1999 by The Board of Regents of the University of Wisconsin System; Reprinted by permission of the Wisconsin Law Review.

Harris, Angela P., Race and Essentialism in Feminist Legal Theory, 42 Stan. L. Rev. 581 (1990). Reprinted with permission of Stanford Law Review.

Hasday, Jill Elaine, Contest and Consent: A Legal History of Marital Rape, 88 Cal. L. Rev. 1373 (2000). Reprinted by permission. ©2000 by the California Law Review. Reprinted from California Law Review vol. 88 no. 5, pp. 1373, 1375-1376, by permission of the Regents of the University of California, Berkeley.

Henderson, Lynne, Honoring Women in Law and Fact, 2 Tex. J. of Women & L. 41 (1993). Reprinted with permission.

Hoppe, Christy, "Man is indicted as rapist who agreed to use condom; 2nd Austin Grand jury takes action after outcry," The Dallas Morning News, Oct. 28, 1992, at 1A. Reprinted by permission.

Hunter, Robert J., et. al., The Death Sentencing of Rapists in Pre-Furman Texas (1942-1971): The Racial Dimension, 20 Am. J. Crim. L. 313 (1993). Reprinted with permission.

"Inferno at the Cocoanut Grove," 20th-Century Memories, Yankee (Nov. 1998). Reprinted by permission of Yankee Publishing, Inc.

"Innocent Plea in Child's Death," May 24, 2000 The Recorder. © 2000 by the Associated Press. Reprinted by permission.

"Jail 'Break-in' a Success, Sort of," Nov. 16, 1992 (The Recorder, San Francisco). Copyright © 1992 by the Associated Press. Reprinted with permission of the Associated Press.

"Judge Agrees to Convict's Death Plea," Jan. 23, 1996 (The Recorder, "In Brief," San Francisco). Copyright © 1996 by the Associated Press. Reprinted with permission of the Associated Press.

"Judge's Comment Raises Cain," Oct. 5, 1994 (The Recorder, San Francisco). Copyright © 1994 by the Associated Press. Reprinted with permission of the Associated Press.

"Judge Sued Over Church Sentences" (The Recorder, San Francisco). Copyright © 1994 by the Associated Press. Reprinted with permission of the Associated Press.

"Jury Recommends 30,000-Year Sentence for Child Rapist," Dec. 16, 1994 (The Recorder, San Francisco). Copyright © 1994 by the Associated Press. Reprinted with permission of the Associated Press.

Kahan, Dan M., Three Conceptions of Federal Criminal-Lawmaking, 1 Buff. Crim. L. Rev. 5, 5-18 (1997).

Kant, Immanuel, The Metaphysical Elements of Justice: Part I of the Metaphysics of Morals (trans. John Ladd 1965). Copyright © 1965 The Bobbs-Merrill Company, Inc. Reprinted by permission of Hackett Publishing Company, Inc. All rights reserved.

Kennedy, Joseph E., Drug Wars in Black and White, 66 Law & Contemp. Probs. 153-154 (2003).

Kids in Cars, statistics reprinted from *http://www.kidsincars.org*. Reprinted with permission.

Kinports, Kit, Rape and Force: The Forgotten Mens Rea, 4 Buff. Crim. L. Rev. 755 (2001). Reprinted by permission.

Kitrosser, Heidi, Meaningful Consent: Toward a New Generation of Statutory Rape Laws, 4 Va. J. of Soc. Pol'y & L. 287, 322-326 (1997).

Klien, Gary, "Teacher Guilty in Fatal Crash," Marin Independent Journal, Oct. 5, 2001, at pp. A1, A9. Reprinted with permission from the Marin Independent Journal.

LaFave, Wayne R., Criminal Law 3rd, ©2000 West Group. Reprinted with the Permission of West, a Thomson business.

LaFave, Wayne R., Hornbook on Criminal Law 4th, ©2003 by West, a Thomson business. Reprinted with Permission.

LaFave, Wayne R. & Austin W. Scott, Jr., Substantive Criminal Law, ©2003 by West, a Thomson business. Reprinted with Permission.

Law, Sylvia A., Commercial Sex: Beyond Decriminalization, 73 S. Cal. L. Rev. 523-610 (2000). Reprinted with the permission of the Southern California Law Review.

Lee, Evan Tsen, Cancelling Crime, 30 Conn. L. Rev. 117 (1997). Reprinted with permission of the author.

"Letters: The Confusion Between Sex and Rape," The Village Voice, Oct. 22, 1979. Copyright ©1979 Village Voice Media, Inc. Reprinted with the permission of The Village Voice.

Little, Rory K., The Federal Death Penalty: History and Some Thoughts About the Department of Justice's Role, 26 Fordham Urb. L.J. 347 (1999). Reprinted with permission.

Luna, Erik, Introduction, 2003 Utah L. Rev. 1, 3. Reprinted by permission of the Utah Law Review.

"Man Convicted for Shooting Arrow into Ex-Lover's Head," Orlando Sentinel, Oct. 24, 1992. Copyright © 1992 the Orlando Sentinel. Reprinted by permission of the Orlando Sentinel.

"Man Convicted of Letting Child Drown, Saving Self," Oct. 12, 2002 (Bakersfield Californian). Copyright © 2002 by the Associated Press. Reprinted by permission.

Markman, Stephen J., & Paul G. Cassell, Protecting the Innocent: A Response to the Bedau-Radelet Study, 41 Stan. L. Rev. 121 (1988). Reprinted by permission of Stanford Law Review.

Massaro, Toni, Shame, Culture, and American Criminal Law, 89 Mich. L. Rev. 1880, 1883 (1991). Reprinted by permission of the author and the Michigan Law Review, June 1991, vol. 89, no. 7. Copyright 1991 by the Michigan Law Review Association.

Massaro, Toni, The Meanings of Shame: Implications for Legal Reform, 3 Psych. Pub. Pol. & L. 645, 649-650 (1997). Reprinted by permission of the author.

Mills, Linda G., Commentary: Killing Her Softly: Intimate Abuse and the Violence of State Intervention, 113 Harv. L. Rev. 550, 554 (1999). Copyright 1999 by the Harvard Law Review Association. Reprinted by permission.

Mison, Robert B., Homophobia In Manslaughter: The Homosexual Advance as Insufficient Provocation, 80 Cal. L. Rev. 133, 133-136 (1992). Reprinted by permission of the author.

"New Proposal for Constitutionalizing Victims' Rights Introduced in Congress," S.J. Res. 35, cited in 71 Criminal Law Reporter 112 (Apr. 24, 2002). Reproduced with permission from Criminal Law Reporter, no. 4, p. 112 (Apr. 24, 2002). Copyright 2002 by The Bureau of National Affairs, Inc. (800-372-1033) http://www.bna.com

Nourse, V.F., Passion's Progress: Modern Law Reform and the Provocation Defense, 106 Yale L.J. 1331-1448 (1997). Reprinted by permission of the author and of the Yale Law Journal Company and the William S. Hein Company from the Yale Law Journal.

Nourse, V.F., Self-Defense and Subjectivity, 68 U. Chi. L. Rev. 1235 (2001). Copyright 2001 by University of Chicago Law School. Reproduced with permission of University of Chicago Law School in the format Textbook via Copyright Clearance Center.

Nugent, William R., et al., Participation in Victim-Offender Mediation and the Prevalence and Severity of Subsequent Delinquent Behavior:

A Meta-Analysis, 2003 Utah L. Rev. 137. Reprinted by permission of the Utah Law Review.

Oberman, Michelle, Girls in the Master's House: Of Protection, Patriarchy and the Potential for Using the Master's Tools to Reconfigure Statutory Rape Law, 50 DePaul L. Rev. 799 (2001). Reprinted with permission.

Ohio Judicial Conference, Ohio Jury Instructions Volume 4—Criminal, Instruction Nos. 409.03 and 409.55 (2004). Reprinted with the permission of Matthew Bender & Company, Inc., a member of the LexisNexis Group.

Oliver, Myrna, Immigrant Crimes, Cultural Defense—A Legal Tactic, LA Times, July 15, 1988, at 1. Copyright 1998, Los Angeles Times. Reprinted by permission.

Pillsbury, Samuel H., Crimes Against the Heart: Recognizing the Wrongs of Forced Sex, 35 Loy. L. Rev. 845, 846-849 (2002). Reprinted by permission of the author.

"Planned Measure Would Stamp Numbers on Ex-Cons' Faces," Feb. 25, 1994 (The Recorder, San Francisco). Copyright © 1994 by the Associated Press. Reprinted with permission of the Associated Press

Punishment: Random House Webster's College Dictionary (2001). Reprinted by permission.

Redding, Richard E., Why It Is Essential to Teach About Mental Health Issues in Criminal Law (And a Primer on How To Do It), 14 Wash. U. J.L. & Pol'y 407, 408-409 (2004). Reprinted by permission of the Washington University Journal of Law & Policy.

Riordan, Dennis, Rosenthal's Reply in Support of Motion for New Trial in United States v. Rosenthal (No. CR-02-0053-CRB) (April 18, 2003). Reprinted by permission of Dennis Riordan, Attorney at Law.

Roberts, Dorothy E., Punishing Drug Addicts Who Have Babies: Women of Color, Equality, and the Right of Privacy, 104 Harv. L. Rev. 1419, 1421, 1428-1430, 1431-1434 (1991). Reprinted by permission of the Harvard Law Review and the author.

Rosenfeld, Megan, "Judge sides with husband in slaying: Is Adultery cause to kill your wife?", San Jose Mercury News, Oct. 19, 1994, 1 & back page. © 1994 The Washington Post, reprinted with permission.

Roth, Nelson E. & Scott E. Sundby, The Felony-Murder Rule: A Doctrine at Constitutional Crossroads, 70 Cornell L. Rev. 446 (1985). Reprinted with permission.

Rychlak, Ronald J., Society's Moral Right to Punish: A Further Exploration of the Denunciation Theory of Punishment, originally published in 65 Tul. L. Rev. 299-338 (1990). Reprinted with permission of the Tulane Law Review Association, which holds the copyright.

San Francisco Department on the Status of Women, Respect Is What's Sexy, © 2000, Poster. Reprinted with permission from the San Francisco Department on the Status of Women.

Sarrel, Philip, M.D. and William H. Masters, M.D., Sexual Molestation of Men by Women, 11 Archives of Sexual Behavior, 117 (1982).

CRIMINAL LAW:
A CONTEMPORARY APPROACH

CHAPTER ONE

OVERVIEW

The Architecture of the Criminal Justice System: Process, Participants, and the Role of Discretion

A. THE START OF A CRIMINAL CASE

Criminal cases typically start when events catch the attention of law enforcement officials. Sometimes the news arrives through reports from others and sometimes through first-hand observations by the police. Once officers receive news of potential criminal activity, they exercise discretion in deciding whether and how to investigate. Police usually react to crimes such as homicide and robbery after their occurrence. In contrast, police are sometimes proactive in investigating crimes like drug and white-collar offenses. Through these exercises of discretion, police control the first portal through which a prospective criminal case must pass. Exercises of discretion pervade the criminal justice system.

Various considerations influence this early exercise of discretion. They include police policy, legal boundaries, the information available about the case, social and cultural perceptions, the gravity of the harm (or threatened harm), any criminal history of the accused, and resources. If law enforcement officials decide to proceed, they may conduct minimal or extensive investigation. Police investigations may employ a host of tools, including search warrants, forensics, sting operations, and surveillance. A typical petty theft from a local retail store involves minimal investigation. The investigation of a theft of computer trade secrets may involve months or years of preparation and be conducted directly under the auspices of the prosecutor.

Both substantive criminal law and criminal procedure have an impact on criminal investigations. Substantive criminal law, the subject of this course, creates and defines criminal offenses such as murder, robbery, and assault. Substantive criminal law determines whether the police need to gather evidence of premeditation to prove a first-degree murder charge. Criminal procedure creates and defines rules for enforcing the laws against criminal offenses. For example, criminal procedure governs the manner in which the police conduct searches and question suspects. The rules of criminal procedure, for instance, determine whether the police properly advised a suspect of her *Miranda* rights.

When the police exercise discretion in ways that coincide with public consensus and constitutional norms on appropriate law enforcement conduct, it rarely

1

generates comment. For example, we generally applaud police pursuit of a hit-and-run driver or investigation of a kidnapping. We find relief in learning that police have succeeded in apprehending an individual wanted in connection with a serious crime or that they have responded to a panicked 911 call.

Sometimes, however, exercises of police discretion generate concern and criticism. We provide two examples below. The first involves a law enforcement approach to domestic violence. The second involves the question of police targeting of homosexual men as potential offenders.

In recent research, almost 1 in 4 women and more than 1 in 20 men reported that they had been physically and/or sexually assaulted by an intimate on at least one occasion.[1] In light of these statistics, consider the following analysis of police responses to domestic violence:

> For many years, societal responses to domestic violence excluded legal intervention. . . . [M]any police departments had "hands off" policies prior to the 1970's, and police training manuals actually specified that arrest was to be avoided whenever possible in responding to domestic disputes.[2]

In the 1970s, 80s, and 90s, scrutiny of and challenges to the lack of police response, in addition to enhanced public understanding of domestic violence and the availability of new legal tools, produced substantial change. From the "hands off" approach, as described above, Professor Cheryl Hanna explains below the nearly complete reversal in approach to preferred or mandatory arrest policies for domestic violence crimes:

> In 1984, the United States Attorney General recommended arrest as the standard police response to domestic violence. This recommendation resulted from a landmark Minneapolis study that compared the deterrent effects of arresting the suspect, mediating the dispute, and requiring the batterer to leave the house for eight hours. The study found that arrest more effectively deterred subsequent violence than did the other courses of action. This study, followed by the Attorney General's recommendation, provided the foundation for nationwide legal reform. . . . All fifty states now provide for warrantless misdemeanor arrests in domestic violence cases.
>
> Since arrest statutes have been broadened, many jurisdictions have moved toward mandatory and pro-arrest policies. Under these policies, an arrest is either required or preferred if there is probable cause to believe that a domestic battery has taken place.[3]

---

1. Patricia Tjaden & Nancy Thoennes, *Extent, Nature, and Consequences of Intimate Partner Violence*, Natl. Inst. Just. & CDC *iii* (2000).

2. Jeffrey Fagan, *The Criminalization of Domestic Violence: Promises and Limits*, Natl. Inst. Just. 4, 8 (Jan. 1996) (citations omitted) [hereinafter Fagan].

3. Cheryl Hanna, *No Right to Choose: Mandated Victim Participation in Domestic Violence Prosecutions*, 109 Harv. L. Rev. 1849, 1859-1860 (1996) (citations omitted) [hereinafter Hanna]. The Attorney General's Task Force on Family Violence lists the following as "Law Enforcement Recommendation 2: Consistent with state law, the chief executive of every law enforcement agency should establish arrest as the preferred response in cases of family violence." Attorney General's Task Force on Family Violence, Final Report 22 (Sept. 1984). Subsequent empirical and theoretical work has caused scholars to revisit the question of whether and when arrest produces deterrence or is the preferred response. *See, e.g.*, Lawrence W. Sherman et al., *Symposium on Domestic Violence: Studies: The Variable Effects of Arrest on Criminal Careers: The Milwaukee Domestic Violence Experiment*, 83 J. Crim. L. & Criminology 137, 139 (1992) ("different kinds of offenders react differently to arrest: some become much more frequently violent, while others become somewhat less frequently violent."); Linda G. Mills, *Commentary: Killing Her Softly: Intimate Abuse and the Violence of State Intervention*, 113 Harv. L. Rev. 550, 554 (1999) (arguing "that such policies as mandatory arrest, prosecution, and reporting, which have become standard legal fare in the fight against domestic violence and which categorically ignore the battered woman's perspective, can themselves be forms of abuse.").

Some challenges to police discretion focus on categories of crime, such as domestic violence, other challenges question police discretion in targeting particular offenders. In one case, a group of defendants challenged their arrests alleging that

> [the] police who arrested them engaged in a pattern of discriminatory arrest and prosecution of homosexuals. . . . In support of their . . . [challenge], defendants presented 10 arrest reports spanning a 2-year period. The reports described decoy officers' arrests of men in and outside an adult bookstore [for soliciting a lewd act to be performed in a public place.] . . . The [trial] court concluded that the operation was focused solely on persons who had a proclivity to engage in homosexual conduct. . . . [The trial court determined] that there was discrimination . . . evidenced by the officers' method of operation; that their method of operation was designed to ferret out homosexuals or those who were likely to engage in homosexual acts, and that it did so without any relationship to the alleged problems at that location for which the citizen complaint had been initially lodged.[4]

As these examples illustrate, police discretion and control over the first portal through which a criminal case must pass play a key role at the outset of a criminal case.

B. CHARGING: THE PROSECUTOR'S OFFICE

If, after investigating an incident, police decide that the case warrants prosecution, they contact a prosecutor's office. Geographic boundaries and the nature of the case can each play a role in determining the jurisdictions of local, state, and federal prosecutors. Sometimes these jurisdictions overlap. Yet, state courts, those in which local and state prosecutors file their cases, hear about 94 percent of criminal cases.[5] Of these, local prosecutors usually handle the overwhelming majority. State prosecutors tend to specialize in particular types of offenses or relieve local prosecutors when they have a conflict of interest and cannot try a case.

Federal jurisdiction arises in a variety of circumstances. For instance, state and local agencies may lack jurisdiction over a crime that occurred on federal land, or a federal statute may preempt state prosecution. Certain categories of crime also garner federal attention. For example, federal, rather than state or local, agencies commonly prosecute bank robberies.

Prosecutors differ in their approach to formally charging an individual with a crime. In Manhattan, prosecutors remain on duty 24 hours a day, seven days a week. Police officers on a case, and sometimes the victims and witnesses, wait in the hallways of the prosecutor's office for the initial processing of the case. This procedure provides prosecutors an excellent opportunity for an early case assessment before moving forward in the charging process, but it is exhausting and time-consuming.

In urban California, by contrast, for many routine cases, one liaison officer from each of the relevant law enforcement agencies brings a stack of cases to the prosecutor's office each morning. The liaison officer collects the relevant paperwork and

---

4. Baluyut v. Superior Court, 12 Cal. 4th 826, 830-831 (1996).
5. Guide to the Criminal Justice System for General Government Elected Officials, Advisory Commission on Intergovernmental Relations (ACIR), M-184, at 24 (1993).

sometimes performs clarifying investigation work but generally is not the arresting or primary investigating officer. Unlike these routine cases, police agencies treat the most serious and most specialized crimes with greater continuity between the police involved in the investigation itself and the prosecutor who handles a particular type of case. In a murder case, for example, the detectives who perform the bulk of the investigation may work directly with a prosecutor assigned to the case shortly after the victim's death. Because individuals cannot generally be held in custody beyond a limited period without formal charges being filed, the accused's custody status often dictates the dispatch with which the prosecutor proceeds.

1. The Charging Decision

Charging a crime affects people's lives. Charging alone can subject the accused to ridicule, shame, alienation, poverty, and imprisonment. The impact on victims and witnesses can also be enormous. Like decisions surrounding an investigation, charging decisions also involve exercises of governmental discretion. Prosecutors control this second portal through which a criminal case generally must pass. To guide the exercise of prosecutorial discretion, prosecutorial organizations, state bar associations, and legislatures have adopted rules, standards, and statutes.

For example, California Rule of Professional Conduct 5-110 requires that "[a] member in government service shall not institute or cause to be instituted criminal charges when the member knows or should know that the charges are not supported by probable cause. . . ."[6] In this context, probable cause may be understood as follows: "a state of facts [that] would lead a [person] . . . of ordinary caution or prudence to believe and conscientiously entertain a strong suspicion of the guilt of the accused."[7] This probable cause standard is equivalent to the standard that police must meet in exercising their discretion to arrest someone. In the range of legal standards, probable cause is not a very demanding one. It requires much less than the "beyond a reasonable doubt" standard necessary for conviction. Similarly, federal prosecutors must, at a minimum, have probable cause to initiate a criminal case.[8]

Sometimes professional organizations promulgate more exacting standards. A statewide prosecutorial association offers the following more detailed and demanding standard.

CALIFORNIA DISTRICT ATTORNEYS ASSOCIATION   Uniform Crime
Charging Standards 13 (1974)

The prosecutor should charge only if the following four basic requirements are satisfied:

a. The prosecutor, based on a complete investigation and a thorough consideration of all pertinent data readily available to him, is satisfied that the evidence shows the accused is guilty of the crime to be charged.

---

6. Rule 5-110, California Rules of Professional Conduct, The State Bar of California (2004) (available on the State Bar of California website, *www.calbar.ca.gov*) (accessed on July 26, 2004).

7. People v. Uhlemann, 9 Cal. 3d 662, 667 (1973).

8. United States Attorneys Manual, Principles of Prosecution, 9-27.200 B (2002), available on the Department of Justice website at *www.usdoj.gov/usao/eousa/foia_reading_room/usam/title9/2mcrm.htm* (accessed on July 31, 2002).

b. There is legally sufficient, admissible evidence of a corpus delicti [this means that, without relying on certain statements that a defendant may have made, there is adequate evidence that a crime took place].

c. There is legally sufficient, admissible evidence of the accused's identity as the perpetrator of the crime charged.

d. The prosecutor has considered the probability of conviction by an objective fact-finder hearing the admissible evidence. The admissible evidence should be of such convincing force that it would warrant conviction of the crime charged by a reasonable and objective fact-finder after hearing all the evidence available to the prosecutor at the time of charging and after hearing the most plausible, reasonably foreseeable defense that could be raised under the evidence presented to the prosecutor.

This standard, unlike the Rules of Professional Conduct, represents a voluntary standard that prosecutors may choose to adopt. It provides more specific guidance than California's Rule 5-110, and it may enhance fairness, consistency, and transparency in the charging decision. Because the statewide organization that published this standard has proven highly influential, through its publications and training of prosecutors, this type of ethical standard, like the professional rules of conduct, may also serve to cabin prosecutorial discretion in charging.

Much to the dismay of many, the fact that police and prosecutors have limited time and resources can also play a substantial role in charging decisions. In addition, prosecutorial perspectives change over time in response to changes in political and social dynamics, new research, education, or information. In California in the early 1990s, police arrested and prosecutors charged and tried individuals who provided clean needles to addicts for the misdemeanor crime of possessing or distributing syringes without a prescription. In contrast, a local San Francisco Bay Area newspaper reported in 2002,

> [i]nstead of arresting people for helping drug addicts get access to clean needles, [one of those California counties] . . . just might start paying for it. . . . Many, especially people in law enforcement, used to view such programs as encouraging drug use. . . . There is now substantial research indicating that needle exchange programs significantly help decrease the rate of HIV and hepatitis C infection without promoting drug use, [said County Health Officer Dr. Scott Morrow.][9]

In the area of domestic violence, like the changes in police policy toward such conduct, prosecutorial policies have also undergone substantial modification. The change from a policy designed to avoid arrest to a preferred or mandatory arrest policy encouraged collection of evidence and passage through the first portal. Following years in which "[p]rosecutors failed to actively pursue cases where victims and offenders had intimate relationships. . . ."[10] "many offices now have pro-prosecution or 'no-drop' policies."[11] Although the specifics vary, "no-drop" policies encourage or require prosecutors to proceed with cases, sometimes even in the face of adamant victim noncooperation.

---

9. Sara Zaske, *County may fund needle exchange*, The Independent, May 18, 2002, at 1A.
10. Fagan, *supra* note 2, at 4.
11. Hanna, *supra* note 3, at 1861-1862.

Professor Cheryl Hanna discusses some of the initial data on the no-drop policies:

> Early data indicate that aggressive prosecution policies can reduce homicides. In San Diego, homicides related to domestic violence fell from thirty in 1985 to seven in 1994, after successful implementation of its . . . no-drop program. Additionally, evaluations suggest that jurisdictions that commit significant resources to domestic violence improve prosecution rates, lower recidivism rates, and communicate a stronger message that domestic violence will not be tolerated.[12]

The current and still evolving approach adopted by police and prosecutors to address domestic violence remains subject to much debate.[13] What is clear is that the discretion once exercised to limit, or exclude, domestic violence from the criminal dockets is now being exercised to emphasize recognition of domestic violence as serious criminal conduct.

Why Did Police and Prosecutorial Policies Toward Domestic Violence Change?

A number of factors, including the results of various studies, may have coalesced to trigger the policy changes. They include:

- *Magnitude of the Crime:* "Nearly 25 percent of surveyed women and 7.6 percent of surveyed men said they were raped and/or physically assaulted by a [partner or date] at some time in their lifetime. . . . " (Patricia Tjaden & Nancy Thoennes, Event, Nature, and Consequences of Intimate Partner Violence, Natl. Inst. Just. & CDC, *iii*, 2000).
- *Widespread Nature of the Crime:* "Domestic violence crosses ethnic, racial, age, national origin, sexual orientation, religious and socioeconomic lines." (American Bar Assn. Comm. on Domestic Violence, *www.abanet.org/domviol/stats.html*, accessed on Nov. 6, 2003).
- *Effect on Observers:* "[G]rowing up in violent homes is detrimental to children, even when children are not direct victims of physical . . . abuse." (Lois Weithorn, *Protecting Children from Exposure to Domestic Violence: The Use and Abuse of Child Maltreatment Statutes*, 53 Hastings L.J. 1, 6 (2001)).
- *Changing Legal Tools:* Jurisdictions have enacted provisions that enable police officers to make arrests in misdemeanor domestic violence cases even when they have not witnessed the assault. (*E.g.*, Cal. Penal Code § 836(d)).
- *Changing Social Attitudes and Successful Law Suits, by Victims, Against Law Enforcement Inaction: E.g.*, In Thurman v. Torrington, 595 F. Supp. 1521, 1529, the Connecticut court refused to dismiss a suit by Tracey Thurman against the Torrington Police Department for its inaction in the face of clear risk and repeated physical violence against her by Thurman's former spouse.
- *Research on the Reasons Why Some Victims Stay or Recant:* (1) Danger of departure — "Empirical research suggests an elevated risk of violence for battered women when they separate from their abusers." David Faigman, et al., Modern Scientific Evidence: The Law and Science of Expert Testimony 361 (West,

continued on next page

---

12. *Id.* at 1864.

13. Among other objections, critics note that mandatory arrest and no-drop policies can undermine the victim's autonomy and place the victim at greater risk (*see* Hanna, *supra* note 3, at 1857-1867), and subsequent studies raise questions about the validity or applicability of some of the early research. (*See* Fagan, *supra* note 2, at 11-15.) *See also supra* note 3.

> 2002); (2) Psychodynamic complexities of battering — an abuser who may be violent one day and extraordinarily loving and contrite the next, convincing the victim that the abuser will never strike the victim again; (3) Pressure batterers apply to control victims; (4) Lack of support for victims to leave; (5) Financial constraints of departure, especially for a parent with young children and no other means of support. *Id.* at 354-362.
>
> Some of the research that advocates have used to support the changes has been strongly criticized. *See, e.g.*, David L. Faigman, The Battered Woman Syndrome and Self-Defense: A Legal and Empirical Dissent, 72 Va. L. Rev. 619, 622, 637 (1986) (critiquing "validity of the research on battered woman syndrome" and arguing that the research contains "methodological and interpretive flaws").

Some types of conduct can result in both civil and criminal liability. For example, while assault and battery are crimes, they are also civil wrongs, called torts. A prosecutor may or may not choose to proceed criminally. Nonetheless, when the conduct constitutes a tort, the aggrieved party can sue the perpetrator civilly regardless of the prosecutor's determination in the criminal domain.

A prosecutor's decision not to prosecute a case is virtually unreviewable, but a prosecutor's decision affirmatively to charge a criminal case is subject to challenge at a variety of stages during the case.

2. The Applicable Law

A key component of the charging decision is determining whether a criminal law has been broken. Our criminal law originated in decisions that English and American judges made in particular cases. Their accumulated decisions, developed over the course of centuries, were known as the "common law." Today, virtually all crimes are created by legislatures through statutes. In fact, Professor Michael Moore contends that "the science of legislation has reached its highest form in criminal legislation."[14] As a consequence, prosecutors most commonly turn to statutes to ascertain the law that is applicable to particular cases. Federal prosecutors charge violations of federal statutes. State and local prosecutors charge violations of state statutes or local laws or ordinances.

A collection of statutes devoted to a particular topic is often called a code. In the 1950s, amidst widespread dissatisfaction with existing criminal codes, a group of criminal law scholars assembled and drafted a detailed new criminal code, the Model Penal Code, to be used as a guide for legislators reforming their states' criminal laws. The Model Penal Code has had, and continues to have, a substantial influence on the statutes to which prosecutors turn in determining the appropriate charge. The Model Penal Code functions as a guide for legislators, but it does not represent the law in any jurisdiction unless the legislature of that jurisdiction adopts its provisions. A number of jurisdictions have, however, revised their penal codes to reflect or incorporate portions, sometimes substantial portions, of the Model Penal Code.

---

14. Michael S. Moore, *Act and Crime: The Philosophy of Action and Its Implications for Criminal Law* 1 (1993).

Once a prosecutor decides that the conduct involved violated a criminal law and the case merits prosecution, she must follow the jurisdiction's charging procedure. The prosecutor's exercise of discretion in favor of proceeding with charging opens the second portal through which a criminal case generally must pass.

3. Grand Jury versus Prosecutorial Charging and Preliminary Hearing

Two procedures dominate charging in the United States. The first, used by the federal government and some states, involves citizens of the community convened as a grand jury. These citizens determine whether a prosecutor can file charges in court. In the second, the prosecutor alone decides whether to charge and files the charges directly with the court, but the court can then conduct a hearing in which it reviews the prosecutor's decision to charge. Thus, within each of these two charging procedures, there is a constraint on prosecutorial discretion. The grand jury or the court hearing serves as a check on the validity of the police and prosecutor's evaluation of the case. The performance of this screening function by the grand jury or by the judge at a preliminary hearing represents another portal through which a criminal case must pass.

a. Grand Jury

A grand jury handling criminal cases has two functions. One is to investigate crime through the grand jury's power to subpoena witnesses, documents, and other evidence. The second is to determine whether there is probable cause that a crime was committed and that the person the prosecution seeks to charge committed it. During a grand jury hearing, the prosecutor brings witnesses to testify before a group of citizens who have been sworn as grand jurors. These jurors decide whether the prosecution has produced adequate proof of the proposed charges. If the grand jurors find the standard has been met as to any or all of the charges, they issue a "true bill of indictment" as to those charges. Grand jurors regularly indict following the recommendations of the presenting prosecutor. For some jurisdictions, this is the only form of charging available for serious cases. Grand jury proceedings are closed and confidential. The target of the proceedings, unless called by or permitted by the prosecutor to testify, is barred from attendance.

b. Preliminary Hearing

In some jurisdictions, prosecutors issue charges directly. Issued charges appear on a formal charging document, sometimes called a "complaint." When the charges in the complaint involve serious offenses, they are usually subject to some preliminary testing in a court procedure, sometimes termed a "preliminary hearing." At the preliminary hearing, the prosecution produces evidence to prove the charges in the complaint. The standard that the prosecution must meet at this early stage generally falls far below the standard used at trial. It is commonly a "probable cause" standard. Unlike grand jury proceedings, preliminary hearings occur in open court in front of a judge or magistrate. Defense counsel may cross-examine witnesses and sometimes presents witnesses. At the conclusion of the evidentiary portion of the hearing, counsel may present arguments. Ultimately, the judge or magistrate determines whether the prosecution's evidence meets the probable cause standard. If the judge finds probable cause, the case moves forward. Usually the case proceeds to a trial or pre-trial docket, and the judge will base future proceedings on a second charging document, called an "information" — much like a grand jury indictment. In some jurisdictions, prosecutors may select between the grand jury or direct charging process for each serious case.

C. IN THE COURTHOUSE

1. Arraignment, Counsel, and Settings

Once the grand jury indicts or the prosecution files a charging document in court, the court arraigns the accused, who then is formally labeled "the defendant" in court papers. "Arraignment" has several functions. The first is to determine whether the defendant has counsel, would like counsel, or wishes to represent himself (known as proceeding "pro se," or "in propria persona," or simply "in pro per"). If the defendant has funds and wishes to hire counsel, the court will usually grant the defendant a short continuance to arrange representation if the attorney is not already present at the arraignment.

The Constitution guarantees counsel to indigent persons accused of serious crimes and to those accused of many types of less serious ones, particularly when incarceration is possible. Some jurisdictions fund an office of attorneys, called public defenders, who represent indigent clients. In other areas, courts appoint or contract with private attorneys to handle cases. Securing representation is often most problematic for defendants whose income is small but is too large to qualify for publicly funded representation. The Constitution also guarantees a defendant the right to represent herself, though courts typically strongly discourage individuals from representing themselves.

At arraignment, the court also informs the defendant of the charges against him and usually inquires whether the defendant wishes to enter a plea of guilty or not guilty. The judge also decides whether the defendant will be held in custody pending trial or allowed to remain free on certain conditions. Often, the court sets the case for further proceedings, which may consist of pre-trial conferences, motions, or even the trial itself.

2. Plea Negotiations

Most criminal cases are not resolved through a trial. Figures vary somewhat, but commonly more than 90 percent of state convictions in criminal cases are based on defendants' pleas of guilty. Similarly, statistics from the year 2000 indicate that, on the federal level, guilty pleas represented approximately 95 percent of federal convictions.[15] In addition, approximately 85 percent of all criminal defendants resolved

---

15. Judicial Business of the United States Courts, Annual Report of the Director 221, tbl. D-4 (2000). This 95 percent statistic measures the percent of convictions that resulted from guilty pleas. Presumably, the remaining 5 percent include convictions resulting from bench or jury trials.

their federal cases by entering guilty pleas.[16] Plea negotiations may begin even before charges are filed. Efforts to dissuade or influence prosecutorial decision making in the pre-charging phase are especially common in white-collar cases, where potential defendants have often engaged defense lawyers long before the final charging decision.[17] Because some jurisdictions do not appoint public defenders until court appearances on a formal charging document begin, the luxury of contacting prosecutors at the pre-charging stage is often reserved for those who can afford private counsel. Most often, then, plea negotiations or plea bargaining begins after the formal filing of charges. Prosecutors and defense counsel may engage in protracted and complex discussions, or the exchange may last but a moment, especially when the prosecutor's office has established a standard offer for certain criminal conduct. Frequently, as a case progresses toward trial, plea negotiations involve a series of brief conversations in which offers change based on the latest ruling in the case or the perceived strength of the evidence and availability of witnesses. Occasionally, cases settle even while jurors are deliberating. To competently advise a client whether to accept a plea, defense counsel sometimes need expertise in domains outside criminal law, criminal procedure, and evidence. For example, defense counsel may need to explore the immigration consequences of accepting a plea.

Judges actively participate in plea negotiations in some courts and not at all in others. Where a judge is actively involved, she may undercut a prosecutor's offer or refuse to accept a plea to the terms of an offer on which the prosecutor and defense counsel have agreed. In the crush of criminal cases in some urban areas, plea negotiations sometimes receive only a few moments of discussion.

Christopher H. Schmitt, 2-MINUTE DISCUSSION DECIDES THE FUTURE FOR MANY DEFENDANTS
San Jose Mercury News, Dec. 8, 1991, at 23A

Behind closed doors, a judge and attorneys for the people and attorneys for the defense gather weekly to grind through a docket that decides plea bargains—who'll get off easy and who'll get hit hard. . . .

The Mercury News observed two . . . sessions in which drug . . . crimes were on the agenda. What follows are vignettes from this front line of justice, where cases rarely get more than a couple of minutes of discussion. . . .

In one form or another, discussions such as these are the backbone of California's jammed judicial system. Without them, the courts would collapse. . . .

A San Jose man is up on drug-dealing charges. Prosecutor Dale Sanderson wants a stiff penalty—three years in state prison.

Defense attorney Gregory M. Alonzo: This is an 18-year-old kid still in high school!
[Judge Ronald] Lisk: But he's selling. . . .
Alonzo (to Sanderson): Do you want an 18-year-old to go to prison?
Sanderson: That's my offer.
Alonzo: Do you want an 18-year-old to go to state prison?
Sanderson: He goes. . . .

---

16. *Id.* This 85 percent statistic measures the percentage of all federal cases that were resolved with guilty pleas. Presumably, the remaining 15 percent included cases that were resolved through trial convictions and acquittals as well as dismissals during the criminal process.
17. Kenneth Mann, *Defending White-Collar Crime: A Portrait of Attorneys at Work* 4 (1985).

Lisk: I have to give him the mandatory minimum — probation and 120 days. And he pleads to both counts.
Alonzo: Six months total?
Lisk: Yes.
Alonzo: OK.

Sometimes there's no room for discussion, as in this drug case.

Lisk: It's a kilo case, guys. Everybody goes to the joint (state prison) for two years for a kilo case. Sorry, there's not much I can do. . . .

In a PCP drug case involving three people, public defender Aram James portrays his client, a San Jose woman, as an innocent bystander.

James: She just happens to be in the bathroom. I don't see how you can tie her to the drugs.
Sanderson: Guilt by history.
James (to Sanderson): I want to know if you'll dismiss. Police break down the (bathroom) door and they find no drugs.
Sanderson: The only problem is (she) is found under the influence.
James: So what are you going to offer her?
Sanderson: As charged — conditional (meaning no state prison time).
Lisk: Six plus six. (Six months in the county jail, six months in a drug program.)
Sanderson: Six plus six is fine with me.

In the case of a Los Gatos man charged with cultivation and possession for sale of marijuana prosecutor Alcala wants to get tough by tacking on another charge: possession of a gun by someone previously convicted of a felony.

Alcala: The guy owns a .22.
Public Defender Yolanda Trevino: He doesn't own a .22. A .22 was in the house. You're jumping to all kinds of conclusions.
Alcala: Call it wild speculation.
Lisk (to Alcala): Are you going to dismiss the felon-with-a-gun (charge)?
Alcala: No.
Lisk: I'll give him four months (in county jail).
Alcala: Four months?!
Lisk: Well, he's not exactly Dillinger.
Alcala: They've spent more time investigating the case than he'll spend in jail!
Trevino: That's right.

The idea behind plea bargaining, of course, is to get early guilty pleas in exchange for lighter sentences than might be true if defendants push their cases through the system. Lisk invokes this hammer often. As he says to one defense attorney in a drug possession and use case:

"Tell him if he doesn't accept that, he's gone (to state prison) for two years. He'll accept it.
"We'll make him an offer he can't refuse."

Substantive criminal law, as well as rules and standards, cabin the discretion exercised by prosecutors during plea negotiations. For example, in some jurisdictions, mandatory minimum sentences both influence the tenor of discussions and

limit the specific offers. Ethical and constitutional rules also affect the negotiation process. Defense counsel must abide by a client's decision to accept an offer
or go to trial. Similarly, ethical rules require defense attorneys to communicate
offers to their clients even if, in particular cases, they would strongly encourage a
client to refuse the offer.

Still, commentators regularly criticize the paucity of regulations on negotiation
tactics. Consider the following perspectives on the institution of plea bargaining:

Jeff Brown, DEALING AWAY THE DEFENSE   The Recorder, Aug. 5, 1991

A criminal defense bar which denies defendants their day in court is a
failure. A bar that conducts fewer and fewer jury trials does not protect the
innocent, and a bar which pleads clients guilty within days of arrest does
not fulfill its constitutional role of checking the power of government. It is
a shocking, but statistically undeniable fact that the American legal system
is in the midst of a dramatic and dangerous shift on the part of defense
attorneys from an adversarial to an accommodational approach . . . . The
number of jury trials conducted in criminal cases in the California superior
courts has declined to the point of insignificance. In 1980, 12.4 percent of the
cases were heard by juries. Today that figure is a miserly 3.9 percent. The
percentage of felony convictions has risen sharply. In 1980, 79.3 percent of
felony cases resulted in convictions. Today it is an astonishing 93 percent.

Christopher H. Schmitt, PLEA BARGAINING FAVORS WHITES AS BLACKS, HISPANICS PAY PRICE   San Jose Mercury News, Dec. 8, 1991, at 1A

In California, justice isn't colorblind. As more and more cases are
decided by plea bargain, whites as a group get significantly better deals
than Hispanics or blacks who are accused of similar crimes and who have
similar criminal backgrounds, a Mercury News analysis of nearly 700,000
cases shows. Such deals between prosecutors and defense lawyers now
occur in more than 95 percent of serious criminal cases, and in the great
bulk of less-serious cases, according to statistics and attorneys. . . .

At virtually every stage of pre-trial negotiation, whites are more successful than non-whites. They do better at getting charges dropped. They're
better able to get charges reduced to lesser offenses. They draw more lenient
sentences and go to prison less often. They get more chances to wipe their
records clean.

Differences in treatment vary by county, by crime and by type of
punishment, but a Mercury News computer-assisted analysis of 683,513
criminal cases from 1981 to 1990 shows a clear pattern of inequity.

3. Discovery

Between the formal filing of the charging document and trial, the prosecution,
and sometimes the defense, provide information about the case to the opposing

side. This process of disclosure and the items disclosed are called "discovery." According to the United States Supreme Court, the Constitution requires that the prosecution disclose "exculpatory" information to the defense.[18] Ethical rules and statutes in some jurisdictions expand that discovery obligation. In some jurisdictions, statutes mandate reciprocal discovery by requiring defense counsel to disclose certain types of information to the prosecution. Statutes or court rules often govern the timing of required disclosures. Failure to disclose or failure to do so in a timely manner forms the basis of numerous trial court proceedings and appeals.

4. Trial

If counsel do not settle a case and the prosecution or the court does not dismiss the charge, the case proceeds to trial. Recall that only a small percentage of criminal cases result in trial, perhaps 5 to 10 percent. For serious criminal charges — and many less serious ones — the Constitution mandates that jurisdictions provide the opportunity for a jury trial. Defendants can waive their right to a jury trial and have, instead, a court or bench trial. In a bench trial, the judge or magistrate acts as both the fact finder and decision maker on legal issues. Jurisdictions differ in the number of jurors required for a jury trial, generally ranging from six to twelve. They usually require that jurors in criminal cases achieve unanimity to reach a verdict of guilty or not guilty. Failure to unanimously agree produces a hung jury. To obtain a conviction, prosecutors must convince jurors of the truth of the charge "beyond a reasonable doubt." The task of furnishing an appropriate definition for this term of art has plagued jurists and legal scholars. However defined, the term does represent the highest legal standard, exceeding other legal standards like "probable cause," "preponderance of evidence," and "clear and convincing."

A trial usually consists of several segments. Following discussions or motions in the trial court out of the presence of prospective jurors, jury selection begins. This process is called "voir dire." The court and, to varying extent, counsel question jurors about their ability to serve in the instant case. Counsel may excuse jurors from service through challenges for cause and peremptory challenges. To prevail on a challenge for cause, counsel must demonstrate to the court that the juror is unlikely to be able to serve impartially. Courts generally allow an unlimited number of challenges for cause. In contrast, counsel using a peremptory challenge need not make any showing to the court of bias; he may simply excuse a juror without articulating a reason. Statutes usually assign a fixed number of peremptory challenges based on the type of case. In addition to the limited number of peremptories, these challenges are subject to attack if counsel exercises one based on an illegal reason. Counsel cannot exclude jurors solely on the basis of certain cognizable group bias. For example, attorneys cannot exclude African Americans from a jury because of their race or men because of their gender.

Following the selection and formal swearing in of the jury, the prosecution typically offers an opening statement. The defense may address the jury immediately after the prosecutor or wait until the beginning of the defendant's case. After opening statements, the prosecutor produces evidence of the crimes alleged in the charging document. Witnesses, both lay and expert, are typically sworn and testify.

---

18. Brady v. Maryland, 373 U.S. 83, 87 (1963).

The prosecutor guides the witnesses through direct examination, and the defense attorney cross-examines the prosecution witnesses. The prosecution also may introduce exhibits, typically documents or objects, such as a weapon. At the conclusion of the prosecution's evidence, the prosecution rests. At this stage, the defense may choose to rest by declining to present evidence, or the defense may present its own evidence. The Constitution reserves for the defendant the decision whether to testify or to exercise her Fifth Amendment right to remain silent.

Ethical rules also govern this portion of the proceedings. For example, both sides are forbidden from presenting testimony that they know to be perjurious. Occasionally, the defendant's right to testify conflicts with counsel's duty to avoid presenting perjured testimony. This conflict has spawned extended discussion in both the scholarly literature and court opinions. We treat the issue at length in Appendix D.

Prosecutors can usually respond to the defense's presentation by furnishing rebuttal evidence and the defense can respond to that with surrebuttal evidence. After the conclusion of the evidentiary portion of the trial, the judge instructs the jurors on the law to apply to the case and each side closes with argument. Again, because the prosecution carries the burden of proof, they argue first and last. After the initial prosecution argument, defense counsel has an opportunity to respond. Following any defense response, prosecutors may make the final closing argument. Judges determine whether arguments precede or follow the judge's instructions to the jury.

Then, the jury retires to deliberate. If the jury reaches a verdict, the foreperson of the jury or clerk of the court announces the verdict. If jurors acquit on the charges, that criminal case ends. The Double Jeopardy Clause of the Constitution prohibits the same sovereignty from prosecuting someone twice for the same offense. As the case involving the assault on Rodney King illustrates, state courts and federal courts are separate sovereignties. State prosecutors tried four officers for offenses related to the assault and the jury acquitted. Following the acquittal, which triggered extensive rioting, the federal government charged the same officers with federal crimes based on the same conduct. The jury in the federal case convicted two of the officers and acquitted the others. As separate sovereignties, both the state and federal courts could prosecute the officers without violating the Double Jeopardy Clause.

In some cases in which jurors find the defendant guilty, jurors participate directly in aspects of the sentencing process. In other cases, the court excuses jurors before undertaking sentencing determinations.

5. Post-Trial: Sentencing and Probation

If the jury finds a defendant guilty, the judge will generally order the preparation of a probation report and set a date for sentencing. For the report, the probation department examines a host of issues that can affect the sentencing decision. Reports commonly include background material on the defendant, the crime, and a proposed sentence. Often judges also have probation reports prepared when there was a plea agreement. Sentencing procedures vary, both from jurisdiction to jurisdiction and from case to case. The procedures may be informal or involve a lengthy hearing with testimony. Criticism reflecting a lack of attention to the needs and treatment of victims in the criminal justice process has resulted in various statutory reforms. As a result of these reforms, in many jurisdictions, victims may participate in the sentencing process.

Two types of sentencing schemes are common. A determinate sentencing scheme prescribes penalties on a relatively detailed level, sometimes imposing severe limitations on a judge's discretion. For example, a sentencing scheme might provide a base term for the offense and very limited ranges to increase or decrease a defendant's sentence based on specific and limited criteria.

In contrast, an indeterminate sentence for first-degree murder might be 25 years to life. Once the minimum sentence has been served, usually some portion of the 25 years, a parole board will determine whether to release the defendant or continue to confine her.

D. PARTICIPANTS

As the description of the process illustrates, many participants play a role in and influence the life cycle of a criminal case. In this section, we concentrate briefly on the role of the following: (1) prosecutor, (2) defense counsel, (3) judge, (4) defendant, (5) victim, (6) court personnel, (7) jurors, (8) probation officers, (9) media.

Prosecutors represent the government. They are entrusted with seeking justice. Their role encompasses decision making on a case from its initial presentation through disposition — dismissal, plea agreement, or trial and sentencing, and sometimes appeal, if a conviction results. Prosecutors wield tremendous power over the lives of others. Most prosecutors strive to apply that power fairly and with integrity.[19] But prosecutors are fallible and often lack resources, particularly on the state and local levels. Even the best-intentioned prosecutors can make mistakes and can succumb to the consequences of a high volume of cases. For example, busy prosecutors may neglect to consult with crime victims regarding the proposed disposition of a criminal case. Moreover, prosecutors must demonstrate constant vigilance against certain pervasive influences, like racism, gender bias, and homophobia.

In addition, because prosecutorial offices sometimes track a prosecutor's career by the number of cases that the prosecutor has tried, and, of those, the number that resulted in jury convictions, prosecutors must reconcile their personal and

---

19. Consider, however, the results of a Chicago Tribune national investigation on prosecutorial misconduct, collated and reprinted in *The Verdict: Dishonor*, by Ken Armstrong & Maurice Possley, from articles originally published Jan. 10–Jan. 14, 1999:

> In the first study of its kind, a Chicago Tribune analysis of thousands of court records, appellate rulings and lawyer disciplinary records from across the United States has found:
>
> - Since a 1962 U.S. Supreme Court ruling designed to curb misconduct by prosecutors, at least 381 defendants nationally have had a homicide conviction thrown out because prosecutors concealed evidence suggesting innocence or presented evidence they knew to be false. Of all the ways that prosecutors can cheat, those two are considered the worst by the courts. And that number represents only a fraction of how often such cheating occurs. . . .
> - Of the 381 defendants, 67 had been sentenced to death. . . .
> - Nearly 30 of those 67 Death Row inmates — about half of those whose cases have been resolved — were subsequently freed. But almost all spent at least five years in prison. One served 26 years before his conviction was reversed and the charges dropped.

A Chicago Tribune Reprint at 3.

professional desire "to win" cases with their overarching mandate to seek justice. For example, prosecutors must guard against both cowardice to go to trial on difficult cases and the inclination to try "easy" cases in which jurors are highly likely to convict but that should have settled before trial. On some days, a prosecutor enjoys the satisfaction of helping those who have been criminally victimized or dismissing a case against someone wrongfully accused. On other days, the work can prove frustrating, when, for example, witnesses fail to appear for court or when cases that have entailed many hours of preparation get continued and continued again.

Defense counsel represent the accused. Defense counsel represent the guilty as well as the innocent. Their success takes many forms. They can succeed, for example, when they thoroughly test the prosecution's case, exposing deficiencies of proof and forcing the prosecution to try to prove the charges beyond a reasonable doubt. They can succeed when gaining a dismissal of the charges or when negotiating a favorable plea disposition for a client. They can succeed when placing a client in rehabilitation to help the client conquer an addiction.

Like prosecutorial work, there are challenges. Defense counsel must, like all the participants, guard against the influences of discrimination that erode fairness in criminal proceedings. In addition, while prosecutors may look to larger institutional issues when handling individual cases, defense counsel must zealously represent each client. Thus, they must resist the temptations that arise from being a repeat player in the system. Even within sizable urban areas, the number of attorneys who regularly practice in the criminal bar may be relatively small. The norm of reciprocity and give and take of daily practice with the same prosecutors and judges may tempt counsel to lose sight of their responsibilities to individual clients. Defense counsel, especially those whose practices involve a high volume of cases, must juggle the needs of, and responsibilities to, many clients simultaneously.

Judges preside over criminal proceedings but their roles vary with different proceedings and different assignments. They determine legal issues, both procedural and substantive. They may actively facilitate settlement or decline to participate in negotiations. They may serve as fact finders in motions or trials without juries. Many judicial tasks, such as some sentencing decisions, involve the exercise of discretion. As is true for prosecutors and defense counsel, ethical standards govern the conduct of judges. They must maintain their impartiality in deciding matters before them. The standards demand that they avoid conflicts of interest and even the mere appearance of impropriety. Holding judicial office can prove prestigious and engaging but it can also isolate the individual judge, who often must confront weighty decisions alone or with very limited outside assistance.

Defendants are the center of a criminal case. The federal Constitution entrusts them with the right to decide whether to settle a case or proceed to trial as well as whether to testify or remain silent. In practice, defendants often follow the advice of their attorneys in most, if not all, major case-related decisions.

Victims, in cases in which identifiable individuals suffer harm, often play crucial, although sometimes peripheral, roles in the criminal justice system. With some exceptions, prosecutors, rather than victims, control the pursuit of the criminal case. Victims may furnish information, testify, and express their views on the outcome of cases. To increase the attention and dignity afforded victims, at least 45 jurisdictions have enacted statutes affording victims certain rights.[20] Similarly,

---

20. ACIR, *supra* note 5, at 26.

on the federal level, senators have introduced legislation to amend the federal Constitution to accord victims a constellation of rights. Consider the text of the proposed constitutional language:[21]

SECTION 1. The rights of victims of violent crime, being capable of protection without denying the constitutional rights of those accused of victimizing them, are hereby established and shall not be denied by any State or the United States and may be restricted only as provided in this article.

SECTION 2. A victim of violent crime shall have the right to reasonable and timely notice of any public proceeding involving the crime and of any release or escape of the accused; the rights not to be excluded from such public proceeding and reasonably to be heard at public release, plea, sentencing, reprieve, and pardon proceedings; and the right to adjudicative decisions that duly consider the victim's safety, interest in avoiding unreasonable delay, and just and timely claims to restitution from the offender. These rights shall not be restricted except when and to the degree dictated by a substantial interest in public safety or the administration of criminal justice, or by compelling necessity.

SECTION 3. Nothing in this article shall be construed to provide grounds for a new trial or to authorize any claim for damages. Only the victim or the victim's lawful representative may assert the rights established by this article, and no person accused of the crime may obtain any form of relief hereunder.

SECTION 4. Congress shall have power to enforce by appropriate legislation the provisions of this article. Nothing in this article shall affect the President's authority to grant reprieves or pardons.

SECTION 5. This article shall be inoperative unless it shall have been ratified as an amendment to the Constitution by the legislatures of three-fourths of the several States within seven years from the date of its submission to the States by the Congress.[22]

Court personnel play a vital role in the criminal justice system. They too exercise discretion and make choices. Clerks handle the administrative business of the courts. Clerks may control the courtroom to which a case is sent or the scheduling of various procedures in a case. Bailiffs control security in the courtroom. They may choose when to bring an in-custody client from the holding cell into the courtroom. Court reporters transcribe the proceedings, producing verbatim accounts of the verbal interactions. Wise attorneys recognize court personnel as individuals whose discretion can impact each criminal case.

Jurors are the fact finders in a criminal case. Their judgment of acquittal frees the accused from those charges and bars further criminal proceedings on them. The jurors' judgment of guilt permits the sovereignty to impose punishment. A jury that fails to reach a verdict hangs. The consequence of a hung jury varies. In some cases, often serious felonies, the prosecution will retry the case to a second jury. In others, the result induces the prosecution to proffer a more favorable settlement or dismiss the charge. Although only a small percentage of cases actually arrive for jury consideration, the impact of jury verdicts pervades the system. In particular, settlement offers depend on the likely response of a jury to the case. Often, jurisdictions develop reputations as leaning strongly toward the prosecution or defense. These perceived leanings also permeate settlement discussions.

---

21. S.J. Res. 35, 107th Cong. (2002).
22. S.J. Res. 35, cited in 71 Criminal Law Reporter 112, Apr. 24, 2002.

A 1993 federal report noted that "[p]robation is the most common criminal sentence, received by almost 2 out of 3 offenders."[23] As a result, busy probation officers serve a multitude of functions. They research and draft probation reports for judges' review in sentencing offenders. Within those reports, they generally recommend sentencing terms. In some jurisdictions, they advise judges on appropriate settlements. They supervise and monitor persons on probation, conducting interviews, searches, and drug checks, as well as facilitating the gain of employment or education. They also participate in hearings and revocations of probation.

From investigation through appeal, the media may influence criminal proceedings. Publicity can provoke outrage at a prosecutor's failure to charge and offers one of the few checks on a prosecutor's otherwise unreviewable discretion to decline to pursue a case. But media attention can also taint the jury pool, resulting in the need to change venue and move a trial to a different location. In these and many other ways, the media exert power over the criminal justice system.

PROBLEMS

1.1 According to a newspaper account,[24] Catherine Sweeney, an Irish schoolteacher, visited the United States. She was driving on a coastal highway and stopped her car at the side of the road to observe birds with her three-year-old daughter. "When she resumed the trip, Sweeney, in the habit of driving on the left side of the road, drove into the wrong lane, [came around a curve and struck a motorcyclist in his own lane, causing his death.] . . . Sweeney remained at the scene of the crash, and investigators determined she showed no signs of intoxication. No blood samples were taken. . . . [Ms. Sweeney] teaches third- and fourth-graders. Her supporters describe her as a peaceful vegetarian so respectful of life that when a bee once strayed into her classroom, she captured and released it because she did not want to teach the children to kill a living thing."

"Nick Calder, a native Londoner and friend of the Sweeneys, said it is commonplace for expatriates and international travelers to get momentarily confused about which side of the road to use. And in Sweeney's case, he said, the hilly terrain and winding roads of [the area in which she was driving] are similar to the geography of Ireland and the United Kingdom."[25]

Assume that the following statutes and jury instructions apply:

Statute: Felony Vehicular Manslaughter is defined as "driving a vehicle in the commission of an unlawful act, not amounting to felony, and with gross negligence."

---

23. ACIR, *supra* note 5, at 28.
24. This Problem is based upon, and quotations in this paragraph are from, Gary Klien, *Teacher guilty in fatal crash*, Marin Independent Journal, Oct. 5, 2001, at A1, A9.
25. *Id.*

Statute: Misdemeanor Vehicular Manslaughter is defined as "driving a vehicle in the commission of an unlawful act, not amounting to felony, without gross negligence."

Instruction: Ordinary negligence "is the doing of something which a reasonably prudent person would not do, or the failure to do something which a reasonably prudent person would do, under similar circumstances. . . . Ordinary or reasonable care is that care which persons of ordinary prudence would use in order to avoid injury to themselves or others under similar circumstances."[26]

Instruction: Gross negligence "means conduct which is more than ordinary negligence . . . . [It] refers to a negligent act which is aggravated, reckless or flagrant and which is such a departure from the conduct of an ordinarily prudent, careful person under the same circumstances as to be contrary to a proper regard for human life or to constitute indifference to the consequences of those acts. The facts must be such that the consequences of the negligent acts could reasonably have been foreseen and it must appear that the death was not the result of inattention, mistaken judgment or misadventure but the natural and probable result of an aggravated, reckless or flagrantly negligent act."[27]

Should the prosecutor charge Ms. Sweeney with homicide in the form of vehicular manslaughter? If you decide that the prosecutor should exercise discretion to charge Ms. Sweeney, should the prosecutor charge the crime as a felony or misdemeanor?

1.2 You are a defense attorney. The prosecution has charged your client with robbery. When you interview your client, she confirms that she committed the offense as detailed in the police report. Your investigation produces nothing to dispute the account in the police report. Your client does not want a felony on her record and would prefer to go to trial and take her chances. She does not plan to testify. She believes that the victim will be too scared to testify or that jurors will feel sorry for her and acquit. You have given her your considered opinion on the likely outcome at trial. Your client insists on going to trial. What should you do?

1.3 Jennifer Johnson was a crack cocaine addict.[28] During both of her pregnancies, she ingested crack cocaine. As a result of her drug use, she experienced at least one crack overdose during her second pregnancy. "Ms. Johnson admitted smoking pot and crack cocaine three to four times every-other-day throughout the duration of her pregnancy with her daughter. Johnson's mother acknowledged that Johnson had been using cocaine for at least three years during the time her daughter and son were born." Each of her two children tested positive for a metabolite or "breakdown" product of cocaine just after birth.

Should a prosecutor charge Ms. Johnson under the following statute?

---

26. California Jury Instructions — Criminal (CALJIC) 8.91 (2003).
27. *Id.* at 3.36.
28. The facts of the Problem are drawn from Johnson v. State, 602 So. 2d 1288 (Fla. 1992).

Florida Statute § 893.13(1)(c)1 (1989)

    c) Except as authorized by this chapter, it is unlawful for any person 18 years of age or older to deliver any controlled substance to a person under the age of 18 years. . . . Any person who violates this provision with respect to:

        1. A controlled substance . . . is guilty of a felony of the first degree. . . .
Cocaine is a controlled substance.

    A Florida prosecutor did charge Ms. Johnson with violating the statute. Consider the perspective provided by Professor Dorothy E. Roberts on the *Johnson* case.

Dorothy E. Roberts, PUNISHING DRUG ADDICTS WHO HAVE BABIES: WOMEN OF COLOR, EQUALITY, AND THE RIGHT OF PRIVACY

104 Harv. L. Rev. 1419, 1421, 1428-1430, 1431-1434 (1991)

    In July 1989, Jennifer Clarise Johnson, a twenty-three-year-old crack addict, became the first woman in the United States to be criminally convicted for exposing her baby to drugs while pregnant. Florida law enforcement officials charged Johnson with two counts of delivering a controlled substance to a minor after her two children tested positive for cocaine at birth. Because the relevant drug law did not apply to fetuses, the prosecution invented a novel interpretation of the statute. The prosecution obtained Johnson's conviction for passing a cocaine metabolite from her body to her newborn infants during the sixty-second period after birth and before the umbilical cord was cut.

    A growing number of women across the country have been charged with criminal offenses after giving birth to babies who test positive for drugs. The majority of these women, like Jennifer Johnson, are poor and Black. Most are addicted to crack cocaine. . . .

    Some experts estimate that as many as 375,000 drug-exposed infants are born every year. In many urban hospitals, the number of these newborns has quadrupled in the last five years. . . .

    Babies born to drug-addicted mothers may suffer a variety of medical, developmental, and behavioral problems, depending on the nature of their mother's substance abuse. Immediate effects of cocaine exposure can include premature birth, low birth weight, and withdrawal symptoms. Cocaine-exposed children have also exhibited neurobehavioral problems such as mood dysfunction, organizational deficits, poor attention, and impaired human interaction, although it has not been determined whether these conditions are permanent. Congenital disorders and deformities have also been associated with cocaine use during pregnancy. According to NAPARE [the National Association for Perinatal Addiction Research and Education], babies exposed to cocaine have a tenfold greater risk of suffering sudden infant death syndrome (SIDS).

    Data on the extent and potential severity of the adverse effects of maternal cocaine use are controversial. The interpretation of studies of cocaine-exposed infants is often clouded by the presence of other fetal risk factors, such as the mother's use of additional drugs, cigarettes, and alcohol and her socioeconomic status. For example, the health prospects of an infant are significantly threatened because pregnant addicts often receive little or no prenatal care and may be malnourished. Moreover, because the medical community has given more attention to studies showing adverse effects of cocaine exposure than to those that deny these effects, the public has a distorted perception of the risks of maternal cocaine use. Researchers have not yet authoritatively determined the percentage of infants exposed to cocaine who actually experience those adverse consequences.

The response of state prosecutors, legislators, and judges to the problem of drug-exposed babies has been punitive. They have punished women who use drugs during pregnancy by depriving these mothers of custody of their children, by jailing them during their pregnancy, and by prosecuting them after their babies are born. . . .

Poor Black women bear the brunt of prosecutors' punitive approach. . . .

To charge drug-addicted mothers with crimes, the state must be able to identify those who use drugs during pregnancy. Because poor women are generally under greater government supervision — through their associations with public hospitals, welfare agencies, and probation officers — their drug use is more likely to be detected and reported. . . . The government's main source of information about prenatal drug use is hospitals' reporting of positive infant toxicologies to child welfare authorities. Hospitals serving poor minority communities implement this testing almost exclusively. Private physicians who serve more affluent women perform less of this screening because they have a financial stake both in retaining their patients' business and securing referrals from them and because they are socially more like their parents. . . .

Health care professionals are much more likely to report Black women's drug use to government authorities than they are similar drug use by their wealthy white patients. A study recently reported in *The New England Journal of Medicine* demonstrated this racial bias in the reporting of maternal drug use. Researchers studied the results of the toxicologic tests of pregnant women who received prenatal care in public health clinics and in private obstetrical offices in Pinellas County, Florida. Little difference existed in the prevalence of substance abuse by pregnant women along either racial or economic lines, nor was there any significant difference between public clinics and private offices. Despite similar rates of substance abuse, however, Black women were *ten times* more likely than whites to be reported to public health authorities for substance abuse during pregnancy. Although several possible explanations can account for this disparate reporting, both public health facilities and private doctors are more inclined to turn in pregnant Black women who use drugs than pregnant white women who use drugs.

In 1992, the Florida Supreme Court reversed Ms. Johnson's convictions.[29]

---

29. Johnson v. State, *supra*.

CHAPTER TWO

PUNISHMENT

A. INTRODUCTION

In this chapter, we study a range of issues related to punishment. First we consider the meaning of the term "punishment." The government, for instance, can confine individuals against their will if they suffer from mental illness and are dangerous. Is this punishment? If not, what distinguishes this governmental restriction of individual freedom from punishment? Once we have explored what constitutes punishment, we turn to why the state punishes and examine several rationales that society relies on to justify punishment. The third portion of this chapter looks at how society punishes and reviews various types of punishment, as well as the process of selecting and implementing punishment. A final section deals with severity: how much punishment should be imposed on an offender.

B. WHAT IS PUNISHMENT?

In 1994, Kansas enacted the following legislation dealing with sexual offenders:

Kansas Statutes Annotated (2002) § 59-29a01

The legislature finds that a small but extremely dangerous group of sexually violent predators exist who do not have a mental disease or defect that renders them appropriate for involuntary treatment pursuant to the treatment act for mentally ill persons defined in K.S.A. 59-2901 et seq. and amendments thereto, which is intended to provide short-term treatment to individuals with serious mental disorders and then return them to the community. In contrast to persons appropriate for civil commitment under K.S.A. 59-2901 et seq. and amendments thereto, sexually violent predators generally have antisocial personality features which are unamenable to existing mental illness treatment modalities and those features render them likely to engage in sexually violent behavior. The legislature further finds that sexually violent predators' likelihood of engaging in repeat acts of predatory sexual violence is high. The existing involuntary commitment procedure pursuant to the treatment act for mentally ill persons defined in K.S.A. 59-2901 et seq. and amendments thereto is inadequate to address the risk these sexually violent predators pose to society. The legislature further finds that the prognosis for rehabilitating sexually violent predators in a prison setting is poor, the treatment needs of this population are very long term and the treatment modalities for this population are very different than the traditional treatment modalities for people appropriate for commitment under the treatment act for mentally ill persons defined in K.S.A. 59-2901 et seq. and amendments thereto, therefore a civil commitment procedure for the long-term care and treatment of the sexually violent predator is found to be necessary by the legislature.

§ 59-29a02

As used in this act: (a) "Sexually violent predator" means any person who has been convicted of or charged with a sexually violent offense and who suffers from a mental abnormality or personality disorder which makes the person likely to engage in the predatory acts of sexual violence.

§ 59-29a05

Upon filing of a petition [by the attorney general], the judge shall determine whether probable cause exists to believe that the person named in the petition is a sexually violent predator. If such determination is made, the judge shall direct that person be taken into custody and the person shall be transferred to an appropriate facility for an evaluation as to whether the person is a sexually violent predator. . . .

§ 59-29a06

Within 45 days after the filing of a petition [by the attorney general], the court shall conduct a trial to determine whether the person is a sexually violent predator. At all stages of the proceedings under this act, any person subject to this act shall be entitled to the assistance of counsel, and if the person is indigent, the court shall appoint counsel to assist such person. . . . The person, the county or district attorney or attorney general, or the judge shall have the right to demand that the trial be before a jury. . . .

§ 59-29a07

The court or jury shall determine whether, beyond a reasonable doubt, the person is a sexually violent predator. If such determination that the person is a sexually violent predator is made by a jury, such determination shall be by unanimous verdict of such jury. Such determination may be appealed. If the court or jury determines that the person is a sexually violent predator, the person shall be committed to the custody of the secretary of social and rehabilitation services for control, care, and treatment until such time as the person's mental abnormality or personality disorder has so changed that the person is safe to be at large. . . . [1]

---

1. The Act also provides additional avenues for someone adjudicated a sexually violent predator to obtain judicial review and release. *Hendricks*, 521 U.S. 346, at 353.

Leroy Hendricks was the first person committed under these provisions. Hendricks challenged his commitment and ultimately sought review of it before the United States Supreme Court.

KANSAS *v.* HENDRICKS
521 U.S. 346 (1997)

Thomas, J. delivered the opinion of the Court, in which Rehnquist, C.J., and O'Connor, Scalia, and Kennedy, JJ. joined. Breyer, J., filed a dissenting opinion, in which Stevens and Souter, JJ., joined and in which Ginsburg, J. joined in parts.

(Thomas, J.) In 1994, Kansas enacted the Sexually Violent Predator Act, which establishes procedures for the civil commitment of persons who, due to a "mental abnormality"[2] or a "personality disorder," are likely to engage in "predatory acts of sexual violence." Kan. Stat. Ann. section 59-29a01 *et seq.* (1994). The State invoked the Act for the first time to commit Leroy Hendricks, an inmate who had a long history of sexually molesting children, and who was scheduled for release from prison shortly after the Act became law. . . . [3]

During the trial, Hendricks' own testimony revealed a chilling history of repeated child sexual molestation and abuse, beginning in 1955. . . . [After convictions for several sex offenses involving children ranging from indecent exposure to molestation, Hendricks was sent to prison. After release, on parole, he was rearrested for another sex offense involving a young child.] Attempts were made to treat him for his sexual deviance, and in 1965 he was considered "safe to be at large," and was discharged from a state psychiatric hospital.

Shortly thereafter, however, Hendricks sexually assaulted another young boy and girl. . . . He was again imprisoned in 1967, but he refused to participate in a sex offender treatment program, and thus remained incarcerated until his parole in 1972. Diagnosed as a pedophile, Hendricks entered into, but then abandoned, a treatment program. He testified that despite having received professional help for his pedophilia, he continued to harbor sexual desires for children. Indeed, soon after his 1972 parole, Hendricks [was convicted of sex offenses involving] his own stepdaughter and stepson. . . . As a result of that conviction, he was once again imprisoned, and was serving that sentence when he reached his conditional release date in September 1994.

Hendricks admitted that he had repeatedly abused children whenever he was not confined. He explained that when he "get[s] stressed out," he "can't control the urge" to molest children. Although Hendricks recognized that his behavior harms children, and he hoped he would not sexually molest children again, he stated that the only sure way he could keep from sexually abusing children in the

---

2. "A 'mental abnormality' was defined, in turn, as a 'congenital or acquired condition affecting the emotional or volitional capacity which predisposes the person to commit sexually violent offenses in a degree constituting such person a menace to the health and safety of others.' "

3. If the custodial agency housing the incarcerated individual notified the local prosecutor of the anticipated release of a person who might have met the Act's criteria, and the prosecutor filed a petition seeking involuntary commitment, and a court determined that there was probable cause to believe that the person was a sexually violent predator, then the individual would be professionally evaluated. Following that evaluation, "a trial would be held to determine beyond a reasonable doubt whether the individual was a sexually violent predator."

future was "to die. . . . " The jury unanimously found beyond a reasonable doubt that Hendricks was a sexually violent predator. The trial court subsequently determined, as a matter of state law, that pedophilia qualifies as a "mental abnormality" as defined by the Act, and thus ordered Hendricks committed to the Secretary's custody. . . .

The thrust of Hendricks' argument is that the Act establishes criminal proceedings; hence confinement under it necessarily constitutes punishment. He contends that where, as here, newly enacted "punishment" is predicated upon past conduct for which he has already been convicted and forced to serve a prison sentence, the Constitution's Double Jeopardy and Ex Post Facto Clauses are violated. We are unpersuaded by Hendricks' argument that Kansas has established criminal proceedings.

The categorization of a particular proceeding as civil or criminal "is first of all a question of statutory construction." We must initially ascertain whether the legislature meant the statute to establish "civil" proceedings. If so, we ordinarily defer to the legislature's stated intent. Here, Kansas' objective to create a civil proceeding is evidenced by its placement of the [Sexually Violent Predator] Act within the Kansas probate code . . . , instead of the criminal code, as well as its description of the Act as creating a " *civil commitment procedure*." Kan. Stat. Ann., Article 29 (1994) ("Care and Treatment for Mentally Ill Persons"), section 59-29a01. Nothing on the face of the statute suggests that the legislature sought to create anything other than a civil commitment scheme designed to protect the public from harm.

Although we recognize that a "civil label is not always dispositive," we will reject the legislature's manifest intent only where a party challenging the statute provides "the clearest proof" that "the statutory scheme [is] so punitive either in purpose or effect as to negate [the State's] intention" to deem it "civil." In those limited circumstances, we will consider the statute to have established criminal proceedings for constitutional purposes. Hendricks, however, has failed to satisfy this heavy burden.

As a threshold matter, commitment under the Act does not implicate either of the two primary objectives of criminal punishment: retribution or deterrence. The Act's purpose is not retributive because it does not affix culpability for prior criminal conduct. Instead such conduct is used solely for evidentiary purposes, either to demonstrate that a "mental abnormality" exists or to support a finding of future dangerousness. . . .

Moreover, unlike a criminal statute, no finding of scienter is required to commit an individual who is found to be a sexually violent predator; instead, the commitment determination is made based on a "mental abnormality" or "personality disorder" rather than on one's criminal intent. The existence of a scienter requirement is customarily an important element in distinguishing criminal from civil statutes. The absence of such a requirement here is evidence that confinement under the statute is not intended to be retributive.

Nor can it be said that the legislature intended the Act to function as a deterrent. Those persons committed under the Act are, by definition, suffering from a "mental abnormality" or a "personality disorder" that prevents them from exercising adequate control over their behavior. Such persons are unlikely to be deterred by the threat of confinement.

QUESTIONS

1. How should "punishment" be defined? What criteria does the Court in *Hendricks* use to define it? What role does the definition of "punishment" play in resolving *Hendricks'* constitutional arguments?

2. Consider the following dictionary definition of punishment: "Punishment: . . . 3. a penalty inflicted for an offense or fault." Random House Webster's College Dictionary (2001). How does the Court's definition of "punishment" compare to this dictionary definition?

3. Section 59-29a01 of the Kansas Sexually Violent Predator Act describes the Act as a "civil commitment procedure for the long term care and treatment of the sexually violent predator." What if Kansas failed to provide treatment to a particular person committed as a sexually violent predator? Would such failure transform that person's commitment into punishment?

PROBLEMS

2.1 Geoffrey is arrested and charged with a violent carjacking. The evidence in the case is strong and the grand jury returns an indictment. Geoffrey asks the trial judge to release him on bail prior to and during his trial. Geoffrey is denied bail and held in the county jail for three and a half months prior to and during his trial. Does his incarceration constitute punishment? What if the reason for the denial is risk of flight? What if the denial is based on the danger of his committing another carjacking or other violent crime? If Geoffrey is convicted, should he receive credit against his carjacking sentence for the three and a half months he spent incarcerated prior to being convicted?

2.2 James and Karen are convicted sex offenders about to be released from prison. Upon release, the state requires each to register as a sexual offender. Because James committed an aggravated sexual offense, his obligation to register continues for the rest of his life. Since Karen's offense was not aggravated, her registration obligation lasts 15 years. Each must register in person four times every year at the local police station and provide detailed current information, including the names and addresses of their places of employment. The state then makes this information available to the public on a Web site. Do these registration requirements constitute punishment? In enacting the registration requirement, the state legislature found that " 'sex offenders posed a high risk of reoffending,' and identified 'protecting the public from sex offenders' as the 'primary governmental interest of the law.' "

2.3 Police find a greenhouse with 100 marijuana plants growing in the backyard of the defendant's $750,000 home. Inside the home, they find marijuana leaves drying on the back porch and in the sunroom. Prosecutors uncover documents indicating that, in addition to serving as the primary residence for the defendant's family, the home has served as the location used for drying the marijuana for the past two years. Prosecutors seek to forfeit the home to the government on the theory that it was being used to facilitate the unlawful processing and distribution of marijuana. Prosecutors indict the defendant for the felony violation of cultivating marijuana. A jury convicts the defendant and the judge sentences the defendant to four years in prison and a fine of $10,000. Subsequent to the sentencing, the prosecution institutes a civil proceeding against the property seeking forfeiture of the home to the government under a statute that reads:

21 United States Code § 881 (2003)

(a) Subject property. The following shall be subject to forfeiture to the United States and no property right shall exist in them: . . .
   (7) All real property, including any right, title, and interest (including any leasehold interest) in the whole of any lot or tract of land and any appurtenances or improvements, which is used, or intended to be used, in any manner or part, to commit, or to facilitate the commission of, a violation of this title punishable by more than one year's imprisonment.

Is forfeiture under this statute punishment for purposes of the Double Jeopardy Clause of the Federal Constitution? If you were the judge in the forfeiture case, how would you rule?

(Problem 2.3 is adapted from United States v. Ursery, 518 U.S. 267 (1996))

C. WHY PUNISH?

PROBLEMS

2.4 Monica was a member in the 1970s of a radical group called the People's Liberation Army (PLA), which was bitterly opposed to the United States war in Vietnam. Monica helped plan the bombing of a police car in retaliation for police killing several PLA members in a shootout at a PLA hideout. She did not actually plant the bomb, but assisted those who did by obtaining materials for the bomb and acting as a lookout when the bomb was placed under a police car. The police discovered the bomb before it exploded and no one was injured. Shortly thereafter, Monica disappeared and remained a fugitive for over 25 years. Recently she was arrested and prosecuted for her part in the attempted bombing. In the past 25 years, Monica changed her name, married, and had three children. She remained a committed social activist, became involved in local politics and community theater, and did charity work such as reading to blind people and serving meals at a local soup kitchen. She engaged in no criminal conduct during the past 25 years. Monica is tried and convicted for her role in the bombing plot and faces a sentence of up to 15 years in prison. Should Monica be punished? If so, what punishment should she receive? Explain.

2.5 Sam is a wealthy businessman charged with felony vehicular homicide, which carries a potential seven-year maximum sentence. The evidence in the case shows that Sam, while driving his Chevy Suburban home from a dinner party at which he had had a great deal to drink, hit a homeless man crossing the street in a pedestrian crosswalk. After realizing he had hit and seriously injured the man, Sam fled, leaving the man to die in the street. A witness saw the accident and gave Sam's license plate number to the police. The typical sentence for such a homicide is two to three years in jail. Although he has previously shown no interest in philanthropy, Sam offers to build a homeless shelter which would house up to 100 men and set up a trust fund to provide food, clothing, medical care, and job training to the shelter's residents. The total cost of Sam's proposed philanthropic project is $15 million. In return, Sam's lawyer asks that Sam be allowed to plead guilty to a misdemeanor drunk driving charge and serve no jail time. The county desperately needs the homeless shelter. Sam has a prior record of three misdemeanor drunk driving convictions. Should the district attorney accept Sam's guilty plea offer? Explain.

2.6 Section 154 of the Imperial Code, enacted by the Inter-Galactic Empire in the year 2041, provides:

> Any adult convicted of possession or sale of a controlled substance is guilty of a felony punishable by between 10 to 20 years imprisonment on a correctional planet doing hard labor.

Controlled substances are defined elsewhere in the Code to include such items as cocaine, heroin, alcohol, and tobacco. The Code also makes clear that the term of imprisonment imposed for violation of the statute is not to be served by the offender, but by a member of the offender's family, such as a spouse, child, or parent. Criteria for choosing the family member to serve the sentence are supplied in the Code with the aim of selecting that person in the offender's family, the imprisonment of whom will cause the most pain and grief to the offender. Can such a sentencing provision be justified in terms of the purposes of punishment?

2.7 Once the decision is made to criminalize the use of a drug such as heroin or cocaine, should those who purchase and use the drug be punished as well as those who distribute and sell the drug? If so, should the punishment be the same for users and sellers? Or should one group be punished more severely than the other?

2.8 John, the priest of the local parish, has admitted molesting five altar boys over the last fifteen years, when the boys were each nine or ten years old. In each instance, he would invite the boy to pray with him and then molest the child. He warned the children not to tell anyone and that the molestation was their penance for misbehavior. The statute of limitations has passed for all but one count of molestation of one of the children. John has pled guilty to that one count. Punishment for that count ranges from probation with no jail time to ten years in state prison. How should the judge sentence John?

2.9   Same facts as in Problem 2.8, but at the sentencing hearing, evidence reveals that John was himself victimized by a priest when John was an altar boy. That priest molested John repeatedly for a period of five years. John had never told anyone of the molestation until he began counseling as a result of the pending criminal case. Should this information affect John's sentencing? If so, how and why? If not, why not?

2.10 Until last month, Larry was the CEO of Oilton, a major corporation in the field of oil and gas. Larry has pled no contest to violating a federal statute that bans trading stock based on insider information. Larry's stock trades totaled a million shares of company stock. He sold the stock the day before the company disclosed its accounting manipulations, which forced it to revise its bottom line from substantial profitability to substantial debt. The stock plummeted from the high of $50 at which Larry sold to 25 cents on the day of the news. Most employees lost their pension plans and their jobs. Larry, on the other hand, made $50 million before resigning as CEO. The crime to which Larry pled no contest has a penalty range from probation with no jail or restitution to ten years in prison. How should Larry be punished?

How would each of the problems above be resolved under the following statutes?

California Penal Code Annotated § 1170(a)(1) (*2002*)

The Legislature finds and declares that the purpose of imprisonment for crime is punishment. This purpose is best served by terms proportionate to the seriousness of the offense with provision for uniformity in the sentences of offenders committing the same offense under similar circumstances. The Legislature further finds and declares that the elimination of disparity and the provision of uniformity of sentences can best be achieved by determinate sentences fixed by statute in proportion to the seriousness of the offense as determined by the Legislature to be imposed by the court with specified discretion.

Edward Livingston   *A System of Penal Law for the United States of America 2 (1828)*

Vengeance is unknown to the law. The only object of punishment is to prevent the commission of offences: it should be calculated to operate,

First, on the delinquent, so as by seclusion to deprive him of the present means, and by habits of industry and temperance, of any future desire to repeat the offence.

Secondly, on the rest of the community, so as to deter them by the example, from a like contravention of the laws. No punishments, greater than are necessary to effect these ends, ought to be inflicted.

Alaska Code of Criminal Procedure § 12.55.65.005   *Declaration of Purpose*

The purpose of this chapter is to provide the means for determining the appropriate sentence to be imposed upon conviction of an offense. The legislature finds that the elimination of unjustified disparity in sentences and the attainment of reasonable uniformity in sentences can best be achieved through a sentencing framework fixed by statute as provided in this chapter. In imposing sentence, the court shall consider

(1) the seriousness of the defendant's present offense in relation to other offenses;

(2) the prior criminal history of the defendant and the likelihood of rehabilitation;

(3) the need to confine the defendant to prevent further harm to the public;

(4) the circumstances of the offense and the extent to which the offense harmed the victim or endangered the public safety or order;

(5) the effect of the sentence to be imposed in deterring the defendant or other members of society from future criminal conduct;

(6) the effect of the sentence to be imposed as a community condemnation of the criminal act and as a reaffirmation of societal norms; and

(7) the restoration of the victim and the community.

One can offer a variety of reasons to punish criminals. We start with a brief overview that defines and contrasts five such rationales: deterrence, incapacitation, rehabilitation, retribution, and denunciation. Later sections of this chapter elaborate on each theory. These justifications, which provide the theoretical underpinnings for criminal law, will be reference points throughout the course.

Retribution seeks to punish a criminal simply because she deserves it. Accordingly, it is often referred to as the "just deserts" theory. As expressed by one of its leading proponents, Immanuel Kant:

> Judicial punishment can never be used merely as a means to promote some other good for the criminal himself or for civil society, but instead must in all cases be imposed on him only on the ground that he has committed a crime; for a human being can never be manipulated merely as a means to the purposes of someone else. . . . He must be found deserving of punishment before any consideration is given to the utility of this punishment for himself or for fellow citizens.[4]

In order for a criminal to receive his just deserts, Kant demanded an "equality" or "sameness of kind" between the crime and the punishment. If, for example, the criminal "has committed murder, he must die."[5]

Deterrence is the notion of reducing crime through the fear of punishment, the "intimidation or terror of the law."[6] The words "deterrence" and "terror" derive from the same Latin verb meaning to frighten or terrify. Specific or special deterrence is the use of punishment to frighten the person actually punished away from reoffending. A five-year prison term imposed on a bank robber for specific deterrence attempts to intimidate the bank robber from robbing another bank after release from prison.

General deterrence aims at frightening potential offenders other than the person punished. At the same time that the bank robber's five-year sentence may specifically deter her from a repeat offense, it may also deter others who learn of her

---

4. Immanuel Kant, *Metaphysical Elements of Justice* 138 (John Ladd Trans., 2d ed. 1999).

5. *Id.*

6. Jeremy Bentham, *Principles of Penal Law* 396 in 1 *The Works of Jeremy Bentham* (John Bowring ed., 1843).

sentence from robbing banks. Under general deterrence, the bank robber's punishment in essence becomes an object lesson to others who are considering following in the bank robber's footsteps. While the five-year sentence cannot specifically deter the bank robber from robbing another bank until after her release from prison, its general deterrent effect should operate on other potential offenders as soon as it is publicly imposed.

Incapacitation similarly seeks to reduce future crime, but operates in a way different from deterrence. Incapacitation aims to deprive the criminal of the ability or opportunity to commit crime. While deterrence assumes its target has the ability and opportunity to commit crime and tries to influence the criminal's choice whether to do so, incapacitation, if successful, denies the offender the choice to commit a crime. Our hypothetical bank robber's five-year jail sentence should incapacitate her for the five years she is in prison, since presumably she will have no opportunity to rob a bank while in prison. Once the robber is released from prison and again has the opportunity to rob a bank, the incapacitating effect of imprisonment ends and, it is hoped, its special deterrent effect begins.

Rehabilitation also seeks to reduce future crime. Rather than intimidating or disabling a criminal, though, rehabilitation seeks to prevent crime by changing the criminal so that he no longer desires to commit crime. If successful, the criminal no longer needs to be deterred or incapacitated.

Deterrence, incapacitation, and rehabilitation have several common features. Each is future-oriented in focusing on what follows from punishment, the *consequences* of its imposition. Each seeks to make punishment *useful* to society by reducing crime. Accordingly, each of these theories is properly described as consequentialist and utilitarian. Jeremy Bentham, the famous nineteenth century philosopher, legal reformer, and originator of modern utilitarianism, for example, proposed preventing a criminal from reoffending "[b]y taking from him the physical power of offending . . . taking away the desire of offending . . . [and] making him afraid of offending."[7] Bentham's proposal, in modern terminology, draws on incapacitation, rehabilitation, and specific deterrence, in that order.

Retribution differs from deterrence, incapacitation, and rehabilitation in several ways. Rather than looking to the future, retribution has a retrospective orientation in that it looks back at the criminal's past acts, mental state, and harm done to assess her just deserts. Second, retribution is not concerned with the consequences or usefulness of punishment, but with the criminal's blameworthiness. Third, where deterrence, incapacitation, and rehabilitation seek to advance society's collective welfare, retribution focuses narrowly on the individual blameworthiness of the criminal.

Denunciation's goal is to express publicly society's disapproval of blameworthy conduct. Accordingly, it shares with retribution a concern with a criminal's blameworthiness, but it also has a utilitarian dimension. Denunciation, for example, seeks through condemnation of a criminal to educate society about and reinforce the norms reflected in the criminal law.

QUESTIONS

1. What theories of punishment are reflected in the statutes that appear earlier in Section C of this chapter?

---

7. *Id.*

2. How are specific deterrence and incapacitation similar? How do they differ?

3. Does prison incapacitate criminals? What crimes does someone in prison retain the capacity to commit? Might a jail sentence have any specific deterrent impact prior to a criminal's release from prison?

4. Reconsider *Kansas v. Hendricks*. What difference would it have made if the Court had determined that incapacitation was a primary purpose of punishment?

5. New York, London, and Tokyo rely on surveillance cameras costing about $56,000 apiece to reduce crime. These cities also deploy fake surveillance cameras, each costing about 10 percent of what a real camera costs. What theories of punishment do the use of real cameras reflect? What about the fake ones?

6. What theories of punishment might be invoked by legislators debating the following:
   (a) abolition of the death penalty.
   (b) a "three strikes" law mandating severe sentences for repeat offenders.
   (c) a statute requiring that adolescents who are charged with violent crimes, such as homicide, be treated in the same way as adult offenders.

PROBLEMS

2.11 Gregory is convicted of using his home computer to receive and exchange child pornography. The judge sentences him to ten years in prison and three years of supervised release. As a condition of his supervised release, the judge bars Gregory from using a computer or the Internet. What theories of punishment might justify this condition?

2.12 A man was convicted in Lahore, Pakistan, of killing 100 children, then mutilating and disposing of their corpses in vats of acid. After conviction, the trial judge announced: "The sentence is that he should be strangled 100 times. . . . His body should be cut in 100 pieces and put in acid, as he did with his victims." Pakistan's Interior Minister expressed doubt that the sentence would actually be carried out because it would offend various international conventions on human rights to which Pakistan is a signatory.[8] What theories of punishment might have motivated the judge to impose such a sentence?

2.13 Paul, a high school wrestling coach, is facing a potential 17-year prison sentence for molesting nearly two dozen boys. To avoid the lengthy prison sentence and convince the judge to put him on probation, Paul tells the judge that "if it means I have to have a surgical procedure so I have no sexuality, I will do that."[9] If such a surgical procedure were imposed as a condition of probation, what theories of punishment might it serve?

2.14 June is convicted of the premeditated murder of her husband. June was having an affair and killed her husband to collect on a large insurance policy and remove him as an obstacle to her being able to marry her lover. The jurisdiction has a death penalty, and the prosecutor

---

8. For Killing 100 Children: *To Be Cut in 100 pieces*, N.Y. Times, March 17, 2000, at A10.

9. James Ewinger, *Sex Offenders Bid for Freedom Rejected*, Cleveland Plain Dealer, Sept. 20, 1995, at 1B.

concludes that June is an appropriate candidate for it. But June's
lawyer approaches the prosecutor with an offer. If the prosecutor forgoes the death penalty, June will agree to life imprisonment. She will
also volunteer to be a subject for dangerous medical experiments the
results of which could ultimately save hundreds of lives. The experiments are so dangerous that medical researchers have so far been
unable find a human subject. According to the theories of punishment,
should the prosecutor accept June's offer?

UNITED STATES *v.* BERGMAN
416 F. Supp. 496 (S.D.N.Y. 1976)

FRANKEL, District Judge.

Defendant is being sentenced upon his plea of guilty to two counts of an 11-
count indictment. The sentencing proceeding is unusual in some respects. It has
been the subject of more extensive submissions, written and oral, than this court
has ever received upon such an occasion. The court has studied some hundreds of
pages of memoranda and exhibits, plus scores of volunteered letters. A broad array
of issues has been addressed. Imaginative suggestions of law and penology have
been tendered. . . . It seems fitting now to report in writing the reasons upon which
the court concludes that defendant must be sentenced to a term of four months in
prison.

I. DEFENDANT AND HIS CRIMES

Defendant appeared until the last couple of years to be a man of unimpeachably
high character, attainments, and distinction. A doctor of divinity and an ordained
rabbi, [people around the world have acclaimed him] for his works of public philanthropy, private charity, and leadership in educational enterprises. Scores of letters
have come to the court from across this and other countries reporting debts of personal gratitude to him for numerous acts of extraordinary generosity. (The court
has also received a kind of petition, with fifty-odd signatures, in which the signers,
based upon learning acquired as newspaper readers, denounce the defendant and
urge a severe sentence. Unlike the pleas for mercy, which appear to reflect unques-
tioned facts inviting compassion, this document should and will be disregarded.) In
addition to his good works, defendant has managed to amass considerable wealth
in the ownership and operation of nursing homes, in real estate ventures, and in a
course of substantial investments.

Beginning about two years ago, investigations of nursing homes in this area,
including questions of fraudulent claims for Medicaid funds, drew to a focus
upon this defendant among several others. The results that concern us were the
present indictment and two state indictments. After extensive pretrial proceedings,
defendant embarked upon elaborate plea negotiations with both state and federal
prosecutors. A state guilty plea and the instant plea were entered in March of this
year. . . .

For purposes of the sentence now imposed, the precise details of the charges,
and of defendant's carefully phrased admissions of guilt, are not matters of prime
importance. Suffice it to say that the plea on Count One (carrying a maximum of

five years in prison and $10,000 fine) confesses defendant's knowing and wilful participation in a scheme to defraud the United States in various ways, including the presentation of wrongfully padded claims for payments under the Medicaid program to defendant's nursing homes. Count Three, for which the guilty plea carries a theoretical maximum of three more years in prison and another $5,000 fine, is a somewhat more "technical" charge. Here, defendant admits to having participated in the filing of a partnership return that was false and fraudulent in failing to list people who had bought partnership interests from him in one of his nursing homes, had paid for such interests, and had made certain capital withdrawals.

The conspiracy to defraud, as defendant has admitted it, is by no means the worst of its kind; it is by no means as flagrant or extensive as has been portrayed in the press; it is evidently less grave than other nursing-home wrongs for which others have been convicted or publicized. At the same time, the sentence, as defendant has acknowledged, is imposed for two federal felonies including, as the more important, a knowing and purposeful conspiracy to mislead and defraud the Federal Government.

THE GUIDING PRINCIPLES OF SENTENCING

Proceeding through the short list of the supposed justifications for criminal sanctions, defense counsel urge that no licit purpose could be served by defendant's incarceration. Some of these arguments are plainly sound; others are not.

The court agrees that this defendant should not be sent to prison for "rehabilitation." Apart from the patent inappositeness of the concept to this individual, this court shares the growing understanding that no one should ever be sent to prison for rehabilitation. That is to say, nobody who would not otherwise be locked up should suffer that fate on the incongruous premise that it will be good for him or her. Imprisonment is punishment. Facing the simple reality should help us to be civilized. It is less agreeable to confine someone when we deem it an affliction rather than a benefaction. If someone must be imprisoned—for other, valid reasons—we should seek to make rehabilitative resources available to him or her. But the goal of rehabilitation cannot fairly serve in itself as grounds for the sentence to confinement. . . .

Equally clearly, this defendant should not be confined to incapacitate him. He is not dangerous. It is most improbable that he will commit similar, or any, offenses in the future. There is no need for "specific deterrence."

Contrary to counsel's submissions, however, two sentencing considerations demand a prison sentence in this case:

First, the aim of *general deterrence*, the effort to discourage similar wrongdoing by others through a reminder that the law's warnings are real and that the grim consequence of imprisonment is likely to follow from crimes of deception for gain like those defendant has admitted.

Second, the related, but not identical, concern that any lesser penalty would, in the words of the Model Penal Code, § 7.01(1)(c), "depreciate the seriousness of the defendant's crime."

Resisting the first of these propositions, defense counsel invoke Immanuel Kant's axiom that "one man ought never to be dealt with merely as a means subservient to the purposes of another." In a more novel, but equally futile, effort, counsel urge that a sentence for general deterrence "would violate the Eighth Amendment proscription against cruel and unusual punishment." Treating the latter point first, because it is a short subject, it may be observed simply that if general deterrence as a sentencing purpose were now to be outlawed, as against a near unanimity of views among state and federal jurists, the bolt would have to come from a place higher than this.

As for Dr. Kant, it may well be that defense counsel mistake his meaning in the present context. Whether or not that is so, and without pretending to authority on that score, we take the widely accepted stance that a criminal punished in the interest of general deterrence is not being employed *"merely* as a means. . . . " Reading Kant to mean that every man must be deemed *more* than the instrument of others, and must "always be treated as an end in himself," the humane principle is not offended here. Each of us is served by the enforcement of the law — not least a person like the defendant in this case, whose wealth and privileges, so long enjoyed, are so much founded upon law. More broadly, we are driven regularly in our ultimate interests as members of the community to use ourselves and each other, in war and in peace, for social ends. One who has transgressed against the criminal laws is certainly among the more fitting candidates for a role of this nature. This is no arbitrary selection. Warned in advance of the prospect, the transgressor has chosen, in the law's premises, "between keeping the law required for society's protection or paying the penalty."

But the whole business, defendant argues further, is guesswork; we are by no means certain that deterrence "works." The position is somewhat overstated; there is, in fact, some reasonably "scientific" evidence for the efficacy of criminal sanctions as deterrents, at least as against some kinds of crimes. Moreover, the time is not yet here when all we can "know" must be quantifiable and digestible by computers. The shared wisdom of generations teaches meaningfully, if somewhat amorphously, that the utilitarians have a point; we do, indeed, lapse often into rationality and act to seek pleasure and avoid pain. It would be better, to be sure, if we had more certainty and precision. Lacking these comforts, we continue to include among our working hypotheses a belief (with some concrete evidence in its support) that crimes like those in this case — deliberate, purposeful, continuing, non-impulsive, and committed for profit — are among those most likely to be generally deterrable by sanctions most shunned by those exposed to temptation.

The idea of avoiding depreciation of the seriousness of the offense implicates two or three thoughts, not always perfectly clear or universally agreed upon, beyond the idea of deterrence. It should be proclaimed by the court's judgment that the offenses are grave, not minor or purely technical. Some attention must be paid to the demand for equal justice; it will not do to leave the penalty of imprisonment a dead letter as against "privileged" violators while it is employed regularly, and with vigor, against others. There probably is in these conceptions an element of retributiveness, as counsel urge. And retribution, so denominated, is in some disfavor as a reason for punishment. It remains a factor, however, as Holmes perceived, and as is known to anyone who talks to judges, lawyers, defendants, or people generally. It may become more palatable, and probably more humanely understood, under the rubric of "deserts" or "just desserts." However the concept is formulated, we have not yet reached a state, supposing we ever should, in which the infliction of punishments for crime may be divorced generally from ideas of blame-worthiness, recompense, and proportionality.

AN ALTERNATIVE, "BEHAVIORAL SANCTION"

Resisting prison above all else, defense counsel included in their thorough memorandum on sentencing two proposals for what they call a "constructive," and therefore a "preferable" form of "behavioral sanction." One is a plan for Dr. Bergman to create and run a program of Jewish vocational and religious high school training. The other is for him to take charge of a "Committee on Holocaust Studies," again concerned with education at the secondary school level.

A third suggestion was made orally at yesterday's sentencing hearing. It was proposed that Dr. Bergman might be ordered to work as a volunteer in some established agency as a visitor and aide to the sick and the otherwise incapacitated. The proposal was that he could read, provide various forms of physical assistance, and otherwise give comfort to afflicted people.

No one can doubt either the worthiness of these proposals or Dr. Bergman's ability to make successes of them. But both of the carefully formulated "sanctions" in the memorandum involve work of an honorific nature, not unlike that done in other projects to which the defendant has devoted himself in the past. It is difficult to conceive of them as "punishments" at all. The more recent proposal is somewhat more suitable in character, but it is still an insufficient penalty. The seriousness of the crimes to which Dr. Bergman has pled guilty demands something more than "requiring" him to lend his talents and efforts to further philanthropic enterprises. It remains open to him, of course, to pursue the interesting suggestions later on as a matter of unforced personal choice.

"MEASURING" THE SENTENCE

In cases like this one, the decision of greatest moment is whether to imprison or not. As reflected in the eloquent submissions for defendant, the prospect of the closing prison doors is the most appalling concern; the feeling is that the length of the sojourn is a lesser question once that threshold is passed. Nevertheless, the setting of a term remains to be accomplished. And in some respects it is a subject even more perplexing, unregulated, and unprincipled.

Days and months and years are countable with a sound of exactitude. But there can be no exactitude in the deliberations from which a number emerges. Without pretending to a nonexistent precision, the court notes at least the major factors.

The criminal behavior, as has been noted, is blatant in character and unmitigated by any suggestion of necessitous circumstance or other pressures difficult to resist. However metaphysicians may conjure with issues about free will, it is a fundamental premise of our efforts to do criminal justice that competent people, possessed of their faculties, make choices and are accountable for them. In this sometimes harsh light, the case of the present defendant is among the clearest and least relieved. Viewed against the maxima Congress ordained, and against the run of sentences in other federal criminal cases, it calls for more than a token sentence.

On the other side are factors that take longer to enumerate. Defendant's illustrious public life and works are in his favor, though diminished, of course, by what this case discloses. This is a first, probably a last, conviction. Defendant is 64 years old and in imperfect health, though by no means so ill, from what the court is told, that he could be expected to suffer inordinately more than many others of advanced years who go to prison.

Defendant invokes an understandable, but somewhat unworkable, notion of "disparity." He says others involved in recent nursing home fraud cases have received relatively light sentences for behavior more culpable than his. He lays special emphasis upon one defendant whose frauds appear indeed to have involved larger amounts and who was sentenced to a maximum of six months' incarceration, to be confined for that time only on week nights, not on week days or weekends. This court has examined the minutes of that sentencing proceeding and finds the case distinguishable in material respects. But even if there were a threat of such disparity as defendant warns against, it could not be a major weight on the scales.

Our sentencing system, deeply flawed, is characterized by disparity. We are to seek to "individualize" sentences, but no clear or clearly agreed standards govern the individualization. The lack of meaningful criteria does indeed leave sentencing judges far too much at large. But the result, with its nagging burdens on conscience, cannot be meaningfully alleviated by allowing any handful of sentences in a short series to fetter later judgments. The point is easy, of course, where Sentence No. 1 or Sentences 1-5 are notably harsh. It cannot be that a later judge, disposed to more leniencies, should feel in any degree "bound." The converse is not identical, but it is not totally different. The net of this is that this court has considered and has given some weight to the trend of the other cited sentences (though strict logic might call for none), but without treating them as forceful "precedents" in any familiar sense.

How, then, the particular sentence adjudged in this case? As has been mentioned, the case calls for a sentence that is more than nominal. Given the other circumstances, however — including that this is a first offense, by a man no longer young and not perfectly well, where danger of recidivism is not a concern — it verges on cruelty to think of confinement for a term of years. We sit, to be sure, in a nation where prison sentences of extravagant length are more common than they are almost anywhere else. By that light, the term imposed today is not notably long. For this sentencing court, however, for a nonviolent first offense involving no direct assaults or invasions of others' security (as in bank robbery, narcotics, etc.), it is a stern sentence. For people like Dr. Bergman, who might be disposed to engage in similar wrongdoing, it should be sufficiently frightening to serve the major end of general deterrence. For all but the profoundly vengeful, it should not depreciate the seriousness of his offenses.

Punishment in or for the Media

Much of defendant's sentencing memorandum is devoted to the extensive barrage of hostile publicity to which he has been subjected during the years before and since his indictment. He argues, and it appears to be undisputed, that the media (and people desiring to be featured in the media) have vilified him for many kinds of evildoing of which he has in fact been innocent. Two main points are made on this score with respect to the problem of sentencing.

First, as has been mentioned, counsel expressed the concern that the court may be pressured toward severity by the force of the seeming public outcry. That the court should not allow itself to be affected in this way is clear beyond discussion. Nevertheless, it is not merely permissible, but entirely wholesome and responsible, for counsel to bring the expressed concern out in the open. Whatever our ideals and mixed images about judges, it would be naïve to doubt that judges have sometimes been swept by a sense of popular demand toward draconian sentencing decisions. It cannot hurt for the sentencing judge to be reminded of this and cautioned about it. There can be no guarantees. The sentencer must confront and regulate himself. But it bears reaffirmance that the court must seek to discount utterly the fact of notoriety in passing its judgment upon the defendant. Defense counsel cite reported opinions of this court reflecting what happens in a large number of unreported cases, by the present sentencer and many others, in which "unknown" defendants have received prison sentences, longer or shorter than today's, for white-collar or comparably nonviolent crimes. The overall run of cases with all their individual variations, will reflect, it is hoped, earnest efforts to hew to the principle of equal treatment, with or without publicity.

Defendant's second point about his public humiliation is the frequently heard contention that he should not be incarcerated because he "has been punished enough." The thought is not without some initial appeal. If punishment were wholly or mainly retributive, it might be a weighty factor. In the end, however, it must be a matter of little or no force. Defendant's notoriety should not in the last analysis serve to lighten, any more than it may be permitted to aggravate, his sentence. The fact that he has been pilloried by journalists is essentially a consequence of the prestige and privileges he enjoyed before he was exposed as a wrongdoer. The long fall from grace was possible only because of the height he had reached. The suffering from loss of public esteem reflects a body of opinion that the esteem had been, in at least some measure, wrongly bestowed and enjoyed. It is not possible to justify the notion that this mode of nonjudicial punishment should be an occasion for leniency not given to a defendant who never basked in such an admiring light at all. The quest for both the appearance and the substance of equal justice prompts the court to discount the thought that the public humiliation serves the function of imprisonment.

Writing, as judges rarely do, about a particular sentence concentrates the mind with possibly special force upon the experience of the sentencer as well as the person sentenced. Consigning someone to prison, this defendant or any other, "is a sad necessity." There are impulses of avoidance from time to time — toward a personally gratifying lenience or toward an opposite extreme. But there is, obviously, no place for private impulse in the judgment of the court. The course of justice must be sought with such objective rationality as we can muster, tempered with mercy, but obedient to the law, which, we do well to remember, is all that empowers a judge to make other people suffer.

QUESTIONS

1. Should any of the following factors have affected Bergman's sentence?
   (a) his age
   (b) his wealth
   (c) the publicity his case attracted
If not, explain why each was irrelevant to the purposes of punishment. If so, should it have increased or decreased his sentence? Explain why in terms of the purposes of punishment.

2. How does Judge Frankel view the question of "free will"?

3. Which theories of punishment depend on a belief in "free will"?

1. Retribution

Immanuel Kant, THE METAPHYSICAL ELEMENTS OF JUSTICE: PART I OF THE METAPHYSICS OF MORALS   100-102 (John Ladd Trans., 1965)

The law concerning punishment is a categorical imperative. . . . If this is so, what . . . of the proposal to permit a criminal who has been condemned to death to remain alive, if, after consenting to allow danger-ous experiments to be made on him, he . . . survives . . . and if doctors thereby obtain new information that benefits the community? Any court of justice would repudiate such a proposal with scorn . . . for [legal] justice ceases to be justice if it can be bought for a price.

What kind and what degree of punishment does public legal justice adopt as its principle and standard? None other than the principle of equal-ity. . . . Accordingly, any undeserved evil that you inflict on someone else among the people is one that you do to yourself. . . . [I]f you steal from him, you steal from yourself. . . . Only the Law of retribution (*jus talio-nis*) can determine exactly the kind and degree of punishment; it must be well understood, however, that this determination [must be made] in the chambers of a court of justice (and not in your private judgment). . . .

But what is meant by the statement: "If you steal from him, you steal from yourself"? Inasmuch as someone steals, he makes the ownership of everyone else insecure, and hence he robs himself (in accordance with the Law of retribution) of the security of any possible ownership.

Consider the following newspaper account of a sentencing hearing in a death penalty case.

Judge Agrees to Convict's Death Plea[10]

A confessed murderer who cooperated with his prosecutor and said he wanted to be sentenced to death has gotten his wish.

After a 7½-day non-jury trial, Santa Clara Superior Court Judge Daniel Creed sentenced Valdamair Fred Morelos to death on Friday. Creed said he was troubled by the process but agreed with Morelos and the prosecutor that death was the proper sentence.

"Mr. Morelos has indicated that if he doesn't receive the death penalty, he intends to kill again," the judge said.

Morelos, 35, admitted the 1992 robbery, rape and torture murder of a 28-year-old man after a dispute over a $40 drug debt.

After his arrest, he expressed a desire to be executed and tried to plead guilty. His public defender refused to consent, saying he had questions about Morelos' mental condition and believed there was a defense to the capital charge.

Prohibited by state law from pleading guilty to a capital crime without his lawyer's consent, Morelos fired his lawyer but was faced with another state law barring a guilty plea to a capital charge without a lawyer. He went to trial but made it clear he was putting up no defense.

---

10. Associated Press, *In Brief*, The Recorder 4 (Jan. 23, 1996).

Morelos provided Deputy District Attorney John Schon with details of the crimes and his motives during the trial. He testified Wednesday that he didn't want to live the rest of his life in prison.

"My personal feelings are, I believe, you kill, you know, the state has a right to retribution: eye for an eye, tooth for a tooth," Morelos said.

Creed said Morelos was mentally competent to stand trial and act as his own lawyer. He scheduled a Feb. 21 hearing for possible motions for a new trial or reconsideration of the verdict, despite Morelos' insistence that he would file no such motions.

David Dolinko, THREE MISTAKES OF RETRIBUTIVISM

39 UCLA L. Rev. 1623, 1629, 1630-1631, 1632-1633, 1635-1636, 1638-1642 (1992)

It is widely acknowledged that retributivism, once treated as an irrational vestige of benighted times, has enjoyed in recent years so vigorous a revival that it can fairly be regarded today as the leading philosophical justification of the institution of punishment. . . .

In general, the sense of "fittingness" or "propriety" inherent in someone's *getting* what she deserves is a very poor guide to whether it is permissible to give her what she deserves. It is "fitting" that proponents of antidemocratic ideologies should themselves be denied freedom of speech, but we do not take such action, nor believe it morally permissible to do so. It is "appropriate" that a law student who cuts classes, reads none of the assigned material, and relics on a commercial outline should do badly in my course — but if he aces my exam, it is not permissible for me to lie about this and flunk him anyway. Roger Wertheimer suggests that "anyone with a sense of justice" would agree "that this would be a better, more fittingly ordered world if the winners [of a state lottery] were the honest, the kind, and the decent rather than the ne'er-do-wells" — yet we do not think it permissible for officials to rig the lottery to ensure such "fitting" results. George Sher, in his booklength study of the concept of desert, isolates the core of the problem: "When we say that persons deserve things, we generally answer questions about what it would be good for them to have; when we attribute rights, we generally answer questions about what others ought to do or refrain from doing." Hence it is entirely possible for a person to deserve treatment which it would nevertheless violate his rights to be given, and which, therefore, no one would be morally at liberty to inflict upon him. . . .

DOES RETRIBUTIVISM "USE" PERSONS?

Retributivists frequently argue that their theory is superior to the deterrence theory because, unlike the latter, it avoids "using" people in a morally improper manner. This argument, which stems from Kant, has been concisely described by Jeffrie Murphy:

[T]he retributivist seeks, not primarily for the socially useful punishment, but for the *just* punishment, the punishment that the criminal (given his wrongdoing) deserves or merits, the punishment that the society has a right to inflict and the criminal a right to demand. Only a theory of punishment built on these values, so a common argument goes, will respect persons as individuals of special worth — a worth that is compromised if we feel free simply to use them (as utilitarian deterrence theory appears willing to use them) for the social good.[30]

. . . [R]etributivism itself can be accused of using convicted offenders, and thus stripped of its cloak of Kantian respectability. This can be done in two ways — by appealing to the inevitability of mistaken convictions, or by attacking the very notion that we can know what the offender truly deserves.

First, since any actual criminal justice system is inherently fallible, any such system will inevitably inflict punishment on some people who are actually innocent and thus do not deserve it. Unless the retributivist rejects all possible systems of legal punishment, therefore, she is endorsing a system that she knows will condemn and punish innocent people. Presumably, she believes that the unjustified punishment of these innocents must be accepted to avoid the far greater injustice that leaving all of the guilty unpunished would produce. But isn't the retributivist then "using" those actually innocent persons who end up wrongly condemned? To be sure, she is ignorant of exactly who these unfortunate persons are. Yet this seems irrelevant: the terrorists who blew up Pan Am Flight 103 over Lockerbie, Scotland in 1988 were "using" the hapless passengers to score a political point even if (as is likely) they were unaware of the passengers' identities. The retributivist remains "willing to trade the welfare of the innocents who are punished by mistake for the greater good of the punishment of the guilty" and thus, it would seem, committed to sacrificing — "using" — the mistakenly convicted for the benefit of society in general. . . .

Even if the retributivist can escape the charge that her willingness to accept a fallible punishment system implies a willingness to "use" the mistakenly convicted, her claim not to use people remains open to attack. For that claim rests on the premise that retributive punishment gives criminals *what they deserve*. It is because punishment gives the criminal what he deserves that the retributivist can insist she is treating the criminal as a full-fledged person, a moral agent, and not a mere tool to be manipulated to deter others or to slake society's thirst for revenge:

> It is the fact that a person has committed a moral offence which, in the first instance, constitutes the justification for his being punished. It is what is due to him, what is his desert. Appeals to grounds other than this amount to denying a person the claim he has to be considered in his own right as a moral subject.[43]

But the credibility of the claim that deserved punishment does not involve "using" the criminal depends on assuming not merely that the criminal deserves some punishment or other, but that he deserves the *quantity* or *degree* of punishment we are inflicting on him. Suppose, for example, that shoplifting became so widespread that deterrence theorists called for punishing it by life imprisonment in order to bring the problem under control. Retributivists would hardly endorse this proposal even though shoplifting deserves to be punished. Rather, they would condemn this exemplary punishment as a clear example of the deterrence theorist's "using" individuals as means to the goal of crime control by punishing them far beyond their "just deserts." Similarly, retributive theorists think that the moral propriety of increased punishment for recidivists turns on whether prior criminal violations alter what the criminal *deserves* for her present transgression. In short,

---

[30] Jeffrie Murphy, *Retributivism and the State's Interest in Punishment*, in Nomos XXVII: Criminal Justice 156, 158-159 (J. Pennock & J. Chapman eds. 1985).

[43] J. Kleinig, *Punishment and Desert* 66 (1973).

the claim that the *amount* of punishment inflicted on offenders must be what they deserve is crucial to the retributivist claim not to use people as mere means.

Yet it has long been a stock objection to retributivism that there is simply no workable way to determine just *what* punishment a criminal deserves. Retributivists very commonly direct us to make punishments "proportional" to crimes by punishing a more serious crime more severely than a less serious one. Unfortunately, this prescription by itself cannot tell us what punishment any particular crime actually deserves, even if we could rank every crime in a single scale from least to most serious. For the prescription requires only that we assign greater penalties as we ascend the scale of crimes, without either supplying a starting point (the penalty for the least serious offense) or telling us *by how much* to increase the penalty as we move from one crime to the next in the scale. . . .

Try, for instance, to rank the following crimes in order of their "seriousness": attempted residential burglary, trading stock on inside information, negligent vehicular homicide, bribing a mine-safety inspector, possessing an ounce of cocaine, and burning a cross on the lawn of black newcomers to a previously all-white neighborhood. To view this motley assortment along a single dimension of "seriousness" would seem no less difficult than to perceive the inner logic behind the apocryphal Chinese encyclopedist of Jorge Luis Borges's imagination. . . .

Most retributivists, confronted with the intractable problem of specifying the "just deserts" properly to be imposed on anyone in the real world, simply label the problem unimportant. . . . Many retributivists profess similar unconcern with the imprecision of judgments about what specific crimes or criminals deserve. . . . Yet retributivists who insist that their theory does not permit "using people" because the punishments it endorses are those that are truly *deserved* cannot blithely admit "Of course, we have no way of ever knowing what punishment anyone actually deserves"!

An example: in 1983, California raised the prescribed "upper term" for voluntary manslaughter — the penalty to be given if aggravating factors are present — from six to eleven years. Is a killer who is sentenced under the current law receiving what he deserves? Or is he receiving nearly twice what he deserves? Five extra years in state prison is simply too great a differential to be dismissed as a mere matter of detail, irrelevant in assessing the justice of the sentence. Or again: what is a first offender's "just desert" for simple possession of a single marijuana cigarette? California authorizes at most a $100 fine, with no jail time, whereas Texas permits a sentence of up to half a year in jail plus a $1,500 fine. Is Texas "using" marijuana offenders to satisfy the public's increasing antidrug hysteria? A theory that cannot answer such questions as these provides no basis for any claims that convicted criminals are not being "used" when they are punished.

As Professor Dolinko notes, figuring out precisely what punishment a criminal deserves can be difficult. But some judges have invented creative sentences to address this apparent difficulty.

Judge's Comment Raises Cain[11]
A judge's sentence allowing a crime victim to take anything she wants from the thief's house amounts to vigilante justice and legal burglary, critics say.

---

11. Associated Press, *The Recorder* 4 (Oct. 5, 1994).

The judge won't comment on the case because it is still pending. But in a transcript of the hearing, he calls his action "an innovative effort" to teach the defendant a lesson and let her "see what it's like to be taken advantage of and have somebody rip you off."

Vista Municipal Judge David Ryan issued the order Sept. 15, allowing crime victim Sarah Land to take whatever she wanted from the home of welfare mother Tyra Ann Veltri, who had fraudulently used Lang's stolen credit cards.

The San Diego County Public Defender's Office is asking that Ryan's order be overturned.

Veltri was in an Escondido supermarket May 9 when one of her three companions stole the purse of Lang, a store employee. Veltri later used some of Lang's credit car[d]s to buy a $300 vacuum cleaner, shoes for her daughter and jewelry.

QUESTIONS

1. A local radio station is about to interview you as a legal expert on retribution. Summarize this theory and give an example as a sound bite so that your description is comprehensible to a layperson and takes no more than two minutes to complete.

2. What does retribution require the state to do? What does it allow the state to do?

3. What limits, if any, should be placed on the retributive theory? For example, could the state kill someone for stealing under the retributive theory?

4. What punishment would retribution dictate in Problems 2.4-2.10 that appear at the beginning of Section C?

5. Rank the crimes Professor Dolinko lists on a scale from 0 to 10, with 0 being the least deserving and 10 being the most deserving of punishment. How do you justify your ranking?

2. Deterrence

Jeremy Bentham, PRINCIPLES OF PENAL LAW   396, 402, 1 The Works of
Jeremy Bentham (John Bowring ed., 1843)

Pain and pleasure are the great springs of human action. When a man perceives or supposes pain to be the consequence of an act, he is acted upon in such a manner as tends, with a certain force, to withdraw him, as it were, from the commission of that act. If the apparent magnitude, or rather value of that pain be greater than the apparent magnitude or value of the pleasure or good he expects to be the consequence of the act, he will be absolutely prevented from performing it. The mischief which would have ensued from the act, if performed, will also by that means be prevented. . . .

The observation of rules of proportion between crimes and punishments has been objected to as useless, because they seem to suppose, that a spirit of calculation has place among the passions of men, who, it is said, never calculate. But dogmatic as this proposition is, it is altogether false. In matters of importance, every one calculates. Each individual calculates with more or less correctness, according to the degrees of his information, and the power of the motives which actuate him; but all calculate. It would be hard to say that a madman does not calculate. Happily, the passion of cupidity, which on account of its power, its constancy, and its extent, is not formidable to society, is the passion which is most given to calculation. This, therefore, will be more successfully combated, the more carefully the law turns the balance of profit against it.

John J. DiIulio, Jr., HELP WANTED: ECONOMISTS, CRIME AND PUBLIC POLICY   10 J. of Econ. Perspectives 3, 16-17 (Winter 1996)

[W]ork by Fleisher (1995) and other urban ethnographers suggests that today's crime-prone boys are too radically present oriented and self-regarding for any type of conventional criminal deterrence to work.

By radically present oriented, I mean that they are almost completely incapable of deferring gratifications for the sake of future rewards. In their lives, there has never been a stable relationship between doing "what's right" and being rewarded and doing "what's wrong" and being punished. Many, in some cases most, of the adults in their lives have been persons who are themselves deviant, delinquent or criminal. Such discipline as they may have received at the hands of parents or other adults has been almost purely arbitrary: the first three times they commit a given prohibited act, nothing happens; the fourth time they get screamed at; the fifth and sixth times nothing happens; the seventh time they get punched in the head; the eighth time nothing happens; and so on. Those crime-prone kids who abuse alcohol or illegal drugs — and many of them do — become even more radically present oriented. Their lived experience, the most powerful teacher of all, counsels that kids who look ahead, stay in school, and "do the right thing" often end up just as jobless, hopeless and miserable as kids who do crime.

Some economists have begun to take such realities into account. For example, in their fine study of work and crime, Witte and Tauchen (1994 p. 4) model the individual as choosing a level of criminal activity rather than the time to allocate to crime "because studies indicate that most criminal acts are unplanned." They also allow for "the possibility of nonmonetary gains from crime." Such work is clearly a step in the right direction. But the extraordinary degree to which today's young street criminals are present oriented, and the extent to which they do crime for fun as well as for profit, has yet to be taken fully into account by economists. "You never think about doing thirty," one young prisoner told me, "when you don't expect to live to thirty."

I suspect that super-impulsive time orientations are analytically tractable. But imagine a radically present-oriented young man who is also unable to feel joy or pain at the joy or pain of others. He is capable of committing the most heinous acts of physical violence for the most trivial reasons (for example, a perception of slight disrespect) without feeling remorse or losing any sleep. He fears neither the stigma of arrest nor the pains of imprisonment. In prison or out, he lives by the code of the streets, a code that reinforces rather than restrains his hair-trigger mentality. If he is part of a gang, then going to prison is very nearly a good "career move." And the things he gets for behaving criminally in a radically present-oriented, totally self-regarding way — money, drugs, status, sex — are their own immediate rewards. So for as long as his youthful energies hold out, he does what comes naturally: murders, assaults, rapes, robs, burglarizes and deals deadly drugs.

I do not have to "imagine" such young men. I have spent years going in and out of county lockups, jails and prisons. These boys are for real, and more are on the way.

If there is a model of criminal deterrence in the literature that mirrors such behavioral propensities, I have yet to come across it. Until economists develop such a model, the suspicion will remain that their notions of deterrence are valuable solely in the seminar room, that their understanding of crime is purely academic. It will not do to make further refinements to conventional deterrence models. Models that assume that young urban street predators are but a highly impulsive breed of middle-aged economics professors are not only intellectually idle, but (should anyone actually be foolish enough to act on them) downright dangerous. The reality simply does not fit the theory; economists need a new theory. . . .

Using the threat of imprisonment to deter makes assumptions about the quality of individuals' lives outside of prison. Consider the following article.

Jail "Break-In" a Success, Sort Of[12]

A former Washoe County jail inmate wasn't too happy with life on the streets. He was hungry. He missed his two buddies who were still in jail. He wanted back in.

Pedro Fernandez, 32, was found late Wednesday on the roof of the minimum security jail, trying to break in with a metal pipe, Undersheriff Dan Coppa said.

Through an interpreter, Coppa said Fernandez told authorities he spent three days on the streets without food since his earlier release, and that two of his friends were still confined there.

"We took him back," Coppa said.

Fernandez was fed, but also faced charges of trespassing, prowling and property damage.

QUESTIONS

1. A local radio station is about to interview you as a legal expert on deterrence. Summarize the theories of general and specific deterrence as a sound bite and provide examples so that your description is comprehensible to a layperson and takes no more than two minutes to complete.

2. What punishment would deterrence dictate in Problems 2.4-2.10 that appear at the beginning of Section C?

3. Incapacitation

Franklin E. Zimring & Gordon Hawkins, INCAPACITATION: PENAL CONFINEMENT AND THE RESTRAINT OF CRIME   3, v, ix (1995)

Incapacitation now serves as the principal justification for imprisonment in American criminal justice: offenders are imprisoned in the United States to restrain them physically from offending again while they are confined. . . .

---

12. Associated Press, *Jail "Break-In" a Success, Sort of*, The Recorder 6 (Nov. 16, 1992).

Of all the justifications for criminal punishment, the desire to incapacitate is the least complicated, the least studied, and often the most important. . . .

Incapacitation is the theory of punishment that seeks to prevent future crime and avoid its attendant personal and social costs by eliminating or restricting the ability and opportunity of a potential criminal to commit crime. Though much present debate focuses on the use of imprisonment to incapacitate, as in California's "three strikes" approach, other forms of punishment may also be motivated by a desire to incapacitate. The death penalty is one example. Conditions of probation that prevent a convicted embezzler from working in a financial institution or prevent a convicted drunk driver from starting his car unless a breath analyzer attached to the ignition reveals a legally acceptable blood alcohol level also qualify as incapacitation measures.

A major concern about incapacitation as a guide to punishment is that incapacitation requires a prediction about the likelihood of the particular offender committing another crime. How accurate are such predictions? This question is the focus of much concern and debate. Every mistaken prediction punishes someone without need and often at great cost to the person punished and to society.

Reliance on incapacitation as the basis of punishment raises a number of problems beyond the accuracy of predictions of future crime. From a retribution perspective, for example, someone can hardly be blamed for something she has not yet done and may not ever do. Another troubling aspect of incapacitation is its open ended nature. According to Professors Zimring and Hawkins, "the topic of incapacitation as a purpose of penal confinement is not well suited to either unqualified acceptance or total rejection. . . . [I]ncapacitation is impossibly open-ended as a general principle of criminal punishment. If persons who present some threat of future crime are to be confined, why not confine all of them indefinitely? The balance of desert and proportionality with preventive potential, as well as rough calculations of cost and benefit — these are the inescapable elements of decisions about the scope of preventive confinement in modern criminal justice."[13]

Incapacitation strategies take two forms, collective incapacitation and selective incapacitation. "Under *collective* strategies, all persons convicted of a designated offense, say robbery or any second felony conviction, would receive the same sentence, say 5 years. . . . *Selective* strategies would involve individualized sentences based on predictions that particular offenders would commit serious offenses at a high rate if not incarcerated."[14]

Scholars have criticized both collective and selective incapacitation approaches. Consider, for example, the concerns identified about selective incapacitation in the excerpt below.

Jacqueline Cohen, INCAPACITATING CRIMINALS: RECENT RESEARCH FINDINGS   U.S. DOJ National Institute of Justice (1983)

. . . 3. Many of the variables in [selective incapacitation] prediction formulas . . . raise other policy or ethical questions. For example . . . the

---

13. Franklin E. Zimring & Gordon Hawkins, *Incapacitation: Penal Confinement and the Restraint of Crime* ix (1995).

14. Jacqueline Cohen, *Incapacitating Criminals: Recent Research Findings*, U.S. DOJ Natl. Inst. Just. (1983).

formula [of an important and often-cited study, the RAND study,] includes employment information, which many would exclude from consideration at sentencing, along with education and similar factors, as class-based variables that, in effect, discriminate against the poor.

4. Many prediction variables, like education, employment, and residential stability, are associated with race: some minorities are on average less well educated and less stably employed than the white majority. Building such variables into sentencing standards, while not intended to punish minorities more severely, would have that effect. . . .

In the next excerpt, Professor Wilson analyzes three conditions on which the theory of incapacitation relies. In reading the passage, consider whether those are the only three conditions upon which the theory depends.

James Q. Wilson, THINKING ABOUT CRIME   145-147 (2d rev. ed. 1983) (1975)

Incapacitation cannot be the sole purpose of the criminal justice system. . . . But there is one great advantage to incapacitation as a crime control strategy — namely, it does not require us to make any assumptions about human nature. . . .

[I]t works provided at least three conditions are met: some offenders must be repeaters, offenders taken off the streets must not be immediately and completely replaced by new recruits, and prison must not increase the post-release criminal activity of those who have been incarcerated sufficiently to offset the crimes prevented by their stay in prison.

The first condition is surely true. Every study of prison inmates shows that a large fraction (recently, about two-thirds) of them had prior criminal records before their current incarceration; every study of ex-convicts shows that a significant fraction (estimates vary from a quarter to a half) are rearrested for new offenses within a relatively brief period. . . .

The second condition . . . seems plausible. . . . For the kinds of predatory street crimes with which we are concerned — robbery, burglary, auto theft, larceny . . . [, as opposed perhaps to crimes, "which are organized along business lines,"] [n]o one need wait for a "vacancy" to appear before he can find an opportunity to become a criminal. . . .

The third condition . . . is that prisons must not be such successful "schools for crime" that the crimes prevented by incarceration are outnumbered by the increased crimes committed after release attributable to what was learned in prison. . . . In general, there is no evidence that the prison experience makes offenders as a whole more criminal. . . .

QUESTION

Professor Wilson's book, from which the above excerpt was drawn, was published in 1983. Reconsider the 1996 excerpt from Professor DiIulio on the radically present oriented offender, for whom prison might be a "good career move." How might these offenders affect the conditions about incapacitation that Professor Wilson posits?

Professor Wilson suggests that to assess the role of incapacitation we must determine, among other things, "how much crime is reduced by sending offenders to prison. . . . " In the next excerpt, Princeton Professor DiIulio summarizes some of the research on that issue.

John J. DiIulio, Jr., PRISONS ARE A BARGAIN, BY ANY MEASURE
New York Times, Jan. 16, 1996, at A17

[I]f incarceration is not the answer, what, precisely, is the question? If the question is how to prevent at-risk youths from becoming stone-cold predators in the first place, then, of course, incarceration is no solution.

But if the question is how to restrain known convicted criminals from murdering, raping, robbing, assaulting and stealing, then incarceration is a solution, and a highly cost-effective one.

On average, it costs about $25,000 a year to keep a convicted criminal in prison. For that money, society gets four benefits: Imprisonment punishes offenders and expresses society's moral disapproval. It teaches felons and would-be felons a lesson: Do crime, do time. Prisoners get drug treatment and education. And, as the columnist Ben Wattenberg has noted, "A thug in prison can't shoot your sister."

All four benefits count. Increased incarceration explains part of the drop in crime in New York and other cities. As some recent studies show, prisons pay big dividends even if all they deliver is relief from the murder and mayhem that incarcerated felons would be committing if free.

In two Brookings Institution studies, in 1991 and 1995, the Harvard economist Anne Piehl and I found that prisoners in New Jersey and Wisconsin committed an average of 12 crimes a year when free, excluding all drug crimes. In other studies, the economist Steven D. Levitt of the National Bureau of Economic Research estimated that "incarcerating one additional prisoner reduces the number of crimes by approximately 13 per year."

The economists Thomas Marvell and Carlisle Moody of William and Mary College found that "a better estimate may be 21 crimes averted per additional prisoner." Patrick A. Langan, senior statistician at the Justice Department's Bureau of Justice Statistics, calculated that tripling the prison population from 1975 to 1989 may have reduced "violent crime by 10 to 15 percent below what it would have been," thereby preventing a "conservatively estimated 390,000 murders, rapes, robberies and aggravated assaults in 1989 alone."

Studies by the Bureau of Justice Statistics found that 94 percent of state prisoners in 1991 had committed a violent crime or been incarcerated or on probation before. Of these prisoners, 45 percent had committed their latest crimes while free on probation or parole. When "supervised" on the streets, they inflicted at least 218,000 violent crimes, including 13,200 murders and 11,600 rapes (more than half of the rapes against children).

Most Americans are more likely to be a victim of violent crime than to suffer injury in a car accident. As estimated in a forthcoming National Institute of Justice study, the violent crimes committed each year will cost victims and society more than $400 billion in medical bills, lost days from work, lost quality of life — and lost life.

Here's the revolving-door rub. Known felons whom the system has put back on the streets are responsible for about one in three violent crimes, and barely one violent crime in a hundred results in imprisonment. On any given day in 1994, about 690,000 people were on probation. About 1.5 times as many convicted violent felons were on probation or parole as were in prison.

All told, research shows it costs society at least twice as much to let a prisoner loose than to lock him up. Compared with the human and financial toll of revolving-door justice, prisons are a real bargain.

Prison definitely pays, but there's one class of criminal that is an arguable exception; low-level, first-time drug offenders.

Most drug felons in state prisons do not fit that description. Instead, they have long adult and juvenile records involving plenty of serious non-drug crimes. And most Federal drug traffickers are not black kids caught with a little crack cocaine or white executives arrested for a small stash of powder cocaine. The average amount of drugs involved in Federal cocaine-trafficking cases is 183 pounds, and the average amount involved in Federal marijuana trafficking cases is 3.5 tons.

Still, though the numbers of petty drug offenders may prove small, it makes no sense to lock away even one drug offender whose case could be adjudicated in special drug courts and handled less expensively through intensively supervised probation featuring no-nonsense drug treatment and community service. . . .

Translations of the costs and benefits of incarceration into monetary values have provoked criticism. Professors Frank Zimring and Gordon Hawkins have argued that "[t]he major strategic problem with this approach is that many of the most significant harms associated with crime have nothing to do with economic efficiency. . . . [O]thers can neither be well measured nor easily translated into public costs. A further problem is that monetized cost estimates add nothing to the proper calculus of choice between the costs of imprisonment and its benefits."[15]

QUESTIONS

1. A local radio station is about to interview you as a legal expert on incapacitation. Summarize this theory and provide an example as a sound bite so that your description is comprehensible to a layperson and takes no more than two minutes to complete.

2. What punishment would incapacitation dictate in Problems 2.4-2.10 that appear at the beginning of Section C?

3. Which of the two questions at the beginning of Professor DiIulio's article on the cost-effectiveness of prisons should we be asking?

Consider the following newspaper account. What theories of punishment does the recommended sentence implicate?

Jury Recommends 30,000-Year Sentence for Child Rapist[16]
A jury fed up with the early release of prisoners has recommended a 30,000-year sentence for a man convicted of raping a 3-year-old girl. But the eight-time felon could be freed in 15 years.

---

15. Zimring & Hawkins, *supra* note 13, at 154.
16. Associated Press, *The Recorder* 14 (Dec. 16, 1994).

"By God we can send a message to the offender that we are not going to tolerate it," jury forewoman Laura Bixler said Wednesday. "We don't want him to have a chance of ever getting out again."

Charles Scott Robinson, 30, whose previous convictions were for nonviolent crimes including burglary and possession of a stolen vehicle, was convicted of six rape counts. The jury sentenced him to 5,000 years on each count; the minimum sentence was 20 years per count.

County Public Defender Bob Ravitz, whose office defended Robinson, called the sentence "utterly ridiculous."

Bixler said the jury would have returned a more realistic sentence if it was assured Robinson wouldn't be released early. The jury was told it could not sentence Robinson to life without parole.

District Judge Dan Owens, who is to sentence Robinson on Dec. 22, has several options, including ordering concurrent or consecutive terms.

The Department of Corrections would consider the 30,000-year sentence to be the same as life. A life sentence is considered 45 years and state law requires that a person be considered for parole after serving one-third of a sentence.

So if the sentences are concurrent, Robinson would come up for parole review after 15 years, said Terry Jenks, the parole board's interim executive director.

4. Rehabilitation

Andrew Von Hirsch & Lisa Maher, SHOULD PENAL REHABILITATIONISM BE REVIVED?

Criminal Justice Ethics 25, 25-29 (Winter/Spring 1992)

Penal rehabilitationism has been in eclipse since the early 1970s. Treatment efforts seemed to offer only limited hope for success. Relying on treatment to decide the sentence seemed also to lead to unjust results — for example, to excessive intrusion into offenders' lives in the name of cure.

Recently, however, there have been hints of an attempted revival. Some researchers claim striking new successes in treatment techniques. These successes, Ted Palmer concludes in a recent survey of treatment methods, suggest that rehabilitative intervention has gained "increased moral and philosophical legitimacy," and that it is no longer the case that rehabilitation "should be secondary to punishment . . . whether for short- or long-term goals." Some penologists — for example, Francis Cullen and Karen Gilbert — argue that a revival of the penal treatment ethic could help lead to a gentler and more caring penal system. Interestingly, such arguments sometimes come from penologists of the left — who once had been so critical of treatment-based punishments. There is by no means unanimity, however, even from these sources. Some researchers — for example, John Whitehead and Steven Lab in their recent survey of juvenile treatments — continue to be quite pessimistic about those treatments' effects. Some writers of the left — for example, Thomas Mathiesen — still strongly resist treatment as the basis for sanctioning. Nevertheless, there is enough ferment to prompt the question in our title, "Should penal rehabilitationism be revived?"

Reinstatement of a treatment ethic would raise a number of questions. How much more is known about the treatment of offenders now than was known a few years ago? How often can treatment give us answers about how severely to sentence convicted offenders? Is treatment really as humane as it is made out to be? How fair is it to base the sentence on an offender's supposed rehabilitative needs? Rehabilitationism went into eclipse some years ago partly because it could not answer those questions satisfactorily. Are better answers available today?

We approach these issues from heterogeneous viewpoints. One of us (von Hirsch) is a philosophical liberal, and has long been an advocate of the desert model. The other (Maher) has a more left and feminist orientation, and is skeptical of a retributive penal ethic. In our present discussion of the new rehabilitationism, we will not be assuming another articulated sentencing philosophy. What we agree on are the questions, not the answers.

QUESTIONS OF EFFECTIVENESS

During the late 60s and the 70s, critics of penal treatment sometimes were tempted to assert that "nothing works."

The phrase now haunts them, and confuses analysis. It implies that the main problem of treatment is that of establishing its effectiveness; and that treatment can be declared a "success" once some programs are shown to work. Both assumptions are erroneous. Even when treatments succeed, their use to decide sentencing questions raises important normative questions (discussed below). And occasional successes are not enough.

The last large-scale survey and analysis of treatments, undertaken by a panel of the National Academy of Sciences, is over a decade old. It was distinctly pessimistic in its conclusions: when subjected to close scrutiny, few programs seemed to succeed in reducing offender recidivism. Since then there has been continued experimentation, and successes have been reported. Some treatment advocates, such as Paul Gendreau and Robert Ross, have suggested that such findings show that rehabilitation has been "revivified."

Perhaps, however, caution is in order. The extent of recent treatment successes remains very much in dispute — as witness a recent debate among researchers who have surveyed juvenile treatment programs. A source of continuing difficulty is that the "whys" of treatment (that is, the processes by which successes are achieved) are seldom understood. Without knowing the processes by which experimental programs produce given outcomes, it is difficult to tell which features "work," and will continue to work, when programs are extended beyond experimental groups and implemented more widely.

Programs appear to have better prospects for success when they focus on selected subgroups of offenders, carefully screened for amenability." Such a screening approach, however, necessarily limits the scope for rehabilitation. Perhaps this or that type of program can be shown to succeed with this or that subgroup of offenders. Treatments do not (and are not likely to) exist, however, that can be relied upon to decide sentences routinely — that can inform the judge, when confronted with the run-of-the-mill robbery, burglary, or drug offense, what the appropriate sanction should be, and can provide even a modicum of assurance that the sanction will contribute to the offender's desistance from crime. Even Palmer concedes that recent treatment surveys do not "indicate that generic types of programs have been found that consistently produce major recidivism reductions"; and that programs that have positive effects for selected offender subgroups "may have limited relevance to the remaining [offender] subtypes — those which might comprise much of the sample." If treatment lacks such routine, predictable applicability, how can it serve as a principal sentencing rationale?

Success depends, also, on the resources available for implementation. The programs that succeed tend to be well-funded, well-staffed, and vigorously implemented. These features are easiest to achieve when the program is tried in an experimental setting. When the same programs are carried out more widely, program quality tends to deteriorate. Even Gendreau and Ross admit that "[we are] still . . . absolutely amateurish at implementing . . . experimentally demonstrated programs within . . . systems provided routinely by government."

QUESTIONS OF HUMANENESS

Some new advocates of penal rehabilitationism, such as Cullen and Gilbert, stress its humaneness. Reemphasizing treatment, they assert, is humane because it is more caring: it looks to the needs of the offender rather than seeking merely to punish or prevent. Is it true that rehabilitation is concerned chiefly with meeting the offender's needs? That depends on whether one is speaking of social service or of measures aimed at preventing recidivism.

Social service is benevolent in intent, if not necessarily in actual application: The aim is to help the offender lead a less deprived life. It can sometimes be achieved by fairly modest interventions: the unskilled offender, for example, might be taught certain skills that make him better able to cope. Providing these services is, we agree, desirable, although it is far from clear to what extent they reduce recidivism. The offender who is taught to read will not necessarily desist from crime as a result.

Treatment programs, however, seldom aim merely at social service. Their objective, instead, is recidivism prevention: protecting us against future depredations on the offender's part. To accomplish that crime-preventive aim, the intervention may well have to be more drastic. It will take more to get the drug-abusing robber to stop committing further robberies than to teach him/her a skill. (A recent review of current research suggests that the best indicator of successful drug treatment outcomes is length of time in treatment.) To describe such strategies as intrinsically humane or caring is misleading: it confuses humanitarian concerns with treatment-as-crime-prevention.

Cullen and Gilbert admit this last point — that rehabilitation is aimed at recidivism prevention. They argue, however, that few people care much about being humane or benevolent to convicted criminals as an end in itself. Rehabilitationism, they argue, offers a more attractive reason — a crime-preventive one — for decent penal policies. There is something circular about this argument. It assumes that rehabilitative punishments are capable of reducing crime significantly, or at least that people will believe they are. And it assumes that treatment-oriented punishments are inherently gentle.

Are rehabilitative responses intrinsically less onerous? Not necessarily. Consider offenders convicted of crimes of intermediate or lesser gravity. A proportionate sanction for such offenses should be of no more than moderate severity. What of a rehabilitative response? That would depend on how much intervention, and how long, is required to alter the offender's criminal propensities — and to succeed, the intervention may have to be quite substantial (as in the just-noted case of drug treatments).

A rehabilitative ethic also tends to shift attention from the offender's actual criminal conduct to his or her lifestyle or social/moral character. For example, the cultural presumption that women are less "rational" often results in their lawbreaking being perceived as symptomatic of social (or biological) pathology. Women found guilty of relatively minor offenses thus may be subjected to substantial treatment interventions. Concerns about offenders' attitudes may elicit intrusive responses aimed at "correcting" individual ways of thinking and feeling.

Cullen and Gilbert, and some other new rehabilitationists, argue for a return to a treatment model, on grounds that other models (for example, desert) have led to harsh results. How supportable are such claims? The severity or leniency with which a given sentencing philosophy is implemented will vary with the manner of its implementation and the criminal justice politics of the jurisdiction involved. That legislatively mandated "deserved" penalties were harsh in California may be attributable, perhaps, to the character of criminal-justice politics in that state, and to having given the legislature the task of setting the specific penalties. A similar philosophy led to different (and less harsh) results in places such as Minnesota and Oregon, where both the form of guidance and the criminal-justice politics were different. Similar considerations apply also to rehabilitationism. Were California to return to a rehabilitative ethos, it is far from certain (given California's politics) how "humane" or benevolent the results would be.

Some new rehabilitationists' rejection of other models, such as desert, is based on a "socially critical" perspective: how the rationale is likely to be implemented in a society characterized by race, class, and gender inequalities. Such a critique, however, cuts both ways: one also needs to consider how rehabilitationism might be implemented in such an unpropitious social setting. It is fallacious to reject desert, for example, because of how "they" might carry it out, and then urge a treatment ethic on the basis of how "we" might implement it — that is, on the assumption of a much more supportive social system and legal culture than exists today. If rehabilitation is kinder, gentler, or better because that is how good people would implement it, then please tell us when and how, in a society such as our own, the good people take over.

While the new rehabilitationists are taking such a critical stance, they might also apply it to the rehabilitative ethic itself. Historically, the treatment ethos supported (as Michel Foucault has pointed out) the expansion of official and expert power/knowledge. If penal rehabilitationism is revived, what checks are there against a further proliferation of these powers?

QUESTIONS OF FAIRNESS

Criminal punishment, by its nature, condemns. The sanction not only visits deprivation but also conveys that the conduct is wrong and the offender to blame for having committed it. This holds whatever purpose is adopted for deciding sentences. Whether the sentence is based on the seriousness of the offender's crime or on his/her need(s) for treatment, it will still imply something about the impropriety of the behavior.

The theoretical basis for the principle of proportionality of sentence is that it comports with the criminal sanction's censuring implications. Conduct that is more blameworthy — in the sense of involving greater harm or culpability — is to be punished (and thereby condemned) more severely; conduct that is less reprehensible is to be punished (and hence censured) more mildly.

Treatment, however, can seldom rely on criteria relating to the blameworthiness of the conduct; whether the offender is amenable to a particular treatment depends, instead, on his/her social and personal characteristics. This creates the potential problem of fairness: one is using criminal punishment, a blame-conveying response, and yet deciding the intervention on the basis of those personal and social variables that have little to do with how reprehensible the behavior is.

How serious is this problem? The answer depends, of course, on how much emphasis proportionality receives. A thoroughgoing desert conception would require the severity of the penal response to depend heavily on the degree of reprehensibleness of the conduct — thus leaving limited scope for rehabilitative considerations (except for deciding among responses of comparable severity). Not everyone supports a desert model, and some new rehabilitationists say they reject it. But then, it needs to be explained what role, if any, the degree of blameworthiness of the conduct should have.

One possibility would be to give proportionality a limiting role: the seriousness of the criminal conduct would set upper and lower bounds on the quantum of punishment within which rehabilitation could be invoked to fix the sentence. That kind of solution requires one to specify how much weight its desert elements should have — that is, how narrow or broad the offense-based limits on the sentence should be. Here, one faces the familiar dilemma; the narrower one sets those limits, the less room there would be for treatment considerations; whereas the wider one sets the limits, the more one would need to worry about seemingly disparate or disproportionate responses.

Another possibility would be to try to dispense with notions of proportionality altogether. Such a strategy, however, would pose its own difficulties. It would, first, have to be explained how it is justifiable to employ punishment — a blaming institution — without regard to the blameworthiness of the conduct. Or, if one proposes to eliminate the censuring element in punishment, it needs to be explained how this may possibly be accomplished. (The juvenile justice system, for example, long purported to convey no blame, but who was fooled?) Second, the absence of significant proportionality constraints could open the way for abuses of the kind that discredited the old rehabilitation — for example, long-term, open-ended intervention against those deemed to be in special need of treatment. (One thinks of the young car thief who was confined for sixteen years at Patuxent Institution because he refused to talk to the therapists.) One might hope that we are more sophisticated now about the therapeutic value of such interventions — but is such hope enough without principled restraints upon rehabilitative responses?

Finally, one could be more ambitious and think of replacing the criminal sanction with a wholly different set of measures. Nils Christie has urged that state punishment be supplanted by communitarian responses aimed at resolution of conflicts. Some feminist writers have been exploring alternative conceptions of justice. These theorists are, however, aware of the scope of this undertaking: it would involve, not a change in sentencing philosophy, but a completely new set of institutions for responding to what is now termed criminal behavior. One would have to consider whether, and how, these new institutions could afford protection against excessive, or seemingly unfair, intrusions. Whatever one thinks of such suggestions (and one of us has been skeptical of Christie's), they constitute a different level of argument, one that concerns basic social and institutional change. These writers are not speaking, as the new rehabilitationists are, about retaining the criminal sanction and merely giving sentencing more of a treatment emphasis.

CONCLUDING THOUGHTS

In offering the foregoing criticisms of the new rehabilitationists, we are not denying that treatment might have a legitimate role in a fair system of sanctions. How large that role should be depends not only on how much is known about treatment but also on what other assumptions one makes — including those regarding proportionality. Rehabilitation, however, cannot be the primary basis for deciding the sentence, nor can it be the rationale for supporting less harsh sanctions than we have today. If we want sanctions scaled down, as they surely should be, the main and explicitly stated reason for so doing should concern equity and the diminution of suffering.

The most dangerous temptation is to treat the treatment ethos as a kind of edifying fiction: If we only act as though we cared—and minister treatment to offenders as a sign of our caring—a more humane penal system will emerge. No serious inquiry is needed, on this view, about the criteria for deciding what constitutes a humane penal system or about how a renewed treatment emphasis could achieve its intended effects or lead to reasonably just outcomes.

Such thinking is a recipe for failure. It is likely to cause the new treatment ethos to be rejected once its specifics (or lack of them) are subject to critical scrutiny. And it could do no more good than the old, largely hortatory treatment ethic: create a facade of treatment behind which decision makers act as they choose. Those who wish to revive penal rehabilitationism have yet to address the hard questions, including the ones we have tried to raise here.

Consider the following discussion of a state study on the impact of rehabilitative drug treatment.

Drug Treatment Saves $1.5 Billion[17]

For every dollar spent on treatment for drug and alcohol abuse, California taxpayers reap $7 in savings, mostly due to reductions in crime and health care costs, a new statewide survey has found.

The cost-benefit analysis, billed as the most comprehensive ever conducted in the United States, also confirmed what smaller studies have already shown: Treatment is highly effective, regardless of the type of program or the drug, and success cuts across all racial and socioeconomic lines.

The study, financed by the state but conducted by an independent research institute, comes at a time of great public skepticism over the benefits of such social programs. . . .

"It's very important that there be a continuously developing data base to demonstrate to the American public the cost effectiveness of drug-abuse treatment," said Alan Leshner, director of the National Institute on Drug Abuse, an arm of the National Institutes of Health. "Most people don't believe treatment works and they're wrong. That's why a study like this is so important." . . .

In the year before treatment, the study found, those enrolled in drug-abuse programs cost state taxpayers $3.1 billion. Of that, $2.4 billion—or 70 percent—was attributed to crime, including the cost of police protection, prosecution and incarceration. Victims of crimes committed by drug abusers, meanwhile, incurred $1.3 billion in medical costs, damaged or stolen property and lost work. Health care for drug abusers totaled $442 million.

Fifteen months after treatment, the cost of crimes tied to the group in treatment had dropped by $1 billion, the study said, accounting for the biggest chunk of savings. The study also found a considerable drop in health care expenditures; emergency room admissions, for instance, decreased by one-third after treatment.

17. Sheryl Stolberg, San Francisco Chronicle Aug. 29, 1994 at A3, describing Dean R. Gerstein, et al., National Opinion Research Center at the University of Chicago, General Report, Evaluating Recovery Services: The California Drug and Alcohol Treatment Assessment (CALDATA) (April 1994).

One sobering finding was that treatment was of little help in getting drug abusers on more stable economic footing. Treatment did not lead to employment, although the research did find that the longer participants stayed in treatment, the more likely they were to find a job afterward. . . .

Although the report's conclusion — that treatment works and saves money — comes as no surprise to those in the field, experts say the study is especially important because it was so rigorously conducted.

While previous research has looked at only a handful of treatment centers — often focusing on those considered model programs — the California study employed random sampling methods to draw a complete picture of 146,515 people enrolled in an array of programs throughout the state's 58 counties.

QUESTIONS

1. A local radio station is about to interview you as a legal expert on rehabilitation. Summarize this theory as a sound bite and provide an example so that your description is comprehensible to a layperson and takes no more than two minutes to complete.

2. On whom does rehabilitation focus? What are its advantages and drawbacks?

3. Reconsider the newspaper clipping about the "jail break-in." What does it suggest about rehabilitation and the allocation of scarce resources?

4. With which theories of punishment is rehabilitation most likely to conflict?

5. What punishment would rehabilitation dictate in Problems 2.4-2.10 that appear at the beginning of Section C?

5. Denunciation

Ronald J. Rychlak, SOCIETY'S MORAL RIGHT TO PUNISH: A FURTHER EXPLORATION OF THE DENUNCIATION THEORY OF PUNISHMENT
65 Tulane L. Rev. 299, 331-332 (1990)

The denunciation theory of punishment says that those who disobey criminal laws should be held up to the rest of society and denounced as violators of the rules that define what the society represents. This theory holds that society must register its disapproval of wrongful acts and reaffirm the values violated by these acts. Punishment declares that this society will not tolerate this conduct, regardless of any future deterrent effect (or lack thereof). Viewed this way, denunciation seems to have much in common with the retributive theory of punishment; however, denunciation does not look only to the wrongdoer's moral culpability. It also looks to certain utilitarian aims or benefits which flow from the infliction of punishment.

One of the most visible aims of denunciation is the maintenance of social cohesion. Punishing those who violate society's rules helps draw law-abiding society together by reaffirming societal values. Denunciation can also serve to educate the public as to social rules or law and to direct community anger away from vengeance. Since each of these benefits can be said to improve the society, denunciation clearly has utilitarian aspects. The most important aim of the denunciatory theory, however, is to reassure the majority of society that the system does work.

Denunciation serves to satisfy the majority's need to know that its rules (reflecting its values and goals) are being enforced. In other words, denunciation shows law-abiding society not only that the criminal law system works, but that the society itself works. Utilitarian principles may lead to a safe society, by discouraging crime, but they do nothing to assure that law-abiding society is satisfied with the criminal law structure that it has put into place. Denunciation is focused on precisely that point.

Consider the following discussion of a ballot initiative.

Planned Measure Would Stamp Numbers on Ex-Cons' Faces[18]

Backers of [a] proposed ballot initiative . . . to . . . implant numbers on parolees' faces have been given permission to seek signatures to put their measures on the . . . ballot. . . .

The implant initiative . . . would require that inmates convicted of violent crimes have facial identification numbers implanted before they are released. It would make it a misdemeanor for anyone to taunt or harass people with facial implants.

The measure needs the signature of 384,974 voters. . . .

Shame may also factor prominently in a denunciatory punishment. But recent writings on shame suggest that it is a complex process that deserves careful scrutiny when it comprises a part of a punishment arsenal.

Toni Massaro, THE MEANINGS OF SHAME: IMPLICATIONS FOR LEGAL REFORM   3 Psych. Pub. Pol. & L. 645, 649-650 (1997)

Shaming will clearly promote one end: communicating the shamer's disgust for the offender and the offense. And it plainly is cheaper than imprisonment and may in some ways be less cruel to offenders. I argue, however, that when judges and other officials express their disgust in this fashion, they risk recommitting the very act that justifies punishment of criminal offenders, that is, the treatment of others as mere objects. These penalties thus may erode important social norms of decency and respect for others' dignity, including criminal offenders' dignity, in ways that even prison does not. Official shaming, ironically, may create less cooperation, not more, in the long run. It may encourage private retaliation against offenders and a kind of "lynch-mob justice" as James Whitman recently explained; it may illumine that for some offenses the penalty is not prison and thus may decrease deterrence; it may raise the spectre of unfairness insofar as it is used only for some offenders; and it may encourage the debasement of norm offenders rather than their reproval and reintegration. . . .

Shame is central to individual emotional development, and doubtless influences the creation and enforcement of social norms; but governmental attempts to manipulate and exploit shame through public humiliation

---

18. Associated Press, *The Recorder* 4 (Feb. 25, 1994).

rituals may be far more complicated, costly, and counterproductive than the reformers seem to appreciate.

In another article on the question of shaming, Dean Massaro suggests that

> shaming practices are most effective and meaningful when five conditions are satisfied. First, the potential offenders must be members of an identifiable group, such as a close-knit religious or ethnic community. Second, the legal sanctions must actually compromise potential offenders' group social standing. That is, the affected group must concur with the legal decisionmaker's estimation of what is, or should be, humiliating to group members. Third, shaming must be communicated to the group and the group must withdraw from the offender—shun her—physically, emotionally, financially or otherwise. Fourth, the shamed person must fear withdrawal by the group. Finally, the shamed person must be afforded some means of regaining community esteem, unless the misdeed is so grave that the offender must be permanently exiled or demoted.[19]

QUESTIONS

1. A local radio station is about to interview you as a legal expert on denunciation. Summarize this theory as a sound bite and provide an example so that your description is comprehensible to a layperson and takes no more than two minutes to complete.

2. Are the five conditions that Dean Massaro describes as important to the efficacy of shaming punishments likely to be present in the United States today? In large urban centers? In smaller towns?

3. What punishment would denunciation dictate in Problems 2.4-2.10 that appear at the beginning of Section C?

4. Reconsider Professor DiIulio's arguments about radically present-oriented youths. How might denunciation and shaming operate in that environment? What type of punishment might a judge impose to invoke shame there?

Jurisprudential scholars often divide the theories of punishment considered in this chapter into two categories, utilitarian and retributivist. Consider Professor Michael Moore's explanation of the dichotomy and his suggestion of a mixed theory of punishment:[20]

> It is common to reduce . . . th[e] list of prima facie justifications of punishment to two general theories, the utilitarian theory and the retributive theory. To see how this is done, one need only consider the good state of affairs that is to be achieved by incapacitation, special deterrence, general deterrence, and rehabilitation. . . . For all four of these rationales for punishment share the prevention of crime as the beneficial end that justifies punishment. . . . In each case, the ultimate justification for inflicting the harm of punishment is that it is outweighed by the good to be achieved, namely, the prevention of future crimes by that offender or others. This justification of an institution by the social welfare it will enhance makes all such theories instances of the utilitarian theory of punishment.
>
> Thus, the denunciation theory of punishment is a second kind of utilitarian theory of punishment, insofar as the good it seeks to achieve is not simply the

19. Toni Massaro, *Shame, Culture, and American Criminal Law*, 89 Mich. L. Rev. 1880, 1883 (1991).
20. Michael S. Moore, *A Taxonomy of Purposes of Punishment, Law and Psychiatry: Rethinking the Relationship* 233-239 (1984) (reprinted in Foundations of Criminal Law).

prevention of crime. To the extent one grants intrinsic value to social cohesion, and does not regard that as a value only because it contributes to the maintenance of public order, the denunciation theory can be distinguished from the other utilitarian theories just considered by the differing social good it seeks to achieve. Nonetheless, it is still a utilitarian theory, since it outweighs the harm that is punishment by some form of net social gain that punishment achieves.

[In a utilitarian theory,] . . . [p]unishment is justified if and only if some net social gain is achieved by it.

A retributivist theory is necessarily nonutilitarian in character, for it eschews justifying punishment by its tendency to achieve any form of net social gain. Rather, retributivism asserts that punishment is properly inflicted because, and only because, the person deserves it. . . .

The Mixed Theory of Punishment

Th[e only mixed theory that] . . . merits any serious attention . . . is . . . the [one] that asserts that punishment is justified if and only if it achieves a net social gain and is given to offenders who deserve it. . . .

QUESTIONS

1. What are the advantages of a mixed theory of punishment? The disadvantages?

2. Can you imagine a situation in which only a retributive theory supports punishment? One in which only utilitarian theories support it?

3. Should the imposition of all punishments require support from a mixed theory?

D. HOW WE PUNISH

This Section examines how the state punishes. We look first at types of punishment through both a brief historical review of punishment in colonial America and a sampling of punishment methods in use today. Our second inquiry involves how states select and implement punishment, where we consider the sometimes disparate impact of prosecution and punishment.

1. Types of Punishment

Nathaniel Hawthorne, THE SCARLET LETTER, FOUR GREAT AMERICAN NOVELS   39-41 (1946)

The door of the jail being flung open from within, there appeared, in the first place, like a black shadow emerging into sunshine, the grim and grisly presence of the town-beadle, with a sword by his side, and his staff of office in his hand. This personage prefigured and represented in his aspect the whole dismal severity of the Puritanic code of law, which it was his business to administer in its final and closest application to the offender. Stretching forth the official staff in his left hand, he laid his right upon the shoulder of a young woman, whom he thus drew forward; until, on the threshold of the prison-door, she repelled him, by an action marked with natural dignity and force of character, and stepped into the open air, as if by her own free will. She bore in her arms a child, a baby of some three months old, who winked and turned aside its little face from the too vivid light of day; because its existence, heretofore, had brought it acquainted only with the gray twilight of a dungeon, or darksome apartment of the prison.

When the young woman — the mother of this child — stood fully revealed before the crowd, it seemed to be her first impulse to clasp the infant closely to her bosom; not so much by an impulse of motherly affection, as that she might thereby conceal a certain token, which was wrought or fashioned to her dress. In a moment, however, wisely judging that one token of her shame would but poorly serve to hide another, she took the baby on her arm, and, with a burning blush, and yet a haughty smile, and a glance that would not be abashed, looked around her at her townspeople and neighbors. On the breast of her gown, in fine red cloth, surrounded with an elaborate embroidery and fantastic flourishes of gold-thread, appeared the letter A. . . . [T]he point which drew all eyes, and, as it were, transfigured the wearer, — so that both men and women, who had been familiarly acquainted with Hester Prynne, were now impressed as if they beheld her for the first time, — was that SCARLET LETTER, so fantastically embroidered and illuminated upon her bosom. It had the effect of a spell, taking her out of the ordinary relations with humanity, and enclosing her in a sphere by herself.

Lawrence Friedman, CRIME AND PUNISHMENT IN AMERICAN HISTORY

19, 37-44 (1993)

European settlers did not come to an empty land. . . . There were native societies in America, old, established societies [with their] own law-ways, [their] own norms, [their] own way of punishing deviants. . . . None of them has left behind a written record of their legal system as it was on the eve of European arrivals.

The [English] settlers of the seventeenth century came at first in dribs and drabs, then in greater numbers; eventually, they overwhelmed the natives and their law. . . . Essentially, . . . this is the law that prevailed, in modified form, along the Atlantic coast, and then, modified again, across the continent. . . .

New England settlements . . . had both the will and the ability to enforce laws against fornication, sins of the flesh, minor vices, and bad behavior. They punished these offenses the way autocratic fathers or mothers punish children; they made heavy use of shame and shaming. The aim was not just to punish, but also to teach a lesson, so that the sinful sheep would want to get back into the flock. Punishment tended to be exceedingly public. The magistrates loved confessions of guilt, open expressions of remorse. They loved to enlist the community, the bystanders; their scorn and the sinners' humiliation, were part of the process. Hundreds of colonial sinners were forced to sit in the stocks — in full public view. Punishment was sometimes tailored to fit the crime, to point up the moral more vividly. Samuel Powell, a servant, stole a pair of breeches in Accomack County, Virginia, in 1638. Part of his punishment was to "sitt in the stocks on the next Sabboth day . . . from the beginninge of morninge prayer until the end of the Sermon with a pair of breeches about his necke."

Severity was not the point in punishing minor sins. The point was repentance and a good swift lesson. Warnings and fines were the punishment of choice for flirting, petting, and other small offenses. More aggravated sins led to the pillory and stocks, and more fines; for still worse cases, a sound whipping was inflicted.

Whipping was an extremely common punishment throughout the colonies, especially for servants and slaves. . . .

Shaming punishments were colorful; they were certainly used with great frequency. But the workaday fine, the drudge-horse of criminal justice was probably the most common form of punishment. Not everybody had money, of course; run-away servants, who would be hard pressed to come up with cash, sometimes atoned for offenses . . . by serving extra time. . . . Thieves were sometimes required to pay extra damages, or to make restitution; restitution was also a way of restoring the equilibrium the thief had disturbed. . . .

Confession and repentance were crucial aims of the criminal process. In Charles County, Maryland, in 1665, Mary Grub accused John Cage of fathering her child; the accusation turned out to be false. The court then forced her "in open Court to Aske him . . . upon her bended knees forgivnes Acknowledging that she hath maliciously wronged him." The system assumed that most offenders would indeed repent and recant. . . . A New Hampshire statute against adultery (1701) neatly illustrates the theory, and suggests the practice. A man and woman convicted of adultery were to be "Sett upon the Gallows" for an hour "with a Rope about their necks and the other [end] . . . cast over the Gallows"; afterwards, they were to be "severely whipt." Moreover, the offenders would "for ever after weare a Capitall Letter: A: of two inches long and proportionable in Bignesse, cutt out in Cloath of a contrary Colour to their Cloaths and Sewed upon their Upper Garments, on the out Side of their Arme or on their Back in open View. . . ."

Branding and letter-wearing were ways of marking an offender publicly — like sitting in the stocks, but far more permanently. The message was that *this* offender was not likely to mend his ways; disgrace would and should last until death. . . . Mutilation was another form of bodily punishment. Graham, the Connecticut burglar, . . . lost an ear. . . .

Branding and mutilation labeled a man or woman a deep-dyed sinner. The next step was banishment: exclusion from the community altogether. A criminal could be banished because (as a heretic, for example) he was a permanent danger, or because of repeated criminality. . . .

Of course, the ultimate form of banishment was death; from this, there was no danger of return. A death sentence meant the gallows; hanging was the usual way of carrying out the sentence. . . . By the standards of the times, and by English standards, the colonies were far from bloody. By our lights, however, it seems barbaric to execute anyone for sodomy or adultery; but colonial leaders thought otherwise. . . .

On the whole, English law was more liberal with capital punishment than colonial law. In England, men and women swung from the gallows for theft, robbery, and burglary; in the colonies, this was exceptionally rare. Property crimes were, on the whole, not capital. . . . There were, it seems, only fifteen executions in Massachusetts Bay before 1660: four for murder, two for infanticide, three for sexual offenses, two for witchcraft; four Quakers were also put to death. . . .

Murder, of course, was a capital crime. So was rape. . . . The death penalty was also imposed on persistent backsliders and incorrigibles. A Virginia statute of 1748 illustrates the point. For stealing a hog, the first offense was worth twenty-five lashes and a fine; the second offense meant two hours in the pillory, nailed by the ears, plus a fine. The third offense brought death. . . . In the South, capital punishment was much more frequent than in the northern colonies; and the burden of it fell most frequently on slaves.

We now turn to current approaches to punishment. Contemporary punishment encompasses a wide array of sanctions. Most of us are familiar with many of them, such as incarceration in state and federal prisons and local jails. Consider the following statistical information regarding incarceration:

U.S. DEPARTMENT OF JUSTICE, BUREAU OF JUSTICE STATISTICS

http://www.ojp.usdoj.gov/bjs/glance/correct.htm (accessed Aug. 14, 2002)

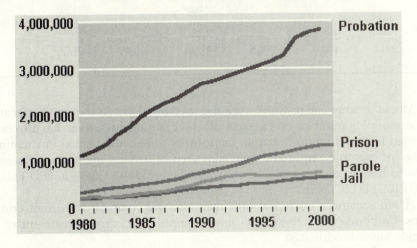

ADULT CORRECTIONAL POPULATIONS

Summary findings

The number of adults in the correctional population has been increasing.

Adult correctional populations, 1980-2000

- In 2000, nearly 6.5 million people were on probation, in jail or prison, or on parole at yearend 2000 — 3.1% of all U.S. adult residents or 1 in every 32 adults.
- State and Federal prison authorities had under their jurisdiction 1,406,031 inmates at yearend 2001: 1,249,038 under State jurisdiction and 156,933 under Federal jurisdiction.
- Local jails held or supervised 702,044 persons awaiting trial or serving a sentence at midyear 2001. About 70,800 of these were persons serving their sentence in the community.

After dramatic increases in the 1980s and 1990s, the incarceration rate has recently leveled off.

Incarceration rate, 1980-2001

- Between 1995 and yearend 2001, the incarcerated population grew an average 3.6% annually. Population growth during the 12-month period ending December 31, 2001 was significantly lower in State prisons (up 0.4%) and local jails (up 1.6%) than in previous years. The Federal prison population rose by 7.0%.

INCARCERATION RATE, 1980-2001
Number of offenders per 100,000 population

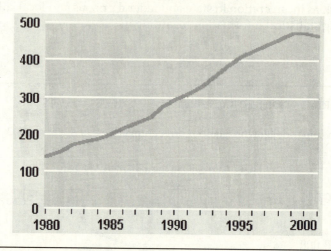

Monetary fines and restitution are also used regularly. As the newspaper article about stamping numbers on the faces of convicts illustrates, there has also been a renewed interest in punishment in the form of public humiliation or shaming. A judge, for example, required a man convicted of driving under the influence to "affix to his personal vehicle a bumper sticker reading, CONVICTED D.U.I.—RESTRICTED LICENSE."[21]

Harsh sentences for repeat offenders also are common in current criminal codes. California's "three strikes" law exemplifies a current treatment of and attitude toward recidivists.

Beyond traditional incarceration and the rebirth of shaming penalties, judges are regularly experimenting with new punishment options, as in the following account:

Judge Sued Over Church Sentences[22]
    A judge who has sentenced at least 350 people to attend church was sued Monday by the American Civil Liberties Union.

---

21. Goldschmitt v. Florida, 490 So. 2d 123, 124 (1986) (the appellate court upheld the condition). For additional examples, *see* Scott E. Sanders, *Scarlet Letters, Bilboes and Cable TV: Are Shame Punishments Cruel and Outdated or Are They a Viable Option for American Jurisprudence?*, 37 Washburn L.J. 359 (1998).
    22. Associated Press, *The Recorder* (1994).

The ACLU challenged the sentence handed to a man accused of drunken driving, saying the punishment was a violation of the separation of church and state.

Thomas P. Quirk, Lake Charles City Court judge, ordered Gregory Thompson to attend church once a week for a year on his no-contest plea in 1993.

"I'm not going to stop until the courts tell me I've got to," Quirk said.

The judge said in an interview that his first church sentence was in 1992. Church is an alternative when someone wants to plead guilty to a minor offense but can't afford a fine, he said.

"Nowadays, we are desperately looking for alternatives to putting people in jail," he said. "We are trying to find things that not only in some way makes them pay . . . but also benefits them."

QUESTIONS

1. Besides constitutional limits, what other constraints should society impose on judges' creativity in inventing punishment alternatives?

2. Should innovative types of punishment be subject to overview or screening, for example, by a panel of judges or community members, before imposition?

3. Has our approach to punishment changed since the colonial era? If so, how?

2. Implementing Punishment

Here we examine how governments in this country implement punishment. Specifically, we look at the distribution of punishment demographically and the architecture of sentencing, with a focus on the federal sentencing guidelines. In the final part of this Section, we study an alternative approach to implementing punishment, called "restorative justice."

The following newspaper account addresses the distribution of punishment.

Charles Finnie, ACCUSED PROSTITUTES WANT BROTHEL'S PRIVILEGED EXPOSED   San Francisco Daily Journal, Sept. 12, 1991, at 1, 6

If police protection is a privilege enjoyed by San Francisco brothel patrons, lawyers for three women facing solicitation charges in a prostitution case aim to change the practice.

A defense request before Municipal Court Judge Jerome Benson today accuses the Police Department of not complying with a June court order that it divulge the names of men at an alleged brothel on Howard Street, which came under police surveillance last October. "San Francisco always has had its bordellos," said Grace L. Suarez, chief of research and a legal strategist for the public defender. "It has always had important men who use them, and cops willing to protect the johns."

Court papers filed last Friday in the case, *People v. Holli Flynn, Sarah Claxton and Carolyn Mann*, ask Benson to sanction the district attorney's office and Police Department by dismissing the charges against the women. "I think it is particularly outrageous," said Deputy Public Defender

Douglas L. Rappaport. "There is no reason in the world why they don't divulge names. They cite a right to privacy, but didn't cite any law to back them up." Rappaport said an inspector told him a membership list of patrons of the Vantage Club, 945 Howard St., "ran from the ceiling to the floor," but that police refuse to turn it over to defense attorneys.

Deputy District Attorney Hugh Donohoe, the prosecutor in the case, could not be reached for comment Wednesday. Previously, Donohoe has said Rappaport is grasping at straws. In court papers, police said Rappaport is "engaging in a fishing expedition."

Police arrested more than a dozen people, including its operator, Thomas Conlon, on suspicion of pimping and pandering, during a Feb. 22 raid at the club, three blocks from the Hall of Justice. The three women represented by Rappaport and Deputy Public Defender Kimiko Burton were arrested after the raid; police say they offered sex to one of three undercover officers who'd been visiting the club from October 1990 through February 1991.

On June 21, Rappaport argued the defense needed the names of club members to build a case of police entrapment or selective prosecution. Benson ruled Rappaport was entitled to the names of all the men on the club's premises during the surveillance, and ordered the prosecution to produce a complete roster. But court papers filed Friday contend the prosecutor produced an incomplete list that included only 17 names. Moreover, Rappaport said, only first names were included.

Rappaport said he believes police are stonewalling, possibly to protect some visitors. "My client has indicated that many influential people frequented the club," Rappaport said. "I have no names."

Rappaport said a second court order requiring police to turn over more names might be fruitless, and that dismissal of the case is warranted.

"My fear is the longer we wait, the more records are being returned to Conlon and the more records are being destroyed."

The relevant statute prohibiting prostitution applies to customers as well as to prostitutes.[23] It reads in pertinent part:

Section 647. Disorderly Conduct[24]

Every person who commits any of the following acts is guilty of disorderly conduct, a misdemeanor:

(b) Who solicits or who agrees to engage in any act of prostitution. A person agrees to engage in an act of prostitution when, with specific intent to so engage, he or she manifests an acceptance of an offer or solicitation to so engage. . . . As used in this subdivision, "prostitution" includes any lewd act between persons for money or other consideration.

---

23. Leffel v. Municipal Court, 54 Cal. App. 3d 569, 576 (1976).
24. Cal. Penal Code § 647 (2003).

QUESTION

What might the conduct of the police and prosecutors in the case as described above suggest about gender, power, and the implementation of punishment?

The chart and statistics that follow on the demographics of prisoners and types of crime resulting in incarceration illustrate some of the disparate impacts produced by the criminal justice system's implementation of punishment.

U.S. DEPARTMENT OF JUSTICE, BUREAU OF JUSTICE STATISTICS (AUG. 12, 2002)

Summary findings

- On December 31, 2001,
  - — 1,962,220 prisoners were held in Federal or State prisons or in local jails — the total increased 1.3% from yearend 2000, less than the average annual growth of 3.6% since yearend 1995.
  - — there were an estimated 470 prison inmates per 100,000 U.S. residents — up from 292 at yearend 1990.
  - — the number of women under the jurisdiction of State or Federal prison authorities decreased — 0.2% from December 31, 2000 to December 31, 2001, reaching 93,031. The number of men rose 1.2%, totaling 1,313,000 at yearend.

- At yearend 2001 there were 3,535 sentenced black male prisoners per 100,000 black males in the United States, compared to 1,177 sentenced Hispanic male inmates per 100,000 Hispanic males and 462 white male inmates per 100,000 white males.

STATE PRISON POPULATION BY OFFENSE TYPE, 1980-2000

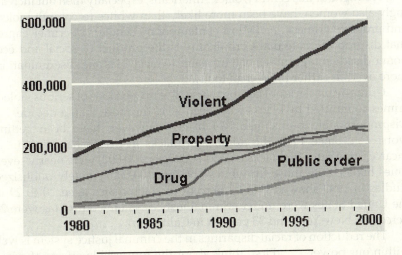

Between 1990 and 2000, the increasing number of violent offenders accounted for 53% of the total growth of the State prison population; 20% of the total growth was attributable to the increasing number of drug offenders.

Percent of Sentenced State inmates

Most serious offense	1990	2000
Total	100%	100%
Violent	46	49
Property	25	20
Drug	22	21
Public-order	7	10

The statistics underscore the proportion of African-American and Hispanic males under the supervision of the criminal justice system. The following excerpt from Professor Michael Tonry addresses the issue of race and the criminal justice system.[25]

Michael Tonry, MALIGN NEGLECT — RACE, CRIME, AND PUNISHMENT IN AMERICA   vii-viii, 3-4, 181 (1995)

[C]rime and drug control policies since 1980 have greatly increased the numbers of young minority citizens, especially males, who are entangled in the justice system's tentacles. . . . [B]y 1990 a quarter of young black males were in jail or prison, on probation or parole. . . . Poor minority communities cannot prosper when so many of their young men are prevented from settling into long-term personal relationships, getting or keeping jobs, and living conventional lives. . . .

Throughout this century, black Americans, especially men but increasingly also women, have been more likely than whites to commit violent and property crimes. . . . [M]ost contemporary scholars of crime[ ] agree that disproportionate black criminality is the product of social and economic disadvantage, much of it traceable to racial bias and discrimination, more overt in earlier times than today. . . .

Crime by blacks is not getting worse. The proportions of serious violent crimes committed by blacks have been level for more than a decade. . . . Disproportionate punishments of blacks, however, have been getting worse. . . . Since 1980, the number of blacks in prison has tripled. . . . Incarceration rates for blacks in 1991 (1,895 per 100,000) were nearly seven times higher than those for whites (293 per 100,000). Widely publicized studies in 1990 showed that 23 percent of black males aged 20 to 29 in the United States were under criminal justice system control (as were 23 percent in New York and 33 percent in California). . . .

The reduction of racial disparities in the criminal justice system is well within our power. . . . First, think about the foreseeable effects of crime

---

25. For more in-depth materials that focus on the impact of a sentencing policy on African-Americans, see the materials on the crack versus powder cocaine debate in Appendix E.

control policy decisions on members of minority groups; when policies are likely to burden members of minority groups disproportionately, reconsider the policies. Second, to guard against racial bias in sentencing and against unjustly severe penalties in general, establish systems of presumptive sentencing guidelines for ordinary cases that set maximum penalties, scaled to the severity of offenders' crimes. Third, recognize the prudence and compassion of our predecessors, and throughout the justice system reestablish presumptions that the least punitive and least restrictive appropriate punishment should be imposed in every case. Fourth, empower judges at sentencing to mitigate sentences for all defendants, irrespective of race, ethnicity, or sex, to take account of individual circumstances. Fifth, celebrate the decent instincts of our predecessors, and reinvest in corrections programs that can help offenders rebuild their lives and enhance their own and their children's life chances. Sixth, most important of all, be honest; for as long as cynical and disingenuous appeals continue to be made by politicians to the deepest fears and basest instincts of the American people, the prospects of reducing racial disparities in the justice system will remain small.

QUESTIONS

1. Do the materials you read earlier in this chapter on why we punish support Professor Tonry's proposals for change?

2. Professor Tonry suggests a return to a more individualized or tailored approach to sentencing. What are the advantages and disadvantages of such individualized sentencing?

In reading the next Section on sentencing discretion and sentencing guidelines, think about how Professor Tonry's recommendations would affect a sentencing guideline scheme.

3. Sentencing Power and Discretion

Who chooses the sentence for a particular offender? Trial judges typically exercise this power subject to constraints that vary from jurisdiction to jurisdiction. Congress dramatically reshaped federal sentencing practices in the 1980s by creating the Federal Sentencing Guidelines, which are representative of a trend in many states. Comparison of the federal trial judge's role in sentencing before and after the Guidelines demonstrates the range of constraints under which a judge may exercise the power to sentence.

The sentencing of a defendant for unarmed bank robbery under 18 United States Code section 2113(a) provides a simple illustration. In the bank robbery statute, Congress explicitly set a maximum penalty of 20 years. Prior to adoption of the Guidelines in the 1980s, a federal judge had the power to impose whatever sentence she felt appropriate — from probation with no term of imprisonment up to a 20 year sentence. In essence, there was no floor to constrain the judge's sentencing discretion, a very high 20 year ceiling, and much room in between. In determining where within such a large discretionary range a particular defendant's sentence should fall, lawyers and judges alike commonly invoked the ideas of just desert and deterrence along with other theories of punishment as reference points.

Judge Frankel's opinion in *Bergman*, written prior to the Guidelines, provides one particularly articulate example. Federal appellate courts showed great deference to the trial judge's choice of sentence and generally treated it as unreviewable.

An offender would not typically be imprisoned, though, for the number of years imposed by the judge. Rather, she was eligible for parole, an early supervised release from prison, after serving one third of her sentence. Parole was mandated after the prisoner had served two thirds of her sentence. If the trial judge, for example, had given our hypothetical bank robber a nine year sentence, she would actually have spent between 3 and 6 years in prison. Executive branch officials of the Parole Commission, not the judge, would have chosen the parole date within that 3 year window.

This approach to federal sentencing is a form of indeterminate sentencing and exhibited a sharing of power among the legislature, judiciary, and the executive branch. The judge and the parole board each exercised great discretion in determining the length of time actually served in prison within broad constraints set by the legislature. Because of parole, it was difficult at the time of the sentencing to determine precisely how long the offender would be in prison. And the time an offender served could vary substantially from the sentence announced in court.

It was this indeterminate sentencing system Judge Frankel described in the *Bergman* case as "deeply flawed," "characterized by disparity" and lacking "clear or agreed standards." His views were widely shared. Responding to such criticism, Congress enacted the Guidelines.

The Guidelines as originally enacted were a form of determinate sentencing. Another form is the "mandatory minimum sentence." A mandatory minimum sets a floor below which the offender's sentence may not drop. As we will see, the guidelines use a sort of bracketing approach, setting both a floor and a ceiling for the offender's sentence.

Rather than enact the Guidelines themselves in the form of a statute, Congress established the United States Sentencing Commission and entrusted its members with that task. In *Mistretta v. United States*, Justice Blackmun described the Commission's composition as follows:

> The Commission is established "as an independent commission in the judicial branch of the United States." § 991(a). It has seven voting members (one of whom is the Chairman) appointed by the President "by and with the advice and consent of the Senate." "At least three of the members shall be Federal judges selected after considering a list of six judges recommended to the President by the Judicial Conference of the United States." No more than four members of the Commission shall be members of the same political party. The Attorney General, or his designee, is an ex officio nonvoting member. The Chairman and other members of the Commission are subject to removal by the President "only for neglect of duty or malfeasance in office or for other good cause shown." Except for initial staggering of terms, a voting member serves for six years and may not serve more than two full terms.[26]

Congress delegated "broad authority to the Commission to review and rationalize the federal sentencing process."

The Guidelines the Commission created changed federal sentencing in several significant ways and were indicative of a national movement toward determinate sentencing. For unarmed bank robbery, rather than choosing whatever sentence from 0 to 20 years she feels is appropriate, a federal trial judge determines the sentence using the following table.

---

26. 488 U.S. 361 (1988).

SENTENCING TABLE (in months of imprisonment)

Criminal History Category (Criminal History Points)

Offense Level	I (0 or 1)	II (2 or 3)	III (4, 5, 6)	IV (7, 8, 9)	V (10, 11, 12)	VI (13 or more)
1	0-6	0-6	0-6	0-6	0-6	0-6
2	0-6	0-6	0-6	0-6	0-6	1-7
3	0-6	0-6	0-6	0-6	2-8	3-9
4	0-6	0-6	0-6	2-8	4-10	6-12
5	0-6	0-6	1-7	4-10	6-12	9-15
6	0-6	1-7	2-8	6-12	9-15	12-18
7	0-6	2-8	4-10	8-14	12-18	15-21
8	0-6	4-10	6-12	10-16	15-21	18-24
9	4-10	6-12	8-14	12-18	18-24	21-27
10	6-12	8-14	10-16	15-21	21-27	24-30
11	8-14	10-16	12-18	18-24	24-30	27-33
12	10-16	12-18	15-21	21-27	27-33	30-37
13	12-18	15-21	18-24	24-30	30-37	33-41
14	15-21	18-24	21-27	27-33	33-41	37-46
15	18-24	21-27	24-30	30-37	37-46	41-51
16	21-27	24-30	27-33	33-41	41-51	46-57
17	24-30	27-33	30-37	37-46	46-57	51-63
18	27-33	30-37	33-41	41-51	51-63	57-71
19	30-37	33-41	37-46	46-57	57-71	63-78
20	33-41	37-46	41-51	51-63	63-78	70-87
21	37-46	41-51	46-57	57-71	70-87	77-96
22	41-51	46-57	51-63	63-78	77-96	84-105
23	46-57	51-63	57-71	70-87	84-105	92-115
24	51-63	57-71	63-78	77-96	92-115	100-125
25	57-71	63-78	70-87	84-105	100-125	110-137
26	63-78	70-87	78-97	92-115	110-137	120-150
27	70-87	78-97	87-108	100-125	120-150	130-162
28	78-97	87-108	97-121	110-137	130-162	140-175
29	87-108	97-121	108-135	121-151	140-175	151-188
30	97-121	108-135	121-151	135-168	151-188	168-210
31	108-135	121-151	135-168	151-188	168-210	188-235
32	121-151	135-168	151-188	168-210	188-235	210-262
33	135-168	151-188	168-210	188-235	210-262	235-293
34	151-188	168-210	188-235	210-262	235-293	262-327
35	168-210	188-235	210-262	235-293	262-327	292-365
36	188-235	210-262	235-293	262-327	292-365	324-405
37	210-262	235-293	262-327	292-365	324-405	360-life
38	235-293	262-327	292-365	324-405	360-life	360-life
39	262-327	292-365	324-405	360-life	360-life	360-life
40	292-365	324-405	360-life	360-life	360-life	360-life
41	324-405	360-life	360-life	360-life	360-life	360-life
42	360-life	360-life	360-life	360-life	360-life	360-life
43	life	life	life	life	life	life

A series of six categories dealing with the offender's criminal history stretch across the top of the table. The worse the history, the higher the number the defendant is assigned and the further the judge moves across the table toward the right and a higher sentence. A series of 43 offense levels based on the details of the offender's crime range along the left side of the table. The more serious the offense, the higher the category assigned and the further the judge moves down the table and toward a higher sentence. Adjustments in offense level are made for factors such as whether the defendant has accepted responsibility and cooperated in the prosecution of others.

The sentencing judge determines the defendant's offense level and criminal history category through a process that can be intricate and subject to dispute. For the first two decades after enactment of the Guidelines, these factors dictated the range within which the judge had to choose a sentence. The two numbers in the table at the intersection of the assigned offense level and criminal history category represented in months the highest and lowest sentences the judge could impose. If our hypothetical bank robber had been assigned an offense level of 20 and a criminal history category of II, the judge had to impose a sentence from 37 to 46 months. The judge could deviate from this range with what is called an upward or downward departure only under limited circumstances.

In effect, the sentencing table imposed on the judge both a floor and a ceiling with little leeway in between. The judge's discretion often operated within a range of months rather than years.

In January of 2005, the United States Supreme Court in *United States v. Booker*, ___ U.S. ___, 125 S. Ct. 738 (2005), held that the mandatory nature of the Guidelines violated a defendant's sixth amendment right to trial by jury since under the Guidelines a judge rather than a jury decided factual questions that trigger a sentence greater than the one that would be imposed based solely on the jury's verdict. The Court did not entirely invalidate the Guidelines. Rather, it stated that the Guidelines are constitutionally valid if treated as advisory rather than mandatory. Federal trial judges must still consult the Guidelines and may use them in the manner described earlier in this Section as a starting point in sentencing but they are no longer required to stay within the Guidelines' limits in imposing sentences.

Many criticized the Guidelines, arguing that they restrict judges too severely and do not allow sufficient individualization to ensure just sentences. The Federal Sentencing Guidelines Manual states that the Guidelines were meant to "further the basic purposes of criminal punishment: deterrence, incapacitation, just punishment, and rehabilitation. . . . " But one rarely hears the purposes of punishment mentioned at a sentencing hearing under the Guidelines. Instead, the courtroom conversation tends to focus on the mechanics of applying the Guidelines' tables, such as resolving factual questions that determine offense level and criminal history category.

Along with enacting the Guidelines, Congress also abolished parole so that the amount of time an offender actually serves in prison is much closer to the amount of time announced by the judge at sentencing than it was prior to the Guidelines. Sentences can be reduced for good behavior in prison by up to 15 percent, but the magnitude of such a reduction is much smaller than that available under parole. The Guidelines represent a dramatic shift in the allocation of sentencing power: They eliminate the executive power exercised by the Parole Commission, reduce judicial power, and consolidate power in the Sentencing Commission and in prosecutors.

QUESTIONS

1. Does the choice to adopt a determinate or indeterminate sentencing scheme reflect a choice about the purposes of punishment underlying sentencing? Does just sentencing require individual consideration of each offender? Each offense?

2. Does the choice to abandon the practice of parole reflect a choice about the purposes of punishment?

3. Is society better served by giving judges discretion in sentencing? Or by restricting it? What are the advantages and disadvantages of giving sentencing discretion to judges?

4. Do you think the average length of sentences imposed under the Guidelines would be about the same as those imposed by judges prior to the Guidelines? More lenient? More severe?

5. Should we be concerned that the rhetoric of sentencing under the Guidelines tends to focus on the mechanics of operating its sentencing table rather than on the underlying purposes of punishment the sentence is supposed to advance?

6. Is it appropriate for legislators to delegate sentencing power to commissioners who are appointed and not elected? What reasons might Congress have had for delegating the task of creating the Guidelines to such a commission?

4. An Alternative Approach to Punishment: Restorative Justice

Restorative justice offers an alternative to the prevailing approach to punishment here in the United States. It can be understood as "a process of bringing together the individuals who have been affected by an offense and having them agree on how to repair the harm caused by the crime. The purpose is to restore victims, restore offenders, and restore communities in a way that all stakeholders can agree is just."[27]

> Substantive restorativism contends that crime is not just an act against the state but against particular victims and the community in general, and for this reason, affected individuals, family members, and supporters are considered central to crime control and appropriate resolutions. . . .
>
> A primary objective of restorativism is making amends for the offending, particularly the harm caused to the victim, rather than inflicting pain upon the offender. Accountability is demonstrated by recognizing the wrongfulness of one's conduct, expressing remorse for the resulting injury, and taking steps to repair any damage. According to restorative justice advocates, crime creates positive obligations that require affirmative action on the part of the offender — most notably, "restoring" victims to their previous status quo by means of financial, physical, or even symbolic reparations.[28]

In the prevailing approach to punishment, victims often have very limited control over the process or outcome of a criminal case. Restorative justice responds to

---

27. John Braithwaite, *A Future Where Punishment Is Marginalized: Realistic or Utopian?*, 46 UCLA L. Rev. 1727, 1743 (1999) (quoted in David Dolinko, *Restorative Justice and the Justification of Punishment*, 2003 Utah L. Rev. 319, 331). There does not appear to be consensus on the definition of "restorative justice." *See* Erik Luna, *Introduction*, 2003 Utah L. Rev. 1, 3. This definition, however, provides a useful starting point for discussion.

28. *See* Luna, *id.*

this concern.[29] For example, victim-offender mediation programs are one "expression of restorative justice."[30] Generally, in such a program the crime victim, the perpetrator, and a mediator or facilitator sit down and meet face-to-face to discuss the crime and try to reach a resolution that embodies appropriate restoration. Such programs often have focused on property crimes and "minor assaults."[31] Authors of a recent analysis of 15 studies of victim-offender mediation in the context of juvenile cases concluded that their "results strongly imply that VOM [victim-offender mediation] is associated with a reduction in delinquent behavior. . . . "[32]

Restorative justice has also provoked criticism. For instance, one scholar notes the approach's

> high potential for giving offenders strikingly disparate treatment. It opens the door to such disparities in two different ways. First, the central aim in its handling of an offender is to repair the harm that her crime inflicted, and the extent of that harm can vary greatly because of factors beyond the offender's foresight or control and irrelevant to her culpability. Second, such forms of restorative justice as mediation and conferencing allow offenders whose behavior and culpability may be quite similar to fare very differently, depending on the temperament and circumstances of their respective victims and on the skills and emotions that they and the victims bring to the negotiating process.[33]

QUESTIONS

1. In addition to those described above, can you identify additional benefits to a restorative justice approach? Additional disadvantages?

2. What considerations should play a role in determining whether restorative justice should be applied in cases involving serious crimes or injuries?

3. Are the considerations different in adult rather than juvenile settings?

E. HOW MUCH PUNISHMENT?

How much punishment should be imposed on a particular defendant? This Section focuses on one way the criminal law has sought to answer this question: the notion of proportional punishment. The principal case, *Ewing v. California*, explores the constitutional dimension of proportionality in a United States Supreme Court decision evaluating California's "three strikes" statute, which imposes lengthy mandatory prison terms on repeat offenders.

Proportionality in punishment is widely viewed as desirable, in addition to being constitutionally required. Legislatures, for example, often make proportionality one of the goals of sentencing, as the following statutes demonstrate:

---

29. Heather Strang & Lawrence W. Sherman, *Repairing the Harm: Victims and Restorative Justice*, 2003 Utah L. Rev. 15-16.

30. William R. Nugent et al., *Participation in Victim-Offender Mediation and the Prevalence and Severity of Subsequent Delinquent Behavior: A Meta-Analysis*, 2003 Utah L. Rev. 137.

31. *Id.*

32. *Id.*

33. Dolinko, *supra* note 27, at 331.

Arkansas Code Annotated § 16-90-801 (2001)   *Statement of sentencing policy*

(b) Purpose of Sentencing Standards.

(1) Though voluntary, the purpose of establishing rational and consistent sentencing standards is to seek to ensure that sanctions imposed following conviction are proportional to the seriousness of the offense of conviction and the extent of the offender's criminal history.

(2) The standards seek to ensure equitable sanctions which provide that offenders similar with respect to relevant sentencing criteria will receive similar sanctions and offenders substantially different with respect to relevant sentencing criteria will receive different sanctions.

(c) Appropriate Use of Sentencing Sanctions.

(1) Rational and consistent sentencing policy requires a continuum of sanctions which increases in direct proportion to the seriousness of the offense and the extent of the offender's criminal history.

New Jersey Code of Criminal Justice § 2C: 1.2 (2003)   *Purposes*

(b) The general purposes of the provisions governing the sentencing of offenders are: . . .

(4) To safeguard offenders against excessive, disproportionate or arbitrary punishment. . . .

Oregon Revised Statutes § 161.025   *Purposes*

(1) The general purposes of chapter 743, Oregon Laws 1971 are: . . .

(f) To prescribe penalties which are proportionate to the seriousness of offenses and which permit recognition of differences in rehabilitation possibilities among individual offenders.

In 2000, by executive order of the governor, Illinois created a commission to revise its criminal code, which issued its final report in January of 2003. As the following excerpt from that report reveals, the commission adopted proportionality as one of its goals.

FINAL REPORT OF THE ILLINOIS CRIMINAL CODE REWRITE AND REFORM COMMISSION, FINAL REPORT

Vol. 1, xxxix-xliii

In developing the Proposed Code, the drafters were guided by . . . general drafting principles, set forth below. . . .

4. GRADE OFFENSES RATIONALLY AND PROPORTIONALLY

For a system of criminal justice to be fair, liability must be assigned according to the relative seriousness of the offense(s) committed. It is critical that a criminal code's system of grading offenses recognize all, and only, suitable distinctions among the relative severity of offenses and develop a scheme to grade each offense proportionally to its gravity in light of those distinctions.

In most cases, determinations of "seriousness" reflect value judgments as to which reasonable people might differ, and as to which the legislature (as the most direct political voice of the people) should have the ultimate authority. Accordingly, the drafters of the Proposed Code have sought to defer to the grading determinations instantiated in existing Illinois law where possible. In some cases, however, broad examination of current grading determinations reveals logical inconsistencies that, it is presumed, the legislature would have sought to avoid had it been aware of them. Such inconsistencies may develop for several reasons. As new offenses are added to a criminal code, the legislature may neglect to consider how the grade of each new offense relates to the grades for other, preexisting offenses. As noted earlier, the sheer increase in the number of offenses, especially offenses outside the criminal code itself, makes it difficult to maintain consistency — assuming one even manages to locate and consider all relevant offenses. In any event, the shared experience of various jurisdictions is that over time, proportionality in the grading of offenses diminishes.

One of the virtues of a broad recodification effort is the opportunity it provides to review the grading system as a whole, considering how all offenses relate to one another rather than considering individual offenses in a vacuum. Following such a review, the drafters have altered the grades of certain offenses where doing so seems necessary to maintain any legitimate sense of proportionality. . . .

C. Maintain Proportionality Between Various Offenses

[An] objective in grading criminal offenses is to ensure that grading remains rational when the grades of different offenses are compared with one another. In other words, a criminal code must maintain *proportionality* of grading across offenses and make certain that the relative level of liability for different offenses parallels the relative harm or wrong they reflect.

Although the drafters of the Proposed Code have deferred, where possible, to the apparent legislative determinations regarding the relative harm of each offense that current grading levels reflect, in a few instances a comparison of different offenses reveals grading discrepancies contrary to any sense of proportionality. For example, consider current law's grading of the theft offenses. The current theft offense aggravates punishment a full grade for thefts from the person and *another* full grade for thefts committed in a school or place of worship. As a result, taking less than $300 in property from a person while in a school or place of worship is a Class 2 felony. Thus a student who takes another student's lunch money out of his pocket is subject to the same punishment as a person who commits kidnapping, aggravated domestic battery, aggravated criminal sexual abuse, or ordinary theft of up to $100,000. The Proposed Code eliminates the full grade aggravation for thefts from the person — whose additional harms are more properly addressed through assault or robbery provisions — and reduces the aggravation for thefts committed in a school or place of worship. . . .

Other examples of disproportionate grading are plentiful. For example, current law grades certain forms of battery more seriously than second-degree murder (and provides no "provocation" mitigation for such batteries). The Proposed Code grades the homicide offense the same as current law, but creates one assault offense whose grade varies depending upon the amount of harm caused, the nature of the conduct, and the status of the victim, but never exceeds the penalty for a deliberate homicide. Likewise, current law grades eavesdropping more seriously than unauthorized videotaping, meaning that someone who videotapes another person undressing in a locker room (or her own home) would be punished less severely than someone who listens to another's phone conversation. The Proposed Code defines a single offense covering violations of this type and imposes a consistent grade.

Why is proportionality in punishment such a widely shared aspiration? From a retributive perspective, disproportional punishment violates the idea that the punishment should be equivalent to the defendant's blameworthiness. In other words, any punishment imposed beyond what is deserved is essentially punishment without blame in violation of the retributive principle. Proportional punishment also makes utilitarian sense. Punishment imposed in excess of what is needed to deter, incapacitate, or rehabilitate has no utility and thus is a waste of public resources. Disproportional punishment may also bring about disrespect for law by the public and by those upon whom it is imposed.

The Oxford English Dictionary defines "proportion" as "[t]he relation existing between things or magnitudes as to size, quantity, number or the like; comparative relation, ratio." Proportionality, then, is a relational concept. Things are not inherently proportional or disproportional. Rather, they have or lack these qualities in relation to something else. In other words, a sentence must be proportional or disproportional to something else. *To what should punishment be proportional?* Is it desert? The need for general deterrence? The defendant's future danger? How do the statutes above answer this question? How do the various opinions that follow in *Ewing* answer it?

The question of whether or not a "three strikes" statute is a good idea is typically resolved by a legislature. In the following case, it was the California legislature. But the United States Supreme Court is the final arbiter of whether such a statute violates the United States Constitution. In the following case, the defendant claimed that the sentence imposed on him violated the Eighth Amendment to the United States Constitution, adopted in 1791, which states:

> Excessive bail shall not be required, nor excessive fines imposed, nor cruel and unusual punishments inflicted.

EWING *v.* CALIFORNIA
538 U.S. 11 (2003)

Justice O'CONNOR announced the judgment of the Court and delivered an opinion in which The Chief Justice and Justice Kennedy join.

In this case, we decide whether the Eighth Amendment prohibits the State of California from sentencing a repeat felon to a prison term of 25 years to life under the State's "Three Strikes and You're Out" law.

I.A

California's three strikes law reflects a shift in the State's sentencing policies toward incapacitating and deterring repeat offenders who threaten the public safety. The law was designed "to ensure longer prison sentences and greater punishment for those who commit a felony and have been previously convicted of serious and/or violent felony offenses." On March 3, 1993, California Assemblymen Bill Jones and Jim Costa introduced Assembly Bill 971, the legislative version of what would later become the three strikes law. The Assembly Committee on Public Safety defeated the bill only weeks later. Public outrage over the defeat sparked a voter initiative to add Proposition 184, based loosely on the bill, to the ballot in the November 1994 general election.

On October 1, 1993, while Proposition 184 was circulating, 12-year-old Polly Klaas was kidnapped from her home in Petaluma, California. Her admitted killer, Richard Allen Davis, had a long criminal history that included two prior kidnapping convictions. Davis had served only half of his most recent sentence (16 years for kidnapping, assault, and burglary). Had Davis served his entire sentence, he would still have been in prison on the day that Polly Klaas was kidnapped.

Polly Klaas' murder galvanized support for the three strikes initiative. Within days, Proposition 184 was on its way to becoming the fastest qualifying initiative in California history. On January 3, 1994, the sponsors of Assembly Bill 971 resubmitted an amended version of the bill that conformed to Proposition 184. On January 31, 1994, Assembly Bill 971 passed the Assembly by a 63 to 9 margin. The Senate passed it by a 29 to 7 margin on March 3, 1994. Governor Pete Wilson signed the bill into law on March 7, 1994. California voters approved Proposition 184 by a margin of 72 to 28 percent on November 8, 1994.

California thus became the second State to enact a three strikes law. . . . Between 1993 and 1995, 24 States and the Federal Government enacted three strikes laws. Though the three strikes laws vary from State to State, they share a common goal of protecting the public safety by providing lengthy prison terms for habitual felons.

B

California's current three strikes law consists of two virtually identical statutory schemes "designed to increase the prison terms of repeat felons." When a defendant is convicted of a felony, and he has previously been convicted of one or more prior felonies defined as "serious" or "violent" in Cal. Penal Code Ann. §§ 667.5 and 1192.7 sentencing is conducted pursuant to the three strikes law. Prior convictions must be alleged in the charging document, and the defendant has a right to a jury determination that the prosecution has proved the prior convictions beyond a reasonable doubt.

If the defendant has one prior "serious" or "violent" felony conviction, he must be sentenced to "twice the term otherwise provided as punishment for the current felony conviction." If the defendant has two or more prior "serious" or "violent" felony convictions, he must receive "an indeterminate term of life imprisonment." Defendants sentenced to life under the three strikes law become eligible for parole on a date calculated by reference to a "minimum term," which is the greater of (a) three times the term otherwise provided for the current conviction, (b) 25 years, or (c) the term determined by the court pursuant to § 1170 for the underlying conviction, including any enhancements.

Under California law, certain offenses may be classified as either felonies or misdemeanors. These crimes are known as "wobblers." Some crimes that would otherwise be misdemeanors become "wobblers" because of the defendant's prior record. For example, petty theft, a misdemeanor, becomes a "wobbler" when the defendant has previously served a prison term for committing specified theft-related crimes. Other crimes, such as grand theft, are "wobblers" regardless of the defendant's prior record. Both types of "wobblers" are triggering offenses under the three strikes law only when they are treated as felonies. Under California law, a "wobbler" is presumptively a felony and "remains a felony except when the discretion is actually exercised" to make the crime a misdemeanor.

In California, prosecutors may exercise their discretion to charge a "wobbler" as either a felony or a misdemeanor. Likewise, California trial courts have discretion to reduce a "wobbler" charged as a felony to a misdemeanor either before preliminary examination or at sentencing to avoid imposing a three strikes sentence. In exercising this discretion, the court may consider "those factors that direct similar sentencing decisions," such as "the nature and circumstances of the offense, the defendant's appreciation of and attitude toward the offense, . . . [and] the general objectives of sentencing."

California trial courts can also vacate allegations of prior "serious" or "violent" felony convictions, either on motion by the prosecution or *sua sponte*. In ruling whether to vacate allegations of prior felony convictions, courts consider whether, "in light of the nature and circumstances of [the defendant's] present felonies and prior serious and/or violent felony convictions, and the particulars of his background, character, and prospects, the defendant may be deemed outside the [three strikes'] scheme's spirit, in whole or in part." Thus, trial courts may avoid imposing a three strikes sentence in two ways: first, by reducing "wobblers" to misdemeanors (which do not qualify as triggering offenses), and second, by vacating allegations of prior "serious" or "violent" felony convictions.

C

On parole from a 9-year prison term, petitioner Gary Ewing walked into the pro shop of the El Segundo Golf Course in Los Angeles County on March 12, 2000. He walked out with three golf clubs, priced at $399 apiece, concealed in his pants leg. A shop employee, whose suspicions were aroused when he observed Ewing limp out of the pro shop, telephoned the police. The police apprehended Ewing in the parking lot.

Ewing is no stranger to the criminal justice system. In 1984, at the age of 22, he pleaded guilty to theft. The court sentenced him to six months in jail (suspended), three years' probation, and a $300 fine. In 1988, he was convicted of felony grand theft auto and sentenced to one year in jail and three years' probation. After Ewing completed probation, however, the sentencing court reduced the crime to a misdemeanor, permitted Ewing to withdraw his guilty plea, and dismissed the case. In 1990, he was convicted of petty theft with a prior and sentenced to 60 days in the county jail and three years' probation. In 1992, Ewing was convicted of battery and sentenced to 30 days in the county jail and two years' summary probation. One month later, he was convicted of theft and sentenced to 10 days in the county jail and 12 months' probation. In January 1993, Ewing was convicted of burglary and sentenced to 60 days in the county jail and one year's summary probation. In February 1993, he was convicted of possessing drug paraphernalia and sentenced to six months in the county jail and three years' probation. In July 1993, he was convicted of appropriating lost property and sentenced to 10 days in the county jail and two years' summary probation. In September 1993, he was convicted of unlawfully possessing a firearm and trespassing and sentenced to 30 days in the county jail and one year's probation.

In October and November 1993, Ewing committed three burglaries and one robbery at a Long Beach, California, apartment complex over a 5-week period. He awakened one of his victims, asleep on her living room sofa, as he tried to disconnect her video cassette recorder from the television in that room. When she screamed, Ewing ran out the front door. On another occasion, Ewing accosted a victim in the mailroom of the apartment complex. Ewing claimed to have a gun and ordered the victim to hand over his wallet. When the victim resisted, Ewing produced a knife and forced the victim back to the apartment itself. While Ewing rifled through the bedroom, the victim fled the apartment screaming for help. Ewing absconded with the victim's money and credit cards.

On December 9, 1993, Ewing was arrested on the premises of the apartment complex for trespassing and lying to a police officer. The knife used in the robbery and a glass cocaine pipe were later found in the back seat of the patrol car used to transport Ewing to the police station. A jury convicted Ewing of first-degree robbery and three counts of residential burglary. Sentenced to nine years and eight months in prison, Ewing was paroled in 1999. Only 10 months later, Ewing stole the golf clubs at issue in this case. He was charged with, and ultimately convicted of, one count of felony grand theft of personal property in excess of $400. As required by the three strikes law, the prosecutor formally alleged, and the trial court later found, that Ewing had been convicted previously of four serious or violent felonies for the three burglaries and the robbery in the Long Beach apartment complex.

At the sentencing hearing, Ewing asked the court to reduce the conviction for grand theft, a "wobbler" under California law, to a misdemeanor so as to avoid a three strikes sentence. Ewing also asked the trial court to exercise its discretion to dismiss the allegations of some or all of his prior serious or violent felony convictions, again for purposes of avoiding a three strikes sentence. Before sentencing Ewing, the trial court took note of his entire criminal history, including the fact that he was on parole when he committed his latest offense. The court also heard arguments from defense counsel and a plea from Ewing himself.

In the end, the trial judge determined that the grand theft should remain a felony. The court also ruled that the four prior strikes for the three burglaries and the robbery in Long Beach should stand. As a newly convicted felon with two or more "serious" or "violent" felony convictions in his past, Ewing was sentenced under the three strikes law to 25 years to life.

The California Court of Appeal affirmed in an unpublished opinion. Relying on our decision in *Rummel v. Estelle*, 445 U.S. 263 (1980), the court rejected Ewing's claim that his sentence was grossly disproportionate under the Eighth Amendment. Enhanced sentences under recidivist statutes like the three strikes law, the court reasoned, serve the "legitimate goal" of deterring and incapacitating repeat offenders. The Supreme Court of California denied Ewing's petition for review, and we granted certiorari. We now affirm.

II.A

The Eighth Amendment, which forbids cruel and unusual punishments, contains a "narrow proportionality principle" that "applies to noncapital sentences." We have most recently addressed the proportionality principle as applied to terms of years in a series of cases beginning with *Rummel v. Estelle, supra.*

In *Rummel*, we held that it did not violate the Eighth Amendment for a State to sentence a three-time offender to life in prison with the possibility of parole. Like Ewing, Rummel was sentenced to a lengthy prison term under a recidivism statute. Rummel's two prior offenses were a 1964 felony for "fraudulent use of a credit card to obtain $80 worth of goods or services," and a 1969 felony conviction for "passing a forged check in the amount of $28.36." His triggering offense was a conviction for felony theft — "obtaining $ 120.75 by false pretenses."

This Court ruled that "[h]aving twice imprisoned him for felonies, Texas was entitled to place upon Rummel the onus of one who is simply unable to bring his conduct within the social norms prescribed by the criminal law of the State." The recidivism statute "is nothing more than a societal decision that when such a person commits yet another felony, he should be subjected to the admittedly serious penalty of incarceration for life, subject only to the State's judgment as to whether to grant him parole." We noted that this Court "has on occasion stated that the Eighth Amendment prohibits imposition of a sentence that is grossly disproportionate to the severity of the crime." But "outside the context of capital punishment, successful challenges to the proportionality of particular sentences have been exceedingly rare." Although we stated that the proportionality principle "would . . . come into play in the extreme example . . . if a legislature made overtime parking a felony punishable by life imprisonment," we held that "the mandatory life sentence imposed upon this petitioner does not constitute cruel and unusual punishment under the Eighth and Fourteenth Amendments."

In *Hutto v. Davis*, 454 U.S. 370 (1982), the defendant was sentenced to two consecutive terms of 20 years in prison for possession with intent to distribute nine ounces of marijuana and distribution of marijuana. We held that such a sentence was constitutional: "In short, *Rummel* stands for the proposition that federal courts should be reluctant to review legislatively mandated terms of imprisonment, and that successful challenges to the proportionality of particular sentences should be exceedingly rare."

Three years after *Rummel*, in *Solem v. Helm*, 463 U.S. 277, 279 (1983), we held that the Eighth Amendment prohibited "a life sentence without possibility of parole for a seventh nonviolent felony." The triggering offense in *Solem* was "uttering a 'no account' check for $100." We specifically stated that the Eighth Amendment's ban on cruel and unusual punishments "prohibits . . . sentences that are disproportionate to the crime committed," and that the "constitutional principle of proportionality has been recognized explicitly in this Court for almost a century." The *Solem* Court then explained that three factors may be relevant to a determination of whether a sentence is so disproportionate that it violates the Eighth Amendment: "(i) the gravity of the offense and the harshness of the penalty; (ii) the sentences imposed on other criminals in the same jurisdiction; and (iii) the sentences imposed for commission of the same crime in other jurisdictions."

Applying these factors in *Solem*, we struck down the defendant's sentence of life without parole. We specifically noted the contrast between that sentence and the sentence in *Rummel*, pursuant to which the defendant was eligible for parole. Indeed, we explicitly declined to overrule *Rummel*: "[O]ur conclusion today is not inconsistent with *Rummel v. Estelle*."

Eight years after *Solem*, we grappled with the proportionality issue again in *Harmelin* [*v. Michigan*, 501 U.S. 987 (1999).] *Harmelin* was not a recidivism case, but rather involved a first-time offender convicted of possessing 672 grams of cocaine. He was sentenced to life in prison without possibility of parole. A majority of the Court rejected *Harmelin*'s claim that his sentence was so grossly disproportionate that it violated the Eighth Amendment. The Court, however, could not agree on why his proportionality argument failed. Justice Scalia, joined by The Chief Justice, wrote that the proportionality principle was "an aspect of our death penalty jurisprudence, rather than a generalizable aspect of Eighth Amendment law." He would thus have declined to apply gross disproportionality principles except in reviewing capital sentences.

Justice Kennedy, joined by two other Members of the Court, concurred in part and concurred in the judgment. Justice Kennedy specifically recognized that "the Eighth Amendment proportionality principle also applies to noncapital sentences."

He then identified four principles of proportionality review — "the primacy of the legislature, the variety of legitimate penological schemes, the nature of our federal system, and the requirement that proportionality review be guided by objective factors" — that "inform the final one: The Eighth Amendment does not require strict proportionality between crime and sentence. Rather, it forbids only extreme sentences that are 'grossly disproportionate' to the crime." Justice Kennedy's concurrence also stated that *Solem* "did not mandate" comparative analysis "within and between jurisdictions."

The proportionality principles in our cases distilled in Justice Kennedy's concurrence guide our application of the Eighth Amendment in the new context that we are called upon to consider.

B

For many years, most States have had laws providing for enhanced sentencing of repeat offenders. Yet between 1993 and 1995, three strikes laws effected a sea change in criminal sentencing throughout the Nation. These laws responded to widespread public concerns about crime by targeting the class of offenders who pose the greatest threat to public safety: career criminals. . . . Though three strikes laws may be relatively new, our tradition of deferring to state legislatures in making and implementing such important policy decisions is longstanding.

Our traditional deference to legislative policy choices finds a corollary in the principle that the Constitution "does not mandate adoption of any one penological theory." A sentence can have a variety of justifications, such as incapacitation, deterrence, retribution, or rehabilitation. Some or all of these justifications may play a role in a State's sentencing scheme. Selecting the sentencing rationales is generally a policy choice to be made by state legislatures, not federal courts.

When the California Legislature enacted the three strikes law, it made a judgment that protecting the public safety requires incapacitating criminals who have already been convicted of at least one serious or violent crime. Nothing in the Eighth Amendment prohibits California from making that choice. To the contrary, our cases establish that "States have a valid interest in deterring and segregating habitual criminals." Recidivism has long been recognized as a legitimate basis for increased punishment.

California's justification is no pretext. Recidivism is a serious public safety concern in California and throughout the Nation. According to a recent report, approximately 67 percent of former inmates released from state prisons were charged with at least one "serious" new crime within three years of their release. In particular, released property offenders like Ewing had higher recidivism rates than those released after committing violent, drug, or public-order offenses. Approximately 73 percent of the property offenders released in 1994 were arrested again within three years, compared to approximately 61 percent of the violent offenders, 62 percent of the public-order offenders, and 66 percent of the drug offenders.

In 1996, when the Sacramento Bee studied 233 three strikes offenders in California, it found that they had an aggregate of 1,165 prior felony convictions, an average of 5 apiece. The prior convictions included 322 robberies and 262 burglaries. About 84 percent of the 233 three strikes offenders had been convicted of at least one violent crime. In all, they were responsible for 17 homicides, 7 attempted slayings, and 91 sexual assaults and child molestations. The Sacramento Bee concluded, based on its investigation, that "in the vast majority of the cases, regardless of the third strike, the [three strikes] law is snaring [the] long-term habitual offenders with multiple felony convictions. . . ."

The State's interest in deterring crime also lends some support to the three strikes law. We have long viewed both incapacitation and deterrence as rationales for recidivism statutes: "[A] recidivist statute['s] . . . primary goals are to deter repeat offenders and, at some point in the life of one who repeatedly commits criminal offenses serious enough to be punished as felonies, to segregate that person from the rest of society for an extended period of time." Four years after the passage of California's three strikes law, the recidivism rate of parolees returned to prison for the commission of a new crime dropped by nearly 25 percent. Even more dramatically:

> [A]n unintended but positive consequence of 'Three Strikes' has been the impact on parolees leaving the state. More California parolees are now leaving the state than parolees from other jurisdictions entering California. This striking turnaround started in 1994. It was the first time more parolees left the state than entered since 1976. This trend has continued and in 1997 more than 1,000 net parolees left California.

To be sure, California's three strikes law has sparked controversy. Critics have doubted the law's wisdom, cost-efficiency, and effectiveness in reaching its goals. This criticism is appropriately directed at the legislature, which has primary responsibility for making the difficult policy choices that underlie any criminal sentencing scheme. We do not sit as a "superlegislature" to second-guess these policy choices. It is enough that the State of California has a reasonable basis for believing that dramatically enhanced sentences for habitual felons "advances the goals of [its] criminal justice system in any substantial way."

III

Against this backdrop, we consider Ewing's claim that his three strikes sentence of 25 years to life is unconstitutionally disproportionate to his offense of "shoplifting three golf clubs." We first address the gravity of the offense compared to the harshness of the penalty. At the threshold, we note that Ewing incorrectly frames the issue. The gravity of his offense was not merely "shoplifting three golf clubs." Rather, Ewing was convicted of felony grand theft for stealing nearly $1,200 worth of merchandise after previously having been convicted of at least two "violent" or "serious" felonies. Even standing alone, Ewing's theft should not be taken lightly. His crime was certainly not "one of the most passive felonies a person could commit." To the contrary, the Supreme Court of California has noted the "seriousness" of grand theft in the context of proportionality review. Theft of $1,200 in property is a felony under federal law, 18 U.S.C. § 641, and in the vast majority of States.

That grand theft is a "wobbler" under California law is of no moment. Though California courts have discretion to reduce a felony grand theft charge to a misdemeanor, it remains a felony for all purposes "unless and until the trial court imposes a misdemeanor sentence." "The purpose of the trial judge's sentencing discretion" to downgrade certain felonies is to "impose a misdemeanor sentence in those cases in which the rehabilitation of the convicted defendant either does not require or would be adversely affected by, incarceration in a state prison as a felon." Under California law, the reduction is not based on the notion that a "wobbler" is "conceptually a misdemeanor." Rather, it is "intended to extend misdemeanant treatment to a potential felon." In Ewing's case, however, the trial judge justifiably exercised her discretion not to extend such lenient treatment given Ewing's long criminal history.

In weighing the gravity of Ewing's offense, we must place on the scales not only his current felony, but also his long history of felony recidivism. Any other approach would fail to accord proper deference to the policy judgments that find expression in the legislature's choice of sanctions. In imposing a three strikes sentence, the State's interest is not merely punishing the offense of conviction, or the "triggering" offense: "It is in addition the interest . . . in dealing in a harsher manner with those who by repeated criminal acts have shown that they are simply incapable of conforming to the norms of society as established by its criminal law." To give full effect to the State's choice of this legitimate penological goal, our proportionality review of Ewing's sentence must take that goal into account.

Ewing's sentence is justified by the State's public-safety interest in incapacitating and deterring recidivist felons, and amply supported by his own long, serious criminal record. . . . Ewing's is not "the rare case in which a threshold comparison of the crime committed and the sentence imposed leads to an inference of gross disproportionality."

We hold that Ewing's sentence of 25 years to life in prison, imposed for the offense of felony grand theft under the three strikes law, is not grossly disproportionate and therefore does not violate the Eighth Amendment's prohibition on cruel and unusual punishments. The judgment of the California Court of Appeal is affirmed.

JUSTICE SCALIA, concurring in the judgment.

In my concurring opinion in *Harmelin v. Michigan*, I concluded that the Eighth Amendment's prohibition of "cruel and unusual punishments" was aimed at excluding only certain modes of punishment, and was not a "guarantee against disproportionate sentences." Out of respect for the principle of stare decisis, I might nonetheless accept the contrary holding of *Solem v. Helm*, — that the Eighth Amendment contains a narrow proportionality principle — if I felt I could intelligently apply it. This case demonstrates why I cannot.

Proportionality — the notion that the punishment should fit the crime — is inherently a concept tied to the penological goal of retribution."[I]t becomes difficult even to speak intelligently of 'proportionality,' once deterrence and rehabilitation are given significant weight," — not to mention giving weight to the purpose of California's three strikes law: incapacitation. In the present case, the game is up once the plurality has acknowledged that "the Constitution does not mandate adoption of any one penological theory," and that a "sentence can have a variety of justifications, such as incapacitation, deterrence, retribution, or rehabilitation." That acknowledgment having been made, it no longer suffices merely to assess "the gravity of the offense compared to the harshness of the penalty," that classic description of the proportionality principle (alone and in itself quite resistant to policy-free, legal analysis) now becomes merely the "first" step of the inquiry. Having completed that step (by a discussion which, in all fairness, does not convincingly establish that 25-years-to-life is a "proportionate" punishment for stealing three golf clubs), the plurality must then *add* an analysis to show that "Ewing's sentence is justified by the State's public-safety interest in incapacitating and deterring recidivist felons."

Which indeed it is — though why that has anything to do with the principle of proportionality is a mystery. Perhaps the plurality should revise its terminology, so that what it reads into the Eighth Amendment is not the unstated proposition that all punishment should be reasonably proportionate to the gravity of the offense, but rather the unstated proposition that all punishment should reasonably pursue the multiple purposes of the criminal law. That formulation would make it clearer than ever, of course, that the plurality is not applying law but evaluating policy.

Because I agree that petitioner's sentence does not violate the Eighth Amendment's prohibition against cruel and unusual punishments, I concur in the judgment.

JUSTICE BREYER, with whom Justice Stevens, Justice Souter, and Justice Ginsburg join, dissenting. . . .

I

This Court's precedent sets forth a framework for analyzing Ewing's Eighth Amendment claim. The Eighth Amendment forbids, as "cruel and unusual punishments," prison terms (including terms of years) that are "grossly disproportionate." In applying the "gross disproportionality" principle, courts must keep in mind that "legislative policy" will primarily determine the appropriateness of a punishment's "severity," and hence defer to such legislative policy judgments. If courts properly respect those judgments, they will find that the sentence fails the test only in *rare* instances. . . . I believe that the case before us is a "rare" case — one in which a court can say with reasonable confidence that the punishment is "grossly disproportionate" to the crime.

II

Ewing's claim crosses the gross disproportionality "threshold." First, precedent makes clear that Ewing's sentence raises a serious disproportionality question. Ewing is a recidivist. Hence the two cases most directly in point are those in which the Court considered the constitutionality of recidivist sentencing: *Rummel* and *Solem*. Ewing's claim falls between these two cases. It is stronger than the claim presented in *Rummel*, where the Court upheld a recidivist's sentence as constitutional. It is weaker than the claim presented in *Solem*, where the Court struck down a recidivist sentence as unconstitutional. . . .

[T]he comparison [of Ewing's sentence with the sentences imposed in *Solem* and *Rummel*] places Ewing's sentence well within the twilight zone between *Solem* and *Rummel* — a zone where the argument for unconstitutionality is substantial, where the cases themselves cannot determine the constitutional outcome. . . .

[S]ome objective evidence suggests that many experienced judges would consider Ewing's sentence disproportionately harsh. The United States Sentencing Commission (having based the federal Sentencing Guidelines primarily upon its review of how judges had actually sentenced offenders) does not include shoplifting (or similar theft-related offenses) among the crimes that might trigger especially long sentences for recidivists, nor did Congress include such offenses among triggering crimes when it sought sentences "at or near the maximum" for certain recidivists.

. . . Ewing's "gross disproportionality" argument is a strong one. That being so, his claim *must* pass the "threshold" test. If it did not, what would be the function of the test? A threshold test must permit *arguably* unconstitutional sentences, not only *actually* unconstitutional sentences, to pass the threshold — at least where the arguments for unconstitutionality are unusually strong ones. A threshold test that blocked every ultimately invalid constitutional claim — even strong ones — would not be a *threshold* test but a *determinative* test. . . .

III

Believing Ewing's argument a strong one, sufficient to pass the threshold, I turn to the comparative analysis. A comparison of Ewing's sentence with other sentences requires answers to two questions. First, how would other jurisdictions (or California at other times, *i.e.*, without the three strikes penalty) punish the same offense conduct? Second, upon what other conduct would other jurisdictions (or California) impose the *same prison term*? Moreover, since hypothetical punishment is beside the point, the relevant prison time, for comparative purposes, is real prison time, *i.e.*, the time that an offender must *actually serve*. . . .

As to California itself, we know the following: First, between the end of World War II and 1994 (when California enacted the three strikes law), *no one* like Ewing could have served more than *10* years in prison. We know that for certain because the maximum sentence for Ewing's crime of conviction, grand theft, was for most of that period 10 years. . . .

[W]e know that California has reserved, and still reserves, Ewing-type prison time, *i.e.*, at least 25 real years in prison, for criminals convicted of crimes far worse than was Ewing's. Statistics for the years 1945 to 1981, for example, indicate that typical (nonrecidivist) male first-degree murderers served between 10 and 15 real years in prison, with 90 percent of all such murderers serving less than 20 real years. Moreover, California, which has moved toward a real-time sentencing system (where the statutory punishment approximates the time served), still punishes far less harshly those who have engaged in far more serious conduct. It imposes, for example, upon nonrecidivists guilty of arson causing great bodily injury a maximum sentence of nine years in prison; it imposes upon those guilty of voluntary manslaughter a maximum sentence of 11 years. It reserves the sentence that it here imposes upon (former-burglar-now-golf-club-thief) Ewing, for nonrecidivist, first-degree murderers.

As to other jurisdictions, we know the following: The United States, bound by the federal Sentencing Guidelines, would impose upon a recidivist, such as Ewing, a sentence that, in any ordinary case, would not exceed 18 months in prison. The Guidelines, based in part upon a study of some 40,000 actual federal sentences, reserve a Ewing-type sentence for Ewing-type *recidivists* who currently commit such crimes as murder, air piracy, robbery (involving the discharge of a firearm, serious bodily injury, and about $1 million), drug offenses involving more than, for example, 20 pounds of heroin, aggravated theft of more than $100 million, and other similar offenses. . . . Ewing also would not have been subject to the federal "three strikes" law, for which grand theft is not a triggering offense.

With three exceptions, we do not have before us information about actual time served by Ewing-type offenders in other States. We do know, however, that the law would make it legally impossible for a Ewing-type offender to serve more than 10 years in prison in 33 jurisdictions, as well as the federal courts, more than 15 years in 4 other States, and more than 20 years in 4 additional States. In nine other States, the law *might* make it legally possible to impose a sentence of 25 years or more, — though that fact by itself, of course, does not mean that judges have actually done so. I say "might" because the law in five of the nine last-mentioned States restricts the sentencing judge's ability to impose a term so long that, with parole, it would amount to at least 25 years of actual imprisonment. . . .

The upshot is that comparison of other sentencing practices, both in other jurisdictions and in California at other times (or in respect to other crimes), validates what an initial threshold examination suggested. Given the information available, given the state and federal parties' ability to provide additional contrary data, and given their failure to do so, we can assume for constitutional purposes that the following statement is true: Outside the California three strikes context, Ewing's recidivist sentence is virtually unique in its harshness for his offense of conviction, and by a considerable degree.

IV

No one argues for Ewing's inclusion within the ambit of the three strikes statute on grounds of "retribution." For reasons previously discussed, in terms of "deterrence," Ewing's 25-year term amounts to overkill. And "rehabilitation" is obviously beside the point. The upshot is that, in my view, the State cannot find in its three strikes law a special criminal justice need sufficient to rescue a sentence that other relevant considerations indicate is unconstitutional.

V

Justice Scalia and Justice Thomas argue that we should not review for gross disproportionality a sentence to a term of years. Otherwise, we make it too difficult for legislators and sentencing judges to determine just when their sentencing laws and practices pass constitutional muster. I concede that a bright-line rule would give legislators and sentencing judges more guidance. But application of the Eighth Amendment to a sentence of a term of years requires a case-by-case approach. And, in my view, like that of the plurality, meaningful enforcement of the Eighth Amendment demands that application — even if only at sentencing's outer bounds.

A case-by-case approach can nonetheless offer guidance through example. Ewing's sentence is, at a minimum, 2 to 3 times the length of sentences that other jurisdictions would impose in similar circumstances. That sentence itself is sufficiently long to require a typical offender to spend virtually all the remainder of his active life in prison. These and the other factors that I have discussed, along with the questions that I have asked along the way, should help to identify "gross disproportionality" in a fairly objective way — at the outer bounds of sentencing.

JUSTICE STEVENS, with whom Justice Souter, Justice Ginsburg, and Justice Breyer join, dissenting.

Justice Breyer has cogently explained why the sentence imposed in this case is both cruel and unusual. The concurrences prompt this separate writing to emphasize that proportionality review is not only capable of judicial application but also required by the Eighth Amendment. "The Eighth Amendment succinctly prohibits 'excessive' sanctions." Faithful to the Amendment's text, this Court has held that the Constitution directs judges to apply their best judgment in determining the proportionality of fines and other forms of punishment, including the imposition of a death sentence. It "would be anomalous indeed" to suggest that the Eighth

Amendment makes proportionality review applicable in the context of bail and fines but not in the context of other forms of punishment, such as imprisonment. Rather, by broadly prohibiting excessive sanctions, the Eighth Amendment directs judges to exercise their wise judgment in assessing the proportionality of all forms of punishment.

The absence of a black-letter rule does not disable judges from exercising their discretion in construing the outer limits on sentencing authority that the Eighth Amendment imposes. After all, judges are "constantly called upon to draw ... lines in a variety of contexts," and to exercise their judgment to give meaning to the Constitution's broadly phrased protections. For example, the Due Process Clause directs judges to employ proportionality review in assessing the constitutionality of punitive damages awards on a case-by-case basis. Also, although the Sixth Amendment guarantees criminal defendants the right to a speedy trial, the courts often are asked to determine on a case-by-case basis whether a particular delay is constitutionally permissible or not.

Throughout most of the Nation's history — before guideline sentencing became so prevalent — federal and state trial judges imposed specific sentences pursuant to grants of authority that gave them uncabined discretion within broad ranges. It was not unheard of for a statute to authorize a sentence ranging from one year to life, for example. In exercising their discretion, sentencing judges wisely employed a proportionality principle that took into account all of the justifications for punishment — namely, deterrence, incapacitation, retribution and rehabilitation. Likewise, I think it clear that the Eighth Amendment's prohibition of "cruel and unusual punishments" expresses a broad and basic proportionality principle that takes into account all of the justifications for penal sanctions. It is this broad proportionality principle that would preclude reliance on any of the justifications for punishment to support, for example, a life sentence for overtime parking.

QUESTIONS

1. Who decides if a defendant falls within California's three strikes statute? The prosecutor? The judge? Or the jury?

2. Justice O'Connor writes: "Recidivism has long been recognized as a legitimate basis for increased punishment." Why is this so? In other words, why should an offender with a prior record receive a harsher sentence than an offender who commits the identical crime but has no prior record? On what ground did the California legislature, in passing the three strikes statute, decide that greater punishment should be given to repeat offenders?

3. Was Ewing punished for his most recent crime of stealing three golf clubs? Or was he punished for both his most recent offense and his prior offenses? Being punished twice for the same offense is typically viewed as unfair and a violation of the Constitution's prohibition against double jeopardy. Are Ewing and other offenders who are sentenced under three strikes laws being punished twice for crimes?

4. Justice Scalia states: "Proportionality — the notion that the punishment should fit the crime — is inherently a concept tied to the penological goal of retribution." Is the idea of proportionality necessarily equivalent to "the notion that the punishment should fit the crime?" Is it inherently tied to retribution?

PROBLEMS

2.15 Leandro was charged and convicted in a California court on two counts of petty theft and received two consecutive terms of 25 years to life under the same three strikes statute at issue in *Ewing*. On one date, Leandro shoplifted five videotapes worth $84.70 from a discount chain store. Two weeks later, he shoplifted four more videotapes worth $68.84 from another branch of the same chain store. Leandro is 37 years old and has been addicted to heroin for the past 20 years. He stole the videotapes to obtain money to purchase heroin. Petty theft is a "wobbler" offense. Typically a misdemeanor, it may be charged as a felony at the discretion of the prosecutor if the defendant has a prior theft conviction. Leandro had a prior theft conviction, and both his petty theft offenses were treated as felonies. Leandro must serve 50 years in prison before becoming eligible for parole. His prior record includes three residential burglaries, two misdemeanor theft convictions, and two convictions for transporting marijuana. Does Leandro's sentence violate the constitutional principle of proportionality?[34]

2.16 In light of the theories of punishment, consider the *Cluff* case:[35]

> Cluff was born in 1951 and was 48 years old at the time of sentencing. His early criminal history consists of a petty theft in 1970, two convictions for indecent exposure in 1972, and a third conviction for indecent exposure in 1973. . . . [A]ll three indecent exposure offenses [involved] children in public areas.
>
> In June, 1984, a jury convicted Cluff of [nine] felony counts of child molestation. . . . With respect to those offenses, the probation report states that while Cluff was residing with his fiancee and two boys (aged five and eight), he frequently molested the boys. In a separate incident in the summer of 1983, Cluff molested the six-year-old son of a visiting friend. Cluff also molested a 7-year-old boy in a similar manner. Cluff received a nine-year prison sentence for these offenses. He was paroled in April 1990.
>
> At that time, prison officials informed him of his lifetime obligation to register as a sex offender. Cluff registered a number of times after changing his residence over the next five years. In October 1995, Cluff moved to San Mateo. On October 18, 1995, he went to the San Mateo police department and registered [as a sex offender] as section 290 requires. . . . When Cluff registered in October 1995, [the registering officer] gave him a form explaining the requirements for registration. Cluff signed the form, which specifically advised him that he was required to update his registration annually within (at that time) 10 days of his birthday. He was not arrested or accused of any further offense until October 1997, when the police arrested him for the registration violation at issue in this case. In October 1997, Sergeant Callagy of the San Mateo Police Department learned that Cluff had not updated his registration during the period around his

---

34. Based on Andrade v. Lockyer, 538 U.S. 68 (2003).
35. Excerpted from People v. Cluff, 2001 Cal. App. LEXIS 200, 105 Cal. Rptr. 2d 80 (2001).

birthday (July 29) in 1996 and 1997. On October 23, 1997, Callagy went to 1408 South Norfolk Street and met with Cluff's landlord. The landlord confirmed that Cluff still lived at that address, and he would have Cluff call Callagy when he returned. Cluff called Callagy the next day, and offered to come in immediately. . . . When Cluff arrived at the police station for his appointment on October 27, Sergeant Callagy immediately arrested him for violating section 290.

The District Attorney charged Cluff in a one-count information as follows: "On or about 10/23/1997, Alan Ross Cluff being a person required to register as a sex offender having been previously convicted of PC section 288A (lewd and lascivious conduct on a child under 14) . . . , did fail to register within the time limits provided, in violation of Penal Code section 290(a)(1), a felony."

The court rendered its verdict in December 1998. . . . The court ruled that Cluff received sufficient notice of the annual registration requirement to satisfy any due process concerns. The court found him guilty as charged. . . . In addition, the court found Cluff had suffered three prior "strikes" under the Three Strikes law and had served a prior prison term.

At the sentencing hearing in February 1999, the court considered the probation officer's report, the report of a court-appointed psychotherapist, and the arguments of counsel. . . . "[W]ith a heavy heart" the court sentenced him to 25 years to life in prison.

Which theories of punishment predominated at the trial level here?

Cluff appealed his sentence and persuaded the appellate court that "there [were] strong arguments that [he] should be treated as though he fell outside the Three Strikes scheme." The appellate court vacated Cluff's sentence and remanded to the trial court. The appellate court instructed the trial court on remand to consider a number of factors "in exercising its discretion to strike one or more of the prior convictions." Which court was right? Does the answer depend on one's choice of a theory of punishment?

CHAPTER THREE

MAKING CRIMINAL LAW

The power to create and define crimes is the power to determine when people will be labeled as criminals, imprisoned, fined, or executed. Who should exercise this power? Who currently does exercise it? These questions lie at the center of the materials in this chapter and will recur throughout your study of criminal law.

Federal and state constitutions divide the power of government among three branches — legislative, executive, and judicial. This division is often referred to as the separation of powers. The conventional concept is that the legislature makes the law, the executive branch enforces the law, and the judiciary applies the law. We will see that today the allocation of power among the three branches is considerably more complex and nuanced than this simple description suggests.

Section A in this chapter focuses on legislators and judges, two groups that play the most visible roles in making criminal law. Sections B and C then address how executive branch officials, such as prosecutors, as well as jurors, participate in shaping the contours of criminal law.

The starting point for assessing criminal liability today is typically a statute enacted by a legislature. Judges exercise great power in shaping modern criminal law through the interpretation of criminal statutes. How do judges go about this task? How should they go about it? We turn to the topic of statutory interpretation and address these questions in Section D, where we examine several different approaches to statutory interpretation.

Section E deals with the final topic in this chapter, specificity. Here, we turn from the question of who makes criminal law to look at what level of clarity and precision should be required of criminal statutes.

A. LEGISLATORS AND JUDGES

The Anglo-American legal system originally relied on judges to formulate criminal law through a body of judicial opinions known as the common law of crimes. *Khaliq*, the first case in this Section, demonstrates that Scotland still recognizes common law crimes. American courts today continue to exercise primary authority as law makers in some fields of law, such as torts. But in the United States, the legislature is now widely viewed as having ultimate authority over the creation and definition of criminal offenses, subject only to constitutional constraints. This modern notion of legislative supremacy in criminal law is reflected in the following passage from a Florida Supreme Court opinion reversing the controversial conviction of a woman for exposing the fetus she was carrying to cocaine:

> Neither judges nor prosecutors can make criminal laws. This is the purview of the Legislature. If the Legislature wanted to punish the uterine transfer of cocaine

from a mother to her fetus, it would be up to the Legislature to consider the attending public policy and constitutional arguments and then pass its legislation. The
Legislature has not done so and the court has no power to make such a law.[1]

The term "legality" is often used to express this preference for legislatively defined
crime. It also expresses a preference for clear and advance definition of crimes,
topics we address below. The *Keeler* case exemplifies the principle of legality.

What position does each of the four states, whose statutes are listed below, take
regarding common law crimes?

New Mexico Statutes Annotated § 30-1-3   *Construction of Criminal Code*

In criminal cases where no provision of this code is applicable, the common law,
as recognized by the United States and the several states of the Union, shall govern.

Florida Statutes § 775.01   *Common law of England*

The common law of England in relation to crimes, except so far as the same
relates to the modes and degrees of punishment, shall be of full force in this state
where there is no existing provision by statute on the subject.

§ 775.02   *Punishment of common-law offenses*

When there exists no such provision by statute, the court shall proceed to punish
such offense by fine or imprisonment, but the fine shall not exceed $500, nor the
imprisonment 12 months.

Arizona Revised Statutes § 13-103   *Abolition of common law offenses and affirmative defenses*

A. All common law offenses and affirmative defenses are abolished. No conduct
or omission constitutes an offense or an affirmative defense unless it is an offense or
an affirmative defense under this title or under another statute or ordinance.

New Hampshire Revised Statutes § 625:6   *All Offenses Defined by Statute*

No conduct or omission constitutes an offense unless it is a crime or violation
under this code or under another statute.

KHALIQ *v.* HER MAJESTY'S ADVOCATE

1983 S.C.C.R. 483 (3 August, 1983)

[The government alleged that Khaliq and another man had sold to a number
of children between the ages of eight and fifteen both glue and paraphernalia for
inhaling vapors from the glue, such as tins, tubes, and plastic bags. The defendants
challenged the indictment on the ground that what they were charged with doing

---

1. Johnson v. Florida, 602 So. 2d 1288, 1294 (Fla. 1992) (quoting People v. Bremer, No. 90-32227-FH
(Mich. Cir. Ct. Jan. 31, 1991).

was not a crime in Scotland. The trial judge ruled on their challenge in the following passages.]

LORD AVONSIDE. . . . [The] charge is claimed to be bad on several grounds, the most important of which is that it 'does not set out a crime known to the law of Scotland'. Argument was presented to the effect that if the crime was a 'new' crime, it could not be introduced into our criminal law by the decision of a single judge. I accept that. It would be a matter for consideration by a quorum of the High Court. . . .

At the outset I was referred by counsel . . . to the fact that while there had been attempts in Parliament to deal — if that be the word — with 'solvent abuse', all that had been achieved was the Solvent Abuse (Scotland) Act 1983. That Act states that a child may be in need of compulsory measures of care within the provisions of the Social Work (Scotland) Act 1968 if 'he has misused a volatile substance by deliberately inhaling, other than for medicinal purposes, that substance's vapour . . . '. I would not brush aside that Act as wholly irrelevant. It does display concern about misuse of volatile substances and shows that there is a defined danger recognised by Parliament.

The initial general approach of counsel for the [defense] was that 'solvents' covered a wide range of substances and that a decision in favour of the Crown in this case could result in many anomalies. There were many types and kinds of 'solvents' legitimately on the public market and open to anyone who wished to buy them. Equally there were many types of drugs which were available without prescription which could be used for wrong and dire purpose and so result in illness or, indeed, death. Cigarettes were dangerous, misused alcohol could lead to death and so on. All that may be so, but I reject argument in terrorem and place no faith in hypotheses of imagination. I am concerned only with the charge before me. Any other case which might arise would depend on the facts and circumstances pertaining to it.

It is not disputed that 'glue' is not listed as a dangerous substance or drug. Nor is it disputed that to possess 'glue' is permissible. Further, in my opinion, it is not a criminal offence for a person who does so to 'misuse glue'. . . . The real or at least the most important issue in this case lies in the assertion that in respect of the first charge of the indictment no crime has been [charged] "which is known to the law of Scotland." In my opinion that assertion is unfounded. . . . The great strength of our common law in criminal matters is that it can be invoked to fill a need. It is not static. Over the centuries it has operated unless its jurisdiction is displaced by statute or by decision of the courts. It did not weaken by time or history. It is as alive today in dealing with the present age as it was in dealing with questions raised in the past.

Hume put it thus: "Let us now attend to those offences against the person, which remain on the footing of the common law, and are punishable only with some inferior pain, at the discretion of the Court. These are various in kind and degree; and the law is provided with sundry corresponding terms for them . . . such as assault, invasion, beating and bruising, blooding and wounding, stabbing, mutilation, demembration, and some others. But although the injury do not come under any of those terms of style, nor be such as can be announced in a single phrase, this circumstance in nowise affects the competency of a prosecution. Let the [charge] . . . give an intelligible account of it in terms at large; and, if it amount to a real injury, it shall be sustained to infer punishment, less or more . . . no matter how new or how strange the wrong."

Alison puts the matter thus: "By the common law every new crime, as it successively arises, becomes the object of punishment, provided it be in itself wrong,
and hurtful to the persons or property of others."

In my opinion, the claim that the first charge sets out an offence which, it is said,
is unknown to 'the law of Scotland' is without substance. The only novelty is that it
[charges] the use and abuse of a solvent. It is only comparatively recently that the
effect of such abuse has become known to the public. That knowledge is significant,
but not decisive in approaching the question of the power of our common law in
criminal matters. It would be strange if the common law cannot deal with a known
danger and the culpability of those who supply for profit the solvents knowing
that abuse and its attendant effects may, in extreme cases, result in the death of the
user.

The common law has been overtaken in some instances by Parliament or the
decisions of the court, but that apart, it can deal with offences which may have
arisen in modern times. The only novelty in the present case is that it involves a
supply to the public, and in particular, children and young people, of a substance
which lends itself to abuse. If the vapour given off by that substance is inhaled,
the user can cause injury to his health and indeed life. This is precisely a situation
with which the common law can deal, where the dangers of such a supply are well
known.

Put in a positive way, if the [defense] were right in their assertion that these
activities did not constitute a crime in the law of Scotland, they can sell or supply
solvents well knowing that their young customers have no intention whatsoever
of using the substances in an ordinary manner, but, packaged in strange containers
as they are, will use the solvents as they might a drug, inhaling the vapours given
off by the solvents to the danger of their health or, indeed, to their lives. It might
seem that Parliament has found difficulty in dealing with that situation, but, if so,
there is all the more reason for applying our common law in criminal matters. I
stress what I have said above. This case is not concerned with a "new" crime. It is
concerned with the breach of existing common law relating to the use of poisonous,
or at least injurious, substances to the danger of health and life. The only novelty
is that the abuse of glue, or other solvent, and the danger of such abuses, has only
been fully recognised fairly recently.

[The trial judge denied the defendant's challenge to the prosecution. The defendants appealed this ruling to the High Court of Judiciary. The High Court affirmed
the trial judge in the following opinion.]

KHALIQ v. HER MAJESTY'S ADVOCATE
1984 S.C.C.R. 23 (17 Nov. 1983)

Lord Justice-General EMSLIE. . . . In introducing the appellants' primary objection to the relevancy of charge 1, Lord McCluskey reminded us quite correctly that
Parliament has not yet subjected solvents to statutory control, fenced by criminal
penalties. There are, further, no statutory provisions restricting the supply of solvents to children. Such provisions have, of course, been made in relation to, for
example, alcohol and tobacco. . . .

The first and perhaps the only critical question to be answered in this case is
whether the Crown's primary submission in support of the relevancy of charge
1 is well founded. The Crown's position is that what is [charged] here is not a

new crime but merely a modern example of conduct which our law has for long regarded as criminal. Such conduct is described by Hume in the passage to which reference has already been made and consists in actions of any kind which cause or are a cause of real injury to the person. The Crown case is, in short, that the actions of the appellants, in the particular circumstances [charged], were a cause of real injury to the children referred to resulting from their inhalation of the intoxicating and dangerous fumes emitted by the solvents supplied to them for that specific purpose. . . .

"It would be a mistake," as the Lord Justice-General (Clyde) observed . . . "to imagine that the criminal common law of Scotland countenances any precise and exact categorisation of the forms of conduct which amount to crime. It has been pointed out many times in this Court that such is not the nature or quality of the criminal law of Scotland. . . .

It is of course not an objection to the relevancy of a charge alleged to be one of criminal conduct merely to say that it is without precise precedent in previous decisions. The categories of criminal conduct are never to this extent closed. "An old crime may certainly be committed in a new way; and a case, though never occurring before on its facts, may fall within the spirit of a previous decision, or within an established general principle." . . . In the case now before us it is to an established general principle that the Lord Advocate resorts in defence of the relevancy and sufficiency of the facts [charged] to constitute an indictable crime, and that general principle is to be found in Hume . . . in the passage quoted by the trial judge in his opinion which I do not find it necessary to repeat. The general principle to be discovered from that passage is that within the category of conduct identified as criminal are acts, whatever their nature may be, which cause real injury to the person. Does this case, though never before occurring on its facts, fall within the general principle as the Lord Advocate contends? In my opinion it does, although the nature of the injury and the act alleged to be a cause of that injury may be new.

Upon the whole matter I am of opinion that the appeals fail and that they should be refused.

QUESTIONS

1. How would the *Khaliq* case be resolved under the New Mexico, Florida, Arizona, and New Hampshire statutes that appear at the beginning of this chapter?

2. Article 7 of the European Convention on Human Rights[2] provides:

> No one shall be held guilty of any criminal offence on account of any act or omission which did not constitute a criminal offence under national or international law at the time when it was committed. Nor shall a heavier penalty be imposed than the one that was applicable at the time the criminal offence was committed.

Would Khaliq's conviction be valid under this provision? In other words, was Khaliq convicted of a new crime? Or had he simply found a new way to commit an old crime? If the latter, what is the name of this old crime?

3. At his sentencing, Khaliq's lawyer claimed that the police had asked Khaliq to stop selling glue and sniffing paraphernalia to children. When Khaliq asked if

---

2. The European Convention on Human Rights was made applicable to Scotland in 1998 by the Human Rights Act 1998, §§ 1(1); 6(1), (2)(a).

what he was doing was a crime, the police told him they "could not say definitely that by doing so [he was] breaking the law." If true, would these facts have any bearing on Khaliq's liability?

4. Khaliq was sentenced by the trial judge to three years' imprisonment. The High Court reduced the sentence to two years, finding that "[a]ll the necessary objectives could have been achieved by a shorter sentence coupled with a clear warning that anyone convicted of a similar crime in the future could expect to be punished more severely."[3] Why should Khaliq receive a lesser sentence than someone who commits the same crime in the future?

KEELER v. SUPERIOR COURT
2 Cal. 3d 619 (1970)

Mosk, J. In this proceeding for writ of prohibition we are called upon to decide whether an unborn but viable fetus is a "human being" within the meaning of the California statute defining murder. We conclude that the Legislature did not intend such a meaning, and that for us to construe the statute to the contrary and apply it to this petitioner would exceed our judicial power and deny petitioner due process of law.

The evidence received at the preliminary examination may be summarized as follows: Petitioner and Teresa Keeler obtained an interlocutory decree of divorce on September 27, 1968. They had been married for 16 years. Unknown to petitioner, Mrs. Keeler was then pregnant by one Ernest Vogt, whom she had met earlier that summer. She subsequently began living with Vogt in Stockton, but concealed the fact from petitioner. . . .

On February 23, 1969, Mrs. Keeler was driving on a narrow mountain road in Amador County . . . She met petitioner driving in the opposite direction; he blocked the road with his car, and she pulled over to the side. He walked to her vehicle and began speaking to her. He seemed calm, and she rolled down her window to hear him. He said, "I hear you're pregnant. If you are you had better stay away from the girls and from here." She did not reply, and he opened the car door; as she later testified, "He assisted me out of the car. . . . [It] wasn't roughly at this time." Petitioner then looked at her abdomen and became "extremely upset." He said, "You sure are. I'm going to stomp it out of you." He pushed her against the car, shoved his knee into her abdomen, and struck her in the face with several blows. She fainted, and when she regained consciousness petitioner had departed.

Mrs. Keeler drove back to Stockton, and the police and medical assistance were summoned. She had suffered substantial facial injuries, as well as extensive bruising of the abdominal wall. A Caesarian section was performed and the fetus was examined *in utero*. Its head was found to be severely fractured, and it was delivered stillborn. The pathologist gave as his opinion that the cause of death was skull fracture with consequent cerebral hemorrhaging, that death would have been immediate, and that the injury could have been the result of force applied to the mother's abdomen. There was no air in the fetus' lungs, and the umbilical cord was intact. . . .

An information was filed charging petitioner, in count I, with committing the crime of murder in that he did "unlawfully kill a human being, to wit Baby Girl

---

3. Khaliq v. Her Majesty's Advocate, 1984 S.C.C.R. 212 (14 June 1984).

Vogt, with malice aforethought." . . . His motion to set aside the information for lack of probable cause was denied, and he now seeks a writ of prohibition; . . .

I

Penal Code Section 187 provides: "Murder is the unlawful killing of a human being, with malice aforethought." The dispositive question is whether the fetus which petitioner is accused of killing was, on February 23, 1969, a "human being" within the meaning of the statute. If it was not, petitioner cannot be charged with its "murder" and prohibition will lie.

Section 187 was enacted as part of the Penal Code of 1872. Inasmuch as the provision has not been amended since that date, we must determine the intent of the Legislature at the time of its enactment. But section 187 was, in turn, taken verbatim from the first California statute defining murder, part of the Crimes and Punishments Act of 1850. Penal Code Section 5 (also enacted in 1872) declares: "The provisions of this code, so far as they are substantially the same as existing statutes, must be construed as continuations thereof, and not as new enactments." We begin, accordingly, by inquiring into the intent of the Legislature in 1850 when it first defined murder as the unlawful and malicious killing of a "human being."

It will be presumed, of course, that in enacting a statute the Legislature was familiar with the relevant rules of the common law, and, when it couches its enactment in common law language, that its intent was to continue those rules in statutory form. This is particularly appropriate in considering the work of the first session of our Legislature: its precedents were necessarily drawn from the common law, as modified in certain respects by the Constitution and by legislation of our sister states.

We therefore undertake a brief review of the origins and development of the common law of abortional homicide. From that inquiry it appears that by the year 1850 — the date with which we are concerned — an infant could not be the subject of homicide at common law *unless it had been born alive*. Perhaps the most influential statement of the "born alive" rule is that of Coke, in mid-17th century: "If a woman be quick with childe,[5] and by a potion or otherwise killeth it in her wombe, or if a man beat her, whereby the childe dyeth in her body, and she is delivered of a dead childe, this is a great misprision [i.e., misdemeanor], and no murder; but if the childe be born alive and dyeth of the potion, battery, or other cause, this is murder; for in law it is accounted a reasonable creature, *in rerum natura*, when it is born alive." In short, "By Coke's time, the common law regarded abortion as murder only if the foetus is (1) quickened, (2) born alive, (3) lives for a brief interval, and (4) then dies." Whatever intrinsic defects there may have been in Coke's work, the common law accepted his views as authoritative. In the 18th century, for example, Coke's requirement that an infant be born alive in order to be the subject of homicide was reiterated and expanded by both Blackstone and Hale. . . .

By the year 1850 this rule of the common law had long been accepted in the United States. As early as 1797 it was held that proof the child was born alive is necessary to support an indictment for murder and the same rule was reiterated on the eve of the first session of our Legislature. . . .

---

[5] "Quickening" is said to occur when movements of the fetus are first sensed or observed, and ordinarily takes place between the 16th and 18th week of pregnancy. Although much of the history of the law of abortion and abortional homicide revolves around this concept, it is of no medical significance and was never adopted into the law of California.

We conclude that in declaring murder to be the unlawful and malicious killing of a "human being" the Legislature of 1850 intended that term to have the settled common law meaning of a person who had been born alive, and did not intend the act of feticide — as distinguished from abortion — to be an offense under the laws of California. . . .

It is the policy of this state to construe a penal statute as favorably to the defendant as its language and the circumstances of its application may reasonably permit; just as in the case of a question of fact, the defendant is entitled to the benefit of every reasonable doubt as to the true interpretation of words or the construction of language used in a statute. We hold that in adopting the definition of murder in Penal Code section 187 the Legislature intended to exclude from its reach the act of killing an unborn fetus.

II

The People urge, however, that the sciences of obstetrics and pediatrics have greatly progressed since 1872, to the point where with proper medical care a normally developed fetus prematurely born at 28 weeks or more has an excellent chance of survival, i.e., is "viable"; that the common law requirement of live birth to prove the fetus had become a "human being" who may be the victim of murder is no longer in accord with scientific fact, since an unborn but viable fetus is now fully capable of independent life; and that one who unlawfully and maliciously terminates such a life should therefore be liable to prosecution for murder under section 187. We may grant the premises of this argument; indeed, we neither deny nor denigrate the vast progress of medicine in the century since the enactment of the Penal Code. But we cannot join in the conclusion sought to be deduced: we cannot hold this petitioner to answer for murder by reason of his alleged act of killing an unborn — even though viable — fetus. To such a charge there are two insuperable obstacles, one "jurisdictional" and the other constitutional.

Penal Code section 6 declares in relevant part that "No act or omission" accomplished after the code has taken effect "is criminal or punishable, except as prescribed or authorized by this code, or by some of the statutes which it specifies as continuing in force and as not affected by its provisions, or by some ordinance, municipal, county, or township regulation. . . . " This section embodies a fundamental principle of our tripartite form of government, i.e., that subject to the constitutional prohibition against cruel and unusual punishment, the power to define crimes and fix penalties is vested exclusively in the legislative branch. Stated differently there are no common law crimes in California. "In this state the common law is of no effect so far as the specification of what acts or conduct shall constitute a crime is concerned. In order that a public offense be committed, some statute, ordinance or regulation prior in time to the commission of the act, must denounce it." . . .

Settled rules of construction implement this principle. Although the Penal Code commands us to construe its provisions "according to the fair import of their terms, with a view to effect its objects and to promote justice" (Pen. Code, § 4), it is clear the courts cannot go so far as to create an offense by enlarging a statute, by inserting or deleting words, or by giving the terms used false or unusual meanings. Penal statutes will not be made to reach beyond their plain intent; they include only those offenses coming clearly within the import of their language. Indeed,

"Constructive crimes — crimes built up by courts with the aid of inference, implication, and strained interpretation — are repugnant to the spirit and letter of English and American criminal law."

Applying these rules to the case at bar, we would undoubtedly act in excess of the judicial power if we were to adopt the People's proposed construction of section 187. As we have shown, the Legislature has defined the crime of murder in California to apply only to the unlawful and malicious killing of one who has been born alive. We recognize that the killing of an unborn but viable fetus may be deemed by some to be an offense of similar nature and gravity; but as Chief Justice Marshall warned long ago, "It would be dangerous, indeed, to carry the principle, that a case which is within the reason or mischief of a statute, is within its provisions, so far as to punish a crime not enumerated in the statute, because it is of equal atrocity, or of kindred character, with those which are enumerated." Whether to thus extend liability for murder in California is a determination solely within the province of the Legislature. For a court to simply declare, by judicial fiat, that the time has now come to prosecute under section 187 one who kills an unborn but viable fetus would indeed be to rewrite the statute under the guise of construing it. Nor does a need to fill an asserted "gap" in the law between abortion and homicide — as will appear, no such gap in fact exists — justify judicial legislation of this nature: to make it "a judicial function 'to explore such new fields of crime as they may appear from time to time' is wholly foreign to the American concept of criminal justice" and "raises very serious questions concerning the principle of separation of powers."

The second obstacle to the proposed judicial enlargement of section 187 is the guarantee of due process of law. Assuming *arguendo* that we have the power to adopt the new construction of this statute as the law of California, such a ruling, by constitutional command, could operate only prospectively, and thus could not in any event reach the conduct of petitioner on February 23, 1969.

The first essential of due process is fair warning of the act which is made punishable as a crime. "That the terms of a penal statute creating a new offense must be sufficiently explicit to inform those who are subject to it what conduct on their part will render them liable to its penalties, is a well-recognized requirement, consonant alike with ordinary notions of fair play and the settled rules of law." "No one may be required at peril of life, liberty or property to speculate as to the meaning of penal statutes. All are entitled to be informed as to what the State commands or forbids." The law of California is in full accord.

This requirement of fair warning is reflected in the constitutional prohibition against the enactment of ex post facto laws. When a new penal statute is applied retrospectively to make punishable an act which was not criminal at the time it was performed, the defendant has been given no advance notice consistent with due process. And precisely the same effect occurs when such an act is made punishable under a preexisting statute but by means of an unforeseeable *judicial* enlargement thereof. . . .

"The fundamental principle that 'the required criminal law must have existed when the conduct in issue occurred,' must apply to bar retroactive criminal prohibitions emanating from courts as well as from legislatures. If a judicial construction of a criminal statute is 'unexpected and indefensible by reference to the law which had been expressed prior to the conduct in issue,' it must not be given retroactive effect." . . .

We conclude that the judicial enlargement of section 187 now urged upon us by the People would not have been forseeable to this petitioner, and hence that its adoption at this time would deny him due process of law.

Let a peremptory writ of prohibition issue restraining respondent court from taking any further proceedings on Count I of the information, charging petitioner with the crime of murder.

BURKE, Acting C.J., dissenting. The majority hold that "Baby Girl" Vogt, who, according to medical testimony, had reached the 35th week of development, had a 96 percent chance of survival, and was "definitely" alive and viable at the time of her death, nevertheless was not a "human being" under California's homicide statutes. In my view, in so holding, the majority ignore significant common law precedents, frustrate the express intent of the Legislature, and defy reason, logic and common sense.

. . . The majority pursue the meaning of the term "human being" down the ancient hallways of the common law, citing Coke, Blackstone and Hale to the effect that the slaying of a "quickened" (i.e. stirring in the womb) child constituted "a great misprision," but not murder. Although, as discussed below, I strongly disagree with the premise that the words of our penal statutes must be construed as of 1648 or 1765, nevertheless, there is much common law precedent which would support the view that a viable fetus such as Baby Girl Vogt is a human being under [California homicide] statutes.

The majority cast a passing glance at the common law concept of quickening, but fail to explain the significance of that concept: At common law, the quickened fetus *was* considered to be a human being, a second life separate and apart from its mother. As stated by Blackstone, in the passage immediately preceding that portion quoted in the majority opinion, "Life is the immediate gift of God, a right inherent by nature in every individual; *and it begins in contemplation of law as soon as an infant is able to stir in the mother's womb."*

Modern scholars have confirmed this aspect of common law jurisprudence. As Means observes, "The common law itself prohibited abortion after quickening and hanging a pregnant felon after quickening, *because the life of a second human being would thereby be taken,* although it did not call the offense murder or manslaughter."

This reasoning explains why the killing of a quickened child was considered "a great misprision," although the killing of an unquickened child was no crime at all at common law Moreover, although the common law did not apply the labels of "murder" or "manslaughter" to the killing of a quickened fetus, it appears that at common law this "great misprision" was severely punished. As late as 1837, the wilful aborting of a woman quick with child was punishable by *death* in England.

Thus, at common law, the killing of a quickened child was severely punished, since that child was considered to be a human being. The majority would have us assume that the Legislature in 1850 and 1872 simply overlooked this "great misprision" in codifying and classifying criminal offenses in California, or reduced that offense to the lesser offense of illegal abortion with its relatively lenient penalties (Pen. Code, § 274).

In my view, we cannot assume that the Legislature intended a person such as defendant, charged with the malicious slaying of a fully viable child, to suffer only the mild penalties imposed upon common abortionists who, ordinarily, procure only the miscarriage of a nonviable fetus or embryo. To do so would completely ignore the important common law distinction between the quickened and unquickened child.

Of course, I do not suggest that we should interpret the term "human being" in our homicide statutes in terms of the common law concept of quickening. At one time, that concept had a value in differentiating, as accurately as was then scientifically possible, between life and nonlife. The analogous concept of viability is clearly more satisfactory, for it has a well defined and medically determinable meaning denoting the ability of the fetus to live or survive apart from its mother.

The majority opinion suggests that we are confined to common law concepts, and to the common law definition of murder or manslaughter. However, the Legislature, in Penal Code Sections 187 and 192, has defined those offenses for us: homicide is the unlawful killing of a "human being." Those words need not be frozen in place as of any particular time, but must be fairly and reasonably interpreted by this court to promote justice and to carry out the evident purposes of the Legislature in adopting a homicide statute. Thus, Penal Code Section 4, which was enacted in 1872 along with sections 187 and 192, provides: "The rule of the common law, that penal statutes are to be strictly construed, has no application to this code. All its provisions are to be construed according to the fair import of their terms, with a view to effect its objects and to promote justice."

As the majority opinion recognizes, "'In this state the common law is of no effect so far as the specification of what acts or conduct shall constitute a crime is concerned.'" Instead, we must construe penal statutes in accordance with the "fair import" of their terms, rather than restrict those statutes to common law principles. . . .

Penal Code section 4 . . . permits this court fairly to construe the terms of those statutes to serve the ends of justice. Consequently, nothing should prevent this court from holding that Baby Girl Vogt was a human ("belonging or relating to man; characteristic of man")[4] being ("existence, as opp. to nonexistence; specif. life")[5] under California's homicide statutes.

We commonly conceive of human existence as a spectrum stretching from birth to death. However, if this court properly might expand the definition of "human being" at one end of that spectrum, we may do so at the other end. Consider the following example: All would agree that "Shooting or otherwise damaging a corpse is not homicide . . . . " In other words, a corpse is not considered to be a "human being" and thus cannot be the subject of a "killing" as those terms are used in homicide statutes. However, it is readily apparent that our concepts of what constitutes a "corpse" have been and are being continually modified by advances in the field of medicine, including new techniques for life revival, restoration and resuscitation such as artificial respiration, open heart massage, transfusions, transplants and a variety of life-restoring stimulants, drugs and new surgical methods. Would this court ignore these developments and exonerate the killer of an apparently "drowned" child merely because that child would have been pronounced dead in 1648 or 1850? Obviously not. Whether a homicide occurred in that case would be determined by medical testimony regarding the capability of the child to have survived prior to the defendant's act. And that is precisely the test which this court should adopt in the instant case.

The common law reluctance to characterize the killing of a quickened fetus as a homicide was based solely upon a presumption that the fetus would have been born dead. This presumption seems to have persisted in this country at least as late

---

[4] Webster's New International Dictionary (2d ed. 1939), page 1211, column 3.
[5] Ibid, at page 247, column 2.

as 1876. Based upon the state of the medical art in the 17th, 18th and 19th centuries, that presumption may have been well-founded. However, as we approach the 21st century, it has become apparent that "This presumption is not only contrary to common experience and the ordinary course of nature, but it is contrary to the usual rule with respect to presumptions followed in this state."

There are no accurate statistics disclosing fetal death rates in "common law England," although the foregoing presumption of death indicates a significantly high death experience. On the other hand, in California the fetal death rate in 1968 is estimated to be 12 deaths in 1,000, a ratio which would have given Baby Girl Vogt a 98.8 percent chance of survival. If, as I have contended, the term "human being" in our homicide statutes is a fluid concept to be defined in accordance with present conditions, then there can be no question that the term should include the fully viable fetus.

The majority suggest that to do so would improperly create some new offense. However, the offense of murder is no new offense. Contrary to the majority opinion, the Legislature has not "defined the crime of murder in California to apply only to the unlawful and malicious killing of one who has been born alive." Instead, the Legislature simply used the broad term "human being" and directed the courts to construe that term according to its "fair import" with a view to effect the objects of the homicide statutes and promote justice. What justice will be promoted, what objects effectuated, by construing "human being" as excluding Baby Girl Vogt and her unfortunate successors? Was defendant's brutal act of stomping her to death any less an act of homicide than the murder of a newly born baby? No one doubts that the term "human being" would include the elderly or dying persons whose potential for life has nearly lapsed; their proximity to death is deemed immaterial. There is no sound reason for denying the viable fetus, with its unbounded potential for life, the same status.

The majority also suggest that such an interpretation of our homicide statutes would deny defendant "fair warning" that his act was punishable as a crime. Aside from the absurdity of the underlying premise that defendant consulted Coke, Blackstone or Hale before kicking Baby Girl Vogt to death, it is clear that defendant had adequate notice that his act could constitute homicide. Due process only precludes prosecution under a new statute insufficiently explicit regarding the specific conduct proscribed, or under a preexisting statute "by means of an unforeseeable *judicial* enlargement thereof."

Our homicide statutes have been in effect in this state since 1850. The fact that the California courts have not been called upon to determine the precise question before us does not render "unforeseeable" a decision which determines that a viable fetus is a "human being" under those statutes. Can defendant really claim suprise that a 5-pound, 18-inch, 34-week-old, living, viable child is considered to be a human being? . . .

In summary, I have shown that at common law, the slaying of a quickened fetus was a "great misprision" and was severely punished, since that fetus was considered to be a human being. We should not presume that the Legislature ignored these common law developments and intended to punish the malicious killing of a viable fetus as the lesser offense of illegal abortion. Moreover, apart from the common law approach, our Legislature has expressly directed us to construe the homicide statutes in accordance with the fair import of their terms. There is no good reason why a fully viable fetus should not be considered a "human being" under those statutes. To so construe them would not create any new offense, and would not deny defendant fair warning or due process. . . .

The trial court's denial of defendant's motion to set aside the information was proper, and the peremptory writ of prohibition should be denied.

The California Legislature responded to the *Keeler* decision by modifying California Penal Code section 187 to explicitly include a fetus as a category of murder victim.

QUESTIONS

1. How would the *Keeler* case be resolved under the New Mexico, Florida, Arizona and New Hampshire statutes that appear at the beginning of this chapter?

2. How would Khaliq have fared if he had been prosecuted in California? How would Keeler have fared in Scotland?

3. Was the prosecution in *Keeler* trying to convict Keeler of a new crime? Or was it prosecuting him for committing an old crime in a new way?

4. Should what Keeler did be treated as a type of homicide? Should feticide be made criminal? Does Justice Mosk directly address either of these questions? On what question does he focus? Why?

PROBLEM

3.1 *Drafting a Feticide Statute*   You are the legislative assistant to a member of the California legislature who, after reading the *Keeler* case, wants to enact legislation making feticide a crime. She asks you to draft a criminal statute. In doing so, how will you address the following:
   (a) a medical doctor performing an abortion;
   (b) a driver who causes an auto accident resulting in a pregnant woman losing the fetus she is carrying;
   (c) a pregnant woman whose fetus dies because she abused cocaine during the pregnancy.

THE RULE OF LENITY

Justice Mosk in *Keeler* writes that "it is the policy of this state to construe a penal statute as favorably to the defendant as its language and the circumstances of its application may reasonably permit; just as in the case of a question of fact, the defendant is entitled to the benefit of every reasonable doubt as to the true interpretation of words or the construction of language used in a statute." This policy regarding the interpretation of criminal statutes is sometimes referred to as the rule of strict construction of criminal statutes or simply the rule of lenity.

UNITED STATES *v.* WILTBERGER   18 U.S. 76, 95 (1820)

MARSHALL, C.J. . . . The rule that penal laws are to be construed strictly, is perhaps not much less old than construction itself. It is founded on the tenderness of the law for the rights of individuals; and on the plain principle that the power of punishment is vested in the legislative, not in the judicial department. It is the legislature, not the Court, which is to define a crime, and ordain its punishment.

Legislatures vary in their attitudes toward the rule of lenity, as the following provisions and case excerpt reveal.

Florida Statutes § 775.021   *Rules of Construction*

(1) The provisions of [the Florida Criminal Code] and offenses defined by other statutes shall be strictly construed; when the language is susceptible of differing constructions, it shall be construed most favorably to the accused.

Arizona Revised Statutes

§ 13-101. Purposes. It is declared that the public policy of this state and the general purposes of the provisions of [the Arizona Criminal Code] are:
    1. To proscribe conduct that unjustifiably and inexcusably causes or threatens substantial harm to individual or public interests;
    2. To give fair warning of the nature of the conduct proscribed and of the sentences authorized upon conviction;
    3. To define the act or omission and the accompanying mental state which constitute each offense and limit the condemnation of conduct as criminal when it does not fall within the purposes set forth;
    4. To differentiate on reasonable grounds between serious and minor offenses and to prescribe proportionate penalties for each;
    5. To insure the public safety by preventing the commission of offenses through the deterrent influence of the sentences authorized;
    6. To impose just and deserved punishment on those whose conduct threatens the public peace; and
    7. To promote truth and accountability in sentencing.

§ 13-104. *Rule of construction.* The general rule that a penal statute is to be strictly construed does not apply to [the Arizona Criminal Code], but the provisions herein must be construed according to the fair meaning of their terms to promote justice and effect the objects of the law, including the purposes stated in section 13-101.

Kentucky Revised Statutes § 446.080 (2002)   *Liberal construction*

(1) All statutes of this state shall be liberally construed with a view to promote their objects and carry out the intent of the legislature. . . .
(2) There shall be no difference in the construction of civil, penal and criminal statutes.

STATE *v*. MAGGIO   Louisiana Supreme Court, 432 So. 2d 854, 856 (1983)

DENNIS, J. . . . [N]umerous state legislatures, frustrated in the field of criminal law, have abrogated or modified the rule [of strict construction of criminal statutes]. Some states expressly repudiated the common law rule of construction and substituted a rule calling for a construction of criminal laws according to the "fair import of their terms." Other states have gone even further and have opted for a "liberal" construction of their criminal laws.

Louisiana took what might be termed a "middle ground" approach somewhere between the old common law rule and the "liberal" rule adopted by other states. At the time of the drafting of the comprehensive criminal code, the members of the Louisiana State Law Institute refused to embrace a rule of either strict or liberal construction. Instead the Law Institute recommended, and the legislature subsequently enacted, a rule of construction which provides:

> The articles of this Code cannot be extended by analogy so as to create crimes not provided for herein; however, in order to promote justice and to effect the objects of the law, all of its provisions shall be given a genuine construction, according to the fair import of their words, taken in their usual sense, in connection with the context, and with reference to the purpose of the provision. Louisiana Revised Statutes 14:3.

Courts often place restrictions on the operation of the rule of lenity, as the following passage reveals.

MUSCARELLO *v*. UNITED STATES   524 U.S. 125, 138 (1998)

BREYER, J. . . . The simple existence of some statutory ambiguity . . . is not sufficient to warrant application of [the rule of lenity], for most statutes are ambiguous to some degree. "'The rule of lenity applies only if, "after seizing everything from which aid can be derived," . . . we can make "no more than a guess as to what Congress intended."'" To invoke the rule, we must conclude that there is a "'grievous ambiguity or uncertainty' in the statute."

QUESTIONS

1. What are the arguments for and against the rule of lenity? Under what circumstances should it apply? Should it apply to all criminal statutes? Or only some?

2. If you were a legislator, would you favor adopting or rejecting the rule of lenity? Would your view change if you were a judge responsible for interpreting and applying criminal statutes?

3. The Louisiana statute mentioned in *Maggio* states that the provisions of the Louisiana Criminal Code "cannot be extended by analogy so as to create crimes not provided for herein." What do you think the legislators meant by using this

language? How would extending homicide "by analogy" have operated in the *Keeler* case?

4. Both the majority and dissent in *Keeler* acknowledge the existence of California Penal Code section 4, which rejects the rule of lenity. Nonetheless, the majority relies on the rule of lenity. Courts often ignore legislative efforts to jettison or modify the rule of lenity. Why do you think they might do so? Is this practice valid?

Most American jurisdictions now recognize only statutory crimes. As the statutes set forth at the beginning of this section reflect, some state legislatures retain common law crimes to supplement statutory crimes. But in the few states to retain common law offenses, courts rarely create or recognize a non-statutory crime. Courts still play a crucial role in the development of criminal law by interpreting and filling gaps in statutes in order to apply them in particular cases. And the common law of crimes remains a historic resource and reference point for legislatures drafting and courts interpreting criminal statutes.

Statutory criminal law in some jurisdictions is simply an accumulation of statutes enacted in piecemeal fashion over many years. Federal criminal law, for example, includes a piracy statute enacted in 1790 along with modern statutes dealing with computer crime and white collar fraud. The piecemeal enactment of such legislation may result in inconsistency, redundancy, and failure to address general questions of criminal law that cut across many statutes, such as issues of interpretation and mental state.

Many state legislatures have replaced an accumulation of criminal provisions with a comprehensive set of simultaneously enacted statutes, often referred to as a code. Jeremy Bentham, an influential proponent of statutory law and critic of common law, coined the term "codification" for this process. When a jurisdiction enacts a criminal code in this fashion, it tends to reduce inconsistency and redundancy and often prompts the legislature to address broad questions that may arise under many statutes. Codification also gives the legislature an opportunity to prune dead wood, outdated statutes no longer enforced, from its criminal laws.

1. Common Law versus Statutes

What explains the modern preference for legislative supremacy in criminal law? The question of whether judges or legislators should create and define crimes necessarily implicates two other questions. One is the *form* that criminal law should take. Legislatures create law in the form of statutes, while judges do so through judicial opinions, sometimes referred to as case law. The second is the *process* by which criminal law should be created. A legislature acts through an overtly political process the sole aim of which is to create statutes. It does not apply the statutes it creates to any particular person or set of facts. Judges, on the other hand, are primarily concerned with adjudicating particular cases and produce law only as necessary to resolve those cases.

One might resort to a variety of criteria to resolve the questions of who should create and define crimes and whether criminal law should take the form of statutes produced by the legislative process or case law resulting from the judicial process of adjudication. Here are a few possibilities. Can you think of others?

a. Legitimacy

Criminal law authorizes imposition of more severe sanctions than civil law. Violation of tort or contract law typically results in an award of money damages. Though a criminal violation can trigger monetary fines and restitution similar in form and function to money damages, it may and often does result in imprisonment and in some cases execution. A criminal conviction also stigmatizes more severely than a civil judgment. Accordingly, it is particularly important that criminal laws be legitimate and viewed as such by those subject to them.

Concern that the judicial branch is undemocratic is a common theme in American law and politics. American colonists, for example, were suspicious of judges and the common law they created because of the judges' allegiance to the English Crown. American judges have referred to themselves as " oligarchic"[4] and "a small and unrepresentative segment of our society."[5]

Legislatures are typically viewed as more representative of the electorate than judges. Voters directly elect legislators, who stand for reelection regularly. Some judges are appointed rather than elected and, in the case of federal judges, are appointed for life and may not be removed from office except for serious misdeeds. Other judges stand for election, but typically serve longer terms than legislators and thus are not as often subject to popular control.

Parts of the legislative process are more open to public scrutiny and input than the judicial process, a fact that may enhance its apparent democratic legitimacy. Candidates for legislative office openly debate the virtues and vices of legislation. After elections, public debate by legislators often continues during the drafting and voting process. Legislative committees regularly hold hearings that are open to the public and press, and they may even be televised. Citizens can and often do contact their representatives and ask them to vote for or against particular legislation.

In comparison, court processes are less open to public scrutiny and input. Appellate courts are the source of most judge-made law. Though not easy to obtain, the public does have access to briefs written by lawyers representing the parties to a case before a court. Hearings are public and are sometimes covered by the press. How judges vote and their supporting reasoning regularly appear in published opinions. But the judges' decision-making process and any debate among judges who disagree are usually shielded from public scrutiny until an opinion is filed. Although courts have discretion to allow those who are not parties to express their views to the court through amicus briefs,[6] judges view as inappropriate the receipt of public comment on a case pending before the court or the legal issues it may resolve. And, in sharp contrast to a legislator, until recently it was a violation of judicial ethics for a judge to express her views on disputed legal and political issues during a campaign.[7]

---

4. American Federation of Labor v. American Sash & Door Co., 335 U.S. 538, 555-556 (1949) (Frankfurter, J., concurring) ("Because the powers exercised by this Court are inherently oligarchic, Jefferson all of his life thought of the Court as 'an irresponsible body' and 'independent of the nation itself.' The Court is not saved from being oligarchic because it professes to act in the service of humane ends. . . . [T]he judiciary is prone to misconceive the public good by confounding private notions with constitutional requirements, and such misconceptions are not subject to legitimate displacement by the will of the people except at too slow a pace.").

5. Thompson v. Oklahoma, 487 U.S. 815, 873 (1988).

6. Courts at times refuse to allow the filing of amicus briefs. See, e.g., Voices for Choices v. Illinois Bell Telephone Co., 339 F.3d 542 (7th Cir. 2003).

7. In Republican Party of Minnesota v. White, 836 U.S. 765 (2002), the Supreme Court found some such restrictions unconstitutional as a violation of the First Amendment.

The idealized image of a legislature as representative of and responsive to the majority of the electorate has suffered in recent decades. Considerable attention has been given to the role of special interest groups in funding campaigns and influencing legislation. And despite the open nature of some aspects of the legislative process, such as debate and voting on the final versions of legislation, much of the legislative process is hidden from public view and subject to complex procedural rules not easily understood. The fate of much legislation is often resolved out of public view and in ways that are far from transparent and subject to accountability.

Electoral accountability and openness suggest that legislators should be more responsive to the majority will than judges. But accountability to the majority raises concerns about the protection of individual rights and the interests of groups such as racial, ethnic, and religious minorities, those suffering social and economic disadvantages, and those holding unconventional views. Criminal sanctions in the United States are imposed disproportionately on minority groups. Will judges or legislators be more likely to protect minority interests from oppression at the hands of the majority?

b. Accessibility and Comprehensibility

Criminal law ideally should be both accessible and comprehensible. In other words, the criminal law should be easy to find and to understand. Accessibility and comprehensibility of criminal law are important for several reasons. "The criminal law is a particularly public and visible part of the law. It is important that its authority and legitimacy should not be undermined by perceptions that it is intelligible only to experts."[8] Accessible and comprehensible criminal law makes it possible for potential offenders to have advance notice about what is and is not criminal. The clearer the threat of punishment, one would presume, the greater the deterrent effect of the criminal law. And blame is easier to assign if the offender acted when he knew or could easily have determined that his conduct violated the law. Increased accessibility and clarity also make it possible for lawyers to advise their clients more accurately and efficiently.

Increased accessibility and comprehensibility are also important for increasing the accuracy and efficiency of those administering the criminal law — police, judges, law clerks, prosecutors, defense counsel and jurors — particularly when dealing with the high volume of cases typical of many modern criminal courts. Obscurity in the definition of offenses, for example, increases the rate of appeals and reversals based on erroneous views of the charged offense.

A standard argument on behalf of statutory law is that it is more accessible than case law. One can locate with relative ease the criminal statutes of a particular jurisdiction. Those of North Carolina and Utah, for example, are found in single volumes. The criminal laws of Illinois and New York each comprise six volumes. Indexes facilitate locating one or more criminal statutes on a particular topic in a matter of minutes. Legal publishers often offer compact, single-volume paperback versions of a jurisdiction's criminal statutes that prosecutors, defense lawyers, and judges can keep at their desks and carry with them to court.

---

8. The Law Commission, A Criminal Code for England and Wales 6 (1989).

Judges, by contrast, typically developed the common law definition of an offense through a gradual, incremental process in a series of opinions over many years. Charting the definition of an offense often required reading numerous cases. Finding these opinions could be a time-consuming and tedious task even for lawyers, and required sophistication in the use of secondary sources and legal research tools. Treatise writers such as Blackstone, for example, summarized the common law to help lawyers find and understand it. Today, although the Internet and its search engines provide greater accessibility to case law, tracking down common law treatment of a particular issue often remains challenging.

With the legislative definition of a crime, a statute provides a useful starting point for determining the definition of offense. But how easy it is to find the full definition of an offense depends on how the legislature drafts the statute. Some criminal statutes are models of clarity. Others simply adopt the common law definition of a crime or do little more than announce the existence of an offense, leaving to the prosecutors, juries, and courts the difficult task of defining its elements. At other times, a statute may be a dense, intimidating text filled with ambiguity and complex, ill-defined terms. Even when the elements are spelled out, the meaning of statutory language must be determined by the judges called on to apply those statutes. Often then the task of learning what an offense requires involves researching case law through a process similar to what the common law required. One clear advantage of statutorily defined crimes is that annotated versions of a jurisdiction's criminal statutes typically collect key cases developing and refining the definition of an offense and place them immediately after the text of the statute.

Are statutes easier to understand than common law? The fact that a legislature is free to use simple, modern language in stating the law while the common law tends to cling tenaciously to outdated terminology would suggest so. At times, the common law camouflaged the substance of criminal law by attaching multiple meanings to well-worn terminology, often meanings at odds with common usage. Also, a statute's only function is to state the law, while a judicial opinion's primary function is to resolve a particular case. In resolving that case, the judge may state the law leading to that resolution clearly. Or she may do so ambiguously, leaving the reader to extrapolate the law from the resolution of the case, a skill referred to in law school as learning how to "read" a case. The meaning of a case is often subject to dispute, such as when judges disagree on the application of prior cases, known as precedent, to a new situation.

These factors suggest that statutes should be more comprehensible than case law. But, as pointed out above, statutes as well as judicial opinions may be poorly drafted. At times, legislatures purposefully leave a certain element vague because of failure to achieve agreement among the legislators regarding that element.

We will leave you to make your own judgments on the relative comprehensibility of statutes and cases as you encounter each type of law in this and other courses.

c. Prospective versus Retrospective Operation

Statutes in theory operate only prospectively. Indeed, retrospective operation of a criminal statute is barred by the United States Constitution's prohibition of ex post facto laws. The common law, by contrast, is typically viewed as being able to create a new crime or expand the definition of an existing crime to meet a new situation and apply it retrospectively. Bentham caustically described the common law as "dog law" because of its retrospective operation:

> When your dog does anything you want to break him of you wait til he does it, and then beat him for it. This is the way you make laws for your dog; and this is the way judges made law for you and me.[9]

The ability of the common law to adapt to new situations is often praised as one of its primary virtues.

Critics of common law respond that as the body of statutory law has grown, society has less need for the common law's ability to create new crimes. An English report recommending the codification of English criminal law adds that

> [t]he common law method of resolving uncertainty by "retrospective" declaration of the law is objectionable in principle. It may lead to the conviction of a defendant on the basis of criminal liability not known to exist in that form before he acted. . . . On the other hand, the effect of an appeal may be to narrow the law retrospectively, either by acknowledging the existence of a defence to criminal liability which was not previously recognised or by altering the definition of a criminal offence. . . . Such a change may give rise to a suggestion not only that the conviction in the earlier case was unsafe but also cast doubt on the validity of the convictions in other cases during the intervening . . . period which had been based on the terms of the direction approved in the earlier case. Such suggestions, which are inherent in the development of the law on a case by case basis, must undermine confidence in this important branch of the law. Statutory changes, on the other hand, do not have retrospective effect. They come into force only after full [legislative] debate with the commencement of the provisions of the statute. Earlier cases are unaffected.[10]

Though statutes in theory do not operate retrospectively, they may do so in practice. If a statute contains ambiguities that are resolved by court interpretation only after the defendant has acted or been convicted, although the statute existed prior to the defendant's act, its meaning was not established until after the fact. A court might remedy this problem by refusing to apply a new interpretation of a statute to a particular case, choosing only to apply it to future cases.

d. Balancing the Particular and the General

Justice Holmes wrote that

> Great cases like hard cases make bad law. For great cases are called great, not by reason of their real importance . . . but because of some accident of immediate overwhelming interest which appeals to the feelings and distorts the judgment. These immediate interests exercise a kind of hydraulic pressure which makes what previously was clear seem doubtful, and before which even well settled principles of law will bend.[11]

Since common law is created in the process of resolving cases, the judges who shape it at times encounter a tension between doing justice to litigants in the cases before them and doing justice to litigants in future cases. Common law courts, then, must simultaneously use two focal points, one narrow and present-oriented, the other broad and future-oriented. Does this responsibility to do justice to particular

---

9. III *The Works of Jeremy Bentham* 235 (Bowring ed., 1838-1843).
10. The Law Commission, A Criminal Code for England and Wales 7-8 (1989).
11. Northern Securities Co. v. United States, 193 U.S. 197, 400-401 (1904).

litigants distort the judgment of common law courts, resulting in the creation of rules unjust to the parties in future cases? Or does the experience of applying rules to actual cases give judges insight and wisdom to help them craft better rules?

Since it does not resolve controversies involving particular parties, a legislature is not subject to a tension between adjudicating a particular case and creating a general rule. Its exclusive role is to create rules to be generally applied in the future. Its focus is solely broad and future oriented.

Particular cases, though, may have a powerful impact on a legislature. High-profile cases at times generate pressures for legislators to enact or revise criminal statutes to respond to public concern about a particular case. In doing so, they may fail to give adequate consideration to a law's long-term impact. John Hinckley's shooting of President Reagan, for example, triggered a wave of legislative activity across the United States restricting access to the insanity defense. And, as Justice O'Connor pointed out in the *Ewing* case in Chapter 2, the well-publicized kidnapping and murder of Polly Klaas in California spurred enactment of California's tough three strikes law.

e. Keeping Criminal Law Current

Are judges or legislators better able to keep the criminal law in touch with current social needs and attitudes? Judges must typically wait for litigants to present a case that gives them the opportunity to change the law. If no such case comes before them, they are unable to reform the law no matter how much it needs to be changed.

Common law also gives great weight to the principle of *stare decisis* — the idea that in determining the law applicable to a particular situation a court is bound by the decisions of earlier courts that have spoken on the issue. Common law judges at times were ingenious at finding ways to evade this principle. They often changed the law without openly acknowledging doing so through a device called the legal fiction. Judges today vary in their fidelity to *stare decisis*. At times, some openly announce that a judicially created rule needs to be changed and then change it. But the principle of *stare decisis* may nonetheless prove a stumbling block to judicial law reform.

Legislators are not bound by *stare decisis*. Nor do they have to wait for a party to a lawsuit to bring a case before them to change the law. They are free to revisit and revise a statute at any time. Also, because of their electoral accountability, they are often thought to be in touch with the needs and attitudes of the electorate and thus have the knowledge of what laws need to be changed.

In practice, though, there are many practical roadblocks to legislative reform. Lack of time due to crowded legislative agendas, lack of consensus within a political party about what shape reform should take, or the fact that different parties control the executive and legislative branches are all potential barriers to legislative law reform.

The English Report on codification mentioned above had the following to say on the issue of reform:

> One commentator wrote to us saying: "The outstanding defect of codes is that, unless they are stated in terms so general as to be unacceptable to the modern codifier, they must inevitably lead to ossification of the law and to the perpetuation

of error . . . (T)he very virtues of codification . . . , especially consistency and certainty, have (as might be expected) their own correlative vice. This is that, for the law to be stated in a form which aspires to consistency and certainty, it must be imprisoned within a framework of principle which is rigid and is also immutable in the sense that it is incapable of gradual development in the light of practical experience. . . . [C]omplete and perfect statement of principle is impossible. . . . "

Although there is force in this view, we feel that it is based on several misconceptions. First, a Code can, whenever necessary, be updated, and made subject to textual amendments. Secondly, the criticism presupposes that the present law is always capable of "gradual development in the light of practical experience." Yet a glance in any criminal law textbook or journal will show that this is not true. The common law often has to struggle on with flaws and "perpetuation of error" until a suitable set of facts arises or until some party decides to take a case to the House of Lords.[12]

f. Institutional Competence

There are a number of additional reasons one might expect a legislature to do a better job of creating law, including criminal law. One is that the legislative process involves deliberation by and input from many more people than the resolution of a court case. This fact, one might argue, should make it less likely that a bad criminal law will be created by a legislature than by a state supreme court.

Also, the legislature can hold hearings through which it gathers facts relevant to proposed legislation. It can also summon experts and those with firsthand experience with the problem the legislation addresses to hear their views. Its committees often have professional staff who can collect data and study an issue. A court may also utilize data about a particular problem that has already been published or otherwise made available. A court can learn the views of experts and others with firsthand experience through the filings of the parties or amici. But courts typically have no ability to generate and an ability inferior to the legislature to gather this sort of information.

But legislatures often fail in actual practice to give careful consideration to the laws they pass. Congressman Dan Rostenkowski, for example, voted for the Federal Sentencing Guidelines both in committee and on the Floor of the House. Later convicted of mail fraud and sentenced to a federal prison, he had the chance firsthand to learn how the Guidelines work. He later admitted in a radio interview that he had been completely unaware of what the Guidelines were about when he voted for them.[13]

B. THE EXECUTIVE BRANCH

The executive branch does not make criminal law. It enforces criminal laws enacted by the legislature. That, at least, is the conventional view of the executive branch's role in the criminal justice system. Closer examination, however, reveals that executive branch officials mold the criminal law in a number of ways.

---

12. *Id.* at 8-9.
13. National Public Radio, "This American Life," Episode 143, "Sentencing" (Oct. 22, 1999).

Executive officials are important players in the political process of creating criminal legislation. Criminal issues sometimes feature prominently in presidential and gubernatorial campaigns and on the legislative agendas of newly elected officials. Both elected and career officials from the federal Department of Justice and state attorney generals' offices can and often do draft and submit proposed criminal statutes to the legislature. They also lobby for or against and provide testimony, empirical data, and advice on criminal statutes the legislature is considering.

Executive clemency — the power to pardon offenders exercised by the president for federal offenses and governors in some states for state offenses — also gives the executive branch power to nullify the application of the criminal law in particular cases.

The executive branch can also influence criminal law in less obvious ways. The positions taken by government lawyers and the arguments they advance play a role in influencing both trial and appellate court interpretation of criminal statutes. Prosecutorial charging policy provides another example. Our criminal justice system gives prosecutors a large measure of discretion whether or not to prosecute a case. A prosecutorial policy not to prosecute a particular crime can effectively nullify an act of the legislature. Fornication and adultery laws still exist in some jurisdictions, for example, but prosecutors largely ignore them. A prosecutorial policy to prosecute offenses recognized by the legislature only under specified conditions effectively "rewrites" a statute. Statutory rape laws, for example, once routinely prohibited sexual intercourse with a female under a certain age even if the female consented and the male was close in age to the victim. Prosecutors, though, often declined to file criminal charges when the intercourse was consensual and occurred between teenagers close in age, in effect creating an age span exemption not found in the language of the statute. Modern legislators have followed the lead set by such prosecutorial policies and now typically incorporate an explicit age span exemption in the statute's language.

Just as with prosecutorial decisions *not* to charge, prosecutorial decisions to charge can also shape the criminal law. Prosecutors in the past, for example, treated dog-mauling cases resulting in death as either accidental killings not warranting prosecution or as meriting a manslaughter charge at best. A recent trend in California to charge such cases as murders reflects in part a prosecutorial strategy to expand the category of murder to encompass such killings. Similarly, skiing accidents resulting in death have traditionally been viewed as not warranting criminal charges. But a recent Colorado case in which a skier was criminally charged and convicted again reveals how prosecutorial charging can expand the boundaries of the criminal law to include cases previously seen as meriting only civil liability.

Executive branch officials also play a role in defining offenses when the legislature explicitly delegates to them the power to create and define crimes. The Massachusetts legislature in 1998 passed a statute restricting gun ownership and making criminal the unlicensed possession of "large capacity weapons."[14] To clarify what constitutes such a weapon, the statute directs an executive official, the Secretary of the Executive Office of Public Safety, to publish and distribute a roster of the weapons that fall within this category. The roster is currently available on a government Web site.

The following case provides another example of such explicit delegation of the power to define what is criminal.

---

14. See Gun Owners' Action League, Inc. v. Jane Swift, 284 F.3d 198 (1st Cir. 2002).

CONNECTICUT *v.* WHITE
204 Conn. 410, 528 A.2d 811 (1987)

SANTANIELLO, J. The defendant, Gordon L. White, was charged ... with three counts of failing to provide a smoke detector in violation of Connecticut state fire safety code §§ 11-1.8.1 and 11-3.3.3.1, and General Statutes §§ 29-292 and 29-295. After a jury trial, the defendant was found guilty .... On appeal, the defendant ... claims ... that the state fire safety code provisions exceed the scope of authority conferred by the code's enabling statute .... We find error.

The jury could reasonably have found the following facts: The defendant owned a three family residential building located at 1387 Corbin Avenue in New Britain. On December 25, 1982, at approximately 5:30 a.m., Edward Ross, an occupant of the first floor apartment, awoke to find smoke filtering into his apartment. After waking up his wife, their child, and his brother-in-law, and escorting them outside, Ross summoned the New Britain fire department. The fire department arrived at the scene almost immediately and began battling a fire which had broken out on the second floor. Several firefighters entered the second floor apartment, which was full of smoke, and discovered the bodies of Maryann Jones and her two young children, Lindsay and Brandy, the occupants of that apartment, lying dead on the floor. The medical examiner concluded that all three had died from asphyxia caused by smoke inhalation.

It was estimated that the fire, apparently caused by an electrical overload from a wall outlet into which a quartz heater had been plugged, began smoldering at approximately 2:30 a.m., but did not break out in the apartment until about 5:30 a.m. As a result of the slow burning nature of the fire, the apartment was covered with soot and was filled with thick smoke. There were no smoke detectors in the building.

At trial, the state introduced evidence regarding how a smoke detector works, the cost of a smoke detector, how it is installed, and its effectiveness. Additionally, testimony was introduced that had smoke detectors been installed in the defendant's building, the occupants would have been alerted to the fire in sufficient time to enable them to escape.

Evidence was also introduced that the defendant owned another multifamily apartment building located in East Hartford. In May, 1982, the defendant received notice from the East Hartford fire marshal informing him that he was required to furnish smoke detectors in his East Hartford building. The defendant installed smoke detectors in the East Hartford building, but he did not install smoke detectors in his New Britain building. Additionally, prior to December, 1982, the defendant undertook renovations on the New Britain property but did not obtain building permits for the work he performed.

At the conclusion of the state's case, the defendant moved for a judgment of acquittal claiming that: ... the state had failed to prove that the defendant had violated Connecticut fire safety code §§ 11-1.8.1 and 11-3.3.3.1 and General Statutes §§ 29-292 and 29-295 because the state did not establish that a building permit had been issued on or after October 1, 1976, for the building in question. The defendant also argued that the fire safety code was inconsistent with its enabling statute in contravention of General Statutes § 29-293. The court denied the defendant's motion. . . .

II

The defendant . . . complains that the fire safety code regulations exceed the scope of authority conferred by § 29-292,[4] the code's enabling legislation. We agree.

It is well established that although the power to make law is vested exclusively in the legislature, the legislature may create a law designed to accomplish a particular purpose and may expressly authorize an administrative agency to "fill up the details" by prescribing rules and regulations for the operation and enforcement of that law. It is necessary, however, that the enabling statute declare legislative policy, establish primary standards or lay down an intelligible principle to which the administrative officer or body must conform. If the legislature fails to prescribe the limits of the power delegated with reasonable clarity, or the power is too broad, its attempt to delegate is a nullity. While the modern trend of the legislature is liberal in approving delegation under broad regulatory standards so as to facilitate the operational functions of administrative agencies; agencies must, nonetheless, act according to the strict statutory authority.

To address the defendant's claim that the fire safety code exceeds the authority conferred by its enabling statute, a review of the original act, its relevant amendment and the relevant code provision is necessary. In 1947, the legislature passed Public Acts 1947, No. 419, which provided that "[t]he state fire marshal shall establish a fire safety code and at any time may amend the same. The regulations in said code shall provide for reasonable safety from fire, smoke, and panic therefrom, in all buildings except in private dwellings occupied by one or two families, and upon

---

[4] "[General Statutes (Rev. to 1983)] Sec. 29-292. (Formerly Sec. 29-40). Fire safety code. Smoke detection and warning equipment. Certificate of occupancy. Review of plans and specifications; fees.

"(a) The state fire marshal and the codes and standards committee shall adopt, promulgate and administer a fire safety code and at any time may amend the same. The regulations in said code shall provide for reasonable safety from fire, smoke and panic therefrom, in all buildings and areas adjacent thereto except in private dwellings occupied by one or two families and upon all premises except those used for manufacturing, and shall include provision for smoke detection and warning equipment in residential buildings designed to be occupied by two or more families for which a building permit is issued on or after October 1, 1976, and in new residential buildings designed to be occupied by one or more families for which a building permit for new occupancy is issued on or after October 1, 1978, to provide Level Four Protection, as defined in the 1974 edition of Number Seventy-four of the National Fire Protection Association. Said regulations shall provide the requirements for markings and literature which shall accompany such equipment sufficient to inform the occupants and owners of such buildings of the purpose, protective limitations and correct installation, operating, testing, maintenance and replacement procedures and servicing instructions for such equipment and shall require that smoke detection and warning equipment which is installed in such residential buildings shall be capable of sensing visible or invisible smoke particles, that the manner and location of installing smoke detectors shall be approved by the local fire marshal or building official, that such installation shall not exceed the standards under which such equipment was tested and approved and that such equipment, when activated, shall provide an alarm suitable to warn the occupants.

"(b) No certificate of occupancy shall be issued for any residential building designed to be occupied by two or more families for which a building permit is issued on or after October 1, 1976, or any new residential building designed to be occupied by one or more families for which a building permit for new occupancy is issued on or after October 1, 1978, unless the local fire marshal or building official has certified that said building is equipped with smoke detection and warning equipment complying with the fire safety code.

"(c) Detailed plans and specifications of structures subject to the state fire safety code may be submitted to the state fire marshal for review and a determination concerning compliance with the state fire safety code. The state fire marshal shall develop a schedule of fees for reviewing such plans and specifications, which schedule shall provide for fees payable to the state treasurer in amounts of not less than ten dollars nor more than one hundred dollars, depending upon the complexity of the review."

all premises except those used for manufacturing." General Statutes (1949 Rev.) § 3665. The purpose of the statute was to give the fire marshal the ability to enact reasonable minimum requirements for safety in new and existing buildings.

For almost thirty years, this act remained substantially unchanged.[5] In 1976, however, the legislature passed No. 76-78 of the 1976 Public Acts (Public Act No. 76-78) which amended § 20-40, the predecessor of § 29-292, mandating, in relevant part, that the regulations "shall include provision for smoke detection systems in residential buildings designed to be occupied by two or more families for which a building permit is issued on or after [October 1, 1976]."

The fire safety code, passed pursuant to § 29-292, requires that smoke detectors be installed in "each guest room, suite or sleeping area of hotels, motels, lodging or rooming houses, and dormitories, and in each dwelling unit within apartment houses and one- and two-family dwellings . . . . " Connecticut State Fire Safety Code (1981) § 11-1.8.1.[6]

The defendant contends that the enabling statute, as amended by Public Act No. 76-78, limits the fire marshal's ability to promulgate regulations concerning smoke detectors in buildings designed to be occupied by two or more families to those buildings for which a building permit has been issued on or after October 1, 1976. Because the fire safety code does not require that smoke detectors be installed only in those buildings, the defendant argues that the code exceeds its express statutory authority.

There is no question that the legislature, in originally enacting § 29-292, conferred upon the fire marshal broad authority to pass rules and regulations to "provide for reasonable safety from fire, smoke and panic therefrom," and that such a conferral was a valid delegation of authority. Had the original statute been in effect during this case, there would be little doubt that the challenged fire safety code regulations would be valid. The legislature, however, amended the enabling statute in 1976. The question thus becomes whether the legislature, in passing Public Act No. 76-78, intended to limit the fire marshal's authority to pass regulations with respect to smoke detectors for residential buildings designed to be occupied by two or more families.

In determining whether the legislature was limiting the authority of the fire marshal to promulgate regulations, we are guided by the well established principles of statutory construction which require us to ascertain and give effect to the apparent intent of the legislature. When the language of the statute is plain and unambiguous, we need look no further than the words themselves because we assume that the language expresses the legislature's intent. If, however, the language is unclear, we must ascertain the intent of the legislature by examining the language of the statute, its legislative history and the purpose the statute is to serve.

An examination of the statute fails to reveal whether the legislature, in enacting Public Act No. 76-78, intended to authorize the fire marshal in promulgating the fire safety code to require smoke detectors only in multifamily buildings for which a building permit was issued after October 1, 1976, as the defendant claims, or, as

[5] In 1958, General Statutes § 3665 was transferred and set out as § 29-40 and in 1983 the statute was transferred and set out as § 29-292.

[6] On March 10, 1987, the Code for Safety to Life from Fire in Buildings and Structures of the National Fire Protection Association, Inc., Standard 101, 1985 edition, was adopted by reference as the Connecticut fire safety code. See Connecticut State Fire Safety Code § 29-292-1. For the purpose of this appeal, however, the code provisions as they existed at the time relevant to this action govern our disposition of the case.

the state argues, intended to set a minimum standard for the installation of smoke detectors and allow the fire marshal to set additional standards regarding smoke detectors.

The state contends that the plain language of the amendment demonstrates that the legislature did not intend to limit the authority of the fire marshal, but rather intended the amendment to direct that "the Code *include* at least that class of buildings." (Emphasis added.) The state argues that the amendment's language that the regulations "shall *include* provision for smoke detection systems" (emphasis added) mandated that the fire marshal *at least include* such a regulation in the code, but did not proscribe him from further regulating in that area. The state claims that the word "include" is a word of enlargement, not one of limitation, and cites to Webster's Third New International Dictionary, which defines "include" as "to place, list or rate as part or component of a whole or larger group, class or aggregate . . . to take in, enfold, or comprise as a discrete or subordinate part or item of a larger aggregate. . . . "

We have recognized in the past, however, that the word "include" may be considered a word of limitation as well as a word of enlargement. In *Hartford Electric Light Co. v. Sullivan*, we recognized that the most likely common use of the term "shall include" is one of limitation. In that case, however, we could not conclude with certainty that it was so employed. Similarly, in the present case we cannot conclude that the word "include" is used as a word of limitation or a word of enlargement.

Because we find the legislative intent unclear from the language of the statute itself, we must turn to other tools of statutory interpretation. Unfortunately the legislative history of Public Act No. 76-78 is of little help. While debate on the amendment indicates that it was enacted to require smoke detectors in all new buildings occupied by two or more families for which a building permit was issued after the enumerated date, it does not indicate whether the legislature intended to preclude the fire marshal from further promulgating regulations for the installation of smoke detectors in other multifamily buildings.

We find it significant, however, that the legislature chose to delineate carefully the types of buildings in which it required the installation of smoke detectors, rather than to mandate generally the installation of smoke detectors and to defer to the fire marshal's authority the promulgation of such regulations. When a statute provides that a thing shall be done in a certain way, it carries with it an implied prohibition against doing that thing a different way. "An enumeration of powers in a statute is uniformly held to forbid things not enumerated. Had the General Assembly intended that the fire marshal be allowed to promulgate more comprehensive regulations, it could easily have broadened the requirements for smoke detector regulations. Instead it specifically set forth that smoke detectors were required in buildings for which building permits were issued on or after October 1, 1976.

Moreover, we agree with the defendant that, because § 29-292 is penal in nature, the statute and the code provision should be construed strictly and we should resolve any ambiguity in the defendant's favor. The fact that this statute has a penal component cannot be seriously doubted, as demonstrated by the defendant's conviction. Thus, because the legislative intent behind Public Act No. 76-78 is not entirely clear, we construe § 29-292 to limit the fire marshal's authority in passing regulations with regard to the installation of smoke detectors. To the extent that fire safety code § 11-1.8.1 regulates beyond that legislative mandate, it exceeds the scope of its statutory authority. The defendant cannot be convicted of violating § 11-1.8.1

unless it is shown that a building permit had been issued for his building on or after the enumerated date. At trial no such evidence was introduced. Accordingly, the defendant's convictions for such violations must be set aside.

QUESTIONS

1. Why do legislatures sometimes expressly authorize administrative agencies to create and define criminal offenses? What are the advantages and disadvantages of such a practice?

2. What is the statutory language at issue in this case? What were the competing positions of the prosecution and defense regarding the meaning of that language? Is the word "include" one of enlargement or limitation? What do you think the legislature intended "include" to mean in this context? Which should control the outcome of the case — what a word means or what the legislature intended it to mean?

In addition to the explicit delegation exemplified in the Massachusetts gun-licensing statute and in *White*, the legislature may also implicitly delegate power to prosecutors by passing a criminal statute that is silent or ambiguous, creating space the executive can fill through the policies it adopts regarding the selection of cases to prosecute. The United States Congress has passed a number of laws that allow federal prosecutors to exercise a large measure of power and effectively transfer to them the task of defining the elements of the offense. Professor Dan Kahan describes this interaction between the legislature and prosecutors in the following passage.

Dan M. Kahan, THREE CONCEPTIONS OF FEDERAL CRIMINAL-LAWMAKING   1 Buff. Crim. L. Rev. 5, 15-16 (1997)

Congress predictably and systematically delegates lawmaking power by drafting criminal statutes in exceedingly general or open-textured terms. . . . The beneficiaries of this lawmaking abdication are individual prosecutors, who as a result of it face little constraint in advancing broad and innovative readings of incompletely specified statutes. If courts disavow the normative discretion to specify what broadly worded statutes do and don't cover, the only sensible limiting principles that will exist are the ones that individual U.S. Attorneys elect to recognize based on their own sense of institutional self-restraint.

And they display precious little of that. Individual U.S. Attorneys are extraordinarily ambitious and routinely enter electoral politics after leaving office. Consequently, while in office, they face significant incentives to advance imaginative readings of vague criminal offenses in order to please influential local interests. Consider Rudolph Giuliani, whose innovative insider-trading prosecutions, it has been alleged, were calculated to win the approval of the established Wall Street firms that were then being routed by Michael Milken and other financial innovators. When Giuliani later ran for Mayor of New York, these firms were among his key supporters.

C. THE JURY

The Sixth Amendment to the United States Constitution provides:

> In all criminal prosecutions, the accused shall enjoy the right to a speedy and
> public trial, by an impartial jury of the State and district wherein the crime shall
> have been committed. . . .

Roughly 90 to 95 percent of criminal cases in both federal and state courts are
resolved without any sort of trial through a guilty plea that is often the result
of negotiation between the prosecution and defense. But because of the Sixth
Amendment, most criminal trials are jury trials. The following excerpt captures
the rationale for trial by jury.

DUNCAN v. LOUISIANA   391 U.S. 145, 156 (1968)

> Providing an accused with the right to be tried by a jury of his peers gave
> him an inestimable safeguard against the corrupt or overzealous prosecu-
> tor and against the compliant, biased, or eccentric judge. If the defendant
> preferred the common-sense judgment of a jury to the more tutored but
> perhaps less sympathetic reaction of the single judge, he was to have it.
> Beyond this, the jury trial provisions in the Federal and State Constitu-
> tions reflect a fundamental decision about the exercise of official power — a
> reluctance to entrust plenary powers over the life and liberty of the citizen
> to one judge or to a group of judges. Fear of unchecked power, so typical
> of our State and Federal Governments in other respects, found expression
> in the criminal law in this insistence upon community participation in the
> determination of guilt or innocence.

The materials in this section address the role of the jury in criminal cases. The
conventional modern view, expressed in the following jury instruction, is that jurors
play no role in making criminal law.

Model Jury Instruction 3.02[15]

It is your duty to find from the evidence what the facts are. You will then apply
the law, as I give it to you, to those facts. You must follow my instructions on the law,
even if you thought the law was different or should be different.

Do not allow sympathy or prejudice to influence you. The law demands of you
a just verdict, unaffected by anything except the evidence, your common sense, and
the law as I give it to you.

In the first selection in this Section, Matthew Harrington describes the historical evolution of the view that jurors are to determine only the facts and not the
law in criminal cases. Jurors do, though, play a role in shaping criminal law in two
primary ways. First, they may do so when required to apply a vague or ambiguous

---

15. Manual of Model Criminal Jury Instructions for the District Courts of the Eighth Circuit (2003).

statute. In the previous Section, we saw how a statute that is silent or ambiguous on a particular point effectively delegates lawmaking power to executive branch officials to exercise through their discretionary power to choose cases for prosecution. Silence or ambiguity in a criminal statute may similarly delegate power to jurors to shape the criminal law through their power to convict or acquit.

Second, even if a statute is clear, jurors may exercise power over the substantive criminal law through nullification. *United States v. Dougherty*, the primary case in this Section, addresses whether jurors should be told they have the power to nullify. This power is similar to the nullification power prosecutors may exercise by refusing to prosecute cases under certain statutes.

Matthew P. Harrington, THE LAW-FINDING FUNCTION OF THE AMERICAN JURY

1999 Wis. L. Rev. 377, 377-380

It has become something of an article of faith in the legal community that it is "the duty of the court to expound the law and that of the jury to apply the law as thus declared." In practice, this is often interpreted to mean that the judge alone has the power to determine the law and the jury is limited to applying the law to the facts. The standard allocation of power between judge and jury is thought to be as old as the common law itself.

In truth, however, this division of labor is of relatively recent origin. Until the early years of this century, many American lawyers and judges believed that juries had the power to declare both the law and the facts. The jury thus had the ability to take upon itself the right to determine the entire controversy. As late as 1895, Supreme Court Justice Shiras asserted:

> The jury . . . are intrusted with the decision of both the law and the facts involved in [the] issue. To assist them in the decision of the facts, they hear the testimony of witnesses; but they are not bound to believe the testimony. To assist them in the decision of the law, they receive the instructions of the judge; but they are not obliged to follow his instructions.[3]

This ability to determine the law was something more than the power to bring in a general verdict, however. American judges actually asserted an almost plenary power in the jury to decide the law as it saw fit. Most recognized that juries might ignore their instructions, and bring in a verdict contrary to the law stated in the charge. For many years, therefore, courts were reluctant to order new trials on the grounds that the verdict was against the law. "It doth not vitiate a verdict," the Connecticut Supreme Court once declared, "that the jury have mistaken the law or the evidence; for . . . they are judges of both."[4]

The jury's power over law has its origins in the struggle against the royal prerogative. In seventeenth-century England, the jury's ability to bring in a general verdict of acquittal was celebrated as a bulwark of liberty. In several notable cases, juries stood up for individual rights against oppressive or unjust prosecutions. This characteristic of jury practice became especially valuable in the colonists' own struggle against the Crown. Colonial juries often refused to convict in cases brought

---

[3] *Sparf*, 156 U.S. at 171 (Shiras, J., dissenting).
[4] Wittner v. Brewster, Kirby 422, 423 (Conn. 1788).

under the navigation acts and sedition laws. Royal officials saw the coercive power of parliamentary legislation hampered by the inability to obtain convictions. The jury's power to nullify unpopular laws made it an important vehicle for the expression of the popular will.

Judges were not alone in their adherence to the jury's law-finding function. Lawyers, too, recognized the jury's power over law, and relied on it in presenting their case. Eighteenth-century lawyers did not hesitate to argue the law to juries, often citing cases and pointing to eminent legal authorities, such as Blackstone, to convince the jury to adopt their own view of the law. This privilege was so jealously guarded that it became the source of a great deal of controversy when judges later attempted to restrict the practice.

The jury's power over law was aided by the fact that few judges in the colonial period had formal legal training; many were simply administrative or legislative officers whose position gave them the right to adjudicate disputes, or prominent members of the community. Knowledge of the law was not a prerequisite to being a judge. As a result, the judge who presided at the trial did not look all that much different from the jury. "In background, experiences, and outlook [juries] were much like the litigants whose disputes they determined, and not very different from the judges who oversaw them."[6] They were neighbors from nearby towns, who shared the same common beliefs and assumptions as the parties before them. Their lack of formal training meant that colonial judges did not usually instruct the jury on the law. Even when they did, judges were quick to advise the jury that they were not bound by the judge's view of the law as stated in the charge.

The relationship between judge and jury did not change much in the years immediately following the Revolution. Although the business of judging was becoming more professionalized, many judges still refused to instruct the jury that it was bound by the charge. This was certainly true in criminal cases, mainly because judges still revered the jury's role as a check on oppressive prosecutions. Nonetheless, many judges refused to instruct the jury on the law in civil suits as well. The jury's power over law in the first decade of the Republic did not, therefore, look very much different than in the colonial era.

In time, however, members of the bench and bar gradually came to the conclusion that the jury's power over law must be restrained. In civil cases, judges and lawyers joined with merchant interests to limit the jury's law-finding function as a means of promoting a stable commercial environment. Such stability was thought necessary to the Republic as a means of putting the new nation on a firm economic footing, allowing it to provide for the welfare of its citizens and assume a place of prominence in the family of nations. This instrumentalist view of the law made judges increasingly willing to devise some means to force juries to adhere to the law as stated in the court's charge. It was not long before American judges resorted to the English doctrine of new trials to reverse verdicts where juries had brought in a verdict contrary to their instructions. This program was so successful that by . . . 1820, [sic] the jury's power over law had all but disappeared.

The jury's law-finding function in criminal cases was to survive much longer, however. Adherence to the view of the jury as a bulwark of liberty meant that many judges were more reluctant to intrude upon the jury's power to bring in a general verdict in criminal trials. Constitutional prohibitions on double jeopardy also meant that the power to grant new trials in criminal cases was severely limited.

---

[6] Bruce H. Mann, *Neighbors and Strangers: Law and Community in Early Connecticut* 71 (1987).

The inability to order a new trial in cases where the jury brought in a verdict of acquittal made it difficult to enforce complete compliance with the court's instructions. The jury's power to acquit "in the teeth of both law and facts" meant that it would always retain some variant of its earlier law-finding function. Nonetheless, by the end of the nineteenth century, judges shed their earlier hesitance and took upon themselves the power to grant new trials in cases of conviction. More importantly, judges also began to instruct juries that they were bound by the law as stated in the charge. They increasingly sought to prevent counsel from advising the jury of its right to nullify and prohibit lawyers from making any sort of legal argument to the jury. In so doing, judges eventually succeeded in burying the jury's law-finding function in the dusts of time. The judges were so successful that few lawyers, and almost no juror, ever has but the faintest inkling of the enormous prerogative that once belonged to the jury.

What is especially striking about the decline of the jury's power over law is the way in which it was carried out. The drive to limit the law-finding function was entirely a judge-led exercise, carried out without legislative warrant and sometimes in the face of legislative enactments to the contrary. Three factors played a role in this effort: Foremost among these was the growing desire for stability in the law. Both judges and lawyers were concerned about the need to provide a stable legal regime. This was so not only to ensure stability in the commercial law, but also to ensure that the criminal law might be fixed and uniform. The increasing diversity of juries was also a factor. The "men of the neighborhood" who adjudicated disputes in the town and county courts were no more. As the nation became diverse and jury service was opened to a wider segment of the population, juries could no longer be counted on to speak from a common set of beliefs and experiences. The way was cleared for inconsistent and contradictory verdicts. Perhaps worse, from the judges' point of view, was the increasing tendency of juries to bring in verdicts at odds with the judges' own views and experiences. Finally, the movement was also fueled by the increasing professionalization of the bench and bar. As legal education became more sophisticated, judges became more convinced that the bench was the proper place in which to lodge the law-finding function.

In the end, the American judiciary succeeded in delegitimizing the jury's power over law by means of a careful and creative reinterpretation of the common law governing the allocation of power between judge and jury. The transformation was long and arduous, marked by a great deal of hesitancy and many missteps; but, the results have been long lasting.

UNITED STATES *v.* DOUGHERTY
473 F.2d 1113 (D.C. Cir. 1972)

Leventhal, Circuit Judge.

Seven of the so-called "D.C. Nine" bring this joint appeal from convictions arising out of their unconsented entry into the Washington offices of the Dow Chemical Company, and their destruction of certain property therein. . . . The undisputed evidence showed that on Saturday, March 22, 1969, appellants broke into the locked fourth floor Dow offices at 1030 15th Street, N.W., Washington, D.C., threw papers and documents about the office and into the street below, vandalized office furniture and equipment, and defaced the premises by spilling about a bloodlike substance. The prosecution proved its case through Dow employees who testified as to the lack of permission and extent of damage, members of the news media who had been summoned to the scene by the appellants and who witnessed the destruction while recording it photographically, and police officers who arrested appellants on the scene. . . .

[The jury acquitted the defendants of burglary but convicted them on unlawful entry and malicious destruction of property.]

III. THE ISSUE OF JURY NULLIFICATION

[Appellants] say that the jury has a well-recognized prerogative to disregard the instructions of the court even as to matters of law, and that they accordingly have the legal right that the jury be informed of its power. . . . There has evolved in the Anglo-American system an undoubted jury prerogative-in-fact, derived from its power to bring in a general verdict of not guilty in a criminal case, that is not reversible by the court. . . .

The pages of history shine on instances of the jury's exercise of its prerogative to disregard uncontradicted evidence and instructions of the judge. Most often commended are the 18th century acquittal of Peter Zenger of seditious libel, on the plea of Andrew Hamilton, and the 19th century acquittals in prosecutions under the fugitive slave law. The values involved drop a notch when the liberty vindicated by the verdict relates to the defendant's shooting of his wife's paramour, or purchase during Prohibition of alcoholic beverages. . . .

Since the jury's prerogative of lenity, again in Learned Hand's words introduces a "slack into the enforcement of law, tempering its rigor by the mollifying influence of current ethical conventions," it is only just, say appellants, that the jurors be so told. It is unjust to withhold information on the jury power of "nullification," since conscientious jurors may come, ironically, to abide by their oath as jurors to render verdicts offensive to their individual conscience, to defer to an assumption of necessity that is contrary to reality.

This so-called right of jury nullification is put forward in the name of liberty and democracy, but its explicit avowal risks the ultimate logic of anarchy. This is the concern voiced by Judge Sobeloff in *United States v. Moylan*:

> To encourage individuals to make their own determinations as to which laws they will obey and which they will permit themselves as a matter of conscience to disobey is to invite chaos. No legal system could long survive if it gave every individual the option of disregarding with impunity any law which by his personal standard was judged morally untenable. Toleration of such conduct would not be democratic, as appellants claim, but inevitably anarchic.

The statement that avowal of the jury's prerogative runs the risk of anarchy, represents, in all likelihood, the habit of thought of philosophy and logic, rather than the prediction of the social scientist. But if the statement contains an element of hyperbole, the existence of risk and danger, of significant magnitude, cannot be gainsaid. In contrast, the advocates of jury "nullification" apparently assume that the articulation of the jury's power will not extend its use or extent, or will not do so significantly or obnoxiously. Can this assumption fairly be made? We know that a posted limit of 60 m.p.h. produces factual speeds 10 or even 15 miles greater, with an understanding all around that some "tolerance" is acceptable to the authorities, assuming conditions warrant. But can it be supposed that the speeds would stay substantially the same if the speed limit were put: Drive as fast as you think appropriate, without the posted limit as an anchor, a point of departure?

Our jury system is a resultant of many vectors, some explicit, and some rooted in tradition, continuity and general understanding without express formulation. A constitution may be meaningful though it is unwritten, as the British have proved for 900 years.

The jury system has worked out reasonably well overall, providing "play in the joints" that imparts flexibility and avoids undue rigidity. An equilibrium has evolved — an often marvelous balance — with the jury acting as a "safety valve" for exceptional cases, without being a wildcat or runaway institution. There is reason to believe that the simultaneous achievement of modest jury equity and avoidance of intolerable caprice depends on formal instructions that do not expressly delineate a jury charter to carve out its own rules of law. We have taken due and wry note that those whose writings acclaim and invoke Roscoe Pound's 1910 recognition of the value of the jury as safety valve, omit mention of the fact that in the same article he referred to "the extreme decentralization that allows a local jury or even a local prosecutor to hold up instead of uphold the law of the state" as one of the conditions that "too often result in a legal paralysis of legal administration," that his writings of that period are expressly concerned with the evils of the "extravagant powers" of juries, and that in 1931 he joined the other distinguished members of the Wickersham Commission in this comment:

> In a number of jurisdictions juries are made judges of the law in criminal cases, thus inviting them to dispense with the rules of law instead of finding the facts. The juror is made judge of the law not to ascertain what it is, but to judge of its conformity to his personal ideals and ascertain its validity on that basis. . . . It is significant that there is most satisfaction with criminal juries in those jurisdictions which have interfered least with the conception of a trial of the facts unburdened with further responsibility and instructed as to the law and advised as to the facts by the judge.

The way the jury operates may be radically altered if there is alteration in the way it is told to operate. The jury knows well enough that its prerogative is not limited to the choices articulated in the formal instructions of the court. The jury gets its understanding as to the arrangements in the legal system from more than one voice. There is the formal communication from the judge. There is the informal communication from the total culture — literature (novel, drama, film, and television); current comment (newspapers, magazines and television); conversation; and, of course, history and tradition. The totality of input generally conveys adequately enough the idea of prerogative, of freedom in an occasional case to depart from what the judge says. Even indicators that would on their face seem too weak to notice — like the fact that the judge tells the jury it must acquit (in case of reasonable doubt) but never tells the jury in so many words that it must convict — are a meaningful part of the jury's total input. Law is a system, and it is also a language, with secondary meanings that may be unrecorded yet are part of its life.

When the legal system relegates the information of the jury's prerogative to an essentially informal input, it is not being duplicitous, chargeable with chicane and intent to deceive. The limitation to informal input is, rather a governor to avoid excess: the prerogative is reserved for the exceptional case, and the judge's instruction is retained as a generally effective constraint. We "recognize a constraint as obligatory upon us when we require not merely reason to defend our rule departures, but damn good reason." The practicalities of men, machinery and rules point up the danger of articulating discretion to depart from a rule, that the breach will be more often and casually invoked. We cannot gainsay that occasionally jurors uninstructed as to the prerogative may feel themselves compelled to the point of rigidity. The danger of the excess rigidity that may now occasionally exist is not as great as the danger of removing the boundaries of constraint provided by the announced rules.

We should also note the inter-relation of the unanimity requirement for petit juries, which was applicable to this trial, and is still the general rule though no longer constitutionally required for state courts. This is an additional reason — a material consideration, though neither a necessary nor sufficient condition — to brake the wheels of those who would tell the petit jurors they are to determine the rules of law, either directly or by telling them they are free to disregard the judge's statement of the rules. The democratic principle would not be furthered, as proponents of jury nullification claim, it would be disserved by investing in a jury that must be unanimous the function not merely of determining facts, hard enough for like-minded resolution, but of determining the rules of law.

Rules of law or justice involve choice of values and ordering of objectives for which unanimity is unlikely in any society, or group representing the society, especially a society as diverse in cultures and interests as ours. To seek unity out of diversity, under the national motto, there must be a procedure for decision by vote of a majority or prescribed plurality — in accordance with democratic philosophy. To assign the role of mini-legislature to the various petit juries, who must hang if not unanimous, exposes criminal law and administration to paralysis, and to a deadlock that betrays rather than furthers the assumptions of viable democracy.

Moreover, to compel a juror involuntarily assigned to jury duty to assume the burdens of mini-legislator or judge, as is implicit in the doctrine of nullification, is to put untoward strains on the jury system. It is one thing for a juror to know that the law condemns, but he has a factual power of lenity. To tell him expressly of a nullification prerogative, however, is to inform him, in effect, that it is he who fashions the rule that condemns. That is an overwhelming responsibility, an extreme burden for the jurors' psyche. And it is not inappropriate to add that a juror called upon for an involuntary public service is entitled to the protection, when he takes action that he knows is right, but also knows is unpopular, either in the community at large or in his own particular grouping, that he can fairly put it to friends and neighbors that he was merely following the instructions of the court.

In the last analysis, our rejection of the request for jury nullification doctrine is a recognition that there are times when logic is not the only or even best guide to sound conduct of government. For machines, one can indulge the person who likes to tinker in pursuit of fine tuning. When men and judicial machinery are involved, one must attend to the many and complex mechanisms and reasons that lead men to change their conduct — when they know they are being studied; when they are told of the consequences of their conduct; and when conduct exercised with restraint as an unwritten exception is expressly presented as a legitimate option.

What makes for health as an occasional medicine would be disastrous as a daily diet. The fact that there is widespread existence of the jury's prerogative, and approval of its existence as a "necessary counter to casehardened judges and arbitrary prosecutors," does not establish as an imperative that the jury must be informed by the judge of that power. On the contrary, it is pragmatically useful to structure instructions in such wise that the jury must feel strongly about the values involved in the case, so strongly that it must itself identify the case as establishing a call of high conscience, and must independently initiate and undertake an act in contravention of the established instructions. This requirement of independent jury conception confines the happening of the lawless jury to the occasional instance that does not violate, and viewed as an exception may even enhance, the over-all normative effect of the rule of law. An explicit instruction to a jury conveys an implied approval that runs the risk of degrading the legal structure requisite for true freedom, for an ordered liberty that protects against anarchy as well as tyranny.

Finally, we are aware that the denial of defendants' request for a nullification instruction will be considered by them to negative some, or perhaps most, of the value of the right of *pro se* representation which we have recognized. This point could be answered in terms of logic: The right of self-representation is given for reasons recognized by the law, and cannot be a springboard to establish the validity of other advantages or conditions that lie in its tactical wake. Thus, a defendant's ability to present his demeanor and often even a kind of testimony, without exposure to impeachment or cross-examination, may be a tactical consequence of *pro se* representation, and even a moving cause of its invocation, but this is not to say it is an objective of the law. But defendants' position merits a more spacious answer, that lies outside the domain of formal logic. It is this. The jury system provides flexibility for the consideration of interests of justice outside the formal rules of law. This embraces whatever extra the defendant conveys by personal representation, whether through demeanor or sincerity of justification. But it is subject to the overriding consideration that what is tolerable or even desirable as an informal, self-initiated exception, harbors grave dangers to the system if it is opened to expansion and intensification through incorporation in the judge's instruction.

[The judgment was reversed on other grounds.]

PROBLEM

3.2 *Cameras in the Jury Room?* You are the judge in a capital murder trial. A public television station files a motion seeking to film the trial, including the jury's deliberation and rendering of its verdict, for later broadcast as part of an award-winning documentary series the station has done on the criminal justice system. The station's purpose is to educate the public on how criminal justice is administered in the courtroom. The state in which you sit has allowed filming of trials for a number of years, but to date cameras have never gone into a jury room in your state. A few other states have allowed filming of jury deliberations in criminal cases for educational purposes. The station proposes to place unattended cameras and microphones in the jury room so that no person other than the jurors would be physically present in the room. The station also suggests that early in the jury selection process any potential juror who objects to being filmed be removed from the potential pool for that case. The defendant, after consulting with his lawyer, consents to having the jury deliberations filmed and agrees to waive any claim of error based on the filming. How would you rule on the television station's motion? What are the potential advantages and disadvantages of allowing cameras into the jury room? Would your ruling depend on whether the prosecuting attorney objects? Would your resolution be different if the case did not involve capital punishment?

QUESTIONS

1. What are the advantages and disadvantages of having jurors rather than judges or legislators define what is criminal? How would Khaliq and Keeler have fared if a jury had been entrusted with the task of defining the criminal law in their respective cases?

2. Does the jury play a role in defining what is criminal under statutes such as the following:

> (a) *It is a third degree felony to kill another negligently. A person acts negligently if she should have been aware of a substantial and unjustifiable risk of death and in so failing grossly deviates from what a reasonable person would have done.*

> (b) *Manslaughter is the intentional killing of another under the influence of actual and reasonable provocation. Reasonable provocation is any provocation which would cause a reasonable person to lose self-control.*

If so, what facets of each statute invite the jury to define the law?

3. How could a judge enforce her view of the criminal law on a jury?

4. Should jurors have power to nullify the application of criminal statutes in particular cases? Is jury nullification always prompted by a disposition toward lenity? How do you think a jury would use that power in the following cases?

> (a) a battered wife is charged with the murder of her abusive husband;

> (b) in a state in which euthanasia is illegal, a husband is charged with the murder by poison of his wife, who suffered from a painful, terminal illness and wished to end her life;

> (c) in a county in which discrimination against a certain minority group is widespread, a young man is charged with assaulting a member of that minority group.

5. Write your own jury instruction informing the jury of their obligations regarding enforcement of the criminal law.

D. STATUTORY INTERPRETATION

Judges exercise significant power to make criminal law through the interpretation of statutes written and enacted by the legislature. Considerable controversy and debate surrounds the question of how judges go about this task, whether they should wield this power to interpret sparingly or expansively. In this Section, we examine three approaches to statutory interpretation. *Church of the Holy Trinity v. United States* exemplifies the "intentionalist" approach to statutory interpretation. In the reading selection following the case, Justice Scalia criticizes *Holy Trinity* and the intentionalist approach it exemplifies and defends a different approach to statutory interpretation known as "textualism." The final excerpt in this Section, by Professor William Eskridge, describes a third view of how judges should interpret statutes, known as "dynamic" statutory interpretation. In the Problems below as well as in much of the rest of the material in this book, you will have opportunities to apply these various approaches.

PROBLEMS

3.3 You are a judge in a city near Mountain View Park, a state park containing several tracts designated as "wilderness areas." In 1964, when the state legislature created wilderness areas, it passed the following statute:

> Use of any motorized vehicle or mechanical transport within any part of a State Park designated as a wilderness area is hereby prohibited. Any person violating this provision is subject to a $1,000 fine and/or 3 months imprisonment.

When the legislature enacted this statute, mountain bikes — bicycles built to climb mountain trails using fat tires with chunky treads — had not been invented. In the past few years, though, mountain bikes have become popular in the park, including its wilderness areas. In response to complaints from hikers and environmental groups, the State Department of Parks and Recreation recently banned mountain bikes from the wilderness areas on the ground that a mountain bike is "mechanical transport" under the above statute.

Keith is an avid mountain biker and owner of a mountain bike shop located near the park. To protest the State's mountain bike ban, Keith and a group of fellow mountain bikers rode their mountain bikes into a wilderness area where they were cited by a Park Ranger for violation of the statute. You are assigned as the trial judge in Keith's case. In a pre-trial motion, Keith's attorney argues that the statute under which Keith has been charged does not apply to mountain bikes. How would you rule?

In making your ruling, consider the following:

(a) Prior to being designated as wilderness areas, hiking, horseback riding, cross-country skiing, as well as canoeing were common in these parklands. The legislative history indicates that the legislature was aware of these uses at the time it passed the statute and indicates no purpose to ban these uses.

(b) Mountain bikers claim that mountain bikers do less damage to wilderness areas than hikers or horses. Hikers typically drive to a trailhead, requiring the establishment of parking and rest rooms. Horses are heavier than mountain bikes and therefore have greater impact on trails. Both hikers and horse riders regularly camp overnight in wilderness areas, requiring the establishment of camping areas and resulting in greater impact from fire rings, trash, and human waste. Mountain bikers rarely camp in a wilderness area.

(c) Participation nationally in mountain biking has increased in the past five years to 7.1 million people.

(d) The Park Service has also banned hang gliders and backcountry skateboards from wilderness areas under the statute.

3.4 Consider the following statute:

> It is unlawful for any person to sell or transfer to a minor any firearm, pistol, Springfield rifle or other repeating rifle, bowie knife or dirk, brass knuckles, slingshot, or electric weapon or device. A person who violates this section commits a felony of the second degree.

(a) Lonnie is arrested and charged with selling aluminum knuckles to a minor. Is he liable under the statute? Would your answer differ if the legislature had added the words "or other" just before the word "knuckles"? Would it be significant if the legislative history revealed that the legislature considered substituting "metal" for "brass" but chose not to do so?

(b) Theresa runs a small fashion boutique selling trendy women's clothes and accessories. One item she brought back from a recent trip to an out-of-state fashion show is advertised as the "brass knuckles" handbag. It is made of snakeskin with a handle of steel knuckles and is described as "a hard-rock mix of sophistication and street style."[16] Theresa sells one such handbag to a minor. Is she liable under the statute? Would it make any difference if the knuckles of the handle were made of brass? What use might the prosecutor make of the advertisement in Lonnie's case in Part (a)?

3.5 Roger forced his way into the apartment of his estranged wife and became involved in a fight with another man present in the apartment. He was arrested and charged under the following statute:

> A person is guilty of assault in the first degree when . . . with intent to cause serious physical injury to another person, he causes such injury to such a person or to a third person by means of a dangerous instrument.

You are the trial judge. Roger moves to dismiss the indictment prior to trial on the ground that no dangerous instrument was used. Assume the government has sufficient evidence in each case to prove that Roger caused physical injury to the victim and did so intentionally. Would you dismiss under the following scenarios?

(a) Assume Roger kicked the victim, who had fallen to the floor, repeatedly in the head and groin with his right foot. Roger was wearing running shoes at the time and the prosecution's position is that the running shoe as used in the fight was a dangerous instrument.

(b) Assume the victim fell to the floor in the bathroom and that Roger grabbed the man's hair and swung his head into the side of a bathtub. The prosecution's position is that the bathtub as used in the fight was a dangerous instrument.

---

16. 32 W, Sept. 2003, at 269.

(c) Roger bit the other man's finger with such force that he severed the nerves in the finger, causing permanent limitation of movement and feeling. The prosecution's position is that Roger's teeth as used in the fight were a dangerous instrument.

(d) Same facts as in (c) except that Roger was HIV positive.

3.6 Jane drove her BMW Z3 southbound on Route 66 intending to turn left at a cross street. The traffic light controlling the intersection turned red as she neared the cross street. Jane pulled into the left-turn lane, braked to a stop, and waited for the green light. A number of cars northbound on Route 66 stopped at the same red light, their drivers also waiting for the light to turn green. When the light did turn green, Jane gunned her engine and quickly executed a left turn directly in front of the cars in the northbound lane but before any of them moved into the intersection. A police officer observed Jane's conduct and cited her. She is now charged under the following statute:

> The driver of a vehicle within an intersection intending to turn to the left shall yield the right of way to any vehicle approaching from the opposite direction [which is within the intersection or so close thereto as to constitute an immediate hazard]. Failure of such a driver to so yield is an offense punishable by up to six months in jail and/or a $1,000 fine.

Did Jane violate the statute? What arguments would you make if you were her defense lawyer? The prosecutor? How would you rule if you were the judge?

1. Intentionalism

CHURCH OF THE HOLY TRINITY *v.* UNITED STATES
143 U.S. 457 (1892)

BREWER, J. Plaintiff in error is a corporation duly organized and incorporated as a religious society under the laws of the state of New York. E. Walpole Warren was, prior to September, 1887, an alien residing in England. In that month the plaintiff in error made a contract with him, by which he was to remove to the city of New York, and enter into its service as rector and pastor; and, in pursuance of such contract, Warren did so remove and enter upon such service. It is claimed by the United States that this contract on the part of the plaintiff in error was forbidden by [the statute below]; and an action was commenced to recover the penalty prescribed by that act. The circuit court held that the contract was within the prohibition of the statute, and rendered judgment accordingly, and the single question presented for our determination is whether it erred in that conclusion.

The first section describes the act forbidden, and is in these words:

Be it enacted by the senate and house of representatives of the United States of America, in congress assembled, that from and after the passage of this act it shall be unlawful for any person, company, partnership, or corporation, in any manner whatsoever, to prepay the transportation, or in any way assist or encourage the importation or migration, of any alien or aliens, any foreigner or foreigners, into the United States, its territories, or the District of Columbia, under contract or agreement, parole or special, express or implied, made previous to the importation or migration of such alien or aliens, foreigner or foreigners, to perform labor or service of any kind in the United States, its territories, or the District of Columbia.

It must be conceded that the act of the corporation is within the letter of this section, for the relation of rector to his church is one of service, and implies labor on the one side with compensation on the other. Not only are the general words labor and service both used, but also, as it were to guard against any narrow interpretation and emphasize a breadth of meaning, to them is added "of any kind"; and, further, as noticed by the circuit judge in his opinion, the fifth section, which makes specific exceptions, among them professional actors, artists, lecturers, singers, and domestic servants, strengthens the idea that every other kind of labor and service was intended to be reached by the first section. While there is great force to this reasoning, we cannot think congress intended to denounce with penalties a transaction like that in the present case. It is a familiar rule that a thing may be within the letter of the statute and yet not within the statute, because not within its spirit nor within the intention of its makers. This has been often asserted, and the Reports are full of cases illustrating its application. This is not the substitution of the will of the judge for that of the legislator; for frequently words of general meaning are used in a statute, words broad enough to include an act in question, and yet a consideration of the whole legislation, or of the circumstances surrounding its enactment, or of the absurd results which follow from giving such broad meaning to the words, makes it unreasonable to believe that the legislator intended to include the particular act. . . .

In *U.S. v. Kirby*, 7 Wall. 482, 486, the defendants were indicted for the violation of an act of congress providing "that if any person shall knowingly and willfully obstruct or retard the passage of the mail, or of any driver or carrier, or of any horse or carriage carrying the same, he shall, upon conviction, for every such offense, pay a fine not exceeding one hundred dollars." The specific charge was that the defendants knowingly and willfully retarded the passage of one Farris, a carrier of the mail, while engaged in the performance of his duty, and also in like manner retarded the steamboat Gen. Buell, at that time engaged in carrying the mail. To this indictment the defendants pleaded specially that Farris had been indicted for murder by a court of competent authority in Kentucky; that a bench-warrant had been issued and placed in the hands of the defendant Kirby, the sheriff of the county, commanding him to arrest Farris, and bring him before the court to answer to the indictment; and that, in obedience to this warrant, he and the other defendants, as his posse, entered upon the steamboat Gen. Buell and arrested Farris, and used only such force as was necessary to accomplish that arrest. The question as to the sufficiency of this plea was certified to this court, and it was held that the arrest of Farris upon the warrant from the state court was not an obstruction of the mail, or the retarding of the passage of a carrier of the mail, within the meaning of the act. In its opinion the court says: "All laws should receive a sensible construction. General terms should be so limited in their application as not to lead to injustice, oppression or an absurd consequence. It will always, therefore, be presumed that the legislature intended exceptions to its language which would avoid results of this character. The reason of the law in such cases should prevail over its letter. The common sense of man approves the judgment mentioned by Puffendorf, that the Bolognian law which enacted 'that whoever drew blood in the streets should be punished with the utmost severity,' did not extend to the surgeon who opened the vein of a person that fell down in the street in a fit. The same common sense accepts the ruling, cited by Plowden, that the statute . . . which enacts that a prisoner who breaks prison shall be guilty of felony, does not extend to a prisoner who breaks out when the prison is on fire, 'for he is not to be hanged because he would not stay to be burnt.' And we think that a like common sense will sanction the ruling we make, that the act of congress which punishes the obstruction or retarding of the passage of the mail, or of its carrier, does not apply to a case of temporary detention of the mail caused by the arrest of the carrier upon an indictment for murder." . . .

Among other things which may be considered in determining the intent of the legislature is the title of the act. We do not mean that it may be used to add to or take from the body of the statute, but it may help to interpret its meaning. . . . "Where the intent is plain, nothing is left to construction. Where the mind labors to discover the design of the legislature, it seizes everything from which aid can be derived; and in such case the title claims a degree of notice, and will have its due share of consideration." . . .

Now, the title of this act is, "An act to prohibit the importation and migration of foreigners and aliens under contract or agreement to perform labor in the United States, its territories, and the District of Columbia." Obviously the thought expressed in this reaches only to the work of the manual laborer, as distinguished from that of the professional man. No one reading such a title would suppose that congress had in its mind any purpose of staying the coming into this country of ministers of the gospel, or, indeed, of any class whose toil is that of the brain. The common understanding of the terms labor and laborers does not include preaching and preachers, and it is to be assumed that words and phrases are used in their ordinary meaning. So whatever of light is thrown upon the statute by the language of the title indicates an exclusion from its penal provisions of all contracts for the employment of ministers, rectors and pastors.

Again, another guide to the meaning of a statute is found in the evil which it is designed to remedy; and for this the court properly looks at contemporaneous events, the situation as it existed, and as it was pressed upon the attention of the legislative body. . . . The situation which called for this statute was briefly but fully stated by Mr. Justice Brown when, as District Judge, he decided the case of *U.S. v. Craig*: "The motives and history of the act are matters of common knowledge. It had become the practice for large capitalists in this country to contract with their agents abroad for the shipment of great numbers of an ignorant and servile class of foreign laborers, under contracts by which the employer agreed, upon the one hand, to prepay their passage, while, upon the other hand, the laborers agreed to work after their arrival for a certain time at a low rate of wages. The effect of this was to break down the labor market, and to reduce other laborers engaged in like occupations to the level of the assisted immigrant. The evil finally became so flagrant that an appeal was made to congress for relief by the passage of the act in question, the design of which was to raise the standard of foreign immigrants, and to discountenance the migration of those who had not sufficient means in their own hands, or those of their friends, to pay their passage."

It appears, also, from the petitions, and in the testimony presented before the committees of congress, that it was this cheap, unskilled labor which was making the trouble, and the influx of which congress sought to prevent. It was never suggested that we had in this country a surplus of brain toilers, and, least of all, that the market for the services of Christian ministers was depressed by foreign competition. Those were matters to which the attention of congress, or of the people, was not directed. So far, then, as the evil which was sought to be remedied interprets the statute, it also guides to an exclusion of this contract from the penalties of the act.

A singular circumstance, throwing light upon the intent of congress, is found in this extract from the report of the senate committee on education and labor, recommending the passage of the bill: "The general facts and considerations which induce the committee to recommend the passage of this bill are set forth in the Report of the Committee of the House. The committee report the bill back without amendment, although there are certain features thereof which might well be changed or modified, in the hope that the bill may not fail of passage during the present session. Especially would the committee have otherwise recommended amendments, substituting for the expression, 'labor and service,' whenever it occurs in the body of the bill, the words 'manual labor' or 'manual service,' as sufficiently broad to accomplish the purposes of the bill, and that such amendments would remove objections which a sharp and perhaps unfriendly criticism may urge to the proposed legislation. The committee, however, believing that the bill in its present form will be construed as including only those whose labor or service is manual in character, and being very desirous that the bill become a law before the adjournment, have reported the bill without change." And, referring back to the report of the Committee of the House, there appears this language: "It seeks to restrain and prohibit the immigration or importation of laborers who would have never seen our shores but for the inducements and allurements of men whose only object is to obtain labor at the lowest possible rate, regardless of the social and material well-being of our own citizens and regardless of the evil consequences which result to American laborers from such immigration." . . .

We find, therefore, that the title of the act, the evil which was intended to be remedied, the circumstances surrounding the appeal to Congress, the reports of the committee of each house, all concur in affirming that the intent of Congress was simply to stay the influx of this cheap, unskilled labor.

But, beyond all these matters, no purpose of action against religion can be imputed to any legislation, state or national, because this is a religious people. This is historically true. From the discovery of this continent to the present hour, there is a single voice making this affirmation. . . .

Suppose, in the Congress that passed this act, some member had offered a bill which in terms declared that, if any Roman Catholic church in this country should contract with Cardinal Manning to come to this country and enter into its service as pastor and priest; or any Episcopal church should enter into a like contract with Canon Farrar; or any Baptist church should make similar arrangements with Rev. Mr. Spurgeon; or any Jewish synagogue with some eminent Rabbi, such contract should be adjudged unlawful and void, and the church making it be subject to prosecution and punishment, can it be believed that it would have received a minute of approving thought or a single vote? Yet it is contended that such was in effect the meaning of this statute. The construction invoked cannot be accepted as correct. It is a case where there was presented a definite evil, in view of which the legislature used general terms with the purpose of reaching all phases of that evil, and thereafter, unexpectedly, it is developed that the general language thus employed is broad enough to reach cases and acts which the whole history and life of the country affirm could not have been intentionally legislated against. It is the duty of the courts, under those circumstances, to say that, however broad the language of the statute may be, the act, although within the letter, is not within the intention of the legislature, and therefore cannot be within the statute.

The judgment will be reversed, and the case remanded for further proceedings in accordance with this opinion.

QUESTIONS

1. In a particular case, if the language of a statute would lead to a different result than the spirit of the statute, which should control? What if the conduct sought to be punished is within the language of the statute but not within its spirit? What if that conduct is within the spirit of the statute but not within its language? In other words, should it make any difference whether use of the spirit of a statute would narrow a criminal statute's scope or expand it? Does the court in *Holy Trinity* use the spirit of the statute at issue in that case to narrow or expand that statute's reach?

2. The statute in *Holy Trinity* contains a specific list of occupations excepted from the statute's prohibition. That list does not include ministers. What inference should the court draw in *Holy Trinity* from the legislature's failure to include ministers on this list?

3. If applying the language of a statute to a particular situation would be absurd, should a judge charged with interpreting the statute create an exception to avoid the absurd result? Or should it be left to the legislature to rewrite the statute to avoid the absurd result?

4. What role does legislative history play in the *Holy Trinity* court's reasoning? In your view, does the court's use of legislative history strengthen or weaken its analysis of the statute?

2. Textualism

Antonin Scalia, A MATTER OF INTERPRETATION   16-37 (1997)

You will find it frequently said in judicial opinions of my court and others that the judge's objective in interpreting a statute is to give effect to "the intent of the legislature." This principle, in one form or another, goes back at least as far as

Blackstone. . . . I think, that it is simply incompatible with democratic government, or indeed, even with fair government, to have the meaning of a law determined by what the lawgiver meant, rather than by what the lawgiver promulgated. . . . It is the *law* that governs, not the intent of the lawgiver. That seems to me the essence of the famous American ideal set forth in the Massachusetts constitution: A government of laws, not of men. Men may intend what they will; but it is only the laws that they enact which bind us.

In reality, however, if one accepts the principle that the object of judicial interpretation is to determine the intent of the legislature, being bound by genuine but unexpressed legislative intent rather than the law is only the *theoretical* threat. The *practical* threat is that, under the guise or even the self-delusion of pursuing unexpressed legislative intents, common-law judges will in fact pursue their own objectives and desires, extending their lawmaking proclivities from the common law to the statutory field. When you are told to decide, not on the basis of what the legislature said, but on the basis of what it *meant*, and are assured that there is no necessary connection between the two, your best shot at figuring out what the legislature meant is to ask yourself what a wise and intelligent person *should* have meant; and that will surely bring you to the conclusion that the law means what you think it *ought* to mean — which is precisely how judges decide things under the common law. As Dean Landis of Harvard Law School (a believer in the search for legislative intent) put it in a 1930 article:

> [T]he gravest sins are perpetrated in the name of the intent of the legislature. Judges are rarely willing to admit their role as actual lawgivers, and such admissions as are wrung from their unwilling lips lie in the field of common and not statute law. . . .

CHURCH OF THE HOLY TRINITY

To give some concrete form to the danger I warn against, let me describe what I consider to be the prototypical case involving the triumph of supposed "legislative intent" (a handy cover for judicial intent) over the text of the law. It is called *Church of the Holy Trinity v. United States* and was decided by the Supreme Court of the United States in 1892. The Church of the Holy Trinity, located in New York City, contracted with an Englishman to come over to be its rector and pastor. The United States claimed that this agreement violated a federal statute that made it unlawful for any person to "in any way assist or encourage the importation or migration of any alien . . . into the United States, . . . under contract or agreement . . . made previous to the importation or migration of such alien . . . , to perform labor or service of any kind in the United States. . . . " . . .

The Court proceeds to conclude from various extratextual indications, including even a snippet of legislative history (highly unusual in those days), that the statute was intended to apply only to manual labor — which renders the exceptions for actors, artists, lecturers, and singers utterly inexplicable. . . . That being so, it says, "[t]he construction invoked [by the prosecution] cannot be accepted as correct." It concludes:

> It is a case where there was presented a definite evil, in view of which the legislature used general terms with the purpose of reaching all phases of that evil, and thereafter, unexpectedly, it is developed that the general language thus employed is broad enough to reach cases and acts which the whole history and life of the country affirm could not have been intentionally legislated against. It is the duty of the

courts, under those circumstances, to say that, however broad the language of the statute may be, the act, although within the letter, is not within the intention of the legislature, and therefore cannot be within the statute.

Well of course I think that the act was within the letter of the statute, and was therefore within the statute: end of case. Congress can enact foolish statutes as well as wise ones, and it is not for the courts to decide which is which and rewrite the former. I acknowledge an interpretative doctrine of what the old writers call *lapsus linguae* (slip of the tongue), and what our modern cases call "scrivener's error," where on the very face of the statute it is clear to the reader that a mistake of expression (rather than of legislative wisdom) has been made. For example, a statute may say "defendant" when only "criminal defendant" (i.e., not "civil defendant") makes sense. The objective import of such a statute is clear enough, and I think it not contrary to sound principles of interpretation, in such extreme cases, to give the totality of context precedence over a single word. But to say that the legislature obviously misspoke is worlds away from saying that the legislature obviously overlegislated. *Church of the Holy Trinity* is cited to us whenever counsel wants us to ignore the narrow, deadening text of the statute, and pay attention to the life-giving legislative intent. It is nothing but an invitation to judicial lawmaking.

There are more sophisticated routes to judicial lawmaking than reliance upon unexpressed legislative intent, but they will not often be found in judicial opinions because they are too obvious a usurpation. Calling the court's desires "unexpressed legislative intent" makes everything seem all right. . . .

[A] modern and forthright approach to according courts the power to revise statutes is set forth in Professor Eskridge's recent book, *Dynamic Statutory Interpretation*. The essence of it is acceptance of the proposition that it is proper for the judge who applies a statute to consider " 'not only what the statute means abstractly, or even on the basis of legislative history, but also what it ought to mean in terms of the needs and goals of our present day society.' " The law means what it ought to mean.

I agree . . . that many decisions can be cited which, by subterfuge, accomplish precisely what . . . Eskridge and other honest nontextualists propose. As I have said, "legislative intent" divorced from text is one of those subterfuges; and as I have described, *Church of the Holy Trinity is* one of those cases. What I think is needed, however, is not rationalization of this process but abandonment of it. It is simply not compatible with democratic theory that laws mean whatever they ought to mean, and that unelected judges decide what that is.

It may well be that the statutory interpretation adopted by the Court in *Church of the Holy Trinity* produced a desirable result; and it may even be (though I doubt it) that it produced the unexpressed result actually intended by Congress, rather than merely the one desired by the Court. Regardless, the decision was wrong because it failed to follow the text. The text is the law, and it is the text that must be observed. . . .

TEXTUALISM

The philosophy of interpretation I have described above is known as textualism. In some sophisticated circles, it is considered simpleminded — "wooden," "unimaginative," "pedestrian." It is none of that. To be a textualist in good standing, one need not be too dull to perceive the broader social purposes that a statute is designed, or could be designed, to serve; or too hidebound to realize that new times require new laws. One need only hold the belief that judges have no authority to pursue those broader purposes or write those new laws.

Textualism should not be confused with so-called strict constructionism, a degraded form of textualism that brings the whole philosophy into disrepute. I am not a strict constructionist, and no one ought to be — though better that, I suppose, than a nontextualist. A text should not be construed strictly, and it should not be construed leniently; it should be construed reasonably, to contain all that it fairly means. . . .

LEGISLATIVE HISTORY

Let me turn now . . . to an interpretive device whose widespread use is relatively new: legislative history, by which I mean the statements made in the floor debates, committee reports, and even committee testimony, leading up to the enactment of the legislation. My view that the objective indication of the words, rather than the intent of the legislature, is what constitutes the law leads me, of course, to the conclusion that legislative history should not be used as an authoritative indication of a statute's meaning. This was the traditional English, and the traditional American, practice. Chief Justice Taney wrote:

> In expounding this law, the judgment of the court cannot, in any degree, be influenced by the construction placed upon it by individual members of Congress in the debate which took place on its passage, nor by the motives or reasons assigned by them for supporting or opposing amendments that were offered. The law as it passed is the will of the majority of both houses, *and the only mode in which that will is spoken is in the act itself;* and we must gather their intention from the language there used, comparing it, when any ambiguity exists, with the laws upon the same subject, and looking, if necessary, to the public history of the times in which it was passed.[40]

That uncompromising view generally prevailed in this country until the present century. The movement to change it gained momentum in the late 1920s and 1930s, driven, believe it or not, by frustration with common-law judges' use of "legislative intent" and phonied-up canons to impose their own views — in those days views opposed to progressive social legislation. I quoted earlier an article by Dean Landis inveighing against such judicial usurpation. The solution he proposed was not the banishment of legislative intent as an interpretive criterion, but rather the use of legislative history to place that intent beyond manipulation. . . .

In the past few decades, however, we have developed a legal culture in which lawyers routinely — and I do mean routinely — make no distinction between words in the text of a statute and words in its legislative history. My Court is frequently told, in briefs and in oral argument, that "Congress said thus-and-so" when in fact what is being quoted is not the law promulgated by Congress, nor even any text endorsed by a single house of Congress, but rather the statement of a single committee of a single house, set forth in a committee report. Resort to legislative history has become so common that lawyerly wags have popularized a humorous quip inverting the oft-recited (and oft-ignored) rule as to when its use is appropriate: "One should consult the text of the statute," the joke goes, "only when the legislative history is ambiguous." Alas, that is no longer funny. Reality has overtaken parody. A few terms ago, I read a brief that *began* the legal argument with a discussion of

---

[40] Aldridge v. Williams, 44 U.S. (3 How.) 9, 24 (1985) (emphasis added).

legislative history and then continued (I am quoting it verbatim): "Unfortunately, the legislative debates are not helpful. Thus, we turn to the other guidepost in this difficult area, statutory language."

As I have said, I object to the use of legislative history on principle, since I reject intent of the legislature as the proper criterion of the law. What is most exasperating about the use of legislative history, however, is that it does not even make sense for those who *accept* legislative intent as the criterion. It is much more likely to produce a false or contrived legislative intent than a genuine one. The first and most obvious reason for this is that, with respect to 99.99 percent of the issues of construction reaching the courts, there is no legislative intent, so that any clues provided by the legislative history are bound to be false. Those issues almost invariably involve points of relative detail, compared with the major sweep of the statute in question. That a majority of both houses of Congress (never mind the President, if he signed rather than vetoed the bill) entertained *any* view with regard to such issues is utterly beyond belief. For a virtual certainty, the majority was blissfully unaware of the *existence* of the issue, much less had any preference as to how it should be resolved.

But assuming, contrary to all reality, that the search for "legislative intent" is a search for something that exists, that something is not likely to be found in the archives of legislative history. In earlier days, when Congress had a smaller staff and enacted less legislation, it might have been possible to believe that a significant number of senators or representatives were present for the floor debate, or read the committee reports, and actually voted on the basis of what they heard or read. Those days, if they ever existed, are long gone. The floor is rarely crowded for a debate, the members generally being occupied with committee business and reporting to the floor only when a quorum call is demanded or a vote is to be taken. And as for committee reports, it is not even certain that the members of the issuing *committees* have found time to read them, . . .

Ironically, but quite understandably, the more courts have relied upon legislative history, the less worthy of reliance it has become. In earlier days, it was at least genuine and not contrived — a real part of the legislation's *history*, in the sense that it was part of the *development* of the bill, part of the attempt to inform and persuade those who voted. Nowadays, however, when it is universally known and expected that judges will resort to floor debates and (especially) committee reports as authoritative expressions of "legislative intent," affecting the courts rather than informing the Congress has become the primary purpose of the exercise. It is less that the courts refer to legislative history because it exists than that legislative history exists because the courts refer to it. One of the routine tasks of the Washington lawyer-lobbyist is to draft language that sympathetic legislators can recite in a prewritten "floor debate" — or, even better, insert into a committee report. . . .

Since there are no rules as to how much weight an element of legislative history is entitled to, it can usually be either relied upon or dismissed with equal plausibility. If the willful judge does not like the committee report, he will not follow it; he will call the statute not ambiguous enough, the committee report too ambiguous, or the legislative history (this is a favorite phrase) "as a whole, inconclusive." It is ordinarily very hard to demonstrate that this is false so convincingly as to produce embarrassment. . . . Legislative history provides, moreover, a uniquely broad playing field. In any major piece of legislation, the legislative history is extensive, and there is something for everybody. . . .

I think it is time to call an end to a brief and failed experiment, if not for reasons of principle then for reasons of practicality. . . . The most immediate and tangible change the abandonment of legislative history would effect is this: Judges, lawyers, and clients will be saved an enormous amount of time and expense. When I was head of the Office of Legal Counsel in the Justice Department, I estimated that 60 percent of the time of the lawyers on my staff was expended finding, and poring over, the incunabula of legislative history. What a waste. We did not use to do it, and we should do it no more.

QUESTIONS

1. Justice Scalia argues that the text of a statute is the only legitimate source for determining what the law is. What if the text is ambiguous? Justice William A. Bablitch of the Wisconsin Supreme Court, for example, has written:

> . . . "That depends on what the meaning of the word 'is' is." William Jefferson Clinton. . . . Language is inherently ambiguous — perhaps not as ambiguous as the quotation above would have us believe, but the quote makes a point: plain meaning is frequently in the eye of the beholder. What is plain to one may be ambiguous to another.[17]

If language is inherently ambiguous, how does reliance on the text of the statute alone, as textualism dictates, provide adequate guidance to judges interpreting statutes?

2. How would a textualist interpret "human being" in the California murder statute in the context of the *Keeler* case? Justice Burke in his *Keeler* dissent argues that the words "human being . . . need not be frozen in place as of any particular time." Would Justice Scalia agree? In other words, if the meaning of words in a statute, such as "human being," changes over time, should courts restrict the statute to the original meaning at the time the statute was enacted? Or should courts use the new meanings the words in the statute acquire over time?

3. What if application of the literal text of a statute to a particular situation would produce an absurd result? How might Justice Scalia respond to this question?

4. Which theory of interpretation puts fewer constraints on judges, intentionalism or textualism? Justice Aharon Barak has written that a judge "who holds that the purpose of the statute may be learned only from its language"[18] has more discretion than the judge "who will seek guidance from every reliable source."[19] How might Justice Scalia reply to this claim?

5. Justice Stevens of the U.S. Supreme Court has written that "[a] method of statutory interpretation that is deliberately uninformed, and hence unconstrained, may produce a result that is consistent with a court's own views of how things should be, but it may also defeat the very purpose for which the provision was enacted."[20] What do you think Justice Stevens meant by the phrase "deliberately uninformed"?

---

17. State v. Peters, 263 Wis. 2d 475, 665 N.W.2d 171 (2003) (Bablitch, J., concurring).
18. Aharon Barak , *Judicial Discretion* 62 (1989).
19. *Id.*
20. Circuit City Stores, Inc. v. Adams, 532 U.S. 105, 133 (2001) (Stevens, J., dissenting).

Stephen Breyer[21], ON THE USES OF LEGISLATIVE HISTORY IN INTERPRETING STATUTES

65 S. Cal. L. Rev. 845, 845-847, 861-865, 872-874 (1992)

I. INTRODUCTION

Until recently an appellate court trying to interpret unclear statutory language would have thought it natural, and often helpful, to refer to the statute's "legislative history." The judges might have examined congressional floor debates, committee reports, hearing testimony, and presidential messages in an effort to determine what Congress really "meant" by particular statutory language. Should courts refer to legislative history as they try to apply statutes correctly? Is this practice wise, helpful, or proper? Lawyers and judges, teachers and legislators, have begun to reexamine this venerable practice, often with a highly critical eye. Some have urged drastically curtailing, or even totally abandoning, its use. Some argue that courts use legislative history almost arbitrarily. Using legislative history, Judge Leventhal once said, is like "looking over a crowd and picking out your friends." Others maintain that it is constitutionally improper to look beyond a statute's language, or that searching for "congressional intent" is a semi-mystical exercise like hunting the snark. . . .

I should like to defend the classical practice and convince you that those who attack it ought to claim victory once they have made judges more sensitive to problems of the abuse of legislative history; they ought not to condemn its use altogether. They should confine their attack to the outskirts and leave the citadel at peace. . . .

I concede at the outset that my arguments are more pragmatic than theoretical. They rest upon two important assumptions. First, I assume that appellate courts are in part administrative institutions that aim to help resolve disputes and, while doing so, interpret, and thereby clarify, the law. Second, I assume that law itself is a human institution, serving basic human or societal needs. It is therefore properly subject to praise, or to criticism, in terms of certain pragmatic values, including both formal values, such as coherence and workability, and widely shared substantive values, such as helping to achieve justice by interpreting the law in accordance with the "reasonable expectations" of those to whom it applies. If you do not accept these assumptions, then I am unlikely to convince you of the legitimate role of legislative history in the judicial process. If you do accept them and if, through example, I can suggest to you that legislative history helps appellate courts reach interpretations that tend to make the law itself more coherent, workable, or fair, then I may convince you that courts should not abandon the practice. . . .

III.   THE CRITICISMS OF THE USE OF LEGISLATIVE HISTORY

. . . Although many of [the criticisms of the use of legislative history] have considerable logical and practical force, the question you should ask is whether they are strong enough to force us to abandon, or significantly to curtail, the often useful practice of looking to legislative history. . . . Why, of all the many tools

---

21. At the time this article was written, Stephen Breyer was the Chief Judge of the United States Court of Appeals for the First Circuit. He is currently an Associate Justice of the United States Supreme Court.

judges use to help interpret unclear statutory language (context, tradition, custom, precedent, dictionary meanings, administrability, and so on), should they not use this one?

A. LACK OF UTILITY

The argument most frequently heard against the use of legislative history is that it does not help. Critics quote Justice Jackson's remark that "legislative history here, as usual, is more vague than the statute we are called upon to interpret." Again they will point to Judge Leventhal's comment that searching congressional documents for a statute's legislative history is like "looking over a crowd and picking out your friends." One can easily find examples of vague or conflicting legislative history. The critics do so, and they cite them.

This kind of argument is strongest when aimed at "misuse" of history. But, how strong a case can it make for abandonment? Logically, the argument is open to the response, "If the history is vague, or seriously conflicting, do not use it." No one claims that history is *always* useful; only that it *sometimes* helps.

Moreover, those who oppose the use of legislative history often illustrate their arguments with Supreme Court cases, for unlike lower courts, the Supreme Court frequently interprets statutory provisions arising out of serious political disagreement. The warring legislative parties, in such cases, often leave no legislative history stone unturned in their efforts to influence subsequent judicial interpretations.

Federal courts of appeals, however, consider many more cases each year, and many more less important cases, than does the Supreme Court. Indeed, they decide about nine thousand cases by written opinion, compared to about 150 in the Supreme Court. Their workload includes many unclear statutory provisions where lack of clarity does *not* reflect major political controversy. Such cases usually do not involve conflicting legislative history; in fact, the history itself often is clear enough to clarify the statute. . . .

B. CONSTITUTIONAL ARGUMENTS

Two types of constitutional arguments are made against the use of legislative history. The first concerns the Constitution's requirements for enacting a law. A bill must pass both houses of Congress and obtain the President's signature or a veto override. The result, says the Constitution, is a statute; and that statute, not a floor speech or committee report or testimony or presidential message or congressional "intent," is the law. The use of legislative history, according to this argument, tends to make these other matters — report language and floor speeches — the "law" even though they had received neither a majority vote nor a presidential signature.

Second, the Constitution vests "legislative" power in a Congress made up of elected members. It does not vest legislative power in congressional staff or in lobbyists. Yet these unelected individuals write the floor statements, testimony, reports, and messages that make up legislative history. Indeed, the elected members may not even read these materials. Thus, to use legislative history not only makes "law" out of that which is not law, but also permits the exercise of legislative power by those who do not constitutionally possess it.

These arguments overstate their case. The "statute-is-the-only-law" argument misses the point. No one claims that legislative history is a statute, or even that, in any strong sense, it is "law." Rather, legislative history is helpful in trying to understand the meaning of the words that do make up the statute or the "law." A judge cannot interpret the words of an ambiguous statute without looking beyond its words for the words have simply ceased to provide univocal guidance to decide the case at hand. Can the judge, for example, ignore a dictionary or the historical interpretive practice of the agency that customarily applies some words? Is a dictionary or an historic agency interpretive practice "law?" It is "law" only in a weak sense that does not claim the status of a statute, and in a sense that violates neither the letter nor the spirit of the Constitution.

The delegation argument ("the Senator did not write, or even read, the report") is susceptible to the same type of criticism. After all, no one elected lexicographers or agency civil servants to Congress. The Constitution nowhere grants them legislative power. Yet, judges universally seek their help in resolving interpretive problems.

More importantly, this argument misunderstands how Congress works as an institution. The relevant point here is that nothing in the Constitution seems to prohibit Congress from using staff and relying upon groups and institutions in the way I have described. And, for purposes of establishing the legislator's personal responsibility, that description does not distinguish between different kinds of documents — between committee reports, floor statements, or statutory text. Rather, it holds the legislator personally responsible for the work of staff, and it correlates the legislator's direct personal involvement, not according to the kind of document, but according to the significance of the decision at issue. That is to say, the personal involvement of the individual legislator in the statute's text itself may or may not be greater than the legislator's involvement with report language or a floor statement. Involvement is a function of the importance of the substantive, procedural, or political issue facing the legislator, not of the "category" of the text that happens to embody that particular issue. It is not obvious that in the late twentieth century there is some better way to organize Congress's work. But regardless of the merits of this process, nothing about it makes a court's reference to legislative history seem *constitutionally* suspect. . . .

The complex legislative process I have described relies heavily upon interactions of legislators, staff, and interest groups to create, review, criticize, and amend legislative language, reports, and floor statements. The process is reasonably open and fair so long as those whom the legislation will likely affect have roughly equal access to the legislative process. However, critics of the congressional process challenge this assumption strongly and often. Most critics concede that trade associations, labor unions, executive departments, and certain public interest groups, all under the watchful eye of the press, participate fully in the process on behalf of those they represent. But they ask several familiar questions. For example, are there not many disadvantaged groups who are excluded from the legislative process? Indeed, is the ordinary citizen adequately represented as a "typical citizen" rather than as a member of some organized interest group? Moreover, does ideology drive congressional staff more than the desire to reflect the will of the voter? Perhaps because we are all familiar with such criticism, my description of the legislative process did not fully dispel doubts about the legitimacy of the use of legislative history.

If these questions disturb you, then you might ask yourself whether judicial abandonment of the use of legislative history would make matters better or worse. Certainly abandonment would eliminate one factor that favors public hearings, public reports vetted by staff, and fairly detailed floor debates. It would also make it easier for legislators to justify amending legislation after it leaves committee, while it is on the floor of the House or Senate, or even while both Houses of Congress confer upon the bill after it passed each in different versions. To the extent that a change weakens the publicly accessible committee system and diminishes the need for public justification, it increases the power of the "special interests" (and here I use that term pejoratively) to secure legislation that is not in the "public interest." Thus, if judges abandon the use of legislative history, Congress will not necessarily produce better laws. . . .

I did not dwell upon the problems of the legislative process . . . because my focus was the judiciary. I have simply argued that, viewed in light of the judiciary's important objective of helping to maintain coherent, workable statutory law, the case for abandoning the use of legislative history has not yet been made. Present practice has proved useful; the alternatives are not promising; radical change is too problematic. The "problem" of legislative history is its "abuse," not its "use." Care, not drastic change, is all that is warranted.

QUESTIONS

1. Justice Breyer does not contest that legislative history can be abused and at times has been abused by courts interpreting statutes. If so, why then shouldn't the use of legislative history be abandoned?

2. Justice Breyer suggests that "judicial abandonment of the use of legislative history" might make the legislative process less open and fair? How so?

3. What do you think Justice Breyer means when he says that "[t]he warring legislative parties, in [cases involving serious political disagreement], often leave no legislative history stone unturned in their efforts to influence subsequent judicial interpretations"?

PROBLEM

3.7 Look back at Problem 3.2, dealing with cameras in the jury room. Assume the jurisdiction in which that Problem occurs has the following statute:

No person shall be permitted to be with a jury while it is deliberating.

Assume also that the case has drawn notoriety and that a member of the state senate has introduced a bill currently being considered by the senate judiciary committee to amend this statute by adding the following language: "Nor shall any camera, microphone, or other recording device be permitted in a jury room while a jury is deliberating." How do you think Justice Brewer would interpret this statute to resolve Problem 3.2? How do you think Justice Scalia would interpret it? How would you interpret the statute? On what basis?

3. Dynamic Statutory Interpretation

William N. Eskridge, Jr., DYNAMIC STATUTORY INTERPRETATION
135 U. Pa. L. Rev. 1479, 1479-1480, 1482-1484, 1496-1497, 1498, 1506-1507 (1987)

Federal judges interpreting the Constitution typically consider not only the constitutional text and its historical background, but also its subsequent interpretational history, related constitutional developments, and current societal facts. Similarly, judges interpreting common law precedents normally consider not only the text of the precedents and their historical context, but also their subsequent history, related legal developments, and current societal context. In light of this, it is odd that many judges and commentators believe judges should consider only the text and historical context when interpreting statutes, the third main source of law. Statutes, however, should — like the Constitution and the common law — be interpreted "dynamically," that is, in light of their present societal, political, and legal context.

Traditional doctrine teaches that statutes should not be interpreted dynamically. Prevailing approaches to statutory interpretation treat statutes as static texts. Thus, the leading treatise states that "[f]or the interpretation of statutes, 'intent of the legislature' is the criterion that is most often cited." This "intentionalist" approach asks how the legislature originally intended the interpretive question to be answered, or would have intended the question to be answered had it thought about the issue when it passed the statute. A "modified intentionalist" approach uses the original purpose of the statute as a surrogate for original intent, especially when the latter is uncertain; the proper interpretation is the one that best furthers the purpose the legislature had in mind when it enacted the statute.

Theoretically, these "originalist" approaches to statutory interpretation assume that the legislature fixes the meaning of a statute on the date the statute is enacted. The implicit claim is that a legislator interpreting the statute at the time of enactment would render the same interpretation as a judge interpreting the same statute fifty years later. This implication seems counterintuitive. Indeed, the legal realists argued this point earlier in the century. For example, gaps and ambiguities exist in all statutes, typically concerning matters as to which there was little legislative deliberation and, hence, no clear intent. As society changes, adapts to the statute, and generates new variations of the problem which gave rise to the statute, the unanticipated gaps and ambiguities proliferate. In such circumstances, it seems sensible that "the quest is not properly for the sense originally intended by the statute, [or] for the sense sought originally to be put into it, but rather for the sense which can be quarried out of it in the light of the new situation." Moreover, as time passes, the legal and constitutional context of the statute may change. Should not an interpreter "ask [her]self not only what the legislation means abstractly, or even on the basis of legislative history, but also what it ought to mean in terms of the needs and goals of our present day society[?]" . . .

I. A MODEL OF DYNAMIC STATUTORY INTERPRETATION

The static vision of statutory interpretation prescribed by traditional doctrine is strikingly outdated. In practice, it imposes unrealistic burdens on judges, asking them to extract textual meaning that makes sense in the present from historical materials whose sense is often impossible to recreate faithfully. As doctrine, it is intellectually antediluvian, in light of recent developments in the philosophy of interpretation. Interpretation is not static, but dynamic. Interpretation is not an archeological discovery,[12] but a dialectical creation. Interpretation is not mere exegesis to pinpoint historical meaning, but hermeneutics to apply that meaning to current problems and circumstances.

The dialectic of statutory interpretation is the process of understanding a text created in the past and applying it to a present problem. This process cannot be described simply as the recreation of past events and past expectations, for the "best" interpretation of a statute is typically the one that is most consonant with our current "web of beliefs" and policies surrounding the statute. That is, statutory interpretation involves the present-day interpreter's understanding and reconciliation of three different perspectives, no one of which will always control. These three perspectives relate to (1) the statutory text, which is the formal focus of interpretation and a constraint on the range of interpretive options available (textual perspective); (2) the original legislative expectations surrounding the statute's creation, including compromises reached (historical perspective); and (3) the subsequent evolution of the statute and its present context, especially the ways in which the societal and legal environment of the statute has materially changed over time (evolutive perspective).

Under dynamic statutory interpretation, the textual perspective is critical in many cases. The traditional understanding of the "rule of law" requires that statutes enacted by the majoritarian legislature be given effect, and that citizens have reasonable notice of the legal rules that govern their behavior. When the statutory text clearly answers the interpretive question, therefore, it normally will be the most important consideration. Exceptions, however, do exist because an apparently clear text can be rendered ambiguous by a demonstration of contrary legislative expectations or highly unreasonable consequences. The historical perspective is the next most important interpretive consideration; given the traditional assumptions that the legislature is the supreme lawmaking body in a democracy, the historical expectations of the enacting legislature are entitled to deference. Hence, when a clear text and supportive legislative history suggest the same answer, they typically will control.

The dynamic model, however, views the evolutive perspective as most important when the statutory text is not clear and the original legislative expectations have been overtaken by subsequent changes in society and law. In such cases, the pull of text and history will be slight, and the interpreter will find current policies and societal conditions most important. The hardest cases, obviously, are those in which a clear text or strong historical evidence or both, are inconsistent with compelling current values and policies. . . .

The three perspectives implicated in dynamic interpretation . . . suggest a continuum. In many cases, the text of the statute will provide determinate answers, though we should trust our reading of the text primarily when the statute is recent and the context of enactment represents considered legislative deliberation and

---

[12] Professor T. Alexander Aleinikoff suggested to me the idea that traditional statutory interpretation is like an archeological expedition. He compares the "archeological metaphor" with a "nautical metaphor," in which Congress turns the statute out to sea and leaves it to drift unpredictably.

decision on the interpretive issue. This is one end of the continuum: the text controls. At the opposite end of the continuum are those cases where neither the text nor the historical context of the statute clearly resolves the interpretive question, and the societal and legal context of the statute has changed materially. In those cases, the evolutive context controls. In general, the more detailed the text is, the greater weight the interpreter will give to textual considerations; the more recent the statute and the clearer the legislative expectations, the greater weight the interpreter will give to historical considerations; the more striking the changes in circumstances (changes in public values count more than factual changes in society), the greater weight the interpreter will give to evolutive considerations. . . .

Historical scholarship suggests that our constitutional system of government was not meant to be one of rigid separation of powers or pure majoritarianism. Instead, the polity created by the Constitution requires a government that is deliberative and promotes the common good, at least on important matters. Judicial lawmaking from statutes has a constructive role to play in such a polity, especially in light of the tendency of the legislature to produce too little up-to-date public-seeking policy and not to produce well-integrated policies. The vision of a tripartite government and the legitimacy of the system are not served by a straitjacketed theory of statutory interpretation but are better served by a flexible approach that is sensitive to current policy concerns. . . .

To a substantial extent, the metaphor of judge as cipher has been replaced with the vision of a creative lawmaker whose judgment in "hard" statutory cases, where the statutory text does not answer the question determinately, rests in large part on the judge's subjective views of the statute and the justice of the particular case. In 1920, Judge Benjamin Cardozo confessed that the nature of the judicial process is "uncertainty" rather than objective answers, and that "the process in its highest reaches is not discovery, but creation." Although Cardozo and his contemporaries usually spoke of judicial creativity in connection with the judge's common law powers, they clearly saw the judge's creative role extending to statutory interpretation as well.

QUESTIONS

1. What meaning would a judge using dynamic statutory interpretation give the words "human being" in the California murder statute in the context of the *Keeler* case? Would the dynamic view be receptive to Justice Burke's argument in his *Keeler* dissent that the words "human being . . . need not be frozen in place as of any particular time?"

2. Which approaches to statutory interpretation do the majority and dissenting opinions in *Keeler* reflect?

PROBLEM

3.8 In the following statutes, legislatures provide guidance to courts on how to interpret statutes. Do these statutes endorse an intentionalist, textualist, or dynamic approach?

Minnesota Statutes § 645.16   *Legislative intent controls*

The object of all interpretation and construction of laws is to ascertain and effectuate the intention of the legislature. Every law shall be construed, if possible, to give effect to all its provisions.

When the words of a law in their application to an existing situation are clear and free from all ambiguity, the letter of the law shall not be disregarded under the pretext of pursuing the spirit.

When the words of a law are not explicit, the intention of the legislature may be ascertained by considering, among other matters:

(1) The occasion and necessity for the law;

(2) The circumstances under which it was enacted;

(3) The mischief to be remedied;

(4) The object to be attained;

(5) The former law, if any, including other laws upon the same or similar subjects;

(6) The consequences of a particular interpretation;

(7) The contemporaneous legislative history; and

(8) Legislative and administrative interpretations of the statute.

§ 645.17   *Presumptions in ascertaining legislative intent*

In ascertaining the intention of the legislature the courts may be guided by the following presumptions:

(1) the legislature does not intend a result that is absurd, impossible of execution, or unreasonable;

(2) the legislature intends the entire statute to be effective and certain;

(3) the legislature does not intend to violate the constitution of the United States or of this state;

(4) when a court of last resort has construed the language of a law, the legislature in subsequent laws on the same subject matter intends the same construction to be placed upon such language; and

(5) the legislature intends to favor the public interest as against any private interest.

Iowa Code § 4.6   *Ambiguous statutes — interpretation*

If a statute is ambiguous, the court, in determining the intention of the legislature, may consider among other matters:

1. The object sought to be attained.

2. The circumstances under which the statute was enacted.

3. The legislative history.

4. The common law or former statutory provisions, including laws upon the same or similar subjects.

5. The consequences of a particular construction.

6. The administrative construction of the statute.

7. The preamble or statement of policy.

Texas Government Code § 311.023 (2004)   *Statute Construction Aids*

In construing a statute, whether or not the statute is considered ambiguous on its face, a court may consider among other matters the:

(1) object sought to be attained;

(2) circumstances under which the statute was enacted;

(3) legislative history;

(4) common law or former statutory provisions, including laws on the same or similar subjects;

(5) consequences of a particular construction;

(6) administrative construction of the statute; and

(7) title (caption), preamble, and emergency provision.

E. SPECIFICITY

Edward Livingston, A SYSTEM OF PENAL LAW FOR THE UNITED STATES OF AMERICA   2 (1828)

Penal laws should be written in plain language, clearly and unequivocally expressed, that they may neither be misunderstood nor perverted; they should be so concise, as to be remembered with ease; and all technical phrases, or words they contain, should be clearly defined. They should be promulgated in such a manner as to force a knowledge of their provisions upon the people; to this end, they should not only be published, but taught in the schools; and publicly read on stated occasions.

In 1992, to combat gang violence and intimidation in some of its neighborhoods, Chicago enacted the following ordinance:

(a) Whenever a police officer observes a person whom he reasonably believes to be a criminal street gang member loitering in any public place with one or more other persons, he shall order all such persons to disperse and remove themselves from the area. Any person who does not promptly obey such an order is in violation of this section.

(b) It shall be an affirmative defense to an alleged violation of this section that no person who was observed loitering was in fact a member of a criminal street gang.

(c) As used in this section:

(1) 'Loiter' means to remain in any one place with no apparent purpose.

(2) 'Criminal street gang' means any ongoing organization, association in fact or group of three or more persons, whether formal or informal, having as one of its substantial activities the commission of one or more of the criminal acts enumerated in paragraph (3), and whose members individually or collectively engage in or have engaged in a pattern of criminal gang activity. . . .

(5) 'Public place' means the public way and any other location open to the public, whether publicly or privately owned.

(e) Any person who violates this Section is subject to a fine of not less than $ 100 and not more than $ 500 for each offense, or imprisonment for not more than six months, or both.

Jesus Morales, convicted under the ordinance, challenged his conviction on appeal and sought review in the United States Supreme Court.

CITY OF CHICAGO *v.* MORALES
527 U.S. 41 (1999)

JUSTICE STEVENS announced the judgment of the Court and delivered the opinion of the Court with respect to Parts I, II, and V, and an opinion with respect to Parts III, IV, and VI, in which Justice Souter and Justice Ginsburg join.

I

Before the ordinance was adopted, the city council's Committee on Police and Fire conducted hearings to explore the problems created by the city's street gangs, and more particularly, the consequences of public loitering by gang members. Witnesses included residents of the neighborhoods where gang members are most active, as well as some of the aldermen who represent those areas. Based on that evidence, the council made a series of findings that are included in the text of the ordinance and explain the reasons for its enactment.

The council found that a continuing increase in criminal street gang activity was largely responsible for the city's rising murder rate, as well as an escalation of violent and drug related crimes. It noted that in many neighborhoods throughout the city, "the burgeoning presence of street gang members in public places has intimidated many law abiding citizens." Furthermore, the council stated that gang members "establish control over identifiable areas. . . . by loitering in those areas and intimidating others from entering those areas; and . . . members of criminal street gangs avoid arrest by committing no offense punishable under existing laws when they know the police are present . . . . " It further found that "loitering in public places by criminal street gang members creates a justifiable fear for the safety of persons and property in the area" and that "aggressive action is necessary to preserve the city's streets and other public places so that the public may use such places without fear." Moreover, the council concluded that the city "has an interest in discouraging all persons from loitering in public places with criminal gang members."

The ordinance creates a criminal offense punishable by a fine of up to $500, imprisonment for not more than six months, and a requirement to perform up to 120 hours of community service. Commission of the offense involves four predicates. First, the police officer must reasonably believe that at least one of the two or more persons present in a "public place" is a "criminal street gang member." Second, the persons must be "loitering," which the ordinance defines as "remaining in any one place with no apparent purpose." Third, the officer must then order "all" of the persons to disperse and remove themselves "from the area." Fourth, a person must disobey the officer's order. If any person, whether a gang member or not, disobeys the officer's order, that person is guilty of violating the ordinance.

Two months after the ordinance was adopted, the Chicago Police Department promulgated General Order 92-4 to provide guidelines to govern its enforcement. That order purported to establish limitations on the enforcement discretion of police officers "to ensure that the anti-gang loitering ordinance is not enforced in an arbitrary or discriminatory way." Chicago Police Department, General Order 92-4. The limitations confine the authority to arrest gang members who violate the ordinance to sworn "members of the Gang Crime Section" and certain other designated officers, and establish detailed criteria for defining street gangs and membership in such gangs. In addition, the order directs district commanders to "designate areas in which the presence of gang members has a demonstrable effect on the activities of law abiding persons in the surrounding community," and provides that the ordinance "will be enforced only within the designated areas." The city, however, does not release the locations of these "designated areas" to the public.

II

During the three years of its enforcement, the police issued over 89,000 dispersal orders and arrested over 42,000 people for violating the ordinance. . . .

The Illinois Supreme Court . . . held "that the gang loitering ordinance violates due process of law in that it is impermissibly vague on its face and an arbitrary restriction on personal liberties." . . .

III

The basic factual predicate for the city's ordinance is not in dispute. As the city argues in its brief, "the very presence of a large collection of obviously brazen, insistent, and lawless gang members and hangers-on on the public ways intimidates residents, who become afraid even to leave their homes and go about their business. That, in turn, imperils community residents' sense of safety and security, detracts from property values, and can ultimately destabilize entire neighborhoods." The findings in the ordinance explain that it was motivated by these concerns. We have no doubt that a law that directly prohibited such intimidating conduct would be constitutional, but this ordinance broadly covers a significant amount of additional activity. Uncertainty about the scope of that additional coverage provides the basis for respondents' claim that the ordinance is too vague.

We are confronted at the outset with the city's claim that it was improper for the state courts to conclude that the ordinance is invalid on its face. The city correctly points out that imprecise laws can be attacked on their face under two different doctrines. First, the overbreadth doctrine permits the facial invalidation of laws that inhibit the exercise of First Amendment rights if the impermissible applications of the law are substantial when "judged in relation to the statute's plainly legitimate sweep." Second, even if an enactment does not reach a substantial amount of constitutionally protected conduct, it may be impermissibly vague because it fails to establish standards for the police and public that are sufficient to guard against the arbitrary deprivation of liberty interests.

While we, like the Illinois courts, conclude that the ordinance is invalid on its face, we do not rely on the overbreadth doctrine. We agree with the city's submission that the law does not have a sufficiently substantial impact on conduct protected by the First Amendment to render it unconstitutional. The ordinance does not prohibit speech. Because the term "loiter" is defined as remaining in one place "with no apparent purpose," it is also clear that it does not prohibit any form of conduct that is apparently intended to convey a message. By its terms, the ordinance is inapplicable to assemblies that are designed to demonstrate a group's support of, or opposition to, a particular point of view. Its impact on the social contact between gang members and others does not impair the First Amendment "right of association" that our cases have recognized.

On the other hand, as the United States recognizes, the freedom to loiter for innocent purposes is part of the "liberty" protected by the Due Process Clause of the

Fourteenth Amendment. We have expressly identified this "right to remove from one place to another according to inclination" as "an attribute of personal liberty" protected by the Constitution. Indeed, it is apparent that an individual's decision to remain in a public place of his choice is as much a part of his liberty as the freedom of movement inside frontiers that is "a part of our heritage" or the right to move "to whatsoever place one's own inclination may direct" identified in Blackstone's Commentaries. 1 W. Blackstone, Commentaries on the Laws of England 130 (1765).

There is no need, however, to decide whether the impact of the Chicago ordinance on constitutionally protected liberty alone would suffice to support a facial challenge under the overbreadth doctrine. For it is clear that the vagueness of this enactment makes a facial challenge appropriate. This is not an ordinance that "simply regulates business behavior and contains a scienter requirement." It is a criminal law that contains no *mens rea* requirement, and infringes on constitutionally protected rights. When vagueness permeates the text of such a law, it is subject to facial attack.

Vagueness may invalidate a criminal law for either of two independent reasons. First, it may fail to provide the kind of notice that will enable ordinary people to understand what conduct it prohibits; second, it may authorize and even encourage arbitrary and discriminatory enforcement. Accordingly, we first consider whether the ordinance provides fair notice to the citizen and then discuss its potential for arbitrary enforcement.

IV

"It is established that a law fails to meet the requirements of the Due Process Clause if it is so vague and standardless that it leaves the public uncertain as to the conduct it prohibits. . . . " The Illinois Supreme Court recognized that the term "loiter" may have a common and accepted meaning, but the definition of that term in this ordinance — "to remain in any one place with no apparent purpose" — does not. It is difficult to imagine how any citizen of the city of Chicago standing in a public place with a group of people would know if he or she had an "apparent purpose." If she were talking to another person, would she have an apparent purpose? If she were frequently checking her watch and looking expectantly down the street, would she have an apparent purpose?

Since the city cannot conceivably have meant to criminalize each instance a citizen stands in public with a gang member, the vagueness that dooms this ordinance is not the product of uncertainty about the normal meaning of "loitering," but rather about what loitering is covered by the ordinance and what is not. The Illinois Supreme Court emphasized the law's failure to distinguish between innocent conduct and conduct threatening harm.[24] Its decision followed the precedent set by a number of state courts that have upheld ordinances that criminalize loitering combined with some other overt act or evidence of criminal intent. However, state courts have uniformly invalidated laws that do not join the term "loitering" with a second specific element of the crime.

---

[24] 177 Ill. 2d at 452, 687 N.E.2d at 61. One of the trial courts that invalidated the ordinance gave the following illustration: "Suppose a group of gang members were playing basketball in the park, while waiting for a drug delivery. Their apparent purpose is that they are in the park to play ball. The actual purpose is that they are waiting for drugs. Under this definition of loitering, a group of people innocently sitting in a park discussing their futures would be arrested, while the 'basketball players' awaiting a drug delivery would be left alone." Chicago v. Youkhana, Nos. 93 MCI 293363 et al. (Ill. Cir. Ct., Cook Cty., Sept. 29, 1993), reprinted in App. to Pet. for Cert. 45a.

The city's principal response to this concern about adequate notice is that loiterers are not subject to sanction until after they have failed to comply with an officer's order to disperse. "Whatever problem is created by a law that criminalizes conduct people normally believe to be innocent is solved when persons receive actual notice from a police order of what they are expected to do." We find this response unpersuasive for at least two reasons.

First, the purpose of the fair notice requirement is to enable the ordinary citizen to conform his or her conduct to the law. "No one may be required at peril of life, liberty or property to speculate as to the meaning of penal statutes." Although it is true that a loiterer is not subject to criminal sanctions unless he or she disobeys a dispersal order, the loitering is the conduct that the ordinance is designed to prohibit. If the loitering is in fact harmless and innocent, the dispersal order itself is an unjustified impairment of liberty. If the police are able to decide arbitrarily which members of the public they will order to disperse, then the Chicago ordinance becomes indistinguishable from the law we held invalid in *Shuttlesworth v. Birmingham*, 382 U.S. 87, 90, 15 L. Ed. 2d 176, 86 S. Ct. 211 (1965).[29] Because an officer may issue an order only after prohibited conduct has already occurred, it cannot provide the kind of advance notice that will protect the putative loiterer from being ordered to disperse. Such an order cannot retroactively give adequate warning of the boundary between the permissible and the impermissible applications of the law.

Second, the terms of the dispersal order compound the inadequacy of the notice afforded by the ordinance. It provides that the officer "shall order all such persons to disperse and remove themselves from the area." This vague phrasing raises a host of questions. After such an order issues, how long must the loiterers remain apart? How far must they move? If each loiterer walks around the block and they meet again at the same location, are they subject to arrest or merely to being ordered to disperse again? As we do here, we have found vagueness in a criminal statute exacerbated by the use of the standards of "neighborhood" and "locality." We remarked in *Connally* [*v. General Constr. Co.*, 269 U.S. 385 (1926)] that "both terms are elastic and, dependent upon circumstances, may be equally satisfied by areas measured by rods or by miles."

Lack of clarity in the description of the loiterer's duty to obey a dispersal order might not render the ordinance unconstitutionally vague if the definition of the forbidden conduct were clear, but it does buttress our conclusion that the entire ordinance fails to give the ordinary citizen adequate notice of what is forbidden and what is permitted. The Constitution does not permit a legislature to "set a net large enough to catch all possible offenders, and leave it to the courts to step inside and say who could be rightfully detained, and who should be set at large." This ordinance is therefore vague "not in the sense that it requires a person to conform his conduct to an imprecise but comprehensible normative standard, but rather in the sense that no standard of conduct is specified at all."

V

The broad sweep of the ordinance also violates " 'the requirement that a legislature establish minimal guidelines to govern law enforcement.' " There are no

---

[29] "Literally read . . . this ordinance says that a person may stand on a public sidewalk in Birmingham only at the whim of any police officer of that city. The constitutional vice of so broad a provision needs no demonstration." 382 U.S. 87 at 90.

such guidelines in the ordinance. In any public place in the city of Chicago, persons who stand or sit in the company of a gang member may be ordered to disperse unless their purpose is apparent. The mandatory language in the enactment directs the police to issue an order without first making any inquiry about their possible purposes. It matters not whether the reason that a gang member and his father, for example, might loiter near Wrigley Field is to rob an unsuspecting fan or just to get a glimpse of Sammy Sosa leaving the ballpark; in either event, if their purpose is not apparent to a nearby police officer, she may — indeed, she "shall" — order them to disperse.

Recognizing that the ordinance does reach a substantial amount of innocent conduct, we turn, then, to its language to determine if it "necessarily entrusts lawmaking to the moment-to-moment judgment of the policeman on his beat." As we discussed in the context of fair notice, the principal source of the vast discretion conferred on the police in this case is the definition of loitering as "to remain in any one place with no apparent purpose."

As the Illinois Supreme Court interprets that definition, it "provides absolute discretion to police officers to determine what activities constitute loitering." We have no authority to construe the language of a state statute more narrowly than the construction given by that State's highest court. "The power to determine the meaning of a statute carries with it the power to prescribe its extent and limitations as well as the method by which they shall be determined."

Nevertheless, the city disputes the Illinois Supreme Court's interpretation, arguing that the text of the ordinance limits the officer's discretion in three ways. First, it does not permit the officer to issue a dispersal order to anyone who is moving along or who has an apparent purpose. Second, it does not permit an arrest if individuals obey a dispersal order. Third, no order can issue unless the officer reasonably believes that one of the loiterers is a member of a criminal street gang.

Even putting to one side our duty to defer to a state court's construction of the scope of a local enactment, we find each of these limitations insufficient. That the ordinance does not apply to people who are moving — that is, to activity that would not constitute loitering under any possible definition of the term — does not even address the question of how much discretion the police enjoy in deciding which stationary persons to disperse under the ordinance.[32] Similarly, that the ordinance does not permit an arrest until after a dispersal order has been disobeyed does not provide any guidance to the officer deciding whether such an order should issue. The "no apparent purpose" standard for making that decision is inherently subjective because its application depends on whether some purpose is "apparent" to the officer on the scene.

Presumably an officer would have discretion to treat some purposes — perhaps a purpose to engage in idle conversation or simply to enjoy a cool breeze on a warm evening — as too frivolous to be apparent if he suspected a different ulterior motive. Moreover, an officer conscious of the city council's reasons for enacting the ordinance might well ignore its text and issue a dispersal order, even though an illicit purpose is actually apparent.

---

[32] It is possible to read the mandatory language of the ordinance and conclude that it affords the police no discretion, since it speaks with the mandatory "shall." However, not even the city makes this argument, which flies in the face of common sense that all police officers must use some discretion in deciding when and where to enforce city ordinances.

It is true, as the city argues, that the requirement that the officer reasonably believe that a group of loiterers contains a gang member does place a limit on the authority to order dispersal. That limitation would no doubt be sufficient if the ordinance only applied to loitering that had an apparently harmful purpose or effect, or possibly if it only applied to loitering by persons reasonably believed to be criminal gang members. But this ordinance, for reasons that are not explained in the findings of the city council, requires no harmful purpose and applies to non-gang members as well as suspected gang members.[34] It applies to everyone in the city who may remain in one place with one suspected gang member as long as their purpose is not apparent to an officer observing them. Friends, relatives, teachers, counselors, or even total strangers might unwittingly engage in forbidden loitering if they happen to engage in idle conversation with a gang member.

Ironically, the definition of loitering in the Chicago ordinance not only extends its scope to encompass harmless conduct, but also has the perverse consequence of excluding from its coverage much of the intimidating conduct that motivated its enactment. As the city council's findings demonstrate, the most harmful gang loitering is motivated either by an apparent purpose to publicize the gang's dominance of certain territory, thereby intimidating nonmembers, or by an equally apparent purpose to conceal ongoing commerce in illegal drugs. As the Illinois Supreme Court has not placed any limiting construction on the language in the ordinance, we must assume that the ordinance means what it says and that it has no application to loiterers whose purpose is apparent. The relative importance of its application to harmless loitering is magnified by its inapplicability to loitering that has an obviously threatening or illicit purpose.

Finally, in its opinion striking down the ordinance, the Illinois Supreme Court refused to accept the general order issued by the police department as a sufficient limitation on the "vast amount of discretion" granted to the police in its enforcement. We agree. That the police have adopted internal rules limiting their enforcement to certain designated areas in the city would not provide a defense to a loiterer who might be arrested elsewhere. Nor could a person who knowingly loitered with a well-known gang member anywhere in the city safely assume that they would not be ordered to disperse no matter how innocent and harmless their loitering might be.

VI

In our judgment, the Illinois Supreme Court correctly concluded that the ordinance does not provide sufficiently specific limits on the enforcement discretion of the police "to meet constitutional standards for definiteness and clarity." We recognize the serious and difficult problems testified to by the citizens of Chicago that led to the enactment of this ordinance. "We are mindful that the preservation of liberty depends in part on the maintenance of social order." However, in this instance the city has enacted an ordinance that affords too much discretion to the police and too little notice to citizens who wish to use the public streets.

Accordingly, the judgment of the Supreme Court of Illinois is
Affirmed.

---

[34] Not all of the respondents in this case, for example, are gang members. The city admits that it was unable to prove that Morales is a gang member but justifies his arrest and conviction by the fact that Morales admitted "that he knew he was with criminal street gang members." Reply Brief for Petitioner 23, n. 14. In fact, 34 of the 66 respondents in this case were charged in a document that only accused them of being in the presence of a gang member. Tr. of Oral Arg. 34, 58.

QUESTIONS

When a court encounters an ambiguous statute, is it preferable for the court to apply the rule of lenity or find the statute void for vagueness? What are the advantages and disadvantages of each?

PROBLEM

3.9 You are the attorney for a city considering enacting the following as a city ordinance. The city council asks you to: (1) provide an opinion about whether the proposed ordinance would be constitutionally valid; (2) review the constitutional strengths and weaknesses of the statute; (3) make suggestions for redrafting the ordinance to cure any constitutional weaknesses.

> A person commits a violation if he loiters or prowls in a place, at a time, or in a manner not usual for law-abiding individuals under circumstances that warrant alarm for the safety of persons or property in the vicinity. Among the circumstances which may be considered in determining whether such alarm is warranted is the fact that the actor takes flight upon appearance of a peace officer, refuses to identify himself, or manifestly endeavors to conceal himself or any object. Unless flight by the actor or other circumstances makes it impracticable, a peace officer shall, prior to any arrest for an offense under this section, afford the actor an opportunity to dispel any alarm which would otherwise be warranted, by requesting him to identify himself and explain his presence and conduct. No person shall be convicted of an offense under this Section if the peace officer did not comply with the preceding sentence, or if it appears at trial that the explanation given by the actor was true and, if believed by the peace officer at the time, would have dispelled the alarm.

A federal statute passed in 1996 has proved to be "the government's favorite tool in fighting terrorism"[22] and has been used in many recent prosecutions, including the case that follows. The relevant text of the statute for purposes of this case is:

18 United States Code § 2339B

Whoever, within the United States or subject to the jurisdiction of the United States, knowingly provides material support or resources to a foreign terrorist organization, or attempts or conspires to do so, shall be [guilty of a crime].

"material support or resources" is defined as:

currency or other financial securities, financial services, lodging, training, safehouses, false documentation or identification, communications equipment, facilities,

---

22. Adam Liptak, *Defending Those Who Defend Terrorists*, The New York Times at § 4, 4 (July 27, 2003).

weapons, lethal substances, explosives, personnel, transportation, and other physical assets.

UNITED STATES *v.* SATTAR
272 F. Supp. 2d 348 (S.D.N.Y. 2003)

KOELTL, D.J. The defendants in this case — Ahmed Abdel Sattar, Yassir Al-Sirri, Lynne Stewart and Mohammed Yousry — were charged [. . .] with conspiring to provide material support and resources to a foreign terrorist organization ("FTO") in violation of 18 U.S.C. § 2339B [. . .] with providing and attempting to provide material support and resources to an FTO in violation of 18 U.S.C. §§ 2339B and 2.

I.

The Indictment alleges the following facts. At all relevant times, the Islamic Group ("IG") existed as an international terrorist group dedicated to opposing nations, governments, institutions, and individuals that did not share IG's radical interpretation of Islamic law. IG considered such parties "infidels" and interpreted the concept of "jihad" as waging opposition against infidels by whatever means necessary, including force and violence. IG regarded the United States as an infidel and viewed the United States as providing essential support to other infidel governments and institutions, particularly Israel and Egypt. IG also opposed the United States because the United States had taken action to thwart IG, including by the arrest, conviction, and continued confinement of its spiritual leader [Sheikh Abdel Rahman].

IG has allegedly operated in the United States from the early 1990s until the date of the filing of the Indictment, particularly in the New York metropolitan area. According to the Indictment, IG's objectives in the United States include (1) the establishment of the United States as a staging ground for violent acts against targets in the United States and abroad; (2) the recruitment and training of members; and (3) fundraising for jihad actions in the United States and overseas. Since Sheikh Abdel Rahman's imprisonment, the Indictment alleges that IG members in the United States have also functioned as a worldwide communications hub for the group, in part by facilitating communications between IG leaders and Sheik Abdel Rahman. IG was designated as a foreign terrorist organization by the Secretary of State . . . .

The Indictment alleges that Sheikh Abdel Rahman has been one of IG's principal leaders and a high-ranking member of jihad organizations based in Egypt and elsewhere since the early 1990s. Sheikh Abdel Rahman allegedly became an "emir" or leader of IG in the United States. Under his leadership, IG subordinates carried out the details of specific jihad operations while shielding Sheikh Abdel Rahman from prosecution. The Indictment charges that Sheik Abdel Rahman, among other things, provided guidance about what actions, including acts of terrorism, were permissible or forbidden under his interpretation of Islamic law; gave strategic advice on how to achieve IG's goals; recruited persons and solicited them to commit violent jihad acts; and sought to protect IG from infiltration by law enforcement.

Sheikh Abdel Rahman was convicted in October 1995 of engaging in a seditious conspiracy to wage a war of urban terrorism against the United States, including the 1993 World Trade Center bombing and a plot to bomb New York City landmarks.

He was also found guilty of soliciting crimes of violence against the United States military and Egyptian President Hosni Mubarak. In January 1996 Sheik Abdel Rahman was sentenced to life imprisonment plus 65 years. His conviction was affirmed on appeal and, on January 10, 2000, the United States Supreme Court denied his petition for a writ of certiorari.

Sheikh Abdel Rahman has been incarcerated at the Federal Medical Center in Rochester, Minnesota since in or about 1997. IG has allegedly taken repeated steps to win Sheikh Abdel Rahman's release. Such steps include the issuance of a statement in response to Sheikh Abdel Rahman's life sentence that warned that "all American interests will be legitimate targets for our struggle until the release of Sheikh Omar Abdel Rahman and his brothers" and that IG "swears by God to its irreversible vow to take an eye for an eye." Also, on or about November 17, 1997, six assassins shot and stabbed a group of tourists at an archeological site in Luxor, Egypt killing fifty-eight tourists and four Egyptians. Before exiting, the Indictment charges, the assassins scattered leaflets calling for Sheikh Abdel Rahman's release and inserted one such leaflet into the slit torso of one victim.

The Bureau of Prisons, at the direction of the Attorney General, imposed Special Administrative Measures ("SAMs") upon Sheikh Abdel Rahman. The SAMs limited certain privileges in order to protect "'persons against the risk of death or serious bodily injury' that might otherwise result." The limitations included restrictions on Sheikh Abdel Rahman's access to the mail, the telephone, and visitors, and prohibited him from speaking with the media. All Counsel for Sheik Abdel Rahman were obligated to sign an affirmation acknowledging that they and their staff would abide fully by the SAMs before being allowed access to their client. In the affirmation, counsel agreed to "only be accompanied by translators for the purpose of communicating with the inmate Abdel Rahman concerning legal matters." Since at least in or about May 1998, counsel agreed not to use "meetings, correspondence, or phone calls with Abdel Rahman to pass messages between third parties (including, but not limited to, the media) and Abdel Rahman."

Defendant Stewart was Sheikh Abdel Rahman's counsel during his 1995 criminal trial and has continued to represent him since his conviction. The Indictment alleges that over the past several years, Stewart has facilitated and concealed messages between her client and IG leaders around the world in violation of the SAMs limiting Sheik Abdel Rahman's communications from prison. During a May 2000 visit to Sheikh Abdel Rahman in prison, Stewart allegedly allowed defendant Yousry, who acted as the Arabic interpreter between Sheikh Abdel Rahman and his attorneys, to read letters from defendant Sattar and others regarding IG matters and to discuss with her client whether IG should continue to comply with a cease-fire that had been supported by factions within IG since in or about 1998. According to the Indictment, Yousry provided material support and resources to IG by covertly passing messages between IG representatives and Sheik Abdel Rahman regarding IG's activities. The Indictment alleges that Stewart took affirmative steps to conceal the May 2000 discussions from prison guards and subsequently, in violation of the SAMs, announced to the media that Sheikh Abdel Rahman had withdrawn his support for the cease-fire. The Indictment charges that in or about May 2000 Stewart submitted an affirmation to the United States Attorney's Office for the Southern District of New York (the "May Affirmation") that falsely stated, among other things, that she agreed to abide by the terms of the SAMs applicable to Sheikh Abdel Rahman and that she would not use her meetings, correspondence or phone calls with Sheikh Abdel Rahman to pass messages between Sheikh Abdel Rahman and third parties including but not limited to the media.

The Indictment also charges that Sattar is an active IG leader who serves as a vital link between Sheik Abdel Rahman and the worldwide IG membership. The Indictment contends that Sattar operates as a communications center for IG from New York City through frequent telephonic contact with IG leaders around the world. More specifically, the Indictment alleges that Sattar provides material support and resources to IG by relaying messages between IG leaders abroad and Sheik Abdel Rahman through visits and phone calls by Sheikh Abdel Rahman's interpreter and attorneys; arranging and participating in three-way phone calls connecting IG leaders around the world to facilitate discussion and coordination of IG activities; passing messages and information from one IG leader and to other group leaders and members; and by providing financial support.

Defendant Al-Sirri was arrested in the United Kingdom in October 2001 until which time, the Indictment alleges, he was the head of the London-based Islamic Observation Center. The Indictment charges that Al-Sirri, like Sattar, facilitated IG communications worldwide and provided material support and resources, including financial support, to the FTO. Al-Sirri was allegedly in frequent telephone contact with Sattar and other IG leaders regarding the dissemination of IG statements on various issues.

The defendants make the following motions. Sattar and Stewart move to dismiss Counts One and Two on the ground that 18 U.S.C. § 2339B is unconstitutionally vague and overbroad. . . .

II.

Section 2339B, which is alleged to have been violated in this case, requires only that a person "knowingly" "provides" "material support or resources" to a "foreign terrorist organization." Section 2339A criminalizes the provision of "material support or resources" "knowing or intending that they are used in preparation for, or in carrying out," a violation of various criminal statutes. No such specific criminal intent provision is included in § 2339B. Section 2339A defines "material support or resources" as indicated above. That definition includes no amount or other measure of magnitude and is carried over into § 2339B.

The Indictment alleges that the defendants conspired to provide and provided communications equipment, personnel, currency, financial securities and financial services (currency, financial securities, and financial services hereinafter "currency"), and transportation to IG.

A.

The defendants argue that 18 U.S.C. § 2339B is unconstitutionally vague specifically with regard to the statute's prohibition on "providing" material support or resources in the form of "communications equipment" and "personnel." With respect to communications equipment, the Indictment alleges, among other things, that "the defendants and the unindicted co-conspirators provided communications equipment and other physical assets, including telephones, computers and telefax machines, owned, operated and possessed by themselves and others, to IG, in order to transmit, pass and disseminate messages, communications and information between and among IG leaders and members in the United States and elsewhere around the world. . . . " The Government has argued that the defendants provided a communications pipeline by which they transmitted messages from Sheikh Abdel Rahman in prison to IG leaders and members throughout the world. Among the specific instances of the use of communications equipment, the Indictment points to the fact that Sattar had telephone conversations with IG leaders in which he related Sheikh Abdel Rahman's instructions to IG leaders and Stewart released Sheikh Abdel Rahman's statement to the press in which Sheikh Abdel Rahman withdrew his support from the then-existing cease-fire. With respect to the provision of personnel, the Indictment alleges that "the defendants and the unindicted co-conspirators provided personnel, including themselves, to IG, in order to assist IG leaders and members in the United States and elsewhere around the world, in communicating with each other. . . . " The defendants argue that the statute fails to provide fair notice of what acts are prohibited by the prohibition against the provision of "communications equipment" and "personnel." A criminal statute implicating First Amendment rights "must 'define the criminal offense with sufficient definiteness that ordinary people can understand what conduct is prohibited and in a manner that does not encourage arbitrary and discriminatory enforcement.'" "In short, the statute must give notice of the forbidden conduct and set boundaries to prosecutorial discretion." When analyzing a vagueness challenge, "[a] court must first determine whether the statute gives the person of ordinary intelligence a reasonable opportunity to know what is prohibited and then consider whether the law provides explicit standards for those who apply it." A "void for vagueness" challenge does not necessarily mean that the statute could not be applied in some cases but rather that, as applied to the conduct at issue in the criminal case, a reasonable person would not have notice that the conduct was unlawful and there are no explicit standards to determine that the specific conduct was unlawful.

First, with regard to the "provision" of "communications equipment," Sattar and Stewart argue that the Indictment charges them with merely talking and that the acts alleged in the Indictment constitute nothing more than using communications equipment rather than providing such equipment to IG. For example, the Indictment charges Sattar with participating in and arranging numerous telephone calls between IG leaders in which IG business was discussed, including the need for "a second Luxor." The Indictment describes numerous other telephone calls in which Sattar participated. Stewart is charged with, among other things, providing communications equipment to IG by announcing Sheikh Abdel Rahman's withdrawal of support for the cease-fire in Egypt and thereby making the statements of the otherwise isolated leader available to the media.

The defendants look to the legislative history of the statute as evidence that Congress did not intend § 2339B to criminalize the mere use of communications equipment, rather than the actual giving of such equipment to IG. The legislative history states:

> The ban does not restrict an organization's or an individual's ability to freely express a particular ideology or political philosophy. Those inside the United States will continue to be free to advocate, think and profess the attitudes and philosophies of the foreign organizations. *They are simply not allowed to send material support or resources to those groups, or their subsidiary groups, overseas.*

H.R. Rep. 104-383 at 45 (emphasis added). Thus, the defendants argue, simply making a phone call or similarly communicating one's thoughts does not fall within the ambit of § 2339B.

The defendants are correct and by criminalizing the mere use of phones and other means of communication the statute provides neither notice nor standards for its application such that it is unconstitutionally vague as applied. The Government argued in its brief that the defendants are charged not merely with using their own phones or other communications equipment but with actively making such equipment available to IG and thus "providing" IG with communications resources that would otherwise be unavailable to the FTO. That argument, however, simply ignores the reality of the facts charged in the Indictment in which various defendants are accused of having participated in the use of communications equipment. The Government subsequently changed course and stated at oral argument that the mere use of one's telephone constitutes criminal behavior under the statute and that, in fact, "use equals provision." The Government also argued that using the conference call feature on a person's phone in furtherance of an FTO was prohibited.

Such changes in the Government's interpretation of § 2339B demonstrate why the provision of communications equipment as charged in the Indictment is unconstitutionally vague: a criminal defendant simply could not be expected to know that the conduct alleged was prohibited by the statute. The defendants were not put on notice that merely using communications equipment in furtherance of an FTO's goals constituted criminal conduct. Moreover, the Government's evolving definition of what it means to provide communications equipment to an FTO in violation of § 2339B reveals a lack of prosecutorial standards that would "permit 'a standardless sweep [that] allows policemen, prosecutors, and juries to pursue their personal predilections.'" For these reasons, § 2339B is void for vagueness as applied to the allegations in the Indictment.

Second, the defendants argue, § 2339B is unconstitutionally vague as applied to the allegations in the Indictment relating to the "provision" of "personnel." The defendants urge the Court to follow the Ninth Circuit Court of Appeals' decision in *Humanitarian Law Project v. Reno*, 205 F.3d 1130, 1137 (9th Cir. 2000), which found that "it is easy to see how someone could be unsure about what [§ 2339B] prohibits with the use of the term 'personnel,' as it blurs the line between protected expression and unprotected conduct." The Court of Appeals thus affirmed the district court's finding that the use of the term "personnel" in § 2339B was unconstitutionally vague.

The Government relies on *United States v. Lindh*, 212 F. Supp. 2d 541, 574 (E.D. Va. 2002), which rejected *Humanitarian Law Project* and found that the alleged plain meaning of personnel — "an employment or employment-like relationship between the persons in question and the terrorist organization" — gave fair notice of what conduct is prohibited under the statute and thus was not unconstitutionally vague. In that case, the court rejected a vagueness challenge in the context of a person who joined certain foreign terrorist organizations in combat against American forces. In defining the reach of the term personnel, the court found that it was not vague because it applied to "employees" or "employee-like operatives" or "quasi-employees" who work under the "direction and control" of the FTO. Whatever the merits of Lindh as applied to a person who provides himself or herself as a soldier in the army of an FTO, the standards set out there are not found in the statute, do not respond to the concerns of the Court of Appeals in *Humanitarian Law Project*, and do not provide standards to save the "provision" of "personnel" from being unconstitutionally vague as applied to the facts alleged in the Indictment. The fact that the "hard core" conduct in *Lindh* fell within the plain meaning of providing personnel yields no standards that can be applied to the conduct by alleged "quasi-employees" in this case. . . .

It is not clear from § 2339B what behavior constitutes an impermissible provision of personnel to an FTO. Indeed, as the Ninth Circuit Court of Appeals stated in *Humanitarian Law Project*, "Someone who advocates the cause of the [FTO] could be seen as supplying them with personnel." The Government accuses Stewart of providing personnel, including herself, to IG. In so doing, however, the Government fails to explain how a lawyer, acting as an agent of her client, an alleged leader of an FTO, could avoid being subject to criminal prosecution as a "quasi-employee" allegedly covered by the statute. At the argument on the motions, the Government expressed some uncertainty as to whether a lawyer for an FTO would be providing personnel to the FTO before the Government suggested that the answer may depend on whether the lawyer was "house counsel" or an independent counsel — distinctions not found in the statute.

The Government concedes that the statute does not prohibit mere membership in an FTO, and indeed mere membership could not constitutionally be prohibited without a requirement that the Government prove the defendants' specific intent to further the FTO's unlawful ends. See *NAACP v. Claiborne Hardware Co.*, 458 U.S. 886, 920 (1982) ("For liability to be imposed by reason of association alone, it is necessary to establish that the group itself possessed unlawful goals and that the individual held a specific intent to further those illegal aims."). The Government attempts to distinguish the provision of "personnel" by arguing that it applies only to providing "employees" or "quasi-employees" and those acting under the "direction and control" of the FTO. But the terms "quasi-employee" or "employee-like operative" or "acting at the direction and control of the organization" are terms that are nowhere found in the statute or reasonably inferable from it.

Moreover, these terms and concepts applied to the prohibited provision of personnel provide no notice to persons of ordinary intelligence and leave the standards for enforcement to be developed by the Government. When asked at oral argument how to distinguish being a member of an organization from being a quasi-employee, the Government initially responded "You know it when you see it." While such a standard was once an acceptable way for a Supreme Court Justice to identify obscenity (see *Jacobellis v. Ohio*, 378 U.S. 184, 197 (1964) (Stewart, J. concurring)), it is an insufficient guide by which a person can predict the legality of that person's conduct.

Moreover, the Government continued to provide an evolving definition of "personnel" to the Court following oral argument on this motion. Added now are "those acting as full-time or part-time employees or otherwise taking orders from the entity" who are therefore under the FTO's "direction or control." (Gov. Letter dated June 27, 2003 at 2 n.1 (quoting the United States Attorneys' Manual definition of "personnel").)

The Government argues, moreover, that the Court should construe the statute to avoid constitutional questions. However, the Court "is not authorized to rewrite the law so it will pass constitutional muster." *Humanitarian Law Project*, 205 F.3d at 1137-38 (rejecting Government's suggestion to construe "personnel" as used in § 2339B as "under the direction or control" of an FTO). The Government also suggested at oral argument that perhaps a heightened scienter standard should be read into the statute, in some circumstances, in defining the provision of personnel. But that specific intent is not contained in the statute and thus could not give notice to persons about their allegedly prohibited conduct. Moreover, the Government subsequently withdrew its suggestion after oral argument. The statute's vagueness as applied to the allegations in the Indictment concerning the provision of personnel is a fatal flaw that the Court cannot cure by reading into the statute a stricter definition of the material support provision than the statute itself provides. . . .

For the reasons explained, Counts One and Two are therefore dismissed.

QUESTIONS

Should courts be equally vigilant in voiding statutes on vagueness grounds regardless of subject matter? In other words, should courts be more tolerant of vagueness in statutes aimed at terrorism than in statutes aimed at loitering? Or should they be less tolerant?

F. SYNTHESIS AND REVIEW

PROBLEM

3.10 Laverne recently gave birth to a baby boy, Earl. Laverne has given birth to two previous babies born with cocaine addictions. Laverne admitted to her pediatrician that she regularly used cocaine while pregnant with Earl and that she used cocaine while in labor just a few hours prior to Earl's delivery. Urine tests demonstrate that Earl has cocaine in his bloodstream, and medical expert testimony will establish that if Laverne took cocaine while in labor it would have remained in her bloodstream until well after Earl was delivered. Laverne is charged with violating the following statute:

It is a felony punishable by up to 15 years imprisonment for anyone to deliver cocaine to a person under the age of 18 years.

The prosecution's theory is that Laverne delivered cocaine to Earl, who was clearly under 18 years of age, through her umbilical cord during the roughly two minutes that passed between his emergence from the birth canal and the severance of the umbilical cord by the obstetrician. Is Laverne liable for violating the statute? What problems would the prosecution encounter in prosecuting Laverne?

Dan M. Kahan, THREE CONCEPTIONS OF
FEDERAL CRIMINAL-LAWMAKING
1 Buff. Crim. L. Rev. 5, 16-18 (1997)

What's needed ideally . . . is a third conception of federal criminal lawmaking — one that conserves the efficiency of delegated criminal lawmaking but that avoids the coordination and the legitimacy problems associated with overt federal common-lawmaking.

III. A REALIZABLE IDEAL: AN ADMINISTRATIVE LAW OF CRIMES

That third conception is what I referred to at the start as the *administrative-law* conception of federal criminal-lawmaking. On this view, filling in incompletely specified criminal statutes is the responsibility not of courts or individual U.S. Attorneys but of an executive agency; that agency could be one newly minted for this purpose, but I'll assume here that it would be the Department of Justice. The Department would exercise its delegated-lawmaking power by issuing formal interpretations of ambiguous or generally worded criminal statutes. For its inter-pretations to be binding on courts, the Department would have to comply with standard administrative-law requirements, including those obliging the agency to justify its position through notice-and-comment rulemaking or its equivalent, and to do so prior to defending its position in litigation.

This administrative-law approach would conserve essentially all of the effi-ciency benefits associated with implied delegation. Congress enjoys the institu-tional economies of incomplete specification regardless of whether it's the Judiciary or an administrative agency that finishes the task. In addition, agencies, like courts, can update the law more quickly than Congress, and can use its contact with actual cases to tailor the law to unforeseen circumstances. Indeed, because the Justice Department has more experience with criminal law enforcement than does any court, and because it is more unified than the Judiciary, an administra-tive regime would likely enhance both the quality and the consistency of federal criminal-lawmaking relative to the existing common-lawmaking baseline.

In addition, an administrative law of crimes would avoid the asserted ten-sions between common-lawmaking and the values of democracy and fair notice. Because the Justice Department is accountable to the President, its judgments on contentious issues are likely to be closer to those of the national electorate than are those of courts. What's more, under the so-called rule against "post hoc ratio-nalizations," the Justice Department would be obliged to issue its interpretations of ambiguous statutes before defending them in court, thus avoiding the unfair surprise sometimes associated with common-lawmaking.

QUESTIONS

Should we openly give the executive branch the power to define crimes as suggested by Professor Kahan? What limits would exist on that power? Would an open grant of such power be better or worse than the current system of implicit delegation?

CHAPTER FOUR

CONDUCT

A. THE ELEMENTS OF AN OFFENSE

One objective of a course in criminal law is to teach the fundamental skill of legal analysis. Much analysis in criminal law focuses on statutes. In analyzing statutes, lawyers generally break them down into parts and refer to those parts as the "elements" of the offense. Distinguishing among the various elements of an offense is critical to clear legal analysis. This chapter focuses on the conduct element.

As an example, consider the following criminal statute:

California Penal Code Annotated § 459 (2003)

Every person who enters any house, room, . . . shop, . . . store, . . . or other building . . . with intent to commit . . . larceny or any felony is guilty of burglary.

"*Enters*" is the conduct element of this statute.

PROBLEM

4.1 Identify the conduct element(s) of each of the following statutes.

1. Computer Trespass

Washington Revised Code § 9A.52.120 (2001)

A person is guilty of computer trespass in the first degree if the person, without authorization, intentionally gains access to a computer system or electronic data base of another; and (a) The access is made with the intent to commit another crime; or (b) The violation involves a computer data base maintained by a government agency.

---

2. Aggravated Assault

Georgia Code Annotated § 16-5-21 (2000)

A person commits the offense of aggravated assault when he or she assaults: (1) With intent to murder, to rape, or to rob; (2) With a deadly weapon or with any object, device, or instrument which, when used offensively against a person, is likely to or actually does result in serious bodily injury; or (3) A person or persons without legal justification by discharging a firearm from within a motor vehicle toward a person or persons.

3. Consumption of Alcoholic Beverage in a Motor Vehicle

Texas Penal Code Annotated § 49.03 (2000) (repealed in 2001)

A person commits an offense if the person consumes an alcoholic beverage while operating a motor vehicle in a public place and is observed doing so by a peace officer.

As the above statutes demonstrate, legislatures typically require some sort of conduct for criminal liability. Lawyers often refer to the conduct element in a criminal statute using the Latin phrase *actus reus.* You should be aware, though, that lawyers vary in their use of the term "actus reus." Some employ "actus reus" in a narrow sense to refer only to the conduct element of a crime. Others give "actus reus" a broader scope, using it to refer not only to the conduct element but collectively to all the non-mental elements of an offense. To avoid this ambiguity and emphasize the importance of distinguishing conduct from other non-mental elements, we use the words "conduct" or "act" rather than "actus reus" in referring to the subject matter of this chapter.

Section B of this chapter examines why conduct is typically viewed as a necessary ingredient in criminal definitions. Section C focuses on what constitutes conduct. Section D then deals with status and the difficulties that may arise in distinguishing status, which generally may not be penalized, from conduct that routinely provides the basis for criminal liability.

Section E treats the common modern code requirement that conduct be voluntary. A defendant may take many steps in a course of conduct leading to a criminal charge. From among those many acts, how should one choose the conduct on which to base criminal liability? This choice in focal point, which is required in some cases, is the subject of Section F on time-framing.

It is sometimes said that there can be no crime without an act. The final three Sections of this chapter will allow you to assess for yourself the validity of this generalization. Section G deals with crimes based on omission, the failure to act. The subject of Section H is possession, a common basis for criminal liability, one that has been described as neither an act nor an omission. This chapter ends with Section I's exploration of the topic of vicarious liability, the controversial practice of imposing criminal punishment on one person based on the actions of another person. As we will see, jurisdictions vary in their acceptance of vicarious liability.

B. WHY REQUIRE CONDUCT?

Why do legislatures routinely include a conduct element in defining crimes? In answering this question, it is helpful to refer back to the purposes of punishment.

From a retributive perspective, criminal punishment requires blameworthiness. Though some religions treat bad thoughts alone as sinful,[1] the criminal law views thoughts alone as insufficiently blameworthy to justify state-imposed criminal punishment. Blame sufficient to warrant criminal sanction attaches only when the person entertaining bad thoughts chooses to act on them.

From a deterrent perspective, the threat of punishment aims to reduce crime by influencing the potential offender in the period between thought and action. Requiring conduct gives that threat the opportunity to dissuade the potential offender from turning bad thoughts into action.

To what extent can we control our thoughts? Without such control, it is hard to find bad thoughts blameworthy. And the threat of punishment, no matter how severe, cannot deter thoughts if they are outside one's control.

From an incapacitation perspective, a conduct requirement may or may not make sense. The person who thinks about crime but poses no risk of acting on her thoughts presents no future danger and accordingly is not in need of incapacitation. A conduct requirement thus protects the idle daydreamer. But what about those who do act on their thoughts? Consider the case of Buford O. Furrow, Jr. According to a newspaper account,[2] he was a heavily armed white supremacist who revealed to psychiatric workers that he was fantasizing about committing a mass killing. A few months later, he shot six people, killing one, at a Jewish community center in Los Angeles.[3] Waiting until someone with bad thoughts does act means losing the opportunity to intervene preemptively and prevent harm.

Defenders of the conduct requirement also frequently rely on practical grounds. If the state were to punish bad thoughts, how would it determine which people were actually thinking bad thoughts? Conduct provides circumstantial evidence to help prove what the offender was thinking.

One way to grasp both the theoretical and practical reasons why criminal law regularly insists on an act is to imagine a criminal justice system without such a requirement. Under such a system, "thinking about killing another human being" or "thinking about stealing the property of another" could be crimes. Under such provisions, who among us would not qualify as a criminal? What means would the police need to adopt to detect such crime? How would the government prove guilt? How could someone charged with such a crime demonstrate her innocence? Imagine also the size and scope of the criminal justice apparatus necessary to enforce such a system.

---

1. *See, e.g.*, Exodus 20:17 ("You shall not covet your neighbor's house; you shall not covet your neighbor's wife or his male servant or his female servant or his ox or his donkey or anything that belongs to your neighbor.") Old Testament (New Amer. Stand.).

2. Barry Meier, *A Violent Creed Is No Bar to Gun Ownership*, N.Y. Times A16 (Aug. 16, 1999).

3. *Id.*

Consider other risks that an "actless" criminal justice system might raise:

SIPRESS

"You look like this sketch of someone who's thinking about committing a crime."

QUESTIONS

1. If scientists could create a complex model of environmental and genetic factors allowing them to predict accurately that a given individual, who has not yet committed a crime, would commit a violent crime sometime in the future, how should that model be used? For example, if scientists used the model to predict that "A" had a 99.9 percent probability of committing a violent crime sometime in the future, would you allow the criminal justice system to imprison or otherwise incapacitate "A" before s/he acted violently? If so, would you permit state intervention at 50 percent? 75 percent? 80 percent? 95 percent? What concerns would such a model raise?

2. Imagine a simple and accurate method for reading someone's thoughts that required no more than touching a person's head. Under what circumstances, if any, would you allow law enforcement to use the method? To screen people to meet with the President? To screen child-care workers? To screen people flying on airplanes? To investigate serial murder cases?

C. WHAT IS AN ACT?

It is not always easy to determine if a defendant fulfills the conduct element of an offense.

PROBLEM

4.2 Consider the following legislative definitions:

New York Penal Law § 15.00 (2000)

"Act" means a bodily movement.

Utah Code Annotated § 76-1-601(1) (2000)

"Act" means a voluntary bodily movement and includes speech.

Evil Emil tells his blind companion that the medicine his companion needs is in the bottle to his companion's left. In fact, the bottle to the left contains poison. Emil's companion picks up and swallows the contents of the bottle on the left and dies. Has Emil acted under these statutes?

QUESTION

What are the benefits of having the legislature define what constitutes an act for purposes of criminal liability? What are the disadvantages?

Limits on the legislative ability to provide a comprehensive definition of an act give rise to the need for judicial interpretation of statutes, as in the following Problem.

PROBLEM

4.3 You are a justice of a state supreme court. You and the other justices have agreed to review a series of cases raising questions about the scope of the following criminal statute:

Driving while under the influence of alcohol or drugs

No person shall operate any vehicle, streetcar, or trackless trolley within this state if the person is under the influence of alcohol, a drug of abuse, or alcohol and a drug of abuse.

The facts in these cases are as follows. Assume the prosecutor can prove that the defendant in each case was under the influence of alcohol at the time he entered his car.

The facts in these cases are as follows: Assume the prosecutor can prove that the defendant in each case was under the influence of alcohol at the time he entered his car.

Case 1. At 1:30 a.m. in the middle of a cold and snowy January night, the sound of a car motor running in his driveway awoke Timothy.

When he investigated, he found that a stranger, Allen, had parked his car in Timothy's driveway with the motor running. Allen was asleep in the driver's seat and did not awaken or stir when Timothy shone a flashlight through the car window into his face. Timothy called the police. The arresting officer concluded that Allen had been in Timothy's driveway a considerable time since no tire tracks were visible behind Allen's car in the freshly fallen snow.

Case 2. After ending a 15-hour work shift at 10 p.m., Michael drove to McDuffie's Bar, parked his car, and went inside, where he stayed until the bar closed at 2:30 a.m. Police found Michael passed out and slumped over the steering wheel of his car, which was still in the same space in McDuffie's lot where he had parked it at 10 p.m. The motor was running at high speed and Michael's foot was on the accelerator. The car was not in gear and the emergency brake was engaged. Michael admitted to the arresting police officers that he was intoxicated and told them he had decided to follow his lawyer's advice not to drive if he "had more than two beers."

Case 3. Police found Bradley asleep in the driver's seat of his car. The car was parked in a lot belonging to a county park. Its motor was not running, but its radio was on. The key was in the ignition, but turned to the left or "ACC" position. The key needs to be turned in the opposite direction, to the right, to start the engine.

Allen, Michael, and Bradley were each charged with violating the above statute. The lower courts have disagreed on whether or not the conduct of Allen, Michael, and Bradley fall within the statute. How would you rule in each case?

D. STATUS

Legislatures typically require that a person do something in order to incur criminal liability. But is it ever permissible to punish a person for *being* rather than *doing* something? This question, which the criminal law frames as whether a person may be punished for his or her *status*, is the focus of this Section. Beyond determining whether someone may be punished for his or her status, courts also struggle to distinguish conduct from status. The United States Supreme Court addresses the distinctions between conduct and status in the following two cases:

ROBINSON *v.* CALIFORNIA

Supreme Court of the United States 370 U.S. 660 (1962)

Mr. Justice STEWART delivered the opinion of the Court.

A California statute makes it a criminal offense for a person to "be addicted to the use of narcotics." This appeal draws into question the constitutionality of that provision of the state law. . . . The appellant was convicted after a jury trial in the Municipal Court of Los Angeles. The evidence against him was given by two Los Angeles police officers. Officer Brown testified that he had had occasion to examine the appellant's arms one evening on a street in Los Angeles some four months before the trial. The officer testified that at that time he had observed "scar tissue and discoloration on the inside" of the appellant's right arm, and "what appeared to be numerous needle marks and a scab which was approximately three inches below the crook of the elbow" on the appellant's left arm. The officer also testified that the appellant under questioning had admitted to the occasional use of narcotics.

Officer Linquist testified that he had examined the appellant the following morning in the Central Jail in Los Angeles. The officer stated that at that time he had observed discolorations and scabs on the appellant's arms, and he identified photographs which had been taken of appellant's arms shortly after his arrest the night before. Based upon more than ten years of experience as a member of the Narcotic Division of the Los Angeles Police Department, the witness gave his opinion that "these marks and the discoloration were the result of the injection of hypodermic needles into the tissue into the vein that was not sterile." He stated that the scabs were several days old at the time of his examination, and that the appellant was neither under the influence of narcotics nor suffering withdrawal symptoms at the time he saw him. This witness also testified that the appellant had admitted using narcotics in the past. . . .

The trial judge instructed the jury that the statute made it a misdemeanor for a person "either to use narcotics, or to be addicted to the use of narcotics. . . . That portion of the statute referring to 'use' of narcotics is based upon the 'act' of using. That portion of the statute referring to 'addicted to the use' of narcotics is based upon a condition or status. They are not identical. . . . To be addicted to the use of narcotics is said to be a status or condition and not an act. It is a continuing offense and differs from most other offenses in the fact that [it] is chronic rather than acute; that it continues after it is complete and subjects the offender to arrest at any time before he reforms. The existence of such a chronic condition may be ascertained from a single examination, if the characteristic reactions of that condition be found present." . . .

This statute . . . is not one which punishes a person for the use of narcotics, for their purchase, sale or possession, or for antisocial or disorderly behavior resulting from their administration. It is not a law which even purports to provide or require medical treatment. Rather, we deal with a statute which makes the "status" of narcotic addiction a criminal offense, for which the offender may be prosecuted "at any time before he reforms." California has said that a person can be continuously guilty of this offense, whether or not he has ever used or possessed any narcotics within the State, and whether or not he has been guilty of any antisocial behavior there.

It is unlikely that any State at this moment in history would attempt to make it a criminal offense for a person to be mentally ill, or a leper, or to be afflicted with a venereal disease. A State might determine that the general health and welfare require that the victims of these and other human afflictions be dealt with by compulsory treatment, involving quarantine, confinement, or sequestration. But, in the light of contemporary human knowledge, a law which made a criminal offense of such a disease would doubtless be universally thought to be an infliction of cruel and unusual punishment in violation of the Eighth and Fourteenth Amendments.

We cannot but consider the statute before us as of the same category. In this Court counsel for the State recognized that narcotic addiction is an illness. Indeed, it is apparently an illness which may be contracted innocently or involuntarily.[9] We hold that a state law which imprisons a person thus afflicted as a criminal, even though he has never touched any narcotic drug within the State or been guilty of any irregular behavior there, inflicts a cruel and unusual punishment in violation of the Fourteenth Amendment. To be sure, imprisonment for ninety days is not, in the abstract, a punishment which is either cruel or unusual. But the question cannot be considered in the abstract. Even one day in prison would be a cruel and unusual punishment for the "crime" of having a common cold.

Reversed.

Mr. Justice HARLAN, concurring.

I am not prepared to hold that on the present state of medical knowledge it is completely irrational and hence unconstitutional for a State to conclude that narcotics addition is something other than an illness nor that it amounts to cruel and unusual punishment for the State to subject narcotics addicts to its criminal law. Insofar as addiction may be identified with the use or possession of narcotics within the State (or, I would suppose, without the State), in violation of local statutes prohibiting such acts, it may surely be reached by the State's criminal law. But in this case the trial court's instructions permitted the jury to find the appellant guilty on no more proof than that he was present in California while he was addicted to narcotics. Since addiction alone cannot reasonably be thought to amount to more than a compelling propensity to use narcotics, the effect of this instruction was to authorize criminal punishment for a bare desire to commit a criminal act.

POWELL v. TEXAS
Supreme Court of the United States 392 U.S. 514 (1968)

Mr. Justice MARSHALL announced the judgment of the Court and delivered an opinion in which the Chief Justice, Mr. Justice Black, and Mr. Justice Harlan join.

In late December 1966, appellant was arrested and charged with being found in a state of intoxication in a public place, in violation of Texas Penal Code, Art. 477 (1952), which reads as follows:

"Whoever shall get drunk or be found in a state of intoxication in any public place, or at any private house except his own, shall be fined not exceeding one hundred dollars."

Appellant was tried in the Corporation Court of Austin, Texas, found guilty, and fined $20. He appealed to the County Court . . . , where a trial de novo was held. His counsel urged that appellant was "afflicted with the disease of chronic alcoholism," that "his appearance in public [while drunk was] . . . not of his own volition," and therefore that to punish him criminally for that conduct would be cruel and unusual, in violation of the Eighth and Fourteenth Amendments to the United States Constitution.

The trial judge in the county court, sitting without a jury, made certain findings of fact, but ruled as a matter of law that chronic alcoholism was not a defense to the charge. . . . [A]ppellant appealed to this Court; we noted probable jurisdiction. . . .

---

[9] Not only may addiction innocently result from the use of medically prescribed narcotics, but a person may even be a narcotics addict from the moment of his birth. Citations omitted.

The principal testimony was that of Dr. David Wade, a Fellow of the American Medical Association, duly certificated in psychiatry. . . . He testified that he had examined appellant, and that appellant is a "chronic alcoholic," who "by the time he has reached [the state of intoxication] . . . is not able to control his behavior, and [who] . . . has reached this point because he has an uncontrollable compulsion to drink." . . .

Appellant testified concerning the history of his drinking problem. He reviewed his many arrests for drunkenness; testified that he was unable to stop drinking; stated that when he was intoxicated he had no control over his actions and could not remember them later, but that he did not become violent; and admitted that he did not remember his arrest on the occasion for which he was being tried. On cross-examination, appellant admitted that he had had one drink on the morning of the trial and had been able to discontinue drinking. . . .

Appellant . . . seeks to come within the application of the Cruel and Unusual Punishment Clause announced in *Robinson v. California*, 370 U.S. 660 (1962). . . . On its face the present case does not fall within that holding, since appellant was convicted, not for being a chronic alcoholic, but for being in public while drunk on a particular occasion. The State of Texas thus has not sought to punish a mere status, as California did in *Robinson*; nor has it attempted to regulate appellant's behavior in the privacy of his own home. Rather, it has imposed upon appellant a criminal sanction for public behavior which may create substantial health and safety hazards, both for appellant and for members of the general public, and which offends the moral and esthetic sensibilities of a large segment of the community. This seems a far cry from convicting one for being an addict, being a chronic alcoholic, being "mentally ill, or a leper. . . . "

Robinson so viewed brings this Court but a very small way into the substantive criminal law. And unless *Robinson* is so viewed it is difficult to see any limiting principle that would serve to prevent this Court from becoming, under the aegis of the Cruel and Unusual Punishment Clause, the ultimate arbiter of the standards of criminal responsibility, in diverse areas of the criminal law, throughout the country.

It is suggested in dissent that *Robinson* stands for the "simple" but "subtle" principle that "[c]riminal penalties may not be inflicted upon a person for being in a condition he is powerless to change. . . . " In that view, appellant's "condition" of public intoxication was "occasioned by a compulsion symptomatic of the disease" of chronic alcoholism, and thus, apparently, his behavior lacked the critical element of *mens rea*. Whatever may be the merits of such a doctrine of criminal responsibility, it surely cannot be said to follow from *Robinson*. The entire thrust of *Robinson*'s interpretation of the Cruel and Unusual Punishment Clause is that criminal penalties may be inflicted only if the accused has committed some act, has engaged in some behavior, which society has an interest in preventing, or perhaps in historical common law terms, has committed some *actus reus*. It thus does not deal with the question of whether certain conduct cannot constitutionally be punished because it is, in some sense, "involuntary" or "occasioned by compulsion." . . .

Mr. Justice WHITE, concurring in the result.

If it cannot be a crime to have an irresistible compulsion to use narcotics, *Robinson v. California*, I do not see how it can constitutionally be a crime to yield to such a compulsion. Punishing an addict for using drugs convicts for addiction under a different name. Distinguishing between the two crimes is like forbidding criminal conviction for being sick with flu or epilepsy but permitting punishment for running a fever or having a convulsion. Unless *Robinson* is to be abandoned, the use of narcotics by an addict must be beyond the reach of the criminal law. Similarly, the chronic alcoholic with an irresistible urge to consume alcohol should not be punishable for drinking or for being drunk.

Powell's conviction was for the different crime of being drunk in a public place. Thus even if Powell was compelled to drink, and so could not constitutionally be convicted for drinking, his conviction in this case can be invalidated only if there is a constitutional basis for saying that he may not be punished for being in public while drunk. The statute involved here, which aims at keeping drunks off the street for their own welfare and that of others, is not challenged on the ground that it interferes unconstitutionally with the right to frequent public places. . . . I cannot say that the chronic alcoholic who proves his disease and a compulsion to drink is shielded from conviction when he has knowingly failed to take feasible precautions against committing a criminal act, here the act of going to or remaining in a public place. On such facts the alcoholic is like a person with smallpox, who could be convicted for being on the street but not for being ill. . . .

The fact remains that some chronic alcoholics must drink and hence must drink *somewhere*. Although many chronics have homes, many others do not. For all practical purposes the public streets may be home for these unfortunates, not because their disease compels them to be there, but because, drunk or sober, they have no place else to go and no place else to be when they are drinking. This is more a function of economic station than of disease, although the disease may lead to destitution and perpetuate that condition. For some of these alcoholics I would think a showing could be made that resisting drunkenness is impossible and that avoiding public places when intoxicated is also impossible. As applied to them this statute is in effect a law which bans a single act for which they may not be convicted under the Eighth Amendment—the act of getting drunk.

Powell modified the protection afforded by *Robinson*. The scope of that remaining protection is at the center of a number of recent legal contests including those involving homelessness and gang affiliation.

Homelessness: In 1992, the United States District Court for the Southern District of Florida addressed the issue of homelessness under the Eighth and Fourteenth Amendments in *Pottenger v. City of Miami*, 810 F. Supp. 1551. The Court noted that:

> Although the law is well-established that a person may not be punished for involuntary status, it is less settled whether involuntary conduct that is inextricably related to that status may be punished. . . . [The City of Miami] has made laudable attempts, particularly in recent years, to assist the homeless. . . . However, many factors have frustrated the City's efforts to alleviate the problem of homelessness. Perhaps the most significant factor is the escalating number of homeless people. . . . The City . . . has arrested thousands of homeless individuals . . . for misdemeanors such as obstructing the sidewalk, loitering, and being in the park after hours.

A number of experts testified on homelessness at the trial. They indicated that "people rarely choose to be homeless. Rather, homelessness is due to various economic, physical or psychological factors that are beyond the homeless individual's control." The Court also noted that "[t]he lack of low-income housing or shelter space cannot be underestimated as a factor contributing to homelessness. At the time of the trial, Miami had fewer than 700 beds available in shelters for the homeless. Except for a fortunate few, most homeless individuals have no alternative to living in public areas." The Court concluded that:

> As long as the homeless . . . do not have a single place where they can lawfully be, the challenged ordinances, as applied to them, effectively punish them for something for which they may not be convicted under the eighth amendment—sleeping, eating and other innocent conduct. Accordingly, the court finds that defendant's conduct violates the eighth amendment ban against cruel and usual punishment. . . . [4]

In 1994, the United States District Court for the Northern District of California also addressed the intersection between homelessness and the Eighth and Fourteenth Amendments. *Joyce v. City and County of San Francisco*, 846 F. Supp. 843. In the San Francisco case, homeless individuals sought to enjoin the City from enforcing part of its Matrix program. "While encompassing a wide range of services to the City's homeless, the Program simultaneously contemplates a rigorous law enforcement component aimed at those violations of state and municipal law which arguably are committed predominantly by the homeless." The homeless individuals seeking the preliminary injunction "endorse[d] much of the Program," but challenged the portion of the Program that "penalize[d] certain 'life-sustaining activities'" engaged in by the homeless.

A memorandum to the Police Department's Southern Station Personnel illustrates the "enforcement efforts characteristic of the Program." It "directs the vigorous enforcement of eighteen specified code sections, including prohibitions against trespassing, public inebriation, urinating or defecating in public, removal and possession of shopping carts, solicitation on or near a highway, erection of tents or structures in parks, obstruction and aggressive panhandling." One "element of the Matrix Program—the Night Shelter Referral Program—attempts to provide temporary housing to those not participating in the longer-term housing program. . . . The Night Referral Program operates by referring women to a women's shelter . . . and by offering to men transportation and a referral slip to the Salvation Army Lifeboat Lodge. . . . The city contends that, of 3,820 referral slips offered to men, only 1,866 were taken, and only 678 actually utilized to obtain a shelter bed reserved for Police referrals." In contrast, those seeking the injunction contend, based on the data from a "survey conducted by Independent Housing Services, . . . [that] from January to July of 1993, [on] average . . . 500 homeless persons [were] turned away nightly from homeless shelters." The "City also contest[ed] the extent to which each" of the four named class members seeking the injunctive relief was actually homeless. The City cited evidence that two had housing, one had declined an invitation to live with his daughter and refused to "sleep at a drop-in shelter." The fourth "had been receiving general assistance from the City, . . . but was . . . suspended for missing appointments."

The Court determined that:

> [a]s an analytical matter, . . . homelessness is not readily classified as a 'status.' Rather, as expressed for the plurality in *Powell* by Justice Marshall, there is a

---

4. Quotations in this and the preceding two paragraphs are from *Pottenger*, 810 F. Supp. 1563, 1558-1559, 1563.

"substantial definitional distinction between a "status" . . . and a 'condition.' . . . " While the concept of status might elude perfect definition, certain factors assist in its determination, such as the involuntariness of the acquisition of that quality (including the presence or not of that characteristic at birth), and the degree to which an individual has control over that characteristic. . . .

Examples of such 'status' characteristics might include age, race, gender, national origin and illness. The reasoning of the Court in including drug addiction as status involved the analogy of drug addiction to a disease or an illness which might be contracted involuntarily. . . . While homelessness can be thrust upon an unwitting recipient, and while a person may be largely incapable of changing that condition, the distinction between the ability to eliminate one's drug addiction as compared to one's homelessness is a distinction in kind as much as in degree. To argue that homelessness is a status and not a condition, moreover, is to deny the efficacy of acts of social intervention to change the condition of those currently homeless. . . .

In addition to the fact that homelessness does not analytically fit into a definition of a status under the contours of governing case law, the effects which would ensue from such a determination by this Court would be staggering. Courts seeking analytical consistency with such a holding would be required to provide constitutional protection to any condition over which a showing could be made that the defendant had no control.[5]

In contrast to the *Pottenger* case, the San Francisco-based District Court found that, on the existing record, those seeking the injunctive relief had not met their burden.

QUESTIONS

1. Why do you think the *Pottenger* and *Joyce* courts reach different results?

2. Does the following additional language from the *Pottenger* decision shed light on the result that court reached?

The evidence presented at trial regarding the magnitude of the homelessness problem was overwhelming in itself. Then, shortly after the trial, one of the worst possible scenarios for homelessness occurred when Hurricane Andrew struck South Florida. Overnight, approximately 200,000 people were left without homes. In sum, this court has no difficulty in finding that the majority of homeless individuals literally have no place to go.[6]

3. Do you think the result in *Joyce* would have been different if a major earthquake had just struck the San Francisco Bay Area, rendering hundreds of thousands of individuals homeless? Or do you think the result was a function of the state of the record developed in the case?

---

5. Quotations in this and preceding paragraphs relating to the *Joyce* case are from *Joyce*, 846 F. Supp. 845-846, 848-850, 875-858.

6. *Supra*, n.4 at 1558-1559.

E. VOLUNTARINESS

PROBLEM

4.4 Consider the following newspaper account:

> On Jan. 31, Chris Doherty, a college student living in a Davis duplex, called the police to complain that his neighbor was making so much noise that he could not sleep. An officer responded to the call and from Mr. Doherty's bedroom, did hear a noise coming through the walls.
>
> It was snoring.
>
> The officer, Van Du Huynh, recommended mediation. But Mr. Doherty, saying he had talked to his neighbor about the problem before, was adamant. He demanded a summons.
>
> . . . Sari Zayed, a 30-year old homemaker and mother of two children, was awakened and handed a ticket for violating the ordinance, which prohibits any willful sound that disturbs the peace.
>
> Snoring? Willful? A court will decide next month, when Mrs. Zayed faces a fine of as much as $135.[7]

The ordinance, under which Mrs. Zayed appears to have been cited, read:

> [I]t is unlawful for any person to wilfully make or continue, or cause to be ma[d]e or continue[d], . . . any noise which unreasonably disturbs the peace and quiet of any neighborhood or which causes discomfort or annoyance to any reasonable person of normal sensitivity residing in the area. [Chapter 16B, Sec. 16B-20. General Prohibition, City of Davis Noise Regulations.]

If you were representing Mrs. Zayed, what arguments would you make on her behalf? If you were the judge in her case, how would you rule? Does this depend on the language of the ordinance? Or on some general principle not found in the language of the ordinance?[8]

In answering these questions, consider the following case and Model Penal Code provisions.

MARTIN v. STATE

Court of Appeals of Alabama 31 Ala. App. 334 (1944)

SIMPSON, Judge.

Appellant was convicted of being drunk on a public highway, and appeals. Officers of the law arrested him at his home and took him onto the highway, where

---

7. *What Is the Sound of Lawlessness? Zzzzzz*, N.Y. Times, Feb. 25, 1994.

8. The case against Mrs. Zayed was later dismissed. Ted Bell, *Court puts Davis snoring case to rest*, The San Francisco Examiner, Mar. 12, 1994 at A3.

he allegedly committed the proscribed acts, viz., manifested a drunken condition by using loud and profane language.

The pertinent provisions of our statute are: "Any person who, while intoxicated or drunk, appears in any public place where one or more persons are present, . . . and manifests a drunken condition by boisterous or indecent conduct, or loud and profane discourse, shall on conviction, be fined," etc. . . .

Under the plain terms of this statute, a voluntary appearance is presupposed. The rule has been declared, and we think it sound, that an accusation of drunkenness in a designated public place cannot be established by proof that the accused, while in an intoxicated condition, was involuntarily and forcibly carried to that place by the arresting officer.

Conviction of appellant was contrary to this announced principle and, in our view, erroneous. It appears that no legal conviction can be sustained under the evidence, so, consonant with the prevailing rule, the judgment of the trial court is reversed and one here rendered discharging appellant.

QUESTIONS

1. Did the language of the statute save Martin? Or a general principle not found in the statute?
2. Would Martin have been liable if the statute had defined the crime he was charged with as "appearing in any public place in a drunken condition"? What if the statute had penalized only "manifesting a drunken condition by boisterous or indecent conduct"?

Model Penal Code § 2.01 (1985)   *Approach to Voluntariness*

(1) A person is not guilty of an offense unless his liability is based on conduct that includes a voluntary act or the omission to perform an act of which he is physically capable.

(2) The following are not voluntary acts within the meaning of this Section:
    (a) a reflex or convulsion;
    (b) a bodily movement during unconsciousness or sleep;
    (c) conduct during hypnosis or resulting from hypnotic suggestion;
    (d) a bodily movement that otherwise is not a product of the effort or determination of the actor, either conscious or habitual.

QUESTIONS

How would Mr. Martin fare under the above Model Penal Code provisions? How about Mrs. Zayed in the snoring problem?

PROBLEM

4.5 As he prepared to leave a wedding reception, Dwight realized he was too inebriated to drive safely and asked a friend for a ride home. In the parking lot, Dwight's friend was drawn into a fist fight with his

> brother. Police arrived and ordered everyone to disperse. Due to his drunken condition, Dwight hesitated. When Dwight failed to respond, a police officer told him that if he failed to get into his truck and drive away, the officer would arrest him. Dwight entered his truck, started the motor and promptly backed his truck into a police car. Dwight was then arrested and charged with driving under the influence. Was Dwight's driving a voluntary act under *Martin*? Under the Model Penal Code?

Martin and the Model Penal Code require that conduct be voluntary to qualify for criminal liability. What, though, does it mean for conduct to be "voluntary"? Students are often led astray when the law uses a familiar word as a term of art, giving it a legal meaning different from the word's meaning in everyday usage. To avoid being misled, it is important to be aware of the special meanings criminal law gives certain words. The word "voluntary" is a good example. In common usage, "voluntary" typically means free from coercion or interference. But in the context of the voluntary act requirement, it has a narrower meaning. Conduct is generally voluntary if the actor made a conscious choice to act, even if coercion influenced the choice. Is it desirable for the criminal law to give words meanings that differ from their common meanings?

In reviewing the common law and MPC positions on voluntariness, consider the circumstances of Kenneth James Parks.

Sometime in the very early hours of May 24th, [Parks] got up from [his living room couch, where he had fallen asleep] and put on a jacket and running shoes. He got his car keys and the key to [his in-laws' home (the Woods family)]. He opened the garage door, got into his car and drove to the Woods' home. . . . There is no evidence of the exact route he followed to travel the 23 kilometres from his home to theirs. If he had taken his usual route, it would have involved some travel on highway 401, a multi-lane highway. He would have used its entrance and exit ramps, negotiated approximately six turns and encountered approximately eight sets of traffic lights. . . .

[Parks] drove to an underground parking area, selected a parking space and parked his car in a somewhat confined area. He then took a tire iron from his car and, using the key entered the Woods' home. . . . He went to the kitchen, got a kitchen knife and went to the bedroom in which Mr. and Mrs. Woods were sleeping.

[Parks] attacked and killed his mother-in-law, Mrs. Woods. He also attacked and injured his father-in-law, Mr. Woods.

Shortly afterwards he left the house, got into his car and drove to a nearby police station. He took the knife with him. At some stage between getting the knife in the kitchen and arriving at the police station, he badly cut both of his own hands. At the police station he made exclamations that were heard variously by different persons as:

'I just killed someone with my bare hands'; 'Oh my God, I just killed someone.' . . . 'I've just killed my mother- and father-in-law. I stabbed and beat them to death. It's all my fault.'[9]

---

9. R. v. Parks, 1990 W.C.B.J. LEXIS 8535, 10 W.C.B. (2d) 236.

Evidence in the case indicated that Parks had been under considerable financial stress caused by his gambling, the loss of his job, and the shadow of an embezzlement charge, but that he had good relationships with his parents-in-law.

> However, his parents-in-law . . . always supported him. He had excellent relations with them: he got on particularly well with his mother-in-law, who referred to him as the "gentle giant."

Parks' defense was sleepwalking, that he had been asleep during the entire violent episode. He claimed to have awakened only after the attacks. At his trial, Parks' defense counsel presented the testimony of a number of doctors, including a neurologist and neuropsychologist with experience in sleep disorders, a psychiatrist, and a forensic psychiatrist, who all testified that Parks was sleepwalking during the episode.

The jury acquitted Parks of the murder of Mrs. Woods and a judge later acquitted Parks of the attempted murder of Mr. Woods.[10]

In the context of the common law approach to voluntariness, were the acquittals legally correct? Under the Model Penal Code? Consider what concerns a sleepwalking defense raises in the context of the *Parks* case and the following excerpt.

When Can Killers Claim Sleepwalking as a Legal Defense?[11]

It is the stuff of television movies and pulp fiction:

A 16-year-old Kentucky girl, dreaming that burglars were breaking into her home and murdering her family, got up in her sleep, picked up two revolvers and fired into the dark house, killing her father and 6-year-old brother and injuring her horrified and bewildered mother.

A vacationing detective, recovering from a nervous breakdown, called upon to help to solve a seemingly motiveless murder of a bather on a beach in France, realized after finding prints in the sand made by a stockinged foot that was missing a toe that he himself was the perpetrator, having shot the man with his pistol while walking in his sleep.

A 23-year-old Toronto man, with a wife and infant daughter, suffering from severe insomnia caused by joblessness and gambling debts, arose in the night and, still asleep, got in his car and drove 14 miles to his in-law's home. He stabbed to death his mother- in-law, whom he loved and who called him "a gentle giant," and tried to kill his father-in-law. He then drove to the police and said "I think I have killed some people . . . my hands," only then realizing he had severely cut his own hands.

Were they legally culpable for their actions? Is someone who kills in his sleep guilty of murder? Perhaps not. The 16-year-old girl and the 23-year-old man were acquitted. The fate of the French detective is not known. And in the current issue of the journal Sleep, which is devoted to the subject of sleep-related violence, Dr. Meir Kryger, director of the Sleep Disorders Center at the St. Boniface Hospital-Research Center in Winnipeg, Canada, wrote, "The potential for sleep disorders to become the 'Twinkie' defense of the 21st century is frightening."

Dr. Kryger said in an interview that in an increasing number of violent crimes, defendants are contending that they were asleep at the time and therefore not accountable for their actions.

---

10. The Crown appealed the acquittals, which were upheld on the appellate level. *Id.*, *R. v. Parks*, 1992 S.C.R. LEXIS 662. Would such an appeal have been possible if Mr. Parks had been tried in the United States?

11. Jane E. Brody, *When Can Killers Claim Sleepwalking as a Legal Defense?*, N.Y. Times, Jan. 16, 1996, C1, C5.

But if a sleep problem is established, said Dr. Clete A. Kushida of the Stanford University Sleep Disorders Clinic, "the courts and the public have to accept that it's a disease like any other disease."

Dr. Kryger added, "In my opinion, a person who commits a violent crime while asleep should not be held responsible for the act, but that person cannot be returned to society without treatment."

These three cases are among the more dramatic examples of a phenomenon known as sleep-related violence, in which part of the brain wakes up enough to allow the person to perform the complex acts while the rest of the brain remains unconscious with sleep. To sleep specialists and increasingly to the law, it is called "noninsane automatism"—an act done by sane persons but without intent, awareness or malice. . . .

[P]sychiatrists and neurologists who specialize in sleep problems insist that most of the disorders that lead to sleep-related aggressive acts are not the result of underlying mental illness. Although severe stress, like having survived a traumatic event, can sometimes trigger the expression of underlying sleep problems, their fundamental cause is a physiological or neurological aberration that disrupts the normal behavior of the brain during sleep and results in partial and often confused arousals.

Researchers have found that the disorders that lead to sleep-related violence can usually be treated effectively with one or more medications, including antiseizure drugs and tranquilizers, that "quiet" the overly active parts of the brain and help to prevent partial arousals during sleep. Patients may also receive counseling to relieve stresses that contribute to their sleep disturbance.

F. TIME-FRAMING[12]

Statutes vary in how they describe the conduct element. The language chosen may give prosecutors and juries leeway in selecting the culpable act. Consider the *Decina* case and the Problem that follows.

PEOPLE *v.* DECINA
Court of Appeals of NewYork 138 N.E.2d 799 (1956)

FROESSEL, JUDGE.

At about 3:30 P.M. on March 14, 1955, a bright, sunny day, defendant was driving, alone in his car. . . . At a point south of an overhead viaduct of the Erie Railroad, defendant's car swerved to the left, across the center line in the street, so that it was completely in the south lane, traveling 35 to 40 miles per hour. It then veered sharply to the right . . . and continued thereafter at a speed estimated to have been about 50 or 60 miles per hour or more. . . .

A group of six schoolgirls were walking north on the easterly side-walk . . . when defendant's car struck them from behind. . . . Three of the children, 6 to 12 years old, were found dead on arrival by the medical examiner, and a fourth child, 7 years old, died in a hospital two days later as a result of injuries sustained in the accident.

---

12. For perhaps the classic exposition of the time frame issue, *see* Mark Kelman, *Interpretive Construction in the Substantive Criminal Law*, 33 Stan. L. Rev. 591 (1981).

After striking the children, defendant's car continued on. . . . With its horn blowing steadily—apparently because defendant was "stooped over" the steering wheel—the car proceeded on the sidewalk until it finally crashed through a 7 1/4-inch brick wall of a grocery store, injuring at least one customer and causing considerable property damage. An injured customer in the store, after receiving first aid, pressed defendant for an explanation of the accident and he told her: "I blacked out from the bridge." . . .

Defendant . . . at the age of 7 . . . was struck by an auto and suffered a marked loss of hearing. In 1946 he was treated in this same hospital for an illness during which he had some convulsions. Several burr holes were made in his skull and a brain abscess was drained. Following this operation defendant had no convulsions from 1946 through 1950. In 1950 he had four convulsions, caused by scar tissue on the brain. From 1950 to 1954 he experienced about 10 or 20 seizures a year, in which his right hand would jump although he remained fully conscious. In 1954, he had 4 or 5 generalized seizures with loss of consciousness, the last being in September, 1954, a few months before the accident. Thereafter he had more hospitalization, a spinal tap, consultation with a neurologist, and took medication daily to help prevent seizures.

On the basis of this medical history, Dr. Wechter made a diagnosis of Jacksonian epilepsy, and was of the opinion that defendant had a seizure at the time of the accident. . . .

We turn first to the [defendant's claim] that his demurrer should have been sustained, since the *indictment* here does not charge a crime. The *indictment* states essentially that defendant, *knowing* "that he was subject to epileptic attacks or other disorder rendering him likely to lose consciousness for a considerable period of time," was culpably negligent "in that he *consciously* undertook to and *did operate* his Buick sedan on a public highway" (emphasis supplied) and "while so doing" suffered such an attack which caused said automobile "to travel at a fast and reckless rate of speed, jumping the curb and driving over the sidewalk" causing the death of 4 persons. In our opinion, this clearly states a violation of section 1053-a of the Penal Law. The statute does not require that a defendant must deliberately intend to kill a human being, for that would be murder. Nor does the statute require that he knowingly and consciously follow the precise path that leads to death and destruction. It is sufficient, we have said, when his conduct manifests a "disregard of the consequences which may ensue from the act, and indifference to the rights of others. No clearer definition, applicable to the hundreds of varying circumstances that may arise, can be given. Under a given state of facts, whether negligence is culpable is a question of judgment." . . .

Assuming the truth of the indictment, as we must on a demurrer, this defendant knew he was subject to epileptic attacks and seizures that might strike *at any time*. He also knew that a moving motor vehicle uncontrolled on a public highway is a highly dangerous instrumentality capable of unrestrained destruction. With this *knowledge*, and without anyone accompanying him, he deliberately took a chance by making a conscious choice of a course of action, in disregard of the consequences which he knew might follow from his conscious act, and which in this case did ensue. How can we say as a matter of law that this did not amount to culpable negligence within the meaning of section 1053-a?

To hold otherwise would be to say that a man may freely indulge himself in liquor in the same hope that it will not affect his driving, and if it later develops that ensuing intoxication causes dangerous and reckless driving resulting in death, his unconsciousness or involuntariness at that time would relieve him from prosecution under the statute. His awareness of a condition which he knows may produce such consequences as here, and his disregard of the consequences, renders him liable for culpable negligence, as the courts below have properly held. . . . To have a sudden sleeping spell, an unexpected heart or other disabling attack, without any prior knowledge or warning thereof, is an altogether different situation . . . and there is simply no basis for comparing such cases with the flagrant disregard manifested here. . . .

DESMOND, Judge. (Concurring in part and dissenting in part.) I think the indictment should be dismissed because it alleges no crime. Defendant's demurrer should have been sustained.

The indictment charges that defendant knowing that "he was subject to epileptic attacks or other disorder rendering him likely to lose consciousness" suffered "an attack and loss of consciousness which caused the said automobile operated by the said defendant to travel at a fast and reckless rate of speed" and to jump a curb and run onto the sidewalk "thereby striking and causing the death" of 4 children. Horrible as this occurrence was and whatever necessity it may show for new licensing and driving laws, nevertheless this indictment charges no crime known to the New York statutes. Our duty is to dismiss it. . . .

Now let us test by its consequences this new construction of section 1053-a. Numerous are the diseases and other conditions of a human being which make it possible or even likely that the afflicted person will lose control of his automobile. Epilepsy, coronary involvements, circulatory diseases, nephritis, uremic poisoning, diabetes, Meniere's Syndrome, a tendency to fits of sneezing, locking of the knee, muscular contractions— any of these common conditions may cause loss of control of a vehicle for a period long enough to cause a fatal accident. An automobile traveling at only 30 miles an hour goes 44 feet in a second. Just what is the court holding here? No less than this: that a driver whose brief blackout lets his car run amuck and kill another has killed that other by reckless driving. But any such "recklessness" consists necessarily not of the erratic behavior of the automobile while its driver is unconscious, but of his driving at all when he knew he was subject to such attacks. Thus, it must be that such a blackout-prone driver is guilty of reckless driving, Vehicle and Traffic Law, § 58, whenever and as soon as he steps into the driver's seat of a vehicle. Every time he drives, accident or no accident, he is subject to criminal prosecution for reckless driving or to revocation of his operator's license. And how many of this State's 5,000,000 licensed operators are subject to such penalties for merely driving the cars they are licensed to drive? No one knows how many citizens or how many or what kind of physical conditions will be gathered in under this practically limitless coverage of section 1053-a of the Penal Law and section 58 and subdivision 3 of section 71 of the Vehicle and Traffic Law. It is no answer that prosecutors and juries will be reasonable or compassionate. A criminal statute whose reach is so unpredictable violates constitutional rights. . . .

PROBLEM

4.6 Mr. Sleepy snores so loudly that, for several hours each night, his snoring exceeds the maximum decibel level proscribed by the local

noise ordinance. The ordinance reads: "Anyone making noise exceeding 85 decibels between 10 P.M. and 6 A.M. shall be in violation of this
ordinance." Mr. Sleepy has a special pillow that enables him to avoid
snoring entirely. His physician prescribed this pillow when Mr. Sleepy
was married and Mrs. Sleepy complained that she couldn't get any
rest. Mr. Sleepy stopped using the pillow after his divorce. Mr. Sleepy's
neighbors have asked him to use the pillow, but he has refused. After
weeks of sleeplessness, Mr. Sleepy's neighbors call the police and have
Mr. Sleepy cited for violating the noise ordinance. Should Mr. Sleepy
be found guilty? If so, for what act is Mr. Sleepy being punished? If the
pillow were no longer effective, but an outpatient surgical procedure
involving local anesthetic and consuming no more than one hour could
cure Mr. Sleepy of snoring, would you hold him liable if he chose not
to have the procedure and continued to snore?

G. OMISSION

Orthodox theory holds that criminal liability may not be imposed without a voluntary act. In the materials that follow, though, you will see that criminal liability
may be imposed for an omission. Can the imposition of liability for *failure to act* be
squared with the principle that criminal liability requires an act?

Criminal laws penalize omissions in two different ways. Some statutes
expressly make failure to act an element of a crime, such as the Deadbeat Parents
Act:

18 United States Code § 228 (2001)

Any person who . . . willfully fails to pay a support obligation with respect to
a child who resides in another State, if such obligation has remained unpaid for a
period longer than 1 year, or is greater than $5,000 . . . shall be punished . . . [by]
a fine . . . , imprisonment for not more than 6 months, or both.

An omission may also be penalized when the language of the relevant statute
speaks in terms of an act, such as killing. As the following case reveals, criminal
law here treats an omission coupled with a duty as the equivalent of an act.

JONES *v.* UNITED STATES

United States Court of Appeals, District of Columbia Circuit 308 F.2d 307 (1962)

WRIGHT, Circuit Judge.

[Jones was convicted at trial of] involuntary manslaughter through failure to
perform [her] legal duty of care for Anthony Lee Green, which failure resulted in
his death. . . . In late 1957, Shirley Green became pregnant, out of wedlock, with
a child, Robert Lee, subsequently born August 17, 1958. Apparently to avoid the
embarrassment of the presence of the child in the Green home, it was arranged that

appellant, a family friend, would take the child to her home after birth. Appellant did so, and the child remained there continuously until removed by the police on August 5, 1960. Initially appellant made some motions toward the adoption of Robert Lee, but these came to nought, and shortly thereafter it was agreed that Shirley Green was to pay appellant $72 a month for his care. According to appellant, these payments were made for only five months. According to Shirley Green, they were made up to July, 1960.

Early in 1959 Shirley Green again became pregnant, this time with the child Anthony Lee, whose death is the basis of appellant's conviction. This child was born October 21, 1959. Soon after birth, Anthony Lee developed a mild jaundice condition, attributed to a blood incompatibility with his mother. The jaundice resulted in his retention in the hospital for three days beyond the usual time, or until October 26, 1959, when, on authorization signed by Shirley Green, Anthony Lee was released by the hospital to appellant's custody. Shirley Green, after a two or three day stay in the hospital, also lived with appellant for three weeks, after which she returned to her parents' home, leaving the children with appellant. She testified she did not see them again, except for one visit in March, until August 5, 1960. Consequently, though there does not seem to have been any specific monetary agreement with Shirley Green covering Anthony Lee's support,[5] appellant had complete custody of both children until they were rescued by the police.

With regard to medical care, the evidence is undisputed. In March, 1960, appellant called a Dr. Turner to her home to treat Anthony Lee for a bronchial condition. Appellant also telephoned the doctor at various times to consult with him concerning Anthony Lee's diet and health. In early July, 1960, appellant took Anthony Lee to Dr. Turner's office where he was treated for "simple diarrhea." At this time the doctor noted the "wizened" appearance of the child and told appellant to tell the mother of the child that he should be taken to a hospital. This was not done.

On August 2, 1960, two collectors for the local gas company had occasion to go to the basement of appellant's home, and there saw the two children. Robert Lee and Anthony Lee at this time were age two years and ten months respectively. Robert Lee was in a "crib" consisting of a framework of wood, covered with a fine wire screening, including the top which was hinged. The "crib" was lined with newspaper, which was stained, apparently with feces, and crawling with roaches. Anthony Lee was lying in a bassinet and was described as having the appearance of a "small baby monkey." One collector testified to seeing roaches on Anthony Lee.

On August 5, 1960, the collectors returned to appellant's home in the company of several police officers and personnel of the Women's Bureau. . . . The officers removed the children to the D. C. General Hospital where Anthony Lee was diagnosed as suffering from severe malnutrition and lesions over large portions of his body, apparently caused by severe diaper rash. Following admission, he was fed repeatedly, apparently with no difficulty, and was described as being very hungry. His death, 34 hours after admission, was attributed without dispute to malnutrition. At birth, Anthony Lee weighed six pounds, fifteen ounces—at death at age ten months, he weighed seven pounds, thirteen ounces. Normal weight at this age would have been approximately 14 pounds. . . .

---

[5] It was uncontested that during the entire period the children were in appellant's home, appellant had ample means to provide food and medical care.

Appellant . . . takes exception to the failure of the trial court to charge that the jury must find beyond a reasonable doubt, as an element of the crime, that appellant was under a legal duty to supply food and necessities to Anthony Lee. . . .

> "The law recognizes that under some circumstances the omission of a duty owed by one individual to another, where such omission results in the death of the one to whom the duty is owing, will make the other chargeable with manslaughter. . . . This rule of law is always based upon the proposition that the duty neglected must be a legal duty, and not a mere moral obligation. It must be duty imposed by law or by contract, and the omission to perform the duty must be the immediate and direct cause of death."

There are at least four situations in which the failure to act may constitute breach of a legal duty. One can be held criminally liable: first, where a statute imposes a duty to care for another; second, where one stands in a certain status relationship to another; third, where one has assumed a contractual duty to care for another; and fourth, where one has voluntarily assumed the care of another and so secluded the helpless person as to prevent others from rendering aid.

It is the contention of the Government that either the third or the fourth ground is applicable here. However, it is obvious that in any of the four situations, there are critical issues of fact which must be passed on by the jury—specifically in this case, whether appellant had entered into a contract with the mother for the care of Anthony Lee or, alternatively, whether she assumed the care of the child and secluded him from the care of his mother, his natural protector. On both of these issues, the evidence is in direct conflict, appellant insisting that the mother was actually living with appellant and Anthony Lee, and hence should have been taking care of the child herself, while Shirley Green testified she was living with her parents and was paying appellant to care for both children.

In spite of this conflict, the instructions given in the case failed even to suggest the necessity for finding a legal duty of care. The only reference to duty in the instructions was the reading of the indictment which charged, inter alia, that the defendants "failed to perform their legal duty." A finding of legal duty is the critical element of the crime charged and failure to instruct the jury concerning it was plain error.

Reversed and remanded.

PROBLEM

4.7 Beverly, a 19-year-old college student, lives in a ten-unit apartment complex. Beverly began dating Sal about six months ago and dated Sal until two weeks ago. Sal has a short temper and is abusive. Beverly had told all the neighbors that last week a court had issued a restraining order requiring Sal to remain at least 100 yards away from Beverly and from the apartment complex. On this evening, Sal, who had been drinking heavily, arrived at the apartment complex and had been let in by one of Beverly's neighbors. Shortly after Sal entered Beverly's apartment, he became violent. As Sal approaches Beverly with a frying pan in his uplifted hand, Beverly begins to scream as loudly as she can. She screams for help, for neighbors to call the police, for someone to stop Sal before he hits her with the frying pan.

> The following neighbors who live in the same apartment complex are home and hear Beverly's screams.
>
> (1) Beverly's bodyguard, whom she had hired to protect her from Sal.
> (2) Beverly's mother.
> (3) A police officer called to the scene of the incident.
> (4) Beverly's landlord.
> (5) The neighbor who had let Sal into the building this evening without consulting Beverly.
> (6) A neighbor who knew that Beverly had sustained serious injury last time Sal had assaulted Beverly.
>
> Which of the above persons could be held criminally accountable if no one intervened or called for help to prevent the assault on Beverly?

The Model Penal Code deals with omissions as follows:

Model Penal Code § 2.01(3) *Omissions*

Liability for the commission of an offense may not be based on an omission unaccompanied by action unless:

(a) the omission is expressly made sufficient by the law defining the offense;

or

(b) a duty to perform the omitted act is otherwise imposed by law.

Subsection (a) refers to statutes such as the Deadbeat Parents Act, discussed above. In accord with *Jones*, Subsection (b) adopts the conventional view that omission plus duty can fulfill the conduct requirement of a statute whose language does not mention omission.

1. Distinguishing Act from Omission

Often it is easy to distinguish an act from a failure to act, an omission. But the line between act and omission is not easily drawn in some cases, and the prosecution and defense may disagree about how to classify a particular case. Characterizing the facts of a case as showing an act by a defendant usually favors the prosecution since that characterization eliminates the need to show the existence of a duty. Showing the existence of a duty may present the prosecutor with both legal and evidentiary challenges.

As *Jones* points out, a "status relationship" such as husband-wife or parent-child typically gives rise to a duty. A case may arise that tests the boundaries of such legal categories. Consider, for example, a recent Connecticut case[13] in which

---

13. State v. Miranda, 715 A.2d 680 (1998).

the defendant, a man, was living with a woman for several years along with her children from a prior relationship. The man and woman had lived together long enough to establish a "common law marriage," a situation in which the law treats a couple as if they were married despite never having gone through any official marriage ceremony. The defendant had not adopted the woman's children. Does a common law marital relationship give rise to a duty on the man's part to rescue or report the woman's severe abuse of her children? This was an issue of first impression in Connecticut, and the prosecutor had to brief and argue for an extension of the duty to rescue at trial and in the appellate and supreme courts before prevailing. The prosecutor also had the burden of obtaining and presenting sufficient evidence at trial to show that a common law relationship existed between the defendant and the woman. None of this would have been necessary if the case had involved action rather than omission on the part of the defendant. In other words, there is simply less for the prosecution to prove in cases involving action rather than omission.

The hypothetical situation in the following Problem illustrates the malleability that may arise in characterizing a set of facts as showing act or omission.

PROBLEMS

4.8 Bill suffers a massive heart attack at his home. When the paramedics arrive, however, there is a misunderstanding regarding the time period that has passed since Bill's heart attack. The paramedics mistakenly believe that Bill's heart attack occurred just 3 minutes before they arrived. In fact, Bill had suffered the heart attack 20 minutes before their arrival, leaving his brain deprived of oxygen for at least 15 minutes. Due to the misunderstanding, the paramedics start CPR. They restart Bill's heart and transport Bill to the hospital. Following an extensive series of tests, Dr. Hall informs the family that Bill will not recover consciousness. Dr. Hall requests the family's permission to unplug the ventilator that forces oxygen into Bill's lungs. Unplugging the ventilator will cause Bill to stop breathing and his heart to stop pumping. The family gives consent and Dr. Hall unplugs the ventilator. Bill ceases to breathe and is declared dead.

Dr. Hall is prosecuted for murder, which is defined here as the purposeful killing of another human being, not under circumstances of self-defense. Did Dr. Hall murder Bill?

4.9 Assume the same facts as in 4.8 above, except that Dr. Hall does not unplug the respirator. Instead, there is an electrical power outage, and Dr. Hall declines to hook Bill's respirator up to the emergency generator. Bill ceases to breathe and is declared dead.

Dr. Hall is prosecuted for murder, as in 4.8 above. Did Dr. Hall murder Bill?

2. Duty to Report or Rescue

Consider the following news account:

Jeremy Strohmeyer walked out of a casino bathroom and matter-of-factly told his friend David Cash that he had just killed 7-year-old Sherrice Iverson, Cash told a Clark County grand jury. . . .

Cash told the panel he didn't react because he was more concerned about being 15 minutes late to meet his father. Later, Cash told the jurors, he worried he would be implicated in the slaying. He said he and Strohmeyer discussed possible alibis and excuses for their behavior.

Strohmeyer, 18, was indicted . . . on charges of murder, first-degree kidnapping and two counts of sexual assault . . . with a minor resulting in substantial bodily harm.

Cash, 18, has not been charged. . . .

Strohmeyer and Sherrice met in the hotel's video arcade and began throwing wet paper towels at each other, Cash told the grand jury. . . .

Cash testified that he got bored in the arcade and went to find Strohmeyer, who was again in the women's bathroom with Sherrice. Cash said their play had turned ugly when Sherrice threw a plastic sign at Strohmeyer.

"Jeremy then grabbed her and took her into one of the stalls in the women's bathroom and he shut the door. And I went over to the door. The door was locked so I went into the stall to the left and boosted myself up on the toilet and looked over," Cash explained to the grand jury.

"I reached over the stall. Jeremy Strohmeyer was restraining her. I believe he had his—I believe it was left hand over her mouth muffling her screams . . .

"My upper torso was over the wall of the stall. I was tapping Jeremy on the head trying to get his attention, telling him to let go, trying to get him to come out of the restroom. I knew at that point that the little game they were playing kind of crossed the line.

"I was tapping on his forehead. At one point I accidentally knocked off his hat. He looked up at me, kind of in a stare, you know, like of—like he didn't care what I was saying."

Cash said he then left the restroom feeling "a small degree" of concern. A few minutes later, he testified, Strohmeyer walked out "looked at me very directly and said, 'I killed her.' "[14]

Cash, who was an undergraduate student at the University of California at Berkeley, neither sought aid to interrupt the event nor did he report what he witnessed to the hotel security or to the police authorities until he was interrogated by the police after his return to California.

Although Cash did say that "he was sorry for the Iverson family,"[15] in a radio interview, Cash is reported to have said:

It's a very tragic event, OK, . . . But the simple fact remains I do not know this little girl. I do not know starving children in Panama. I do not know people that die of disease in Egypt. The only person I knew in this event was Jeremy Strohmeyer and I know as his best friend that he had potential.[16]

---

14. These paragraphs of indented material relating to David Cash's grand jury testimony are quoted from Caren Benjamin, *Strohmeyer confided to friend he killed girl, grand jury told*, Las Vegas Review-Journal, Aug. 15, 1997, 1A.

15. Lynda Gorov, *Outrage Follows Cold Reply to Killing*, The Boston Globe, Aug. 7, 1998, at A1.

16. *Id.*

"Strohmeyer pleaded guilty to the girl's murder and was sentenced to life in prison."[17] Cash was never charged with any criminal conduct in connection with the event. But his behavior engendered substantial public outcry that resulted in legislative reform:

Davis Signs Child Assault 'Good Samaritan' Bill[18]

Gov. Gray Davis signed a bill [in September of 2000] requiring witnesses of a violent or sexual assault on a child under 14 to notify the police.

The bill was introduced in response to the 1997 killing of 7-year old Sherrice Iverson in a Nevada casino by Jeremy Strohmeyer.

Strohmeyer's best friend, David Cash, knew about the assault but did not contact authorities.

Tolakson [the assemblyman who sponsored the bill said], "Sometimes people don't have their internal compass set right and don't report. But this law will help if they don't want to get in trouble."

California Penal Code § 152.3 (2003), reads in pertinent part:

(a) Any person who reasonably believes that he or she has observed the commission of any of the following offenses where the victim is a child under the age of 14 years shall notify a peace officer. . . .

(1) Murder.

(2) Rape.

(3) [Lewd & Lascivious Act on a child]. . . .

(c) The duty to notify a peace officer imposed pursuant to subdivision (a) is satisfied if the notification or an attempt to provide notice is made by telephone or any other means.

(d) Failure to notify as required . . . is a misdemeanor and is punishable by a fine or not more than one thousand five hundred dollars ($1,500), by imprisonment in a county jail for not more than six months, or by both that fine and imprisonment.

(e) The requirements of this section shall not apply to the following:

(1) A person who is related to either the victim or the offender, including a husband, wife, parent, child, brother, sister, grandparent, grandchild, or other person related by consanguinity or affinity.

(2) A person who fails to report based on a reasonable mistake of fact.

(3) A person who fails to report based on a reasonable fear for his or her own safety or for the safety of his or her family.[19]

Laws requiring reporting or actual rescue have been in effect in several jurisdictions for decades. For example, the Vermont Statutory Code reads:

A person who knows that another is exposed to grave physical harm shall, to the extent that [aid] can be rendered without danger or peril to himself or without interference with important duties owed to others, give reasonable assistance to the exposed person unless . . . care is being provided by others.
[Vt. Stat. Ann. tit. 12, § 519 (2002).]

In evaluating such duties, consider the following:

---

17. Lynda Gledhill & Greg Lucas, *Davis Signs Child Assault 'Good Samaritan' Bill*, San Francisco Chronicle, Sept. 19, 2000, at A3.

18. *Id.*

19. Cal. Penal Code § 152.3. Observations of offenses against children (2003).

Eugene Volokh, DUTIES TO RESCUE AND THE ANTICOOPERATIVE EFFECTS OF LAW

88 Geo. L.J. 105, 105–108 (1999)

Samaritans come in at least five different stripes:

The Good Samaritan helps the victim by calling the police. He might even help by physically interceding while the crime is happening. . . .

The Hopelessly Bad Samaritan refuses to help—perhaps because of loyalty to the criminal, unreasonable fear of retaliation, or callousness coupled with a perceived improbability of being identified and prosecuted even if a duty-to-rescue/report law exists—and can't be budged from this by conscience, threat of punishment, or the law's normative force.

The Legally Swayable Samaritan would be Bad in the absence of the duty-to-rescue/report law, but would be swayed by such a law's coercive or normative effect.

The Delayed Samaritan initially does nothing—because of loyalty, panic, hurry, fear, or uncertainty—but later changes his mind (perhaps prompted by a day's contemplation or by hearing that the police are looking for information about the crime) and wants to report what he saw.

The Passive Samaritan never reports the crime, but when the police come to his door looking for witnesses, he is willing—because of remorse, a felt duty to answer questions, fear of lying to the police, or just the natural tendency to respond to questions asked by those in authority—to tell them what he saw.

This typology tells us two things. First, and most obvious, duty-to-rescue/report laws by definition won't do much about the Hopelessly Bad Samaritan. The laws will affect those who are Bad enough that they act wrongly on their own, but are nonetheless so sensitive to the law's normative effect that they are Legally Swayable to being Good. Some people will fall into this category, but I doubt many will . . . This suggests that the laws will do relatively little good, something the laws' supporters do not deny; the laws, they often agree, will influence only a few people, but they argue that even this small benefit is justification enough.

The trouble, though, is that as to the Delayed Samaritan and the Passive Samaritan— two groups usually forgotten in the outrage at the genuinely Bad—the laws may actually be counterproductive. Imagine a person who sees a neighbor seriously abusing the neighbor's child. Though the Good Samaritan would intervene or at least call authorities, some otherwise decent people fail to do this. Some might be afraid, reasonably or not, that the abusive parent will physically hurt them if they intercede. Others may wrongly feel a sense of loyalty to their neighbor or wrongly conclude that it's none of their business. Others may misperceive the magnitude of the abuse, thinking that it might be permissible parental discipline; people are often reluctant to get the police involved unless they're sure that a serious crime is taking place. Still others may be paralyzed with indecision.

These are generally unworthy responses, but fortunately, after reflection or after observing other events, some witnesses may change their minds. A gnawing conscience may move them to call the police a day later. Witnessing a second (or tenth) incident of abuse may finally drive them to action. Seeing the child the next day with a black eye may convince them that the abuse was serious and that they are morally obligated to act to stop it. And even if they don't come forward on their own, a visit from the police or from child welfare officials investigating the matter may prompt them to disclose what they saw, thus helping save the child from further abuse.

People who react this way may still be morally culpable for their initial failure to aid or to report, but the more practically important fact is that the legal system—and the victim and possible future victims—can nonetheless use their belated help. Delayed Samaritanism and Passive Samaritanism aren't as good as Good Samaritanism, but they are much better than nothing, and shouldn't be discouraged.

Under a duty-to-rescue/report law, though, both the Delayed and the Passive Samaritans in such a situation have already committed a crime by not helping or responding "as soon as reasonably practicable." By the time the remorse sets in, the Delayed and Passive Samaritans are legally guilty, and either volunteering or honestly answering police questions will incriminate them.

The Delayed and Passive Samaritans therefore have a choice; continue to keep quiet and likely never be conclusively found out to have been a witness, or speak up and risk a criminal prosecution or perhaps a civil lawsuit for their initial failure to act. . . .

Thus, in trying to achieve a procooperative effect, duty-to-rescue/report laws may inadvertently cause an anticooperative effect.

QUESTIONS

What are the advantages and disadvantages of rescue and reporting duties? If you were a legislator, would you vote in favor of imposing such duties?

H. POSSESSION

In this Section, we consider the use of possession as the conduct element of an offense. Possession is the basis of a number of offenses. Possession of narcotics, possession of burglar's tools, and possession of an illegal firearm, such as a sawed-off shotgun, are common examples. At times, determining whether a defendant possessed something seems quite straightforward. A defendant, for example, might have been videotaped holding a sawed-off shotgun during a bank robbery or arrested after handing narcotics to an undercover police officer in exchange for money. But closer examination reveals that the use of possession poses both theoretical and practical difficulties.

> At least two conceptual problems result from the use of possession as a basis for imposing any sort of criminal liability. First, the creation of such liability is at odds with the notion that the criminal law should proscribe only an act or the failure to perform an act which it was physically possible to perform—in short, an act or omission. Strictly speaking, possession is neither. Second, possession crimes are somewhat anomalous. Possession of an object in and of itself is not the law's real concern. The law forbids possession of counterfeit dies or narcotics because the government wants to preclude their use. Criminalization of possession allows the police to arrest and convict an individual before he can use the prescribed object. Moreover, possession statutes provide a pragmatic means of facilitating law enforcement. In the drug area, for example, it is easier to show possession than to prove use, distribution, or sale.[20]

If possession is neither act nor omission, what is it?

---

20. Charles H. Whitebread & Ronald Stevens, *Constructive Possession in Narcotics Cases: To Have and Have Not*, 58 Va. L. Rev. 751, 752-754 (1972) (citations omitted).

One practical problem in the criminal law's use of possession is how to limit it. The criminal law recognizes that more than one person can possess the same item, a concept known as "joint" possession. It also recognizes a concept known as "constructive" possession. Actual possession usually means something is on someone's person, in their clothing, or within their physical custody.[21] Courts have found defining "constructive" possession a more complex endeavor. Typically, constructive possession is found when actual possession is lacking but the person nonetheless exercises some sort of control over the item. According to scholars in the field, "[t]he apparent purpose of a constructive possession doctrine is expansion of the scope of possession statutes to encompass those cases where actual possession at the time of arrest can not be shown, but 'where the inference that there has been possession at one time is exceedingly strong.'"[22] Should constructive possession be sufficient to establish criminal liability?

PROBLEMS

Consider the following jury instructions on possession and apply them to the Problems below.

Possession   Actual physical custody, or knowledge of the substance's presence, as well as power and intent to control its use or disposition. [Oklahoma Uniform Jury Instructions (2d ed. including 1997 supplement).]

Possession: [A] person is aware of the presence and character of the substance and has [a]ctual physical possession means that the substance is found on the person. Constructive possession means that the person has dominion or control over the substance. Mere proximity is not enough. [Virginia, Title 21: Controlled Substances, Chapter 8: Possession, 201. Michie's Jury Instructions § 21-8-201[2], Definition (Virginia Model Jury Instructions—Criminal (repl. ed. 1993).]

Possession – Defined.   A person has possession of something if the person knows of its presence and has physical control of it, or knows of its presence and has the power and intention to control it.

More than one person can be in possession of something if each knows of its presence and has the power and intention to control it. [Ninth Circuit Pattern Jury Instructions (Criminal Cases), Chapter 3. § 3.16 Instructions at end of case.]

4.10 Officer Careful has pulled a car over for speeding. As she speaks with Driver Sam, she smells a strong odor of marijuana emanating from the car. She asks Sam's permission to search the car. Sam agrees. He

---

21. *See, e.g., Possession*, Drug Offenses—Definitions, Oklahoma Jury Instructions (2d edition, including 1997 supplement), OUJI-CR 6-9.
22. *Supra* note 20, at 755 (quoting the First Report of the Natl. Comm. on Marihuana and Drug Abuse, Appendix 139 (1972)).

and Sally, the front seat passenger, step out. On the armrest between the two front bucket seats, Officer Careful finds a package containing $60.00 worth of tar heroin. Officer Careful understands that tar heroin can be ingested in at least two ways: It can be smoked or injected. Officer Careful notes that both Sam and Sally have symptoms of being under the influence of heroin. In addition, Sally has track marks on her arms from multiple injections, of which at least one has not yet successfully scabbed. Officer Careful also finds a marijuana joint on the floor in front of the right front passenger seat. In this jurisdiction, possession of heroin and possession of marijuana are criminal. Possession of heroin is a felony and possession of marijuana is a misdemeanor. What information would you consider important in deciding whether to charge Sam and Sally with possession of either drug under the definitions of possession given above? If you were the defense attorney for Sam, what arguments would you make to the prosecutor to dissuade the prosecutor from charging? For Sally?

4.11 Dwayne is a drug dealer and a felon, having served time for possession of a controlled substance with intent to distribute. Dwayne is arrested one day trying to sell drugs to an undercover police officer. A criminal statute forbids a felon from possessing a firearm. Would Dwayne be liable under any of the following circumstances?

(a) Dwayne is arrested with a 9 mm pistol in his hand, which he was using to threaten the undercover police officer.

(b) Police find the gun in Dwayne's pocket when they search him at the time of arrest.

(c) Dwayne is arrested in his truck and police find the gun under the driver's seat.

(d) Same as (c), except police find the gun in the truck's unlocked glove box. What if the glove box was locked?

(e) Same as (c), except that police find the gun in a closed zippered bag along with money and drug scales under a tarp in the bed of the truck.

(f) Police obtain a warrant and search the apartment Dwayne shares with his girlfriend, Rose. During the search, the police find the gun under some clothes on a shelf in a closet shared by Dwayne and Rose. Rose tells the police that the gun is hers and that she keeps it for protection when Dwayne is not at home. Police find one of Dwayne's fingerprints on the gun.

The Model Penal Code offers the following provision on possession:

Model Penal Code § 2.01 (1985)

(4) Possession is an act, within the meaning of this Section, if the possessor knowingly procured or received the thing possessed or was aware of his control thereof for a sufficient period to have been able to terminate his possession.

QUESTIONS

1. How does the MPC approach differ from the jury instructions given above for constructive possession?

2. What concerns do you think the MPC drafters were trying to address through the language of the provision?

I. VICARIOUS LIABILITY

The word "vicarious" is derived from a Latin word, "vicar," meaning the representative of another person. Webster's defines "vicarious" as meaning "endured, suffered, or performed by one person in place of another." Webster's New World Dictionary of the American Language—College Edition 1624 (1968). Vicarious authority, for example, is authority exercised by one person on behalf of another.

Should the criminal law recognize vicarious liability, punishing one person based on the conduct of another? The materials in this Section address this controversial question.

PROBLEMS

4.12 You are counsel to the judiciary committee of a state legislature. In response to a series of newspaper stories about young teens joining street gangs and becoming involved with drugs, weapons, and violence, the legislature is considering enacting new legislation that would make a parent criminally liable for an offense involving drugs, weapons, or violence committed by his or her child if: (a) the child is under 16; (b) the child is a member of a street gang; and (c) the parent knows of the child's gang membership. The chair of the judiciary committee asks for your advice. What are the arguments for and against such a law? Are there alternative ways to write such a statute that would address any constitutional concerns?

4.13 Reread Problem 2.6. Is section 154 of the Imperial Code consistent with the idea that crime requires some sort of conduct? Is section 154 constitutional?

PEOPLE *v.* JACKSON

Michigan Court of Appeals 176 Mich. App. 620 (1989)

PER CURIAM. The people appeal [an] opinion and order of the Kalamazoo Circuit Court reversing defendant's misdemeanor conviction. . . .

The record reveals that defendant, Philip C. Jackson, a certified commercial applicator of pesticides under the Pesticide Control Act, is the branch manager of the Kalamazoo outlet of the Orkin Company, a nationwide pest control service. In May, 1987, James A. Gregart, who happens to be the prosecuting attorney for Kalamazoo County, contracted with the Orkin Company to treat his home with chlordane, a pesticide regulated under the Pesticide Control Act. Defendant dispatched Andrew Price, a noncertified applicator of pesticides, to the Gregart home to apply the chlordane. Price's failure to follow the recommended and accepted procedures for use of the chemical prompted a complaint. Apparently, Price sprayed chlordane on the lawn of the Gregart home. When the complaint was verified, defendant discharged Price and, with an associate, properly applied the pesticide at the Gregart household. In addition, the Orkin Company refunded the downpayment of $167, cancelled the remaining balance of $930, added one year to the warranty period, paid $1,321 to replace carpeting in the downstairs area of the Gregart home, and paid $807 for medical examinations and testing for Gregart, his wife and his children.

Gregart subsequently applied for the appointment of a special prosecutor who would seek to impose criminal sanctions against defendant under the Pesticide Control Act. As a result, a misdemeanor warrant was issued against defendant naming Gregart as the victim and a representative of the Michigan Department of Agriculture as the complaining witness. . . . [A] plea of nolo contendere was entered pursuant to a plea bargain under the terms of which the issue of defendant's vicarious liability under the Pesticide Control Act was preserved for appeal. A fine of $100, costs of $50, and a fee of $5 were levied. . . . The circuit court reversed defendant's misdemeanor conviction and the present appeal by the people ensued.

The sections of the Pesticide Control Act pertinent to this appeal, being §§ 12(5) and (6), 26(1), and 29(1), provide as follows:

(5) A pesticide applicator shall follow recommended and accepted good practices in the use of pesticides including use of a pesticide in a manner consistent with its labeling.

(6) A certified applicator shall be responsible for the application of a pesticide by a noncertified applicator under his instruction and control even though the certified applicator is not physically present. A certified applicator shall be physically present during the application of a pesticide if prescribed by the label. [MCL 286.562(5) and (6); MSA 12.340(12)(5) and (6).]

(1) A person who violates this act is guilty of a misdemeanor and shall be fined not more than $500.00 for each offense. [MCL 286.576(1); MSA 12.340(26)(1).]

(1) This act shall not terminate or in any way modify any liability, civil or criminal, which is in existence on the effective date of this act. [MCL 286.579(1); MSA 12.340(29)(1).]. . . .

The district court, in ruling that the responsibility or vicarious liability established in § 12(6) of the act regarding certified applicators included criminal responsibility and vicarious liability for such applicators, stated:

It is [defendant's] claim that . . . Section [12(6)] makes him only civilly responsible for what his non-certified applicator did. . . .

[I]t is my opinion that the Act provides for both civil and criminal responsibility because to say otherwise will be to say that the Act cannot perform the purpose for which it was intended and that is to control the application of pesticides, such as Chlordane, by hiring a non-certified person and tell[ing] him to go do it, turn[ing] him loose.

The circuit court, in reversing the district court, concluded that § 12(6) of the act does not subject certified applicators to vicarious criminal responsibility for the acts of noncertified applicators because such responsibility would be in derogation of the common law and was not specifically provided for in § 12(6). . . . .

It is true that "[criminal] liability does not arise vicariously unless the Legislature so provides," *People v. Wilcox*, 83 Mich. App. 654 (1978), that in exercising its authority to abrogate the common law the Legislature must speak with specificity and in no uncertain terms, and that, in general, criminal statutes are to be strictly construed.[2] However, we do not believe that these principles work in this case to shield defendant from vicarious criminal liability under the Pesticide Control Act.

The general rule that criminal statutes are to be strictly construed is inapplicable when the general purpose of the Legislature is manifest and is subserved by giving the words used in the statute their ordinary meaning. In addition, statutory language which is clear and unambiguous should be given its plain meaning by the judiciary.

In the Pesticide Control Act the Legislature provided that any person who violates a provision of the act is guilty of a misdemeanor. . . . One provision of the act, § 12(5), requires a pesticide applicator to follow the recommended and accepted good practices in the use of pesticides, and another provision of the act, § 12(6), makes a certified applicator "responsible" for the application of a pesticide by a noncertified applicator under his instruction and control. While, as the circuit court stressed, the Legislature did not insert the modifier "criminally" before the operative word "responsible" in § 12(6), neither did it insert the word "civilly." The effect of the circuit court's ruling, however, is to limit the plain meaning of the term used by the Legislature so that the unlimited term "responsible" may mean only civilly, not criminally, responsible. We see no need to so qualify, circumscribe or restrict the plain meaning of the word chosen by the Legislature in drafting § 12(6) of the Pesticide Control Act. . . . The statute itself provides that a certified applicator "shall be responsible" for the application of a pesticide by a noncertified applicator under his instruction and control, and further provides that a violation of the act constitutes a misdemeanor. Thus, by its own terms, the statute imposes vicarious criminal liability upon a certified applicator for actions in violation of the act performed by a noncertified applicator working under the instruction and control of the certified applicator. . . .

Our analysis and conclusion in this case are consistent with the comments of other legal authorities.

[I]n LaFave & Scott, [Criminal Law § 32], pp. 224-225, it is stated:

> Some criminal statutes, generally containing no language of fault, specifically impose criminal liability upon the employer for the bad conduct of his employee—e.g., "whoever, by himself or by his agent, sells articles at short weight shall be punished by . . . . "
>
> Often statutes are not that specific as to whether or not they impose vicarious liability. In such a case, if the statutory crime is worded in language requiring

---

[2] We note that in the Michigan Penal Code it is provided:

The rule that a penal statute is to be strictly construed shall not apply to this act or any of the provisions thereof. All provisions of this act shall be construed according to the fair import of their terms, to promote justice and to effect the objects of the law. [MCL 750.2; MSA 28.192.]

some type of fault ("knowingly," "wilfully," "with intent to," etc.), then . . . the employer is not criminally liable unless he knew of or authorized that action. . . .
[For statutes that do not explicitly impose vicarious liability nor use terms of fault,] . . . [t]he question is one of construction of the statute. . . . If the authorized punishment is light—a fine or perhaps a short imprisonment—the statute is likely to be construed to impose vicarious liability on a faultless employer. But if the permitted punishment is severe—a felony or a serious misdemeanor—the statute is not apt to be so construed in the absence of an express provision for vicarious responsibility.

Even if we were to agree with defendant that the language in the Pesticide Control Act regarding the vicarious criminal responsibility of certified applicators is ambiguous and, thus, requires construction, we believe that the intent of the Legislature is to impose such responsibility. The authorized punishment is light, a fine of not more than $500 for each offense. . . . Moreover, only by imposing vicarious criminal responsibility can the full intent of the legislation, to protect the public health and safety from deliberate as well as negligent environmental degradation, effectively be carried out. The Pesticide Control Act allows the hiring of uncertified applicators to apply pesticides, but places on the certified applicators the responsibility for selecting, training, and instructing such uncertified applicators. To allow the certified applicator to escape vicarious criminal responsibility under these circumstances would be to preclude employment of the law's most puissant implement of public protection and to diminish the statute's deterrent effect. To hold that a certified applicator may be held criminally responsible for violations of the act only when he himself, and not a noncertified applicator under his instruction and control, has committed those violations "would be to prepare a way of easy escape" and "would go a long way . . . toward destroying the beneficial effects and purposes of this law." *Groff v. State*, 171 Ind. 547; 85 N.E. 769, 770-771 (1908). . . .

A major purpose of the Pesticide Control Act is to regulate the release of such poisons so as to reduce the possibility of deleterious effects on the public health. We believe that our holding in this case is consistent with that purpose and is mandated under the language of the Pesticide Control Act.

Reversed.

QUESTIONS

1. What are the advantages and disadvantages of vicarious criminal liability? Why do you think a legislature might choose to use it? What objective does vicarious liability serve in the context of pesticide use?

2. Is vicarious liability consistent with the purposes of punishment we studied in Chapter 2? Is vicarious liability fair?

3. What could Mr. Jackson have done to avoid prosecution in this case?

In 1988, shortly before the publication of this case, the Environmental Protection Agency banned all uses of chlordane. The Agency for Toxic Substances and Disease Registry, a division of the United States Department of Health and Human Services, provides information about chlordane. Consider the excerpt that follows:

CHLORDANE CAS #57-74-9

ToxFAQS™ for Chlordane, Agency for Toxic Substances and Disease Registry
http://www.atsdr.cdc.gov/tfacts31.html (accessed Oct. 18, 2004)

Chlordane is a manufactured chemical that was used as a pesticide in the United States from 1948 to 1988. . . . It doesn't occur naturally in the environment. It is a thick liquid whose color ranges from colorless to amber. Chlordane has a mild, irritating smell. . . .

Because of concern about damage to the environment and harm to human health, the Environmental Protection Agency (EPA) banned all uses of chlordane in 1983 except to control termites. In 1988, EPA banned all uses. . . .

- Chlordane entered the environment when it was used as a pesticide on crops, on lawns and gardens, and to control termites. . . .
- It can stay in the soil for over 20 years. . . .
- It breaks down very slowly. . . .
- It builds up in the tissues of fish, birds, and mammals.

[People may be exposed to chlordane:]

- By eating crops grown in soil that contains chlordane.
- By eating fish or shellfish caught in water that is contaminated by chlordane.
- By breathing air or touching soil near homes treated for termites with chlordane. . . .

Chlordane affects the nervous system, the digestive system, and the liver in people and animals. Headaches, irritability, confusion, weakness, vision problems, vomiting, stomach cramps, diarrhea, and jaundice have occurred in people who breathed air containing high concentrations of chlordane or accidentally swallowed small amounts of chlordane. Large amounts of chlordane taken by mouth can cause convulsions and death in people.

Do the risks associated with chlordane affect your view of the court's interpretation of the statute at issue in *Jackson*?

In the employer-employee context, courts that impose vicarious liability commonly apply a version of the tort doctrine of *respondeat superior*. This doctrine holds the employer to answer for the agent or employee's conduct if the conduct was within the agent's or employee's scope of employment. Consider the excerpts from the jury instructions that follow, representing a Wisconsin court's explanation of employer/employee liability:

STATE *v.* BEAUDRY

Supreme Court Wisconsin 123 Wis. 2d 40, 46-47 (1985)

[I]f a person employs another to act for him in the conduct of his business, and such servant or agent violates the law, . . . then the employer is guilty of that violation as if he had been present or had done that act himself, if such act was within the scope of the employment of the servant or agent. It is no defense to prosecution under the statute that the employer was not upon the premises, did not know of the acts of his servant or agent, had not consented thereto, or even had expressly forbidden such act.

"A servant or agent is within the scope of his employment when he is performing work or rendering services he was hired to perform and render within the time and space limits of his authority and is actuated by a purpose in serving his employer in doing what he is doing. He is within the scope of his employment when he is performing work or rendering services in obedience to the express orders or directions of his master or doing that which is warranted within the express or implied authority, considering the nature of the services required, the instructions which he has received, and the circumstances under which his work is being done or the services are being rendered.["]

"A servant or agent is outside the scope of his employment when he deviates or steps aside from the prosecution of his master's business for the purpose of doing an act or rendering a service intended to accomplish an independent purpose of his own, or for some other reason or purpose not related to the business of his employer.["]

"Such deviation or stepping aside from his employer's business may be momentary and slight, measured in terms of time and space, but if it involves a change of mental attitude in serving his personal interests, or the interests of another instead of his employer's, then his conduct falls outside the scope of his employment.["]

Vicarious liability in criminal law represents the exception rather than the rule. When it appears, it commonly involves employer/employee or agency relationships. But some courts outlaw vicarious criminal liability, even within the confines of the employer/employee context, as a constitutional violation.

STATE *v.* GUMINGA
Minnesota Supreme Court 395 N.W.2d 344 (1986)

YETKA, Justice. On May 29, 1985, the state filed a criminal complaint in Hennepin County Municipal Court against George Joseph Guminga, defendant. . . .

On March 29, 1985, in the course of an undercover operation, two investigators for the City of Hopkins entered Lindee's Restaurant, Hopkins, Minnesota, with a 17-year-old woman. All three ordered alcoholic beverages. The minor had never been in Lindee's before, and the waitress did not ask the minor her age or request identification. When the waitress returned with their orders, the minor paid for all the drinks. After confirming that the drink contained alcohol, the officers arrested the waitress for serving intoxicating liquor to a minor in violation of Minn.Stat. § 340.73 (1984). The owner of Lindee's, defendant George Joseph Guminga, was subsequently charged with violation of section 340.73 pursuant to Minn. Stat. § 340.941 (1984), which imposes vicarious criminal liability on an employer whose employee serves intoxicating liquor to a minor. The state does not contend that Guminga was aware of or ratified the waitress's actions. . . .

The certified question of law before this court is as follows:

Whether Minn. Stat. § 340.941, on its face, violates the defendant's right to due process of law under the Fourteenth Amendment to the United States Constitution and analogous provisions of the Constitution of the State of Minnesota.

We find that the statute in question does violate the due process clauses of the Minnesota and the United States Constitutions and thus answer the question in the affirmative. . . .

Minn. Stat. § 340.73 (1984) provides . . .

It is unlawful for any person, except a licensed pharmacist to sell, give, barter, furnish, deliver, or dispose of, in any manner, either directly or indirectly, any intoxicating liquors or nonintoxicating malt liquors in any quantity, for any purpose, to any person under the age of 19 years. . . .

Whoever in any way procures intoxicating liquor or nonintoxicating malt liquor for the use of any person named in this section shall be deemed to have sold it to that person. Any person violating any of the provisions of this section is guilty of a gross misdemeanor.

Minn. Stat. § 340.941 (1984) imposes vicarious criminal liability on the employer for an employee's violation of section 340.73:

Any sale of liquor in or from any public drinking place by any clerk, barkeep, or other employee authorized to sell liquor in such place is the act of the employer as well as that of the person actually making the sale; and every such employer is liable to all the penalties provided by law for such sale, equally with the person actually making the same.

Under Minn. Stat. § 609.03 (1984), a defendant who commits a gross misdemeanor may be sentenced to "imprisonment for not more than one year or to payment of a fine of not more than $3,000 or both." In addition, a defendant convicted under section 340.941 may, at the discretion of the licensing authority, have its license suspended, revoked or be unable to obtain a new license. . . . As a gross misdemeanor, a conviction under section 340.941 would also affect a defendant's criminal history score were he or she to be convicted of a felony in the future. . . .

Since this is not an appeal from a conviction, we do not yet know whether, if found guilty, Guminga would be subjected to imprisonment, a suspended sentence, or a fine. . . .

We find that criminal penalties based on vicarious liability under Minn. Stat. § 340.941 are a violation of substantive due process and that only civil penalties would be constitutional. A due process analysis of a statute involves a balancing of the public interests protected against the intrusion on personal liberty while taking into account any alternative means by which to achieve the same end. . . . The private interests affected, however, include liberty, damage to reputation and other future disabilities arising from criminal prosecution for an act which Guminga did not commit or ratify. Not only could Guminga be given a prison sentence or a suspended sentence, but, in the more likely event that he receives only a fine, his liberty could be affected by a longer presumptive sentence in a possible future felony conviction. Such an intrusion on personal liberty is not justified by the public interest protected, especially when there are alternative means by which to achieve the same end, such as civil fines or license suspension, which do not entail the legal and social ramifications of a criminal conviction. . . .

The dissent's citation to an article by Sayre, *Criminal Responsibility for the Acts of Another*, 43 Harv. L. Rev. 689 (1930), is . . . inapposite. After finding numerous opinions on *both* sides of the question of whether to impose vicarious criminal liability, Professor Sayre states: "The liquor cases embody numerous diverging and conflicting views, and cannot be reconciled." Professor Sayre noted:

> The danger is that criminal courts may forget the fundamental distinctions between criminal and civil liability for another's acts, and begin to use as precedents for true-crime cases those liquor cases which virtually adopt the doctrine of *respondeat superior.*

Professor Sayre went on to summarize the appropriate legal principle in these terms:

> As the decisions indicate, a sharp line must be drawn between true crimes involving serious punishments and petty misdemeanors involving only light monetary fines. Where the offense is in the nature of a true crime, that is, where it involves moral delinquency or is punishable by imprisonment or a serious penalty, it seems clear that the doctrine of *respondeat superior* must be repudiated as a foundation for criminal liability.

. . . Yet, it must be recognized that the imposition of criminal liability for fault-less conduct is contrary to the basic Anglo-American premise of criminal justice that crime requires personal fault on the part of the accused. Perhaps the answer should be the same as the answer proposed in the case of strict-liability crimes: it is proper for the legislature to single out some special areas of human activity and impose vicarious liability on employers who are without personal fault, but the matter should not be called a "crime" and the punishment should not include more than a fine or forfeiture or other civil penalty; that is, it should not include imprisonment. As the law now stands, however, in almost all jurisdictions imprisonment and the word "criminal" may be visited upon perfectly innocent employers for the sins of their employees.

LaFave & Scott, Handbook on Criminal Law § 32 at 227-28 (1972). . . .

The dissent argues that vicarious liability is necessary as a deterrent so that an owner will impress upon employees that they should not sell to minors. However, it does not distinguish between an employer who vigorously lectures his employees and one who does not. According to the dissent, each would be equally guilty. We believe it is a deterrent enough that the employee who sells to the minor can be charged under the statute and that the business is subject to fines or suspension or revocation of license.

In this last quarter of the twentieth century, there is doubt whether the United States Supreme Court would uphold a conviction under the provisions of the United States Constitution. Even if it were to do so, the statute we hold violates Minn. Const. art. I, § 7, which states:

> [No] person shall be held to answer for a criminal offense without due process of law . . . nor be deprived of life, liberty or property without due process of law.

We specifically and exclusively decide the question under the provisions of the Minnesota Constitution herein cited. We find that, in Minnesota, no one can be convicted of a crime punishable by imprisonment for an act he did not commit, did not have knowledge of, or give expressed or implied consent to the commission thereof.

QUESTIONS

1. Did Guminga "sell, give, barter, furnish, deliver or dispose of" liquor to a minor? If not, on what basis was he charged with violating Minnesota § 340.73?

2. The Minnesota legislature in § 340.941 chose to create vicarious criminal liability for employers who own and operate businesses that sell liquor. How is it that the Minnesota Supreme Court can override this legislative choice? Is such an override consistent with the notion of legislative supremacy in making criminal law? Could the state have sought review in the United States Supreme Court of the Minnesota Supreme Court's decision in *Guminga*?

3. How might the Minnesota legislature rewrite the statutes at issue to remedy the constitutional defect found by the *Guminga* court and still create an incentive for employers to prevent their employees from selling liquor to minors?

PROBLEM

4.14 JB was the co-owner of a tavern, which has a liquor license. The following law is in effect in the town in which the tavern operates:

> No licensed tavern may remain open between the hours of 1 A.M. and 8 A.M. Any person who violates this provision shall be fined not more than $500 or imprisoned for not more than 90 days or both.

At 3:45 A.M., a law enforcement officer noticed that the tavern seemed better-lighted than usual, that two persons were seated inside, that music was playing, that someone was standing behind the bar, and that there were glasses on the bar. The door was locked, but upon knocking, the officer was admitted by the tavern manager, who, along with the other two persons, were drinking.

After learning of the incident, JB's spouse, and co-owner of the tavern, discharged the tavern manager. At JB's trial for violation of the law, the tavern manager testified that he had not been authorized to stay open after 1:00 A.M. nor to throw a party for his friends. Instead, he had been instructed to close promptly at 1:00 A.M. The tavern manager explained that he kept the tavern open simply to throw a private party for friends and to benefit himself, not the tavern owners. He also explained that he had not charged his friends for any of the drinks he served after 1:00 A.M.[23]

Should a jury convict JB under the statute?

---

23. Adapted from State v. Beaudry, 123 Wis. 2d 40 (1985).

J. SYNTHESIS AND CHALLENGES

PROBLEMS

4.15 Daniel is severely allergic to bee stings. His doctor told him a bee sting could kill him by causing a reaction severe enough to close down his airways and suffocate him in minutes unless he gives himself an injection of epinephrine. The doctor gives Daniel an epinephrine injection kit and advises Daniel to keep it with him at all times. One day Daniel is driving at about 45 m.p.h in his car with the windows open on a busy street in the middle of the day when a bee flies in the window and starts buzzing around his head. Upon hearing the bee, Daniel realizes he left his injection kit at home. Daniel panics and starts wildly waving his arms around his head to shoo the bee away. In doing so, he lets go of the steering wheel of his car, which crashes into and demolishes a new police car worth $40,000. Luckily no one is hurt, but Daniel is charged under the following statute:

> Anyone who damages property of another in excess of $1,000 is guilty of a misdemeanor punishable by 6 months in jail or a $5,000 fine.

Is Daniel liable for violating the statute?[24]

4.16 Siamese twin girls were born conjoined at the chest in the summer of 2000. The weaker of the twins, "Mary," relied "on her sister's heart and lungs to survive." This reliance was causing substantial strain on "Jodie's," the stronger twin's, organs. Surgical separation of the twins would kill Mary. Failure to separate the twins meant that both were "likely to perish within three to six months because of the extra strain on Jodie's organs."[25] According to Jodie's representative, "medical experts believed that she would not face significant problems," upon separation. If the parents had succeeded in preventing the doctors from separating the twins and both had perished within three months, what legal arguments might be raised about the conduct requirement in a prosecution of the parents for homicide?

In the real case, courts did order separation. As predicted, Jodie survived and Mary died as a result of the operation.

4.17 With current technology, it is possible for a person to control a computer purely through brain waves.[26] Electrodes can be planted in the brain that transmit the brain's electrical impulses to a receiver that then translates those signals into digital information that can drive the computer.[27] Let's hypothesize that, with additional refinement, the

---

24. Adapted from *Police forgive beeline crash into 3 cop cars* (Associated Press, Sept. 15, 1993).

25. Quotations in Problem 4.16 are from *Court orders second medical exam*, Associated Press Newswires (Associated Press, Sept. 4, 2000).

26. The technology is currently being used by persons who have suffered severe damage to the brain stem, eliminating effective communication with the spinal cord. *See* Bruce Headlam, *The Mind That Moves Objects*, N.Y. Times Magazine 63 (June 11, 2000).

27. Id.

> computer to which the receiver sends the information is a robot. Let
> us further imagine that Horrible Hilda, whose brain waves control the
> robot, concentrates on poisoning Jolly John by putting hemlock into
> his afternoon smoothie. As a result, the robot responding to Hilda's
> input, adds hemlock to John's afternoon smoothie, causing John's
> death.
>
> Did Hilda commit an act? Consider the New York and Utah
> statutes in Section C above. Do they provide guidance? How would a
> prosecutor approach charging under the statutes in Section C? How
> should a court interpret these statutes? As technology advances, dis-
> tinguishing between thought and act may become progressively more
> challenging.

Rethinking the Conduct Requirement. In recent years, scholars have focused on rethinking the conduct element of crimes. Consider the proposals in the two excerpts below.

It is often stated that criminal liability requires an act, and many scholars adhere to this view. Professor Douglas Husak, though, takes the position that criminal liability does not depend on an act, but on what he calls the "control requirement."[28] He explains the notion of control as follows:

> The core idea behind the control requirement is that a person lacks responsibility
> for those states of affairs he or she is unable to prevent from taking place or obtain-
> ing. . . . I propose to explicate control in terms of what it is reasonable to expect of
> persons. A person lacks control over a state of affairs and neither is nor ought to be
> criminally liable for it if it is unreasonable to expect him or her to have prevented
> that state of affairs from obtaining. . . . [29]
>
> Defenders of the act requirement must strain to explain liability for omissions.
> *Some* explanation is required, if the act requirement is to be preserved. . . . I believe
> that this normative basis is easily described. Criminal liability should sometimes
> be imposed for omissions because persons are able to exercise control over a state
> of affairs by not acting, and persons may be subject for moral and criminal con-
> demnation for some of those untoward states of affairs over which they exercise
> sufficient control. This basis can be extended far beyond the category of omissions,
> thus opening the door to further kinds of exceptions to the act requirement.[30]

As indicated at the beginning of this chapter, it is typically thought to be improper to punish thoughts. What implications does Professor Husak's control requirement have for punishing thoughts? He maintains that the control requirement exempts most thoughts from punishment:

> [T]he best reason to resist criminal liability for the vast majority of thoughts is that
> persons lack the requisite degree of control over most of their mental processes to
> be responsible for them. Consider beliefs. A person cannot control whether or not
> he or she believes the Earth to be round, for example. A person simply evaluates the

---

28. Douglas Husak, *Does Criminal Liability Require an Act? In Philosophy and the Criminal Law: Principle and Critique* 60 (Antony Duff ed., 1998).
29. *Id.* at 77-78.
30. *Id.* at 82.

evidence and forms a judgment about the shape of the Earth, without exercising much if any control over the outcome. For this reason, liability for beliefs would be unjustifiable.[31]

But Professor Husak contends that the control requirement supports punishment for thoughts a person controls:

> I will call those thoughts that are sufficiently under the control of persons "mental acts." Clearly, some mental acts exist. For example, whether a person decides to rob a bank, deliberates over time, anticipates every contingency, and carefully plans an escape seems no less under individual control than whether he or she commits any number of acts that unquestionably are the proper objects of criminal liability.[32]

QUESTIONS

1. Look back over the criminal law's treatment of the issues you studied in this chapter, such as status, omission, and possession. Does Professor Husak's principle of control provide a more convincing explanation of the criminal law's treatment of these issues than an act requirement? Does a control requirement better serve the purposes of the criminal law than an act requirement?

2. Do you agree with Professor Husak that a person lacks control over her beliefs?

Deborah W. Denno, CRIME AND CONSCIOUSNESS: SCIENCE AND INVOLUNTARY ACTS

87 Minn. L. Rev. 269, 269-272, 274-275, 361, 369 (2002)

In 1906 Edouard Claparede experimented with the mind. He pricked the hand of a memory-impaired patient while greeting her with a pin concealed between his fingers. As always, the patient failed to recognize Claparede when the two met again; yet, she refused to shake his hand, explaining that it might be unpleasant but she did not know why. With this test, Claparede revealed the dynamics of "covert awareness"—the inconsistency between individuals' conscious acts and their unconscious memories, perceptions, and judgments.

Claparede's research was unusual for its time. For most of the twentieth century, the topic of consciousness, apart from Freudian theory, was not considered fit for serious scientific study. Consciousness was the "ghost in the machine," an unobservable, immeasurable, phenomenon rendered irrelevant to objective science. Starting in the 1970s, however, interest in the topic surged to the current point of "explosion." The scientific "race" to understand consciousness is on and the potential for discovery seems boundless.

The race within science has far-reaching legal implications. Criminal law, in particular, presumes that most human behavior is voluntary and that individuals are consciously aware of their acts. On the other hand, it also presumes that individuals who act unconsciously, such as sleepwalkers, are not "acting" at all. Under the criminal law's voluntary act requirement, unconscious individuals can be totally acquitted even if their behavior causes serious harm.

---

31. *Id.* at 87.
32. *Id.*

In contrast to these legal "dichotomies" (voluntary/involuntary, conscious/unconscious), modern neuroscientific research has revealed a far more fluid and dynamic relationship between conscious and unconscious processes. If such fluidity exists, human behavior is not always conscious or voluntary in the "either/or" way that the voluntary act requirement presumes. Rather, consciousness manifests itself in degrees that represent varying levels of awareness. [My writing] . . . confronts this clash between legal and scientific perspectives on consciousness by proposing new ways to structure the voluntary act requirement so that it incorporates the insights of modern science on the human mind. . . .

Despite the differences and debates among cognitive scientists on the topic, one idea becomes clear: No consensus of scientific support exists for the concept of a conscious/unconscious dichotomy. [In my writing, I propose] . . . that the voluntary act requirement should be simplified and consist of three parts: (1) voluntary acts, (2) involuntary acts, and (3) semi-voluntary acts. Semi-voluntary acts would incorporate cases that have previously been shoehorned into the first two categories. . . . Semi-voluntary acts would include . . . those who acted involuntarily or semi-voluntarily but demonstrate the potential to be dangerous again [for example, a violent sleepwalker]. . . . Classifying [a violent sleepwalker's, like Kenneth] Parks' behavior as semi-voluntary would preclude an unqualified acquittal for him, but, at the same time, avoid the injustice or putting someone like Parks in an institution for the criminally insane. . . . The result of integrating increasing knowledge about the unconscious into the criminal law will mean that individuals will be held both more and less responsible than the conventional understanding. . . .

If the criminal law can confront and modify the chimera of "either/or" embedded in the voluntary act requirement, it can join science with a more nuanced, and more just, view of the human mind.

QUESTIONS

1. What expectations about the legal system and juries would adding a category of semivoluntary acts invoke?
2. How would jurors or judges make such a determination in a trial setting?
3. How should punishment for semivoluntary acts be graded?

CHAPTER FIVE

MENTAL STATES

Legislatures regularly include one or more mental state requirements in defining crimes. This mental element is often referred to by the Latin phrase *mens rea*, meaning guilty mind. Consider, for example, the following criminal statutes and identify the mental state or states each requires for conviction.

New York Penal Law § 140.25 *Burglary*

A person is guilty of burglary in the second degree when he knowingly enters or remains unlawfully in a building with intent to commit a crime therein, and when:

    1. In effecting entry or while in the building or in immediate flight therefrom, he or another participant in the crime:

        (a) Is armed with explosives or a deadly weapon; or

        (b) Causes physical injury to any person who is not a participant in the crime; or

        (c) Uses or threatens the immediate use of a dangerous instrument; or

        (d) Displays what appears to be a pistol, revolver, rifle, shotgun, machine gun or other firearm; or

    2. The building is a dwelling.

Colorado Revised Statutes § 18-3-205 *Vehicular Assault*

If a person operates or drives a motor vehicle in a reckless manner, and this conduct is the proximate cause of serious bodily injury to another, such person commits vehicular assault.

Alabama Criminal Code § 13A-6-4 *Criminally Negligent Homicide*

A person commits the crime of criminally negligent homicide if he causes the death of another person by criminal negligence.

This chapter focuses on the mental state element in crime. The first Section describes how legislatures use mental states to define and grade crimes. It identifies common problems and sources of confusion regarding mental states. Section A also introduces basic concepts and vocabulary, comparing the Model Penal Code's use of the words "purpose," "knowledge," "recklessness" and "negligence," with the more traditional term "intent." At times, legislatures do create crimes that dispense in whole or in part with mental state. We examine this controversial practice, known as *strict* or *absolute* liability, in Section B.

Legislatures often draft statutes that are silent or otherwise ambiguous regarding mental state, leaving it to the courts to decide what mental states should apply or if strict liability should be imposed. Such statutes are a perennial source of uncertainty and confusion in criminal law and create challenging issues of statutory interpretation for judges, a topic we examine in Section C.

Sections D and E address how the criminal law responds to a defendant's claim that she was ignorant or mistaken about a matter of fact or law. Questions of ignorance and mistake can often be resolved easily if the legislature has been clear in defining the mental states required for conviction. But, as mentioned in the previous paragraph, legislatures unfortunately often draft statutes that are ambiguous on mental states, causing considerable confusion in the treatment of ignorance and mistake.

Sections F and G deal with two mental states encountered less often than those covered in Section A. Section F treats "willful blindness," a term used to describe a person who goes out of his way to avoid knowledge. In the *Jewell* case in Section F, for example, the defendant consciously avoided knowledge that a car he was paid to drive across an international border contained marijuana. Section G deals with the notion of conditional purpose, the idea that one may have the purpose to do an act or cause a result only if some condition is fulfilled, such as using force only if the victim of the crime resists. Jurisdictions vary on whether they find conditional purpose sufficient for liability under a statute that requires purpose.

What impact should intoxication by alcohol or drugs have on criminal liability? Should the fact that a defendant was drunk when he killed someone, for example, aggravate or mitigate his punishment? Or should it be treated as irrelevant? Section H, on intoxication, looks at these and related questions.

Finally, Section I gives detailed attention to the common law classifications of specific and general intent crimes. A number of jurisdictions, such as Florida and California, continue to rely on the specific and general intent categories. But many jurisdictions, along with the Model Penal Code, have abandoned this common law terminology and classification scheme.

A. INTRODUCTION

1. Functions of Mental States

a. Distinguishing Criminal from Non-Criminal Conduct

Why do legislatures use mental state as an ingredient in defining crimes? Justice Jackson offered the following explanation:

> The contention that an injury can amount to a crime only when inflicted by intention is no provincial or transient notion. It is as universal and persistent in mature systems of law as belief in freedom of the human will and a consequent ability and

duty of the normal individual to choose between good and evil. A relation between some mental element and punishment for a harmful act is almost as instinctive as the child's familiar exculpatory "But I didn't mean to". . . . [1]

As this passage suggests, a defendant's mental state is closely tied to our intuitive sense of blameworthiness. Therefore, from a retributive perspective, it makes sense to rely on mental state to indicate conduct that is blameworthy and should be criminally sanctioned.

Compare, for example, a political extremist who sends a letter containing anthrax to a government office and the mail carrier who delivers the letter. The terrorist's purpose is to infect and kill a legislator whom the terrorist has targeted because of the legislator's support of abortion rights. The mail carrier, by contrast, does not know the letter is contaminated. His only purpose is to deliver mail, not hurt anyone. The legislator opens the letter, is infected, and dies. We think of the terrorist as a blameworthy criminal because she had the purpose to kill, and the mail carrier as innocent because he did not, regardless of the fact that the actions of each played a role in bringing about the legislator's death.

b. Grading Offenses

Mental state may also be used to establish the relative blameworthiness of and severity of punishment for crimes. The architecture of the law of homicide, for example, is built on gradations of mental state regarding the victim's death. The Model Penal Code's homicide hierarchy places those who kill with purpose or knowledge regarding the death, such as the terrorist who mailed anthrax in the previous hypothetical, in its highest homicide category, murder. Those who kill recklessly—by consciously engaging in highly risky conduct, such as drag racing—typically fall into a homicide category just below murder, called "manslaughter," and are exposed to proportionally less punishment than those convicted of murder. The Model Penal Code creates a third homicide category of negligent homicide for those who kill by engaging in highly risky conduct when they should be but are not aware of the risk of death. Negligent homicide usually entails lesser punishment than manslaughter.

2. Sources of Difficulty

Despite the intuitive appeal of mental states in marking the boundaries of the criminal law and grading offenses, the treatment of mental states is the source of considerable confusion and difficulty in criminal law. Three aspects of mental state regularly cause trouble.

a. Mental State Is a Question of Degree

As the Model Penal Code's homicide hierarchy illustrates, a variety of mental states, which vary in blameworthiness, may qualify a defendant for criminal sanctions. Early criminal law, though, failed to recognize such variation. It treated mental state as a simple black and white proposition. Just as the power switch on a television set has only on and off positions, the criminal law originally took the

---

1. Morissette v. United States, 342 U.S. 246, 250 (1952).

simplistic view that a person either had *mens rea* or did not. Virtually any sort of moral blameworthiness sufficed.

Modern criminal law recognizes a range of possible mental states that correlate with different degrees of blameworthiness, shadings of grey rather than black or white. It views mental state as analogous to a radio's volume control rather than its power switch. As one moves up the hierarchy of mental states from negligence to purpose, for example, blame increases, just as the sound coming from a radio increases as one moves the volume control from left to right.

Despite this modern view, the failure to recognize the fact that mental state can take a variety of forms with varying degrees of blameworthiness and the failure to distinguish clearly among those mental states has been and continues to be a common problem in the criminal law's treatment of mental state.

b. Multiple Mental States

Criminal statutes may and often do require more than one mental state for conviction. The New York burglary statute at the outset of this chapter is an example. It requires both *knowledge* about entering or remaining in a building and *intent* to commit a crime.

As such statutes implicitly recognize, a person is capable of simultaneously having more than one mental state. Take, for example, someone transporting stolen archaeological artifacts into the United States. One mental state the person may possess is *purpose* to transport the objects at issue, the objective of moving them from one place to another. At the same time, the person may have a second mental state, *knowledge* that the objects are archaeological artifacts. While having such purpose and knowledge, the person may at the same time have a third mental state, *recklessness* regarding the fact that the artifacts are stolen. A person might have all three of these mental states at the same time or lack one or more of them.

Failure to distinguish clearly among multiple mental states required by a statute for conviction and among multiple mental states possessed by a particular defendant has also been and continues to be a common problem in the criminal law's treatment of mental state.

c. Mental State Is Relational

A third critical aspect of mental state is that it is relational, an idea we encountered in studying proportionality. Suppose someone asked you, "Do you belong?" You would be unable to respond unless the questioner provided a reference point by answering a second question, "to what?" Your answers to the first question would vary with the reference point — for example, your family, the Sierra Club, your law school class, the mafia.

The same is true with mental state. If we were to ask, "What was the mental state of the defendant?" in our stolen artifacts hypothetical, it would be impossible to answer the question clearly without specifying the reference point for the mental state — the act of transporting the artifacts, their status as artifacts, or their status as stolen. The defendant may have purpose to transport the objects but not realize that they are artifacts or that they are stolen. Or he might know they are artifacts but not know they are stolen. That a crime may require and a criminal may possess more than one mental state make it critical to specify to what the mental state pertains in order to avoid confusion. Unfortunately, legislators, judges, and criminal lawyers often fail to specify mental state in dealing with mental state issues.

Criminal law's treatment of mental state has evolved from rudimentary to relatively sophisticated by recognizing (1) that mental state is a question of degree, (2) that crimes and criminals can have more than one mental state, and (3) that mental state is relational. The level of sophistication and clarity in dealing with these topics, though, still varies greatly from one legislature, judge, and lawyer to the next.

3. The Vocabulary of Mental States

The criminal law's traditional treatment of mental state resulted in widespread confusion and discontent. Consider, for example, the following passage from a 1977 Senate report proposing reform of the federal criminal law's handling of mental state:

> Present Federal criminal law is composed of a bewildering array of terms used to describe the mental element of an offense. The National Commission's consultant on this subject identified 78 different terms used in present law. These range from the traditional "knowingly," "willfully," and "maliciously," to the redundant "willful, deliberate, malicious, and premeditated," to the conclusory "unlawfully," "improperly," and "feloniously," to the self-contradictory "wilfully neglects." No Federal statute attempts a comprehensive and precise definition of the terms used to describe the requisite state of mind. Nor are the terms defined in the statutes in which they are used. Instead the task of giving substance to the "mental element" used in a particular statute has been left to the courts.[2]

This report identifies two problems in the treatment of *mens rea*. One is the sheer number and variety of mental state terms. The second is the fact that these terms are either poorly defined or not defined at all. The lack of clarity in the language of mental state reflected an underlying conceptual failure to divide mental states into separate categories. In other words, lack of clarity in *speaking* about mental state often reflected a more basic problem of lack of precision in *thinking* about mental state.

a. Model Penal Code Terminology

The Model Penal Code exemplifies a more recent stage in the evolution of the criminal law's treatment of mental states. The Model Penal Code seeks to remedy the vocabulary problems described in the report quoted above by using four primary mental states — purpose, knowledge, recklessness, and negligence — and attempting to define each with precision. It recognizes that a person may simultaneously entertain more than one mental state and that the definition of a crime often entails use of multiple mental states. It also insists on specifying what the mental state pertains to and analyzing mental state separately for each non-mental element of an offense.

The Model Penal Code defines these four mental states in section 2.02. The following Comment to that section explains the drafters' goals.

---

2. Criminal Code Reform Act of 1977, S. Rep. No. 605, 95th Cong., 1st Sess. at 55 (1977).

Model Penal Code § 2.02   *General Requirements of Culpability*

Comment

[This] section . . . attempts the extremely difficult task of articulating the kinds of culpability that may be required for the establishment of liability. It delineates four levels of culpability: purpose, knowledge, recklessness and negligence. It requires that one of these levels of culpability must be proved with respect to each "material element" of the offense, which may involve (1) the nature of the forbidden conduct, (2) the attendant circumstances, or (3) the result of conduct. The question of which level of culpability suffices to establish liability must be addressed separately with respect to each material element, and will be resolved either by the particular definition of the offense or the general provisions of this Section.

The purpose of articulating these distinctions in detail is to advance the clarity of draftsmanship in the delineation of the definitions of specific crimes, to provide a distinct framework against which those definitions may be tested, and to dispel the obscurity with which the culpability requirement is often treated when such concepts as "general criminal intent," "*mens rea*," "presumed intent," "malice," "wilfulness," "scienter," and the like have been employed. What Justice Jackson called "the variety, disparity and confusion" of judicial definitions of "the requisite but elusive mental element" in crime should, insofar as possible, be rationalized by a criminal code.

The Model Code's approach is based upon the view that clear analysis requires that the question of the kind of culpability required to establish the commission of an offense be faced separately with respect to each material element of the crime.

Under the Code, therefore, the problem of the kind of culpability that is required for conviction must be faced separately with respect to each material element of the offense, although the answer may in many cases be the same with respect to each element.

In contrast with the legislative approach before the Model Code, virtually all recent legislative revisions and proposals follow it in setting up general standards of culpability.

Examine the following Model Penal Code provisions to see how they define "purpose," "knowledge," "recklessness," and "negligence."

Model Penal Code § 2.02   *General Requirements of Culpability*

(2) Kinds of Culpability Defined.
   (a) Purposely.
   A person acts purposely with respect to a material element of an offense when:
         (i) if the element involves the nature of his conduct or a result thereof, it is his conscious object to engage in conduct of that nature, or to cause such result; and
         (ii) if the element involves the attendant circumstances, he is aware of the existence of such circumstances or he believes or hopes that they exist.
   (b) Knowingly.
   A person acts knowingly with respect to a material element of an offense when:
         (i) if the element involves the nature of his conduct or the attendant circumstances, he is aware that his conduct is of that nature or that such circumstances exist; and
         (ii) if the element involves a result of his conduct, he is aware that it is practically certain that his conduct will cause such a result.

Comment

Purpose and Knowledge. In defining the kinds of culpability, the Code draws a narrow distinction between acting purposely and knowingly, one of the elements of ambiguity in legal usage of the term "intent." Knowledge that the requisite external circumstances exist is a common element in both conceptions. But action is not purposive with respect to the nature or result of the actor's conduct unless it was his conscious object to perform an action of that nature or to cause such a result. It is meaningful to think of the actor's attitude as different if he is simply aware that his conduct is of the required nature or that the prohibited result is practically certain to follow from his conduct. . . .

Most recent legislative revisions and proposals have adopted, though with varying terminology, the Model Code's distinction between purpose and knowledge. They, like the Code, have made these levels of culpability depend on the actual state of mind of the actor rather than on what a reasonable man in the circumstances would have contemplated.

(c) Recklessly.

A person acts recklessly with respect to a material element of an offense when he consciously disregards a substantial and unjustifiable risk that the material element exists or will result from his conduct. The risk must be of such a nature and degree that, considering the nature and purpose of the actor's conduct and the circumstances known to him, its disregard involves a gross deviation from the standard of conduct that a law-abiding person would observe in the actor's situation.

Comment

Recklessness. An important discrimination is drawn between acting either purposely or knowingly and acting recklessly. As the Code uses the term, recklessness involves conscious risk creation. It resembles acting knowingly in that a state of awareness is involved, but the awareness is of risk, that is of a probability less than substantial certainty; the matter is contingent from the actor's point of view. Whether the risk relates to the nature of the actor's conduct, or to the existence of the requisite attendant circumstances, or to the result that may ensue, is immaterial; the concept is the same, and is thus defined to apply to any material element.

The risk of which the actor is aware must of course be substantial in order for the recklessness judgment to be made. The risk must also be unjustifiable. Even substantial risks, it is clear, may be created without recklessness when the actor is seeking to serve a proper purpose, as when a surgeon performs an operation that he knows is very likely to be fatal but reasonably thinks to be necessary because the patient has no other, safer chance. Some principle must, therefore, be articulated to indicate the nature of the final judgment to be made after everything has been weighed. Describing the risk as "substantial" and "unjustifiable" is useful but not sufficient, for these are terms of degree, and the acceptability of a risk in a given case depends on a great many variables. Some standard is needed for determining *how* substantial and *how* unjustifiable the risk must be in order to warrant a finding of culpability. There is no way to state this value judgment that does not beg the question in the last analysis; the point is that the jury must evaluate the actor's conduct and determine whether it should be condemned. The Code proposes, therefore, that this difficulty be accepted frankly, and that the jury be asked to measure the substantiality and unjustifiability of the risk by asking whether its disregard, given the actor's perceptions, involved a gross deviation from the standard of conduct that a law-abiding person in the actor's situation would observe.

Ultimately, then, the jury is asked to perform two distinct functions. First, it is to examine the risk and the factors that are relevant to how substantial it was and to the justifications for taking it. In each instance, the question is asked from the point of view of the actor's perceptions, i.e., to what extent he was aware of risk, of factors relating to its substantiality and of factors relating to its unjustifiability. Second, the jury is to make the culpability judgment in terms of whether the defendant's conscious disregard of the risk justifies condemnation. Considering the nature and purpose of his conduct and the circumstances known to him, the question is whether the defendant's disregard of the risk involved a gross deviation from the standards of conduct that a law-abiding person would have observed in the actor's situation. . . .

Most recent undertakings to revise criminal codes have substantially accepted the Model Code's formulation of recklessness.

(d) Negligently.

A person acts negligently with respect to a material element of an offense when he should be aware of a substantial and unjustifiable risk that the material element exists or will result from this conduct. The risk must be of such a nature and degree that the actor's failure to perceive it, considering the nature and purpose of his conduct and the circumstances known to him, involves a gross deviation from the standard of care that a reasonable person would observe in the actor's situation.

Comment

Negligence. The fourth kind of culpability is negligence. It is distinguished from purposeful, knowing or reckless action in that it does not involve a state of awareness. A person acts negligently under this subsection when he inadvertently creates a substantial and unjustifiable risk of which he ought to be aware. . . . As in the case of recklessness, both the substantiality of the risk and the elements of justification in the situation form the relevant standards of judgment. And again it is quite impossible to avoid tautological articulation of the final question. The tribunal must evaluate the actor's failure of perception and determine whether, under all the circumstances, it was serious enough to be condemned. The jury must find fault, and must find that it was substantial and unjustified; that is the heart of what can be said in legislative terms.

As with recklessness, the jury is asked to perform two distinct functions. First, it is to examine the risk and the factors that are relevant to its substantiality and justifiability. In the case of negligence, these questions are asked not in terms of what the actor's perceptions actually were, but in terms of an objective view of the situation as it actually existed. Second, the jury is to make the culpability judgment, this time in terms of whether the failure of the defendant to perceive the risk justifies condemnation. Considering the nature and purpose of his conduct and the circumstances known to him, the question is whether the defendant's failure to perceive a risk involves a gross deviation from the standard of care that a reasonable person would observe in the actor's situation.

Formulation of the standard in these terms is believed to be a substantial improvement over the traditional approach to defining negligence for purposes of criminal liability. Much of this confusion is dispelled by a clear-cut distinction between recklessness and negligence in terms of the actor's awareness of the risk involved. Clarity is also promoted by formulating the inquiry in terms of the specific factors to which attention is directed in the Model Code.

A further point in the Code's concept of negligence merits attention. The standard for ultimate judgment invites consideration of the "care that a reasonable person would observe in the actor's situation." There is an inevitable ambiguity in "situation." If the actor were blind or if he had just suffered a blow or experienced a heart attack, these would certainly be facts to be considered in a judgment involving criminal liability, as they would be under traditional law. But the heredity, intelligence or temperament of the actor would not be held material in judging negligence, and could not be without depriving the criterion of all its objectivity. The Code is not intended to displace discriminations of this kind, but rather to leave the issue to the courts.

No one has doubted that purpose, knowledge, and recklessness are properly the basis for criminal liability, but some critics have opposed any penal consequences for negligent behavior. Since the actor is inadvertent by hypothesis, it has been argued that the "threat of punishment for negligence must pass him by, because he does not realise that it is addressed to him." So too, it has been urged that education or corrective treatment, not punishment, is the proper social method for dealing with persons with inadequate awareness, since what is implied is not a moral defect. This analysis, however, oversimplifies the issue. When people have knowledge that conviction and sentence, not to speak of punishment, may follow conduct that inadvertently creates improper risk, they are supplied with an additional motive to take care before acting, to use their faculties and draw on their experience in gauging the potentialities of contemplated conduct. To some extent, at least, this motive may promote awareness and thus be effective as a measure of control. Moreover, moral defect can properly be imputed to instances where the defendant acts out of insensitivity to the interests of other people, and not merely out of an intellectual failure to grasp them. In any event legislators act on these assumptions in a host of situations, and it would be dogmatic to assert that they are wholly wrong. Accordingly, negligence, as here defined, should not be wholly rejected as a ground of culpability that may suffice for purposes of penal law, though it should properly not generally be deemed sufficient in the definition of specific crimes and it should often be differentiated from conduct involving higher culpability for the purposes of sentence. . . .

Most recent legislative revisions and proposals have adopted definitions of negligence similar to that of the Model Code.

(5) Substitutes for Negligence, Recklessness and Knowledge. When the law provides that negligence suffices to establish an element of an offense, such element also is established if a person acts purposely or knowingly, or recklessly. When recklessness suffices to establish an element, such element also is established if a person acts purposefully or knowingly. When acting knowingly suffices to establish an element, such element also is established if a person acts purposely.

QUESTIONS

1. What distinguishes each Model Penal Code mental state from the others?

2. Jerome Hall has referred to the phrase "wilful, wanton negligence" as "the apex of [judicial] infelicity" in defining "mental state" and described it as suggesting "a triple contradiction."[3] What is the triple contradiction in the phrase?

3. Does the Model Penal Code satisfactorily define each mental state? Do these definitions delegate any lawmaking to judges? To jurors? If so, how are they consistent with the idea of legislative supremacy in criminal lawmaking that we studied in Chapter 3?

4. The Model Penal Code Comment on negligence states:

If the actor were blind or if he had just suffered a blow or experienced a heart attack, these would certainly be facts to be considered in a judgment involving criminal liability, as they would be under traditional law. But the heredity, intelligence or temperament

---

3. Jerome Hall, General Principles of the Criminal Law 124 (2d ed. 1960).

of the actor would not be held material in judging negligence, and could not be without depriving the criterion of all its objectivity.

Why are the facts listed in the first sentence of this quotation relevant to criminal liability? Why are the facts listed in the second sentence irrelevant?

5. Should criminal liability be imposed based on negligence? What are the arguments for and against such liability? How do those arguments relate to the purposes of punishment we studied in Chapter 2?

PROBLEMS

5.1 Late one evening from the window of his apartment several stories above the street, Dino observes two men beating a third man on the sidewalk. One of the assailants is kicking the victim and the other is beating him about the head with a pipe. The victim screams for help and pleads with the men not to hurt or kill him. Dino fetches his 25 caliber automatic handgun but by the time he returns to the window the beating has stopped. The victim is standing on the sidewalk and the former assailants are walking away. Dino yells at the men to halt. When they begin to run, despite seeing other people on the street near the men, Dino fires several "warning shots" to frighten the men as they flee. One of Dino's bullets nearly strikes an innocent passerby. What is Dino's mental state regarding injury to the passerby?

5.2 Lorna is having an affair with Jerome. Together they plan to kill Lorna's husband to remove him as an obstacle to their relationship and to collect on a $1 million insurance policy. One evening shortly thereafter, Lorna and her husband are returning by car to their house. Lorna is behind the wheel. When they arrive home, her husband gets out and walks in front of the car to open the garage door. When he does so, Lorna hits the gas, running over him and killing him. What is Lorna's mental state regarding the death of her husband?

5.3 Rich is a member of a radical animal rights group. Karen, another member of the group, is incarcerated in the county jail awaiting trial on charges of having broken into a research lab at a local university and freed a number of research animals. Rich decides to spring Karen from jail. To do so he plans to use a powerful explosive to dismantle the main door to the jail. Rich is experienced in the use of explosives from his days working in the mining industry. He calculates that the explosive will do great damage to anything within 50 feet of the door, but he knows that Karen's cell is several hundred feet away from the door, far enough away so that the explosive will not injure her. Rich plants the explosive charge and as he does so he observes that a deputy sheriff is sitting just inside the door. Although Rich would prefer not to hurt the deputy, he nonetheless sets off the charge, killing the deputy, and then frees Karen. What is Rich's mental state regarding the death of the deputy?

5.4 Kathleen is a research doctor conducting a cancer study on human volunteer subjects. The information obtained from the study could save thousands of lives, but Kathleen is informed that there is a 10 percent chance that one or more of the subjects could die. Kathleen conducts the study, during which one of the subjects does in fact die. What is Kathleen's mental state regarding the subject's death?

5.5 Terry is an electrician and owner of an electrical supply company. He is certified as an electrical inspector by the state and works in that capacity for several towns near the town in which he lives. One day Terry installs some electric heaters in the basement of an elderly neighbor's house in return for $1,200. Shortly afterward, a fire breaks out in the basement of the neighbor's house and one of the neighbor's grandchildren dies in the fire. The local fire marshal testifies that the heaters Terry installed caused the fire. He also testifies that Terry's installation of the heaters resulted in numerous violations of the electrical code. One heater was installed directly beneath an outlet in violation of the manufacturer's instructions. The heater was also stamped as being a 120 volt unit but was wired to a 240 volt circuit. The heater was not properly grounded, and the heater's internal thermostat did not function properly. The fire marshal also testified that these violations were uncommon and that he had never witnessed so many violations at one site. Terry admits his electrical work for his neighbor violated the electrical code. But he testifies that these violations were only to save his neighbor money and that he believed his work on the house was safe. What was Terry's mental state regarding the death of his neighbor's grandchild?

5.6 Christine decides to end a troubled relationship with Randall, her boyfriend of several months. The day after informing Randall of her decision, Christine heads to work in her car. While driving to work, she notices Randall following her in his car. Christine tries to lose him by making several detours from her usual route. Randall runs several stop signs to keep up with Christine and drives his car within a few feet of the rear of her car while going over 40 miles per hour. Christine eventually loses sight of Randall, arrives at work, and starts to walk across the parking lot outside the building in which she works. As she does so, she see Randall's car speeding toward her across the parking lot and freezes. Randall continues toward her, honking his horn and swerving to avoid her by about two feet at the last minute. What is Randall's mental state regarding injury to Christine?

5.7 Make a list of the items of evidence you might offer as prosecutor to prove and as defense counsel to disprove mental state in each of the following:

(a) Purposeful destruction of property;
(b) Receiving money known to be stolen or embezzled;
(c) Reckless assault;
(d) Negligently discharging a harmful quantity of oil into a navigable water.

b. Traditional Terminology: Intent

Of all the words used to describe the mental component in crime, the one most frequently used is probably "intent." At times intent is used to mean purpose, which conforms to the meaning of "intent" in common usage. Some criminal codes, for example, explicitly define intent in this way:

Maine Criminal Code Chapter 15, § 352

"Intent to deprive" means to have the conscious object . . . [t]o withhold property permanently or for so extended a period or to use under such circumstances that a substantial portion of its economic value, or the use and benefit thereof, would be lost; . . .

Alabama Criminal Code § 13A-2-2

Intentionally. A person acts intentionally with respect to a result or to conduct described by a statute defining an offense, when his purpose is to cause that result or to engage in that conduct.

But judges often stretched the word "intent" and gave it other meanings at odds with its meaning in common usage, as in the following cases.

STATE *v.* ROUFA   241 La. 474, 476-477, 484-485, 487 (1961)

Maurice L. Roufa was charged by bill of information with a violation of LSA-R.S. 14:106(2), the Louisiana Obscenity Statute. . . . Paragraph Two of the Louisiana Obscenity Statute recites:

"Obscenity is the intentional . . . [p]roduction, sale, exhibition, possession with intention to display, exhibit, or sell, or the advertisement of, any obscene, lewd, lascivious, filthy, or sexually indecent print, picture, motion picture, written composition, model, instrument, contrivance or thing of whatsoever description."

. . . We conclude that the word "Intentional" and the phrase "With Intention" in the Louisiana Obscenity Statute mean that knowledge is implied where one has criminal intent. It leaps to the mind that knowledge is necessary to intention and that one cannot have intention without knowledge. . . . The actual obscenity of the publications allegedly intentionally possessed by the defendant will be a question of fact for the trial court's determination. The criminal intent or guilty knowledge of the defendant will also be a question of fact for the trial court's determination.

REGINA *v.* FAULKNOR   13 Cox Crim. Cases 550 (1877)

[T]o constitute an offense under the Malicious Injuries to Property Act, the act done must be in fact intentional and wilful, although the intention and will may (perhaps) be held to exist in, or be proved by, the fact that the accused knew that the injury would be the probable result of his unlawful act, and yet did the act reckless of such consequences.

WOODWARD v. STATE   144 So. 895, 896 (1932)

Intent is a necessary element of assault and battery. . . . 'An assault and battery is the unlawful touching of another by the aggressor himself or by any other substance put in motion by him.' An assault and battery may be committed with a motor vehicle by striking a person, or a vehicle in which he is riding, either intentionally or by driving so negligently as to constitute a reckless disregard of human life and safety. Of course, mere negligence would not impute an intent. If negligence be relied on, then it must amount to reckless, willful, and wanton disregard of the rights of others, in which state of case the intent is imputed to the accused.

STATE v. CLARDY   73 S.C. 340, 358 (1905)

The Court charged that "a criminal intent is attributed to a person who even does a grossly careless act," which in light of the undisputed facts, meant, that "a criminal intent is attributed to a person who kills another with a deadly weapon from gross carelessness," but the jury were left to determine whether such act was done with gross carelessness. So the language of the charge, "the law presumes that he intended to do what he actually did do," in the light of the facts, simply means, "the law, in the case of a homicide with a deadly weapon under circumstances showing gross carelessness, presumes that he intended to do what he actually did do." . . . The Circuit Judge, recognizing the rule that there must be a criminal intent for every common law crime, and having previously clearly stated the law concerning murder and voluntary manslaughter, was submitting to the jury the law as to voluntary manslaughter, in which gross negligence supplies the place of criminal intent.

Model Penal Code § 2.02   *General Requirements of Culpability*

Comment

The Model Code's approach to purpose and knowledge is in fundamental disagreement with the position of the House of Lords in *Director of Public Prosecutions v. Smith.* That case effectively equated "intent to inflict grievous bodily harm" with what the defendant as a reasonable man must be taken to have contemplated, thus erecting an objective instead of a subjective inquiry to determine what the defendant "intended." In the Code's formulation, both "purposely" and "knowingly," as well as "recklessly," are meant to ask what, in fact, the defendant's mental attitude was. It was believed to be unjust to measure liability for serious criminal offenses on the basis of what the defendant should have believed or what most people would have intended.

Legislators have also given the word "intent" many meanings, as in the following Kansas statute.

Kansas Criminal Code Annotated § 21-3201   *Criminal Intent*

(a) Except as otherwise provided, a criminal intent is an essential element of every crime defined by this code. Criminal intent may be established by proof that the conduct of the accused person was intentional or reckless. Proof of intentional conduct shall be required to establish criminal intent, unless the statute defining the crime expressly provides that the prohibited act is criminal if done in a reckless manner.

(b) Intentional conduct is conduct that is purposeful and willful and not accidental. As used in this code, the terms "knowing," "willful," "purposeful," and "on purpose" are included within the term "intentional."

(c) Reckless conduct is conduct done under circumstances that show a realization of the imminence of danger to the person of another and a conscious and unjustifiable disregard of that danger. The terms "gross negligence," "culpable negligence," "wanton negligence" and "wantonness" are included within the term "recklessness" as used in this code.

QUESTIONS

1. Which Model Penal Code mental state is closest to the definition of "intent" given in each of the above cases and statutes?

2. Why do you think those who drafted the Model Penal Code chose not to use intent as one of its mental states?

3. The *Roufa* case states that "one cannot have intention without knowledge." Is this true?

4. What does it mean in *Woodward* and *Clardy* to impute, attribute, or presume intent?

As treatment of mental states evolved, a classification scheme still used today in many states emerged that is sometimes referred to as "offense analysis."[4] Common law judges developed two categories — "specific intent" and "general intent" crimes — as means for dealing in part with cases of intoxication and mistake. Section I deals with this terminology in detail. Here we briefly describe that scheme to help you understand its place in the evolution of the criminal law's treatment of mental states.

Offense analysis divides crimes into those of "specific intent" and "general intent" as well as implicitly recognizing a third residual category of strict liability crimes. This classification system represents an advance over prior treatment of *mens rea* in that it recognizes the existence of two different types of mental state. But it commonly fails to recognize that a single offense may entail more than one mental state, and, with general intent offenses, often fails to specify to what the intent pertains. This classification scheme also often fails to effectively define either specific intent or general intent or to provide clear criteria for distinguishing between them.

---

4. *See* Paul A. Robinson & Jane A. Grall, *Element Analysis in Defining Criminal Liability: The Model Penal Code and Beyond*, 35 Stan. L. Rev. 681 (1983).

The definition of these terms varies from jurisdiction to jurisdiction and can even vary from case to case, resulting in much confusion and dissatisfaction. Despite this confusion, one particular type of crime is consistently classified as a specific intent offense — one that requires intent regarding something not included in the non-mental elements of the offense. Assume, for example, burglary is breaking and entering the dwelling of another *with intent to commit a felony therein.* In offense analysis, the italicized intent is referred to as a "specific intent."

In contrast to offense analysis, the Model Penal Code breaks crimes down into elements and examines mental state separately for each element. This approach is sometimes called "element analysis."[5]

4. The "Other Minds" Question

"The sphygmograph records with graphic certainty the fluctuations of the pulse. There is no instrument yet invented that records with equal certainty the fluctuations of the mind." — *People v. Zackowitz,* 254 N.Y. 192, 195 (1930) (Cardozo, J.).

How can we discover the internal mental state of another person? Can we determine whether or not someone acts with *purpose* to kill? Whether someone crossing a border *knows* that a package contains an illegal narcotic? Whether a gun dealer *knows* that the person he sells a firearm to is a minor? Whether a parent is *aware* of the risk that striking a small child with a fist might kill the child? How does a prosecutor months or years after the fact manage to prove such mental states beyond a reasonable doubt? How can we expect juries to resolve such issues? Philosophers refer to this as the "other minds" problem — the difficulty in determining what is going on inside the mind of another.[6]

The law of evidence recognizes two types of evidence — direct and circumstantial. Direct evidence is evidence that if believed establishes the point it is offered to prove without the necessity of drawing any inferences. Circumstantial evidence, by contrast, requires the use of one or more inferences to prove the point. Imagine you wish to prove to a jury that it snowed between midnight and sunrise on a particular day. First, you call a witness who was awake and outside at 2 A.M. on the date in question, and she testifies that she saw and felt the snow coming down. Second, you call a witness who testifies that the ground and streets around his house were completely dry and without a trace of snow when he went to bed at midnight but that he saw and drove through a foot of snow at sunrise the next day as he went to work. The first witness provides direct evidence. If believed, her testimony establishes your point without the jury having to draw any inferences. The second witness provides circumstantial evidence. In order to conclude that it snowed between midnight and sunrise, the jury must draw an inference: if there was no snow on the ground at midnight and a foot of snow on the ground at sunrise, then it must have snowed between midnight and sunrise.

Circumstantial evidence is often referred to as if it is necessarily weaker than direct evidence, but this is not so. Direct evidence may be weak or strong depending on the particular witness. Qualities such as a witness's sincerity and capacity to

---

5. *Id.*
6. *See* Rebecca Dresser, *Culpability and Other Minds,* 2 Law and: 41 (1992).

accurately perceive, remember, and recount events about which the witness testifies vary from witness to witness. And circumstantial evidence may be weak or strong depending on the strength of the inferences it supports.

Prosecutors and defense lawyers draw on both sorts of evidence in criminal cases in general and to prove or disprove subjective mental states in particular. At times, the prosecutor will have access to direct evidence. The defendant may have made a statement of his mental state to another person, such as the victim. The statement may have been recorded by an undercover informant or a court-authorized telephone wiretap or heard by an accomplice who agrees to cooperate and testify for the government. The defendant may have made a confession after the crime, including a statement of her mental state at the time of the offense. The defense may also rely on direct evidence, such as the defendant taking the stand and testifying that he did not have the requisite mental state.

Both sides also typically rely heavily on circumstantial evidence to establish a required internal mental state or lack thereof. In a homicide case, for example, the use of a deadly weapon pointed at a vital part of the victim's body such as the head, neck, or heart, the firing of multiple shots, or the presence of a motive such as revenge or financial gain would help a prosecutor prove purpose to kill.

The use of evidence that a reasonable person *would have known* something or *would have been aware* of a risk in a particular situation as circumstantial evidence that a defendant *actually knew* something or *actually realized* a risk is often the source of confusion between the objective standard of negligence and internal mental states such as knowledge or awareness of risk. For example, if the minor who purchased a gun from a gun dealer was so small in stature and young in appearance that a reasonable person would have concluded he was underage, then the jury may infer that the defendant actually was aware that the purchaser was underage. If all that was required regarding the purchaser's age was simple negligence, the jury would not need to draw any inference. But if knowledge regarding age is required to convict, the jury must take an additional inferential step from what *a reasonable person would have known* to what *the defendant actually did know* about the purchaser's being underage. If the jury refuses to take that step, perhaps concluding that the defendant is not as perceptive or intelligent as a reasonable person or simply believing the defendant's testimony that he did not know, they should acquit.

B. STRICT LIABILITY

According to Justice Jackson, crime is "a compound concept, *generally* constituted only from concurrence of an evil-meaning mind with an evil-doing hand." (Emphasis added). But there exists a category of crimes that require no evil-meaning mind, no mental state, as the following statute reveals:

Colorado Revised Statutes § 18-1-502   *Requirements for criminal liability in general and for offenses of strict liability and of mental culpability*

The minimum requirement for criminal liability is the performance by a person of conduct which includes a voluntary act or the omission to perform an act which he is physically capable of performing. If that conduct is all that is required for commission of a particular offense, or if an offense or some material element thereof does not require a culpable mental state on the part of the actor, the offense is one of "strict liability." If a culpable mental state on the part of the actor is required with respect to any material element of an offense, the offense is one of "mental culpability."

Strict liability is sometimes referred to as absolute liability. The statutory definitions of strict liability crimes often read like their civil counterparts in torts and lack any mental state terminology. If one does an act and any remaining non-mental elements are fulfilled, one is liable. We start this Section with the *Balint* case, one of the earliest Supreme Court analyses of strict liability crimes.

UNITED STATES *v.* BALINT
258 U.S. 250 (1922)

TAFT., C.J. Defendants were indicted for a violation of the Narcotic Act of December 17, 1914. The indictment charged them with unlawfully selling to another a certain amount of a derivative of opium and a certain amount of a derivative of coca leaves, not in pursuance of any written order on a form issued in blank for that purpose by the Commissioner of Internal Revenue, contrary to provisions of § 2 of the act. The defendants demurred to the indictment on the ground that it failed to charge that they had sold the inhibited drugs knowing them to be such. The statute does not make such knowledge an element of the offense. The District Court sustained the demurrer and quashed the indictment. The correctness of this ruling is the question before us.

While the general rule at common law was that the scienter was a necessary element in the indictment and proof of every crime, and this was followed in regard to statutory crimes even where the statutory definition did not in terms include it there has been a modification of this view in respect to prosecutions under statutes the purpose of which would be obstructed by such a requirement. It is a question of legislative intent to be construed by the court. It has been objected that punishment of a person for an act in violation of law when ignorant of the facts making it so, is an absence of due process of law. But that objection was considered and overruled in *Shevlin-Carpenter*, in which it was held that in the prohibition or punishment of particular acts, the State may in the maintenance of a public policy provide "that he who shall do them shall do them at his peril and will not be heard to plead in defense good faith or ignorance." Many instances of this are to be found in regulatory measures in the exercise of what is called the police power where the emphasis of the statute is evidently upon achievement of some social betterment rather than the punishment of the crimes as in cases of mala in se. So, too, in the collection of taxes, the importance to the public of their collection leads the legislature to impose on the taxpayer the burden of finding out the facts upon which his liability to pay depends and meeting it at the peril of punishment. Again where one deals with others and his mere negligence may be dangerous to them, as in selling diseased food or poison, the policy of the law may, in order to stimulate proper care, require the punishment of the negligent person though he be ignorant of the noxious character of what he sells.

The question before us, therefore, is one of the construction of the statute and of inference of the intent of Congress. The Narcotic Act has been held by this court to be a taxing act with the incidental purpose of minimizing the spread of addiction to the use of poisonous and demoralizing drugs.

Section 2 of the Narcotic Act [reads:]

> Part of § 2 of an act entitled An Act To Provide for the registration of, with collectors of internal revenue, and to impose a special tax upon all persons who produce, import, manufacture, compound, deal in, dispense, sell, distribute, or give away opium or coca leaves, their salts, derivatives, or preparations, and for other purposes.
>
> Sec. 2. That it shall be unlawful for any person to sell, barter, exchange, or give away any of the aforesaid drugs except in pursuance of a written order of the person to whom such article is sold, bartered or exchanged, or given, on a form to be issued in blank for that purpose by the Commissioner of Internal Revenue.

It is very evident from a reading of it that the emphasis of the section is in securing a close supervision of the business of dealing in these dangerous drugs by the taxing officers of the Government and that it merely uses a criminal penalty to secure recorded evidence of the disposition of such drugs as a means of taxing and restraining the traffic. Its manifest purpose is to require every person dealing in drugs to ascertain at his peril whether that which he sells comes within the inhibition of the statute, and if he sells the inhibited drug in ignorance of its character, to penalize him. Congress weighed the possible injustice of subjecting an innocent seller to a penalty against the evil of exposing innocent purchasers to danger from the drug, and concluded that the latter was the result preferably to be avoided. Doubtless considerations as to the opportunity of the seller to find out the fact and the difficulty of proof of knowledge contributed to this conclusion. We think the demurrer to the indictment should have been overruled.

QUESTIONS

1. Why don't we have many of the the facts concerning Balint's alleged commission of the charged offense in this opinion? What role does a demurrer serve?

2. What are the non-mental elements required for violation of Section 2 of the Narcotic Act? Balint's mental state about which of these non-mental elements is at issue?

3. Chief Justice Taft uses the word "scienter" in his opinion. Like the noun "science" ("a systematically organized body of knowledge on a particular subject"),[7] scienter derives from a latin verb meaning to know. "Scienter" literally means "knowingly." What meaning does the context suggest Chief Justice Taft gives to "scienter"? You may remember that Justice Thomas also used the word "scienter" in his opinion in *Hendricks*, where he took the lack of a scienter requirement in the Kansas Sexually Violent Predator Act as indicating a lack of intent on the part of the Kansas legislature to punish those falling under that act. What does the context suggest Justice Thomas meant by "scienter" in *Hendricks*?

4. Chief Justice Taft states: "It is a question of legislative intent to be construed by the court." What is the "it" to which this statement refers?

---

7. The New Oxford American Dictionary 1526 (2001).

5. The phrase "at his peril" is often used especially by courts to describe strict liability. What does the phrase mean? Try writing a sentence that clearly and completely expresses the thinking behind this phrase.

6. The *Balint* opinion indicates that strict liability is sometimes objected to as "an absence of due process of law ." What connection is there between the presence or absence of a mental state and due process? Remember that the Minnesota Supreme Court in *Guminga* found vicarious liability a violation of due process. What parallels are there between strict liability and vicarious liability?

7. Was the purpose of Congress to impose strict liability in Section 2 of the Narcotic Act "manifest"—that is, "clear or obvious to the eye or mind?"[8] If so, what is it about the statute that makes this legislative purpose easy to understand?

8. How do the rationales for strict liability examined in *Balint* relate to the purposes of punishment? Are they retributive? Utilitarian?

In contrast to *Balint*, the Model Penal Code rejects the use of strict liability in crimes, as reflected in the following provisions.

Model Penal Code § 2.02(1)   *Minimum Requirements of Culpability.*

Except as provided in Section 2.05, a person is not guilty of an offense unless he acted purposely, knowingly, recklessly or negligently, as the law may require, with respect to each material element of the offense. . . .

Comment

Objective. This section expresses the Code's basic requirement that unless some element of mental culpability is proved with respect to each material element of the offense, no valid criminal conviction may be obtained. This requirement is subordinated only to the provision of Section 2.05 for a narrow class of strict liability offenses that are limited to those for which no severer sentence than a fine may be imposed.

Model Penal Code § 2.05   *When Culpability Requirements Are Inapplicable to Violations and to Offenses Defined by Other Statutes; Effect of Absolute Liability in Reducing Grade of Offense to Violation*

(1) The requirements of culpability prescribed by Sections 2.01 and 2.02 do not apply to:

(a) offenses that constitute violations, unless the requirement involved is included in the definition of the offense or the Court determines that its application is consistent with effective enforcement of the law defining the offense; or

(b) offenses defined by statutes other than the Code, insofar as a legislative purpose to impose absolute liability for such offenses or with respect to any material element thereof plainly appears.

(2) Notwithstanding any other provision of existing law and unless a subsequent statute otherwise provides:

(a) when absolute liability is imposed with respect to any material element of an offense defined by a statute other than the Code and a conviction is based upon such liability, the offense constitutes a violation; and

---

8. *Id.* at 1039.

(b) although absolute liability is imposed by law with respect to one or more of the material elements of an offense defined by a statute other than the Code, the culpable commission of the offense may be charged and proved, in which event negligence with respect to such elements constitutes sufficient culpability and the classification of the offense and the sentence that may be imposed therefor upon conviction are determined by Section 1.04 and Article 6 of the Code.

The Strict Liability Debate

Should mental state be eliminated in certain criminal offenses? This question is the source of considerable debate. The arguments in favor of strict liability are primarily utilitarian. Proponents claim that strict liability makes enforcement easier, cheaper, and more effective, protects society by increasing deterrence, and addresses special needs in the area of regulatory or public welfare crimes. Critics advance both retributive and utilitarian arguments to attack strict liability.

Eliminating mental state does make enforcement easier and cheaper. Requiring the prosecution to prove fewer elements means the government needs to invest fewer resources investigating, preparing, and trying cases. Echoing the "other minds" problem, the argument can be made that internal mental state is hard to investigate and prove, particularly in regulatory crimes. Such proof problems give defendants opportunities to falsely claim lack of any culpable mental state.

Those in favor of strict liability often argue that it increases the deterrent effect of a criminal prohibition compared with a similar prohibition requiring proof of mental state. The thinking here is that jettisoning mental state increases certainty of conviction, in turn increasing deterrence. As deterrence increases, harm to society from the criminal behavior should correspondingly decrease.

Special need in the area of regulatory crimes is also frequently invoked in defense of strict liability. As the Supreme Court stated in *United States v. Morissette,*

> The industrial revolution multiplied the number of workmen exposed to injury from increasingly powerful and complex mechanisms, driven by freshly discovered sources of energy, requiring higher precautions by employers. Traffic of velocities, volumes and varieties unheard of came to subject the wayfarer to intolerable casualty risks if owners and drivers were not to observe new cares and uniformities of conduct. Congestion of cities and crowding of quarters called for health and welfare regulations undreamed of in simpler times. Wide distribution of goods became an instrument of wide distribution of harm when those who dispersed food, drink, drugs, and even securities, did not comply with reasonable standards of quality and integrity, disclosure and care. Such dangers have engendered increasingly numerous and detailed regulations which heighten the duties of those in control of particular industries, trades, properties or activities that affect public health, safety or welfare.

Strict liability can be criticized by drawing on the retributive limiting principle we encountered at the outset of the course — that there should be no criminal punishment without blame and that there is no blame without a culpable mental state. Critics of strict liability also counter the utilitarian argument for increased deterrence by pointing out the lack of empirical support for the claimed increase in deterrence. Dissociating criminal punishment from blame may also breed disrespect for and cynicism toward the criminal law among the group one seeks to deter and among the public in general. Such disrespect and cynicism might well decrease deterrence. They also might increase jury nullification, resulting in less certainty of conviction and thus undermining deterrence.

The assumption underlying the deterrence argument is that those in a regulated area will respond to the imposition of strict liability by expending extra effort to adhere to the law. But a utilitarian argument against strict liability challenges this assumption. It asserts that strict liability deters more than we want it to by discouraging not only criminal conduct but also socially desirable conduct.[9] Imposing strict liability on food distributors, for example, for selling contaminated food in addition to deterring sale of contaminated food may also drive people out of the food distribution business. Such over-deterrence may produce the unintended consequence of increasing the very harm it seeks to prevent. If strict liability does in fact drive some people to abandon entirely the regulated activity on which strict liability is imposed, who will choose to leave? One possibility is that careful business people will decide to abandon the activity since they are exposed to liability even if they act without culpability. Who then is likely to remain? The careless — those who are poor risk calculators and non-calculators — may disproportionately choose to stay in the field. If the careful leave and the careless remain, the harm the strict liability measure seeks to avoid may well increase.[10]

In response to the retributive argument against strict liability as imposing punishment without blame, a strict liability proponent might argue that the punishments imposed in strict liability offenses are typically small, usually limited to fines, so lack of blame is not critical. A critic might counter that if the punishments are limited to monetary fines, then civil enforcement is a more appropriate route to imposition of a monetary penalty. Imposition of a civil penalty is also more certain than imposition of a criminal sanction because the civil system has a lower burden of proof than the criminal system and poses fewer barriers to enforcement. Civil liability, for example, unlike criminal liability, gives rise to no constitutional privilege against self-incrimination. Thus the threat of a civil monetary penalty may be a more certain and thus a more effective deterrent than a criminal fine.

The strict liability advocate may also argue that just because mental state and blame are not required to be proven as an element of the offense does not mean convicted defendants are necessarily blameless. The criminal justice system might choose to rely on the police and prosecutors to exercise their discretion to prosecute only cases in which they are convinced there is blame, even if they are not required to prove it. The police and prosecutors' sense of retributive justice might lead them to do this. But self-interest may also dictate prosecuting only people with culpable mental states, since police and prosecutors may fear jury nullification unless the evidence strongly suggests some level of blame. The criminal justice system might also choose to rely on juries to nullify and judges to impose only monetary punishment unless blame is shown.

The notion that the burden of ensuring culpability should be entrusted to police and prosecutors raises serious questions of whether we can trust police and prosecutors to perform this task. It also raises the possibility of discriminatory enforcement. Jury nullification may not be reliable for protecting blameless defendants because the judge may choose not to admit defense evidence showing lack of

9. Phillip Johnson, *Strict Liability: The Prevalent View*, Encyclopedia of Crime and Justice 1518, 1520-1521 (1983).
10. Stephen J. Schulhofer, *Harm and Punishment: A Critique of Emphasis on the Results of Conduct in the Criminal Law*, 122 U. Pa. L. Rev. 1497, 1586-1587 (1974).

mental state on the ground that such evidence is irrelevant because mental state is not an element of the crime and therefore not an issue in the case. The existence of mandatory sentencing guidelines may severely curtail the judge's ability to make sure that strict liability crimes are never punished with imprisonment.

A compromise position between requiring the government to prove a subjective mental state and abandoning mental state entirely through strict liability is the idea of lowering the culpability requirement to simple negligence and shifting the burden of proof to the defendant. If the defendant can prove by a preponderance of the evidence that she acted reasonably, then no liability is imposed. This remedies the difficulties of proving subjective mental state on the part of the government by changing from a subjective standard to an objective standard and putting the burden of proving reasonableness on the defendant.

C. RESOLVING STATUTORY AMBIGUITY

As we pointed out in the introduction to this chapter, legislatures often draft statutes that are silent or otherwise ambiguous regarding mental state. Prosecutors, defense lawyers, and judges are then left to decide what mental state should be applied or if strict liability should be imposed. Statutes that are silent or ambiguous regarding mental state are a regular source of uncertainty and confusion in criminal law and create challenging issues of statutory interpretation for lawyers to argue and for judges to decide. We examine such statutes and how judges interpret them in this Section.

PROBLEM

5.8 Amanda is a private security guard at a military base that provides housing for United States Coast Guard personnel and their families. In a parking area Amanda regularly patrols, there is an old camper-trailer of the sort that is towed behind a car or truck and can be opened into a large canvas tent and platform upon reaching a camping area. The camper-trailer has not been moved in over two years. It has a flat tire and no license plate. One day Amanda decides to take the camper trailer and use it for her family. She takes it home, cleans it, repairs the tire, and begins using it with her family. A few months later, she is arrested and charged under the statute below. Amanda claims that she thought the camper trailer had been abandoned. It turns out that the camper-trailer belongs to a Coast Guard enlisted man. Because he has been on several long tours of duty, he has had no opportunity to use the camper-trailer in recent years.

Assume that the military base where Amanda was employed is within the special maritime and territorial jurisdiction of the United States and that the trailer's value is $1200. Is Amanda liable under the following statute? If you represented Amanda, what arguments would you make on her behalf? If you were the prosecutor, what evidence would help you to convict?

18 United States Code § 661

Whoever, within the special maritime and territorial jurisdiction of the United States, takes and carries away, with intent to steal or purloin, any personal property of another shall be punished as follows:

If the property taken is of a value exceeding $ 1,000, or is taken from the person of another, by a fine under this title, or imprisonment for not more than five years, or both; in all other cases, by a fine under this title or by imprisonment not more than one year, or both.

If the property stolen consists of any evidence of debt, or other written instrument, the amount of money due thereon, or secured to be paid thereby and remaining unsatisfied, or which in any contingency might be collected thereon, or the value of the property the title to which is shown thereby, or the sum which might be recovered in the absence thereof, shall be the value of the property stolen.

Would the following facts make a difference in determining Amanda's liability? If so, why?

(a) Amanda took the camper-trailer off the base in the middle of the day.
(b) Amanda took the camper-trailer off the base in the middle of the night.
(c) Amanda made several attempts to identify and locate the owner.
(d) Amanda made no attempt to identify or locate the owner.

MORISSETTE v. UNITED STATES

342 U.S. 246 (1952)

JACKSON, J. . . . . On a large tract of uninhabited and untilled land in a wooded and sparsely populated area of Michigan, the Government established a practice bombing range over which the Air Force dropped simulated bombs at ground targets. These bombs consisted of a metal cylinder about forty inches long and eight inches across, filled with sand and enough black powder to cause a smoke puff by which the strike could be located. At various places about the range signs read "Danger — Keep Out — Bombing Range." Nevertheless, the range was known as good deer country and was extensively hunted.

Spent bomb casings were cleared from the targets and thrown into piles "so that they will be out of the way." They were not stacked or piled in any order but were dumped in heaps, some of which had been accumulating for four years or upwards, and were exposed to the weather and rusting away.

Morissette, in December of 1948, went hunting in this area but did not get a deer. He thought to meet expenses of the trip by salvaging some of these casings. He unloaded three tons of them on his truck and took them to a nearby farm, where they were flattened by driving a tractor over them. After expending this labor and trucking them to market in Flint, he realized $84. . . .

The loading, crushing and transporting of these casings were all in broad daylight, in full view of passersby, without the slightest effort at concealment. When an investigation was started, Morissette voluntarily, promptly and candidly told the whole story to the authorities, saying that he had no intention of stealing but thought the property was abandoned, unwanted and considered of no value to the government. He was indicted, however, on the charge that he "did unlawfully, wilfully and knowingly steal and convert" property of the United States of a value of $84, in violation of 18 U.S.C. § 641, which provides that "whoever embezzles, steals, purloins, or knowingly converts" government property is punishable by fine and imprisonment. Morissette was convicted and sentenced to imprisonment for two months or to pay a fine of $200.[11] . . .

On his trial, Morissette, as he had at all times told investigating officers, testified that from appearances he believed the casings were cast-off and abandoned, that he did not intend to steal the property, and took it with no wrongful or criminal intent. The trial court, however, was unimpressed, and ruled: "He took it because he thought it was abandoned and he knew he was on government property. . . . That is no defense. . . . I don't think anybody can have the defense they thought the property was abandoned on another man's piece of property." The court stated: "I will not permit you to show this man thought it was abandoned. . . . I hold in this case that there is no question of abandoned property." The court refused to submit or to allow counsel to argue to the jury whether Morissette acted with innocent intention. . . .

I.

The contention that an injury can amount to a crime only when inflicted by intention is no provincial or transient notion. It is as universal and persistent in mature systems of law as belief in freedom of the human will and a consequent ability and duty of the normal individual to choose between good and evil. A relation between some mental element and punishment for a harmful act is almost as instinctive as the child's familiar exculpatory "But I didn't mean to," and has afforded a rational basis for a tardy and unfinished substitution of deterrence and reformation in place of retaliation and vengeance as the motivation for public prosecution. Unqualified acceptance of this doctrine by English common law in the Eighteenth Century was indicated by Blackstone's sweeping statement that to constitute any crime there must first be a "vicious will." Common-law commentators of the Nineteenth Century early pronounced the same principle, although a few exceptions not relevant to our present problem came to be recognized.

Crime, as a compound concept, generally constituted only from concurrence of an evil-meaning mind with an evil-doing hand, was congenial to an intense individualism and took deep and early root in American soil. As the states codified the common law of crimes, even if their enactments were silent on the subject, their courts assumed that the omission did not signify disapproval of the principle

---

11. 18 U.S.C. § 641, so far as pertinent, reads: Whoever embezzles, steals, purloins, or knowingly converts to his use or the use of another, or without authority, sells, conveys, or disposes of any record, voucher, money, or thing of value of the United States [] [s]hall be fined not more than $10,000 or imprisoned not more than ten years, or both; but if the value of such property does not exceed the sum of $100, he shall be fined not more than $1,000 or imprisoned not more than one year, or both.

but merely recognized that intent was so inherent in the idea of the offense that it required no statutory affirmation. Courts, with little hesitation or division, found an implication of the requirement as to offenses that were taken over from the common law. The unanimity with which they have adhered to the central thought that wrongdoing must be conscious to be criminal is emphasized by the variety, disparity and confusion of their definitions of the requisite but elusive mental element. However, courts of various jurisdictions, and for the purposes of different offenses, have devised working formulae, if not scientific ones, for the instruction of juries around such terms as "felonious intent," "criminal intent," "malice aforethought," "guilty knowledge," "fraudulent intent," "wilfulness," "scienter," to denote guilty knowledge, or "mens rea," to signify an evil purpose or mental culpability. By use or combination of these various tokens, they have sought to protect those who were not blameworthy in mind from conviction of infamous common-law crimes.

However, the *Balint* . . . [offense] . . . belong[s] to a category of another character, with very different antecedents and origins. The [crime] . . . there involved depend[s] on no mental element but consist[s] only of forbidden acts or omissions. This, while not expressed by the Court, is made clear from examination of a century-old but accelerating tendency, discernible both here and in England, to call into existence new duties and crimes which disregard any ingredient of intent. . . .

While many of these duties are sanctioned by a more strict civil liability, lawmakers, whether wisely or not, have sought to make such regulations more effective by invoking criminal sanctions to be applied by the familiar technique of criminal prosecutions and convictions. This has confronted the courts with a multitude of prosecutions, based on statutes or administrative regulations, for what have been aptly called "public welfare offenses." These cases do not fit neatly into any of such accepted classifications of common-law offenses, such as those against the state, the person, property, or public morals. Many of these offenses are not in the nature of positive aggressions or invasions, with which the common law so often dealt, but are in the nature of neglect where the law requires care, or inaction where it imposes a duty. Many violations of such regulations result in no direct or immediate injury to person or property but merely create the danger or probability of it which the law seeks to minimize. While such offenses do not threaten the security of the state in the manner of treason, they may be regarded as offenses against its authority, for their occurrence impairs the efficiency of controls deemed essential to the social order as presently constituted. In this respect, whatever the intent of the violator, the injury is the same, and the consequences are injurious or not according to fortuity. Hence, legislation applicable to such offenses, as a matter of policy, does not specify intent as a necessary element. The accused, if he does not will the violation, usually is in a position to prevent it with no more care than society might reasonably expect and no more exertion than it might reasonably exact from one who assumed his responsibilities. Also, penalties commonly are relatively small, and conviction does no grave damage to an offender's reputation. Under such considerations, courts have turned to construing statutes and regulations which make no mention of intent as dispensing with it and holding that the guilty act alone makes out the crime. This has not, however, been without expressions of misgiving. . . .

After the turn of the Century, a new use for crimes without intent appeared when New York enacted numerous and novel regulations of tenement houses, sanctioned by money penalties. Landlords contended that a guilty intent was essential to establish a violation. Judge Cardozo wrote the answer:

"The defendant asks us to test the meaning of this statute by standards applicable to statutes that govern infamous crimes. The analogy, however, is deceptive. The element of conscious wrongdoing, the guilty mind accompanying the guilty act, is associated with the concept of crimes that are punished as infamous. . . . Even there it is not an invariable element. . . . But in the prosecution of minor offenses, there is a wider range of practice and of power. Prosecutions for petty penalties have always constituted in our law a class by themselves. . . . That is true though the prosecution is criminal in form."

Tenement House Department v. McDevitt, 215 N.Y. 160, 168 (1915).

Soon, employers advanced the same contention as to violations of regulations prescribed by a new labor law. Judge Cardozo, again for the court, pointed out, as a basis for penalizing violations whether intentional or not, that they were punishable only by fine "moderate in amount," but cautiously added that in sustaining the power so to fine unintended violations "we are not to be understood as sustaining to a like length the power to imprison. We leave that question open." . . .

Neither this Court nor, so far as we are aware, any other has undertaken to delineate a precise line or set forth comprehensive criteria for distinguishing between crimes that require a mental element and crimes that do not. We attempt no closed definition, for the law on the subject is neither settled nor static. The conclusion reached in the *Balint* case . . . has our approval and adherence for the circumstances to which it was there applied. A quite different question here is whether we will expand the doctrine of crimes without intent to include those charged here.

Stealing, larceny, and its variants and equivalents, were among the earliest offenses known to the law that existed before legislation; they are invasions of rights of property which stir a sense of insecurity in the whole community and arouse public demand for retribution, the penalty is high and, when a sufficient amount is involved, the infamy is that of a felony, which, says Maitland, is " . . . as bad a word as you can give to man or thing." State courts of last resort, on whom fall the heaviest burden of interpreting criminal law in this country, have consistently retained the requirement of intent in larceny-type offenses. If any state has deviated, the exception has neither been called to our attention nor disclosed by our research.

Congress, therefore, omitted any express prescription of criminal intent from the enactment before us in the light of an unbroken course of judicial decision in all constituent states of the Union holding intent inherent in this class of offense, even when not expressed in a statute. Congressional silence as to mental elements in an Act merely adopting into federal statutory law a concept of crime already so well defined in common law and statutory interpretation by the states may warrant quite contrary inferences than the same silence in creating an offense new to general law, for whose definition the courts have no guidance except the Act. Because the [offense] . . . before this Court in the *Balint* . . . case . . . [was] of this latter class, we cannot accept . . . [it] as authority for eliminating intent from offenses incorporated from the common law. . . .

[W]here congress borrows terms of art in which are accumulated the legal tradition and meaning of centuries of practice, it presumably knows and adopts the cluster of ideas that were attached to each borrowed word in the body of learning from which it was taken and the meaning its use will convey to the judicial mind unless otherwise instructed. In such case, absence of contrary direction may be taken as satisfaction with widely accepted definitions, not as a departure from them.

We hold that mere omission from § 641 of any mention of intent will not be construed as eliminating that element from the crimes denounced. . . .

Knowledge, of course, is not identical with intent and may not have been the most apt words of limitation. But knowing conversion requires more than knowledge that defendant was taking the property into his possession. He must have had knowledge of the facts, though not necessarily the law, that made the taking a conversion. In the case before us, whether the mental element that Congress required be spoken of as knowledge or as intent, would not seem to alter its bearing on guilt. For it is not apparent how Morissette could have knowingly or intentionally converted property that he did not know could be converted, as would be the case if it was in fact abandoned or if he truly believed it to be abandoned and unwanted property.

Of course, the jury, considering Morissette's awareness that these casings were on government property, his failure to seek any permission for their removal and his self-interest as a witness, might have disbelieved his profession of innocent intent and concluded that his assertion of a belief that the casings were abandoned was an afterthought. Had the jury convicted on proper instructions it would be the end of the matter. But juries are not bound by what seems inescapable logic to judges. They might have concluded that the heaps of spent casings left in the hinterland to rust away presented an appearance of unwanted and abandoned junk, and that lack of any conscious deprivation of property or intentional injury was indicated by Morissette's good character, the openness of the taking, crushing and transporting of the casings, and the candor with which it was all admitted. They might have refused to brand Morissette as a thief. Had they done so, that too would have been the end of the matter.

Reversed.

QUESTIONS

1. Was Morissette's case more difficult to resolve than Amanda's case in Problem 5.8? How does the text of 18 U.S.C. § 641 differ from the text of 18 U.S.C. § 661?

2. The *Morissette* Court distinguishes between traditional common law crimes and new public welfare or regulatory crimes. What significance does the court attach to this distinction?

3. Rewrite § 641 to reflect the *Morissette* Court's interpretation of that statute. What changes would you make to the language of § 641?

Model Penal Code Interpretation Rules

Statutory ambiguity about mental state is such a common problem in criminal law that the Model Penal Code created several specific rules for resolving such confusion. Those rules and their explanatory comments appear below.

Model Penal Code § 2.02   *General Requirements of Culpability*

(1) *Minimum Requirements of Culpability.* Except as provided in Section 2.05, a person is not guilty of an offense unless he acted purposely, knowingly, recklessly or negligently, as the law may require, with respect to each material element of the offense. . . .

Comment

Objective. This section expresses the Code's basic requirement that unless some element of mental culpability is proved with respect to each material element of the offense, no valid criminal conviction may be obtained. This requirement is subordinated only to the provision of Section 2.05 for a narrow class of strict liability offenses that are limited to those for which no severer sentence than a fine may be imposed.

(3) *Culpability Required Unless Otherwise Provided.* When the culpability sufficient to establish a material element of an offense is not prescribed by law, such element is established if a person acts purposely, knowingly or recklessly with respect thereto.

Comment

Offense Silent as to Culpability. Subsection (3) provides that unless the kind of culpability sufficient to establish a material element of an offense has been prescribed by law, it is established if a person acted purposely, knowingly or recklessly with respect thereto. This accepts as the basic norm what usually is regarded as the common law position. More importantly, it represents the most convenient norm for drafting purposes. When purpose or knowledge is required, it is conventional to be explicit. And since negligence is an exceptional basis of liability, it should be excluded as a basis unless explicitly prescribed.

(4) *Prescribed Culpability Requirement Applies to All Material Elements.* When the law defining an offense prescribes the kind of culpability that is sufficient for the commission of an offense, without distinguishing among the material elements thereof, such provision shall apply to all the material elements of the offense, unless a contrary purpose plainly appears. . . .

Comment

Ambiguous Culpability Requirements. Subsection (4) seeks to assist in the resolution of a common ambiguity in penal legislation, the statement of a particular culpability requirement in the definition of an offense in such a way that it is unclear whether the requirement applies to all the elements of the offense or only to the element that it immediately introduces. The draftsmen of the Wisconsin revision posed the problem in these terms: "When, for example, a statute says that it is unlawful to 'wilfully, maliciously, or wantonly destroy, remove, throw down or injure any . . . [property] . . . upon the land of another,' do the words denoting the requirement of intent apply only to the doing of the damage or do they also modify the phrase 'upon the land of another,' thus requiring knowledge or belief that the property is located upon land which belongs to another?" The Model Penal Code agrees with their view that these "problems can and should be taken care of in the definition of criminal intent."

The Code proceeds in the view that if a particular kind of culpability has been articulated at all by the legislature as sufficient with respect to any element of the offense, the assumption is that it was meant to apply to all material elements. Hence this construction is required, unless a "contrary purpose plainly appears." When a distinction is intended, as it often is, proper drafting ought to make it clear.

[An example] may help to clarify the intended scope of the provision and to illustrate its relationship with Subsection 3. False imprisonment is defined by Section 212.3 of the Model Code to include one who "knowingly restrains another unlawfully so as to interfere substantially with his liberty." Plainly, the word "knowingly" is intended to modify the restraint, so that the actor must, in order to be convicted under this section, know that he is restraining his victim. The question whether "knowingly" also qualifies the unlawful character of the restraint is not clearly answered by the definition of the offense, but is answered in the affirmative by the subsection under discussion. . . .

PROBLEMS

5.9 The Criminal Code of the State of Imagination has the following burglary statute:

> It is a crime to purposely enter a residence at night to steal.

Assume that the State of Imagination has adopted the MPC approach to mental states. Decide whether D would be guilty of burglary in each of the following sets of facts.

(a) D walks into a store at night intending to steal and it turns out, unbeknownst to D, that the upstairs rooms of the store are actually the living quarters of the store clerk, which qualifies the building as a residence.

(b) D intends to and does enter a residence at night intending to steal, but the sun comes up before D can steal anything.

5.10 Another jurisdiction, the State of Confusion, has the following burglary statute:

> It is a crime to enter a residence at night to steal.

Assume that the State of Confusion has adopted the MPC approach to mental states. Decide whether D is guilty of burglary under the following facts.

> D walks into a store at night intending to steal and it turns out, unbeknownst to D, that the upstairs rooms of the store are actually the living quarters of the store clerk, which qualifies the building as a residence.

Now try a more challenging version of the burglary statute Problems:

5.11 You are a public defender in the State of New York and have been appointed to represent a client charged with second-degree burglary under the New York statute that appears below. Your client admits entering the building in question, a warehouse, intending to steal some property inside the building.

New York Penal Law § 140.25   *Burglary in the Second Degree*

> A person is guilty of burglary in the second degree when he knowingly enters or remains unlawfully in a building with intent to commit a crime therein, and when:
>
>> 1. In effecting entry or while in the building or in immediate flight therefrom, he or another participant in the crime:

(a) Is armed with explosives or a deadly weapon; or

(b) Causes physical injury to any person who is not a participant in the crime; or

(c) Uses or threatens the immediate use of a dangerous instrument; or

(d) Displays what appears to be a pistol, revolver, rifle, shotgun, machine gun or other firearm; or

2. The building is a dwelling.

Burglary in the second degree is a class C felony.

(a) Your client did not know that the warehouse in question was a dwelling. He carefully surveyed the warehouse for several weeks prior to his entry and accurately determined that the warehouse closes each day at 5 P.M. and that all employees appear to leave at that time. Your client checked with the city and found that no residential occupancy permit had been issued for the warehouse. Your client even went so far as to ask some of the employees at the warehouse, whom he met at local bar, and they informed him that the building was not used as a dwelling. Unfortunately for your client, it turns out that a small section of an upper floor in the rear of the building serves as an apartment for a watchman who lives in the building and uses a rear entrance to enter and to exit. Do the facts related in this paragraph affect your client's liability under the burglary statute?

(b) Assume for this part that the warehouse was *not* a dwelling. Your client agreed with a friend together to steal some laptop computers and cash from a shipping office inside the warehouse and split the proceeds of the theft. Your client did not know that the friend was carrying a loaded handgun in a jacket pocket at the time they entered the warehouse. Do the facts related in this paragraph affect your client's liability under the statute?

(c) Assume for this part that the warehouse was *not* a dwelling and that your client acted *alone* and was *unarmed*. Your client thought that there was no one in the warehouse at the time he entered it. As he was rummaging about the warehouse looking for property to steal, a watchman appeared, turning on lights and demanding to know who was in the building. Your client hid behind some crates until the watchman passed his hiding place, then bolted for the door to make his escape. The watchman heard your client fleeing and gave chase. In doing so, he slipped and fell, breaking an arm and spraining his knee. Do the facts related in this paragraph affect your client's liability under the statute?

(d) You have been hired as counsel for the committee of the New York legislature responsible for drafting and amending New York's criminal laws. You are directed by the committee chair to propose amendments to New York Penal Law Section 140.25 to clarify its application to situations such as those presented in Part A of this Problem. What amendments do you suggest?

A common statutory ambiguity arises when a statute lacks mental state terminology. Courts must then determine whether the legislature intended to impose strict liability. Professor Wayne LaFave identifies a series of factors that courts use in interpreting criminal statutes to resolve this ambiguity. These include:[12]

1. Legislative history and context.
2. Guidance from other statutes.
3. "The severity of the punishment."
4. The seriousness of the public harm the statute seeks to prevent.
5. "The defendant's opportunity to ascertain the true facts."
6. The difficulty of proving mental state.
7. "The number of prosecutions to be expected" under the statute.

The California Court of Appeals applies these factors in the following case.

PEOPLE v. TAYLOR

93 Cal. App. 4th 933 (2001)

SCOTLAND, P.J. Among the crimes of violence, illicit drugs, and illegal possession of weapons of which defendant James Patrick Taylor was convicted is the possession of a cane sword.

[W]e agree with defendant that the trial court erred in failing to instruct the jury that, to be guilty of possessing a cane sword, a person must know the cane actually conceals a sword. As we will explain, the application of factors considered in determining whether the Legislature intended a criminal statute to impose liability without proof of scienter leads us to conclude that possession of a cane sword is not a strict liability offense. In order to protect against the significant possibility of punishing innocent possession by one who believes he or she simply has an ordinary cane, we infer the Legislature intended a scienter requirement of knowledge that the cane conceals a sword. . . .

When officers searched the residence occupied by defendant, a convicted felon, they found 72 grams of methamphetamine, 102.8 grams of marijuana, 49 grams of psilocybin mushrooms, a firearm, and $8,150 in cash. Six months later, during the search of a storage room leased by defendant, officers found marijuana and psilocybin mushrooms, numerous firearms and types of ammunition, and a cane sword. When defendant was arrested that day, he had a small amount of marijuana in his sock. . . . Defendant was convicted of . . . possessing a cane sword [and several other offenses].

Section 12020, subdivision (a) provides in pertinent part: "Any person in this state who does any of the following is punishable by imprisonment in a county jail not exceeding one year or in the state prison: (1) . . . possesses any cane gun or wallet gun, any undetectable firearm, any firearm which is not immediately recognizable as a firearm, any camouflaging firearm container, any ammunition which contains or consists of any flechette dart, any bullet containing or carrying an explosive agent, any ballistic knife, any multiburst trigger activator, any nunchaku, any short-barreled shotgun, any short-barreled rifle, any metal knuckles, any belt buckle knife, any leaded cane, any zip gun, any shuriken, any unconventional pistol, any lipstick case knife, *any cane sword*, any shobi-zue, any air gauge knife,

---

12. Wayne R. LaFave, *Criminal Law* 274-276 (4th ed. 2003).

any writing pen knife, any metal military practice hand grenade or metal replica hand grenade, or any instrument or weapon of the kind commonly known as a blackjack, slung shot, billy, sand club, sap, or sandbag." (Italics added.)

Thus, included in this menagerie of unusual, sophisticated weapons, some with mysterious and evil-sounding names, is a cane sword, which is defined as "a cane, swagger stick, stick, staff, rod, pole, umbrella, or similar device, having concealed within it a blade that may be used as a sword or stiletto." From outward appearance, a cane sword seems to be a common walking cane. Its unlawful component — the sword blade — is neatly concealed inside the cane, with a fitting and seal keeping the curved handle locked in position while the cane is used for walking. The blade is ejected with the twist of the handle.

Defendant contends that an element of the crime of possessing a cane sword in violation of section 12020, subdivision (a)(1) is knowledge that the cane conceals a sword. Accordingly, he argues, his conviction for violating that section must be reversed because the trial court did not instruct the jury on the knowledge element of the crime and because the prosecutor failed to present evidence from which the jurors could infer defendant had the requisite knowledge that the cane he possessed concealed a sword. Although we disagree with the second point, we find merit in the first.

As acknowledged by our dissenting colleague, "the requirement that, for a criminal conviction, the prosecution prove some form of guilty intent, knowledge, or criminal negligence is of such long standing and so fundamental to our criminal law that penal statutes will often be construed to contain such an element despite their failure expressly to state it." This generally is so because "the existence of a *mens rea* is the rule of, rather than the exception to, the principles of Anglo-American criminal jurisprudence." In other words, there must be a union of act and wrongful intent, or criminal negligence. "So basic is this requirement that it is an invariable element of every crime unless excluded expressly or by necessary implication."

There is, however, an exception for certain types of penal laws, often referred to as public welfare offenses, for which the Legislature has intended that proof of scienter or wrongful intent is not necessary for conviction. "Such offenses generally are based upon the violation of statutes which are purely regulatory in nature and involve widespread injury to the public. 'Under many statutes enacted for the protection of the public health and safety, e.g., traffic and food and drug regulations, criminal sanctions are relied upon even if there is no wrongful intent. These offenses usually involve light penalties and no moral obloquy or damage to reputation. Although criminal sanctions are relied upon, the primary purpose of the statutes is regulation rather than punishment or correction. The offenses are not crimes in the orthodox sense, and wrongful intent is not required in the interest of enforcement.'"

Where legislative intent is not readily discerned from the text of a statute, the California Supreme Court has applied a framework that considers seven factors "courts have commonly taken into account in deciding whether a statute should be construed as a public welfare offense. . . ." [The court here recites the seven LaFave factors.]

Considering these factors, the dissent concludes "the Legislature did not intend that the prosecution prove defendant knew the characteristics that bring the weapon within the proscription of section 12020 (a)(1)," i.e., that the cane concealed a sword. In our colleague's view, it is a defendant's burden to raise as a defense that he or she did not know the unlawful characteristic of the cane. We cannot agree.

In *In re Jorge M.*, the Supreme Court interpreted section 12280 (b), which, among other things, prohibits the possession of an unregistered "assault weapon" as defined in sections 12276 and 12276.1. The specific weapon at issue in that case was an "SKS-45 semiautomatic rifle with a detachable 'banana clip' magazine." Considering the seven factors . . . the court concluded that the assault weapon statute is not a strict liability crime. Nevertheless, the court held that, due to gravity of the public safety threat addressed by the statute and the need for effective enforcement of the law, the assault weapon statute does not require actual knowledge of the weapon's unlawful characteristics. Rather, guilt can be established by proof that the person charged with unlawfully possessing an assault weapon "knew or reasonably should have known the firearm possessed the characteristics [that make it an assault weapon]."

Four of the factors considered by the Supreme Court appear to have weighed most heavily in its decision: the serious threat of harm posed by the unlawful possession of semiautomatic firearms in the form of assault weapons (factor four); the potential difficulty of routinely proving actual knowledge on the part of defendants in the substantial number of prosecutions to be expected under the assault weapon statute (factors six and seven); and the opportunity of the defendant to have ascertained the true facts about the weapon (factor five). Of significance to its holding is the Supreme Court's observation that, because of the general principle that all persons are obligated to learn of and comply with the law, it ordinarily is reasonable to conclude that, absent "exceptional cases in which the salient characteristics of the firearm are extraordinarily obscure, or the defendant's possession of the gun was so fleeting or attenuated as not to afford an opportunity for examination," a person who knowingly possesses a semiautomatic firearm reasonably would investigate and determine whether the gun's characteristics make it an assault weapon.

None of these factors applies to a cane sword. Common sense indicates that a cane sword does not present the serious threat of harm posed by the unlawful possession of a semiautomatic assault weapon (factor four). And common experience indicates that there will not be a substantial number of prosecutions for cane sword possession such that prosecutors will have difficulty routinely proving actual knowledge of the unlawful characteristic of a cane sword (factors six and seven). For example, in this case, the location of the cane sword among the cache of other weapons unlawfully possessed by the able-bodied defendant was circumstantial evidence of his knowledge of the cane sword's unlawful characteristic.

It also is very significant that, unlike a semiautomatic firearm the outward nature of which reasonably would lead the person possessing it to investigate and determine whether the firearm has the characteristics of an assault weapon, a cane sword is an object the unlawful nature of which is extraordinarily, and intentionally, obscure (factor five). As we have noted, from outward appearance, a traditional curved cane sword seems to be a common walking cane. Its unlawful component — the sword blade — is neatly concealed inside the cane, with a fitting and seal keeping the curved handle locked in position while the cane is used for walking. The blade is ejected with the twist of the handle. . . .

Certainly, the unlawful characteristic of a cane sword is far more obscure than that of a dirk or dagger, the possession of which concealed upon one's person also is prohibited by section 12020, subdivision (a).

"Because the dirk or dagger portion of section 12020 criminalizes " 'traditionally lawful conduct' " [possessing a knife], the California Supreme Court has construed that statute to "contain a 'knowledge' element." "Thus, to commit the offense, a defendant must . . . have the requisite *guilty mind*: that is, the defendant must knowingly and intentionally carry concealed upon his or her person an instrument 'that is capable of ready use as a stabbing weapon.' § 12020, subds. (a), (c)(24).) A defendant who does not know that he is carrying the weapon or that the concealed instrument may be used as a stabbing weapon is therefore not guilty of violating section 12020."

So it should be with a cane sword due to the obscure nature of its unlawful characteristic. In order to protect against the significant possibility of punishing innocent possession by one who believes he or she simply has an ordinary cane, we infer the Legislature intended a scienter requirement of actual knowledge that the cane conceals a sword.

The three other factors identified by the Supreme Court support our conclusion. The rationales of *In re Jorge M.* and *People v. Rubalcava* suggest the context of the statute (factor one) favors a *mens rea* requirement for the possession of a cane sword, as it does for the possession of a dirk or dagger. And, as acknowledged by the dissent, the general provisions on *mens rea* and strict liability crimes (factor two) and the severity of punishment (factor three) support a *mens rea* requirement.

Since the trial court did not instruct the jury that actual knowledge the cane conceals a sword is an element of the crime and the People make no effort to demonstrate how the error may have been harmless, we shall reverse defendant's conviction for possessing a cane sword.

Near the end of the majority opinion, Judge Scotland refers to passages from Judge Morrison's dissent in *Taylor* dealing with factors two and three on the LaFave list. Here are those passages:

General Provision on *Mens Rea*

Penal Code section 20 provides: "In every crime or public offense there must exist a union, or joint operation of act and intent, or criminal negligence." While this rule is not inflexible — public welfare offenses are the principal exception — the *Jorge M.* court found it to "establish a presumption against criminal liability without mental fault or negligence, rebuttable only by compelling evidence of legislative intent to dispense with *mens rea* entirely. This factor favors a finding of a *mens rea* requirement.

Severity of Punishment

Penal Code section 12020(a)(1) is an alternative felony/misdemeanor. As such, it is punished as a felony unless charged as a misdemeanor or reduced to a misdemeanor by the sentencing court. (Pen. Code, § 17, subd. (b).) The felony sentence is 16 months, two years, or three years. (Pen. Code, § 18.)

The United States Supreme Court has emphasized that the severe punishment of a felony suggests the Legislature did not intend to eliminate the *mens rea* requirement. (*Staples v. United States, supra,* 511 U.S. 600, 618 128 L. Ed. 2d 608, 624.) This factor, therefore, favors finding a *mens rea* requirement.

PROBLEM

5.12 Which of the following statutes is likely to concern a strict liability crime? What additional information would facilitate your decision?

(a) It shall be unlawful for any person to receive or possess a firearm capable of fully automatic operation which is not registered to him/her in the National Firearms Registration and Transfer Record. Violation of this Act is a felony punishable by a maximum of five years imprisonment.

(b) The introduction or delivery for introduction into interstate commerce of any drug that is adulterated or misbranded is prohibited. Any person who violates this provision is guilty of a misdemeanor.

(c) Anyone who operates a motor vehicle in a manner which causes the death of another person is subject to imprisonment for a maximum of two years.

D. MISTAKE OF FACT

What does a defendant mean when she makes a claim of ignorance, mistake, or accident regarding a factual matter relevant to a crime? Is she saying that she did not commit the crime in question? Or is she saying that she did commit the crime, but should nonetheless be relieved of liability because of ignorance, mistake, or accident? Consider the following definitions.

Vol VII The Oxford English Dictionary 640 (2d ed. 1989): **ignorance**: the fact or condition of being ignorant; want of knowledge . . .

Webster's New Collegiate Dictionary 736, 7 (1977): **mistake**: a misunderstanding of the meaning or implication of something; a wrong action or statement proceeding from faulty judgment, inadequate knowledge, or inattention.

accident: an event occurring by chance . . . ; lack of intention . . . ; an unfortunate event resulting from carelessness, unawareness, ignorance or a combination of causes . . .

Ninth Circuit Manual of Model Jury Instructions — Criminal (2003) § 5.6
Knowingly Defined

An act is done knowingly if the defendant is aware of the act and does not act through ignorance, mistake, or accident. . . . You may consider evidence of the defendant's words, acts, or omissions, along with all the other evidence, in deciding whether the defendant acted knowingly.

Assume Problems 5.13 through 5.16 arise in a Model Penal Code jurisdiction.

PROBLEMS

5.13 Knowing possession of cocaine is a crime. Janet is a cocaine dealer. Janet has regular runners she uses to deliver cocaine around town. One day, though, Janet gets a call from a customer who wants some cocaine in a hurry, but none of her regular runners is available. Janet decides to use a legitimate local delivery service to get the cocaine to her customer. Ivan, an employee of the delivery company, responds to Janet's call in his delivery truck. Janet gives him a box of groceries, tells him she wants them delivered to a friend, and provides the address. Included in the box is a clear jar of white powder, which is marked "sugar" but actually contains cocaine. It turns out that police have had Janet under surveillance for some time. They follow Ivan and arrest him just after he delivers the box including the cocaine to Janet's customer. Is Ivan liable for knowing possession of cocaine?

Should it make any difference how Ivan describes his mental state? Consider the following variations:

(a) "I didn't know the white stuff in the jar was cocaine."
(b) "I thought the white stuff in the jar was sugar. The label said sugar."
(c) "I was mistaken about what the white powder was."
(d) "I was ignorant of the true nature of the white powder."

5.14 Assume possession of a sword cane is a crime and that strict liability applies to whether or not the cane contains a sword. When her father dies, Shelly inherits his entire estate. She cleans out his attic and discards many items, but retains a number of things, including a cane she thinks would look great hanging on the wall of her library. Shelly is unaware that the cane from her father's attic is a sword cane. Before hanging it on the wall, she takes it, along with some other items, to an antique dealer for an appraisal. The antique dealer discovers the true nature of the cane when he inspects it. He calls the police, who charge Shelly. Is Shelly liable for possession of the sword cane?

Should it make any difference how Shelly describes her mental state? Consider the following variations:

(a) "I didn't know it was a sword cane."
(b) "I thought it was simply a cane."
(c) "I was mistaken about the nature of the cane."
(d) "I was ignorant of the nature of the cane."

5.15 Assume that killing another person with purpose to cause that death is murder. Silvia and her friend Vince often play practical jokes on one another. One night Silvia decides to frighten Vince by pointing her revolver, which she thinks is unloaded, at Vince's head and pulling the trigger. Silvia usually keeps the revolver empty. But just to be sure, she opens the gun and quickly checks the chambers. In doing so, she fails to notice a single bullet in the chamber just to the left of the firing pin. Silvia puts the gun to Vince's head, pulls the trigger, and the gun fires.

Vince drops dead and Silvia collapses in shock and remorse. Is Silvia liable for murder on the basis of purposefully causing Vince's death?

Should it make any difference how Silvia describes her mental state? Consider the following variations:

(a) "It wasn't my purpose to kill Vince. I just wanted to scare him."
(b) "I thought the gun was unloaded."
(c) "I was mistaken about whether the gun was loaded."
(d) "I was ignorant of the fact that a bullet was in the gun."

5.16 Assume that killing another human being with negligence regarding the death is negligent homicide. Perry and Ann are the parents of Jack, a three-year-old boy. One day Jack comes home from school with a sore throat, fever, and runny nose. Perry and Ann treat Jack with cold medicine and decide to keep him home from school the next day. The next morning, Ann wakes up, goes into Jack's room, and finds him dead in his bed. An autopsy reveals that Jack had a rare allergy and that his symptoms were the result of his having eaten some unusual food at school. Inflammation in his throat had become so severe that Jack was unable to breathe. The medical examiner determines that if Perry and Ann had brought Jack to a hospital emergency room as soon as he came home from school, Jack could have been saved through the administration of medicine to counter his allergic reaction. Are Perry and Ann liable for negligent homicide for their failure to take Jack to an emergency room?

Should it make any difference how Perry and Ann describe their mental states? Consider the following variations:

(a) "We didn't know he had an allergy or was suffering an allergic reaction."
(b) "We thought he just had a cold."
(c) "We were mistaken about what he was suffering from and how much danger it posed."
(d) "We were ignorant of how serious Jack's condition was."

Assume Problem 5.17 arises in a non-Model Penal Code jurisdiction.

5.17 John was arrested after police saw him leave a clandestine laboratory set up in a garage to extract pseudoephedrine from cold pills, a step in the process of manufacturing methamphetamine. John received $500 for "washing" cold pills to extract the pseudoephedrine but claims he was unaware that it was to be used to make methamphetamine. He had seen ephedrine advertised as a diet and body-building agent and thought the extracted pseudoephedrine was to be resold for such a purpose. When John asked and was told the pseudoephedrine was to be used to make methamphetamine, he got scared, stopped work, and left the garage where the pills were being washed. John is charged under the following statute:

Every person who manufactures methamphetamine shall be punished in the state prison by a term of up to ten years.

At trial, John's wife testifies that John does not use or have any involvement with methamphetamine or any other illegal drug. A former work supervisor testifies that John is an honest and conscientious worker, does not drink or use illegal drugs, and is somewhat naïve about worldly matters.

Possession or sale of methamphetamine is also a crime. The statute penalizing possession and sale makes no mention of mental state, but the courts have required knowledge that the substance possessed or sold is methamphetamine in order to sustain a criminal conviction. The manufacturing of methamphetamine at one time was covered by the same statute that penalizes possession and sale. But the legislature made manufacturing a separate offense in order to impose a higher penalty on manufacturing. Assume that a person who extracts pseudoephedrine is engaged in the process of manufacturing methamphetamine. Is John liable? Should it make any difference how John describes his mental state? Consider the following variations:

(a) "I didn't know the pseudophedrine was to be used for making methamphetamine."
(b) "I thought the pseudophedrine was to be sold for dieting."
(c) "I was mistaken about how the pseudophedrine was to be used."
(d) "I was ignorant of how the pseudophedrine was to be used."

1. Mistake as Evidence of Mental State

The preferable way to approach claims of mistake, ignorance, or accident is to treat such claims as evidence regarding mental state, or, more precisely, as evidence that the defendant may have lacked a particular mental state. When a defendant claims to have lacked a mental state required for conviction of a crime, it raises a factual issue for the jury to resolve. Both the prosecution and the defense can present direct and circumstantial evidence on such a question. The defendant may testify, for example, that he lacked a mental state — that is, that he was ignorant or mistaken or caused some result by accident. Such testimony qualifies as direct evidence. The defendant may also offer circumstantial evidence to prove the same point. In Problem 5.15, for example, the fact that the victim was a friend of the defendant, Silvia, makes it less likely that Silvia purposefully killed him. If Janet, in Problem 5.13, paid Ivan only his normal fee to deliver the box containing the jar of white powder, it makes it less likely that Ivan knew the jar contained cocaine. The prosecution may also offer direct evidence of the defendant's mental state, such as a confession or a tape-recorded phone call in which the defendant admitted having the required mental state. Often the prosecution must use circumstantial evidence of mental state. In Problem 5.15, a recent quarrel between Silvia and her victim would be a piece of circumstantial evidence tending to show that Silvia did have purpose to kill. In Problem 5.13, if Janet had paid Ivan a very large sum above his normal fee to deliver the box, it would tend to show that Ivan knew or was aware of a substantial risk that the box contained something illegal. A useful exercise is to review each of the problems from 5.13 through 5.17 and identify the various pieces of evidence to see what, if any, bearing each has on the mental-state issue presented in that problem.

After evaluating and weighing the evidence presented by both sides, direct and circumstantial, the jury finally determines whether the government has met its burden of proving beyond reasonable doubt that the defendant did have the required mental state. Thus, a defendant should prevail if the jury concludes that there exists reasonable doubt about whether he or she had a required mental state.

PROBLEM

5.18 Would the defendants in Problems 5.13 through 5.17 above be held liable under the following statutes?

Iowa Criminal Code § 701.6   *Ignorance or mistake*

. . . Evidence of an accused person's ignorance or mistake as to a matter of . . . fact . . . shall be admissible in any case where it shall tend to prove the existence or nonexistence of some element of the crime with which the person is charged.

Model Penal Code § 2.04   *Ignorance or Mistake*

(1) Ignorance or mistake as to a matter of fact or law is a defense if:

(a) the ignorance or mistake negatives the purpose, knowledge, belief, recklessness or negligence required to establish a material element of the offense; or

(b) the law provides that the state of mind established by such ignorance or mistake constitutes a defense.

Comment

Relation of Ignorance or Mistake to Culpability Requirements. Subsection (1) states the conventional position under which the significance of ignorance by the defendant of a matter of fact or law, or a mistake as to such matters, is determined by the mental state required for the commission of the offense involved. Thus ignorance or mistake is a defense when it negatives the existence of a state of mind that is essential to the commission of an offense, or when it establishes a state of mind that constitutes a defense under a rule of law relating to defenses. In other words, ignorance or mistake has only evidential import; it is significant whenever it is logically relevant, and it may be logically relevant to negate the required mode of culpability or to establish a special defense.

The critical legislative decisions, therefore, relate to the establishment of the culpability for specific offenses as they are defined in the criminal code. . . . To put the matter as this subsection does is not to say anything that would not otherwise be true, even if no provision on the subject were made. As Glanville Williams has summarized the matter, the rule relating to mistake "is not a new rule; and the law could be stated equally well without reference to mistake. . . . [I]t is impossible to assert that a crime requiring intention or recklessness can be committed although the accused laboured under a mistake negativing the requisite intention or recklessness. Such an assertion carries its own refutation."

PROBLEM

5.19 The following jury instructions are pattern instructions for use in cases of mistake of fact. The bracketed words and blank spaces in each mark the language the trial judge tailors to the charge in the particular case. If you were the trial judge in Problems 5.13 through 5.17 above, in which cases would it be appropriate to give either instruction? How would you tailor the language of each instruction to the charge in each problem? Would the defendants in those problems be held liable under either instruction?

Ohio Jury Instructions Volume 4 — Criminal § 409.03   *Mistake of fact*

1. Unless the defendant had the required _____ [mental state] he is not guilty of the crime of _____.

2. In determining whether the defendant had the required _____ [mental state], you will consider whether he acted under a mistake of fact regarding

_____.

3. If the defendant had an honest belief arrived at in good faith in the existence of such facts and acted in accordance with the facts as he believed them to be, he is not guilty of _____ as _____ [mental state] is an essential element of that offense.

Pattern Jury Instructions (Criminal Cases) Prepared by the Committee on Pattern Criminal Jury Instructions, First Circuit (1998) § 5.02   *Mental State That Is Inconsistent With the Requisite Culpable State of Mind*

Evidence has been presented of defendant's mistake. Such mistake may be inconsistent with _____ [the requisite culpable state of mind for the charged offense]. If after considering the evidence of mistake, together with all the other evidence, you have a reasonable doubt that defendant acted with _____ [the requisite culpable state of mind], then you must find defendant not guilty.

PEOPLE *v.* RYPINSKI
157 A.D.2d 260, 555 N.Y.S.2d 500 (1990)

Pine, J. Defendant was convicted, after a jury trial, of reckless assault in the second degree (Penal Law § 120.05 [4]), as a purported lesser included offense of reckless assault in the first degree (Penal Law § 120.10 [3]). He was acquitted of two companion counts of intentional assault and one count of criminal possession of a weapon. He contends on appeal that the court erroneously refused to charge that a mistake of fact is a defense to reckless assault. No issue is raised with respect to the propriety of charging assault in the second degree as a lesser included offense.

The evidence established that defendant, who had been drinking all evening, shot Gordon Ulrich above the left knee in the early morning hours of January 1, 1985 after an argument concerning defendant's girlfriend. Prosecution witnesses testified that, before defendant got a rifle from his car, he threatened to blow the victim's brains out. They also testified that, after the gun discharged, defendant said "I'm sorry, it was an accident. I didn't mean to hurt anybody."

Defendant testified that he was a member of a conservation society and used its rifle range. He said that he intended to go there on January 1st, that he had cleaned the rifle the day before, that he always kept three rounds of ammunition in the rifle (one in the chamber and two in the clip), and that he had removed and replaced the three rounds while cleaning the gun. He said he had thrown it in the back seat of his car because he was having trouble opening his trunk.

He testified that he was drunk and that, when he knew there would be trouble, he pulled the rifle from the back seat of his car. He further testified that: "as I stood by the door, I ejected it three times. And the gun was unloaded as far as I knew because I always had the three rounds in it. And I turned away from my car. I had the rifle in my right hand, and I was hanging on to the car with my left as I was walking. I didn't even reach to the end of the car and the rifle discharged. I don't know how it went off. It was unloaded as far as I knew. And I was surprised as everybody else. I was in shock that it went off. I looked around. I heard people screaming, and I looked and I seen somebody on the ground. I walked over to the person and I seen him bleeding. I put my hand on him and I says, I'm sorry, it was an accident."

Defendant conceded that he did not look in the chamber to see whether the gun was unloaded. He testified that the only way the gun could have been loaded was that he had not put one bullet in the chamber and two "in the ready" as he thought, but had mistakenly put three "in the ready." If he had done that, there would still have been a bullet in the chamber after he cocked the rifle three times.

Defendant requested the court to charge that the jury could consider whether a mistake of fact negated the culpable mental state required for each of the three assault counts charged in the indictment. His request was granted with respect to the intentional counts only. Although there was no specific request for a mistake of fact charge on the purported lesser included reckless assault crime of which defendant was convicted, we find that the issue whether a mistake of fact defense applies to reckless conduct is preserved on this record.

The mistake of fact defense is found in Penal Law § 15.20 (1) (a), which provides:

"A person is not relieved of criminal liability for conduct because he engages in such conduct under a mistaken belief of fact, unless:
    "(a) Such factual mistake negatives the culpable mental state required for the commission of an offense."

Recklessness is a culpable mental state defined in Penal Law § 15.05 (3). It requires that the actor be aware of and consciously disregard a substantial and unjustifiable risk that a result will occur or that a circumstance exists.

In *People v. Marrero*, the Court of Appeals . . . held: "Although the drafters of the New York statute did not adopt the precise language of the Model Penal Code provision . . . it is evident and has long been believed that the Legislature intended the New York statute to be similarly construed. In fact, the legislative history of section 15.20 is replete with references to the influence of the Model Penal Code provision."

Section 2.04 (1) (a) of the Model Penal Code provides:

"(1) Ignorance or mistake as to a matter of fact or law is a defense if:

"(a) the ignorance or mistake negatives the purpose, knowledge, belief, *reck-lessness* or negligence required to establish a material element of the offense" (emphasis added).

The commentary notes that the mistake of fact need not be reasonable in order to exculpate a defendant of a crime requiring intentional or knowing action. The commentary also notes that New York is in accord with the Model Penal Code in not requiring that the mistake be reasonable.

It is clear that Penal Law § 15.20(1)(a), in referring to a culpable mental state required for the commission of an offense, included recklessness as a culpable mental state because that mental state is defined as such in Penal Law § 15.05(3) and recklessness is specifically mentioned in Model Penal Code § 2.04. Therefore, the court erred in refusing to so charge the jury. Defendant's conviction must be reversed, the sentence thereon vacated, and the indictment dismissed. The People may re-present appropriate charges to another Grand Jury if so advised.

Here is the New York statute under which Rypinski was convicted:

New York Penal Code § 120.05   *Assault in the second degree*

A person is guilty of assault in the second degree when: . . .

4. He recklessly causes serious physical injury to another person by means of a deadly weapon or a dangerous instrument; . . .

QUESTIONS

1. Assume Rypinski is retried on a charge of reckless assault. Draft the instruction on mistake of fact the trial judge should give the jury at the retrial.

2. Rypinski claimed to have been mistaken about the gun being loaded. What evidence supports his claim? What evidence tends to disprove his claim? If you were a juror at a retrial, would you convict or acquit?

3. Why did the appellate court in *Rypinski* not simply remand the case for a new trial? Why did the court dismiss the indictment and require the prosecutor to re-present the case to another grand jury?

2. Reasonableness

Wayne R. LaFave   Criminal Law 282 (4th ed. 2003)

"Uncertainty as to the precise significance of the defendant's mistake or ignorance of the surrounding facts is attributable in part to assertions, usually unexplained, in some decisions that the error must be a reasonable one. . . . "

Model Penal Code § 2.04   *Ignorance or Mistake of Law*

Comment

There is no justification . . . for requiring that ignorance or mistake be reasonable if the crime or the element of the crime involved requires acting purposely or knowingly for its commission.

It is true, of course, that whether recklessness or negligence suffices as a mode of culpability with respect to a given element of an offense is often raised for the first time in dealing with a question of mistake. That this may happen emphasizes the importance of perceiving that the question relates to the underlying rule as to the kind of culpability required with respect to the particular element of the offense involved. Generalizations about mistake of fact and mistake of law, or about honest and reasonable mistakes as relevant to general and specific intent crimes, tend to obscure rather than clarify that simple point.

Texas Penal Code § 8.02   *Mistake of Fact*

(a) It is a defense to prosecution that the actor through mistake formed a reasonable belief about a matter of fact if his mistaken belief negated the kind of culpability required for commission of the offense.

New Jersey Code of Criminal Justice § 2C:2-4   *Ignorance or mistake*

a. Ignorance or mistake as to a matter of fact . . . is a defense if the defendant reasonably arrived at the conclusion underlying the mistake and:

(1) It negatives the culpable mental state required to establish the offense; or

(2) The law provides that the state of mind established by such ignorance or mistake constitutes a defense.

PROBLEMS

5.20 What effect does the inclusion of a reasonableness requirement have on the operation of the Texas and New Jersey mistake statutes that appear above?

5.21 If the defendants in Problems 5.13 through 5.17 that appear at the outset of this section were required to prove that their mistakes were reasonable in order to be acquitted, what impact would such a requirement have on the definition of the offense in each statute? How would it affect the liability of the defendants in those Problems?

5.22 Jane was convicted after a jury trial under a statute that states: "It is a felony punishable by 10 years' imprisonment knowingly to sell crack cocaine within 1,000 feet of any school." The school in question was a preschool serving children of families with working parents and located in a light-industry building in a primarily commercial area. Jane was arrested by an undercover police officer in front of the building in which the preschool was located. Jane testified at trial and admitted that she did in fact sell a small amount of crack cocaine within 1,000 feet of the preschool, but claimed that she was mistaken about whether the building in question contained a school. She believed the building and the surrounding area were strictly commercial.

At Jane's trial, the judge gave the following instruction on mistake of fact:

> Ladies and gentlemen of the jury, Jane, the defendant, has admitted in her testimony selling the crack cocaine in question within a prohibited distance from a school but claims to have been mistaken about whether the building in question contained a school. Now the statute in question punishes only knowingly selling crack cocaine within 1,000 feet of a school, and the defendant has admitted that she knew she was selling the crack cocaine in question. If you find that the defendant's mistake negates the knowledge required by the statute, then you should acquit her. However, you should acquit her on the basis of her mistake only if you find her mistake is one for which you think there is a reasonable explanation or excuse.

Assume the preschool qualifies as a "school" and the amount of crack cocaine qualifies for prosecution under the statute. You are an appellate judge reviewing Jane's conviction. Should you reverse Jane's conviction? Why? What, if anything, did the trial judge do wrong in instructing the jury? Write the instruction the trial judge should give to the jury if you reverse and grant Jane a new trial.

What explains the tendency of legislators and judges to add a reasonableness requirement for mistake to exculpate even if the statute requires knowledge for conviction? One possible explanation is the intuitive allure of reasonableness. It may just seem reasonable to require a defendant's mistake to be reasonable.

Another possible explanation is semantic — the failure to appreciate that claims of mistake or ignorance are ways of talking about mental state. Because the vocabulary is different — using terms such as "ignorance" and "mistake" rather than "knowledge," "purpose" or "intent" — some legislators and judges seem not to realize that requiring the government to prove knowledge and simultaneously insisting that the defendant be reasonable are inconsistent. When legislators and judges use two different "languages" regarding mental state they may fail to see inconsistencies that would be more apparent if only one language were used. Imagine if a contractor in building a house were forced simultaneously to use both feet and inches and metric units of measurement. Using two different standards requiring conversion increases the risk of error. The same is true when legislators and judges address mental state using two different languages — the standard vocabulary of mental state and the vocabulary of mistake and ignorance.

The way lawyers tend to frame issues of mistake and ignorance may also contribute to the confusion. Typically the topic of ignorance and mistake is introduced by asking whether either "is a defense." Due to imprecision in the use of the term "defense," as described in the next paragraph, this way of posing the question may mask the connection between mental state and mistake and can prompt lawyers, judges, and legislators to view them as unrelated.

The term "defense" is used by lawyers, legislators, and judges to refer to two different ways of defeating liability. At times they use it to refer to defense strategies in which the defendant is contesting one of the elements of the offense. Examples are alibi and mistaken identity. Each essentially attempts to establish that the defendant did not engage in the prohibited conduct. In an alibi defense, the defendant tries to show that he could not have committed the act because he was elsewhere at the time of the offense. A mistaken identity defense tries to show that one or more witnesses has wrongly identified the defendant as the person who committed the act. Mistake and ignorance properly fall within this broad use of "defense." Just as alibi and mistaken identity contest the conduct element, an assertion of ignorance or mistake in a case contests mental state.

But "defense" is also often used to refer to strategies, such as self-defense and necessity, in which the defendant admits fulfillment of the elements of the offense but nonetheless seeks to avoid liability by asserting a principle that justifies or excuses the defendant despite an admission that he committed the acts and had the requisite mental states. This second meaning of "defense" is sometimes referred to as "confession and avoidance" — confessing fulfillment of the elements but avoiding liability through assertion of an overriding principle. If a defendant uses self-defense to try to defeat liability for an aggravated assault, the defendant admits the elements of the crime — conduct, injury to the victim, causation and purpose to injure — but argues that she should nonetheless be exonerated because she had a good reason for doing so: to prevent the victim from injuring her or another.

Necessity provides another example of a defense in which the defendant confesses fulfillment of the offense elements. For example, there is the famous case of *The Queen v. Dudley and Stephens* (reproduced in Chapter 8 on the necessity defense). In that case, after having been shipwrecked and stranded in a lifeboat for many days without food and water, Dudley killed and cannabalized a member of his crew. Dudley admitted the elements of murder — conduct, death, causation, and the purpose to kill — but nonetheless sought to avoid liability by arguing that the intentional killing of the victim was justified in order to save others.

As discussed above, when a defendant makes a claim of mistake in a case in which the government is required to prove the defendant's knowledge, the defendant is contesting fulfillment of an element of the crime rather than using confession and avoidance. Nonetheless, judges and legislators who are not careful in their use of the term "defense" may equate a defense of mistake or ignorance with confession and avoidance, prompting them to fail to see the relation between mistake or ignorance claims and the mental elements of the offense.

Such imprecise use of the term "defense" should be distinguished from legislators making a conscious choice to shift the burden of proof regarding mental state to a defendant, as discussed in Section B on strict liability.

Another reason judges and legislators may tend to add a reasonableness requirement is the legacy of the common law's treatment of mistake. The common law took an evidentiary approach to specific intent crimes. If the mistake negated the specific intent required, then there was no liability. But with general intent crimes, at times the common law required that the defendant's mistake be both honest and reasonable. By adding this reasonableness requirement, what meaning was the common law effectively giving to the word "intent"? Where else have you seen that meaning given to "intent"?

QUESTION

In *Balint*, 258 U.S. 250, in Section B of this chapter, Chief Justice Taft quoted an earlier Supreme Court case approving strict liability that stated that the government "may in the maintenance of a public policy provide "that he who shall do [particular acts] shall do them at his peril and will not be heard to plead in *defense* good faith or ignorance." (Emphasis added.) Which meaning of "defense" is being used in this quotation?

3. Liability for "Lesser Legal Wrongs"

Although the overarching Model Penal Code principle allows mistake to exonerate if it negates the mental state required to prove a material element of a crime, an important limitation to that principle appears in the MPC section below.

Model Penal Code § 2.04(2)

(2) Although ignorance or mistake would otherwise afford a defense to the offense charged, the defense is not available if the defendant would be guilty of another offense had the situation been as he supposed. In such case, however, the ignorance or mistake of the defendant shall reduce the grade and degree of the offense of which he may be convicted to those of the offense of which he would be guilty had the situation been as he supposed.

E. MISTAKE OF LAW

1. The Law Defining the Charged Offense

PROBLEMS

5.23 Jane is the leader of a community organization for girls in a western state. The group is trying to raise money for a trip to Disney World. As a fund-raising venture, Jane and some of the other mothers silk-screen t-shirts to sell to summer visitors to a nearby national park. On the t-shirts, Jane uses the image of Smokey the Bear, a figure popular with tourists because of the many forest fires that have plagued the western United States in recent years. Jane and the other mothers are arrested and charged under the following statute:

Whoever reproduces for monetary gain the image of Smokey the Bear without the prior written permission of the United States Forest

Service is punishable by a fine of up to $1,000 and six months imprisonment.

Jane and the other mothers did not obtain permission from the Forest Service and were unaware of the existence of this statute. Are they liable?

5.24 Leonard moves to the State of Imagination from a foreign country to be near his children and grandchildren. He is 70 years old and speaks little English. He spends most of his time at a community center with other elderly men from his native land. They pass much time playing card games in which substantial sums change hands. This type of gambling is a common and completely acceptable pastime for elderly gentlemen in Leonard's native land. One day, the community center is raided and Leonard and his fellow card players are indicted and charged under the following statute.

It is a misdemeanor to participate in gambling, including playing card games for money, betting on horses, or other forms of lottery or chance without a state license.

Leonard and his colleagues had no idea that gambling was illegal here without a license. Moreover, Leonard reads no English. Is Leonard liable under the statute?

a. The Conventional Position

UNITED STATES v. BAKER
807 F.2d 427 (1986)

REAVLEY, J. Paul Baker appeals his conviction for trafficking in counterfeit goods, claiming that an element of the offense is knowledge of the criminality of the conduct and that the jury should have been so charged. We reject his contention and affirm his conviction. . . .

. . . [The Trademark Counterfeiting Act] subjects to criminal penalties anyone who

intentionally traffics or attempts to traffic in goods or services and knowingly uses a counterfeit mark on or in connection with such goods or services. (codified at 18 U.S.C. § 2320).

Paul Baker was convicted under this new statute for dealing in counterfeit watches. He does not dispute that he intentionally dealt in the watches. He also admits that he knew the "Rolex" watches he sold were counterfeit. His contention is that the statute requires that he act with knowledge that his conduct is criminal . . . and that he would not have done so had he known he was committing a crime.

Although this is a case of first impression as to this statute, the underlying legal principles are well established. "The definition of the elements of a criminal offense is entrusted to the legislature, particularly in the case of federal crimes, which are solely creatures of statute." Thus our job on this appeal is to determine what Congress intended when it enacted the statute under which Baker was convicted.

Both the language of the statute and the legislative history lead to the inescapable conclusion that Baker need not have known that his conduct was a crime. . . .

The statute clearly sets out the elements of the crime and the mental state required for each element. The defendant must intentionally deal in goods and he must knowingly use a counterfeit mark in connection with those goods. There is no ambiguity in this language and nothing in the statute suggests that any other mental state is required for conviction. . . .

Our reading of the statute is confirmed by resort to the legislative history. The committee reports on the bill contain detailed descriptions of the mental states required for conviction, yet nowhere do they state that knowledge of illegality is an element of the crime. . . .

It is not surprising that Congress would allow conviction of one who knows that he is selling bogus "Rolex" watches even though he does not know his conduct is punishable as a crime. While it is true that the "general principle that ignorance or mistake of law is no excuse is usually greatly overstated," the principle continues to be valid to the extent that ordinarily "the criminal law does not require knowledge that an act is illegal, wrong, or blameworthy."[1] Baker's claim is merely that, even though he had the mental states required by the face of the statute, he should not be convicted because he did not know that Congress had passed a statute criminalizing his conduct. This clearly is not the law. A defendant cannot "avoid prosecution by simply claiming that he had not brushed up on the law."

QUESTIONS

1. The *Baker* court states that "[b]oth the language of the statute and the legislative history" lead the court to reject Baker's argument. How does the language of the statute help the court resolve the case? To what language is the court referring? How does the statute's legislative history help the court?

2. The Model Penal Code Comment that follows refers to "the conventional position" on mistake of law. What is this conventional position according to the *Baker* court? To what law does this conventional position refer?

3. How would the *Baker* case be resolved under the following Model Penal Code provisions?

Model Penal Code Mistake of Law Provisions § 2.02(9)   *Culpability as to Illegality of Conduct.*

Neither knowledge nor recklessness or negligence as to whether conduct constitutes an offense or as to the existence, meaning or application of the law determining

---

[1] A noted treatise in the area summarizes this principle as follows:

> It bears repeating here that the cause of much confusion concerning the significance of the defendant's ignorance or mistake of law is the failure to distinguish two quite different situations: (1) that in which the defendant consequently lacks the mental state required for commission of the crime and thus . . . has a valid defense; and (2) that in which the defendant still had whatever mental state is required for commission of the crime and only claims that he was unaware that such conduct was proscribed by the criminal law, which . . . is ordinarily not a recognized defense.

W. LaFave & A. Scott, Criminal Law § 47, at 362-363 (1972).
Baker's contention clearly falls within the second of the situations described.

the elements of an offense is an element of such offense, unless the definition of the offense or the Code so provides.

Comment

Culpability as to Illegality of Conduct. Subsection (9) states the conventional position that knowledge of the existence, meaning or application of the law determining the elements of an offense is not an element of that offense, except in the unusual situations where the law defining the offense or the Code so provides. . . .

The proper arena for the principle that ignorance or mistake of law does not afford an excuse is thus with respect to the particular law that sets forth the definition of the crime in question. It is knowledge of *that* law that is normally not a part of the crime, and it is ignorance or mistake as to *that* law that is denied defensive significance by this subsection of the Code and by the traditional common law approach to the issue.

Model Penal Code § 2.04 *Ignorance or Mistake*

(1) Ignorance or mistake as to a matter of fact or law is a defense if:
(a) the ignorance or mistake negatives the purpose, knowledge, belief, recklessness or negligence required to establish a material element of the offense; or
(b) the law provides that the state of mind established by such ignorance or mistake constitutes a defense.

Iowa Criminal Code § 701.6 *Ignorance or Mistake*

All persons are presumed to know the law. Evidence of an accused person's ignorance or mistake as to a matter of fact or law shall be admissible in any case where it shall tend to prove the existence or nonexistence of some element of the crime with which the person is charged.

QUESTION

Do the MPC and Iowa provisons on mistake of law differ? If so, how?

b. Special Cases

i. Statutes Requiring Culpability Regarding Illegality

Model Penal Code § 2.02(9) *Culpability as to Illegality of Conduct*

Comment

It needs to be recognized, however, that there may be *special cases* where *knowledge of the law defining the offense should be part of the culpability requirement for its commission,* i.e., where a belief that one's conduct is not a violation of the law or, at least, such a belief based on reasonable grounds, ought to engender a defense. Such a result might be brought about directly by the definition of the crime, e.g., by explicitly requiring awareness of a regulation, violation of which is denominated as an offense. It also may be brought about by a general provision in the Code indicating circumstances in which mistakes about the law defining an offense will constitute a defense. In either case, the result is exceptional and arises only when the governing law "so provides." (Emphasis added.)

RATZLAF *v.* UNITED STATES

510 U.S. 135 (1994)

GINSBURG, J. Federal law requires banks and other financial institutions to file reports with the Secretary of the Treasury whenever they are involved in a cash transaction that exceeds $10,000. . . . It is illegal to "structure" transactions—i.e., to break up a single transaction above the reporting threshold into two or more separate transactions—for the purpose of evading a financial institution's reporting requirement. . . . "A person willfully violating" this antistructuring provision is subject to criminal penalties. . . . This case presents a question on which Courts of Appeals have divided: Does a defendant's purpose to circumvent a bank's reporting obligation suffice to sustain a conviction for "willfully violating" the antistructuring provision? We hold that the "willfulness" requirement mandates something more. To establish that a defendant "willfully violated" the antistructuring law, the Government must prove that the defendant acted with knowledge that his conduct was unlawful.

I

On the evening of October 20, 1988, defendant. . . . Waldemar Ratzlaf ran up a debt of $160,000 playing blackjack at the High Sierra Casino in Reno, Nevada. The casino gave him one week to pay. On the due date, Ratzlaf returned to the casino with cash of $100,000 in hand. A casino official informed Ratzlaf that all transactions involving more than $10,000 in cash had to be reported to state and federal authorities. The official added that the casino could accept a cashier's check for the full amount without triggering any reporting requirement. The casino helpfully placed a limousine at Ratzlaf's disposal, and assigned an employee to accompany him to banks in the vicinity. Informed that banks too, are required to report cash transactions in excess of $10,000, Ratzlaf purchased cashier's checks, each for less than $10,000 and each from a different bank. He delivered these checks to the High Sierra Casino.

Based on this endeavor, Ratzlaf was charged with "structuring transactions" to evade the banks' obligation to report cash transactions exceeding $10,000. . . . The trial judge instructed the jury that the Government had to prove defendant's knowledge of the banks' reporting obligation and his attempt to evade that obligation, but did not have to prove that the defendant knew the structuring was unlawful. Ratzlaf was convicted, fined, and sentenced to prison.

Ratzlaf maintained on appeal that he could not be convicted of "willfully violating" the antistructuring law solely on the basis of his knowledge that a financial institution must report currency transactions in excess of $10,000 and his intention to avoid such reporting. To gain a conviction for "willful" conduct, he asserted, the Government must prove he was aware of the illegality of the "structuring" in which he engaged. The Ninth Circuit upheld the trial court's construction of the legislation and affirmed Ratzlaf's conviction. . . . We granted certiorari . . . and now conclude that, to give effect to the statutory "willfulness" specification, the

Government had to prove Ratzlaf knew the structuring he undertook was unlawful. We therefore reverse the judgment of the Court of Appeals. . . .

II

A

Congress enacted the Currency and Foreign Transactions Reporting Act in response to increasing use of banks and other institutions as financial intermediaries by persons engaged in criminal activity. The Act imposes a variety of reporting requirements on individuals and institutions regarding foreign and domestic financial transactions. The reporting requirement relevant here, § 5313(a), applies to domestic financial transactions. Section 5313(a) reads:

"When a domestic financial institution is involved in a transaction for the payment, receipt, or transfer of United States coins or currency (or other monetary instruments the Secretary of the Treasury prescribes), in an amount, denomination, or amount and denomination, or under circumstances the Secretary prescribes by regulation, the institution and any other participant in the transaction the Secretary may prescribe shall file a report on the transaction at the time and in the way the Secretary prescribes. . . . "[3]

To deter circumvention of this reporting requirement, Congress enacted an antistructuring provision, 31 U.S.C. § 5324, as part of the Money Laundering Control Act of 1986. Section 5324, which Ratzlaf is charged with "willfully violating," reads:

"No person shall for the purpose of evading the reporting requirements of section 5313(a) with respect to such transaction — . . .
(3) structure or assist in structuring, or attempt to structure or assist in structuring, any transaction with one or more domestic financial institutions."

The criminal enforcement provision at issue, 31 U.S.C. § 5322(a), sets out penalties for "a person willfully violating," *inter alia*, the anti-structuring provision. Section 5322(a) reads:

"A person willfully violating this subchapter . . . or a regulation prescribed under this subchapter . . . shall be fined not more than $250,000, or imprisoned for not more than five years, or both."

Section 5324 forbids structuring transactions with a "purpose of evading the reporting requirements of section 5313(a)." Ratzlaf admits that he structured cash transactions, and that he did so with knowledge of, and a purpose to avoid, the banks' duty to report currency transactions in excess of $10,000. The statutory formulation (§ 5322) under which Ratzlaf was prosecuted, however, calls for proof of "willfulness" on the actor's part. The trial judge in Ratzlaf's case, with the Ninth Circuit's approbation, treated § 5322(a)'s "willfulness" requirement essentially as surplusage — as words of no consequence. Judges should hesitate so to treat statutory terms in any setting, and resistance should be heightened when the words describe an element of a criminal offense. . . .

"Willful," this Court has recognized, is a "word of many meanings," and "its construction is often . . . influenced by its context." . . . Accordingly, we view

---

[3] By regulation, the Secretary ordered reporting of "transaction[s] in currency of more than $10,000." 31 CFR § 103.22 (a) (1993). . . .

§§ 5322(a) and 5324(3) mindful of the complex of provisions in which they are embedded. In this light, we count it significant that § 5322(a)'s omnibus "willfulness" requirement, when applied to other provisions in the same subchapter, consistently has been read by the Courts of Appeals to require both "knowledge of the reporting requirement" and a "specific intent to commit the crime," i.e., "a purpose to disobey the law." . . .

Undoubtedly there are bad men who attempt to elude official reporting requirements in order to hide from Government inspectors such criminal activity as laundering drug money or tax evasion. But currency structuring is not inevitably nefarious. Consider, for example, the small business operator who knows that reports filed under [the relevant section] are available to the Internal Revenue Service. To reduce the risk of an IRS audit, she brings $9,500 in cash to the bank twice each week, in lieu of reporting over $10,000 once each week. That person, if the United States is right, has committed a criminal offense, because she structured cash transactions "for the specific purpose of depriving the Government of the information that [the relevant section] is designed to obtain." . . . Nor is a person who structures a currency transaction invariably motivated by a desire to keep the Government in the dark. . . . But under the Government's construction an individual would commit a felony against the United States by making cash deposits in small doses, fearful that the bank's reports would increase the likelihood of burglary, or in an endeavor to keep a former spouse unaware of his wealth. . . .

In § 5322, Congress subjected to criminal penalties only those "willfully violating" § 5324, signaling its intent to require for conviction proof that the defendant knew not only of the bank's duty to report cash transactions in excess of $10,000, but also of his duty not to avoid triggering such a report. There are, we recognize, contrary indications in the statute's legislative history. But we do not resort to legislative history to cloud a statutory text that is clear. Moreover, were we to find [the relevant section's] "willfulness" requirement ambiguous as applied . . . , we would resolve any doubt in favor of the defendant. . . .

We do not dishonor the venerable principle that ignorance of the law generally is no defense to a criminal charge. . . . In particular contexts, however, Congress may decree otherwise. That, we hold, is what Congress has done with respect to [this statute] and the provisions it controls. To convict Ratzlaf of the crime with which he was charged, . . . the jury had to find he knew the structuring in which he engaged was unlawful. Because the jury was not properly instructed in this regard, we reverse the judgment of the Ninth Circuit and remand this case for further proceedings consistent with this opinion.

Dissent, BLACKMUN, J.

On October 27, 1988, . . . Waldemar Ratzlaf arrived at a Nevada casino with a shopping bag full of cash to pay off a $160,000 gambling debt. He told casino personnel he did not want any written report of the payment to be made. The casino vice president informed Ratzlaf that he could not accept a cash payment of more than $10,000 without filing a report.

Ratzlaf, along with his wife and a casino employee, then proceeded to visit several banks in and around Stateline, Nevada and South Lake Tahoe, California, purchasing separate cashier's checks, each in the amount of $9,500. At some banks the Ratzlafs attempted to buy two checks — one for each of them — and were told that a report would have to be filed; on those occasions they canceled the transactions. Ratzlaf then returned to the casino and paid off $76,000 of his debt in cashier's checks. A few weeks later, Ratzlaf gave three persons cash to purchase cashier's checks in amounts less than $10,000. The Ratzlafs themselves also bought five more such checks in the course of a week.

A jury found beyond a reasonable doubt that Ratzlaf knew of the financial institutions' duty to report cash transactions in excess of $10,000 and that he structured transactions for the specific purpose of evading the reporting requirements.

The Court today, however, concludes that these findings are insufficient . . . because a defendant also must have known that the structuring in which he engaged was illegal. Because this conclusion lacks support in the text of the statute, conflicts in my view with the basic principles governing the interpretation of criminal statutes, and is squarely undermined by the evidence of congressional intent, I dissent.

I

"The general rule that ignorance of the law or a mistake of law is no defense to criminal prosecution is deeply rooted in the American legal system." . . . Thus, the term "willfully" in criminal law generally "refers to consciousness of the act but not to consciousness that the act is unlawful." . . .

Unlike other provisions of the subchapter, the antistructuring provision identifies the purpose that is required for a . . . violation: "evading the reporting requirements." The offense of structuring, therefore, requires (1) knowledge of a financial institution's reporting requirements, and (2) the structuring of a transaction for the purpose of evading those requirements. These elements define a violation that is "willful" as that term is commonly interpreted. The majority's additional requirement that an actor have actual knowledge that structuring is prohibited strays from the statutory text, as well as from our precedents interpreting criminal statutes generally and "willfulness" in particular. . . .

In interpreting federal criminal tax statutes, this Court has defined the term "willfully" as requiring the "voluntary, intentional violation of a known legal duty." . . . Our rule in the tax area, however, is an "exception to the traditional rule," applied "largely due to the complexity of the tax laws." . . . The rule is inapplicable here, where, far from being complex, the provisions involved are perhaps among the simplest in the United States Code.

Although I believe the statutory language is clear in light of our precedents, the legislative history confirms that Congress intended to require knowledge of (and purpose to evade) the reporting requirements but not specific knowledge of the illegality of structuring.

QUESTIONS

1. Didn't Ratzlaf make the same argument as Baker did? If so, why did Ratzlaf win and Baker lose? Has Justice Ginsburg in *Ratzlaf* turned the conventional position on mistake of law on its head? Or can the *Ratzlaf* case be squared with the conventional position? How do you think Justice Ginsburg would rule on Baker's argument?

2. Do you believe that the Court's interpretation of "willfully" effectuated congressional intent? Consider the following:

In direct response to the *Ratzlaf* decision, Congress amended § 5324 effective September 23, 1994, by deleting the statutory "willfulness" requirement for *all* criminal prosecutions brought under 31 U.S.C. § 5324. . . . The effect of this legislative "fix" was to *eliminate entirely* the statutory willfulness requirement in all criminal prosecutions for violation of the "structuring" provisions of Section 5324(a)(3). Under the *"Ratzlaf fix"* — applicable to offenses *completed* after the statute's effective date — it is only necessary to prove that criminal defendants prosecuted under 31 U.S.C. § 5324 acted for the purpose of evading the CTR reporting requirements.[13]

3. Justice Blackmun in his dissent indicates that he differs with Justice Ginsburg in his approach to: (a) the text of the statute, (b) statutory interpretation, and (c) use of legislative intent. What approach does each Justice take to each of these topics?

4. The lower courts in *Ratzlaf* apparently treated "willfulness" as surplusage. Why would judges at both the trial and appellate levels treat a word placed in a statute by a legislature as being of "no consequence"?

5. Note that Ratzlaf — or actually Ratzlaf's lawyers — admitted in the Supreme Court that Ratzlaf met all the statutory elements except "willfulness." Why would a lawyer do such a thing? If Ratzlaf is retried after the Supreme Court's reversal of his conviction, does the prosecutor still have to prove the elements Ratzlaf admitted? If so, can she use Ratzlaf's admission to prove them?

6. How would the *Ratzlaf* case be resolved under the Model Penal Code?

ii. Reliance on Official Interpretation

The conventional view, exemplified by *Baker*, is that no mental state is required regarding the existence or meaning of the criminal law a defendant is charged with violating. But some statutes are written or interpreted as adopting the unconventional position of requiring the prosecution to prove some mental state regarding illegality. The tax statute at issue in *Ratzlaf* is an example of such an unconventional statute.

What happens, though, if a government agent, such as a police officer, misleads a defendant about the illegality of his conduct? If the statute under which the defendant is charged adopts the unconventional position, for instance by requiring knowledge of illegality, and the defendant lacks the required knowledge due to his reliance on a statement by a government agent, the question of liability is easy to resolve. The defendant would lack a required mental state and would not be liable.

But what if such a defendant is charged under a statute adopting the conventional position? Should the fact that the defendant was misled by a government agent be treated as irrelevant? Or should the defendant be relieved of liability? The materials in this Section address this problem.

COX *v.* LOUISIANA
379 U.S. 559 (1965)

GOLDBERG, J. [Defendant] was convicted of violating a Louisiana statue which provides:

"Whoever, with the intent of interfering with, obstructing, or impeding the administration of justice, or with the intent of influencing any judge, juror, witness, or court officer, in the discharge of his duty pickets or parades in or near a building housing a court of the State of Louisiana . . . shall be fined not more than

---

13. Criminal Resource Manual, Department of Justice, §2033 Structuring, *http://www.usdoj.gov/usao/eousa/foia_reading_room/usam/title9/crm02033.htm* (accessed 9/21/2002).

five thousand dollars or imprisoned not more than one year, or both." La. Rev. Stat. § 14:401 (Cum. Supp. 1962). [Defendant] was . . . sentenced to the maximum penalty under the statute of one year in jail and a $5,000 fine . . .

The record here clearly shows that the officials present gave permission for the demonstration to take place across the street from the courthouse. Cox testified that they gave him permission to conduct the demonstration on the far side of the street. This testimony is not only uncontradicted but is corroborated by the State's witnesses who were present. Police Chief White testified that he told Cox "he must confine" the demonstration "to the west side of the street." James Erwin, news director of radio station WIBR, agreed that Cox was given permission for the assembly as long as it remained within a designated time. When Sheriff Clemmons sought to break up the demonstration, he first announced, "now, you have been allowed to demonstrate." The Sheriff testified that he had "no objection" to the students "being assembled on that side of the street." . . .

[Defendant] was convicted for demonstrating not "in," but "near" the courthouse. It is undisputed that the demonstration took place on the west sidewalk, the far side of the street, exactly 101 feet from the courthouse steps and, judging from the pictures in the record, approximately 125 feet from the courthouse itself. The question is raised as to whether the failure of the statute to define the word "near" renders it unconstitutionally vague. . . . It is clear that there is some lack of specificity in a word such as "near." While this lack of specificity may not render the statute unconstitutionally vague, at least as applied to a demonstration within the sight and hearing of those in the courthouse, it is clear that the statute, with respect to the determination of how near the courthouse a particular demonstration can be, foresees a degree of on-the-spot administrative interpretation by officials charged with responsibility for administering and enforcing it. It is apparent that demonstrators, such as those involved here, would justifiably tend to rely on this administrative interpretation of how "near" the courthouse a particular demonstration might take place. Louisiana's statutory policy of preserving order around the courthouse would counsel encouragement of just such reliance. This administrative discretion to construe the term "near" concerns a limited control of the streets and other areas in the immediate vicinity of the courthouse and is the type of narrow discretion which this Court has recognized as the proper role of responsible officials in making determinations concerning the time, place, duration, and manner of demonstrations. . . . Obviously, telling demonstrators how far from the courthouse steps is "near" the courthouse for purposes of a permissible peaceful demonstration is a far cry from allowing one to commit, for example, murder, or robbery.

Thus, the highest police officials of the city, in the presence of the Sheriff and Mayor, in effect told the demonstrators that they could meet where they did, 101 feet from the courthouse steps, but could not meet closer to the courthouse. In effect, [defendant] was advised that a demonstration at the place it was held would not be one "near" the courthouse within the terms of the statute. . . . The Due Process Clause does not permit convictions to be obtained under such circumstances. . . .

Reversed.

QUESTIONS

1. Was the defendant incorrect about the law? About which law was there a question?

2. Did the error negate the defendant's *mens rea* with respect to the statute? If not, then why did the court reverse the conviction?

HOPKINS *v.* STATE
193 Md. 489 (1949)

DeLaPlaine, J. This appeal was taken by the Rev. William F. Hopkins, of Elkton, from the judgment of conviction entered upon the verdict of a jury in the Circuit Court for Cecil County for violation of the statute making it unlawful to erect or maintain any sign intended to aid in the solicitation or performance of marriages. . . .

The State charged that on September 1, 1947, defendant maintained a sign at the entrance to his home at 148 East Main Street in Elkton, and also a sign along a highway leading into the town, to aid in the solicitation and performance of marriages. Four photographs were admitted in evidence. One photograph, taken on an afternoon in September, 1947, shows the sign in Elkton containing the name "Rev. W.F. Hopkins, Notary Public, Information." The fourth shows this sign illuminated at night.

The State showed that during the month of August, 1947, thirty ministers performed 1,267 marriages in Cecil County, and of this number defendant performed 286, only three of which were ceremonies in which the parties were residents of Cecil County. . . .

Defendant did not testify. Several witnesses, however, testified that, though he has been residing in Elkton, he has been serving as the pastor of a church with about 40 members in Middletown, Delaware, known as the First Home Missionary Church. . . .

The Act of 1943, now under consideration, was passed by the Legislature of Maryland to curb the thriving businesses which unethical ministers had built up as a result of the tremendous increase in the number of couples coming into the State to be married following the passage of stringent marriage laws in nearby States. The first measure passed by the Legislature to suppress these unethical practices was the Act of 1922 making it unlawful for any minister to give or offer to give any money, present or reward to any hotel porter, railroad porter, or any other person as an inducement to direct to said minister any person contemplating matrimony. . . . [The Legislature subsequently passed at least two additional restrictions.]

After the passage of these restrictive Acts, there were still signs in Elkton and along the highways offering information to couples contemplating matrimony. Accordingly in 1943 the Legislature passed the Act, which is now before us, to prohibit billboards, signs, posters or display advertising of any kind, or information booths, intended to aid in the solicitation or performance of marriages. . . .

Defendant contended that the judge erred in excluding testimony offered to show that the State's Attorney advised him in 1944 before he erected the signs, that they would not violate the law. It is generally held that the advice of counsel, even though followed in good faith, furnishes no excuse to a person for violating the law and cannot be relied upon as a defense in a criminal action. . . . Moreover, advice given by a public official, even a State's Attorney, that a contemplated act is not criminal will not excuse the offender if, as a matter of law, the act performed did amount to a violation of the law. . . . These rules are founded upon the maxim that ignorance of the law will not excuse its violation. If an accused could be exempted from punishment for crime by reason of the advice of counsel, such advice would become paramount to the law.

While ignorance of fact may sometimes be admitted as evidence of lack of criminal intent, ignorance of the law ordinarily does not give immunity from punishment for crime, for every man is presumed to intend the necessary and legitimate consequences of what he knowingly does. In the case at bar defendant did not claim that the State's Attorney misled him regarding any facts of the case, but only that the State's Attorney advised him as to the law based upon the facts. Defendant was aware of the penal statute enacted by the Legislature. He knew what he wanted to do, and he did the thing he intended to do. He claims merely that he was given advice regarding his legal rights. If there was any mistake, it was mistake of law and not of fact. If the right of a person to erect a sign of a certain type and size depends upon the construction and application of a penal statute, and the right is somewhat doubtful, he erects the sign at his peril. In other words, a person who commits an act which the law declares to be criminal cannot be excused from punishment upon the theory that he misconstrued or misapplied the law. . . . For these reasons the exclusion of the testimony offered to show that defendant had sought and received advice from the State's Attorney was not prejudicial error.

Judgment affirmed, with costs.

Model Penal Code § 2.04   *Ignorance or Mistake*

(3) A belief that conduct does not legally constitute an offense is a defense to prosecution for that offense based upon such conduct when:

(a) the statute or other enactment defining the offense is not known to the actor and has not been published or otherwise made reasonably available prior to the conduct alleged; or

(b) he acts in reasonable reliance upon an official statement of the law, afterward determined to be invalid or erroneous, contained in

(i)   a statute or other enactment;

(ii) a judicial decision, opinion or judgment;

(iii) an administrative order or grant of permission; or

(iv) an official interpretation of the public officer or body charged by law with responsibility for the interpretation, administration or enforcement of the law defining the offense.

Texas Penal Code § 8.03   *Mistake of Law*

(a) It is no defense to prosecution that the actor was ignorant of the provisions of any law after the law has taken effect.

(b) It is an affirmative defense to prosecution that the actor reasonably believed the conduct charged did not constitute a crime and that he acted in reasonable reliance upon:

(1) an official statement of the law contained in a written order or grant of permission by an administrative agency charged by law with responsibility for interpreting the law in question; or

(2) a written interpretation of the law contained in an opinion of a court of record or made by a public official charged by law with responsibility for interpreting the law in question.

QUESTION

Does the Texas statute differ from the Model Penal Code? If so, how?

PROBLEM

5.25 Should the defendant be exonerated under the following circumstances?

Dr. Rosenthal cultivated medical marijuana for distribution to individuals who suffered from illnesses, like AIDS and cancer. He believed that he was legally authorized to do so under both federal and state law. His belief, as described in one of his court submissions, is excerpted below:[14]

> [H]e relied on a federal statute, 21 U.S.C. § 885(d), which states that "no criminal or civil liability shall be imposed . . . upon any duly authorized officer of . . . any state [or] political subdivision thereof . . . who shall be lawfully engaged in the enforcement of any law or municipal ordinance relating to controlled substances," along with Oakland Municipal Ordinance No. 12076, which is intended to provide immunity to medical cannabis provider associations pursuant to § 885(d); that the Oakland Cannabis Buyer's Cooperative was designated by Oakland to provide medical marijuana; deputized Rosenthal to act as its agent, and provided him with a letter informing him that he was a duly authorized officer of the City of Oakland and "as such [was] immune from civil and criminal liability under section 885(d);" that Rosenthal relied on that deputization in considering himself immune from federal prosecution; that the defendant discussed his cultivation activities with various local officials and the San Francisco District Attorney, all of whom told him that they supported his activities; that Mary Pat Jacobs, spokesperson for the Sonoma Alliance for Medical Marijuana, had told Rosenthal that she in turn had been told by DEA Supervisor Mike Heald that the DEA was not interested in interfering with the efforts of California counties to provide medical marijuana to seriously ill California patients; and that Rosenthal relied on these conversations with Jacobs to reinforce his conclusion that he was immunized from prosecution under federal law.

---

2. Mistake Regarding Circumstances that Include a Legal Element

Model Penal Code § 2.02   *General Requirements of Culpability*

---

14. The problem is based on Rosenthal's Reply in Support of Motion for New Trial in United States v. Rosenthal (No. CR-02-0053-CRB) (April 18, 2003) by Dennis Riordan, Attorney at Law. The quoted material is at 11-12.

Comment

It should be noted that the general principle that ignorance or mistake of law is no excuse is greatly overstated; it has no application, for example, *when the circumstances made material by the definition of the offense include a legal element.* Thus it is immaterial in theft, when claim of right is adduced in defense, that the claim involves a legal judgment as to the right of property. Claim of right is a defense because the property must belong to someone else for the theft to occur and the defendant must have culpable awareness of that fact. Insofar as this point is involved, there is no need to state a special principle; the legal element involved is simply an aspect of the attendant circumstances, with respect to which knowledge, recklessness or negligence, as the case may be, is required for culpability by Subsections (1) and (3). The law involved is not the law defining the offense; it is some other legal rule that characterizes the attendant circumstances that are material to the offense. (Emphasis added.)

REGINA *v.* SMITH (DAVID)

[1974] Q.B. 354 (1973)

On June 26, 1973, . . . the appellant, David Raymond Smith, pleaded not guilty to an indictment charging him . . . with contravening section 1 (1) of the Criminal Damage Act 1971. On June 28, 1973, the jury . . . convicted the appellant and he was discharged conditionally for 12 months and was ordered to pay £ 40 compensation. He appealed against conviction. . . .

. . . In 1970 the appellant became the tenant of a ground-floor flat. . . . The letting included a conservatory. In the conservatory the appellant and his brother, who lived with him, installed some electric wiring for use with stereo equipment. Also, with the landlord's permission, they put up roofing material and asbestos wall panels and laid floor boards. There is no dispute that the roofing, wall panels and floor boards became part of the house and, in law, the property of the landlord. Then in 1972 the appellant gave notice to quit and asked the landlord to allow the appellant's brother to remain as tenant of the flat. On September 18, 1972, the landlord informed the appellant that his brother could not remain. On the next day the appellant damaged the roofing, wall panels and floorboards he had installed in order — according to the appellant and his brother — to gain access to and remove the wiring. The extent of the damage was £ 130. When interviewed by the police, the appellant said: "Look, how can I be done for smashing my own property. I put the flooring and that in, so if I want to pull it down it's a matter for me." . . .

The appellant's defence was that he honestly believed that the damage he did was to his own property, that he believed that he was entitled to damage his own property and therefore he had a lawful excuse for his actions causing the damage. In the course of his summing up the deputy judge directed the jury in these terms:

"Now, in order to make the offence complete, the person who is charged with it must destroy or damage that property belonging to another, 'without lawful excuse,' and that is something that one has got to look at a little more, members of the jury, because you have heard here that, so far as each defendant was concerned, it never occurred to them, and, you may think, quite naturally never occurred to either of them, that these various additions to the house were anything but their own property. . . . But members of the jury, the Act is quite specific, and so far as the defendant David Smith is concerned lawful excuse is the only defence which has been raised. It is said that he had a lawful excuse by reason of his belief, his honest and genuinely held belief that he was destroying property which he had a right to destroy if he wanted to. But, members of the jury, I must direct you as a matter of law, and you must, therefore, accept it from me, that belief by the defendant David Smith that he had the right to do what he did is not lawful excuse within the meaning of the Act. Members of the jury, it is an excuse, it may even be a reasonable excuse, but it is not, members of the jury, a lawful excuse, because, in law, he had no right to do what he did. Members of the jury, as a matter of law, the evidence, in fact, discloses, so far as David Smith is concerned, no lawful excuse at all, because, as I say, the only defence which he has raised is the defence that he thought he had the right to do what he did. I have directed you that that is not a lawful excuse, and, members of the jury, it follows from that that so far as David Smith is concerned, I am bound to direct you as a matter of law that you must find him guilty of this offence with which he is charged."

It is contended for the appellant that that is a misdirection in law, and that, as a result of the misdirection, the entire defence of the appellant was wrongly withdrawn from the jury.

Section 1 of the Criminal Damage Act 1971 reads:

"(1) A person who without lawful excuse destroys or damages any property belonging to another intending to destroy or damage any such property or being reckless as to whether any such property would be destroyed or damaged, shall be guilty of an offence." . . .

It is argued for the appellant that an honest, albeit erroneous, belief that the act causing damage or destruction was done to his own property provides a defence to a charge brought under section 1 (1). The argument is . . . that the offence charged includes the act causing the damage or destruction and the element of mens rea. The element of mens rea relates to all the circumstances of the criminal act. The criminal act in the offence is causing damage to or destruction of "property belonging to another" and the element of mens rea, therefore, must relate to "property belonging to another." Honest belief, whether justifiable or not, that the property is the defendant's own negatives the element of mens rea. . . .

It is conceded by Mr. Gerber that there is force in the argument that the element of mens rea extends to "property belonging to another." But, it is argued, the section creates a new statutory offence and that it is open to the construction that the mental element in the offence relates only to causing damage to or destroying property. That if in fact the property damaged or destroyed is shown to be another's property the offence is committed although the defendant did not intend or foresee damage to another person's property. . . .

If the direction given by the deputy judge in the present case is correct, then the offence created by section 1 (1) of the Act of 1971 involves a considerable extension of the law in a surprising direction. Whether or not this is so depends upon the construction of the section. Construing the language of section 1 (1) we have no doubt that the actus reus is "destroying or damaging any property belonging to another." It is not possible to exclude the words "belonging to another" which describes the "property." Applying the ordinary principles of mens rea, the intention and recklessness and the absence of lawful excuse required to constitute the offence have reference to property belonging to another. It follows that in our judgment no offence is committed under this section if a person destroys or causes damage to property belonging to another if he does so in the honest though mistaken belief that the property is his own, and provided that the belief is honestly held it is irrelevant to consider whether or not it is a justifiable belief.

In our judgment, the direction given to the jury was a fundamental misdirection in law. The consequence was that the jury were precluded from considering facts capable of being a defence to the charge and were directed to convict.

For these reasons on November 5 at the conclusion of argument we allowed the appeal and ordered that the conviction be quashed.

QUESTIONS

1. About what law was Smith mistaken? The criminal law he was charged with violating? Or some other law?

2. The *Smith (David)* opinion refers to Smith's mistake claim several times as a "defence". Was Smith's mistake claim an example of "confession and avoidance"? Or was he simply contesting whether the government had proven an element of the charged offense?

3. How would the *Smith (David)* case be resolved under the Model Penal Code?

F. WILLFUL BLINDNESS

PROBLEM

5.26 Gwen is a bank trust officer. One day she approaches her friend Richard, a stockbroker and sometime art dealer, to ask for his help. Gwen tells Richard that the beneficiary of one of the trusts she administers is an older man, Bob, who has become quite fond of her. Bob's older brother died and left stock in a trust for Bob, which has increased enormously in value. Bob is a man of simple tastes who withdraws only a few hundred dollars a month from the thousands of dollars in interest available to him. The rest of the trust's income just keeps accumulating. Gwen tells Richard that Bob wants to make a gift to her because she has been so kind to him over the years but bank regulations will not let her take the money directly from Bob. Gwen proposes to write Richard a series of ten checks for $3,000 each. All Richard has to do is deposit the checks in his account and then write a check to Gwen. For his help, Gwen offers to allow Richard to keep half the money. Gwen will wind up with $15,000 and Richard will wind up with $15,000. Gwen offers to further explain the bank regulations and to have Richard meet Bob, but Richard indicates that he doesn't want to know any more than Gwen has told him. Gwen and Richard go ahead with the transaction. Six months later, an FBI agent calls on Richard. It turns out that Gwen was embezzling the money from Bob's trust account without Bob's knowledge or consent. Richard is charged with a felony under a statute that reads:

> Anyone who receives money in excess of $1,000 knowing that it is either stolen or embezzled is guilty of a felony punishable by up to five years in prison.
>
> Is Richard criminally liable under the statute?

PATTERN JURY INSTRUCTIONS (CRIMINAL CASES)

Prepared by the Committee on Pattern Criminal Jury Instructions, First Circuit (1998)

2.14 "WILLFUL BLINDNESS" AS A WAY OF SATISFYING KNOWINGLY

In deciding whether the defendant acted knowingly, you may infer that the defendant had knowledge of a fact if you find that he/she deliberately closed his/her eyes to a fact that otherwise would have been obvious to him/her. In order to infer knowledge, you must find that two things have been established. First, that the defendant was aware of a high probability of the fact in question. Second, that the defendant consciously and deliberately avoided learning of that fact. That is to say, the defendant willfully made himself blind to that fact. It is entirely up to you to determine whether he deliberately closed his eyes to the fact and, if so, what inference, if any, should be drawn. However, it is important to bear in mind that mere negligence or mistake in failing to learn the fact is not sufficient. There must be a deliberate effort to remain ignorant of the fact.

Comment

. . . "The danger of an improper willful blindness instruction is 'the possibility that the jury will be led to employ a negligence standard and convict a defendant on the impermissible ground that he should have known [an illegal act] was taking place.' " [*United States v. Brandon*, 17 F.3d 409, 453 (1st Cir. 1994).]

QUESTION

Why is it impermissible to convict someone on the ground that he should have known an illegal act was taking place when knowledge is the required mental state?

UNITED STATES *v.* JEWELL

532 F.2d 697 (1976)

BROWNING, J. . . . It is undisputed that [Jewell] entered the United States driving an automobile in which 110 pounds of marihuana worth $6,250 had been concealed in a secret compartment between the trunk and rear seat. [Jewell] testified that he did not know the marihuana was present. There was circumstantial evidence from which the jury could infer that appellant had positive knowledge of the presence of the marihuana, and that his contrary testimony was false.

[Jewell] testified that a week before the incident in question he sold his car for $100 to obtain funds "to have a good time." He then rented a car for about $100, and he and a friend drove the rented car to Mexico. [Jewell] and his friend were unable to explain their whereabouts during the period of about 11 hours between the time they left Los Angeles and the time they admitted arriving in Mexico.

Their testimony regarding acquisition of the load car follows a pattern common in these cases: they were approached in a Tijuana bar by a stranger who identified himself only by his first name "Ray." He asked them if they wanted to buy marihuana, and offered to pay them $100 for driving a car north across the border. [Jewell] accepted the offer and drove the load car back, alone. [Jewell's] friend drove the . . . rented car back to Los Angeles.

[Jewell] testified that the stranger instructed him to leave the load car at the address on the car registration slip with the keys in the ashtray. The person living at that address testified that he had sold the car a year earlier and had not seen it since. When the Customs agent asked [Jewell] about the secret compartment in the car, [Jewell] did not deny knowledge of its existence, but stated that it was in the car when he got it. . . .

On the other hand there was evidence from which the jury could conclude that appellant spoke the truth—that although appellant knew of the presence of the secret compartment and had knowledge of facts indicating that it contained marihuana, he deliberately avoided positive knowledge of the presence of the contraband to avoid responsibility in the event of discovery. . . . The Drug Enforcement Administration agent testified that [Jewell] stated "he thought there was probably something wrong and something illegal in the vehicle, but that he checked it over. He looked in the glove box and under the front seat and in the trunk, prior to driving it. *He didn't find anything and therefore he assumed that the people at the border wouldn't find anything either*" (emphasis added). [Jewell] was asked at trial whether he had seen the special compartment when he opened the trunk. He responded, "Well, you know, I saw a void there, but I didn't know what it was." He testified that he did not investigate further. . . . The jury would have been justified in accepting all of the testimony as true and concluding that although [defendant] was aware of facts making it virtually certain that the secret compartment concealed marihuana, he deliberately refrained from acquiring positive knowledge of the fact. If the jury concluded the latter was indeed the situation, and if positive knowledge is required to convict, the jury would have no choice consistent with its oath but to find appellant not guilty even though he deliberately contrived his lack of positive knowledge.

[The jury convicted Jewell under the following statutes: (1) knowingly or intentionally importing a controlled substance, 21 U.S.C. §§ 952(a), 960(a)(1); (2) knowingly or intentionally possessing, with intent to distribute, a controlled substance, 21 U.S.C. 841(a)(1).]

[Jewell] tendered an instruction that to return a guilty verdict the jury must find that the defendant knew he was in possession of marihuana. The trial judge rejected the instruction. . . .

The court instructed the jury that "knowingly" meant voluntarily and intentionally and not by accident or mistake. . . . The court continued: The Government can complete their burden of proof by proving, beyond a reasonable doubt, that if the defendant was not actually aware that there was marijuana in the vehicle he was driving when he entered the United States his ignorance in that regard was solely and entirely a result of his having made a conscious purpose to disregard the nature of that which was in the vehicle, with a conscious purpose to avoid learning the truth.

The legal premise of these instructions is firmly supported by leading commentators here and in England. Professor Rollin M. Perkins writes, "One with a
deliberate antisocial purpose in mind . . . may deliberately 'shut his eyes' to avoid
knowing what would otherwise be obvious to view. In such cases, so far as criminal
law is concerned, the person acts at his peril in this regard, and is treated as having 'knowledge' of the facts as they are ultimately discovered to be." . . . Professor
Glanville Williams states, on the basis of both English and American authorities,
"To the requirement of actual knowledge there is one strictly limited exception. . . .
[The] rule is that if a party has his suspicion aroused but then deliberately omits to
make further enquiries, because he wishes to remain in ignorance, he is deemed to
have knowledge." Professor Williams concludes, "The rule that wilful blindness is
equivalent to knowledge is essential, and is found throughout the criminal law. . . .
It is, at the same time, an unstable rule, because judges are apt to forget its very
limited scope. A court can properly find wilful blindness only where it can almost
be said that the defendant actually knew. . . . It requires in effect a finding that
the defendant intended to cheat the administration of justice. Any wider definition would make the doctrine of wilful blindness indistinguishable from the civil
doctrine of negligence in not obtaining knowledge.

The substantive justification for the rule is that deliberate ignorance and positive knowledge are equally culpable. The textual justification is that in common
understanding one "knows" facts of which he is less than absolutely certain. To act
"knowingly," therefore, is not necessarily to act only with positive knowledge, but
also to act with an awareness of the high probability of the existence of the fact in
question. When such awareness is present, "positive" knowledge is not required.

This is the analysis adopted in the Model Penal Code. Section 2.02(7) states:
"When knowledge of the existence of a particular fact is an element of an offense,
such knowledge is established if a person is aware of a high probability of its
existence, unless he actually believes that it does not exist." . . .

"Deliberate ignorance" instructions have been approved in prosecutions under
criminal statutes prohibiting "knowing" conduct by the Courts of Appeals of the
Second, Sixth, Seventh, and Tenth Circuits. In many other cases, Courts of Appeals
reviewing the sufficiency of evidence have approved the premise that "knowingly"
in criminal statutes is not limited to positive knowledge, but includes the state of
mind of one who does not possess positive knowledge only because he consciously
avoided it. These lines of authority appear unbroken. Neither the dissent nor the
briefs of either party has cited a case holding that such an instruction is error or
that such evidence is not sufficient to establish "knowledge."

There is no reason to reach a different result under the statute involved in
this case. Doing so would put this court in direct conflict with Courts of Appeals
in two other circuits that have approved "deliberate ignorance" instructions in
prosecutions under 21 U.S.C. § 841(a), or its predecessor, 21 U.S.C. § 174. Nothing
is cited from the legislative history of the Drug Control Act indicating that Congress
used the term "knowingly" in a sense at odds with prior authority. Rather, Congress
is presumed to have known and adopted the "cluster of ideas" attached to such a
familiar term of art. *Morissette v. United States*, 342 U.S. 246 (1952). . . .

Appellant's narrow interpretation of "knowingly" is inconsistent with the Drug
Control Act's general purpose to deal more effectively "with the growing menace of
drug abuse in the United States." Holding that this term introduces a requirement
of positive knowledge would make deliberate ignorance a defense. It cannot be
doubted that those who traffic in drugs would make the most of it. This is evident

from the number of appellate decisions reflecting conscious avoidance of positive knowledge of the presence of contraband—in the car driven by the defendant or in which he is a passenger, in the suitcase or package he carries, in the parcel concealed in his clothing. . . .

It is worth emphasizing that the required state of mind differs from positive knowledge only so far as necessary to encompass a calculated effort to avoid the sanctions of the statute while violating its substance. "A court can properly find wilful blindness only where it can almost be said that the defendant actually knew." . . .

No legitimate interest of an accused is prejudiced by such a standard, and society's interest in a system of criminal law that is enforceable and that imposes sanctions upon all who are equally culpable requires it.

The conviction is affirmed.

KENNEDY, J., dissenting.

[One] problem [with the willful blindness doctrine] is that the English authorities seem to consider wilful blindness a state of mind distinct from, but equally culpable as, "actual" knowledge. When a statute specifically requires knowledge as an element of a crime, however, the substitution of some other state of mind cannot be justified even if the court deems that both are equally blameworthy. . . .

Finally, the wilful blindness doctrine is uncertain in scope. There is disagreement as to whether reckless disregard for the existence of a fact constitutes wilful blindness or some lesser degree of culpability. Some cases have held that a statute's scienter requirement is satisfied by the constructive knowledge imputed to one who simply fails to discharge a duty to inform himself. There is also the question of whether to use an "objective" test based on the reasonable man, or to consider the defendant's subjective belief as dispositive.

The approach adopted in section 2.02(7) of the Model Penal Code clarifies, and, in important ways restricts the English doctrine. . . . This provision requires an awareness of a high probability that a fact exists, not merely a reckless disregard, or a suspicion followed by a failure to make further inquiry. It also establishes knowledge as a matter of subjective belief, an important safeguard against diluting the guilty state of mind required for conviction. It is important to note that section 2.02(7) is a definition of knowledge, not a substitute for it. . . .

In light of the Model Penal Code's definition, the "conscious purpose" jury instruction is defective in three respects. First, it fails to mention the requirement that Jewell have been aware of a high probability that a controlled substance was in the car. It is not culpable to form "a conscious purpose to avoid learning the truth" unless one is aware of facts indicating a high probability of that truth. To illustrate, a child given a gift-wrapped package by his mother while on vacation in Mexico may form a conscious purpose to take it home without learning what is inside; yet his state of mind is totally innocent unless he is aware of a high probability that the package contains a controlled substance. Thus, a conscious purpose instruction is only proper when coupled with a requirement that one be aware of a high probability of the truth.

The second defect in the instruction as given is that it did not alert the jury that Jewell could not be convicted if he "actually believed" there was no controlled substance in the car. The failure to emphasize, as does the Model Penal Code, that subjective belief is the determinative factor, may allow a jury to convict on an objective theory of knowledge—that a reasonable man should have inspected the car and would have discovered what was hidden inside. One recent decision reversed a jury instruction for this very deficiency—failure to balance a conscious purpose instruction with a warning that the defendant could not be convicted if he actually believed to the contrary.

Third, the jury instruction clearly states that Jewell could have been convicted even if found ignorant or "not actually aware" that the car contained a controlled substance. This is unacceptable because true ignorance, no matter how unreasonable, cannot provide a basis for criminal liability when the statute requires knowledge. A proper jury instruction based on the Model Penal Code would be presented as a way of defining knowledge, and not as an alternative to it.

QUESTIONS

1. What is willful blindness? Is it a substitute for or a type of knowledge? Should courts substitute willful blindness for knowledge when a statute calls for knowledge? Why does Judge (now Justice) Kennedy emphasize that willful blindness is "a way of defining knowledge, and not . . . an alternative to it"?

2. What are the difficulties in treating willful blindness as a proxy for knowledge? Is there another mental state that better captures willful blindness? If so, why don't courts or the MPC use that mental state?

3. In *Keeler*, the court interpreted the word "human being" not to include a fetus. In *Martin*, the court interpreted the word "appear" to include a voluntariness requirement. Is the *Jewell* court's interpretation of the word "knowingly" similar to or different from the interpretation in *Keeler* and in *Martin*?

4. Judge Browning cites the *Morissette* case in support of his interpretation of the statutes under which Jewell was charged. How does *Morissette* support Judge Browning's interpretation?

The Model Penal Code Approach to Willful Blindness

The willful blindness problem proved important enough to merit special attention in the Model Penal Code provisions on culpability.

§ 2.02(7) *Requirement of Knowledge Satisfied by Knowledge of High Probability.* When knowledge of the existence of a particular fact is an element of an offense, such knowledge is established if a person is aware of a high probability of its existence, unless he actually believes it does not exist.

The following commentary to the Model Penal Code explains the MPC position.

Comment

Knowledge Satisfied by High Probability. Subsection (7) deals with the situation that British commentators have denominated "wilful blindness" or "connivance," the case of the actor who is aware of the probable existence of a material fact but does not determine whether it exists or does not exist. Whether such cases should be viewed as instances of acting recklessly or knowingly presents a subtle but important question.

The Code proposes that the case be viewed as one of acting knowingly when what is involved is a matter of existing fact, but not when what is involved is the result of the defendant's conduct, necessarily a matter of the future at the time of acting. The position reflects what was believed to be the normal policy of criminal enactments that rest liability on acting "knowingly." The inference of "knowledge" of an existing fact is usually drawn from proof of notice of high probability of its existence, unless the defendant establishes an honest, contrary belief. Subsection (7) solidifies this usual result and clarifies the terms in which the issue is submitted to the jury.

Some recently revised and proposed codes have included similar language. . . .

QUESTIONS

1. Is the instruction given by the trial court in *Jewell* consistent with the MPC standard in 2.02(7)?

2. Why should it matter whether the non-mental element the knowledge relates to occurs in the present or the future? How would the MPC Commentary apply to the facts in the *Jewell* case?

3. Which defines "willful blindness" most clearly? Judge Browning's opinion in *Jewell*? Judge Kennedy's dissent in *Jewell*? The Model Penal Code? Or the First Circuit Pattern jury instruction that appears at the outset of this Section?

G. CONDITIONAL PURPOSE/INTENT

PROBLEM

5.27 Sheila is charged under a burglary statute that reads:

> It is a felony to enter a residence at night with intent to steal.

Sheila concedes that she intended to enter a residence at night, but contends that she intended to steal only if no one were home.[15] After entering, Sheila discovered that someone was at home and left without taking anything. Is she liable under the statute?

5.28 You are a lawyer working at a law firm that represents a shelter for homeless men as a pro bono client. The executive director of the shelter informs you that a large percentage of the homeless men who frequent the shelter are heroin addicts and that the incidence of HIV infection among such men has been growing due to the multiple re-use of dirty hypodermic needles to inject heroin. The executive director tells you that the shelter wants to begin a program distributing clean hypodermic needles to its residents to help prevent or reduce the spread of HIV infection, but he is concerned that they may encounter legal problems. Assume the state in which you live makes it a crime to use drugs such as heroin and that one is an accomplice to a crime if one assists another to commit a crime with the purpose that the crime be committed. Are the workers at the shelter criminally liable if they hand out clean hypodermic needles?

---

15. Example based on MPC Comment 2.02(8).

HOLLOWAY *v.* UNITED STATES

526 U.S. 1 (1999)

STEVENS. J. Carjacking "with the intent to cause death or serious bodily harm" is a federal crime.[1] The question presented in this case is whether that phrase requires the Government to prove that the defendant had an unconditional intent to kill or harm in all events, or whether it merely requires proof of an intent to kill or harm if necessary to effect a carjacking. Most of the judges who have considered the question have concluded, as do we, that Congress intended to criminalize the more typical carjacking carried out by means of a deliberate threat of violence, rather than just the rare case in which the defendant has an unconditional intent to use violence regardless of how the driver responds to his threat.

I

A jury found petitioner guilty on three counts of carjacking, as well as several other offenses related to stealing cars.[2] In each of the carjackings, petitioner and an armed accomplice identified a car that they wanted and followed it until it was parked. The accomplice then approached the driver, produced a gun, and threatened to shoot unless the driver handed over the car keys.[3] The accomplice testified that the plan was to steal the cars without harming the victims, but that he would have used his gun if any of the drivers had given him a "hard time." When one victim hesitated, petitioner punched him in the face but there was no other actual violence.

The District Judge instructed the jury that the Government was required to prove beyond a reasonable doubt that the taking of a motor vehicle was committed with the intent "to cause death or serious bodily harm to the person from whom the car was taken." After explaining that merely using a gun to frighten a victim was not sufficient to prove such intent, he added the following statement over the defendant's objection:

"In some cases, intent is conditional. That is, a defendant may intend to engage in certain conduct only if a certain event occurs.

"In this case, the government contends that the defendant intended to cause death or serious bodily harm if the alleged victims had refused to turn over their cars. If you find beyond a reasonable doubt that the defendant had such an intent, the government has satisfied this element of the offense. . . . "

---

[1] As amended by the Violent Crime Control and Law Enforcement Act of 1994, § 60003(a) (14), 108 Stat. 1970, and by the Carjacking Correction Act of 1996, § 2, 110 Stat. 3020, the statute provides:

"Whoever, with the intent to cause death or serious bodily harm takes a motor vehicle that has been transported, shipped, or received in interstate or foreign commerce from the person or presence of another by force and violence or by intimidation, or attempts to do so, shall —
  "(1) be fined under this title or imprisoned not more than 15 years, or both,
  "(2) if serious bodily injury (as defined in section 1365 of this title, including any conduct that, if the conduct occurred in the special maritime and territorial jurisdiction of the United States, would violate section 2241 or 2242 of this title) results, be fined under this title or imprisoned not more than 25 years, or both, and
  "(3) if death results, be fined under this title or imprisoned for any number of years up to life, or both, or sentenced to death." 18 U.S.C. § 2119 (1994 ed. and Supp. III) (emphasis added).

[2] He was also charged with conspiring to operate a "chop shop" in violation of 18 U.S.C. § 371, operating a chop shop in violation of § 2322, and using and carrying a firearm in violation of § 924(c).

[3] One victim testified that the accomplice produced his gun and threatened, "'Get out of the car or I'll shoot.'" App. 51. Another testified that he said, "'Give me your keys or I will shoot you right now.'" *Id.* at 52.

In his postverdict motion for a new trial, petitioner contended that this instruction was inconsistent with the text of the statute. The District Judge denied the motion, stating that there "is no question that the conduct at issue in this case is precisely what Congress and the general public would describe as carjacking, and that Congress intended to prohibit it in § 2119." 921 F. Supp. 155, 156 (EDNY 1996). He noted that the statute as originally enacted in 1992 contained no intent element but covered all carjackings committed by a person "possessing a firearm." A 1994 amendment had omitted the firearm limitation, thus broadening the coverage of the statute to encompass the use of other weapons, and also had inserted the intent requirement at issue in this case. The judge thought that an "odd result" would flow from a construction of the amendment that "would no longer prohibit the very crime it was enacted to address except in those unusual circumstances when carjackers also intended to commit another crime—murder or a serious assault." *Id.* at 159. Moreover, the judge determined that even though the issue of conditional intent has not been discussed very often, at least in the federal courts, it was a concept that scholars and state courts had long recognized.

Over a dissent that accused the majority of "a clear judicial usurpation of congressional authority," *United States v. Arnold*, 126 F.3d 82, 92 (CA2 1997) (opinion of Miner, J.), the Court of Appeals affirmed. The majority was satisfied that "the inclusion of a conditional intent to harm within the definition of specific intent to harm" was not only "a well-established principle of common law," but also, and "most importantly," comported "with a reasonable interpretation of the legislative purpose of the statute." The alternative interpretation, which would cover "only those carjackings in which the carjacker's sole and unconditional purpose at the time he committed the carjacking was to kill or maim the victim," the court concluded, was clearly at odds with the intent of the statute's drafters.

To resolve an apparent conflict with a decision of the Ninth Circuit, *United States v. Randolph*, 93 F.3d 656 (1996),[4] we granted certiorari.

II

Writing for the Court in *United States v. Turkette*, 452 U.S. 576, 593, 69 L. Ed. 2d 246, 101 S. Ct. 2524 (1981), Justice White reminded us that the language of the statutes that Congress enacts provides "the most reliable evidence of its intent." For that reason, we typically begin the task of statutory construction by focusing on the words that the drafters have chosen. In interpreting the statute at issue, "we consider not only the bare meaning" of the critical word or phrase "but also its placement and purpose in the statutory scheme."

The specific issue in this case is what sort of evil motive Congress intended to describe when it used the words "with the intent to cause death or serious bodily harm" in the 1994 amendment to the carjacking statute. More precisely, the question is whether a person who points a gun at a driver, having decided to pull the trigger if the driver does not comply with a demand for the car keys, possesses

---

[4] The Ninth Circuit held that neither a person's mere threat to the driver that " 'she would be okay if she [did] what was told of her' " nor "the brandishing of a weapon, without more" constituted an intent to cause death or serious bodily harm under the amended version of § 2119. 93 F.3d at 664-665. The court therefore reversed the defendant's carjacking conviction on the ground of insufficient evidence. In the course of its opinion, the Ninth Circuit also stated more broadly that "the mere conditional intent to harm a victim if she resists is simply not enough to satisfy § 2119's new specific intent requirement." *Id.* at 665. It is this proposition with which other courts have disagreed. . . .

the intent, at that moment, to seriously harm the driver. In our view, the answer to that question does not depend on whether the driver immediately hands over the keys or what the offender decides to do after he gains control over the car. At the relevant moment, the offender plainly does have the forbidden intent.

The opinions that have addressed this issue accurately point out that a carjacker's intent to harm his victim may be either "conditional" or "unconditional."[5] The statutory phrase at issue theoretically might describe (1) the former, (2) the latter, or (3) both species of intent. Petitioner argues that the "plain text" of the statute "unequivocally" describes only the latter: that the defendant must possess a specific and unconditional intent to kill or harm in order to complete the proscribed offense. To that end, he insists that Congress would have had to insert the words "if necessary" into the disputed text in order to include the conditional species of intent within the scope of the statute. Because Congress did not include those words, petitioner contends that we must assume that Congress meant to provide a federal penalty for only those carjackings in which the offender actually attempted to harm or kill the driver (or at least intended to do so whether or not the driver resisted).

We believe, however, that a commonsense reading of the carjacking statute counsels that Congress intended to criminalize a broader scope of conduct than attempts to assault or kill in the course of automobile robberies. As we have repeatedly stated, " 'the meaning of statutory language, plain or not, depends on context.' " When petitioner's argument is considered in the context of the statute, it becomes apparent that his proffered construction of the intent element overlooks the significance of the placement of that element in the statute. The carjacking statute essentially is aimed at providing a federal penalty for a particular type of robbery. The statute's mens rea component thus modifies the act of "taking" the motor vehicle. It directs the factfinder's attention to the defendant's state of mind at the precise moment he demanded or took control over the car "by force and violence or by intimidation." If the defendant has the proscribed state of mind at that moment, the statute's scienter element is satisfied.

Petitioner's reading of the intent element, in contrast, would improperly transform the mens rea element from a modifier into an additional actus reus component of the carjacking statute; it would alter the statute into one that focuses on attempting to harm or kill a person in the course of the robbery of a motor vehicle.[6] Indeed, if we accepted petitioner's view of the statute's intent element, even Congress' insertion of the qualifying words "if necessary," by themselves, would not have solved the deficiency that he believes exists in the statute. The inclusion of those words after the intent phrase would have excluded the unconditional species of intent—the intent to harm or kill even if not necessary to complete a carjacking. Accordingly, if Congress had used words such as "if necessary" to describe the conditional species of intent, it would also have needed to add something like "or even if not necessary" in order to cover both species of intent to harm. Given the fact that the actual text does not mention either species separately—and thus does not expressly exclude either—that text is most naturally read to encompass the mens

---

[5] *See, e.g.*, Williams, 136 F.3d at 550-551; Anderson, 108 F.3d at 481.

[6] Although subsections (2) and (3) of the carjacking statute envision harm or death resulting from the crime, subsection (1), under petitioner's reading, would have to cover attempts to harm or kill when no serious bodily harm resulted.

rea of both conditional and unconditional intent, and not to limit the statute's reach to crimes involving the additional actus reus of an attempt to kill or harm.

Two considerations strongly support the conclusion that a natural reading of the text is fully consistent with a congressional decision to cover both species of intent. First, the statute as a whole reflects an intent to authorize federal prosecutions as a significant deterrent to a type of criminal activity that was a matter of national concern.[7] Because that purpose is better served by construing the statute to cover both the conditional and the unconditional species of wrongful intent, the entire statute is consistent with a normal interpretation of the specific language that Congress chose. Indeed, petitioner's interpretation would exclude from the coverage of the statute most of the conduct that Congress obviously intended to prohibit.

Second, it is reasonable to presume that Congress was familiar with the cases and the scholarly writing that have recognized that the "specific intent" to commit a wrongful act may be conditional. The facts of the leading case on the point are strikingly similar to the facts of this case. In *People v. Connors*, 253 Ill. 266, 97 N.E. 643 (1912), the Illinois Supreme Court affirmed the conviction of a union organizer who had pointed a gun at a worker and threatened to kill him forthwith if he did not take off his overalls and quit work. The Court held that the jury had been properly instructed that the "specific intent to kill" could be found even though that intent was "coupled with a condition" that the defendant would not fire if the victim complied with his demand. That holding has been repeatedly cited with approval by other courts and by scholars. Moreover, it reflects the views endorsed by the authors of the Model Criminal Code.[11] The core principle that emerges from these sources is that a defendant may not negate a proscribed intent by requiring the victim to comply with a condition the defendant has no right to impose; "an intent to kill, in the alternative, is nevertheless an intent to kill."[12]

This interpretation of the statute's specific intent element does not, as petitioner suggests, render superfluous the statute's "by force and violence or by intimidation" element. While an empty threat, or intimidating bluff, would be sufficient to satisfy the latter element, such conduct, standing on its own, is not enough to satisfy § 2119's specific intent element. In a carjacking case in which the driver surrendered or otherwise lost control over his car without the defendant attempting to inflict, or

---

[7] Although the legislative history relating to the carjacking amendment is sparse, those members of Congress who recorded comments made statements reflecting the statute's broad deterrent purpose. See 139 Cong. Rec. 27867 (1993) (statement of Sen. Lieberman) ("Th[e 1994] amendment will broaden and strengthen the [carjacking] law so our U.S. attorneys will have every possible tool available to them to attack the problem"); 140 Cong. Rec. E858 (May 5, 1994) (extension of remarks by Rep. Franks) ("We must send a message to [carjackers] that committing a violent crime will carry a severe penalty"). There is nothing in the 1994 amendment's legislative history to suggest that Congress meant to create a federal crime for only the unique and unusual subset of carjackings in which the offender intends to harm or kill the driver regardless of whether the driver accedes to the offender's threat of violence.

[11] Section 2.02(6) of the Model Penal Code provides:

"Requirement of Purpose Satisfied if Purpose Is Conditional.

When a particular purpose is an element of an offense, the element is established although such purpose is conditional, unless the condition negatives the harm or evil sought to be prevented by the law defining the offense."

American Law Institute, Model Penal Code (1985).

Of course, in this case the condition that the driver surrender the car was the precise evil that Congress wanted to prevent.

[12] Perkins & Boyce, Criminal Law, at 647.

actually inflicting, serious bodily harm, Congress' inclusion of the intent element requires the Government to prove beyond a reasonable doubt that the defendant would have at least attempted to seriously harm or kill the driver if that action had been necessary to complete the taking of the car.

In short, we disagree with petitioner's reading of the text of the Act and think it unreasonable to assume that Congress intended to enact such a truncated version of an important criminal statute.[14] The intent requirement of § 2119 is satisfied when the Government proves that at the moment the defendant demanded or took control over the driver's automobile the defendant possessed the intent to seriously harm or kill the driver if necessary to steal the car (or, alternatively, if unnecessary to steal the car). Accordingly, we affirm the judgment of the Court of Appeals.

It is so ordered.

SCALIA, J. dissenting.

The issue in this case is the meaning of the phrase, in 18 U.S.C. § 2119, "with the intent to cause death or serious bodily harm." (For convenience' sake, I shall refer to it in this opinion as simply intent to kill.) As recounted by the Court, petitioner's accomplice, Vernon Lennon, "testified that the plan was to steal the cars without harming the victims, but that he would have used his gun if any of the drivers had given him a 'hard time.' " The District Court instructed the jury that the intent element would be satisfied if petitioner possessed this " conditional" intent. Today's judgment holds that instruction to have been correct.

I dissent from that holding because I disagree with the following, utterly central, passage of the opinion:

"[A] carjacker's intent to harm his victim may be either 'conditional' or 'unconditional.' The statutory phrase at issue theoretically might describe (1) the former, (2) the latter, or (3) both species of intent."

I think, to the contrary, that in customary English usage the unqualified word "intent" does not usually connote a purpose that is subject to any conditions precedent except those so remote in the speaker's estimation as to be effectively nonexistent—and it *never* connotes a purpose that is subject to a condition which the speaker hopes will not occur. (It is this last sort of "conditional intent" that is at issue in this case, and that I refer to in my subsequent use of the term.) "Intent" is "[a] state of mind in which a person seeks to accomplish a given result through a course of action." Black's Law Dictionary 810 (6th ed. 1990). One can hardly "seek to accomplish" a result he hopes will not ensue.

The Court's division of intent into two categories, conditional and unconditional, makes the unreasonable seem logical. But Aristotelian classification says nothing about linguistic usage. Instead of identifying two categories, the Court might just as readily have identified three: unconditional intent, conditional intent, and feigned intent. But the second category, like the third, is simply not conveyed by the word "intent" alone. There is intent, conditional intent, and feigned intent, just as there is agreement, conditional agreement, and feigned agreement— but to say that in either case the noun alone, without qualification, "theoretically

---

[14] We also reject petitioner's argument that the rule of lenity should apply in this case. We have repeatedly stated that " 'the rule of lenity applies only if, after seizing everything from which aid can be derived, . . . we can make no more than a guess as to what Congress intended.' " Muscarello v. United States, 524 U.S. 125, 1998 U.S. LEXIS 3879 at *24, 141 L. Ed. 2d 111, 118 S. Ct. 1911 (1998) (quoting United States v. Wells, 519 U.S. 482, 499, 137 L. Ed. 2d 107, 117 S. Ct. 921 (1997)) (additional quotations and citations omitted).

might describe" all three phenomena is simply false. Conditional intent is no more embraced by the unmodified word "intent" than a sea lion is embraced by the unmodified word "lion."

If I have made a categorical determination to go to Louisiana for the Christmas holidays, it is accurate for me to say that I "intend" to go to Louisiana. And that is so even though I realize that there are some remote and unlikely contingencies—"acts of God," for example—that might prevent me. (The fact that these remote contingencies are always implicit in the expression of intent accounts for the humorousness of spelling them out in such expressions as "if I should live so long," or "the Good Lord willing and the creek don't rise.") It is less precise, though tolerable usage, to say that I "intend" to go if my purpose is conditional upon an event which, though not virtually certain to happen (such as my continuing to live), is reasonably likely to happen, and which I hope will happen. I might, for example, say that I "intend" to go even if my plans depend upon receipt of my usual and hoped-for end-of-year bonus.

But it is not common usage—indeed, it is an unheard-of usage—to speak of my having an "intent" to do something, when my plans are contingent upon an event that is not virtually certain, and that I hope will not occur. When a friend is seriously ill, for example, I would not say that "I intend to go to his funeral next week." I would have to make it clear that the intent is a conditional one: "I intend to go to his funeral next week if he dies." The carjacker who intends to kill if he is met with resistance is in the same position: he has an "intent to kill if resisted"; he does not have an "intent to kill." No amount of rationalization can change the reality of this normal (and as far as I know exclusive) English usage. The word in the statute simply will not bear the meaning that the Court assigns.

The Government makes two contextual arguments to which I should respond. First, it points out that the statute criminalizes not only carjackings accomplished by "force and violence" but also those accomplished by mere "intimidation." Requiring an unconditional intent, it asserts, would make the number of covered carjackings accomplished by intimidation "implausibly small." That seems to me not so. It is surely not an unusual carjacking in which the criminal jumps into the passenger seat and forces the person behind the wheel to drive off at gunpoint. A carjacker who intends to kill may well use this modus operandi, planning to kill the driver in a more secluded location. Second, the Government asserts that it would be hard to imagine an unconditional-intent-to-kill case in which the first penalty provision of § 2119 would apply, i.e., the provision governing cases in which no death or bodily harm has occurred. That is rather like saying that the crime of attempted murder should not exist, because someone who intends to kill always succeeds.

Notwithstanding the clear ordinary meaning of the word "intent," it would be possible, though of course quite unusual, for the word to have acquired a different meaning in the criminal law. The Court does not claim—and falls far short of establishing—such "term-of-art" status. It cites five state cases (representing the majority view among the minority of jurisdictions that have addressed the question) saying that conditional intent satisfies an intent requirement; but it acknowledges that there are cases in other jurisdictions to the contrary. As I understand the Court's position, it is not that the former cases are right and the latter wrong, so that "intent" in criminal statutes, a term of art in that context, includes conditional intent; but rather that "intent" in criminal statutes may include conditional intent, depending upon the statute in question. That seems to me not an available option. It is so utterly clear in normal usage that "intent" does not include conditional intent, that only an accepted convention in the criminal law could give the word a different meaning. And an accepted convention is not established by the fact that some courts have thought so some times. One must decide, I think, which line of cases is correct, and in my judgment it is that which rejects the conditional-intent rule.

There are of course innumerable federal criminal statutes containing an intent requirement, ranging from intent to steal, see 18 U.S.C. § 2113, to intent to defeat the provisions of the Bankruptcy Code, see § 152(5), to intent that a vessel be used in hostilities against a friendly nation, see § 962, to intent to obstruct the lawful exercise of parental rights, see § 1204. Consider, for example, 21 U.S.C. § 841, which makes it a crime to possess certain drugs with intent to distribute them. Possession alone is also a crime, but a lesser one, see § 844. Suppose that a person acquires and possesses a small quantity of cocaine for his own use, and that he in fact consumes it entirely himself. But assume further that, at the time he acquired the drug, he told his wife not to worry about the expense because, if they had an emergency need for money, he could always resell it. If conditional intent suffices, this person, who has never sold drugs and has never "intended" to sell drugs in any normal sense, has been guilty of possession with intent to distribute. Or consider 18 U.S.C. § 2390, which makes it a crime to enlist within the United States "with intent to serve in armed hostility against the United States." Suppose a Canadian enlists in the Canadian army in the United States, intending, of course, to fight all of Canada's wars, including (though he neither expects nor hopes for it) a war against the United States. He would be criminally liable. These examples make it clear, I think, that the doctrine of conditional intent cannot reasonably be applied across-the-board to the criminal code. I am unaware that any equivalent absurdities result from reading "intent" to mean what it says—a conclusion strongly supported by the fact that the Government has cited only a single case involving another federal statute, from over two centuries of federal criminal jurisprudence, applying the conditional-intent doctrine (and that in circumstances where it would not at all have been absurd to require real intent).[1] The course selected by the Court, of course—"intent" is sometimes conditional and sometimes not—would require us to sift through these many statutes one-by-one, making our decision on the basis of such ephemeral indications of "congressional purpose" as the Court has used in this case, to which I now turn.

Ultimately, the Court rests its decision upon the fact that the purpose of the statute—which it says is deterring carjacking—"is better served by construing the statute to cover both the conditional and the unconditional species of wrongful intent." It supports this statement, both premise and conclusion, by two unusually uninformative statements from the legislative history (to stand out in that respect in that realm is quite an accomplishment) that speak generally about strengthening

---

[1] The one case the Government has come up with is Shaffer v. United States, 308 F.2d 654 (CA5 1962), cert. denied, 373 U.S. 939, 10 L. Ed. 2d 694, 83 S. Ct. 1544 (1963), which upheld a conviction of assault "with intent to do bodily harm" where the defendant had said that if any persons tried to leave the building within five minutes after his departure "he would shoot their heads off," 308 F.2d at 655. In my view, and in normal parlance, the defendant did not "intend" to do bodily harm, and there would have been nothing absurd about holding to that effect.

The Government cites six other federal cases, Brief for United States 14-15, n. 5, but they are so inapposite that they succeed only in demonstrating the weakness of its assertion that conditional intent is the federal rule. . . .

and broadening the carjacking statute and punishing carjackers severely. But every statute intends not only to achieve certain policy objectives, but to achieve them by the means specified. Limitations upon the means employed to achieve the policy goal are no less a "purpose" of the statute than the policy goal itself. Under the Court's analysis, any interpretation of the statute that would broaden its reach would further the purpose the Court has found. Such reasoning is limitless and illogical.

The Court confidently asserts that "petitioner's interpretation would exclude from the coverage of the statute most of the conduct that Congress obviously intended to prohibit." It seems to me that one can best judge what Congress "obviously intended" not by intuition, but by the words that Congress enacted, which in this case require intent (not conditional intent) to kill. Is it implausible that Congress intended to define such a narrow federal crime? Not at all. The era when this statute was passed contained well publicized instances of not only carjackings, and not only carjackings involving violence or the threat of violence (as of course most of them do); but also of carjackings in which the perpetrators senselessly harmed the car owners when that was entirely unnecessary to the crime. I have a friend whose father was killed, and whose mother was nearly killed, in just such an incident—after the car had already been handed over. It is not at all implausible that Congress should direct its attention to this particularly savage sort of carjacking—where killing the driver is part of the intended crime.[2]

Indeed, it seems to me much more implausible that Congress would have focused upon the ineffable "conditional intent" that the Court reads into the statute, sending courts and juries off to wander through "would-a, could-a, should-a" land. It is difficult enough to determine a defendant's actual intent; it is infinitely more difficult to determine what the defendant planned to do upon the happening of an event that the defendant hoped would not happen, and that he himself may not have come to focus upon. There will not often be the accomplice's convenient confirmation of conditional intent that exists in the present case. Presumably it will be up to each jury whether to take the carjacker ("Your car or your life") at his word. Such a system of justice seems to me so arbitrary that it is difficult to believe Congress intended it. Had Congress meant to cast its carjacking net so broadly, it could have achieved that result—and eliminated the arbitrariness—by defining the crime as "carjacking under threat of death or serious bodily injury." Given the language here, I find it much more plausible that Congress meant to reach—as it said—the carjacker who intended to kill.

In sum, I find the statute entirely unambiguous as to whether the carjacker who hopes to obtain the car without inflicting harm is covered. Even if ambiguity existed, however, the rule of lenity would require it to be resolved in the defendant's favor The Government's statement that the rule of lenity "has its *primary* application in

---

[2] Note that I am discussing what was a plausible congressional purpose in enacting this language— not what I necessarily think was the real one. I search for a plausible purpose because a text without one may represent a "scrivener's error" that we may properly correct. There is no need for such correction here; the text as it reads, unamended by a meaning of "intent" that contradicts normal usage, makes total sense. If I were to speculate as to the real reason the "intent" requirement was added by those who drafted it, I think I would select neither the Court's attribution of purpose nor the one I have hypothesized. Like the District Court, see 921 F. Supp. 155, 158 (EDNY 1996), and the Court of Appeals for the Third Circuit, see United States v. Anderson, 108 F.3d 478, 482-483 (1997), I suspect the "intent" requirement was inadvertently expanded beyond the new subsection 2119(3), which imposed the death penalty—where it was thought necessary to ensure the constitutionality of that provision. Of course the actual intent of the draftsmen is irrelevant; we are governed by what Congress enacted.

cases in which there is some doubt whether the legislature intended to criminalize conduct that might otherwise appear to be innocent," Brief for United States 31 (emphasis added), is carefully crafted to conceal the fact that we have repeatedly applied the rule to situations just like this. For example, in *Ladner v. United States*, 358 U.S. 169, 3 L. Ed. 2d 199, 79 S. Ct. 209 (1958), the statute at issue made it a crime to assault a federal officer with a deadly weapon. The defendant, who fired one shotgun blast that wounded two federal officers, contended that under this statute he was guilty of only one, and not two, assaults. The Court said, in an opinion joined by all eight Justices who reached the merits of the case:

> "This policy of lenity means that the Court will not interpret a federal criminal statute so as to increase the penalty that it places on an individual when such an interpretation can be based on no more than a guess as to what Congress intended. If Congress desires to create multiple offenses from a single act affecting more than one federal officer, Congress can make that meaning clear. We thus hold that the single discharge of a shotgun alleged by the petitioner in this case would constitute only a single violation of § 254."

In *Bell v. United States*, 349 U.S. 81, 99 L. Ed. 905, 75 S. Ct. 620 (1955), the issue was similar: whether transporting two women, for the purpose of prostitution, in the same vehicle and on the same trip, constituted one or two violations of the Mann Act. In an opinion authored by Justice Frankfurter, the Court said:

> "When Congress leaves to the Judiciary the task of imputing to Congress an undeclared will, the ambiguity should be resolved in favor of lenity. And this is not out of any sentimental consideration, or for want of sympathy with the purpose of Congress in proscribing evil or antisocial conduct. It may fairly be said to be a presupposition of our law to resolve doubts in the enforcement of a penal code against the imposition of a harsher punishment."

If that is no longer the presupposition of our law, the Court should say so, and reduce the rule of lenity to an historical curiosity. But if it remains the presupposition, the rule has undeniable application in the present case. If the statute is not, as I think, clear in the defendant's favor, it is at the very least ambiguous and the defendant must be given the benefit of the doubt. . . .

This seems to me not a difficult case. The issue before us is not whether the "intent" element of some common-law crime developed by the courts themselves—or even the "intent" element of a statute that replicates the common-law definition—includes, or should include, conditional intent. Rather, it is whether the English term "intent" used in a statute defining a brand new crime bears a meaning that contradicts normal usage. Since it is quite impossible to say that long-standing, agreed-upon legal usage has converted this word into a term of art, the answer has to be no. And it would be no even if the question were doubtful. I think it particularly inadvisable to introduce the new possibility of " conditional-intent" prosecutions into a modern federal criminal-law system characterized by plea bargaining, where they will predictably be used for in terrorem effect. I respectfully dissent.

THOMAS, J. dissenting.

I cannot accept the majority's interpretation of the term "intent" in 18 U.S.C. § 2119 (1994 ed. and Supp. III) to include the concept of conditional intent. The central difficulty in this case is that the text is silent as to the meaning of "intent"— the carjacking statute does not define that word, and Title 18 of the United States

Code, unlike some state codes, lacks a general section defining intent to include conditional intent. See, e.g., Del. Code Ann., Tit. 11, § 254 (1995); Haw. Rev. Stat. § 702-209 (1993); 18 Pa. Cons. Stat. § 302(f) (1998). As the majority notes, there is some authority to support its view that the specific intent to commit an act may be conditional. In my view, that authority does not demonstrate that such a usage was part of a well-established historical tradition. Absent a more settled tradition, it cannot be presumed that Congress was familiar with this usage when it enacted the statute. For these reasons, I agree with Justice Scalia the statute cannot be read to include the concept of conditional intent and, therefore, respectfully dissent.

QUESTIONS

1. What approach to statutory interpretation does Justice Stevens employ? What approach did the trial judge use? What about Justices Scalia and Thomas?

2. Does the text of the carjacking statute support the majority's interpretation of the carjacking statute? Or Justice Scalia's? Is the statute's language clear or ambiguous?

3. Is conditional intent a type of intent? Or not?

4. If a word used in a criminal statute has achieved what Justice Scalia calls "term of art" status and acquired a meaning in the criminal law different from its meaning in ordinary usage, which meaning should a judge use in interpreting and applying the statute?

H. INTOXICATION

Should the fact that someone was intoxicated with alcohol or another drug play a role in determining criminal liability or punishment? If so, should it mitigate or aggravate?

The criminal law's answers to these questions have changed over time and vary significantly today from jurisdiction to jurisdiction. *Montana v. Egelhoff*, found later in this Section, traces the evolution of the common law's position and describes recent legislative developments on intoxication. As described in *Egelhoff*, the common law moved to a compromise position on intoxication, allowing mitigation in one category of offenses, specific intent crimes, but disallowing it in another category, general intent crimes. *Egelhoff* also describes a recent legislative trend of returning toward an earlier common law position of severely restricting the use of intoxication. Legislatures in most states have dealt with the subject of intoxication by statute. The selection of statutes that appears after *Egelhoff* represents a range of approaches found in current statutory provisions.

The criminal law's vacillation and variation in dealing with intoxication is partly a product of our society's ambivalence about alcohol. Though intoxication statutes do not distinguish among intoxicants, alcohol is by far the most popular drug in the United States and the most frequent source of intoxication problems in criminal law. Accordingly, our views about alcohol have played a dominant role in shaping our attitudes about the impact of intoxication on criminal liability. Consider the following data about alcohol use and its costs in the United States.

UNITED STATES DEPARTMENT OF HEALTH AND HUMAN SERVICES
10th Annual Report to the U.S. Congress on Alcohol and Health 1 (2000)

Forty-four percent of the adult U.S. population (aged 18 and over) are current drinkers who have consumed at least 12 drinks in the preceding year. While most people who drink do so safely, the minority who consume alcohol heavily produce an impact that ripples outward to encompass their families, friends, and communities. The following statistics give a glimpse of the magnitude of problem drinking:

- Approximately 14 million Americans—7.4 percent of the population—meet the diagnostic criteria for alcohol abuse or alcoholism.
- More than one-half of American adults have a close family member who has or has had alcoholism.
- Approximately one in four children younger than 18 years old in the United States is exposed to alcohol abuse or alcohol dependence in the family.
- Of 11.1 million victims of violent crime each year, almost one in four, or 2.7 million, report that the offender had been drinking alcohol prior to committing the crime.
- Traffic crashes involving alcohol killed more than 16,000 people in 1997 alone.
- The estimated economic cost of alcohol abuse was $184.6 billion for 1998 alone, or roughly $638 for every man, woman, and child living in the United States that year.

Alcohol is legal, widely accepted, and typically used without negative consequences. At the same time, alcohol has a high correlation with crime and imposes significant human and economic costs. So is drinking blameworthy? Is it something the criminal law should seek to deter? Our culture's schizophrenic views about alcohol are captured in the following statement from a congressman asked to explain his attitude toward whiskey:

If you mean the demon drink that poisons the mind, pollutes the body, desecrates family life and inflames sinners, then I'm against it. But if you mean the elixir of Christmas cheer, the shield against winter chill, the taxable potion that puts needed funds into public coffers to comfort little crippled children, then I'm for it. This is my position, and I will not compromise.[16]

What view, then, should the criminal law take toward alcohol? As you read *Hood* and *Egelhoff* and the statutes on intoxication below, try to articulate the policies underlying various legal rules about intoxication. Do you think the differences result from disagreement about the relevance of intoxication in proving or disproving the elements of a charged offense? Or do policies unrelated to relevance explain the divergence in approaches to intoxication? The following passage, written by Chief Justice Traynor, is a useful starting point in answering these questions.

---

16. M. Lender & J. Martin, *Drinking in America: A History* 169 (1982).

PEOPLE *v.* HOOD   1 Cal. 3d 444 (1969)

A significant effect of alcohol is to distort judgment and relax the controls on aggressive and anti-social impulses. Alcohol apparently has less effect on the ability to engage in simple goal-directed behavior, although it may impair the efficiency of that behavior. In other words, a drunk man is capable of forming an intent to do something simple, such as strike another, unless he is so drunk that he has reached the stage of unconsciousness. What he is not as capable as a sober man of doing is exercising judgment about the social consequences of his acts or controlling his impulses toward anti-social acts. He is more likely to act rashly and impulsively and to be susceptible to passion and anger.

MONTANA *v.* EGELHOFF
518 U.S. 37 (1996)

SCALIA, J. We consider in this case whether the Due Process Clause is violated by Montana Code Annotated § 45-2-203, which provides, in relevant part, that voluntary intoxication "may not be taken into consideration in determining the existence of a mental state which is an element of [a criminal] offense."

I

In July 1992, while camping out in the Yaak region of northwestern Montana to pick mushrooms, respondent made friends with Roberta Pavola and John Christenson, who were doing the same. On Sunday, July 12, the three sold the mushrooms they had collected and spent the rest of the day and evening drinking, in bars and at a private party in Troy, Montana. Some time after 9 P.M., they left the party in Christenson's 1974 Ford Galaxy station wagon. The drinking binge apparently continued, as respondent was seen buying beer at 9:20 P.M. and recalled "sitting on a hill or a bank passing a bottle of Black Velvet back and forth" with Christenson.

At about midnight that night, officers of the Lincoln County, Montana, sheriff's department, responding to reports of a possible drunk driver, discovered Christenson's station wagon stuck in a ditch along U.S. Highway 2. In the front seat were Pavola and Christenson, each dead from a single gunshot to the head. In the rear of the car lay respondent, alive and yelling obscenities. His blood-alcohol content measured .36 percent over one hour later. On the floor of the car, near the brake pedal, lay respondent's .38 caliber handgun, with four loaded rounds and two empty casings; respondent had gunshot residue on his hands.

Respondent was charged with two counts of deliberate homicide, a crime defined by Montana law as "purposely" or "knowingly" causing the death of another human being. Mont. Code Ann. § 45-5-102 (1995). A portion of the jury charge, uncontested here, instructed that "[a] person acts purposely when it is his conscious object to engage in conduct of that nature or to cause such a result," and that "[a] person acts knowingly when he is aware of his conduct or when he is aware under the circumstances his conduct constitutes a crime; or, when he is aware there exists the high probability that his conduct will cause a specific result." Respondent's defense at trial was that an unidentified fourth person must have committed the murders; his own extreme intoxication, he claimed, had rendered him physically incapable of committing the murders, and accounted for his inability to recall the events of the night of July 12. Although respondent was allowed to make this use of the evidence that he was intoxicated, the jury was instructed, pursuant to Mont. Code Ann. § 45-2-203 (1995), that it could not consider respondent's "intoxicated condition . . . in determining the existence of a mental state which is an element of the offense." The jury found respondent guilty on both counts, and the court sentenced him to 84 years' imprisonment.

The Supreme Court of Montana reversed. It reasoned (1) that respondent "had a due process right to present and have considered by the jury all relevant evidence to rebut the State's evidence on all elements of the offense charged," and (2) that evidence of respondent's voluntary intoxication was "clearly . . . relevant to the issue of whether [respondent] acted knowingly and purposely." Because § 45-2-203 prevented the jury from considering that evidence with regard to that issue, the court concluded that the State had been "relieved of part of its burden to prove beyond a reasonable doubt every fact necessary to constitute the crime charged," and that respondent had therefore been denied due process. We granted certiorari.

II

The cornerstone of the Montana Supreme Court's judgment was the proposition that the Due Process Clause guarantees a defendant the right to present and have considered by the jury " *all relevant evidence* to rebut the State's evidence on all elements of the offense charged." Respondent does not defend this categorical rule; he acknowledges that the right to present relevant evidence "has not been viewed as absolute." That is a wise concession, since the proposition that the Due Process Clause guarantees the right to introduce all relevant evidence is simply indefensible. As we have said: "The accused does not have an unfettered right to offer [evidence] that is incompetent, privileged, or otherwise inadmissible under standard rules of evidence." Relevant evidence may, for example, be excluded on account of a defendant's failure to comply with procedural requirements. And any number of familiar and unquestionably constitutional evidentiary rules also authorize the exclusion of relevant evidence. For example, Federal (and Montana) Rule of Evidence 403 provides: "*Although relevant*, evidence may be excluded if its probative value is substantially outweighed by the danger of unfair prejudice, confusion of the issues, or misleading the jury, or by considerations of undue delay, waste of time, or needless presentation of cumulative evidence" (emphasis added). Hearsay rules similarly prohibit the introduction of testimony which, though unquestionably relevant, is deemed insufficiently reliable. Of course, to say that the right to introduce relevant evidence is not absolute is not to say that the Due Process Clause places *no* limits upon restriction of that right. But it is to say that the defendant asserting such a limit must sustain the usual heavy burden that a due process claim entails:

> "Preventing and dealing with crime is much more the business of the States than it is of the Federal Government, and . . . we should not lightly construe the Constitution so as to intrude upon the administration of justice by the individual States. Among other things, it is normally 'within the power of the State to regulate procedures under which its laws are carried out,' . . . and its decision in this regard is not subject to proscription under the Due Process Clause unless 'it offends some principle of justice so rooted in the traditions and conscience of our people as to be ranked as fundamental.' "

Respondent's task, then, is to establish that a defendant's right to have a jury consider evidence of his voluntary intoxication in determining whether he possesses the requisite mental state is a "fundamental principle of justice."

Our primary guide in determining whether the principle in question is fundamental is, of course, historical practice. Here that gives respondent little support. By the laws of England, wrote Hale, the intoxicated defendant "shall have no privilege by this voluntary contracted madness, but shall have the same judgment as if he were in his right senses." According to Blackstone and Coke, the law's condemnation of those suffering from *dementia affectata* was harsher still: Blackstone, citing Coke, explained that the law viewed intoxication "as an aggravation of the offence, rather than as an excuse for any criminal misbehaviour." This stern rejection of inebriation as a defense became a fixture of early American law as well. The American editors of the 1847 edition of Hale wrote:

> "Drunkenness, it was said in an early case, can never be received as a ground to excuse or palliate an offence: this is not merely the opinion of a speculative philosopher, the argument of counsel, or the *obiter dictum* of a single judge, but it is a sound and long established maxim of judicial policy, from which perhaps a single dissenting voice cannot be found. But if no other authority could be adduced, the uniform decisions of our own Courts from the first establishment of the government, would constitute it now a part of the common law of the land."

The historical record does not leave room for the view that the common law's rejection of intoxication as an "excuse" or "justification" for crime would nonetheless permit the defendant to show that intoxication prevented the requisite *mens rea*. Hale, Coke, and Blackstone were familiar, to say the least, with the concept of *mens rea*, and acknowledged that drunkenness "deprive[s] men of the use of reason." It is inconceivable that they did not realize that an offender's drunkenness might impair his ability to form the requisite intent; and inconceivable that their failure to note this massive exception from the general rule of disregard of intoxication was an oversight. Hale's statement that a drunken offender shall have the same judgment "as if he were in his right senses" must be understood as precluding a defendant from arguing that, because of his intoxication, he could not have possessed the *mens rea* required to commit the crime. And the same must be said of the exemplar of the common-law rule cited by both Hale and Blackstone. . . .

Against this extensive evidence of a lengthy common-law tradition decidedly against him, the best argument available to respondent is the one made by his *amicus* and conceded by the State: Over the course of the 19th century, courts carved out an exception to the common law's traditional across-the-board condemnation of the drunken offender, allowing a jury to consider a defendant's intoxication when assessing whether he possessed the mental state needed to commit the crime charged, where the crime was one requiring a "specific intent." The emergence of this new rule is often traced to an 1819 English case, in which Justice Holroyd is reported to have held that "though voluntary drunkenness cannot excuse from the commission of crime, yet where, as on a charge of murder, the material question is, whether an act was premeditated or done only with sudden heat and impulse, the fact of the party being intoxicated [is] a circumstance proper to be taken into consideration." 1 W. Russell, Crimes and Misdemeanors 8 (citing *King v. Grindley*, Worcester Sum Assizes 1819, MS). This exception was "slow to take root," however, even in England. Indeed, in the 1835 case of *King v. Carroll*, Justice Park claimed that Holroyd had "retracted his opinion" in *Grindley*, and said "there is no doubt that

that case is not law." In this country, as late as 1858 the Missouri Supreme Court could speak as categorically as this:

> "To look for deliberation and forethought in a man maddened by intoxication is vain, for drunkenness has deprived him of the deliberating faculties to a greater or less extent; and if this deprivation is to relieve him of all responsibility or to diminish it, the great majority of crimes committed will go unpunished. This however is not the doctrine of the common law; and to its maxims, based as they obviously are upon true wisdom and sound policy, we must adhere."

And as late as 1878, the Vermont Supreme Court upheld the giving of the following instruction at a murder trial:

> " 'The voluntary intoxication of one who without provocation commits a homicide, although amounting to a frenzy, that is, although the intoxication amounts to a frenzy, does not excuse him from the same construction of his conduct, and the same legal inferences upon the question of premeditation and intent, as affecting the grade of his crime, which are applicable to a person entirely sober.' "

Eventually, however, the new view won out, and by the end of the 19th century, in most American jurisdictions, intoxication could be considered in determining whether a defendant was capable of forming the specific intent necessary to commit the crime charged.

On the basis of this historical record, respondent's *amicus* argues that "the old common-law rule...was no longer deeply rooted at the time the Fourteenth Amendment was ratified." That conclusion is questionable, but we need not pursue the point, since the argument of *amicus* mistakes the nature of our inquiry. It is not the State which bears the burden of demonstrating that its rule is "deeply rooted," but rather respondent who must show that the principle of procedure *violated* by the rule (and allegedly required by due process) is " 'so rooted in the traditions and conscience of our people as to be ranked as fundamental.' " Thus, even assuming that when the Fourteenth Amendment was adopted the rule Montana now defends was no longer generally applied, this only cuts off what might be called an *a fortiori* argument in favor of the State. The burden remains upon respondent to show that the "new common-law" rule—that intoxication may be considered on the question of intent—was so deeply rooted at the time of the Fourteenth Amendment (or perhaps has become so deeply rooted since) as to be a fundamental principle which that Amendment enshrined.

That showing has not been made. Instead of the uniform and continuing acceptance we would expect for a rule that enjoys "fundamental principle" status, we find that fully one-fifth of the States either never adopted the "new common-law" rule at issue here or have recently abandoned it.[17]

---

17. Besides Montana, those States are Arizona, *see* State v. Ramos, 133 Ariz. 4, 6, 648 P.2d 119, 121 (1982) (upholding statute precluding jury consideration of intoxication for purposes of determining whether defendant acted "knowingly"); Ariz. Rev. Stat. Ann. § 13-503 (Supp. 1995-1996) (voluntary intoxication "is not a defense for any criminal act or requisite state of mind"); Arkansas, *see* White v. State, 290 Ark. 130, 134-137, 717 S.W.2d 784, 786-788 (1986) (interpreting Ark. Code Ann. § 5-2-207 (1993)); Delaware, *see* Wyant v. State, 519 A.2d 649, 651 (1986) (interpreting Del. Code. Ann., Tit. 11, § 421 (1995)); Georgia, *see* Foster v. State, 258 Ga. 736, 742-745, 374 S.E.2d 188, 194-196 (1988) (interpreting Ga. Code Ann. § 16-3-4 (1992)), cert. denied, 490 U.S. 1085, 104 L. Ed. 2d 671, 109 S. Ct. 2110 (1989); Hawaii, *see* Haw. Rev. Stat. § 702-230(2) (1993), State v. Souza, 72 Haw. 246, 248, 813 P. 2d 1384, 1386 (1991) (§ 702-230(2) is constitutional); Mississippi, *see* Lanier v. State, 533 So. 2d 473, 478-479 (1988); Missouri, *see* Mo. Rev. Stat. § 562.076 (1994), State v. Erwin, 848 S.W.2d 476, 482 (§ 562.076 is constitutional), cert. denied, 510 U.S. 826, 126 L. Ed. 2d 56, 114 S. Ct. 88 (1993); South Carolina, *see* State v. Vaughn, 268 S.C.

It is not surprising that many States have held fast to or resurrected the common-law rule prohibiting consideration of voluntary intoxication in the determination of *mens rea*, because that rule has considerable justification—which alone casts doubt upon the proposition that the opposite rule is a "fundamental principle." A large number of crimes, especially violent crimes, are committed by intoxicated offenders; modern studies put the numbers as high as half of all homicides, for example. Disallowing consideration of voluntary intoxication has the effect of increasing the punishment for all unlawful acts committed in that state, and thereby deters drunkenness or irresponsible behavior while drunk. The rule also serves as a specific deterrent, ensuring that those who prove incapable of controlling violent impulses while voluntarily intoxicated go to prison. And finally, the rule comports with and implements society's moral perception that one who has voluntarily impaired his own faculties should be responsible for the consequences.

There is, in modern times, even more justification for laws such as § 45-2-203 than there used to be. Some recent studies suggest that the connection between drunkenness and crime is as much cultural as pharmacological—that is, that drunks are violent not simply because alcohol makes them that way, but because they are behaving in accord with their learned belief that drunks are violent. This not only adds additional support to the traditional view that an intoxicated criminal is not deserving of exoneration, but it suggests that juries—who possess the same learned belief as the intoxicated offender—will be too quick to accept the claim that the defendant was biologically incapable of forming the requisite *mens rea*. Treating the matter as one of excluding misleading evidence therefore makes some sense.

In sum, not every widespread experiment with a procedural rule favorable to criminal defendants establishes a fundamental principle of justice. Although the rule allowing a jury to consider evidence of a defendant's voluntary intoxication where relevant to *mens rea* has gained considerable acceptance, it is of too recent vintage, and has not received sufficiently uniform and permanent allegiance, to qualify as fundamental, especially since it displaces a lengthy commonlaw tradition which remains supported by valid justifications today. . . .

"The doctrines of *actus reus, mens rea,* insanity, mistake, justification, and duress have historically provided the tools for a constantly shifting adjustment of the tension between the evolving aims of the criminal law and changing religious, moral, philosophical, and medical views of the nature of man. This process of adjustment has always been thought to be the province of the States." The people of Montana have decided to resurrect the rule of an earlier era, disallowing consideration of voluntary intoxication when a defendant's state of mind is at issue. Nothing in the Due Process Clause prevents them from doing so, and the judgment of the Supreme Court of Montana to the contrary must be reversed.

QUESTIONS

1. Which of the following statements is accurate? The Montana intoxication statute:

      (a) eliminates an affirmative defense

119, 124-126, 232 S.E.2d 328, 330-331 (1977); and Texas, *see* Hawkins v. State, 605 S.W.2d 586, 589 (Tex. Crim. App. 1980) (interpreting Tex. Penal Code Ann. § 8.04).

    (b) excludes evidence regarding mental state
    (c) redefines the mental state element of an offense

2. Which theories of punishment support the Montana intoxication statute? Which theories of punishment support the common law position of allowing the defendant to introduce intoxication evidence in cases involving specific intent crimes?

As *Egelhoff* illustrates, criminal defendants frequently seek to use intoxication as evidence that they lacked a mental state required for liability, such as purpose to kill. Resolving such a claim is not an easy task. Alcohol produces its physiological effects on both body and mind in degrees that range from barely perceptible to coma, with many gradations in between. The extent of both intoxication and impairment of mental function can often be difficult to determine with precision. Common experience and research have shown that alcohol affects perception, memory, and cognition. Evidence of alcohol use by a witness is routinely admitted at trial for jurors to use in assessing the ability of the witness to perceive and remember what she recounts in her testimony. But precisely how and to what degree alcohol affects mental function is not entirely clear and is still the subject of much research. Alcohol's effects are subject to significant variation depending on a multitude of factors such as body weight, gender, food consumption, rate of drinking and drinking experience. The same amount of alcohol, for example, can intoxicate a novice drinker but have much less effect on a person with a history of heavy drinking.

For these reasons, claims about how much a defendant drank and how it affected his mental processes may be easy to make but difficult for the government to refute. If a defendant is arrested at the time of the crime, blood-alcohol level evidence may be obtained. But if no such timely arrest is made, it may be hard to disprove false claims about drinking and its effect on the mind. These practical problems in accurately assessing intoxication claims provide one set of reasons a legislature might resist allowing defendants to use intoxication evidence to disprove a mental state.

The effects of alcohol are also subject to much public misunderstanding. A leading pharmacology treatise, for example, reports that "[t]he public often views alcoholic drinks as stimulating, but [alcohol] is primarily a central nervous system depressant."[18] Justice Scalia stated in *Egelhoff* that recent studies suggest that the correlation of crime with intoxication "is as much cultural as pharmacological." One of the articles he cited explains this cultural phenomenon:

> Although popular thought may hold that alcohol makes people behave in out-of-character ways, recent research suggests that it does not. MacAndrew and Edgerton, in their cross-cultural review of drunken comportment and its consequences, concluded that the pharmacological action of ethanol cannot account for the transformations in social behavior that occur when people drink, as those transformations vary widely from culture to culture and in the same culture across time periods. Their contention that the effects of alcohol are instead culturally learned spurred research showing that certain of these effects are exhibited by people who only think that they have imbibed.[19]

---

18. Goodman & Gilman's *The Pharmacological Basis of Therapeutics* 430 (10th ed. 2001).
19. Barbara Critchlow, *The Powers of John Barleycorn: Beliefs About the Effects of Alcohol on Social Behavior*, 41 No. 7, American Psychologist 751, 751 (1986).

The MacAndrew and Edgerton study referred to in this passage concludes by describing the authors' thesis that

> the way people comport themselves when they are drunk is determined not by alcohol's toxic assault upon the seat of moral judgment, conscience, or the like, but by what their society makes of and imparts to them concerning the state of drunkenness. . . . The moral, then, is this. Since societies, like individuals, get the sorts of drunken comportment they allow, they deserve what they get.[20]

QUESTIONS

1. Justice Scalia argues in *Egelhoff* that public misperceptions provide support for restricting evidence of intoxication because jurors, based on their learned beliefs that drunks are violent "will be too quick to accept the claim that the defendant was biologically incapable of forming the requisite *mens rea.*" Does the Montana rule protect against this danger?

2. Does the existence of such "learned beliefs" about alcohol provide a rationale for restricting evidence of intoxication aside from the possibility of jurors being misled by the evidence? Are there steps the criminal law should take to address such beliefs in addition to restricting the uses that can be made of intoxication in criminal cases?

3. If violent behavior is the result of "learned beliefs" about alcohol rather than a pharmacological "assault" on the brain, does that fact change the blameworthiness of drinking? Does it make drinking more or less dangerous?

PROBLEMS

Should evidence that the defendant was intoxicated be admitted in the following Problems? In answering this question, apply the statutes below.

5.29 Paul is charged with stealing a car from the parking lot of a convenience store located a few blocks from his apartment. The victim left the keys in the car while she went into the convenience store. As she was standing at the checkout counter, the victim saw a man of Paul's approximate height, weight, and hair color sprint across the parking lot, quickly jump into her car and drive it away. The theft took place at 11:30 P.M., and the parking lot was poorly lit. The victim of the crime picked out Paul from a photospread and later identified him in a lineup. Paul claims the victim is mistaken in her identification and offers the testimony of two friends that they observed Paul consume a large quantity of alcohol from 8 to 11 P.M. on the night of the car theft and that Paul was barely able to stand or speak when they left him at 11:15 that night.

5.30 Alan goes to a party at the apartment of Chris, an acquaintance of one of Alan's friends. Alan wears to the party his ten-year-old black leather

---

20. Craig MacAndrew & Robert B. Edgerton, *Drunken Comportment: A Social Explanation* 165, 173 (1969).

jacket. When he arrives at the party, Chris hangs Alan's jacket, along with those of his other guests, in a hall closet outside his bedroom. At the party, Alan consumes a large quantity of alcohol. Just before midnight, Alan decides to leave the party. Alan walks to the closet where Chris hung his jacket. When Alan opens the closet door, instead of taking his own jacket, he takes a similar brand new black leather jacket belonging to Chris and leaves the party. Someone observes Alan's conduct and calls the police, who arrest Alan a few hours later and charge him with theft. Assume Alan is charged under the following statute:

Anyone who knowingly and unlawfully takes the property of another with intent to permanently deprive the owner of it is guilty of theft.

Alan admits that he took Chris's jacket, but argues that because of the alcohol he had drunk he thought the jacket he took was in fact his.

5.31 After several hours of drinking, James begins bragging to Michael about his lack of fear of firearms. Michael decides to test James's claim with a revolver he recently purchased. While showing the gun to James, Michael puts the gun to James's head. To Michael's amazement, the gun goes off, killing James.

(a) Michael claims he was simply trying to frighten James and believed that when he pulled the trigger the gun was unloaded. He argues that because of the alcohol he had consumed, he failed to remember that he had placed bullets in the gun a few days earlier. Does it make any difference if:

(1) Michael is charged with reckless homicide?
(2) Michael is charged with negligent homicide?

(b) Michael claims that he did not intend to pull the trigger of the gun but merely meant to place it against James's head to frighten him. He argues that because of the alcohol he had consumed, his motor skills were impaired and he wasn't in control of his trigger finger.

5.32 Joel is on a business trip to a large city. One night after he has had quite a few drinks in the bar of the hotel where he is staying, a young woman approaches him and engages him in conversation. Joel buys her several drinks. About an hour later, Joel offers the young woman $100 to go to his room with him and have sex. She agrees. As they leave the bar together, both are arrested by an undercover police officer who overheard their conversation. Joel is charged under the following statute:

A person is guilty of patronizing a prostitute in the third degree when, being over twenty-one years of age, he patronizes a prostitute and the person patronized is less than seventeen years of age.

Joel is 30 years old. The young woman turns out to be 16 years old. Joel wants to introduce evidence of his drinking to show he lacked the required mental state regarding the prostitute being less than 17.

> (a) Assume the statute requires knowledge regarding the prostitute's being less than 17.
> (b) Assume the statute requires recklessness regarding the prostitute's being less than 17.
> (c) Assume the statute requires negligence regarding the prostitute's being less than 17.

Montana Code Annotated § 45-2-203   *Responsibility—intoxicated condition*

A person who is in an intoxicated condition is criminally responsible for his conduct and an intoxicated condition is not a defense to any offense and may not be taken into consideration in determining the existence of a mental state which is an element of the offense unless the defendant proves that he did not know that it was an intoxicating substance when he consumed, smoked, sniffed, injected, or otherwise ingested the substance causing the condition.

Ohio Revised Code § 2901.21   *Requirements for criminal liability*

(C) Voluntary intoxication may not be taken into consideration in determining the existence of a mental state that is an element of a criminal offense. Voluntary intoxication does not relieve a person of a duty to act if failure to act constitutes a criminal offense. Evidence that a person was voluntarily intoxicated may be admissible to show whether or not the person was physically capable of performing the act with which the person is charged.

Minnesota Statutes § 609.075   *Intoxication as defense*

An act committed while in a state of voluntary intoxication is not less criminal by reason thereof, but when a particular intent or other state of mind is a necessary element to constitute a particular crime, the fact of intoxication may be taken into consideration in determining such intent or state of mind.

Iowa Code § 701.5   *Intoxicants or drugs*

The fact that a person is under the influence of intoxicants or drugs neither excuses the person's act nor aggravates the person's guilt, but may be shown where it is relevant in proving the person's specific intent or recklessness at the time of the person's alleged criminal act or in proving any element of the public offense with which the person is charged.

Model Penal Code § 2.08   *Intoxication*

(1) Except as provided in Subsection (4) of this Section, intoxication of the actor is not a defense unless it negatives an element of the offense.

(2) When recklessness establishes an element of the offense, if the actor, due to self-induced intoxication, is unaware of a risk of which he would have been aware had he been sober, such unawareness is immaterial.

(3) Intoxication does not, in itself, constitute mental disease within the meaning of Section 4.01.

QUESTIONS

1. How does each of these statutes differ from the original common law position on intoxication described in *Egelhoff*?

2. Why does the Model Penal Code's intoxication provision devote a separate section to recklessness? What is the effect of that section? Why does the Model Penal Code's intoxication provision not specifically address negligence?

3. We learned in dealing with the subject of mistake that the term "defense" is used to encompass two different ways of defeating liability. One is by contesting an element of the offense. The other is when the defendant admits the elements but seeks to avoid liability by asserting some other principle. The word "defense" is often used in referring to intoxication. With which meaning is this term used in the context of intoxication?

4. A number of jurisdictions have left the law on intoxication to judges to develop through a common law process. Should legislators or judges be making the law in this area? Or should the significance of intoxication be left to the jury to handle in its role as the finder of fact?

I. SPECIFIC AND GENERAL INTENT

1. Defining Specific and General Intent

As discussed in the introduction to this chapter, jurisdictions commonly classify crimes into categories based on mental state. A substantial number of jurisdictions have used general and specific intent as primary mental state rubrics. Legislatures and courts have imbued them with multiple and sometimes conflicting meanings. To provide some guidance in this realm, we employ a less conventional approach and, in this Section, offer a series of three hypothetical opinions, along with other related materials, in which an imaginary state court analyzes the distinctions between specific intent and general intent and their application to mistakes and intoxication.

In the first hypothetical *Mistook* opinion, we select and discuss what are probably the most common meanings of specific and general intent, and then apply them to the three statutes involved in the case. In the second *Mistook* opinion, we explore the effect of mistake of fact on specific and general intent. The materials that follow this exploration include an analysis of two doctrines related to mistake of fact, the moral and legal wrong doctrines, as well as the *Gordon* case from 1875, in which the Alabama Supreme Court analyzed the effect of mistake in a non-MPC context. From mistake of fact, we turn to the third *Mistook* opinion, which focuses on the intersection of mistake of law and specific and general intent. Finally, the *Williams* case delves into the relationship between intoxication and specific intent.

PEOPLE *v.* SALLY MISTOOK

1 Imagination Cases 1
Supreme Court of the State of Imagination (2003)

REVEL, J. In this appeal, we must first decide whether the trial court properly held the defendant to answer at the conclusion of the preliminary hearing. In order to hold the defendant to answer, the law requires that the evidence convince the judge that there was probable cause to believe that the defendant committed each of the offenses. In order to determine whether there was adequate probable cause, we must first ascertain the mental state required for each offense. The prosecution charged the defendant with burglary, trespass, and abandoning an unsecured refrigerator. The statutes read in pertinent part as follows:

(1) Burglary: Every person who enters any building or part of a building at night with intent to commit grand or petit larceny or any felony is guilty of burglary.[21]

(2) Trespass: Every person who willfully commits a trespass by any of the following is guilty of a misdemeanor:

(a) Entering and occupying real property or structures of any kind without the consent of the owner, the owner's agent, or the person in lawful possession.[22]

(3) Abandoned Refrigerators: Any person who discards or leaves in any place accessible to children any refrigerator, having a capacity of one and one-half cubic feet or more, which is no longer in use, and which has not had the door removed or the hinges and such portion of the latch mechanism removed to prevent latching or locking of the door, is guilty of an infraction.[23]

We begin by reviewing the evidence presented at the preliminary hearing. As is typical at a preliminary hearing, only the prosecution called witnesses. The defendant, Sally Mistook, was a student at the local law school. The victim of the first two offenses, Professor Jessie Earnest, taught first-year Criminal Law, a class in which Sally was enrolled. On the date in question, school security apprehended Sally at 6:45 P.M. in the stairwell between the floor housing faculty offices and the building exit. She was holding a folder containing a draft of the class examination. Professor Earnest testified that at 6:30 P.M. on that evening, she had left two folders on the table just inside the door to her office. One was a draft of the final exam. The other contained the class roster and lecture notes. She further testified that she had not given Sally Mistook permission to enter her office and take any folders. Professor Earnest also testified that when she left the building just after 6:30 P.M., she observed that it was sunset.

During a consensual search conducted at Sally's student residence, just after Sally's arrest, police observed two children playing with a full-size, old, empty, unplugged refrigerator left on the street outside Sally's ground-floor residence. One child had climbed into the refrigerator and was closing the door as part of the game in which the children were engaged. The refrigerator had Sally's name on it. The incident occurred on a Monday. Regular campus trash collection occurs on Tuesday mornings.

---

21. We note that this statute mirrors in pertinent part California Penal Code § 459, except that it retains the common law requirement of nighttime and explicitly includes the language "part of a building," which has been developed by the California courts in interpreting their statute.

22. We note that this statute mirrors in pertinent part California Penal Code § 602(l).

23. We note that this statute mirrors in pertinent part California Penal Code § 402b, except that our statute is punishable as an infraction, while the California equivalent is punishable as a misdemeanor.

To determine whether the court properly found probable cause, we must consider these offenses in light of our jurisdiction's law on mental states. Unlike those jurisdictions that have adopted the Model Penal Code approach to mental states, our jurisdiction, like a number of others, has maintained the terminology of a more traditional approach to mental states. Two categories of mental state dominate here, specific intent and general intent. Our legislature also creates some crimes that require no mental state. These exceptions to the rule are known as strict or absolute liability offenses. In addition to specific and general intent, we have a collection of special mental states that may appear within specific or general intent crimes. These mental states include, for example, maliciously and willfully.

As our colleagues on the California Supreme Court lamented over 30 years ago, "specific and general intent have been notoriously difficult terms to define and apply. . . . "[24] As Professor Joshua Dressler has noted: "The terms 'specific intent' and 'general intent' are the bane of criminal law students and lawyers. This is because the terms are critical to understanding various common law rules of criminal responsibility, yet the concepts are so 'notoriously difficult . . . to define and apply . . . [that] a number of text writers recommend that they be abandoned altogether.' "[25] We join these laments and encourage our legislators to revise our archaic and confusing approach to mental states. Like our colleagues, we object to the specific and general intent approach on several grounds. First, the meanings of the terms vary. It is therefore difficult to understand or apply the terms consistently. Second, they fail to distinguish clearly among the gradations of available mental states. Third, by categorizing offenses under one of only two labels, they generally fail to recognize that actors can possess multiple mental states concurrently. Finally, this approach also fails to recognize the relational quality of mental states — that mental states relate to particular components of offenses rather than to the offense as a whole.

We have studied the treatises and prior case law on the specific and general intent terms. Over the decades, jurisdictions have assigned them many meanings. Among others, some jurisdictions use the term "general intent" to mean a mental state of recklessness or negligence or even knowledge while "specific intent" is used to denote purpose.[26] Other jurisdictions use "general intent" "in the same way as 'criminal intent' to mean the general notion of *mens rea*, while 'specific intent' is taken to mean the mental state required for a particular crime."[27] Having acknowledged the flawed nature of the specific and general intent approach, we must nonetheless attempt to determine the mental state required for each of the three crimes involved in this case using that framework. Among the numerous definitions, for purposes of this case, we have chosen to apply here what appear to be the most commonly invoked definitions of the terms:
Definition #1:

> The most common usage of "specific intent" is to designate a special mental element which is required above and beyond any mental state required with respect to the actus reus of the crime. Common law larceny, for example, requires the taking and carrying away of the property of another, and the defendant's mental state

---

24. People v. Hood, 1 Cal. 3d 444 (1969).
25. Joshua Dressler, *Understanding Criminal Law* 135-136 (2001).
26. *Id.*
27. 1 Wayne R. LaFave & Austin W. Scott, Jr., *Substantive Criminal Law* [3.5(e)] (3d ed. 2000).

as to this act must be established, but in addition it must be shown that there was an "intent to steal" the property. . . . The same situation prevails with many statutory crimes: . . . confining another "for the purpose of ransom or reward" in kidnapping; making an untrue statement "designedly, with intent to defraud" in the crime of false pretenses. . . ."[28]

Definition #2:

When the definition of a crime consists of only the description of a particular act, without reference to intent to do a further act or achieve a future consequence, we ask whether the defendant intended to do the proscribed act. This intention is deemed to be a general criminal intent. When the definition refers to defendant's intent to do some further act or achieve a future consequence, the crime is deemed to be one of specific intent.[29]

In ascertaining whether the offenses fall under either category, we begin by examining the language of the statute.

Burglary: Every person who enters any building or part of a building at night with intent to commit grand or petit larceny or any felony is guilty of burglary.

Under our statute, burglary requires an intent to commit any felony or to commit larceny, also known as theft. According to Definition #1, a specific intent "designates a special mental element . . . beyond that required for the actus reus of the crime." Although we have found courts and legislators use the term "actus reus" to mean a variety of things, everything from the conduct elements alone to all non-mental state elements, we understand it to refer here to the conduct and circumstance elements of the offense. Here the conduct is a person's entry into a building or part of a building. The circumstance element is whether the entry occurs at night. If we eliminate the conduct and circumstance the language remaining in the statute is "with intent to commit grand or petit larceny or any felony." Like the example of larceny above, this remaining language refers to a special mental element beyond that required for the actus reus of the crime. Under Definition #1, burglary is a specific intent crime. The legislature has enhanced our confidence in this result by using the language common in specific intent crimes, "with intent to."

Similarly, under Definition #2, the "with intent to" language refers to a future act or further consequence beyond the entry of the building or part of a building at night, therefore rendering burglary a specific intent crime.

The plain language of the statute enables us to conclude that burglary is a specific intent crime. Had we any remaining doubts, a quick review of the legislative history would reassure. The burglary statute has been in effect for over 100 years. The legislative history indicates that its enactment represented the codification of the traditional common law crime of burglary, historically a specific intent offense. The sole modification to the statute occurred in 1972, when the legislature added the terms "or part of a building." At that time, the legislative materials reaffirmed that the purpose behind the law was to codify the old common law crime of burglary. In addition, the legislative materials noted that burglary differed from offenses like trespass, because burglary required that the accused possess the intent to commit a felony or steal at the time the accused entered the part of the building. Thus, we find that burglary is a specific intent crime.

---

28. *Id.*
29. People v. Hood, *supra* note 25.

The question then before the trial judge was whether the evidence revealed probable cause to believe that Sally Mistook entered the law school building or some part of that building at night and that, at the time she entered, she entertained the intent to commit a felony or theft. Security apprehended Sally in the stairwell leading to an exit of the building with Professor Earnest's folder containing a draft of the final examination. A fact finder could reasonably infer that Sally had entered the building or the professor's office with the specific intent to steal that exam. The late hour of the day and the fact that Professor Earnest had already left her office support that inference. A fact finder could also determine that probable cause existed to believe that night had fallen by the time Sally entered the office, presumably sometime between 6:30 and 6:45 P.M., in light of Professor Earnest's testimony about the sunset she observed when exiting the building just after 6:30 P.M.

Using this circumstantial evidence, the trial judge correctly applied our specific intent burglary law to the facts presented at the preliminary hearing in the probable cause finding.

We turn now to the language of the trespass statute:

Trespass: Every person who willfully commits a trespass by any of the following is guilty of a misdemeanor:
a. Entering and occupying real property or structures of any kind without the consent of the owner, the owner's agent, or the person in lawful possession.

In applying Definition #1, we look for any special mental state terminology. The only term referring to a mental state is "willfully." We must determine whether this mental state applies to the actus reus of the crime or is a special mental state beyond the actus reus. To violate the trespass law, a person must commit the trespass willfully by entering and occupying the structure without the owner's consent. The most logical construction of the language of the statute suggests that one must willfully enter and occupy the structure. Under this construction, "willfully" refers to the mental state required with respect to the conduct element of the crime. It does not appear to refer to a special mental state beyond the actus reus.

Our Criminal Code also defines the term "willfully" as follows: "A person acts willfully when he or she does an act on purpose or willingly." "Willfully" implies a level of conscious awareness of one's conduct. "Willfully" precludes liability for an accidental or unconscious act. As one of our colleagues on the Florida Supreme Court noted in his criticism of the specific and general intent dichotomy: "The word 'willful' does not signal a specific intent requirement, instead meaning no more than 'a willingness to do the proscribed act.'"[30]

"Willfully" seems to be an extension of the foundational criminal law prerequisite that the act be voluntary and does not connote a special mental state separate from the actus reus in this context. We are aware that in some very limited circumstances, usually involving complex financial transactions or taxes, the United States Supreme Court has held that "willfully" can mean that the actor must know that he is violating a legal duty. But "trespass" involves neither complex financial transactions nor taxes.

---

30. Frey v. Florida, 708 So. 2d 918, 923 (1998) (Justice Anstead dissenting) (citing United States v. Manganellis, 864 F.2d 528, 536 (7th Cir. 1988)).

Under Definition #2, "trespass" seems to consist of "only the description of a particular act, without reference to intent to do a further act or achieve a future consequence." If the person willfully enters and occupies the structure without consent, the crime is complete. Trespass, then, is not a specific intent crime. Rather, it meets the definition of a general intent crime. While it is possible that the legislature could have categorized "trespass" as a strict or absolute liability crime, we consider that highly unlikely for the reasons we discuss below in our analysis of the third offense.

Having concluded that trespass is a general intent crime, we must determine if the trial judge properly found that there was probable cause to believe that Sally Mistook committed trespass. In light of the testimony that she entered Professor Earnest's office when Professor Earnest was not present and Professor Earnest had not given Sally permission to enter the office to take the folder, we find the evidence adequate to hold Sally to answer on this count.

Finally, we turn to the third offense involving the abandoned refrigerator. Let us begin with the statutory language:

Criminal Code § 402 — Abandoned Refrigerators: Any person who discards or leaves in any place accessible to children any refrigerator, having a capacity of one and one-half cubic feet or more, which is no longer in use, and which has not had the door removed or the hinges and such portion of the latch mechanism removed to prevent latching or locking of the door, is guilty of an infraction.

This statute is silent on the question of mental states. It refers to no intent to do a future act or achieve a future consequence. It is not a specific intent statute. Because its language is "only the description of a particular act," it meets the definition of a general intent crime. Nonetheless, for the reasons we detail below, we believe that the legislature intended Criminal Code § 402 to fall into the rare class of strict liability statutes.

Beyond the absence of explicit mental states, a feature also common in general intent crimes, the statute relates to conduct involving the public health and safety. Abandoned refrigerators whose doors can seal in a child represent a public safety hazard. The statute transfers responsibility for risky conduct from those unable to protect themselves to those able to protect against the hazard. In this, it resembles a tort statute but comes with a criminal sanction. We contrast our statute with the almost identical California statute, California Penal Code § 402b (2001). The California statute is a misdemeanor, while ours is an infraction. The legislature's decision to classify this as the least culpable form of criminal conduct, an infraction, also suggests the possibility of strict liability.

The language of the statute, its public welfare overtones, and its status as an infraction all suggest that the proper category for it would be strict liability. We consider now the legislative history. Although the legislative history is sparse, it does include reference to the responsibility of the refuse collection industry to include a warning in the material that it sends with customers' bills that alerts the customers of their responsibility to secure refrigerators left out for collection.

The history also includes remarks by the sponsoring legislator, emphasizing the importance of shifting the burden for protecting our children to those who leave out such appliances regardless of their culpability.

"We don't care what they were thinking. We must protect the children. We need a criminal enforcement mechanism." The legislator also compared this bill to those statutes that protect against adulterated drugs and food.

Before reaching our conclusion, we compare this statute to the trespass statute that we considered earlier. The trespass statute did have a mental state term, "willfully." Even though "willfully" may duplicate the general voluntary act requirement, it is an indication that the legislature anticipated that some general criminal intent would be required. The abandoned refrigerator statute lacks even such a limited mental state term. Trespass is a traditional common law crime. Common law and early statutory crimes usually required some culpable mental state. The abandoned refrigerator statute is not a common law crime; it is a creature of statute. It is a creature of the age of statutes protecting public welfare. Trespass is a misdemeanor. Abandoning a refrigerator is an infraction.

Cumulatively, these indicia, along with the legislative history, indicate the legislature's desire to create a strict liability statute. We conclude that the third offense is a strict liability statute.

The trial judge could reasonably infer that a full-size refrigerator met the size requirements of the statute. The evidence indicates that it was large enough to fit a child inside. From the location of the refrigerator outside Sally's campus residence and the fact that her name was on it, the trial judge could conclude that Sally owned the refrigerator and had put out the refrigerator for collection. Because the statute declares a strict liability offense, the prosecution need prove no mental state. From the description given of the location and condition of the refrigerator, the judge could conclude that the prosecution had presented adequate evidence of any remaining elements of the statute.

We affirm the order of the trial court holding Ms. Mistook to answer for each of the three offenses. The case may proceed to trial.

So ordered.

QUESTIONS

Reconsider the seven factors, listed in Section C, that Professor LaFave identified as important in determining whether a statute is a strict liability offense. Which of those factors did the *Mistook* court consider? For each factor the *Mistook* opinion discusses, did the factor weigh in favor of or against the finding of strict liability?

2. Mistake of Fact: Specific and General Intent

PEOPLE *v.* SALLY MISTOOK

2 Imagination Cases 5 (2004)
Supreme Court of the State of Imagination

REVEL, J. In this appeal, we review the trial court's instructions to the jury on the question of mistake. Initially, we reviewed this case upon a challenge to the trial court's decision to hold the defendant to answer following the preliminary examination. At that time, we assessed the requisite mental states for the three offenses with which Ms. Mistook was charged. We determined that burglary is a specific intent offense; trespass is a general intent offense; abandoning a refrigerator is a strict liability offense.

Following our decision upholding the trial court's order, the case proceeded to jury trial. The jury convicted Ms. Mistook on all three counts. Ms. Mistook brings this appeal challenging the trial court's instructions to the jury on the question of mistake.

We review the evidence adduced at the trial, including that presented by the defense. This more extensive presentation provides a more detailed and somewhat different picture than was available at the time of the preliminary hearing.

With some additions, the People's evidence is the same as that presented at the preliminary hearing:

The defendant, Sally Mistook, was a student at the local law school. The victim of the first two offenses, Professor Jessie Earnest, taught first-year Criminal Law, a class in which Sally was enrolled. On the date in question, school security apprehended Sally at 6:45 P.M. in the stairwell between the floor housing faculty offices and the building exit. She was holding a folder containing a draft of the class examination belonging to Professor Earnest. Professor Earnest testified that at 6:30 P.M. on that evening, she had left two folders on the table just inside the door to her office. One folder contained a draft of the final exam. The other contained the class roster and lecture notes. She further testified that she had not given Sally Mistook permission to enter her office and take any folders. Professor Earnest also testified that when she left the building just after 6:30 P.M., she observed the sun set.

Just as police arrived to conduct a search at Sally's student residence, they noticed two children playing with a full-size, old, empty, unplugged refrigerator left on the street outside Sally's ground-floor residence. One child had climbed into the refrigerator and was closing the door as part of the game in which the children were engaged. The refrigerator had Sally's name on it. The incident occurred on a Monday. Regular campus trash collection occurs on Tuesday mornings. The police investigator testified that the refrigerator could contain two cubic feet of contents.

Here, we summarize the evidence presented by the defense. Sally Mistook admitted being a student in Professor Earnest's class. Ms. Mistook explained that she feared being called on by Professor Earnest. Professor Earnest was the only first-year professor at the law school who still required students to stand when called on. She often grilled the selected student for upwards of 20 minutes. Although Professor Earnest was unfailingly polite and never tried to humiliate students, she asked hard questions and did not allow students to pass or request the assistance of co-counsel. Ms. Mistook dreaded being called on. She explained that on the day in question, she became especially fearful of being called on. The class was beginning the study of mental states, and Ms. Mistook found them quite confusing. Because Professor Earnest called on students alphabetically and the last student on whom she had called was Mr. Mayes, Ms. Mistook knew her turn could not be far away. After class, back at the student residences, Ms. Mistook resolved to make the class roster disappear. Ms. Mistook consulted her classmate, Harry Hellper, an especially astute classmate, about the legality of her plan. Harry informed Sally that he thought her plan was sneaky and unethical but not illegal. He suggested that perhaps Sally could find a way of avoiding entry into the office. He remembered flipping to somewhere near the end of the text and reading something about unauthorized entry. He promised not to disclose her secret.

Professor Earnest normally held office hours on Mondays from 4:00 P.M. to 6:40 P.M. Professor Earnest had told students that, unless she had cancelled her office hours, if students arrived during those hours and she was not there, they were welcome to go in and make themselves comfortable and wait for her return. Professor Earnest explained that, occasionally, she printed out a case or statute in response to a student's question and needed to pick up the printout from the central printer in the office just across from hers. Ms. Mistook arrived outside Professor Earnest's office at 6:35 P.M. Ms. Mistook noticed that the door was partially open but that no one was inside. She could see the folder in which Professor Earnest kept the class roster on a table just inside the office. Ms. Mistook realized that she didn't need to set foot into the office to get the folder. She reached her arm inside the office and grabbed the folder. Ms. Mistook took the folder to the stairwell where school security personnel, who had been monitoring her on their cameras, apprehended her. In her distressed state, Ms. Mistook had neglected to read the class handout from Professor Earnest, distributed in class earlier that day, indicating that Professor Earnest had cancelled her regular office hours that Monday.

Ms. Mistook further testified that she had left the refrigerator outside for collection. She claimed, however, although she was unaware of the law, she had removed one set of hinges to use for another purpose and believed that that would prevent the door from latching.

In rebuttal, the prosecution brought the refrigerator to court and demonstrated that it continued to latch. We discuss below any remaining relevant evidence as it relates to each claim of mistake.

In Ms. Mistook's first argument, she complains that the judge's refusal to give a mistake instruction regarding the burglary charge was error. Ms. Mistook claims that she never intended to steal the class examination. She took the exam folder by mistake.

We must determine whether the judge should have instructed the jury on the effect of mistake on a specific intent crime. To do so, we engage in a two-step analysis. In the first step, we classify the type of mistake. Our jurisdiction continues to distinguish between mistakes of fact and mistakes of law. In this instance, Ms. Mistook claims that she took the wrong folder. She entertained no confusion or mistake about a legal issue. Hers was a simple mistake of fact.

In the second step, we assess whether her mistake negated the mental state required for the crime. Applied here, did her selection of the wrong folder negate her intent to commit theft at the time of entry? "Theft" is defined as the taking and carrying away of the personal property of another with the intent to permanently deprive the owner of the property. Did Ms. Mistook's selection of the wrong folder mean that at the time she entered Professor Earnest's office, she lacked the intent to permanently deprive Professor Earnest of the class roster? Our answer is no. Ms. Mistook's selection of the wrong folder has no bearing on whether, at the time she reached into the office, she intended to deprive Professor Earnest permanently of the class roster by making it "disappear." Her mistake of fact does not and could not negate the mental state required by the definition of "burglary." Thus, the trial court correctly refused to instruct the jury on mistake of fact on the burglary charge.

Next, Ms. Mistook argues that the trial court should have instructed the jury on mistake of fact regarding the trespass charge. Here she argues that she was mistaken about whether she had permission to enter. She bases her claim of permission on Professor Earnest's encouragement to students that they make themselves welcome in Professor Earnest's office during Professor Earnest's office hours. Ms. Mistook argues that any entry occurred during the window of permission during office hours. Ms. Mistook believed, in error, that she had permission to enter based on these circumstances. Her mistake was her failure to read the class handout advising students that Professor Earnest had cancelled her office hours.

To determine whether the judge should have instructed on mistake for trespass, a general intent crime, we engage in a two-step analysis. In the first step, we determine whether the mistake was one of fact or law. Her belief that she had permission to enter, based on her failure to read the handout, relates to no legal issue. Like the earlier mistake, it is a simple mistake of fact.

In our jurisdiction, in step two, for a general intent crime we must consider whether a jury could have found that her mistake was both honest and reasonable. In effect, we imply a mental state of negligence for a general intent crime. If the mistake negates the mental state of negligence, then the mistake exonerates.

Given her preoccupation with being called on in class, a jury could have found that Ms. Mistook honestly failed to read the handout and believed that she had permission. Whether it was reasonable for Ms. Mistook to fail to read the handout strikes us as an appropriate determination for a jury to make. Ms. Mistook might point out to the jury that Professor Earnest's door was open and unlocked, leading a reasonable person to believe that she had stepped away temporarily to collect a printout — that is, that Professor Earnest was holding office hours. Or Ms. Mistook might describe the circumstances surrounding the general distribution of handouts that might suggest it would be reasonable for a student to delay reading the handout until later in the week, before the next class session. If the jury concluded that Ms. Mistook honestly and reasonably believed that she had permission to enter when she took the folder, she cannot be convicted of trespass in our jurisdiction. Consequently, we find that the trial court erred by failing to instruct the jury on the effect of mistake of fact on the general intent offense of trespass.

Finally, Ms. Mistook argues that the trial court should have instructed the jury on mistake of fact with respect to the count involving the abandoning of a refrigerator. Again, our first step is to determine whether the mistake is one of law or fact. We agree with Ms. Mistook that her mistaken belief that removing one set of latches would disable the door was a mistake of fact. Abandoning a refrigerator is, however, a strict liability crime. There is no mental state to negate. Therefore, a mistake of fact has no impact on Ms. Mistook's liability for the strict liability offense of abandoning a refrigerator. The trial court correctly refused to instruct the jury on mistake of fact on this charge.

QUESTIONS

1. What are the basic principles that govern mistakes of fact and the three categories of offenses here?

2. Which treatment of mistakes makes more sense, the traditional one illustrated here, or the MPC approach?

The Moral Wrong and Legal Wrong Doctrines

While the basic principle regarding general intent crimes and mistakes of fact allows an honest and reasonable mistake to negate the imputed negligence, sometimes jurisdictions have applied other hurdles before making exoneration available. These hurdles are known as the moral wrong and legal wrong doctrines. The moral wrong doctrine can be explained as follows: Although ignorance or mistake would otherwise exonerate (because the ignorance/mistake was reasonable), that exoneration is not available if the defendant's conduct, with the facts as the defendant believed them to be, would still be morally wrong.[31] The legal wrong doctrine can be explained as follows: Although ignorance or mistake would otherwise exonerate (because the ignorance/mistake was reasonable), that exoneration is not available if the defendant's conduct, with the facts as the defendant believed them to be, still constitutes a legal wrong, even though it may be a lesser legal wrong.[32] The traditional legal wrong doctrine holds the offender culpable for the greater offense, even though his mental state corresponds only to the lesser offense.

PROBLEM

5.33 In the State of Imagination, there are two crimes related to abandoning one's underage children without support. The Code defines and classifies them as follows:

> Abandonment in the first degree: It is a crime to abandon your child when that child is under the age of ten. This crime is a felony and punishable by five years in the state prison.

> Abandonment in the second degree: It is a crime to abandon your child when that child is at least ten years old but not yet fourteen. This crime is a misdemeanor and punishable by not more than one year in the county jail.

Mr. Hale is the sole supporter of his young son. His child is nine years old and will turn ten in two weeks. Mr. Hale believes that the child is already ten years old. Mr. Hale was overseas serving in the military at the time of the child's birth. The letter he received from his wife and mother of the child mistakenly gave the child's birthday as two weeks earlier than the child's actual birthday. Unfortunately, the child's mother died shortly after Mr. Hale's return home and she never informed Mr. Hale of the child's true birth date. Mr. Hale has never checked the birth certificate, which was sent directly to the various authorities who needed it for school admission and similar circumstances.

Mr. Hale receives a letter from an old love who wants to marry Mr. Hale, but only if he has no children. Mr. Hale decides that a ten-year-old can fend for himself. Mr. Hale abandons his child to find his old love.

Mr. Hale is caught and charged with abandonment in the first degree, the felony of abandoning a child under the age of ten.

(a) What type of mistake has Mr. Hale made?

---

31. Joshua Dressler, *Understanding Criminal Law* 157-159 (3d ed. 2001).
32. *Id.*

(b) Assume that the State of Imagination does not apply either the moral or legal wrong doctrine. Of what would Mr. Hale be guilty?

(c) Now assume that the State of Imagination applies the moral wrong doctrine. Of what would Mr. Hale be guilty?

(d) Now assume that instead of the moral wrong doctrine, the State applies the legal wrong doctrine. Of what would Mr. Hale be guilty?

(e) How would the moral and legal wrong doctrines apply to Ms. Mistook?

3. Mistake of Law: Specific and General Intent

In this next opinion, the Supreme Court of the State of Imagination returns to Sally Mistook's case to consider her claims of mistake of law.

PEOPLE v. SALLY MISTOOK

2 Imagination Cases 10 (2004)
Supreme Court of the State of Imagination

REVEL, J. In this portion of our opinion, we consider Ms. Mistook's claim that the trial judge failed to properly instruct the jury on the impact of her mistakes of law on her liability for burglary, a specific intent offense, Trespass, a general intent offense, and abandoning a refrigerator, a strict liability offense.

(1) Burglary: Every person who enters any building or part of a building at night with intent to commit grand or petit larceny or any felony is guilty of burglary.

(2) Trespass: Every person who willfully commits a trespass by any of the following is guilty of a misdemeanor: . . .

> (b) Entering and occupying real property or structures of any kind without the consent of the owner, the owner's agent, or the person in lawful possession.

(3) Abandoned refrigerators: Any person who discards or leaves in any place accessible to children any refrigerator having a capacity of one and one-half cubic feet or more, which is no longer in use and which has not had the door removed or the hinges and such portion of the latch mechanism removed to prevent latching or locking of the door, is guilty of an infraction.

With respect to the burglary count, Ms. Mistook contends that, prior to the offense, she sought legal advice from Harry Hellper about the legality of her conduct. He gave her incorrect advice. She relied on his mistaken "legal" advice. Ms. Mistook sought to have the trial court instruct the jury on the "official reliance" exception, one of the rare situations in which a mistake of law, which may not negate a mental state required for the crime, can nonetheless exonerate. The "official reliance" exception permits defendants to shield themselves from culpability only under very limited conditions, like those in *Cox v. Louisiana*. These conditions do not include reliance on private counsel, even those who have been duly admitted to the Bar. Advice from a would-be lawyer, even an able and astute law student, does not qualify. We note in passing that Harry Hellper should resist the temptation to furnish any advice that a listener might interpret as legal advice. Our jurisdiction, like a number of others, prohibits practicing law without a license.

Thus the trial court correctly instructed the jury with respect to the reliance on the official interpretation mistake of law issue on the burglary count.

We turn now to Ms. Mistook's next claim. The trial court instructed the jury that "entry" for purposes of both the crime of burglary and the crime of trespass meant "any intrusion that breaks the airspace of the structure." Here, Ms. Mistook argues she made a mistake of law. She believed that "entry" required that she "set foot on the premises," the legal definition of "entry" in the jurisdiction in which she grew up. By merely reaching her arm into the office without setting foot on the premises, she would not have committed "entry" in her hometown.

We note that Ms. Mistook's claim of mistake with respect to "entry" applies only to any entry into the professor's office. The jury may have found the requisite entry for the burglary charge to have been Ms. Mistook's entry into the building itself. In the interests of fairness and to provide greater clarity, however, we analyze the possible application of mistake of law to Ms. Mistook's actions within the airspace of the professor's office.

To ascertain whether our jurisdiction entitles Ms. Mistook to a mistake of law instruction with respect to the burglary charge, we perform a two-step analysis. First, we classify the type of mistake. Ms. Mistook's mistake involves the legal definition of "entry" and qualifies as a mistake of law. In step two, with a specific intent crime, we must decide whether her mistake negates the mental state required for burglary. The statute does not suggest that awareness of the legal definition of "entry" is required. Nor does Ms. Mistook's mistake regarding the definition of "entry" negate the mental state required by the specific intent portion of the statute.[33] When Ms. Mistook voluntarily engaged in the act of breaking the airspace by inserting her arm into the office, she did so with the purpose of reaching inside the office and committing theft. Her mistake does not negate her intent to commit theft.

With respect to trespass, the general rule for mistakes of law and general intent crimes appears to be that mistakes of law do not exonerate,[34] except perhaps in *Lambert* or official reliance circumstances. But Ms. Mistook argues that trespass has a special mental state, "willfully." She insists therefore that we should consider not only the *Lambert* and official reliance exceptions, but also whether "willfully" entitles her to a special mistake of law defense. In this sense, she urges us to consider trespass like a specific intent crime for the analysis of mistakes of law, in which her mistake might negate the required mental state of "willfully."

We consider the question of a special mistake of law defense first. Ms. Mistook urges that the inclusion of the term "willfully" in the trespass statute provides a special ignorance or mistake of law exception. She analogizes her situation to that in *Ratzlaf*. She argues that "willfully" means that she had to understand the legal definition of "entry." We disagree. We understand the United States Supreme Court's *Ratzlaf* and related decisions to apply only in unusual circumstances, where the charges involve complex tax or financial regulations. The common law crime of trespass is not such a circumstance. Therefore, we do not construe

33. Dressler, *Understanding Criminal Law, supra* note 32, at 174-176.
34. *See id.*

"willfully" as imposing on prosecutors a special duty to prove an awareness of the law of trespass or a specific understanding of the legal definition of "entry" in the trespass context. Thus, her mistake does negate the mental state required by the offense.

The second exception is the official reliance exception. That is also not applicable here. As explained above, Harry Hellper's advice would not protect Ms. Mistook. The third exception is known as the due process or *Lambert* exception. Very rarely, prosecution for a crime, defined by the actor's status and involving an omission, can violate the Constitution if adequate notice of the offense was not provided prior to the violation and no opportunity to comply followed notice. That is not the case with the traditional common law offense of trespass. Trespass here is not a crime of omission or status. None of the exceptions applies.

Finally, with respect to the charge of abandoning a refrigerator, Ms. Mistook says she did not know such a crime existed. Here, she asserts a classic ignorance of the law defense. Ignorance of the law almost never exonerates. As explained in the preceding paragraph, as in the case of mistake, three exceptions exist. The first, discussed above, occurs when the ignorance or mistake negates the mental state required by the crime. This does not apply here. Abandoning a refrigerator is a strict liability crime. There is no mental state to negate. The second is the official reliance exception. That is also not applicable here. It is not clear she even consulted her colleague, Harry Hellper, about this offense. Even if she did, as explained above, his advice would not protect her. The third exception, the *Lambert* exception, also does not apply as abandoning a refrigerator is neither a crime of omission nor a crime based on the status of the actor.

The old maxim does apply in this case: Ignorance of the law is no excuse. Appeal on the mistake of law issues denied.

QUESTIONS

1. What are the traditional approaches to mistake of law for specific intent, general intent, and strict liability crimes, as illustrated in the third *Mistook* opinion?

2. Which approach makes more sense in the context of mistakes — the MPC or the traditional approach?

PROBLEMS

For each of the following scenarios, consider whether the accused would be held liable under a traditional approach.

5.34 Mr. Social is charged with violating the following statute in the state vehicle code:

It is illegal to drive with more than .08 percent of alcohol in a person's bloodstream.

Under this statute, the prosecutor has charged and proven that Mr. Social was driving with more than .08 percent of alcohol in his bloodstream. In a separate section, the vehicle code defines "driving" as having control over a car with the motor running.

Mr. Social's argument: "I knew it was against the law to drive with more than .08 percent of alcohol, but since I'd just started the ignition and hadn't put the car into drive yet, I didn't think I was driving."

Does Mr. Social's mistake save him from conviction?

5.35 Ms. Counsel is charged with violating the following statute in the state vehicle code:

It is illegal to drive with more than .08 percent of alcohol in a person's bloodstream.

Under this statute, the prosecutor has charged and proven that Ms. Counsel was driving with a .09 percent of alcohol in her bloodstream. In a separate section, the vehicle code defines "driving" as having control over a car with the motor running.

Ms. Counsel's argument: Before I went to the party and drank alcohol, I consulted with my attorney. My attorney told me that the legal limit was .10. I carefully calculated how many drinks I could have based on my weight and tolerance. I drank less than would put me at the legal limit. Then I got into my car and started driving. I was arrested just a few minutes after I got on the road.

Does Ms. Counsel's mistake save her from conviction?

5.36 Same as 5.35 except for the following facts. In addition, during the party, neighbors called the police because some people at the party were playing the music too loudly. Before Ms. Counsel left the party, she asked one of the officers if he thought that she was too inebriated to drive. He gave her three field sobriety tests and said she was fine.

5.37 In 1986, the State of Imagination enacted the following law:

To protect the health and welfare of the residents of the State of Imagination, all persons planning to be married must be tested for certain contagious diseases before the marriage ceremony. Failure to comply with this act will render the marriage void.

Sally, who did not know of this law, married Jeff in 1987 without undergoing any of the required tests. Sally subsequently purchased a home and represented on the loan application, which required sworn signatures under penalty of perjury, that she was married to Jeff. When Sally defaulted on the loan and Jeff could not pay, the district attorney charged Sally with perjury, which reads as follows:

Every person who declares under penalty of perjury and willfully states as true any material matter which he or she knows to be false is guilty of perjury.

Does Sally's mistake save her from conviction under the statute?

GORDON *v*. STATE   Alabama Supreme Court, 52 Ala. 308 (1875)

BRICKELL, C.J. This indictment is founded on the fortieth section of the statute, approved April 22, 1873, entitled, "An act to regulate elections in the State of Alabama," which declares "That any person voting more than once at any election held in this State, or depositing more than one ballot for the same office at such election, or is guilty of any other kind of illegal or fraudulent voting, shall be deemed guilty of a felony." . . . The first count charges that the [defendant], not being of the age of twenty-one years, voted at the last general election in this State. . . . Two witnesses were examined on the behalf of the defendant; one, his mother, and the other an acquaintance who had known him from his birth, and resided in the same neighborhood, and for a long time a member of the same family with defendant, and they testified the defendant was of the age of twenty-one years, in the August preceding the election. That they had frequently told defendant he would be of full age in that month, and subsequently and before the election told him he was of age. The court refused to charge the jury that if defendant, in reliance on these statements, honestly believed he was of full age when he voted, he should not be convicted. . . .

How would a traditional court analyze Mr. Gordon's mistake argument? How would an MPC jurisdiction analyze it?

The Alabama Supreme Court's analysis follows:

"All crime exists, primarily, in the mind." A wrongful act and a wrongful intent must concur, to constitute what the law deems a crime. When an act denounced by the law is proved to have been committed, in the absence of countervailing evidence, the criminal intent is inferred from the commission of the act. The inference may be, and often is removed by the attending circumstances, showing the absence of a criminal intent. Ignorance of law is never an excuse, whether a party is charged civilly or criminally. Ignorance of fact may often be received to absolve a party from civil or criminal responsibility. On the presumption that everyone capable of acting for himself knows the law, courts are compelled to proceed. If it should be abandoned, the administration of justice would be impossible, as every cause would be embarrassed with the collateral inquiry of the extent of legal knowledge of the parties seeking to enforce or avoid liability and responsibility.

The criminal intention being of the essence of crime, if the intent is dependent on a knowledge of particular facts, a want of such knowledge, not the result of carelessness or negligence, relieves the act of criminality. An illustration may be found in the vending of obscene or immoral publications. A knowledge of the character of such publications is an indispensable ingredient of the offence. From the vending it would be inferable; but if it appeared the vendor was blind, and in the course of his trade happened innocently to make the sale, a want of knowledge of the character of the publication would relieve him from criminal responsibility. . . . Illegal voting, when it is supposed to arise from a want of legal qualifications, is dependent on the voter's knowledge of the particular facts which make up the qualification. Every man is bound to know the law requires that every voter shall be a native born or naturalized citizen of the United States, of the age of twenty-one years, and have resided in the State six months, and the county in which he offers to vote, three months next preceding the election, and must not have been convicted of the offenses mentioned in the Constitution as the disqualification of an elector. He is bound to exercise reasonable diligence, if he resided near the boundary line of a county, and should be informed by those having the means of knowledge that his residence was within the county, and he, without a knowledge of the real facts, honestly acting on this information should vote, he could not fairly be charged with illegal voting, though on a subsequent survey or on some other evidence, it should be ascertained his residence was not within the county. The precise time when a man arrives at the age of twenty-one years is a fact, knowledge of which he derives necessarily from his parents, or other relatives or acquaintances having knowledge of the time of his birth. If acting in good faith, on information fairly obtained from them under an honest belief that he had reached the age, he votes, having the other necessary qualifications, illegal voting should not be imputed to him. The intent which makes up the crime cannot be affirmed. Whether he had the belief that he was a qualified voter, and the information was fairly obtained, should be referred to, and determined by the jury. The whole inquiry should be directed to the voter's knowledge of facts, and to his diligence in acquiring the requisite knowledge. If he votes recklessly or carelessly, when the facts are doubtful or uncertain, his ignorance should not excuse him, if the real facts show he was not qualified. If ignorant of the disqualifying fact, and without a want of diligence, under an honest belief of his right to vote, he should be excused, though he had not the right.

The charge [jury instruction] given by the [trial] court, and several of the refusals to charge, were according to these views erroneous, and the judgment must be reversed, and the cause remanded.

QUESTIONS

1. How did the Alabama Court analyze Mr. Gordon's claim?
2. Did the court treat the statute as a specific or general intent crime, or did the court use another framework for analysis?

Although the authors have been unable to ascertain who Mr. Gordon was and why the question arose about knowledge of his age, consider the historical context of birth records in Alabama in the mid-1800s. Where were children born? Why might individuals not have official records or not have access to official records of their birth?

Consider the following account:

> I was born in Tuckahoe, near Hillsborough, and about twelve miles from Easton, in Talbot county, Maryland. I have no accurate knowledge of my age, never having seen any authentic record containing it. By far the larger part of the slaves know as little of their ages as horses know of theirs, and it is the wish of most masters within my knowledge to keep their slaves thus ignorant. I do not remember to have ever met a slave who could tell of his birthday. They seldom come nearer to it than planting-time, harvest-time, cherrytime, spring-time, or fall-time. A want of information concerning my own was a source of unhappiness to me even during childhood. The white children could tell their ages. I could not tell why I ought to be deprived of the same privilege. I was not allowed to make any inquiries of my master concerning it. He deemed all such inquiries on the part of a slave improper and impertinent, and evidence of a restless spirit. The nearest estimate I can give makes me now between twenty-seven and twenty-eight years of age. I come to this, from hearing my master say, some time during 1835, I was about seventeen years old.

Frederick Douglass, *Narrative of the Life of Frederick Douglass* 21 (1845) (Signet ed. 1968).

4. Intoxication: Specific and General Intent

In the opinion below, the *Williams* court addresses the effect of intoxication in a jurisdiction that uses the traditional specific and general intent rubrics. As you read the case, consider whether the court would have reached a different result in an MPC jurisdiction.

UNITED STATES *v.* WILLIAMS
332 F. Supp. 1 (1971)

MURRAY, J. In this case the defendant was charged . . . with robbery of a branch of the Maryland National Bank in Cambridge, Maryland on December 4, 1970. The case was tried non-jury on September 13 and 14, 1971.

The basic facts are not in dispute. In a stipulation signed by government counsel, the defendant and his counsel, it was agreed that on the date set out in the indictment, the defendant went into the bank in Cambridge, Maryland and requested a loan from a branch officer of the bank. The officer declined to grant the defendant a loan. Thereafter the defendant walked up to Mrs. Martina Bennett, a teller, and handed to her a note stating "This is a stickup." Mrs. Bennett gave him all her cash, and defendant then left the bank with the money. It was also stipulated that Mrs. Bennett was intimidated by defendant giving her the note and for that reason turned over to defendant the funds in her drawer. An audit made immediately after the robbery showed the defendant had taken $4,727 of the bank's money.

While defendant thus does not contest the fact that a robbery occurred and he committed it, his counsel urges upon the Court that an essential element of the crime is lacking. It is contended that the two sections of the bank robbery statute on which the counts in the indictment are based both require a specific intent to steal, and that at the time of the robbery defendant was so intoxicated from alcohol and drugs that he was incapable of forming such specific intent.

The threshold legal questions thus are whether voluntary intoxication can negative specific intent as an element of crime and, if so, whether the offense . . . charged . . . [in] the indictment require[s] proof of specific intent. If specific intent is an element . . . the factual question then arises as to whether on all the evidence the degree of defendant's intoxication was such as to create a reasonable doubt that defendant had a specific intent to steal when the robbery took place.

It is clear from the cases that while voluntary intoxication is ordinarily no defense to crime, it may have that effect if specific intent is an element of the crime. . . .

Thus in the area of criminal responsibility as affected by voluntary intoxication, a distinction must be drawn between so-called "general intent" to commit a crime and a "specific intent" to do a particular criminal act. . . .

[T]here are certain crimes such as burglary and larceny where the act must be accompanied with a specific intent. Thus at common law in larceny there must be a taking and carrying away of the property of another *with the intent* to permanently deprive that person of his ownership of the goods. In burglary there must be a breaking and entry of a dwelling house in the night-time *with the intent* to commit a felony therein. Holmes in his work *The Common Law* suggests (p. 74) that the object of punishing such breaking and entering is not to prevent trespasses, even when committed by night, but only such trespasses as are the first step to wrongs of a greater magnitude, like robbery or murder. . . .

[T]he Court feels that historically and legally . . . a specific intent to steal is an element of the crime. The Court on a review of all the evidence in the case is satisfied beyond a reasonable doubt that defendant when he took and carried away money belonging to the bank exceeding $100 in value did so with the intent to steal or purloin.

The Court in finding as a fact that defendant had the intent to steal is not unmindful of the fact that there was substantial evidence to show that defendant had imbibed significant quantities of alcohol and drugs, but the Court from all the evidence finds beyond a reasonable doubt that he both had the capacity to and did intend to steal when he took the bank's money. The basis for the Court's finding in this regard requires some reference to the evidence of defendant's taking of alcohol and drugs and his condition at the time of the robbery.

In testifying on his own behalf, defendant claimed that as a result of an argument with his wife he started drinking with a companion around 9:00 A.M. on December 3, 1970, the day before the robbery and over the next fourteen hours the two consumed three fifths of whiskey, of which defendant had about half. During this period defendant also took 6 or 7 "yellow jackets" or barbiturate pills. Between midnight on December 3 and the occurrence of the robbery around 1:00 P.M. on December 4, defendant claims that he and a companion drank an additional one or one and a half fifths of whiskey, of which defendant had all but half a pint. In addition, sometime in this latter period defendant took some LSD pills, with the result that he had only "spotty" recollection of events the morning of the robbery. Defendant does recall going into the bank and talking with the branch officer, and leaving the bank stuffing money under his jacket, but disclaims any recollection of confronting the teller, presenting her with a "stickup" note and actually receiving from her over $4,000 in cash.

The witnesses who actually observed the defendant on the day of the robbery indicate he had been drinking but not that he was drunk. A cab driver named Hopkins who drove the defendant at 6:00 A.M. to redeem his watch and then to a drive-in said his eyes were red and he had been drinking. His speech was "heavy" and he did not seem to walk normally.

Mrs. Florence Brannock, a teller in the bank, spoke briefly with defendant when he asked for the loan department and directed him to the branch officer. She felt he smelled strongly of cheap wine or alcohol and that his speech while understandable was not normal — it was a little "slurred" or "thick."

Branch Officer John Bramble testified that the defendant came into his office seeking a $400 loan for Christmas. In their conversation defendant gave his place of employment, said he owned a 1969 Chevrolet and had an account in the Farmer's and Merchant's bank across the street. The witness said he could smell a strong odor of alcohol on the defendant's breath and felt he was under the influence of liquor and that he also appeared somewhat nervous. After declining to grant the defendant a loan, the witness watched the defendant walk towards the lobby of the bank and could not remember anything unusual about the defendant's walk.

Mrs. Martina Bennett, a cash teller, recalled that a little after 1:00 P.M. a man approached from the side aisle of the bank. She recalled having seen him previously at Mrs. Brannock's desk. He put a note on her counter and said nothing. At first she thought he might be deaf and read the note. It was printed in pencil on a torn piece of paper and read "This is a stickup." She noticed that he had his right hand in his jacket pocket which was thrust forward pointing at her as though he had a gun. She was terrified and afraid he was going to shoot her. She put all her money on the counter, but she did not see what he did with it, although she believes he dropped some and then picked it up. She noticed nothing unusual about the defendant's appearance and did not smell any alcohol. When he was standing before her he did not appear to waver, but his eyes did appear sleepy. She watched him walk away from her counter and down a flight of four steps leading to the lobby entrance. . . .

The testimony as to acts of the defendant closest in time to the robbery was given by the owner of a small store in Cambridge, George Heist. His store is located about two blocks from the bank. He recalled that the defendant came into his store about noon and asked for a piece of paper to figure a bill. The defendant reached for a sales pad but the witness did not want the defendant to use the pad and gave him a piece of paper instead. The defendant turned around with his back to the witness and put the piece of paper on top of some stocking boxes and started to write. Apparently dissatisfied, he balled up the piece of paper and threw it on the floor. Defendant reached again for the witness' sales pad, which the witness again refused to give him, tearing off a piece of old calendar paper instead. Defendant again turned around and wrote some more, and then left the store.

The witness said that the defendant while in his store seemed coherent, didn't stagger, and acted normally except for trying to take his sales pad twice. However, because the defendant "seemed a little high on something" he decided, after the defendant left the store, to read what was on the balled up piece of paper. It read "This is a stick." Although defendant on leaving the store walked away from and not towards the bank, the witness appropriately concluded a robbery might be in prospect and got a policeman to whom he gave a description of the defendant. Later he heard the fire whistle blow about 1:00 P.M., which was a signal that the bank had been robbed.

Dr. Leonard Rothstein, a private psychiatrist called by defendant, had an interview examination with defendant on May 24, 1971 and also talked to defendant's wife. The defendant gave the doctor a history of abusing alcohol since age 19, and told the doctor he was drinking beer all day before the robbery and took some "yellow jackets" in the evening, and some LSD in the morning before the robbery. Dr. Rothstein found no significant evasiveness in the defendant and no discrepancies between defendant's account and his wife's.

On the basis of defendant's account to him and his examination the doctor expressed the opinion that at the time of the offense the defendant had no psychosis or structural alteration in the brain. However, the doctor concluded from what the defendant told him of his ingestion of alcohol and drugs that the higher centers governing the making of judgments, control of behavior and retention of experience in memory had been affected. While the defendant knew what he was doing, his judgment about the appropriateness of his actions and his ability to control them were severely impaired. From the history the doctor concluded the defendant had taken the alcohol and drugs voluntarily and with knowledge from previous experience of their probable effect. In response to a hypothetical question asked on cross examination by counsel for the government, the doctor admitted that if the defendant had not taken alcohol and drugs before the offense, he would at the time have had no psychiatric illness and would have had the capacity to conform his conduct to the requirements of the law.

Dr. William Fitzpatrick, who had examined the defendant on July 15, 1971 at the request of the government, was called as an expert psychiatric witness by the defense. He related a personal history and account of the offense given him by the defendant very similar to that related by defendant's own expert, Dr. Rothstein. He found the defendant of normal intelligence with no evidence of psychosis or structural brain disorder. From the history he judged defendant to be a passive dependent personality of the type more likely to abuse alcohol than the average person. Although from defendant's own account he was an episodic heavy user of alcohol and drugs, he did not find evidence that he was an alcoholic or a drug addict. He felt that because defendant was a passive dependent type he had a condition something short of total mental health. However, had the defendant not taken alcohol and drugs at time of the offense, he would not consider that defendant lacked criminal responsibility or capacity to conform his conduct to the requirements of the law. Although the doctor did not know the quantity of alcohol or drugs defendant consumed before the offense, he assumed the defendant was intoxicated at the time and that his intoxication was self-induced with knowledge on the part of the defendant that he would get drunk if he drank. He admitted that if he assumed a lesser degree of intoxication he would have to alter his opinion, but his opinion that defendant at the time of the offense could not conform his conduct to the requirements of the law was based on assumed intake of large quantities of alcohol. However, the doctor honestly disclaimed any opinion on whether defendant could specifically intend to rob a bank.

In expressing their conclusions, both psychiatrists obviously had in mind the ALI formulation contained in Model Penal Code, Section 4.01, approved in this circuit in *United States v. Chandler*, 393 F.2d 920 (1968). However, defense counsel disclaimed any contention that this standard was applicable in determining the issue of the criminal responsibility of this defendant. In this connection it is noted that Section 2.08(3) of the Model Penal Code provides "Intoxication does not, in itself, constitute mental disease within the meaning of Section 4.01."

As then Circuit Judge Burger stated in *Heideman v. United States*, 104 U.S. App. D.C. 128, 259 F.2d 943, at p. 946 (1958): "Drunkenness, while efficient to reduce or remove *inhibitions*, * does not readily negate *intent*.*" (* Footnotes omitted.)

The Court believes that the defendant had taken alcohol and drugs to the point of being "under the influence" but that he was not so intoxicated as not to understand what he was doing or to not have the intention to steal from the bank. There is a marked difference between the accounts of the persons who observed defendant and defendant's own account as to his condition. It appears from a witness called by the defense that he was able to write a "stickup" note shortly before the robbery, to go into the bank, hold a coherent conversation about a loan, present the note, obtain over $4,000 in cash, none of which has been returned, and make good his escape. The Court concludes beyond a reasonable doubt that defendant had the intent to steal from the bank as required for conviction. . . .

QUESTIONS

1. Why did the court conclude that robbery was a specific intent crime?
2. How intoxicated must a defendant be to find relief under the federal court's approach?
3. What evidence do you think the court found persuasive? Why should general intent crimes exclude consideration of intoxication?

J. SYNTHESIS AND CHALLENGES

Consider the statutory interpretation issue presented by the excerpt below from the *People v. Ryan* case, 82 N.Y.2d 497, 499-501 (1993).

[T]he trial evidence revealed that on October 2, 1990, defendant asked his friend David Hopkins to order and receive a shipment of hallucinogenic mushrooms on his behalf. Hopkins agreed, and adhering to defendant's instructions placed a call to their mutual friend Scott in San Francisco and requested the "usual shipment." Tipped off to the transaction, on October 5 State Police Investigator Douglas Vredenbrugh located the package at a Federal Express warehouse in Binghamton. The package was opened (pursuant to a search warrant) and resealed after its contents were verified. The investigator then borrowed a Federal Express uniform and van and delivered the package to Hopkins, the addressee, who was arrested upon signing for it.

Hopkins explained that the package was for defendant and agreed to participate in a supervised delivery to him. In a telephone call recorded by the police, Hopkins notified the defendant that he got the package, reporting a "shit load of mushrooms in there." Defendant responded, "I know, don't say nothing." At another point Hopkins referred to the shipment containing two pounds. The men agreed to meet later that evening at the firehouse in West Oneonta.

At the meeting after a brief conversation, Hopkins handed defendant a . . . package. Moments after taking possession, defendant was arrested. He was later indicted for . . . criminal possession of a controlled substance in the second degree. . . .

Additionally [at trial], the police chemist testified that the total weight of the mushrooms in Hopkins' package was 932.8 grams (about two pounds), and that a 140-gram sample of the package contents contained 796 milligrams of psilocybin, a hallucinogen. He did not know, however, the process by which psilocybin appears in mushrooms, whether naturally, by injection or some other means. Nor was there any evidence as to how much psilocybin would typically appear in two pounds of mushrooms.

At the close of the People's case, defendant moved to dismiss for insufficient proof that he knew the level of psilocybin in the mushrooms, and also requested a charge-down to seventh degree attempted criminal possession, which has no weight element. Both applications were denied, defendant was convicted as charged and he was sentenced as a second felony offender to 10 years-to-life.

The defendant was charged under the following statute:

Penal Law § 220.18(5)

A person is guilty of criminal possession of a controlled substance in the second degree when he knowingly and unlawfully possesses: . . . Six hundred twenty-five milligrams of a hallucinogen.

The *Ryan* court stated that the question of statutory interpretation before [the court] is whether "knowingly" applies to the weight of the controlled substance.

Using a non-MPC approach to *mens rea*, how would you answer this question? Using an MPC approach, how would you answer it?

South African criminal law recognizes the concept of "conscious negligence," described as follows:

> Conscious negligence exists where the accused foresees only a remote possibility of a consequence resulting and fails to take the steps that a reasonable man would have taken to guard against this possibility.
>
> For instance, in *R v Hedley* the accused was found guilty of culpable homicide where he fired a rifle shot at a cormorant near the edge of a dam. The bullet ricocheted off the surface of the water, near some huts which the accused admitted seeing before he fired, and killed a woman. Broome JP said: "He knew that the bullet he was firing would strike the water and might ricochet, and that if it did ricochet it might pass near the huts and so might hit someone. It is true that the likelihood of harm was small, but on the other hand the harm, if it resulted, would be very serious."
>
> In other words, Hedley foresaw the remote possibility that he might kill someone when he fired the shot. Since a reasonable person would not have fired the shot in these circumstances, he was consciously negligent in doing so.[35]

What similarities does conscious negligence have to the mental states recognized by the MPC? How does it differ from those mental states? Should conscious negligence be a basis for criminal liability?

———————————————

The Restatement Second of Torts gives the following definitions:

§ 8A   *Intent*

The word "intent" is used throughout the Restatement of this Subject to denote that the actor desires to cause consequences of his act, or that he believes that the consequences are substantially certain to result from it.

§ 500   *Reckless Disregard of Safety Defined*

The actor's conduct is in reckless disregard of the safety of another if he does an act or intentionally fails to do an act which it is his duty to the other to do, knowing or having reason to know of facts which would lead a reasonable man to realize, not only that his conduct creates an unreasonable risk of physical harm to another, but also that such risk is substantially greater than that which is necessary to make his conduct negligent.

§ 282   *Negligence Defined*

In the Restatement of this Subject, negligence is conduct which falls below the standard established by law for the protection of others against unreasonable risk of harm. It does not include conduct recklessly disregardful of an interest of others.

How do the tort law definitions of each of these terms compare with the criminal law's definitions? Is it desirable for mental state terminology to be consistent across different areas of substantive law?

———————————————

———————————————

35. Jonathan Burchell & John Milton, *Principles of Criminal Law* 321-322 (2d ed. 1997).

It is sometimes said to be a "maxim" of criminal law that "ignorance or mistake of law is never a defense." As the cases and Problems in Section E demonstrate, though, ignorance or mistake of law at times does insulate a defendant from liability. Rewrite the "ignorance of the law" maxim so that it accurately reflects the nuances of the law you learned in Section E.

Although scholars often view the MPC approach to mental states one of the MPC's greatest achievements, consider the following critiques.

Harold Edgar, MENS REA   Encyclopedia of Crime and Justice 1037-1039 (1983)

What the Code does, then, is to deprive the system of the ambiguous terms, such as *intent* and *willful*. . . . The existence of seventy-six mens rea formulas in the federal criminal law may be taken as evidence of legislative failure. Some of the variety in culpability language, however, may reflect not follies but an inchoate understanding that the ways we use language to describe motives and purposes vary from one context to another. If this is true, and if the problems are ones of cultural intuition about language, the wise legislative response may be to free courts to let similar words adapt to their different settings. . . .

The problem, then, is that the Model Penal Code, and the states that follow it, are at risk by employing uniform culpability language if the single standard does not fit the common patterns of various crimes and the defensive settings that the Code encompasses. . . .

[T]he psychological model of conduct underlying the Code, the idea that we act by willing discrete behaviors, reflects ancient psychology. Surely it is a fiction; no homunculus lives inside the brain, sending out orders to animate the limbs. Although the law can live happily with fictions, the acceptance of fictions usually marks issues the law seeks to avoid, not ones it confronts.

It has been argued, for example, that the affirmative common-law terms denoting culpability (intent, malice, and so on) are basically fictions. The law handled the problems of proving these mental states by extensive use of presumptions: for example, a man intends the natural and probable consequences of his acts. . . .

The Model Penal Code, however, gives precise definitions of purpose, knowledge, and recklessness on the supposition that these are provable occurrences. The supposition is very questionable. It is implausible to assume that persons always think of the kind of results they will cause in committing crime. In the typical homicide case growing out of an argument with family or friends, an actor reacts with explosive rage. If he says that he gave absolutely no thought to consequences, is he guilty only of negligent homicide because the thought of "death" or "risk of death" never went through his mind?. . . .

To be sure, the Code, although it makes no use of the common-law presumptions, can rely on juries to determine that people had a "conscious objective," even though their own daily experience shows that this often misdescribes human behavior. Nonetheless, is a body of law seriously flawed if it provides an elaborate set of precise rules whose operability depends upon the jury's willingness to make artificial characterizations?

George P. Fletcher, DOGMAS OF THE MODEL PENAL CODE

2 Buff. Crim. L. Rev. 3-5, 6-8 (1998) (citations omitted)

The Model Penal Code has become the central document of American criminal justice. It has had some effect on law reform in over 35 states. More significantly, it provides the lingua franca of most people who teach criminal law in the United States. Most academics think the precise definitions of culpability states in section 2.02(2) are really neat. . . .

The downside of the Model Penal Code's influence is that it has come to shape our understanding of what a code should do in the field of criminal justice. The resulting assumptions are what I call the dogmas of the Model Penal Code. I formulate these assumptions as propositions of ironic advice to a legislature.

Dogma I: Define as many concepts as you can — whether you are competent to do so or not

The Code ventures precise definitions on matters where many philosophers fear to tread. . . .

One of the celebrated achievements of the Model Penal Code is the definition of the four mental states — purpose, knowledge, recklessness, and negligence — section 2.02(2). These are highly complex definitions, hardly worth repeating here. Suffice it to say that the definitions are so complicated that one wonders whether any judge has ever mastered them. But even if they could be easily mastered, my objection is worth repeating. Are these matters really within the province of legislative wisdom and authority? After all, is there one accessible truth about the distinction between intentional and negligent conduct? Is the matter appropriately subject to legislative will?

My doubts about legislative competence in th[is area] . . . mental states — are nourished by a glance at the 1975 German Criminal Code. The German statute makes no effort whatsoever to define these contested concepts. . . .

Why then, might the Model Penal Code venture definitions where the German drafters wisely abstain? The simple explanation is that the American approach to drafting of a code proceeds on the assumption that the code must rest on its bottom. It is not embedded in a theoretical literature that elaborates the essential concepts necessary for working with the code. We might call a code of this sort imperialistic. It seeks to displace not only the encrustation of the case law but also the teachings of scholars. It purports to be a comprehensive guide to the solution of the problems it addresses. Of course, the courts must apply the code and resolve some problems in the interstices of its provisions. Scholars are left with the residual task of writing commentary on the code and the case law.

Dogma II: Write provisions that seem precise but that judges could never understand

A good example of this tendency are the provisions on culpability states already mentioned. Two provisions that could be very simple — those on purposely and knowingly committing offenses — depend on the subtle classification of each criminal act into the elements of the nature of the conduct, the consequences, and the circumstances. Each of these three categories require a different mental element for each of the two types of culpability. In all, then, the Model Penal Code uses four, perhaps five, different mental attitudes to describe two forms of culpability:

1. awareness of the element
2. practical certainty of the element
3. conscious object of the element
4. believes or hopes that the element exists

Needless to say that these four mental states could be allocated to the categories of nature, consequences, and circumstances of offenses in any number of ways. There is nothing in the Model Penal Code to suggest that the present allocation is rational or coherent. As a result it is very difficult to remember which mental attitude goes with which category and which level of culpability. I would be greatly surprised if more than a handful of sophisticated judges actually understood and applied these overly complex provisions.

QUESTIONS

1. Are Professor Edgar's criticisms persuasive? If so, why? If not, why not?
2. Do Professor Fletcher's criticisms of the MPC differ from Professor Edgar's? If so, how? In what ways are they similar?
3. Does Professor Fletcher underestimate the ability of judges to parse the MPC provisions?
4. Is the MPC's treatment of mental states preferable to the traditional one?

CHAPTER SIX

HOMICIDE

A. INTRODUCTION

Although homicides represent a relatively small percentage of overall crime, the topic of homicide draws a level of popular and academic attention disproportional to that percentage. Portrayals of crime on television and in the movies commonly focus on homicide. Homicides receive extensive news coverage. Academics also give a great deal of attention to the law of homicide. A number of factors may explain this level of attention. The crimes of murder and manslaughter were among the first recognized by the common law. The criminal justice system's most severe sanctions are imposed in homicide cases, including the death penalty. Homicide can also have a devastating impact on family members and other surviving victims. Because of the attention given homicides in both the news and other popular media, homicides also seriously undermine society's sense of security.

The architecture of the law of homicide throughout American jurisdictions has many common features. All homicides require the same three non-mental elements — (1) some form of conduct, (2) a resulting death, and (3) a causative link between the conduct and the death. The law of homicide revolves in large measure around the actor's mental state regarding the death. So another common feature across jurisdictions is the role played by the mental element pertaining to the death. Someone who causes death with purpose to kill will initially qualify for murder in virtually every jurisdiction. A killing done with recklessness regarding the death initially qualifies as manslaughter. Someone who causes a death with simple negligence as to the death will often escape criminal homicide liability.

Because of the role played by mental state in the hierarchy of homicide, the organization of this chapter is keyed to the actor's mental state regarding death. We start with premeditation and deliberation, a standard that is widely considered the most demanding and blameworthy. In many jurisdictions, proof of premeditation and deliberation raises an "ordinary" murder that was committed with purpose from second-degree to first-degree murder. Next we turn to provocation, a doctrine that can lower an actor's liability from murder to manslaughter, even though the actor killed purposely. The Section following our discussion of provocation deals with reckless murder, cases in which the degree of recklessness regarding death is so extreme that a killing that normally would be treated as manslaughter will be raised to murder. We then continue down the mental state continuum and treat reckless and negligent killings. The chapter's final two categories of homicide are usually understood to incorporate a strict liability component with respect to the actor's mental state regarding the death. They are the felony murder and misdemeanor manslaughter rules. The chapter ends with an analysis of the death penalty, a punishment for which homicide may be a prerequisite.

As noted previously, the law of homicide has a number of features that are fairly uniform from jurisdiction to jurisdiction, such as a purposeful killing initially qualifying for murder, recognition of some sort of extreme reckless murder, and provocation reducing murder to manslaughter. But there are some aspects of the law of homicide that vary dramatically from jurisdiction to jurisdiction. What qualifies as provocation, for example, can differ widely from state to state. Jurisdictions are also divided on questions such as whether and how to divide murder into degrees and whether to subsume negligent killing along with reckless killing under the rubric of manslaughter or to create a separate crime of negligent homicide with a lesser penalty.

Our federal system of government is responsible for jurisdictional variation in the criminal law. States are allowed and encouraged to shape their criminal law as they see fit within the bounds of the Constitution. You will encounter jurisdictional variation not just in homicide but in many other areas throughout the rest of this book. Try to spot such variations and decipher what policy or political issues may cause states to differ. At the same time, note jurisdictional uniformity when you find it. In the law of homicide, there are some points on which jurisdictions vary, but don't let this variation mask the fact that there are many points on which jurisdictions are quite uniform. You will need to recognize both jurisdictional uniformity as well as variation to master criminal law.

What significance do the purposes of punishment you studied in Chapter 2 play in homicide? A premeditated and deliberate killing, such as a murder for hire, seems so blameworthy and the killer so dangerous that there might be no doubt that the killer should be punished under at least four of the theories we studied: under a retributive theory for just deserts, to deter him and other potential killers, to incapacitate him, and to denounce his conduct. In homicide, the purposes of punishment serve primarily to provide guidance on grading homicide offenses — how and where lines should be drawn that dictate the range of potential punishment. So the purposes of punishment help determine not only whether the actor should be punished but also how much punishment the actor deserves. One example is the treatment of negligent killing. Should we create for it a separate category with a different name, such as "negligent homicide," and give it a lesser punishment than reckless killing? Or should both negligent and reckless killing be called "manslaughter" and be given the same potential punishment? Another example is whether extreme reckless killings should be classified and punished as murder or manslaughter.

B. PURPOSEFUL KILLINGS

1. Degrees of Murder

Do the following statutes recognize degrees of murder? If so, on what bases do they distinguish between degrees of murder?

California Penal Code Annotated § 189 (2003)   *Murder; degrees*

All murder which is perpetrated by means of a destructive device or explosive, a weapon of mass destruction, knowing use of ammunition designed primarily to penetrate metal or armor, poison, lying in wait, torture, or by any other kind of willful, deliberate, and premeditated killing, or which is committed in the perpetration of, or attempt to perpetrate arson, rape, carjacking, robbery, burglary, mayhem, kidnapping, train wrecking, or any act punishable under [enumerated sexual offenses], or any murder which is perpetrated by means of discharging a firearm from a motor vehicle, intentionally at another person outside of the vehicle with the intent to inflict death, is murder of the first degree. All other kinds of murders are of the second degree.

To prove the killing was "deliberate and premeditated," it shall not be necessary to prove the defendant maturely and meaningfully reflected upon the gravity of his or her act.

California Penal Code Annotated § 190 (2003)   *Penalty for murder in the first degree*

(a) Every person guilty of murder in the first degree shall be punished by death, imprisonment in the state prison for life without the possibility of parole, or imprisonment in the state prison for a term of 25 years to life . . . .

[With specified exceptions,] . . . every person guilty of murder in the second degree shall be punished by imprisonment in the state prison for a term of 15 years to life.

Kansas Statutes Annotated § 21-3401 (2003)   *Murder in the first degree*

Murder in the first degree is the killing of a human being committed:

(a) Intentionally and with premeditation; or

(b) in the commission of, attempt to commit, or flight from an inherently dangerous felony as defined in K.S.A. 21-3436 and amendments thereto.

Murder in the first degree is an off-grid person felony.

Kansas Statutes Annotated § 21-3402 (2003)   *Murder in the second degree*

Murder in the second degree is the killing of a human being committed:

(a) Intentionally; or

(b) unintentionally but recklessly under circumstances manifesting extreme indifference to the value of human life.

Murder in the second degree as described in subsection (a) is a severity level 1, person felony. Murder in the second degree as described in subsection (b) is a severity level 2, person felony.

Model Penal Code § 210.2 (1985)   *Murder*

(1) Except as provided in Section 210.3(1)(b), criminal homicide constitutes murder when:

(a) it is committed purposely or knowingly; or

(b) it is committed recklessly under circumstances manifesting extreme indifference to the value of human life. Such recklessness and indifference are presumed if the actor is engaged or is an accomplice in the commission of, or an attempt to commit, or flight after committing or attempting to commit robbery, rape or deviate sexual intercourse by force or threat of force, arson, burglary, kidnapping or felonious escape.

(2) Murder is a felony of the first degree [but a person convicted of murder may be sentenced to death, as provided in Section 210.6].

PROBLEM

6.1 James and Penny, both regular users of heroin, have been dating for several years. One evening James arrives at Penny's apartment with some heroin he received as a gift from a friend. After dinner, at Penny's request, James injects Penny with some of the heroin. A few minutes later, James injects himself. The amount of heroin James injects into both Penny and himself is the same as that which he and Penny regularly use. It turns out, however, that the heroin his friend gave him is much more potent than James realizes. Penny dies of a heroin overdose. James, who is considerably taller and heavier than Penny, becomes quite ill from the heroin but eventually recovers. Under the statutes above, is James liable for murder based on Penny's death? If so, for what degree of murder?

---

2. Premeditation and Deliberation

Murder historically required "malice aforethought." The meaning of this term has varied over time and still engenders debate. Courts usually interpret this phrase to encompass intent to kill. The intent to kill is referred to as express malice. Malice aforethought also encompasses three other categories that the law treats as legally equivalent to intent to kill. These are referred to as implied malice. The first is intent to do serious bodily injury. The second is extreme recklessness that reveals an indifference to the value of human life. The common law used terms such as "abandoned and malignant heart" or "depraved heart" to capture this level of indifference and risk. The third category is known as felony murder.

Each of the four categories that comprise malice aforethought — (1) intent to kill, (2) intent to do serious bodily injury, (3) extreme recklessness, and (4) felony murder — can support a charge of murder. When one of these is established, many jurisdictions elevate an "ordinary" murder to aggravated murder if additional circumstances or mental states are present. Perhaps the most common of these are premeditation and deliberation.

The materials below compare the definitions and applications of premeditation and deliberation. If you were a legislator, which approach would you favor?

STATE *v.* BINGHAM
Court of Appeals of Washington 40 Wash. App. 553 (1985)

Worswick, C.J. — We are asked to decide whether the time to effect death by manual strangulation is alone sufficient to support a finding of premeditation in the absence of any other evidence supporting such a finding. We hold it is not. Accordingly, we reverse the conviction of Charles Dean Bingham for aggravated first degree murder. . . .

Leslie Cook, a retarded adult living at the Laurisden Home in Port Angeles, was raped and strangled on February 15, 1982. Bingham was the last person with whom she was seen. The two of them got off the Port Angeles-Sequim bus together at Sequim about 6 p.m. on February 15. They visited a grocery store and two residences. The last of these was Enid Pratt's where Bingham asked for a ride back to Port Angeles. When he was refused, he said they would hitchhike. They took the infrequently traveled Old Olympic Highway. Three days later, Cook's body was discovered in a field approximately 1/4 mile from the Pratt residence.

At trial, the State's expert testified that, in order to cause death by strangulation, Cook's assailant would have had to maintain substantial and continuous pressure on her windpipe for 3 to 5 minutes. The State contended that this alone was enough to raise an inference that the murder was premeditated. . . . Therefore, it allowed the issue of premeditation to go to the jury. The jury convicted Bingham of aggravated first degree murder, rape being the aggravating circumstance. On appeal, counsel for Bingham concedes that a finding of guilty of murder was justified; he challenges only the finding of premeditation, contending that the evidence was insufficient to support it. We agree.

Premeditation is a separate and distinct element of first degree murder. It involves the mental process of thinking over beforehand, deliberation, reflection, weighing or reasoning for a period of time, however short, after which the intent to kill is formed. The time required for manual strangulation is sufficient to permit deliberation. However, time alone is not enough. The evidence must be sufficient to support the inference that the defendant not only had the time to deliberate, but that he actually did so. To require anything less would permit a jury to focus on the method of killing to the exclusion of the mental process involved in the separate element of premeditation.

The concept of premeditation had a slow but sure beginning in Anglo-American legal history. More than 500 years ago, English jurists arrived at the not surprising conclusion that the worst criminals — and those most deserving of the ultimate punishment — were those who planned to kill and then did so. Thus began the movement toward classification of homicides that resulted in restriction of the death penalty to those involving "malice prepensed" or "malice aforethought." When Washington's first criminal code was enacted in 1854, the Territorial Legislature abandoned this archaic language and used the phrase "deliberate and premeditated malice" in defining first degree murder. It thereby made a clear separation between a malicious intent and the process of deliberating before arriving at that intent.

Our Supreme Court recognized the need for evidence of both time for and fact of deliberation in *State v. Arata*, 56 Wash. 185, 189, 105 P. 227 (1909). Although it reversed a first degree murder conviction because a portion of an instruction was erroneous, it approved the remainder of the instruction, saying:

> [I]n substance, the law knows no specific time; if the man reflects upon the act a moment antecedent to the act, it is sufficient; the time of deliberation and premeditation need not be long; if it furnishes room for reflection *and the facts show that such reflection existed*, then it is sufficient deliberation, and closed the instruction upon this point with the statement: "There need be no appreciable space of time between the formation of the intention to kill and the killing." By these few last words the court destroyed at once all that was good in the entire statement, and

gave the jury a rule which this court has frequently held was erroneous. This was reversible error.

. . . The subject of premeditation appears frequently in Washington cases. However, it is seldom discussed in a way that affords clear, objective guidance to trial judges in determining the sufficiency of the evidence to support it. Nevertheless, review of these cases reveals that in each one where the evidence has been found sufficient, there has been some evidence beyond time from which a jury could infer the fact of deliberation. This evidence has included, *inter alia*, motive, acquisition of a weapon, and planning directly related to the killing.

Unless evidence of both time for and fact of deliberation is required, premeditation could be inferred in any case where the means of effecting death requires more than a moment in time. For all practical purposes, it would merge with intent; proof of intent would become proof of premeditation. However, the two elements are separate. Premeditation cannot be inferred from intent.

Premeditation can be proved by direct evidence, or it can be proved by circumstantial evidence where the inferences drawn by the jury are reasonable and the evidence supporting the jury's findings is substantial. There was no such evidence here, either direct or circumstantial.

There was no evidence that Bingham had known Cook before February 15 or that he had a motive to kill her. By chance, they took the same bus. When Cook's companion on the bus refused to go to Sequim with her, Bingham offered to see that Cook got back to the Laurisden Home later. That was apparently still his intention when he asked for a ride at the Pratt residence. It could be inferred that between there and the field 1/4 mile away, he decided to rape her. A reasonable jury could not infer from this beyond a reasonable doubt that he also planned to kill her. There is no other evidence to support a finding of premeditation. The fact of strangulation, without more, leads us to conclude that the jury only speculated as to the mental process involved in premeditation. This is not enough. The premeditation finding cannot stand. . . .

Reversed. Remanded for entry of judgment and sentence for second degree murder.

PEOPLE *v.* MORRIN

Court of Appeals of Michigan 187 N.W.2d 434 (1971)

First-degree and second-degree murder are separate offenses, carrying vastly different penalties, distinguished only by the requirement that a homicide punishable as first-degree murder be committed with premeditation and deliberation. If premeditation and deliberation are ill-defined, the jury is left with no objective standards upon which to base its verdict. Convictions of the two offenses will be distributed not on the basis of ascertainable criteria, but entirely as products of the subjective, wholly individualist determinations of different juries.

The United States Supreme Court has frequently ruled that juries cannot be permitted to determine criminal liability without a reasonably ascertainable standard of guilt. Absent such standards, the jury has the sort of naked and arbitrary power which is inconsistent with due process.

Accordingly, it underscores the difference between the statutory degrees of murder to emphasize that premeditation and deliberation must be given independent meaning in a prosecution for first-degree murder. The ordinary meaning of the terms will suffice. To premeditate is to think about beforehand; to deliberate is to measure and evaluate the major facets of a choice or problem. As a number of courts have pointed out, premeditation and deliberation characterize a thought process undisturbed by hot blood. While the minimum time necessary to exercise this process is incapable of exact determination, the interval between initial thought and ultimate action should be long enough to afford a reasonable man time to subject the nature of his response to a "second look."[46]

QUESTIONS

1. Should courts or legislatures specify a minimum amount of time required to establish premeditation and deliberation?
2. What criteria beyond time should courts consider in determining whether the killer premeditated and deliberated?

Courts take disparate approaches to the definition and application of the term "premeditation and deliberation." Compare the approaches in *Bingham* and *Morrin* above with those in *Carroll*, *Young*, and *Carmichael* below.

COMMONWEALTH v. CARROLL

Supreme Court of Pennsylvania 412 Pa. 525 (1963)

Opinion by Mr. Chief Justice BELL, November 12, 1963:

The defendant, Carroll, pleaded guilty generally to an indictment charging him with the murder of his wife, and was tried by a Judge without a jury in the Court of Oyer and Terminer of Allegheny County. That Court found him guilty of

---

[46] Perkins sums up:

"An additional requirement of this particular clause ["willful, deliberate and premeditated"] is that this intent be formed by a mind free from undue excitement. 'Deliberation means that the act is done in a cool state of blood.'

" 'Premeditation means "thought of beforehand" for some length of time, however short.' . . . The notion that a fully-formed intent is always deliberate and premeditated, no matter how short the time between the first thought of the matter and the execution of the plan, is preposterous.

"The sound interpretation of such a statute is that a killing is deliberate and premeditated if, and only if, it results from real and substantial reflection. It is not sufficient that the idea be fully formed and acted upon; it must be pondered over and weighed in the mind. The intent to kill must be turned over in the mind and given a 'second thought'. It is true the law does not attempt to set a period of time for this requirement in terms of hours, or minutes or even seconds; but premeditation takes 'some appreciable time'.

"[T]here are three basic requirements for murder in the first degree, in addition to the requirement that the homicide must be murder within the rules of the common law. The first of these is that the homicide be intentional; the second is that the intent to kill must be formed by a mind that is cool rather than one that is unreasonably inflamed or excited; and the third is that the thought of taking the victim's life must have been reflected upon for some appreciable length of time *before* it was carried into effect, although not necessarily *after* the fatal decision was made. Needless to add, deliberation, premeditation and malice may all be inferred from sufficiently probative facts and circumstances."

Perkins on Criminal Law (2d ed.), pp. 91-93 (Emphasis by author).

first-degree murder and sentenced him to life imprisonment. Following argument and denial of motions in arrest of judgment and for a new trial, defendant took this appeal. The only questions involved are thus stated by the appellant:

(1) "Does not the evidence sustain a conviction no higher than murder in the second degree?"

(2) "Does not the evidence of defendant's good character, together with the testimony of medical experts, including the psychiatrist for the Behavior Clinic of Allegheny County, that the homicide was not premeditated or intentional, *require* the Court below to fix the degree of guilt of defendant no higher than murder in the second degree?"

The defendant married the deceased in 1955, when he was serving in the Army in California. Subsequently he was stationed in Alabama, and later in Greenland. During the latter tour of duty, defendant's wife and two children lived with his parents in New Jersey. Because this arrangement proved incompatible, defendant returned to the United States on emergency leave in order to move his family to their own quarters. On his wife's insistence, defendant was forced to secure a "compassionate transfer" back to the States, and subsequently to resign from the Army in July of 1960, by which time he had attained the rank of Chief Warrant Officer. Defendant was a hard worker, earned a substantial salary and bore a very good reputation among his neighbors.

In 1958, decedent-wife suffered a fractured skull while attempting to leave defendant's car in the course of an argument. Allegedly this contributed to her mental disorder, which was later diagnosed as a schizoid personality type. In 1959 she underwent psychiatric treatment at the mental hygiene clinic in Aberdeen, Maryland. She complained of nervousness and told the examining doctor "I feel like hurting my children." This sentiment sometimes took the form of sadistic "discipline" toward their very young children. Nevertheless, upon her discharge from the clinic, the doctors considered her much improved. With this background we come to the immediate events of the crime.

In January, 1962, defendant was selected to attend an electronics school in Winston-Salem, North Carolina, for nine days. His wife greeted this news with violent argument. Immediately prior to his departure for Winston-Salem, at the suggestion and request of his wife, he put a *loaded* .22 caliber pistol on the windowsill at the head of their common bed, so that she would feel safe. On the evening of January 16, 1962, defendant returned home and told his wife that he had been temporarily assigned to teach at a school in Chambersburg, which would necessitate his absence from home four nights out of seven for a ten week period. A violent and protracted argument ensued at the dinner table and continued until four o'clock in the morning.

Defendant's own statement after his arrest details the final moments before the crime: "We went into the bedroom a little before 3 o'clock on Wednesday morning where we continued to argue in short bursts. Generally she laid with her back to me facing the wall in bed and would just talk over her shoulder to me. I became angry and more angry especially what she was saying about my kids and myself, and sometime between 3 and 4 o'clock in the morning I remembered the gun on the window sill over my head. I think she had dozed off. *I reached up and grabbed the pistol and brought it down and shot her twice in the back of the head.*"[1]

---

[1] When pressed on cross-examination defendant approximated that five minutes elapsed between his wife's last remark and the shooting.

Defendant's testimony at the trial elaborated this theme. He started to think about the children, "seeing my older son's feet what happened to them. I could see the bruises on him and Michael's chin was split open, four stitches. I didn't know what to do. I wanted to help my boys. Sometime in there she said something in there, she called me some kind of name. I kept thinking of this. *During this time I either thought or felt — I thought of the gun, just thought of the gun.* I am not sure whether I felt my hand move toward the gun — I saw my hand move, the next thing — the only thing I can recollect after that is right after the shots or right during the shots I saw the gun in my hand just pointed at my wife's head. She was still lying on her back — I mean her side. I could smell the gunpowder and I could hear something — it sounded like running water. I didn't know what it was at first, didn't realize what I'd done at first. Then I smelled it. I smelled blood before . . . ."

"Q. At the time you shot her, Donald, were you fully aware and intend to do what you did? A. I don't know positively. All I remember hearing was two shots and feeling myself go cold all of a sudden."

Shortly thereafter defendant wrapped his wife's body in a blanket, spread and sheets, tied them on with a piece of plastic clothesline and took her down to the cellar. He tried to clean up as well as he could. That night he took his wife's body, wrapped in a blanket with a rug over it to a desolate place near a trash dump. He then took the children to his parents' home in Magnolia, New Jersey. He was arrested the next Monday in Chambersburg where he had gone to his teaching assignment.

Although defendant's brief is voluminous, the narrow and only questions which he raises on this appeal are as hereinbefore quoted. Both are embodied in his contention that the crime amounted only to second degree murder and that his conviction should therefore be reduced to second degree or that a new trial should be granted. . . .

The specific intent to kill which is necessary to constitute in a nonfelony murder, murder in the first degree, may be found from a defendant's words or conduct or from the attendant circumstances together with all reasonable inferences therefrom, and may be inferred from the intentional use of a deadly weapon on a vital part of the body of another human being.

It is well settled that a jury or a trial Court can believe all or a part of or none of a defendant's statements, confessions or testimony, or the testimony of any witness.

If we consider only the evidence, which is favorable to the Commonwealth, it is without the slightest doubt sufficient in law to prove first degree. However, even if we believe all of defendant's statements and testimony, there is no doubt that this killing constituted murder in the first degree. Defendant first urges that there was insufficient time for premeditation in the light of his good reputation. This is based on an isolated and oft repeated statement in *Commonwealth v. Drum*, that " 'no time is too short for a wicked man to frame in his mind his scheme of murder.' " Defendant argues that, conversely, a long time is necessary to find premeditation in a "good man." We find no merit in defendant's analogy or contention. As Chief Justice Maxey appropriately and correctly said in *Commonwealth v. Earnest*: "Whether the intention to kill and the killing, that is, the premeditation and the fatal act, were within a brief space of time or a long space of time is immaterial if the killing was in fact intentional, willful, deliberate and premeditated . . . . As Justice Agnew said in *Com. v. Drum*: 'The law fixes upon no length of time as necessary to form the intention to kill, but leaves the existence of a fully formed intent as a fact to be determined by the jury, from all the facts and circumstances in the evidence.' "

Defendant further contends that the time and place of the crime, the enormous difficulty of removing and concealing the body, and the obvious lack of an escape plan, militate against and make a finding of premeditation legally impossible. This is a "jury argument"; it is clear as crystal that such circumstances do not negate premeditation. This contention of defendant is likewise clearly devoid of merit.

Defendant's most earnestly pressed contention is that the *psychiatrist's opinion* of what *defendant's state of mind must have been and was at the time of the crime,* clearly establishes not only the lack but also the legal impossibility of premeditation. Dr. Davis, a psychiatrist of the Allegheny County Behavior Clinic, testified that defendant was "for a number of years . . . passively going along with a situation which he . . . [was] not controlling and he . . . [was] not making any decisions, and finally a decision . . . [was] forced on him. . . . He had left the military to take this assignment, and he was averaging about nine thousand a year; he had a good job. He knew that if he didn't accept this teaching assignment in all probability he would be dismissed from the Government service, and at his age and his special training he didn't know whether he would be able to find employment. More critical to that was the fact that at this point, as we understand it, his wife issued an ultimatum that if he went and gave this training course she would leave him . . . . He was so dependent upon her he didn't want her to leave. He couldn't make up his mind what to do. He was trapped . . . ."

The doctor then gave *his opinion* that "rage," "desperation," and "panic" produced "an impulsive automatic reflex type of homicide, . . . as opposed to an intentional premeditated type of homicide. . . . Our feeling was that if this gun had fallen to the floor he wouldn't have been able to pick it up and consummate that homicide. And I think if he had to load the gun he wouldn't have done it. This is a matter of opinion, but this is our opinion about it."

There are three answers to this contention. First, as we have hereinbefore stated, neither a Judge nor a jury has to believe all or any part of the testimony of the defendant or of any witness. Secondly, the opinion of the psychiatrists was based to a large extent upon statements made to them by the defendant, which need not be believed and which are in some instances opposed by the facts themselves. Thirdly, a psychiatrist's opinion of a defendant's impulse or lack of intent or state of mind is, in this class of case, entitled to very little weight, and this is especially so when defendant's own actions, or his testimony or confession, or the facts themselves, belie the opinion. . . .

Defendant's *own statement* after his arrest, upon which his counsel so strongly relies, *as well as his testimony at his trial,* clearly convict him of first degree murder and justify the finding and sentence of the Court below. Defendant himself described his actions at the time he killed his wife. From his own statements and from his own testimony, it is clear that, terribly provoked by his allegedly nagging, belligerent and sadistic wife,[2] defendant remembered the gun, deliberately took it down, and deliberately fired two shots into the head of his sleeping wife. There is no doubt that this was a wilful, deliberate and premeditated murder.

---

[2] While this picture of his wife is different from that depicted by her neighbors, if defendant's version is true, the remedy lies in a commutation by the Board of Pardons and not by a disregard of the law by the Courts.

YOUNG *v*. STATE   Alabama Crim. App., 428 So. 2d 155 (1982)[1]

Premeditation and deliberation in the law of homicide are synonymous terms meaning simply that the accused, before he committed the fatal act, intended that he would commit the act at the time that he did and that death would result. It does not mean that the accused "must have sat down and reflected over it or thought over it for any appreciable length of time."

Premeditation and deliberation may be formed while the killer is "pressing the trigger that fired the fatal shot." There need be no "appreciable space of time between the formation of the intention to kill and the act of killing." Such space of time is "immaterial." "It was possible for the defendant to have framed a premeditated as well as a malicious design to kill after taking up the gun and before it was fired."

CARMICHAEL *v*. STATE   Supreme Court of Arkansas, 340 Ark. 598, 602 (2000)

Premeditated and deliberated murder occurs when it is the killer's conscious object to cause death and he forms that intention before he acts and as a result of a weighing of the consequences of his course of conduct. Premeditation is not required to exist for a particular length of time. It may be formed in an instant and is rarely capable of proof by direct evidence but must usually be inferred from the circumstances of the crime. Similarly, premeditation and deliberation may be inferred from the type and character of the weapon, the manner in which the weapon was used, the nature, extent, and location of the wounds, and the accused's conduct. One can infer premeditation from the method of death itself where the cause of death is strangulation.

QUESTIONS

1. How do the "premeditation and deliberation" standards in *Carroll, Young,* and *Carmichael* differ from those in *Bingham* and *Morrin*?
2. Which is preferable?

PROBLEMS

6.2 You are on an advisory committee to the judicial council of your state. The council is formulating definitions of "premeditation" and "deliberation" to be added to the first-degree murder statute. That statute specifies that premeditation and deliberation qualify for first-degree murder but does not define either word. Draft a list of factors that

---

1. All citations omitted.

courts should consider when determining whether the requirements of premeditation and deliberation are satisfied. Then formulate definitions of "premeditation" and "deliberation" to be added to the first-degree murder statute. The current statute reads:

> All murder committed with premeditation and deliberation is murder of the first degree.

6.3 Martha and Jim have been a devoted married couple for 42 years. They have three children and five grandchildren. Two years ago Jim was diagnosed with terminal bone cancer. Martha has been a loving caregiver, attending to Jim's every need and wish. Despite radiation, chemotherapy, and various experimental medical procedures, the cancer continues to progress, causing Jim enormous pain. Jim has been bed-bound for three months. He is in almost constant pain and is paralyzed from the neck down. Martha administers morphine in liquid form to Jim several times a day to try to manage the pain. Because some of Jim's bones are very fragile, when Martha moves Jim to change the linens or wash him, it can cause Jim's bones to fracture, producing excruciating pain. Jim's doctor tells Martha that, although one cannot predict with certainty, because Jim is still able to eat and none of his vital organs has failed, Jim is likely to live anywhere from three months to a year more. When Jim learns of the doctor's prognosis, he begs Martha to help him end his suffering. Martha believes that if she steadily increases the amount of morphine she gives Jim, he will die a painless death while asleep or in a coma. On a calm day, when Jim's pain seems under better control, she discusses her plan with Jim. Jim readily agrees. The next morning, Martha begins increasing the morphine dosage. Martha's objective is to eliminate Jim's pain and provide him peace. She continues to increase the morphine dosage, adjusting it five times over the following 24 hours. She sits with Jim, holding his hand, and singing their favorite songs. Finally, Jim drifts into a coma and dies 12 hours later. The coroner determines that the cause of death was morphine overdose. What was Martha's mental state with respect to Jim's death? Should Martha's conduct be treated as a crime? If so, of what crime should Martha be convicted? How does motive relate to mental state?

3. The Provocation Doctrine

The provocation doctrine typically reduces murder to manslaughter. It developed as a common law response to the severity of the punishment that followed a murder conviction. If the gradations in the law of homicide were a series of floors in a building with an elevator, we would travel to the top floor for the most serious and severely punished murders, such as those done with premeditation and deliberation. As the previous Section illustrates, jurisdictions often title these killings first-degree murders. One floor below, we would find "ordinary" murder, a murder that lacks any aggravating element. A jurisdiction that recognizes degrees of murder will commonly label this second-degree murder. If we traveled down another floor, we would find voluntary manslaughter based on provocation. Voluntary manslaughter usually triggers a less severe, sometimes substantially less severe, penalty than second-degree murder. Voluntary manslaughter generally involves an intentional killing. To distinguish voluntary manslaughter from ordinary murder, the provocation doctrine uses certain criteria. In this section, we study the evolution of those criteria from a rigid traditional multi-part test to the more flexible Model Penal Code approach.

a. The Traditional Approach

The traditional approach restricts the use of provocation to cases in which the circumstances satisfy a rigorous multi-part test. The *Lawton* case, which follows, illustrates this traditional test.

STATE *v.* LAWTON

Superior Court of New Jersey, Appellate Division 298 N.J. Super. 27 (1997)

HUMPHREYS, J.A.D. Defendant appeals the denial of his motion for post-conviction relief. He asserts that his 1987 conviction for first degree murder and possession of a handgun should be vacated. . . .

We conclude that errors in the charge to the jury caused a fundamental injustice and a deprivation of constitutional rights. We therefore reverse and remand for a new trial on the murder conviction. We do not reach the other issues raised by the defendant.

I

Defendant was beaten in a bar in 1986. He went home, got a handgun, went back to the bar, and shot and killed a person he thought was one of his assailants. Only ten minutes elapsed between the end of the beating and the shooting. The critical issue in the case was whether defendant acted in the heat of passion with reasonable provocation. If he did so act, the offense would be manslaughter, not murder.

The defendant was tried in 1987. The jury convicted the defendant of murder. . . .

II

The crucial issue in this case is whether defendant's crime was murder or manslaughter.

Former Chief Justice Weintraub defined voluntary manslaughter as

> a slaying committed in a transport of passion or heat of blood induced by an adequate provocation, provided the killing occurs before the passage of time sufficient for an ordinary person in like circumstances to cool off. The common law deemed such circumstances to negate the malice required for murder. Involved is a concession to the frailty of man, a recognition that the average person can understandably react violently to a sufficient wrong and hence some lesser punishment is appropriate.

Under the New Jersey Code of Criminal Justice, a homicide which would otherwise be murder is manslaughter if it is "committed in the heat of passion resulting
from a reasonable provocation." N.J.S.A. 2C:11-4(b)(2).

In *State v. Mauricio*, 117 N.J. 402, 568 A.2d 879 (1990), the Court said:

> [p]assion/provocation manslaughter has four elements: the provocation must be
> adequate; the defendant must not have had time to cool off between the provocation
> and the slaying; the provocation must have actually impassioned the defendant;
> and the defendant must not have actually cooled off before the slaying. The first
> two criteria are objective, the other two subjective. If a slaying does not include
> all of those elements, the offense of passion/provocation manslaughter cannot be
> demonstrated.

[*Id.* at 411, 568 A.2d 879 (citations omitted).]

Words alone do not constitute adequate provocation. A threat with a gun or
a knife may constitute adequate provocation. A battery, except for a light blow,
has traditionally been considered "almost as a matter of law," to constitute adequate provocation. *State v. Mauricio, supra*, 117 N.J. at 414. In *Mauricio*, the Court
concluded that where defendant had an altercation with a bouncer, was later
forcibly evicted from a tavern, and then shot and killed a person he erroneously
believed to be the bouncer some fifteen minutes later, a jury could reasonably find
passion/provocation manslaughter. *Id.* at 415.

A battery unquestionably occurred in the present case. The defendant was
severely beaten by perhaps as many as eight to ten persons. A police officer observed
that the defendant's face was "swollen," an eye was apparently closed and his face
appeared "deformed." The defendant's wife testified that he had been beaten so
badly that the swelling in his face made his eyes appear "like they were sitting on the
side of his head." The severity of the beating coupled with the defendant's committing the crime only ten minutes later offer strong support for the contention that this
was a crime resulting from passion/provocation and therefore was manslaughter
not murder.

When the evidence warrants a passion/provocation charge, as it certainly does
here, the trial judge must charge the jury that the State bears the burden of proving
beyond a reasonable doubt the absence of "passion/provocation." *State v. Heslop*,
135 N.J. 318, 322, 639 A.2d 1100 (1994).

The Court stated in *State v. Heslop, supra*: "[w]e have held that if a court fails
to indicate *clearly* that the burden is on the State to prove beyond a reasonable
doubt that a defendant did not act with passion or provocation, such a failure will
constitute error." . . .

The judge did not charge the jury that the State had the burden of proving that the defendant did not act from passion/provocation. The judge did
not charge that the State's burden on this issue was proof beyond a reasonable
doubt. . . .

The cumulative impact of these errors was likely to cause confusion in the
jurors' minds and also to suggest to the jury that the defendant, not the State, had
the burden of proof on the issue of passion/provocation. . . .

The defendant testified and admitted that he shot the victim. The only real
issue is whether the offense is murder or manslaughter. The State may therefore elect to consent to the entry of a judgment of manslaughter in lieu of a
retrial. If the State does so consent, the judge should conduct a new sentencing
proceeding. . . .

QUESTIONS

1. List the parts of the traditional test for manslaughter as described in *Lawton*. Are these consistent with the New Jersey manslaughter statute?

2. Can you explain why the law required each part of the test?

i. Legally Adequate Provocation

As *Lawton* illustrates, under the traditional approach, access to the provocation doctrine was limited to certain categories often referred to as "legally adequate" provocation. Only cases falling within these categories qualified for mitigation. One example of such a category is battery. If a defendant killed a victim in response to the victim battering the defendant, the defendant could make use of the provocation doctrine. The Maryland case below involves the treatment of another common category of legally adequate provocation, adultery.

DENNIS *v.* STATE

Court of Special Appeals of Maryland 105 Md. App. 687 (1995)

WILNER, Chief Judge.

On the evening of August 21, 1993, appellant, armed with a handgun, went to the home of Mark Bantz, apparently kicked in the door, entered the house, and shot Mr. Bantz nine times — in the chest, in the head, and in the back. At least three of the wounds were fatal.

As a consequence of this conduct, a jury in the Circuit Court for Baltimore County convicted appellant of premeditated first degree murder, burglary, and unlawful use of a handgun, for which substantial sentences were imposed. Appellant complains in this appeal that the court refused to instruct the jury properly on the crime of manslaughter. . . . We find no merit in these complaints and shall therefore affirm the judgments entered by the circuit court.

FACTUAL BACKGROUND

Although appellant claimed to have no memory of the actual killing, his defense was that it must have occurred in the heat of passion, as the result of a dual, or mixed, provocation — . . . [a] two-month adulterous relationship [between defendant's wife, Robin, and Bantz], culminating in the sight of seeing them in an amorous embrace; and knowledge gained earlier in the day that, on the previous evening, Bantz had smoked cocaine in the presence of appellant's 12-year-old son.

Appellant and Robin met while they were teenagers; they began to live together and married when Robin became pregnant. Appellant worked hard to support his family, and all, apparently, went well until late 1990 or early 1991, when they began to suffer financial difficulties due, according to appellant, to Robin's spending habits. . . .

[O]n June 26, 1993, Robin left the marital home, telling appellant that she was going to live with a female friend. About a week later, Robin confessed that she was, in fact, living with Mr. Bantz. Appellant became "emotionally upset" at this news, at least in part because he knew that Bantz was "involved with drugs." This concern heightened when he learned, in mid-July, that Robin too had begun smoking cocaine. She rejected his pleas to come home, "because of the drugs and the sex." Appellant then made two threats against Bantz — one in a conversation with Bantz's parents and one in a letter he wrote to Robin.

By late July or early August, appellant began to accept the situation. Although still professing strong feelings for Robin, he said that he "was starting to learn to accept the fact that she wasn't going to come home" and to focus his attention on raising his son. By August, he continued, "I was doing fairly good with all of this. I was pretty much coming back to earth." On Tuesday, August 17, however, Robin told appellant that she wanted to return. The next day, appellant picked her up from work, took her to Bantz's house to get some of her belongings, and had dinner and spent the night with her.

Notwithstanding this romantic interlude and the representation that her affair with Bantz was over, Robin asked for a little more time to make up her mind. She said that Bantz had moved back with his parents and allowed her to remain in the home they had shared until she could decide what she wanted to do. It is not clear whether appellant and Robin had contact the next day, but on Thursday, August 19, they again spent the evening together. On Friday evening, at Robin's request, appellant allowed his son to stay with Robin. When appellant took his son to the house, Bantz was not there.

On Saturday, appellant learned from his son that Bantz had come to the house on Friday evening, and that, as they were watching television, Bantz smoked cocaine. Appellant decided to investigate. He tried to reach Robin by telephone, but, when there was no answer, he drove to Bantz's house. He had with him in the car a .22 caliber handgun, allegedly because of a hunting trip planned for the next day[1] Appellant stopped on the way and called Robin again, this time getting through to her; stating that she was going out with a girlfriend, she asked him to stay away, but he told her he was coming.

When he arrived at the home, appellant saw Bantz's father's truck, thereby indicating Bantz's presence. He approached the house, opened the screen door, and looked through the window. He described in his testimony what he saw:

> "I seen [Bantz] standing there, and he had his hands around my wife, and they were kind of, like embraced in, I don't know, some kind of mood, I guess.
> He had her dress all hiked up around her. I could see her, you know. It was kind of hard to take. . . .
> She was — it was, like, her back and [Bantz's] belly. He had her kind of around in front of him, and the best way I can say it, he had her all hooked up . . .
> He had her dress kind of hiked up around her and it just looked like he was maybe feeling her private parts or so. . . .
> It looked like they were getting ready to engage in some kind of sex act."

Appellant claimed to have no memory of what next occurred, and, because he and Robin reconciled, she refused to testify. Testimony from two police officers who responded to the scene in response to emergency calls from Robin indicate that the front door had been kicked in and that the nine bullets fired into Bantz's head and body had been fired from at least 18 inches away; they were not contact wounds.

---

[1] In fact, a hunting trip, as such, was not planned. Hunting was not allowed in August. Testimony by appellant's friend, who was to accompany him, indicated that they were intending to "scout out" areas for a future hunting trip, and that appellant was bringing his pistol for "snakes or wild dogs."

MANSLAUGHTER INSTRUCTIONS

When counsel and the court first conferred on jury instructions, the court indicated that it proposed to give the Pattern Jury Instruction on voluntary manslaughter drafted by the Maryland State Bar Association Committee on Criminal Pattern Jury Instructions (MPJI-Cr 4:17.4C). In pertinent part, that instruction states that a killing in hot blooded response to "legally adequate provocation" is a mitigating circumstance, that in order for such a mitigating circumstance to exist in the particular case, five factors must be present: (1) the defendant reacted to something in "a hot blooded rage"; (2) the rage was caused by something "the law recognizes as legally adequate provocation" and that the only act the jury could find to be adequate provocation under the evidence in this case is "the sudden discovery of the defendant's spouse in an act of sexual intercourse"; (3) the defendant was still enraged when he killed the victim; (4) there was not enough time between the provocation and the killing for a reasonable person's rage to cool; and (5) the victim was the person who provoked the rage.

Appellant raised no objection then, and raises no complaint now, about any aspect of that proposed instruction other than the language in element (2) declaring that the only adequate provocation under the facts of this case would be if appellant suddenly discovered Robin "in an act of sexual intercourse." . . . [T]he court . . . agreed to modify the instruction . . . to read "sudden discovery by the Defendant of the Defendant's spouse in the act of sexual intercourse or his having strong reason to believe that it recently took place." It gave the instruction in that form. . . .

After some period of deliberation, the jury sent a note asking the court to "clarify the term recent in the description of legal provocation in terms of recently had sexual intercourse, and must it be intercourse?" That provoked another discussion between counsel and the court . . . [after which the Court] instructed the jury that "recent is a term which is imprecise, and its meaning is within your sound discretion" and "intercourse is to be interpreted as having its usual and generally accepted meaning."

In this appeal, appellant complains that the court erred in limiting the provocation to the discovery of actual sexual intercourse, i.e., coition. He urges that (1) the conduct observed by him "was sufficient to constitute an 'act of sexual intercourse' necessary to form legally adequate provocation for the killing," (2) even if it was not, the law should recognize "significant sexual contact" or "sexual intimacy" as sufficient provocation, and (3) in any event, the jury should have been instructed to consider "the victim's illicit drug use in the presence of appellant's child" as sufficient provocation.

To constitute a mitigating factor sufficient to negate the element of malice, and thereby reduce murder to manslaughter, the provocation must be "adequate." In *Girouard, supra*, 321 Md. at 539, the Court explained that, for a provocation to be "adequate," it must be "calculated to inflame the passion of a *reasonable* [person] and tend to cause [that person] to act for the moment from passion rather than reason." (Emphasis added.) That describes one aspect of "adequacy." There is another, which flows from the requirement that the passion be that of a reasonable person; the provocation must be one the law is prepared to recognize as minimally sufficient, in proper circumstances, to overcome the restraint normally expected from reasonable persons. There are many "slings and arrows of outrageous fortune" that people either must tolerate or find an alternative way, other than homicide, to redress.

Judge Moylan commented on this in *Tripp v. State*, 36 Md. App. 459, 473 (1977):

> "We begin with the proposition that there must be not simply provocation in psychological fact, but one of certain fairly-well defined classes of provocation recognized as being adequate as a matter of law. . . . "

We are not dealing here with the entire universe of situations that might have the required effect. One type of conduct that the common law has long and consistently recognized as legally adequate is observing one's spouse in an act of adultery. The *Girouard* Court confirmed that "discovering one's spouse in the act of sexual intercourse with another" constitutes sufficient provocation.[3] 321 Md. at 538. In *Tripp, supra*, 36 Md. App. at 475, we allowed a modest expansion. We there observed:

> "The law anciently required a spouse unexpectedly to discover the erring spouse *in flagrante delicto.* In its more modern and liberalized manifestations, it has been extended to situations where the spouse has suddenly been told of the other spouse's infidelity or has strong reason to believe that there has been such infidelity. *Even in the liberalized forms, however, the indispensable predicate is sexual intercourse."*

(Emphasis added.)

We need not determine here whether the term "sexual intercourse" might properly include any conduct other than coition. It is enough for us to reject the proposition that mere "sexual intimacy" or "significant sexual contact" — the standard urged by appellant — suffices. Those terms are much too general and cover far too great a range of conduct to be legally acceptable. It is clear that the kind of conduct allegedly observed by appellant as he peered through the window does not fall within any reasonable definition of "sexual intercourse."

Appellant's alternative assertion is that legally adequate provocation can be fashioned from the combination of Robin's earlier adultery, Bantz's corruption of her and appellant's son with drugs, and the suggestive embrace that he actually witnessed. That argument, though couched in terms of expanding the concept of adequate provocation, more significantly implicates, and fails to satisfy, the required causation between the provocation, the passion, and the killing.

By his own testimony, any passion generated by the knowledge that Robin had been engaged in an adulterous affair had cooled long before appellant appeared at Bantz's house. He had, in effect, forgiven Robin for her past infidelity and agreed to resume the marital relationship. Nor can provocation be found from the revelation of Bantz's drug use on Friday evening. . . . [A]lthough appellant testified that he "didn't like it," he offered no evidence that he was, in any way, enraged by that revelation. . . .

---

[3] At a more ancient time, it appears that the killing of a man caught in the act of adultery with the defendant's wife was regarded as entirely justifiable. Blackstone notes in his discussion of the crime of manslaughter that

> "if a man takes another in the act of adultery with his wife and kills him directly on the spot, though this was allowed by the laws of Solon, as likewise by the Roman civil law, (if the adulterer was found in the husband's own house,) and also among the ancient Goths, yet in England it is not absolutely ranked in the class of justifiable homicide . . . but it is manslaughter. It is, however, the lowest degree of it; and therefore in such a case the court directed the burning in the hand to be gently inflicted, because there could not be a greater provocation."

W. Blackstone, *Commentaries on the Laws of England*, Book IV * 191-92 (Lewis ed., 1922) (footnotes omitted). As Judge Moylan noted in *Tripp*, we have advanced somewhat in the past 200 years.

What appellant seeks to do is to combine three separate grievances, arising or occurring at different times, none of which individually can constitute legally adequate provocation as of the time appellant actually shot Bantz, and make the combination suffice as provocation. A few States, notably California and Pennsylvania, have apparently found sufficient provocation from what appears to be "the last straw" theory — a smoldering resentment or pent-up rage resulting from earlier insults or humiliating events culminating in a triggering event that, by itself, might be insufficient. Maryland has not adopted that view; nor, apparently, have most other States. In *Tripp*, we rejected the "long smoldering grudge" or "slow burn" as adequate. 36 Md. App. at 471-72. In *Girouard*, the Court of Appeals rejected taunts and verbal assaults as adequate provocation, even when taking on their humiliating and enraging character from antecedent events.

Antecedent events may be relevant in determining whether the triggering event in fact produced the hot blood necessary to rebut malice — they may support or detract from that nexus — but they do not suffice to give the triggering event a legal quality it does not otherwise have. Discovering one's spouse in an embrace with a paramour will not constitute adequate provocation because at some earlier time he or she committed adultery with that paramour. That is a matter for the divorce court; it does not reduce murder to some lesser offense. . . . We find no error in the court's instructions. . . .

QUESTIONS

1. What significance should the criminal law attach to the fact that a defendant was provoked? Should it mitigate or aggravate liability? Or should it be treated as irrelevant? In answering these questions, is your rationale based on retributive or utilitarian thinking?

2. Should the law allow adultery to reduce murder to manslaughter? Do reasonable people respond to adultery with lethal force? If so, why doesn't the doctrine provide for complete acquittal? If reasonable people don't respond with lethal force, why reduce the charge from murder to manslaughter?

3. If adultery is legally adequate provocation, should sexual infidelity in non-marital relationships also qualify as legally adequate provocation?

Professor Joshua Dressler explains the rationale for the mitigation of murder to voluntary manslaughter as follows:

> The true reason for the law's "concession to human weakness" — the reason why, if A kills P in sudden rage at his actions, the law will likely allow A to argue that the jury should reduce homicide to manslaughter — is that the homicide is the result of an understandable and *excusable* loss of self-control arising from his anger. Common experience teaches that, at some point, anger becomes so intense that people find it extremely difficult to control themselves and respond constructively rather than violently, to the anger-producing stimulus. Therefore, when A kills P because his reason is "disturbed or obscured by passion to an extent which *might render* ordinary men, of fair average disposition, *liable* to act rashly or without due deliberation or reflection, and from passion, rather than judgment," he is less to blame than if he killed P while he was calm. This is because it is harder for A to control his actions when he is angry than when he is calm.[2]

---

2. Joshua Dressler, *When "Heterosexual" Men Kill "Homosexual" Men: Reflections on Provocation Law, Sexual Advances, and the "Reasonable Man" Standard*, 85 J. Crim. L. & Criminology 726, at 747-748 (1995).

The *Dennis* case reflects a traditional approach to voluntary manslaughter. Only certain categories of conduct qualify as legally adequate: mutual combat, assault, battery, illegal arrest, adultery,[3] and "violent or sexual . . . assault on a close relative."[4] The judge, as opposed to the jury, determines whether conduct falls within these categories.

In 1997, the Maryland legislature enacted the following statute.

Maryland Criminal Law Code Annotated § 2-207(b) (2002)

(b) Spousal adultery not a mitigating factor. — The discovery of one's spouse engaged in sexual intercourse with another person does not constitute legally adequate provocation for the purpose of mitigating a killing from the crime of murder to voluntary manslaughter even though the killing was provoked by that discovery.

To understand why the Maryland legislature might have taken this action, consider the following three items: an article about a 1994 Maryland case involving Kenneth Peacock, a newspaper account of the legislative response, and the history of voluntary manslaughter as described in the excerpt from the *Shane* case below.

Judge sides with husband in slaying: Is Adultery cause to kill your wife?[5]

Towson Md. — The thing is, the prosecutor said, it was only a single shot.

Kenneth Lee Peacock, 36, a long-distance trucker, came home unexpectedly one night last February to find his wife, Sandra Kaye, in bed with another man. His late wife, that is. After several hours of drinking and arguing, he took down his hunting rifle and shot her in the head. Monday he was sentenced to 18 months in jail with possible work release, and 50 hours of community service in an unspecified domestic violence program.

And Judge Robert Cahill probably has been added to the "They Just Don't Get It" hall of fame.

"I seriously wonder how many married men — married five, four years — would have the strength to walk away without inflicting some corporal punishment," the judge said during the hourlong sentencing hearing in Baltimore County Circuit Court, as reported in the Baltimore Sun. "I'm forced to impose a sentence . . . only because I think I must do it to make the system honest. . . . "

Peacock was allowed to plead guilty to manslaughter even though hours had passed between the time he discovered his wife *in flagrante* — hours during which he drank both beer and wine — and the time of the killing. Peacock chased the lover off at gunpoint, according to court documents, and then shot his wife about 4 A.M. . . . [6]

After a 3-Year Fight, Murder Is Finally Murder in Maryland[7]

Maryland lawmaker Joan Pitkin was tired of watching men get away with murder. In 1994, she watched Kenneth Lee Peacock receive a sentence of less than two years for killing his wife hours after finding her in bed with another man. A year later,

---

3. Wayne R. LaFave, *Criminal Law* 706-709 (3d ed. 2000).

4. Model Penal Code § 210.3 (1985) (Commentaries, p.58).

5. Megan Rosenfeld, San Jose Mercury News (Oct. 19, 1994), 1 & back page.

6. According to Maryland newspaper accounts, Judge Cahill did face a disciplinary inquiry regarding his comments at the sentencing in the *Peacock* matter, Elaine Tassy, *Cahill Says Remarks at Killer's Sentencing Not Meant to Offend; Testifying for 2 Hours, Judge Acknowledges Comments Were Imperfect*, The Baltimore Sun (Feb. 2, 1996), at 2B, but the Judicial Disabilities Commission dismissed the allegations against him by a 5 to 2 vote. Deirdre M. Childress, *Md. Judge Cleared of Bias in Remarks at Sentencing; He Expressed Degree of Understanding Toward Trucker Convicted of Killing Unfaithful Wife*, The Washington Post, May 4, 1996, at 803.

7. Kimberly Wilmot-Weidman, Chicago Tribune, Nov. 23, 1997.

Brian Nalls received a 10-year sentence for killing his wife after suspecting that she may have been unfaithful. . . .

Both men based their defense on a Maryland law, similar to ones of other states, that labels infidelity or the mere suspicion of infidelity as sufficient provocation for a spousal killing, reducing the charge to manslaughter, with a maximum sentence of 10 years. . . .

The revised law, which passed in May 1997, removed spousal adultery from the list of provocations that can trigger deadly rage and lead to the lesser manslaughter charge.

OHIO v. SHANE
Supreme Court of Ohio 63 Ohio St. 3d 630 (1992)

The case before us involves a defendant who allegedly was provoked to act under the influence of sudden passion or in a sudden fit of rage by his fiancée's words informing him of her sexual infidelity. Therefore, we consider only whether the provocation alleged in such a situation is reasonably sufficient so that a voluntary manslaughter instruction should have been given.

Many courts have adopted a rule that "mere words" can not be sufficient provocation to reduce a murder charge to voluntary manslaughter, no matter how insulting or inciteful. This general rule usually applies even if the spoken words have the effect of informing the defendant of some provocative event that has taken place. . . . It appears, however, that courts are generally more inclined to give a manslaughter instruction when the alleged provocation is a victim-spouse's confession of adultery. The typical scenario is a wife's confession of adultery which allegedly so provokes a husband that he kills her in a sudden fit of rage. Some courts have limited this infidelity exception to the acts between spouses, but have not applied it when the parties are romantically involved but are not married, even when the relationship is similar to a marriage. This adultery exception has been totally rejected by some courts, unless the situation is where the spouse discovers the other spouse in the act of adultery itself, or immediately thereafter. Finally, a few courts have not followed a "mere words" rule, but, instead, have approved a manslaughter jury instruction when words alone were the only provocation alleged, and no relationship existed between victim and assailant.

While the "mere words" rule is attractive — it has the advantage of offering a bright line test which eliminates an entire class of cases — the rule has been criticized as imposing an "unnecessary limitation on the use of voluntary manslaughter as a mitigating defense." Romero, Sufficiency of Provocation for Voluntary Manslaughter in New Mexico: Problems in Theory and Practice (1982), 12 New Mex. L. Rev. 747, 776. It is argued that such a rule ignores the fact that sometimes words may be even more inflammatory than aggressive actions, and that the rule keeps from the jury some situations that should qualify for a manslaughter instruction. Nevertheless, we do not believe that words alone are generally as inflammatory as aggressive actions. Further, it is only when a jury could reasonably find that the defendant was incited by sufficient provocation brought on by the victim that an instruction on voluntary manslaughter should be given in a murder prosecution.

We disapprove of a rule which does not allow "mere words" to be sufficient provocation to reduce murder to manslaughter generally, but which makes a specific exception where the provocation consists of mere words by one spouse informing the other spouse of infidelity. This exception to the general rule has its foundation in the ancient common-law concept that the wife is the property of the husband. See *Regina v. Mawgridge* (1707), Kelyng, J. 119, 137, 84 Eng. Rep. 1107, 1115: "When a man is taken in adultery with another man's wife, if the husband shall stab the adulterer, or knock out his brains, that is bare manslaughter: for jealousy is the rage of a man, and adultery is the highest invasion of property. . . . " (Citations omitted.) This archaic rule has no place in modern society. Words informing another of infidelity should not be given special treatment by courts trying to determine what provocation is reasonably sufficient provocation. The killing of a spouse (usually a wife) by a spouse (usually a husband) who has just been made aware of the victim spouse's adultery simply is not an acceptable response to the confession of infidelity.

We hold that words alone will not constitute reasonably sufficient provocation to incite the use of deadly force in most situations. Rather, in each case, the trial judge must determine whether evidence of reasonably sufficient provocation occasioned by the victim has been presented to warrant a voluntary manslaughter instruction. The trial judge is required to decide this issue as a matter of law, in view of the specific facts of the individual case. The trial judge should evaluate the evidence in the light most favorable to the defendant, without weighing the persuasiveness of the evidence.

QUESTIONS

1. Should words alone ever trigger the provocation doctrine? What if the words themselves enraged a defendant, as in the case of an insult or racial slur? What if the words informed the defendant of an act, such as a battery of a family member or adultery? Should the criminal law require that a defendant witness a provoking act first hand in order to claim provocation?

2. Who should decide whether "mere words" are sufficient to invoke provocation and mitigate murder to manslaughter? The legislature? The trial judge? Jurors?

In the following excerpt Professor Joshua Dressler addresses the gender orientation of the provocation doctrine:

> In today's more gender-sensitive era, courts increasingly use the term "Reasonable *Person*" in instructions to juries on provocation. But this gender-neutrality disguises an important fact, which is that the provocation defense itself is a male-oriented doctrine. That is, while women are often the victims of provoked killings or the stimulus for them, . . . men are the predominant beneficiaries of a doctrine that mitigates intentional homicide to manslaughter.
>
> Of course, as long as males are defendants in criminal homicide prosecutions more often than women, men are the primary beneficiaries of *all* criminal law defenses. But having said this, if ever the criminal law follows "boys" rules, it does here. Consider, first, that men are far more prone to violence than women. Both daily experience and crime statistics support this claim. Although the number of women sentenced for violent offenses has risen slightly in recent years, it is still true that "[w]omen rarely kill," and, to the extent that they do, "female homicide is so different from male homicide that women and men may be said to live in two different cultures, each with its own 'subculture of violence.' "[8]

---

8. Quoting Laurie J. Taylor, Comment, *Provoked Reason in Men and Women: Heat-of-Passion Manslaughter and Imperfect Self-Defense*, 33 UCLA L. Rev. 1679, 1680-1681 (1986) (footnotes omitted).

What is important here, however, is not simply that the average male is more susceptible to violent loss of self-control than is the average woman. It is also necessary to consider how men and women respond to affronts, *i.e.*, to provocations. Women usually submit stoically to their victimization or deny their status as victims by blaming themselves ("I deserve this treatment"); men are more likely to characterize themselves as victims of injustice, or to think that their self-worth has been attacked, and to act offensively as a result. One glance at the common law categories of "adequate provocation" shows that the defense has served a male interest, by mitigating the predominantly male reaction of retaliating for affronts and other "injustices."

The preceding observations might lead to the conclusion that courts should abolish the provocation defense. Arguably, the defense removes an important incentive for persons — primarily men — to learn self-control. And from a feminist perspective, the doctrine specifically "reinforces the conditions in which men are perceived and perceive themselves as natural aggressors, and in particular women's natural aggressors."[9]

3. Do Professor Dressler's comments affect your thinking about provocation? If so, how? If the provocation doctrine "has served a male interest," should that lead to abolition or modification of the doctrine? If the latter, what modifications should be made?

ii. Actual Provocation

The second part of the traditional provocation test requires that the defendant actually be provoked. Consider this Pennsylvania statute:

18 Pennsylvania Consolidated Statutes Annotated § 2503 (1998)   *Voluntary Manslaughter*

(a) **General Rule** — A person who kills an individual without lawful justification commits voluntary manslaughter if at the time of the killing he is acting under a sudden and intense passion resulting from serious provocation by:

(1) the individual killed; or

(2) another whom the actor endeavors to kill, but he negligently or accidentally causes the death of the individual killed.

QUESTIONS

1. What does the Pennsylvania statute require for voluntary manslaughter?

2. For those of you acquainted with the Star Trek® character "Data," consider his dilemma in the context of voluntary manslaughter. Could he ever invoke the provocation doctrine? Contrast the behavior of Captain James T. Kirk, from the original series.

iii. The Cooling Questions

Traditional doctrine puts time limits on the anger and loss of control that can qualify for mitigation under the provocation theory. The following Louisiana statute provides an example:

---

9. Dressler, *supra* note 2, at 735-737 (citation omitted).

Louisiana Statutes Annotated § 14:31 (2001)   *Manslaughter*

A. Manslaughter is:

   (1) A homicide which would be murder under either Article 30 (first degree murder) or Article 30.1 (second degree murder), but the offense is committed in sudden passion or heat of blood immediately caused by provocation sufficient to deprive an average person of his self-control and cool reflection. Provocation shall not reduce a homicide to manslaughter if the jury finds that the offender's blood had actually cooled, or that an average person's blood would have cooled, at the time the offense was committed.

QUESTIONS

1. What does the Louisiana statute require for manslaughter? Who decides if these requirements are met? The trial judge? Or the jury?
2. Compare the Louisiana and Pennsylvania statutes. Which gives judges and lawyers better guidance?

In the Ohio case that follows, what role does time play in the court's analysis?

STATE *v.* PIERCE

Supreme Court of Ohio 64 Ohio St. 2d 281 (1980)

APPEAL from the Court of Appeals for Stark County.

This appeal arises from the conviction of Homer C. Pierce, Jr. (hereinafter "defendant-appellant"), for the December 23, 1976, aggravated murder of Jeffrey LaPorte in Massillon, Ohio.

The relevant facts are not in dispute. As early as November 11, 1976, defendant, by his own admission, threatened LaPorte with serious bodily harm because LaPorte was spending time with defendant's wife. Also, as of that same date, defendant and his wife were contemplating legal separation. Several days later, defendant agreed to a divorce on the condition that his wife would not see LaPorte or any other man for two months. Shortly thereafter, defendant agreed to permit his wife to see LaPorte in public. Upon seeing them together in public, however, defendant became upset and decided to leave Massillon for a while.

On the night of December 16, 1976, contemporaneous with his return to Massillon, defendant admitted telephoning his wife at her home. Upon determining that LaPorte was then in her company, defendant further admitted threatening LaPorte with serious bodily harm. After defendant hung up, his wife telephoned the police who thereupon arrived at her home. A December 16, 1976, police report includes (1) defendant's wife's statement that defendant was holding a gun to the telephone and clicking it during his conversation with her; and (2) LaPorte's statement that defendant had threatened to kill him. While the police were still on the scene, defendant telephoned a second time. Defendant admitted that he conversed with the police during this second call and that he informed them that he owned a .22 caliber weapon.

At least four witnesses, in addition to defendant's wife, testified that defendant had threatened LaPorte sometime during the months of November and December, 1976.

In a handwritten last will and testament dated December 18, 1976, defendant left his property to his sisters and his life insurance to his stepdaughter. A Firearms Transaction Record of December 19, 1976, indicates that defendant purchased a Winchester 30-30 rifle from a local store. . . .

On the evening of December 22, 1976, defendant spoke to his wife, LaPorte and some of his wife's relatives and friends on the telephone. During these calls, a fight between defendant and LaPorte, which never materialized, was discussed.

At approximately 6:00 A.M. on the next morning, December 23, defendant visited a restaurant where both LaPorte and his brother were employed. There, defendant learned from LaPorte's brother that LaPorte was still at home where he was preparing to depart for the restaurant. Defendant left the restaurant and drove to LaPorte's home. When defendant arrived at LaPorte's home (approximately 6:30 A.M.), LaPorte had just entered his vehicle which was parked in front of his home. Defendant thereupon repeatedly fired a long-barreled automatic weapon containing 30-30 ammunition at LaPorte, killing him. The killing was witnessed by LaPorte's mother. . . .

The grand jury indicted defendant for aggravated murder, R. C. 2903.01, to which defendant pleaded not guilty and not guilty by reason of insanity. Subsequent to trial, the jury was instructed on aggravated murder; on the lesser-included offenses of murder, R. C. 2903.02; on voluntary manslaughter, R. C. 2903.03; and on the defense of insanity. On August 1, 1979, the jury found defendant guilty of aggravated murder, and conviction and sentence were entered accordingly. On appeal, the Court of Appeals affirmed this conviction.

The cause is now before this court pursuant to an allowance of a motion for leave to appeal.

I.

In proposition of law number three, defendant-appellant argues that the trial court's instruction on voluntary manslaughter was prejudicial because it included inadequate definitions of both extreme emotional distress and serious provocation.

The Court of Appeals found it unnecessary to consider this argument, ruling that defendant was not entitled to an instruction on voluntary manslaughter. We agree.

R. C. 2903.03, in part, provides:

"(A) No person, while under extreme emotional stress brought on by serious provocation reasonably sufficient to incite him into using deadly force, shall knowingly cause the death of another."

State v. Muscatello (1978), 55 Ohio St. 2d 201, paragraph four of the syllabus, provides that in a prosecution for aggravated murder, an instruction on the lesser-included offense of voluntary manslaughter must be submitted to the jury if "the defendant produces or elicits some evidence on the mitigating circumstance of extreme emotional stress described in R. C. 2903.03." *State v. Muscatello*, supra, paragraph five of the syllabus, however, defines an act committed under extreme emotional stress as "one performed under the influence of sudden passion or in the heat of blood without time and opportunity for reflection or for passions to cool."

Further, under Ohio law, the lesser-included offense of voluntary manslaughter does not embrace "a deliberate, calculated homicide [merely] . . . because extreme emotional stress brought on by the requisite provocation caused the laying of plans for the killing, as well as the killing itself . . . ." "It is upon just such fact-patterns that defendants enjoy the opportunity of obtaining relief by means other than a resort to deadly force." *Id.* at page 205.

Defendant introduced evidence of his emotional stress which he alleged was caused by the breakdown of his marriage; his contact with his wife, LaPorte and others during the six weeks preceding the killing; and a number of idiosyncratic personality traits. Further, defendant introduced evidence of his telephone conversations on the night before the killing, December 22, 1976, with his wife, some of his wife's relatives and friends, and LaPorte, in which a fight between defendant and LaPorte, which never materialized, was discussed.

Even assuming that these telephone conversations on the night before the killing could constitute requisite provocation, defendant was not entitled to an instruction on voluntary manslaughter. Given the period of time which elapsed between these telephone conversations and the killing on the next morning (during which there is no evidence of provocation), such killing was not, as a matter of law, committed under extreme emotional stress, since no finder of fact could possibly conclude that the killing was "performed under the influence of sudden passion or in the heat of blood, *without time and opportunity for reflection or for passions to cool." State v. Muscatello, supra,* paragraph five of the syllabus. (Emphasis added.) Therefore, we conclude that defendant was not entitled to an instruction on voluntary manslaughter.

QUESTIONS

1. What time limit does the *Pierce* court place on provocation? What rationale supports this limit?

2. What if Pierce had encountered LaPorte two hours after the telephone conversations? Would he have been able to claim provocation in Ohio? Should he have been able to claim provocation? Upon what factors should it depend?

b. The Traditional Approach in Transition

i. Redefining "Reasonable Person"

Some courts and legislatures have moved away from the rigidity of the traditional test. Although it is from an 1862 decision, the excerpt below offers a more modern and expansive view of provocation than the traditional test.

MAHER *v.* PEOPLE
Supreme Court of Michigan 10 Mich. 212 (1862)

To the question, what shall be considered in law a reasonable or adequate provocation for such state of mind, so as to give to a homicide, committed under its influence, the character of manslaughter? On principle, the answer, as a general rule, must be, anything the natural tendency of which would be to produce such a state of mind in ordinary men, and which the jury are satisfied did produce it in the case before them — not such a provocation as must, by the laws of the human mind, produce such an effect with the *certainty that physical effects follow from physical causes*; for then the individual could hardly be held morally accountable. Nor, on the other hand, must the provocation, in every case, be held sufficient or reasonable, because such a state of excitement has followed from it; for then, by habitual and long continued indulgence of evil passions, a bad man might acquire a claim to mitigation which would not be available to better men, and on account of that very wickedness of heart which, in itself, constitutes an aggravation both in morals and in law.

In determining whether the provocation is sufficient or reasonable, *ordinary human nature*, or the average of men recognized as men of fair average mind and disposition, should be taken as the standard — unless, indeed, the person whose guilt is in question be shown to have some peculiar weakness of mind or infirmity of temper, not arising from wickedness of heart or cruelty of disposition.

It is, doubtless, in one sense, the province of the court to define what, in law, will constitute a reasonable or adequate provocation, but not, I think, in ordinary cases, to determine whether the provocation proved in the particular case is sufficient or reasonable. . . .

The judge, it is true, must, to some extent, assume to decide upon the sufficiency of the alleged provocation, when the question arises upon the admission of testimony; and when it is so clear as to admit of no reasonable doubt upon any theory, that the alleged provocation could not have had any tendency to produce such state of mind, in ordinary men, he may properly exclude the evidence; but, if the alleged provocation be such as to admit of any reasonable doubt, whether it might not have had such tendency, it is much safer, I think, and more in accordance with principle, to let the evidence go to the jury under the proper instructions. . . . The law can not with justice assume, by the light of past decisions, to catalogue all the various facts and combinations of facts which shall be held to constitute reasonable or adequate provocation. Scarcely two past cases can be found which are identical in all their circumstances; and there is no reason to hope for greater uniformity in future. Provocations will be given without reference to any previous model, and the passions they excite will not consult the precedents.

The same principles which govern, as to the extent to which the passions must be excited and reason disturbed, apply with equal force to the time during which its continuance may be recognized as a ground for mitigating the homicide to the degree of manslaughter, or, in other words, to the question of cooling time. This, like the provocation itself, must depend upon the nature of man and the laws of the human mind, as well as upon the nature and circumstances of the provocation, the extent to which the passions have been aroused, and the fact, whether the injury inflicted by the provocation is more or less permanent or irreparable. . . . No precise time, therefore, *in hours or minutes*, can be laid down by the court, as a rule of law, within which the passions *must be held* to have subsided and reason to have resumed its control, without setting at defiance the laws of man's nature, and ignoring the very principle on which provocation and passion are allowed to be shown, at all, in mitigation of the offense. The question is one of reasonable time, depending upon all the circumstances of the particular case; and where the law has not defined, and can not without gross injustice define the precise time which shall be deemed reasonable.

QUESTIONS

1. How does the *Maher* court's approach to provocation differ from the traditional approach? Is the *Maher* approach preferable? How might this last question

be answered from the point of view of a defendant? From the point of view of the victim? From society's point of view?

2. Which theories of punishment support the modern, expansive approach to provocation? Does the following Georgia statute reflect a narrow or expansive attitude toward provocation? Is it closer to the traditional approach or the *Maher* view?

Georgia Code Annotated § 16-5-2 (2001)   *Voluntary Manslaughter*

(a) A person commits the offense of voluntary manslaughter when he causes the death of another human being under circumstances which would otherwise be murder and if he acts solely as the result of a sudden, violent, and irresistible passion resulting from serious provocation sufficient to excite such passion in a reasonable person; however, if there should have been an interval between the provocation and the killing sufficient for the voice of reason and humanity to be heard, of which the jury in all cases shall be the judge, the killing shall be attributed to deliberate revenge and be punished as murder.

PROBLEM

6.4 Consider the excerpted facts below from *People v. Nesler*, 16 Cal. 4th 561, 941 P.2d 87 (1997):

Daniel Driver allegedly raped defendant's son, W., at a Christian camp where Driver worked. Driver told W., who was then seven years of age, that Driver would kill him, his sister, and defendant if W. told anyone what had happened. Several months later, W. disclosed to defendant what Driver had done. In May 1989, a complaint was filed against Driver, alleging seven counts of child molestation involving four boys, including W. Driver, however, had fled and was not apprehended until late 1992 or early 1993.

During this period, W. became hypervigilant and expected Driver to kidnap and kill him. He also began asking defendant questions about suicide, and once defendant found him with a gun. Fearing that W. would kill himself, she obtained counseling for him. Defendant told her sister, Jannette Martinez, that when defendant was a child she had been raped in the same manner as W., and that there was a time when she, too, wanted to die.

Before Driver's preliminary hearing took place in April 1993, defendant protested when she learned that W. would have to face Driver at the hearing. She suggested videotaping W.'s testimony, but that alternative was unavailable; defendant then asked that the hearing at least be closed to the public. On the morning of the hearing, W. began vomiting and continued to do so after he arrived at the courthouse. Defendant appeared nervous, upset, and extremely anxious about W. She told an investigator that W. might not be able to testify, and she attempted to reassure and encourage the boy. When Driver arrived at the courthouse for the hearing, he looked at W. and grinned with a mean, disgusted, and haughty look. Defendant lunged for Driver, but Martinez grabbed her arm. Defendant again asked someone from the district attorney's office whether the courtroom could be closed, but an open hearing was held.

After W. entered the waiting room for witnesses, he continued to vomit. The mother of one of the other boys said that she did not believe her testimony had gone well, and that Driver had smirked at her and her son when they testified. This woman also said that she was convinced Driver was "going to walk," and that she wanted to get a gun and kill him. She told defendant to try to do better than she and her son had done. After this exchange, defendant became nervous and started pacing.

Defendant and W. were to be the last witnesses to testify at the preliminary hearing. Just before they were called, defendant asked the investigator whether he and other employees in the district attorney's office would get in trouble if "something happened" to Driver. Believing that defendant was referring to a previous assault upon Driver by another inmate in the jail, the investigator gave a negative response. Defendant and Martinez entered the courtroom, and the prosecutor told them to take a seat. The judge was not present, and a shackled Driver was sitting in a chair approximately one foot from defense counsel. Defendant stood behind the defense attorney, drew a gun she had taken from Martinez's purse, and shot Driver five times in the left side of the head and neck; a sixth bullet missed Driver and was found in the wall. The gun's muzzle was within two to three feet of Driver's head, and the shots were fired in rapid succession. Driver was killed almost instantly.

Defendant was taken into custody. She remarked, "You don't understand. He has raped hundreds of boys." The same day, in a tape-recorded statement, defendant said that she had not intended to kill Driver at the hearing and did not know whether she had done the right thing, but was tired of all the pain Driver had caused, and that he deserved to die. Defendant thought that W.'s pain had destroyed her sense of right and wrong. She said that when Driver smirked at her son outside the courthouse, she would have killed him right there had she already taken possession of the gun. . . .

After completion of the guilt phase of the trial, the jury found defendant not guilty of first or second degree murder, but returned a verdict of guilt on the lesser included offense of voluntary manslaughter. . . .

Do the facts described above support mitigation to voluntary manslaughter under the traditional approach to provocation? If so, what was the legally adequate provocation? If not, what modification to the traditional approach does the *Nesler* verdict imply?

How should a court or a jury measure cooling time?

ii. Battered Woman's Syndrome and Legal Provocation

BROOKS *v.* STATE

Court of Criminal Appeals of Alabama 630 So. 2d 160 (1993)

BOWEN, Presiding Judge

The appellant, Marguerite Louise Brooks, was convicted of the murder of her husband, Lewis Brooks, and was sentenced to life imprisonment.

I . . .

The evidence presented at trial tended to show that on September 18, 1992, the appellant was walking down the street with her friend Jeanette McLendon when Lewis Brooks, the appellant's husband, who was accompanied by his friend Yancey Davis, accosted the appellant and told her to "bring [her] ass here." Brooks began "cussing and fussing" at the appellant, grabbed the appellant's blouse, and jerked her toward him. The appellant pulled free. Then she and Ms. McLendon, pursued by Lewis Brooks and Yancey Davis, ran across the street to Ms. McLendon's house. Brooks was drunk and angry and he told Yancey Davis that he was "going to kill that bitch," referring to the appellant.

According to Ms. McLendon, the appellant said "that she needed something . . . she wasn't going to come out that door empty-handed." When McLendon informed the appellant that there was a gun in the dresser drawer, the appellant took the gun and went outside. Seeing her husband, the appellant told him that "she wasn't going to let him hurt her no more and [to] stay back." R. 498. Lewis Brooks advanced toward the appellant with his hands raised and she told him again, "Stay back; I will shoot." Brooks said, "You got the gun; go on and do what you got to do." When Brooks continued to move toward the appellant with his hands up, the appellant shot him.

The undisputed evidence at trial established that the appellant was a battered wife who had suffered physical abuse not only at the hands of her current husband, Lewis Brooks, but also at the hands of her former husband and another male companion with whom she had once cohabited. The State's expert witness, Dr. Karl Kirkland, a psychologist and certified forensics examiner, testified that the appellant suffered from "battered woman syndrome," a type of post-traumatic stress disorder characterized by the following symptoms:

> "Depression, a feeling of restricted choice, chronic apprehensiveness, a great deal of anxiety, a tendency to blame oneself, increased dependency. Some people describe a psychological paralysis of the will. That is, it causes a person to stay in a battering relationship. For a long time women who stayed in battering relationships were felt to be either masochistic or to be emotionally disturbed or else why would they stay. And the literature has not supported either of those theories. It basically says they stay because they are afraid."

Dr. Kirkland testified that the appellant's "status as an abused woman or wife played a major role in her behavior at the time of the offense." . . .

II

The appellant . . . contends that the trial court erred by instructing the jury that "battered woman syndrome" did not constitute legal provocation sufficient to reduce murder to manslaughter.

After the jury had been deliberating for some time, it returned to the court-room to ask the trial judge the following questions: (1) "What is the definition of murder by law?" (2) "What is the definition of manslaughter by law?" (3) "Is 'battered woman syndrome' grounds for manslaughter?" and (4) "Is 'battered woman syndrome' considered provocation?" The court answered the first two questions by reinstructing the jury on murder and heat-of-passion manslaughter. The court answered the third and fourth questions simply by stating, "No."

We note that other jurisdictions considering this issue have found provocation and heat-of-passion manslaughter instructions to be appropriate in prosecutions of battered victims who kill their batterers.

In *State v. Vigilante*, 257 N.J. Super. 296, 608 A.2d 425 (1992), the court held that a battered child prosecuted for killing his father was entitled to a heat-of-passion manslaughter instruction. The New Jersey court concluded that the child's past abuse and his contemplation of future abuse, combined with the father's threat to kill the child presented grounds for a provocation and heat-of-passion manslaughter charge.

> "It seems to us that a course of ill treatment which can induce a homicidal response in a person of ordinary firmness and which the accused reasonably believes is likely to continue, should permit a finding of provocation. In taking this view, we merely acknowledge the undoubted capacity of events to accumulate a detonating force, no different from that of a single blow or injury. The question is simply one of fact, whether the accused did, because of such prolonged oppression and the prospect of its continuance, experience a sudden episode of emotional distress which overwhelmed her reason, and whether, if she did, she killed because of it and before there had passed time reasonably sufficient for her emotions to yield to reason."

Vigilante, . . . 257 N.J Super at 304, 608 A.2d at 429-30 (quoting *State v. Guido*, 40 N.J. 191, 211, 191 A.2d 45, 56 (1963). . . .

In the present case, however, we need not decide this issue because defense counsel made no objection to the court's answers regarding manslaughter and the battered woman syndrome. The appellant has therefore failed to preserve this issue for review. See Rule 21.2, A.R. Crim. P. ("No party may assign as error the court's giving . . . of an erroneous, misleading, incomplete, or otherwise improper oral charge, unless he objects thereto before the jury retires to consider its verdict, stating the matter to which he objects and the grounds of his objection").

The judgment of the circuit court is affirmed.

QUESTIONS

1. Under a traditional approach, was there legally adequate provocation in *Brooks*? Was there sufficient cooling time?

2. Why did Judge Bowen discuss, but not decide, whether an instruction allowing provocation to mitigate murder to manslaughter should be given in a case involving a battered woman?

Do the following statistics influence whether and how a court should consider domestic violence in the context of the provocation doctrine?

**AMERICAN BAR ASSOCIATION, COMMISSION
ON DOMESTIC VIOLENCE**

(excerpted statistics) *http://www.abnet.org/domviol/stats.html* (accessed Oct. 25, 2004)

DOMESTIC VIOLENCE CROSSES ETHNIC, RACIAL, AGE, NATIONAL ORIGIN, SEXUAL
ORIENTATION, RELIGIOUS AND SOCIOECONOMIC LINES.

- by the most conservative estimate, each year 1 million women suffer nonfatal violence by an intimate. (Bureau of Justice Statistics Special Report: Violence Against Women: Estimates from the Redesigned Survey (NCJ-154348) August 1995, p.3.)
- by other estimates, 4 million American women experience a serious assault by an intimate partner during an average 12-month period. (American Psychl. Ass'n, Violence and the Family: Report of the American Psychological Association Presidential Task Force on Violence and the Family (1996), p.10.)
- 70% of intimate homicide victims are female. (Bureau of Justice Statistics Selected Findings: Violence Between Intimates (NCJ-149259), November 1994.)
- 37% of women injured by violence and treated in an emergency room were injured by an intimate; less than 5% of men injured by violence and treated in an emergency room were injured by an intimate. (Bureau of Justice Statistics: Violence-Related Injuries Treated in Hospital Emergency Departments (NCJ-156921), August 1997 p.5)
- 47% of men who beat their wives do so at least 3 times per year. (AMA Diagnostic & Treatment Guidelines on Domestic Violence, SEC: 94-677:3M:9/94 (1994).)

4. Killings Under the Model Penal Code's Extreme Mental or Emotional Disturbance Provision

Model Penal Code § 210.3 (1985)   *Manslaughter*

(1) Criminal homicide constitutes manslaughter when: . . .

(b) a homicide which would otherwise be murder is committed under the influence of extreme mental or emotional disturbance for which there is reasonable explanation or excuse. The reasonableness of such explanation or excuse shall be determined from the viewpoint of a person in the actor's situation under the circumstances as he believes them to be.

(2) Manslaughter is a felony of the second degree.[10]

The MPC's formulation of the extreme mental or emotional disturbance (EMED) doctrine raises the question of how we should understand "the actor's situation." The drafters offer the following commentary:[11]

Comment

The critical element in the Model Penal Code formulation is the clause requiring that reasonableness be assessed "from the viewpoint of a person in the actor's situation."

---

10. Model Penal Code §§ 210.0 to 213.6 (1985).
11. *Id.* at § 210.3 (Commentary, p.62-63).

The word "situation" is designedly ambiguous. On the one hand, it is clear that personal handicaps and some external circumstances must be taken into account. Thus, blindness, shock from traumatic injury, and extreme grief are all easily read into the term "situation." This result is sound, for it would be morally obtuse to appraise a crime for mitigation of punishment without reference to these factors. On the other hand, it is equally plain that idiosyncratic moral values are not part of the actor's situation. An assassin who kills a political leader because he believes it is right to do so cannot ask that he be judged by the standard of a reasonable extremist. Any other result would undermine the normative message of the criminal law. In between these two extremes, however, there are matters neither as clearly distinct from individual blameworthiness as blindness or handicap nor as integral a part of moral depravity as a belief in the rightness of killing. Perhaps the classic illustration is the unusual sensitivity to the epithet "bastard" of a person born illegitimate. An exceptionally punctilious sense of personal honor or an abnormally fearful temperament may also serve to differentiate an individual actor from the hypothetical reasonable man, yet none of these factors is wholly irrelevant to the ultimate issue of culpability. The proper role of such factors cannot be resolved satisfactorily by abstract definition of what may constitute adequate provocation. The Model Code endorses a formulation that affords sufficient flexibility to differentiate in particular cases between those special aspects of the actor's situation that should be deemed material for purpose of grading and those that should be ignored. There thus will be room for interpretations of the word "situation," and that is precisely the flexibility desired. There will be opportunity for argument about the reasonableness of explanation or excuse, and that too is a ground on which argument is required. In the end the question is whether the actor's loss of self-control can be understood in terms that arouse sympathy in the ordinary citizen. Section 210.3 faces this issue squarely and leaves the ultimate judgment to the ordinary citizen in the function of a juror assigned to resolve the specific case.

QUESTION

Does this formulation provide adequate guidance?

PROBLEMS

6.5 What are the elements of the Model Penal Code's EMED doctrine? How do they differ from traditional provocation doctrine?

6.6 Stephen Carr was hiking and arrived at a campsite where he observed two lesbians making love. Upset by what he observed, he killed one woman and wounded the other. He offers the following evidence, inter alia, in support of a manslaughter charge:

(a) "a history of constant rejection by women, including his mother, who may have been involved in a lesbian relationship," and

(b) evidence that he had been subject to "sexual abuse while in prison."[12]

What happens under the traditional approach? What happens under the MPC?

---

12. Problem 6.6 is based on and quotations are from Commonwealth v. Carr, 580 A.2d 1362, 1363-1364 (Pa. Super. Ct. 1990).

6.7 Jane had been abused by Tom for many years. Tom's abuse of Jane resulted in six separate hospitalizations for serious injuries, including a broken rib and cuts requiring multiple stitches. Jane shoots Tom while he is sleeping. Tom had been asleep for four hours prior to the killing. The most recent physical abuse occurred more than two days prior to the homicide. What happens under the traditional approach? What happens under the MPC?

6.8 The defendant and the victim had "met in a bar earlier in the night and returned to the victim's apartment, where they engaged in consensual sexual relations. Thereafter, the defendant struck the victim on the head repeatedly with a heavy glass bottle filled with pennies, and strangled her to death with a brassiere. Later in the day, the defendant went to the police and confessed to the killing. At trial, the defendant proffered the affirmative defense of extreme emotional disturbance, admitting that he had killed the victim as alleged by the prosecution, but seeking to have the jury find him guilty of manslaughter instead of murder."

"At his second trial, the defendant's defense was that he had 'snapped' and was 'totally out of control' at the time of the killing because of an extreme emotional disturbance triggered by his dissatisfaction with the victim who reportedly turned her back on him and went to sleep after they engaged in sexual intercourse. In connection with the affirmative defense, the defendant contended that his extreme emotional disturbance was explained or excused by several personality disorders, most prominent among them, post traumatic stress disorder arising from his service in the Vietnam war."[13]

What happens under the traditional approach? What happens under the MPC? What are the advantages of the traditional approach? The disadvantages? What are the advantages of the MPC approach? The disadvantages?

The appropriate approach to and boundaries of the provocation doctrine have incited much scholarly discussion. For an argument from one such discussion, consider the excerpt below.

Robert B. Mison, HOMOPHOBIA IN MANSLAUGHTER: THE HOMOSEXUAL ADVANCE AS INSUFFICIENT PROVOCATION   80 Cal. L. Rev. 133, 133-136
(1992) (citations omitted)

The question is simple: Should a nonviolent sexual advance in and of itself constitute sufficient provocation to incite a reasonable man to lose his self-control and kill in the heat of passion? If so, the defendant will be guilty of voluntary manslaughter, not murder. This sexual-advance defense could be used by a male or a female who claims that he or she killed in reaction

---

13. Based on and quotations from People v. Wood, 568 N.Y.S.2d 651, 652 (1991).

to the victim's sexual advance. As the law now stands, however, only a homosexual advance can mitigate murder to manslaughter.

Consider the following story in which the defendant successfully raised the homosexual-advance defense to mitigate his crime. A young man is out drinking heavily with his friends. His car breaks down and he hitches a ride with another man, the victim. Together they drive around looking for women for sex. After a while, the young man asks, "Where can I get a blow job?" The victim-to-be responds, "I can handle that." They continue to drive around, stopping at a convenience store for some cigarettes before going to a baseball field at a local school. They wander into the shadows where the victim pulls down his pants and underwear and attempts to embrace the young man. But the young man kicks him, stomps on him, takes his money, and leaves the victim to die on the isolated field. Before leaving the scene, the young man returns to the victim's car and carefully wipes it clean of his fingerprints.

At his trial, the young man claims that the victim's homosexual overture provoked him to lose his self-control and kill. He took the money and wiped his fingerprints from the car only as an afterthought. Defense counsel argues that a reasonable jury could find the victim's homosexual advance sufficient provocation for the defendant's acts and requests the judge to instruct the jury on the lesser included offense of voluntary manslaughter. The prosecution does not object. The judge, satisfied that a reasonable jury could find the victim's sexual advance adequate provocation, permits defense counsel to argue provocation and agrees to instruct the jury on voluntary manslaughter. The jury finds the young man guilty — of voluntary manslaughter. . . .

The continued use and acceptance of this defense sends a message to juries and the public that if someone makes a homosexual overture, such an advance may be sufficient provocation to kill that person. This reinforces both the notions that gay men are to be afforded less respect than heterosexual men, and that revulsion and hostility are natural reactions to homosexual behavior. . . .

The homosexual advance defense is a misguided application of provocation theory and a judicial institutionalization of homophobia. . . . [J]udges should hold, as a matter of law, that a homosexual advance is not sufficient provocation to incite a "reasonable man" to kill.

QUESTIONS

Should judges exclude certain categories of behavior from the provocation doctrine? If not, why not? If so, how should judges select the categories? Should the choice, instead, rest with the legislature? Or with jurors?

5. Synthesis and Challenge

PROBLEMS

6.9 Stanley lost both legs at his hip joints five years ago following a terrible auto accident. After the accident, Stanley became bitter. He lost his job. His relationship with his wife, June, and his son, James, became distant and tense. Several years ago, Stanley learned from a friend that June was having an affair with another man.

One day Stanley finds a letter written by June to her paramour. That evening, when June returns from work, Stanley confronts her with the letter. June admits the adultery and angrily begins taunting Stanley, calling him "only half a man." Furious, Stanley pulls out a loaded handgun and fires away at June, screaming "you're a dead woman, June." June, however, manages to dive for cover without being hit by any bullets. Unfortunately, though, James walks through the door at this very moment, is hit in the head by one of Stanley's bullets, and is killed instantly. Discuss the homicide liability of Stanley for the death of James.

(1) Assume a non-Model Penal Code jurisdiction.
(2) Would your analysis be different if Stanley were prosecuted in a Model Penal Code jurisdiction?

6.10 Consider the following excerpted facts from the Michigan case of *People v. Schmitz*:[14]

> This case arises from defendant's killing of Scott Amedure with a shotgun on March 9, 1995. Three days before the shooting, defendant appeared with Amedure and Donna Riley in Chicago for a taping of an episode of the Jenny Jones talk show, during which defendant was surprised by Amedure's revelation that he had a secret crush on [the defendant]. After the taping, defendant told many friends and acquaintances that he was quite embarrassed and humiliated by the experience and began a drinking binge.
>
> On the morning of the shooting, defendant found a sexually suggestive note from Amedure on his front door. Defendant then drove to a local bank, withdrew money from his savings account, and purchased a 12-gauge pump-action shotgun and some ammunition. Defendant then drove to Amedure's trailer, where he confronted Amedure about the note. When Amedure just smiled at him, defendant walked out of the trailer, stating that he had to shut off his car. Instead, defendant retrieved the shotgun and returned to the trailer. Standing at the front door, defendant fired two shots into Amedure's chest, leaving him with no chance for survival. Defendant left the scene and telephoned 911 to confess to the shooting.

Under the traditional approach, about which types of homicide should the jury have been instructed? Under the MPC approach?

6.11 You are legislative counsel to the judiciary committee of a state senate. The committee has decided to propose new legislation on provocation for consideration by the state legislature. The senator who chairs the committee has asked you to do the following:

(a) Summarize the arguments for and against the provocation doctrine.

---

14. 231 Mich. App. 521 (1998).

(b) Make a recommendation about whether the provocation doctrine should be eliminated entirely, made applicable only to homicide, or expanded as a mitigating factor in all criminal offenses.

(c) After reviewing the statutes and cases that appear in the provocation portion of this chapter and the excerpt from the United States Sentencing Guidelines that appears below, summarize the key issues that the new provocation statute should address and make a recommendation to the committee on each issue.

(d) Draft a proposed provocation statute for the committee to consider.

United States Sentencing Guidelines § 5k2.10 (18 U.S.C. Appx.) (LEXIS 2004)
Victim's Conduct (Policy Statement)

If the victim's wrongful conduct contributed significantly to provoking the offense behavior, the court may reduce the sentence below the guideline range to reflect the nature and circumstances of the offense. In deciding . . . the extent of a sentence reduction, the court should consider:

1. The size and strength of the victim, or other relevant physical characteristics, in comparison with those of the defendant.

2. The persistence of the victim's conduct and any efforts by the defendant to prevent confrontation.

3. The danger reasonably perceived by the defendant, including the victim's reputation for violence.

4. The danger actually presented to the defendant by the victim.

5. Any other relevant conduct by the victim that substantially contributed to the danger presented.

6. The proportionality and reasonableness of the defendant's response to the victim's provocation.

Victim misconduct ordinarily would not be sufficient to warrant application of this provision in the context of offenses under Chapter Two, Part A, Subpart 3 (Criminal Sexual Abuse). In addition, this provision usually would not be relevant in the context of non-violent offenses. There may, however, be unusual circumstances in which substantial victim misconduct would warrant a reduced penalty in the case of a non-violent offense. For example, an extended course of provocation and harassment might lead a defendant to steal or destroy property in retaliation.

Consider Professor Victoria Nourse's proposed reconstruction and defense of the provocation doctrine.

Victoria Nourse, PASSION'S PROGRESS: MODERN LAW REFORM AND THE PROVOCATION DEFENSE
106 Yale L.J. 1331, 1389-1393 (1997)

Why do we partially excuse some defendants who kill even though we know that no "reasonable person" kills? My proposal seeks to reconstruct, rather than abolish, the defense. . . .

A. Emotions and Reasons

Advocates of abolition face an obvious question: If we abolish the defense, what becomes of the woman who, distraught and enraged, kills her stalker, her rapist, or her batterer? I suspect that many would say that these women deserve our compassion. The most persuasive scholarly defenses of provocation have all invoked examples, like these, in which the defendant's emotion reflects the outrage of one responding to a grave wrong that the law otherwise punishes. Commentators frequently use examples of men killing their wives' rapists or children who kill abusive parents as clear cases of provoked murder. When, for example, the MPC drafters sought to justify their expansion of the defense, they relied on a case involving forcible sodomy.

The problem comes when we focus on cases in which the emotion is based on less compelling "reasons" — when women kill their departing husbands or men kill their complaining wives. Under conventional liberal theory, if extreme emotion is shown, these cases should be handled no differently from cases where victims kill their rapists and stalkers and batterers. The quantity or intensity of the emotion provides the excuse, not the reasons for the emotion. This focus on emotion, to the exclusion of reason, reflects a very important assumption made by liberal theories of the defense, that emotion obscures reason. When we distinguish the rapist killer from the departing wife killer, we acknowledge a very different view of emotion, one in which emotion is imbued with meaning. Both the departing wife killer and the rapist killer may be upset, but the meanings embodied in their claims for emotional understanding are quite different. In distinguishing these cases based on the reasons for the claimed emotion, we acknowledge a view of emotion in which emotion is not the enemy of reason but, instead, its embodiment. . . .

In the past two decades, the idea of emotion as the natural enemy of reason has been seriously questioned by brain scientists and psychologists, by rhetoricians and philosophers, by classicists and even by legal scholars. That both brain scientists and philosophers may now agree that emotion reflects or assists our reasoning processes tells us something that law, and life, already reflect. When we see that someone is angry, we do not call [a] psychiatric expert for a diagnosis, we simply ask "why?" We expect reasons, and they are typically attributions of wrongdoing and blame. This intuition is reflected in almost all versions of the provocation defense. No form of the defense excuses, even partially, based on emotion alone. Even the MPC's version of the defense, the defense most devoted to behavioral explanation, nevertheless assumes that it is possible to have reasons for emotions. . . .

B. A Proposal for a "Warranted Excuse"

Where does this understanding of emotion lead us? It helps us to see why we might distinguish intuitively the rapist killer from the departing wife killer. In the first case, we feel "with" the killer because she is expressing outrage in ways that communicate an emotional judgment (about the wrongfulness of rape) that is uncontroversially shared, indeed, that the law itself recognizes. Such claims resonate because we cannot distinguish the defendant's sense of emotional wrongfulness from the law's own sense of appropriate retribution. The defendant's emotional judgments are the law's own. In this sense, the defendant is us. By contrast, the departing wife killer cannot make such a claim. He asks us to share in the idea that leaving merits outrage, a claim that finds no reflection in the law's mirror.

In fact, the law tells us quite the opposite: that departure, unlike rape and battery and robbery, merits protection rather than punishment.

This understanding finally allows us to suggest an answer to the paradox with which we continually confront our law students: How can it be that a reasonable person kills in these circumstances and, if a reasonable person would, why not completely exonerate him? The short answer is that "reasonable men and women" do not kill in these circumstances, but reasonable men and women may well possess emotions that the law needs to protect. Without protecting some emotions, the criminal law contradicts itself. It punishes the very emotions implicit in the law's own judgments that killing and raping and robbing are both wrong and merit retribution. At the same time, protecting emotion does not require us to protect the deed. If we protect the act of killing, the criminal law commits itself to a different contradiction, one in which the State embraces or at least tolerates vigilantism.

We can now see why the provocation defense has always stood on the fence, partially . . . [condemning], yet partially exculpating. In every provoked murder case the law risks the embrace of revenge. To maintain its monopoly on violence, the State must condemn, at least partially, those who take the law into their own hands. At the same time, however, some provoked murder cases temper our feelings of revenge with the recognition of tragedy. Some defendants who take the law into their own hands respond with a rage shared by the law. In such cases, we "understand" the defendant's emotions because these are the very emotions to which the law appeals for the legitimacy of its own use of violence. At the same time, we continue to condemn the act because the defendant has claimed a right to use violence that is not his own.

The important point to see here is that the provoked killer's claim for our compassion is not simply a claim for sympathy; it is a claim of authority and a demand for our concurrence. The defendant who asks for our compassion, that we feel "with him," asks that we "share the state of mind that [he] express[es]." He asks that we share his judgments of emotional blame. Precisely because he asks us to embrace those emotional judgments, he asks us to embrace him as legislator, as one who rightly sets the emotional terms of blame and wrongdoing vis-à-vis his victim. . . . [W]hen a defendant responds with outrage to conduct society protects, he seeks to supplant the State's normative judgment, to impose his individual vision of blame and wrongdoing not only on the victim, but also on the rest of us.

PROBLEM

6.12 Evaluate Professor Nourse's proposal. Now, imagine that you are in a country in which adultery can be punished as a capital offense.[15] How would Professor Nourse's proposal apply to a husband who killed his wife or his wife's lover after discovering their adultery?

---

15. In 2002, in a case that gained international attention, a Nigerian court sentenced Amina Lawal to the penalty of death by stoning for the crime of adultery. In September of 2003, the highest court of Nigeria overturned the conviction. Somini Sengupta, *Death by stoning sentence overturned*, San Francisco Chronicle, Sept. 26, 2003, A12.

C. RECKLESS KILLINGS

1. Reckless Murder

In this Section, our homicide elevator goes from manslaughter back up to murder. Here, the focus is on murder based on extreme recklessness. The common law treated this sort of extreme recklessness as a type of "implied malice" and used a collection of colorful verbiage in referring to it, such as "abandoned and malignant heart." As you read the materials that follow, compare the various formulations of the required mental state. On what factors do courts rely in assessing whether the defendant possessed extreme recklessness or an "abandoned and malignant heart"? Are those who kill with extreme recklessness as blameworthy as those who kill with purpose or knowledge? Are they as dangerous?

PROBLEM

6.13 Craig and Andy are friends. One night at Craig's house, Craig suggests a game of Russian roulette. Andy agrees. Craig fetches his handgun, places it against Andy's head and pulls the trigger. The gun fires and Andy is instantly killed. Is Craig liable for homicide? For murder? Would the following factual variations make a difference in his liability?

(a) Craig thinks the gun is empty when he pulls the trigger, though he failed to check it before pulling the trigger.

(b) Craig thinks the gun is empty when he fetches it and fails to check all the chambers of the gun's barrel. The gun is a six-chambered revolver that rotates clockwise. Craig places a single bullet in the chamber immediately to the right of the firing pin. He then closes the barrel, puts the gun to Andy's head, and pulls the trigger. The bullet that kills Andy is not the one Craig placed in the chamber to the right of the firing pin. It turns out that Craig's brother earlier that day had placed several other bullets in the gun. It is one of these that kills Andy.

(c) There is only one bullet in the gun, which Craig places there before firing. Craig spins the barrel once, then fires three times with the gun placed against Andy's head. The third shot kills Andy.

(d) There is only one bullet in the gun, which Craig places there before firing. Craig places the gun against Andy's head and fires three times. Craig spins the barrel prior to each shot. The third shot kills Andy.

(e) Craig and Andy take turns putting the gun to their own heads and firing, spinning the barrel before each pull of the trigger. Andy goes first and Craig second. Nothing happens on either of these pulls of the trigger. Andy then takes another turn placing the gun against his own head and firing. On this third turn, the gun goes off, killing Andy.

Before reading the *Fleming* case, read the federal statute under which Fleming was tried and convicted. Does it set forth a category of reckless murder? If so, what language does it use to do so? Is reckless murder first degree or second degree?

18 United States Code § 1111 (1994)   *Murder*

(a) Murder is the unlawful killing of a human being with malice aforethought. Every murder perpetrated by poison, lying in wait, or any other kind of willful, deliberate, malicious, and premeditated killing; or committed in the perpetration of, or attempt to perpetrate, any arson, escape, murder, kidnaping, treason, espionage, sabotage, aggravated sexual abuse or sexual abuse[,] burglary, or robbery; or perpetrated from a premeditated design unlawfully and maliciously to effect the death of any human being other than him who is killed, is murder in the first degree.

Any other murder is murder in the second degree.

(b) Within the special maritime and territorial jurisdiction of the United States,

Whoever is guilty of murder in the first degree shall suffer death unless the jury qualifies its verdict by adding thereto "without capital punishment," in which event he shall be sentenced to imprisonment for life;

Whoever is guilty of murder in the second degree, shall be imprisoned for any term of years or for life.

UNITED STATES *v.* FLEMING
739 F.2d 945 (4th Cir. 1984)

Harrison L. WINTER, Chief Judge:

This case requires us to decide whether a non-purposeful vehicular homicide can ever amount to murder. We conclude that it can.

I.

Defendant David Earl Fleming was convicted of second-degree murder, in violation of 18 U.S.C. § 1111, in the death of Margaret Jacobsen Haley. Mrs. Haley was the driver of an automobile with which an automobile operated by the defendant collided when defendant lost control while traveling at a high rate of speed.

Fleming's car was observed at about 3:00 p.m. on June 15, 1983, traveling southbound on the George Washington Memorial Parkway in northern Virginia at speeds variously estimated by witnesses as between 70 and 100 miles per hour. The speed limit on the Parkway is, at most points, 45 miles per hour. Fleming several times directed his southbound car into the northbound lanes of the Parkway in order to avoid traffic congestion in the southbound lanes. Northbound traffic had to move out of his way in order to avoid a head-on collision. At one point, a pursuing police officer observed Fleming steer his car into the northbound lanes, which were separated from the southbound lanes at that point and for a distance of three-tenths of a mile by a raised concrete median, and drive in the northbound lanes, still at a high rate of speed, for the entire length of the median. At two other points, Fleming traveled in northbound lanes that were separated from the southbound lanes by medians.

Approximately six miles from where his car was first observed traveling at excessive speed, Fleming lost control of it on a sharp curve. The car slid across the northbound lanes, striking the curb on the opposite side of the highway. After striking the curb, Fleming's car straightened out and at that moment struck the car driven by Mrs. Haley that was coming in the opposite direction. Fleming's car at the moment of impact was estimated by witnesses to have been traveling 70 to 80 miles per hour; the speed limit at that point on the Parkway was 30 miles per hour. Mrs. Haley received multiple severe injuries and died before she could be extricated from her car.

Fleming was pulled from the wreckage of his car and transported to a Washington hospital for treatment. His blood alcohol level was there tested at .315 percent.

Fleming was indicted by a grand jury on a charge of second-degree murder and a number of other charges which are not relevant to this appeal. He was tried before a jury on the murder charge and convicted.

II.

Defendant maintains that the facts of the case cannot support a verdict of murder. Particularly, defendant contends that the facts are inadequate to establish the existence of malice aforethought, and thus that he should have been convicted of manslaughter at most.

Malice aforethought, as provided in 18 U.S.C. § 1111(a), is the distinguishing characteristic which, when present, makes a homicide murder rather than manslaughter.[2] Whether malice is present or absent must be inferred by the jury from the whole facts and circumstances surrounding the killing.

Proof of the existence of malice does not require a showing that the accused harbored hatred or ill will against the victim or others. Neither does it require proof of an intent to kill or injure. Malice may be established by evidence of conduct which is "reckless and wanton and a gross deviation from a reasonable standard of care, of such a nature that a jury is warranted in inferring that defendant was aware of a serious risk of death or serious bodily harm." To support a conviction for murder, the government need only have proved that defendant intended to operate his car in the manner in which he did with a heart that was without regard for the life and safety of others.[3]

We conclude that the evidence regarding defendant's conduct was adequate to sustain a finding by the jury that defendant acted with malice aforethought.

---

[2] Malice aforethought is a concept that originated with the common law and is used in 18 U.S.C. § 1111(a) in its common law sense. The statute's terms, since known to and derived from the common law, are referable to it for interpretation. Accordingly, we do not confine our consideration of the precedents to decisions of federal courts interpreting the federal statute, but rather consider other sources which may shed light on the issues of this case.

[3] We note that, even assuming that subjective awareness of the risk is required to establish murder where the killing resulted from reckless conduct, an exception to the requirement of subjective awareness of risk is made where lack of such awareness is attributable solely to voluntary drunkenness . . . . Defendant's state of voluntary intoxication thus would not have been relevant to whether the jury could have inferred from the circumstances of the crime that he was aware of the risk created by his conduct.

It is urged upon us, however, that a verdict of murder in this case should be precluded by the existence of a statute defining and proscribing involuntary manslaughter, 18 U.S.C. § 1112(a).[4] Defendant maintains that vehicular homicide where no purpose on the part of the accused to have caused death or injury has been shown should result only in conviction of involuntary manslaughter. Otherwise, defendant argues, all drunk driving homicides and many reckless driving ones will be prosecutable as murder. We are not persuaded by the argument.

The difference between malice, which will support conviction for murder, and gross negligence, which will permit of conviction only for manslaughter, is one of degree rather than kind. See, e.g., *United States v. Dixon*, 135 U.S. App. D.C. 401, 419 F.2d 288, 292-293 (D.C. Cir. 1969) (Leventhal, J., concurring) (difference between murder and manslaughter lies in the quality of the accused's awareness of the risk). See also Holmes, The Common Law 59 (1881) (The difference between murder and manslaughter lies "in the degree of danger attaching to the act in the given state of facts."). In the vast majority of vehicular homicides, the accused has not exhibited such wanton and reckless disregard for human life as to indicate the presence of malice on his part. In the present case, however, the facts show a deviation from established standards of regard for life and the safety of others that is markedly different in degree from that found in most vehicular homicides. In the average drunk driving homicide, there is no proof that the driver has acted while intoxicated with the purpose of wantonly and intentionally putting the lives of others in danger. Rather, his driving abilities were so impaired that he recklessly put others in danger simply by being on the road and attempting to do the things that any driver would do. In the present case, however, danger did not arise only by defendant's determining to drive while drunk. Rather, in addition to being intoxicated while driving, defendant drove in a manner that could be taken to indicate depraved disregard of human life, particularly in light of the fact that because he was drunk his reckless behavior was all the more dangerous.

III. . . .

Defendant also contends that the district court erred in admitting into evidence defendant's driving record which showed previous convictions for driving while intoxicated. The driving record would not have been admissible to show that defendant had a propensity to drive while drunk. However, the driving record was relevant to establish that defendant had grounds to be aware of the risk his drinking and driving while intoxicated presented to others. It thus was properly admitted.

AFFIRMED.

---

4. 18 U.S.C. § 1112(a) provides:

> Manslaughter is the unlawful killing of a human being without malice. It is of two kinds:
> Voluntary — Upon a sudden quarrel or heat of passion.
> Involuntary — In the commission of an unlawful act not amounting to a felony, or in the commission in an unlawful manner, or without due caution and circumspection, of a lawful act which might produce death.

QUESTIONS

1. What distinguishes reckless murder from manslaughter?
2. Are the criteria for reckless murder objective or subjective?
3. What should distinguish reckless murder from manslaughter?

Fleming was one of a series of cases across the country in which prosecutors sought and courts upheld a murder, rather than manslaughter, conviction in cases of non-purposeful killings by intoxicated drivers. Consider the facts from the California case of *People v. Watson*, below, in determining whether murder was the appropriate charge in that case:

> In the late night and early morning hours of January 2 and 3, 1979, defendant Robert Watson consumed large quantities of beer in a Redding bar. Approximately an hour and a half after leaving the bar, defendant drove through a red light on a Redding street and avoided a collision with another car only by skidding to a halt in the middle of the intersection. After this near collision, defendant drove away at high speed, approached another intersection and, although he again applied his brakes struck a Toyota sedan. Three passengers in the Toyota were ejected from the vehicle and the driver and her six-year-old daughter were killed. Defendant left 112 feet of skid marks prior to impact, and another 180 feet of skid marks to the vehicle's point of rest.
>
> The applicable speed limit at the accident scene was 35 miles per hour. Expert testimony based on the skid marks and other physical evidence estimated defendant's speed immediately prior to applying his brakes at 84 miles per hour. At point of impact, the experts concluded that defendant's speed was approximately 70 miles per hour. Eyewitness Henke testified that defendant's car passed him "real fast" (estimated by Henke at 50 to 60 miles per hour) shortly before the collision. According to Henke, defendant swerved from the slow lane into the fast lane, suddenly braked and skidded into the intersection, and thereupon struck the other vehicle. Henke believed that the traffic light was green when defendant entered the intersection.
>
> Defendant's blood alcohol content one-half hour after the collision was .23 percent, more than twice the percentage necessary to support a finding that he was legally intoxicated.[16]
>
> [The Court also noted that the defendant] . . . had driven his car to the establishment where he had been drinking, and he must have known that he would have to drive it later. It also may be presumed that defendant was aware of the hazards of driving while intoxicated."[17]

The *Watson* court described the standard that the prosecution had to prove in order for a court to uphold a murder charge:

> [w]hen a person does " 'an act, the natural consequences of which are dangerous to life, which act was deliberately performed by a person who knows that his conduct endangers the life of another and who acts with conscious disregard for life' . . . ." Phrased a different way, malice may be implied when defendant does an act with a high probability that it will result in death and does it with a base antisocial motive and with a wanton disregard for human life.[18]

---

16. People v. Watson, 30 Cal. 3d 290, 293-294 (1981).
17. *Id.* at 300.
18. *Id.*

QUESTIONS

1. Are the two descriptions of implied malice by the *Watson* court above the same? If not, how do they differ?

2. Could a court uphold a murder conviction under either description based on the facts of *Watson* given above?

Consider the excerpt that follows from then California Chief Justice Bird's dissent in the *Watson* case. How might the estimate of the number of intoxicated drivers who arrive home safely affect the analysis of probability of death?

> The fact that [defendant] was under the influence of alcohol made his driving more dangerous. A high percentage of accidents are caused by such drivers. No one holds a brief for this type of activity. However, a rule should not be promulgated by this court that driving while under the influence of alcohol is sufficient to establish an act "likely to kill." Death or injury is not the probable result of driving while under the influence of alcohol. "Thousands, perhaps hundreds of thousands, of Californians each week reach home without accident despite their driving intoxicated." [Citing *Taylor v. Superior Court*, 24 Cal. 3d 890, at 907, dissenting opinion of Clark, J.]
>
> The majority also fail to demonstrate that it is reasonable to infer that [defendant] had a conscious disregard for life. Can a conscious disregard for life be established by the fact that several hours *before* the accident [defendant] drove his car to a bar? The majority hold as a matter of law that he "must have known" he would have to drive his car later and that he wilfully drank alcohol until he was under its influence.
>
> . . . The majority's reasoning also perpetuates the fiction that when a person drinks socially, he wilfully drinks to come under the influence of alcohol and with this knowledge drives home at a later time. This unfounded conclusion ignores social reality. "[T]ypically [a person] sets out to drink without becoming intoxicated, and because alcohol distorts judgment, he overrates his capacity, and misjudges his driving ability after drinking too much." (*Taylor, supra*, 24 Cal. 3d at p. 908, dissenting opinion of Clark, J.)[19]

BERRY v. SUPERIOR COURT

208 Cal. App. 3d 783 (1989)

NOT CITABLE — ORDERED NOT PUBLISHED

Agliano, P. J. — The People have charged Michael Patrick Berry, defendant, with the murder of two and one-half-year-old James Soto who was killed by Berry's pit bull dog. Defendant also stands accused of negligent keeping of a mischievous animal which kills a human being (Pen. Code, § 399); marijuana cultivation (Health & Saf. Code, § 11358); and misdemeanor keeping of a fighting dog. (Pen. Code, § 597.5, subd. (a)(1).) By this statutorily authorized petition for a writ of prohibition (Pen. Code, § 999a), defendant seeks dismissal of the charges of murder and Penal Code section 399. He claims the evidence taken at the preliminary hearing falls legally short of establishing implied malice sufficient to bind over for murder; the factual findings of the magistrate rule out malice; and there is no evidence that the animal was mischievous or was kept without ordinary care.

---

19. *Id.* at 305-306 (Bird, C.J. dissenting).

A reviewing court may not substitute its judgment as to the weight of the evidence for that of the magistrate, and, if there is some evidence to support the information, the court will not inquire into its sufficiency . . . . Every legitimate inference that may be drawn from the evidence must be drawn in favor of the information." Our task is to decide whether "a person of ordinary caution or prudence would be led to believe and conscientiously entertain a strong suspicion that defendant committed the crime charged."

We have concluded, for reasons we shall state, that judged by this standard of review the record here will support a prosecution for murder. The other charges may also go forward.

RECORD OF THE PRELIMINARY HEARING

In the municipal court, defendant was charged with three counts: Involuntary manslaughter (Pen. Code, § 192, subd. (b)); Penal Code section 399; and marijuana cultivation (Health & Saf. Code, § 11358). Although murder was not alleged, the People may charge it in the information if the evidence developed at the preliminary hearing supports the charge.

The record shows that on June 13, 1987, James Soto, then aged two years and eight months, was killed by a pit bull dog named "Willy" owned by defendant. The animal was tethered near defendant's house but no obstacle prevented access to the dog's area. The victim and his family lived in a house which stood on the same lot, sharing a common driveway. The Soto family had four young children, then aged ten, four and one-half, two and one-half, and one year.

On the day of the child's death, his mother, Yvonne Nunez, left the child playing on the patio of their home for a minute or so while she went into the house, and when she came out the child was gone. She was looking for him when within some three to five minutes her brother-in-law, Richard Soto, called her and said defendant's dog had attacked James. Meanwhile the father, Arthur Soto, had come upon the dog Willy mauling his son. He screamed for defendant to come get the dog off the child; defendant did so. The child was bleeding profusely. Although an on-call volunteer fireman with paramedical training who lived nearby arrived within minutes and attempted to resuscitate the child, James died before an emergency crew arrived at the scene.

There was no evidence that Willy had ever before attacked a human being, but there was considerable evidence that he was bred and trained to be a fighting dog and that he posed a known threat to people. Defendant bought Willy from a breeder of fighting dogs, who informed defendant of the dog's fighting abilities, his gameness, wind, and exceptionally hard bite. The breeder told defendant that in a dog fight "a dog won't go an hour with Willy and live."

The police searched defendant's house after the death of James and found many underground publications about dog fighting; a pamphlet entitled "42 day keep" which set out the 6-week conditioning procedures used to prepare a dog for a match; a treadmill used to condition a dog and increase its endurance; correspondence with Willy's breeder, Gene Smith; photographs of dog fights; and a "break stick," used to pry fighting dogs apart since they will not release on command. One of Smith's letters dated December 7, 1984, described Willy as having an exceptionally hard bite.

Two women who knew defendant testified he told them he had raised dogs for fighting purposes and had fought pit bulls.

Richard Soto testified defendant told him he used the treadmill to increase the strength and endurance of his dogs. Defendant also told both Arthur and Richard Soto that he would not fight his dogs for less than $500 and he told Richard Willy had had matches as far away as South Carolina.

The victim's mother testified defendant had several dogs. He told her not to be concerned about the dogs, that they would not bother her children, except for "one that he had on the side of the house" which was behind a six-foot fence. Defendant further said this dangerous dog was Willy but that she need not be concerned since he was behind a fence. There was a fence where the dog was tethered on the west side of defendant's house, but the fence was not an enclosure and did not prevent access to the area the dog could reach.

The police found some 243 marijuana plants growing behind defendant's house. Willy was tethered in such location that anyone wanting to approach the plants would have to cross the area the dog could reach. That area was readily accessible to anyone.

An animal control officer qualified as an expert on fighting dogs testified. He said pit bull dogs are selectively bred to be aggressive towards other animals. They give no warning of their attack, attack swiftly, silently and tenaciously. Although many recently bred pit bulls have good dispositions near human beings and are bred and raised to be pets, there are no uniform breeding standards for temperament and the animal control officers consider a pit bull dangerous unless proved otherwise.

Defendant's counsel placed great emphasis on certain testimony of the animal control officer, Miller. Counsel claimed that Miller testified Willy's attack on James was completely unpredictable, and that the People are bound by this testimony and therefore cannot argue that defendant ought to have foreseen what would happen. The testimony occurred during cross-examination, as follows: defendant's counsel asked Miller whether he knew of any prior attacks by Willy, and he said no. Then counsel quoted from an article written by Miller saying that even pit bulls with no prior history of aggression have been known to become highly aggressive "when at large, when in a pack, when confronted by any aggressive dog or under other unpredictable situations." Miller affirmed he believed this. Then counsel ruled out such factors as the dog being at large, in a pack, and so forth, and then said the dog being confronted by the little boy "would come under this unpredictable situation then, wouldn't he?" and Miller said yes. Counsel then asked, "So then what you are saying is is [sic] that without any prior knowledge of unpredictability, Willy could cause an attack such as this, isn't that true?" and Miller said yes.

When testifying, Arthur Soto denied having told any investigator that defendant had warned him about Willy. Counsel interrogating him insinuated that he was afraid to testify about prior warnings because he might jeopardize his civil lawsuit against defendant. Later an officer who had investigated the death and had interviewed Arthur testified pursuant to Evidence Code section 1237 that Arthur had told the officer defendant had warned Arthur to "keep the kids away from the killer dog," meaning Willy.

DISCUSSION

WHETHER EVIDENCE IS SUFFICIENT TO BIND OVER ON MURDER CHARGE

First, defendant claims that as a matter of law the record does not show implied malice sufficient to require him to stand trial for a charge of second degree murder.

As stated above, the issue at this stage of the proceedings is not whether the evidence establishes guilt beyond a reasonable doubt, but rather whether the evidence is sufficient to lead a man of ordinary caution or prudence to believe and conscientiously entertain a strong suspicion of his guilt of this offense, or whether there is some rational ground for assuming the possibility of his guilt.

The case of *People v. Watson, supra*, 30 Cal. 3d 290, a case involving reckless driving under the influence, states that the test of implied malice in an unintentional killing is actual appreciation of a high degree of risk that is objectively present. There must be a high probability that the act done will result in death and it must be done with a base antisocial motive and with wanton disregard for life. The conduct in *Watson*, held sufficient to ground a finding of malice, was reckless speeding while intoxicated. Defendant had prior knowledge of the hazards of drunk driving.

The recent decision in *People v. Protopappas* (1988) 201 Cal. App. 3d 152 further elaborates the definition of implied malice. That case found sufficient evidence of implied malice to support the defendant dentist's convictions of the murders of three of his patients, who died because of his recklessness. He clearly did not intend to kill them; as the decision pointed out, it was in his interests to keep them alive so that he could continue to collect fees from them. Further, his failure to provide proper treatment for them could be characterized as an act of omission or neglect rather than an affirmative act of homicide. But the appellate court found sufficient evidence of malice because the jury could infer from his conduct that he actually appreciated the risk to his patients and exhibited extreme indifference to their welfare in failing to provide the proper treatment and care and in administering anesthesia to them in grossly negligent fashion. The court found substantial evidence Protopappas's treatment of his patients was " ' "aggravated, culpable, gross, or reckless" neglect . . . [which] involved such a high degree of probability that it would result in death that it constituted "a wanton disregard for human life" making it second degree murder.' " The *Protopappas* court further elaborated the requirements of implied malice thus: "wantonness, an extreme indifference to [the victim's] life, and subjective awareness of the very high probability of her death." (201 Cal. App. 3d p. 168.)

Interestingly, the court in *Protopappas* referred to the dentist's conduct as "the health care equivalent of shooting into a crowd or setting a lethal mantrap in a dark alley." Similarly here, the People seek to analogize defendant's manner of keeping Willy as the equivalent of setting a lethal mantrap, since anyone could have approached the dog and been at risk of attack. (Cases holding second degree murder may rest on the setting of a lethal trap include *People v. Ceballos* (1974) 12 Cal. 3d 470, 477.)

Another decision which thoughtfully explores the nature of implied malice is *People v. Love* (1980) 111 Cal. App. 3d 98. . . .

Love observes that the "continuum of death-causing behavior for which society imposes sanctions is practically limitless with the gradations of more culpable conduct imperceptibly shading into conduct for the less culpable. Our high court has drawn this line placing in the more culpable category not only those deliberate life-endangering acts which are done with a subjective awareness of the risk involved, but also life-endangering conduct which is 'only' done with the awareness the conduct is contrary to the laws of society. . . .

The decision in *Love* sets forth two prerequisites for affixing second degree murder liability upon an unintentional killing. One requirement is the defendant's extreme indifference to the value of human life, a condition which must be demonstrated by showing the probability that the conduct involved will cause death. Another requirement is awareness either (1) of the risks of the conduct, *or* (2) that the conduct is contrary to law. Here, evidence of the latter requirement is first, that the very possession of Willy may have constituted illegal keeping of a fighting dog. (Pen. Code, § 597.5.) Second, there is evidence that defendant kept Willy to guard marijuana plants, also conduct with elements of illegality and antisocial purpose. Thus the second element which *Love* required could be satisfied here in a number of ways.

Defendant argues that the elements posited in *Love* — awareness of high risk of antisocial or illegal conduct — are insufficient. He says a further requirement is that the defendant have actively killed the victim, rather than being guilty of passive omissions which result in the death. . . .

However, despite defendant's argument that all second degree murders involve acts of commission rather than omission, at least two cases of second degree murder, *Protopappas* and *Burden,* arguably rest on reckless failure to provide proper care or treatment. The *Protopappas* court described the defendant's conduct there in precisely those terms. *Burden* rests on a father's neglect in caring for his son, namely, allowing him to starve to death. The *Burden* court said that "the common law does not distinguish between homicide by act and homicide by omission." " ' "Willful failure of a person to perform a legal duty, whereby the death of another is caused, is murder. . . . " ' "

Almost any behavior can alternately be stated as a sin of omission or of commission. Therefore the distinction of active and passive behavior is not a reliable means of distinguishing intentional and unintentional homicide. For example defendant seeks to distinguish the spring gun case (*People v. Ceballos*) as one involving an active act of setting the trap; but his conduct could equally be described as stationing the dog in a dangerous location. Rather, as the cases hold, attention is best focused on the difference in mental state, in the defendant's intent. Death by agency of an "abandoned and malignant heart," more precisely defined in *Watson,* as a subjective appreciation of a high risk of death, is murder; by gross negligence alone is manslaughter.

Have we here evidence of the elements of second degree murder as described in these decisions, namely, the high probability the conduct will result in the death of a human being, a subjective appreciation of the risk, and a base antisocial purpose or motive? The People point to these facts: The homes of defendant and the victim's family shared a lot and were in close proximity, the Soto family had four very young children and defendant knew this; defendant knew the dog Willy was dangerous to the children, as evidenced by the mother's testimony that he told her that dog could be dangerous but was behind a fence; defendant in fact lulled Yvonne into a false sense of security by assuring her the dangerous dog was behind a fence when he was in fact accessible; defendant bred fighting dogs and had knowledge of the nature and characteristics of fighting pit bulls; defendant had referred to Willy as a "killer dog"; pit bulls in fact are sometimes dangerous and will attack unpredictably and without warning; and Willy was a proven savage fighting dog.

From this mass of evidence it is possible to isolate facts which standing alone would not suffice as the basis of a murder charge. For example, we do not believe that a showing that Willy was dangerous to other dogs, without more, would be sufficient to bind over his owner on a murder charge; there is no evidence in this record that dogs who are dangerous to their own kind are ipso facto dangerous to human beings and therefore there is no support for an inference that the owner of such a dog should be aware of any such danger. But the evidence amassed here goes beyond demonstrating that Willy was aggressive towards his own kind. We believe this record shows first, that Willy's owner may have been actually aware of the dog's potential danger to human beings. This mental state may be proved by showing he kept the dog chained, he warned the child's parents that the dog was dangerous to children, and he spoke of the dog as dangerous. Second, the testimony of the animal control officer could support an inference that fighting pit bull dogs are dangerous to human beings, and the record of defendant's extensive knowledge of the breed could support an inference that he knew such dogs are dangerous.

Defendant argues that the testimony of the animal control officer, Miller, regarding the dangerousness of pit bulls, conclusively establishes that Willy's attack was "unpredictable" in the sense that it could not reasonably have been anticipated. This interpretation is not compelled. Some of that testimony consists of responses to ungrammatical questions and as such does not establish any proposition with certainty.[1] But a possible fair reading of Miller's testimony is that he used "unpredictable" not in the sense that no one could predict whether the dog would ever attack, but rather, in the sense that the dog could be expected to attack without advance warning or apparent cause. Thus Miller's testimony could support an inference that pit bulls are known to be liable to attack human beings. There is also evidence, consisting mainly of physical evidence seized from defendant's home, showing that defendant is a connoisseur of fighting pit bull dogs and had sought out a vicious dog in order to have him fight successfully.

Thus there is a basis from which the trier of fact could derive the two required elements of implied malice, namely existence of an objective risk and subjective awareness of that risk. Additionally, there is arguably some base and antisocial purpose involved in keeping the dog (1) because harboring a fighting dog is illegal and (2) because there is some evidence the dog was kept to guard an illegal stand of marijuana. Illegality of the underlying conduct is not an element of the charge, but may be relevant on the issue of subjective intent.

We do not know the actual probability that a death could result from defendant's conduct in keeping the dog. Presumably that is a question of fact to be submitted to the court or jury upon appropriate instructions requiring that it find a high probability that death would result from the circumstances before it can convict of murder.

Defendant emphasizes the facts that Willy had never before attacked a human being and that he was kept chained on the premises. First, the fact that the dog was kept chained lessened little the risk which he posed, in view of the close proximity of very young children, the obvious risk of a child's wandering near, and indeed being attracted to a seemingly harmless pet, and the easy accessibility to his vicinity. The mere fact he was chained clearly cannot, under the circumstances of record, absolve the owner of blame. Also, the fact that defendant took the precaution of restraining the dog is a fact which might show he knew the dog was dangerous. . . . A similar inference may rest on the facts the dog was a pit bull, bought for his fighting ability,

---

[1] The question counsel asked Miller was "So then what you are saying is is [sic] that without any prior knowledge of unpredictability, Willy could cause an attack such as this, isn't that true?" to which he said yes. As a matter of English grammar there is no reliable inference that can be based on this interrogation.

bred and conditioned as a fighting dog, kept chained, and described by defendant as a killer. . . . These circumstances clearly support an inference defendant knew his dog was dangerous to humans. . . .

We conclude that it is for the jury to resolve the factual issues of probability of death and subjective mental state. There is sufficient evidence to justify trial for murder on an implied malice theory. . . .

The petition for writ of prohibition is denied.

Willy

QUESTIONS

1. Should animal owners ever be liable for homicide based on the actions of their animals? For murder? Should it matter what type of animal it is?

2. Is the owner's presence or absence at the time of the attack relevant? Imagine that Mr. Berry saw his pit bull attack his neighbor's child and ran outside screaming "Release" to the dog, but the dog failed to release the child. Should that affect the defendant's liability?

3. The *Berry* court refers to the "high probability of death" standard for implied malice as described by *Watson*. Is a high probability of death an appropriate standard? What does high probability mean? 10 percent? 20 percent? 90 percent?

4. In the *Berry* case, the jury ultimately acquitted the defendant of murder but convicted him of manslaughter. What factors might have influenced the jury to convict him of manslaughter rather than murder?

The *Berry* case is not the only case in which prosecutors have charged murder when a dog fatally attacked a person. For example, in a highly-publicized San Francisco case, the prosecutor charged the defendant, Majorie Knoller, with murder when a Presa Canario dog in her care attacked and killed her neighbor, Diane Whipple. In that case, the jury convicted Marjorie Knoller of the murder charge. Subsequent to the trial, however, the trial court judge granted a new trial motion overturning the murder conviction. Appendix C contains an excerpt from the transcript explaining the judge's reasoning and analyzing the murder standard in that case.

PROBLEMS

6.14 Based on the information reported in the following news account, are the parents guilty of homicide? If so, what type of homicide?

> [According to the Associated Press report, Joseph and Deborah Thompson were charged] after their 3-year-old nephew drank a fatal dose of methadone that had been stored in his plastic juice cup. . . . Traces of cocaine were also found in the boy's system, which police said could have been due to secondhand smoke from others smoking crack cocaine in the apartment. . . .   Attorney Charles Jameson, who is representing Deborah Thompson, has said she was devastated by the death of the boy, whom she took in at the age of 6 months. . . . Police said the Thompsons are on methadone, a synthetic narcotic used to wean addicts from heroin. They said Deborah Thompson had asked her husband to store some extra methadone in the refrigerator and he used Joecorri's cup. Thompson apparently forgot that the methadone, which had been mixed with cranberry juice, was in the cup. Joecorri came in from play, he drank the methadone and fell asleep. Deborah Thompson was away from home at the time. She called authorities after she was unable to rouse the boy later that evening.[20]

6.15 From the following news account, can you determine whether Troy Carlisle should be convicted of a crime? If so, what crime?

> Troy Carlisle, 28, told authorities he was trying to save Dallas Reinhardt when he removed her life jacket to pull her to shore. But Carlisle also testified that he knew the girl would die. . . .   He originally was charged under a 130-year-old Mississippi law called "depraved heart murder," which is filed when someone is suspected of placing another person in imminent danger of death. The charge carries a penalty of life in prison. Prosecutors said Dallas would likely have survived had Carlisle not taken the life jacket to save himself. But defense attorney Jack Jones told jurors it was unreasonable to apply normal standards to the situation. "How do you judge a drowning man? You can't do it," he said. In a taped interview played

---

20. Associated Press, *Innocent Plea in Child's Death*, "The Recorder," May 24, 2000 at p.7.

to the jury, Carlisle said the child's jacket could not support the two of them so he decided to take it off her and wrap it around his arm. He said he then tried to pull her to safety. Carlisle said he became tired and the water either yanked the girl from his grasp or he let go. "I was thinking I was gonna die or she was gonna die," Carlisle said. "I didn't really want both of us to die, so I'd figured I'd take it off her and put it around my arm . . . but she slipped out of my hand." Later he told deputies he felt "scared, ashamed and disappointed" as he thought back on the scene.[21]

6.16 News accounts paint the following picture of Chante Mallard when she killed Gregory Biggs: She had spent the evening with friends, drinking alcohol and taking Ecstasy. She was driving home when she hit Biggs, a pedestrian on the highway. He landed stuck in her windshield, head first to the floorboard inside the car, with one leg nearly severed. After attempting unsuccessfully to remove Biggs at an intersection, Mallard chose to drive to her home and park in her garage. There, with Biggs still alive but trapped in the windshield, she apologized to him and lamented that she did not know what to do, but she did not remove him from the windshield nor seek medical attention for him. Apparently, Biggs was alive for some time in her garage, perhaps a number of hours, moaning or talking as he bled to death. Later that day, friends of Mallard helped her dispose of Biggs' dead body in a park. The prosecution argued that, because his injuries were not immediately life threatening, he could have lived had Mallard sought medical attention in a timely fashion. Mallard's lawyer agreed with much of the factual story presented by the prosecution but contended that Mallard had hit Biggs by accident and then simply panicked; that she should not be held liable for murder.[22] For what crime regarding Biggs' death should Mallard be held liable? What was her mental state? What act did she perform?

2. The Model Penal Code Approach to Reckless Murder

Model Penal Code § 210.2 (1985)   *Murder*

(1) Except as provided in Section 210.3(1) (b), criminal homicide constitutes murder when: . . .

---

21. Associated Press, *Man convicted of letting child drown, saving self*, Bakersfield Californian, Oct. 12, 2002, at p.A11.

22. The factual details for Problem 6.16 are based on reports from Associated Press, *Driver Hit Man and Let Him Die in Her Garage, Police Say*, New York Times, Mar. 7, 2003; CNN, *Woman panicked after touching man in windshield*, http://www.cnn.com/2003/LAW/06/26/windshield.death/ (accessed May 25, 2003), Associated Press, *Timeline of Events in the Chante Mallard Windshield Death Case*, wysiwyg://7/http://www.foxnews.com/story/0,2933,90498,00.html (accessed Aug. 6, 2003); CNN, *Woman in Windshield Murder Trial Says She Left Man to Die*, http://www.cnn.com/Transcripts/ 0306/23/lol.02.html (accessed May 25, 2003).

(b) it is committed recklessly under circumstances manifesting extreme indifference to the value of human life . . . .

QUESTIONS

1. Does the MPC formulation of reckless murder differ from that in the *Fleming* case? In the *Berry* case?
2. What does it mean to "manifest extreme indifference to the value of human life"?
3. Imagine that you are a legislator in a jurisdiction that is redrafting its murder law. How would you phrase the description of reckless murder?
4. Apply the MPC approach to reckless murder to Problems 6.13-6.16. Based on the reported events, would the defendants in those problems qualify for reckless murder under the MPC standard?

3. Manslaughter

In this Section we descend down the homicide elevator from murder to manslaughter. Unlike voluntary manslaughter, the focus here is not on provocation but on issues of risk. What was the probability that death would occur? Was there a legitimate reason for taking the risk? Was the defendant aware of the risk? The analysis often resembles that done in extreme reckless murder cases. While jurisdictions often require a subjective awareness of the risk of death, others permit a finding of manslaughter without subjective awareness. They rely instead on some form of negligence.

18 Pennsylvania Consolidated Statute Annotated § 2504 (1998)

Involuntary manslaughter

(a) General Rule—A person is guilty of involuntary manslaughter when as a direct result of the doing of an unlawful act in a reckless or grossly negligent manner, or the doing of a lawful act in a reckless or grossly negligent manner, he causes the death of another person.

(b) Grading—Involuntary manslaughter is a misdemeanor of the first degree. [Punishable by up to five years' imprisonment.]

Model Penal Code § 210.3 (1985)   *Manslaughter*

(1) Criminal homicide constitutes manslaughter when:
    (a) it is committed recklessly; . . .
(2) Manslaughter is a felony of the second degree.

New York Penal Law § 125.15 (1998)   *Manslaughter in the Second Degree*

A person is guilty of manslaughter in the second degree when:
    1. He recklessly causes the death of another person; . . .
Manslaughter in the second degree is a class C felony. [Punishable by up to 15 years' imprisonment.]

QUESTIONS

1. How do the above statutes differ from one another in defining manslaughter?

2. Based on the statutes above, how does manslaughter differ from reckless murder?

COMMONWEALTH *v.* WELANSKY

Supreme Court of Massachusetts 316 Mass. 383 (1944)

LUMMUS, J. On November 28, 1942, and for about nine years before that day, a corporation named New Cocoanut Grove, Inc., maintained and operated a "night club" in Boston, having an entrance at 17 Piedmont Street, for the furnishing to the public for compensation of food, drink, and entertainment consisting of orchestra and band music, singing and dancing. It employed about eighty persons. The corporation, its officers and employees, and its business, were completely dominated by the defendant Barnett Welansky, who is called in this opinion simply the defendant, since his codefendants were acquitted by the jury. He owned, and held in his own name or in the names of others, all the capital stock. He leased some of the land on which the corporate business was carried on, and owned the rest, although title was held for him by his sister. He was entitled to, and took, all the profits. Internally, the corporation was operated without regard to corporate forms, as though the business were that of the defendant as an individual. It was not shown that responsibility for the number or condition of safety exits had been delegated by the defendant to any employee or other person.

The defendant was accustomed to spend his evenings at the night club, inspecting the premises and superintending the business. On November 16, 1942, he became suddenly ill, and was carried to a hospital, where he was in bed for three weeks and remained until discharged on December 11, 1942. During his stay at the hospital, although employees visited him there, he did not concern himself with the night club, because, as he testified, he "knew it would be all right" and that "the same system . . . [he] had would continue" during his absence. There is no evidence of any act, omission or condition at the night club on November 28, 1942, (apart from the lighting of a match hereinafter described), that was not within the usual and regular practice during the time before the defendant was taken ill when he was at the night club nearly every evening. . . .

[There were only two entrances and exits intended for the normal use of the night club's patrons. There were also five emergency exits, described as follows.]

(1) A door, opening outward to Piedmont Street, two and one half feet wide, at the head of the stairway leading to and from the basement Melody Lounge. That door apparently was not visible from the greater part of the foyer, for it was in a passageway that ran from one end of the foyer past the office to the stairway. That door was marked "Exit" by an electric sign. It was equipped with a "panic" or "crash" bar, intended to unbolt and open the door upon pressure from within the building. But on the evidence it could have been found that the device just mentioned was regularly made ineffective by having the door locked by a separate lock operated by a key that was kept in a desk in the office. Late in the evening of November 28, 1942, firemen found that door locked and had to force it open with an axe. The jury were entitled to disbelieve the testimony of the defendant that he

had instructed the head waiter, who died in the occurrence of that evening, always to keep that door unlocked. It may be observed that if that door should be left so that it could be opened by means of the panic bar, a patron might leave through that door without paying his bill. It does not appear that anyone watched that door to prevent patrons from so doing.

(2) A door two and one third feet wide leading from the foyer, near the revolving door, into the small vestibule adjoining the office, already described. From that vestibule another similar door, swinging inward, gave egress to Piedmont Street, near the revolving door. The door to Piedmont Street could not be opened fully, because of a wall shelf. And that door was commonly barred in the evening, as it was on November 28, 1942, by a removable board with clothing hooks on it, and by clothing, for in the evening the office and vestibule were used for checking clothing.

(3) A door, opening outward, from the middle of the wall of the main dining room to Shawmut Street, and marked "Exit" by an electric sign. The opening was about three and two thirds feet wide. The defendant testified that this was the principal exit provided for emergencies. From the sides of the opening hung double doors, equipped with "panic" bars intended to unbolt and open the doors upon pressure from within. But on the evening of November 28, 1942, one of the two doors did not open upon pressure, and had to be hammered with a table before it would open. Besides, the "panic" doors were hidden from the view of diners by a pair of "Venetian" wooden doors, swinging inward, and fastened by a hook, which had to be opened before one could operate the "panic" doors. In addition, dining tables were regularly placed near the Venetian doors, one of them within two feet, and these had to be moved away in order to get access to the doors. That condition prevailed on the evening of November 28, 1942.

(4) The service door, two and one half feet wide, swinging inward, leading to Shawmut Street at 8 Shawmut Street. This door was . . . in a part of the premises to which patrons were not admitted and which they could not see. This door was known to employees, but doubtless not to patrons. It was kept locked by direction of the defendant, and the key was kept in a desk in the office.

(5) The door, two and three fourths feet wide, swinging inward, leading from a corridor into which patrons had no occasion to go, to Shawmut Street at 6 Shawmut Street. No patron was likely to know of this door. It was kept locked by direction of the defendant, but he ordered the key placed in the lock at seven every evening.

We now come to the story of the fire. A little after ten o'clock on the evening of Saturday, November 28, 1942, the night club was well filled with a crowd of patrons. It was during the busiest season of the year. An important football game in the afternoon had attracted many visitors to Boston. Witnesses were rightly permitted to testify that the dance floor had from eighty to one hundred persons on it, and that it was "very crowded." Witnesses were rightly permitted to give their estimates, derived from their observations, of the number of patrons in various parts of the night club. Upon the evidence it could have been found that at that time there were from two hundred fifty to four hundred persons in the Melody Lounge, from four hundred to five hundred in the main dining room and the Caricature Bar, and two hundred fifty in the Cocktail Lounge. Yet it could have been found that the crowd was no larger than it had been on other Saturday evenings before the defendant was taken ill, and that there had been larger crowds at earlier times. . . .

A bartender in the Melody Lounge noticed that an electric light bulb which was in or near the cocoanut husks of an artificial palm tree in the corner had been turned off and that the corner was dark. He directed a sixteen year old bar boy who was waiting on customers at the tables to cause the bulb to be lighted. A soldier sitting with other persons near the light told the bar boy to leave it unlighted. But the bar boy got a stool, lighted a match in order to see the bulb, turned the bulb in its socket, and thus lighted it. The bar boy blew the match out, and started to walk away. Apparently the flame of the match had ignited the palm tree and that had speedily ignited the low cloth ceiling near it, for both flamed up almost instantly. The fire spread with great rapidity across the upper part of the room, causing much heat. The crowd in the Melody Lounge rushed up the stairs, but the fire preceded them. People got on fire while on the stairway. The fire spread with great speed across the foyer and into the Caricature Bar and the main dining room, and thence into the Cocktail Lounge. Soon after the fire started the lights in the night club went out. The smoke had a peculiar odor. The crowd was panic stricken, and rushed and pushed in every direction through the night club, screaming, and overturning tables and chairs in their attempts to escape.

The door at the head of the Melody Lounge stairway was not opened until firemen broke it down from outside with an axe and found it locked by a key lock, so that the panic bar could not operate. Two dead bodies were found close to it, and a pile of bodies about seven feet from it. The door in the vestibule of the office did not become open, and was barred by the clothing rack. The revolving door soon jammed, but was burst out by the pressure of the crowd. The head waiter and another waiter tried to get open the panic doors from the main dining room to Shawmut Street, and succeeded after some difficulty. The other two doors to Shawmut Street were locked, and were opened by force from outside by firemen and others. Some patrons escaped through them, but many dead bodies were piled up inside them. A considerable number of patrons escaped through the Broadway door, but many died just inside that door. Some employees, and a great number of patrons, died in the fire. Others were taken out of the building with fatal burns and injuries from smoke, and died within a few days.

I. THE PLEADINGS, VERDICTS, AND JUDGMENTS.

The defendant [was] indicted for manslaughter . . . . [The Commonwealth specified] among other things that the alleged misconduct of the defendant consisted in causing or permitting or failing reasonably to prevent defective wiring, the installation of inflammable decorations, the absence of fire doors, the absence of "proper means of egress properly maintained" and "sufficient proper" exits, and overcrowding. . . .

The defendant was found guilty . . . [and] sentenced to imprisonment in the State prison upon each count for a term of not less than twelve years and not more than fifteen years, the first day of said term to be in solitary confinement and the residue at hard labor.

II. THE PRINCIPLES GOVERNING LIABILITY.

The Commonwealth disclaimed any contention that the defendant intentionally killed or injured the persons named in the indictments as victims. It based its case on involuntary manslaughter through wanton or reckless conduct. The judge instructed the jury correctly with respect to the nature of such conduct.

Usually wanton or reckless conduct consists of an affirmative act, like driving an automobile or discharging a firearm, in disregard of probable harmful consequences to another. But where, as in the present case, there is a duty of care for the safety of business visitors invited to premises which the defendant controls, wanton or reckless conduct may consist of intentional failure to take such care in disregard of the probable harmful consequences to them or of their right to care.

To define wanton or reckless conduct so as to distinguish it clearly from negligence and gross negligence is not easy. Sometimes the word "wilful" is prefaced to the words "wanton" and "reckless" in expressing the concept. That only blurs it. Wilful means intentional. In the phrase "wilful, wanton or reckless conduct," if "wilful" modifies "conduct" it introduces something different from wanton or reckless conduct, even though the legal result is the same. Wilfully causing harm is a wrong, but a different wrong from wantonly or recklessly causing harm. If "wilful" modifies "wanton or reckless conduct" its use is accurate. What must be intended is the conduct, not the resulting harm. The words "wanton" and "reckless" are practically synonymous in this connection, although the word "wanton" may contain a suggestion of arrogance or insolence or heartlessness that is lacking in the word "reckless." But intentional conduct to which either word applies is followed by the same legal consequences as though both words applied.

The standard of wanton or reckless conduct is at once subjective and objective. . . . Knowing facts that would cause a reasonable man to know the danger is equivalent to knowing the danger. The judge charged the jury correctly when he said, "To constitute wanton or reckless conduct, as distinguished from mere negligence, grave danger to others must have been apparent, and the defendant must have chosen to run the risk rather than alter his conduct so as to avoid the act or omission which caused the harm. If the grave danger was in fact realized by the defendant, his subsequent voluntary act or omission which caused the harm amounts to wanton or reckless conduct, no matter whether the ordinary man would have realized the gravity of the danger or not. But even if a particular defendant is so stupid [or] so heedless . . . that in fact he did not realize the grave danger, he cannot escape the imputation of wanton or reckless conduct in his dangerous act or omission, if an ordinary normal man under the same circumstances would have realized the gravity of the danger. A man may be reckless within the meaning of the law although he himself thought he was careful."

The essence of wanton or reckless conduct is intentional conduct, by way either of commission or of omission where there is a duty to act, which conduct involves a high degree of likelihood that substantial harm will result to another. . . .

The words "wanton" and "reckless" are thus not merely rhetorical or vituperative expressions used instead of negligent or grossly negligent. They express a difference in the degree of risk and in the voluntary taking of risk so marked, as compared with negligence, as to amount substantially and in the eyes of the law to a difference in kind. For many years this court has been careful to preserve the distinction between negligence and gross negligence, on the one hand, and wanton or reckless conduct on the other. In pleadings as well as in statutes the rule is that "negligence and willful and wanton conduct are so different in kind that words properly descriptive of the one commonly exclude the other."

Notwithstanding language used commonly in earlier cases, and occasionally in later ones, it is now clear in this Commonwealth that at common law conduct does not become criminal until it passes the borders of negligence and gross negligence and enters into the domain of wanton or reckless conduct. There is in Massachusetts at common law no such thing as "criminal negligence." . . .

Judgments affirmed.

QUESTIONS

1. How does the Massachusetts definition of manslaughter compare with the Pennsylvania, MPC, and New York definitions in the statutes that precede the *Welansky* case?

2. Does Massachusetts allow a manslaughter conviction based on negligence?

PROBLEM

6.17 After graduating from law school and passing the bar exam, you are working as counsel to the Judiciary Committee of the Senate of the State of Massachusetts. Assume that *Commonwealth v. Welansky* is currently the controlling case on the definition of "manslaughter" in Massachusetts. The senator who chairs the Judiciary Committee is troubled by the *Welansky* case's imprecision in defining "manslaughter." She wants you to draft a statute to rectify *Welansky's* ambiguities and clarify how manslaughter is defined in Massachusetts. She asks you to write her a short memo on *Welansky* in two parts: (1) In the first part, identify the analytical and logical weaknesses in the opinion by Justice Lummus in *Welansky*; (2) draft a statute that remedies these weaknesses.

Consider the following excerpt:

Inferno at the Cocoanut Grove
"20th Century Memories," Yankee at pps. 49, 125 (Nov. 1998)

On November 28, 1942, a fire at the Cocoanut Grove nightclub in Boston killed 492 persons. Unable to escape because of locked or jammed exit doors, most died from inhaling poisonous gases. Th[is] eyewitness account[] [was] . . . culled from hundreds of responses from readers, whose memories of that terrible night are still fresh.

Like Toothpaste Out of a Tube
JOHN D. QUINN *was on a two-week leave from the Naval Training Center in Newport, Rhode Island. He was in the Melody Lounge with his date, Gerry Whitehead, and their friends Dick and Marion Luby.*

We hadn't been there more than two or three minutes when one side of the room suddenly lit up. Looking to my left, I saw a fake palm tree on fire. At that time, the blaze was about 18 inches high and dangerously close to the red or orange ceiling-to-floor drapes.

I said, "Let's go." Thinking that things would soon be under control, we started up the stairs. A man in a tuxedo (I think he was a bouncer) ran down the stairs past us, holding a fire extinguisher. It must have been only seconds later that the same man rushed up the stairs past us with a look of horror and fear on his blackened face.

With Dick and Marion just ahead of us, Gerry and I were about 12 feet into the corridor beyond the stairs, which led to the dining room, when I felt a tremendous heat on the back of my neck. When I turned around, I saw a sheet of flame that reached from ceiling to stairs and wall to wall. That's the last time I looked back.

When we reached the dining room, Dick and Marion were still ahead of us. They were holding hands. It appeared as though she wanted to go back to the booth to get her new coat. That's the last I ever saw of them, because just then the lights went out.

Just before they went out, I saw to my right a group of people gathered. I remembered that the revolving door was there. Knowing that equal pressure on each side of that door would let nobody through, I had to think of some other way if we were going to get out of there alive.

With the light of the fire behind us, I could just barely make out a group of people to my left, all the way across the dining room, approximately 40 to 50 feet away. That became the target, I told Gerry, "Do exactly as I tell you and don't say anything until we get out."

My thought was to head for the middle of the pack and, with equal pressure from both sides and back, the mob would squeeze us out like toothpaste out of a tube — if indeed there was an opening to get out.

I encircled her waist with my right arm and hand; with my left hand, I kept reaching out in front of her, knocking over tables and chairs and anything else that might slow us down. Once we were in the mob, breathing became extremely difficult, not only from the tremendous pressure of the packed bodies, but also from the black smoke. It seemed Gerry would take a couple of steps then trip over something, presumably a body. Every time she would trip, I would go down on one knee to bring her back up. When I did that, I also had to lift one or more people who had climbed on my back in their desperate effort to get out. I saw two men in tuxedoes trying to, for lack of a better word, swim out. They had climbed up on the backs of people until they reached the heads. Then they would reach forward with one hand, grab some hair, and pull themselves forward, then reach with the other hand and repeat the stroke.

I could feel myself getting weaker and weaker. Between helping Gerry up, the people on my back, and breathing the poisonous smoke, I knew I couldn't last much longer. I was on one knee with my right hand on Gerry's back. I knew I had given it my best shot, and the only thing left for me to do was to push her as hard as I possibly could. As I tensed my muscles for the push, she broke the code of silence with one word: "Air!"

I gathered what little strength I had left and stood up. Just as I reached my feet, the "tube of toothpaste" theory worked. We were squirted out the opening, both of us landing on the hood of a car parked at the curb. I don't remember my feet touching the sidewalk.

As we slid off the hood and turned to face the opening, the only people I saw moving were two men dragging out bodies. To the best of my knowledge, I was the last one out alive . . . .

How Did It Start?

Although investigators blamed a busboy who, while trying to replace a light bulb, struck a match near the paper decorations on the ceiling of the Melody Lounge, former Boston firefighter Charles Kenney of Harwich, Massachusetts, believes the club was rapidly engulfed in flames because of the presence of methyl chloride gas in the cooling system. During the war years, almost all Freon was allocated to the military, and the highly flammable methyl chloride was used as a substitute cooling chemical. According to Kenney, investigators in 1942 mistakenly concluded that the refrigerant was not a factor because they assumed the system was filled with either Freon or sulfur dioxide, both nonflammable substances. Witnesses have recently come forward confirming that the Cocoanut Grove was using methyl chloride in the system that cooled their beer and food that fateful night.

According to news accounts, in February 2003, 100 people died in a nightclub fire in Rhode Island after pyrotechnics for a band performance apparently ignited the flammable soundproofing foam around the stage.[23] In reports of the indictments, the Attorney General of Rhode Island explained that the defendants, who were the club owners and the band's tour manager, "were charged with two types of involuntary manslaughter: one for 'gross negligence,' the other for committing a misdemeanor such as a fire code violation that led to a death."[24] How do these charges compare to those in *Welansky*?

As you read the *Hall* case, which follows, think about how the definition and analysis of "manslaughter" in *Hall* differs from that in *Welansky*. If you were a legislator, which approach to manslaughter would you adopt?

PEOPLE v. HALL
Colorado Supreme Court 999 P.2d 207 (2000)

Justice BENDER delivered the Opinion of the Court.

I. INTRODUCTION

We hold that Nathan Hall must stand trial for the crime of reckless manslaughter. While skiing on Vail mountain, Hall flew off of a knoll and collided with Allen Cobb, who was traversing the slope below Hall. Cobb sustained traumatic brain injuries and died as a result of the collision. The People charged Hall with felony reckless manslaughter.

At a preliminary hearing to determine whether there was probable cause for the felony count, the county court found that Hall's conduct "did not rise to the level of dangerousness" required under Colorado law to uphold a conviction for manslaughter, and the court dismissed the charges. On appeal, the district court affirmed the county court's decision. The district court determined that in order for Hall's conduct to have been reckless, it must have been "at least more likely than not" that death would result. Because the court found that "skiing too fast for the conditions" is not "likely" to cause a another person's death, the court concluded that Hall's conduct did not constitute a "substantial and unjustifiable" risk of death. Thus, the district court affirmed the finding of no probable cause.

The charge of reckless manslaughter requires that a person "recklessly cause[] the death of another person." § 18-3-104(1)(a), 6 C.R.S. (1999). For his conduct to be reckless, the actor must have consciously disregarded a substantial and unjustifiable risk that death could result from his actions. See § 18-1-501(8). We hold that, for the purpose of determining whether a person acted recklessly, a particular result does not have to be more likely than not to occur for the risk to be substantial and unjustifiable. A risk must be assessed by reviewing the particular facts of the individual case and weighing the likelihood of harm and the degree of harm that

---

23. Associated Press, *Three charged in Rhode Island nightclub fire*, http://www.kvia.com/Global/story.asp?S=1557764&na v=AbC0JZvP (accessed May 25, 2003).
    24. *Id.*

would result if it occurs. Whether an actor consciously disregarded such a risk may be inferred from circumstances such as the actor's knowledge and experience, or from what a similarly situated reasonable person would have understood about the risk under the particular circumstances.

We hold that under the particular circumstances of this case, whether Hall committed the crime of reckless manslaughter must be determined by the trier of fact. Viewed in the light most favorable to the prosecution, Hall's conduct — skiing straight down a steep and bumpy slope, back on his skis, arms out to his sides, off-balance, being thrown from mogul to mogul, out of control for a considerable distance and period of time, and at such a high speed that the force of the impact between his ski and the victim's head fractured the thickest part of the victim's skull — created a substantial and unjustifiable risk of death to another person. A reasonable person could infer that the defendant, a former ski racer trained in skier safety, consciously disregarded that risk. For the limited purposes of a preliminary hearing, the prosecution provided sufficient evidence to show probable cause that the defendant recklessly caused the victim's death. Thus, we reverse the district court's finding of no probable cause and we remand the case to that court for trial.

II. FACTS AND PROCEDURAL HISTORY

On April 20, 1997, the last day of the ski season, Hall worked as a ski lift operator on Vail mountain. When he finished his shift and after the lifts closed, Hall skied down toward the base of the mountain. The slopes were not crowded.

On the lower part of a run called "Riva Ridge," just below where the trail intersects with another called "North Face Catwalk," Hall was skiing very fast, ski tips in the air, his weight back on his skis, with his arms out to his sides to maintain balance. He flew off of a knoll and saw people below him, but he was unable to stop or gain control because of the moguls.

Hall then collided with Cobb, who had been traversing the slope below Hall. The collision caused major head and brain injuries to Cobb, killing him. Cobb was taken to Vail Valley Medical Center, where efforts to resuscitate him failed. Hall's blood alcohol level was .009, which is less than the limit for driving while ability impaired. A test of Hall's blood for illegal drugs was negative.

The People charged Hall with manslaughter (a class 4 felony) and misdemeanor charges that are not relevant to this appeal. At the close of the prosecution's case at the preliminary hearing, the People requested that, with respect to the manslaughter count, the court consider the lesser-included charge of criminally negligent homicide (a class 5 felony).

The county court held a preliminary hearing to determine whether there was probable cause to support the felony charges against Hall. At the preliminary hearing, the People presented testimony from an eyewitness, the coroner who conducted the autopsy on Cobb's body, an investigator from the District Attorney's office, and the detective who investigated the accident for the Eagle County Sheriff's department.

Judge Buck Allen, who serves as a judge for several mountain towns and lives in Vail, testified that he is an expert skier and familiar with Vail's slopes. He was making a final run for the day when he first noticed Hall on the slope. Allen was on part of the run called "Lower Riva," which is just below the "North Face Catwalk." From that part of the slope, Allen had a direct line of sight to the bottom of the run. Allen said that he could see other skiers traversing the slope below him at least from their waists up and that there were no blind spots on that part of the run.

Hall passed Allen skiing "at a fairly high rate of speed." Allen estimated that Hall was skiing about three times as fast as he was. Allen stated that Hall was "sitting back" on his skis, tips in the air, with his arms out to his sides in an effort to maintain his balance. Hall was skiing straight down the fall line; that is, he was skiing straight down the slope of the mountain without turning from side-to-side or traversing the slope. Hall "bounded off the bumps as he went," and "the terrain was controlling [Hall]" rather than the other way around. In Allen's opinion, Hall was skiing too fast for the skill level he demonstrated, and Hall was out of control "if you define 'out of control' as [not] being able to stop or avoid someone." Although he watched Hall long enough to note Hall's unsafe skiing — approximately two or three seconds — Allen did not see the collision.

Detective McWilliam investigated the collision for the Eagle County Sheriff's office. McWilliam testified that Deputy Mossness said that while Hall could not remember the collision, Hall admitted that as he flew off a knoll and looked down, he saw people below him but could not stop because of the bumps:

Mr. Hall told [the deputy] that he had been skiing that day, he was an employee of Vail Associates. That he was coming down the mountain and that he — he said he flew off of a knoll, looked down and saw some people below him down the slope, tried to slow down, and that because of the bumps, he wasn't able to stop. And he doesn't remember beyond that point. But he was told that somebody — that he had collided with someone.

McWilliam testified that he interviewed Jonathan Cherin, an eyewitness to the collision between Hall and Cobb. Cherin stated that he saw Hall skiing straight down the slope at a high speed and out of control. He said that Cobb, who appeared to be an inexperienced skier, traversed the slope below Hall when Hall hit some bumps, became airborne, and struck Cobb.

McWilliam testified that Deputy Bishop, an officer on the scene, told McWilliam about the observations of other witnesses to the collision. Bruce Yim said that Hall was skiing too fast, that he was out of control, and that Hall collided with Cobb as Cobb traversed the slope. Loic Lemaner, who was skiing below Cobb at the time of the collision, saw Hall after the collision. Lemaner said that after the collision, Hall struck Lemaner's skis and poles, breaking one of Lemaner's poles in half.

McWilliam said that the trail was 156 feet across at the point of the collision. Cobb's body came to rest slightly to the right of the center of the slope. Hall came to rest in the center of the trail, approximately eighty-three feet below Cobb's body.

Upon cross-examination, McWilliam testified that in eleven years' experience in Eagle County, he was aware of two other collisions between skiers on Vail mountain that resulted in the death of a skier. McWilliam said that deaths on Vail mountain from such collisions are rare.

Sandberg, an investigator for the District Attorney's office, testified that he spoke with Mark Haynes, who had been Hall's high school ski coach. Haynes told Sandberg that in the years he coached Hall, Hall was one of the top two or three skiers on the team and that Hall was "talented and aggressive." Haynes said that Hall participated in slalom and giant slalom races when he was in high school. Haynes taught his skiers to ski safely and under control.

Dr. Ben Galloway, the coroner who performed the autopsy on Cobb's body, testified that Cobb died from a single and traumatic blow to his head that fractured his skull and caused severe brain injuries. The coroner said that the injury was consistent with the impact from an object, such as a ski, striking Cobb's head on a perpendicular plane. In addition to the skull fractures and brain injuries, Cobb had a contusion or bruise around his right eye and had an abrasion across his nose. Although he noted the effects of the failed resuscitation efforts, Galloway saw no signs of trauma to any other parts of Cobb's body, indicating that Cobb's head was the sole area of contact.

Galloway testified that Hall struck Cobb just below his right ear, in an area of the skull where the bones are thickest and "it takes more force to fracture those areas" than other areas of the skull. Galloway described the injury as an "extensive basal skull fracture" with "components" or smaller fractures that extended from the major fracture. The damage to Cobb's skull resulted in "contusions or bruises" on Cobb's brain, a subdural hemorrhage near the brain stem, and "marked swelling of the brain due to cerebral edema." This trauma to Cobb's brain led to cardiorespiratory failure, the cause of Cobb's death. Galloway noted that as a result of the bleeding from Cobb's brain, Cobb aspirated blood into his lungs, "which certainly compromised his ability to breathe." Galloway found that the severe head injury was the sole cause of Cobb's death.

Galloway testified that "it would take considerable force" to cause such an injury: . . .

> In my experience in my practice spanning some 25 years, you most commonly see this type of fracturing when someone is thrown out of an automobile or a moving vehicle and sustains a basal skull fracture.

Following the presentation of these witnesses, the county court considered whether there was sufficient evidence to find probable cause that Hall recklessly caused Cobb's death. The county court reviewed other Colorado manslaughter cases where courts found substantial and unjustified risks of death resulting from conduct such as firing a gun at a person or kicking an unconscious person in the head. The court found that Hall's conduct — which the court characterized as skiing "too fast for the conditions" — did not involve a substantial and unjustifiable risk of death and "does not rise to the level of dangerousness required under the current case law" to sustain a count of manslaughter. Because Hall's conduct did not, in the court's view, involve a substantial and unjustifiable risk of death, the court found that the prosecution failed to provide sufficient proof that Hall acted recklessly. The county court therefore dismissed the manslaughter count.

The prosecution appealed the county court's decision to the district court pursuant to Crim. P. 5(a)(4)(IV). The district court agreed with the county court that the prosecution failed to establish probable cause. The court held that Hall's conduct did not involve a substantial risk of death because any risk created by Hall had a less than fifty percent chance of causing another's death . . . .

The People petitioned this court pursuant to C.A.R. 49, and we granted certiorari to consider the following:

> (1) Whether the district court erred by establishing "more likely than not" as the level of substantial risk of death that a defendant must disregard for a finding of probable cause that he caused the death of another recklessly; and
> (2) Whether the district court reviewed the wrong criteria and neglected the evidence relating specifically to this case in affirming the county court's dismissal of a manslaughter charge at preliminary hearing.

III. Discussion . . .

B. Manslaughter and Recklessness . . .

To demonstrate that Hall committed the crime of manslaughter, the prosecution must provide sufficient evidence to show that the defendant's conduct was reckless. Thus, we focus on describing the mental state of recklessness and determining whether Hall's conduct meets that definition.

As Colorado's criminal code defines recklessness, "A person acts recklessly when he consciously disregards a substantial and unjustifiable risk that a result will occur or a that circumstance exists." § 18-1-501(8). Thus, in the case of manslaughter, the prosecution must show that the defendant's conduct caused the death of another and that the defendant:

1) consciously disregarded
2) a substantial and
3) unjustifiable risk that he would
4) cause the death of another.

We examine these elements in detail.

Substantial and Unjustifiable Risk

To show that a person acted recklessly, the prosecution must establish that the person's conduct created a "substantial and unjustifiable" risk. The district court construed some of our earlier cases as requiring that the risk of death be "at least more likely than not" to constitute a substantial and unjustifiable risk of death. In interpreting our cases, the court relied on an erroneous definition of a "substantial and unjustifiable" risk. Whether a risk is substantial must be determined by assessing both the likelihood that harm will occur and the magnitude of the harm should it occur. We hold that whether a risk is unjustifiable must be determined by assessing the nature and purpose of the actor's conduct relative to how substantial the risk is. Finally, in order for conduct to be reckless, the risk must be of such a nature that its disregard constitutes a gross deviation from the standard of care that a reasonable person would exercise.

A risk does not have to be "more likely than not to occur" or "probable" in order to be substantial. A risk may be substantial even if the chance that the harm will occur is well below fifty percent. Some risks may be substantial even if they carry a low degree of probability because the magnitude of the harm is potentially great. For example, if a person holds a revolver with a single bullet in one of the chambers, points the gun at another's head and pulls the trigger, then the risk of death is substantial even though the odds that death will result are no better than one in six. As one court remarked,

> If the potential of a risk is death, that risk is always serious. Therefore, only some likelihood that death will occur might create for most people a "substantial and unjustifiable" risk. . . .

State v. Standiford, 769 P.2d 254, 263 n.9 (Utah 1988) . . . . Conversely, a relatively high probability that a very minor harm will occur probably does not involve a "substantial" risk. Thus, in order to determine whether a risk is substantial, the court must consider both the likelihood that harm will occur and the magnitude of potential harm, mindful that a risk may be "substantial" even if the odds of the harm occurring are lower than fifty percent.

Whether a risk is substantial is a matter of fact that will depend on the specific circumstances of each case. Some conduct almost always carries a substantial risk of death, such as engaging another person in a fight with a deadly weapon or firing a gun at another. In such instances, the substantiality of the risk may be evident from the nature of the defendant's conduct and the court will not have to examine the specific facts in detail.

Other conduct requires a greater inquiry into the facts of the case to determine whether it creates a substantial risk of death. . . .

As well as being substantial, a risk must be unjustifiable in order for a person's conduct to be reckless. Whether a risk is justifiable is determined by weighing the nature and purpose of the actor's conduct against the risk created by that conduct. If a person consciously disregards a substantial risk of death but does so in order to advance an interest that justifies such a risk, the conduct is not reckless. For example, if a surgeon performs an operation on a patient that has a seventy-five percent chance of killing the patient, but the patient will certainly die without the operation, then the conduct is justified and thus not reckless even though the risk is substantial.

In addition to the separate analyses that are applied to determine whether a risk is both "substantial" and "unjustified," the concept of a "substantial and unjustifiable risk" implies a risk that constitutes a gross deviation from the standard of care that a reasonable law-abiding person would exercise under the circumstances. . . . A substantial and unjustifiable risk must constitute a "gross deviation" from the reasonable standard of care in order to justify the criminal sanctions imposed for criminal negligence or reckless conduct, as opposed to the kind of deviation from the reasonable standard of care that results in civil liability for ordinary negligence.

Whether a risk is substantial and unjustified is a question of fact. Hence, at trial, the trier of fact must determine whether the facts presented prove beyond a reasonable doubt that the risk was substantial and unjustified. In the limited context of a preliminary hearing, the court must determine whether a risk was substantial and unjustified by considering the evidence presented in the light most favorable to the prosecution, and the court must ask whether a reasonable person could "entertain" the belief — though not necessarily conclude beyond a reasonable doubt — that the defendant's conduct was reckless based on that evidence.

Conscious Disregard

In addition to showing that a person created a substantial and unjustifiable risk, the prosecution must demonstrate that the actor "consciously disregarded" the risk in order to prove that she acted recklessly. A person acts with a conscious disregard of the risk created by her conduct when she is aware of the risk and chooses to act despite that risk. In contrast to acting "intentionally" or "knowingly," the actor does not have to intend the result or be "practically certain" that the result will occur, he only needs to be "aware" that the risk exists.

Although recklessness is a less culpable mental state than intentionally or knowingly, it involves a higher level of culpability than criminal negligence. Criminal negligence requires that, "through a gross deviation from the standard of care that a reasonable person would exercise," the actor fails to perceive a substantial and unjustifiable risk that a result will occur or a circumstance exists. An actor is criminally negligent when he should have been aware of the risk but was not, while recklessness requires that the defendant actually be aware of the risk but disregard it. Thus, even if she should be, a person who is not actually aware that her conduct creates a substantial and unjustifiable risk is not acting recklessly.

A court or trier of fact may infer a person's subjective awareness of a risk from the particular facts of a case, including the person's particular knowledge or expertise. . . .

In addition to the actor's knowledge and experience, a court may infer the actor's subjective awareness of a risk from what a reasonable person would have understood under the circumstances. When a court infers the defendant's subjective awareness of a risk from what a reasonable person in the circumstances would have known, the court may consider the perspective of a reasonable person in the situation and with the knowledge and training of the actor. Although a court can infer what the defendant actually knew based on what a reasonable person would have known in the circumstances, a court must not confuse what a reasonable person would have known in the circumstances with what the defendant actually knew. See *id.* Thus, if a defendant engaged in conduct that a reasonable person would have understood as creating a substantial and unjustifiable risk of death, the court may infer that the defendant was subjectively aware of that risk, but the court cannot hold the defendant responsible if she were actually unaware of a risk that a reasonable person would have perceived.

Hence, in a reckless manslaughter case, the prosecution must prove that the defendant acted despite his subjective awareness of a substantial and unjustifiable risk of death from his conduct. Because absent an admission by the defendant such awareness cannot be proven directly, the court or trier of fact may infer the defendant's awareness of the risk from circumstances such as the defendant's training, knowledge, and prior experiences, or from what a reasonable person would have understood under the circumstances.

Risk of Death

The final element of recklessness requires that the actor consciously disregard a substantial and unjustifiable risk of a particular result, and in the case of manslaughter the actor must risk causing death to another person. The risk can be a risk of death to another generally; the actor does not have to risk death to a specific individual. Because the element of a "substantial and unjustifiable risk" measures the likelihood and magnitude of the risk disregarded by the actor, any risk of death will meet the requirement that the actor, by his conduct, risks death to another. That is, only a slight risk of death to another person is necessary to meet this element.

IV. APPLICATION OF LEGAL PRINCIPLES TO HALL'S CONDUCT . . .

The district court's conclusion that Hall's conduct did not represent a substantial and unjustifiable risk of death rested on an erroneous construction of recklessness. Relying on two of our earlier cases, the court found that for a risk to be "substantial" it must "be at least more likely than not that death would result." As discussed, a risk of death that has less than a fifty percent chance of occurring may nonetheless be a substantial risk depending on the circumstances of the particular case. Because the district court applied a flawed interpretation of the law, we hold that the district court's assessment of probable cause was in error. . . .

We first ask whether the prosecution presented sufficient evidence to show that Hall's conduct created a substantial and unjustifiable risk of death. Like other activities that generally do not involve a substantial risk of death, such as driving a car or installing a heater, "skiing too fast for the conditions" is not widely considered behavior that constitutes a high degree of risk. However, we hold that the specific facts in this case support a reasonable inference that Hall created a substantial and unjustifiable risk that he would cause another's death.

Several witnesses stated that Hall was skiing very fast. Allen and the other eyewitnesses all said that Hall was travelling too fast for the conditions, at an excessive rate of speed, and that he was out of control. Allen said that Hall passed him on the slope travelling three times faster than Allen, himself an expert skier. Sandberg presented testimony that Hall was a ski racer, indicating that Hall was trained to attain and ski at much faster speeds than even skilled and experienced recreational skiers. The witnesses said that Hall was travelling straight down the slope at such high speeds that, because of his lack of control, he would not have been able to stop or avoid another person.

In addition to statements of witnesses, the nature of Cobb's injuries and other facts of the collision support the inference that Hall was skiing at an inordinately high speed when he struck Cobb. . . . Thus, based on the testimony of the witnesses and the coroner's examination of Cobb's body, a reasonable person could conclude that Hall was skiing at very high speeds, thereby creating a risk of serious injury or death in the event of a skier-to-skier collision.

In addition to Hall's excessive speed, Hall was out of control and unable to avoid a collision with another person. . . . [A] reasonably prudent person could have concluded that Hall was unable to anticipate or avoid a potential collision with a skier on the trail below him.

While skiing ordinarily carries a very low risk of death to other skiers, a reasonable person could have concluded that Hall's excessive speed, lack of control, and improper technique for skiing bumps significantly increased both the likelihood that a collision would occur and the extent of the injuries that might result from such a collision, including the possibility of death, in the event that a person like Cobb unwittingly crossed Hall's downhill path. McWilliam testified that he was aware of only two other deaths from skier collisions on Vail mountain in the past eleven years, but a reasonable person could have determined that Hall's conduct was precisely the type of skiing that risked this rare result.

We next ask whether a reasonable person could have concluded that Hall's creation of a substantial risk of death was unjustified. To the extent that Hall's extremely fast and unsafe skiing created a risk of death, Hall was serving no direct interest other than his own enjoyment. . . .

In addition to our conclusion that a reasonable person could have entertained the belief that Hall's conduct created a substantial and unjustifiable risk, we must ask whether Hall's conduct constituted a "gross deviation" from the standard of care that a reasonable law-abiding person (in this case, a reasonable, law-abiding, trained ski racer and resort employee) would have observed in the circumstances.

As we noted, the nature of the sport involves moments of high speeds and temporary losses of control. See also § 33-44-102 (recognizing "the dangers that inhere in the sport of skiing"). However, the General Assembly imposed upon a skier the duty to avoid collisions with any person or object below him. See § 33-44-109(2).[14]

---

[14] Section 33-44-109(2) states:

Each skier has the duty to maintain control of his speed and course at all times when skiing and to maintain a proper lookout so as to be able to avoid other skiers and objects. However, the primary duty shall be on the person skiing downhill to avoid collision with any person or objects below him.

Although this statute may not form the basis of criminal liability, it establishes the minimum standard of care for uphill skiers and, for the purposes of civil negligence suits, creates a rebuttable presumption that the skier is at fault whenever he collides with skiers on the slope below him. A violation of a skier's duty in an extreme fashion, such as here, may be evidence of conduct that constitutes a "gross deviation" from the standard of care imposed by statute for civil negligence. Hall admitted to Deputy Mossness that as he flew off a knoll, he saw people below him but was unable to stop; Hall was travelling so fast and with so little control that he could not possibly have respected his obligation to avoid skiers below him on the slope. Additionally, Hall skied in this manner for some time over a considerable distance, demonstrating that his high speeds and lack of control were not the type of momentary lapse of control or inherent danger associated with skiing. Based on the evidence, a reasonable person could conclude that Hall's conduct was a gross deviation from the standard of care that a reasonable, experienced ski racer would have exercised knowing that other people were on the slope in front of him and that he could not see the area below the knolls and bumps over which he was jumping.

Having determined that Hall's conduct created a substantial and unjustified risk of death that is a gross deviation from the reasonable standard of care under the circumstances, we next ask whether a reasonably prudent person could have entertained the belief that Hall consciously disregarded that risk. Hall is a trained ski racer who had been coached about skiing in control and skiing safely. Further, he was an employee of a ski area and had a great deal of skiing experience. Hall's knowledge and training could give rise to the reasonable inference that he was aware of the possibility that by skiing so fast and out of control he might collide with and kill another skier unless he regained control and slowed down. . . .

Although the risk that he would cause the death of another was probably slight, Hall's conduct created a risk of death. Hall's collision with Cobb involved enough force to kill Cobb and to simulate the type of head injury associated with victims in car accidents. Even though it is a rare occurrence, the court heard testimony that two skiers in the past eleven years died on Vail mountain alone from skier-to-skier collisions. Based on the evidence presented at the preliminary hearing, a reasonable person could conclude that Hall's conduct involved a risk of death.

Thus, interpreting the facts presented in the light most favorable to the prosecution, we hold that a reasonably prudent and cautious person could have entertained the belief that Hall consciously disregarded a substantial and unjustifiable risk that by skiing exceptionally fast and out of control he might collide with and kill another person on the slope.

Obviously, this opinion does not address whether Hall is ultimately guilty of any crime. Rather, we hold only that the People presented sufficient evidence to establish probable cause that Hall committed reckless manslaughter, and the court should have bound Hall's case over for trial.

QUESTIONS

1. How does the mental state standard in *Hall* differ from that in *Welansky*? Which is preferable? Why?

2. How might Hall's conviction affect the behavior of skiers in Colorado? Of resort operators?

D. NEGLIGENT KILLING

The type of negligence that the criminal law requires for a negligent homicide commonly exceeds simple or ordinary negligence, the kind that may give rise to tort liability in a civil law suit. Such negligence is often termed "gross negligence." Some jurisdictions do, however, impose homicide liability based on simple or ordinary negligence. Should negligent killing ever be a criminal offense? Or should liability for negligent killing be limited to civil money damages? What are the comparative advantages and disadvantages of criminal and civil liability as a deterrent to negligent killing?

STATE *v.* WILLIAMS
Court of Appeals of Washington 4 Wash. App. 908 (1971)

HOROWITZ, Chief Judge.

Defendants, husband and wife, were charged by information filed October 3, 1968, with the crime of manslaughter for negligently failing to supply their 17-month child with necessary medical attention, as a result of which he died on September 12, 1968. Upon entry of findings, conclusions and judgment of guilty, sentences were imposed on April 22, 1969. Defendants appeal.

The defendant husband, Walter Williams, is a 24-year-old full-blooded Sheshont Indian with a sixth-grade education. His sole occupation is that of laborer. The defendant wife, Bernice Williams, is a 20-year-old part Indian with an 11th grade education. At the time of the marriage, the wife had two children, the younger of whom was a 14-month-old son. Both parents worked and the children were cared for by the 85-year-old mother of the defendant husband. The defendant husband assumed parental responsibility with the defendant wife to provide clothing, care and medical attention for the child. Both defendants possessed a great deal of love and affection for the defendant wife's young son.

The court expressly found:

> That both defendants were aware that William Joseph Tabafunda was ill during the period September 1, 1968 to September 12, 1968. The defendants were ignorant. They did not realize how sick the baby was. They thought that the baby had a toothache and no layman regards a toothache as dangerous to life. They loved the baby and gave it aspirin in hopes of improving its condition. They did not take the baby to a doctor because of fear that the Welfare Department would take the baby away from them. They knew that medical help was available because of previous experience. They had no excuse that the law will recognize for not taking the baby to a doctor.

The defendants Walter L. Williams and Bernice J. Williams were negligent in not seeking medical attention for William Joseph Tabafunda.

That as a proximate result of this negligence, William Joseph Tabafunda died. . . .

From these and other findings, the court concluded that the defendants were each guilty of the crime of manslaughter as charged. . . .

Defendants take no exception to findings but contend that the findings do not support the conclusions that the defendants are guilty of manslaughter as charged. . . .

Parental duty to provide medical care for a dependent minor child was recognized at common law and characterized as a natural duty. In Washington, the existence of the duty is commonly assumed and is stated at times without reference to any particular statute. The existence of the duty also is assumed, but not always defined, in statutes that provide special criminal and civil sanctions for the performance of that duty. . . . [A]t common law, in the case of involuntary manslaughter, the breach [of the duty to provide medical care] had to amount to more than mere ordinary or simple negligence — gross negligence was essential. In Washington, however, RCW 9.48.060[2] (since amended by Laws of 1970, ch. 49, § 2) and RCW 9.48.1503 supersede both voluntary and involuntary manslaughter as those crimes were defined at common law. Under these statutes the crime is deemed committed even though the death of the victim is the proximate result of only simple or ordinary negligence.

The concept of simple or ordinary negligence describes a failure to exercise the "ordinary caution" necessary to make out the defense of excusable homicide. RCW 9.48.150.[3] Ordinary caution is the kind of caution that a man of reasonable prudence would exercise under the same or similar conditions. If, therefore, the conduct of a defendant, regardless of his ignorance, good intentions and good faith, fails to measure up to the conduct required of a man of reasonable prudence, he is guilty of ordinary negligence because of his failure to use "ordinary caution." If such negligence proximately causes the death of the victim, the defendant, as pointed out above, is guilty of statutory manslaughter. . . .

In the instant case . . . the defendant husband is not the father of the minor child, nor has he adopted that child. Nevertheless, the evidence shows that he had assumed responsibility with his wife for the care and maintenance of the child, whom he greatly loved. Such assumption of responsibility, characterized in the information as that required of a "guardian and custodian," is sufficient to impose upon him the duty to furnish necessary medical care.

The remaining issue of proximate cause requires consideration of the question of when the duty to furnish medical care became activated. If the duty to furnish such care was not activated until after it was too late to save the life of the child, failure to furnish medical care could not be said to have proximately caused the child's death. Timeliness in the furnishing of medical care also must be considered in terms of "ordinary caution." The law does not mandatorily require that a doctor be called for a child at the first sign of any indisposition or illness. The indisposition or illness may appear to be of a minor or very temporary kind, such as a toothache or cold. If one in the exercise of ordinary caution fails to recognize that his child's symptoms require medical attention, it cannot be said that the failure to obtain such medical attention is a breach of the duty owed. In our opinion, the duty as formulated in *People v. Pierson*, 176 N.Y. 201, 68 N.E. 243 (1903) . . . properly defines the duty contemplated by our manslaughter statutes RCW 9.48.060 and RCW 9.48.150. The court there said:

> We quite agree that the Code does not contemplate the necessity of calling a physician for every trifling complaint with which the child may be afflicted which in most instances may be overcome by the ordinary household nursing by members

---

[2] RCW 9.48.060 provided in part: "In any case other than those specified in RCW 9.48.030, 9.48.040 and 9.48.050, homicide, not being excusable or justifiable, is manslaughter."

[3] RCW 9.48.150 provides: "Homicide is excusable when committed by accident or misfortune in doing any lawful act by lawful means, with ordinary caution and without any unlawful intent."

of the family; that a reasonable amount of discretion is vested in parents, charged with the duty of maintaining and bringing up infant children; and that the standard is at what time would an ordinarily prudent person, solicitous for the welfare of his child and anxious to promote its recovery, deem it necessary to call in the services of a physician.

It remains to apply the law discussed to the facts of the instant case. . . .

Dr. Gale Wilson, the autopsy surgeon and chief pathologist for the King County Coroner, testified that the child died because an abscessed tooth had been allowed to develop into an infection of the mouth and cheeks, eventually becoming gangrenous. This condition, accompanied by the child's inability to eat, brought about malnutrition, lowering the child's resistance and eventually producing pneumonia, causing the death. Dr. Wilson testified that in his opinion the infection had lasted for approximately 2 weeks, and that the odor generally associated with gangrene would have been present for approximately 10 days before death. He also expressed the opinion that had medical care been first obtained in the last week before the baby's death, such care would have been obtained too late to have saved the baby's life. Accordingly, the baby's apparent condition between September 1 and September 5, 1968 became the critical period for the purpose of determining whether in the exercise of ordinary caution defendants should have provided medical care for the minor child.

The testimony concerning the child's apparent condition during the critical period is not crystal clear, but is sufficient to warrant the following statement of the matter. The defendant husband testified that he noticed the baby was sick about 2 weeks before the baby died. The defendant wife testified that she noticed the baby was ill about a week and a half or 2 weeks before the baby died. The evidence showed that in the critical period the baby was fussy; that he could not keep his food down; and that a cheek started swelling up. The swelling went up and down, but did not disappear. In that same period, the cheek turned "a bluish color like." The defendants, not realizing that the baby was as ill as it was or that the baby was in danger of dying, attempted to provide some relief to the baby by giving the baby aspirin during the critical period and continued to do so until the night before the baby died. The defendants thought the swelling would go down and were waiting for it to do so; and defendant husband testified, that from what he had heard, neither doctors nor dentists pull out a tooth "when it's all swollen up like that." There was an additional explanation for not calling a doctor given by each defendant. Defendant husband testified that "the way the cheek looked, . . . and that stuff on his hair, they would think we were neglecting him and take him away from us and not give him back." Defendant wife testified that the defendants were "waiting for the swelling to go down," and also that they were afraid to take the child to a doctor for fear that the doctor would report them to the welfare department, who, in turn, would take the child away. "It's just that I was so scared of losing him." They testified that they had heard that the defendant husband's cousin lost a child that way. The evidence showed that the defendants did not understand the significance or seriousness of the baby's symptoms. However, there is no evidence that the defendants were physically or financially unable to obtain a doctor, or that they did not know an available doctor, or that the symptoms did not continue to be a matter of concern during the critical period. Indeed, the evidence shows that in April 1968 defendant husband had taken the child to a doctor for medical attention.

In our opinion, there is sufficient evidence from which the court could find, as it necessarily did, that applying the standard of ordinary caution, *i.e.*, the caution exercisable by a man of reasonable prudence under the same or similar conditions, defendants were sufficiently put on notice concerning the symptoms of the baby's illness and lack of improvement in the baby's apparent condition in the period from September 1 to September 5, 1968 to have required them to have obtained medical care for the child. The failure so to do in this case is ordinary or simple negligence, and such negligence is sufficient to support a conviction of statutory manslaughter.

The judgment is affirmed.

QUESTIONS

1. Were Walter and Bernice Williams blameworthy? Were their actions dangerous? What if their failure to recognize the baby's condition was the result of lack of medical sophistication? Or lack of education?

2. Would Walter and Bernice Williams have had a better chance of acquittal under the Model Penal Code's definition of "negligence"? Why?

Consider the following excerpt in evaluating whether the parents in the *Williams* case were negligent:[25]

William Byler, *Removing Children: The Destruction of American Indian Families*, 9 Civil Rights 19 (Summer 1977).

Surveys of States with large Indian populations conducted by the Association on American Indian Affairs (AAIA) in 1969 and again in 1974 indicate that approximately 25-35 percent of all Indian children are separated from their families and placed in foster homes, adoptive homes, or institutions. . . .

The disparity in placement rates for Indian[s] and non-Indians is shocking. . . . In the state of Washington, the Indian adoption rate is 19 times greater and the foster care rate ten times greater [than for non-Indians]. . . .

How are we to account for this disastrous situation? The reasons appear very complex. . . . [They] include a lack of rational federal and state standards governing child welfare matters, a breakdown in due process, economic incentives, and the harsh social conditions in so many Indian communities. . . .

Very few Indian children are removed from their families on the grounds of physical abuse. One study of a North Dakota reservation showed that these grounds were advanced in only 1 per cent of the cases. . . .

In judging the fitness of a particular family, many social workers, ignorant of Indian cultural values and social norms, . . . frequently discover neglect or abandonment where none exists.

For example, the dynamics of the Indian extended families are largely misunderstood. An Indian child may have scores of, perhaps more than a hundred, relatives who are counted as close, responsible members of the family. Many social workers . . . consider leaving the child with persons outside the nuclear family as neglect and thus as grounds for terminating parental rights. . . .

[In one case,] social workers asserted . . . , although they had no evidence that the mother was unfit, it was their belief that an Indian reservation is an unsuitable environment for a child and that the pre-adoptive parents were financially able to provide a home and a way of life superior to the one furnished by the natural mother. . . .

25. We express here our appreciation to Professors John Kaplan and Robert Weisberg. It was through an early edition of their text that we became acquainted with the materials from Willam Byler and the Indian Child Welfare Act.

The abusive actions of social workers would largely be nullified if more judges were themselves knowledgeable about Indian life and required a sharper definition of standards of child abuse and neglect. . . .

It is an unfortunate fact of life for many Indian parents that the primary service agency to which they must turn for financial help also exercises police powers over their family life and is, most frequently, the agency that initiates custody proceedings. . . .

Congress recognized the concerns raised in William Byler's work and enacted the Indian Child Welfare Act of 1978, 25 U.S.C. §§ 1901-1963, to address unwarranted removal of children from American Indian homes and the failure to place children with families that share the values of Indian culture.

In particular, the Act acknowledged

that an alarmingly high percentage of Indian families are broken up by the removal, often unwarranted, of their children from them by nontribal public and private agencies and that an alarmingly high percentage of such children are placed in non-Indian foster and adoptive homes and institutions; and . . . that the States . . . have often failed to recognize the essential tribal relations of Indian people and the cultural and social standards prevailing in Indian communities and families. 25 U.S.C. § 1901(4), (5) (1990). [The Act aimed to establish] minimum Federal standards for the removal of Indian children from their families and the placement of such children in foster or adoptive homes which will reflect the unique values of Indian culture . . . . *Id.* at § 1902.

Reconsider *Williams.* Does the additional information from William Byler and the Indian Child Welfare Act affect your assessment of negligence? If so, how? If not, why not?

1. The Model Penal Code Approach to Negligent Killing

The Model Penal Code provision on negligent killing reads as follows:

§ 210.4   *Negligent Homicide*

(1) Criminal homicide constitutes negligent homicide when it is committed negligently.

(2) Negligent homicide is a felony of the third degree.

QUESTIONS

1. What type of negligence does the MPC require to satisfy its negligent homicide provision?

2. How does the MPC's definition of "negligence" differ from that in *Williams?*

In the following Problems, would the defendants be held liable under the *Williams* standard? What about that of the MPC?

PROBLEMS

6.18 A construction crew is working at night on a seldom-used road. They have dug a trench to access electrical connections underground. Before their break at 2:00 A.M., they place reflective orange cones around the trench and hang reflective tape from cone to cone so that it encircles the trench at a height of 12 inches. Car headlights would clearly reveal and highlight the reflective tape, warning drivers to beware. A bicyclist cycles by in the dark. When his tire hits the reflective tape, he is thrown into the trench and dies.

6.19 Nathaniel and Alexa have been trying to have a child since they were first married ten years ago. Both believe in a religion that eschews most contemporary medical intervention. Prayer is the only permitted intervention for physical ailments. For ten years, they prayed for a baby. A year ago, Alexa became pregnant. After the baby was born, it began to show signs of cystic fibrosis. As the baby's condition deteriorated, Nathaniel and Alexa and other members of their religion began a 24-hour prayer vigil at the baby's bedside. The baby's condition continued to worsen over the next few days, with the baby turning blue and then dying. After the baby's death, the coroner performed an autopsy and determined that the baby suffocated on the thick mucus secretions that cystic fibrosis caused in the baby's lungs. The coroner determined that the baby's life could have been saved during this episode had the parents taken the baby to a pediatrician, who would have intervened to loosen the mucus through massage or medication and provide adequate oxygen to enable the baby to breathe. With what, if any, crime should Nathaniel and Alexa be charged?

6.20 You are a law clerk working in the district attorney's office. Police incident reports reveal the facts as described below about the deaths of two infants. Your supervisor asks you to provide a memo evaluating whether charges should be filed in each case and describing the charges you considered. Your jurisdiction follows the Model Penal Code. Your supervisor expects that your memo will provide a thorough and balanced evaluation of both the doctrinal and policy implications of your recommendations. Policy considerations here include both those relating to the purposes of punishment and to any strategic considerations that stem from the anticipated jury responses to the incidents.

Incident #1. Ruth gave birth to her daughter, Tabitha, three months ago. The pregnancy was difficult. Ruth developed gestational diabetes during the pregnancy. The pregnancy-related diabetes did not disappear after Tabitha's birth. Instead, it became a life-threatening form of adult onset diabetes. For Ruth, this means that she must inject herself with insulin twice a day and carefully monitor her food and drink consumption. Ruth knows that when she begins feeling weak, she must eat or drink immediately to avoid fainting. On this afternoon, Ruth planned to take Tabitha to the park. Usually, Ruth packs high-carbohydrate energy bars and a high-sugar juice drink in case she feels faint. Today, however, she was running late to meet her friend and her friend's infant daughter at the park. Ruth glanced in the diaper bag before she left and noticed that there was only an empty energy bar wrapper in the space she reserved for the energy bars and juice drinks. Because Ruth had just eaten lunch and planned to stay at the park for only an hour, until Tabitha fell asleep for her afternoon nap, Ruth hurried Tabitha into the rear-facing car seat and drove to the park. Once there, Ruth and her friend played with the babies on the swings and strolled them around the park for an hour. Both babies fell asleep. Ruth and her friend became engaged in conversation. Before Ruth noticed, she had been at the park for two hours. She returned quickly to the car and buckled Tabitha into her car seat. As Ruth drove toward home, she began to feel weak. She parked in the driveway and tried to hurry into the house. It was too late. She had waited too long and she fainted just inside the front door. Four hours later, Ruth's husband arrived to find Tabitha in her car seat, dead from heat exposure. Ruth's husband was able to revive Ruth. Ruth recovered. The police have asked that your supervisor issue criminal charges against Ruth for the death of Tabitha. The incident occurred on a breezy, partly sunny day. The high temperature was 67 degrees Fahrenheit. All the windows in the car were rolled shut.

Incident #2.   One afternoon, Bob was taking care of his three-month-old daughter, Jillian. In the three months since Jillian was born, Bob had only had sole care of Jillian on one other occasion. Usually, Bob's wife was the primary caretaker of Jillian. Jillian loved to ride in the car as it helped her fall asleep. Because Jillian had been cranky all day, Bob placed Jillian in her rear-facing car seat and drove her all around the town until she fell comfortably asleep. Once she was asleep, Bob called his best friend on his cell phone. Bob's best friend invited Bob to drop by and play cards. Bob agreed. On the way to his best friend's home, Bob stopped at the grocery store and picked up some snacks. Jillian was sleeping so quietly that Bob forgot that she was in the back seat. Bob drove to his best friend's home and parked in the driveway. He headed into the house and played cards for two hours, until he heard a commotion outside. He saw neighbors trying to break the window of his car. He ran outside and opened the car door. The police and an ambulance were called and Jillian was pronounced dead from heat exposure at the scene. The police have asked that your supervisor issue criminal charges against Bob for Jillian's death. It was a breezy, partly sunny day. The high temperature was 67 degrees Fahrenheit. All the windows in the car were shut.

In recent years, parents and other caregivers leaving infants and young children unattended in cars has caused a substantial number of deaths.[26] Sometimes the

---

26. One author reports in a 2002 law review article that "sixty children have died in California as a direct result of being left unattended in or near motor vehicles. These children died as a result of exposure to extreme heat or because they accessed the vehicle's controls and caused the vehicle to move." Jaeson D. White, *Sit Right Here Honey, I'll Be Right Back: The Unattended Child in Motor Vehicle Safety Act*, 33 McGeorge L. Rev. 343 (2002). For a focus specifically on the issue of children's death from hyperthermia, *see* Stephanie Armagost, *An Innocent Mistake or Criminal Conduct: Children Dying of Hyperthermia in Hot Vehicles*, 23 Hamline J. Pub. L. & Poly. 109, 111 (2001) ("Since 1980, Kids 'N Cars, a

parent or caregiver may forget that the child, perhaps buckled into a rear-facing car seat, is in the car. Sometimes the parent or caregiver may leave the child due to failure to recognize that hyperthermia may occur even on a temperate day. In response to preventable car-related tragedies involving children, effective January 2002, California enacted "Kaitlyn's Law." It reads in pertinent part as follows:

California Vehicle Code Annotated § 15620

(a) A parent, legal guardian, or other person responsible for a child who is 6 years of age or younger may not leave that child inside a motor vehicle without being subject to the supervision of a person who is 12 years of age or older, under either of the following circumstances:
　　　(1) Where there are conditions that present a significant risk to the child's health or safety.
　　　(2) When the *vehicle's* engine is running or the vehicle's keys are in the ignition, or both.
(b) A violation of subdivision (a) is an infraction punishable by a fine of one hundred dollars ($100).
(c) Nothing in this section shall preclude prosecution under both this section and . . . [the manslaughter section or the child endangerment sections of the Penal Code], or any other provision of law.

QUESTIONS

1. What arguments might be made for and against Kaitlyn's Law?
2. What mental states does Kaitlyn's Law require?
3. Would the existence of a statute such as Kaitlyn's Law affect the assessment of liability in Problem 6.20 above?

E. FELONY MURDER

The felony-murder doctrine holds a felon and her accomplices liable for murder when a killing is committed in the perpetration of or attempt to perpetrate a felony. The original common law doctrine was extremely broad. Liability attached even if the killing was accidental or the fatal blow was struck by the intended victim or a police officer responding to the felony. Over time, courts and legislatures contracted the doctrine. We treat felony murder and its misdemeanor parallel, misdemeanor manslaughter, here because they are usually understood to incorporate a strict liability component with respect to the actor's mental state regarding the death.

After an introductory Problem, we begin with the basic felony-murder rule. This first Subsection contrasts West Virginia's relatively broad felony-murder rule in the *Sims* case with Michigan's rejection of the rule in *Aaron.* Following commentary debating the merits of the doctrine, we study five common limitations on felony murder — enumeration, the inherent dangerousness requirement, the merger doctrine, the agency rule, and the res gestae or duration requirement.

---

nonprofit organization that monitors child vehicle-related deaths, has documented 178 cases of heat-related deaths of children in automobiles. Charges were filed in 65 of these cases, and of those, only 26 ended in convictions.")

At the conclusion of these limitations, we examine the Model Penal Code treatment of felony murder. Before turning to misdemeanor manslaughter, we discuss the provocative act doctrine, a particular application of reckless murder that was developed in the context of felony-murder cases. We then consider felony murder's cousin, misdemeanor manslaughter.

PROBLEM

6.21 As a result of a downturn in the local economy, Henry recently lost his job as an associate in a small law firm. To make some much needed cash, Henry has been earning money gardening in yards around town. One day, Henry goes to the back door of the home of the Juarez family, for whom he gardens, to ask a question. Henry notices a bank envelope with a large sum of money on the kitchen table. His rent is due and he feels desperate. Henry tries the kitchen door and finds it unlocked. He walks quietly into the kitchen, intending to take $400, just enough to pay his rent. Just as he steps toward the table and puts his hand on the envelope, he slips and falls on the freshly waxed floor. Mrs. Juarez hears the noise and comes running into the kitchen. She too slips on the waxed floor. Unfortunately, Mrs. Juarez hits her head on a granite counter as she slides to the floor. As a result of the fall, Mrs. Juarez suffers a severe concussion from which she dies a week later. Henry makes a full recovery from his fall.

Is Henry liable for felony murder? The state in which he is prosecuted has the following statute:

> Murder by means of poison, lying in wait, a destructive device, torture, or by any willful, deliberate and premeditated killing, or in the perpetration of, or attempt to perpetrate, arson, kidnapping, sexual assault, robbery, burglary, breaking and entering, or extortion is murder of the first degree. All other murder is murder of the second degree.

> Assume that burglary is defined as "entry into a structure with the intent to commit theft."

---

1. The Basic Rule

STATE *v.* SIMS

Supreme Court of Appeals of West Virginia 162 W. Va. 212 (1978)

MILLER, Justice:

Paul Sims, after pleading guilty to first degree murder, contends that he was coerced into the plea as a result of the trial court's ruling in connection with the felony-murder rule.

The claimed coercion occurred when the trial court ruled preliminarily to the trial that as a matter of law Sims' defense of an accidental discharge of his shotgun during the commission of a burglary would not permit the jury to reduce the crime below first degree murder. We refuse to overturn the guilty plea.

The operative facts are these: Around 2:00 A.M. on January 16, 1976, the defendant Paul Sims, Clay Grimmer and Arthur Burns went to the home of Mr. and Mrs. Oscar Schmidt located in Brooke County, West Virginia. After cutting the telephone wires on the outside of the house, Sims and Burns proceeded onto the front porch of the home. Both men were armed. Sims carried a 20-gauge sawed-off shotgun and Burns had a pistol.

The Schmidts' bedroom adjoined the porch. While Sims remained on the porch adjacent to the windows, his companion Burns broke the windows and stepped through them into the bedroom. Sims pointed his shotgun and a flashlight into the bedroom. Shortly after Burns had entered the bedroom, Walter Schmidt, the son of Oscar Schmidt, entered the bedroom from another portion of the house.

Apparently as a result of this distraction, Oscar Schmidt was able to seize his pistol and fire it at Sims. The bullet struck Sims' right arm, and he claimed this caused an involuntary muscle spasm in his trigger finger which resulted in the discharge of the shotgun, killing Walter Schmidt.

In support of the defendant's theory that the bullet wound caused an involuntary muscle reaction, his attorneys took a deposition from the neurologist who treated him for the injury. Since the doctor was not available for testimony at the trial, the prosecuting and defense attorneys stipulated that his deposition would be read at trial.

Based upon his examination and treatment of the defendant's wound, together with his expert knowledge of the involved nerves and muscles, the doctor concluded it was possible that the bullet wound caused an involuntary muscle reflex resulting in the discharge of the shotgun.

It is to be noted that the State did not agree with the involuntary reflex theory and vigorously cross-examined the doctor, who conceded that the same type of wound might instead have caused the defendant to drop the gun.

The trial court proceeded to rule *in limine* that even assuming the defendant's theory to be true, it would not present a factual defense to mitigate the first degree murder verdict required under this State's felony-murder rule.

I

The issue before us on this direct appeal relates to the voluntariness of the guilty plea based on the theory that the plea was coerced as a result of the court's preliminary ruling that deprived the defendant of a key factual defense. However, the focus is not upon the court's ruling, but the competency of defendant's counsel in advising the guilty plea in light of the court's ruling.

II

[T]he guilty plea in this case can only be invalidated if it can be found that Sims' counsel was not acting with reasonable competency when he advised that an involuntary homicide would not mitigate the crime of felony-murder. There is no dispute that the killing occurred during the course of an attempted burglary. There is also no dispute that the guilty plea was prompted by defendant's belief that he had no defense to the felony-murder crime.

Our inquiry is narrowed to a consideration of whether our felony-murder rule, which by statute makes the crime first degree murder, admits any amelioration from first degree by virtue of the fact that the homicide was accidental.

Our felony-murder statute alters the scope of the common law rule by confining its application to the crimes of arson, rape, robbery and burglary or the attempt to commit such crimes. W.Va. Code, 61-2-1.[5] Traditionally at common law, the commission of, or the attempt to commit, any felony which resulted in a homicide was deemed murder.[6] . . .

Our statute enumerates three broad categories of homicide constituting first degree murder: (1) murder by poison, lying in wait, imprisonment, starving; (2) by any wilful, deliberate and premeditated killing; (3) in the commission of, or attempt to commit, arson, rape, robbery or burglary. . . .

It is defendant's contention that this State's felony-murder statute warrants the conclusion that malice is an element of the crime and that an accidental homicide committed during one of the designated felonies will not invoke the felony-murder rule. The third syllabus of *State ex rel. Peacher v. Sencindiver*, — W.Va. — 233 S.E.2d 425 (1977), is cited as supporting this point. . . .

[But i]n each of [the] . . . cases cited by *Peacher* the courts found that the felony-murder crime historically did not require malice, premeditation or deliberate intent to kill as an element of proof. . . .

[From a review of the law of other jurisdictions, t]wo salient facts emerge. . . . First, in those jurisdictions having felony-murder statutes similar to ours, the courts recognize that their statutes embody the common law concept of the crime of felony-murder. Second, the common law created this substantive crime so as not to include the element that the homicide has to be committed with malice or an intent to kill.

The defendant argues, however, that a literal reading of our statute would suggest that by the use of the term "murder" as the initial subject of the sentence setting out the categories of first degree murder, it was intended that the State must initially prove what amounts to a common law murder before it can invoke the felony-murder rule. Stripping the statute of its other categories of first degree murder, the defendant presents the statute as follows:

"Murder . . . in the commission of, or attempt to commit, arson, rape, robbery or burglary, is murder of the first degree." [Code 61-2-1.]

He submits that this is a fair reading of the third syllabus of *Peacher*. From a purely grammatical standpoint, it would have been better usage to begin the independent clause defining the crime of felony-murder with the term "homicide." However this may be, we do not approach the question of what the statute means as if we were on a maiden voyage and were forced upon uncharted seas without compass or sextant.

The felony-murder rule was a part of our substantive criminal law long before this State was formed. No case, either from this Court or from the Virginia court, has ever broken from the historical common law precedent to suggest that proof of an intentional killing is an element of the felony-murder crime. This principle is

---

[5] "Murder by poison, lying in wait, imprisonment, starving, or by any wilful, deliberate and pre-meditated killing, or in the commission of, or attempt to commit, arson, rape, robbery or burglary, is murder of the first degree. All other murder is murder of the second degree."

[6] W. LaFave & A. Scott, *Handbook on Criminal Law* § 71, at 545 (1972); R. Perkins, *Criminal Law* 37-38 (2d ed. 1969); 40 Am. Jur. 2d *Homicide* § 72; Annot., 50 A.L.R.2d 397.

not only settled in the Virginias, but exists uniformly in all other states which have similar statutes.

In the few cases where such argument, as here advanced, has been considered, it has been flatly rejected as violating the historical common law concepts of the crime of felony-murder. . . .

The use of the term "murder" in the statute, W.Va. Code, 61-2-1, and in the third syllabus of *Peacher* as it relates to the crime of felony-murder, means nothing more than it did at common law — a homicide.

The defendant's trial counsel competently advised him as to the guilty plea, as there could be no reasonable expectation under the settled principles of our law that an unintended homicide committed in the course of an attempted burglary would constitute a defense to first degree murder arising out of the felony-murder rule.[12]

For these reasons, we affirm the judgment of the Circuit Court of Brooke County.

QUESTIONS

1. If Sims had not been engaged in a felony, would he be liable under any category of homicide? If so, what category?

2. Was the firing of the gun a voluntary act by Sims? If not, would that negate his liability? On what conduct by Sims is his homicide liability based?

Consider the following facts from *People v. Stamp*, 2 Cal. App. 3d 203, 208-209 (1969):

> Defendant Koory and Stamp, armed with a gun and a blackjack, entered the rear of a building housing the offices of General Amusement Company, ordered the employees they found there to go to the front of the premises, where the two secretaries were working. Stamp, the one with the gun, then went into the office of Carl Honeyman, the owner and manager. Thereupon, Honeyman, looking very frightened and pale, emerged from the office in a "kind of hurry." He was apparently propelled by Stamp, who had hold of him by an elbow.
>
> The robbery victims were required to lie down on the floor while the robbers took the money and fled out the back door. As the robbers, who had been on the premises 10 to 15 minutes, were leaving, they told the victims to remain on the floor for five minutes so that no one would "get hurt."
>
> Honeyman, who had been lying next to the counter, had to use it to steady himself in getting up off the floor. Still pale, he was short of breath, sucking air, and pounding and rubbing his chest. As he walked down the hall, in an unsteady manner, still breathing hard and rubbing his chest, he said he was having trouble "keeping the pounding down inside" and that his heart was "pumping too fast for him" . . . 15 or 20 minutes after the robbery had occurred, he collapsed on the floor. . . . [H]e was pronounced dead on arrival at the hospital. The coroner's report listed the immediate cause of death as heart attack. . . .
>
> The victim was an obese, 60-year-old man, with a history of heart disease, who was under a great deal of pressure due to the intensely competitive nature of his business. Additionally, he did not take good care of his heart.

---

[12] It should be noted that under defendant's plea bargain, he was sentenced to life with a recommendation of mercy, which is the most reduced sentence a jury might have returned.

> Three doctors . . . testified that although Honeyman had an advanced case of atherosclerosis, a progressive and ultimately fatal disease, there must have been some immediate upset to his system which precipitated the attack. It was their conclusion in response to a hypothetical question that but for the robbery there would have been no fatal seizure at that time. . . .   There was opposing testimony to the effect that it could not be said with reasonable medical certainty that fright could ever be fatal.

Following the principles of the *Sims* case, what result should the Court in *Stamp* have reached?

The court did hold Stamp liable. It noted the following general principles about felony murder:

> Under the felony-murder rule of section 189 of the Penal Code, a killing committed in either the perpetration of or an attempt to perpetrate robbery is murder of the first degree. This is true whether the killing is wilfull, deliberate and premeditated, or merely accidental or unintentional, and whether or not the killing is planned as part of the commission of the robbery. . . .
>
> The doctrine presumes malice aforethought on the basis of the commission of a felony inherently dangerous to human life. . . .   This is a rule of substantive law in California and not merely an evidentiary shortcut to finding malice as it withdraws from the jury the requirement that they find either express malice or the implied malice which is manifested in an intent to kill. . . .   Under this rule no intentional act is necessary other than the attempt to or the actual commission of the robbery itself. . . .
>
> There is no requirement that the killing occur, "while committing" or "while engaged in" the felony, or that the killing be "a part of" the felony, other than that the few acts be a part of one continuous transaction. . . .
>
> The doctrine is not limited to those deaths which are foreseeable. . . .   As long as the homicide is the direct causal result of the robbery the felony-murder rule applies whether or not the death was a natural or probable consequence of the robbery. . . .   So long as life is shortened as a result of the felonious act, it does not matter that the victim might have died soon anyway.[27]

In contrast to the *Sims* and *Stamp* courts' approval of the felony-murder doctrine, the Michigan Supreme Court rejects the doctrine in the *Aaron* case below.

PEOPLE *v.* AARON

Supreme Court of Michigan 409 Mich. 672 (1980)

FITZGERALD, J. The existence and scope of the felony-murder doctrine have perplexed generations of law students, commentators and jurists in the United States and England, and have split our own Court of Appeals. In these cases, we must decide whether Michigan has a felony-murder rule which allows the element of malice required for murder to be satisfied by the intent to commit the underlying felony or whether malice must be otherwise found by the trier of fact. We must also determine what is the *mens rea* required to support a conviction under Michigan's first-degree murder statute.

---

27. *Stamp*, 2 Cal. App. 3d 203, at 209-210.

FACTS . . .

Defendant Aaron was convicted of first-degree felony murder as a result of a homicide committed during the perpetration of an armed robbery. The jury was instructed that they could convict defendant of first-degree murder if they found that defendant killed the victim during the commission or attempted commission of an armed robbery. . . .

II. HISTORY OF THE FELONY-MURDER DOCTRINE

Felony murder has never been a static, well-defined rule at common law, but throughout its history has been characterized by judicial reinterpretation to limit the harshness of the application of the rule. Historians and commentators have concluded that the rule is of questionable origin and that the reasons for the rule no longer exist, making it an anachronistic remnant, "a historic survivor for which there is no logical or practical basis for existence in modern law." . . .

At early common law, the felony-murder rule went unchallenged because at that time practically all felonies were punishable by death.[33] It was, therefore, "of no particular moment whether the condemned was hanged for the initial felony or for the death accidentally resulting from the felony." Thus, as Stephen and Perkins point out, no injustice was caused directly by application of the rule at that time. . . .

Case law of Nineteenth-Century England reflects the efforts of the English courts to limit the application of the felony-murder doctrine. . . .

In this century, the felony-murder doctrine was comparatively rarely invoked in England[44] and in 1957 England abolished the felony-murder rule. Section 1 of England's Homicide Act, 1957, 5 & 6 Eliz 2, c 11, § 1, provides that a killing occurring in a felony-murder situation will not amount to murder unless done with the same malice aforethought as is required for all other murder . . . .

III. LIMITATION OF THE FELONY-MURDER DOCTRINE IN THE UNITED STATES

While only a few states have followed the lead of Great Britain in abolishing felony murder, various legislative and judicial limitations on the doctrine have effectively narrowed the scope of the rule in the United States. Perkins states that the rule is "somewhat in disfavor at the present time" and that "courts apply it where the law requires, but they do so grudgingly and tend to restrict its application where circumstances permit".[46]

The draftsmen of the Model Penal Code have summarized the limitations imposed by American courts as follows:[47]

(1) "The felonious act must be dangerous to life."

(2) and (3) "The homicide must be a natural and probable consequence of the felonious act." "Death must be 'proximately' caused." Courts have also required that

---

[33] By a practice known as "benefit of clergy" a defendant could avoid the death penalty. At early law, members of the clergy could be tried only by an ecclesiastical court. The test for determining entitlement to the benefit was the ability to read. The effect of the benefit was to shield from the death penalty those who qualified for its protection since a court of the Church could not pronounce a judgment of blood. However, a series of statutes in the late Fifteenth and early Sixteenth Centuries removed the more culpable homicides from the protection of the benefit of clergy. [citations omitted].

[44] Preveser, *The English Homicide Act: A New Attempt to Revise the Law of Murder*, 57 Colum L Rev 624, 635 (1957).

[46] Perkins, [*Criminal Law* (2d ed.)].

[47] Model Penal Code (Tentative Draft No 9, 1959), § 201.2, Comment 4, p 37.

the killing be the result of an act done in the furtherance of the felonious purpose and not merely coincidental to the perpetration of a felony. These cases often make distinctions based on the identity of the victim (*i.e.*, whether the decedent was the victim of the felony or whether he was someone else, *e.g.*, a policeman or one of the felons) and the identity of the person causing the death.

(4) "The felony must be *malum in se.*"

(5) "The act must be a common-law felony."

(6) "The period during which the felony is in the process of commission must be narrowly construed."

(7) "The underlying felony must be 'independent' of the homicide."

Some courts, recognizing the questionable wisdom of the rule, have refused to extend it beyond what is required. . . .

Other courts have required a finding of a separate *mens rea* connected with the killing in addition to the intent associated with the felony. . . .

Kentucky and Hawaii have specifically abolished the felony-murder doctrine.

Ohio has effectively abolished the felony-murder rule.

Seven states have downgraded the offense and consequently reduced the punishment.

Three states require a demonstration of *mens rea* beyond the intent to cause the felony. . . .

Other restrictions of the common-law rule include the enumeration of felonies which are to be included within the felony-murder category, and the reduction to manslaughter of killings in the course of non-enumerated felonies. . . .

Finally, a limitation of relatively recent origin is the availability of affirmative defenses where a defendant is not the only participant in the commission of the underlying felony. The New York statute provides, as do similar statutes of nine other states, an affirmative defense to the defendant when he:

"(a) Did not commit the homicidal act or in any way solicit, request, command, importune, cause or aid the commission thereof; and

"(b) Was not armed with a deadly weapon, or any instrument, article or substance readily capable of causing death or serious physical injury and of a sort not ordinarily carried in public places by law-abiding persons; and

"(c) Had no reasonable ground to believe that any other participant was armed with such a weapon, instrument, article or substance; and

"(d) Had no reasonable ground to believe that any other participant intended to engage in conduct likely to result in death or serious physical injury."[83]

. . . The numerous modifications and restrictions placed upon the common-law felony-murder doctrine by courts and legislatures reflect dissatisfaction with the harshness and injustice of the rule. Even though the felony-murder doctrine survives in this country, it bears increasingly less resemblance to the traditional felony-murder concept. To the extent that these modifications reduce the scope and significance of the common-law doctrine, they also call into question the continued existence of the doctrine itself.

---

[83] NY Penal Law § 125.25.

IV. The Requirement of Individual Culpability for Criminal Responsibility

"If one had to choose the most basic principle of the criminal law in general . . . it would be that criminal liability for causing a particular result is not justified in the absence of some culpable mental state in respect to that result. . . . "[86]

The most fundamental characteristic of the felony-murder rule violates this basic principle in that it punishes all homicides, committed in the perpetration or attempted perpetration of proscribed felonies whether intentional, unintentional or accidental, without the necessity of proving the relation between the homicide and the perpetrator's state of mind. This is most evident when a killing is done by one of a group of co-felons. . . .

The felony-murder rule's most egregious violation of basic rules of culpability occurs where felony murder is categorized as first-degree murder. All other murders carrying equal punishment require a showing of premeditation, deliberation and willfulness while felony murder only requires a showing of intent to do the underlying felony. Although the purpose of our degree statutes is to punish more severely the more culpable forms of murder, an accidental killing occurring during the perpetration of a felony would be punished more severely than a second-degree murder requiring intent to kill, intent to cause great bodily harm, or wantonness and willfulness. Furthermore, a defendant charged with felony murder is permitted to raise defenses only to the mental element of the felony, thus precluding certain defenses available to a defendant charged with premeditated murder who may raise defenses to the mental element of murder (*e.g.*, self-defense, accident). Certainly, felony murder is no more reprehensible than premeditated murder.

LaFave & Scott explain the felony-murder doctrine's failure to account for a defendant's moral culpability as follows:

> "The rationale of the doctrine is that one who commits a felony is a bad person with a bad state of mind, and he has caused a bad result, so that we should not worry too much about the fact that the fatal result he accomplished was quite different and a good deal worse than the bad result he intended. Yet it is a general principle of criminal law that one is not ordinarily criminally liable for bad results which differ greatly from intended results."[88]

The failure of the felony-murder rule to consider the defendant's moral culpability is explained by examining the state of the law at the time of the rule's inception. The concept of culpability was not an element of homicide at early common law. The early definition of malice aforethought was vague. The concept meant little more than intentional wrongdoing with no other emphasis on intention except to exclude homicides that were committed by misadventure or in some otherwise pardonable manner. Thus, under this early definition of malice aforethought, an intent to commit the felony would in itself constitute malice. Furthermore, as all felonies were punished alike, it made little difference whether the felon was hanged for the felony or for the death. . . .

Today, however, malice is a term of art. It does not include the nebulous definition of intentional wrongdoing. Thus, although the felony-murder rule did not broaden the definition of murder at early common law, it does so today. We find this enlargement of the scope of murder unacceptable, because it is based on a

---

[86] Gegan, *Criminal Homicide in the Revised New York Penal Law*, 12 NY L Forum 565, 586 (1966). . . .

[88] LaFave & Scott, [*Criminal Law*] p 560.

concept of culpability which is "totally incongruous with the general principles of our jurisprudence"[97] today.

V. The Felony-Murder Doctrine in Michigan

A. Murder and Malice Defined

In order to understand the operation of any state's felony-murder doctrine, initially it is essential to understand how that state defines murder and malice.

In Michigan, murder is not statutorily defined. This Court early defined the term as follows:

> "Murder is where a person of sound memory and discretion unlawfully kills any reasonable creature in being, in the peace of the state, with malice prepense or aforethought, either express or implied." *People v Potter*, 5 Mich 1 (1858). . . .

We agree with the following analysis of murder and malice aforethought presented by LaFave & Scott:

> "Though murder is frequently defined as the unlawful killing of another 'living human being' with 'malice aforethought', in modern times the latter phrase does not even approximate its literal meaning. Hence it is preferable not to rely upon that misleading expression for an understanding of murder but rather to consider the various types of murder (typed according to the mental element) which the common law came to recognize and which exist today in most jurisdictions:
>
>> "(1) intent-to-kill murder;
>> "(2) intent-to-do-serious-bodily-injury murder;
>> "(3) depraved-heart murder [wanton and willful disregard that the natural tendency of the defendant's behavior is to cause death or great bodily harm]; and
>> "(4) felony murder."[101]

Our focus in this opinion is upon the last category of murder, *i.e.*, felony murder. We do not believe the felony-murder doctrine, as some courts and commentators would suggest, abolishes the requirement of malice, nor do we believe that it equates the *mens rea* of the felony with the *mens rea* required for a non-felony murder. We construe the felony-murder doctrine as providing a separate definition of malice, thereby establishing a fourth category of murder. The effect of the doctrine is to recognize the intent to commit the underlying felony, in itself, as a sufficient *mens rea* for murder. This analysis of the felony-murder doctrine is consistent with the historical development of the doctrine.

The question we address today is whether Michigan recognizes the felony-murder doctrine and, accordingly, the category of malice arising from the underlying felony. The relevant inquiry is first whether Michigan has a statutory felony-murder doctrine. If it does not, it must then be determined whether Michigan has or should have a common-law felony-murder doctrine.

B. Statutory Felony Murder

Michigan does not have a statutory felony-murder doctrine which designates as murder any death occurring in the course of a felony without regard to whether it was the result of accident, negligence, recklessness or willfulness. Rather, Michigan

---

[97] First Report From His Majesty's Commissioners on Criminal Law (1834), p 29. (In: Parliamentary Papers [1834], Vol 26, p 105.)

[101] LaFave & Scott, *Criminal Law*, p 528.

has a statute which makes a *murder* occurring in the course of one of the enumerated felonies a first-degree murder:

"Murder which is perpetrated by means of poison, lying in wait, or other wilful, deliberate, and premeditated killing, or which is committed in the perpetration, or attempt to perpetrate arson, criminal sexual conduct in the first or third degree, robbery, breaking and entering of a dwelling, larceny of any kind, extortion, or kidnapping, is murder of the first degree, and shall be punished by imprisonment for life." MCL 750.316; MSA 28.548.

. . . Thus, we conclude that Michigan has not codified the common-law felony-murder rule. The use of the term "murder" in the first-degree statute requires that a murder must first be established before the statute is applied to elevate the degree.

C. COMMON-LAW FELONY MURDER IN MICHIGAN

The prosecution argues that even if Michigan does not have a statutory codification of the felony-murder rule, the common-law definition of murder included a homicide in the course of a felony. Thus, the argument continues, once a homicide in the course of a felony is proven, under the common-law felony-murder rule a murder has been established and the first-degree murder statute then becomes applicable. . . .

Our research has uncovered no Michigan cases, nor do the parties refer us to any, which have expressly considered whether Michigan has or should continue to have a common-law felony-murder doctrine. . . .

However, our finding that Michigan has never specifically adopted the doctrine which defines malice to include the intent to commit the underlying felony is not the end of our inquiry. In Michigan, the general rule is that the common law prevails except as abrogated by the Constitution, the Legislature or this Court. Const 1963, art 3, § 7. . . .

The cases before us today squarely present us with the opportunity to review the doctrine and to consider its continued existence in Michigan. Although there are no Michigan cases which specifically abrogate the felony-murder rule, there exists a number of decisions of this Court which have significantly restricted the doctrine in Michigan and which lead us to conclude that the rule should be abolished. . . .

Accordingly, we hold today that malice is the intention to kill, the intention to do great bodily harm, or the wanton and willful disregard of the likelihood that the natural tendency of defendant's behavior is to cause death or great bodily harm. We further hold that malice is an essential element of any murder, as that term is judicially defined, whether the murder occurs in the course of a felony or otherwise. The facts and circumstances involved in the perpetration of a felony may evidence an intent to kill, an intent to cause great bodily harm, or a wanton and willful disregard of the likelihood that the natural tendency of defendant's behavior is to cause death or great bodily harm; however, the conclusion must be left to the jury to infer from all the evidence. . . .

VI. PRACTICAL EFFECT OF ABROGATION OF THE COMMON-LAW FELONY-MURDER DOCTRINE

From a practical standpoint, the abolition of the category of malice arising from the intent to commit the underlying felony should have little effect on the result of the majority of cases. In many cases where felony murder has been applied, the use of the doctrine was unnecessary because the other types of malice could have been inferred from the evidence.

Abrogation of this rule does not make irrelevant the fact that a death occurred in the course of a felony. A jury can properly infer malice from evidence that a defendant intentionally set in motion a force likely to cause death or great bodily harm. . . . If the jury concludes that malice existed, they can find murder and, if they determine that the murder occurred in the perpetration or attempted perpetration of one of the enumerated felonies, by statute the murder would become first-degree murder.

The difference is that the jury may not find malice from the intent to commit the underlying felony alone. The defendant will be permitted to assert any of the applicable defenses relating to *mens rea* which he would be allowed to assert if charged with premeditated murder. . . .

In the past, the felony-murder rule has been employed where unforeseen or accidental deaths occur and where the state seeks to prove vicarious liability of co-felons. In situations involving the vicarious liability of co-felons, the individual liability of each felon must be shown. It is fundamentally unfair and in violation of basic principles of individual criminal culpability to hold one felon liable for the unforeseen and unagreed-to results of another felon. In cases where the felons are acting intentionally or recklessly in pursuit of a common plan, the felony-murder rule is unnecessary because liability may be established on agency principles.

Finally, in cases where the death was purely accidental, application of the felony-murder doctrine is unjust and should be precluded. The underlying felony, of course, will still be subject to punishment. . . .

QUESTIONS

1. Do you support retention or abolition of the felony-murder rule? Is your reasoning retributive? Or utilitarian?

2. Despite extensive criticism, many jurisdictions retain the felony-murder rule. What do you think explains its continued vitality?

David Crump & Susan Waite Crump, IN DEFENSE OF THE FELONY MURDER DOCTRINE

8 Harv. J.L. & Pub. Poly. 359, 362-368, 370-371, 374-375 (Spring 1985)

Differences in result must be taken into account as part of actus reus if classification and grading are to be rational. For example, murder and attempted murder may require similar mental states (indeed, attempted murder generally requires proof of a higher mental element), but no common law jurisdiction treats the two offenses as one, and certainly none treats attempted murder more severely. The only difference justifying this classification is that death results in one offense but not in the other. Similarly, it is a misdemeanor for a person to operate a motor vehicle while impaired by drugs or alcohol, but if this conduct causes the death of a human being, the offense in some jurisdictions is elevated to the status of homicide. Most jurisdictions treat vehicular homicide more severely than the misdemeanor of alcohol-impaired driving, even though the actions and mental states of the defendant may be equivalent or identical. . . .

The classification and grading of offenses so that the entire scheme of defined crimes squares with societal perceptions of proportionality — of "just deserts" — is a fundamental goal of the law of crimes.

The felony murder doctrine serves this goal, just as do the distinctions inherent in the separate offenses of attempted murder and murder, or impaired driving and vehicular homicide. Felony murder reflects a societal judgment that an intentionally committed robbery that causes the death of a human being is qualitatively more serious than an identical robbery that does not. Perhaps this judgment could have been embodied in a newly defined offense called "robbery-resulting-in-death"; but while a similar approach has been adopted in some areas of the criminal law, such a proliferation of offense definitions is undesirable. Thus the felony murder doctrine reflects the conclusions that a robbery that causes death is more closely akin to murder than to robbery. If this conclusion accurately reflects societal attitudes, and if classification of crimes is to be influenced by such attitudes in order to avoid depreciation of the seriousness of the offense and to encourage respect for the law, then the felony murder doctrine is an appropriate classificatory device. . . .

Juries provide another index of the public's attitude toward felony murder. Kalven and Zeisel [researchers on jury issues] were surprised to find that jurors faced with actual felony murder cases agreed with the doctrine. The jury research revealed in public attitudes a resistance to the criminalization of many kinds of socially disapproved events (including some homicides), but *not* felony murder. . . .

Scholarly criticisms of felony murder have tended to neglect its relationship to proportionality and grading. The criticisms erroneously tend to regard mens rea as the only legitimate determinant of the grade of a homicide resulting from a felony. This reasoning sometimes leads modern writers into the same rigid formalism, divorced from policy, that they rightly reject in historical justifications of the rule. Mens rea is not a "unified field theory" of homicide, and while such a theory might make the subject artificially "logical" or "consistent," it does not reflect our society's more complex understanding of the nature, function, and purpose of criminal law. The fallacy of this approach is its denigration of actus reus and its failure to include the result of defendant's conduct as a determinant of just disposition. The importance of this factor is demonstrated by the attempted murder and alcohol-impaired driving examples given above. Simply put, if one must categorize a robbery causing death as either a robbery or a murder, it is the latter category that is the "better fit"; calling such a crime robbery, and robbery only, would distort its significance in the scheme of crime grading. . . .

A purpose of sentencing closely related to proportionality is that of condemnation. . . .

Condemnation itself is a multifaceted idea. It embodies the notion of reinforcement of societal norms and values as a guide to the conduct of upright persons, as opposed to less upright ones who presumably require the separate prod of "deterrence." The felony murder rule serves this purpose by distinguishing crimes that cause human deaths, thus reinforcing the reverence for human life. To put the argument differently, characterizing a robbery-homicide solely as robbery would have the undesirable effect of communicating to the citizenry that the law does not consider a crime that takes a human life to be different from one that does not — a message that would be indistinguishable, in the minds of many, from a devaluation of human life.

Another aspect of condemnation is the expression of solidarity with the victims of crime. If we as a society label a violent offense in a manner that depreciates its significance, we communicate to the victim by implication that we do not understand his suffering. He may be left with the impression that he is unprotected — or even that he is disoriented, having himself failed to understand the rules of the game. Felony murder is a useful doctrine because it reaffirms to the surviving family of a felony-homicide victim the kinship the society as a whole feels with him by denouncing in the strongest language of the law the intentional crime that produced the death. . . .

Deterrence is the policy most often recognized in the cases. Scholars, however, tend to dismiss this rationale, using such arguments as the improbability that felons will know the law, the unlikelihood that a criminal who has formed the intent to commit a felony will refrain from acts likely to cause death, or the assertedly small number of felony-homicides.

The trouble with these criticisms is that they underestimate the complexity of deterrence. There may be more than a grain of truth in the proposition that felons, if considered as a class, evaluate risks and benefits differently than members of other classes in society. The conclusion does not follow, however, that felons cannot be deterred, or that criminals are so different from other citizens that they are impervious to inducements or deterrents that would affect people in general. There is mounting evidence that serious crime is subject to deterrence if consequences are adequately communicated. The felony murder rule is just the sort of simple, commonsense, readily enforceable, and widely known principle that is likely to result in deterrence. . . .

The argument against deterrence often proceeds on the additional assumption that felony murder is addressed only to accidental killings and cannot result in their deterrence. By facilitating proof and simplifying the concept of liability, however, felony murder may deter intentional killings as well. The robber who kills intentionally, but who might claim under oath to have acted accidentally, is thus told that he will be deprived of the benefit of this claim. By institutionalizing this effect and consistently condemning robbery-homicides as qualitatively more blameworthy than robberies, the law leads the robber who kills intentionally to expect this treatment for himself. Furthermore, the contrary argument proves too much even as to robbery-killings that are factually accidental. The proposition that accidental killings cannot be deterred is inconsistent with the widespread belief that the penalizing of negligence, and even the imposition of strict liability, may have deterrent consequences. . . .

Another advantage of the felony murder rule . . . is that it may aid in the optimal allocation of criminal justice resources. A small minority of cases is tried before juries. The efforts of judges, courtroom time, lawyering on both sides, and support services are all scarce resources. Although we resist thinking of criminal justice in these terms, and few would be willing to put a specific dollar price upon its proper function, the quality of our justice is limited by the scarcity of these resources and by the efficiency with which we allocate them. . . .

One of our choices might be to improve the allocation of criminal justice resources by adopting some version of the felony murder rule. The rule has beneficial allocative consequences because it clearly defines the offense, simplifies the task of the judge and jury with respect to questions of law and fact, and thereby promotes efficient administration of justice. . . .

Obviously, reliance upon this policy should be limited carefully. The failure to recognize the effects of our decisions upon the use of scarce resources, however, would be equally dangerous, threatening to lower the quality of criminal justice generally.

Before we turn to several of the more common limitations on the doctrine, consider the constitutional criticisms of the felony-murder doctrine in the following excerpt from an article by Professors Scott Sundby and Nelson Roth:[28]

> The felony-murder rule has been criticized almost from its inception as a harsh legal doctrine with insufficient policy justifications. Two basic conceptualizations of felony murder have emerged: the rule is viewed either as providing a conclusive presumption of the culpability required for murder, or as a distinct crime for which the killing does not have a separate mens rea element apart from the felony.
>
> The Supreme Court's holding in *Sandstrom v. Montana* constitutionally prohibits conclusive presumptions because they violate a defendant's presumption of innocence and because they intrude upon the jury's duty to affirmatively find each element of the offense. The felony-murder rule violates both rationales of [a] defendant's culpability for murder . . . .
>
> Those courts that have attempted to avoid the due process problems of mandatory presumptions have characterized the felony-murder rule as a distinct crime without a separate mens rea element for the homicide. The Supreme Court has recently indicated, however, that eighth amendment and due process restrictions limit the ability of legislatures and courts to create and sanction nonregulatory crimes that do not contain a requirement of culpability. In *Enmund v. Florida* and *United States v. United States Gypsum Co.*, the Court has noted that a relationship between culpability and punishment is intrinsic to our criminal system. The felony-murder rule violates this basic principle of our legal system when justified as a strict liability crime.
>
> The felony-murder rule arose from obscure historical origins and has developed haphazardly into a harsh and unjust legal doctrine. It is perhaps fitting, therefore, that two separate lines of constitutional doctrines, developing independently, have come together in such a way that it is impossible to conceptualize felony murder in a manner that does not run afoul of constitutional guarantees.

2. The Model Penal Code and Felony Murder

Model Penal Code § 210.2 (1985)   *Murder*

(1) Except as provided in Section 210.3(1)(b), criminal homicide constitutes murder when:

(b) it is committed recklessly under circumstances manifesting extreme indifference to the value of human life. Such recklessness and indifference are presumed if the actor is engaged or is an accomplice in the commission of, or an attempt to commit, or flight after committing or attempting to commit robbery, rape or deviate sexual intercourse by force or threat of force, arson, burglary, kidnapping or felonious escape.

The Model Penal Code approach to felony murder incorporates a presumption that someone committing or attempting to commit the listed felonies manifests

---

28. Nelson E. Roth & Scott E. Sundby, *The Felony-Murder Rule: A Doctrine at Constitutional Crossroads*, 70 Cornell L. Rev. 446, 491-492 (1985).

extreme indifference, a mental state that qualifies for murder. This presumption is rebuttable. In other words, under the MPC, a defendant may introduce evidence and attempt to prove that she did not in fact have extreme indifference to the value of human life. In a burglary case, what evidence might a defendant offer to rebut the presumption of extreme indifference? What about in a robbery case? An arson case?

QUESTIONS

1. Does the MPC accept the felony-murder rule? Reject it? Or something in between?

2. Is the MPC provision immune from the constitutional criticism of Professors Sundby and Roth?

3. How would the defendants in the felony-murder cases described earlier in this chapter have fared under the MPC approach?

4. How does the MPC approach compare to that in *Aaron*?

3. Limitations on the Felony-Murder Rule

The history of the felony-murder rule, particularly in this century, is one of restrictions. The Sections that follow address five of the most common limitations.

a. Enumeration

Legislatures can limit the scope of the felony-murder rule by enumerating or listing the felonies that can support a felony-murder conviction. The absence of a felony from the list excludes it as a possible basis for a felony-murder charge under that statute.

Below is an example:

Wisconsin Statutes § 940.03 (1994)   *Felony Murder*

Whoever causes the death of another human being while committing or attempting to commit a crime specified in s. 940.225(1) or (2)(a) [first degree sexual assault and second degree sexual assault with use or threat of force or violence], 943.02 [arson], 943.10(2) [armed burglary] or 943.32(2) [armed robbery] may be imprisoned for not more than 20 years in excess of the maximum period of imprisonment provided by law for that crime or attempt.

Under this statute, a prosecutor could not base a felony-murder charge on the felony of unarmed robbery, unarmed burglary, grand theft, or dozens of other felonies.

Sometimes legislatures enumerate felonies for only one of the jurisdictions' degrees of murder. Enumeration is perhaps most common when legislatures seek to limit liability for first-degree murder. Legislatures may enumerate felonies that qualify for first-degree murder but leave unspecified the felonies that may qualify for second-degree murder. The Delaware Code below is an example:

Delaware Code Annotated, Title 11, § 635 (2001)   *Murder in the second degree; class B felony*

A person is guilty of murder in the second degree when:

(2) In the course of and in furtherance of the commission or attempted commission of any felony not specifically enumerated in § 636 of this title or immediate flight therefrom, the person, with criminal negligence, causes the death of another person.

Murder in the second degree is a class B felony. Notwithstanding any provision of this title to the contrary, the minimum sentence for a person convicted of murder in the second degree in violation of this section shall be 10 years at Level V.

These unspecified felonies are then often subject to some or all of limitations described below.

b. Inherently Dangerous Felony

Courts use the inherently dangerous felony rule to limit the types of felonies on which the prosecution can base a charge of felony murder. What felonies or types of felonies would you consider to be inherently dangerous? How do you assess the inherent dangerousness of a felony? Should it matter if the felon is very careful during the felony?

PEOPLE *v.* SANCHEZ

Court of Appeal of California 86 Cal. App. 4th 970 (2001)

Opinion certified for partial publication.

SCOTLAND, P.J. One passenger was killed and two were seriously injured when defendant Refugio Anthony Sanchez crashed his car while trying to elude pursuing police officers. Criminal charges were filed, and defendant was convicted of a number of offenses, including second degree murder. (Pen. Code, § 187, subd. (a).) Sentenced to state prison, he appeals.

In the published portion of this opinion, we agree with defendant that his murder conviction must be reversed because the trial court erred in instructing the jury, pursuant to the felony-murder doctrine, that a person who kills a human being while violating Vehicle Code section 2800.3 is guilty of second degree murder. . . . As we shall explain, in determining whether the felonious violation of section 2800.3 is inherently dangerous to human life as required for application of the second degree felony-murder doctrine, we must look to the elements of the statute in the abstract, rather than to defendant's specific conduct. In doing so, we conclude that, because dispositive elements of section 2800.3 can be satisfied by conduct that does not necessarily pose a high probability of death, it is not a felony inherently dangerous to human life. Thus, section 2800.3 cannot serve as the predicate crime for application of the second degree felony-murder doctrine. . . .

FACTS

Around 2:00 A.M. on March 1, 1998, Officer John Morris saw defendant's car run a stop sign and two red lights at speeds between 35 to 55 miles per hour. Morris turned on the red lights and siren of his marked patrol vehicle and pursued the car, which barely missed colliding with another vehicle while speeding through an intersection. Goldie McCowan, one of three passengers in defendant's car, told defendant to pull over because police were behind them. Defendant refused to do so, claiming he could get away. Eventually, all the passengers pleaded for defendant to pull over. But "[h]e just turned up the music" and drove faster.

Defendant accelerated to speeds between 85 to 100 miles per hour. As he drove down a residential street at high speed, defendant came to a 90-degree turn in the road. Unable to make the turn, defendant lost control of the car, the right rear of which "swung out" and "clipped the guardrail." After hitting the guardrail, the car flipped upside down and crashed into a house. Skid marks indicated that defendant's car was traveling at approximately 84 miles per hour when he lost control at the turn in the road.

Officer Morris stopped to render aid and arrest the driver. Flames were coming out of the front of the car, and smoke and gasoline pouring out of the back. A car door was open, and one of the passengers was facedown on the ground, with the vehicle partially on top of her. Morris heard a woman in the back of the car screaming for help.

As others who had joined the pursuit attended to the passengers, Officer Bobby Daniels and another officer pulled defendant from the car. Defendant, who did not appear to be injured, was belligerent and continually screamed at the officers. Noticing that defendant had a strong odor of alcohol on his breath and was unable to stand on his own, Officer Daniels concluded that defendant was under the influence of alcohol. Subsequent testing revealed that defendant had a blood-alcohol level of .18 percent.

One of the passengers, Lakisha Davis, died as a result of the crash. Goldie McCowan suffered a broken right arm, a fractured collarbone, and injuries to her hip. Shanise Shaver was cut and bruised on her hand, head, and stomach.

Prior to the fatal crash, defendant had been convicted of driving under the influence of alcohol and his driver's license had been suspended. . . .

III

The jury was presented with two alternative theories to support defendant's conviction of second degree murder: (1) he acted with implied malice in unlawfully killing Lakisha Davis, or (2) he caused her death while committing a felony that is inherently dangerous to human life but is not enumerated in Penal Code section 189 (the second degree felony-murder rule).[3] . . .

The second degree felony-murder theory applies when a defendant commits a homicide during the perpetration of a felony that is inherently dangerous to human life but is not enumerated in Penal Code section 189. " 'The felony-murder doctrine, whose ostensible purpose is to deter those engaged in felonies from killing negligently or accidentally, operates to posit the existence of that crucial mental state — and thereby to render irrelevant evidence of actual malice or the lack thereof — when the killer is engaged in a felony whose inherent danger to human life renders logical an imputation of malice on the part of all who commit it.' " In other words, a defendant who kills a human being during the commission of a felony that is inherently dangerous to human life is deemed to have acted with malice aforethought, i.e., committed murder. A felony is inherently dangerous to

---

[3] A person who kills a human being during the commission of a felony enumerated in Penal Code section 189 is guilty of first degree felony murder.

human life when it "carr[ies] 'a high probability' that death will result." (*People v. Patterson* (1989) 49 Cal. 3d 615, 627 italics omitted.) . . .

[T]he difference between implied malice and felony murder is that, under the implied malice theory, when the defendant kills a person while committing an act which, by its nature, poses a high probability that the act will result in death, the trier of fact *may infer* the defendant killed with malice aforethought; whereas, under the felony-murder theory, if the inherently dangerous act is a felony, the defendant is *deemed* to have killed with malice aforethought as a matter of law.

In this case, defendant's appeal addresses only the second theory tendered by the prosecutor, that defendant was guilty of felony murder based upon his violation of section 2800.3, which was charged as a felony.[4]

Over defendant's objection, the trial court agreed with the prosecutor that the felonious violation of section 2800.3 is an inherently dangerous felony that can support a murder conviction via the second degree felony-murder doctrine. Consequently, the court instructed the jury as follows: "Every person who unlawfully kills a human being with malice aforethought *or during the commission or attempted commission of evading a peace officer, a felony inherently dangerous to human life*, is guilty of the crime of murder in violation of Section 187 of the Penal Code. In order to prove this crime, each of the following elements must be proved: One, a human being was killed; and two, the killing was unlawful; and three, the killing was done with malice aforethought *or occurred during the commission or attempted commission of evading a peace officer, a felony inherently dangerous to human life. Evading a peace officer is a felony inherently dangerous to human life.*" (Italics added.) The court further instructed that "[t]he unlawful killing of a human being whether intentional, unintentional, or accidental, *which occurs during the commission or attempted commission of a crime of evading a peace officer is murder of the second degree when the perpetrator had the specific intent to commit that crime.*" (Italics added.)

Defendant contends "it was error for the court to predicate a felony[-]murder instruction upon a violation of section 2800.3." We agree for reasons that follow.

Under specified conditions satisfied by the evidence in this case, "[a]ny person who, while operating a motor vehicle and with the intent to evade, willfully flees or otherwise attempts to elude a pursuing peace officer's motor vehicle, is guilty of a misdemeanor. . . . " (§ 2800.1.) Section 2800.3 provides that "[w]henever willful flight or attempt to elude a pursuing peace officer in violation of Section 2800.1 proximately causes death or serious bodily injury to any person, the person driving the pursued vehicle, upon conviction, shall be punished by [confinement in state prison or county jail]. . . . "

[T]o serve as the basis for the second degree felony-murder rule, the predicate crime must be a felony inherently dangerous to human life, i.e., there must be a high probability that death will result from its commission. "In determining whether a felony is inherently dangerous [to human life], the court looks to the elements of the felony *in the abstract*, 'not the "particular" facts of the case,' i.e., not to the defendant's specific conduct.[6]

---

[4] Section 2800.3 is not a felony enumerated in Penal Code section 189.

[6] "This form of analysis is compelled because there is a killing in every case where the [felony-murder] rule might potentially be applied. If in such circumstances a court were to examine the particular facts of the case prior to establishing whether the underlying felony is inherently dangerous [to human life], . . . the existence of the dead victim might appear to lead inexorably to the conclusion that the underlying felony is exceptionally hazardous. [But such an analysis would be] unjustifiable bootstrapping." (*People v. Burroughs, supra*, 35 Cal. 3d at p. 830.)

In *People v. Burroughs*, the Supreme Court laid out the analytical model for determining whether, in the abstract, the elements of a felony make the crime inherently dangerous to human life. Courts "look first to the primary element of the offense at issue, then to the 'factors elevating the offense to a felony.' . . . In this examination we are required to view the statutory definition of the offense as a whole, taking into account even nonhazardous ways of violating the provisions of the law which do not necessarily pose a threat to human life." Thus, if dispositive elements of the statute may be established by conduct that does not endanger human life, it is not a felony inherently dangerous to human life.

As can be seen from the statutory language quoted above, the primary element of section 2800.3 is that, while operating a motor vehicle and with the intent to evade, a person willfully flees or otherwise attempts to elude a pursuing peace officer's motor vehicle. Common sense and common experience indicate that attempts by drivers to flee or otherwise elude pursuing peace officers often involve conduct that is inherently dangerous to human life. This case is a prime example of such reprehensible misconduct. But, as the Supreme Court has instructed, we must examine the crime in the abstract. And, as can be attested to by those who watched the ludicrous pursuit of Orenthal James Simpson in his white Bronco, a driver can flee or otherwise attempt to elude pursuing officers in a manner that does not pose a high probability of death to anyone. Hence, the primary element of section 2800.3 fails to support a determination that the offense is an inherently dangerous felony.

Therefore, we turn to the factor that elevates the misconduct from a misdemeanor to a felony, i.e., when the person driving the pursued vehicle proximately causes death "or" serious bodily injury to any person while fleeing or otherwise attempting to elude a pursuing peace officer. " 'Serious bodily injury' means a serious impairment of physical condition, including, but not limited to, the following: loss of consciousness; concussion; bone fracture; protracted loss or impairment of function of any bodily member or organ; a wound requiring extensive suturing; and serious disfigurement." (Pen. Code, § 243, subd. (f)(4).)

That "death" and "serious bodily injury" are identified in the disjunctive as separate risks in section 2800.3 indicates the Legislature intended that a person may violate the section without necessarily endangering human life. . . .

Because dispositive elements of the statute can be satisfied by conduct that does not necessarily pose a high probability of death, the violation of section 2800.3, in the abstract, is not a felony inherently dangerous to human life. Consequently, it cannot serve as the predicate crime for application of the second degree felony-murder rule.

QUESTIONS

1. How does the *Sanchez* court determine if a felony is inherently dangerous? What probability of death is required?

2. What does it mean for a felony to be inherently dangerous in the abstract?

3. Unlike California courts, some courts assess inherent danger based on the facts of the case. What is the significance of assessing the inherent danger of a felony in the context of the facts of the particular case rather than in the abstract?

4. Should shooting into an inhabited dwelling qualify as an inherently dangerous felony?

5. Should the felony described below qualify?

Except as otherwise authorized by law, any person who willfully discharges a firearm in a grossly negligent manner which could result in injury or death to a person is guilty of a public offense. . . . Cal. Penal Code Ann. § 246.3 (1999).

c. The Merger Doctrine

Like the inherent danger limitation, courts use the merger doctrine to limit the types of felonies upon which the prosecution can base a felony-murder charge. If a felony "merges" with a homicide, that means it cannot support a felony murder charge. This doctrine is sometimes referred to as the "independent" felony rule. A felony must be independent of the homicide in order to support a felony-murder charge. In other words, a felony that "merges" is not "independent."

BARNETT v. STATE

Court of Criminal Appeals of Alabama 783 So. 2d 927 (2000)

COBB, Judge.

The appellant, Andrae Barnett, was indicted and convicted of felony murder, a violation of § 13A-6-2(a)(3), Ala. Code 1975. Barnett was sentenced to 50 years in the state penitentiary. . . .

On the afternoon of October 17, 1998, Morris Givens and his brother Andrae Barnett went to Daphne Golson's house to pick up Givens's three-year old daughter Jamari and take her to the fair. Daphne Golson is Jamari's mother and Givens's former girlfriend. Golson, her mother, her daughter Jamari, and her boyfriend Kevon Moses were at the home when Givens and Barnett arrived. . . .

Golson stepped off the porch. . . . She then began to argue with Givens. While Golson and Givens were arguing, a separate altercation began between Moses and Barnett. Golson heard a noise behind her and turned; Barnett was holding a garden hoe. According to Golson, Barnett had the hoe in his hands and Moses was backing away from Barnett. As he backed away, Moses tripped over Givens's feet, fell on his stomach, and was hit in the back of the head with the hoe by Barnett. Moses died as a result of the blow to the head. Subsequently, Barnett was arrested and indicted on the charge of felony murder.

On appeal, Barnett asserts that the trial court erred by allowing him to be charged with felony murder when the underlying felony was assault, because he argues, assault was an essential part of the homicide itself. . . .

Barnett's felony-murder conviction was premised on the underlying felony of assault in the first degree. Whether felony murder can be premised on a murder resulting from a first degree assault is a question of first impression in Alabama. The indictment stated that Barnett

"did commit or attempt to commit the crime of Assault First Degree, a felony clearly dangerous to human life and, in the furtherence [sic] of committing or attempting to commit Assault in the First Degree on KEVON MOSES did cause the death of KEVON MOSES by striking him with a garden hoe, in violation of Section 13A-6-2, Code of Alabama, 1975."

Under Alabama law, a person commits the crime of felony murder when

"he commits or attempts to commit arson in the first degree, burglary in the first or second degree, escape in the first degree, kidnapping in the first degree, rape in the first degree, robbery in any degree, sodomy in the first degree, or any other felony clearly dangerous to human life and, in the course of and in furtherance of the crime that he is committing or attempting to commit, or in immediate flight therefrom, he, or another participant if there be any, causes the death of any person."

See § 13A-6-2(a)(3), Ala. Code 1975. Assault in the first degree is defined at § 13A-6-20(a)(1), Ala. Code 1975:

"(a) A person commits the crime of assault in the first degree if:
    (1) With intent to cause serious physical injury to another person, he causes serious physical injury to any person by means of a deadly weapon or a dangerous instrument."

In *People v. Ireland*, 70 Cal. 2d 522 (Cal. 1969), the Supreme Court of California addressed whether assault with a deadly weapon could constitute the predicate felony for a felony-murder charge. The appellant in *Ireland* shot and killed his wife. During the trial, the trial court instructed the jury that it could convict Ireland of felony murder if it determined that he committed the underlying felony of assault with a deadly weapon. In discussing this issue, the Supreme Court of California stated:

"We have concluded that the utilization of the felony-murder rule in circumstances such as those before us extends the operation of that rule 'beyond any rational function it is designed to serve.' (*People v. Washington* (1965) 62 Cal. 2d 777, 783) To allow such use of the felony-murder rule would effectively preclude the jury from considering the issue of malice aforethought in all cases wherein homicide has been committed as a result of a felonious assault — a category which includes the great majority of all homicides. This kind of bootstrapping finds support neither in logic nor in law. We therefore hold that a second degree felony-murder instruction may not properly be given when it is based upon a felony which is an integral part of the homicide and which the evidence produced by the prosecution shows to be an offense included in fact within the offense charged."

Other jurisdictions have construed their felony-murder laws in a similar manner, and have held that felonious assault merges into the homicide. . . .

Conceived in the nineteenth century, the merger doctrine bars the use of the felony-murder rule when the underlying felony directly results in, or is an integral part of, the homicide. . . . Thus, under the merger doctrine, the elements of the underlying felony must be independent of the homicide. We believe that the California Supreme Court's rationale in *Ireland* is sound and that the "merger doctrine" should be applied in felony-murder cases in which the underlying felony is the assault that results in the victim's death.

To read the "clearly dangerous to human life" language in the felony murder rule as allowing an assault on the homicide victim to be the predicate felony for felony murder would offend the statutory construction of Alabama's homicide laws. The Legislature has defined those acts that constitute murder as well as those acts that constitute manslaughter. See §§ 13A-6-2 and 13A-6-3, Ala. Code 1975. If prosecutors could prove murder by proving the intent element of assault as opposed to the requisite mens rea for murder or manslaughter, §§ 13A-6-2(a)(1) and (2), 13A-6-2(b), and 13A-6-3, Ala. Code 1975 would effectively be eliminated. Clearly, such a result would be contrary to legislative intent. . . .

REVERSED AND REMANDED.

QUESTIONS

1. Should the felony of shooting into an inhabited dwelling merge? Reconsider your analysis of whether shooting into an inhabited dwelling constitutes an inherently dangerous felony.

2. Is there a relationship between felonies that qualify as inherently dangerous and those that merge? If so, what is it?

As noted above, legislatures commonly designate particular felonies as ones that can support a first-degree murder conviction. These enumerated felonies are not generally subject to the inherent danger or merger limitations. Rather, courts often treat such enumerated felonies as having a legislative exemption from the inherent danger and merger requirements. In contrast, both enumerated felonies and unenumerated felonies may be subject to other limitations, such as the agency and res gestae limitations discussed below.

d. Agency or "In Furtherance"

Unlike the inherent danger and merger limitations, the agency limitation does not focus on the type of felony. Instead, it narrows felony murder by restricting the circumstances under which a felon can be held liable for felony murder. These cases typically involve shooting deaths. The analysis tends to focus on two issues: (1) was the shooter a felon? And (2) was the victim a felon? As you read the materials in this Subsection, ask yourself whether and why these issues are important. Is the identity of the shooter or the victim significant from the perspective of the purposes of punishment?

Consider the Delaware statute that follows:

Delaware Code Annotated, Title 11, § 635 (2001) *Murder in the second degree; class B felony*

A person is guilty of murder in the second degree when:

(2) In the course of and in furtherance of the commission or attempted commission of any felony not specifically enumerated in § 636 of this title or immediate flight therefrom, the person, with criminal negligence, causes the death of another person.

Murder in the second degree is a class B felony. Notwithstanding any provision of this title to the contrary, the minimum sentence for a person convicted of murder in the second degree in violation of this section shall be 10 years at Level V.

QUESTION

What does the statutory language "in furtherance of the commission" mean?

WEICK v. STATE

Supreme Court of Delaware 420 A.2d 159 (1980)

HERRMANN, Chief Justice.

On appeal, the defendants petition this court to reverse their convictions for Murder in the Second Degree under 11 Del. C. § 635(2); and Conspiracy in the Second Degree under 11 Del. C. § 512(1). . . .

I.

The facts giving rise to the indictments were stipulated for the purposes of trial as follows:

> In November, 1977, the defendants agreed with each other and with a fifth person, Eugene Edgar Weick, to seize by force a quantity of marijuana held illegally by Robert and Kathy Fitzgerald. To this end, the defendants Frank Weick, Eugene Weick and Messick armed themselves with loaded sawed-off shotguns. Then they and the defendants Jerry and Gary Connelly proceeded to the Fitzgerald residence.
>
> Messick, his shotgun hidden under his coat, was admitted to the house by Robert Fitzgerald. Once inside, Messick produced the shotgun and forced Fitzgerald into a rear room of the house. At that point, Frank Weick trained his shotgun on Fitzgerald through a window in that room.
>
> Simultaneously, Kathy Fitzgerald came out of a bedroom and observed what was occurring in the rear of the house. She returned to the bedroom and obtained a 30-30 caliber rifle. On re-exiting from the bedroom she observed Eugene Weick breaking through the kitchen door. She fired the rifle at Eugene and the bullet struck him in the face. Messick and Frank Weick retreated from the house, taking Eugene with them, and met the Connellys, who had been awaiting them in the getaway car. They placed their injured cohort in the car and fled the scene, failing to consummate the intended drug theft. Eugene subsequently died of the bullet wound he received at the hands of Mrs. Fitzgerald. The criminal charges brought against the defendants were based upon that homicide.

The defendants contend: (1) that § 635(2) was applied to them improperly in that it was used as the basis for convictions and sentences for the killing of a co-felon by the intended victim of the felony. . . .

II.

Under § 635(2), the Statute upon which the Murder convictions were based, a person is guilty of Murder in the Second Degree when:

> "(i)n the course of and in furtherance of the commission or attempted commission of any felony not specifically enumerated in § 636 of this title or immediate flight therefrom, he, with criminal negligence, causes the death of another person."

The defendants contend that this section was improperly applied to them because, manifestly, § 635(2) was not intended to punish one who commits a felony for a homicide that occurs during the perpetration of that felony but is not committed by him, his agent, or some one under his control. We agree.

Section 635(2) is the statutory substitute for the common-law felony-murder rule. *Delaware Criminal Code Commentary* 192 (1973). . . .

"[W]ith the general trend toward mitigation in the severity of punishment for many felonies, and with the addition of many statutory felonies of a character less dangerous than was typical of most common law felonies, the irrationality and unfairness of an unlimited felony-murder rule become increasingly apparent." 230 A.2d at 268. Consequently, limitations were placed on the scope of the rule. One such restriction was the requirement of a causal connection between the felony and the murder. Another restraint placed on the rule by some courts was the requirement that the killing be performed by the felon, his accomplices, or one associated with the felon in his unlawful enterprise.

In the development of the felony-murder rule through the common law and by statute, the latter limitation has become the majority rule. . . .   The parameters of this rule are probably best defined by *Commonwealth v. Redline*, Pa. Supr., 391 Pa. 486, 137 A.2d 472, 476 (1958) in which it was stated:

> "In adjudging a felony-murder, it is to be remembered at all times that the thing which is imputed to a felon for a killing incidental to his felony is *malice* and *not the act of killing*. The mere coincidence of homicide and felony is not enough to satisfy the requirements of the felony murder doctrine. It is necessary . . . to show that the conduct causing death was done in furtherance of the design to commit the felony. Death must be a consequence of the felony . . . and not merely coincidence."

We think that this rule clearly applies to § 635(2). That section requires that the homicide be committed "in the course of and in furtherance" of the commission or attempted commission of any felony not enumerated in § 636. Certainly the killing of a co-felon by the victim or a police officer, or the accidental killing of an innocent bystander by the victim or a police officer, can hardly be considered to be "in furtherance" of the commission or attempted commission of a felony. Indeed, the homicide in the instant case was an attempt to prevent the felony. . . .

The case is remanded to the Superior Court for further proceedings in accordance herewith. . . .

Compare the position taken in the above decision with that taken below in *Oimen*:

STATE *v.* OIMEN

Supreme Court of Wisconsin 184 Wis. 2d 423 (1994)

HEFFERNAN, CHIEF JUSTICE. . . . We accepted review limited to the following two issues: whether the felony murder statute, sec. 940.03, Stats., applies to a defendant whose co-felon is killed by the intended felony victim; and whether the circuit court erred in instructing the jury on the elements of felony murder.

We conclude that under sec. 940.03, a defendant can be charged with felony murder for the death of a co-felon when the killing was committed by the victim of the underlying felony. Sec. 940.03 limits liability to those deaths caused by a defendant committing or attempting to commit a limited number of inherently dangerous felonies, but it contains no other limitations on liability. The state need only prove that the defendant caused the death, and that the defendant caused the death while committing or attempting to commit one of the five listed felonies. The defendant's acts need not be the sole cause of death. Thus, Oimen was appropriately charged with felony murder for the death of a co-felon, Shawn Murphy McGinnis, who was killed by Tom Stoker, the victim of the underlying felony. . . .

[Evidence suggested that Oimen helped plan the robbery and provided information about the victim and the sums of money the victim kept at his home as well as a diagram of the intended victim's house. Oimen waited up the street in the getaway vehicle until the shooting of McGinnis by the intended victim, at which time, Oimen apparently drove away.]

The jury found Oimen guilty on all counts. . . .

The first issue we address on review is whether a defendant may be charged with felony murder under sec. 940.03, Stats., when that defendant's co-felon is killed by the intended victim of the underlying felony. Statutory construction is a question of law that this court determines de novo. The principal objective of statutory construction is to ascertain and give effect to the legislature's intent. In determining that intent, we first resort to the language of the statute.

Section 940.03, Stats., states:

> Whoever causes the death of another human being while committing or attempting to commit a crime specified in s. 940.225(1) or (2)(a) [first degree sexual assault and second degree sexual assault with use or threat of force or violence], 943.02 [arson], 943.10(2) [armed burglary] or 943.32(2) [armed robbery] may be imprisoned for not more than 20 years in excess of the maximum period of imprisonment provided by law for that crime or attempt.

We conclude that the plain meaning of sec. 940.03, Stats., allows a defendant to be charged with felony murder when a co-felon is killed by the intended felony victim. Section 940.03, Stats., contains two elements, which were set forth in the jury instructions: the defendant must cause a death and the defendant must cause the death while committing or attempting to commit one of the five listed felonies. "Causes" has a consistent, well-established meaning in Wisconsin criminal law. An actor causes death if his or her conduct is a "substantial factor" in bringing about that result. As long as an actor's conduct is a "substantial factor" in bringing about a death, the plain language of sec. 940.03 places no limits on whose death it is that results. Under sec. 940.03, it is irrelevant that McGinnis, the person who was killed, was a co-felon. It is also irrelevant for purposes of sec. 940.03 that the rifle shot fired by Stoker was the immediate cause of McGinnis's death. A "substantial factor" need not be the sole cause of death. . . .

The conclusion we reach regarding the elements of felony murder liability, based on the plain language of sec. 940.03, is supported by the legislative history. Sec. 940.03 became law when the legislature revised the law of homicide. These revisions were drafted by the Wisconsin Judicial Council's Special Committee on Homicide and Lesser Included Offenses ["Homicide Law Committee"]. . . . [8] The Homicide Law Committee discussions indicate that the Judicial Council decided to recommend only one limitation on liability — the major limitation of restricting felony murder liability to killings that occur during the course of five listed felonies.

The Homicide Law Committee discussed and rejected other limitations on felony murder liability. . . .

A brief discussion by members of the Homicide Law Committee indicates that sec. 940.03 was not meant to be restricted to situations in which the person killed was the victim of the underlying felony. A member of the committee raised the possibility of having a longer list of underlying felonies and limiting the statute's coverage to killings of the victim of those crimes. However, another committee member stated the victim limitation could present problems and asked whether patrons at a retail store would be "victims" if killed in an armed robbery when only cash register proceeds had been taken. The other committee member agreed that limiting the statute's coverage to death of victims of the underlying felony could prove to be complicated. We could find no further discussion suggesting that sec. 940.03 was to apply only to murders of certain individuals such as bystanders or victims of the underlying felony. No such limiting language was proposed. . . .

---

[8] The Wisconsin Judicial Council is a body of twenty members that has powers and duties set forth in sec. 758.13(2), Stats., including:

> (d) Receive, consider and in its discretion investigate suggestions from any source pertaining to the administration of justice and to make recommendations.

[T]he committee [also] made no effort to . . . limit liability to the "trigger person" when it developed the fall back provision that became sec. 940.03.

Oimen points out that the vast majority of state courts that have addressed this issue have concluded that the applicable statute does not make a felon liable for murder when the killing was done by a victim of the felony. These states take what has been termed the "agency approach" to felony murder liability, under which a felon can only be liable for death when the killing was committed by an individual acting in concert with him, i.e. acting in furtherance of the underlying felony. We believe that sec. 940.03 and the accompanying legislative history indicate that the legislature did not intend to impose liability only when there is an "agency" relationship. . . . . [W]e note that the cases adopting the agency approach appear to be grounded in policy concerns — dissatisfaction with the strict liability aspect of felony murder, or a concern that liability in such cases "erodes the relation between criminal liability and moral culpability." [*People v.*] *Washington*, 402 P.2d [130] at 134 [(1965)]. While that concern is not unreasonable, that policy determination is one for the legislature to make and the Wisconsin legislature's determination is to the contrary.

Realizing that application of the felony murder statute could lead to harsh results in some cases, the Homicide Law Committee explained that any potential harshness can be mitigated at sentencing. . . . *By the court.* — Decision affirmed.

QUESTIONS

1. The "in furtherance" limitation is often known as the "agency" rule. Why might that label be used?

2. How would you describe the "in furtherance" or "agency" limitation in your own words? Write a brief description of it and a few hypotheticals to illustrate how it works.

3. How and why might an enumerated felony be subject to an agency limitation? How does an agency limitation differ from an inherent danger limitation?

PROBLEM

6.22[29] During the confusion in the aftermath of a burglary of a commercial building by several individuals, a police officer shoots and kills someone. The officer saw the victim running with a handgun in the direction that two of the individuals, believed to be perpetrators of the burglary, had fled. The victim failed to halt upon being ordered to do so. The victim was later identified as another law enforcement officer.

The court must determine whether there is an agency limitation on the state's felony-murder doctrine.

Here is the text of the statute:

"(a) A person who kills an individual without lawful justification commits murder if, in performing the acts which cause the death:

---

29. The facts in this problem are based on and the quotations are from People v. Hickman, 12 Ill. App. 3d 412 (1973).

(3) He is attempting or committing a forcible felony other than manslaughter."

(Assume that the burglary here is a forcible felony.)

Based on the text of the statute, what conclusion should the court reach?

If, in addition to the text of the statute, the court had available, as described below, the "notes and reports of the commission pursuant to which the statutory provision was adopted," should the court consider them? If so, what conclusion should the court reach on the question at issue?

> We find on page 9 of Illinois Annotated Statute chapter 38 the following comments in regard to application . . . of the felony-murder provision:
>
> > "It is immaterial whether the killing in such a case is intentional or accidental, or is committed by a confederate without the connivance of the defendant . . . or even by a third person trying to prevent the commission of the felony."

e. Res Gestae Limits

The fifth limitation on the felony-murder rule we will examine, the res gestae restriction, analyzes how closely tied the killing is to the felony. Courts here often focus on time, whether the felony was still in progress at the time of the killing or, if the felony had been completed, how much time had transpired between completion of the felony and the death. Courts applying the res gestae limitation also consider the distance between the place of the felony and the place of the death as well as the strength of the causal connection between the felony and the death. Again, as you read the materials that follow, ask yourself if and why time, space, and causal connection are important in establishing the bounds of murder liability.

STATE v. ADAMS

Supreme Court of Missouri 339 Mo. 926 (1936)

ELLISON, J. — The appellant was convicted of murder in the first degree, the jury inflicting the death penalty, for the fatal shooting of Clarence Green, night marshal of the town of Campbell in Dunklin County, in March, 1934. It was not controverted at the trial that just preceding the homicide the appellant and two accomplices were engaged in burglarizing a filling station at Campbell. But he contended the burglarious enterprise had been abandoned, that he was in flight, and that Green was shot by another of the burglars for which he is not responsible. . . .

Summarizing the evidence as briefly as possible, it was conceded by appellant's counsel in open court at the trial, and the undisputed evidence showed it, that he and two accomplices had broken into a White Eagle gasoline filling station at

Campbell about eleven o'clock at night and had carried out and deposited on the ground certain articles of property which they were stealing, and had gone back presumably for more loot when the deceased Clarence Green, together with Rodney Brown, city marshal, and two other men, drove up to the filling station. The three burglars fled across lots into a wooded section behind the station. Green and Brown followed in pursuit, being guided mainly by sound since it was too dark to see the fugitives in the woods, though the moon was shining. How far from the filling station the chase continued the record does not clearly show — perhaps several hundred feet — but at any rate, Brown testified that Green was about twenty feet ahead of him and some fifty feet from what the witnesses called "the fourth fence" when suddenly one gunshot was fired by someone straight ahead of Green who sagged down and then started to straighten up. Several more shots came from an oblique direction. From their rapid succession it appeared they had been fired from an automatic shotgun. Green reeled in a semicircle for about fifteen feet, fell, and died without uttering a word. . . .

[W]e must . . . pass on the assignments in [the] motion for new trial charging the homicide was not committed in the perpetration or attempted perpetration of the burglary — this because the court gave instructions authorizing a conviction on that theory, and the appellant complains there was no evidence to support them. The seventh instruction declared any homicide committed in the perpetration or attempted perpetration of a burglary is murder in the first degree, and the eighth instruction told the jury the perpetration or attempted perpetration of a burglary consists not only in burglariously breaking and entering a building and seizing property therein with intent to steal and carry it away, but includes also the act of asportation, and continues until the property has been reduced to the unmolested dominion of the burglars. This instruction then went on to advise the jury that if they found the killing of Green was done by the appellant, or others with whom he knowingly acted in joint concert, while the appellant and such others were engaged in the perpetration or attempted perpetration of a burglary as above defined, the law would presume and supply the several mental ingredients necessary to make the homicide murder in the first degree.

The appellant's motion points to the undisputed evidence showing that when the officers approached the filling station the three accomplices abandoned the burglary and all dominion over the property they had seized, and fled from the premises, the fatal shooting occurring thereafter. He maintains that under these facts the homicide was not committed in the perpetration or attempted perpetration of the burglary within the meaning of the statute; and that he cannot be held guilty of murder in the first degree on that theory, either as the actual killer, or as a co-conspirator in the antecedent burglary if the fatal shot was fired by another of the trio. . . .

It is held in many jurisdictions, including Missouri, that when the homicide is within the *res gestae* of the initial crime and is an emanation thereof, it is committed in the *perpetration* of that crime in the statutory sense. Thus it has been often ruled that the statute applies where the initial crime and the homicide were parts of one continuous transaction, and were closely connected in point of time, place and causal relation, as where the killing was done in flight from the scene of the crime to prevent detection, or promote escape. The same rule has been followed in cases of *attempted* robbery where there was no asportation, the robbers being compelled to flee without obtaining any property. [T]his is the prevailing doctrine in this country. . . .

The undisputed evidence in this case shows the killing of Green was of the *res gestae* of the burglary. Instruction No. 8, if it was erroneous in the respect above pointed out, was error in favor of the appellant, rather than against him, because it allowed a conviction on the theory that the homicide was committed in the perpetration or attempted perpetration of the burglary, only if the jury found the killing was done during the actual burglary or the asportation of the property sought to be taken. . . .

But the instruction could have done no harm in this case, because, as we have shown, the undisputed evidence shows the homicide was committed within the *res gestae* of the burglary, and the question of asportation and possession was immaterial. . . .

Date of execution set for December 18, 1936.

How far does the res gestae of a felony extend? Consider the following standard from *State v. Williams*, 776 So. 2d 1066 (2001):

> The crux of this case is the breadth of the phrase "engaged in the perpetration of . . . any felony" in the felony murder statute. . . .
>
> In deciding whether a killing falls under the felony murder statute, the more recent supreme court case of *Parker v. State*, 641 So. 2d 369, 376 (Fla. 1994), looked for a "break in the chain of circumstances" between the killing and the underlying felony. . . .
>
> To find what the supreme court calls "a break in the chain of circumstances" between the killing and the underlying felony, courts focus on the time, distance, and causal relationship between the underlying felony and the killing. "Neither the passage of time nor separation in space from the felonious act to the killing precludes a felony murder conviction when it can be said . . . that the killing is a predictable result of the felonious transaction."
>
> [O]ne of the most important factors to consider in deciding if there has been a "break in the chain of circumstances" is whether the "fleeing felon has reached a place of temporary safety." *Parker*, 570 So. 2d at 1051 (quoting LaFave, Substantive Criminal Law, § 7.5 (1986)). If the felon has gained a place of temporary safety after commission of the felony and before the death of the victim, the felony murder rule generally does not apply.

F. THE PROVOCATIVE ACT DOCTRINE

Imagine a bank robber who unwittingly trips a silent alarm and finds himself surrounded in the bank lobby by a phalanx of armed police. The robber takes a hostage and emerges from the bank shouting threats and firing his gun in the direction of the police, who fire back at the robber and accidentally kill the hostage.

Could the defendant be liable under the felony-murder rule? Not if the jurisdiction has adopted the "in furtherance" limitation, also known as the "agency" rule. The police shooting was in opposition to, not in furtherance of, the robbery. The agency rule typically requires that the shooter be a felon. In our hypothetical, the shooter was a police officer.

The provocative act doctrine, however, may enable prosecutors to nonetheless charge first-degree murder in those felony cases. To succeed, a prosecutor must satisfy at least three criteria. First, she must prove that the felon(s) harbored malice aforethought. In this case, it is the "extreme recklessness" form of implied malice. A classic example of such malice is initiating a gun battle, as in our hypothetical. Note that the provocative act doctrine is distinct from felony murder and relies on a different theory of malice—namely, extreme recklessness.

Second, the prosecutor must prove that the "killing [was] attributable to the act of the defendant or his accomplice. When the defendant or his accomplice, with a conscious disregard for life, intentionally commits an act that is likely to cause death, [like initiating a gun battle] and his victim or a police officer kills in reasonable response to such act, the defendant is guilty of murder."[30]

Generally, an extreme reckless killing qualifies as second-degree murder in a jurisdiction that divides murder into degrees. Thus, using this analysis so far, the prosecutor has proven ordinary or second-degree murder. To reach first-degree murder, the prosecutor must prove, as the third requirement, that the now-established murder was committed during one of the felonies enumerated in the first-degree murder statute. If the murder was committed during one of those listed felonies, the statute "may properly be invoked to determine the degree [of the] murder."[31] The California courts, for example, have read the enumeration language in its first-degree murder statute as having a "grading" function separate from its function of creating a felony-murder rule. Thus, the felony-murder provision of the first-degree murder statute elevates the degree of an extreme reckless murder from second to first.[32]

QUESTIONS

1. How does the provocative act doctrine differ from felony murder?
2. Are there any similarities between the provocative act doctrine and the Michigan case, *Aaron*, which rejected felony murder?

G. MISDEMEANOR MANSLAUGHTER

Misdemeanor manslaughter offers prosecutors a shortcut similar to felony murder. If the prosecutor proves that the defendant caused a death as a result of committing or attempting to commit a misdemeanor, the defendant may be liable for misdemeanor manslaughter. The doctrine saves the prosecution the need to prove a mental state beyond that required for the misdemeanor. As with the felony-murder doctrine, some courts narrow the doctrine through the imposition of various limitations.

---

30. People v. Gilbert, 63 Cal. 2d 690, 704 (1965). In People v. Antick, 539 P.2d 43 (Cal. Sup. Ct. 1975), the court modified the provocative act doctrine to exclude homicide liability under certain circumstances when a felon is the one killed.

31. *Gilbert*, 63 Cal. 2d, at 705.

32. *Id.* (if the killing was committed by an accomplice, the prosecution must also prove that the "accomplice [caused] the death of another human being by an act committed in furtherance of the common design").

UNITED STATES *v.* WALKER

District of Columbia Court of Appeals 380 A.2d 1388 (1977)

Opinion:

KERN, Associate Judge:

Appellee was charged with two counts of involuntary manslaughter and one count of carrying a pistol without a license (D.C. Code 1973, § 22-3204). The government appeals from the trial court's dismissal of the count in the indictment which charged that appellee

> feloniously, in perpetrating and attempting to perpetrate the crime of carrying a pistol without a license, involving danger of injury, did shoot Ernestine Curry with a pistol, thereby causing injuries from which the said Ernestine Curry died. . . .

At the hearing on appellee's motion to dismiss this count of the indictment, the government's proffer of evidence was that appellee, while carrying a pistol without a license, dropped it in the stairwell of an apartment building, and that the gun went off, fatally wounding a bystander. Appellee's proffer was that a firearms expert had determined that when the hammer of the pistol was not cocked, it would fire on impact only if dropped at a particular angle. These proffers constitute the only explanation in the record of the incident underlying the indictment.

There is no statutory definition of manslaughter in this jurisdiction. . . . [In an earlier opinion on] involuntary manslaughter, we said:

> Involuntary manslaughter is an unlawful killing which is unintentionally committed. By unintentionally it is meant that there is no intent to kill or to do bodily injury. The crime may occur as the result of an unlawful act which is a *misdemeanor involving danger of injury*. . . . The requisite intent in involuntary manslaughter is supplied by the intent to commit the misdemeanor, or by gross or criminal negligence. . . .

The state of mind in involuntary manslaughter is characterized, on the one hand, by a lack of intent to cause death or injury and, on the other, by a lack of awareness of the consequences of the act amounting to an unreasonable failure of perception [criminal negligence] . . . *or the intention to do an act which is a misdemeanor and is in some way dangerous.* . . . [*Id.* at 215]

We defined the elements of involuntary manslaughter as: "(1) an unlawful killing of a human being (2) with either (a) *the intent to commit a misdemeanor dangerous in itself* or (b) an unreasonable failure to perceive the risk of harm to others." *Id.* at 216; emphasis added.

This appeal therefore presents for our determination the question whether the unlawful act of carrying a pistol without a license is also a dangerous act. *Id.* at 216 n.24. The pertinent statute provides:

> No person shall within the District of Columbia carry either openly or concealed on or about his person, except in his dwelling house or place of business or on other land possessed by him, a pistol without a license therefor issued as hereinafter provided. . . . [D.C. Code 1973, § 22-3204.]

Appellee, citing *Mitchell v. United States*, argues that the plain intent of Section 3204 is to stop the prohibited conduct *before* danger of injury arises, and that such danger is not a necessary concomitant of the offense.[3] Appellee proceeds to illustrate what he deems to be the "essence" of the offense of carrying a pistol without a license by the following hypothetical:

> [Two] persons [are] walking peaceably on a public street carrying holstered pistols. One . . . has a license to carry a pistol, but the other has *no* license. The second person is violating section 3204, and the first is *not*. Yet there is no difference between them in terms of the danger presented to others.

Appellee's hypothetical and argument notwithstanding, we conclude that carrying a pistol without a license exposes the community to such inherent risk of harm that when death results, even though an unintended consequence, the defendant may be nonetheless charged with involuntary manslaughter. Appellee in the instant case was carrying a loaded handgun, which, so far as the record shows, had no purpose other than its use as a weapon. Implicit in the statutory proscription of carrying a pistol without a license outside the possessor's "dwelling house or place of business" is a congressional recognition of the inherent risk of harm to the public of such dangerous instrumentality being carried about the community and away from the residence or business of the possessor. Indeed, the history of the statute evinces congressional concern with the need to control the introduction of pistols into the community by licensing all those who do so. . . .

Additionally, we think it significant in assessing the dangerousness *vel non* of the unlawful act of carrying a pistol without a license that Congress has expressly required one who seeks the license to be "a suitable person to be so licensed." D.C. Code 1973, § 22-3206. Issuance of these licenses is the responsibility of the Chief of the Metropolitan Police Department, *id.*, and is subject to restrictive regulations which, among other things, require the applicant to be of sound mind, to be without a prior criminal record, not to be an alcoholic or user of narcotics, to "be trained and experienced in the use, functioning and safe operation of the pistol," and finally, "to be free from physical defects which would impair his safe use of the weapon." 21 D.C. Reg. 413-21 (1974).

Thus, taking up appellee's hypothetical of the two persons carrying pistols on a public street, one of whom is licensed and the other of whom is not, we conclude that Congress intended to preclude the non-licensee from being on the street with his weapon because of the danger he posed to the community as a result (1) of the inherent dangerousness of the weapon he carried, and (2) of the absence of any evidence of his capability to carry safely such a dangerous instrumentality.

To summarize, this court in [*United States v. Bradford*], defined involuntary manslaughter as the killing of another "as the result of an unlawful act which is a misdemeanor involving danger of injury." In *Mitchell*, we declared the object of Section 3204, which proscribes carrying a pistol outside the residence or place of business without a license, to be "to forestall the temptation to use it [the pistol] as such," thereby recognizing the danger of injury arising from the unlicensed carrying of the pistol. We now hold that a charge of violation of Section 3204 resulting in the shooting and death of another validly charges involuntary manslaughter because the misdemeanor of carrying a pistol without a license is dangerous in and of itself. Accordingly, the

---

[3] In *Mitchell* we concluded that "the object of the statute [section 3204] is not to prohibit the carrying of a pistol with intent to use it as a weapon, but to *forestall the temptation to use it* as such by forbidding possession of such an object *outside the possessor's home or place of business*." emphasis added.

trial court's order must be reversed and the count at issue restored to the indictment.

So ordered.

QUESTIONS

1. What limitation does *Walker* recognize on misdemeanor manslaughter?

2. Would limitations similar to those imposed in some jurisdictions on felony murder be appropriate for misdemeanor manslaughter?

H. SYNTHESIS AND REVIEW

PROBLEM

6.23 Sarah is a member of a radical white supremacist group dedicated to ridding the United States of "the pernicious influences" of
"alien" racial and religious groups. In order to help fund her group's
activities, she decides to kidnap for ransom Stephen, the son of a
prominent newspaper owner. The family's newspaper is liberal in
its political point of view and has been highly critical of the white
supremacist movement. Sarah and a group of confederates abduct
Stephen early one morning while he is on his way to work and take
him to a remote wooded area in the countryside. In order to keep
Stephen out of sight and out of trouble while negotiating the group's
$1 million ransom demand, Sarah and her confederates bury Stephen
alive in a wooden box, the dimensions of which are roughly six
feet by four feet by four feet. The box is buried by Sarah approximately three feet underground in a sandy, wooded area. In the
box, Sarah leaves a small bulb connected to several car batteries.
In order to provide Stephen with air, Sarah buries next to the box
an air tank with a day's supply of air in it. A mouthpiece is connected from the tank to the box for Stephen to breathe through.
One of her confederates asks Sarah, "Don't you think he might
suffocate? He's not worth anything to us dead." Sarah replies, "It
is a risk worth taking. Their newspaper has tried to suffocate our
movement."

The next day, Sarah makes several telephone calls to Stephen's
family demanding $1 million in ransom. Acting on the advice of the
FBI and local police, Stephen's family initially stalls for several hours
and resists Sarah's ransom demands. During the delay, the FBI traces
the calls to the telephone booth Sarah has been using to make the
ransom calls. While Sarah is making her final ransom call for the
day, the FBI arrests her. At the time of her arrest, she is alone. Her
confederates hear of the arrest and, afraid that Sarah may talk, head

for Canada, leaving Stephen buried in the box. At the border her confederates are all killed in a shoot-out with Canadian and United States police.

During intense interrogation in the days following her arrest, Sarah refuses to reveal the whereabouts of Stephen. The police inform Sarah that Stephen has not been found and that her confederates have all been killed. A week after Sarah's arrest, while Sarah is still in custody and refusing to talk, police dogs locate the site at which Stephen had been buried alive. When the box is uncovered, Stephen is found dead. A medical examiner later determines: (1) that Stephen died from suffocation two days before the police discovered the location of the box, and (2) that Stephen would have lived if his location had been discovered two days earlier.

Is Sarah liable for homicide based on Stephen's death? If so, what type of homicide? Assessing Sarah's homicide liability will require you to draw on some of the materials you studied in chapters prior to the one on homicide, such as those dealing with conduct.

I. CAPITAL PUNISHMENT: CONSTITUTIONAL DIMENSIONS

1. Introduction

Deprivation of life is the ultimate penalty imposed by the state for criminal conduct. As of May 2004, more than two-thirds of the states as well as the federal government had statutes authorizing imposition of the death penalty.[33]

UNITED STATES DEPARTMENT OF JUSTICE, OFFICE OF JUSTICE PROGRAMS, BUREAU OF JUSTICE STATISTICS, CAPITAL PUNISHMENT STATISTICS

http://www.ojp.usdoj.gov/bjs/cp.htm (Mar. 22, 2004)

- In 2002, 71 persons in 13 States were executed.
- Lethal injection accounted for 70 of the executions; 1 was carried out by electrocution.
- Of the persons under sentence of death in 2001:

  — 1,931 were white
  — 1,554 were black

---

33. Death Penalty Information Center Web site, *http://www.deathpenaltyinfo.org/article.php?scid=121 & scid=11#with* (accessed May 14, 2004). This number is similar to the United States Department of Justice, Office of Justice Programs, Bureau of Justice Statistics' Web site total of jurisdictions with prisoners under sentence of death, given above. *http://www.ojp.usdoj.gov/bjs/abstract/cp01.htm* (accessed Mar. 22, 2004).

— 27 were American Indian
— 33 were Asian
— 12 were of unknown race

- The 364 Hispanic inmates under sentence of death accounted for 12% of inmates with a known ethnicity.
- Fifty-one women were under sentence of death.
- At yearend 2002, 37 States and the Federal prison system held 3,557 prisoners under sentence of death, 20 fewer than at yearend 2001. All had committed murder.

Debate about the wisdom and constitutionality of capital punishment focuses on both the state-sanctioned execution itself as well as the process that the state must follow to exact such a penalty. The United States Supreme Court has played a substantial role in defining this process through its interpretation of the federal Constitution. In this Section of the chapter, we study that evolving constitutional framework. We begin with the text of the federal Constitution and Bill of Rights, followed by an overview of the Court's interpretation of the relevant constitutional provisions. We then engage in a detailed reading of some of the most significant cases in the Court's death penalty jurisprudence.

2. Constitutional Text

The original Constitution did not explicitly mention capital punishment. Specific mention first appeared in the Bill of Rights, which was ratified in 1791, four years after the Constitution itself. Within the Bill of Rights, the Fifth Amendment makes three direct references to capital punishment. It reads:

> No person shall be held to answer for a capital, or otherwise infamous crime, unless on a presentment or indictment of a Grand Jury, except in cases arising in the land or naval forces, or in the Militia, when in actual service in time of War or public danger; nor shall any person be subject for the same offence to be twice put in jeopardy of life or limb; nor shall be compelled in any criminal case to be a witness against himself, nor be deprived of life, liberty, or property, without due process of law; nor shall private property be taken for public use, without just compensation.[34]

In analyzing the approach taken by the Framers of the Constitution to the federal death penalty, Professor Rory Little explains:

> When establishing the Union in 1787, the Framers appear to have given little attention to the death penalty. This is unsurprising. Death as a penalty for serious felonies was common in the eighteenth century, and the Constitution simply assumes, without ever stating expressly, that capital punishment will be imposed. For example, the Fifth Amendment explicitly assumes that there will be "capital" crimes and suggests that persons may be deprived of "life," if such is accomplished with due process of law.
> In the body of the Constitution itself, the death penalty is never mentioned. However treason, traditionally a capital offense, is mentioned in Article III, and Congress is expressly authorized to "declare the punishment of treason." The debate regarding this clause in the Constitutional Convention strongly indicates that the Framers

---

34. U.S. Const. amend. V.

assumed that treason would be punished by death, and the First Congress soon so provided.[35]

The Supreme Court has exercised control over the death penalty through its interpretation of the Due Process guarantee that appears in the Fifth Amendment and through the Eighth Amendment's ban on the infliction of "cruel and unusual punishments."[36] The Eighth Amendment, perhaps to an even greater extent than the Due Process Clause, has provided the constitutional language that has proven the primary vehicle for shaping constitutional death penalty law.

3. Is the Death Penalty Itself a Constitutional Form of Punishment?

We consider first the facial constitutionality of the death penalty. In other words, is the death penalty unconstitutional per se? The Court, confronting the question directly in its 1976 opinion, *Gregg v. Georgia*, held that the death penalty for the crime of murder did not per se violate the Eighth Amendment's "cruel and unusual punishments" provision.

In its *Gregg* opinion, the Court explained that "the Eighth Amendment has not been regarded as a static concept . . . '[t]he Amendment must draw its meaning from the evolving standards of decency that mark the progress of a maturing society.' "[37] These evolving standards of decency require an assessment of society's contemporary values. Here, the Court emphasized the importance of relying upon "objective indicia that reflect the public attitude toward a given sanction."[38] In addition to being consistent with these contemporary values, the "penalty also must accord with 'the dignity of man,' which is the 'basic concept underlying the Eighth Amendment.' "[39] For the first part of the constitutional analysis, to assess contemporary values, the Court turned to the historical treatment of the death penalty, past and current legislative judgment as expressed through statutes, a state public referendum on the death penalty, and jury response to the death penalty. After reviewing these indicia and despite vehement dissent, the Court concluded that the death penalty was not inconsistent with contemporary values.

For the second part of the analysis, the question of the dignity of man, the Court considered whether the sanction was "so totally without penological justification that it results in the gratuitous infliction of suffering."[40] Here, the Court focused on the "two principal social purposes: retribution and deterrence"[41] that the sanction "is said to serve."[42] The Court observed:

> The instinct for retribution is part of the nature of man, and channeling that instinct in the administration of criminal justice serves an important purpose in promoting the stability of a society governed by law. When people begin to believe that

---

35. Rory K. Little, *The Federal Death Penalty: History and Some Thoughts About the Department of Justice's Role*, 26 Fordham Urb. L.J. 347, 360-361 (1999).

36. U.S. Const. amend VIII. Some of the Court's death penalty jurisprudence also relies on the Equal Protection Clause.

37. 428 U.S. 153, 172-173 (1976).

38. *Id.* at 173.

39. *Id.*

40. *Id.* at 183.

41. *Id.*

42. *Id.*

organized society is unwilling or unable to impose upon criminal offenders the punishment they "deserve," then there are sown the seeds of anarchy — of self-help,
vigilante justice, and lynch law.[43]

The Court then noted that

"[r]etribution is no longer the dominant objective of the criminal law, . . . but
neither is it a forbidden objective nor one inconsistent with our respect for the
dignity of men. Indeed, the decision that capital punishment may be the appropriate
sanction in extreme cases is an expression of the community's belief that certain
crimes are themselves so grievous an affront to humanity that the only adequate
response may be the penalty of death."[44]

Having affirmed the legitimacy of retribution as an objective of the death
penalty, the Court then examined deterrence: "Statistical attempts to evaluate the
worth of the death penalty as a deterrent to crimes by potential offenders have
occasioned a great deal of debate. The results simply have been inconclusive. As
one opponent of capital punishment has said:

"[A]fter all possible inquiry, including the probing of all possible methods of
inquiry, we do not know, and for systematic and easily visible reasons cannot know,
what the truth about this "deterrent" effect may be. . . . ' "[45]

Ultimately on the issue of deterrence, the Court deferred to the judgment of
the legislatures. The Court wrote that they "can evaluate the results of statistical
studies in terms of their own local conditions and with a flexibility of approach
that is not available to the courts."[46]

Thus, the Court found that "the infliction of death as a punishment for murder is not without justification and thus is not unconstitutionally severe . . . [or]
disproportionate in relation to the crime [of murder] for which it is imposed."[47]

Although the Court has not found the death penalty unconstitutional per se,
it has held that unconstitutionality may lie in the administration or application of
capital punishment. In the next Section, we examine the competing values at the
heart of this debate.

4. Competing Values: Discretion versus Standards

Competing values emerge from the Court's interpretation of constitutional
doctrine. On the one hand, there is the value of individualized consideration and
discretion to choose the appropriate punishment in each case. On the other, there is
the value of standards that can enhance uniformity and mitigate arbitrariness. Over
the years, the Court has emphasized the importance of each of these values. In the
1978 *Lockett* decision, the Court underscored the need for individual consideration
of each case and each accused defendant. As the Court explained in *Lockett*, "[g]iven
that the imposition of death by public authority is so profoundly different from all
other penalties, we cannot avoid the conclusion that an individualized decision is
essential in capital cases."[48] The Court therefore determined that "the sentencer,

---

43. *Id.* (quoting Furman v. Georgia, 408 U.S. 238, 308 (1972)).
44. *Id.* at 183-184.
45. *Id.* (quoting C. Black, *Capital Punishment: The Inevitability of Caprice and Mistake* 25-26 (1974)),
at 184-185.
46. *Id.* at 186.
47. *Id.* at 187.
48. Lockett v. Ohio, 438 U.S. 586, 605 (1978).

in all but the rarest kind of capital case, not be precluded from considering, *as a mitigating factor*, any aspect of a defendant's character or record and any of the circumstances of the offense that the defendant proffers as a basis for a sentence less than death."[49] A plurality of the Court viewed individualized consideration, in which discretion plays a fundamental role, as necessary to enhance the reliability of the sentence — whether "death is the appropriate punishment in the specific case"[50] and to respect the uniqueness of each individual defendant.[51]

But unbridled or standardless discretion and individualized consideration open the door to arbitrary applications of the sentence of death. Balancing the importance of individualized consideration, the Court now requires guidance or standards that cabin its exercise. This guidance limits the scope of discretion and aims to increase fairness and consistency in the application of the death penalty. This guidance surfaces in at least two forms.

First, the Court has provided generalized guidance on how states may, and may not, shape their death penalty law. States usually translate this guidance into statutes that govern the imposition of the death penalty. These statutes circumscribe the universe of circumstances upon which a fact finder may base a death sentence in a particular case. Commonly, these statutes also require particular factual findings before the fact finder may select death. For example, before an individual convicted of murder becomes eligible for the death penalty, the statute can require that the jury must find one or more aggravating circumstances present. These might include, for example, that the defendant had prior felony convictions or that the defendant committed more than one murder in the case. Some statutes require that the jury make findings not only about aggravating but also about mitigating factors and that the jury then weigh them against one another in determining sentence. Mitigators might relate, for example, to a defendant's youth or minor role in the crime. In this way, legislatures have sought to navigate a course that minimizes unfairness in the application of the death penalty while permitting fact finders to evaluate each accused individual and his situation.

Second, in addition to generalized guidance, the Court has created explicit bright and quasi bright-line rules about how and when the fact finder may impose a sentence of death. For example, as analyzed in greater detail later in the chapter, the Court determined, in *Coker v. Georgia*,[52] that the Eighth Amendment prohibits capital punishment for the rape of an adult woman. Thus, such a crime cannot serve as the basis on which a sentencing authority relies to impose a sentence of death.[53]

The importance of discretion and of standards for guiding that discretion create ongoing tension. Before we turn to cases that identify and address these competing tensions in the Court's death penalty matrix, we introduce you to some of the concepts and complexities by asking you to participate as a juror in the Problem that follows.

---

49. *Id.* at 604-605.

50. *Id.* at 601 (quoting Roberts (Harry) v. Louisiana, 431 U.S. 633, 637 (1977)).

51. *Id.* at 605.

52. 433 U.S. 584 (1977).

53. Whether a crime, other than murder, can serve as the basis of a death sentence is a current issue. In a 2003 Louisiana case, State v. Kennedy, 98-1425, the defendant was sentenced to death for the sexual assault of a child under the age of 12. *See* Lisa Stansky, *Death Sentence for Child Rape Could Go to Supreme Court*, The Recorder (Sept. 16, 2003).

PROBLEM

6.24[54] Imagine that you were selected as an alternate juror in the jointly
charged and tried cases of *People v. Helton & Raft*. To qualify as a juror
(and this may or may not require some mental gymnastics on your
part), you agreed that your views on the death penalty would not
" 'prevent or substantially impair the performance of [your] duties as
a juror in accordance with [your] instructions and [your] oath.' "[55] As
is commonly the procedure, this trial is a bifurcated proceeding. In the
first phase, the jury determines whether the defendants committed the
crimes with which they are charged. In the second, if the jury has found
the defendants guilty of a crime for which a death sentence is possible,
they proceed to a penalty phase. As we discuss in greater detail below,
the first phase in this case concluded with convictions on each count
of the charging document. After the jury reached its verdicts in the
first phase of the case, one juror became ill and you then became a
juror for the penalty phase of the case. The facts that follow represent
the consensus among all the jurors of what happened in the first phase
of the case.

Facts: In January of 2004, Frederick Helton, a 25-year-old male, was
serving a 25-year-to-life sentence for mayhem, second-degree murder,
and aggravated battery. Those convictions involved Helton's violent
assault on a driver who had cut him off on the highway. In that incident, Helton repeatedly beat and ultimately decapitated the driver
with a switch-blade knife and the car jack designed for changing flat
tires. He also severely injured a passerby who had stopped to render
assistance.

   While serving his sentence, Helton worked in the prison kitchen.
There, Helton secured a carving knife and hid it in his clothes and
then in the pillow in his cell. His cellmate, Jeremiah Raft, a 23-year-old
male, saw Helton drawing diagrams and plans and realized that Helton was planning an escape. Raft threatened to tell prison authorities.
In exchange for silence, Helton promised to include Raft in the escape.
Raft questioned Helton about the specifics of the plan, reminding Helton that prisoners had no fire power and that the guards did. Helton
assured Raft that "it was under control; that we will use our brains to
get out."

   On the day of the escape, Helton and Raft went to the kitchen
at the time of their shift. Helton and Raft began unloading supplies
from the delivery truck. Only one guard supervised the unloading.
While Raft was carrying sacks of rice into the kitchen pantry, Helton
grabbed the guard and cut out her tongue so that the guard could not
cry for help and then tied up the guard with some rope and placed her

---

54. Although this problem was developed by the authors, its content was influenced by a number
of real death penalty cases.
55. The United States Supreme Court held in Wainwright v. Witt, 469 U.S. 412, 424 (1985), that this
was the appropriate standard to apply to jury selection.

in the truck. He then took the guard's gun and, when Raft returned, closed the truck's doors and held the gun to the truck driver's head. On Helton's orders, the truck driver drove the truck out of the prison facility. When they had driven 25 miles into the desert surrounding the prison, Helton forced the truck driver out, shot him multiple times in both feet to prevent him from walking and left him to die of exposure. The driver did die some four days later of exposure and blood loss from the wounds. Helton then returned to the back of the truck. There he found the guard, conscious but bleeding. While Raft watched, Helton ordered the guard to beg for mercy and laughed when the guard tried. Helton then took the guard's money and credit cards and drove the truck on through the desert. Helton used the guard's money to buy whatever he or Raft needed or wanted during the trip through the desert. During the three days of the journey, Helton kept the guard in the back of the truck trailer. Helton and Raft ate and drank in front of the conscious and bleeding guard but gave her nothing to eat or drink. At the end of the three days, Helton kicked the guard out of the trailer and left her to die on the side of the road. When Helton and Raft reached the next town, they encountered a police roadblock. Helton took careful aim and fired his remaining three bullets toward a police officer on a motorcycle, striking and killing the officer instantly. Then he drove the truck at full speed into a line of motorcycle officers, killing two and injuring three others. Finally a police sharpshooter shot Helton, causing him to fall from the truck. The police located Raft asleep in the back of the truck's cab. Helton made a full recovery from his injuries.

Based on this information, in the guilt phase, the jury convicted both Helton and Raft of the following charges:

(1) First-degree murder of the truck driver
(2) First-degree murder of the prison guard
(3) First-degree murder of a police officer (Motorcycle Officer #1)
(4) First-degree murder of a police officer (Motorcycle Officer #2)
(5) First-Degree murder of a police officer (Motorcycle Officer #3)
(6) Attempted first-degree murder of a police officer (Motorcycle Officer #4)
(7) Attempted first-degree murder of a police officer (Motorcycle Officer #5)
(8) Attempted first-degree murder of a police officer (Motorcycle Officer #6)
(9) Mayhem on the prison guard
(10) Kidnapping by force of the prison guard
(11) Kidnapping by force of the truck driver
(12) Torture of the prison guard
(13) Torture of the truck driver
(14) Armed robbery of the prison guard

In the penalty phase, both the prosecution and the defense offered additional evidence. With respect to Helton, the prosecution entered his criminal history ("rap sheet") into evidence. In addition to the crimes for which he was serving a sentence at the time of his escape, his rap sheet listed four armed robberies, ten separate convictions for drug dealing, all when Helton was an adult, as well as several car thefts and residential burglaries committed when Helton was a juvenile. The prosecution also introduced a videotape of Helton's statement to the police, one that the judge had excluded during the first phase of the trial. In it, Helton said that he "would never stop killing. It's the ultimate rush. No prison can hold me and no one can stop me."

Raft's rap sheet showed two voluntary manslaughter convictions and twenty drug possession convictions. The prosecution also proved that Raft was a member of a violent gang.

The families of two of the victims testified. In addition to their horror, shock, and grief, they explained that the truck driver, a 24-year-old male, left behind two daughters, aged two and seven years. They explained that he had been attending community college and been the sole bread winner in his family as his wife had been fighting ovarian cancer. The prison guard, a 23-year-old female, was working her way through night law school.

On behalf of the defense, Helton's attorney documented, through testimony and records, an extensive pattern of abuse toward Helton by his father. According to the evidence, Helton's mother had died when Helton was five years old. Helton's father had raised Helton, leaving him unsupervised much of the time when Helton's father was working. Helton's father used a belt regularly in enforcing discipline. Helton's lawyer had Helton raise his shirt and show a series of deep scars on his back. Helton dropped out of school at 12 and lived most of his life on the streets. Helton's sister, who had given evidence of Helton's childhood, begged the jury to spare his life.

Raft's defense counsel offered evidence that Raft's intelligence was at the lowest end of the normal range, barely above the developmentally disabled (or "mentally retarded") range. He was a follower rather than a leader. He was 23 years old and had suffered from a drug addiction for ten of those years. Raft had grown up in a poverty-ridden and violent neighborhood, where gang loyalty was the only hope of survival. Raft testified on his own behalf, admitting the crimes and saying he had wanted to escape but had only gone along with the torture so that Helton wouldn't turn the gun on Raft.

(a) You must decide whether to recommend a sentence of death or life without parole for Helton and for Raft. The court will provide you no further guidance. What sentences would you impose?

(b) As in part (a) you must decide whether to recommend a sentence of death or life without parole for Helton and for Raft. But the court instructs you to apply the following statute[56] to the case:

At the sentence hearing the state shall have the burden of proving beyond a reasonable doubt the existence of any aggravating circumstances. Provided, however, any aggravating circumstance which the verdict convicting the defendant establishes was proven beyond a

---

56. Excerpts (1), (3), and (4) are from the Alabama Criminal Code §§ 13A-5-45; 13A-5-49; 13A-5-51; 13A-5-52 (Alabama Code 2003).

reasonable doubt at trial shall be considered as proven beyond a reasonable doubt for purposes of the sentence hearing. Unless at least one aggravating circumstance, as defined [below] exists, the sentence shall be life imprisonment without parole.

Aggravating circumstances shall be the following:

(1) The capital offense was committed by a person under sentence of imprisonment;

(2) The defendant was previously convicted of another capital offense or a felony involving the use or threat of violence to the person;

(3) The defendant knowingly created a great risk of death to many persons;

(4) The capital offense was committed while the defendant was engaged or was an accomplice in the commission of, or an attempt to commit, or flight after committing, or attempting to commit, rape, robbery, burglary or kidnapping;

(5) The capital offense was committed for the purpose of avoiding or preventing a lawful arrest or effecting an escape from custody;

(6) The capital offense was committed for pecuniary gain;

(7) The capital offense was committed to disrupt or hinder the lawful exercise of any governmental function or the enforcement of laws;

(8) The capital offense was especially heinous, atrocious, or cruel compared to other capital offenses;

(9) The defendant intentionally caused the death of two or more persons by one act or pursuant to one scheme or course of conduct; or

(10) The capital offense was one of a series of intentional killings committed by the defendant.

Aggravating circumstances shall also be:

(1) The capital offense was "'outrageously or wantonly vile, horrible or inhuman.'"[57]

(2) "[B]y the murder, or circumstances surrounding its commission, the defendant exhibited utter disregard for human life."[58]

(3) The capital offense caused the death of a law enforcement official engaged in the performance of his/her duties.

Mitigating circumstances shall include, but not be limited to, the following:[59]

(1) The defendant has no significant history of prior criminal activity;

(2) The capital offense was committed while the defendant was under the influence of extreme mental or emotional disturbance;

57. Godfrey v. Georgia, 446 U.S. 420, 428 (1980).
58. Arave v. Creech, 507 U.S. 463, 465 (1993) (citing Idaho Code § 19-2515(g)(6) (1987)).
59. Based on Alabama Criminal Code § 13A-5-51 (Alabama Code 2003).

> (3) The victim was a participant in the defendant's conduct or consented to it;
> (4) The defendant was an accomplice in the capital offense committed by another person and his participation was relatively minor;
> (5) The defendant acted under extreme duress or under the substantial domination of another person;
> (6) The capacity of the defendant to appreciate the criminality of his conduct or to conform his conduct to the requirements of law was substantially impaired; and
> (7) The age of the defendant at the time of the crime.
> In addition to the mitigating circumstances specified [above], mitigating circumstances shall include any aspect of a defendant's character or record and any of the circumstances of the offense that the defendant offers as a basis for a sentence of life imprisonment without parole instead of death, and any other relevant mitigating circumstance which the defendant offers as a basis for a sentence of life imprisonment without parole instead of death.

Which, if any, aggravating factors did you find present? Which, if any, mitigating circumstances were present? What sentences would you impose?

Was your task easier in (a) or (b)? Would the approach in (a) or (b) lead to fairer results?

5. Discretion versus Standards: The Competition Defined

In 1971 the Court decided *McGautha v. California*. In *McGautha*, the Court evaluated the then-existing California approach to capital cases, in which the legislature furnished juries with no guidance in choosing between life and death once a jury had convicted the defendant of the requisite charge(s). In that case, relying on "history, experience, and the present limitations of human knowledge, [the Court found] it quite impossible to say that committing to the untrammeled discretion of the jury the power to pronounce life or death in capital cases is offensive to anything in the Constitution."[60]

Just one year after *McGautha*, in 1972, the Court in *Furman*, below, effectively overruled *McGautha*. It rejected unfettered jury discretion by reversing the death sentences of three men, whose juries had operated without legislative guidelines in selecting between life and death. Only one paragraph in *Furman* garnered sufficient votes to represent the controlling decision. From there, the opinion splinters into a series of separate concurrences and dissents.

---

60. McGautha v. California, 402 U.S. 183, 207 (1971).

FURMAN *v.* GEORGIA

Supreme Court of the United States 408 U.S. 238 (1972)

[Together with *Jackson v. Georgia* and *Branch v. Texas.*]

Opinion; Per Curiam:

Petitioner [Furman] was convicted of murder in Georgia and was sentenced to death . . . . [Petitioners Jackson and Branch were convicted of rape and sentenced to death in Georgia and Texas respectively.] Certiorari was granted limited to the following question: "Does the imposition and carrying out of the death penalty in [these cases] constitute cruel and unusual punishment in violation of the Eighth and Fourteenth Amendments?" The Court holds that the imposition and carrying out of the death penalty in these cases constitute cruel and unusual punishment in violation of the Eighth and Fourteenth Amendments. The judgment in each case is therefore reversed insofar as it leaves undisturbed the death sentence imposed, and the cases are remanded for further proceedings.

So ordered.

Mr. Justice STEWART, concurring.

The penalty of death differs from all other forms of criminal punishment, not in degree but in kind. It is unique in its total irrevocability. It is unique in its rejection of rehabilitation of the convict as a basic purpose of criminal justice. And it is unique, finally, in its absolute renunciation of all that is embodied in our concept of humanity. . . .

These death sentences are cruel and unusual in the same way that being struck by lightning is cruel and unusual. For, of all the people convicted of rapes and murders in 1967 and 1968, many just as reprehensible as these, the petitioners are among a capriciously selected random handful upon whom the sentence of death has in fact been imposed. My concurring Brothers have demonstrated that, if any basis can be discerned for the selection of these few to be sentenced to die, it is the constitutionally impermissible basis of race. But racial discrimination has not been proved, and I put it to one side. I simply conclude that the Eighth and Fourteenth Amendments cannot tolerate the infliction of a sentence of death under legal systems that permit this unique penalty to be so wantonly and so freakishly imposed.

For these reasons I concur in the judgments of the Court.

DISSENT:

Mr. Chief Justice BURGER, with whom Mr. Justice Blackmun, Mr. Justice Powell and Mr. Justice Rehnquist join dissenting. . . .

I

If we were possessed of legislative power, I would either join with Mr. Justice Brennan and Mr. Justice Marshall or, at the very least, restrict the use of capital punishment to a small category of the most heinous crimes. Our constitutional inquiry, however, must be divorced from personal feelings as to the morality and efficacy of the death penalty, and be confined to the meaning and applicability of the uncertain language of the Eighth Amendment. . . .

II

Counsel for petitioners properly concede that capital punishment was not impermissibly cruel at the time of the adoption of the Eighth Amendment. Not only do the records of the debates indicate that the Founding Fathers were limited in their concern to the prevention of torture, but it is also clear from the language of the Constitution itself that there was no thought whatever of the elimination of capital punishment. . . .

In the 181 years since the enactment of the Eighth Amendment, not a single decision of this Court has cast the slightest shadow of a doubt on the constitutionality of capital punishment. In rejecting Eighth Amendment attacks on particular modes of execution, the Court has more than once implicitly denied that capital punishment is impermissibly "cruel" in the constitutional sense. . . .

III

There are no obvious indications that capital punishment offends the conscience of society to such a degree that our traditional deference to the legislative judgment must be abandoned. . . .   Capital punishment is authorized by statute in 40 States, the District of Columbia, and in the federal courts for the commission of certain crimes. On four occasions in the last 11 years Congress has added to the list of federal crimes punishable by death. In looking for reliable indicia of contemporary attitude, none more trustworthy has been advanced.

One conceivable source of evidence that legislatures have abdicated their essentially barometric role with respect to community values would be public opinion polls, of which there have been many in the past decade addressed to the question of capital punishment. Without assessing the reliability of such polls, or intimating that any judicial reliance could ever be placed on them, it need only be noted that the reported results have shown nothing approximating the universal condemnation of capital punishment that might lead us to suspect that the legislatures in general have lost touch with current social values.

Counsel for petitioners rely on a different body of empirical evidence. They argue, in effect, that the number of cases in which the death penalty is imposed, as compared with the number of cases in which it is statutorily available, reflects a general revulsion toward the penalty that would lead to its repeal if only it were more generally and widely enforced. It cannot be gainsaid that by the choice of juries — and sometimes judges — the death penalty is imposed in far fewer than half the cases in which it is available. To go further and characterize the rate of imposition as "freakishly rare," as petitioners insist, is unwarranted hyperbole. And regardless of its characterization, the rate of imposition does not impel the conclusion that capital punishment is now regarded as intolerably cruel or uncivilized. . . .

The selectivity of juries in imposing the punishment of death is properly viewed as a refinement on, rather than a repudiation of, the statutory authorization for that penalty. . . .

Statistics are also cited to show that the death penalty has been imposed in a racially discriminatory manner. Such statistics suggest, at least as a historical matter, that Negroes have been sentenced to death with greater frequency than whites in several States, particularly for the crime of interracial rape. If a statute that authorizes the discretionary imposition of a particular penalty for a particular crime is used primarily against defendants of a certain race, and if the pattern of use can be fairly explained only by reference to the race of the defendants, the Equal Protection Clause of the Fourteenth Amendment forbids continued enforcement of that statute in its existing form.

To establish that the statutory authorization for a particular penalty is inconsistent with the dictates of the Equal Protection Clause, it is not enough to show how it was applied in the distant past. The statistics that have been referred to us cover periods when Negroes were systematically excluded from jury service and when racial segregation was the official policy in many States. Data of more recent vintage are essential. While no statistical survey could be expected to bring forth absolute and irrefutable proof of a discriminatory pattern of imposition, a strong showing would have to be made, taking all relevant factors into account.

It must be noted that any equal protection claim is totally distinct from the Eighth Amendment question to which our grant of certiorari was limited in these cases. Evidence of a discriminatory pattern of enforcement does not imply that any use of a particular punishment is so morally repugnant as to violate the Eighth Amendment. . . .

While I would not undertake to make a definitive statement as to the parameters of the Court's ruling, it is clear that if state legislatures and the Congress wish to maintain the availability of capital punishment, significant statutory changes will have to be made. Since the two pivotal concurring opinions turn on the assumption that the punishment of death is now meted out in a random and unpredictable manner, legislative bodies may seek to bring their laws into compliance with the Court's ruling by providing standards for juries and judges to follow in determining the sentence in capital cases or by more narrowly defining the crimes for which the penalty is to be imposed. . . .

VI

Since there is no majority of the Court on the ultimate issue presented in these cases, the future of capital punishment in this country has been left in an uncertain limbo. . . . While I cannot endorse the process of decisionmaking that has yielded today's result and the restraints that that result imposes on legislative action, I am not altogether displeased that legislative bodies have been given the opportunity, and indeed unavoidable responsibility, to make a thorough re-evaluation of the entire subject of capital punishment. If today's opinions demonstrate nothing else, they starkly show that this is an area where legislatures can act far more effectively than courts. . . .

Mr. Justice BLACKMUN, dissenting.

I join the respective opinions of The Chief Justice, Mr. Justice Powell, and Mr. Justice Rehnquist, and add only the following, somewhat personal, comments.

1. Cases such as these provide for me an excruciating agony of the spirit. I yield to no one in the depth of my distaste, antipathy, and, indeed, abhorrence, for the death penalty, with all its aspects of physical distress and fear and of moral judgment exercised by finite minds. That distaste is buttressed by a belief that capital punishment serves no useful purpose that can be demonstrated. For me, it violates childhood's training and life's experiences, and is not compatible with the philosophical convictions I have been able to develop. It is antagonistic to any

sense of "reverence for life." Were I a legislator, I would vote against the death penalty. . . .

10. It is not without interest, also, to note that, although the several concurring opinions acknowledge the heinous and atrocious character of the offenses committed by the petitioners, none of those opinions makes reference to the misery the petitioners' crimes occasioned to the victims, to the families of the victims, and to the communities where the offenses took place. The arguments for the respective petitioners, particularly the oral arguments, were similarly and curiously devoid of reference to the victims. There is risk, of course, in a comment such as this, for it opens one to the charge of emphasizing the retributive. Nevertheless, these cases are here because offenses to innocent victims were perpetrated. This fact, and the terror that occasioned it, and the fear that stalks the streets of many of our cities today perhaps deserve not to be entirely overlooked. . . .

Although personally I may rejoice at the Court's result, I find it difficult to accept or to justify as a matter of history, of law, or of constitutional pronouncement. . . .

QUESTIONS

1. What are the risks of discretion in the capital context?
2. What are its benefits?
3. Can discretion and standards be effectively reconciled?

Furman indicated that the "untrammeled discretion,"[61] *McGautha* had approved was now unconstitutional. In reaction, some states enacted laws that eliminated discretion entirely. Still others developed statutes that guided discretion of jurors' choices between life and death. Four years after *Furman*, the Court issued a series of decisions addressing statutes that legislatures had enacted in response to the *Furman* decision. One of these was *Woodson v. North Carolina*, 428 U.S. 280 (1976). Woodson was convicted of first-degree murder and sentenced to death under North Carolina's new mandatory death penalty statute. Once the jury determined guilt, the statute automatically required a penalty of death, thus eliminating any jury discretion on the issue of penalty. The Court analyzed the question of the constitutionality of such a mandatory death penalty using its Eighth Amendment framework.

First, it assessed the contemporary standards by looking at "history and traditional usage, legislative enactments, and jury determinations."[62] On the historical front, the Court found that such mandatory impositions of death had "been rejected as unduly harsh and unworkably rigid" by both juries and legislatures. Over the course of United States history, juries had often refused to convict "palpably guilty men of first-degree murder" in order to avoid an automatic death sentence. Legislators responded by authorizing jury discretion. In light of "the evolving standards of decency that mark the progress of a maturing society," the Court concluded that "North Carolina's mandatory death penalty statute for first-degree murder departs markedly from contemporary standards . . . and thus cannot be applied consistent[ly] with the Eighth and Fourteenth Amendments' requirement[s]. . . . " The Court found additional constitutional flaws in the North Carolina statute. One

---

61. McGautha, 402 U.S. at 207.
62. Quotations in this paragraph are from *Woodson*, 428 U.S. at 288, 293, 301 (quoting Trop v. Dulles, 356 U.S. at 101) (plurality opinion), 301, 303, 304.

of these was the obvious inability of the jury to consider "relevant aspects of the character and record of each convicted defendant. . . . " "It treats all persons convicted of a designated offense not as uniquely individual human beings, but as members of a faceless, undifferentiated mass to be subjected to the blind infliction of the penalty of death."

Gregg v. Georgia was a second important decision issued in the 1976 term that addressed a state's response to *Furman*. As you read the excerpt from *Gregg* below, consider the differences between the North Carolina mandatory death penalty and the Georgia approach.

GREGG *v.* GEORGIA

Supreme Court of the United States 428 U.S. 153 (1976)

Judgment of the Court, and opinion of Mr. Justice Stewart, Mr. Justice Powell, and Mr. Justice Stevens, announced by Mr. Justice STEWART. . . .

[Petitioner Gregg was sentenced to death under the Georgia statute enacted in response to *Furman*.] . . .

B

We now turn to consideration of the constitutionality of Georgia's capital-sentencing procedures. In the wake of *Furman*, Georgia amended its capital punishment statute, but chose not to narrow the scope of its murder provisions. Thus, now as before *Furman*, in Georgia "[a] person commits murder when he unlawfully and with malice aforethought, either express or implied, causes the death of another human being." Ga. Code Ann., § 26-1101(a) (1972). All persons convicted of murder "shall be punished by death or by imprisonment for life." § 26-1101(c) (1972).

Georgia did act, however, to narrow the class of murderers subject to capital punishment by specifying 10 statutory aggravating circumstances, one of which must be found by the jury to exist beyond a reasonable doubt before a death sentence can ever be imposed. In addition, the jury is authorized to consider any other appropriate aggravating or mitigating circumstances. § 27-2534.1 (b) (Supp. 1975).[63] The jury is not required to find any mitigating circumstance in order to make a recommendation of mercy that is binding on the trial court, but it must find a *statutory* aggravating circumstance before recommending a sentence of death.

These procedures require the jury to consider the circumstances of the crime and the criminal before it recommends sentence. No longer can a Georgia jury do as Furman's jury did: reach a finding of the defendant's guilt and then, without guidance or direction, decide whether he should live or die. Instead, the jury's attention is directed to the specific circumstances of the crime: Was it committed in the course of another capital felony? Was it committed for money? Was it committed upon a peace officer or judicial officer? Was it committed in a particularly heinous way or in a manner that endangered the lives of many persons? In addition, the jury's attention is focused on the characteristics of the person who committed the crime: Does he have a record of prior convictions for capital offenses? Are there any special facts about this defendant that mitigate against imposing capital punishment

---

63. [Ga. Code Ann. § 27-2534.1 (1975).]

(*e.g.*, his youth, the extent of his cooperation with the police, his emotional state at the time of the crime). As a result, while some jury discretion still exists, "the discretion to be exercised is controlled by clear and objective standards so as to produce non-discriminatory application." *Coley v. State*, 231 Ga. 829, 834, 204 S.E. 2d 612, 615 (1974). . . .

[T]he concerns expressed in *Furman* that the penalty of death not be imposed in an arbitrary or capricious manner can be met by a carefully drafted statute that ensures that the sentencing authority is given adequate information and guidance. As a general proposition these concerns are best met by a system that provides for a bifurcated proceeding at which the sentencing authority is apprised of the information relevant to the imposition of sentence and provided with standards to guide its use of the information.[64]

As an important additional safeguard against arbitrariness and caprice, the Georgia statutory scheme provides for automatic appeal of all death sentences to the State's Supreme Court. That court is required by statute to review each sentence of death and determine whether it was imposed under the influence of passion or prejudice, whether the evidence supports the jury's finding of a statutory aggravating circumstance, and whether the sentence is disproportionate compared to those sentences imposed in similar cases. . . .

The petitioner contends, however, that the changes in the Georgia sentencing procedures are only cosmetic, that the arbitrariness and capriciousness condemned by *Furman* continue to exist in Georgia—both in traditional practices that still remain and in the new sentencing procedures adopted in response to *Furman*.

1

First, the petitioner focuses on the opportunities for discretionary action that are inherent in the processing of any murder case under Georgia law. He notes that the state prosecutor has unfettered authority to select those persons whom he wishes to prosecute for a capital offense and to plea bargain with them. Further, at the trial the jury may choose to convict a defendant of a lesser included offense rather than find him guilty of a crime punishable by death, even if the evidence would support a capital verdict. And finally, a defendant who is convicted and sentenced to die may have his sentence commuted by the Governor of the State and the Georgia Board of Pardons and Paroles.

The existence of these discretionary stages is not determinative of the issues before us. At each of these stages an actor in the criminal justice system makes a decision which may remove a defendant from consideration as a candidate for the death penalty. *Furman*, in contrast, dealt with the decision to impose the death sentence on a specific individual who had been convicted of a capital offense. Nothing in any of our cases suggests that the decision to afford an individual defendant mercy violates the Constitution. *Furman* held only that, in order to minimize the risk that the death penalty would be imposed on a capriciously selected group of offenders, the decision to impose it had to be guided by standards so that the sentencing authority would focus on the particularized circumstances of the crime and the defendant. . . .

---

64. This paragraph was inserted here although it appears in an earlier portion of the original opinion at 428 U.S. 153, 195.

V

The basic concern of *Furman* centered on those defendants who were being condemned to death capriciously and arbitrarily. Under the procedures before the Court in that case, sentencing authorities were not directed to give attention to the nature or circumstances of the crime committed or to the character or record of the defendant. Left unguided, juries imposed the death sentence in a way that could only be called freakish. The new Georgia sentencing procedures, by contrast, focus the jury's attention on the particularized nature of the crime and the particularized characteristics of the individual defendant. . . . No longer can a jury wantonly and freakishly impose the death sentence; it is always circumscribed by the legislative guidelines. . . . [T]he concerns that prompted our decision in *Furman* are not present to any significant degree in the Georgia procedure applied here.

[W]e hold that the statutory system under which Gregg was sentenced to death does not violate the Constitution.

QUESTIONS

1. Is the Court correct when it states that "Nothing in any of our cases suggests that the decision to afford an individual defendant mercy violates the Constitution"? Is the Court overlooking risks to consistency or fairness that mercy might generate?

2. Reconsider the discussion in Chapter 3, Making Criminal Law, of dynamic statutory interpretation. Does the "evolving standards" approach, applied in constitutional interpretation to the Eighth Amendment, resemble dynamic statutory interpretation?

In theory, guided discretion meant that jurors could consider the circumstances of each case on an individualized basis but did so only within a statutory framework of standards designed to mitigate arbitrariness. Concerns, however, arose about whether the standards or guidance had succeeded in mitigating arbitrariness. One critical concern involved whether the remaining discretion left open a window for illegal biases to play a role in the jury's choice between life and death. The *McCleskey* case addresses that concern. It is one of the most controversial in the matrix of the Court's death penalty jurisprudence.

McCLESKEY *v.* KEMP

Supreme Court of the United States 481 U.S. 279 (1987)

Justice POWELL delivered the opinion of the Court.

This case presents the question whether a complex statistical study that indicates a risk that racial considerations enter into capital sentencing determinations proves that petitioner McCleskey's capital sentence is unconstitutional under the Eighth or Fourteenth Amendment.

I

McCleskey, a black man, was convicted of two counts of armed robbery and one count of murder in the Superior Court of Fulton County, Georgia, on October 12, 1978. McCleskey's convictions arose out of the robbery of a furniture store and the killing of a white police officer during the course of the robbery. The evidence at trial indicated that McCleskey and three accomplices planned and carried out the robbery. All four were armed. McCleskey entered the front of the store while the other three entered the rear. McCleskey secured the front of the store by rounding up the customers and forcing them to lie face down on the floor. The other three rounded up the employees in the rear and tied them up with tape. The manager was forced at gunpoint to turn over the store receipts, his watch, and $6. During the course of the robbery, a police officer, answering a silent alarm, entered the store through the front door. As he was walking down the center aisle of the store, two shots were fired. Both struck the officer. One hit him in the face and killed him. . . .

Under Georgia law, the jury could not consider imposing the death penalty unless it found beyond a reasonable doubt that the murder was accompanied by one of the statutory aggravating circumstances. The jury in this case found two aggravating circumstances to exist beyond a reasonable doubt: the murder was committed during the course of an armed robbery, and the murder was committed upon a peace officer engaged in the performance of his duties. In making its decision whether to impose the death sentence, the jury considered the mitigating and aggravating circumstances of McCleskey's conduct. McCleskey offered no mitigating evidence. The jury recommended that he be sentenced to death on the murder charge and to consecutive life sentences on the armed robbery charges. The court followed the jury's recommendation and sentenced McCleskey to death. . . .

In support of his claim [of unconstitutionality], McCleskey proffered a statistical study performed by Professors David C. Baldus, Charles Pulaski, and George Woodworth (the Baldus study) that purports to show a disparity in the imposition of the death sentence in Georgia based on the race of the murder victim and, to a lesser extent, the race of the defendant. The Baldus study is actually two sophisticated statistical studies that examine over 2,000 murder cases that occurred in Georgia during the 1970's. The raw numbers collected by Professor Baldus indicate that defendants charged with killing white persons received the death penalty in 11% of the cases, but defendants charged with killing blacks received the death penalty in only 1% of the cases. The raw numbers also indicate a reverse racial disparity according to the race of the defendant: 4% of the black defendants received the death penalty, as opposed to 7% of the white defendants.

Baldus also divided the cases according to the combination of the race of the defendant and the race of the victim. He found that the death penalty was assessed in 22% of the cases involving black defendants and white victims; 8% of the cases involving white defendants and white victims; 1% of the cases involving black defendants and black victims; and 3% of the cases involving white defendants and black victims. Similarly, Baldus found that prosecutors sought the death penalty in 70% of the cases involving black defendants and white victims; 32% of the cases involving white defendants and white victims; 15% of the cases involving black defendants and black victims; and 19% of the cases involving white defendants and black victims.

Baldus subjected his data to an extensive analysis, taking account of 230 variables that could have explained the disparities on nonracial grounds. One of his models concludes that, even after taking account of 39 nonracial variables, defendants charged with killing white victims were 4.3 times as likely to receive a death sentence as defendants charged with killing blacks. According to this model, black defendants were 1.1 times as likely to receive a death sentence as other defendants. Thus, the Baldus study indicates that black defendants, such as McCleskey, who kill white victims have the greatest likelihood of receiving the death penalty. . . .

II

McCleskey's first claim is that the Georgia capital punishment statute violates the Equal Protection Clause of the Fourteenth Amendment. He argues that race has infected the administration of Georgia's statute in two ways: persons who murder whites are more likely to be sentenced to death than persons who murder blacks, and black murderers are more likely to be sentenced to death than white murderers. As a black defendant who killed a white victim, McCleskey claims that the Baldus study demonstrates that he was discriminated against because of his race and because of the race of his victim. In its broadest form, McCleskey's claim of discrimination extends to every actor in the Georgia capital sentencing process, from the prosecutor who sought the death penalty and the jury that imposed the sentence, to the State itself that enacted the capital punishment statute and allows it to remain in effect despite its allegedly discriminatory application. We agree with the Court of Appeals, and every other court that has considered such a challenge, that this claim must fail.

A

Our analysis begins with the basic principle that a defendant who alleges an equal protection violation has the burden of proving "the existence of purposeful discrimination." *Whitus v. Georgia*, 385 U.S. 545, 550 (1967). A corollary to this principle is that a criminal defendant must prove that the purposeful discrimination "had a discriminatory effect" on him. *Wayte v. United States*, 470 U.S. 598, 608 (1985). Thus, to prevail under the Equal Protection Clause, McCleskey must prove that the decisionmakers in *his* case acted with discriminatory purpose. He offers no evidence specific to his own case that would support an inference that racial considerations played a part in his sentence. Instead, he relies solely on the Baldus study. McCleskey argues that the Baldus study compels an inference that his sentence rests on purposeful discrimination. McCleskey's claim that these statistics are sufficient proof of discrimination, without regard to the facts of a particular case, would extend to all capital cases in Georgia, at least where the victim was white and the defendant is black.

The Court has accepted statistics as proof of intent to discriminate in certain limited contexts. First, this Court has accepted statistical disparities as proof of an equal protection violation in the selection of the jury venire in a particular district. Although statistical proof normally must present a "stark" pattern to be accepted as the sole proof of discriminatory intent under the Constitution,[65] "[b]ecause of the

---

[65]. Gomillion v. Lightfoot, 364 U.S. 339 (1960), and Yick Wo v. Hopkins, 118 U.S. 356 (1886), are examples of those rare cases in which a statistical pattern of discriminatory impact demonstrated a constitutional violation. In *Gomillion*, a state legislature violated the Fifteenth Amendment by altering the boundaries of a particular city "from a square to an uncouth twenty-eight-sided figure." 364 U.S., at 340. The alterations excluded 395 of 400 black voters without excluding a single white voter. *Id.* at 341. In *Yick Wo*, an ordinance prohibited operation of 310 laundries that were housed in wooden buildings, but allowed such laundries to resume operations if the operator secured a permit from the government.

nature of the jury-selection task, . . . we have permitted a finding of constitutional violation even when the statistical pattern does not approach [such] extremes." [citation omitted.] Second, this Court has accepted statistics in the form of multiple-regression analysis to prove statutory violations under Title VII of the Civil Rights Act of 1964.

But the nature of the capital sentencing decision, and the relationship of the statistics to that decision, are fundamentally different from the corresponding elements in the venire-selection or Title VII cases. Most importantly, each particular decision to impose the death penalty is made by a petit jury selected from a properly constituted venire. Each jury is unique in its composition, and the Constitution requires that its decision rest on consideration of innumerable factors that vary according to the characteristics of the individual defendant and the facts of the particular capital offense. Thus, the application of an inference drawn from the general statistics to a specific decision in a trial and sentencing simply is not comparable to the application of an inference drawn from general statistics to a specific venire-selection or Title VII case. . . .

Because discretion is essential to the criminal justice process, we would demand exceptionally clear proof before we would infer that the discretion has been abused. . . . Accordingly, we hold that the Baldus study is clearly insufficient to support an inference that any of the decisionmakers in McCleskey's case acted with discriminatory purpose.

B

McCleskey also suggests that the Baldus study proves that the State as a whole has acted with a discriminatory purpose. He appears to argue that the State has violated the Equal Protection Clause by adopting the capital punishment statute and allowing it to remain in force despite its allegedly discriminatory application. But "'[d]iscriminatory purpose' . . . implies more than intent as volition or intent as awareness of consequences. It implies that the decisionmaker, in this case a state legislature, selected or reaffirmed a particular course of action at least in part 'because of,' not merely 'in spite of,' its adverse effects upon an identifiable group." *Personnel Administrator of Massachusetts v. Feeney*, 442 U.S. 256, 279 (1979) (footnote and citation omitted). For this claim to prevail, McCleskey would have to prove that the Georgia Legislature enacted or maintained the death penalty statute *because of* an anticipated racially discriminatory effect. In *Gregg v. Georgia, supra*, this Court found that the Georgia capital sentencing system could operate in a fair and neutral manner. There was no evidence then, and there is none now, that the Georgia Legislature enacted the capital punishment statute to further a racially discriminatory purpose. . . .

Accordingly, we reject McCleskey's equal protection claims.

III

McCleskey also argues that the Baldus study demonstrates that the Georgia capital sentencing system violates the Eighth Amendment. . . .

When laundry operators applied for permits to resume operation, all but one of the white applicants received permits, but none of the over 200 Chinese applicants were successful. In those cases, the Court found the statistical disparities "to warrant and require," Yick Wo v. Hopkins, *supra*, at 373, a "conclusion [that was] irresistible, tantamount for all practical purposes to a mathematical demonstration," Gomillion v. Lightfoot, *supra*, at 341, that the State acted with a discriminatory purpose.

IV

B

Although our decision in *Gregg* as to the facial validity of the Georgia capital punishment statute appears to foreclose McCleskey's disproportionality argument, he further contends that the Georgia capital punishment system is arbitrary and capricious in *application*, and therefore his sentence is excessive, because racial considerations may influence capital sentencing decisions in Georgia. We now address this claim.

To evaluate McCleskey's challenge, we must examine exactly what the Baldus study may show. Even Professor Baldus does not contend that his statistics *prove* that race enters into any capital sentencing decisions or that race was a factor in McCleskey's particular case.[29] Statistics at most may show only a likelihood that a particular factor entered into some decisions. There is, of course, some risk of racial prejudice influencing a jury's decision in a criminal case. There are similar risks that other kinds of prejudice will influence other criminal trials. The question "is at what point that risk becomes constitutionally unacceptable," *Turner v. Murray*, 476 U.S. 28, 36, n.8 (1986). McCleskey asks us to accept the likelihood allegedly shown by the Baldus study as the constitutional measure of an unacceptable risk of racial prejudice influencing capital sentencing decisions. This we decline to do. . . .

C

At most, the Baldus study indicates a discrepancy that appears to correlate with race. Apparent disparities in sentencing are an inevitable part of our criminal justice system. The discrepancy indicated by the Baldus study is "a far cry from the major systemic defects identified in *Furman*," *Pulley v. Harris*, 465 U.S., at 54 . . . . Despite these imperfections, our consistent rule has been that constitutional guarantees are met when "the mode [for determining guilt or punishment] itself has been surrounded with safeguards to make it as fair as possible." *Singer v. United States*, *supra*, at 35. Where the discretion that is fundamental to our criminal process is involved, we decline to assume that what is unexplained is invidious. . . .

V

Two additional concerns inform our decision in this case. First, McCleskey's claim, taken to its logical conclusion, throws into serious question the principles that underlie our entire criminal justice system. The Eighth Amendment is not limited in application to capital punishment, but applies to all penalties. Thus, if we accepted McCleskey's claim that racial bias has impermissibly tainted the capital sentencing decision, we could soon be faced with similar claims as to other types of penalty. Moreover, the claim that his sentence rests on the irrelevant factor of race easily could be extended to apply to claims based on unexplained discrepancies that correlate to membership in other minority groups, and even to gender. Similarly, since McCleskey's claim relates to the race of his victim, other claims could apply with equally logical force to statistical disparities that correlate with the race or sex of other actors in the criminal justice system, such as defense attorneys or

---

[29] According to Professor Baldus:

"McCleskey's case falls in [a] grey area where . . . you would find the greatest likelihood that some inappropriate consideration may have come to bear on the decision.

"In an analysis of this type, obviously one cannot say that we can say to a moral certainty what it was that influenced the decision. We can't do that." App. 45-46.

judges. Also, there is no logical reason that such a claim need be limited to racial or sexual bias. If arbitrary and capricious punishment is the touchstone under the Eighth Amendment, such a claim could — at least in theory — be based upon any arbitrary variable, such as the defendant's facial characteristics, or the physical attractiveness of the defendant or the victim, that some statistical study indicates may be influential in jury decisionmaking. As these examples illustrate, there is no limiting principle to the type of challenge brought by McCleskey. . . .   Second, McCleskey's arguments are best presented to the legislative bodies. It is not the responsibility — or indeed even the right — of this Court to determine the appropriate punishment for particular crimes. . . .   Despite McCleskey's wide-ranging arguments that basically challenge the validity of capital punishment in our multiracial society, the only question before us is whether in his case, the law of Georgia was properly applied. We agree with the District Court and the Court of Appeals for the Eleventh Circuit that this was carefully and correctly done in this case.

Dissent:

Justice BRENNAN, with whom Justice Marshall joins, and with whom Justice Blackmun and Justice Stevens join in all but Part I, dissenting. . . .

II

At some point in this case, Warren McCleskey doubtless asked his lawyer whether a jury was likely to sentence him to die. A candid reply to this question would have been disturbing. First, counsel would have to tell McCleskey that few of the details of the crime or of McCleskey's past criminal conduct were more important than the fact that his victim was white. Furthermore, counsel would feel bound to tell McCleskey that defendants charged with killing white victims in Georgia are 4.3 times as likely to be sentenced to death as defendants charged with killing blacks. In addition, frankness would compel the disclosure that it was more likely than not that the race of McCleskey's victim would determine whether he received a death sentence: 6 of every 11 defendants convicted of killing a white person would not have received the death penalty if their victims had been black, while, among defendants with aggravating and mitigating factors comparable to McCleskey's, 20 of every 34 would not have been sentenced to die if their victims had been black. Finally, the assessment would not be complete without the information that cases involving black defendants and white victims are more likely to result in a death sentence than cases featuring any other racial combination of defendant and victim. The story could be told in a variety of ways, but McCleskey could not fail to grasp its essential narrative line: there was a significant chance that race would play a prominent role in determining if he lived or died.

The Court today holds that Warren McCleskey's sentence was constitutionally imposed. . . .   The Court reaches this conclusion by placing four factors on the scales opposite McCleskey's evidence: the desire to encourage sentencing discretion, the existence of "statutory safeguards" in the Georgia scheme, the fear of encouraging widespread challenges to other sentencing decisions, and the limits of the judicial role. The Court's evaluation of the significance of petitioner's evidence is fundamentally at odds with our consistent concern for rationality in capital sentencing, and the considerations that the majority invokes to discount that evidence cannot justify ignoring its force.

III

A

It is important to emphasize at the outset that the Court's observation that McCleskey cannot prove the influence of race on any particular sentencing decision is irrelevant in evaluating his Eighth Amendment claim. Since *Furman v. Georgia*, 408 U.S. 238 (1972), the Court has been concerned with the *risk* of the imposition of an arbitrary sentence, rather than the proven fact of one. *Furman* held that the death penalty "may not be imposed under sentencing procedures that create a substantial risk that the punishment will be inflicted in an arbitrary and capricious manner." *Godfrey v. Georgia, supra,* at 427. . . . This emphasis on risk acknowledges the difficulty of divining the jury's motivation in an individual case. In addition, it reflects the fact that concern for arbitrariness focuses on the rationality of the system as a whole, and that a system that features a significant probability that sentencing decisions are influenced by impermissible considerations cannot be regarded as rational.[1] . . .

B

The Baldus study indicates that, after taking into account some 230 nonracial factors that might legitimately influence a sentencer, the jury *more likely than not* would have spared McCleskey's life had his victim been black. The study distinguishes between those cases in which (1) the jury exercises virtually no discretion because the strength or weakness of aggravating factors usually suggests that only one outcome is appropriate; and (2) cases reflecting an "intermediate" level of aggravation, in which the jury has considerable discretion in choosing a sentence. McCleskey's case falls into the intermediate range. In such cases, death is imposed in 34% of white-victim crimes and 14% of black-victim crimes, a difference of 139% in the rate of imposition of the death penalty. In other words, just under 59% — almost 6 in 10 — defendants comparable to McCleskey would not have received the death penalty if their victims had been black. . . .

Of the more than 200 variables potentially relevant to a sentencing decision, race of the victim is a powerful explanation for variation in death sentence rates — as powerful as nonracial aggravating factors such as a prior murder conviction or acting as the principal planner of the homicide.[5] . . .

[B]lacks who kill whites are sentenced to death at nearly *22 times* the rate of blacks who kill blacks, and more than *7 times* the rate of whites who kill blacks. In addition, prosecutors seek the death penalty for 70% of black defendants with white victims, but for only 15% of black defendants with black victims, and only 19% of white defendants with black victims. Since our decision upholding the Georgia

---

[1] Once we can identify a pattern of arbitrary sentencing outcomes, we can say that a defendant runs a risk of being sentenced arbitrarily. It is thus immaterial whether the operation of an impermissible influence such as race is intentional. While the Equal Protection Clause forbids racial discrimination, and intent may be critical in a successful claim under that provision, the Eighth Amendment has its own distinct focus: whether punishment comports with social standards of rationality and decency. It may be, as in this case, that on occasion an influence that makes punishment arbitrary is also proscribed under another constitutional provision. That does not mean, however, that the standard for determining an Eighth Amendment violation is superseded by the standard for determining a violation under this other provision. Thus, the fact that McCleskey presents a viable equal protection claim does not require that he demonstrate intentional racial discrimination to establish his Eighth Amendment claim.

[5] The fact that a victim was white accounts for a nine percentage point difference in the rate at which the death penalty is imposed, which is the same difference attributable to a prior murder conviction or the fact that the defendant was the "prime mover" in planning a murder. Supp. Exh. 50.

capital sentencing system in *Gregg*, the State has executed seven persons. All of the seven were convicted of killing whites, and six of the seven executed were black. Such execution figures are especially striking in light of the fact that, during the period encompassed by the Baldus study, only 9.2% of Georgia homicides involved black defendants and white victims, while 60.7% involved black victims. . . .

The statistical evidence in this case thus relentlessly documents the risk that McCleskey's sentence was influenced by racial considerations. . . . In light of the gravity of the interest at stake, petitioner's statistics on their face are a powerful demonstration of the type of risk that our Eighth Amendment jurisprudence has consistently condemned.

C

Evaluation of McCleskey's evidence cannot rest solely on the numbers themselves. We must also ask whether the conclusion suggested by those numbers is consonant with our understanding of history and human experience. Georgia's legacy of a race-conscious criminal justice system, as well as this Court's own recognition of the persistent danger that racial attitudes may affect criminal proceedings, indicates that McCleskey's claim is not a fanciful product of mere statistical artifice.

For many years, Georgia operated openly and formally precisely the type of dual system the evidence shows is still effectively in place. The criminal law expressly differentiated between crimes committed by and against blacks and whites, distinctions whose lineage traced back to the time of slavery. . . .

By the time of the Civil War, a dual system of crime and punishment was well established in Georgia. The state criminal code contained separate sections for "Slaves and Free Persons of Color," and for all other persons. The code provided, for instance, for an automatic death sentence for murder committed by blacks, but declared that anyone else convicted of murder might receive life imprisonment if the conviction were founded solely on circumstantial testimony *or* simply if the jury so recommended. The code established that the rape of a free white female by a black "shall be" punishable by death. However, rape by anyone else of a free white female was punishable by a prison term not less than 2 nor more than 20 years. The rape of *blacks* was punishable "by fine and imprisonment, at the discretion of the court." . . .

In more recent times, some 40 years ago, Gunnar Myrdal's epochal study of American race relations produced findings mirroring McCleskey's evidence:

> "As long as only Negroes are concerned and no whites are disturbed, great leniency will be shown in most cases. . . . The sentences for even major crimes are ordinarily reduced when the victim is another Negro. . . .
>
> "For offenses which involve any actual or potential danger to whites, however, Negroes are punished more severely than whites. . . .
>
> "On the other hand, it is quite common for a white criminal to be set free if his crime was against a Negro." G. Myrdal, An American Dilemma 551-553 (1944). . . .

This historical review of Georgia criminal law is not intended as a bill of indictment calling the State to account for past transgressions. . . . But it would be unrealistic to ignore the influence of history in assessing the plausible implications of McCleskey's evidence. . . .

The ongoing influence of history is acknowledged, as the majority observes, by our "'unceasing efforts' to eradicate racial prejudice from our criminal justice system." These efforts, however, signify not the elimination of the problem but its persistence. . . .

[W]e have demanded a uniquely high degree of rationality in imposing the death penalty. A capital sentencing system in which race more likely than not plays a role does not meet this standard. . . .

IV

The Court cites four reasons for shrinking from the implications of McCleskey's evidence: the desirability of discretion for actors in the criminal justice system, the existence of statutory safeguards against abuse of that discretion, the potential consequences for broader challenges to criminal sentencing, and an understanding of the contours of the judicial role. While these concerns underscore the need for sober deliberation, they do not justify rejecting evidence as convincing as McCleskey has presented.

The Court maintains that petitioner's claim "is antithetical to the fundamental role of discretion in our criminal justice system." . . .

Reliance on race in imposing capital punishment, however, is antithetical to the very rationale for granting sentencing discretion. Discretion is a means, not an end. It is bestowed in order to permit the sentencer to "trea[t] each defendant in a capital case with that degree of respect due the uniqueness of the individual." *Lockett v. Ohio*, 438 U.S. 586, 605 (1978). . . .

Considering the race of a defendant or victim in deciding if the death penalty should be imposed is completely at odds with this concern that an individual be evaluated as a unique human being. Decisions influenced by race rest in part on a categorical assessment of the worth of human beings according to color, insensitive to whatever qualities the individuals in question may possess. Enhanced willingness to impose the death sentence on black defendants, or diminished willingness to render such a sentence when blacks are victims, reflects a devaluation of the lives of black persons. When confronted with evidence that race more likely than not plays such a role in a capital sentencing system, it is plainly insufficient to say that the importance of discretion demands that the risk be higher before we will act—for in such a case the very end that discretion is designed to serve is being undermined. . . .

The Court also declines to find McCleskey's evidence sufficient in view of "the safeguards designed to minimize racial bias in the [capital sentencing] process." . . .

It has now been over 13 years since Georgia adopted the provisions upheld in *Gregg*. Professor Baldus and his colleagues have compiled data on almost 2,500 homicides committed during the period 1973-1979. . . . The challenge to the Georgia system is not speculative or theoretical; it is empirical. As a result, the Court cannot rely on the statutory safeguards in discounting McCleskey's evidence, for it is the very effectiveness of those safeguards that such evidence calls into question. . . .

The Court next states that its unwillingness to regard petitioner's evidence as sufficient is based in part on the fear that recognition of McCleskey's claim would open the door to widespread challenges to all aspects of criminal sentencing. Taken on its face, such a statement seems to suggest a fear of too much justice. Yet surely the majority would acknowledge that if striking evidence indicated that other minority groups, or women, or even persons with blond hair, were disproportionately sentenced to death, such a state of affairs would be repugnant to deeply rooted conceptions of fairness. . . .

In fairness, the Court's fear that McCleskey's claim is an invitation to descend a slippery slope also rests on the realization that any humanly imposed system of penalties will exhibit some imperfection. Yet to reject McCleskey's powerful evidence on this basis is to ignore both the qualitatively different character of the death penalty and the particular repugnance of racial discrimination, considerations which may properly be taken into account in determining whether various punishments are "cruel and unusual." . . .

[T]he Court's fear of the expansive ramifications of a holding for McCleskey in this case is unfounded because it fails to recognize the uniquely sophisticated nature of the Baldus study. . . . Acceptance of petitioner's evidence would therefore establish a remarkably stringent standard of statistical evidence unlikely to be satisfied with any frequency. . . .

Finally, the Court justifies its rejection of McCleskey's claim by cautioning against usurpation of the legislatures' role in devising and monitoring criminal punishment. The Court is, of course, correct to emphasize the gravity of constitutional intervention and the importance that it be sparingly employed. The fact that "capital punishment is now the law in more than two thirds of our States," however, does not diminish the fact that capital punishment is the most awesome act that a State can perform. The judiciary's role in this society counts for little if the use of governmental power to extinguish life does not elicit close scrutiny. . . .

The Court thus fulfills, rather than disrupts, the scheme of separation of powers by closely scrutinizing the imposition of the death penalty, for no decision of a society is more deserving of "sober second thought." Stone, *The Common Law in the United States*, 50 Harv. L. Rev. 4, 25 (1936).

V . . .

The Court's decision today will not change what attorneys in Georgia tell other Warren McCleskeys about their chances of execution. Nothing will soften the harsh message they must convey, nor alter the prospect that race undoubtedly will continue to be a topic of discussion. McCleskey's evidence will not have obtained judicial acceptance, but that will not affect what is said on death row. However many criticisms of today's decision may be rendered, these painful conversations will serve as the most eloquent dissents of all.

QUESTIONS

1. What type of showing should the Eighth Amendment require to demonstrate unconstitutional bias based on race?
2. Why might McCleskey's lawyer have offered no evidence in mitigation?

The Court's opinion expresses concern that there is "no limiting principle to the type of challenge brought by McCleskey." Among the influences on which a defendant might base a claim, the Court includes the characteristic of "the physical attractiveness of the defendant or the victim." Consider the following excerpt:

David L. Wiley, BEAUTY AND THE BEAST: PHYSICAL APPEARANCE DISCRIMINATION IN AMERICAN CRIMINAL TRIALS   27 St. Mary's L.J. 193, 194, 202-203, 211-215 (1995) (citations omitted)
___

Physical appearance discrimination, or corporeal attribution, the process of judging a person's disposition on the basis of his or her physical appearance, is one of the most commonly practiced forms of discrimination in the world. . . . [R]esearchers have found that humans associate physical attractiveness with positive personal characteristics and physical unattractiveness with socially deviant behavior. . . . Social psychology teaches that humans make false substantive assumptions about other people's dispositions based on image alone. . . .

Physical appearance discrimination plays a substantive and all-too-frequent role in American criminal trials. Research suggests that people viewed as facially unattractive are more likely to be perceived as criminal than are facially attractive persons. Similarly, physically unattractive people are more likely to be reported for committing a crime than are their physically attractive counterparts. . . . Moreover, simulated juries tend to recommend lighter sentences for physically attractive defendants and harsher sentences for physically unattractive defendants, regardless of the severity of the crime. . . .

In several ways, physical appearance discrimination parallels race discrimination. . . . [R]esearch suggests that jurors are more lenient with attractive defendants because jurors seem to identify more closely with them. In other words, it is easier for jurors to imagine themselves as the defendant when the defendant is attractive; attractiveness equates with familiarity, which in turn results in empathy. This same premise underlies racial discrimination in juror judgments: it is easier for jurors to imagine themselves in the defendant's situation when the defendant is of the same race as the juror.

If the research and the author's interpretation of it in the above excerpt are correct, what does that suggest about the Court's fears? Is race distinguishable from physical attractiveness in Eighth Amendment terms?

In 1988, as part of the Anti-Drug Abuse Act, Congress commissioned the United States General Accounting Office (GAO) "to study capital sentencing procedures to determine if the race of either the victim or the defendant influences the likelihood that defendants will be sentenced to death."[66] In 1990, the GAO published a report to the Senate and House Committees on the Judiciary discussing the "evaluation synthesis—a review and critique of existing research"—that it had conducted and the conclusions it had reached. "First, [the GAO] identified and collected all potentially relevant studies done at the national, state, and local levels from both published and unpublished sources. . . . " [After additional surveying and filtering with a focus on] "both appropriateness and overall quality of the research,"[67] the GAO identified 28 studies on which it based its conclusions. Consider the following excerpt from the GAO findings:

> Our synthesis of the 28 studies shows a pattern of evidence indicating racial disparities in the charging, sentencing, and imposition of the death penalty after the *Furman* decision.
>
> In 82 percent of the studies, race of the victim was found to influence the likelihood of being charged with capital murder or receiving the death penalty, i.e., those who murdered whites were found to be more likely to be sentenced to death than those who murdered blacks. This finding was remarkably consistent across data sets, states, data collection methods, and analytic techniques. . . .

---

66. United States Accounting Office, *Death Penalty Sentencing: Research Indicates Pattern of Racial Disparities*, 1 (Feb. 26, 1990).
    67. *Id.* at 1-2.

The evidence for the influence of the race of defendant on death penalty outcomes was equivocal. Although more than half of the studies found that race of defendant influenced the likelihood of being charged with a capital crime or receiving the death penalty, the relationship between race of defendant and outcome varied across studies. . . .

Finally, more than three-fourths of the studies that identified a race of defendant effect found that black defendants were more likely to receive the death penalty. However, the remaining studies found that white defendants were more likely to be sentenced to death.

To summarize, the synthesis supports a strong race of victim influence. The race of the offender influence is not as clear cut and varies across a number of dimensions. Although there are limitations to the studies' methodologies, they are of sufficient quality to support the synthesis findings.[68]

CALLINS *v.* COLLINS

Supreme Court of the United States 510 U.S. 1141 (1994)

Opinion:

The petition for a writ of certiorari is denied.

Justice BLACKMUN, dissenting.

On February 23, 1994, at approximately 1:00 a.m., Bruce Edwin Callins will be executed by the State of Texas. Intravenous tubes attached to his arms will carry the instrument of death, a toxic fluid designed specifically for the purpose of killing human beings. The witnesses, standing a few feet away, will behold Callins, no longer a defendant, an appellant, or a petitioner, but a man, strapped to a gurney, and seconds away from extinction . . . .

From this day forward, I no longer shall tinker with the machinery of death. For more than 20 years I have endeavored — indeed, I have struggled — along with a majority of this Court, to develop procedural and substantive rules that would lend more than the mere appearance of fairness to the death penalty endeavor. Rather than continue to coddle the Court's delusion that the desired level of fairness has been achieved and the need for regulation eviscerated, I feel morally and intellectually obligated simply to concede that the death penalty experiment has failed. It is virtually self-evident to me now that no combination of procedural rules or substantive regulations ever can save the death penalty from its inherent constitutional deficiencies. The basic question — does the system accurately and consistently determine which defendants "deserve" to die? — cannot be answered in the affirmative. It is not simply that this Court has allowed vague aggravating circumstances to be employed, relevant mitigating evidence to be disregarded, and vital judicial review to be blocked. The problem is that the inevitability of factual, legal, and moral error gives us a system that we know must wrongly kill some defendants, a system that fails to deliver the fair, consistent, and reliable sentences of death required by the Constitution. . . .

F

In the years since *McCleskey*, I have come to wonder whether there was truth in the majority's suggestion that discrimination and arbitrariness could not be purged from the administration of capital punishment without sacrificing the equally essential component of fairness — individualized sentencing. Viewed in this way,

---

68. *Id.* at pps. 5, 6.

the consistency promised in *Furman* and the fairness to the individual demanded in *Lockett* are not only inversely related, but irreconcilable in the context of capital punishment. . . .

The path the Court has chosen lessens us all. I dissent.

Justice SCALIA, concurring [in the denial of certiorari].

Justice Blackmun dissents from the denial of certiorari in this case with a statement explaining why the death penalty "as currently administered," is contrary to the Constitution of the United States. That explanation often refers to "intellectual, moral and personal" perceptions, but never to the text and tradition of the Constitution. It is the latter rather than the former that ought to control. The Fifth Amendment provides that "[n]o person shall be held to answer for a capital . . . crime, unless on a presentment or indictment of a Grand Jury, . . . nor be deprived of life . . . without due process of law." This clearly permits the death penalty to be imposed, and establishes beyond doubt that the death penalty is not one of the "cruel and unusual punishments" prohibited by the Eighth Amendment.

As Justice Blackmun describes, however, over the years since 1972 this Court has attached to the imposition of the death penalty two quite incompatible sets of commands: The sentencer's discretion to impose death must be closely confined, but the sentencer's discretion *not* to impose death (to extend mercy) must be unlimited. These commands were invented without benefit of any textual or historical support; they are the product of just such "intellectual, moral, and personal" perceptions as Justice Blackmun expresses today, some of which (*viz.*, those that have been "perceived" simultaneously by five Members of the Court) have been made part of what is called "the Court's Eighth Amendment jurisprudence."

Though Justice Blackmun joins those of us who have acknowledged the incompatibility of the Court's *Furman* and *Lockett-Eddings* lines of jurisprudence, he unfortunately draws the wrong conclusion from the acknowledgment. He says:

> "The proper course when faced with irreconcilable constitutional commands is not to ignore one or the other, nor to pretend that the dilemma does not exist, but to admit the futility of the effort to harmonize them. This means accepting the fact that the death penalty cannot be administered in accord with our Constitution."

Surely a different conclusion commends itself — to wit, that at least one of these judicially announced irreconcilable commands which cause the Constitution to prohibit what its text explicitly permits must be wrong.

Convictions in opposition to the death penalty are often passionate and deeply held. That would be no excuse for reading them into a Constitution that does not contain them, even if they represented the convictions of a majority of Americans. Much less is there any excuse for using that course to thrust a minority's views upon the people. Justice Blackmun begins his statement by describing with poignancy the death of a convicted murderer by lethal injection. He chooses, as the case in which to make that statement, one of the less brutal of the murders that regularly come before us — the murder of a man ripped by a bullet suddenly and unexpectedly, with no opportunity to prepare himself and his affairs, and left to bleed to death on the floor of a tavern. The death-by-injection which Justice Blackmun describes looks pretty desirable next to that. It looks even better next to some of the other cases currently before us which Justice Blackmun did not select as the vehicle for his announcement that the death penalty is always unconstitutional — for example, the case of the 11-year-old girl raped by four men and then killed by stuffing her panties down her throat. How enviable a quiet death by lethal injection compared with that! If the people conclude that such more brutal deaths may be deterred by capital punishment; indeed, if they merely conclude that justice requires such brutal deaths to be avenged by capital punishment; the creation of false, untextual and unhistorical contradictions within "the Court's Eighth Amendment jurisprudence" should not prevent them.

QUESTIONS

1. In comparing Justice Blackmun's dissent in *Furman* with his dissent from the denial of certiorari in *Callins*, what appears to have changed his mind?

2. Is Justice Blackmun's blanket rejection of the death penalty a proper application of *stare decisis*? Consider the Court's description of *stare decisis* from a 1991 ruling on the admissibility of certain evidence in a capital case:

> *Stare decisis* is the preferred course because it promotes the evenhanded, predictable, and consistent development of legal principles, fosters reliance on judicial decisions, and contributes to the actual and perceived integrity of the judicial process. Adhering to precedent "is usually the wise policy, because in most matters it is more important that the applicable rule of law be settled than it be settled right." Nevertheless, when governing decisions are unworkable or are badly reasoned, "this Court has never felt constrained to follow precedent." *Stare decisis* is not an inexorable command; rather, it "is a principle of policy and not a mechanical formula of adherence to the latest decision." This is particularly true in constitutional cases, because in such cases "correction through legislative action is practically impossible." Considerations in favor of *stare decisis* are at their acme in cases involving property and contract rights, where reliance interests are involved; the opposite is true in cases such as the present one involving procedural and evidentiary rules.[69]

6. Bright-Line and Quasi-Bright-Line Rules

In addition to generalized guidance, the Court has established certain bright-line or quasi-bright-line rules under the "guided" portion of the "guided discretion" approach. Here are some of the most significant of those rules:

a. Type of Offense

In *Coker v. Georgia*, the Court focused on whether rape of an adult woman could serve as the basis for a sentence of death. At the time of Coker's conviction, the Georgia Code provided that rape could be punished by (1) death, (2) life imprisonment, or (3) by "imprisonment for not less than one nor more than 20 years. Punishment [was] determined by a jury in a separate sentencing proceeding in which at least one of [a list] of statutory aggravating circumstances [had to] be found before" death could be imposed.[70]

On the day of the rape, Coker escaped from prison where he had been serving sentences for murder, rape, kidnaping, and aggravated assault. That evening, initially threatening the couple into whose house he entered with a board and then a knife, Coker robbed them, raped the woman and took her with him in the couple's car. "The jury returned a verdict of guilty. . . . A sentencing hearing was then conducted. . . ."[71] The jury found two aggravating factors, namely that the "rape had

---

69. Payne v. Tennessee, 501 U.S. 808, 827-828 (1991) (citations omitted).
70. Coker v. Georgia, 433 U.S. 584, 586 (1977).
71. *Id.* at 587.

been committed by a person with a prior record of conviction for a capital felony" and that it "had been committed in the course of committing another capital felony, namely, [an] armed robbery. . . . "[72]

The Court used the framework developed in its Eighth Amendment jurisprudence to conclude that "a sentence of death is grossly disproportionate and excessive punishment for the crime of rape."[73]

Consider the dissent's position below:

> On December 5, 1971, the petitioner, Ehrlich Anthony Coker, raped and then stabbed to death a young woman. Less than eight months later Coker kidnaped and raped a second young woman. After twice raping this 16-year-old victim . . . [he] severely beat her with a club, and dragged her into a wooded area where he left her for dead. He was apprehended and pleaded guilty to offenses stemming from these incidents. He was sentenced by three separate courts to three life terms, two 20-year terms, and one 8-year term of imprisonment. Each judgment specified that the sentences it imposed were to run consecutively rather than concurrently. Approximately 1½ years later, on September 2, 1974, petitioner escaped from the state prison where he was serving these sentences. He promptly raped another 16-year-old woman in the presence of her husband, abducted her from her home, and threatened her with death and serious bodily harm. It is this crime for which the sentence now under review was imposed.
>
> The Court today holds that the State of Georgia may not impose the death penalty on Coker. In so doing, it prevents the State from imposing any effective punishment upon Coker for his latest rape. The Court's holding, moreover, bars Georgia from guaranteeing its citizens that they will suffer no further attacks by this habitual rapist. In fact, given the lengthy sentences Coker must serve for the crimes he has already committed, the Court's holding assures that petitioner — as well as others in his position — will henceforth feel no compunction whatsoever about committing further rapes as frequently as he may be able to escape from confinement and indeed even within the walls of the prison itself. To what extent we have left States "elbow room" to protect innocent persons from depraved human beings like Coker remains in doubt.[74] . . .
>
> Apart from the reality that rape is inherently one of the most egregiously brutal acts one human being can inflict upon another, there is nothing in the Eighth Amendment that so narrowly limits the factors which may be considered by a state legislature in determining whether a particular punishment is grossly excessive. Surely recidivism, especially the repeated commission of heinous crimes, is a factor which may properly be weighed as an aggravating circumstance, permitting the imposition of a punishment more severe than for one isolated offense.[75]

QUESTION

From the dissenting Justices' perspective in the above excerpt, for what was Coker punished with a death sentence?

b. Mens Rea

In two important bright-line or quasi-bright-line decisions, the Court considered the availability of the death penalty in felony-murder cases where the

72. *Id.* at 588-589.
73. *Id.* at 592.
74. *Id.* at 605-607.
75. *Id.* at 608.

defendant participated in the felony but did not personally kill the victim nor have express malice with respect to the victim's death.

In the first of these, *Enmund v. Florida*, 458 U.S. 782 (1982), the Court answered the question of "whether death is a valid penalty under the Eighth and Fourteenth Amendments for one who neither took life, attempted to take life, nor intended to take life."[76] The evidence at Enmund's trial suggests that he was the lookout and getaway driver in a residential armed robbery. It appears that Enmund was waiting outside in the car for his co-felons during the robbery, in which a co-defendant shot and killed both of the robbery victims. After conducting its Eighth Amendment inquiry, the Court concluded:

> Although the judgments of legislatures, juries, and prosecutors weigh heavily in the balance, it is for us ultimately to judge whether the Eighth Amendment permits imposition of the death penalty on one such as Enmund who aids and abets a felony in the course of which a murder is committed by others but who does not himself kill, attempt to kill, or intend that a killing take place or that lethal force will be employed. We have concluded, along with most legislatures and juries, that it does not.[77]

In support of its conclusion, the Court also considered whether either deterrence or retribution supported imposition of the death penalty in Enmund's circumstances. Here, the Court wrote:

> We are quite unconvinced, however, that the threat that the death penalty will be imposed for murder will measurably deter one who does not kill and has no intention or purpose that life will be taken. Instead, it seems likely that "capital punishment can serve as a deterrent only when murder is the result of premeditation and deliberation," (citation omitted) for if a person does not intend that life be taken or contemplate that lethal force will be employed by others, the possibility that the death penalty will be imposed for vicarious felony murder will not "enter into the cold calculus that precedes the decision to act." (citation omitted)
>
> It would be very different if the likelihood of a killing in the course of a robbery were so substantial that one should share the blame for the killing if he somehow participated in the felony. But competent observers have concluded that there is no basis in experience for the notion that death so frequently occurs in the course of a felony for which killing is not an essential ingredient that the death penalty should be considered as a justifiable deterrent to the felony itself. Model Penal Code § 201.2, Comment, p. 38, and n. 96. This conclusion was based on three comparisons of robbery statistics, each of which showed that only about one-half of one percent of robberies resulted in homicide. The most recent national crime statistics strongly support this conclusion.[24] In addition to the evidence that killings only rarely occur during robberies is the fact, already noted, that however often death occurs in the course of a felony such as robbery, the death penalty is rarely imposed on one only vicariously guilty of the murder, a fact which further attenuates its possible utility as an effective deterrent.
>
> As for retribution as a justification for executing Enmund, we think this very much depends on the degree of Enmund's culpability—what Enmund's intentions, expectations, and actions were. . . .

---

76. 458 U.S. at 787.

77. *Id.* at 797.

[24] An estimated total of 548,809 robberies occurred in the United States in 1980. U.S. Dept. of Justice, Federal Bureau of Investigation, Uniform Crime Reports 17 (1981). Approximately 2,361 persons were murdered in the United States in 1980 in connection with robberies, *id.*, at 13, and thus only about 0.43% of robberies in the United States in 1980 resulted in homicide. . . .

Putting Enmund to death to avenge two killings that he did not commit and had no intention of committing or causing does not measurably contribute to the retributive end of ensuring that the criminal gets his just deserts.[78]

The second case, *Tison v. Arizona*,[79] involved the prosecution of two sons of Gary Tison. Both sons, along with other family members, had facilitated Gary Tison's escape from prison. They entered the prison and armed Gary Tison and his cellmate. They "locked the prison guards and visitors in a storage closet." After hiding out for two nights, the group drove through the desert toward another city. They "decided to flag down a passing motorist and steal a car." The car that stopped held a husband, his wife, their 2-year-old son, and the husband's 15-year-old niece. After the plot to steal the motorist family's car became clear, the father of the motorist family begged for life. Gary Tison sent his sons to the car to get water for the motorist's family who, the sons believed, were to be left in the desert. The sons headed toward the car and then heard shots. They turned to see their father and his cellmate "brutally murder their four captives with repeated blasts from their shotguns. Neither made an effort to help the victims, though both later stated they were surprised by the shooting." All the members of the Tison group then got into the car and continued to flee. The police later apprehended the sons after a shoot-out. Gary Tison escaped into the desert where he died of exposure.

The Court addressed the question of whether death could be imposed on a "defendant whose participation [in serious felonies] is major [but] whose mental state is one of reckless indifference to the value of human life." Using the framework developed for evaluating Eighth Amendment claims, the Court held that "major participation in the felony committed, combined with reckless indifference to human life, is sufficient to satisfy the *Enmund* culpability requirement."[80]

QUESTIONS

1. How do *Enmund* and *Tison* differ?
2. Was the death penalty warranted in the *Tison* case on the basis of retribution? On the basis of deterrence?

c. Offender Characteristics

i. Insanity

In its 1986 decision in *Ford v. Wainwright*, 477 U.S. 399 (1986), the Court affirmed the longtime common law rule against executing insane individuals. In these cases, there is generally a post-conviction assessment or finding of insanity during the period of pre-execution confinement. The Court noted that the "bar against executing a prisoner who has lost his sanity bears impressive historical credentials; the practice consistently has been branded 'savage and inhuman.'"[81] Rationales that have been advanced for this rule include: (1) "the execution of an insane person simply offends humanity," (2) "it provides no example to others and thus contributes nothing to whatever deterrence value is intended to be served by capital punishment," (3) "madness is its own punishment," (4) "the community's quest

---

78. 458 U.S. at 800-801.
79. The quotations in this paragraph and the next come from Tison v. Arizona, 481 U.S. 137 (1987) at 139, 139-141, 158.
80. *Id.* at 145.
81. 477 U.S. at 406.

for 'retribution' — the need to offset a criminal act by a punishment of equivalent 'moral quality' — is not served by execution of an insane person, which has a 'lesser value' than that of the crime for which he is to be punished."[82]

ii. Mental Retardation

In 2002, in *Atkins v. Virginia* the Court addressed whether the Eighth Amendment prohibited execution of persons with certain intellectual disabilities. The Court noted that

> [t]hose mentally retarded persons who meet the law's requirements for criminal responsibility should be tried and punished when they commit crimes. Because of their disabilities in areas of reasoning, judgment, and control of their impulses, however, they do not act with the level of moral culpability that characterizes the most serious adult criminal conduct. Moreover, their impairments can jeopardize the reliability and fairness of capital proceedings against mentally retarded defendants."[83]

The Court noted that "[m]entally retarded persons frequently know the difference between right and wrong and are competent to stand trial. Because of their impairments, however, by definition they have diminished capacities to understand and process information, to communicate, to abstract from mistakes and learn from experience, to engage in logical reasoning, to control impulses, and to understand the reactions of others. There is no evidence that they are more likely to engage in criminal conduct than others, but there is abundant evidence that they often act on impulse rather than pursuant to a premeditated plan, and that in group settings they are followers rather than leaders. Their deficiencies do not warrant an exemption from criminal sanctions, but they do diminish their personal culpability."[84] Thus, the Court held: "Construing and applying the Eighth Amendment in light of our 'evolving standards of decency,' we therefore conclude that such punishment is excessive and that the Constitution 'places a substantive restriction on the State's power to take the life' of a mentally retarded offender."[85]

QUESTIONS

What arguments about retribution and deterrence might you make that are relevant to the *Atkins* holding?

iii. Age

On March 1, 2005, the United States Supreme Court invoked the Eighth and Fourteenth Amendments to "forbid imposition of the death penalty on offenders who were under the age of 18 when their crimes were committed." *Roper v. Simmons*, 2005 U.S. LEXIS 2200, **49-50. The majority focused on "[t]hree general differences between juveniles under 18 and adults". The differences involved (1) "comparative immaturity and irresponsibility", (2) a vulnerability to "negative influences and outside pressures", and (3) the less well-formed character of a juvenile in comparison with that of an adult. *Id.* at **33-34. The Court found that these differences "demonstrate that juvenile offenders cannot with reliability be classified among

---

82. *Id.* at 407-408.
83. 536 U.S. 304, 306-307 (2002).
84. *Id.* at 318.
85. *Id.* at 321.

the worst offenders." *Id.* In light of the "diminished culpability of juveniles", the majority concluded that neither retribution nor deterrence justified imposition of the death penalty on juvenile offenders. *Id.* at **35-36.

d. Method of Execution

In the challenges to execution methods that the United States Supreme Court has addressed thus far, it has declined to outlaw any particular method of execution as violating the Eighth Amendment. In 1996, however, the Ninth Circuit affirmed a district court ruling outlawing execution by lethal gas.[86] Note, from the empirical data at the start of the chapter, that states employed only two methods of execution in 2002: lethal injection and electrocution. Of those, 70 executions involved lethal injection and 1 involved electrocution. Using the Supreme Court's Eighth Amendment jurisprudence, what factors should a court consider to determine if a method of execution violates the "cruel and unusual punishment" clause?

e. Constitutional and Constitutionally Suspect Aggravating Circumstances

Since *Furman*, the Court has addressed whether particular aggravating circumstances are unconstitutional under the Eighth Amendment. The Court determines whether the statutory language itself is "too vague to provide any guidance to the sentencer."[87] If it is that vague, "then the federal court must attempt to determine whether the state courts have further defined the vague terms and, if they have done so, whether those definitions are constitutionally sufficient — *i.e.*, whether they provide *some* guidance to the sentencer."[88] With adequate guidance, a state court can salvage facially vague language. Compare the three aggravating circumstances described below.

In the first of the three cases, *Godfrey v. Georgia*,[89] the Court evaluated an aggravating circumstance that permitted a sentence of death if the fact finder found the offense "outrageously or wantonly vile, horrible and inhuman."[90] Unlike in earlier cases where juries had found this circumstance true, the Georgia Supreme Court did not limit this aggravating circumstance to those situations in which there was torture or aggravated battery or depravity of mind. Without such a limiting construction, the United States Supreme Court found that "[t]here is nothing in these few words, standing alone, that implies any inherent restraint on the arbitrary and capricious infliction of a death sentence. A person of ordinary sensibility could fairly characterize almost every murder as 'outrageously or wantonly vile, horrible and inhuman.' "[91] Describing the discretion in the choice of sentence as "standardless and unchanneled," the Court held that "[t]here is no principled way to distinguish this case, in which the death penalty was imposed, from the many cases in which it was not."[92]

---

86. Fierro v. Gomez, 77 F.3d 301 (1996).
87. Walton v. Arizona, 497 U.S. 639, 654 (1990).
88. *Id.*
89. 446 U.S. 420 (1980).
90. *Id* at 428.
91. *Id.*
92. *Id.* at 429, 433.

In the second case, *Walton v. Arizona*,[93] the Court considered Arizona's "especially heinous, cruel, or depraved" aggravating circumstance. The Arizona Supreme Court had provided the following limiting construction: "a crime is committed in a 'depraved' manner when the perpetrator 'relishes' the murder, evidencing debasement or perversion,' or 'shows an indifference to the suffering of the victim and evidences a sense of pleasure' in the killing."[94] The Court "concluded that this construction adequately guided sentencing discretion, even though 'the proper degree of definition of an aggravating factor of this nature is not susceptible of mathematical precision.' "[95]

In the third case, *Arave v. Creech*,[96] the Court evaluated the constitutionality of an aggravating circumstance that read: " 'by the murder, or circumstances surrounding its commission, the defendant exhibited utter disregard for human life.' "[97] The Idaho Supreme Court had construed "utter disregard" as "reflective of other acts or circumstances surrounding the crime which exhibit the highest, the utmost, callous disregard for human life, i.e., the cold-blooded, pitiless slayer."[98] The Court determined that "the phrase 'cold-blooded, pitiless slayer' refers to a killer who kills without feeling or sympathy . . . . [These terms] describe the defendant's state of mind: not his *mens rea* but his attitude toward his conduct and his victim."[99] The Court held that this was "not a 'subjective' matter, but a *fact* to be inferred from the surrounding circumstances." Although the Court characterized this as a close question, it found that the language was adequately "clear and objective" and passed constitutional muster.

QUESTIONS

1. Are the constructions of the aggravating circumstances from the three cases summarized above reconcilable?

2. Should a state supreme court's limiting construction control whether an aggravating circumstance is too vague to meet Eighth Amendment requirements?

f. Victim Impact Statements

For a number of years, the United States Supreme Court required the exclusion of "victim impact evidence during the penalty phase of a capital trial."[100] In the following case, the Court reconsidered that position.

---

93. 497 U.S. 639 (1990). In its 2002 decision in Ring v. Arizona, 536 U.S. 584, 589, the United States Supreme Court overruled a portion of *Walton* and held that "[c]apital defendants . . . are entitled to a jury determination of any fact on which the legislature conditions an increase in their maximum punishment." Following *Ring*, juries, rather than judges, must serve as the fact finders in determining whether aggravating circumstances apply when such circumstances can increase the defendant's total punishment.

94. *Walton*, 497 U.S. at 655 (quoting State v. Walton, 159 Ariz. 571, 587 (1989)).

95. *Arave*, 507 U.S. 473 (quoting *Walton*, 159 Ariz. at 655) (1989)).

96. 507 U.S. 463.

97. *Id*. at 465, citing Idaho Code § 19-2515(g)(6) (1987).

98. State v. Osborn, 102 Idaho 405, 418-419 (1981).

99. This and remaining quotations in this paragraph are from *Arave*, 507 U.S. 463 at 472-473, 474 (1993).

100. Payne v. Tennessee, 501 U.S. at 808.

PAYNE *v.* TENNESSEE

United States Supreme Court 501 U.S. 808, 811 (1991)

Payne . . . was convicted by a jury on two counts of first-degree murder and one count of assault with intent to commit murder in the first degree. He was sentenced to death for each of the murders and to 30 years in prison for the assault.

The victims of Payne's offenses were 28-year-old Charisse Christopher, her 2-year-old daughter Lacie, and her 3-year-old son Nicholas. The three lived together in an apartment in Millington, Tennessee, across the hall from Payne's girl-friend. . . .

Payne . . . entered the Christophers' apartment, and began making sexual advances towards Charisse. Charisse resisted and Payne became violent. A neighbor who resided in the apartment directly beneath the Christophers heard Charisse screaming. " 'Get out, get out,' as if she were telling the children to leave." The noise briefly subsided and then began, " 'horribly loud.' " The neighbor called the police after she heard a "blood curdling scream" from the Christophers' apartment.

When the first police officer arrived at the scene, he immediately encountered Payne, who was leaving the apartment building, so covered with blood that he appeared to be " 'sweating blood. . . .' "

Inside the apartment, the police encountered a horrifying scene. Blood covered the walls and floor throughout the unit. Charisse and her children were lying on the floor in the kitchen. Nicholas, despite several wounds inflicted by a butcher knife that completely penetrated through his body from front to back, was still breathing. Miraculously, he survived, but not until after undergoing seven hours of surgery and a transfusion of 1,700 cc's of blood — 400 to 500 cc's more than his estimated normal blood volume. Charisse and Lacie were dead. . . .

During the sentencing phase of the trial, . . . [t]he State presented the testimony of Charisse's mother, Mary Zvolanek. When asked how Nicholas had been affected by the murders of his mother and sister, she responded:

> He cries for his mom. He doesn't seem to understand why she doesn't come home. And he cries for his sister Lacie. He comes to me many times during the week and asks me, Grandmama, do you miss my Lacie. And I tell him yes. He says, I'm worried about my Lacie.

In arguing for the death penalty during closing argument, the prosecutor commented on the continuing effects of Nicholas' experience, stating:

> But we do know that Nicholas was alive. And Nicholas was in the same room. Nicholas was still conscious. His eyes were open. He responded to the paramedics. He was able to follow their directions. He was able to hold his intestines in as he was carried to the ambulance. So he knew what happened to his mother and baby sister.
>
> There is nothing you can do to ease the pain of any of the families involved in this case. . . . But there is something that you can do for Nicholas.
>
> Somewhere down the road Nicholas is going to grow up, hopefully. He's going to want to know what happened. And he is going to know what happened to his baby sister and his mother. He is going to want to know what type of justice was done. He is going to want to know what happened. With your verdict, you will provide the answer. . . .

[In reconsidering its position on victim impact evidence, the Court observed that] the assessment of harm caused by the defendant as a result of the crime charged has understandably been an important concern of the criminal law, both in determining the elements of the offense and in determining the appropriate punishment. Thus, two equally blameworthy criminal defendants may be guilty of different offenses solely because their acts cause differing amounts of harm. . . . [If each of two defendants] participates in a robbery, and each of whom acts with reckless disregard for human life; if the robbery in which the first defendant participated results in the death of a victim, he may be subjected to the death penalty, but if the robbery in which the second defendant participates does not result in the death of a victim, the death penalty may not be imposed. . . .

Wherever judges in recent years have had discretion to impose sentence, the consideration of the harm caused by the crime has been an important factor in the exercise of that discretion. . . .

In the majority of cases, and in this case, victim impact evidence serves entirely legitimate purposes. In the event that evidence is introduced that is so unduly prejudicial that it renders the trial fundamentally unfair, the Due Process Clause of the Fourteenth Amendment provides a mechanism for relief. Courts have always taken into consideration the harm done by the defendant in imposing sentence, and the evidence adduced in this case was illustrative of the harm caused by Payne's double murder.

We are now of the view that a State may properly conclude that for the jury to assess meaningfully the defendant's moral culpability and blameworthiness, it should have before it at the sentencing phase evidence of the specific harm caused by the defendant. "[T]he State has a legitimate interest in counteracting the mitigating evidence which the defendant is entitled to put in, by reminding the sentencers that just as the murderer should be considered as an individual, so too the victim is an individual whose death represents a unique loss to society and in particular to his family."

g. Innocence

In the 1993 *Herrera v. Collins* decision,[101] the Supreme Court considered whether a claim of "actual innocence" could trigger relief in a death penalty context, after all of the defendant's appeals and collateral avenues of attack have been exhausted. Does the Eighth Amendment "prohibit the execution of a person who is innocent of the crime for which he was convicted?"[102] The Court explained that "a claim of 'actual innocence' is not itself a constitutional claim, but instead a gateway through which a habeas petitioner must pass to have his otherwise barred constitutional claim considered on the merits."[103] Herrera, however, did "not seek excusal of a procedural error so that he [could] bring an independent constitutional claim challenging his conviction or sentence. . . . [Rather, he argued that he was] entitled to habeas relief because newly discovered evidence show[ed] that his conviction [was] factually incorrect."[104] The Court suggested that the proper route for rectifying any such error was executive clemency. Nonetheless, in the end, the Court left open a very limited window for actual innocence claims. It concluded:

---

101. 506 U.S. 390 (1993).
102. *Id.* at 398.
103. *Id.* at 404.
104. *Id.*

We may assume, for the sake of argument in deciding this case, that in a capital case a truly persuasive demonstration of "actual innocence" made after trial would render the execution of a defendant unconstitutional, and warrant federal habeas relief if there were no state avenue open to process such a claim. But because of the very disruptive effect that entertaining claims of actual innocence would have on the need for finality in capital cases, and the enormous burden that having to retry cases based on often stale evidence would place on the States, the threshold showing for such an assumed right would necessarily be extraordinarily high.[105]

QUESTIONS

1. What concerns should courts have in considering claims of "actual innocence" ten years after a conviction?
2. What arguments favor such reconsideration?
3. What standard should a convicted individual have to meet to receive such review?

The specter of executing an innocent person fuels much public and legal debate over the death penalty. Researchers and commentators dispute whether or when such an execution has actually taken place in modern times here in the United States.[106] Whatever the result of that debate, particularly with the advent of DNA testing, a number of death row inmates, some of whom spent considerable time in prison under threat of capital punishment, have been exonerated.[107] In this context, consider the response to the concern about innocence and wrongful convictions by then Governor George Ryan of Illinois. After courts determined that 13 inmates on Illinois' death row had been wrongly convicted in the period between 1977 and 2000,[108] then Governor Ryan imposed a moratorium on executions.[109] Three years later, Governor Ryan indicated that he "was not prepared to take the risk that we may execute an innocent person"[110] and commuted

---

105. *Id.* at 417.
106. Hugo Adam Bedau & Michael L. Radelet, *Miscarriages of Justice in Potentially Capital* Cases, 40 Stan. L. Rev. 21, 72-75 (1987) (listing "twenty-three cases of persons we believe to be innocent defendants who were executed" from 1905 through 1974); Stephen J. Markman & Paul G. Cassell, *Protecting the Innocent: A Response to the Bedau-Radelet Study*, 41 Stan. L. Rev. 121, 124 (1988) ("Bedau and Radelet have made no persuasive showing that anyone has been wrongly executed since new capital punishment procedures were instituted in the wake of *Furman v. Georgia*.").
107. The Innocence Project homepage, *www.innocenceproject.org* (accessed July 30, 2004). The effect of lingering doubt about the defendant's culpability may play a significant role in the exercise of jurors' sentencing discretion. *See* Margery M. Koosed, *Averting Mistaken Executions by Adopting the Model Penal Code's Exclusion of Death in the Presence of Lingering Doubt*, 21 No. Ill. U. L. Rev. 41, 60 (2001). Researchers on the Capital Jury Project, which conducted post-trial capital juror interviews in more than ten states, noted that "[t]he haunting possibility of an erroneous capital murder conviction, and even more so, the prospect of condemning and even executing an innocent person, is more formidable in jurors' decision making than any of the other mitigating considerations" and that lingering doubt "is the strongest influence in support of a final life punishment vote." William J. Bowers et al., *Foreclosed Impartiality in Capital Sentencing: Jurors' Predispositions, Guilt-Trial Experience and Premature Decisionmaking*, 83 Cornell L. Rev. 1476, 1534, 1536 (1998) (cited in Koosed, *supra*, at 56 n.60.). The error rate in capital cases is a subject of current and continuing debate. *Compare, e.g.*, James S. Liebman, et al., *Symposium: Restructuring Federal Courts: Habeas: Capital Attrition: Error Rates in Capital Cases, 1973-1995*, 78 Tex. L. Rev. 1839 (2000) *with* Joseph L. Hoffman, *Violence and Truth*, 76 Ind. L.J. 939 (2001).
108. *See Ryan Clearing Death Row*, CBSNEWS.com (Jan. 11, 2003) at *cbsnews.co . . . tional/main534639.shtml?cmp=EM8707* (accessed June 3, 2004).
109. *Id.*
110. *Id.*

the death sentences of all death row inmates on the Illinois death row at the time, more than 150 condemned individuals.[111]

PROBLEM

6.25 In *Herrera*, the United States Supreme Court described the standard that the defense would have to meet to demonstrate actual innocence in a case in which innocence was the appellate focus. Would the facts in the following case rise to the showing of innocence required in *Herrera*?[112]

"Shortly before 11 P.M. in late September 1981, the body of Public Safety Officer David Rucker was found on the highway." He was lying next to his patrol car and had been shot in the head. "At about the same time . . . Officer Carrisalez observed a speeding vehicle traveling . . . away from the place where Rucker's body had been found along the same road." Carrisalez and his partner Hernandez stopped the speeding vehicle. When Carrisalez spoke with the driver, the driver shot Carrisalez in the chest, a wound from which he died nine days later.

The evidence at trial on the murder of Officer Carrisalez consisted of Hernandez's identification of the defendant as the shooter and an affidavit from Carrisalez, made before he died, that the defendant was the shooter. In addition, the speeding car "was registered to the [defendant's] 'live-in' girlfriend. [Defendant] was known to drive this car and had a set of keys in his pants pocket when he was arrested" several days after the shootings. "Hernandez identified the car involved . . . [and] testified that there had been found only one person in the car that night. . . . [Defendant's] Social Security card had been alongside Rucker's patrol car, . . . [s]platters of blood on the car [involved] . . . and on [defendant's] blue jeans and wallet were identified as type A blood — the same type which Rucker had. ([Defendant] has type O blood.) Similar evidence with respect to strands of hair found in the car indicated that the hair was Rucker's and not [defendant's]. A handwritten letter was also found on the person of [defendant] when he was arrested, which strongly implied that he had killed Rucker." It read in part as follows:

> What happened to Rucker was for a certain reason. I knew him as Mike Tatum. He was in my business, and he violated some of its laws and suffered the penalty, like the one you have for me when the time comes.
>
> My personal life, which has been a conspiracy since my high school days, has nothing to do with what has happened. The other officer that became part of our lives, me and Rucker's (Tatum), that night had not to do with this [*sic*]. He was out to do what he had to

---

111. *Illinois Supreme Court upholds commuted death sentences*, CNN.com (Jan. 23, 2004) at *cnn.com/20 . . . W01/23/death.penalty.illinois.ap/* (accessed June 3, 2004).

112. Facts and quoted material in the Problem are drawn from 506 U.S. 390, 393 (1993).

do, protect, but that's life. . . . I will present myself if this is read word for word over the media. . . .

The letter was signed with the defendant's name.

The defendant was convicted of first-degree murder for the killing of Officer Carrisalez and sentenced to death.

Ten years after his conviction, the defendant claimed he was "actually innocent" of the murder. He claimed that his brother, who was now dead, had been the killer.

Defendant submitted four affidavits in support of his claim.

The first was from the attorney who had represented the defendant's brother. His affidavit, dated 1990, claimed that his client, the defendant's brother, had confessed to the killings of Rucker and Carrisalez. Similarly, defendant's brother's former cellmate claimed that the brother had confessed to killing Rucker and Carrisalez. The third affidavit came from the brother's son, the defendant's nephew, who claimed that at the time of the shootings, when the nephew was nine years old, he had been present and seen his father shoot both officers. Finally, the defendant offered an affidavit from a schoolmate of both the defendant and his brother, who claimed that the brother had also confessed to him in 1983.

CHAPTER SEVEN

CAUSATION

A. INTRODUCTION

Legislatures often include a result element when defining crimes. The various categories of homicide, for example, all require a "death." Other examples of result elements found in criminal statutes are "serious bodily injury" and "damage to property." When a crime requires a result, the prosecution must prove not only that the result occurred but also that the defendant's conduct *caused* that result. By contrast, crimes without a result element do not require proof of causation. Theft, reckless driving, and attempt are examples of crimes that lack result elements and accordingly do not require proof of causation.

This chapter focuses on two central questions. First, why is causation ever a prerequisite for criminal liability? Second, what is required to satisfy causation? In answering the first, think about the following scenario. Defendant Uno, intending to kill victim Quatro, sprinkles a fatal dose of cyanide poison on the brownies that Uno knows Quatro will eat at lunch. Meanwhile, en route home from the gym early that same morning, Quatro's car is struck by a drunk driver, killing both Quatro and the drunk driver. Should Uno be liable for Quatro's death? Intuition may suggest that Uno should not be held liable for a death he played no role in bringing about, and the criminal law accords with your intuition. Uno would not be held liable for Quatro's death because of a lack of causation between Uno's conduct and Quatro's death. What underlies this intuition? In answering this question, look back to the purposes of punishment. Does a retributive concern about blame explain causation requirements? Does it make any difference if one measures blame by reference to mental state or by reference to any harm that actually occurs? Or do utilitarian concerns about danger drive causation?

Consider, however, a second scenario. A and B leave a bar one minute apart. Both are severely intoxicated and drive at 75 m.p.h. to their respective homes, which are just a few houses apart. A and B run the same multiple stop signs and red lights along the way. A arrives home without causing any harm. B, just one minute behind A, hits a school bus carrying a soccer team returning from a game. B survives but several young people on the bus are killed. Who should be punished? A, who caused no harm? B, who caused several deaths? If both should be punished, should B be punished more severely than A?

If one uses harm to assess blame, it makes sense to punish *B* more severely than *A* from a retributive perspective because *B*'s driving brought about several deaths. But what if one uses mental state rather than harm to assess blame? Is *A*'s mental state any less blameworthy than *B*'s? If one relies on the utilitarian purposes of punishment to determine whether and how severely *A* and *B* should be punished, it is difficult to distinguish between *A* and *B*. *A*'s conduct was just as dangerous as *B*'s. Both seem equally in need of deterrence and incapacitation. Which theories of punishment, then, support treating *A* and *B* differently? Should homicide liability and severity of punishment hinge on *B*'s "bad luck" in striking or *A*'s "good luck" in missing the bus? What does this hypothetical scenario suggest about the use of causation as an ingredient in formulating criminal liability?

To answer the second inquiry and determine what is required to satisfy causation, we begin with a typical criminal jury instruction succinctly stating the basic law of causation and a Problem asking you to apply the instruction to the facts of a number of cases you have already studied. The jury instruction reveals that the test for causation has two components. The prosecution must prove both. The first is often referred to as "cause in fact" or "but for cause" and the second as "proximate cause." The materials that follow the introductory problem examine both cause in fact and proximate cause in detail.

The law of causation is often criticized as murky and indeterminate. See if you agree with this assessment as you attempt to decide whether causation is fulfilled in each of these cases.

Although legislatures have primary authority in criminal law, they have shown little interest in the law of criminal causation. Most states do not have a statute addressing causation. Rather, judges largely control the development of the law of causation through a common law process. The law you will encounter in this chapter, unlike most of the other chapters in this book, is almost exclusively in the form of judicial opinions. Why might legislators have chosen not to deal with causation by statute?

PROBLEM

7.1   **Jury Instruction on Causation**[1]
        The state alleges that the defendant's act caused the death at issue in this case. Cause is an essential element in a homicide offense. An act causes death if (1) without the act the death would not have occurred and (2) the act produces the death in a natural and continuous sequence. The defendant's responsibility is not limited to the immediate or most obvious result of the defendant's act. The defendant is also responsible for the natural and foreseeable consequences that follow, in the ordinary course of events, from the act.

   (a) Put yourself in the role of a juror and apply the above instruction to the following cases.

---

1. This instruction is based on Ohio Jury Instructions — Criminal, 409.55 (2004).

(1) *Keeler v. Superior Court* (Chapter 3) (in utero fetus dies after defendant, with the goal of killing the fetus, assaults pregnant ex-wife). Did Keeler's conduct cause the death of the fetus his former wife was carrying?

(2) *Jones v. United States* (Chapter 4) (ten-month-old infant, Anthony Lee, who had been in the defendant's care, dies of malnutrition). Did Jones' failure to act cause the death of Anthony Lee?

(3) *Commonwealth v. Carroll* (Chapter 6) (defendant shoots wife after argument about defendant taking teaching position that would require his absence from the home several nights a week). Did Carroll's conduct cause his wife's death?

(4) *United States v. Fleming* (Chapter 6) (victim dies after intoxicated defendant collides with victim's car on wrong side of highway). Did Fleming's conduct cause the death of the woman who died in the collision?

(5) *Berry v. Superior Court* (Chapter 6) (child dies after being mauled by defendant's pit bull, Willy). Did Berry's conduct cause the death of his neighbor's child?

(6) *Commonwealth v. Welansky* (Chapter 6) (many victims are unable to escape and die in a fire at the Cocoanut Grove nightclub). Did Welansky's conduct cause the deaths of those who died in the Cocoanut Grove fire?

(7) *People v. Hall* (Chapter 6) (victim skier dies after being struck in the head by defendant skier). Did Hall's conduct cause the death of the skier he struck?

(8) *State v. Williams* (Chapter 6) (17-month-old child, William, dies after parents fail to provide medical attention). Did his parents' failure to provide medical attention cause William's death?

(b) What is required under this jury instruction for a jury to find that someone caused a death?

(c) Who is making the law of criminal causation under an instruction such as the one that appears above? The legislature? The judge? The jury?

B. CAUSE IN FACT

Cause in fact is sometimes referred to as factual or "but for" cause. The jury instruction in Problem 7.1 above uses the standard test for cause in fact, whether "without the [defendant's] act the death would not have occurred." This same test is often expressed using the phrase "but for." That is, if the result would not have occurred but for the defendant's act, then cause in fact is fulfilled. Recall the *Stamp* felony murder case in which the victim of a robbery died from a heart attack less than one hour after the robbery. The medical expert's testimony that "but for the robbery there would have been no fatal seizure at that time" provided the evidentiary basis for the jury to find that the robbery was a cause in fact of the victim's death, fulfilling the first component of causation.

The test described in the previous paragraph is effective in assessing this first prong of causation in the vast majority of cases. As Professor Joshua Dressler has explained, however, there are occasional cases in which the unmodified version given in the preceding paragraph fails to produce a satisfactory or just result.[2] These cases involve situations in which there are "multiple actual causes."[3] For example, in the rare case when two acts combine to bring about a particular result and each act on its own would have produced that result, neither act would meet the standard test for cause in fact. In such circumstances, the criminal law can modify the "but for" test by adding additional language—for example, without the defendant's act, the death would not have occurred "as it did" or "when it did."[4]

To illustrate the application of the modified test, imagine that A puts a slow-acting poison in B's coffee. This poison would kill B in six hours. While B is drinking the poisoned coffee, B eats a pastry, to which C, completely independently of A, has added poison. C's poison alone would kill B in six hours. In combination, the two poisons cause B to die in 30 minutes. Under the unmodified standard test (without C's poison, would B have died?), the answer is: "Yes, B would have died even without C's poison." Applying just the standard test, then, would suggest that C's poison was not a cause in fact of B's death. After all, B would have died from A's poison, even without C's conduct. Applying the same standard test to A (without A's poison, would B have died?), we would again answer: "Yes, B would have died even without A's poison." Under the standard test, it would appear that neither A nor C was a cause in fact of B's death. These results seem counterintuitive and inconsistent with the theories of punishment that we have studied. If we modify the standard test, however, to read: without C's poison, would B have died when B did?, we would answer in the negative: No, B would not have died in 30 minutes without C's poison. Similarly, B would not have died in 30 minutes without A's poison. With the modified test, consistent with our intuition, both A and C are causes in fact of B's death. Sometimes, instead of the modified standard test, courts employ an alternative test, one that holds each act sufficient if it was a "substantial factor" in bringing about the result.[5]

The cause in fact inquiry is a factual one, whether or not the defendant's conduct in some way contributed to the result. This component of causation has been described as adopting a "scientific notion of causation. Whether cigarette smoking causes cancer, whether the presence of hydrogen or helium caused an explosion, are factual questions to be resolved by the best science the courts can muster."[6]

You should keep in mind that cause in fact is a necessary but not sufficient condition for criminal liability. Many acts fulfill the test for cause in fact even though they do not warrant criminal punishment. A, for example, hires B to work as a sales clerk in A's store. During a robbery of the store, B is shot and killed. If A had not hired B, B would not have been killed in the robbery. A's act of hiring B thus meets the test for cause in fact of B's homicide though it does not merit criminal punishment. The second component of causation—proximate cause—serves an important limiting function by sifting, from the many acts that fulfill cause in fact, those on which criminal liability may be imposed.

2. Joshua Dressler, *Understanding Criminal Law*, 184-187 (3d ed. 2001).
3. *Id.* at 184.
4. *Id.* at 184-187.
5. See Wayne LaFave, *Criminal Law* 334 (4th ed. 2003)
6. Michael S. Moore, *Causation* in 1 Encyclopedia of Crime and Justice 152 (2d ed. 2002).

PROBLEMS

7.2 Was cause in fact fulfilled in each of the scenarios mentioned in Problem 7.1?

7.3 Mary and Jim recently refinanced their mortgage with a new bank. Mary takes care of the couple's banking chores and did most of the work on the refinancing. One evening, because Mary knows she has a busy schedule the following day, she asks Jim to stop by the bank during his lunch hour to pick up a form to have their monthly mortgage payment automatically deducted from their joint checking account. Jim's typical routine is to exercise during his lunch hour by running or lifting weights at a gym. The next day, Jim goes to the bank during his lunch hour and happens to arrive in the middle of a bank robbery. Police surround the bank and the robbers take Jim hostage and flee. Jim is shot and killed in an exchange of gunfire between the robbers and pursuing police. Is Mary's act of asking Jim to visit the bank during his lunch hour a cause in fact of Jim's death?

7.4 Stephen was recently fired from a position as a nursing home administrator. His employers discovered that in order to increase profits, Stephen had drastically cut the nursing home staff while simultaneously increasing the number of residents. After Stephen made the staff cuts, Geraldine, an elderly resident of the nursing home, wandered outside during the night, where she died of exposure. You are the local prosecutor. Public attention is focused on Geraldine's death, and her relatives demand that you charge Stephen with manslaughter based on her death. What problems might you encounter in proving beyond a reasonable doubt that Stephen's conduct was a cause in fact of Geraldine's death?

7.5 Recall that, in the *Stamp* felony murder case, the victim of the robbery died less than an hour after the robbery, and a medical expert attributed his death to the robbery. What if his death were not the result of a heart attack induced by the stress of the robbery? Rather, he had a fatal reaction to the cinnamon that was inadvertently added to his café latte at lunch. Are the actions of the bank robbers a cause in fact of the victim's death? Should the victim's death play a role in determining the criminal liability or punishment of Stamp and the other bank robbers? Apply the theories of punishment in answering this question.

7.6 *V* is an undercover agent who has investigated wrongdoing by various criminal organizations in the United States and around the world. One such organization hires *A*, an assassin, to kill *V*. Another criminal organization separately hires *B*, a hit man, to kill *V*. *A* lies in wait for *V*, intending to surprise and stab him. At the same time, *B* takes up a sniper position nearby, armed with a high-powered rifle, intending to shoot and kill *V*. *A* and *B* are unaware of each other's conduct or intentions. As *V* comes into view, *A* jumps out and stabs *V* in the heart, inflicting a mortal wound. At the same moment, *B* shoots *V* through the head, also inflicting a mortal wound. Is the act of either *A* or *B* a cause in fact of *V*'s death?

7.7 Jeffrey and Jennifer are charged with manslaughter based on the death of Jeffrey's six-year-old son, Billy. Jennifer is Jeffrey's girlfriend and lived with Jeffrey and Billy. On the evening prior to Billy's death, Jennifer beat Billy and left him severely bruised. During this beating, she struck Billy several times forcefully on the head. The following morning, Billy was slow to get out of bed. Jeffrey then beat Billy again, delivering a number of blows to Billy's head. Later that afternoon, Billy lost consciousness and was taken to the emergency room of a local hospital, where he died. The prosecution calls the coroner as an expert witness. She testifies that one particularly severe blow to the head appears to have caused Billy's death, but she is unable to determine whether the blow was one struck by Jennifer the evening prior to Billy's death or by Jeffrey on the morning of Billy's death. Both Jeffrey and Jennifer ask the trial judge to grant a motion for acquittal for failure to prove causation. How should the judge rule?

7.8 Ernestina is jealous of her sister Chloe and Chloe's success as an actress. Ernestina puts slow-acting poison in Chloe's morning tea. The poison takes six hours to cause death. On Chloe's way to the studio later that morning, a car strikes and kills her instantly. Is Ernestina's act of poisoning Chloe a cause in fact of Choe's death?

7.9 Imagine that after Ernestina poisons Chloe's tea, Prunella, Chloe's older sister, who is also jealous of Chloe, stabs Chloe in the leg with a paring knife. Ernestina's poison alone would have taken six hours to cause death. The stab wound inflicted by Prunella alone would have taken three hours to cause death. Together they cause Chloe to die in one hour. Is Ernestina's conduct a cause in fact of Chloe's death? Is Prunella's?

C. PROXIMATE CAUSE

Proximate cause is sometimes referred to as legal cause or cause in law. As the jury instruction in Problem 7.1 exemplifies, the test for proximate cause is vague. That instruction uses several phrases to guide the jury in resolving the proximate cause question. The result must occur "in a natural and continuous sequence," though causation is "not limited to the immediate or most obvious result." The defendant is "responsible for the natural and foreseeable consequences that follow, in the ordinary course of events, from the act."

Use of the words "natural" and "foreseeable" and the phrase "in the ordinary course of events" indicate that probability plays an important role in determining proximate cause. Generally, the higher the probability that a result will follow from the defendant's act, the greater the likelihood that the defendant's act will be found to have proximately caused that result. The probability issue in causation is often addressed in terms of foreseeability, the most frequently invoked test for determining proximate cause. A defendant is usually held to have proximately caused a foreseeable result and not to have proximately caused an unforeseeable result. What, though, must be foreseeable? The result? The manner in which the result occurred? Both? And how foreseeable must the result and/or the manner of its occurrence be? In other words, what level of probability is required for a finding of proximate cause? The law on proximate cause typically is not clear in answering these questions, giving judges and juries considerable latitude in determining the boundaries of proximate cause.

If a second person is involved in bringing about a result required for criminal liability, the causation analysis often becomes more complex, and issues other than foreseeability may play a role. A subsequent actor sometimes insulates a prior actor from criminal liability. In the jargon of causation, the second actor is often referred to as an "intervening cause" who may "break the causal chain" between the first actor and the result. Saying that a second actor breaks the causal chain between a prior actor's conduct and a result means that the first actor will not be found to have proximately caused the result.

The precise conditions under which a subsequent actor's conduct breaks the causal chain are the source of considerable confusion in the law of causation. Courts are often neither clear nor consistent in their treatment of intervening cause cases. The mental state and blameworthiness of the second actor play major roles in determining whether or not the second actor will relieve a first actor of causal responsibility. Take, for example, a case in which A wishes to kill C. A disguises a bomb as a toy, wraps it in a package, and sends it to C using a courier, B. B, who works for a courier service and is paid by A to deliver the package, is unaware of A's plan and the content of the package. B delivers the package to C, who opens it and is killed. In this hypothetical, B's conduct did in fact play a role in bringing about C's death, but because B had an innocent mental state and no blame in relation to C's death, B's act will not relieve A of liability. In other words, B's conduct does not break the causal chain between A's conduct and C's death. The higher the intervenor's mental state and blame, the greater the chance that the intervenor will break the causal chain.

In contrast to the inquiry underlying cause in fact, which was factual in nature, the proximate cause inquiry asks the jury to assess blame and responsibility. In other words, while cause in fact is concerned with finding out what happened, proximate cause is concerned with determining who should be held responsible for what happened.

Keep in mind that a finding of causation alone is not equivalent to a finding of criminal liability. The other elements of the offense, such as mental state and voluntary act, must also be satisfied.

PROBLEMS

7.10 Robert is a freshman in college. One afternoon after classes he goes to the college gym and plays in a pick-up basketball game. During the game, Robert gets into a shoving match with Steve, another player. After the game, Steve continues to verbally spar with Robert and the two wind up in a fistfight. Robert prevails in the altercation and walks away when Steve is on the ground and unable to fight anymore. That evening, Steve and several of his friends go to Robert's dorm to retaliate. They plan to gang up on Robert and allow Steve to assault

Robert in fashion similar to the beating Robert gave Steve earlier in the day. Robert hears a knock on his door. When he looks through the peephole he sees Steve and his friends, who begin to pound on the door shouting that they are going to beat Robert and challenging him to come outside. They also attempt to force the door open. Meanwhile, Robert goes to the window of his dorm room and attempts to leap to the ground to escape. In doing so, he falls badly and breaks his neck. An ambulance is called, but Robert is dead by the time help arrives. Is the conduct of Steve and his friends a proximate cause of Robert's death? Consider the following variables. Would any of them make a difference in your determination of proximate causation?

(a) Robert's room is on the second floor of the dorm.
(b) Robert's room is on the fourth floor of the dorm.
(c) Robert's room is on the eighth floor of the dorm.
(d) Steve was accompanied by two friends.
(e) Steve was accompanied by four friends.
(f) Steve was accompanied by eight friends.
(g) Steve and his friends were brandishing baseball bats.
(h) Steve and his friends were carrying knives hidden in their pockets.

7.11 *D* was convicted at trial for armed robbery. *A* testified as an expert witness for the prosecution at trial. In a subsequent audit of the police forensic science laboratory, it is determined that *A* committed perjury at *D*'s trial when he testified that *D*'s fingerprint matched a fingerprint found on a gun used in the robbery. Without this evidence, it is unlikely the jury would have convicted *D*. *D* later dies. Could *A* be held liable for homicide under any of the following scenarios?

(a) *D* was killed when a state-owned and operated bus transporting him to prison crashed. Assume the driver of the bus was negligent.
(b) *D* was purposefully killed by another prisoner once he arrived at prison.
(c) Assume *D*'s case involved a capital homicide rather than an armed robbery. *D* was executed by the state following his conviction.

STATE *v.* JENKINS

276 S.C. 209, 277 S.E.2d 147 (1981)

Per Curiam

Robert Hamilton Jenkins was convicted of murder and sentenced to life imprisonment. His grounds for this appeal include the assertion that the trial judge erred in failing to submit to the jury as possible verdicts assault and battery with intent to kill and assault and battery of a high and aggravated nature. We find no reversible error and affirm.

Appellant's indictment for murder followed the death of a stabbing victim. The evidence reflects that the victim identified the appellant as the assailant before being rushed to a hospital for treatment of serious wounds to the neck and arms.

The victim lost substantial amounts of blood and was in a state of shock before reaching the hospital.

In order to determine the extent of the victim's injuries to the major blood vessels, an arteriogram was performed. Although the arteriogram is a common procedure, the victim suffered a rare, fatal reaction to the dye used in the arteriogram procedure. The evidence includes medical testimony that the victim's immediate cause of death was the reaction to the dye, that she probably would have survived absent the reaction, but that she probably would not have survived without medical treatment.

The trial judge submitted to the jury three possible verdicts — murder, manslaughter, and not guilty. He properly instructed the jury that there must be a causal relationship between the defendant's act and the death of the deceased before criminal liability may be imposed. The jury's verdict of guilty of murder necessarily included a finding adverse to appellant on the causation issue, which finding excluded a verdict for an offense not involving the victim's death.

Additionally, appellant does not in this Court challenge the sufficiency of the evidence to sustain the conviction of murder. Under such circumstances, we conclude there was no prejudicial error in refusing to submit to the jury the two degrees of assault and battery. The verdict in this case is consistent with those cases holding that one who inflicts an injury on another is deemed by law to be guilty of homicide where the injury contributes mediately or immediately to the death of the other.

. . . Accordingly, we affirm the lower court's determination of those issues under Rule 23 of the Rules of Practice of this Court.

QUESTIONS

1. How likely was it that the victim would die? How likely was it that the victim would die *from a fatal reaction to the arteriogram dye*? Which is the relevant inquiry for determining proximate cause?

2. *Jenkins* provides an example of what is often called the "eggshell victim" rule. Is this rule consistent with the requirement of foreseeability?

PEOPLE v. FLENON
42 Mich. App. 457 (1972)

V. J. BRENNAN, P.J., and McGREGOR and BRONSON, JJ. All concurred.

Defendant was convicted by jury verdict of murder in the first degree and sentenced to life imprisonment. He appeals this conviction as a matter of right. . . .

In the early morning hours of March 21, 1970, defendant left a house in Detroit carrying a shotgun for the avowed purpose of "getting back" at an unidentified person. He proceeded down the street until he encountered a group of persons including Carl Johnson, the deceased. Upon realizing the defendant had a gun, the group dispersed. Defendant chased the deceased, cornered him behind a parked car and shot him in the upper part of his leg.

Carl Johnson was rushed to a hospital where his right leg was amputated high above the knee because of the severity of the wound. Five weeks later, Carl Johnson was released and returned home. Within a short period of time he substantially weakened and was readmitted to the hospital where he died. The cause of death was found by the doctor performing the autopsy to be serum hepatitis and pneumonia.

Defendant's first allegation of error is that there was an insufficient causal connection between the gunshot wound and death by serum hepatitis to sustain his conviction. . . .

The causation problem in the instant case is compounded by defendant's allegation that serum hepatitis constituted an independent intervening cause suspending his liability. The concept of medical mistreatment becoming an intervening cause was considered in *People v Cook*, 39 Mich 236 (1878). There the victim received medical treatment including the administration of morphine after being shot by defendant. Since the victim's death was attributed to the morphine, defendant claimed that this medicine produced death independent of the wound and suspended his liability. The *Cook* Court found that morphine was a proper and appropriate medicine given by competent and skillful physicians. The legal principles applied by the *Cook* Court depended upon whether the wound was considered mortal and were summarized by its statement that:

> "In a case where the *wound is not mortal*, the injured person may recover, and thus no homicide have been committed. If, however, death do result, the accused will be held responsible, unless it was occasioned, not by the wound, but by *grossly erroneous medical treatment*. But where the *wound is a mortal one*, there is no chance for the injured person to recover, and therefore the reason which permits the showing of death from medical treatment does not exist."[7] (Emphasis added.)

Although the *Cook* Court did not clearly indicate the nature of the wound at issue, it concluded that the victim's death could not be attributed to the independent act of a third person. Failing to find the wound inflicted in the present case from which the deceased initially recovered to be mortal, the type of medical treatment rendered requires further inquiry.

The Court in *People v Cook, supra*, terminated the defendant's responsibility only if the medical treatment was *grossly erroneous*. This principle was affirmed by the Court's statement in *People v Townsend*, 214 Mich 267, 278-279 (1921), that:

> " 'He who inflicted the injury is liable even though the medical or surgical treatment which was the direct cause of the death was *erroneous* or *unskilful*, or although the death was due to the negligence or failure by the deceased to procure treatment or take proper care of the wound.' " (Emphasis added.)

This standard which requires something more than ordinary negligence before exculpating a defendant is sound. The concept of an intervening cause is predicated upon foreseeability. Since humans are not infallible, a doctor's negligence is foreseeable and cannot be used by a defendant to exonerate himself from criminal liability.

An application of these standards to the instant case requires an understanding of the alleged intervening cause. The only expert witness testifying at trial was offered by the people. This witness discussed the disease of serum hepatitis and opined that the deceased contracted this disease from the blood transfusion received during the operation to amputate his leg. After indicating that the deceased received a total of 11 pints of blood during medical treatment, he testified that there was a 100% possibility of *exposure* to the disease after receipt of six pints of blood.

---

[7] People v Cook, 39 Mich 236, 240 (1878).

The incidence of death after such exposure is .01% to 3%.[10] This testimony leads us to the conclusion that the victim's exposure to serum hepatitis upon receiving a blood transfusion necessitated by the injury inflicted by the defendant is clearly foreseeable. Whether the victim contracts the disease and dies depends upon his susceptibility to it. Defendant must take his victim as he finds him and may not escape liability because a majority of the people are able to withstand contraction of the disease or death following such contraction. This disease injected through medical intervention is similar to the injection of morphine causing death in the *Cook* case and cannot itself constitute an intervening cause.

The medical evidence concerning this disease similarly precludes a finding that the medical profession's inability to prevent or cure such a prevailing disease constitutes gross mistreatment or an intervening cause. This disease cannot be cultured, precluding experimental testing except by human volunteers, is impossible to detect or screen out from blood, and its cause is currently unknown. The justifiable conclusion based upon this data is that serum hepatitis is an unavoidable risk indigenous to blood transfusions. . . .

Affirmed.

QUESTIONS

1. Should causation analysis in cases such as *Flenon* depend on whether or not the initial wound was mortal? Do any theories of punishment justify distinguishing between mortal and non-mortal wounds?

2. Should causation analysis turn on the distinction between negligence and gross negligence? Or should the chain of causation be severed when a subsequent actor displays recklessness? Knowledge? Purpose?

STATE *v.* ECHOLS   919 S.W.2d 634 (1995)

SUMMERS, J. The defendant Robert L. Echols was convicted by a jury of aggravated robbery, and the trial court entered judgment. On appeal, he claims that the evidence is insufficient to support his conviction because his conduct was not the cause of the victim's injury. We affirm the judgment of the trial court.

Shortly after 6:00 a.m. on June 17, 1993, the victim unlocked her door and an outer wrought iron security door to take out the garbage. Meanwhile, the defendant who had "been up all night smoking drugs" was walking home. As he walked past the victim's house he saw her purse. While the victim was gathering the garbage, the defendant opened the door and grabbed the victim's purse. When the victim went outside to scream for help and look for the defendant, she fell. She was later admitted to the hospital where she was diagnosed with a fractured bone in her hip. The victim remained in the hospital for four days and later underwent three weeks of rehabilitation. She testified that she was in a "lot of pain."

---

[10] The mortality rate increases with age and may go as high as 20% or 30%. 2 Gray, Attorneys' Textbook of Medicine (3d ed), § 38.36, p 38-53.

One element of aggravated robbery is that the alleged victim suffer serious bodily injury. This offense requires a defendant to cause a certain result — serious bodily injury. The necessary causal relationship between the conduct and the result is that the defendant's conduct be both 1) the "but for" cause or "cause in fact" and 2) the "proximate" or "legal cause" of the result.

The defendant essentially contends that the evidence fails to establish that his conduct was the proximate cause of the victim's serious bodily injury. Rather, he appears to assert that the victim's own conduct was the cause of her injury. A defendant's conduct is the proximate cause of the natural and probable consequences of his conduct.

Where sufficiency of the evidence is challenged, the relevant question for an appellate court is whether, after viewing the evidence in the light most favorable to the prosecution, any rational trier of fact could have found the essential elements of the crime or crimes beyond a reasonable doubt. This standard applies to evidence of causation. The evidence amply supports a finding that the defendant's conduct was the proximate cause of the victim's injury. The victim's act of quickly exiting the house to scream for help and look for the defendant is a natural and probable response to the defendant's conduct. Her actions were normal and instinctive under the circumstances. That the victim's own conduct may also be a proximate cause of her injury is of no consequence to the defendant's situation. "One whose wrongdoing is a concurrent proximate cause of an injury may be criminally liable the same as if his wrongdoing were the sole proximate cause of the injury."

Affirmed.

QUESTIONS

1. Can the victim of a crime be an intervenor who breaks the causal chain between a defendant's conduct and the victim's injury or death?

2. The court emphasizes that the victim's conduct was a *response* to the defendant's conduct. Why is this significant?

3. The court also emphasizes that the victim's conduct was "normal and intuitive." Why is this significant?

4. How would the approach taken by the *Flenon* court apply to the facts in *Echols*?

PEOPLE *v.* KIBBE
35 N.Y.2d 407 (1974)

GABRIELLI, J. Subdivision 2 of section 125.25 of the Penal Law provides, in pertinent part, that "[a] person is guilty of murder" when "[under] circumstances evincing a depraved indifference to human life, he recklessly engages in conduct which creates a grave risk of death to another person, and thereby causes the death of another person."

The factual setting of the bizarre events of a cold winter night of December 30, 1970, as developed by the testimony, . . . reveal the following: During the early evening the defendants were drinking in a Rochester tavern along with the victim, George Stafford. The bartender testified that Stafford was displaying and "flashing" one hundred dollar bills, was thoroughly intoxicated and was finally "shut off" because of his inebriated condition. At some time between 8:15 and 8:30 P.M., Stafford inquired if someone would give him a ride to Canandaigua, New York, and the defendants, who, according to their statements, had already decided to steal Stafford's money, agreed to drive him there in Kibbe's automobile. The three men left the bar and proceeded to another bar where Stafford was denied service due to his condition. The defendants and Stafford then walked across the street to a third bar where they were served, and each had another drink or two.

After they left the third bar, the three men entered Kibbe's automobile and began the trip toward Canandaigua. Krall drove the car while Kibbe demanded that Stafford turn over any money he had. In the course of an exchange, Kibbe slapped Stafford several times, took his money, then compelled him to lower his trousers and to take off his shoes to be certain that Stafford had given up all his money; and when they were satisfied that Stafford had no more money on his person, the defendants forced Stafford to exit the Kibbe vehicle.

As he was thrust from the car, Stafford fell onto the shoulder of the rural two-lane highway on which they had been traveling. His trousers were still down around his ankles, his shirt was rolled up towards his chest, he was shoeless and he had also been stripped of any outer clothing. Before the defendants pulled away, Kibbe placed Stafford's shoes and jacket on the shoulder of the highway. Although Stafford's eyeglasses were in the Kibbe vehicle, the defendants, either through inadvertence or perhaps by specific design, did not give them to Stafford before they drove away. It was sometime between 9:30 and 9:40 P.M. when Kibbe and Krall abandoned Stafford on the side of the road. The temperature was near zero, and, although it was not snowing at the time, visibility was occasionally obscured by heavy winds which intermittently blew previously fallen snow into the air and across the highway; and there was snow on both sides of the road as a result of previous plowing operations. The structure nearest the point where Stafford was forced from the defendants' car was a gasoline service station situated nearly one half of a mile away on the other side of the highway. There was no artificial illumination on this segment of the rural highway.

At approximately 10:00 p.m. Michael W. Blake, a college student, was operating his pickup truck in the northbound lane of the highway in question. Two cars, which were approaching from the opposite direction, flashed their headlights at Blake's vehicle. Immediately after he had passed the second car, Blake saw Stafford sitting in the road in the middle of the northbound lane with his hands up in the air. Blake stated that he was operating his truck at a speed of approximately 50 miles per hour, and that he "didn't have time to react" before his vehicle struck Stafford. After he brought his truck to a stop and returned to try to be of assistance to Stafford, Blake observed that the man's trousers were down around his ankles and his shirt was pulled up around his chest. A Deputy Sheriff called to the accident scene also confirmed the fact that the victim's trousers were around his ankles, and that Stafford was wearing no shoes or jacket.

At the trial, the Medical Examiner of Monroe County testified that death had occurred fairly rapidly from massive head injuries. In addition, he found proof of a high degree of intoxication with a .25%, by weight, of alcohol concentration in the blood.

For their acts, the defendants were convicted of murder, robbery in the second degree and grand larceny in the third degree. However, the defendants basically challenge only their convictions of murder, claiming that the People failed to establish beyond a reasonable doubt that their acts "caused the death of another". . . . [W]e are required to determine whether the defendants may be convicted of murder for the occurrences which have been described. They contend that the actions of Blake, the driver of the pickup truck, constituted both an intervening and superseding cause which relieves them of criminal responsibility for Stafford's death. There is, of course, no statutory provision regarding the effect of an intervening cause of injury as it relates to the criminal responsibility of one who sets in motion the machinery which ultimately results in the victim's death; and there is surprisingly little case law dealing with the subject. Moreover, analogies to causation in civil cases are neither controlling nor dispositive, since, as this court has previously stated: "A distance separates the negligence which renders one criminally liable from that which establishes civil liability"; and this is due in large measure to the fact that the standard or measure of persuasion by which the prosecution must convince the trier of all the essential elements of the crime charged, is beyond a reasonable doubt. . . . However, to be a sufficiently direct cause of death so as to warrant the imposition of a criminal penalty therefor, it is not necessary that the ultimate harm be intended by the actor. It will suffice if it can be said beyond a reasonable doubt, as indeed it can be here said, that the ultimate harm is something which should have been foreseen as being reasonably related to the acts of the accused.

In *People v. Kane*, the defendant inflicted two serious pistol shot wounds on the body of a pregnant woman. The wounds caused a miscarriage; the miscarriage caused septic peritonitis, and the septic peritonitis, thus induced, caused the woman's death on the third day after she was shot. Over the defendant's insistence that there was no causal connection between the wounds and the death and, in fact, that the death was due to the intervention of an outside agency, namely, the negligent and improper medical treatment at the hospital, this court affirmed the conviction "even though the medical treatment may also have had some causative influence."

We subscribe to the requirement that the defendants' actions must be a *sufficiently direct cause* of the ensuing death before there can be any imposition of criminal liability, and recognize, of course, that this standard is greater than that required to serve as a basis for tort liability. Applying these criteria to the defendants' actions, we conclude that their activities on the evening of December 30, 1970 were a sufficiently direct cause of the death of George Stafford so as to warrant the imposition of criminal sanctions. In engaging in what may properly be described as a despicable course of action, Kibbe and Krall left a helplessly intoxicated man without his eyeglasses in a position from which, because of these attending circumstances, he could not extricate himself and whose condition was such that he could not even protect himself from the elements. The defendants do not dispute the fact that their conduct evinced a depraved indifference to human life which created a grave risk of death, but rather they argue that it was just as likely that Stafford would be miraculously rescued by a good samaritan. We cannot accept such an argument. There can be little doubt but that Stafford would have frozen to death in his state of undress had he remained on the shoulder of the road. The only alternative left to him was the highway, which in his condition, for one reason or another, clearly foreboded the probability of his resulting death.

Under the conditions surrounding Blake's operation of his truck (i.e., the fact that he had his low beams on as the two cars approached; that there was no artificial lighting on the highway; and that there was insufficient time in which to react to Stafford's presence in his lane), we do not think it may be said that any supervening wrongful act occurred to relieve the defendants from the directly foreseeable consequences of their actions. In short, we will not disturb the jury's determination that the prosecution proved beyond a reasonable doubt that their actions came clearly within the statute and "[caused] the death of another person". . . .

Orders affirmed.

QUESTIONS

1. Who were potential intervenors in *Kibbe*? Stafford, the victim? Blake, the driver of the truck that hit the victim?

2. Was Stafford's conduct responsive to the defendants' initial conduct or coincidental? What about Blake's conduct?

3. Was the result in *Kibbe* (*i.e.*, Stafford's death) foreseeable? Was the manner in which it occurred foreseeable? How likely does the result and/or manner have to be in order to be foreseeable?

4. How much deference should courts give jurors on questions of proximate causation?

COMMONWEALTH *v.* ROOT
403 Pa. 571, 170 A.2d 310 (1961)

JONES, C.J. The appellant was found guilty of involuntary manslaughter for the death of his competitor in the course of an automobile race between them on a highway. The trial court overruled the defendant's demurrer to the Commonwealth's evidence and, after verdict, denied his motion in arrest of judgment. On appeal from the judgment of sentence entered on the jury's verdict, the Superior Court affirmed. We granted allocatur because of the important question present as to whether the defendant's unlawful and reckless conduct was a sufficiently direct cause of the death to warrant his being charged with criminal homicide.

The testimony, which is uncontradicted in material part, discloses that, on the night of the fatal accident, the defendant accepted the deceased's challenge to engage in an automobile race; that the racing took place on a rural 3-lane highway; that the night was clear and dry, and traffic light; that the speed limit on the highway was 50 miles per hour; that, immediately prior to the accident, the two automobiles were being operated at varying speeds of from 70 to 90 miles per hour; that the accident occurred in a no-passing zone on the approach to a bridge where the highway narrowed to two directionally-opposite lanes; that, at the time of the accident, the defendant was in the lead and was proceeding in his right-hand lane of travel; that the deceased, in an attempt to pass the defendant's automobile, when a truck was closely approaching from the opposite direction, swerved his car to the left, crossed the highway's white dividing line and drove his automobile on the wrong side of the highway head-on into the oncoming truck with resultant fatal effect to himself.

This evidence would of course amply support a conviction of the defendant for speeding, reckless driving and, perhaps, other violations of The Vehicle Code. . . . In any event, unlawful or reckless conduct is only one ingredient of the crime of involuntary manslaughter. Another essential and distinctly separate element of the crime is that the unlawful or reckless conduct charged to the defendant was the direct cause of the death in issue. The first ingredient is obviously present in this case but, just as plainly, the second is not.

While precedent is to be found for application of the tort law concept of "proximate cause" in fixing responsibility for criminal homicide, the want of any rational basis for its use in determining criminal liability can no longer be properly disregarded. When proximate cause was first borrowed from the field of tort law and applied to homicide prosecutions in Pennsylvania, the concept connoted a much more direct casual relation in producing the alleged culpable result than it does today. Proximate cause, as an essential element of a tort founded in negligence, has undergone in recent times, and is still undergoing, a marked extension. More specifically, this area of civil law has been progressively liberalized in favor of claims for damages for personal injuries to which careless conduct of others can in some way be associated. To persist in applying the tort liability concept of proximate cause to prosecutions for criminal homicide after the marked expansion of *civil* liability of defendants in tort actions for negligence would be to extend possible *criminal* liability to persons chargeable with unlawful or reckless conduct in circumstances not generally considered to present the likelihood of a resultant death.

In this very case the Superior Court mistakenly opined that "The concept of proximate cause as applied in tort cases is applicable to similar problems of causation in criminal cases. *Commonwealth v. Almeida*." It is indeed strange that the *Almeida* case should have been cited as authority for the above quoted statement; the rationale of the *Almeida* case was flatly rejected by this Court in *Commonwealth v. Redline*, where we held that the tort liability concept of proximate cause is not a proper criterion of causation in a criminal homicide case. True enough, *Commonwealth v. Redline* was a murder case, but the distinction between murder and involuntary manslaughter does not rest upon a differentiation in causation; it lies in the state of mind of the offender. If one kills with malice aforethought, he is chargeable with murder; and if death, though unintentional, results directly from his unlawful or reckless conduct, he is chargeable with involuntary manslaughter. In either event, the accused is not guilty unless his conduct was a cause of death sufficiently direct as to meet the requirements of the *criminal*, and not the *tort*, law.

The instant case is one of first impression in this State; and our research has not disclosed a single instance where a district attorney has ever before attempted to prosecute for involuntary manslaughter on facts similar to those established by the record now before us. The closest case, factually, would seem to be *Commonwealth v. Levin*, which affirmed the defendant's conviction of involuntary manslaughter. In the *Levin* case two cars were racing on the streets of Philadelphia at speeds estimated at from 85 to 95 miles per hour. The defendant's car, in the left-hand lane, was racing alongside of the car in which the deceased was a passenger when the defendant turned his automobile sharply to the right in front of the other car, thereby causing the driver of the latter car to lose control and smash into a tree, the passenger being thrown to the road and killed as a result of the impact. It is readily apparent that the elements of causation in the *Levin* case were fundamentally different from those in the present case. Levin's act of cutting his automobile sharply in front of the car in which the deceased was riding directly forced that car off of the road and into the tree. The defendant's reckless and unlawful maneuver was the direct cause of the crucial fatality. In the instant case, the defendant's conduct was not even remotely comparable. Here, the action of the deceased driver in recklessly and suicidally swerving his car to the left lane of a 2-lane highway into the path of an oncoming truck was not forced upon him by any act of the defendant; it was done by the deceased and by him alone, who thus directly brought about his own demise. The *Levin* case was properly decided but it cannot, by any ratiocination, be utilized to justify a conviction in the present case.

Legal theory which makes guilt or innocence of criminal homicide depend upon such accidental and fortuitous circumstances as are now embraced by modern tort law's encompassing concept of proximate cause is too harsh to be just. . . .

Even if the tort liability concept of proximate cause were to be deemed applicable, the defendant's conviction of involuntary manslaughter in the instant case could not be sustained under the evidence. The operative effect of a supervening cause would have to be taken into consideration. *Commonwealth v. Redline.* But, the trial judge refused the defendant's point for charge to such effect and erroneously instructed the jury that "negligence or want of care on the part of [the deceased] is no defense to the criminal responsibility of the defendant. . . . "

The Superior Court, in affirming the defendant's conviction in this case, approved the charge above mentioned, despite a number of decisions in involuntary manslaughter cases holding that the conduct of the deceased victim must be considered in order to determine whether the defendant's reckless acts were the proximate (i.e., sufficiently direct) cause of his death. The Superior Court dispensed with th[e] decisional authority by expressly overruling [past decisions] . . . on the ground that there can be more than one proximate cause of death. The point is wholly irrelevant. Of course there can be more than one proximate cause of death just as there can also be more than one direct cause of death. For example, in the so-called "shield" cases where a felon interposes the person of an innocent victim between himself and a pursuing officer, if the officer should fire his gun at the felon to prevent his escape and fatally wound the person used as a shield, the different acts of the policeman and the felon would each be a direct cause of the victim's death.

If the tort liability concept of proximate cause were to be applied in a criminal homicide prosecution, then the conduct of the person whose death is the basis of the indictment would have to be considered, not to prove that it was merely an *additional* proximate cause of the death, but to determine, under fundamental and long recognized law applicable to proximate cause, whether the subsequent wrongful act *superseded* the original conduct chargeable to the defendant. If it did in fact supervene, then the original act is so insulated from the ensuing death as not to be its proximate cause.

Under the uncontradicted evidence in this case, the conduct of the defendant was not the proximate cause of the decedent's death as a matter of law. In *Kline v. Moyer and Albert*, the rule is stated as follows: "Where a second actor has become aware of the existence of a potential danger created by the negligence of an original tortfeasor, and thereafter, by an independent act of negligence, brings about an accident, the first tortfeasor is relieved of liability, because the condition created by him was merely a circumstance of the accident and not its proximate cause.

In the case last above cited, while Angretti was driving his truck eastward along a highway, a bus, traveling in the same direction in front of him, stopped to take on a passenger. Angretti swerved his truck to the left into the lane of oncoming traffic in an attempt to pass the bus but collided with a tractor-trailer driven by the plaintiff's decedent, who was killed as a result of the collision. In affirming the entry of judgment n.o.v. in favor of the defendant bus company, we held that any negligence on the part of the bus driver, in suddenly bringing his bus to a halt in order to pick up a passenger, was not a proximate cause of the death of the plaintiff's decedent since the accident "was due entirely to the intervening and superseding negligence of Angretti in allowing his truck to pass over into the pathway of the westbound tractor-trailer. . . . "

In the case now before us, the deceased was aware of the dangerous condition created by the defendant's reckless conduct in driving his automobile at an excessive rate of speed along the highway but, despite such knowledge, he recklessly chose to swerve his car to the left and into the path of an oncoming truck, thereby bringing about the head-on collision which caused his own death.

To summarize, the tort liability concept of proximate cause has no proper place in prosecutions for criminal homicide and more direct casual connection is required for conviction. In the instant case, the defendant's reckless conduct was not a sufficiently direct cause of the competing driver's death to make him criminally liable therefor.

The judgment of sentence is reversed and the defendant's motion in arrest of judgment granted.

EAGEN, J., dissenting.

The opinion of the learned Chief Justice admits, under the uncontradicted facts, that the defendant, at the time of the fatal accident involved, was engaged in an unlawful and reckless course of conduct. Racing an automobile at 90 miles per hour, trying to prevent another automobile going in the same direction from passing him, in a no-passing zone on a two-lane public highway, is certainly all of that. Admittedly also, there can be more than one direct cause of an unlawful death. To me, this is self-evident. But, says the majority opinion, the defendant's recklessness was not a direct cause of the death. With this, I cannot agree.

If the defendant did not engage in the unlawful race and so operate his automobile in such a reckless manner, this accident would never have occurred. He helped create the dangerous event. He was a vital part of it. The victim's acts were a natural reaction to the stimulus of the situation. The race, the attempt to pass the other car and forge ahead, the reckless speed, all of these factors the defendant himself helped create. He was part and parcel of them. That the victim's response was normal under the circumstances, that his reaction should have been expected and was clearly foreseeable, is to me beyond argument. That the defendant's recklessness was a substantial factor is obvious. All of this, in my opinion, makes his unlawful conduct a direct cause of the resulting collision.

The cases cited in support of the majority opinion are not in point. For instance, in *Johnson v. Angretti,* this Court, in affirming the trial court, found that the bus driver *was not guilty of any negligence or violation of The Vehicle Code*[1] in bringing the bus to a stop. The Court, as dicta, then went on to say, "Moreover it is clear that such alleged violation bore no casual relation whatever to the happening of the accident which was due entirely to the intervening and superseding negligence of Angretti in allowing his truck to pass over into the pathway of the westbound tractor-trailer

---

[1] Emphasis throughout, ours.

instead of bringing his vehicle to a stop as Osterling [the driver of the truck directly behind the bus and in front of Angretti] had done and *as he admitted he could readily have done without colliding with the truck ahead of him.* The situation created by the stopping of the bus was merely a circumstance of the accident and not its proximate cause: (citing cases)." It is readily apparent that the instant case and the Angretti case are distinguishable in all the important factors. In the present case there was, (1) recklessness and a violation of The Vehicle Code; (2) a joint venture or common enterprise of racing; (3) no proof that Hall could have guided his car back into the right-hand lane behind Root after he became aware of the danger of the oncoming truck. . . .

In the present case, there wasn't any evidence that Hall saw the oncoming truck when he pulled out to pass Root. This would have been suicide, against which there is a presumption. The act of passing was not an "extraordinary negligent" act, but rather a "normal response" to the act of "racing." Furthermore, as Hall pulled out to pass, Root "dropped off" his speed to 90 miles an hour. Such a move probably prevented Hall from getting back into the right-hand lane since he was alongside of Root at the time and to brake the car at that speed would have been fatal to both himself and Root. Moreover, the dangerous condition of which the deceased had to become aware of before the defendant was relieved of his direct casual connection with the ensuing accident, was not the fact that the defendant was driving at an excessive rate of speed along the highway. He knew that when the race began many miles and minutes earlier. *The dangerous condition necessary was an awareness of the oncoming truck and the fact that at the rate of speed Root was traveling he couldn't safely pass him.* This important fact was not shown and, therefore, was a question for the fact-finders and not a question that could be decided as a matter of law.

The majority opinion states, "Legal theory which makes guilt or innocence of criminal homicide depend upon such *accidental and fortuitous circumstances* as are now embraced by modern tort law's encompassing concept is . . . too harsh to be just." If the resulting death had been dependent upon "accidental and fortuitous circumstances" or, as the majority also say, "in circumstances not generally considered to present the likelihood of a resultant death," we would agree that the defendant is not criminally responsible. However, acts should be judged by their tendency under the known circumstances, not by the actual intent which accompanies their performance. Every day of the year, we read that some teen-agers, or young adults, somewhere in this country, have been killed or have killed others, while racing their automobiles. Hair-raising, death-defying, lawbreaking rides, which encompass "racing" are the rule rather than the exception, and endanger not only the participants, but also every motorist and passenger on the road. To call such resulting accidents "accidental and fortuitous," or unlikely to result in death, is to ignore the cold and harsh reality of everyday occurrences. Root's actions were as direct a cause of Hall's death as those in the "shield" cases. Root's shield was his high speed and any approaching traffic in his quest to prevent Hall from passing, which he knew Hall would undertake to do, the first time he thought he had the least opportunity. . . .

But, says the majority opinion, these are principles of tort law and should not in these days be applied to the criminal law. But such has been the case since the time of Blackstone. These same principles have always been germane to both crimes and tort. They have been repeatedly so applied throughout the years and were employed in a criminal case in Pennsylvania as long as one hundred and seventeen years ago. . . .

While the victim's foolhardiness in this case contributed to his own death, he was not the only one responsible and it is not he alone with whom we are concerned. It is the people of the Commonwealth who are harmed by the kind of conduct the defendant pursued. Their interests must be kept in mind.

QUESTIONS

1. The conduct of the defendants in *Kibbe* was found to have proximately caused the victim's death in that case. The conduct of the defendant in *Root*, however, was determined not to have proximately caused the victim's death. What explains the different outcomes in the two cases in terms of proximate cause?

2. Was the result in *Root* foreseeable? What about the manner in which it occurred? Were the victim driver's actions foreseeable? Were they a response to Root's actions? What was the blameworthiness of Root? Of the victim driver?

3. Does time-framing play a role in the outcome of *Root*? Which opinion uses narrow time-framing and which uses broad time-framing? How does choice about time-framing affect causation analysis?

D. THE MODEL PENAL CODE AND CAUSATION

Model Penal Code § 2.03   *Causal Relationship Between Conduct and Result; Divergence Between Result Designed or Contemplated and Actual Result or Between Probable and Actual Result*

(1) Conduct is the cause of a result when:

(a) it is an antecedent but for which the result in question would not have occurred; and

(b) the relationship between the conduct and result satisfies any additional causal requirements imposed by the Code or by the law defining the offense.

(2) When purposely or knowingly causing a particular result is an element of an offense, the element is not established if the actual result is not within the purpose or the contemplation of the actor unless:

(a) the actual result differs from that designed or contemplated, as the case may be, only in the respect that a different person or different property is injured or affected or that the injury or harm designed or contemplated would have been more serious or more extensive than that caused; or

(b) the actual result involves the same kind of injury or harm as that designed or contemplated and is not too remote or accidental in its occurrence to have a [just] bearing on the actor's liability or on the gravity of his offense.

(3) When recklessly or negligently causing a particular result is an element of an offense, the element is not established if the actual result is not within the risk of which the actor is aware or, in the case of negligence, of which he should be aware unless:

(a) the actual result differs from the probable result only in the respect that a different person or different property is injured or affected or that the probable injury or harm would have been more serious or more extensive than that caused; or

(b) the actual result involves the same kind of injury or harm as the probable result and is not too remote or accidental in its occurrence to have a [just] bearing on the actor's liability or on the gravity of the offense.

(4) When causing a particular result is a material element of an offense for which absolute liability is imposed by law, the element is not established unless the actual result is a probable consequence of the actor's conduct.

QUESTIONS

1. Does the MPC simply state the law of criminal causation reflected in the other materials in this chapter? Or does the MPC change the law of criminal causation? If so, what does it change? Are these changes an improvement? Apply the MPC to each of the cases and problems in this chapter. Would any come out differently?

2. Does causation determine what is just? Or does what is just determine causation?

PROBLEM

7.12 Draft a jury instruction on causation for use in a jurisdiction that has adopted the MPC provision on causation. Does your MPC instruction differ from the jury instruction on causation that appears in Problem 7.1 at the outset of this chapter? If so, how?

E. SYNTHESIS AND REVIEW

1. In most cases requiring proof of causation, proximate cause is resolved quite easily. But in a small number of cases, proximate cause is highly problematic. How is it that proximate cause is usually easy to resolve but occasionally very difficult? What distinguishes easy causation cases from difficult ones?

2. Are the problems that exist in the law of causation due to the fact that causation doctrine was developed by judges through a common law process? If legislatures had addressed causation through statutes, is it likely the law of causation would be in better shape? How might such a statute read?

3. In *Commonwealth v. Root*, Justice Jones argues for a more limited approach to causation in criminal law than in tort law. Based on what you have studied in your torts course, are the requirements for causation in tort law different than the requirements for causation in criminal law? If so, how do they differ? Should causation standards in criminal law be more demanding than in tort law? If so, why?

4. As stated at the outset of this chapter, the conventional view is that only crimes requiring a result also require causation. Professor Michael Moore has written that this "dogma . . . is manifestly false."[7] He argues that "a causal judgment is involved in all actions prohibited or required by the criminal law." Theft, for example, is typically viewed as a crime that does not require a result, and thus does not require causation. But Professor Moore argues that "a theft occurs . . . only when an actor's voluntary act *causes* movement ('asportation') of the goods stolen." Do you agree with Professor Moore? How could a crime such as burglary be analyzed as involving a causal element?

PROBLEM

7.13 Alex ambushes John and beats him with metal knuckles. John suffers severe brain damage and enters a vegetative coma. After three months in the hospital with no change in his condition or hope for improvement, John develops pneumonia, an illness not uncommon to bedridden and comatose individuals. Without antibiotics, John will die. John's parents and doctors decide to withhold antibiotic treatment. Two days later, John dies.[8] Who caused John's death? Who, if anyone, should be held criminally liable for John's death?

---

7. Michael S. Moore, *id.* at 151.
8. Adapted from People v. Funes, 23 Cal. App. 4th 1506 (1994).

CHAPTER EIGHT

JUSTIFICATIONS AND EXCUSES

A. INTRODUCTION

Justifications and excuses are ways of defeating criminal liability. "A justification renders a nominal violation of the criminal law lawful and therefore exempt from criminal sanctions. . . . Those who act [with a legal justification] exercise a privilege and act in conformity with the law."[1] In contrast, an excuse

> concedes that the violation is unjustified, but seeks to exempt the particular actor from responsibility for the unjustified act. A claim of justification maintains that the act is right; a claim of excuse concedes that the act in the abstract is wrong, but argues that the actor is not personally responsible for having committed the act. Injuring an innocent person is wrong, but if the actor is insane, his condition precludes his being held responsible for the wrongful act.[2]

The distinction between a justification and an excuse can be important. For example, someone who aids a criminal act for which a justification exists will also usually have the benefit of that justification. Excuse, however, typically is personal to the actor. A sane person who aids an insane person to kill cannot make use of the insanity excuse.

Both justifications and excuses are defenses. The term "defense" can encompass two different ways of defeating liability. Sometimes it is used to refer to defense strategies, such as alibi, mistaken identity, mistake of fact, and intoxication, in which a defendant is essentially contesting the prosecution's proof of one of the elements of the offense. Alibi and mistaken identity, for example, are ways of arguing that the defendant did not engage in the prohibited conduct — someone else did. Mistake of fact and intoxication are typically used to show that the defendant lacked a required mental state.

But "defense" is also used to refer to strategies such as self-defense and necessity in which the defendant admits fulfillment of the elements but nonetheless seeks to avoid liability by asserting some other principle. This second meaning is sometimes referred to as "confession and avoidance" — confessing to fulfilling the

---

1. George P. Fletcher, *Justification, Theory*, 3 Encyclopedia of Crime and Justice, 941 (Sanford H. Kadish ed., 1983).
2. *Id.* at 942.

elements but avoiding liability through assertion of an overriding principle.[3] Under this latter meaning of "defense," even if the prosecution proves every element of the crime, the jury should acquit the defendant if it finds the defense applicable. This is often called a "true" or "affirmative" defense. Commonly, this type of affirmative defense places some burden on the defendant to demonstrate the existence of the circumstances that trigger the defense. This burden may require, for example, only the production of some evidence or require the defense to prove the existence of the defense by a standard such as a preponderance of the evidence.

In this chapter, we focus on four affirmative defenses. We begin with a combined treatment of self-defense and its twin, defense of others, and then turn to the defense of necessity. These defenses are regularly accorded the status of justifications. The chapter concludes with duress and insanity, defenses that represent excuses.

B. SELF-DEFENSE AND DEFENSE OF OTHERS

1. Introduction

A legal system is possible only if the state enjoys a monopoly of force. When private individuals appeal to force and decide who shall enjoy the right to "life, liberty and the pursuit of happiness," there can be no pretense of the rule of law. Yet the state's monopoly also entails an obligation to secure its citizens against violence. When individuals are threatened with immediate aggression, when the police cannot protect them, the monopoly of the state gives way. The individual right of survival reasserts itself.[4]

The use of force in response to the aggression of another raises a constellation of legal issues. What do jurisdictions generally require for a successful assertion of self-defense and defense of others? In answering this question, we begin by analyzing a series of self-defense problems and statutes. Look for the similarities and the differences in what these statutes require for a successful self-defense claim. In particular, focus on the issues of reasonableness and imminence. Each is critical in the law of defensive force.

Following the Problems and statutes, we study the issue of reasonableness, also commonly termed "a reasonable person standard," in the controversial case of *People v. Goetz*. In that case, we consider the perspective from which self-defense must be asserted, that of a hypothetical reasonable person in the defendant's situation or that of the defendant himself. Recall the importance of the question of "reasonableness" and perspective from our earlier study of homicide law. After the *Goetz* case, we look at both reasonableness and imminence in the context of domestic violence in *State v. Norman*. We then turn to the rules on retreat and the potential

---

3. A Dictionary of Law 96 (Elizabeth A. Martin ed., 1997) ("confession and avoidance A pleading in the defence that, while admitting or assuming the truth of the material facts alleged in the statement of the claim (the confession), seeks to avoid or destroy the legal consequences of those facts by alleging further facts constituting some defence to the claim (the avoidance). An example is a plea of self-defence to an action for assault."); Black's Law Dictionary 293 (Bryan A. Garner ed., 1997) ("confession and avoidance. A plea in which a defendant admits allegations but pleads additional facts that deprive the admitted facts of an adverse legal effect.").

4. George P. Fletcher, *A Crime of Self-Defense* 18 (1988).

right of self-defense for an initial aggressor. Finally, we examine the Model Penal Code approach on defensive force.

PROBLEMS

8.1 One Halloween, when Fred was a child, he knocked on the door of a house while trick-or-treating. A man with red hair in an elaborate vampire costume opened the door. Fred was terrified. Since that time, Fred has been frightened of red-haired men. Fred works as a repossession agent, a job in which he is often threatened by those whose cars he has been hired to repossess. Earlier today, Fred was repossessing a car when a red-haired man confronted Fred and demanded that Fred cease his repossession. The man was much larger than Fred and yelled and cursed at Fred in an angry tone of voice. The man displayed no weapon nor did he threaten Fred with physical harm. Nonetheless, Fred flashed back to his childhood terror and pulled out his .22 semi-automatic. As the man came within arm's length of Fred, Fred became convinced he was in mortal danger and fired three shots, killing the man. Does Fred have a viable self-defense claim under any of the statutes below?

8.2 Sheila and her neighbor Yolanda have been feuding for years. Their dispute has grown quite acrimonious. Since they are both fencing enthusiasts, Yolanda challenges Sheila to a fencing match. Sheila accepts. As part of the match, Yolanda stabs Sheila in the leg. Does Yolanda have a viable self-defense claim?

8.3 Consider the following news account of a California trial case:

> "The defendant, from the Eritrea region of Ethiopia, claimed that he suffered headaches and stomachaches because an Ethiopian woman he had dated was a *bouda* controlled by the Evil Spirit and inflicting pain on him. After begging her several times to stop, he said, he went to her apartment with a gun, intending only to frighten her, but shot her twice. . . . [The defense attorney] presented testimony from UC Berkeley anthropology professor William Shack, who said Ethiopians from the Eritrea area do indeed believe that the Evil Spirit inflicts pain through a woman selected as a *bouda*. . . . A psychologist also testified that because of the defendant's war-torn background he was unusually likely to interpret physical pain according to the culture of his upbringing."[5]

Based on the events as reported in the news account, would the defendant have a viable self-defense claim?

Based on the statutes below, under which, if any, would the defendants in the Problems above have viable self-defense claims?

---

5. Myrna Oliver, *Immigrant Crimes, Cultural Defense — A Legal Tactic*, LA Times, July 15, 1988, 1.

Arkansas Code Annotated § 5-2-607 (2001)   *Justification*

Use of deadly physical force in defense of a person

(a) A person is justified in using deadly physical force upon another person if he reasonably believes that the other person is:

(1) Committing or about to commit a felony involving force or violence;

(2) Using or about to use unlawful deadly physical force; or

(3) Imminently endangering his or her life or imminently about to victimize [any family or household members] from the continuation of a pattern of domestic abuse.

Illinois Compiled Statute 5/7-1 (2001)   *Use of Force in Defense of Person*

A person is justified in the use of force against another when and to the extent that he reasonably believes that such conduct is necessary to defend himself or another against such other's imminent use of unlawful force. However, he is justified in the use of force which is intended or likely to cause death or great bodily harm only if he reasonably believes that such force is necessary to prevent imminent death or great bodily harm to himself or another, or the commission of a forcible felony.

Nebraska Revised Statute § 28-1409 (2001)   *Use of force in self-protection*

(1) Subject to the provisions of this section and of section 28-1414, the use of force upon or toward another person is justifiable when the actor believes that such force is immediately necessary for the purpose of protecting himself against the use of unlawful force by such other person on the present occasion. . . .

(4) The use of deadly force shall not be justifiable under this section unless the actor believes that such force is necessary to protect himself against death, serious bodily harm, kidnapping or sexual intercourse compelled by force or threat. . . .

Nebraska Revised Statute § 28-1414 (2001)   *Mistake of law; reckless or negligent use of force*

(1) The justification afforded by sections 28-1409 . . . is unavailable when:

(2) [T]he actor believes that the use of force upon or toward the person of another is necessary for any of the purposes for which such belief would establish a justification under section [28-1409] but the actor is reckless or negligent in having such belief or in acquiring or failing to acquire any knowledge or belief which is material to the justifiability of his use of force, the justification afforded by those sections is unavailable in a prosecution for an offense for which recklessness or negligence, as the case may be, suffices to establish culpability.

(3) When the actor is justified under section [28-1409] in using force upon or toward the person of another but he recklessly or negligently injures or creates a risk of injury to innocent persons, the justification afforded by those sections is unavailable in a prosecution for such recklessness or negligence towards innocent persons.

Colorado Revised Statute § 18-1-704 (2001)   *Use of Physical Force in Defense of a Person*

(1) Except as provided . . . a person is justified in using physical force upon another person in order to defend himself or a third person from what he reasonably

believes to be the use or imminent use of unlawful physical force by that other person, and he may use a degree of force which he reasonably believes to be necessary for that purpose.

(2) Deadly physical force may be used only if a person reasonably believes that a lesser degree of force is inadequate and:

(a) The actor has reasonable grounds to believe, and does believe, that he or another person is in imminent danger of being killed or of receiving great bodily injury; . . .

(4) Notwithstanding the provisions of subsection (1) of this section, a person is not justified in using physical force if: . . .

(c) The physical force involved is the product of a combat by agreement not specifically authorized by law.

QUESTIONS

1. How do the Arkansas and Illinois statutes differ? How are they alike?

2. How do the Arkansas, Colorado, and Illinois statutes differ from the Nebraska statute?

3. How do these statutes distinguish between deadly and nondeadly force? Are the differences significant?

4. Why does the Colorado statute prevent a defendant from prevailing on a self-defense claim if s/he engaged in combat by agreement? Why don't the other statutes have a similar provision?

5. Are the terms "about to" and "imminent" synonymous?

2. The *Goetz* Case

The *Goetz* case attained great notoriety and provoked a powerful response throughout the nation and particularly among New Yorkers. As you read the case, try to determine why it had this impact. Does something seem to be missing from the opinion?

PEOPLE *v.* GOETZ

New York Court of Appeals 68 N.Y.2d 96 (1986)

Chief Judge WACHTLER

A Grand Jury has indicted defendant on attempted murder, assault, and other charges for having shot and wounded four youths on a New York City subway train after one or two of the youths approached him and asked for $5. The lower courts, concluding that the prosecutor's charge to the Grand Jury on the defense of justification was erroneous, have dismissed the attempted murder, assault and weapons possession charges. We now reverse and reinstate all counts of the indictment.

I.

The precise circumstances of the incident giving rise to the charges against defendant are disputed. . . . [W]e have summarized the facts as they appear from the evidence before the Grand Jury. . . .

On Saturday afternoon, December 22, 1984, Troy Canty, Darryl Cabey, James Ramseur, and Barry Allen boarded an IRT express subway train in The Bronx and headed south toward lower Manhattan. The four youths rode together in the rear portion of the seventh car of the train. Two of the four, Ramseur and Cabey, had screwdrivers inside their coats, which they said were to be used to break into the coin boxes of video machines.

Defendant Bernhard Goetz boarded this subway train at 14th Street in Manhattan and sat down on a bench towards the rear section of the same car occupied by the four youths. Goetz was carrying an unlicensed .38 caliber pistol loaded with five rounds of ammunition in a waistband holster. The train left the 14th Street station and headed towards Chambers Street.

It appears from the evidence before the Grand Jury that Canty approached Goetz, possibly with Allen beside him, and stated "give me five dollars." Neither Canty nor any of the other youths displayed a weapon. Goetz responded by standing up, pulling out his handgun and firing four shots in rapid succession. The first shot hit Canty in the chest; the second struck Allen in the back; the third went through Ramseur's arm and into his left side; the fourth was fired at Cabey, who apparently was then standing in the corner of the car, but missed, deflecting instead off of a wall of the conductor's cab. After Goetz briefly surveyed the scene around him, he fired another shot at Cabey, who then was sitting on the end bench of the car. The bullet entered the rear of Cabey's side and severed his spinal cord.

All but two of the other passengers fled the car when, or immediately after, the shots were fired. The conductor, who had been in the next car, heard the shots and instructed the motorman to radio for emergency assistance. The conductor then went into the car where the shooting occurred and saw Goetz sitting on a bench, the injured youths lying on the floor or slumped against a seat, and two women who had apparently taken cover, also lying on the floor. Goetz told the conductor that the four youths had tried to rob him.

While the conductor was aiding the youths, Goetz headed towards the front of the car. The train had stopped just before the Chambers Street station and Goetz went between two of the cars, jumped onto the tracks and fled. Police and ambulance crews arrived at the scene shortly thereafter. Ramseur and Canty, initially listed in critical condition, have fully recovered. Cabey remains paralyzed, and has suffered some degree of brain damage.

On December 31, 1984, Goetz surrendered to police in Concord, New Hampshire, identifying himself as the gunman being sought for the subway shootings in New York nine days earlier. Later that day, after receiving *Miranda* warnings, he made two lengthy statements, both of which were tape recorded with his permission. In the statements, which are substantially similar, Goetz admitted that he had been illegally carrying a handgun in New York City for three years. He stated that he had first purchased a gun in 1981 after he had been injured in a mugging. Goetz also revealed that twice between 1981 and 1984 he had successfully warded off assailants simply by displaying the pistol.

According to Goetz's statement, the first contact he had with the four youths came when Canty, sitting or lying on the bench across from him, asked "how are you," to which he replied "fine." Shortly thereafter, Canty, followed by one of the other youths, walked over to the defendant and stood to his left, while the other two youths remained to his right, in the corner of the subway car. Canty then said "give me five dollars." Goetz stated that he knew from the smile on Canty's face that they wanted to "play with me." Although he was certain that none of the youths had a gun, he had a fear, based on prior experiences, of being "maimed."

Goetz then established "a pattern of fire," deciding specifically to fire from left to right. His stated intention at that point was to "murder [the four youths], to hurt them, to make them suffer as much as possible." When Canty again requested money, Goetz stood up, drew his weapon, and began firing, aiming for the center of the body of each of the four. Goetz recalled that the first two he shot "tried to run through the crowd [but] they had nowhere to run." Goetz then turned to his right to "go after the other two." One of these two "tried to run through the wall of the train, but . . . he had nowhere to go." The other youth (Cabey) "tried pretending that he wasn't with [the others]" by standing still, holding on to one of the subway hand straps, and not looking at Goetz. Goetz nonetheless fired his fourth shot at him. He then ran back to the first two youths to make sure they had been "taken care of." Seeing that they had both been shot, he spun back to check on the latter two. Goetz noticed that the youth who had been standing still was now sitting on a bench and seemed unhurt. As Goetz told the police, "I said '[you] seem to be all right, here's another,' " and he then fired the shot which severed Cabey's spinal cord. Goetz added that "if I was a little more under self-control . . . I would have put the barrel against his forehead and fired." He also admitted that "if I had had more [bullets], I would have shot them again, and again, and again."

II.

After waiving extradition, Goetz was brought back to New York and arraigned on a felony complaint charging him with attempted murder and criminal possession of a weapon. The matter was presented to a Grand Jury in January 1985, with the prosecutor seeking an indictment for attempted murder, assault, reckless endangerment, and criminal possession of a weapon. Neither the defendant nor any of the wounded youths testified before this Grand Jury. On January 25, 1985, the Grand Jury indicted defendant on one count of criminal possession of a weapon in the third degree, for possessing the gun used in the subway shootings, and two counts of criminal possession of a weapon in the fourth degree, for possessing two other guns in his apartment building. It dismissed, however, the attempted murder and other charges stemming from the shootings themselves.

Several weeks after the Grand Jury's action, the People, asserting that they had newly available evidence, moved for an order authorizing them to resubmit the dismissed charges to a second Grand Jury. Supreme Court, Criminal Term, after conducting an in camera inquiry, granted the motion. . . . Two of the four youths, Canty and Ramseur, testified. Among the other witnesses were four passengers from the seventh car of the subway who had seen some portions of the incident. . . .

On March 27, 1985, the second Grand Jury filed a 10-count indictment, containing four charges of attempted murder, four charges of assault in the first degree, one charge of reckless endangerment in the first degree, and one charge of criminal possession of a weapon in the second degree [possession of loaded firearm with intent to use it unlawfully against another]. . . .

On October 14, 1985, Goetz moved to dismiss the charges contained in the second indictment alleging, among other things, that the evidence before the second Grand Jury was not legally sufficient to establish the offenses charged, and that the prosecutor's instructions to that Grand Jury on the defense of justification were erroneous and prejudicial to the defendant so as to render its proceedings defective.

On November 25, 1985, . . . a column appeared in the *New York Daily News* containing an interview which the columnist had conducted with Darryl Cabey the previous day in Cabey's hospital room. The columnist claimed that Cabey had told him in this interview that the other three youths had all approached Goetz with the intention of robbing him. The day after the column was published, a New York City police officer informed the prosecutor that he had been one of the first police officers to enter the subway car after the shootings, and that Canty had said to him "we were going to rob [Goetz]". . . .

III.

Penal Law article 35 recognizes the defense of justification, which "permits the use of force under certain circumstances." One such set of circumstances pertains to the use of force in defense of a person, encompassing both self-defense and defense of a third person (Penal Law § 35.15). Penal Law § 35.15 (1) sets forth the general principles governing all such uses of force: "[a] person may . . . use physical force upon another person when and to the extent he *reasonably believes* such to be necessary to defend himself or a third person from what he *reasonably believes* to be the use or imminent use of unlawful physical force by such other person" (emphasis added).

Section 35.15 (2) sets forth further limitations on these general principles with respect to the use of "deadly physical force": "A person may not use deadly physical force upon another person under circumstances specified in subdivision one unless (a) He *reasonably believes* that such other person is using or about to use deadly physical force . . . or (b) He *reasonably believes* that such other person is committing or attempting to commit a kidnapping, forcible rape, forcible sodomy or robbery" (emphasis added).[4]

Thus, consistent with most justification provisions, Penal Law § 35.15 permits the use of deadly physical force only where requirements as to triggering conditions and the necessity of a particular response are met. As to the triggering conditions, the statute requires that the actor "reasonably believes" that another person either is using or about to use deadly physical force or is committing or attempting to commit one of certain enumerated felonies, including robbery. As to the need for the use of deadly physical force as a response, the statute requires that the actor "reasonably believes" that such force is necessary to avert the perceived threat.[5]

Because the evidence before the second Grand Jury included statements by Goetz that he acted to protect himself from being maimed or to avert a robbery, the prosecutor correctly chose to charge the justification defense in section 35.15 to the Grand Jury. The prosecutor properly instructed the grand jurors to consider whether the use of deadly physical force was justified to prevent either serious physical injury or a robbery, and, in doing so, to separately analyze the defense with respect to each of the charges. . . .

---

[4] Section 35.15 (2) (a) further provides, however, that even under these circumstances a person ordinarily must retreat "if he knows that he can with complete safety as to himself and others avoid the necessity of [using deadly physical force] by retreating."

[5] While the portion of section 35.15 (2) (b) pertaining to the use of deadly force to avert a felony such as robbery does not contain a separate "retreat" requirement, it is clear from reading subdivisions (1) and (2) of section 35.15 together, as the statute requires, that the general "necessity" requirement in subdivision (1) applies to all uses of force under section 35.15, including the use of deadly physical force under subdivision (2) (b).

When the prosecutor had completed his charge, one of the grand jurors asked for clarification of the term "reasonably believes." The prosecutor responded by instructing the grand jurors that they were to consider the circumstances of the incident and determine "whether the defendant's conduct was that of a reasonable man in the defendant's situation." It is this response by the prosecutor — and specifically his use of "a reasonable man" — which is the basis for the dismissal of the charges by the lower courts. As expressed repeatedly in the Appellate Division's plurality opinion, because section 35.15 uses the term *"he* reasonably believes," the appropriate test, according to that court, is whether a defendant's beliefs and reactions were "reasonable *to him*." Under that reading of the statute, a jury which believed a defendant's testimony that he felt that his own actions were warranted and were reasonable would have to acquit him, regardless of what anyone else in defendant's situation might have concluded. Such an interpretation defies the ordinary meaning and significance of the term "reasonably" in a statute, and misconstrues the clear intent of the Legislature, in enacting section 35.15, to retain an objective element as part of any provision authorizing the use of deadly physical force.

Penal statutes in New York have long codified the right recognized at common law to use deadly physical force, under appropriate circumstances, in self-defense. These provisions have never required that an actor's belief as to the intention of another person to inflict serious injury be correct in order for the use of deadly force to be justified, but they have uniformly required that the belief comport with an objective notion of reasonableness. The 1829 statute, using language which was followed almost in its entirety until the 1965 recodification of the Penal Law, provided that the use of deadly force was justified in self-defense or in the defense of specified third persons "when there shall be a reasonable ground to apprehend a design to commit a felony, or to do some great personal injury, and there shall be imminent danger of such design being accomplished". . . .

In 1961 the Legislature established a Commission to undertake a complete revision of the Penal Law and the Criminal Code. The impetus for the decision to update the Penal Law came in part from the drafting of the Model Penal Code by the American Law Institute, as well as from the fact that the existing law was poorly organized and in many aspects antiquated. . . . While using the Model Penal Code provisions on justification as general guidelines, however, the drafters of the new Penal Law did not simply adopt them verbatim.

The provisions of the Model Penal Code with respect to the use of deadly force in self-defense reflect the position of its drafters that any culpability which arises from a mistaken belief in the need to use such force should be no greater than the culpability such a mistake would give rise to if it were made with respect to an element of a crime. Accordingly, under Model Penal Code § 3.04(2)(b), a defendant charged with murder (or attempted murder) need only show that he *"believe[d]* that [the use of deadly force] was necessary to protect himself against death, serious bodily injury, kidnapping or [forcible] sexual intercourse" to prevail on a self-defense claim (emphasis added). If the defendant's belief was wrong, and was recklessly, or negligently formed, however, he may be convicted of the type of homicide charge requiring only a reckless or negligent, as the case may be, criminal intent.

The drafters of the Model Penal Code recognized that the wholly subjective test set forth in section 3.04 differed from the existing law in most States by its omission of any requirement of reasonableness. The drafters were also keenly aware that requiring that the actor have a "reasonable belief" rather than just a "belief" would alter the wholly subjective test. . . .

New York did not follow the Model Penal Code's equation of a mistake as to the need to use deadly force with a mistake negating an element of a crime, choosing instead to use a single statutory section which would provide either a complete defense or no defense at all to a defendant charged with any crime involving the use of deadly force. The drafters of the new Penal Law adopted in large part the structure and content of Model Penal Code § 3.04, but, crucially, inserted the word "reasonably" before "believes". . . .

We cannot lightly impute to the Legislature an intent to fundamentally alter the principles of justification to allow the perpetrator of a serious crime to go free simply because that person believed his actions were reasonable and necessary to prevent some perceived harm. To completely exonerate such an individual, no matter how aberrational or bizarre his thought patterns, would allow citizens to set their own standards for the permissible use of force. It would also allow a legally competent defendant suffering from delusions to kill or perform acts of violence with impunity, contrary to fundamental principles of justice and criminal law. . . .

Nowhere in the legislative history is there any indication that "reasonably believes" was designed to change the law on the use of deadly force or establish a subjective standard. To the contrary, the Commission, in the staff comment governing arrests by police officers, specifically equated "[he] reasonably believes" with having a reasonable ground for believing. . . .

Goetz also argues that the introduction of an objective element will preclude a jury from considering factors such as the prior experiences of a given actor and thus, require it to make a determination of "reasonableness" without regard to the actual circumstances of a particular incident. This argument, however, falsely presupposes that an objective standard means that the background and other relevant characteristics of a particular actor must be ignored. To the contrary, we have frequently noted that a determination of reasonableness must be based on the "circumstances" facing a defendant or his "situation." Such terms encompass more than the physical movements of the potential assailant. As just discussed, these terms include any relevant knowledge the defendant had about that person. They also necessarily bring in the physical attributes of all persons involved, including the defendant. Furthermore, the defendant's circumstances encompass any prior experiences he had which could provide a reasonable basis for a belief that another person's intentions were to injure or rob him or that the use of deadly force was necessary under the circumstances.

Accordingly, a jury should be instructed to consider this type of evidence in weighing the defendant's actions. The jury must first determine whether the defendant had the requisite beliefs under section 35.15, that is, whether he believed deadly force was necessary to avert the imminent use of deadly force or the commission of one of the felonies enumerated therein. If the People do not prove beyond a reasonable doubt that he did not have such beliefs, then the jury must also consider whether these beliefs were reasonable. The jury would have to determine, in light of all the "circumstances," as explicated above, if a reasonable person could have had these beliefs.

The prosecutor's instruction to the second Grand Jury that it had to determine whether, under the circumstances, Goetz's conduct was that of a reasonable man in his situation was thus essentially an accurate charge. . . .

It will now be for the petit jury to decide whether the prosecutor can prove beyond a reasonable doubt that Goetz's reactions were unreasonable and therefore excessive. . . .

Accordingly, the order of the Appellate Division should be reversed, and the dismissed counts of the indictment reinstated.

QUESTIONS

1. What does New York law require for self-defense?

2. What characteristics does the "reasonable person" share with the defendant in assessing a claim of self-defense under New York law?

3. Would you describe the definition of "reasonable person" in the *Goetz* case as closer to an "objective reasonable man" standard or an "individualized" standard?

4. In what other areas of the course have we encountered similar issues?

5. Two of the victims were carrying screwdrivers when the incident occurred. Is this fact relevant? If so, why? On what does its relevance to a self-defense claim depend?

One of the primary issues that influenced public opinion about the case was the issue of race. Although it is difficult to discern from the appellate opinion, Goetz was white and the four shooting victims were black. As is often the case in jury trials, various evidentiary rules result in information being kept from the jury. In this trial, jurors were not told of a racist comment allegedly made by Goetz some years before the shooting.[6] If you had been a juror, would such a comment have influenced your view of the self-defense claim?

What are the advantages and disadvantages of an "objective" standard? What are the advantages and disadvantages of an individualized standard?

Consider the following excerpt from Professor George Fletcher's book on the *Goetz* case:[7]

> [After the shooting s]omeone pulls the emergency brake and the train screeches to a halt. The passengers flee the car, but two women remain, immobilized by fear. Goetz says some soothing words to the fearful women, and then a conductor approaches and asks him whether he is a cop. The gunman replies, "They tried to rip me off." He refuses to hand over his gun and quietly walks to the front of the car . . . and disappears into the dark of the subway tunnel. Three young black kids lie bleeding on the floor of the train; Darrell Cabey sits wounded and paralyzed in the end seat.
>
> A mythical figure is born — an unlikely avenger for the fear that both unites and levels all urban dwellers in the United States. If the four kids had mugged a passenger, newspaper reporters would have sighed in boredom. There are, on average, 38 crimes a day on the New York subways. If a police officer had intervened and shot four kids who were hassling a rider for money, protests of racism and police brutality would have been the call of the day. This was different. A common man had emerged from the shadows of fear. He shot back when others only fantasize their responses to shakedowns on the New York subways. . . .
>
> With no offender to bear down on, the press has only the four black kids to portray in the news. . . . Uneducated, with criminal records, on the prowl for a few dollars, they exemplify the underclass of teenage criminals feared by both blacks and whites. . . .

---

6. George P. Fletcher, *A Crime of Self-Defense: Bernhard Goetz and the Law on Trial* at 136 (1988).
7. *Id.* at 2, 4.

From the very beginning, the Goetz proceedings are caught in a political dialectic between the rush of popular support for the "subway vigilante" and the official attitude of outrage that anyone would dare usurp the state's task of keeping law and order. While the public calls into the newly established police hotline to express support for the wanted man, public officials . . . come out strongly against "vigilantism" on the streets.

Ultimately, the jury in the criminal trial acquitted Goetz of all the charges except criminal possession of a weapon in the third degree. One of the victims of the shooting, Darrell Cabey, who remained paralyzed, sued Goetz. The jury found in favor of Mr. Cabey and awarded him the sum of $43,000,000.[8] What might explain these profoundly disparate results?

As the statutes earlier in the chapter and the New York statute in the *Goetz* case illustrate, the doctrine of defense of others largely parallels that of self-defense. Commonly, a defendant must meet the same requirements for each. But sometimes courts have distinguished a self-defense claim from one for defense of others. For example, under a traditional self-defense claim, if the defendant made an honest but reasonable error about the need to use deadly defensive force, the defendant generally still benefited from a defensive force defense. If the defendant used deadly force against a gun-wielding assailant but the assailant turned out to be a police officer engaged in a legitimate arrest and a person in the defendant's situation could have reasonably mistaken the officer for someone intending unlawful deadly harm, the defendant could still usually invoke a self-defense claim. In contrast, some courts have not upheld such a claim when the defendant misperceived the situation and was acting in defense of a third party.[9]

Historically, some courts have also limited the right to use deadly force to defend third parties to those to whom the defendant has a specified relationship, like a spousal or parental relationship.[10]

3. Self-Defense and Domestic Violence

The issue of self-defense arises in many factual contexts. Much debate over the past several decades has focused on its use in the domestic violence context. A substantial portion of this debate revolves around the effects of domestic violence on the person battered and the requirements of reasonableness and imminence. Contrast the majority and dissent approaches to these issues in the *Norman* case below.

STATE *v.* NORMAN
Supreme Court of North Carolina 324 N.C. 253 (1989)

MITCHELL, Justice.

The defendant was tried . . . upon a proper indictment charging her with the first degree murder of her husband. The jury found the defendant guilty of

---

8. Associated Press, Arizona Daily Wildcat, *Jury hands down $43M verdict in lawsuit against Goetz*, http://wildcat.arizona.edu//papers/89/144/11_1_m.html (accessed Aug. 2, 2004).

9. Wayne R. LaFave, *Criminal Law* 550-552 (4th ed. 2000).

10. *Id.* at 553.

voluntary manslaughter. The defendant appealed from the trial court's judgment sentencing her to six years imprisonment.

The Court of Appeals granted a new trial, citing as error the trial court's refusal to submit a possible verdict of acquittal by reason of perfect self-defense. Notwithstanding the uncontroverted evidence that the defendant shot her husband three times in the back of the head as he lay sleeping in his bed, the Court of Appeals held that the defendant's evidence that she exhibited what has come to be called "the battered wife syndrome" entitled her to have the jury consider whether the homicide was an act of perfect self-defense and, thus, not a legal wrong.

We conclude that the evidence introduced in this case would not support a finding that the defendant killed her husband due to a reasonable fear of imminent death or great bodily harm, as is required before a defendant is entitled to jury instructions concerning either perfect or imperfect self-defense. Therefore, the trial court properly declined to instruct the jury on the law relating to self-defense. Accordingly, we reverse the Court of Appeals.

At trial, the State presented the testimony of Deputy Sheriff R. H. Epley of the Rutherford County Sheriff's Department, who was called to the Norman residence on the night of 12 June 1985. Inside the home, Epley found the defendant's husband, John Thomas Norman, lying on a bed in a rear bedroom with his face toward the wall and his back toward the middle of the room. He was dead, but blood was still coming from wounds to the back of his head. A later autopsy revealed three gunshot wounds to the head, two of which caused fatal brain injury. The autopsy also revealed a .12 percent blood alcohol level in the victim's body.

Later that night, the defendant related an account of the events leading to the killing, after Epley had advised her of her constitutional rights and she had waived her right to remain silent. The defendant told Epley that her husband had been beating her all day and had made her lie down on the floor while he slept on the bed. After her husband fell asleep, the defendant carried her grandchild to the defendant's mother's house. The defendant took a pistol from her mother's purse and walked the short distance back to her home. She pointed the pistol at the back of her sleeping husband's head, but it jammed the first time she tried to shoot him. She fixed the gun and then shot her husband in the back of the head as he lay sleeping. After one shot, she felt her husband's chest and determined that he was still breathing and making sounds. She then shot him twice more in the back of the head. The defendant told Epley that she killed her husband because "she took all she was going to take from him so she shot him."

The defendant presented evidence tending to show a long history of physical and mental abuse by her husband due to his alcoholism. At the time of the killing, the thirty-nine-year-old defendant and her husband had been married almost twenty-five years and had several children. The defendant testified that her husband had started drinking and abusing her about five years after they were married. His physical abuse of her consisted of frequent assaults that included slapping, punching and kicking her, striking her with various objects, and throwing glasses, beer bottles and other objects at her. The defendant described other specific incidents of abuse, such as her husband putting her cigarettes out on her, throwing hot coffee on her, breaking glass against her face and crushing food on her face. Although the defendant did not present evidence of ever having received medical treatment for any physical injuries inflicted by her husband, she displayed several scars about her face which she attributed to her husband's assaults.

The defendant's evidence also tended to show other indignities inflicted upon her by her husband. Her evidence tended to show that her husband did not work and forced her to make money by prostitution, and that he made humor of that fact to family and friends. He would beat her if she resisted going out to prostitute herself or if he was unsatisfied with the amounts of money she made. He routinely called the defendant "dog," "bitch" and "whore," and on a few occasions made her eat pet food out of the pets' bowls and bark like a dog. He often made her sleep on the floor. At times, he deprived her of food and refused to let her get food for the family. During those years of abuse, the defendant's husband threatened numerous times to kill her and to maim her in various ways.

The defendant said her husband's abuse occurred only when he was intoxicated, but that he would not give up drinking. She said she and her husband "got along very well when he was sober," and that he was "a good guy" when he was not drunk. She had accompanied her husband to the local mental health center for sporadic counseling sessions for his problem, but he continued to drink.

In the early morning hours on the day before his death, the defendant's husband, who was intoxicated, went to a rest area off I-85 near Kings Mountain where the defendant was engaging in prostitution and assaulted her. While driving home, he was stopped by a patrolman and jailed on a charge of driving while impaired. After the defendant's mother got him out of jail at the defendant's request later that morning, he resumed his drinking and abuse of the defendant.

The defendant's evidence also tended to show that her husband seemed angrier than ever after he was released from jail and that his abuse of the defendant was more frequent. That evening, sheriff's deputies were called to the Norman residence, and the defendant complained that her husband had been beating her all day and she could not take it anymore. The defendant was advised to file a complaint, but she said she was afraid her husband would kill her if she had him arrested. The deputies told her they needed a warrant before they could arrest her husband, and they left the scene.

The deputies were called back less than an hour later after the defendant had taken a bottle of pills. The defendant's husband cursed her and called her names as she was attended by paramedics, and he told them to let her die. A sheriff's deputy finally chased him back into his house as the defendant was put into an ambulance. The defendant's stomach was pumped at the local hospital, and she was sent home with her mother.

While in the hospital, the defendant was visited by a therapist with whom she discussed filing charges against her husband and having him committed for treatment. Before the therapist left, the defendant agreed to go to the mental health center the next day to discuss those possibilities. The therapist testified at trial that the defendant seemed depressed in the hospital, and that she expressed considerable anger toward her husband. He testified that the defendant threatened a number of times that night to kill her husband and that she said she should kill him "because of the things he had done to her."

The next day, the day she shot her husband, the defendant went to the mental health center to talk about charges and possible commitment, and she confronted her husband with that possibility. She testified that she told her husband later that day: "J. T., straighten up. Quit drinking. I'm going to have you committed to help you." She said her husband then told her he would "see them coming" and would cut her throat before they got to him.

The defendant also went to the social services office that day to seek welfare benefits, but her husband followed her there, interrupted her interview and made her go home with him. He continued his abuse of her, threatening to kill and to maim her, slapping her, kicking her, and throwing objects at her. At one point, he took her cigarette and put it out on her, causing a small burn on her upper torso. He would not let her eat or bring food into the house for their children.

That evening, the defendant and her husband went into their bedroom to lie down, and he called her a "dog" and made her lie on the floor when he lay down on the bed. Their daughter brought in her baby to leave with the defendant, and the defendant's husband agreed to let her baby-sit. After the defendant's husband fell asleep, the baby started crying and the defendant took it to her mother's house so it would not wake up her husband. She returned shortly with the pistol and killed her husband.

The defendant testified at trial that she was too afraid of her husband to press charges against him or to leave him. She said that she had temporarily left their home on several previous occasions, but he had always found her, brought her home and beaten her. Asked why she killed her husband, the defendant replied: "Because I was scared of him and I knowed when he woke up, it was going to be the same thing, and I was scared when he took me to the truck stop that night it was going to be worse than he had ever been. I just couldn't take it no more. There ain't no way, even if it means going to prison. It's better than living in that. That's worse hell than anything."

The defendant and other witnesses testified that for years her husband had frequently threatened to kill her and to maim her. When asked if she believed those threats, the defendant replied: "Yes. I believed him; he would, he would kill me if he got a chance. If he thought he wouldn't a had to went to jail, he would a done it."

Two expert witnesses in forensic psychology and psychiatry who examined the defendant after the shooting, Dr. William Tyson and Dr. Robert Rollins, testified that the defendant fit the profile of battered wife syndrome. This condition, they testified, is characterized by such abuse and degradation that the battered wife comes to believe she is unable to help herself and cannot expect help from anyone else. She believes that she cannot escape the complete control of her husband and that he is invulnerable to law enforcement and other sources of help.

Dr. Tyson, a psychologist, was asked his opinion as to whether, on 12 June 1985, "it appeared reasonably necessary for Judy Norman to shoot J. T. Norman?" He replied: "I believe that . . . Mrs. Norman believed herself to be doomed . . . to a life of the worst kind of torture and abuse, degradation that she had experienced over the years in a progressive way; that it would only get worse, and that death was inevitable. . . . " Dr. Tyson later added: "I think Judy Norman felt that she had no choice, both in the protection of herself and her family, but to engage, exhibit deadly force against Mr. Norman, and that in so doing, she was sacrificing herself, both for herself and for her family."

Dr. Rollins, who was the defendant's attending physician at Dorothea Dix Hospital when she was sent there for evaluation, testified that in his opinion the defendant was a typical abused spouse and that "[s]he saw herself as powerless to deal with the situation, that there was no alternative, no way she could escape it." Dr. Rollins was asked his opinion as to whether "on June 12th, 1985, it appeared reasonably necessary that Judy Norman would take the life of J. T. Norman?" Dr. Rollins replied that in his opinion, "that course of action did appear necessary to Mrs. Norman."

Based on the evidence that the defendant exhibited battered wife syndrome, that she believed she could not escape her husband nor expect help from others, that her husband had threatened her, and that her husband's abuse of her had worsened in the two days preceding his death, the Court of Appeals concluded that a jury reasonably could have found that her killing of her husband was justified as an act of perfect self-defense. The Court of Appeals reasoned that the nature of battered wife syndrome is such that a jury could not be precluded from finding the defendant killed her husband lawfully in perfect self-defense, even though he was asleep when she killed him. We disagree.

The right to kill in self-defense is based on the necessity, real or reasonably apparent, of killing an unlawful aggressor to save oneself from *imminent* death or great bodily harm at his hands. Our law has recognized that self-preservation under such circumstances springs from a primal impulse and is an inherent right of natural law.

In North Carolina, a defendant is entitled to have the jury consider acquittal by reason of *perfect* self-defense when the evidence, viewed in the light most favorable to the defendant, tends to show that at the time of the killing it appeared to the defendant and she believed it to be necessary to kill the decedent to save herself from imminent death or great bodily harm. That belief must be reasonable, however, in that the circumstances as they appeared to the defendant would create such a belief in the mind of a person of ordinary firmness. Further, the defendant must not have been the initial aggressor provoking the fatal confrontation. A killing in the proper exercise of the right of *perfect* self-defense is always completely justified in law and constitutes no legal wrong.

Our law also recognizes an *imperfect* right of self-defense in certain circumstances, including, for example, when the defendant is the initial aggressor, but without intent to kill or to seriously injure the decedent, and the decedent escalates the confrontation to a point where it reasonably appears to the defendant to be necessary to kill the decedent to save herself from imminent death or great bodily harm. Although the culpability of a defendant who kills in the exercise of *imperfect* self-defense is reduced, such a defendant is *not justified* in the killing so as to be entitled to acquittal, but is guilty at least of voluntary manslaughter.

The defendant in the present case was not entitled to a jury instruction on either perfect or imperfect self-defense. The trial court was not required to instruct on *either* form of self-defense unless evidence was introduced tending to show that at the time of the killing the defendant reasonably believed herself to be confronted by circumstances which necessitated her killing her husband to save herself from *imminent* death or great bodily harm. No such evidence was introduced in this case, and it would have been error for the trial court to instruct the jury on *either* perfect or imperfect self-defense. . . .

The killing of another human being is the most extreme recourse to our inherent right of self-preservation and can be justified in law only by the utmost real or apparent necessity brought about by the decedent. For that reason, our law of self-defense has required that a defendant claiming that a homicide was justified and, as a result, inherently lawful by reason of perfect self-defense must establish that she reasonably believed at the time of the killing she otherwise would have immediately suffered death or great bodily harm. Only if defendants are required to show that they killed due to a reasonable belief that death or great bodily harm was imminent can the justification for homicide remain clearly and firmly rooted in necessity. . . .

The term "imminent," as used to describe such perceived threats of death or great bodily harm as will justify a homicide by reason of perfect self-defense, has been defined as "immediate danger, such as must be instantly met, such as cannot be guarded against by calling for the assistance of others or the protection of the law." Black's Law Dictionary 676 (5th ed. 1979). Our cases have sometimes used the phrase "about to suffer" interchangeably with "imminent" to describe the immediacy of threat that is required to justify killing in self-defense.

The evidence in this case did not tend to show that the defendant reasonably believed that she was confronted by a threat of imminent death or great bodily harm. The evidence tended to show that no harm was "imminent" or about to happen to the defendant when she shot her husband. The uncontroverted evidence was that her husband had been asleep for some time when she walked to her mother's house, returned with the pistol, fixed the pistol after it jammed and then shot her husband three times in the back of the head. The defendant was not faced with an instantaneous choice between killing her husband or being killed or seriously injured. Instead, *all* of the evidence tended to show that the defendant had ample time and opportunity to resort to other means of preventing further abuse by her husband. There was no action underway by the decedent from which the jury could have found that the defendant had reasonable grounds to believe either that a felonious assault was imminent or that it might result in her death or great bodily injury. Additionally, no such action by the decedent had been underway immediately prior to his falling asleep. . . .

The reasoning of our Court of Appeals in this case proposes to change the established law of self-defense by giving the term "imminent" a meaning substantially more indefinite and all-encompassing than its present meaning. This would result in a substantial relaxation of the requirement of real or apparent necessity to justify homicide. Such reasoning proposes justifying the taking of human life not upon the reasonable belief it is necessary to prevent death or great bodily harm — which the imminence requirement ensures — but upon purely subjective speculation that the decedent probably would present a threat to life at a future time and that the defendant would not be able to avoid the predicted threat.

The Court of Appeals suggests that such speculation would have been particularly reliable in the present case because the jury, based on the evidence of the decedent's intensified abuse during the thirty-six hours preceding his death, could have found that the decedent's passive state at the time of his death was "but a momentary hiatus in a continuous reign of terror by the decedent [and] the defendant merely took advantage of her first opportunity to protect herself." 89 N.C. App. at 394. Requiring jury instructions on perfect self-defense in such situations, however, would still tend to make opportune homicide lawful as a result of mere subjective predictions of indefinite future assaults and circumstances. Such predictions of future assaults to justify the defendant's use of deadly force in this case would be entirely speculative, because there was no evidence that her husband had ever inflicted any harm upon her that approached life-threatening injury, even during the "reign of terror." It is far from clear in the defendant's poignant evidence that any abuse by the decedent had ever involved the degree of physical threat required to justify the defendant in using deadly force, even when those threats were imminent. The use of deadly force in self-defense to prevent harm other than death or great bodily harm is excessive as a matter of law.

As we have stated, stretching the law of self-defense to fit the facts of this case would require changing the "imminent death or great bodily harm" requirement to something substantially more indefinite than previously required and would weaken our assurances that justification for the taking of human life remains firmly rooted in real or apparent necessity. That result in principle could not be limited to a few cases decided on evidence as poignant as this. The relaxed requirements for perfect self-defense proposed by our Court of Appeals would tend to categorically legalize the opportune killing of abusive husbands by their wives solely on the basis of the wives' testimony concerning their subjective speculation as to the probability of future felonious assaults by their husbands. Homicidal self-help would then become a lawful solution, and perhaps the easiest and most effective solution, to this problem. . . .

For the foregoing reasons, we conclude that the defendant's conviction for voluntary manslaughter and the trial court's judgment sentencing her to a six-year term of imprisonment were without error. Therefore, we must reverse the decision of the Court of Appeals which awarded the defendant a new trial.

Reversed.

Justice MARTIN dissenting.

At the outset it is to be noted that the peril of fabricated evidence is not unique to the trials of battered wives who kill. The possibility of invented evidence arises in all cases in which a party is seeking the benefit of self-defense. Moreover, in this case there were a number of witnesses other than defendant who testified as to the actual presence of circumstances supporting a claim of self-defense. This record contains no reasonable basis to attack the credibility of evidence for the defendant. . . .

At the heart of the majority's reasoning is its unsubstantiated concern that to find that the evidence presented by defendant would support an instruction on self-defense would "expand our law of self-defense beyond the limits of immediacy and necessity." Defendant does not seek to expand or relax the requirements of self-defense and thereby "legalize the opportune killing of allegedly abusive husbands by their wives," as the majority overstates. Rather, defendant contends that the evidence as gauged by the existing laws of self-defense is sufficient to require the submission of a self-defense instruction to the jury. The proper issue for this Court is to determine whether the evidence, viewed in the light most favorable to the defendant, was sufficient to require the trial court to instruct on the law of self-defense. I conclude that it was. . . .

A defendant is entitled to an instruction on self-defense when there is evidence, viewed in the light most favorable to the defendant, that these four elements existed at the time of the killing:

(1) it appeared to defendant and he believed it to be necessary to kill the deceased in order to save himself from death or great bodily harm; and

(2) defendant's belief was reasonable in that the circumstances as they appeared to him at the time were sufficient to create such a belief in the mind of a person of ordinary firmness; and

(3) defendant was not the aggressor in bringing on the affray, i.e., he did not aggressively and willingly enter into the fight without legal excuse or provocation; and

(4) defendant did not use excessive force, i.e., did not use more force than was necessary or reasonably appeared to him to be necessary under the circumstances to protect himself from death or great bodily harm. . . .

Evidence presented by defendant described a twenty-year history of beatings and other dehumanizing and degrading treatment by her husband. In his expert testimony a clinical psychologist concluded that defendant fit "and exceed[ed]" the profile of an abused or battered spouse, analogizing this treatment to the dehumanization process suffered by prisoners of war under the Nazis during the Second World War and the brainwashing techniques of the Korean War. The psychologist described the defendant as a woman incarcerated by abuse, by fear, and by her conviction that her husband was invincible and inescapable:

> Mrs. Norman didn't leave because she believed, fully believed that escape was totally impossible. There was no place to go. [S]he had left before; he had come and gotten her. She had gone to the Department of Social Services. He had come and gotten her. The law, she believed the law could not protect her; no one could protect her, and I must admit, looking over the records, that there was nothing done that would contradict that belief. She fully believed that he was invulnerable to the law and to all social agencies that were available; that nobody could withstand his power. As a result, there was no such thing as escape.

When asked if he had an opinion whether it appeared reasonably necessary for Judy Norman to shoot her husband, this witness responded:

> Yes. . . . I believe that in examining the facts of this case and examining the psychological data, that Mrs. Norman believed herself to be doomed . . . to a life of the worst kind of torture and abuse, degradation that she had experienced over the years in a progressive way; that it would only get worse, and that death was inevitable; death of herself, which was not such, I don't think was such an issue for her, as she had attempted to commit suicide, and in her continuing conviction of J. T. Norman's power over her, and even failed at that form of escape. I believe she also came to the point of beginning to fear for family members and her children, that were she to commit suicide that the abuse and the treatment that was heaped on her would be transferred onto them.

This testimony describes defendant's perception of circumstances in which she was held hostage to her husband's abuse for two decades and which ultimately compelled her to kill him. This testimony alone is evidence amply indicating the first two elements required for entitlement to an instruction on self-defense.

In addition to the testimony of the clinical psychologist, defendant presented the testimony of witnesses who had actually seen defendant's husband abuse her. These witnesses described circumstances that caused not only defendant to believe escape was impossible, but that also convinced *them* of its impossibility. Defendant's isolation and helplessness were evident in testimony that her family was intimidated by her husband into acquiescing in his torture of her. Witnesses also described defendant's experience with social service agencies and the law, which had contributed to her sense of futility and abandonment through the inefficacy of their protection and the strength of her husband's wrath when they failed. Where torture appears interminable and escape impossible, the belief that only the death of the oppressor can provide relief is reasonable in the mind of a person of ordinary firmness, let alone in the mind of the defendant, who, like a prisoner of war of some years, has been deprived of her humanity and is held hostage by fear. . . .

Evidence presented in the case sub judice revealed no letup of tension or fear, no moment in which the defendant felt released from impending serious harm, even while the decedent slept. . . . Psychologists have observed and commentators have described a "constant state of fear" brought on by the cyclical nature of battering as well as the battered spouse's perception that her abuser is both "omnipotent and unstoppable." *See* Comment, *The Admissibility of Expert Testimony on the Battered Woman Syndrome in Support of a Claim of Self-Defense*, 15 Conn. L. Rev. 121, 131 (1982). Constant fear means a perpetual anticipation of the next blow, a perpetual expectation that the next blow will kill. "[T]he battered wife is constantly in a heightened state of terror because she is certain that one day her husband will kill her during the course of a beating. . . . Thus from the perspective of the battered wife, the danger is constantly 'immediate.' " Eber, *The Battered Wife's Dilemma: To Kill or To Be Killed*, 32 Hastings L.J. 895, 928-29 (1981). For the battered wife, if there is no escape, if there is no window of relief or momentary sense of safety, then the next attack, which could be the fatal one, is imminent. In the context of the doctrine of self-defense, "imminent" is a term the meaning of which must be grasped from the defendant's point of view. Properly stated, the second prong of the question is not whether the threat was *in fact* imminent, but whether defendant's belief in the impending nature of the threat, given the circumstances as she saw them, was reasonable in the mind of a person of ordinary firmness.[1]

Defendant's intense fear, based on her belief that her husband intended not only to maim or deface her, as he had in the past, but to kill her, was evident in the testimony of witnesses who recounted events of the last three days of the decedent's life. This testimony could have led a juror to conclude that defendant reasonably perceived a threat to her life as "imminent," even while her husband slept. Over these three days, her husband's anger was exhibited in an unprecedented crescendo of violence. The evidence showed defendant's fear and sense of hopelessness similarly intensifying, leading to an unsuccessful attempt to escape through suicide and culminating in her belief that escape would be possible only through her husband's death.

Defendant testified that on 10 June, two days before her husband's death, he had again forced her to go to a rest stop near Kings Mountain to make money by prostitution. Her daughter Phyllis and Phyllis's boyfriend Mark Navarra accompanied her on this occasion because, defendant said, whenever her husband took her there, he would beat her. Phyllis corroborated this account. She testified that her father had arrived some time later and had begun beating her mother, asking how much money she had. Defendant said they all then drove off. Shortly afterwards an officer arrested defendant's husband for driving under the influence. He spent the night in jail and was released the next morning on bond paid by defendant's mother.

Defendant testified that her husband was argumentative and abusive all through the next day, 11 June. Mark Navarra testified that at one point defendant's husband threw a sandwich that defendant had made for him on the floor. She made another; he threw it on the floor, as well, then insisted she prepare one without touching it. Defendant's husband had then taken the third sandwich, which defendant had wrapped in paper towels, and smeared it on her face. Both Navarra and Phyllis testified that they had later watched defendant's husband seize defendant's

---

[1] This interpretation of the meaning of "imminent" is reflected in the Comments to the Model Penal Code: "The actor must believe that his defensive action is immediately necessary and the unlawful force against which he defends must be force that he apprehends will be used on the present occasion, but he need not apprehend that it will be immediately used." Model Penal Code § 3.04 comment (ALI 1985).

cigarette and put it out on her neck, the scars from which defendant displayed to the jury.

A police officer testified that he arrived at defendant's home at 8:00 that evening in response to a call reporting a domestic quarrel. Defendant, whose face was bruised, was crying, and she told the officer that her husband had beaten her all day long and that she could not take it any longer. The officer told her that he could do nothing for her unless she took out a warrant on her husband. She responded that if she did, her husband would kill her. The officer left but was soon radioed to return because defendant had taken an overdose of pills. The officer testified that defendant's husband was interfering with ambulance attendants, saying "Let the bitch die." When he refused to respond to the officer's warning that if he continued to hinder the attendants, he would be arrested, the officer was compelled to chase him into the house.

Defendant's mother testified that her son-in-law had reacted to the discovery that her daughter had taken the pills with cursing and obscenities and threats such as, "Now, you're going to pay for taking those pills," and "I'll kill you, your mother and your grandmother." His rage was such that defendant's mother feared he might kill the whole family, and knowing defendant's sister had a gun in her purse, she took the gun and placed it in her own.

Defendant was taken to the hospital, treated, and released at 2:30 A.M. She spent the remainder of the night at her grandmother's house. Defendant testified that the next day, 12 June, she felt dazed all day long. She went in the morning to the county mental health center for guidance on domestic abuse. When she returned home, she tried to talk to her husband, telling him to "straighten up. Quit drinking. . . . I'm going to have you committed to help you." Her husband responded, "If you do, I'll see them coming and before they get here, I'll cut your throat."

Later, her husband made her drive him and his friend to Spartanburg to pick up the friend's paycheck. On the way, the friend testified, defendant's husband "started slapping on her" when she was following a truck too closely, and he periodically poured his beer into a glass, then reached over and poured it on defendant's head. At one point defendant's husband lay down on the front seat with his head on the arm rest, "like he was going to go to sleep," and kicked defendant, who was still driving, in the side of the head.

Mark Navarra testified that in the year and a half he had lived with the Normans, he had never seen defendant's husband madder than he was on 12 June, opining that it was the DUI arrest two days before that had ignited J.T.'s fury. Phyllis testified that her father had beaten her mother "all day long." She testified that this was the third day defendant's husband had forbidden her to eat any food. Phyllis said defendant's family tried to get her to eat, but defendant, fearing a beating, would not. Although Phyllis's grandmother had sent over a bag of groceries that day, defendant's husband had made defendant put them back in the bag and would not let anyone eat them.

Early in the evening of 12 June, defendant's husband told defendant, "Let's go to bed." Phyllis testified that although there were two beds in the room, her father had forbidden defendant from sleeping on either. Instead, he had made her lie down on the concrete floor between the two beds, saying, "Dogs don't lay in the bed. They lay in the floor." Shortly afterward, defendant testified, Phyllis came in and asked her father if defendant could take care of her baby while she went to the store. He assented and eventually went to sleep. Defendant was still on the floor, the baby on the small bed. The baby started to cry and defendant "snuck up and took him out there to [her] mother's [house]." She asked her mother to watch the baby, then asked if her mother had anything for headache, as her head was "busting." Her mother responded that she had some pain pills in her purse. Defendant went in to get the pills, "and the gun was in there, and I don't know, I just seen the gun, and I took it out, and I went back there and shot him."

From this evidence of the exacerbated nature of the last three days of twenty years of provocation, a juror could conclude that defendant believed that her husband's threats to her life were viable, that serious bodily harm was imminent, and that it was necessary to kill her husband to escape that harm. And from this evidence a juror could find defendant's belief in the necessity to kill her husband not merely reasonable but compelling.

The third element for entitlement to an instruction on self-defense requires that there be evidence that the defendant was not the aggressor in bringing on the affray. If the defendant was the aggressor and killed with murderous intent, that is, the intent to kill or inflict serious bodily harm, then she is not entitled to an instruction on self-defense. A hiatus between provocation by the decedent and the killing can mark the initiation of a new confrontation between the defendant and the decedent, such that the defendant's earlier perception of imminent danger no longer appears reasonable and the defendant becomes the aggressor. . . .

Where the defendant is a battered wife, there is no analogue to the victim-turned-aggressor. . . . Where the defendant is a battered wife, the affray out of which the killing arises can be a continuing assault. There was evidence before the jury that it had not been defendant but her husband who had initiated "the affray," which the jury could have regarded as lasting twenty years, three days, or any number of hours preceding his death. And there was evidence from which the jury could infer that in defendant's mind the affray reached beyond the moment at which her husband fell asleep. Like the ongoing threats of death or great bodily harm, which she might reasonably have perceived as imminent, her husband continued to be the aggressor and she the victim.

Finally, the fourth element of self-defense poses the question of whether there was any evidence tending to show that the force used by defendant to repel her husband was not excessive, that is, more than reasonably appeared to be necessary under the circumstances. This question is answered in part by abundant testimony describing defendant's immobilization by fear caused by abuse by her husband. Three witnesses, including the decedent's best friend, all recounted incidents in which defendant passively accepted beating, kicks, commands, or humiliating affronts without striking back. From such evidence that she was paralyzed by her husband's presence, a jury could infer that it reasonably appeared to defendant to be necessary to kill her husband in order ultimately to protect herself from the death he had threatened and from severe bodily injury, a foretaste of which she had already experienced. . . .

It is to be remembered that defendant does not have the burden of persuasion as to self-defense; the burden remains with the state to prove beyond a reasonable doubt that defendant intentionally killed decedent without excuse or justification. If the evidence in support of self-defense is sufficient to create a reasonable doubt in the mind of a rational juror whether the state has proved an intentional killing without justification or excuse, self-defense must be submitted to the jury. This is such a case. . . .

QUESTIONS

1. What is the rule regarding self-defense in North Carolina as expressed in the *Norman* case?
2. Why do the majority and dissent come to different conclusions?
3. To which requirements of self-defense is battered woman syndrome testimony relevant?

Consider the Utah self-defense statute and legislative intent information on the 1994 revision to that statute below. How might a court using this statute have resolved the issues in *Norman*?

Utah Code Annotated § 76-2-402 (2001)   *Force in defense of a person — Forcible felony defined*

(1) A person is justified in threatening or using force against another when and to the extent that he or she reasonably believes that force is necessary to defend himself or a third person against such other's imminent use of unlawful force. However, that person is justified in using force intended or likely to cause death or serious bodily injury only if he or she reasonably believes that force is necessary to prevent death or serious bodily injury to himself or a third person as a result of the other's imminent use of unlawful force, or to prevent the commission of a forcible felony. . . .

(5) In determining imminence or reasonableness under Subsection (1), the trier of fact may consider, but is not limited to, any of the following factors:

    (a) the nature of the danger;
    (b) the immediacy of the danger;
    (c) the probability that the unlawful force would result in death or serious bodily injury;
    (d) the other's prior violent acts or violent propensities; and
    (e) any patterns of abuse or violence in the parties' relationship.

Legislative Intent. — Laws 1994, Chapter 26, § 2 provides: Amendments made by this act to Section 76-2-402, regarding self-defense, are intended to clarify that justification of the use of force in defense of a person applies equally to all persons including victims of abuse in ongoing relationships. It is intended that otherwise competent evidence regarding a victim's response to patterns of domestic abuse or violence be considered by the trier of fact in determining imminence or reasonableness in accordance with that section, and that the evidence be considered when useful in understanding the perceptions or conduct of a witness.

4. Retreat

Traditionally, a nonaggressor was not required to retreat before employing force, even deadly force, if the requirements of self-defense were otherwise met. More recently, however, particularly following promulgation of the Model Penal Code, a number of jurisdictions adopted retreat requirements.[11] What rationales support

---

11. *See* Model Penal Code § 3.04 (Commentaries at 55) (1985).

a no-retreat approach? Which support a retreat requirement? If safe retreat is available, is deadly defensive force ever necessary?

PROBLEM

8.4 Bob and Judy are arguing about division of property in anticipation of their legal separation. Bob insists on keeping the antique rifle that Judy inherited from her father before she and Bob married. The argument gets so heated that Judy pulls a knife and threatens Bob with serious injury if he does not give her the rifle. Bob responds by pointing the rifle at Judy and firing, causing her serious injury. Does Bob have a viable self-defense claim under the statutes below?

Arkansas Code Annotated § 5-2-607 (2001) *Use of deadly physical force in defense of a person*

(a) A person is justified in using deadly physical force upon another person if he reasonably believes that the other person is: . . .
(2) Using or about to use unlawful deadly physical force. . . .
(b) A person may not use deadly physical force in self-defense if he knows that he can avoid the necessity of using that force with complete safety:
(1) By retreating, except that a person is not required to retreat if he is in his dwelling and was not the original aggressor, or . . .
(2) By surrendering possession of property to a person claiming a lawful right thereto.

Nebraska Revised Statute § 28-1409 (2001) *Use of force in self-protection*

(4) The use of force shall not be justifiable under this section . . . if: . . .
(b) The actor knows that he can avoid the necessity of using such force with complete safety by retreating or by surrendering possession of a thing to a person asserting a claim of right thereto or by complying with a demand that he abstain from any action which he has no duty to take, except that:
(i) The actor shall not be obliged to retreat from his dwelling or place of work, unless he was the initial aggressor or is assailed in his place of work by another person whose place of work the actor knows it to be. . . .

Montana Code Annotated § 45-3-102 (2001) *Use of force in defense of person*

A person is justified in the use of force or threat to use force against another when and to the extent that he reasonably believes that such conduct is necessary to defend himself or another against such other's imminent use of unlawful force. However, he is justified in the use of force likely to cause death or serious bodily harm only if he reasonably believes that such force is necessary to prevent imminent death or serious bodily harm to himself or another or to prevent the commission of a forcible felony.

QUESTIONS

1. What rules about retreat do the statutes illustrate?
2. How do the concepts of necessity of using force and retreat relate to one another?
3. How did retreat rules apply to the *Goetz* case? To the *Norman* case?

Even when jurisdictions require retreat, it is not typically required within one's residence. This exception to the retreat requirement is known as the "castle exception." As the Nebraska Code above illustrates, some jurisdictions, following the Model Penal Code approach, extend the castle exception beyond the home to a non-aggressor's place of work.

QUESTIONS

1. What purposes might the castle exception serve?
2. What risks might it present?

5. Initial Aggressor Rules

Defensive force implies a response needed to protect against aggression by another. Initial aggressors generally lack the right to resort to defensive force. Nonetheless, under certain circumstances, an initial aggressor can gain the right to use defensive force. According to the two statutes that follow, under what circumstances may an initial aggressor make use of defensive force? How do these apply to Problem 8.5 below?

PROBLEM

8.5 Candace discovers that Sammie was intimate with Candace's boyfriend earlier in the week. Candace encounters Sammie at a party and begins an argument with Sammie. Candace hurls nasty racial and gender-based epithets at Sammie. Sammie pokes Candace on her arm with the thin metal pick used for removing clam hors d'oeuvres from their shells. Candace responds by grabbing her clam pick and stabbing Sammie in her leg. Candace continues her assault on Sammie. Sammie, still holding the metal pick in a threatening manner toward Candace, says: "Wait, I'm bleeding." Can Sammie or Candace prevail on a self-defense claim under the statutes that follow?

Texas Penal Code Annotated § 9.31 (2002) *Self-Defense*

(a) Except as provided in Subsection (b), a person is justified in using force against another when and to the degree he reasonably believes the force is immediately necessary to protect himself against the other's use or attempted use of unlawful force.

    (b) The use of force against another is not justified:

        (1) in response to verbal provocation alone; . . .

        (3) if the actor consented to the exact force used or attempted by the other.

        (4) if the actor provoked the other's use or attempted use of unlawful force, unless:

            (A) the actor abandons the encounter, or clearly communicates to the other his intent to do so reasonably believing he cannot safely abandon the encounter; and

            (B) the other nevertheless continues or attempts to use unlawful force against the actor. . . .

Colorado Revised Statute § 18-1-704 (2001)   *Use of physical force in defense of a person*

    (1) Except as provided in subsections (2) and (3) of this section, a person is justified in using physical force upon another person in order to defend himself or a third person from what he reasonably believes to be the use or imminent use of unlawful physical force by that other person, and he may use a degree of force which he reasonably believes to be necessary for that purpose.

    (2) Deadly physical force may be used only if a person reasonably believes a lesser degree of force is inadequate and:

        (a) The actor has reasonable ground to believe, and does believe, that he or another person is in imminent danger of being killed or of receiving great bodily injury; or

        (b) The other person is using or reasonably appears about to use physical force against the occupant of a dwelling or business establishment while committing or attempting to commit burglary. . . .

        (c) The other person is committing or reasonably appears about to commit kidnapping, . . . robbery, . . . sexual assault . . . or assault. . . .

    (3) Notwithstanding the provisions of subsection (1) of this section, a person is not justified in using physical force if:

        (a) With intent to cause bodily injury or death to another person, he provokes the use of unlawful force by that other person; or

        (b) He is the initial aggressor; except that his use of physical force upon another person under the circumstances is justifiable if he withdraws from the encounter and effectively communicates to the other person his intent to do so, but the latter nevertheless continues or threatens the use of unlawful physical force; or

        (c) The physical force involved is the product of a combat by agreement not specifically authorized by law.

QUESTIONS

    1. What does the Texas statute require for an initial aggressor to gain the right to self-defense?

2. Is the statute's use of the phrase "he reasonably believes the force is immediately necessary to protect himself against the other's use or attempted use of force" different from the formulation in earlier statutes of "he reasonably believes that such conduct is necessary to defend himself . . . against such other's imminent use of unlawful force"?

3. How does the Colorado statute differ from the Texas statute on the requirements for gaining the right to self-defense by an initial aggressor?

4. Apply the language of each of the statutes excerpted in Question 2 above to the *Norman* case. What result would each produce?

6. Model Penal Code Treatment of Self-Defense

Apply the excerpts of the Model Penal Code provisions below on self-protection to Problems 8.1-8.3 at the beginning of the self-defense Section.

Model Penal Code § 3.04 (1985)   *Use of Force in Self-Protection*

(1) *Use of Force Justifiable for Protection of the Person.* Subject to the provisions of this Section and of Section 3.09, the use of force upon or toward another person is justifiable when the actor believes that such force is immediately necessary for the purpose of protecting himself against the use of unlawful force by such other person on the present occasion.

(2) *Limitations on Justifying Necessity for Use of Force.* . . .

(b) The use of deadly force is not justifiable under this Section unless the actor believes that such force is necessary to protect himself against death, serious bodily injury, kidnapping or sexual intercourse compelled by force or threat; nor is it justifiable if:

(i) the actor, with the purpose of causing death or serious bodily injury provoked the use of force against himself in the same encounter; or

(ii) the actor knows that he can avoid the necessity of using such force with complete safety by retreating or by surrendering possession of a thing to a person asserting a claim of right thereto or by complying with a demand that he abstain from any action that he has no duty to take, except that:

(A) the actor is not obliged to retreat from his dwelling or place of work, unless he was the initial aggressor or is assailed in his place of work by another person whose place of work the actor knows it to be. . . .

(c) Except as required by paragraph . . . (b) of this Subsection, a person employing protective force may estimate the necessity thereof under the circumstances as he believes them to be when the force is used, without retreating, surrendering possession, or doing any other act that he has no legal duty to do or abstaining from any lawful action.

Model Penal Code § 3.09 (1985)   *Reckless or Negligent Use of Otherwise Justifiable Force.* . . .

(2) When the actor believes that the use of force upon or toward the person of another is necessary for any of the purposes for which such belief would establish a justification under Sections 3.03 to 3.08 but the actor is reckless or negligent in having such belief or in acquiring or failing to acquire any knowledge or belief that is material to the justifiability of his use of force, the justification afforded by those Sections is

unavailable in a prosecution for an offense for which recklessness or negligence, as the case may be, suffices to establish culpability.

QUESTIONS

1. What happens under the Model Penal Code provisions when the defendant genuinely but erroneously believes in the need for self-defense?

2. From reading the statutes listed earlier in this chapter, which jurisdiction do you think has adopted the MPC approach?

7. Synthesis and Review

PROBLEMS

8.6 Tyler is waiting at a red light. When the light turns green, he sees a family of ducks from the local pond crossing in front of his vehicle. While he is waiting for them to cross, Marsha, whose car is behind Tyler's, begins honking at Tyler. Because Tyler has a very large car, Marsha does not see the ducks. Marsha becomes so irate that she gets out of her car to threaten Tyler. She brings her vicious, snarling pit bull dog with her. Tyler and Marsha engage in a loud and nasty argument, with the pit bull straining at its leash. The pit bull is quite frightening, and Tyler is terrified. Marsha threatens to unleash her dog if Tyler does not apologize. Tyler pulls a gun and shoots Marsha. Does Tyler have a viable self-defense claim?

8.7 Jim belongs to a local gang called the "Tips." A rival gang, the "Coolers," have been driving in Tips' territory. Jim understands this intrusion into his gang's territory as an invitation to fight and a precursor to a drive-by shooting. There have been two drive-by shootings by the Coolers in the past month and two retaliatory shootings by the Tips. Jim just saw a car full of Coolers about a mile away. He did not see any exposed weapons, but Jim knows that the Coolers always travel well-armed. In anticipation of the violence to come, Jim heads home for his gun. On his way back out his front door, he sees the Coolers' car heading down his block. He raises his gun and aims at the front-seat passenger. The backseat passenger sticks a gun out the window and shoots Jim. Do any of the involved persons have a viable self-defense claim?

8.8 John Rowe and Michael Evans are prison inmates. The prison changes Evans' cell assignment so that he has a cell adjacent to Rowe. Rowe complains "that Evans' proximity might cause trouble. Rowe's fears [are] soon substantiated." "Evans [writes] Rowe a note demanding that Rowe go to Evans' cell the next morning and engage in sexual activities with him. In the note, Evans . . . threaten[s] that if Rowe [does] not meet Evans's . . . expectations, 'someone will get hurt and perhaps even die.' The next morning . . . , Evans enter[s] Rowe's cell. Rowe claims that Evans physically attacked him and attempted to rape him [at that time]. Rowe yelled out for help, and in an alleged attempt to repel Evans, struck him repeatedly with . . . an unheated hot pot."[12] Does Rowe have a viable self-defense claim?

8.9 Jaclyn Kurr "killed her boyfriend, Antonio Pena, with a knife . . . on October 9, 1999. According to a Kalamazoo police officer, defendant told him that she and Pena had argued that day over Pena's cocaine use. Defendant told the officer that Pena subsequently punched her two times in the stomach and that she warned Pena not to hit her because she was carrying his babies. Defendant stated that when Pena came toward her again, she stabbed him in the chest. He died as a result of the stab wound."[13] Assume that she was in the first trimester of pregnancy, should she be entitled to a defense-of-others claim? If so, under what circumstances? If not, why not?

The cases involving battered women and the use of the battered woman syndrome have generated extensive scholarly discussion. The excerpts below briefly explore two dimensions of that discussion.

Anne M. Coughlin, EXCUSING WOMEN   82 Cal. L. Rev. 1, 4-7 (1994)

While many feminist scholars conclude that the courts cannot justly blame an accused woman without considering abuse that she endured at the hands of her husband, several others have expressed uneasiness with the battered woman syndrome defense because it institutionalizes within the criminal law negative stereotypes of women. I agree with this criticism; in particular, the defense is objectionable because it relieves the accused woman of the stigma and pain of criminal punishment only if she embraces another kind of stigma and pain: she must advance an interpretation of her own activity that labels it the irrational product of a "mental health disorder."

However, this criticism leaves off precisely where the most profound feminist objection to the defense should begin. It is my thesis that the existing feminist critique of the battered woman syndrome defense is inadequate because the negative implications for women go far beyond the reinforcement of particular aspects of stereotyped gender roles that some of us may wish to shed. None of those who advocate, or, for that matter, criticize, adoption of the battered woman syndrome defense has noticed that, for many centuries, the criminal law has been content to excuse women for criminal misconduct on the ground that they cannot be expected to, and, indeed, should not, resist the influence exerted by their husbands. No similar excuse has ever been afforded to men; to the contrary, the criminal law

---

12. Based on and quotations from Rowe v. DeBruyn, 17 F.3d 1047, 1049 (7th Cir. 1994).
13. Quoted from People v. Kurr, 253 Mich. App. 317, 318 (2002).

consistently has demanded that men withstand any pressures in their lives that compel them to commit crimes, including pressures exerted by their spouses. In this way, the theory of criminal responsibility has participated in the construction of marriage and, indeed, of gender, as a hierarchical relationship. By construing wives as incapable of choosing lawful conduct when faced with unlawful influence from their spouses, the theory invests men with the authority to govern both themselves and their irresponsible wives.

The battered woman syndrome defense rests on and reaffirms this invidious understanding of women's incapacity for rational self-control. For the sake of clarity, I must emphasize that my argument is not that the battered woman syndrome defense is illegitimate merely because it fails to hold women to the same demanding standard against which men are measured. Rather, my claim is that, by denying that women are capable of abiding by criminal prohibitions, in circumstances said to afflict many women at some point during their lives, the defense denies that women have the same capacity for self-governance that is attributed to men, and, if the theory of responsibility operates in practice as its proponents claim, the defense thereby exposes women to forms of interference against which men are safe.

The existing feminist critique of the battered woman syndrome defense is inadequate in another significant respect. The scholars who worry that the defense may reinforce negative stereotypes of women have assigned the problem to the manner in which the courts are interpreting the defense, rather than to the values embraced by the defense itself. Proponents of the defense assert that the expert psychological testimony supporting the defense is not offered to prove that battered women are mentally ill or psychologically incompetent, as the language of many appellate opinions suggests, but to expose the underlying conditions of gender inequality that cause women's criminal misconduct and to refute sexist assumptions that blame women for falling victim to domestic violence. While it would not be surprising to discover that the courts have exacerbated the most negative aspects of the battered woman syndrome defense, I do not agree with the commentators who assign to the courts and to defense lawyers the primary fault for the failures of this defense. The defense itself defines the woman as a collection of mental symptoms, motivational deficits, and behavioral abnormalities; indeed, the fundamental premise of the defense is that women lack the psychological capacity to choose lawful means to extricate themselves from abusive mates.

V. F. Nourse, SELF-DEFENSE AND SUBJECTIVITY   68 U. Chi. L. Rev. 1235, 1237-1239, 1240-1242 (2001)

A. TIME, SUBJECTIVITY, AND SELF-DEFENSE

If there is a debate within the criminal law academy about self-defense today, it does not focus on the content of the doctrine. Instead, it focuses on whether the legal standard should be more "objective" or "subjective."

Conventional wisdom has it that the principal issue in self-defense cases is whether we should apply a rule that focuses on the particular defendant or one that imposes the standards of the "reasonable person." This apparent dichotomy has had an enormous influence on modern teaching and case law. In many a self-defense case, defendants argue that the jury instructions granted were too "objective," the State responds that they were "subjective" enough, and the court most often concludes that the standard requires both objectivity and subjectivity.

This dichotomy between subjective and objective approaches has, in turn, come to shape our vision of the problems of self-defense law. In an attempt to generate discussion about the wisdom of a more or less subjective standard, casebooks routinely juxtapose a case involving a battered woman claiming a subjective rule with a case that pushes that rule to encompass a far less sympathetic defendant. The central image of the debate is often the sad tale of Judy Norman, or a case like hers, of a woman who killed her partner while asleep or hours after the last bout of violence. Often, the foil to this drama is the unpalatable racist, such as Bernhard Goetz, the subway vigilante. Students who sympathize with the battered woman are questioned about whether they are prepared to defend a subjectified legal standard if they know that this will mean aid for those, such as Goetz, to whom they are generally unsympathetic.

The debate over the "subjective" is often associated with an empirical assumption about the nature of battered woman cases — that the facts don't quite measure up. In particular, the facts are thought not to "measure up" primarily because they fail to meet the legal doctrine's requirement for an imminent threat. Given this, it is not surprising that the legal concept of imminence has come to occupy a "central" place in the debate over the law and theory of self-defense. That debate, as currently envisioned, pits "objectivists," who argue that a strict imminence requirement is important to the law of self-defense, against "subjectivists," who appear to argue that the law should be "loosened" for battered women.

B. Time as Meaningful

Much of this debate appears to proceed on the assumption that the meaning of the term "imminence" is self-evident. Treatises and law reviews tell us that "the requirement of imminence means that the time for defense is *now*. The defender cannot wait *any longer*." Similarly, force is "imminent" if it will occur "almost immediately," "upon the instant," or "at once." "Legitimate self-defense must be neither too soon nor too late." Although the Model Penal Code sought to change this rule, and potentially soften it, by shifting the requirement from the threat (as "imminent") to the response (as "immediately necessary"), this approach has done little to change the basic assumption that we are still talking about temporal matters. . . .

It turns out that the battered woman cases in my survey, like their male counterparts, raise imminence most often in confrontational situations, where the defendant kills when she sees a gun, where the victim is advancing, or during an actual brawl. If that is right, then the problem of the battered woman case may not be one of fact, but of law. We do not ask of the man in the barroom brawl that he leave the bar before the occurrence of an anticipated fight, but we do ask the battered woman threatened with a gun why she did not leave the relationship. If, when courts are saying "imminence," they import meanings that demand retreat *before* the confrontation, they are applying a rule that the law itself disavows (for any defendant). And, if that is right, we need not subjectify the law for the disfavored; instead, we must deal with the potential for objective rules to contradict themselves, to perpetuate meanings that they disavow.

C. NECESSITY

1. Introduction

A necessity defense may be triggered when an actor engages in what would otherwise be a crime in order to avoid a greater harm. Trespassing onto someone's land to avoid being struck by a speeding automobile is a classic example. Trespass is a crime. But avoiding the greater harm of serious bodily injury justifies the trespass and exonerates the actor.

Necessity is a justification. Someone acting under the pressure of necessity engages in conduct of which society approves and which it encourages. Someone aiding in the criminal activity of an individual with a valid necessity defense usually may also avail herself of the defense.

Commentators and courts commonly view necessity as a "true affirmative" defense. As the introductory materials to this chapter indicate, asserting a true affirmative defense means that the actor admits the elements that constitute the offense, but then offers a rationale justifying his conduct and asks the fact-finder to acquit him.

We begin our study of necessity by analyzing statutory approaches to the defense and applying them to a series of Problems. We then turn to the common law approach to necessity and to perhaps the most famous case taught in Anglo-American criminal law, *The Queen v. Dudley & Stephens*. Next we examine application of the necessity defense to civil disobedience and prison escapes. Finally, we explore the Model Penal Code approach to necessity, known as the "choice of evils."

PROBLEMS

8.10 Mr. and Mrs. Smith become convinced that their daughter is being brainwashed by a satanic cult. The cult forbids family visitors. The Smiths hire a private detective who, by spying through an open window, videotapes some of the cult's practices. The video reveals worship services in which Adolf Hitler is revered as a deity and initiation ceremonies that involve forced fasting for periods of up to 21 days. The video shows the Smiths' daughter looking very gaunt and dazed. The Smiths estimate that their daughter has lost 20 pounds in the two weeks that she has lived at the complex. They fear for her physical and mental well being. They hire a deprogramming service to kidnap their daughter and work with her to unlearn the cult's message. During the kidnaping, the Smiths' daughter resists violently. Neighbors call the police because of the commotion. The Smiths and the deprogrammers are arrested and charged with kidnaping and trespass. Would the Pennsylvania or Wisconsin statutes below provide the Smiths or the deprogrammers with a necessity defense?

8.11 "On July 22, 1992, [Arlin] Budoo was a passenger in a car whose other occupants were Monte Glen, Sean Branch, Isaiah Taylor, and Michael Douglas. When Glen became aware that Branch, Taylor, and Douglas planned to kill him, he fled the car. However, Taylor followed and shot him ten times. Budoo witnessed the murder. Budoo initially refused to provide any information about the murder because he was afraid for himself and his family. Eventually he gave a statement to [the police] . . . , but declined any police protection." The prosecution granted him immunity, but he refused to testify before the grand jury. The government offered to protect Budoo and discuss "witness security with him [. He] declined to even discuss what his options would be under the Witness Protection Program.

"Despite his refusal to testify before the grand jury, Budoo was subpoenaed to appear as a witness at the trial of Taylor on July 24, 1993. However, upon learning that a witness who testified the previous day had been murdered, Budoo once again refused to testify. . . . Budoo was charged with contempt . . . in that he willfully and knowingly disobeyed an order of the Court to testify, thereby causing an obstruction of the orderly administration of justice."[14] Would the Arizona statute below afford Mr. Budoo a necessity defense?

8.12 Same as 8.11, except imagine that the defendant belongs to a gang in which killings of gang members are common to enforce order and loyalty within the gang. Would the Arizona statute below afford the defendant a defense under these circumstances?

8.13 Anti-abortion protestors block the entrance to a clinic that offers medical services to women. Of the services offered, 5 percent involve abortion procedures. Police arrest the protestors for trespassing and blocking a public sidewalk. At trial, the protestors prove that their efforts on the day in question prevented three women from obtaining abortions. The government proves that 50 other women were denied non-abortion-related medical services. Would the New York statute below provide a necessity defense for the protestors?

8.14 "Richard J. Anthuber is a heroin addict. . . . [P]rison officers found him injecting himself in his cell at the Racine Correctional Institution. . . . He specifically asserts that his illegal drug use was made necessary by the Department of Corrections (DOC) depriving him of the methadone it promised to provide. . . ."[15] "Unfortunately, as a result of what the State acknowledges was a 'mistake' by DOC personnel, Anthuber was not provided with methadone when he entered Racine. Although he tried, through counsel, to get the DOC to live up to the transfer agreement, the health officers at Racine could not cooperate because the

---

14. Quoted from Budoo v. United States, 677 A.2d 51, 52-54 (1996).
15. Quoted from Wisconsin v. Anthuber, 201 Wis. 2d 512, 515 (1996).

facility was not certified to administer methadone. . . . On August 7, a prison guard caught Anthuber injecting heroin into his foot."[16] Would the Arizona or Wisconsin statutes below provide a necessity defense for Mr. Anthuber?

8.15 A wildfire is roaring up the hillside toward seven houses at the top of the hillside and a small enclave of ten houses on the far side of the hill. George burns down the seven houses at the top of the hillside to create a firebreak and prevent the fire from reaching the enclave of ten houses. Would the New York or Wisconsin statutes provide George with a necessity defense?

8.16 Reconsider the problem from the Conduct chapter (Chapter 4) in which the parents of conjoined twins, Jody and Mary, tried to prevent their physical separation. In that case, doctors anticipated that, without separation, both twins would perish in a matter of months due to the strain on Jody's heart, which Mary's body caused. With surgery, Mary, who relied on Jody's heart to survive, would perish, but Jody was likely to survive and flourish. Had the doctors not first sought a court order to resolve the question of separation but instead had separated the twins on their own, would they have had a viable necessity defense to murder under the Arizona or New York statutes?

Arizona Revised Statute § 13-417 (2001)   *Necessity Defense*

A. Conduct that would otherwise constitute an offense is justified if a reasonable person was compelled to engage in the proscribed conduct and the person had no reasonable alternative to avoid imminent public or private injury greater than the injury that might reasonably result from the person's own conduct.

B. An accused person may not assert the defense under subsection A if the person intentionally, knowingly or recklessly placed himself in the situation in which it was probable that the person would have to engage in the proscribed conduct.

C. An accused person may not assert the defense under subsection A for offenses involving homicide or serious physical injury.

New York Penal Law § 35.05 (2001)   *Justification; generally*

[C]onduct which would otherwise constitute an offense is justifiable and not criminal when. . . .

2. Such conduct is necessary as an emergency measure to avoid an imminent public or private injury which is about to occur by reason of a situation occasioned or developed through no fault of the actor, and which is of such gravity that, according to ordinary standards of intelligence and morality, the desirability and urgency of avoiding such injury clearly outweigh the desirability of avoiding the injury sought to be prevented by the statute defining the offense in issue. The necessity and justifiability of such conduct may not rest upon considerations pertaining only to the morality and advisability of the statute, either in its general application or with respect to an application to a particular class of cases arising thereunder.

---

16. *Id.* at 516.

18 Pennsylvania Consolidated Statute Annotated § 503 (2002) *Justification generally*

(a) General rule. — Conduct which the actor believes to be necessary to avoid a harm or evil to himself or another is justifiable if:

(1) the harm or evil sought to be avoided by such conduct is greater than that sought to be prevented by the law defining the offense charged;

(2) neither this title nor other law defining the offense provides exceptions or defenses dealing with the specific situation involved; and

(3) a legislative purpose to exclude the justification claimed does not otherwise plainly appear.

(b) Choice of evils. — When the actor was reckless or negligent in bringing about the situation requiring a choice of harms or evils or in appraising the necessity for his conduct, the justification afforded by this section is unavailable in a prosecution for any offense for which recklessness or negligence, as the case may be, suffices to establish culpability.

Wisconsin Statute § 939.47 (2001) *Necessity*

Pressure of natural physical forces which causes the actor reasonably to believe that his or her act is the only means of preventing imminent public disaster, or imminent death or great bodily harm to the actor or another and which causes him or her so to act, is a defense to a prosecution for any crime based on that act, except that if the prosecution is for first-degree intentional homicide, the degree of the crime is reduced to 2nd-degree intentional homicide.

QUESTIONS

1. Are there any features common to all of the statutes above?
2. Are there any features unique to only one of the statutes?

PROBLEM

8.17 You are a state legislator. A committee on which you serve has been assigned the task of writing a necessity statute. Draft the statute. What elements would your statute have? Why?

---

2. Necessity and the Common Law

"Leading cases are the very stuff of which the common law is made, and [according to one of its historians] no leading case in the common law is better known than that of *Regina v. Dudley and Stephens.*"[17]

---

17. A.W. Brian Simpson, *Cannibalism and the Common Law: The Story of the Tragic Last Voyage of the Mignonette and the Strange Legal Proceedings to Which It Gave Rise* ix (1984).

THE QUEEN *v.* DUDLEY AND STEPHENS

14 Law Reports 273 Dec. 9, 1884

INDICTMENT for the murder of Richard Parker on the high seas within the jurisdiction of the Admiralty.

At the trial before Huddleston, B., at the Devon and Cornwall Winter Assizes, November 7, 1884, the jury, at the suggestion of the learned judge, found the facts of the case in a special verdict which stated "that, on July 5, 1884, the prisoners, Thomas Dudley and Edward Stephens, with one Brooks, all able-bodied English seamen, and the deceased also an English boy, between seventeen and eighteen years of age, . . . were cast away in a storm on the high seas 1600 miles from the Cape of Good Hope, and were compelled to put into an open boat belonging to the said yacht. That in this boat they had no supply of water and no supply of food, except two 1 lb. tins of turnips, and for three days they had nothing else to subsist upon. That on the fourth day they caught a small turtle, upon which they subsisted for a few days, and this was the only food they had up to the twentieth day when the act now in question was committed. That on the twelfth day the remains of the turtle were entirely consumed, and for the next eight days they had nothing to eat. That they had no fresh water, except such rain as they from time to time caught in their oilskin capes. That the boat was drifting on the ocean, and was probably more than 1000 miles away from land. That on the eighteenth day, when they had been seven days without food and five without water, the prisoners spoke to Brooks as to what should be done if no succour came, and suggested that some one should be sacrificed to save the rest, but Brooks dissented, and the boy, to whom they were understood to refer, was not consulted. That on the 24th of July, the day before the act now in question, the prisoner Dudley proposed to Stephens and Brooks that lots should be cast who should be put to death to save the rest, but Brooks refused to consent, and it was not put to the boy, and in point of fact there was no drawing of lots. That on that day the prisoners spoke of their having families, and suggested it would be better to kill the boy that their lives should be saved, and Dudley proposed that if there was no vessel in sight by the morrow morning, the boy should be killed. That next day, the 25th of July, no vessel appearing, Dudley told Brooks that he had better go and have a sleep, and made signs to Stephens and Brooks that the boy had better be killed. The prisoner Stephens agreed to the act, but Brooks dissented from it. That the boy was then lying at the bottom of the boat quite helpless, and extremely weakened by famine and by drinking sea water, and unable to make any resistance, nor did he ever assent to his being killed. The prisoner Dudley offered a prayer asking forgiveness for them all if either of them should be tempted to commit a rash act, and that their souls might be saved. That Dudley, with the assent of Stephens, went to the boy, and telling him that his time was come, put a knife into his throat and killed him then and there; that the three men fed upon the body and blood of the boy for four days; that on the fourth day after the act had been committed the boat was picked up by a passing vessel, and the prisoners were rescued, still alive, but in the lowest state of prostration. That they were carried to the port of Falmouth, and committed for trial at Exeter. That if the men had not fed upon the body of the boy they would probably not have survived to be so picked up and rescued, but would within the four days have died of famine. That the boy, being in a much weaker condition, was likely to have died before them. That at the time of the act in question there was no sail in sight, nor any reasonable prospect of relief. That under these circumstances there appeared to the prisoners every probability that unless they then fed or very soon fed upon the boy or one of themselves they would die of starvation. That there was no appreciable chance of saving life except by killing some one for the others to eat. That assuming any necessity to kill anybody, there was no greater necessity for killing the boy than any of the other three men." But whether upon the whole matter by the jurors found the killing of Richard Parker by Dudley and Stephens be felony and murder the jurors are ignorant, and pray the advice of the Court thereupon, and if upon the whole matter the Court shall be of opinion that the killing of Richard Parker be felony and murder, then the jurors say that Dudley and Stephens were each guilty of felony and murder as alleged in the indictment. . . .

Lord COLERIDGE, C.J. The two prisoners, Thomas Dudley and Edwin Stephens, were indicted for the murder of Richard Parker on the high seas. . . . They were tried before my Brother Huddleston . . . and, under the direction of my learned Brother, the jury returned a special verdict, the legal effect of which has been argued before us, and on which we are now to pronounce judgment.

The special verdict as, after certain objections by Mr. Collins to which the Attorney General yielded, it is finally settled before us is as follows. [His Lordship read the special verdict as above set out.] From these facts, stated with the cold precision of a special verdict, it appears sufficiently that the prisoners were subject to terrible temptation, to sufferings which might break down the bodily power of the strongest man, and try the conscience of the best. Other details yet more harrowing, facts still more loathsome and appalling, were presented to the jury, and are to be found recorded in my learned Brother's notes. But nevertheless this is clear, that the prisoners put to death a weak and unoffending boy upon the chance of preserving their own lives by feeding upon his flesh and blood after he was killed, and with the certainty of depriving *him*, of any possible chance of survival. The verdict finds in terms that "if the men had not fed upon the body of the boy they would *probably* not have survived," and that "the boy being in a much weaker condition was *likely* to have died before them." They might possibly have been picked up next day by a passing ship; they might possibly not have been picked up at all; in either case it is obvious that the killing of the boy would have been an unnecessary and profitless act. It is found by the verdict that the boy was incapable of resistance, and, in fact, made none; and it is not even suggested that his death was due to any violence on his part attempted against, or even so much as feared by, those who killed him. Under these circumstances the jury say that they are ignorant whether those who killed him were guilty of murder, and have referred it to this Court to determine what is the legal consequence which follows from the facts which they have found. . . .

There remains to be considered the real question in the case — whether killing under the circumstances set forth in the verdict be or be not murder. The contention that it could be anything else was, to the minds of us all, both new and strange, and we stopped the Attorney General in his negative argument in order that we might hear what could be said in support of a proposition which appeared to us to be at once dangerous, immoral, and opposed to all legal principle and analogy. . . . First it is said that it follows from various definitions of murder in books of authority, which definitions imply, if they do not state, the doctrine, that in order to save your own life you may lawfully take away the life of another, when that other is neither attempting nor threatening yours, nor is guilty of any illegal act whatever towards you or any one else. But if these definitions be looked at they will not be found to sustain this contention. . . .

[T]he doctrine contended for receives no support from the great authority of Lord Hale. . . . [H]e says that "the necessity which justifies homicide is of two kinds: (1) the necessity which is of a private nature; (2) the necessity which relates to the public justice and safety. The former is that necessity which obligeth a man to his own defence and safeguard. . . . " "As touching the first of these — viz., homicide in defence of, a man's own life, which is usually styled se defendendo." It is not possible to use words more clear to shew that Lord Hale regarded the private necessity which justified, and alone justified, the taking the life of another for the safeguard of one's own to be what is commonly called "self-defence." (Hale's Pleas of the Crown, i. 478.)

But if this could be even doubtful upon Lord Hale's words, Lord Hale himself has made it clear. For in the chapter in which he deals with the exemption created by compulsion or necessity he thus expresses himself: — "If a man be desperately assaulted and in peril of death, and cannot otherwise escape unless, to satisfy his assailant's fury, he will kill an innocent person then present, the fear and actual force will not acquit him of the crime and punishment of murder, if he commit the fact, for he ought rather to die himself than kill an innocent; but if he cannot otherwise save his own life the law permits him in his own defence to kill the assailant, for by the violence of the assault, and the offence committed upon him by the assailant himself, the law of nature, and necessity, hath made him his own protector. . . . " (Hale's Pleas of the Crown, vol. i. 51.). . . .

Now, except for the purpose of testing how far the conservation of a man's own life is in all cases and under all circumstances, an absolute, unqualified, and paramount duty, we exclude from our consideration all the incidents of war. We are dealing with a case of private homicide, not one imposed upon men in the service of their Sovereign and in the defence of their country. Now it is admitted that the deliberate killing of this unoffending and unresisting boy was clearly murder, unless the killing can be justified by some well-recognised excuse admitted by the law. It is further admitted that there was in this case no such excuse, unless the killing was justified by what has been called "necessity." But the temptation to the act which existed here was not what the law has ever called necessity. Nor is this to be regretted. Though law and morality are not the same, and many things may be immoral which are not necessarily illegal, yet the absolute divorce of law from morality would be of fatal consequence; and such divorce would follow if the temptation to murder in this case were to be held by law an absolute defence of it. It is not so. To preserve one's life is generally speaking a duty, but it may be the plainest and the highest duty to sacrifice it. War is full of instances in which it is a man's duty not to live, but to die. The duty, in case of shipwreck, of a captain to his crew, of the crew to the passengers, of soldiers to women and children . . . ; these duties impose on men the moral necessity, not of the preservation, but of the sacrifice of their lives for others from which in no country, least of all, it is to be hoped, in England, will men ever shrink, as indeed, they have not shrunk. It is not correct, therefore, to say that there is any absolute or unqualified necessity to preserve one's life. . . . Who is to be the judge of this sort of necessity? By what measure is the comparative value of lives to be measured? Is it to be strength, or intellect, or what? It is plain that the principle leaves to him who is to profit by it to determine the necessity which will justify him in deliberately taking another's life to save his own. In this case the weakest, the youngest, the most unresisting, was chosen. Was it more necessary to kill him than one of the grown men? The answer must be "No." . . .

There is no safe path for judges to tread but to ascertain the law to the best of their ability and to declare it according to their judgment; and if in any case the law appears to be too severe on individuals, to leave it to the Sovereign to exercise that prerogative of mercy which the Constitution has intrusted to the hands fittest to dispense it.

It must not be supposed that in refusing to admit temptation to be an excuse for crime it is forgotten how terrible the temptation was; how awful the suffering; how hard in such trials to keep the judgment straight and the conduct pure. We are often compelled to set up standards we cannot reach ourselves, and to lay down rules which we could not ourselves satisfy. But a man has no right to declare temptation to be an excuse, though he might himself have yielded to it, nor allow compassion for the criminal to change or weaken in any manner the legal definition of the crime. It is therefore our duty to declare that the prisoners' act in this case was wilful murder, that the facts as stated in the verdict are no legal justification of the homicide; and to say that in our unanimous opinion the prisoners are upon this special verdict guilty of murder.[1] THE COURT then proceeded to pass sentence of death upon the prisoners.[2]

QUESTIONS

1. What does the *Dudley & Stephens* case illustrate about the common law approach to the defense of necessity?

2. Is the situation of being without food and water for an extended period of time unique to shipwrecks of the 1800s? Are you aware of any modern examples of this situation?

3. Is the result in *Dudley and Stephens* too harsh? Is the approach the case takes to necessity too harsh?

4. What does the fact that the sentence of death was later commuted to six months' imprisonment suggest about the purposes behind the sentences in this case?

5. Why did Brooks escape prosecution?

6. Would any of the statutes at the start of the chapter have provided Dudley and Stephens with a necessity defense?

Consider the following comments from historian, A. W. Brian Simpson:

> In effect, all the witnesses to the killing of Richard Parker were defendants. In the contemporary state of the law, it was quite out of the question for them to be required to give their account of what happened or give sworn evidence in court and thereby expose themselves to cross-examination to elicit the facts. . . . It was plain, too, that the defense of necessity would be raised; the legal status of this

---

[1] My brother Grove has furnished me with the following suggestion, too late to be embodied in the judgment but well worth preserving: "If the two accused men were justified in killing Parker, then if not rescued in time, two of the three survivors would be justified in killing the third, and of the two who remained the stronger would be justified in killing the weaker, so that three men might be justifiably killed to give the fourth a chance of survival." —C.

[2] This sentence was afterwards commuted by the Crown to six months' imprisonment.

defense was problematical, and its application might well depend on the precise conditions in the *Mignonette*'s dinghy. Only a witness who had actually been there could speak convincingly about them.

[The prosecutor,] Mr. Danckwerts therefore needed such a witness, and the only candidates were Dudley, Stephens, and Brooks. One of them must appear for the crown, and the obvious choice was Brooks, who was of subordinate status and had taken no active part in the killing.[18]

According to Simpson, records indicate that public opinion strongly supported Dudley and Stephens during much of the pre-trial and trial phase of the case.[19] In explaining the context of the times regarding cannibalism by stranded seafarers, Simpson explains: "[M]aritime survival cannibalism, preceded by the drawing of lots and killing, was a socially accepted practice among seamen until the end of the days of sail. . . . "[20] "In spite of the frequent occurrence of survival cannibalism, often preceded by deliberate killing, and the abundant evidence of a nautical custom legitimating the practice of killing under necessity, the survivors of the *Mignonette* have always been regarded as the first and indeed only individuals who have ever faced trial for murder for a killing committed in such circumstances."[21] Simpson suggests that British authorities had been seeking a case "to bring the custom of the sea before a court of law for condemnation"[22] for some time.

PROBLEM

8.18 The elements of a necessity defense vary. Compare the elements as enumerated below from the Ohio case of *Spingola*[23] with the statutes that appear at the start of this chapter:

> (1) [T]he harm must be committed under the pressure of physical or natural force, rather than human force; (2) the harm sought to be avoided is greater than, or at least equal to that sought to be prevented by the law defining the offense charged; (3) the actor reasonably believes at that moment that his act is necessary and is designed to avoid the greater harm; (4) the actor must be without fault in bringing about the situation; and (5) the harm threatened must be imminent, leaving no alternative by which to avoid the greater harm.

---

3. Civil Disobedience

Defendants have raised the necessity defense in a host of contexts. Two common ones are civil disobedience and prison escapes. The *Schoon* case that follows deals with civil disobedience.

---

18. *Supra* note 17 at 90.
19. *Id.* at 87.
20. *Id.* at 145.
21. *Id.* at 161.
22. *Id.* at 195.
23. Columbus v. Spingola, 144 Ohio App. 3d 76, 83 (2001).

UNITED STATES *v.* SCHOON
971 F.2d 193 (9th Cir. 1992)

BOOCHEVER, Circuit Judge:

Gregory Schoon, Raymond Kennon, Jr., and Patricia Manning appeal their convictions for obstructing activities of the Internal Revenue Service Office in Tucson, Arizona, and failing to comply with an order of a federal police officer. Both charges stem from their activities in protest of United States involvement in El Salvador. They claim the district court improperly denied them a necessity defense. Because we hold the necessity defense inapplicable in cases like this, we affirm.

I.

On December 4, 1989, thirty people, including appellants, gained admittance to the IRS office in Tucson, where they chanted "keep America's tax dollars out of El Salvador," splashed simulated blood on the counters, walls, and carpeting, and generally obstructed the office's operation. After a federal police officer ordered the group, on several occasions, to disperse or face arrest, appellants were arrested.

At a bench trial, appellants proffered testimony about conditions in El Salvador as the motivation for their conduct. They attempted to assert a necessity defense, essentially contending that their acts in protest of American involvement in El Salvador were necessary to avoid further bloodshed in that country. While finding appellants motivated solely by humanitarian concerns, the court nonetheless precluded the defense as a matter of law, relying on Ninth Circuit precedent. The sole issue on appeal is the propriety of the court's exclusion of a necessity defense as a matter of law.

II.

A district court may preclude a necessity defense where "the evidence, as described in the defendant's offer of proof, is insufficient as a matter of law to support the proffered defense." *United States v. Dorrell*, 758 F.2d 427, 430 (9th Cir. 1985). To invoke the necessity defense, therefore, the defendants colorably must have shown that: (1) they were faced with a choice of evils and chose the lesser evil; (2) they acted to prevent imminent harm; (3) they reasonably anticipated a direct causal relationship between their conduct and the harm to be averted; and (4) they had no legal alternatives to violating the law. *U.S. v. Aguilar*, 883 F.2d 662, 693 (9th Cir. 1989), cert. denied. We review *de novo* the district court's decision to bar a necessity defense.

The district court denied the necessity defense on the grounds that (1) the requisite immediacy was lacking; (2) the actions taken would not abate the evil; and (3) other legal alternatives existed. Because the threshold test for admissibility of a necessity defense is a conjunctive one, a court may preclude invocation of the defense if "proof is deficient with regard to any of the four elements." *Id.* ·

While we could affirm substantially on those grounds relied upon by the district court, we find a deeper, systemic reason for the complete absence of federal case law recognizing a necessity defense in an indirect civil disobedience case. As used in this opinion, "civil disobedience" is the wilful violation of a law, undertaken for the purpose of social or political protest. . . . Indirect civil disobedience involves violating a law or interfering with a government policy that is not, itself, the object of protest. Direct civil disobedience, on the other hand, involves protesting the existence of a law by breaking that law or by preventing the execution of that law in a specific instance in which a particularized harm would otherwise follow. This case involves indirect civil disobedience because these protestors were not challenging the laws under which they were charged. In contrast, the civil rights lunch counter sit-ins, for example, constituted direct civil disobedience because the protestors were challenging the rule that prevented them from sitting at lunch counters. Similarly, if a city council passed an ordinance requiring immediate infusion of a suspected carcinogen into the drinking water, physically blocking the delivery of the substance would constitute direct civil disobedience: protestors would be preventing the execution of a law in a specific instance in which a particularized harm — contamination of the water supply — would otherwise follow.

While our prior cases consistently have found the elements of the necessity defense lacking in cases involving indirect civil disobedience, we have never addressed specifically whether the defense is available in cases of indirect civil disobedience. Indeed, some other courts have appeared doubtful. Today, we conclude, for the reasons stated below, that the necessity defense is inapplicable to cases involving indirect civil disobedience.

III.

Necessity is, essentially, a utilitarian defense. It therefore justifies criminal acts taken to avert a greater harm, maximizing social welfare by allowing a crime to be committed where the social benefits of the crime outweigh the social costs of failing to commit the crime. Pursuant to the defense, prisoners could escape a burning prison, a person lost in the woods could steal food from a cabin to survive; an embargo could be violated because adverse weather conditions necessitated sale of the cargo at a foreign port; a crew could mutiny where their ship was thought to be unseaworthy; and property could be destroyed to prevent the spread of fire.

What all the traditional necessity cases have in common is that the commission of the "crime" averted the occurrence of an even greater "harm." In some sense, the necessity defense allows us to act as individual legislatures, amending a particular criminal provision or crafting a one-time exception to it, subject to court review, when a real legislature would formally do the same under those circumstances. For example, by allowing prisoners who escape a burning jail to claim the justification of necessity, we assume the lawmaker, confronting this problem, would have allowed for an exception to the law proscribing prison escapes.

Because the necessity doctrine is utilitarian, however, strict requirements contain its exercise so as to prevent nonbeneficial criminal conduct. For example, " 'if the criminal act cannot abate the threatened harm, society receives no benefit from the criminal conduct.' " *Applying the Necessity Defense*, 64 N.Y.U. L. Rev. at 102 (quoting *United States v. Gant*, 691 F.2d 1159, 1164 (5th Cir. 1982)). Similarly, to forgive a crime taken to avert a lesser harm would fail to maximize social utility. The cost of the crime would outweigh the harm averted by its commission. Likewise, criminal acts cannot be condoned to thwart threats, yet to be imminent, or those for which there are legal alternatives to abate the harm.

Analysis of three of the necessity defense's four elements leads us to the conclusion that necessity can never be proved in a case of indirect civil disobedience. We do not rely upon the imminent harm prong of the defense because we believe there can be indirect civil disobedience cases in which the protested harm is imminent.

A.

1. Balance of Harms

It is axiomatic that, if the thing to be averted is not a harm at all, the balance of harms necessarily would disfavor any criminal action. Indirect civil disobedience seeks first and foremost to bring about the repeal of a law or a change of governmental policy, attempting to mobilize public opinion through typically symbolic action. These protestors violate a law, not because it is unconstitutional or otherwise improper, but because doing so calls public attention to their objectives. Thus, the most immediate "harm" this form of protest targets is the *existence* of the law or policy. However, the mere existence of a constitutional law or governmental policy cannot constitute a legally cognizable harm. *See* Comment, *Political Protest and the Illinois Defense of Necessity*, 54 U. Chi. L. Rev. 1070, 1083 (1987) ("In a society based on democratic decision making, this is how values are ranked — a protester cannot simply assert that her view of what is best should trump the decision of the majority of elected representatives."). . . .

The protest in this case was in the form of indirect civil disobedience, aimed at reversal of the government's El Salvador policy. That policy does not violate the Constitution, and appellants have never suggested as much. There is no evidence that the procedure by which the policy was adopted was in any way improper; nor is there any evidence that appellants were prevented systematically from participating in the democratic processes through which the policy was chosen. The most immediate harm the appellants sought to avert was the existence of the government's El Salvador policy, which is not in itself a legally cognizable harm. Moreover, any harms resulting from the operation of this policy are insufficiently concrete to be legally cognizable as harms for purposes of the necessity defense.

Thus, as a matter of law, the mere existence of a policy or law validly enacted by Congress cannot constitute a cognizable harm. If there is no cognizable harm to prevent, the harm resulting from criminal action taken for the purpose of securing the repeal of the law or policy necessarily outweighs any benefit of the action.

2. Causal Relationship Between Criminal Conduct and Harm to Be Averted

This inquiry requires a court to judge the likelihood that an alleged harm will be abated by the taking of illegal action. In the sense that the likelihood of abatement is required in the traditional necessity cases, there will never be such likelihood in cases of indirect political protest. In the traditional cases, a prisoner flees a burning cell and averts death, or someone demolishes a home to create a firebreak and prevents the conflagration of an entire community. The nexus between the act undertaken and the result sought is a close one. Ordinarily it is the volitional illegal act alone which, once taken, abates the evil.

In political necessity cases involving indirect civil disobedience against congressional acts, however, the act alone is unlikely to abate the evil precisely because the action is indirect. Here, the IRS obstruction, or the refusal to comply with a federal officer's order, are unlikely to abate the killings in El Salvador, or immediately change Congress's policy; instead, it takes another *volitional* actor not controlled by the protestor to take a further step; Congress must change its mind.

3. Legal Alternatives

A final reason the necessity defense does not apply to these indirect civil disobedience cases is that legal alternatives will never be deemed exhausted when the harm can be mitigated by congressional action. As noted above, the harm indirect civil disobedience aims to prevent is the continued existence of a law or policy. Because congressional action can *always* mitigate this "harm," lawful political activity to spur such action will always be a legal alternative. On the other hand, we cannot say that this legal alternative will always exist in cases of direct civil disobedience, where protestors act to avert a concrete harm flowing from the operation of the targeted law or policy.

The necessity defense requires the absence of any legal alternative to the contemplated illegal conduct which could reasonably be expected to abate an imminent evil. A prisoner fleeing a burning jail, for example, would not be asked to wait in his cell because someone might conceivably save him; such a legal alternative is ill-suited to avoiding death in a fire. In other words, the law implies a reasonableness requirement in judging whether legal alternatives exist.

Where the targeted harm is the existence of a law or policy, our precedents counsel that this reasonableness requirement is met simply by the possibility of congressional action. For example, in *Dorrell*, [758 F.2d 427 (9th Cir. 1985),] an indirect civil disobedience case involving a trespass on Vandenburg Air Force Base to protest the MX missile program, we rejected Dorrell's claims that legal alternatives, like lobbying Congress, were unavailable because they were futile. . . . Without expressly saying so, *Dorrell* decided that petitioning Congress to change a policy is *always* a legal alternative in such cases, regardless of the likelihood of the plea's success. Thus, indirect civil disobedience can never meet the necessity defense requirement that there be a lack of legal alternatives.

B.

As have courts before us, we could assume, as a threshold matter, that the necessity defense is conceivably available in these cases, but find the elements never satisfied. Such a decision, however, does not come without significant costs. First, the failure of the federal courts to hold explicitly that the necessity defense is unavailable in these cases results in district courts expending unnecessary time and energy trying to square defendants' claims with the strict requirements of the doctrine. Second, such an inquiry oftentimes requires the courts to tread into areas constitutionally committed to other branches of government. For example, in *May*, [622 F.2d 1000 (1980),] which involved trespass on a naval base to protest American nuclear weapons policy, we noted that, "[t]o consider defendants' argument [that trespassing was justified by the nefariousness of the Trident missile] would put us in the position of usurping the functions that the Constitution has given to the Congress and to the President." *May*, 622 F.2d at 1009. Third, holding out the possibility of the defense's applicability sets a trap for the unwary civil disobedient, rather than permitting the individual to undertake a more realistic cost-benefit analysis before deciding whether to break the law in political protest. Fourth, assuming the applicability of the defense in this context may risk its distortion in traditional cases. Finally, some commentators have suggested that the courts have sabotaged the usually low threshold for getting a defense theory before the jury as a means of keeping the necessity defense from the jury.

The real problem here is that litigants are trying to distort to their purposes an age-old common law doctrine meant for a very different set of circumstances. What these cases are really about is gaining notoriety for a cause — the defense allows protestors to get their political grievances discussed in a courtroom. It is precisely this political motive that has left some courts, like the district court in this case, uneasy. Because these attempts to invoke the necessity defense "force the courts to choose among causes they should make legitimate by extending the defense of necessity," *Dorrell*, 758 F.2d at 432, and because the criminal acts, themselves, do not maximize social good, they should be subject to a *per se* rule of exclusion.

Thus, we see the failure of any federal court to recognize a defense of necessity in a case like ours not as coincidental, but rather as the natural consequence of the historic limitation of the doctrine. Indirect protests of congressional policies can never meet all the requirements of the necessity doctrine. Therefore, we hold that the necessity defense is not available in such cases. . . .

Affirmed.

QUESTIONS

What if animal rights protestors free all the animals used for experimentation in a college laboratory, arguing that they were saving the animals from pain and suffering in lab cages and undergoing the process of experimentation? Should these protestors have a necessity defense?

4. Prison Escape

Hawaii Revised Statute § 703-302 (2001) *Choice of Evils*

(1) Conduct which the actor believes to be necessary to avoid an imminent harm or evil to the actor or to another is justifiable provided that:

(a) The harm or evil sought to be avoided by such conduct is greater than that sought to be prevented by the law defining the offense charged; and

(b) Neither the Code nor other law defining the offense provides exceptions or defenses dealing with the specific situation involved; and

(c) A legislative purpose to exclude the justification claimed does not otherwise plainly appear.

(2) When the actor was reckless or negligent in bringing about the situation requiring a choice of harms or evils or in appraising the necessity for the actor's conduct, the justification afforded by this section is unavailable in a prosecution for any offense for which recklessness or negligence, as the case may be, suffices to establish culpability.

(3) In a prosecution for escape . . . the defense available under this section is limited to an affirmative defense consisting of the following elements:

(a) The actor receives a threat, express or implied, of death, substantial bodily injury, or forcible sexual attack;

(b) Complaint to the proper prison authorities is either impossible under the circumstances or there exists a history of futile complaints;

(c) Under the circumstances there is no time or opportunity to resort to the courts;

(d) No force or violence is used against prison personnel or other innocent persons; and

(e) The actor promptly reports to the proper authorities when the actor has attained a position of safety from the immediate threat.

PROBLEM

8.19[24] "On November 5, 1986, Ronald J. McIntosh landed a helicopter on the grounds of the Federal Correctional Institution at Pleasanton ("FCI Pleasanton") in order to effect the escape of his girlfriend, Samantha D. Lopez. Although the escape was initially successful, the two were apprehended ten days later near Sacramento. . . . At 11:15, the helicopter approached FCI Pleasanton. McIntosh [an experienced helicopter pilot] landed the helicopter on the prison athletic field, and Lopez, who had been waiting there for McIntosh, got into it. . . . Lopez and McIntosh defended on the ground that Lopez' escape was necessary because her life had been threatened by prison authorities and was in immediate danger.

According to Lopez, her problems at the prison began in early 1986. At that time, Lopez was a member of the Inmate Council, a group organized to act as liaison between the prisoners and the administration. She also worked in the business office at FCI Pleasanton where she often handled the prison's financial records. Lopez testified that she went to the warden in March 1986 with a long list of prisoner complaints. She claims that the warden responded to her concerns by stating that he did not care about the prisoners' problems and that no one else cared either. Lopez allegedly then told the warden that, while people on the outside might not care about the prisoners' complaints, they would probably be interested in the evidence of misappropriation and mismanagement of funds that she had uncovered while working in the business office. According to Lopez, the warden responded by threatening her life, intimating that she might not live long enough to take her case before the parole board and remarking that 'accidents happen in prisons every day.'

In the months following her interview with the warden, various other prison officials allegedly began to torment and threaten Lopez. Lopez contends that the situation grew so intolerable that she feared her life was in immediate danger and that the only alternative available to her was escape. . . .

[As examples of the threats, Lopez contended that] in December 1985, one prison guard allegedly told Lopez that if she continued to make waves, she was going to 'drown.' That same officer allegedly entered her room in May, told her he ought to slap some sense into her and pushed her to the ground. When the guard learned of her later complaint to an associate warden, Lopez claims he threatened to 'fix' her."

Assume further that Ms. Lopez made efforts to contact her attorney during the period between her escape and her capture.

24. Quoted facts in this Problem are drawn from United States v. Lopez, 885 F.2d 1428, 1431-1432 (9th Cir. 1989).

> The prosecution presented extensive evidence refuting Ms. Lopez's claims. If you assume, however, that Ms. Lopez's claims are true, should she be acquitted under the Hawaii statute above?

QUESTION

The jury instructions in the *Lopez* case read as follows:

"Legal justification" means that an otherwise criminal act may not be punished, if that act was necessary in order to avoid a significantly greater evil. The four elements of Ms. Lopez's necessity defense are:

One, that the threat or threats to Ms. Lopez, and the fear which the threats caused, were immediate, and involved death or serious bodily injury;

Second, that Ms. Lopez['s] fear was well-grounded. This means that Ms. Lopez had a good-faith belief in the imminence and severity of the threat, and that belief must also have been objectively reasonable;

Three, that there was no reasonable and legal opportunity to avoid or escape the threatened harm; and

Four, that Ms. Lopez made a bona fide good-faith effort to surrender to authorities after she reached a position of safety.[25]

Do the elements of the necessity defense in these instructions differ from those in the Hawaii statute?

5. Model Penal Code Treatment of Choice of Evils

Model Penal Code § 3.02 (1985)   *Justification Generally: Choice of Evils*

(1) Conduct which the actor believes to be necessary to avoid a harm or evil to himself or another is justifiable, provided that:

(a) the harm or evil sought to be avoided by such conduct is greater than that sought to be prevented by the law defining the offense charged; and

(b) neither the Code nor other law defining the offense provides exceptions or defenses dealing with the specific situation involved; and

(c) a legislative purpose to exclude the justification claimed does not otherwise plainly appear.

(2) When the actor was reckless or negligent in bringing about the situation requiring a choice of harms or evils or in appraising the necessity for his conduct, the justification afforded by this Section is unavailable in a prosecution for any offense for which recklessness or negligence, as the case may be, suffices to establish culpability.

QUESTIONS

1. What do you see as the advantages of the MPC approach to necessity? What are its limitations?

2. Which statute at the start of the Necessity Section reflects the MPC treatment of necessity?

---

25. *Lopez*, 885 F.2d 1428, 1433.

PROBLEMS

8.20 Doctors are able to recover a viable liver from a recently deceased individual. The liver is needed for a patient on the transplant list in a hospital in a nearby city. As soon as the recipient hospital hears that a liver is available, they begin preparing the recipient patient for surgery. An ambulance from the donor hospital begins the journey of 50 miles, with the liver packed for transportation. The ambulance turns on its lights and travels at 100 miles an hour in a posted 70 mile an hour zone. Just before it reaches the recipient hospital, the local police pull the ambulance over and charge the driver with a speeding violation.

Assume that the speeding statute reads as follows: "It is unlawful to exceed the posted speed limit. This section does not apply to law enforcement vehicles. Nor does it apply to fire trucks when they are proceeding to the scene of an emergency. Nor does this section apply to ambulances that are proceeding to the scene of an accident or carrying a patient to the hospital."[26]

You represent the ambulance driver. What arguments would you make on the driver's behalf? How would your arguments change, if, unlike the situation in the real case on which the Problem is based, the ambulance driver had caused an accident in which someone was injured? What if the accident caused someone's death?

8.21 In the summer of 2003, a pizza deliveryman delivered pizza to a remote location. Shortly thereafter, he entered a bank with a bulge under his t-shirt and presented a note demanding cash. The teller gave him the cash. Shortly thereafter, the police arrested him. The bulge turned out to be a bomb that the deliveryman begged police to remove.[27] In the real case, the bomb detonated and killed the deliveryman. Imagine instead that the deliveryman had survived the detonation and further that shortly before the bank robbery, he had delivered pizza to would-be bank robbers who had attached the bomb to his chest and told him to rob the bank or they would detonate the bomb. As directed, he completed the robbery and brought the proceeds to the would-be bank robbers, who removed the bomb. Subsequently, the government prosecuted the pizza deliveryman. As his attorney, what arguments would you raise in his defense?

---

26. This Problem is adapted from news accounts reporting a case in England in 2003 in which an ambulance driver was cited for speeding while carrying a liver from a hospital in Leeds to one in Cambridge for a transplant operation.
Associated Press, Star Tribune, *Ambulance driver charged with speeding while delivering liver*, http://www.startribune.com/viewers/story.php?template=print_a&story=39308 23 (accessed June 16, 2003); itv.com news, *Speeding charge for ambulance*, http://www.itv.com/news/38417.html (accessed June 16, 2003).
27. *See* CBS Evening News, *Forced to Become Human Bomb?* (accessed Sept. 1, 2003) http://www.cbsnews.com/stories/2003/09/01/eveningnews/main57 (accessed July 20, 2004).

D. DURESS

1. Introduction

"The defense of duress ... serves to excuse behavior where extrinsic circumstances compel a person to perform unlawful acts which he did not otherwise wish to do."[28] In a classic example of duress, a stranger holds a gun to an actor's temple and threatens the actor with instant death if the actor does not commit a crime — for example, a battery by hitting an innocent third party. The actor must choose between the risk that the stranger will carry out the threat and committing the crime of battery. If the actor chooses to strike the innocent third party, all the elements of the crime of battery will be fulfilled. The actor here makes a reluctant but conscious decision and corresponding physical movement to strike another. She therefore has done a voluntary act. In addition, assume battery requires no more mental state than a purpose to do the act with knowledge that the act is likely to cause the offensive physical contact with the third party. Consequently, with both the conduct and mental state elements satisfied, absent the duress defense, the actor would be guilty of battery.[29]

The argument in favor of this excuse defense is that "[t]here is no just reason to impose criminal sanctions, or try to reform a man, because he committed unlawful acts which anyone else, given the circumstances, would also have committed."[30] The theories of punishment we have studied fail to justify punishment here. Retributivism fails, as there is little to suggest moral blameworthiness in the actor's response to the threat. Similarly, when the actor's plight meets the requirements of the defense, she has, in society's cost-benefit calculus, chosen an acceptable response, one we would not wish to deter her or someone else from choosing. Nor do incapacitation, rehabilitation, or denunciation seem appropriate responses. We would be removing the actor from society, trying to alter her response, or publicly denouncing her to prevent her from engaging in conduct that society finds acceptable and no different from what we would expect from others similarly situated.

Because courts and legislators have usually treated duress as an excuse rather than a justification, they often place a burden on the defense to raise a reasonable doubt, to produce evidence, or to prove duress by a preponderance of evidence. Duress and necessity share a number of characteristics. Consequently, some jurisdictions treat them as overlapping defenses. Others consider them distinct.

In this Section we begin by studying a group of statutes that define the defense of duress. Using a series of four Problems, we analyze the similarities and differences among various statutory treatments of this defense. Following the Problems, we consider the *Contento-Pachon* case, which explores both the elements of duress and one court's view of the differences between duress and necessity.

---

28. Working Papers of The National Commission on Reform of Federal Criminal Laws, Vol. 1, 273 (U.S. Gov. Printing Office 1970).
29. *Id.*
30. *Id.*

Oregon Revised Statute Annotated § 161.270 (2001)   *Duress*

(1) The commission of acts which would otherwise constitute an offense, other than murder, is not criminal if the actor engaged in the proscribed conduct because the actor was coerced to do so by the use or threatened use of unlawful physical force upon the actor or a third person, which force or threatened force was of such nature or degree to overcome earnest resistance.

(2) Duress is not a defense for one who intentionally or recklessly places oneself in a situation in which it is probable that one will be subjected to duress.

Arizona Revised Statute § 13-412 (2002)   *Duress*

A. Conduct which would otherwise constitute an offense is justified if a reasonable person would believe that he was compelled to engage in the proscribed conduct by the threat or use of immediate physical force against his person or the person of another which resulted or could result in serious physical injury which a reasonable person in the situation would not have resisted.

B. The defense provided by subsection A is unavailable if the person intentionally, knowingly or recklessly placed himself in a situation in which it was probable that he would be subjected to duress.

C. The defense provided by subsection A is unavailable for offenses involving homicide or serious physical injury.

Washington Revised Code § 9A.16.060 (2000)   *Duress*

(1) In any prosecution for a crime, it is a defense that:

(a) The actor participated in the crime under compulsion by another who by threat or use of force created an apprehension in the mind of the actor that in case of refusal he or she or another would be liable to immediate death or immediate grievous bodily injury; and

(b) That such apprehension was reasonable upon the part of the actor; and

(c) That the actor would not have participated in the crime except for the duress involved.

(2) The defense of duress is not available if the crime charged is murder, manslaughter, or homicide by abuse.

(3) The defense of duress is not available if the actor intentionally or recklessly places himself or herself in a situation in which it is probable that he or she will be subject to duress.

(4) The defense of duress is not established solely by showing that a married person acted on the command of his or her spouse.

Model Penal Code § 2.09 (1985)   *Duress*

(1) It is an affirmative defense that the actor engaged in the conduct charged to constitute an offense because he was coerced to do so by the use of, or a threat to use, unlawful force against his person or the person of another, that a person of reasonable firmness in his situation would have been unable to resist.

(2) The defense provided by this Section is unavailable if the actor recklessly placed himself in a situation in which it was probable that he would be subjected to duress. The defense is also unavailable if he was negligent in placing himself in

such a situation, whenever negligence suffices to establish culpability for the offense charged.

PROBLEMS

8.22 The 18-year old defendant had worked at Floyd Culver's garage and become acquainted with both Mr. & Mrs. Culver. One night, according to the defendant, Mrs. Culver, a woman of 45, "came in an automobile [to the park where the defendant was located] and asked him to go down town with her. While driving along she told him that she wanted him to break into the filling station. She also drew a pistol and told him that if he did not do so she would kill him. She had the pistol on him until the automobile stopped across the street. She then got out of the car and followed him to the station and kept the pistol pointed at him until he broke into the station. He did not want to break in, but was afraid of [Mrs.] Culver. . . . The mother of the [defendant] testified that after her son was arrested [Mrs.] Culver came to her home and told her that it was all her fault, that she had told her son that if he did not break into the building she would blow his brains out, and showed [the] witness the gun she had used. [The defendant's mother] was corroborated by her daughter, who claims to have been present when the conversation occurred."[31] Should the defendant be excused on the basis of duress?

8.23 Defendant, a taxi driver, was hired by several men to transport them to the country at the rate of $3 per hour on September 16, 1919. He was unaware of the nature of their business in the country. At a farm house five miles outside Grand Rapids, the men informed defendant that they were proceeding on to Grand Rapids to commit some crime, which he later learned was a bank robbery. From the time the men disclosed their intentions, the defendant was in

> actual present fear of his immediate death by their use of revolvers which they had in their possession, and which at times they held at his head; that from the moment of disclosure until after the robbery of the bank he was at all times under the control of one or more of [the men]; and that he believed if he made any attempt whatever to escape, . . . he would pay for the same by his death; that said [men] told him after leaving said farm house that he might as well make up his mind, if he hoped to live to return to his wife, to obey orders . . . that after the robbery he was ordered by one of the robbers to drive on certain roads . . . , where the said robbers left him, and for the first time defendant was free to act; that he thereupon returned to his home in Detroit with his car, and, after telling his wife what had happened, went to the police headquarters in Detroit and informed the officials of the facts, and delivered over to them intact the money that he received for his services, which was much less than had been

---

31. Based on and quotation from *Nall v. Commonwealth*, 208 Ky. 700, 701-702 (1925).

agreed upon. . . . Defendant was charged with robbery for driving the getaway car.[32]

Should defendant be acquitted on the basis of duress?

8.24 The victim, a 14-year-old, discussed selling drugs for LaMacey Woods. Woods gave the victim $80 worth of crack cocaine to sell, which the victim did sell and then provided the proceeds to Woods. The victim was subsequently subjected to torture by several individuals, including the defendant, Sedrick Scott. Woods told Scott to hit the victim and Scott did. "At Woods' direction, Scott tied [the victim's] hands behind his back" and the beating and kicking of the victim continued, although Scott was not a direct perpetrator. Scott took off the victim's shirt and told the victim to lie on his back. Upon Woods' instructions, Scott told the victim to turn over and Woods then burned the victim's back with a clothes iron. "Scott cut [the victim's] arm with a razor blade." Scott then took a more passive role, observing the remaining members of "the family" torturing the victim during what appeared to be an initiation process into the Crips gang. "Woods [then] told Scott that the victim was now Scott's 'man' or 'shadow.' [The victim] was directed to do whatever Scott told him to do." Scott took the victim to a club where he bought the victim something to eat and drink. Scott then disappeared and the victim went home and to the hospital. The victim did not disclose the source of his injuries. The victim subsequently went to Woods' house to look for Scott. Several days later, the victim was at a club and Scott arrived and put a gun to the victim's "side, and told the victim that Woods was waiting for him outside." Woods had sent Scott into the club to summon the victim. Several men including Scott went in the car with the victim. According to the victim, nothing prevented Scott from shooting Woods at that time. They arrived at Woods' house and Woods told everyone to wait in the car. Again, according to the victim, nothing prevented Scott from leaving. Woods returned and everyone got out. Another man beat the victim with a pole. Inside the house, Woods told the victim that "they were going to kill him this time." When Woods was not in the room, Scott tied the victim's hands behind his back and ripped off the victim's shirt. "Woods returned with a clothes iron and burned [the victim] on his chest and stomach. [Another] man stabbed [the victim] with a knife. Woods shocked [the victim] with the extension cord device. Scott was '[j]ust standing around watching.'" At one point, Woods "returned with a .38 revolver and played Russian roulette with [the victim]. Woods pulled the trigger four or five times with the weapon pointed at [the victim's] head and then fired the final bullet into the floor. [The victim explained] . . . that Scott appeared to be frightened of Woods while this was happening." Eventually, the victim was forced to disrobe and locked in a car trunk. Scott later checked on the victim "to see if he was okay." After learning that the victim was cold, Scott subsequently brought food and clothing.

32. Based on and quotations from People v. Merhige, 212 Mich. 601 (1920).

The victim described Scott as "concerned and . . . the only one trying to help him." Ultimately, the victim was taken to a motel by Woods and when no one arrived to pick him up, he called a family member who took him to the hospital where he spent six days. In describing his captivity, the victim explained that "Woods told people what to do and that he punished people who did not act accordingly." Recruits and gang members "were not allowed to see their own families." Scott contends that "he held essentially the same position in the Insanes or Crips organization" as the victim, except that Scott "was already a member of the group, whereas [the victim] was still in the recruitment state."[33] Should Scott be acquitted of the charges of kidnapping and assault on the grounds of duress?

8.25 "Defendant and Ms. Wynashe were inmates of the California Rehabilitation Center. They departed from that institution and were promptly captured in a hayfield a few yards away. . . .

"They had been in the institution about two and one-half months and during that time they had been threatened continuously by a group of lesbian inmates who told them they were to perform lesbian acts. . . . [T]hey complained to the authorities several times but nothing was done about their complaints. On the day of the escape, 10 or 15 of these lesbian inmates approached them and again offered them the alternative [to engage in sexual acts or fight]. This time there was a fight. . . . After the fight, Ms. Wynashe and defendant were told by this group of lesbians that they 'would see the group again.' At this point, both defendant and Ms. Wynashe feared for their lives. Ms. Wynashe was additionally motivated by a protective attitude toward [the defendant,] who had the intelligence of a 12-year old. It was represented that a psychiatrist would testify as to defendant's mental capacity. On the basis of what had occurred, the threats made, the fact that officials had not done anything for their protection, Ms. Wynashe and defendant felt they had no choice but to leave the institution in order to save themselves."[34]

Should the defendant be acquitted on the grounds of duress?

2. The *Contento-Pachon* Case

UNITED STATES *v.* CONTENTO-PACHON

723 F.2d 691 (9th Cir. 1984)

BOOCHEVER, Circuit Judge. This case presents an appeal from a conviction for unlawful possession with intent to distribute a narcotic controlled substance in

---

33. This Problem is based on and quotations are from State v. Scott, 250 Kan. 350, 352, 353, 354, 355, 359 (1992).

34. Quoted from People v. Lovercamp, 43 Cal. App. 3d 823, 825 (1974).

violation of 21 U.S.C. § 841(a)(1) (1976). At trial, the defendant attempted to offer evidence of duress and necessity defenses. The district court excluded this evidence on the ground that it was insufficient to support the defenses. We reverse because there was sufficient evidence of duress to present a triable issue of fact.

I. FACTS

The defendant-appellant, Juan Manuel Contento-Pachon, is a native of Bogota, Colombia and was employed there as a taxicab driver. He asserts that one of his passengers, Jorge, offered him a job as the driver of a privately-owned car. Contento-Pachon expressed an interest in the job and agreed to meet Jorge and the owner of the car the next day.

Instead of a driving job, Jorge proposed that Contento-Pachon swallow cocaine-filled balloons and transport them to the United States. Contento-Pachon agreed to consider the proposition. He was told not to mention the proposition to anyone, otherwise he would "get into serious trouble." Contento-Pachon testified that he did not contact the police because he believes that the Bogota police are corrupt and that they are paid off by drug traffickers.

Approximately one week later, Contento-Pachon told Jorge that he would not carry the cocaine. In response, Jorge mentioned facts about Contento-Pachon's personal life, including private details which Contento-Pachon had never mentioned to Jorge. Jorge told Contento-Pachon that his failure to cooperate would result in the death of his wife and three-year-old child.

The following day the pair met again. Contento-Pachon's life and the lives of his family were again threatened. At this point, Contento-Pachon agreed to take the cocaine into the United States.

The pair met two more times. At the last meeting, Contento-Pachon swallowed 129 balloons of cocaine. He was informed that he would be watched at all times during the trip, and that if he failed to follow Jorge's instruction he and his family would be killed.

After leaving Bogota, Contento-Pachon's plane landed in Panama. Contento-Pachon asserts that he did not notify the authorities there because he felt that the Panamanian police were as corrupt as those in Bogota. Also, he felt that any such action on his part would place his family in jeopardy.

When he arrived at the customs inspection point in Los Angeles, Contento-Pachon consented to have his stomach x-rayed. The x-rays revealed a foreign substance which was later determined to be cocaine.

At Contento-Pachon's trial, the government moved to exclude the defenses of duress and necessity. The motion was granted. We reverse.

A. DURESS

There are three elements of the duress defense: (1) an immediate threat of death or serious bodily injury, (2) a well-grounded fear that the threat will be carried out, and (3) no reasonable opportunity to escape the threatened harm. Sometimes a fourth element is required: the defendant must submit to proper authorities after attaining a position of safety.

Factfinding is usually a function of the jury, and the trial court rarely rules on a defense as a matter of law. If the evidence is insufficient as a matter of law to support a duress defense, however, the trial court should exclude that evidence.

The trial court found Contento-Pachon's offer of proof insufficient to support a duress defense because he failed to offer proof of two elements: immediacy and inescapability. We examine the elements of duress.

Immediacy: The element of immediacy requires that there be some evidence that the threat of injury was present, immediate, or impending. "[A] veiled threat of future unspecified harm" will not satisfy this requirement. *Rhode Island Recreation Center v. Aetna Casualty and Surety Co.*, 177 F.2d 603, 605 (1st Cir. 1949). The district court found that the initial threats were not immediate because "they were conditioned on defendant's failure to cooperate in the future and did not place defendant and his family in immediate danger."

Evidence presented on this issue indicated that the defendant was dealing with a man who was deeply involved in the exportation of illegal substances. Large sums of money were at stake and, consequently, Contento-Pachon had reason to believe that Jorge would carry out his threats. Jorge had gone to the trouble to discover that Contento-Pachon was married, that he had a child, the names of his wife and child, and the location of his residence. These were not vague threats of possible future harm. According to the defendant, if he had refused to cooperate, the consequences would have been immediate and harsh.

Contento-Pachon contends that he was being watched by one of Jorge's accomplices at all times during the airplane trip. As a consequence, the force of the threats continued to restrain him. Contento-Pachon's contention that he was operating under the threat of immediate harm was supported by sufficient evidence to present a triable issue of fact.

Escapability: The defendant must show that he had no reasonable opportunity to escape. The district court found that because Contento-Pachon was not physically restrained prior to the time he swallowed the balloons, he could have sought help from the police or fled. Contento-Pachon explained that he did not report the threats because he feared that the police were corrupt. The trier of fact should decide whether one in Contento-Pachon's position might believe that some of the Bogota police were paid informants for drug traffickers and that reporting the matter to the police did not represent a reasonable opportunity of escape.

If he chose not to go to the police, Contento-Pachon's alternative was to flee. We reiterate that the opportunity to escape must be reasonable. To flee, Contento-Pachon, along with his wife and three year-old child, would have been forced to pack his possessions, leave his job, and travel to a place beyond the reaches of the drug traffickers. A juror might find that this was not a reasonable avenue of escape. Thus, Contento-Pachon presented a triable issue on the element of escapability.

Surrender to Authorities: As noted above, the duress defense is composed of at least three elements. The government argues that the defense also requires that a defendant offer evidence that he intended to turn himself in to the authorities upon reaching a position of safety. Although it has not been expressly limited, this fourth element seems to be required only in prison escape cases. Under other circumstances, the defense has been defined to include only three elements.

The Supreme Court in *United States v. Bailey*, 444 U.S. 394, 413 (1980), noted that "escape from federal custody . . . is a continuing offense and . . . an escapee can be held liable for failure to return to custody as well as for his initial departure." This factor would not be present in most crimes other than escape.

In cases not involving escape from prison there seems little difference between the third basic requirement that there be no reasonable opportunity to escape the threatened harm and the obligation to turn oneself in to authorities on reaching a point of safety. Once a defendant has reached a position where he can safely turn himself in to the authorities he will likewise have a reasonable opportunity to escape the threatened harm.

That is true in this case. Contento-Pachon claims that he was being watched at all times. According to him, at the first opportunity to cooperate with authorities without alerting the observer, he consented to the x-ray. We hold that a defendant who has acted under a well-grounded fear of immediate harm with no opportunity to escape may assert the duress defense, if there is a triable issue of fact whether he took the opportunity to escape the threatened harm by submitting to authorities at the first reasonable opportunity.

B. Necessity

The defense of necessity is available when a person is faced with a choice of two evils and must then decide whether to commit a crime or an alternative act that constitutes a greater evil. Contento-Pachon has attempted to justify his violation of 21 U.S.C. § 841(a)(1) by showing that the alternative, the death of his family, was a greater evil.

Traditionally, in order for the necessity defense to apply, the coercion must have had its source in the physical forces of nature. The duress defense was applicable when the defendant's acts were coerced by a human force. W. LaFave & A. Scott, *Handbook on Criminal Law* § 50 at 383 (1972). This distinction served to separate the two similar defenses. But modern courts have tended to blur the distinction between duress and necessity. . . .

The defense of necessity is usually invoked when the defendant acted in the interest of the general welfare. For example, defendants have asserted the defense as a justification for (1) bringing laetrile into the United States for the treatment of cancer patients, (2) unlawfully entering a naval base to protest the Trident missile system, (3) burning Selective Service System records to protest United States military action.

Contento-Pachon's acts were allegedly coerced by human, not physical forces. In addition, he did not act to promote the general welfare. Therefore, the necessity defense was not available to him. Contento-Pachon mischaracterized evidence of duress as evidence of necessity. The district court correctly disallowed his use of the necessity defense.

II. Conclusion

Contento-Pachon presented credible evidence that he acted under an immediate and well-grounded threat of serious bodily injury, with no opportunity to escape. Because the trier of fact should have been allowed to consider the credibility of the proffered evidence, we reverse. The district court correctly excluded Contento-Pachon's necessity defense.

REVERSED and REMANDED.

Coyle, District Judge (dissenting in part and concurring in part):
[I]n its Order the district court stated:

> The first threat made to defendant and his family about three weeks before the flight was not immediate; the threat was conditioned upon defendant's failure to cooperate in the future and did not place the defendant and his family in immediate danger or harm. Moreover, after the initial threat and until he went to the house where he ingested the balloons containing cocaine, defendant and his family were

not physically restrained and could have sought help from the police or fled. No such efforts were attempted by defendant. Thus, defendant's own offer of proof negates two necessary elements of the defense of duress.

In cases where the defendant's duress has been raised, the courts have indicated that the element of immediacy is of crucial importance. The trial court found that the threats made against the defendant and his family lacked the requisite element of immediacy. This finding is adequately supported by the record. The defendant was outside the presence of the drug dealers on numerous occasions for varying lengths of time. There is no evidence that his family was ever directly threatened or even had knowledge of the threats allegedly directed against the defendant.

Moreover, the trial court found that the defendant and his family enjoyed an adequate and reasonable opportunity to avoid or escape the threats of the drug dealers in the weeks before his flight. Until he went to the house where he ingested the balloons containing cocaine, defendant and his family were not physically restrained or prevented from seeking help. The record supports the trial court's findings that the defendant and his family could have sought assistance from the authorities or have fled. Cases considering the defense of duress have established that where there was a reasonable legal alternative to violating the law, a chance to refuse to do the criminal act and also to avoid the threatened danger, the defense will fail. Duress is permitted as a defense only when a criminal act was committed because there was no other opportunity to avoid the threatened danger.

QUESTIONS

1. How should "immediacy" be defined in the context of duress?

2. Would the *Contento-Pachon* case have come out differently if those threatening Contento-Pachon had urged him to commit robbery? How about kidnapping a child?

3. If no one had been on the airplane watching Contento-Pachon, would the immediacy criterion have been satisfied?

E. INSANITY AND MENTAL ILLNESS

1. Introduction

Mental illness is an important issue in the criminal justice system. Some research suggests that defendants in a substantial portion of criminal cases suffer from some form of mental illness.[35]

---

35. One scholar describes the situation and some of the studies as follows:

> The prevalence of mental disorders among persons with criminal justice involvement is staggering. Each year about 700,000 adults with serious mental illness come into contact with the criminal justice system. Justice Department statistics indicate that sixteen percent of jail and prison inmates have a serious mental illness but these estimates rise to 35% when they include less serious disorders. . . . Indeed, a recent study in Michigan found that 31% of its prison population required psychiatric care. The largest study to date, sampling 3,332 inmates

Although mental illness may be part of the subtext in many cases, formal recognition of mental illness in criminal cases generally falls under three rubrics: (1) insanity, (2) effect on required mental state (diminished capacity), and (3) incompetence. Insanity and diminished capacity, as used here, relate to the defendant's mental state at the time of the offense.[36] For competence, we look instead at the defendant's mental condition and ability to understand the criminal proceedings. Before turning to the focal point of this section, insanity, we briefly describe and contrast insanity, diminished capacity, and competence.

Of the three, insanity is perhaps the most widely known. In a criminal case, the presumption is that the defendant was sane at the time of the commission of the act. As a result, the law commonly treats insanity as an affirmative defense. Even if the defendant succeeds and the fact finder declares the defendant not guilty by reason of insanity, this insanity acquittal, unlike other acquittals, does not necessarily result in release. Instead, courts regularly commit defendants for evaluation and treatment of the underlying mental illness. The court may ultimately commit a defendant to a mental institution for a longer period of time than he would have served had the defendant been convicted and sentenced.

The insanity defense has provoked substantial controversy over the course of its existence. It appears to be raised, however, in only a small percentage of cases. According to one multi-jurisdictional study, "the insanity defense was raised in approximately one percent of all felony cases."[37] Of these, the study indicates that only 26 percent were successful.[38]

The criminal justice system also sometimes recognizes the impact of mental illness on the defendant's capacity to entertain the required mental state for the crime.[39] For example, theft requires that the defendant believe that the property taken belongs to another. If a defendant's mental illness makes him incapable of understanding that the property belongs to someone else, the defendant would lack

---

in New York prisons, found that 80% had severe disorders requiring treatment and another 16% had mental disorders requiring periodic mental health services.

Richard E. Redding, *Why It Is Essential to Teach About Mental Health Issues in Criminal Law (And a Primer on How To Do It)*, 14 Wash. U. J.L. & Pol'y 407, 408-409 (2004).

36. Courts sometimes use the term "insanity" interchangeably with "competency" when describing issues of competence, *e.g.*, competence to be executed. (*See, e.g.*, Ford v. Wainwright, 477 U.S. 399, 410 n.2 (1986)). For purposes of clarity in this chapter, we use the term "competency" to refer to any assessment or description of the defendant's mental condition during a stage of the criminal proceedings. This approach reflects the influence of a guide for mental health professionals and lawyers. Gary B. Melton et al., *Psychological Evaluations for the Courts*, 182 (1997).

37. Lisa A. Callahan et al., *The Volume and Characteristics of Insanity Defense Pleas: An Eight-State Study*, 19 Bull. Am. Acad. Psych. & Law, 331, 334 (1991).

38. *Id.*

39. Some jurisdictions distinguish between the defendant's capacity to entertain the required mental state ("diminished capacity") and her actually having possessed the required mental state at the time of the offense ("diminished actuality"). In jurisdictions that do not recognize diminished capacity but do recognize diminished actuality, instead of asking whether the defendant had the capacity to entertain the mental state, the question becomes whether, as a result of the mental illness, the circumstances demonstrate that the defendant in fact lacked the mental state at the time of the offense. California Penal Code § 28 provides a statutory example of how a jurisdiction may draw the distinction:

California Penal Code § 28 (2003). *Mental Disease.*

(a) Evidence of mental disease, mental defect, or mental disorder shall not be admitted to show or negate the capacity to form any mental state, including, but not limited to, purpose, intent, knowledge, premeditation, deliberation, or malice aforethought, with which the accused committed the act. Evidence of mental disease . . . is admissible solely on the issue of whether or not the accused actually formed a required specific intent, premeditated, deliberated, or harbored malice aforethought, when a specific intent crime is charged.

E. Insanity and Mental Illness 555 on>egment>

the mental state required for the crime. Courts and commentators sometimes refer to this as "diminished capacity."[40] Instead of serving as a true affirmative defense, the mental illness affects evaluation of whether the prosecution has proven the requisite mental state for one or more of the charges.[41] Both insanity and diminished capacity involve an evaluation of the defendant's state of mind at the time of the offense.

Competence relates to the defendant's ability to understand the proceedings and assist in the defense. The question of competence may arise at many points in a criminal case. It focuses on a different period of time than insanity. Competence deals with the defendant's ability to understand the legal proceedings at the time they occur. Unlike insanity, lack of competence is not a defense. While insanity can extinguish liability, lack of competence bars prosecution while the defendant is incompetent. A court may delay or suspend criminal proceedings while the defendant is incompetent. If a court has suspended proceedings due to the defendant's incompetence, proceedings can resume if the defendant (re)gains competence and is able to understand the criminal proceedings. Tests for determining competence vary, depending on the stage of the proceedings.[42] Recent competency litigation has revolved around the state's ability to medicate defendants against their will in order to return them to competence and continue legal proceedings against them, including execution.[43]

Almost all criminal codes in the United States have provisions on insanity and competence. Fewer jurisdictions permit mental illness evidence to be introduced under a diminished capacity theory.

The next Section reviews one state's struggle to select a definition of insanity. A series of opinions reflect the evolution of the state's insanity law. Following those opinions, we focus on a quandary in the law of insanity. To qualify as insane, must the individual lack knowledge that her conduct is *morally* wrong? Or must she lack knowledge that her conduct is *legally* wrong? The Section then proceeds to canvass several of the most common legal definitions of insanity and presents a set of Problems to which those definitions can be applied. We then focus on the rationales for and critiques of an insanity defense. Before the final synthesis and review material, we consider briefly two applications of the insanity defense in recent decades, post-traumatic stress disorder and postpartum psychosis.

2. Case Study: One State's Struggle to Choose an Insanity Test

Over the past centuries, English and American courts and commentators have developed several definitions of "insanity." Perhaps the most famous and widely used is the *M'Naghten* test, to which the English House of Lords gave its imprimatur in 1843. The Model Penal Code standard, developed by experts under the auspices of the American Law Institute (ALI), represents another highly influential test. Both of these tests are discussed in the following opinion.

---

40. For a discussion of the related doctrine of "partial responsibility," *see* Wayne LaFave, *Criminal Law* 451-460 (4th ed. 2003).

41. For an analysis of the implications of a diminished-capacity approach, *see* State v. Wilcox, 70 Ohio St. 2d 182 (Sup. Ct. Ohio 1982).

42. Melton, et al., *supra* note 36, at 119-185.

43. *See, e.g.*, Singelton v. Norris, 319 F.3d 1018 (2003).

PEOPLE *v.* DREW

Supreme Court of California 22 Cal. 3d 333 (1978)

TOBRINER, J. — For over a century California has followed the M'Naghten[1] test to define the defenses of insanity and idiocy. The deficiencies of that test have long been apparent, and judicial attempts to reinterpret or evade the limitations of M'Naghten have proven inadequate. We shall explain why we have concluded that we should discard the M'Naghten language, and update the California test of mental incapacity as a criminal defense by adopting the test proposed by the American Law Institute. . . .

The purpose of a legal test for insanity is to identify those persons who, owing to mental incapacity, should not be held criminally responsible for their conduct. The criminal law rests on a postulate of free will — that all persons of sound mind are presumed capable of conforming their behavior to legal requirements and that when any such person freely chooses to violate the law, he may justly be held responsible. From the earliest days of the common law, however, the courts have recognized that a few [categories of] persons lack the mental capacity to conform to the strictures of the law. . . . The principle that mental incapacity constitutes a defense to crime is today accepted in all American jurisdictions.

The California Penal Code codifies the defense of mental incapacity. . . . [S]ection 26 specifies that "All persons are capable of committing crimes except those belonging to the following classes" and includes among those classes "Idiots" and "Lunatics"* and "insane persons."

Although the Legislature has thus provided that "insanity" is a defense to a criminal charge, it has never attempted to define that term. The task of describing the circumstances under which mental incapacity will relieve a defendant of criminal responsibility has become the duty of the judiciary.

Since *People v. Coffman* (1864) 24 Cal. 230, 235, the California courts have followed the M'Naghten rule to define the defense of insanity. The curious origin of the M'Naghten rule has been frequently recounted. In 1843 Daniel M'Naghten, afflicted with paranoia, attempted to assassinate the Prime Minister of England, and succeeded in killing the Prime Minister's secretary. M'Naghten's acquittal on grounds of insanity so disturbed Queen Victoria that she summoned the House of Lords to obtain the opinion of the judges on the law of insanity. The 15 judges of the common law courts were called in an extraordinary session, "under a not subtle atmosphere of pressure" to answer five hypothetical questions on the law of criminal responsibility.

In response to two of the questions propounded the judges stated that "to establish a defence on the ground of insanity, it must be clearly proved that, at the time of the committing the act, the party accused was labouring under such a defect of reason, from disease of the mind, as not to know the nature and quality of the act he was doing; or, if he did know it, that he did not know he was doing what was wrong." Although an advisory opinion, and thus most questionable authority, this language became the basis for the test of insanity in all American states except New Hampshire.

---

[1] Daniel M'Naghten was inconsistent in the spelling of his name, and courts and commentators ever since have shared in that inconsistency. We follow the spelling in the Clark and Finnelly report of the M'Naghten case.

* The term "lunatics" . . . probably referred to persons who had lucid intervals; "insane persons" to those who lacked lucid intervals. The cases do not distinguish between the two terms.

Despite its widespread acceptance, the deficiencies of M'Naghten have long been apparent. Principal among these is the test's exclusive focus upon the cognitive capacity of the defendant, an outgrowth of the then current psychological theory under which the mind was divided into separate independent compartments, one of which could be diseased without affecting the others. As explained by Judge Ely of the Ninth Circuit: "The M'Naghten rules fruitlessly attempt to relieve from punishment only those mentally diseased persons who have no cognitive capacity. . . . This formulation does not comport with modern medical knowledge that an individual is a mentally complex being with varying degrees of awareness. It also fails to attack the problem presented in a case wherein an accused may have understood his actions but was incapable of controlling his behavior. Such a person has been allowed to remain a danger to himself and to society whenever, under M'Naghten, he is imprisoned without being afforded such treatment as may produce rehabilitation and is later, potentially recidivistic, released."[7]

M'Naghten's exclusive emphasis on cognition would be of little consequence if all serious mental illness impaired the capacity of the affected person to know the nature and wrongfulness of his action. . . . Current psychiatric opinion, however, holds that mental illness often leaves the individual's intellectual understanding relatively unimpaired, but so affects his emotions or reason that he is unable to prevent himself from committing the act. "[I]nsanity does not only, or primarily, affect the cognitive or intellectual faculties, but affects the whole personality of the patient, including both the will and the emotions. An insane person may therefore often know the nature and quality of his act and that it is wrong and forbidden by law, and yet commit it as a result of the mental disease." (Rep. Royal Com. on Capital Punishment, 1949-1953, p. 80.)

The annals of this court are filled with illustrations of the above statement: the deluded defendant in *People v. Gorshen* who believed he would be possessed by devilish visions unless he killed his foreman; the schizophrenic boy in *People v. Wolff*, who knew that killing his mother was murder but was unable emotionally to control his conduct despite that knowledge; the defendant in *People v. Robles* (1970), suffering from organic brain damage, who mutilated himself and killed others in sudden rages. To ask whether such a person knows or understands that his act is "wrong" is to ask a question irrelevant to the nature of his mental illness or to the degree of his criminal responsibility.

Secondly, "M'Naghten's single track emphasis on the cognitive aspect of the personality recognizes no degrees of incapacity. Either the defendant knows right from wrong or he does not. . . . But such a test is grossly unrealistic. . . . As the commentary to the American Law Institute's Model Penal Code observes, 'The law must recognize that when there is no black and white it must content itself with different shades of gray.' "

In short, M'Naghten purports to channel psychiatric testimony into the narrow issue of cognitive capacity, an issue often unrelated to the defendant's illness or crime. The psychiatrist called as a witness faces a dilemma: either he can restrict his testimony to the confines of M'Naghten, depriving the trier of fact of a full presentation of the defendant's mental state, or he can testify that the defendant cannot tell "right" from "wrong" when that is not really his opinion because by so

---

[7] Numerous other cases and writers have cited M'Naghten's failure to include a volitional element in its test of insanity.

testifying he acquires the opportunity to put before the trier of fact the reality of defendant's mental condition. . . .

Even if the psychiatrist is able to place before the trier of fact a complete picture of the defendant's mental incapacity, that testimony reaches the trier of fact weakened by cross-examination designed to show that defendant knew right from wrong. As a result, conscientious juries have often returned verdicts of sanity despite plain evidence of serious mental illness and unanimous expert testimony that the defendant was insane.

[Over the years, innovative modifications to the M'Naghten rule set forth by California courts have failed] to cure its basic defects. . . .

In our opinion the continuing inadequacy of M'Naghten as a test of criminal responsibility cannot be cured by further attempts to interpret language dating from a different era of psychological thought, nor by the creation of additional concepts designed to evade the limitations of M'Naghten. It is time to recast M'Naghten in modern language, taking account of advances in psychological knowledge and changes in legal thought.

The definition of mental incapacity appearing in section 4.01 of the American Law Institute's Model Penal Code represents the distillation of nine years of research, exploration, and debate by the leading legal and medical minds of the country. It specifies that "A person is not responsible for criminal conduct if at the time of such conduct as a result of mental disease or defect he lacks substantial capacity either to appreciate the criminality [wrongfulness] of his conduct or to conform his conduct to the requirements of law."[8]

Adhering to the fundamental concepts of free will and criminal responsibility, the American Law Institute test restates M'Naghten in language consonant with current legal and psychological thought. . . .

The advantages [of the ALI test] may be briefly summarized. First, the ALI test adds a volitional element, the ability to conform to legal requirements, which is missing from the M'Naghten test. Second, it avoids the all-or-nothing language of M'Naghten and permits a verdict based on lack of substantial capacity. Third, the ALI test is broad enough to permit a psychiatrist to set before the trier of fact a full picture of the defendant's mental impairments and flexible enough to adapt to future changes in psychiatric theory and diagnosis. Fourth, by referring to the defendant's capacity to "appreciate" the wrongfulness of his conduct the test confirms our holding in *People v. Wolff*, that mere verbal knowledge of right and wrong does not prove sanity. . . .

In light of the manifest superiority of the ALI test, the only barrier to the adoption of that test we perceive lies in the repeated judicial declarations that any change in the M'Naghten rule requires legislative action. This pronouncement rests on two bases: the lengthy history of the M'Naghten rule in California and the failure of the 1927 Legislature, when it revised the procedures for pleading and trying the defense of insanity, to overturn the M'Naghten test.

---

[8] The American Law Institute takes no position as to whether the term "criminality" or the term "wrongfulness"' best expresses the test of criminal responsibility; we prefer the term "criminality." Subdivision 2 of the American Law Institute test provides that "the terms 'mental disease or defect' do not include an abnormality manifested only by repeated criminal or otherwise anti-social conduct." The language, designed to deny an insanity defense to psychopaths and sociopaths, is not relevant to the present case. The question whether to adopt subdivision 2 of the ALI test is one which we defer to a later occasion.

The concept that an extended line of judicial decisions, accompanied by leg-islative inaction, can freeze the evolution of judicial principles, divesting the courts of authority to overturn their prior decisions, is not in good repute. . . . [T]he judiciary has the responsibility for legal doctrine which it has created.[11] The power of the court to reshape judicial doctrine does not authorize us to overturn constitutionally valid statutes. But as Justice Mosk explained in his con-curring opinion in *People v. Kelly*, the M'Naghten rule is not an integral part of the statutory structure of California criminal law. The Legislature has never enacted the M'Naghten rule as a test of insanity, and its provisions relating to criminal responsibility do not incorporate the M'Naghten formula. Thus replacement of the M'Naghten rule with the ALI test will not contradict or nullify any legislative enactment.

QUESTIONS

1. Why did the court rather than the legislature undertake changing the insanity standard from *M'Naghten* to the ALI test?
2. What advantages does change by the court have? What disadvantages?
3. Should there be a different standard for insanity for medical diagnosis than for legal attribution of responsibility? Or should the standards be the same?
4. What does Justice Tobriner imply about the dilemma of a psychiatrist testifying under the *M'Naghten* standard?
5. What, according to the court, does the ALI test purport to do in relation to the old *M'Naghten* standard?
6. How is mental disease determined under *M'Naghten*? Under the ALI test? Who should determine whether the defendant's mental condition qualifies as a mental disease or defect?

PEOPLE *v.* FIELDS

Supreme Court of California 35 Cal. 3d 329 (1983)

(A) "ANTISOCIAL PERSONALITY" AS A FORM OF INSANITY

Defendant, after presenting no defense of significance at the guilt phase of the trial, offered a defense of insanity. He presented evidence that he had an "antisocial personality" which, he claimed, constituted a form of insanity under the American Law Institute (ALI) test we endorsed in *People v. Drew* (1978). . . . [19]

[In *Drew*, we deferred the question of whether to adopt subdivision 2 of the American Law Institute test because it was not relevant to that case. Subdivi-sion 2] provides that "the terms 'mental disease or defect' do not include an

---

[11] When the law governing a subject has been shaped and guided by judicial decision, legislative inaction does not necessarily constitute a tacit endorsement of the precise stage in the evolution of the law extant at the time when the Legislature did nothing; it may signify that the Legislature is willing to entrust the further evolution of legal doctrine to judicial development.

[19] An initiative measure effective June 8, 1982, enacted a statutory definition of insanity (see Pen. Code, § 25, subd. (b)) which resembles the M'Naghten test rejected by this court in People v. Drew. The considerations of policy barring extension of the insanity defense to psychopaths discussed in this opinion apply with equal force to cases arising under the new statutory definition.

abnormality manifested only by repeated criminal or otherwise antisocial conduct." This language [was] designed to deny an insanity defense to psychopaths and sociopaths. . . . Forecasting that the California Supreme Court would adopt subdivision 2 of the ALI test, the trial judge in the present case instructed the jury in accord with that provision. The present case thus presents the issue we deferred deciding in *Drew*.

Defense counsel called as his only expert witness Dr. Ronald Markman, who testified that defendant suffered from an "antisocial personality" (the current psychiatric term for psychopaths and sociopaths),[20] that this condition is a "mental disease," and that because of this disease defendant was unable to conform his behavior to legal requirements. He described defendant as a person who lacks the interest, concern, or ability to conform to social roles, and was unable to benefit from experience. On cross-examination, however, he was asked whether his views would change if the term "mental disease" did not include an abnormality "manifested only by repeated or otherwise antisocial conduct." Markman replied that under this definition defendant would not be insane.

When the trial judge, over defendant's objection, instructed the jury on subdivision 2 of the ALI test, the defense case was destroyed. As the prosecutor pointed out to the jury, under subdivision 2's definition of mental disease, Dr. Markman agreed with the prosecution experts that defendant was sane, and no testimony whatever supported the insanity defense.

Before explaining our reasons for approving the court's instruction based on subdivision 2, it is important to note what that subdivision does and does not do. Although it was designed to deny an insanity defense to psychopaths and sociopaths, it does not have that precise effect. What it does is prevent consideration of a mental illness if that illness is manifested only by a series of criminal or antisocial acts. If that illness manifests itself in some other way as well, then it can be considered as a "mental disease" under the ALI test, and instances of criminal or antisocial conduct can be ascribed to that disease or cited as evidence of its severity. (Thus Dr. Markham may have been mistaken when, in response to a question excluding consideration of "an abnormality manifested only by repeated or otherwise antisocial conduct," he stated that "by definition, you are excluding the antisocial personality.")

In effect, subdivision 2 operates to define a prima facie case for an insanity defense: if the defense expert can point to no symptom, no manifestation, of defendant's condition except repeated criminal or antisocial acts, that condition cannot be considered grounds for finding defendant insane. Whether this requirement denies the insanity defense to a person with an "antisocial personality" will depend upon the individual case, and on the ability of the psychiatrist to base a diagnosis upon facts additional to a list of defendant's criminal or antisocial acts.

We advance three reasons for approving subdivision 2 of the ALI test. First, that provision has been endorsed by the overwhelming weight of authority. [S]even federal circuits have considered the issue, with five adopting subdivision 2 and two rejecting that provision; fourteen states have adopted subdivision 2 either through legislation or judicial decision. No state has rejected it.

---

[20] The terms "psychopath" and "sociopath" are used interchangeably in the psychiatric literature; the newer term "antisocial personality" is roughly equivalent although, as we will explain later in this opinion, the profession has attempted to establish specific criteria for use of this term which may make it narrower than the earlier designations.

Second, subdivision 2 is consistent with the majority view of psychiatrists and psychologists that proof of a series of criminal or antisocial acts is insufficient to demonstrate mental disease. The standard authority for classification and diagnosis of mental illness is the American Psychiatric Association's Diagnostic and Statistical Manual. The term "antisocial personality" first appeared in the second edition of this manual (DSM-II) in 1968. In defining that term, the manual stated explicitly that "[a] mere history of repeated legal or social offenses is not sufficient to justify this diagnosis."[24] . . .

[W]e foresee harmful legal and social consequences if an expert's diagnosis of mental illness and opinion of insanity could be based solely on recidivist behavior. If a pattern of antisocial behavior is sufficient basis for an insanity defense, then a substantial proportion of serious criminal offenders would be able to assert this defense. It may be that few would succeed in persuading a jury. But the assertion of the insanity defense by recidivists with no apparent sign of mental illness except their penchant for criminal behavior would burden the legal system, bring the insanity defense itself into disrepute, and imperil the ability of persons with definite mental illness to assert that defense.

We have considered carefully the views of the Ninth Circuit in *Wade v. United States* (9th Cir. 1970), the leading decision rejecting subdivision 2 of the ALI test. The *Wade* court reasoned that it was preferable for dangerous psychopaths to be found insane, because a defendant convicted of crime must be released when he has served his sentence but one found insane could be confined indefinitely. . . .

Against this asserted advantage of an insanity finding — an advantage which is nonexistent when the underlying crime carries a sentence of life imprisonment — we must balance a substantial disadvantage. To classify persons with "antisocial personality" as insane would put in the mental institutions persons for whom there is currently no suitable treatment and who would be a constant danger to the staff and other inmates. Mental hospitals are not designed for this type of person; prisons are.

Indeed, the "antisocial personality" is the classic criminal; our prisons are largely populated by such persons. To classify such persons as insane would radically revise the criminal law — insanity, instead of a rare exception to the rule of criminal accountability, would become the ordinary defense in a felony trial. Absent a better understanding of the disorder of "antisocial personality" and some effective treatment for this condition, such an expansive role for the insanity defense would work more harm than good.

QUESTIONS

1. Should the insanity defense include psychopaths?
2. Which theories of punishment support the result reached by the Court?

---

[24] The description of antisocial personality in DSM-II states that persons with this illness are those "who are basically unsocialized and whose behavior pattern brings them repeatedly into conflict with society. They are incapable of significant loyalty to individuals, groups, or social values. They are grossly selfish, callous, irresponsible, impulsive, and unable to feel guilt or to learn from experience and punishment. Frustration tolerance is low. They tend to blame others or offer plausible rationalizations for their behavior. A mere history of repeated legal or social offenses is not sufficient to justify this diagnosis."

PEOPLE *v.* SKINNER

Supreme Court of California 39 Cal. 3d 765 (1985)

GRODIN, J. For over a century prior to the decision in *People v. Drew* (1978), California courts framed this state's definition of insanity, as a defense in criminal cases, upon the two-pronged test adopted by the House of Lords in *M'Naghten's* Case (1843). . . .

Over the years the *M'Naghten* test became subject to considerable criticism and was abandoned in a number of jurisdictions. In *Drew* this court followed suit, adopting the test for mental incapacity proposed by the American Law Institute. . . .

In June 1982 the California electorate adopted an initiative measure, popularly known as Proposition 8, which (among other things) for the first time in this state established a statutory definition of insanity: "In any criminal proceeding . . . in which a plea of not guilty by reason of insanity is entered, this defense shall be found by the trier of fact only when the accused person proves by a preponderance of the evidence that he or she was incapable of knowing or understanding the nature and quality of his or her act and of distinguishing right from wrong at the time of the commission of the offense." (Penal Code, § [25 (b)).] . . .

We conclude, as did the Court of Appeal in *Horn* that section 25(b) reinstated the *M'Naghten* test as it was applied in California prior to *Drew* as the test of legal insanity in criminal prosecutions in this state.

IV

Although the People agree that the purpose of section 25(b) was to return the test of legal insanity in California to the pre-ALI-*Drew* version of the *M'Naghten* test, they argue that reversal of this judgment is not required because both prongs of that test are actually the same. The findings of the trial judge in this case illustrate the fallacy inherent in this argument. It is true that a person who is unaware of the nature and quality of his act by definition cannot know that the act is wrong. In this circumstance the "nature and quality" prong subsumes the "right and wrong" prong.

The reverse does not necessarily follow, however. The expert testimony in this case supported the findings of the trial court that this defendant was aware of the nature and quality of his homicidal act. He knew that he was committing an act of strangulation that would, and was intended to, kill a human being. He was not able to comprehend that the act was wrong because his mental illness caused him to believe that the act was not only morally justified but was expected of him. He believed that the homicide was "right." . . .

Courts in a number of jurisdictions which have considered the question have come to the conclusion as we do, that a defendant who is incapable of understanding that his act is morally wrong is not criminally liable merely because he knows the act is unlawful. Justice Cardozo, in an opinion for the New York Court of Appeal, eloquently expressed the underlying philosophy: "In the light of all these precedents, it is impossible, we think, to say that there is any decisive adjudication which limits the word 'wrong' in the statutory definition to legal as opposed to moral wrong. . . . The interpretation placed upon the statute by the trial judge may be tested by its consequences. A mother kills her infant child to whom she has been devotedly attached. She knows the nature and quality of the act; she knows that the law condemns it; but she is inspired by an insane delusion that God has appeared to her and ordained the sacrifice. It seems a mockery to say that, within the meaning of the statute, she knows that the act is wrong. If the definition propounded by the trial judge is right, it would be the duty of a jury to hold her responsible for the crime. We find nothing either in the history of the rule, or in its reason or purpose, or in judicial exposition of its meaning, to justify a conclusion so abhorrent. . . . Knowledge that an act is forbidden by law will in most cases permit the inference of knowledge that, according to the accepted standards of mankind, it is also condemned as an offense against good morals. Obedience to the law is itself a moral duty. If, however, there is an insane delusion that God has appeared to the defendant and ordained the commission of a crime, we think it cannot be said of the offender that he knows the act to be wrong." . . .

Kaus, J., Broussard, J., Reynoso, J., and Lucas, J., concurred. . . .

Bird, C.J., Dissenting. — In June of 1982, the voters adopted a ballot measure which radically altered the test for criminal insanity in this state. (Pen. Code, § [25 (b)] . . . popularly known as Prop. 8.) I cannot ignore the fact that they adopted language which unambiguously requires the accused to demonstrate that "he or she was incapable of knowing or understanding the nature and quality of his or her act and of distinguishing right from wrong at the time of the commission of the offense." There is nothing in the statute, in Proposition 8 as a whole, or in the ballot arguments that implies that the electorate intended "and" to be "or." However unwise that choice, it is not within this court's power to ignore the expression of popular will and rewrite the statute.

Since appellant failed to establish his insanity under the test enunciated in Penal Code section [25 (b),] I cannot join the decision of my brethren.

QUESTIONS

1. Why, in 1982, might the electorate have reinstated a more restrictive definition of insanity than the court's then applicable *Drew* definition?

2. Should the court have followed the literal language of the statute? What theories of statutory construction, if any, support the court's decision here?

One of the most controversial issues of the *M'Naghten* definition involves the distinction between moral and legal wrong, discussed briefly in the *Skinner* case. The Washington Supreme Court addresses this issue in the *Crenshaw* case below.

3. Moral Wrong versus Legal Wrong

STATE v. CRENSHAW

Supreme Court of Washington 98 Wash. 2d 78 (1983)

Brachtenbach, J. Petitioner Rodney Crenshaw pleaded not guilty and not guilty by reason of insanity to the charge of first degree murder of his wife, Karen Crenshaw. A jury found him guilty. . . .

[Here, we consider] the propriety of the insanity defense instruction which explained the right-wrong standard in the *M'Naghten* test in terms of "legal" right and wrong. . . .

Before turning to the legal issues, the facts of the case must be recounted. While defendant and his wife were on their honeymoon in Canada, petitioner was deported as a result of his participation in a brawl. He secured a motel room in Blaine, Washington, and waited for his wife to join him. When she arrived 2 days later, he immediately thought she had been unfaithful — he sensed "it wasn't the same Karen . . . she'd been with someone else."

Petitioner did not mention his suspicions to his wife; instead he took her to the motel room and beat her unconscious. He then went to a nearby store, stole a knife, and returned to stab his wife 24 times, inflicting a fatal wound. He left again, drove to a nearby farm where he had been employed and borrowed an ax. Upon returning to the motel room, he decapitated his wife with such force that the ax marks cut into the concrete floor under the carpet and splattered blood throughout the room.

Petitioner then proceeded to conceal his actions. He placed the body in a blanket, the head in a pillowcase, and put both in his wife's car. Next, he went to a service station, borrowed a bucket and sponge, and cleaned the room of blood and fingerprints. Before leaving, petitioner also spoke with the motel manager about a phone bill, then chatted with him for awhile over a beer.

When Crenshaw left the motel he drove to a remote area 25 miles away where he hid the two parts of the body in thick brush. He then fled, driving to the Hoquiam area, about 200 miles from the scene of the crime. There he picked up two hitchhikers, told them of his crime, and enlisted their aid in disposing of his wife's car in a river. The hitchhikers contacted the police and Crenshaw was apprehended shortly thereafter. He voluntarily confessed to the crime.

The defense of not guilty by reason of insanity was a major issue at trial. Crenshaw testified that he followed the Moscovite religious faith, and that it would be improper for a Moscovite not to kill his wife if she committed adultery. Crenshaw also has a history of mental problems, for which he has been hospitalized in the past. The jury, however, rejected petitioner's insanity defense, and found him guilty of murder in the first degree.

A INSANITY DEFENSE INSTRUCTION

Insanity is an affirmative defense the defendant must establish by a preponderance of the evidence. Sanity is presumed, even with a history of prior institutional commitments from which the individual was released upon sufficient recovery.

The insanity defense is not available to all who are mentally deficient or deranged; legal insanity has a different meaning and a different purpose than the concept of medical insanity. *State v. White*, 60 Wn.2d 551, 589, 374 P.2d 942 (1962). A verdict of not guilty by reason of insanity completely absolves a defendant of any criminal responsibility. Therefore, "the defense is available only to those persons who have lost contact with reality so completely that they are beyond any of the influences of the criminal law."

Petitioner assigned error to insanity defense instruction 10 which reads:

> In addition to the plea of not guilty, the defendant has entered a plea of insanity existing at the time of the act charged.
> Insanity existing at the time of the commission of the act charged is a defense.

> For a defendant to be found not guilty by reason of insanity you must find that, as a result of mental disease or defect, the defendant's mind was affected to such an extent that the defendant was unable to perceive the nature and quality of the acts with which the defendant is charged or was unable to tell right from wrong with reference to the particular acts with which defendant is charged.
>
> What is meant by the terms "right and wrong" refers to knowledge of a person at the time of committing an act that he was acting contrary to the law.

Clerk's Papers, at 27. But for the last paragraph, this instruction tracks the language of WPIC 20.01, which is the *M'Naghten* test as codified in RCW 9A.12.010. Petitioner contends, however, that the trial court erred in defining "right and wrong" as legal right and wrong rather than in the moral sense.

We find this instruction was not reversible error on . . . alternative grounds: (1) The *M'Naghten* opinion amply supports the "legal" wrong definition as used in this case, (2) under these facts, "moral" wrong and "legal" wrong are synonymous, therefore the "legal" wrong definition did not alter the meaning of the test. . . .

I

The definition of the term "wrong" in the *M'Naghten* test has been considered and disputed by many legal scholars. In Washington, we have not addressed this issue previously.

The confusion arises from apparent inconsistencies in the original *M'Naghten* case. In response to the House of Lords first question, the justices replied that if an accused knew he was acting contrary to law but acted under a partial insane delusion that he was redressing or revenging some supposed grievance or injury, or producing some supposed public benefit, "he is nevertheless punishable . . . if he knew at the time of committing such crime that he was acting *contrary to law;* . . . *the law of the land.*" (Italics ours.) *M'Naghten's Case,* 8 Eng. Rep. 718, 722 (1843). In this answer, the justices appear to approve the legal standard of wrong when there is evidence that the accused knew he was acting contrary to the law.

This has been characterized as inconsistent with the justices' response to the second and third questions, regarding how a jury should be instructed on the insanity defense:

> If the question were to be put [to a jury] as to the knowledge of the accused solely and exclusively with reference to the law of the land, it might tend to confound the jury, by inducing them to believe that an actual knowledge of the law of the land was essential in order to lead to a conviction; whereas the law is administered upon the principle that every one must be taken conclusively to know it, without proof that he does know it. If the accused was conscious that the act was one which he ought not to do, and if that act was at the same time contrary to the law of the land, he is punishable; and the usual course therefore has been to leave the question to the jury, whether the party accused had a sufficient degree of reason to know that he was doing an act that was wrong: and this course we think is correct, accompanied with such observations and explanations as the circumstances of each particular case may require.

M'Naghten, at 723. This response appears to require both that the accused be "conscious that the act was one which he ought not to do" and that the act be "contrary to the law."

A close examination of these answers, however, shows they are reconcilable in the context of this case. First, the similarities between the hypothetical in the first question and Crenshaw's situation should afford that answer great weight. If, arguendo, Crenshaw was delusional, his delusion was only partial, for it related only to his perceptions of his wife's infidelity. His behavior towards others, *i.e.*, the motel manager and the woman who loaned him the ax, at the time of the killing was normal. Crenshaw also "knew he was acting contrary to law," as evidenced by his sophisticated attempts to hide his crime and by the expert, psychiatric testimony. Furthermore, he acted with a view "of redressing or revenging [the] supposed grievance" of his wife's infidelity. Thus, the Crenshaw situation fits perfectly into the first hypothetical, and the trial court understandably relied on this passage in approving the challenged instruction. . . .

II

Alternatively, the statement in instruction 10 may be approved because, in this case, legal wrong is synonymous with moral wrong. This conclusion is premised on two grounds.

First, in discussing the term "moral" wrong, it is important to note that it is society's morals, and not the individual's morals, that are the standard for judging moral wrong under *M'Naghten*. If wrong meant moral wrong judged by the individual's own conscience, this would seriously undermine the criminal law, for it would allow one who violated the law to be excused from criminal responsibility solely because, in his own conscience, his act was not morally wrong. This principle was emphasized by Justice Cardozo:

> The anarchist is not at liberty to break the law because he reasons that all government is wrong. The devotee of a religious cult that enjoins polygamy or human sacrifice as a duty is not thereby relieved from responsibility before the law. . . .

People v. Schmidt, 216 N.Y. 324, 340, 110 N.E. 945, 950 (1915). . . .

There is evidence on the record that Crenshaw knew his actions were wrong according to society's standards, as well as legally wrong. Dr. Belden testified:

> I think Mr. Crenshaw is quite aware on one level that he is in conflict with the law *and with people*. However, this is not something that he personally invests his emotions in.

(Italics ours.) We conclude that Crenshaw knew his acts were morally wrong from society's viewpoint and also knew his acts were illegal. His personal belief that it was his duty to kill his wife for her alleged infidelity cannot serve to exculpate him from legal responsibility for his acts.

A narrow exception to the societal standard of moral wrong has been drawn for instances wherein a party performs a criminal act, knowing it is morally and legally wrong, but believing, because of a mental defect, that the act is ordained by God: such would be the situation with a mother who kills her infant child to whom she is devotedly attached, believing that God has spoken to her and decreed the act. Although the woman knows that the law and society condemn the act, it would be unrealistic to hold her responsible for the crime, since her free will has been subsumed by her belief in the deific decree.

This exception is not available to Crenshaw, however. Crenshaw argued only that he followed the Moscovite faith and that Moscovites believe it is their duty to kill an unfaithful wife. This is not the same as acting under a deific command. Instead, it is akin to "[t]he devotee of a religious cult that enjoins . . . human sacrifice as a duty [and] is *not* thereby relieved from responsibility before the law." (Italics ours.) Crenshaw's personal "Moscovite" beliefs are not equivalent to a deific decree and do not relieve him from responsibility for his acts.

Once moral wrong is equated with society's morals, the next step, equating moral and legal wrong, follows logically. The law is, for the most part, an expression of collective morality.

Most cases involving the insanity defense involve serious crimes for which society's moral judgment is identical with the legal standard.

Therefore, a number of scholars have concluded that, as a practical matter, the way in which a court interprets the word "wrong" will have little effect on the eventual outcome of a case.

QUESTION

The *Crenshaw* case describes what Professors Kadish and Schulhofer call the "deific decree" exception (Criminal Law and Its Processes 941 (6th ed. 1995)). Based on your reading of *Crenshaw*, what are the requirements for this exception? Why were they not met in *Crenshaw*?

PROBLEMS

M'Naghten and four other influential definitions appear following the Problems below. Apply each to the Problems. Consider their similarities and their differences. Which one is preferable?

8.26 Andrea Yates, the mother of five young children between the ages of six months and seven years, drowned each of her children, one after the other, in the bathtub of their family home in June of 2001. In response to questioning about the acts, Mrs. Yates indicated that the children had not done anything to make her angry and that she had been considering drowning them for some time. She explained that her thoughts about drowning her children were part of her realization that she had "not been a good mother to them." She explained this by noting that "[t]hey weren't developing correctly." They had, in her view, behavioral and learning problems. She stated that she "realized it was time to be punished . . . [f]or not being a good mother."[44] She explained: "After I kill them, they would go up to heaven and be with God and be safe."[45] Two years earlier, she had attempted suicide and been treated for depression.

Assume that Mrs. Yates suffered from postpartum psychosis, a severe mental disease. Should the jury have found her insane under any of the definitions in Section 4 below or under Texas Penal Code § 8.01, immediately below?

---

44. This problem is based on the transcript of Andrea Yates's statement to the police reported in the Associated Press, Houston Chronicle, *Transcript of Andrea Yates' confession*, *wysiwg://41/http://www.chron.com/. . . story.mpl/special/drownings/1266294* (accessed July 28, 2004) and on the Teachey article cited in the next footnote.

45. Lisa Teachey, *DA releases video of Yates talking about drownings*, Houston Chronicle, June 15, 2002, at A1.

Texas Penal Code Annotated § 8.01 (2003)   *Insanity*

(a) It is an affirmative defense to prosecution that, at the time of the conduct charged, the actor, as a result of severe mental disease or defect, did not know that his conduct was wrong.

(b) The term "mental disease or defect" does not include an abnormality manifested only by repeated criminal or otherwise antisocial conduct.

PROBLEM

8.27   The defendant, John Hinckley, shot then President Ronald Reagan. Assume that evidence presented at trial suggested that Hinckley was obsessed with the actress Jodi Foster and that he believed that killing President Reagan would impress her. Assume also that Hinckley suffered from psychosis, a severe mental illness, and genuinely believed that President Reagan's death would produce his desired result. Under the tests below, should the fact finder acquit Hinckley?

---

4. Insanity Definitions

(1) Federal Test: "It is an affirmative defense to a prosecution under any Federal statute that, at the time of the commission of the acts constituting the offense, the defendant, as a result of a severe mental disease or defect, was unable to appreciate the nature and quality or the wrongfulness of his acts. Mental disease or defect does not otherwise constitute a defense." 18 U.S.C.S. § 17 (2003).

(2) M'Naghten Test: "[T]o establish a defence on the ground of insanity, it must be clearly proved that, at the time of the committing of the act, the party accused was labouring under such a defect of reason, from disease of the mind, as not to know the nature and quality of the act he was doing; or, if he did know it, that he did not know he was doing what was wrong." *M'Naghten's Case*, 8 Eng. Rep. 718, 722 (1843).

(3) Model Penal Code Test: "A person is not responsible for criminal conduct if at the time of such conduct as a result of mental disease or defect he lacks substantial capacity either to appreciate the criminality [wrongfulness] of his conduct or to conform his conduct to the requirements of law.[46]

" . . . [A]s used in this Article, the terms 'mental disease or defect' do not include an abnormality manifested only by repeated criminal or otherwise antisocial conduct." Model Penal Code § 4.01 (1985).

(4) Irresistible Impulse Test: "[T]he degree of insanity which will relieve the accused of the consequences of a criminal act must be such as to create in his mind an

---

46. The Model Penal Code drafters explain the inclusion of the alternatives of "criminality" and "wrongfulness" as follows: "Wrongfulness is suggested as a possible alternative to criminality, though it is recognized that few cases are likely to arise in which the variation will be determinative." Model Penal Code, Commentaries, Complete Statutory Text, art. 4, p.62.

uncontrollable impulse to commit the offense charged. This impulse must be such as to override the reason and judgment and obliterate the sense of right and wrong to the extent that the accused is deprived of the power to choose between right and wrong. The mere ability to distinguish right from wrong is no longer the correct test either in civil or criminal cases, where the defense of insanity is interposed. . . . [T]he accused must be capable, not only of distinguishing between right and wrong, but that he was not impelled to do the act by an irresistible impulse, which means before it will justify a verdict of acquittal that his reasoning powers were so far dethroned by his diseased mental condition as to deprive him of the will power to resist the insane impulse to perpetrate the deed, though knowing it to be wrong." *Smith v. United States*, 36 F.2d 548, 549 (1929).

(5) Durham Test: "[A]n accused is not criminally responsible if his unlawful act was the product of mental disease or mental defect." *Durham v. United States*, 214 F.2d 862, 874-875 (1954).

5. Rationales for and Against an Insanity Defense

Despite overwhelming acceptance under federal and state law of some version of an insanity defense, its utility, desirability, and scope remain controversial. Particular cases often spark renewed debate about the defense. For instance, the jury's acquittal of John Hinckley by reason of insanity on the charge of the attempted assassination of President Reagan had a profound effect on the treatment of legal insanity in this country.

> During the three-year period following the *Hinckley* acquittal, Congress and half the states enacted changes in the insanity defense, all designed to limit it in some respect. Congress and nine states narrowed the substantive test of insanity; Congress and seven states shifted the burden of proof to the defendant; eight states supplemented the insanity verdict with a separate verdict of guilty but mentally ill; and one state (Utah) abolished the defense altogether.[47]

In 1966, Congress established a commission to "undertake a complete review and recommend revision of the federal criminal laws."[48] As part of its task, the commission reviewed a host of arguments about potential abolition of the insanity defense. In reading those arguments that follow from the commission's report, consider which you find most persuasive.

WORKING PAPERS OF THE NATIONAL COMMISSION ON REFORM OF FEDERAL CRIMINAL LAW
Vol. 1 pps. 248–253 (1970)

IN SUPPORT OF ABOLISHING THE INSANITY DEFENSE:

* There is a shortage of "[t]rained mental health personnel." Their time should be devoted to serving "in disposition and treatment of persons who have

---

47. Peter W. Low et al., *The Trial of John W. Hinckley, Jr.: A Case Study in the Insanity Defense*, 126-127 (1986). The Model Penal Code test applied in the federal courts at the time of Hinckley's trial.
48. *Supra* note 28 at 248-253 (1970).

engaged in criminal conduct" rather than "in courthouses so that they will be available to engage in retrospective reconstructions of criminal responsibility." (noting the "fairly extreme example [of] *Wright v. United States*, in which eleven psychiatrists examined the defendant and testified before the jury.").

* "Insanity is frequently and properly called a 'rich man's defense,' for the wealthy can sift the pool of potential expert witnesses for those who will produce favorable testimony in a convincing manner."

* "Key terms in the conventionally utilized insanity tests (particularly when one goes beyond *M'Naghten*) such as 'mental disease,' 'capacity to conform,' are vague at best, and perhaps meaningless. The insanity defenses invite semantic jousting, metaphysical speculation, intuitive moral judgments in the guise of factual determinations."

* "The literature reveals great uncertainty as to the function of insanity defenses. Currently, it perhaps is most commonly stated as designed to remove from the criminal process those who are deemed to be not blameworthy. Left unclear is the establishment of criteria for determining blameworthiness and the identification of persons meeting such criteria."

* "The crucial decisions with respect to persons, including mentally abnormal persons, who commit criminal acts involve disposition. An insanity defense is a poor device for determination of whether persons ought to be institutionalized and if so, to what facility they are to be directed. It is far more rational to face this question frankly and directly. Large numbers of defendants who could present effective insanity defenses under present standards do not do so either because the possibility is not recognized or because it is avoided, commonly out of fear of more lengthy detention and/or more painful stigmatization."

* "The criminal process has the advantages of determinate maximum periods of detention, proportionality between the seriousness of the offense and the penalty. Persons channeled out of the criminal system by the insanity defense are subject to incarceration, possibly for life. The criteria for release such as 'recovered sanity,' no longer 'dangerous' are subject to such wide variations of meaning as to afford little protection to the 'patient.' "

* "A number of informed observers believe that it is therapeutically desirable to treat behavioral deviants as responsible for their conduct rather than as involuntary victims playing a sick role."

In Support of Retaining the Insanity Defense:

* "There is a powerful root feeling in our culture tha[t] an 'insane' person is not appropriately subject to the condemnation implicit in criminal conviction and sentencing. We sense a lack of culpability. . . . In part these feelings may be attributable to a subjective sense of freedom to avoid criminal conduct ourselves and our lack of identification with grossly abnormal offenders, whom we feel to be different from ourselves in the sense of being less free."

* "To abolish the insanity defense would be to seem to recognize that criminal sanction may be imposed irrespective of whether the defendant freely chose his course of conduct, thus weakening what is at least a useful myth."

* "Criminal convictions carry added sanctions of loss of reputation, self-deprecation, and (frequently) civil legal liabilities."

* "If a special insanity defense is eliminated, there will be greater need to provide means for channeling mentally abnormal persons away from correctional institutions and into mental hospitals."

QUESTION

Which argument do you find most convincing?

6. Recent Application of the Insanity Defense

In recent decades, defendants have raised the insanity defense in a number of different contexts. We consider two that have been the subject of academic and court commentary. The first is "post-traumatic stress disorder," a psychological condition associated with significant stressful events, such as some types of military service. The second is "postpartum psychosis." Brief descriptions of each follow. Consider whether or how the descriptions apply to Problems 8.28 and 8.29, which appear below the descriptions.

a. Post-Traumatic Stress Disorder

In the following excerpt, Professor C. Peter Erlinder discusses formal recognition of post-traumatic stress disorder in the early 1980s.

Post Traumatic Stress Disorder (PTSD) is the designation assigned to a group of symptoms in the current edition of the Diagnostic and Statistical Manual of the American Psychiatric Association. (DSM III). Prior to 1980, when the most recent edition of the manual was published, the symptoms that are now grouped under PTSD were not included under a single diagnostic heading. Consequently, prior to 1980, mental health professionals and attorneys lacked an identifiable and accepted description of the symptoms now known as PTSD that could be employed in diagnosis, treatment, or legal proceedings. . . .

Any principled description of PTSD must begin with the clear recognition that it is not a *new* phenomenon in combat veterans, nor is it limited to veterans. A substantial body of research suggests that stress reactions among veterans have resulted from every major conflict in this century, and, perhaps, are an unavoidable consequence of war. In addition, over the past several decades research has indicated that reactions similar to the PTSD diagnostic criteria can be seen in such apparently diverse groups as rape victims, World War II (WW II) and Korean War survivors, Holocaust survivors, Hiroshima atomic blast victims, and survivors of other catastrophic events. . . .

The fact that PTSD encompasses reactions to stressful events other than combat in Vietnam is recognized in the diagnostic criteria for PTSD set forth by the American Psychiatric Association in DSM III. In that discussion, DSM III states that "[t]he essential feature is the development of characteristic symptoms following a psychologically traumatic event that is generally outside the range of normal human experience. . . .

Following the traumatic event, a person who suffers from PTSD may have a number of symptoms that include: self medication through substance or alcohol abuse, memory loss, loss of sleep, nightmares reliving the original traumatic event, intrusive thoughts, exaggerated startle response, reduction in emotional response, a feeling of alienation, and "disassociative states" during which the original event is relived and *"the individual behaves as though experiencing the event of the moment."* . . . The . . . difficult aspect of PTSD for many to accept is that the *symptoms of PTSD can occur long after the original traumatic event has ended.* . . .

For those trained to survive in combat, a "reexperiencing" of the original event may include combat-like reactions. Accordingly, DSM III specifically mentions "unpredictable explosions of aggressive behavior" as characteristic of war veterans with PTSD. . . .

It is crucial for attorneys to understand that the effects of PTSD while widespread, may be subtle. . . .

Another important aspect of PTSD that attorneys should recognize is that PTSD *is a psychological condition brought about by factors external to the person who experiences symptoms.* . . .

Perhaps most importantly, and perhaps because PTSD is brought about by external factors, many health professionals agree that PTSD is highly amenable to treatment.[49]

Although more recent revisions of the Diagnostic and Statistical Manual of Mental Disorders (DSM-IV-TR) may have clarified or revised some aspects of the diagnostic criteria for PTSD,[50] the understanding remains that PTSD is a mental disorder that can provoke "disassociative states . . . during which components of the event are relived and the person behaves as though experiencing the event at that moment. . . . "[51]

b. Postpartum Psychosis

According to scholarship on legal issues related to postpartum disorders, "[p]ostpartum psychosis exists when the mother loses her ability to distinguish reality from fantasy. She may experience visual or auditory hallucinations. The postpartum psychotic suffers from delusions that may include guilt concerning her child or her husband, anxiety about not being capable or caring for the baby properly, concern that something is wrong with the baby, and infanticidal or suicidal thoughts. She may hear voices telling her that her child is a demon, or that she must die. She experiences her delusions and hallucinations as reality."[52]

Postpartum psychosis generally qualifies as a recognized mental illness.

PROBLEMS

8.28   Jerold was a Korean War veteran who saw extensive combat. When he returned from his tour of duty, he felt proud that he had served his country but has always refused to discuss his war experiences. For a period of months after his return, Jerold seemed uninterested in civilian life. He began drinking and seemed unwilling to return to work. He often suffered from graphic combat nightmares from which he

---

49. C. Peter Erlinder, *Paying the Price for Vietnam: Post-Traumatic Stress Disorder and Criminal Behavior*, 25 B.C. L. Rev. 305, 308, 310-313 (1984).

50. *See* DSM-IV-TR, 463-468 (American Psychiatric Assn. 4th ed. 2000).

51. *Id.*at 464.

52. Laura E. Reece, *Comment: Mothers Who Kill: Postpartum Disorders and Criminal Infanticide*, 38 UCLA L. Rev. 699, 712 (1991).

awoke sweating and disoriented. After eight months, however, Jerold decided to go back to school to become an architect. Jerold struggled through school, taking two leaves of absence to deal with his insomnia and nightmares. He finally completed the program two years ago. Since then, Jerold has slowly developed an architectural practice. He works out of a renovated loft that overlooks a quiet park in a peaceful suburb of a large city. Six months ago, he landed a contract to design a new entertainment complex in the heart of the city. While he was working on those designs, his longtime lover left him, claiming that Jerold had become very withdrawn and uncommunicative. Although Jerold regularly visits the scenes of his architectural projects, because loud noises often startle him, he does so in the evening after construction work has been completed for the day. Unexpectedly, a problem develops on the construction site of the entertainment complex for which Jerold drew the blueprints. The foreman asks Jerold to resolve an issue regarding the blueprints. When Jerold arrives, construction is in full swing. The noise of the jackhammering is deafening, and vibrations from the machinery cause the ground to rumble and shake. Jerold discovers that the construction crew has misinterpreted his drawings and made serious errors in the foundation of the new complex. Jerold and the foreman begin arguing. Jerold leans over the blueprints, grabs a metal pipe, and begins pounding the foreman's head. Other workers pull Jerold away, but the injuries inflicted by Jerold are fatal and the foreman dies. As Jerold's defense attorney in the murder trial, what theories would you employ in Jerold's defense? What facts might be critical to those theories?

8.29 "On March 17, 1987, Massip gave birth to a son, Michael. Although she was a caring, loving mother, Michael cried 15-18 hours a day. At first, doctors believed he suffered from colic, but suspected later that it was something more. He was in a great deal of pain and nothing Massip did helped to alleviate it. She tried feeding him different formulas but he just vomited.

"Before giving birth, Massip was a happy, healthy, nonviolent person who looked forward to motherhood. However, after Michael was born, she began feeling confused and worthless; and during the next six weeks she could neither sleep nor eat. She began having suicidal thoughts, such as jumping off a building or out of a window. She also experienced hallucinations; voices were telling her the baby was in pain.

"On April 25, Massip experienced a blackout or seizure. Believing she needed rest, she went to her mother's house for the weekend, leaving Michael with his father. However, she could still hear Michael's cries in her mind. She felt the room was moving, the walls and ceiling waving, even when she was sitting down. On April 27, she went to see her obstetrician, who believed she was having a nervous breakdown and prescribed tranquilizers.

"On April 29, when Michael began crying again, Massip took him for a walk. During the walk, she heard voices telling her the baby was in pain and to put him out of his misery; she felt as if she were in a tunnel and everything was moving slowly. She was watching her own actions from outside of herself. At one point during the walk, she saw herself throw the baby in front of a car. The driver did not recognize the bundle as a baby, but was able to swerve and missed it. Massip later that day placed Michael under the tire of her car and drove over him. She then picked him up and walked with him, but did not remember what he looked like. At that time, she saw him as a doll or an object, not a person.

"In fact, Massip had run over her baby, afterward placing him in a trash can, where he was later discovered. She told her husband the baby had been kidnapped and gave a description of the kidnapper. Later, when they were at the police station, she admitted to her husband she had killed Michael."[53]

Assume that Massip suffered from postpartum psychosis. Should she be acquitted by reason of insanity?

7. Synthesis and Review of Insanity Issues

PROBLEMS

8.30 Defendant Bruce suffers from a severe form of paranoid schizophrenia. He can, however, control his mental illness through daily ingestion of medication. Because the medication makes Bruce sleepy and he dislikes that groggy feeling, Bruce stops taking his medication. Several weeks later, while driving to the supermarket, Bruce has a schizophrenic episode in which he believes that aliens are taking over the earth. He rams the car ahead of him, believing that the driver of that car is an alien carrying weapons of mass destruction and that Bruce must save the world. Bruce's actions result in the death of both the driver and passenger of the car ahead of him.

Assume that psychiatrists are prepared to testify at Bruce's trial that he satisfied the criteria for insanity under the *M'Naghten* test in use in the jurisdiction at the time of the killing. They also would testify that, had Bruce taken his medication, he would have been able to avoid the episode entirely. What should the criminal justice system do?

8.31 According to an account of the incident:

> On January 3, 1999, Kendra Webdale, an aspiring writer who had moved to [New York City] from Buffalo, was waiting for the N train on the 23rd Street platform. [Andrew] Goldstein was there, too, pacing erratically and acting enough like a crazy man that several passengers turned away. Goldstein wound up behind Webdale

---

53. Quoted from People v. Massip, 235 Cal. App. 3d 1884, 1888-1889 (1990).

and as the train raced into the station[, h]e grabbed her and shoved her onto the track, where she was crushed to death by the 80,000 pound subway traveling at 35 miles per hour. . . . [54]

Just prior to pushing Ms. Webdale, the defendant explained later, in a January 4, 1999 videotaped interview with the prosecutor, that he experienced a sensation of losing control of his motor systems, like he was "being inhabited." He felt an "overwhelming urge to strike out or push or punch." Assume that the defendant knew, at the time, that pushing someone onto the tracks would result in death, and that it was wrong (legally and morally) to kill someone in this way.

According to his attorney, Mr. Goldstein suffered from a severe form of the mental illness known as schizophrenia and had been in and out of mental institutions repeatedly over the decade preceding the offense. About six months prior to this fatal assault, Mr. Goldstein claimed that responding medical workers had brought Mr. Goldstein to a mental institution after he had attacked a woman on the subway. According to his attorney, the records of Mr. Goldstein's struggle with mental illness reflect numerous unprovoked assaults; And that he had sought medical attention for his mental illness many times; but that he was repeatedly turned away or released after a short period of time.[55]

Should Goldstein be held criminally accountable for homicide? Under which of the five definitions of insanity given earlier in this chapter should a jury acquit Goldstein? Should Goldstein be acquitted under the applicable New York statute, which reads as follows:

New York Penal Code Ann. § 40.15 (1998)   *Mental Disease or Defect*

In any prosecution for an offense, it is an affirmative defense that when the defendant engaged in the proscribed conduct, he lacked criminal responsibility by reason of mental disease or defect. Such lack of criminal responsibility means that at the time of such conduct, as a result of mental disease or defect, he lacked substantial capacity to know or appreciate either:

    1. The nature and consequences of such conduct; or
    2. That such conduct was wrong.

In light of the language of the New York statute, what result do you think the jury reached?

Over the years, scholars have proposed substantial reconceptions of the role of insanity in criminal law. In the following excerpt, Professor Christopher Slobogin offers such a reconception.

---

54. Quoted from Dan Ackman, *Goldstein Lawyers Put Mental Healthcare System on Trial,* *http://www.dackman.homestead.com/files/GoldsteinTrial.htm* (accessed July 28, 2004).
55. Information in this paragraph is based on *id.*

Christopher Slobogin, AN END TO INSANITY: RECASTING THE ROLE OF MENTAL DISABILITY IN CRIMINAL CASES

86 Va. L. Rev. 1199, 1199-1200, 1202-1207 (2000) (citations omitted)

INSANITY defense jurisprudence has long been in a state of chaos. Some have responded to this unfortunate situation by calling for abolition of the defense, while others have tinkered further with its scope. This Article proposes what amounts to an intermediate position. It argues that insanity should be eliminated as a separate defense, but that the effects of mental disorder should still carry significant moral weight. More specifically, mental illness should be relevant in assessing culpability only as warranted by general criminal law doctrines concerning mens rea, self-defense and duress.

While a few scholars and courts have toyed with this idea, it has yet to be fully endorsed or coherently defended by any of them. This Article provides such a defense. It contends that, both morally and practically, the most appropriate manner of recognizing mental illness's mitigating impact in criminal cases is to recast mental disorder as a factor relevant to the general defenses, rather than treat it as a predicate for a special defense. . . .

Accepting blameworthiness as the touchstone of the criminal law means that individual culpability must be assessed. That is where the kind of inquiry the insanity defense mandates comes into play. It is meant to help us decide who among those who commit criminal acts deserve to be the subject of criminal punishment.

The central assertion of this Article, however, is that the insanity defense does not adequately carry out this definitional task. At least in its modern guises, the insanity defense is overbroad. Instead, mental disorder should be relevant to criminal culpability only if it supports an excusing condition that, under the subjective approach to criminal liability increasingly accepted today, would be available to a person who is *not* mentally ill. The three most prominent such conditions would be: (1) a mistaken belief about circumstances that, had they occurred as the person believed, would amount to a legal justification; (2) a mistaken belief that conditions exist that amount to legally recognized duress; and (3) the absence of intent to commit crime (that is, the lack of mens rea, defined subjectively in terms of what the defendant actually knew or was aware of).

Before justifying this position, some examples of how it would apply in well-known actual and hypothetical cases should be provided. As a prime example of the first excusing condition, consider the famous *M'Naghten* case, from whence much of current insanity defense jurisprudence derives. In 1843, Daniel M'Naghten killed the secretary of Prime Minister Peel, apparently believing the secretary was Peel and that killing Peel would bring an end to a campaign of harassment against him. He was found insane by the trial court judges. Whether M'Naghten would have been acquitted under the proposed approach would depend upon whether he believed the harassment would soon lead to his death or serious bodily harm and whether he thought there was any other way to prevent that occurrence. Because in his paranoid state he feared he would be assassinated by his enemies and had on several occasions unsuccessfully applied to the police for protection, he may have had such a defense. But if the circumstances in which he thought he was involved would not amount to self-defense, no acquittal would result (although a conviction of manslaughter rather than murder might have been appropriate, analogous to the result under the modern theory of "imperfect" self-defense as it has developed in connection with provocation doctrine).

Now consider the case of John Hinckley, who convinced a jury that he was insane when he tried to kill President Reagan. If, as even his defense attorneys asserted, John Hinckley shot President Reagan simply because he believed Reagan's death would somehow unite him with actress Jodi Foster, he would be convicted under the proposed approach. Regardless of how psychotic Hinckley may have been at the time of the offense, he would not have an excuse under the proposed regime, because killing someone to consummate a love affair is never justified, nor is it deserving even of a reduction in charge.

[Another recent case furnishes an additional exemplar] of how the proposed regime might work in practice. Jeffrey Dahmer killed and cannibalized thirteen individuals. The jury was right to convict him. As sick as his actions were, even he never thought they were justified, and he would not be excused under the proposal. . . .

In these cases, then, whether a defense existed under the proposed approach would depend upon self-defense principles, applied to the circumstances as the defendant believed them to be. A second variety of cases can be analyzed in terms of a similarly subjectified version of duress, which traditionally has excused crimes that are coerced by serious threats to harm the perpetrator. For instance, some people with mental illness who commit crimes claim they were commanded by God to do so. If the perceived consequences of disobeying the deity were lethal or similarly significant, such a person would deserve acquittal, perhaps even if the crime charged were homicide. On the other hand, . . . the mere fact that the defendant honestly believed God ordained a crime would not automatically be an excuse.

The third type of excuse that might apply when people with mental illness commit crime — lack of mens rea — is extremely rare. M'Naghten, Hinckley, [and] Dahmer . . . all intended to carry out their criminal acts. Indeed, most people with mental disorder who cause harm mean to do so, albeit sometimes for reasons that seem irrational. Nonetheless, when mens rea is defined subjectively, there are at least four possible lack-of-mens rea scenarios: involuntary action, mistake as to results, mistake as to circumstances, and ignorance of the law.

First, a person may engage in motor activity without intending it to occur (for example, a reflex action which results in a gun firing and killing someone). The criminal law typically classifies such events as involuntary acts. Although mental disorder usually does not eliminate conscious control over bodily movements associated with crime, when it does (for example, in connection with epileptic seizures), a defense would exist if one accepts the premise that culpability requires intent.

Second, a person may intentionally engage in conduct but intend a different result than that which occurs (such as when firing a gun at a tree kills a person due to a ricochet). Distortions of perception caused by mental illness might occasionally lead to such accidental consequences; for instance, a mentally ill person driving a car may inadvertently hit someone because his "voices" and hallucinations prevent him from perceiving the relevant sounds and visual cues. In such situations a subjectively defined mens rea doctrine would absolve him of criminal liability for any harm caused.

Closely related is the situation in which a person intentionally engages in conduct and intends the physical result that occurs, but is under a misapprehension as to the attendant circumstances (such as when a person intentionally shoots a gun at what he thinks is a dummy but which in fact is a real person). Of the various mens rea defenses, mental illness is most likely to play a role here (in what has sometimes been labeled the "mistake of fact" defense). For instance, a person who believes he is shooting the devil when in fact he is killing a person, or a person who exerts control over property he delusionally believes to be his, would be acquitted of homicide and theft, respectively, if mens rea is subjectively defined. . . .

Finally, a person may intentionally engage in conduct and intend the result, under no misapprehension as to the attendant circumstances, but still not intend to commit a crime because of an inadequate understanding of what crime is. There are actually two versions of this type of mens rea requirement. First, the person may not be aware of the *concept* of crime (as might be true of a three-year-old). Second, the person may understand that criminal prohibitions exist but believe that his specific act is legally permissible (such as might occur when a person from a different country commits an act that would be perfectly legal in his culture, although illegal in ours). The first situation might be called "general" ignorance of the law, while the second might be called "specific" ignorance of the law. Outside of the insanity and infancy contexts, neither type of ignorance has been recognized as an excuse for *mala in se* crimes. However, . . . a subjectively defined mens rea doctrine should excuse at least general ignorance of the law, a position that would acquit those rare individuals who intentionally carry out criminal acts without understanding the concepts of good and evil.

In short, the proposal would treat people with mental disorder no differently from people who are not mentally ill, assuming (and this is admittedly a big assumption) a modern criminal justice system that adopts a subjective approach to culpability.

QUESTIONS

What would be the advantages of adopting Professor Slobogin's approach? The disadvantages?

CHAPTER NINE

RAPE

A. INTRODUCTION

In his 1760s Commentaries, William Blackstone defined common law "rape" as the "carnal knowledge of a woman forcibly and against her will."[1] In recent decades, many state legislatures have sought to redefine rape, making it, according to Professor Susan Estrich, the "subject of substantive criminal law in great[est] ferment."[2] Widespread criticism of the traditional approach to defining the crime of rape and the criminal justice system's treatment of rape victims fuels this ferment.

Much of the criticism centers on a deep distrust of rape complainants that permeates the history of rape law.[3] For example, until reforms in recent decades, unlike other crime victims, judges routinely instructed jurors to be wary of the testimony of rape complainants.[4] Although much rarer today, at least in some circumstances, a number of jurisdictions still authorize the use of such a cautionary instruction. Similarly, courts commonly treated rape complainants like accomplices to the crime by requiring corroboration of their testimony. This meant that, for almost every other crime, a victim's testimony by itself could support a conviction, but for rape, victim testimony alone was, as a matter of law, insufficient.

---

1. William Blackstone, IV *Commentaries on the Laws of England*, ch. 15 at 208 (Thomas M. Cooley ed., 1879).
2. Susan Estrich, *Teaching Rape Law*, 102 Yale L.J. 509, 516 (1992).
3. The causes of this distrust are the subject of debate. *See, e.g.,* Anne M. Coughlin, *Sex and Guilt*, 84 Va. L. Rev. 1 (1998) (Professor Coughlin, offering "an alternative account of rape doctrine," argues that this distrust is a function of the historical context in which rape law developed. In a society in which all intercourse outside of marriage was criminal, rape victims, by acknowledging intercourse, were admitting elements of criminal conduct. Accordingly, Professor Coughlin contends that the legal barriers for victims were consistent with treatment of them as accomplices, who were generally distrusted. She concludes that society's rejection of the view that all intercourse outside of marriage is criminal underscores the need for rape law reform and consequently elimination of those legal barriers for victims).
4. Consider the Model Penal Code's proposed caution to the jury on the credibility of a rape victim:
   Model Penal Code § 213.6 (1985), *Provisions Generally Applicable to Article 213*

(5) In any prosecution before a jury for an offense under this Article, the jury shall be instructed to evaluate the testimony of a victim or complaining witness with special care in view of the emotional involvement of the witness and the difficulty of determining the truth with respect to alleged sexual activities carried out in private.

In addition, rape complainants had to report the offense promptly, a rule that became known as the "prompt complaint" rule. Although statutes of limitations existed for rape, like other offenses, failure to report promptly under the common law, even if the report fell well within the statute of limitations, created " 'a strong but not conclusive presumption against a woman.' "[5] Some jurisdictions, following the lead of the Model Penal Code in the 1950s, went further and enacted a complete bar to rape prosecutions when the victim did not report promptly.[6]

In the wake of rape law reform, jurisdictions have largely eliminated the formal doctrinal requirement of prompt complaint. Still, in modified forms, the rule remains in a number of jurisdictions.[7]

The cautionary instruction, the corroboration requirement, and the prompt complaint rule are three transparent manifestations of the criminal law's distrust of rape victims. That distrust continues to influence today's legal discourse on rape law and reform efforts.

This section begins with background information about rape. We consider statistics, studies, demographics, and accounts of rape—several by survivors. Although the accounts can be painful to read, these graphic descriptions provide critical insight into the crime and its impact. Following the background information, we turn to the elements of rape. Starting with Blackstone's formulation, we look at what has changed and what has remained unchanged about rape law since Blackstone's time.

Our study of the definition of rape begins with the conduct element—how legislatures have altered Blackstone's "carnal knowledge of a woman" as the starting point in defining "rape." We then turn to two other elements of Blackstone's formulation, "forcibly and against her will." The crime of rape has historically required, and in many jurisdictions continues to require, proof of both force and lack of consent. In defining and applying force and lack of consent, courts have focused on whether and to what extent the victim resisted. Accordingly we study force, lack of consent, and resistance together. Afterwards, we review the current status of rape law reform and consider perspectives on its evolution. In the last section, we analyze the crime of statutory rape, where, rather than focusing on consent or force, the ages of the involved parties generally control whether the sexual conduct qualifies as criminal.

---

5. Model Penal Code Commentaries, § 420-421, citing 4 W. Blackstone Commentaries * 211; 1 W. Hawkins, Pleas of the Crown 170 (3d ed. 1788). The Model Penal Code's provision on Prompt Complaint reads:

No prosecution may be instituted or maintained under this Article unless the alleged offense was brought to the notice of public authority within [3] months of its occurrence or, where the alleged victim was less than [16] years old or otherwise incompetent to make complaint, within [3] months after a parent, guardian or other competent person specially interested in the victim learns of the offense.

Contrast the MPC position with the language of the Montana statute, which declares: "(4) Evidence of failure to make a timely complaint or immediate outcry does not raise any presumption as to the credibility of the victim." Mont. Code Ann. § 45-5-511(4).
6. Model Penal Code Commentaries § 213.6, *supra* note 5, at 420-421.
7. *See, e.g.,* Tex. Code Crim. Proc. art. 38.07 (2004) (requiring that the victim have informed a person, other than the defendant, within one year of the sexual offense in order for his/her uncorroborated testimony to support a conviction, and providing for three very limited exceptions, *e.g.,* the victim being 17 years of age or younger).

B. CONTEXT: STATISTICS, STUDIES, AND DEMOGRAPHICS

Patricia Tjaden & Nancy Thoennes, PREVALENCE, INCIDENCE, AND CONSEQUENCES OF VIOLENCE AGAINST WOMEN: FINDINGS FROM THE NATIONAL VIOLENCE AGAINST WOMEN SURVEY   2, 3 National Institute of Justice Centers for Disease Control and Prevention (Nov. 1998)

[From late 1995 through May, 1996, the National Institute of Justice and the Centers for Disease Control and Prevention sponsored a national survey of 8,000 men and 8,000 women about their experiences with rape. They found the following:]

> Using a definition of rape that includes forced vaginal, oral, and anal sex, the survey found that 1 of 6 U.S. women and 1 of 33 U.S. men has experienced an attempted or completed rape as a child and/or an adult; specifically, 18 percent of surveyed women and 3 percent of surveyed men said they experienced a completed or attempted rape at some time in their life.

Lawrence A. Greenfeld, SEX OFFENSES AND OFFENDERS: AN ANALYSIS OF DATA ON RAPE AND SEXUAL ASSAULT   U.S. DOJ NCJ-163392 (Feb. 1997)

According to the National Crime Victim Survey, "[t]hree out of four rape/sexual assault victimizations involved offenders . . . with whom the victim had a prior relationship as a family member, intimate, or acquaintance."

Ted R. Miller et al., VICTIM COSTS AND CONSEQUENCES: A NEW LOOK   U.S. DOJ, Natl Inst. of Justice, Table 5, p. 17 (excerpted) (1996)

ANNUAL LOSSES DUE TO CRIME (M = MILLIONS, IN 1993 DOLLARS)

	Medical	Other Tangible	Quality of Life	Total
Rape and Sexual Assault	4,000M	3,500M	119,000M	127,000M

Susan Estrich, REAL RAPE   19-20 (1987)

In their landmark study of jury trials, Kalven and Zeisel found not only that juries tend to be prejudiced against the prosecution in rape cases, but that they will go to great lengths to be lenient with defendants if there is any suggestion of "contributory behavior" on the part of the victim. "Contributory behavior" warranting leniency includes the victim's hitchhiking, dating, and talking with men at parties.

Kalven and Zeisel divided their rape cases into two categories, aggravated and simple. . . . "Aggravated" rape, according to them, includes cases with extrinsic violence, multiple assailants, or no prior relationship between victim and offender (strangers). "Simple" rape includes cases in which none of these "aggravating circumstances" is present. Jury conviction rates were nearly four times as high in the aggravated cases. Kalven and Zeisel asked judges if they agreed or disagreed with the jury's verdict in particular cases. The percentage of judges in disagreement with the jury jumped from 12 percent in the aggravated cases to 60 percent in the simple cases, with the bulk of the disagreement explained by the jury's absolute determination not to convict of rape if there was any sign of contributory fault by the woman, despite enough evidence of guilt to satisfy the judge.

Barbara W. Girardin et al., FINDINGS IN SEXUAL ASSAULT AND CONSENSUAL INTERCOURSE, COLOR ATLAS OF SEXUAL ASSAULT   22-24 (1997)

Slaughter and Brown (1992) found genital injury in 87% of the patients reporting within 48 hours after nonconsensual penile vaginal penetration ($n = 238$) when examined by a prepared sexual assault examiner and with colposcopic magnification. Genital injury may be present even when there are no subjective symptoms reported by the patient (Rambow and others, 1992). . . .

However, the prevalence of serious injury requiring medical care, hospitalization, or surgery is less then 5%. . . .

Physical injury, including genital injury, is not an inevitable consequence of rape and the absence of genital injury does not provide proof of consent. . . .

Lack of magnification can drop the probability of detecting injury from 87% with colposcopy and a trained examiner, to 10% to 30% by gross visualization alone.

Patricia A. Resnick & Monica K. Schnicke, COGNITIVE PROCESSING THERAPY FOR RAPE VICTIMS: A TREATMENT MANUAL   4 (1993)

Sexual assault . . . is a traumatic event from which many victims never fully recover. Many victims develop problems with depression, poor self-esteem, interpersonal difficulties, and sexual dysfunctions. . . . However, the most frequently observed disorder that develops as a result of sexual assault is post-traumatic stress disorder (PTSD).

Angela P. Harris, RACE AND ESSENTIALISM IN FEMINIST LEGAL THEORY   42 Stan. L. Rev. 581, 598-599, 600 (1990)

[T]he paradigm experience of rape for black women has historically involved the white employer in the kitchen or bedroom as much as the strange black man in the bushes. During slavery, the sexual abuse of black women by white men was commonplace. Even after emancipation, the majority of working black women were domestic servants for white families, a job which made them uniquely vulnerable to sexual harassment and rape.

Moreover, as a legal matter, the experience of rape did not even exist for black women. During slavery, the rape of a black woman by any man, white or black, was simply not a crime. Even after the Civil War, rape laws were seldom used to protect black women against either white or black men, since black women were considered promiscuous by nature. In contrast to the partial or at least formal protection white women had against sexual brutalization, black women frequently had no legal protection whatsoever. "Rape," in this sense, was something that only happened to white women; what happened to black women was simply life.

Finally, for black people, male and female, "rape" signified the terrorism of black men by white men, aided and abetted, passively (by silence) or actively (by "crying rape"), by white women. . . .

Nor has this aspect of rape become purely historical curiosity. Susan Estrich reports that between 1930 and 1967, 89 percent of the men executed for rape in the United States were black; a 1968 study of rape sentencing in Maryland showed that in all 55 cases where the death penalty was imposed the victim had been white, and that between 1960 and 1967, 47 percent of all black men convicted of criminal assaults on black women were immediately released on probation.

Ben Schmitt, DNA COMES TO DEFENSE'S RESCUE
The Recorder 1, 6 (June 18, 1999)

On November 14, 1983, Calvin C. Johnson Jr. swore that he was innocent of the rape for which a jury had convicted him and a judge sentenced him to life in prison. The victim of the rape had identified Mr. Johnson from a photo spread two weeks after the attack and again at the trial, although, in between, she had identified someone else in a separate photo identification. Sixteen years later, on June 15, 1999, DNA testing exonerated Mr. Johnson and he was released from prison. Mr. Johnson explained: "I love Georgia, but I had an all-white jury. The victim was white and I'm black. There's no way when I walked in that I was going to walk out of the courtroom."

Robert J. Hunter et al., THE DEATH SENTENCING OF RAPISTS
IN PRE-FURMAN TEXAS (1942-1971): THE RACIAL
DIMENSION   20 Am. J. Crim. L. 313, 336 (1993)

**RAPIST AND VICTIM RACIAL COMBINATION COMPARISON
OF DEATH- AND TERM-SENTENCED RAPISTS (1942-1971)
(RESTRICTED POPULATION)**

Rapist Race By Victim Race	Percent of Death-Sentenced Rapists (n = 74)	Percent of Term-Sentenced Rapists (n = 87)
White X White	21.6%	56.9%
White X Black	0.0%	1.1%
White X Hispanic	0.0%	0.0%
Black X White	70.2%	2.3%
Black X Black	1.3%	0.0%
Black X Hispanic	1.3%	0.0%
Hispanic X White	4.0%	2.3%
Hispanic X Black	0.0%	1.1%
Hispanic X Hispanic	1.3%	13.9%

People *v.* Liberta, New York Court of Appeals   64 N.Y.2d 152,
n. 8 (1984) (citations omitted)

The stigma and other difficulties associated with a woman reporting a rape
and pressing charges probably deter most attempts to fabricate an incident;
rape remains a grossly under-reported crime.

Linda Fairstein, SEXUAL VIOLENCE: OUR WAR AGAINST
RAPE   229 (1993)

[M]ost law enforcement officials equate the amount of false reporting of
sex offenses with that of every other category of crime, at approximately
5 percent of the total number of reports.

C. WHAT IS RAPE?

1. Women as Victims: Two Women's Accounts

Forcible rape is not in any normal sense intercourse. . . . I believe that it is
the most physically painful ordeal that an individual can undergo and still live

afterward. When I was being raped I felt as though I were being repeatedly stabbed with a knife in one of the most sensitive areas of my body. Near the end, I was in shock. I felt numb and could feel no pain, but I knew that the rapist was tearing me apart inside. Hours after the attack the pain returned, and I felt as though I had been set on fire. Although I bled for only a few days, the pain lasted for weeks. . . . "[T]here is no 'sex' in rape. There is only pain. . . . "[8]

He wasn't just my Uncle. He was my favorite uncle. The one I liked seeing the most at family functions. Now he's the devil.

When you are molested by a family member, raped by an acquaintance or sexually abused by someone you know, it wrecks the way you perceive the world.

I have no reason to fear the man waiting in the bushes. MY boogie man has a face I have to look at every day in family photos that hang in my grandma's house. The man in the bushes has never hurt me, a man I loved hurt me. I have to listen to family members who don't know, talk about him and how "wonderful" he is. Even my Mom who did know about what he did pushed it so far back in her memory it's like I made it up. Twice. If she did something the first time I would probably have forgotten it because I was so young.

I'm not saying that what happens to a woman when they are raped by a stranger is any less than when you are raped by an acquaintance. What I am saying though is that the stranger in the bushes is not more culpable than an acquaintance. . . . [An acquaintance] may be in my opinion even more culpable and blameworthy.

People who trust and love you are supposed to protect you, care for you, and prevent other people from doing bad things to you. They are not supposed to be the bad people you have to watch out for.

I don't trust men anymore. When I get a hug from my Dad, the person who means the most to me in the whole world, I think about was that hug too long? When I go to a male friend's house for the first time or he drives me home I check for exits and look for things I could use to protect myself. My body sometimes freezes when someone touches me and I wasn't expecting it. At movies I shake and cry when someone is violated. I relive my experience.

I have nightmares and flashbacks whenever I can smell alcohol on someone who kisses me. I see my scared little ghost-white face looking in the mirror trying to figure out what to do to stop what was happening. Imagine what that does to a relationship when you're trying to be intimate. It's hard to be intimate with a person when you're getting a flashback.

This memory isn't something that only comes into your head once in a while. It's persistent. You think about was it my fault, could I have done something different to prevent it. What if this, what if that. I think about my two girl cousins and am scared to death he may hurt them too. But because most people don't know I can't do anything to protect them without tearing up my family.

I can't be in a closed room with a man who is around seven years older than me. I get nervous and fidgety. Even if that man is my boss at work.

---

8. Village Voice (Letter to the Editor) (Oct. 22, 1979), *quoted in* Elizabeth Stanko, *Intimate Intrusions, Women's Experience of Male Violence*, 34-35 (1985), *quoted in* Nancy S. Erickson, *Final Report: "Sex Bias in the Teaching of Criminal Law,"* 42 Rutgers L. Rev. 309, 342 (1990).

My Uncle took something away from me that no matter what I do I can't get back. He took my faith in the people I love and care about and he makes me on a daily basis doubt their integrity and morals.[9]

2. Men as Victims: Two Men's Accounts

In the summer of 1973 a 28-year-old Quaker pacifist named Robert A. Martin, a former seaman with a background in journalism, held a stunning press conference in Washington, D.C. Arrested during a peace demonstration in front of the White House, Martin had chosen to go to prison rather than post a $10 bond. His first week in the District of Columbia jail, Martin told reporters, passed uneventfully enough in a quiet cellblock populated by older prisoners including Watergate burglar C. Gordon Liddy, but then he was transferred to Cellblock 2, a tier of "predominantly young . . . prisoners, many of them in jail for serious crimes of violence." During his first evening recreation period on the new tier, the boyish-looking pacifist was invited into a cell on the pretext that some of the men wanted to talk with him. Once inside, he said, "My exit was blocked and my pants were forcibly taken off me, and I was raped. Then I was dragged from cell to cell all evening." Martin was promised protection from further assaults by two of his violators. The next night his "protectors" initiated a second general round of oral and rectal rape. The pair stood outside his cell and collected packs of cigarettes from other prisoners wanting a turn. When his attackers gave him a brief rest period to overcome his gagging and nausea, Martin made his escape and alerted a guard. He was taken to D.C. General Hospital where he underwent VD tests and a rectal examination. The following morning a Quaker friend posted his bond.[10]

In the absence of prior documentation that men or boys can be and are sexually assaulted by women, there has been the widespread belief that it would be almost impossible for a man to achieve or maintain an erection when threatened or attacked by a woman. Widespread acceptance of this sexual myth has had unfortunate implications for medicine, psychology, and law. Its persistence in our culture has meant that male victims of sexual assault have not been identified and that their psychotherapeutic needs have remained unmet.

Sexual abuse of men by women has been an integral but little publicized part of many cultures. Most of the sexual abuse has been committed by older females on young males. . . . What has not been really understood is the fact that sexual dysfunction or disorder can occur as a consequence of the male sexual abuse. . . .

. . . The first case is that of a 27-year-old, 178-pound male truck driver, married at 21 and divorced at 25 years of age. After the divorce, he socialized primarily in a bar society, occasionally patronizing prostitutes. He estimated approximately 30 different female sex partners before the sexual assault. . . .

---

9. C. H., a female student in one of the authors' Criminal Law classes, writing in response to the excerpt from Professor Joshua Dressler's article, in Section D.2.b.

10. Susan Brownmiller, *Against Our Will: Men, Women, and Rape*, 258-259 (1975) (listing as sources: Robert A. Martin press conference: Jared Stout, "Quaker Tells of Rape in D.C. Jail," Washington Star-News, Aug. 25, 1973; David L. Aiken, "Ex-Sailor Charges Jail Rape, Stirs up Storm," The Advocate Sept. 26, 1973, p.5).

One night he had been drinking in a bar with a woman companion he had not known previously. They went to a motel where he was given another drink and shortly thereafter fell asleep. He awoke to find himself naked, tied hand and foot to a bedstead, gagged, and blindfolded. As he listened to voices in the room, it was evident that several women were present.

When the women realized that he was awake, he was told that he had to "have sex with all of them." He thinks that during his period of captivity four different women used him sexually, some of them a number [of] times. . . . Following the first two coital episodes, he did not ejaculate again until he was seen in therapy. After several more coital experiences, it became increasingly difficult for him to maintain an erection. When he couldn't function well, he was threatened with castration and felt a knife held to his scrotum. He was terrified that [he] would be cut and did have some brief improvement in erective quality. . . .

He believes that the period of forcible restraint and repeated sexual assaults continued for more than 24 hours. . . . The man did not report the episode to the police or tell anyone of his experience. He was terrified that if his friends found out about his "disgrace" they would think him "less than a man" because he had been "raped by women. . . ."

In subsequent months, [he] attempted sexual intercourse with several different women, but he was never able to achieve or maintain an erection sufficient for vaginal penetration, nor did he ejaculate. The man married about a year before he sought professional support but was unable to consummate the marriage. When he and his wife were seen in therapy, she was unaware of his history of sexual assault.[11]

QUESTIONS

1. The national survey on rape cited above indicates that 18 percent of women and 3 percent of men have been victims of rape or attempted rape. What might those statistics suggest about the experiences, in regard to such crimes, of the student population of a law school class studying rape law?

2. The table above showing the death penalty, rape, and race is based on data from before 1977, the year in which the United States Supreme Court held that a death sentence for rape committed on an adult female violates the constitutional prohibition on cruel and unusual punishments.[12] Compare, though, the statistics about white rapists and black victims with those of black rapists and white victims. What do the disparities suggest?

D. EVOLVING DEFINITIONS

1. Conduct

Blackstone defined "rape" as the "carnal knowledge of a woman forcibly and against her will." Carnal knowledge meant sexual intercourse involving at least

---

11. Philip M. Sarrel & William H. Masters, *Sexual Molestation of Men by Women*, 11 Archives of Sexual Behavior 117-118, 120-121, 123 (1982).
12. Coker v. Georgia, 433 U.S. 584 (1977).

slight penile penetration of the vaginal area. This definition of rape required a male perpetrator and a female victim. Reform efforts led many legislatures to define the primary conduct more broadly. Modern legislatures have also attached a variety of labels to current versions of the common law crime of rape. These include, for example, sexual assault, sexual abuse, criminal sexual assault, as well as rape.

PROBLEM

9.1 Consider the four factual scenarios described below and the statutes that follow them. Then apply each statute to each of the scenarios. Assume that all other elements are fulfilled. Which of the statutes cover the conduct described?

(a) John has sexual intercourse with Karen.
(b) Arthur anally penetrates Fred.
(c) Karen engages in oral sex with Jessica.
(d) Jill masturbates Tom.

Idaho Code § 18-6101 (2004)   *Rape defined*

Rape is defined as the penetration, however slight, of the oral, anal or vaginal opening with the perpetrator's penis accomplished with a female . . .
    (3) Where she resists but her resistance is overcome by force or violence. . . .

New York Criminal Law § 130.35 (2003)   *Rape in the first degree*

A male is guilty of rape in the first degree when he engages in sexual intercourse with a female:
    1. By forcible compulsion. . . .

720 Illinois Compiled Statute 5/12-13 (2001)   *Criminal Sexual Assault*

(a) The accused commits criminal sexual assault if he or she:
    (1) commits an act of sexual penetration by the use of force or threat of force. . . .

720 Illinois Compiled Statues 5/12-12(f) (2001)

"Sexual penetration" means any contact, however slight, between the sex organ or anus of one person by an object, the sex organ, mouth or anus of another person, or any intrusion, however slight, or any part of the body of one person or of any animal or object into the sex organ or anus of another person, including but not limited to cunnilingus, fellatio or anal penetration.

Iowa Code Annotated § 709.1 (2002) *Sexual abuse defined*

Any sex act between persons is sexual abuse by either of the persons when the act is performed with the other person in any of the following circumstances:
1. The act is done by force or against the will of the other. . . .

Model Penal Code § 213.0 (1985) *Definitions*

(2) "Sexual intercourse" includes intercourse per os or per anum, with some penetration however slight; emission is not required.

Massachusetts General Laws Annotated chapter 265 § 22 (2000) *Rape, generally* . . .

(b) Whoever has sexual intercourse or unnatural sexual intercourse with a person and compels such person to submit by force and against his will. . . .

QUESTIONS

1. Which statute provides the broadest coverage of conduct?
2. Assume that the Massachusetts Criminal Code fails to define "unnatural sexual intercourse." What concerns would that failure raise?
3. Which statutory language regarding conduct would you choose as a state legislator? Why?

2. Force, Resistance, and Consent

In addition to the conduct element of carnal knowledge, Blackstone's definition of rape required that the act be committed "forcibly and against her will." In defining and applying these elements to the facts of rape cases, courts looked to the resistance of rape victims. Courts gauged the existence and extent of force by analyzing how much resistance the defendant had overcome. Similarly, resistance communicated that the contact was against the victim's will, that she had not consented. Since consent was presumed absent a physical manifestation of nonconsent, resistance disproved the presumption. Actual physical force was not necessarily required. Threats and fear of serious bodily injury could serve as constructive force, a proxy for actual physical force. In such circumstances, a court might find resistance unnecessary. In this section, we study the interaction among these components of rape law.

a. Force or Fear

PEOPLE *v.* WARREN
Illinios Appellate Court 113 Ill. App. 3d 1 (1983)

KARNS, Justice:
Defendant, Joel F. Warren, was charged by information with two counts of deviate sexual assault. Following a bench trial, defendant was convicted on both counts and was sentenced to a term of six years in prison.

On appeal, defendant contends that the State did not prove him guilty of deviate sexual assault beyond a reasonable doubt. Specifically, defendant argues that the State failed to prove that the acts complained of were committed by force or threat of force or against the will of the complainant. Defendant further contends that he was denied due process of law when the court convicted him on the basis of an improper standard of guilt.

At the time of the incident, defendant, Joel Warren, was 30 years of age and was a student at Southern Illinois University. Complainant was 32 years of age and worked as a volunteer at Synergy, an organization located in Carbondale, Illinois.

Complainant testified that on the afternoon of July 1, 1980, she rode her bicycle to Horstman's Point, which overlooks the Carbondale City Reservoir in Carbondale. While complainant was standing alone at Horstman's Point, defendant approached her and initiated and engaged in a conversation with her. Although complainant did not know defendant, she responded to his conversation which was general in nature.

Complainant started to walk away from the lake in the direction of her bicycle which was at the top of the hill. While she walked up the hill, defendant continued talking as he walked alongside of her. Complainant testified that when she got on her bicycle defendant placed his hand on her shoulder. At this time, complainant stated, "No, I have to go now," to which defendant responded, "This will only take a minute. My girlfriend doesn't meet my needs." Defendant also told her that "I don't want to hurt you."

According to complainant, defendant then lifted her off the ground and carried her into a wooded area adjacent to the reservoir. Upon entering the woods, defendant placed complainant on the ground and told her to put her head on his backpack. Defendant then told her to take her pants down which she did part way. Defendant pulled her pants completely off and placed them underneath her. He then proceeded to pull up complainant's tank top shirt and began kissing her breasts and vaginal area. After he finished kissing complainant, defendant sat up and unzipped his pants and complainant performed an act of fellatio upon him.

At the completion of this second act, defendant gave complainant an article of clothing to wipe her mouth. Complainant then dressed and defendant picked her up again and carried her back to her bicycle. Defendant testified that complainant asked him, "Is that all?" to which he answered, "Yes."

Complainant got on her bicycle and rode to Synergy, where she spoke to a volunteer worker who referred her to the Women's Center in Carbondale. At the Women's Center, she spoke with Mary Kay Bachman, with whom she went to the Carbondale Police Department. Complainant related the incident to Officer William Kilquist, who testified that complainant appeared to be very upset. Officer Kilquist further testified that no formal report was prepared at the request of complainant.

On February 15, 1981, complainant saw defendant while she was jogging and reported him to the police as the man with whom she had sexual relations. Defendant was arrested at his home later that day by Officers Hunziker and Hawk of the Southern Illinois Police Department and charged with deviate sexual assault.

At the outset, we note that there are no significant inconsistencies in the testimony of the two parties. Instead, we are faced with facts which are susceptible of more than one reading. Defendant admits that he performed the acts upon which the deviate sex charges are based. He contends, however, that the acts complained of were performed without force or threat of force.

Reviewing courts are especially charged with the duty of carefully examining the evidence in rape or deviate sexual assault cases and it is the duty of the reviewing court to reverse the judgment unless the evidence is sufficient to remove all reasonable doubt of defendant's guilt and create an abiding conviction that he is guilty of the crime charged. The ultimate issue presented for review in the instant case is whether the State satisfactorily proved that the acts complained of were committed by force or threat of force as required to constitute deviate sexual assault.

To sustain a conviction for deviate sexual assault, there must be evidence that defendant, by force or threat, compelled another to perform or submit to any act of deviate sexual conduct. There is, however, no definite standard which fixes the amount of force which is required to sustain the charge of rape or deviate sexual assault. Each case must be examined on the basis of its own particular facts.

In the present case, the State contends that defendant coerced complainant into engaging in deviate sexual acts by threatening to use physical force. The State maintains that this threat was conveyed by defendant's statement that "I don't want to hurt you," the implication being that he would hurt her if she did not comply. Although this interpretation has some merit, we do not believe that it is the most reasonable conclusion drawn from the facts. Defendant did not make the above statement while brandishing a weapon or applying physical force, a circumstance which would support the State's construction. Instead, we find that the record is devoid of any attendant circumstances which suggest that complainant was compelled to submit to defendant.

In addition, the State argues that the threat of force was conveyed by the disparity of size and strength between the parties. The record shows that at the time of the incident complainant was 5'2" tall weighing 100 to 105 pounds, whereas defendant was 6'3" and 185 pounds. The State further maintains that the seclusion of the woods contributed to this threat of force. Although it is proper to consider such factors in weighing the evidence, we do not believe that the evidence taken as a whole supports the State's conclusion. Aside from picking up complainant and carrying her into and out of the woods, defendant did not employ his superior size and strength. Furthermore, complainant did not attempt to flee or in any meaningful way resist the sexual advances of defendant.

Much of the State's case rests upon its contention that complainant's absence of effort in thwarting defendant's advances was motivated by her overwhelming fear. In support of this position, the State offers complainant's statement that she did not attempt to flee because, "it was in the middle of the woods and I didn't feel like I could get away from him and I thought he'd kill me." Moreover, complainant stated that she did not yell or scream because the people she had seen in the area were too far away and that under the circumstances she felt that screaming "would be bad for me."

Despite professing fear for her safety, complainant concedes that defendant did not strike her or threaten to strike her or use a weapon. When defendant picked up complainant and carried her into the wooded area, she did not protest but merely stated, "I can walk." Although she maintained that she stiffened up to make it harder for him to carry her, defendant did not recall any resistance. At no time did complainant tell defendant to leave her alone or put her down. Furthermore, complainant did not object when defendant instructed her to take off her pants, but instead she complied with his request by pulling down her pants part way. . . .

In the case before us, defendant maintains that once complainant became aware that defendant intended to engage in sexual relations it was incumbent upon her to resist. This resistance would have the effect of giving defendant notice that his acts were being performed without her consent. It is well settled that if complainant had the use of her faculties and physical powers, the evidence must show such resistance as will demonstrate that the act was against her will. If the circumstances show resistance to be futile or life endangering or if the complainant is overcome by superior strength or paralyzed by fear, useless or foolhardy acts of resistance are not required. We cannot say that any of the above factors are present here. Complainant's failure to resist when it was within her power to do so conveys the impression of consent regardless of her mental state, amounts to consent and removes from the act performed an essential element of the crime. We do not mean to suggest, however, that the complainant did in fact consent; however, she must communicate in some objective manner her lack of consent.

Defendant's second contention is that the trial court violated his due process by applying an erroneous standard of guilt. Defendant maintains that the trial court created a new standard of guilt in determining that defendant used "psychological force" to overcome the will of complainant. . . .

Although the trial court employed a new term in entering its judgment, we believe it is clear that the court applied the statutory standard of guilt. We believe, however, that the State has not proved that defendant committed deviate sexual acts by force or threat of force as required by statute. Consequently, the judgment of conviction for deviate sexual assault is reversed.

Reversed.

HARRISON, Presiding Justice:

I respectfully dissent.

It is well settled that a victim need not resist when to do so would be futile or life endangering, or where she is overcome by superior strength or paralyzed by fear. Such was the case here. The victim testified that she did not scream because there was no one in the vicinity to hear her screams. She considered escaping but decided that an attempt would be futile because she could not outrun the defendant in the woods. She testified that she resisted when he carried her into the woods, although she did not strike or otherwise physically assault him because of the likelihood that such behavior would anger him. She was overpowered by him physically (compare 5 ft. 2 in., 100 lbs. to 6 ft. 3 in., 185 lbs.) and felt extremely vulnerable in such an isolated area where no one was around to help her. Under these circumstances, where violent resistance might only have provoked the defendant, her acquiescence was reasonable and did not constitute consent.

In addition, the victim made an immediate complaint to a counseling center and to the police. A prompt complaint to authorities has been held sufficient corroboration. And even if uncorroborated, the testimony of the witness alone can be sufficient to justify the conviction if that testimony is clear and convincing. In my view, her account of the episode and the reasons explaining her behavior were clear and convincing. Therefore, I would affirm the defendant's conviction for deviate sexual assault.

QUESTIONS

1. Why is the majority unpersuaded that physically lifting a stranger off her feet and carrying her some distance to an isolated wooded area is force? Should the relative sizes of the defendant and the complainant play a role in determining whether force was used?

2. How is "force" defined here? How is it related to a threat? Why does the court conclude that a threat was not present?

3. Is consent relevant to the legal issue the court sets itself to resolve? How does resistance relate to consent in the *Warren* case?

4. What role does the fact that the complainant complained promptly play in the dissent's analysis?

5. From the dissent's discussion, what appears to be the role of corroboration in sexual offenses in Illinois in 1983?

PROBLEM

9.2 Consider the following account:

> The complainant, a female college student, left her class, went to her dormitory room where she drank a martini, and then went to a lounge to await her boyfriend. When her boyfriend failed to appear, she went to another dormitory to find a friend, Earl Hassel. She knocked on the door, but received no answer. She tried the door-knob and, finding it unlocked, entered the room and discovered a man sleeping on the bed. The complainant originally believed the man to be Hassel, but it turned out to be Hassel's roommate, [the Defendant. He] asked her to stay for a while and she agreed. He requested a back-rub and she declined. He suggested that she sit on the bed, but she declined and sat on the floor.
>
> [Defendant] then moved to the floor beside her, lifted up her shirt and bra and massaged her breasts. He then unfastened his pants and unsuccessfully attempted to put his penis in her mouth. They both stood up, and he locked the door. He returned to push her onto the bed, and removed her undergarments from one leg. He then pene-trated her vagina with his penis. After withdrawing and ejaculating on her stomach, he stated, "Wow, I guess we just got carried away," to which she responded, "No, we didn't get carried away, you got carried away."
>
> The complainant repeatedly said "no" throughout the encounter, but took no physical action to discourage or impede the defendant. She states that the defendant "put me down on the bed. He didn't throw me on the bed. It was kind of like a push." She also states that the defendant's hands were not restraining her in any manner, though the weight of his body was on top of her. The evidence also shows that the door could have been easily unlocked and that the complainant was aware of this but did not attempt to unlock the door or leave the room.[13]

Has the defendant violated the following statutes?

---

13. Based on and quoted from Commonwealth v. Berkowitz, 415 Pa. Super. 505 (1992).

18 Pennsylvania Consolidated Statues Annotated § 3121 (2001)   *Rape*

A person commits a felony of the first degree when he or she engages in sexual intercourse with a complainant:
    (1) By forcible compulsion. . . .

18 Pennsylvania Consolidated Statutes Annotated. § 3124.1 (2001)   *Sexual Assault*

Except as provided in section 3121 (relating to rape) or 3123 (relating to involuntary deviate sexual intercourse), a person commits a felony of the second degree when that person engages in sexual intercourse or deviate sexual intercourse with a complainant without the complainant's consent.

Idaho Code § 16101 (2001)   *Rape defined*

Rape is defined as the penetration, however slight, of the oral, anal or vaginal opening with the perpetrator's penis accomplished with a female . . .
    (3) Where she resists but her resistance is overcome by force or violence. . . .

QUESTIONS

1. What are the elements of each statute? What are the differences among the statutes?
2. How should "forcible compulsion" be interpreted? Is "forcible compulsion" something distinct from lack of consent? Or does it incorporate lack of consent?
3. Reconsider the *Warren* case. Would Warren be liable under either Pennsylvania or Idaho law?

b. New Perspectives on Force

STATE IN INTEREST OF M.T.S.
Supreme Court of New Jersey 129 N.J. 422 (1992)

HANDLER, J.
Under New Jersey law a person who commits an act of sexual penetration using physical force or coercion is guilty of second-degree sexual assault. The sexual assault statute does not define the words "physical force." The question posed by this appeal is whether the element of "physical force" is met simply by an act of non-consensual penetration involving no more force than necessary to accomplish that result.

That issue is presented in the context of what is often referred to as "acquaintance rape." The record in the case discloses that the juvenile, a seventeen-year-old boy, engaged in consensual kissing and heavy petting with a fifteen-year-old girl and thereafter engaged in actual sexual penetration of the girl to which she had not consented. There was no evidence or suggestion that the juvenile used any unusual or extra force or threats to accomplish the act of penetration.

The trial court determined that the juvenile was delinquent for committing a sexual assault. The Appellate Division reversed the disposition of delinquency, concluding that non-consensual penetration does not constitute sexual assault unless it is accompanied by some level of force more than that necessary to accomplish the penetration. We granted the State's petition for certification. . . .

II

The New Jersey Code of Criminal Justice, N.J.S.A. 2C:14-2c(1), defines "sexual assault" as the commission "of sexual penetration" "with another person" with the use of "physical force or coercion."[1] An unconstrained reading of the statutory language indicates that both the act of "sexual penetration" and the use of "physical force or coercion" are separate and distinct elements of the offense. Neither the definitions section of N.J.S.A. 2C:14-1 to -8, nor the remainder of the Code of Criminal Justice provides assistance in interpreting the words "physical force." The initial inquiry is, therefore, whether the statutory words are unambiguous on their face and can be understood and applied in accordance with their plain meaning. . . .

The parties offer two alternative understandings of the concept of "physical force" as it is used in the statute. The State would read "physical force" to entail any amount of sexual touching brought about involuntarily. A showing of sexual penetration coupled with a lack of consent would satisfy the elements of the statute. The Public Defender urges an interpretation of "physical force" to mean force "used to overcome lack of consent." That definition equates force with violence and leads to the conclusion that sexual assault requires the application of some amount of force in addition to the act of penetration.

Current judicial practice suggests an understanding of "physical force" to mean "any degree of physical power or strength used against the victim, even though it entails no injury and leaves no mark." Model Jury Charges, Criminal 3 (revised Mar. 27, 1989). . . . The dictionary provides several definitions of "force," among which are the following: (1) "power, violence, compulsion, or constraint exerted upon or against a person or thing," (2) "a general term for exercise of strength or power, esp. physical, to overcome resistance," or (3) "strength or power of any degree that is exercised without justification or contrary to law upon a person or thing." *Webster's Third New International Dictionary* 887 (1961).

Thus, as evidenced by the disagreements among the lower courts and the parties, and the variety of possible usages, the statutory words "physical force" do not evoke a single meaning that is obvious and plain. Hence, we must pursue avenues of construction in order to ascertain the meaning of that statutory language. Those avenues are well charted. When a statute is open to conflicting interpretations, the court seeks the underlying intent of the legislature, relying on legislative history and the contemporary context of the statute. With respect to a law, like the sexual assault statute, that "alters or amends the previous law or creates or abolishes types of actions, it is important, in discovering the legislative intent, to ascertain the old law, the mischief and the proposed remedy." We also remain mindful of the basic

---

[1] The sexual assault statute, N.J.S.A.: 2C:14-2c(1), reads as follows:

c. An actor is guilty of sexual assault if he commits an act of sexual penetration with another person under any one of the following circumstances:

(1) The actor uses physical force or coercion, but the victim does not sustain severe personal injury; . . . Sexual assault is a crime of the second degree.

tenet of statutory construction that penal statutes are to be strictly construed in favor of the accused. Nevertheless, the construction must conform to the intent of the Legislature. . . .

Under traditional rape law, in order to prove that a rape had occurred, the state had to show both that force had been used and that the penetration had been against the woman's will. Force was identified and determined not as an independent factor but in relation to the response of the victim, which in turn implicated the victim's own state of mind. "Thus, the perpetrator's use of force became criminal only if the victim's state of mind met the statutory requirement. The perpetrator could use all the force imaginable and no crime would be committed if the state could not prove additionally that the victim did not consent." Although the terms "non-consent" and "against her will" were often treated as equivalent, under the traditional definition of rape, both formulations squarely placed on the victim the burden of proof and of action. Effectively, a woman who was above the age of consent had actively and affirmatively to withdraw that consent for the intercourse to be against her will. As a Delaware court stated, "If sexual intercourse is obtained by milder means, or with the consent or silent submission of the female, it cannot constitute the crime of rape."

The presence or absence of consent often turned on credibility. To demonstrate that the victim had not consented to the intercourse, and also that sufficient force had been used to accomplish the rape, the state had to prove that the victim had resisted. According to the oft-quoted Lord Hale, to be deemed a credible witness, a woman had to be of good fame, disclose the injury immediately, suffer signs of injury, and cry out for help. Courts and commentators historically distrusted the testimony of victims, "assuming that women lie about their lack of consent for various reasons: to blackmail men, to explain the discovery of a consensual affair, or because of psychological illness." Evidence of resistance was viewed as a solution to the credibility problem; it was the "outward manifestation of nonconsent, [a] device for determining whether a woman actually gave consent."

The resistance requirement had a profound effect on the kind of conduct that could be deemed criminal and on the type of evidence needed to establish the crime. . . . In many jurisdictions the requirement was that the woman have resisted to the utmost. . . . "[A] mere tactical surrender in the face of an assumed superior physical force is not enough. Where the penalty for the defendant may be supreme, so must resistance be unto the uttermost." Other states followed a "reasonableness" standard, while some required only sufficient resistance to make non-consent reasonably manifest. . . .

That the law put the rape victim on trial was clear.

The resistance requirement had another untoward influence on traditional rape law. Resistance was necessary not only to prove non-consent but also to demonstrate that the force used by the defendant had been sufficient to overcome the victim's will. The amount of force used by the defendant was assessed in relation to the resistance of the victim. In New Jersey, the amount of force necessary to establish rape was characterized as "'the degree of force sufficient to overcome any resistance that had been put up by the female.'" *State v. Terry*, 89 N.M. Super. [445] at 451 [(1965).] Resistance, often demonstrated by torn clothing and blood, was a sign that the defendant had used significant force to accomplish the sexual intercourse. Thus, if the defendant forced himself on a woman, it was her responsibility to fight back, because force was measured in relation to the resistance she put forward. Only if she resisted, causing him to use more force than was necessary to achieve penetration, would his conduct be criminalized. Indeed, the significance of resistance as the proxy for force is illustrated by cases in which victims were unable to resist; in such cases the force incident to penetration was deemed sufficient to establish the "force" element of the offense.

The importance of resistance as an evidentiary requirement set the law of rape apart from other common-law crimes, particularly in the eyes of those who advocated reform of rape law in the 1970s. . . .

They emphasized that rape had its legal origins in laws designed to protect the property rights of men to their wives and daughters. Although the crime had evolved into an offense against women, reformers argued that vestiges of the old law remained, particularly in the understanding of rape as a crime against the purity or chastity of a woman. The burden of protecting that chastity fell on the woman, with the state offering its protection only after the woman demonstrated that she had resisted sufficiently. . . .

Critics of rape law agreed that the focus of the crime should be shifted from the victim's behavior to the defendant's conduct, and particularly to its forceful and assaultive, rather than sexual, character. Reformers also shared the goals of facilitating rape prosecutions and of sparing victims much of the degradation involved in bringing and trying a charge of rape. . . . [A]ll proponents of reform shared a central premise: that the burden of showing non-consent should not fall on the victim of the crime. In dealing with the problem of consent the reform goal was not so much to purge the entire concept of consent from the law as to eliminate the burden that had been placed on victims to prove they had not consented.

Similarly, with regard to force, rape law reform sought to give independent significance to the forceful or assaultive conduct of the defendant and to avoid a definition of force that depended on the reaction of the victim. Traditional interpretations of force were strongly criticized for failing to acknowledge that force may be understood simply as the invasion of "bodily integrity." In urging that the "resistance" requirement be abandoned, reformers sought to break the connection between force and resistance.

III

The history of traditional rape law sheds clearer light on the factors that became most influential in the enactment of current law dealing with sexual offenses. . . .

Since the 1978 reform, the Code has referred to the crime that was once known as "rape" as "sexual assault." The crime now requires "penetration," not "sexual intercourse." It requires "force" or "coercion," not "submission" or "resistance." It makes no reference to the victim's state of mind or attitude, or conduct in response to the assault. . . . It emphasizes the assaultive character of the offense by defining sexual penetration to encompass a wide range of sexual contacts, going well beyond traditional "carnal knowledge."[2] Consistent with the assaultive character, as opposed to the traditional sexual character, of the offense, the statute also renders the crime gender-neutral: both males and females can be actors or victims. . . .

---

[2] The reform replaced the concept of carnal abuse, which was limited to vaginal intercourse, with specific kinds of sexual acts contained in a broad definition of penetration: Sexual penetration means vaginal intercourse, cunnilingus, fellatio or anal intercourse between persons or insertion of the hand, finger or object into the anus or vagina either by the actor or upon the actor's instruction. [N.J.S.A. 2C:14-1.]

The Legislature's concept of sexual assault and the role of force was significantly colored by its understanding of the law of assault and battery. As a general matter, criminal battery is defined as "the unlawful application of force to the person of another." The application of force is criminal when it results in either (a) a physical injury or (b) an offensive touching. *Id.* at 301-02. Any "unauthorized touching of another [is] a battery. Thus, by eliminating all references to the victim's state of mind and conduct, and by broadening the definition of penetration to cover not only sexual intercourse between a man and a woman but a range of acts that invade another's body or compel intimate contact, the Legislature emphasized the affinity between sexual assault and other forms of assault and battery. . . .

The understanding of sexual assault as a criminal battery, albeit one with especially serious consequences, follows necessarily from the Legislature's decision to eliminate nonconsent and resistance from the substantive definition of the offense. Under the new law, the victim no longer is required to resist and therefore need not have said or done anything in order for the sexual penetration to be unlawful. The alleged victim is not put on trial, and his or her responsive or defensive behavior is rendered immaterial. We are thus satisfied that an interpretation of the statutory crime of sexual assault to require physical force in addition to that entailed in an act of involuntary or unwanted sexual penetration would be fundamentally inconsistent with the legislative purpose to eliminate any consideration of whether the victim resisted or expressed non-consent. . . .

We conclude, therefore, that any act of sexual penetration engaged in by the defendant without the affirmative and freely-given permission of the victim to the specific act of penetration constitutes the offense of sexual assault. Therefore, physical force in excess of that inherent in the act of sexual penetration is not required for such penetration to be unlawful. The definition of "physical force" is satisfied under N.J.S.A. 2C:14-2c(1) if the defendant applies any amount of force against another person in the absence of what a reasonable person would believe to be affirmative and freely-given permission to the act of sexual penetration.

Under the reformed statute, permission to engage in sexual penetration must be affirmative and it must be given freely, but that permission may be inferred either from acts or statements reasonably viewed in light of the surrounding circumstances. . . .

Our understanding of the meaning and application of "physical force" under the sexual assault statute indicates that the term's inclusion was neither inadvertent nor redundant. The term "physical force," like its companion term "coercion," acts to qualify the nature and character of the "sexual penetration." Sexual penetration accomplished through the use of force is unauthorized sexual penetration. That functional understanding of "physical force" encompasses the notion of "unpermitted touching" derived from the Legislature's decision to redefine rape as a sexual assault. As already noted, under assault and battery doctrine, any amount of force that results in either physical injury or offensive touching is sufficient to establish a battery. Hence, as a description of the method of achieving "sexual penetration," the term "physical force" serves to define and explain the acts that are offensive, unauthorized, and unlawful.

That understanding of the crime of sexual assault fully comports with the public policy sought to be effectuated by the Legislature. In redefining rape law as sexual assault, the Legislature adopted the concept of sexual assault as a crime against the bodily integrity of the victim. Although it is possible to imagine a set of rules in which persons must demonstrate affirmatively that sexual contact is unwanted or not permitted, such a regime would be inconsistent with modern principles of personal autonomy. The Legislature recast the law of rape as sexual assault to bring that area of law in line with the expectation of privacy and bodily control that long has characterized most of our private and public law. In interpreting "physical force" to include any touching that occurs without permission we seek to respect that goal. . . .

Each person has the right not only to decide whether to engage in sexual contact with another, but also to control the circumstances and character of that contact. No one, neither a spouse, nor a friend, nor an acquaintance, nor a stranger, has the right or the privilege to force sexual contact.

We emphasize as well that what is now referred to as "acquaintance rape" is not a new phenomenon. Nor was it a "futuristic" concept in 1978 when the sexual assault law was enacted. Current concern over the prevalence of forced sexual intercourse between persons who know one another reflects both greater awareness of the extent of such behavior and a growing appreciation of its gravity. Notwithstanding the stereotype of rape as a violent attack by a stranger, the vast majority of sexual assaults are perpetrated by someone known to the victim. One respected study indicates that more than half of all rapes are committed by male relatives, current or former husbands, boyfriends or lovers. Similarly, contrary to common myths, perpetrators generally do not use guns or knives and victims generally do not suffer external bruises or cuts. Although this more realistic and accurate view of rape only recently has achieved widespread public circulation, it was a central concern of the proponents of reform in the 1970s.

The insight into rape as an assaultive crime is consistent with our evolving understanding of the wrong inherent in forced sexual intimacy. . . .

IV

In a case such as this one, in which the State does not allege violence or force extrinsic to the act of penetration, the factfinder must decide whether the defendant's act of penetration was undertaken in circumstances that led the defendant reasonably to believe that the alleged victim had freely given affirmative permission to the specific act of sexual penetration. . . .

In these cases neither the alleged victim's subjective state of mind nor the reasonableness of the alleged victim's actions can be deemed relevant to the offense. The alleged victim may be questioned about what he or she did or said only to determine whether the defendant was reasonable in believing that affirmative permission had been freely given. . . .

If there is evidence to suggest that the defendant reasonably believed that such permission had been given, the State must demonstrate either that defendant did not actually believe that affirmative permission had been freely-given or that such a belief was unreasonable under all of the circumstances. Thus, the State bears the burden of proof throughout the case. . . .

Because "physical force" as an element of sexual assault in this context requires the *absence* of affirmative and freely-given permission, the "consent" necessary to negate such "physical force" under a defense based on consent would require the *presence* of such affirmative and freely-given permission. Any lesser form of consent would render the sexual penetration unlawful and cannot constitute a defense. . . .

We acknowledge that cases such as this are inherently fact sensitive and depend on the reasoned judgment and common sense of judges and juries. The trial court concluded that the victim had not expressed consent to the act of intercourse, either through her words or actions. We conclude that the record provides reasonable support for the trial court's disposition.

Accordingly, we reverse the judgment of the Appellate Division and reinstate the disposition of juvenile delinquency for the commission of second-degree sexual assault.

Consider Professor Joshua Dressler's criticism of *M.T.S.*:

Joshua Dressler, WHERE WE HAVE BEEN, AND WHERE WE MIGHT BE GOING: SOME CAUTIONARY REFLECTIONS ON RAPE LAW REFORM   46 Clev. St. L. Rev. 410, 410, 421-423, 426-428 (1998)

[A] few states are taking reform to another, I believe more questionable level. Consider the *M.T.S.* case. A 17-year-old boy, M.T.S., lived in the same house as C.G., a fifteen-year-old girl, and her parents. On the critical night, the two participated in consensual "kissing and heavy petting." Ultimately, intercourse occurred in the girl's bedroom. C.G. testified that M.T.S. had intercourse with her while she was asleep. He claimed an entirely consensual enterprise. The court, as trier of fact, "did not find that C.G. had been sleeping at the time of penetration, but nevertheless found that she had not consented to the actual sexual act." There was no evidence that M.T.S. threatened C.G. in any manner, nor did she physically resist his actions. Nonetheless, the defendant was convicted of forcible rape, according to a statute that, by its terms, required evidence that the sexual penetration occurred as the result of "physical force or coercion."

Now, what is wrong with convicting M.T.S.? There is *nothing* wrong with convicting M.T.S. of a crime. If C.G. truly did not consent to the intercourse, as the judge found, she *was* wronged. Her right of sexual autonomy *was* violated. But, let's put the case in perspective. At an earlier time, in many jurisdictions, if the teenagers' sexual activities had been brought to the attention of prosecutors, the matter would have been handled as a case of statutory rape, and probably treated leniently given the boy's age and lack of criminal record. But, here the prosecutor sought to prove *forcible* rape. . . .

What is wrong, first of all, is that the court effectively redrafted the statute. . . .

Not only has the court acted as a super-legislature, but by treating sexual intercourse as "force" it invites disproportional punishment. Can there be any doubt that forcible nonconsensual intercourse is a worse harm than *non*forcible, nonconsensual intercourse and, therefore, should be punished more severely? Yet, as interpreted, the New Jersey rape statute treats alike the rapist who jumps out from the bushes with a knife or gun and threatens the victim, the rapist who uses mild physical force to secure intercourse with an unwilling partner, and the teenage boy who has ordinary intercourse after consensual petting, without obtaining permission for the act. . . .

Let's start with the proposition that "no means no." This has become the mantra of the rape reform movement, and it is an excellent one. It is a clear and proper message. *Any* person who has sexual contact with a person who does not want it has violated the latter's sexual autonomy and, therefore, has wronged that individual. But, that only begins, it does not end, the analysis.

The first issue is whether intercourse following a "no" should constitute a crime. Not all wrongs are sufficiently egregious to justify the criminal (as distinguished from a civil) sanction. . . . I have no difficulty saying — it isn't a close issue — that a person who has nonforcible intercourse following a "no" — *however that "no" is expressed, whether in words or conduct* — has wronged that individual in a serious manner and (*mens rea* issues aside for now) deserves to be treated as a criminal. But, that being said, his conduct should constitute a . . . lesser sexual offense than rape, in a thoughtful reformed system.

But *M.T.S.* does not say, simply, "no means no." It says that the *actus reus* of forcible rape occurs in the absence of a "yes" in words or action. . . .

It is certainly *wiser* for a male to obtain permission rather than to rely on a female's lack of objection as grounds for proceeding. We would be better off if the culture taught boys that permission is required before having sexual contact with a female, *and* if girls were taught to make their wishes known — yes or no — plainly and truthfully to males. But, should we go so far as to treat the act of sexual intercourse, performed *non*forcibly with an adult female in full control of her faculties, as rape for want of a "yes," when the female could as easily have said "no"? . . .

When a female says "no," she is an active and equal participant in the story. She has made her wishes known. If the male proceeds against her expressed wishes, his actions justify condemnation. But, in the case of a female who says nothing — perhaps, as in *M.T.S.*, the parties are involved in heavy petting or some romantic interlude and the male nonforcibly, but unilaterally, proceeds to a greater degree of sexual intimacy — is not the female also responsible for what occurs? This is not to hearken back to a physical resistance requirement; this is simply to say that verbal resistance is resistance. As Vivian Berger has written "overprotection risks enfeebling instead of empowering women." Men should be taught in our culture to seek permission; but women should also be taught in our culture to express their wishes, whether it is to invite or reject sexual contact.

QUESTIONS

1. What are the consequences of the definition of "force" that the Supreme Court of New Jersey adopted in *M.T.S.*?

2. Is Professor Dressler correct when he says that "forcible nonconsensual intercourse is a worse harm than *non*forcible nonconsensual intercourse"? Does it depend on how "force" is defined?

3. Are force and nonconsent redundant in New Jersey in sexual assault cases involving intercourse after *M.T.S.*?

The highest courts of other jurisdictions have not rushed to adopt the *M.T.S.* court's view of force. Still, at least one other appellate court has concluded that force means no more force than that inherent in penetration. In *State v. Sedra*, 614 So. 2d 533 (1993), a Florida appellate court interpreted the following statute to require no more force than that inherent in penetration.

Florida Statute § 794.011(5) (2001)

A person who commits sexual battery upon a person 12 years of age or older, without that person's consent, and in the process thereof uses physical force and violence not likely to cause serious personal injury is guilty of a felony of the second degree.

The court based its conclusion on a legislative amendment enacted shortly after the statute in question. The amendment read: "The legislature . . . *never intended* that the sexual battery offense described in 794.011(5) require any force or violence beyond the force and violence that is inherent in the accomplishment of 'penetration' or 'union'. . . . "[14]

In addition, some jurisdictions have enacted graded sexual assault provisions in which at least one grade does not require proof of force. Consider the text of the Nevada statute below:

Nevada Revised Statute Annotated § 200.366 (2001)   *Sexual assault: Definition; penalties*

1. A person who subjects another person to sexual penetration, or who forces another person to make a sexual penetration on himself or another, or on a beast, against the will of the victim or under conditions in which the perpetrator knows or should know that the victim is mentally or physically incapable of resisting or understanding the nature of his conduct, is guilty of sexual assault.

QUESTION

Is the Nevada Statute subject to the same criticisms as the *M.T.S.* case? If not, what distinguishes the two?

c. Mental State Regarding Force or Fear

Statutes are frequently silent on the issue of mental state concerning force. What inference should be drawn from this legislative silence? How would that silence be treated under the Model Penal Code? The question of the accused's mental state regarding force rarely arises in cases involving guns, knives, other weapons, or even explicit threats of violence. In those circumstances, it is highly likely that the accused had purpose with respect to the use of force. In other circumstances, the issue of mental state proves more difficult. For example, when the case involves the accused acting in a sexually aggressive manner and using a threatening tone of voice in pursuing sexual contact and when the accused is substantially larger than the victim, should prosecutors in rape cases have to prove a particular mental state

---

14. Fla. Stat. § 794.005, quoted in Florida v. Sedra, 614 So. 2d 533, 535 (1993).

regarding force? What mental state should the law require that the defendant have with respect to force?

Sometimes courts do articulate a mental state requirement regarding force. For example, in Maryland, courts have looked to whether " 'the acts and threats of the defendant were reasonably calculated to create in the mind of the victim . . . a real apprehension, due to fear, of imminent bodily harm. . . . ' "[15] What does "reasonably calculated" mean?

Professor Kit Kinports explains that "[v]ery little attention has been paid to the mens rea applicable to the element of force, that is, the defendant's state of mind with respect to the presence of force."[16] She concludes that

> the elements of force and nonconsent are duplicative of one another. A woman who did not consent to intercourse was, by definition, forced, and one who was forced did not consent. By the same token, a defendant who knew (or should have known) that the victim did not consent also knew (or should have known) that he was forcing her to submit. Therefore, proof of either lack of consent on the part of the victim or the use of force on the part of the defendant — plus the accompanying mens rea — ought to suffice to support a rape conviction. And the fact that courts routinely ignore questions of mens rea and force, in contravention of the general criminal law presumption that a mens rea requirement attaches to every material element of the crime, demonstrates that they too recognize, at least implicitly, that the traditional "conjunction of force and nonconsent" is . . . "redundant."[17]

PROBLEM

9.3 What if the accused in a rape case normally, and on the occasion at issue, wore a pen knife on a belt but never intended to frighten or intimidate the victim with the knife. The accused was substantially larger than the victim and very aggressive in his pursuit of her. The victim felt frightened and submitted against her will to sexual penetration. Should a court focus on mental state of the force circumstance?

A fair number of courts have focused on and evaluated the victim's fear. For example, in the Maryland case quoted above, *Rusk*, the court reported the results of its findings on the question of victim fear as follows: "The vast majority of jurisdictions have required that the victim's fear be reasonably grounded in order to obviate the need for either proof of actual force on the part of the assailant or physical resistance on the part of the victim."[18]

---

15. State v. Rusk, 289 Md. 230, 242 (1981) (quoting Hazel v. State, 221 Md. 464 (1960)).
16. Kit Kinports, *Rape and Force: The Forgotten Mens Rea*, 4 Buff. Crim. L. Rev. 755, 759 (2001).
17. *Id.* at 798-799.
18. *Rusk*, 289 Md. 230, at 244.

QUESTIONS

1. What does "reasonably grounded" mean?
2. Should courts focus on the victim's fear or the defendant's mental state, or both? What are the consequences of focusing on the victim's fear? On the defendant's mental state?

3. Other Types of Coercion

Scholarship on the question of coercion indicates that, except in limited circumstances, the law of rape has historically declined to recognize coercion as sufficient for a rape conviction absent physical harm or threats or fear of such harm.[19] As an example, consider Professor Schulhofer's discussion of the *Biggs* case.

> In Pennsylvania, John Biggs repeatedly had sex with his seventeen-year-old daughter. He told her that if she told anyone, he would show people nude pictures of her. If he had forced her to pay him in cash for not showing the pictures, he would be guilty of blackmail, a serious felony in nearly all states. But Biggs could not be convicted of blackmail because he obtained sex, not money, and he could not be convicted of rape, because, as the appellate court put it, he obtained his daughter's compliance "by threats, not of force, but of humiliation."[20]

But the statutes of some jurisdictions now permit convictions for sexual offenses when coercion involves pressure other than threats of physical force. Professor Patricia J. Falk notes that a New Hampshire statute punishes a defendant who obtains sexual intercourse by "threat to retaliate," where retaliation includes "public humiliation or disgrace."[21]

4. Fraud: An Alternative to Force

To induce participation, apart from force, perpetrators sometimes employ fraud. The traditional law of rape permitted convictions based on fraud only in limited circumstances. The first generally involved medical examinations when the doctor deceived the woman into believing that he was using an appropriate medical instrument to examine her, but instead he penetrated her with his penis. In these cases, courts have treated women as deceived about the essential fact of intercourse — that is, that the patient consented to a medical exam but not to intercourse. The second type of case that courts recognize as a rape case happens when the perpetrator deceives the woman into believing he is her husband. Although the law found this harder to classify as deception regarding the essential fact of intercourse, courts have, although not consistently, convicted defendants of rape in this circumstance.[22] Some states include such circumstances in the language of one of the jurisdiction's statutes on sexual offenses:

---

19. *See* Stephen Schulhofer, *Unwanted Sex: The Culture of Intimidation and the Failure of Law*, 101, 114, 279 (1998).
20. *Id.*
21. Patricia J. Falk, *Rape by Fraud and Rape by Coercion*, 64 Brook. L. Rev. 39, 120 (1998).
22. Wayne LaFave, *Criminal Law* 767 (3d ed. 2000) The law often labeled these types of fraud, "fraud in the factum."

Colorado Revised Statute Annotated § 18-402 (2001)   *Sexual assault*

(1) Any actor who knowingly inflicts sexual intrusion or sexual penetration on a victim commits sexual assault if: . . .

      c) The actor knows that the victim submits erroneously, believing the actor to be the victim's spouse; or

      g) The actor, while purporting to offer a medical service, engages in treatment or examination of a victim for other than a bona fide medical purpose or in a manner substantially inconsistent with reasonable medical practices.

In contrast, the law historically refused to recognize as rape those types of deception used to persuade the complainant to consent to intercourse with knowledge that it was intercourse to which the complainant was consenting.[23] According to Professor Falk, in an article published in 1998,

> [t]he legislative prohibition of sexual penetration or contact accomplished by fraud that occurs outside of professional treatment contexts continues to be a difficult problem. No doubt wary of casting their nets too wide, state legislatures have been quite conservative, tending to enact very specific provisions to cover a few factual scenarios rather than passing more global fraud statutes.[24]

Professor Falk points out that the Tennessee and Alabama statutes are exceptions. They

> provide for a global treatment of fraud in relation to rape or other sexual offense. . . . The distinguishing characteristic of both states' statutes is that they do not specifically set forth the exact types of fraud at issue. . . . [In the Tennessee circumstance,] [s]uch fraud is defined as 'used in normal parlance and includes, but is not limited to, deceit, trickery, misrepresentation and subterfuge, and shall be broadly construed to accomplish the purposes of this title. . . . ' Finally, Tennessee provides that consent is not effective when it is induced by deception.[25]

Tennessee Code Annotated § 39-13-503 (2001)   *Rape*

(a) Rape is unlawful sexual penetration of a victim by the defendant or of the defendant by a victim accompanied by any of the following circumstances: . . .

      (4) The sexual penetration is accomplished by fraud.

In 1999, a man convicted of rape and attempted rape under the Tennessee statute excerpted above challenged the validity of the rape-by-fraud provision.[26] The appellant, who "came to be known as the 'Fantasy Man,' would call young women late at night, impersonating their fiancé or lover." He would tell the woman that "he had a special fantasy from the movie, Nine 1/2 Weeks, and that he wanted her to act out a scene from the movie with him." The fantasy involved the women blindfolding themselves and waiting unclothed for the appellant with the understanding that they would then "act out the fantasy and have sexual intercourse. . . ." Was appellant's conduct covered by the statute?

Defining "fraud" challenges legislators and scholars. Should fraud encompass a defendant who falsely promises to marry the complainant if the complainant

---

23. *Id.* This type of fraud generally fell under the rubric, "fraud in the inducement."
24. Patricia J. Falk, *supra* note 21 at 118-119.
25. *Id.* at 109-110.
26. Tennessee v. Mitchell, 1999 Tenn. Crim. App. LEXIS 772 (1999). Quotations in this paragraph are all from the *Mitchell* case.

agrees to intercourse? With respect to drawing the necessary lines on fraud, consider Professor Schulhofer's proposal in Section H of this chapter.

5. Consent

Although the materials already presented in this chapter raise issues related to consent, we examine the issue in greater depth in the materials that follow. Recall that the common law definition of rape required that the act be committed both "forcibly" — the subject covered in depth earlier in the chapter — and "against her will" — the subject of this section. The presentation begins with the traditional view of consent and its relationship to resistance and progresses to more modern treatments of consent.

a. The Traditional View

BROWN *v.* STATE
Supreme Court of Wisconsin 127 Wis. 193 (1906)

Dodge, J. . . . As the statement of facts discloses, the only mooted question was that of prosecutrix's physical resistance to the act of intercourse, and, as to this, counsel for plaintiff in error urges, with great force, that there was not evidence sufficient to satisfy any reasonable mind, beyond reasonable doubt, of such resistance as the law makes sine qua non to the crime of rape. We need not reiterate those considerations of the ease of assertion of the forcible accomplishment of the sexual act, with impossibility of defense save by direct denial, or of the proneness of the woman, when she finds the fact of her disgrace discovered or likely of discovery, to minimize her fault by asserting vis major, which have led courts, and none more strenuously than this, to hold to a very strict rule of proof in such cases. Not only must there be entire absence of mental consent or assent, but there must be the most vehement exercise of every physical means or faculty within the woman's power to resist the penetration of her person, and this must be shown to persist until the offense is consummated. We need not mention the exception where the power of resistance is overcome by unconsciousness, threats, or exhaustion, for, in this case, there is no proof of any of those things. Further, it is settled in this state that no mere general statements of the prosecutrix, involving her conclusions, that she did her utmost and the like, will suffice to establish this essential fact, but she must relate the very acts done, in order that the jury and the court may judge whether any were omitted. Turning to the testimony of prosecutrix, we find it limited to the general statement, often repeated, that she tried as hard as she could to get away. Except for one demand, when first seized, to "let me go," and inarticulate screams, she mentions no verbal protests. While we would reasonably recognize the limitations resting on many people in attempting expression and description, we cannot conceive it possible that one whose mind and exertions had, during an encounter of this sort, been set on resistance, could or would in narrative mention nothing but escape or withdrawal. A woman's means of protection are not limited to that, but she is equipped to interpose most effective obstacles by means of hands and limbs and pelvic muscles. Indeed, medical writers insist that these obstacles are practically insuperable in absence of more than the usual relative disproportion of age and strength between man and woman, though no such impossibility is recognized as a rule of law. In addition to the interposition of such obstacles is the ability and tendency of reprisal, of counter physical attack. It is hardly within the range of reason that a man should come out of so desperate an encounter as the determined normal woman would make necessary, without signs thereof upon his face, hands, or clothing. Yet this prosecutrix, of at least fair intelligence, education, and ability of expression, in her narrative mentions no single act of resistance or reprisal. It is inconceivable that such efforts should have been forgotten if they were made, or should fail of prominence in her narrative. The distinction between escape and resistance is admirably discussed by Ryan, C. J., in *State v. Welch*, 37 Wis. 201. Resistance is opposing force to force (Bouvier), not retreating from force. These illustrations but serve to point the radical difference between the mental conception of resistance and escape and emphasize the improbability that if the former existed only the latter would have been mentioned. This court does not hold, with some, that, as matter of law, rape cannot be established by the uncorroborated testimony of the sufferer, but, in common with all courts, recognizes that, without such corroboration, her testimony must be most clear and convincing. Among the corroborating circumstances almost universally present in cases of actual rape are the signs and marks of the struggle upon the clothing and persons of the participants, and the complaint by the sufferer at the earliest opportunity. In the present case the former is absolutely wanting, for the one-inch rip in prosecutrix's underwear was not shown to be of a character or location significant of force or violence. Not a bruise or scratch on either was proved, and none existed on prosecutrix, for she was carefully examined by physicians. Her outer clothing not only presented no tearing, but no disarray, so far as the testimony goes. When one pauses to reflect upon the terrific resistance which the determined woman should make, such a situation is well-nigh incredible. The significance of the other corroborative circumstance, that of immediate disclosure, is much weakened in this case by the fact that prosecutrix turned from her way to friends and succor to arrange her underclothing and there discovered a condition making silence impossible. Such facts cannot but suggest a doubt whether her encounter would ever have been disclosed had not the discovery of blood aroused her fear that she was injured and must seek medical aid, or at least that she could not conceal from her family what had taken place. Nor is this thoughtfulness of the disarrangement of her clothing consistent with the outraged woman's terror-stricken flight to friends to give the alarm and seek aid which is to be expected. We are convinced that there was no evidence of the resistance which is essential to the crime of rape, and that the motion for new trial should have been granted on that ground.

By the Court. — Judgment and sentence reversed, and cause remanded for a new trial.

QUESTIONS

1. What purposes does a resistance requirement serve?

2. What might the blood that the prosecutrix in *Brown* discovers suggest? Should this matter to the court's analysis? Is the court correct in suggesting that the discovery of blood made the silence impossible?

3. Were the judges' assumptions about female behavior realistic in 1906? Are they realistic today?

With respect to early cases such as *Brown*, Professor Susan Estrich notes:

> The resistance requirement may have been more accurate as a description not of the reactions of women, but of the projected reactions of men to the rape of their wives and daughters. Certainly they, who knew how to fight, would have. They would have punched and kicked and screamed and maybe even killed. Or at least they thought they would. And maybe it was better for the judges to think that their wives would, too. . . .
>
> A system of law which at that time treated women, in matters ranging from ownership of property to the pursuit of the professions to participation in society, as passive and powerless, nonetheless demanded that in matters of sex they be strong and aggressive and powerful. . . .
>
> The reasonable woman, it seems, is not a schoolboy "sissy"; she is a real man.
>
> The requirement that a victim of a simple rape do more than say no was virtually without precedent in the criminal law. Many other crimes encompass a consent defense; none other has defined it so as to mandate actual physical resistance. In trespass, the posting of a sign or the offering of verbal warnings generally suffices to meet the victim's burden of nonconsent. . . . In robbery, claims that the victim cooperated with the taking of the money or eased the way, and thus consented, have been generally unsuccessful. Only where the owner of the property actively participates in planning and committing the theft will consent be found; mere "passive submission" or "passive assent" does not amount to consent — except in the law of rape.[27]

b. Consent in Transition

PEOPLE *v.* BARNES
Supreme Court of California 42 Cal. 3d 284 (1986)

BIRD, Chief Justice.

At common law, the crime of rape was defined as "the carnal knowledge of a woman forcibly and against her will." Historically, it was considered inconceivable that a woman[14] who truly did not consent to sexual intercourse would not meet force with force. The law originally demanded "utmost resistance" from the woman to ensure she had submitted rather than consented.

California long ago rejected this "primitive rule" of utmost resistance. "A woman who is assaulted need not resist to the point of risking being beaten into insensibility. If she resists to the point where further resistance would be useless or, . . . until her resistance is overcome by force or violence, submission thereafter is not consent." In our state, it had long been the rule that the resistance required by former section 261, subdivision 2, was only that which would reasonably manifest refusal to consent to the act of sexual intercourse.

Nevertheless, courts refused to uphold a conviction of rape by force where the complainant had exhibited little or no resistance. The law demanded some measure of resistance, for it remained a tenet that a virtuous woman would by nature resist a sexual attack.

---

27. Estrich, *Real Rape, supra* Section B, at 31, 40-41, 65.

[14] Although the balance of this opinion frequently refers to the rape complainant as female, the discussion applies equally to male rape complainants.

The requirement that a woman resist her attacker appears to have been grounded in the basic distrust with which courts and commentators traditionally viewed a woman's testimony regarding sexual assault. . . .

Such wariness of the complainant's credibility created "an exaggerated insistence on evidence of resistance." As an objective indicator of nonconsent, the requirement of resistance insured against wrongful conviction based solely on testimony the law considered to be inherently suspect. In our state, it supplied a type of intrinsic corroboration of the prosecuting witness's testimony, a collateral demanded even when extrinsic corroboration was not required. Thus did the resistance requirement continue even in its modified form, to nurture and reflect the perspective, still held by some modern commentators, that "human nature will impel an unwilling woman to resist unlawful sexual intercourse with great effort."

Recently, however, the entire concept of resistance to sexual assault has been called into question. . . . It has been suggested that while the presence of resistance may well be probative on the issue of force or nonconsent, its absence may not.

For example, some studies have demonstrated that while some women respond to sexual assault with active resistance, others "freeze." One researcher found that many women demonstrate "psychological infantilism" — a frozen fright response — in the face of sexual assault. The "frozen fright" response resembles cooperative behavior. Indeed, as Symonds notes, the "victim may smile, even initiate acts, and may appear relaxed and calm." Subjectively, however, she may be in a state of terror.[16] Symonds also reports that the victim may make submissive signs to her assailant and engage in propitiating behavior in an effort to inhibit further aggression. These findings belie the traditional notion that a woman who does not resist has consented. They suggest that lack of physical resistance may reflect a "profound primal terror" rather than consent.

Additionally, a growing body of authority holds that to resist in the face of sexual assault is to risk further injury.[17]

In a 1976 study of rape victims and offenders, the Queen's Bench Foundation found that over half of the sexual assault offenders studied reported becoming more violent in response to victim resistance. Injury as reported by victims correlated with some form of resistance, including verbal stalling, struggling and slapping. Those victims who resisted during coitus suffered increased violence as the assailant forced compliance. Victim resistance, whether passive or active, tended to precede an increase or intensification of the assailant's violence.

On the other hand, other findings indicate that resistance has a direct correlation with *deterring* sexual assault. Of the 75 convicted rapists the Queen's Bench Foundation questioned, half believed that their sexual assaults could have been deterred by active victim resistance. [Susan] Brownmiller argues that submissive behavior is *not* necessarily helpful to a rape victim and suggests that strong resistance on the part of women can thwart rape. She suggests it would be well for women to undergo systematic training in self-defense in order to fight back against their attackers.

Reflecting the foregoing uncertainties about the advisability of resistance, the Queen's Bench Foundation concluded: "Overall, the research findings suggest that

---

[16] Symonds writes: "In light of the traumatic psychological infantalism . . . that most victims of violent crime undergo, it is surprising we see any resisting patterns at all." [citations omitted]

[17] One author strongly discourages any type of resistance in sexual assault, including screaming, weapon use, self-defense and even feigned fainting. (Storaska, *How to Say No to a Rapist and Survive* (1975) pp. 30-49.)

rape prevention is more possible through vigorous resistance[;] however, resistance incurs greater risk of injury. When confronted with attack, each woman must make a choice which is highly personal and may be affected by situational factors beyond her control." These conclusions are also contained in a pamphlet for distribution to the general public in which the reader is advised that physical resistance may increase the danger or may thwart the attack; the woman must therefore evaluate the threat she faces and decide how to react based on the kind of person she is.

In sum, it is not altogether clear what the absence of resistance indicates in relation to the issue of consent. Nor is it *necessarily* advisable for one who is assaulted to resist the attack. It is at least arguable that if it fails to deter, resistance may well increase the risk of bodily injury to the victim. This possibility, as well as the evolution in societal expectations as to the level of danger a woman should risk when faced with sexual assault, are reflected in the Legislature's elimination of the resistance requirement. In so amending section 261, subdivision (2), the Legislature has demonstrated its unwillingness to dictate a prescribed response to sexual assault. For the first time, the Legislature has assigned the decision as to whether a sexual assault should be resisted to the realm of personal choice.

The elimination of the resistance requirement is also consistent with the modern trend of removing evidentiary obstacles unique to the prosecution of sexual assault cases. For example, in enacting section 1112 in 1980, the Legislature barred psychiatric examinations of rape complainants which had been authorized. . . . In recent years, the Legislature has also prohibited the instructional admonition that an "unchaste woman" is more likely to consent than her chaste counterpart . . . and has largely precluded the use of evidence of a complaining witness's sexual conduct to prove consent.

This court has made similar strides. Over a decade ago, the use of CALJIC No. 10.22, embodying the deprecatory "Hale instruction,"[18] was disapproved. That holding laid to juridical rest the notion that "those who claim to be victims of sexual offenses are presumptively entitled to less credence than those who testify as the alleged victims of other crimes." . . .

By removing resistance as a prerequisite to a rape conviction, the Legislature has brought the law of rape into conformity with other crimes such as robbery, kidnapping and assault, which require force, fear, and nonconsent to convict. In these crimes, the law does not expect falsity from the complainant who alleges their commission and thus demand resistance as a corroboration and predicate to conviction. Nor does the law expect that in defending oneself or one's property from these crimes, a person must risk injury or death by displaying resistance in the face of attack. The amendment of section 261, subdivision (2), acknowledges that previous expectational disparities, which singled out the credibility of rape complainants as suspect, have no place in a modern system of jurisprudence.

This court therefore concludes that the Legislature's purposes in amending section 261 were (1) to relieve the state of the need to establish resistance as a

---

[18] Former CALJIC No. 10.22 read: " 'A charge such as that made against the defendant in this case is one which is easily made and, once made, difficult to defend against, even if the person accused is innocent. [¶.] Therefore, the law requires that you examine the testimony of the female person named in the information with caution.' " (*People v. Rincon-Pineda, supra*, 14 Cal.3d at p. 871.) The instruction was based on Sir Matthew Hale's well-worn 17th century admonition that the testimony of "sometimes . . . malicious and false" rape complainants must be cautiously scrutinized since rape " 'is an accusation easily to be made and hard to be proved, and harder to be defended by the party accused, tho never so innocent.' [Citation.]" (*Id.*, at pp. 873, 874, 875.)

prerequisite to a rape conviction, and (2) to release rape complainants from the potentially dangerous burden of resisting an assailant in order to substantiate allegations of forcible rape.

As noted, it is no longer proper to instruct the jury that it must find the complainant resisted before it may return a verdict of guilt. Nor may lack of resistance be employed by courts — like the Court of Appeal here — to support a finding of insufficient evidence of rape under section 261, subdivision (2).[19]

Although resistance is fading from rape statutes, it has not disappeared. Reconsider the Idaho statute found earlier in the chapter and reprinted below. In some jurisdictions, rape continues to be formally defined in terms of resistance:

Idaho Code § 18-6101 (2004)

Rape is defined as the penetration, however slight, of the oral, anal or vaginal opening with the perpetrator's penis accomplished with a female under any one (1) of the following circumstances: . . .

> 3. Where she resists but her resistance is overcome by force or violence.
>
> 4. Where she is prevented from resistance by the infliction, attempted infliction, or threatened infliction of bodily harm, accompanied by apparent power of execution. . . .

The statutes of some jurisdictions now explicitly provide that "[a] victim need not prove physical resistance to the offender"[28] in rape or sexual offense prosecutions.

QUESTIONS

1. How was "consent" defined in the *Brown* case?

2. Do you find Professor Estrich's explanation for the kind of resistance required in the early cases persuasive?

3. Should consent be presumed or should lack of consent be presumed in a sexual encounter? If lack of consent should be presumed, how should "consent" be defined?

Consider the following definitions of "consent." The first three are excerpts from statutes. The fourth is from the Antioch College Sexual Offense Policy. On whom does the burden regarding consent fall in each?

Wisconsin Statute Annotated § 940.225 (2002)

(4) "Consent," as used in this section, means words or overt actions by a person who is competent to give informed consent indicating a freely given agreement to have sexual intercourse or sexual contact.

---

[19] The statutory change does not mean that when resistance does exist, it is irrelevant to nonconsent. Absence of resistance may also continue to be probative of whether the accused honestly and reasonably believed he was engaging in consensual sex. (*See People v. Mayberry,* (1975) 15 Cal.3d 143, 155 [125 Cal. Rptr. 745, 542 P.2d 1337].)

28. Ohio Rev. Code Ann. § 2907.02 (2001).

Florida Statute Annotated § 794.011 (2001)

(a) "Consent" means intelligent, knowing, and voluntary consent and does not include coerced submission. "Consent" shall not be deemed or construed to mean the failure by the alleged victim to offer physical resistance to the offender.

720 Illinois Compiled Statute 5/12-17 (2001)   *Defenses*

(a) It shall be a defense to any offense under [the sexual offense section of this Code] . . . where force or threat of force is an element of the offense that the victim consented. "Consent" means a freely given agreement to the act of sexual penetration or sexual conduct in question. Lack of verbal or physical resistance or submission by the victim resulting from the use of force or threat of force by the accused shall not constitute consent. The manner of dress of the victim at the time of the offense shall not constitute consent.

The Antioch College Sexual Offense Policy (Consent)

1. For the purpose of this policy, "consent" shall be defined as follows: the act of willingly and verbally agreeing to engage in specific sexual contact or conduct. 2. If sexual contact and/or conduct is not mutually and simultaneously initiated, then the person who initiates sexual contact/conduct is responsible for getting the verbal consent of the other individual(s) involved.

In deciding how the law should treat consent, consider the following study:

Charlene L. Muehlenhard & Lisa C. Hollabaugh, DO WOMEN SOMETIMES SAY NO WHEN THEY MEAN YES? THE PREVALENCE AND CORRELATES OF WOMEN'S TOKEN RESISTANCE TO SEX
54 J. Personality & Soc. Psychol. 872, 872-874 (1988)

There is a common belief that many women offer token resistance to sex; that they say no even when they mean yes and that their protests are not to be taken seriously. This belief is based on the traditional sexual script in which women's role is to act resistant to sex and men's role is to persist in their sexual advances despite women's resistance. . . .

Research supports the idea that many men do not believe it when women say no to sex. In one study, men read a scenario in which a woman dressed and behaved "modestly" on a date; when her date made a sexual advance, she said no three times and tried to move away. In spite of this, men's mean ratings of how much she wanted sex were almost at the middle of the scale. After the men were told to assume that the woman really did not want to have sex, their ratings of various aspects of the scenario (e.g., how justified the man was in forcing the woman to have sex) changed significantly, providing additional evidence that the men had not initially believed the woman's protests. . . .

Thus, there is documentation that many men believe that women follow this sexual script, but is this belief founded in fact? Do women ever engage in token resistance to sex: If so, how often and why?

This study investigated women's token resistance to sex, which we defined as a woman's indicating that she did not want to have sex even though she had every intention and was willing to engage in sexual intercourse. . . . Subjects were 610 female introductory psychology students from Texas A& M University. . . . Their mean age was 19 years. . . .

Of the 601 women who completed the Situation Questionnaire, 39.3% ($n = 240$) reported saying no to sexual intercourse when they meant yes. Of these women, 32.5% reported engaging in token resistance only once, 45.6% reported doing this 2 to 5 times, 11.2% reported 6 to 10 times, 7.8% reported 11 to 20 times, and 2.9% reported more than 20 times.

QUESTIONS

The Mullenhard and Hollabaugh study indicates that, of the population they studied, almost 40 percent of the women had said "no" to sexual intercourse at least once when they meant "yes." Although the study indicates that about one-third of those women reported using token resistance only once, imagine hypothetically that 40 percent of women systematically used token resistance in all their sexual encounters and did not later indicate "yes" or demonstrate consent prior to sexual intercourse. Imagine also that the remaining 60 percent who said "no" meant "no." If the men in those circumstances had respected the token resistance and desisted, 40 percent of women and their partners would have missed the opportunity for an ultimately "consensual" sexual encounter. What if, however, the men, having read the study, decided to proceed despite the "no"? In 60 percent of the cases, the men would have compelled nonconsenting women to have sex. Which conduct should the law encourage?

The issue of consent is, of course, also an issue of perception and cultural standards. In the following excerpt, Robin Weiner critiques the "reasonable person" standard.

Robin Weiner, SHIFTING THE COMMUNICATION BURDEN: A MEANINGFUL CONSENT STANDARD IN RAPE, 6 Harv. Women's L.J. 143, 147-149 (1983)

Because both men and women are socialized to accept coercive sexuality as the norm in sexual behavior, men often see extreme forms of this behavior as seduction, rather than rape. A great many incidents women consider rape are, in effect, considered "normal" by both male perpetrators and the male-dominated legal system. Even convicted rapists tend to test as "sexually and psychologically normal" according to the male social norms. Thus, what is "normal" according to male social norms and reasonable according to male communication patterns and expectations does not accord with what women believe to be reasonable. Men are also more likely than women to view behaviors by the woman as contributing to a rape.

The man's failure to ensure consent to sex may be normal, and hence reasonable by male standards, although unreasonable by female standards. The man of "reasonable prudence and intelligence" in our society may not actively seek overt consent because he may assume that a nonconsenting woman will make her lack of consent known. A reasonable woman, however, may perceive certain behavior as indicating that the man plans to have sex with her whether she consents or not, although the man may not have meant to communicate with such an intent.

Miscommunication of this sort may create a situation where submission would be reasonable behavior for a woman but would not indicate voluntary consent. A woman may believe she has communicated her unwillingness to have sex — and other women would agree, thus making it a "reasonable" female expression. Her male partner might still believe she is willing — and other men would agree with his interpretation. The woman, who believes that she has conveyed her lack of consent, may interpret the man's persistence as an indication that he does not care if she objects and plans to have sex despite her lack of consent. She may then feel frightened by the man's persistence, and may submit against her will.

The use of the reasonable person standard thus has a basic flaw. Courts do not clarify the perspective from which the "reasonableness" standard should be applied.

QUESTIONS

1. How could courts or legislatures be more specific about the perspective from which reasonableness should be judged?
2. What choices about such perspectives are available?
3. What might be the consequences of each of those choices?

PROBLEM

9.4 D is accused of rape under the following statute:

Texas Penal Code Annotated § 22.011 (1992)   *Sexual Assault*

(a) A person commits an offense if the person:
   (1) intentionally or knowingly:
      (A) causes the penetration of the anus or female sexual organ of another person by any means, without the person's consent.

Is D liable based on the following facts?

Complainant's account: The complainant returns home just before 3:00 A.M. She encounters a stranger in her hallway, wielding a knife. She screams, slams the bedroom door, locks it, and tries to dial 911. The drunk stranger breaks down the door and knocks the phone out of the complainant's hand. "Threatening her with a knife, 'he ordered her to take his pants off.' The complainant said, 'If you're going to rape me, I want you to use a condom because I don't want to die of AIDS.'" He said, "I don't have AIDS," and she said, "How do you know I don't?" The complainant "got a condom and placed it on him and then he assaulted her," by sexually penetrating her. She "tried several times to escape, but the [stranger] followed her with a knife. Finally, when he set the knife down after about an hour, she grabbed it and fled naked to a neighbor's apartment to call the police."

D's account: D, who lives elsewhere in the same apartment complex, says that he "wandered into the wrong apartment and, alarmed by the woman's barking dog, took a knife from the kitchen. He

> went upstairs. And there's a dog barking, her screaming, she turns on the light and says put down the knife." "From there, there's some discussion, and she asks him to use a condom, provides him with a condom, takes his pants off and puts it on him. After they finish, she goes downstairs to get a glass of water, and then runs out."[29]

6. The Model Penal Code

The Model Penal Code sets forth a series of sex offenses. Unlike traditional approaches to rape, they do not explicitly include a consent provision. Instead, they focus on force and compulsion. The Code provisions defining rape and related offenses follow:

Model Penal Code § 213.1 (1985)   *Rape and Related Offenses*

(1) *Rape.* A male who has sexual intercourse with a female not his wife is guilty of rape if:

a) he compels her to submit by force or by threat of imminent death, serious bodily injury, extreme pain or kidnapping, to be inflicted on anyone; or

b) he has substantially impaired her power to appraise or control her conduct by administering or employing without her knowledge drugs, intoxicants or other means for the purpose of preventing resistance; or

c) the female is unconscious; or

d) the female is less than 10 years old.

Rape is a felony of the second degree unless i) in the course thereof the actor inflicts serious bodily injury upon anyone, or ii) the victim was not a voluntary social companion of the actor upon the occasion of the crime and had not previously permitted him sexual liberties, in which cases the offense is a felony of the first degree.

(2) *Gross Sexual Imposition.* A male who has sexual intercourse with a female not his wife commits a felony of the third degree if:

a) he compels her to submit by any threat that would prevent resistance by a woman of ordinary resolution; or

b) he knows she suffers from a mental disease or defect which renders her incapable of appraising the nature of her conduct; or

c) he knows that she is unaware that a sexual act is being committed upon her or that she submits because she mistakenly supposes that he is her husband.

QUESTION

How does the MPC provision on rape differ from the approach in Blackstone's day?

---

29. Based on and quotations from Christy Hoppe, *Man is indicted as rapist who agreed to use condom; 2nd Austin grand jury takes action after outcry*, The Dallas Morning News, Oct. 28, 1992, at 1A.

Some jurisdictions emulate the MPC in its formal elimination of consent. Consider the Ohio rape provision, reproduced in relevant part below:

Ohio Revised Code Annotated § 2907.02 (2001)   *Rape*

(2) No person shall engage in sexual conduct with another when the offender purposely compels the other person to submit by force or threat of force.

QUESTIONS

1. What are the consequences of eliminating consent as an element? What are the disadvantages of eliminating consent and instead focusing on force? What impact might the absence have on information about the victim's prior sexual history?

2. Do the MPC provisions focus more on the defendant or on the victim?

3. Under the MPC provisions, would it matter if the victim had been out drinking at a bar or had worn revealing clothing?

4. Under the Code, would it matter if the individual had had a prior relationship but had not had sexual contact?

5. Compare the effect of the decision in *M.T.S* with the approaches taken by the MPC and the Ohio statute above. Which is the best approach?

7. Mental State Regarding Consent

Should the prosecution be required to prove that the defendant had a culpable mental state regarding the victim's lack of consent? Consider the following problem in deciding what, if any, mental state the prosecution should have to prove.

PROBLEM

9.5 Consider the case that follows.

> The complainant was a tenant in a farmhouse owned by the defendant's parents. She had occasion to meet defendant several times when he did some repair work around the premises for his parents. The two had also met several times at a local bar and at least one party which both had attended. Their acquaintance was casual and limited to an exchange of pleasantries. They had never been out together nor had defendant ever visited at complainant's home as a guest. On one occasion defendant suggested that the two "get together for a private party." The complainant declined by suggesting that "some other time" might be more appropriate.
>
> On the night of the crime, the complainant . . . went out for the evening. She returned home alone around midnight, locked the doors, and opened a window in the living room, where she slept. Sometime around 2:00 A.M. she was awakened by someone who kissed her on the lips and said, "Kathy, how are you doing?" Because of the darkness, she was unable to identify her visitor and asked who it was. He responded, "it is me. Who did you think it was?"

The testimony concerning what happened thereafter is in dispute. The defendant says that the two held hands, continued to kiss, and engaged in conversation. The complainant denies there was any further conversation or embracing. Instead, she testified defendant removed his trousers, lay down on top of her on the couch where she had been sleeping, and started to remove her underpants. She made no resistance and voiced no objection except to say, "Don't. I am on the rag." Defendant said, "Don't worry about it." He continued with the removal of her undergarment.

Defendant thereafter had sexual intercourse with the complainant twice. During these occasions she made neither verbal nor physical protest. At one time she actively assisted him when he was having difficulty in achieving penetration. After the second act of intercourse, the complainant asked if she could get a cigarette and defendant consented. She went to the kitchen, lit a cigarette, and returned to the living room. Again asking permission first, she then went upstairs to the bathroom, dressed, and upon her return, found defendant asleep. It was only then, aided by a light from the kitchen, and peering closely at her sleeping assailant, that she identified him as the defendant. Satisfying herself that he was surely asleep, she left the premises, got in her car, and drove to the home of a friend. . . . At defendant's trial . . . [the friend] testified that complainant was "pretty hysterical" when she arrived, that she was "shaking real bad," and that she kept repeating, "[defendant] raped me." . . .

At trial, the complainant explained her failure to offer more direct and positive resistance by saying she was afraid to do so. She said she did not make an outcry because there was no one to hear her. She did not attempt to repel defendant because she was frightened. She described herself as being "scared to death." She felt "paralyzed" as far as physical resistance was concerned. A recent incident in which the body of a murdered woman was found in a ditch "flashed across [her] mind." She related this to her own plight.[30]

(a) What mental state does the defendant's account suggest he had regarding consent?

(b) What mental state does the complainant's account suggest that the defendant had regarding consent?

(c) What mental state should the prosecution have to prove regarding consent?

(d) Should a jury convict the defendant under the portion of the Tennessee statute that follows?

Tennessee Code Annotated § 39-13-503 (2001)   *Rape*

a) Rape is unlawful sexual penetration of a victim by the defendant or of the defendant by a victim accompanied by any of the following circumstances:

(1) Force or coercion is used to accomplish the act;

(2) The sexual penetration is accomplished without the consent of the victim and the defendant knows or has reason to know at the time of the penetration that the victim did not consent; . . .

---

30. Iowa v. Bauer, 324 N.W.2d 320 (1982).

(e) What definition of "consent" should the court use? Does the choice of definition affect your analysis about the defendant's mental state regarding consent?

(f) Consider the English statute that follows. Should the defendant be convicted under this statute?

Sexual Offences Act 1956 § 1   [*Rape of woman or man*]

Date-In-Force: 3 November 1994
Text:
It is an offence for a man to rape a woman.
[A] man commits rape if

(1) he has sexual intercourse with a woman [whether vaginal or anal] who at the time of the intercourse does not consent to it; and
(2) at the time he knows that she does not consent to the intercourse or is reckless as to whether she consents to it.

(g) How does the Tennessee statute differ from the English statute?

Consider the following case on the question of mistake and consent in the rape context:

COMMONWEALTH *v.* LOPEZ

Supreme Judicial Court of Massachusetts 433 Mass. 722 (2001)

SPINA, J.

The defendant, Kenny Lopez, was convicted on two indictments charging rape and one indictment charging indecent assault and battery on a person over the age of fourteen years. We granted his application for direct appellate review. The defendant claims error in the judge's refusal to give a mistake of fact instruction to the jury. He asks us to recognize a defendant's honest and reasonable belief as to a complainant's consent as a defense to the crime of rape, and to reverse his convictions and grant him a new trial. Based on the record presented, we decline to do so, and affirm the convictions.

1. *Background.* We summarize facts that the jury could have found. On May 8, 1998, the victim, a seventeen year old girl, was living in a foster home in Springfield. At approximately 3 P.M., she started walking to a restaurant where she had planned to meet her biological mother. On the way, she encountered the defendant. He introduced himself, asked where she was going, and offered to walk with her. The victim met her mother and introduced the defendant as her friend. The defendant said that he lived in the same foster home as the victim and that "they knew each other from school." Sometime later, the defendant left to make a telephone call. When the victim left the restaurant, the defendant was waiting outside and offered to walk her home. She agreed.

The two walked to a park across the street from the victim's foster home and talked for approximately twenty to thirty minutes. The victim's foster sisters were within earshot, and the victim feared that she would be caught violating her foster mother's rules against bringing "a guy near the house." The defendant suggested that they take a walk in the woods nearby. At one point, deep in the woods, the victim said that she wanted to go home. The defendant said, "trust me," and assured her that nothing would happen and that he would not hurt her. The defendant led the victim down a path to a secluded area.

The defendant asked the victim why she was so distant and said that he wanted to start a relationship with her. She said that she did not want to "get into any relationship." The defendant began making sexual innuendos to which the victim did not respond. He grabbed her by her wrist and began kissing her on the lips. She pulled away and said, "No, I don't want to do this." The defendant then told the victim that if she "had sex with him, [she] would love him more." She repeated, "No, I don't want to. I don't want to do this." He raised her shirt and touched her breasts. She immediately pulled her shirt down and pushed him away.

The defendant then pushed the victim against a slate slab, unbuttoned her pants, and pulled them down. Using his legs to pin down her legs, he produced a condom and asked her to put it on him. The victim said, "No." The defendant put the condom on and told the victim that he wanted her to put his penis inside her. She said, "No." He then raped her, and she began to cry. A few minutes later, the victim made a "jerking move" to her left. The defendant became angry, turned her around, pushed her face into the slate, and raped her again. The treating physician described the bruising to the victim's knees as "significant." The physician opined that there had been "excessive force and trauma to the [vaginal] area" based on his observation that there was "a lot of swelling" in her external vaginal area and her hymen had been torn and was "still oozing." The doctor noted that in his experience it was "fairly rare" to see that much swelling and trauma.

The defendant told the victim that she "would get in a lot of trouble" if she said anything. He then grabbed her by the arm, kissed her, and said, "I'll see you later." The victim went home and showered. She told her foster mother, who immediately dialed 911. The victim cried hysterically as she spoke to the 911 operator.

The defendant's version of the encounter was diametrically opposed to that of the victim. He testified that the victim had been a willing and active partner in consensual sexual intercourse. Specifically, the defendant claimed that the victim initiated intimate activity, and never once told him to stop. Additionally, the defendant testified that the victim invited him to a party that evening so that he could meet her friends. The defendant further claimed that when he told her that he would be unable to attend, the victim appeared "mildly upset."

Before the jury retired, defense counsel requested a mistake of fact instruction as to consent.[1] The judge declined to give the instruction, saying that, based "both on the law, as well as on the facts, that instruction is not warranted." Because the defendant's theory at trial was that the victim actually consented and not that the defendant was "confused, misled, or mistaken" as to the victim's willingness to engage in sexual intercourse, the judge concluded that the ultimate question for the jury was simply whether they believed the victim's or the defendant's version of the encounter. The decision not to give the instruction provides the basis for this appeal.

---

[1] The defendant proposed the following instruction: "If the Commonwealth has not proved beyond a reasonable doubt that the defendant was not motivated by a reasonable and honest belief that the complaining witness consented to sexual intercourse, you must find the defendant not guilty."

2. *Mistake of fact instruction.* . . . In *Commonwealth v. Ascolillo*, 405 Mass. 456, 541 N.E.2d 570 (1989), we held that the defendant was not entitled to a mistake of fact instruction, and declined to adopt a rule that "in order to establish the crime of rape the Commonwealth must prove *in every case* not only that the defendant intended intercourse but also that he did not act pursuant to an honest and reasonable belief that the victim consented" (emphasis added). Neither the plain language of our rape statute nor this court's decisions prior to the *Ascolillo* decision warrant a different result.

A fundamental tenet of criminal law is that culpability requires a showing that the prohibited conduct (actus reus) was committed with the concomitant mental state (mens rea) prescribed for the offense. The mistake of fact "defense" is available where the mistake negates the existence of a mental state essential to a material element of the offense.[3] In determining whether the defendant's honest and reasonable belief as to the victim's consent would relieve him of culpability, it is necessary to review the required elements of the crime of rape. . . .

The current rape statute, G. L. c. 265, § 22 (b), provides in pertinent part:

"Whoever has sexual intercourse or unnatural sexual intercourse with a person and compels such person to submit by force and against his will, or compels such person to submit by threat of bodily injury, shall be punished by imprisonment in the state prison for not more than twenty years."

This statute follows the common-law definition of rape, and requires the Commonwealth to prove beyond a reasonable doubt that the defendant committed (1) sexual intercourse (2) by force or threat of force and against the will of the victim.

As to the first element, there has been very little disagreement. Sexual intercourse is defined as penetration of the victim, regardless of degree. The second element has proven to be more complicated. We have construed the element, "by force and against his will," as truly encompassing two separate elements each of which must independently be satisfied. Therefore, the Commonwealth must demonstrate beyond a reasonable doubt that the defendant committed sexual intercourse (1) by means of physical force; nonphysical, constructive force; or threats of bodily harm, either explicit or implicit; and (2) at the time of penetration, there was no consent.

Although the Commonwealth must prove lack of consent, the "elements necessary for rape do not require that the defendant intend the intercourse be without consent." Historically, the relevant inquiry has been limited to consent in fact, and no mens rea or knowledge as to the lack of consent has ever been required.

A mistake of fact as to consent, therefore, has very little application to our rape statute. Because G. L. c. 265, § 22, does not require proof of a defendant's knowledge of the victim's lack of consent or intent to engage in nonconsensual intercourse as a material element of the offense, a mistake as to that consent cannot, therefore, negate a mental state required for commission of the prohibited conduct. Any perception (reasonable, honest, or otherwise) of the defendant as to the victim's consent is consequently not relevant to a rape prosecution.

---

[3] Thus understood, a mistake of fact is not truly a defense, but rather a means of demonstrating that the prosecution has failed to prove beyond a reasonable doubt the essential elements of the crime. . . .

This is not to say, contrary to the defendant's suggestion, that the absence of any mens rea as to the consent element transforms rape into a strict liability crime. It does not. Rape, at common law and pursuant to G. L. c. 265, ?§ 22, is a general intent crime, and proof that a defendant intended sexual intercourse by force coupled with proof that the victim did not in fact consent is sufficient to maintain a conviction.

Other jurisdictions have held that a mistake of fact instruction is necessary to prevent injustice. New Jersey, for instance, does not require the force necessary for rape to be anything more than what is needed to accomplish penetration. Thus, an instruction as to a defendant's honest and reasonable belief as to consent is available in New Jersey to mitigate the undesirable and unforeseen consequences that may flow from this construction. By contrast, in this Commonwealth, unless the putative victim has been rendered incapable of consent, the prosecution must prove that the defendant compelled the victim's submission by use of physical force; nonphysical, constructive force; or threat of force. Proof of the element of force, therefore, should negate any possible mistake as to consent.

We also have concerns that the mistake of fact defense would tend to eviscerate the long-standing rule in this Commonwealth that victims need not use any force to resist an attack. A shift in focus from the victim's to the defendant's state of mind might require victims to use physical force in order to communicate an unqualified lack of consent to defeat any honest and reasonable belief as to consent. The mistake of fact defense is incompatible with the evolution of our jurisprudence with respect to the crime of rape.

We are cognizant that our interpretation is not shared by the majority of other jurisdictions. States that recognize a mistake of fact as to consent generally have done so by legislation. . . .

The mistake of fact "defense" has been recognized by judicial decision in some States. In 1975, the Supreme Court of California became the first State court to recognize a mistake of fact defense in rape cases. . . .[5]

Other State courts have employed a variety of different constructions in adopting the mistake of fact defense. . . .

However, the minority of States sharing our view is significant. Whether such a defense might, in some circumstances, be appropriate is a difficult question that we may consider on a future case where a defendant's claim of reasonable mistake of fact is at least arguably supported by the evidence. This is not such a case.

Judgments affirmed.

---

[5] Since that time, the Supreme Court of California has retreated from its original holding and steadily has eroded the defense. Today, the defense is available only if there is "substantial evidence of equivocal conduct that would have led a defendant to reasonably and in good faith believe consent existed where it did not." People v. Williams, 4 Cal. 4th 354, 362, (1992). Thus, as a threshold matter, the judge, not the jury, must find that the evidence with respect to consent is equivocal. Unless this showing is made, the "jury will be foreclosed from considering evidence that the defendant honestly and reasonably believed that there was consent, even if that jury would have credited such evidence." Cavallaro, [A Big Mistake: Eroding the Defense of Mistake of Fact About Consent in Rape, 86 J. Crim. L. & Criminology 815] at 852 [(1996)]. This requirement, in effect, virtually eliminates the mistake of fact doctrine because "[t]hose defendants who, as a factual matter, would present the strongest mistake case, by testifying to conduct that could be characterized as 'unequivocal,' are precluded by the rule of *Williams* from presenting that defense to the jury." *Id.* at 838. On the other hand, a "defendant who describes an encounter in which the complainant's conduct was admittedly equivocal as to consent essentially concedes that point and is doomed to almost certain conviction." *Id.* at 838-839.

QUESTIONS

1. Is the treatment of mistake in rape consistent with the treatment of mistake of fact that we studied earlier in the course?

2. If a statute requires force beyond the act of penetration itself, what are the risks of eliminating a mental state requirement regarding consent?

3. If the statutory definition of "consent" is the one in effect in Wisconsin, what would it mean to be negligent about the absence of consent? To be reckless about the absence of consent? To lack knowledge about the absence of consent?

4. In contrast, if consent is presumed, absent some clear physical manifestation of nonconsent, what does it mean to be negligent about the absence of consent? To be reckless about the absence of consent? To lack knowledge about the absence of consent?

In the excerpt that follows, Professor Lynne Henderson comments on the appropriate mens rea regarding consent:[31]

First, the minimum culpable mens rea requirement as to consent should be negligence, as Susan Estrich has argued. But, . . . simply using the reasonable man, or the reasonable man in the defendant's circumstances, standard is not enough. . . . Thus, I would argue that the law impose strict liability as soon as the woman says no or indicates that she does not want to engage in sexual activity. This essentially creates a conclusive presumption of recklessness. Once the man is told no, he is alerted to the risk of lack of consent and should bear the risk if he continues despite the no. No should mean no. Stop should mean stop. Crying should negate consent. Similarly, screaming and silence are negations. Further, a woman's lack of positive cooperation in sexual activity is a signal of nonconsent, not her natural passivity. If the man is under the influence, it should not negate his mens rea; many jurisdictions already presume recklessness as mens rea when the defendant is voluntarily intoxicated, and the presumption should be equally applicable to culpability for rape.

I believe imposing a conclusive presumption of recklessness in such instances would cover the so-called "ambiguous" situation, in which the man claims he had "mixed signals" or that the woman seemed to be "going along" because he is on notice to ascertain whether his partner is willing to continue, and if he does not stop and clarify things, he is reckless. But even if the presumption does not work in the ambiguous case, the benefits of this presumption are several. First, it displaces focus from the male standard as to what constitutes consent and what does not. Second, a conclusive presumption would at least make those instances in which there were threats or where a woman's refusal to consent was ignored easier to prosecute. Third, a presumption of recklessness when a man is on notice speaks to the specific event and at the specific time more than the current practice does. While it may be true that the victim's credibility can still be attacked with prior acts of consent, in the instance of an acquaintance rape it is less relevant that she consented in the past if she said no at the time in question, because what he believed or presumed would be irrelevant to his being on notice at the time of the interaction that led him to rape. Of course, the woman's credibility as to whether she signaled no in such a way as to put the man on notice still can be attacked in a number of ways — by innuendo if nothing else — but at least the law would not be telling the jury that it does not matter if she said no, or cried, or froze in terror. Finally, a conclusive presumption really does give women some power to determine whether or not they wish to engage in heterosexual activity. At present, if their voices can be ignored, if their silence can be ignored, by men and by the law, it makes no sense for women to take

---

31. Lynne Henderson, *Honoring Women in Law and Fact*, 2 Tex. J. Women & L. 41, 67 (1993).

any affirmative responsibility in sexual encounters. And if this is the case, then the old no-means-yes, just-overpower-me model of heterosexuality remains firmly in place in law and in fact.

Professor Stephen Schulhofer has expressed concern about mistakes with respect to consent:

> What seems certain is that miscommunication about sexual desires is entirely commonplace. If we consider actual behavior of real people in our world as it stands, mistakes about consent, including mistakes about the meaning of "no," are undoubtedly frequent. And *sometimes*, in *some* settings, those mistakes will be "reasonable," even from the perspective of many women. . . . The messy facts of a no-means-yes culture spell danger for women. . . .
>
> In determining "consent," as in making judgments about force, fear, intimidation, and "reasonableness," law's vague, abstract standards are especially troubling in this respect. Law has not simply opted for a neutral solution to these socially contested issues. In each instance, law has chosen sides. The law gives priority to the interest (the predominantly male interest) in seeking sexual gratification through advances backed by physical strength and social power. And the law gives priority to protecting sexually assertive individuals (predominantly men) from the risk of conviction without clear warning in advance. At the same time the law denies protection to women, whose sexual independence is so often at risk, and leaves them to fend off sexual pressure as best they can, with self-help their only remedy.[32]

One additional consideration about consent underscores its temporal nature. If initially valid consent is withdrawn during sexual intercourse, does continuing penetration constitute rape? Consider a 2001 court's conclusion on this issue:[33]

> [F]orcible rape occurs when the act of sexual intercourse is accomplished against the will of the victim by force or threat of bodily injury, and it is immaterial at what point the victim withdraws her consent, so long as that withdrawal is communicated to the male and he thereafter ignores it.

QUESTION

In light of the excerpts by Professors Henderson and Schulhofer, how should a legislature treat consent?

8. Incapacity to Consent

Modern rape statutes commonly prohibit intercourse when there is a proxy for force and/or lack of consent, such as the administration of certain intoxicants, unconsciousness of the victim, and lack of legal capacity to consent.[34] The Kansas statute below provides an example.

---

32. *Supra* note 19 at 65-67.
33. In re John Z., 94 Cal. App. 4th 33 (2001).
34. For a cogent analysis of consent and mental retardation, *see* Deborah W. Denno, *Sexuality, Rape, and Mental Retardation*, 1997 U. Ill. L. Rev. 315.

Kansas Statute Annotated § 21-3502 (2000)   *Rape*

(a) Rape is: (1) Sexual intercourse with a person who does not consent to the sexual intercourse, under any of the following circumstances:

B) when the victim is unconscious or physically powerless; or

C) when the victim is incapable of giving consent because of mental deficiency or disease, or when the victim is incapable of giving consent because of the effect of any alcoholic liquor, narcotic, drug or other substance, which condition was known by the offender or was reasonably apparent to the offender. . . .

E. RAPE SHIELD STATUTES

At one time, a defendant in a rape case could admit into evidence the sexual history of the complainant under two different theories. First, it was admissible on the issue of consent. The assumption was that if a woman had consented to sexual intercourse on prior occasions, that earlier consent made it more likely that she consented to sexual intercourse on the occasion at issue in the rape charge. Second, courts admitted it on the issue of credibility. The assumption was that a woman who had engaged in past consensual intercourse was less credible than a woman who had not.

The admission of sexual history in rape cases resulted in humiliation and embarrassment of the complainant, effectively discouraging victims from reporting or agreeing to cooperate in the prosecution of rapes. Sexual history evidence also tended to trigger in juries the passing of harsh judgments on the complainant and the acquittal of defendants who had in fact committed rape if the jury found moral fault with the complainant's sexual history. In addition, the inferences underlying the traditional theories of admissibility on consent as well as credibility came to be viewed as based on gender stereotypes rather than reality. In other words, there typically is no correlation between sexual history and either consent or credibility. Accordingly, legislatures in virtually all jurisdictions altered the rules on admissibility of sexual history in rape cases by enacting what are commonly called "rape shield" statutes. The scope of protection provided by these statutes, however, varies substantially.

Consider the Problem that follows and apply the Rhode Island and Nevada rape shield statutes below to the Problem.

Rhode Island General Laws § 11-37-13 (2002)   *Prior sexual conduct of complainant — Admissibility of Evidence*

If a defendant who is charged with the crime of sexual assault intends to introduce proof that the complaining witness has engaged in sexual activities with other persons, he or she shall give notice of that intention to the court and the attorney for the state. The notice shall be given prior to the introduction of any evidence of that fact. It shall be given orally out of the hearing of spectators and, if the action is being tried by a jury, out of hearing of the jurors. Upon receiving this notice, the court shall order the defendant to make a specific offer of the proof that he or she intends to introduce in support of this issue. The offer of proof, and all arguments relating to it, shall take place outside the hearing of spectators and jurors. The court shall then rule upon the admissibility of the evidence offered.

Nevada Revised Statute § 28-321 (2001) *Sexual Assault; evidence of past sexual behavior; when admissible; procedure*

(1) If the defendant intends to offer evidence of specific instances of the victim's past sexual behavior, notice of such intention shall be given to the prosecuting attorney and filed with the court not later than fifteen days before trial.

(2) Upon motion to the court by either party in a prosecution in a case of sexual assault, an in camera hearing shall be conducted in the presence of the judge, under guidelines established by the judge, to determine the relevance of evidence of the victim's or the defendant's past sexual behavior. Evidence of a victim's past sexual behavior shall not be admissible unless such evidence is: (a) Evidence of past sexual behavior with persons other than the defendant, offered by the defendant upon the issue of whether the defendant was or was not, with respect to the victim, the source of any physical evidence including but not limited to, semen, injury, blood, saliva, and hair; or (b) evidence of past sexual behavior with the defendant when such evidence is offered by the defendant on the issue of whether the victim consented to the sexual behavior upon which the sexual assault is alleged if it is first established to the court that such activity shows such a relation to the conduct involved in the case and tends to establish a pattern of conduct or behavior on the part of the victim as to be relevant to the issue of consent.

QUESTIONS

1. What are the differences between these two statutes?
2. What are the advantages of the Rhode Island statute? The disadvantages?
3. What are the advantages of the Nevada statute? The disadvantages?

PROBLEM

9.6 Harold is the defendant in a rape case. He and the complainant, Susan, were classmates in college. Several years after graduation, each returned to the college campus for the weekend to attend a football game and class reunion. During the weekend, Harold and Susan attended the same reunion party. When the party was over, Susan gave Harold a ride to his hotel, where the act of sexual intercourse on which the rape charge is based took place. Harold admits that he had sexual intercourse with Susan on the evening in question, but asserts that she consented. Susan states that she did not consent, that Harold forced her to have sexual intercourse. Harold wishes to introduce the following items of evidence on the issue of consent.

(a) The testimony of Thomas that two weeks prior to the evening of the incident giving rise to the charges against Harold, Thomas met Susan in a bar on campus and later the same evening had consensual sexual intercourse with her in his hotel room.
(b) The testimony of Jane, a friend of Harold's, that, at the reunion party on the evening in question, Susan was "snuggling up to Harold, you know, kind of hanging all over him."

(c) The testimony of George that Susan is, in his view, "very sexually active."

(d) The testimony of Maria that Susan is "widely known as promiscuous."

(e) The testimony of Harold that he and Susan had consensual sexual intercourse several times in the weeks prior to the reunion weekend.

(f) The testimony of Susan's doctor that Susan was wearing an IUD contraceptive device on the evening in question and had been for several years prior to that evening.

F. RAPE TRAUMA SYNDROME

Rape Trauma Syndrome (RTS) describes a collection of common reactions that a sexual assault survivor may manifest.[35] It can serve to explain the conduct of a survivor that might be perceived by laypersons as inconsistent with how they expect a sexual assault survivor to act. In this way, it might be used to explain unanticipated conduct, like a delay in reporting a rape or the calm demeanor of a survivor after a rape. Prosecutors often seek to admit it to undermine a defense theory that the complainant in fact consented. The *Taylor* case that follows offers an overview and application of RTS.

PEOPLE *v.* TAYLOR
Court of Appeals of New York 75 N.Y.2d 277 (1990)

OPINION . . . In these two cases, we consider whether expert testimony that a complaining witness has exhibited behavior consistent with "rape trauma syndrome" is admissible at the criminal trial of the person accused of the rape. Both trial courts admitted the testimony and the Appellate Division affirmed in both cases. We now affirm in *People v Taylor* and reverse in *People v Banks*. . . .

I. *PEOPLE v TAYLOR*

On July 29, 1984, the complainant, a 19-year-old Long Island resident, reported to the town police that she had been raped and sodomized at gunpoint on a deserted beach near her home. The complainant testified that at about nine that evening she had received a phone call from a friend, telling her that he was in trouble and asking her to meet him at a nearby market in half an hour. Twenty minutes later, the same person called back and changed the meeting place. The complainant arrived at the agreed-upon place, shut off the car engine and waited. She saw a man approach her car and she unlocked the door to let him in. Only then did she realize that the person who had approached and entered the car was not the friend she had come to meet. According to the complainant, he pointed a gun at her, directed her to nearby Clarke's Beach, and once they were there, raped and sodomized her.

---

35. David Faigman et al., *Science in the Law, Social and Behavioral Science Issues* 270 (2002).

The complainant arrived home around 11:00 P.M., woke her mother and told her about the attack. Her mother then called the police. Sometime between 11:30 P.M. and midnight, the police arrived at the complainant's house. At that time, the complainant told the police she did not know who her attacker was. She was taken to the police station where she described the events leading up to the attack and again repeated that she did not know who her attacker was. At the conclusion of the interview, the complainant was asked to step into a private room to remove the clothes that she had been wearing at the time of the attack so that they could be examined for forensic evidence. While she was alone with her mother, the complainant told her that the defendant, John Taylor, had been her attacker. The time was approximately 1:15 A.M. The complainant had known the defendant for years, and she later testified that she happened to see him the night before the attack at a local convenience store.

Her mother summoned one of the detectives and the complainant repeated that the defendant had been the person who attacked her. The complainant said that she was sure that it had been the defendant because she had had ample opportunity to see his face during the incident. The complainant subsequently identified the defendant as her attacker in two separate lineups. He was arrested on July 31, 1984, and was indicted by the Grand Jury on one count of rape in the first degree, two counts of sodomy in the first degree and one count of sexual abuse in the first degree.

The defendant's first trial ended without the jury being able to reach a verdict. At his second trial, the Judge permitted Eileen Treacy, an instructor at the City University of New York, Herbert Lehman College, with experience in counseling sexual assault victims, to testify about rape trauma syndrome. The prosecutor introduced this testimony for two separate purposes. First, Treacy's testimony on the specifics of rape trauma syndrome explained why the complainant might have been unwilling during the first few hours after the attack to name the defendant as her attacker where she had known the defendant prior to the incident. Second, Treacy's testimony that it was common for a rape victim to appear quiet and controlled following an attack, responded to evidence that the complainant had appeared calm after the attack and tended to rebut the inference that because she was not excited and upset after the attack, it had not been a rape. At the close of the second trial, the defendant was convicted of two counts of sodomy in the first degree and one count of attempted rape in the first degree and was sentenced to an indeterminate term of 7 to 21 years on the two sodomy convictions and 5 to 15 years on the attempted rape conviction.

II. PEOPLE V BANKS

On July 7, 1986, the defendant Ronnie Banks approached the 11-year-old complainant, who was playing with her friends in the City of Rochester. The complainant testified that the defendant told her to come to him and when she did not, he grabbed her by the arm and pulled her down the street. According to the complainant, the defendant took her into a neighborhood garage where he sexually assaulted her. The complainant returned to her grandmother's house, where she was living at the time. The next morning, she told her grandmother about the incident and the police were contacted. The defendant was arrested and charged with three counts involving forcible compulsion — rape in the first degree, sodomy in the first degree and sexual abuse in the first degree — and four counts that were based solely on the age of the victim — rape in the second degree, sodomy in the second degree, sexual abuse in the second degree and endangering the welfare of a child.

At trial, the complainant testified that the defendant had raped and sodomized her. In addition, she and her grandmother both testified about the complainant's behavior following the attack. Their testimony revealed that the complainant had been suffering from nightmares, had been waking up in the middle of the night in a cold sweat, had been afraid to return to school in the fall, had become generally more fearful and had been running and staying away from home. Following the introduction of this evidence, the prosecution sought to introduce expert testimony about the symptoms associated with rape trauma syndrome.

Clearly, the prosecution, in an effort to establish that forcible sexual contact had in fact occurred, wanted to introduce this evidence to show that the complainant was demonstrating behavior that was consistent with patterns of response exhibited by rape victims. The prosecutor does not appear to have introduced this evidence to counter the inference that the complainant consented to the incident, since the 11-year-old complainant is legally incapable of consent (Penal Law § 130.05 [3] [a]). Unlike *Taylor*, the evidence was not offered to explain behavior exhibited by the victim that the jury might not understand; instead, it was offered to show that the behavior that the complainant had exhibited after the incident was consistent with a set of symptoms commonly associated with women who had been forcibly attacked. The clear implication of such testimony would be that because the complainant exhibited these symptoms, it was more likely than not that she had been forcibly raped.

The Judge permitted David Gandell, an obstetrician-gynecologist on the faculty of the University of Rochester, Strong Memorial Hospital, with special training in treating victims of sexual assault, to testify as to the symptoms commonly associated with rape trauma syndrome. After Gandell had described rape trauma syndrome he testified hypothetically that the kind of symptoms demonstrated by the complainant were consistent with a diagnosis of rape trauma syndrome. At the close of the trial, the defendant was acquitted of all forcible counts and was convicted on the four statutory counts. He was sentenced to indeterminate terms of 3-1/2 to 7 years on the rape and sodomy convictions and to definite one-year terms on the convictions of sexual abuse in the second degree and endangering the welfare of a child.

III. RAPE TRAUMA SYNDROME

In a 1974 study rape trauma syndrome was described as "the acute phase and long-term reorganization process that occurs as a result of forcible rape or attempted forcible rape. This syndrome of behavioral, somatic, and psychological reactions is an acute stress reaction to a life-threatening situation" (Burgess & Holmstrom, *Rape Trauma Syndrome, 131 Am J Psychiatry* 981, 982 [1974]). Although others had studied the reactions of rape victims prior to this publication, the Burgess and Holmstrom identification of two separate phases in a rape victim's recovery has proven enormously influential.

According to Burgess and Holmstrom, the rape victim will go through an acute phase immediately following the incident. The behavior exhibited by a rape victim after the attack can vary. While some women will express their fear, anger and anxiety openly, an equal number of women will appear controlled, calm, and subdued (Burgess & Holmstrom, *op. cit.,* at 982). Women in the acute phase will also experience a number of physical reactions. These reactions include the actual physical trauma that resulted from the attack, muscle tension that could manifest itself in tension headaches, fatigue, or disturbed sleep patterns, gastrointestinal irritability and genitourinary disturbance *(id.)*. Emotional reactions in the acute phase generally take the form of fear, humiliation, embarrassment, fear of violence and death, and self-blame *(id.,* at 983).

As part of the long-term reorganizational phase, the victim will often decide to make a change in her life, such as a change of residence. At this point, the woman will often turn to her family for support *(id.)*. Other symptoms that are seen in this phase are the occurrence of nightmares and the development of phobias that relate to the circumstances of the rape *(id.,* at 984). For instance, women attacked in their beds will often develop a fear of being indoors, while women attacked on the street will develop a fear of being outdoors *(id.)*.

While some researchers have criticized the methodology of the early studies of rape trauma syndrome, Burgess and Holmstrom's model has nonetheless generated considerable interest in the response and recovery of rape victims and has contributed to the emergence of a substantial body of scholarship in this area. . . .

We realize that rape trauma syndrome encompasses a broad range of symptoms and varied patterns of recovery. . . . We are satisfied, however, that the relevant scientific community has generally accepted that rape is a highly traumatic event that will in many women trigger the onset of certain identifiable symptoms.

We note that the American Psychiatric Association has listed rape as one of the stressors that can lead to posttraumatic stress disorder (American Psychiatric Association, Diagnostic & Statistical Manual of Mental Disorders 247, 248 [3d ed. rev. 1987] [DSM III-R]). According to DSM III-R, there is an identifiable pattern of responses that can follow an intensely stressful event. The victim who suffers from posttraumatic stress disorder will persistently reexperience the traumatic event in a number of ways, as through dreams, flashbacks, hallucinations, or intense distress at exposure to events that resemble or symbolize the traumatic event *(id.,* at 250). The victim will also avoid stimuli that he or she associates with the trauma *(id.)*. Finally, the victim will experience "persistent symptoms of increased arousal," which could include difficulty in falling or staying asleep, sudden outbursts of anger, or difficulty concentrating *(id.)*. While the diagnostic criteria for posttraumatic stress disorder that are contained in DSM III-R have convinced us that the scientific community has accepted that rape as a stressor can have marked, identifiable effects on a victim's behavior, we would further note that although rape trauma syndrome can be conceptualized as a posttraumatic stress disorder *(see,* Nadelson, Notman, Zackson & Gornick, *op. cit.,* at 1267), victims of rape will often exhibit peculiar symptoms — like a fear of men — that are not commonly exhibited by victims of other sorts of trauma. . . .

IV. THE LAW

Having concluded that evidence of rape trauma syndrome is generally accepted within the relevant scientific community, we must now decide whether expert testimony in this area would aid a lay jury in reaching a verdict. "[Expert] opinion is proper when it would help to clarify an issue calling for professional or technical knowledge, possessed by the expert and beyond the ken of the typical juror" *(De Long v County of Erie,* 60 NY2d 296, 307). . . .

[R]ape is a crime that is permeated by misconceptions. Society and law are finally realizing that it is an act of violence and not a sexual act. . . . Studies have shown that one of the most popular misconceptions about rape is that the victim by behaving in a certain way brought it on herself. For that reason, studies have demonstrated that jurors will under certain circumstances blame the victim for the attack and will refuse to convict the man accused. Studies have also shown that jurors will infer consent where the victim has engaged in certain types of behavior prior to the incident. . . .

Because cultural myths still affect common understanding of rape and rape victims and because experts have been studying the effects of rape upon its victims only since the 1970's, we believe that patterns of response among rape victims are not within the ordinary understanding of the lay juror. For that reason, we conclude that introduction of expert testimony describing rape trauma syndrome may under certain circumstances assist a lay jury in deciding issues in a rape trial. . . .

Among those States that have allowed such testimony to be admitted, the purpose for which the testimony was offered has proven crucial. A number of States have allowed testimony of rape trauma syndrome to be admitted where the defendant concedes that sexual intercourse occurred, but contends that it was consensual. . . .

Other States have permitted the admission of this testimony where it was offered to explain behavior exhibited by the complainant that might be viewed as inconsistent with a claim of rape. In *People v Hampton* (746 P2d 947), the Colorado Supreme Court held that in a case where the complainant waited 89 days to report an attack, expert testimony that a rape victim who is assaulted by someone she knows is more reluctant to report an attack was admissible to explain the delay in reporting (*id.*, at 952). . . . Other States that have permitted the admission of expert testimony of this type to explain inconsistencies in the behavior of the complainant, especially where a child is involved. . . .

Having concluded that evidence of rape trauma syndrome can assist jurors in reaching a verdict by dispelling common misperceptions about rape, and having reviewed the different approaches taken by the other jurisdictions that have considered the question, we too agree that the reason why the testimony is offered will determine its helpfulness, its relevance and its potential for prejudice. In the two cases now before us, testimony regarding rape trauma syndrome was offered for entirely different purposes. We conclude that its admission at the trial of John Taylor was proper, but that its admission at the trial of Ronnie Banks was not.

As noted above, the complaining witness in *Taylor* had initially told the police that she could not identify her assailant. Approximately two hours after she first told her mother that she had been raped and sodomized, she told her mother that she knew the defendant had done it. The complainant had known the defendant for years and had seen him the night before the assault. We hold that under the circumstances present in this case, expert testimony explaining that a rape victim who knows her assailant is more fearful of disclosing his name to the police and is in fact less likely to report the rape at all was relevant to explain why the complainant may have been initially unwilling to report that the defendant had been the man who attacked her. Behavior of this type is not within the ordinary understanding of the jury and testimony explaining this behavior assists the jury in determining what effect to give to the complainant's initial failure to identify the defendant . This evidence provides a possible explanation for the complainant's behavior that is consistent with her claim that she was raped. As such, it is relevant.

Rape trauma syndrome evidence was also introduced in *Taylor* in response to evidence that revealed the complainant had not seemed upset following the attack. We note again in this context that the reaction of a rape victim in the hours following her attack is not something within the common understanding of the average lay juror. Indeed, the defense would clearly want the jury to infer that because the victim was not upset following the attack, she must not have been raped. This inference runs contrary to the studies cited earlier, which suggest that half of all women who have been forcibly raped are controlled and subdued following the attack. Thus, we conclude that evidence of this type is relevant to dispel misconceptions that jurors might possess regarding the ordinary responses of rape victims in the first hours after their attack. We do not believe that evidence of rape trauma syndrome, when admitted for that express purpose, is unduly prejudicial.

The admission of expert testimony describing rape trauma syndrome in *Banks*, however, was clearly error. As we noted earlier, this evidence was not offered to explain behavior that might appear unusual to a lay juror not ordinarily familiar with the patterns of response exhibited by rape victims. We conclude that evidence of rape trauma syndrome is inadmissible when it inescapably bears solely on proving that a rape occurred, as was the case here.

QUESTIONS

1. Should courts prohibit introduction of RTS to prove that a rape occurred? Why?

2. Is there a distinction between proving that a rape occurred and that a victim did not act inconsistently with having been raped?

G. SPECIAL HURDLES: THE MARITAL EXEMPTION AND ACQUAINTANCE RAPE

As discussed at the outset of this chapter, based on a deep distrust of rape complainants, the law created substantial hurdles for victims of rape, such as cautionary instructions, the corroboration requirement, and the prompt complaint rule. In addition, for the crime of rape, the law discriminated against victims based on their relationship with their assailants. It refused to recognize the crime of rape by a husband of his wife. It has also discriminated informally, and sometimes formally, against victims who were acquainted with their assailants in other social contexts or relationships. In this Section of the chapter, we explore the marital exemption to the crime of rape and also focus specifically on the issue of acquaintance rape.

1. The Marital Exemption

The criminal law has been slow to protect wives from the sexual violence of their husbands. For example, although the Model Penal Code offered a progressive approach to many vexing criminal law issues, it retained a marital exemption.

Model Penal Code § 213.1 (1985)   *Rape and Related Offenses*

(1) *Rape.* A male who has sexual intercourse with a female not his wife is guilty of rape if:

(a) he compels her to submit by force or by threat of imminent death, serious bodily injury, extreme pain or kidnapping to be inflicted on anyone; . . .

Model Penal Code § 213.6 (1985)   *Provisions Generally Applicable to Article 213*

(2) *Spouse Relationships.* Whenever in this Article the definition of an offense excludes conduct with a spouse, the exclusion shall be deemed to extend to persons living as man and wife, regardless of the legal status of their relationship. The exclusion shall be inoperative as respects spouses living apart under a decree of judicial separation.

The comments to the Model Penal Code's provision on rape include the following as part of the discussion of forcible rape in the domestic rape context:[36]

At common law a man could not commit rape by forcing his wife to engage in intercourse. This rule prevailed at the time the Model Penal Code was drafted and [as of 1980] has been continued in most revised penal laws. . . .

First, marriage or equivalent relationship, while not amounting to a legal waiver of the woman's right to say "no," does imply a kind of generalized consent that distinguishes some versions of the crime of rape from parallel behavior by a husband. The relationship itself creates a presumption of consent, valid until revoked. At a minimum, therefore, husbands must be exempt from those categories of liability based not on force or coercion but on a presumed incapacity of the woman to consent. For example, a man who has intercourse with his unconscious wife should scarcely be condemned to felony liability on the ground that the woman in such circumstances is incapable of consenting to sex with her own husband, at least unless there are aggravating circumstances. The same holds true for intercourse with a wife who for some reason other than unconsciousness is not aware that a sexual act is committed upon her. . . .

The major context of which those who would abandon the spousal exclusion are thinking, however, is the situation of rape by force or threat. . . .

Here the law already authorizes a penalty for assault. If the actor causes serious bodily injury, the punishment is quite severe. The issue is whether the still more drastic sanctions of rape should apply. The answer depends on whether the injury caused by forcible intercourse by a husband is equivalent to that inflicted by someone else. The gravity of the crime of forcible rape derives not merely from its violent character but also from its achievement of a particularly degrading kind of unwanted intimacy. Where the attacker stands in an ongoing relation of sexual intimacy, that evil, as distinct from the force used to compel submission, may well be thought qualitively different. The character of the voluntary association of husband and wife, in other words, may be thought to affect the nature of the harm involved in unwanted intercourse. That, in any event, is the conclusion long endorsed by the law of rape and carried forward in the Model Penal Code provision.

---

36. Model Penal Code and Commentaries, art. 213, 341, 344-346 (1985).

QUESTIONS

1. Do you agree with the MPC Comment's reasoning?
2. What explains the attitudes reflected in that reasoning? Is the following information from Professor Stephen Schulhofer of importance to your analysis? "Seventeen people served as reporters, associate reporters, or special consultants for the Model Penal Code project; none was a woman. Of the forty lawyers and professors who served on the institute's Criminal Law Advisory Committee, only one was a woman."[37]

PEOPLE *v.* LIBERTA
Court of Appeals of New York 64 N.Y.2d 152 (1984)

OPINION OF THE COURT

WACHTLER, Judge.

The defendant, while living apart from his wife pursuant to a Family Court order, forcibly raped and sodomized her in the presence of their 2-1/2 year old son. Under the New York Penal Law a married man ordinarily cannot be prosecuted for raping or sodomizing his wife. The defendant, however, though married at the time of the incident, is treated as an unmarried man under the Penal Law because of the Family Court order. On this appeal, he contends that because of the exemption for married men, the statutes for rape in the first degree (Penal Law, § 130.35) and sodomy in the first degree (Penal Law, § 130.50) violate the equal protection clause of the Federal Constitution (US Const., 14th Amdt). The defendant also contends that the rape statute violates equal protection because only men, and not women, can be prosecuted under it.

I

Defendant Mario Liberta and Denise Liberta were married in 1978. Shortly after the birth of their son, in October of that year, Mario began to beat Denise. In early 1980 Denise brought a proceeding in the Family Court in Erie County seeking protection from the defendant. On April 30, 1980 a temporary order of protection was issued to her by the Family Court. Under this order, the defendant was to move out and remain away from the family home, and stay away from Denise. The order provided that the defendant could visit with his son once each weekend.

On the weekend of March 21, 1981, Mario, who was then living in a motel, did not visit his son. On Tuesday, March 24, 1981 he called Denise to ask if he could visit his son on that day. Denise would not allow the defendant to come to her house, but she did agree to allow him to pick up their son and her and take them both back to his motel after being assured that a friend of his would be with them at all times. The defendant and his friend picked up Denise and their son and the four of them drove to defendant's motel.

When they arrived at the motel the friend left. As soon as only Mario, Denise, and their son were alone in the motel room, Mario attacked Denise, threatened to kill her, and forced her to perform fellatio on him and to engage in sexual intercourse

---

37. *Supra* note 19 at 286.

with him. The son was in the room during the entire episode, and the defendant forced Denise to tell their son to watch what the defendant was doing to her.

The defendant allowed Denise and their son to leave shortly after the incident. Denise, after going to her parents' home, went to a hospital to be treated for scratches on her neck and bruises on her head and back, all inflicted by her husband. She also went to the police station, and on the next day she swore out a felony complaint against the defendant. On July 15, 1981 the defendant was indicted for rape in the first degree and sodomy in the first degree.

II

Section 130.35 of the Penal Law provides in relevant part that "A male is guilty of rape in the first degree when he engages in sexual intercourse with a female . . . by forcible compulsion." "Female," for purposes of the rape statute, is defined as "any female person who is not married to the actor" (Penal Law, § 130.00, subd 4). Section 130.50 of the Penal Law provides in relevant part that "a person is guilty of sodomy in the first degree when he engages in deviate sexual intercourse with another person . . . by forcible compulsion." "Deviate sexual intercourse" is defined as "sexual conduct between persons not married to each other consisting of contact between the penis and the anus, the mouth and penis, or the mouth and the vulva" (Penal Law, § 130.00, subd 2). Thus, due to the "not married" language in the definitions of "female" and "deviate sexual intercourse," there is a "marital exemption" for both forcible rape and forcible sodomy. The marital exemption itself, however, has certain exceptions. For purposes of the rape and sodomy statutes, a husband and wife are considered to be "not married" if at the time of the sexual assault they "are living apart . . . pursuant to a valid and effective: (i) order issued by a court of competent jurisdiction which by its terms or in its effect requires such living apart, or (ii) decree or judgment of separation, or (iii) written agreement of separation" (Penal Law, § 130.00, subd 4). . . .

The defendant was . . . convicted of rape in the first degree and sodomy in the first degree and the conviction was affirmed by the Appellate Division. . . . Defendant . . . asserts, assuming that because of the Family Court order he is treated just as any unmarried male would be, that he cannot be convicted of either rape in the first degree or sodomy in the first degree because both statutes are unconstitutional. Specifically, he contends that both statutes violate equal protection because they burden some, but not all males (all but those within the "marital exemption"), and that the rape statute also violates equal protection for burdening only men, and not women. The lower courts rejected the defendant's constitutional arguments, finding that neither statute violated the equal protection clause in the Fourteenth Amendment. Although we affirm the conviction of the defendant, we do not agree with the constitutional analysis of the lower courts and instead conclude that the marital and gender exemptions must be read out of the statutes prohibiting forcible rape and sodomy. . . .

IV

The defendant's constitutional challenges to the rape and sodomy statutes are premised on his being considered "not married" to Denise and are the same challenges as could be made by any unmarried male convicted under these statutes. The defendant's claim is that both statutes violate equal protection because they are underinclusive classifications which burden him, but not others similarly situated. . . .

A. The Marital Exemption

As noted above, under the Penal Law a married man ordinarily cannot be convicted of forcibly raping or sodomizing his wife. This is the so-called marital exemption for rape (see 1881 Penal Code, tit. X, ch II, § 278). Although a marital exemption was not explicit in earlier rape statutes (see 1863 Rev. Stats. part 4, ch I, tit. 2, art. 2, § 22), an 1852 treatise stated that a man could not be guilty of raping his wife (Barbour, Criminal Law of State of New York [2d ed.], p. 69). The assumption, even before the marital exemption was codified, that a man could not be guilty of raping his wife, is traceable to a statement made by the 17th century English jurist Lord Hale, who wrote: "[T]he husband cannot be guilty of a rape committed by himself upon his lawful wife, for by their mutual matrimonial consent and contract the wife hath given up herself in this kind unto her husband, which she cannot retract" (1 Hale, History of Pleas of the Crown, p. 629). Although Hale cited no authority for his statement it was relied on by State Legislatures which enacted rape statutes with a marital exemption and by courts which established a common-law exemption for husbands. . . .

Presently, over 40 States still retain some form of marital exemption for rape. While the marital exemption is subject to an equal protection challenge, because it classifies unmarried men differently than married men, the equal protection clause does not prohibit a State from making classifications, provided the statute does not arbitrarily burden a particular group of individuals. . . . Where a statute draws a distinction based upon marital status, the classification must be reasonable and must be based upon "some ground of difference that rationally explains the different treatment."

We find that there is no rational basis for distinguishing between marital rape and nonmarital rape. The various rationales which have been asserted in defense of the exemption are either based upon archaic notions about the consent and property rights incident to marriage or are simply unable to withstand even the slightest scrutiny. We therefore declare the marital exemption for rape in the New York statute to be unconstitutional.

Lord Hale's notion of an irrevocable implied consent by a married woman to sexual intercourse has been cited most frequently in support of the marital exemption. Any argument based on a supposed consent, however, is untenable. Rape is not simply a sexual act to which one party does not consent. Rather, it is a degrading, violent act which violates the bodily integrity of the victim and frequently causes severe, long-lasting physical and psychic harm. To ever imply consent to such an act is irrational and absurd. Other than in the context of rape statutes, marriage has never been viewed as giving a husband the right to coerced intercourse on demand. Certainly, then, a marriage license should not be viewed as a license for a husband to forcibly rape his wife with impunity. A married woman has the same right to control her own body as does an unmarried woman. . . . If a husband feels "aggrieved" by his wife's refusal to engage in sexual intercourse, he should seek relief in the courts governing domestic relations, not in "violent or forceful self-help" (State v. Smith, 85 N.J. 193, 206).

The other traditional justifications for the marital exemption were the common-law doctrines that a woman was the property of her husband and that the legal existence of the woman was "incorporated and consolidated into that of the husband" (1 Blackstone's Commentaries [1966 ed.], p. 430; . . .) Both these doctrines, of course, have long been rejected in this State. Indeed, "[n]owhere in the common-law world — [or] in any modern society — is a woman regarded as chattel or demeaned by denial of a separate legal identity and the dignity associated with recognition as a whole human being" (*Trammel v. United States*, 445 U.S. 40, 52).

Because the traditional justifications for the marital exemption no longer have any validity, other arguments have been advanced in its defense. The first of these recent rationales, which is stressed by the People in this case, is that the marital exemption protects against governmental intrusion into marital privacy and promotes reconciliation of the spouses, and thus that elimination of the exemption would be disruptive to marriages. While protecting marital privacy and encouraging reconciliation are legitimate State interests, there is no rational relation between allowing a husband to forcibly rape his wife and these interests. The marital exemption simply does not further marital privacy because this right of privacy protects consensual acts, not violent sexual assaults. Just as a husband cannot invoke a right of marital privacy to escape liability for beating his wife,[7] he cannot justifiably rape his wife under the guise of a right to privacy.

Similarly, it is not tenable to argue that elimination of the marital exemption would disrupt marriages because it would discourage reconciliation. Clearly, it is the violent act of rape and not the subsequent attempt of the wife to seek protection through the criminal justice system which "disrupts" a marriage. Moreover, if the marriage has already reached the point where intercourse is accomplished by violent assault it is doubtful that there is anything left to reconcile. This, of course, is particularly true if the wife is willing to bring criminal charges against her husband which could result in a lengthy jail sentence.

Another rationale sometimes advanced in support of the marital exemption is that marital rape would be a difficult crime to prove. A related argument is that allowing such prosecutions could lead to fabricated complaints by "vindictive" wives. The difficulty of proof argument is based on the problem of showing lack of consent. Proving lack of consent, however, is often the most difficult part of any rape prosecution, particularly where the rapist and the victim had a prior relationship. Similarly, the possibility that married women will fabricate complaints would seem to be no greater than the possibility of unmarried women doing so. . . . [8] The criminal justice system, with all of its built-in safeguards, is presumed to be capable of handling any false complaints. Indeed, if the possibility of fabricated complaints were a basis for not criminalizing behavior which would otherwise be sanctioned, virtually all crimes other than homicides would go unpunished.

The final argument in defense of the marital exemption is that marital rape is not as serious an offense as other rape and is thus adequately dealt with by the possibility of prosecution under criminal statutes, such as assault statutes, which provide for less severe punishment. The fact that rape statutes exist, however, is a recognition that the harm caused by a forcible rape is different, and more severe, than the harm caused by an ordinary assault. "Short of homicide, [rape] is the 'ultimate violation of self.'" Under the Penal Law, assault is generally a misdemeanor unless either the victim suffers "serious physical injury" or a deadly weapon or dangerous instrument is used (Penal Law, §§ 120.00,

---

[7] A wife may sue her husband for torts he commits against her, including assault and battery (General Obligations Law, 3-313).

[8] The stigma and other difficulties associated with a woman reporting a rape and pressing charges probably deter most attempts to fabricate an incident; rape remains a grossly under-reported crime (see Note, Rape Reform and a Statutory Consent Defense, 74 J. Crim. L. & Criminology 1518, 1519, n.7. . . .)

120.05, 120.10). Thus, if the defendant had been living with Denise at the time he forcibly raped and sodomized her he probably could not have been charged with a felony, let alone a felony with punishment equal to that for rape in the first degree.

Moreover, there is no evidence to support the argument that marital rape has less severe consequences than other rape. On the contrary, numerous studies have shown that marital rape is frequently quite violent and generally has *more* severe, traumatic effects on the victim than other rape.

Among the recent decisions in this country addressing the marital exemption, only one court has concluded that there is a rational basis for it. We agree with the other courts which have analyzed the exemption, which have been unable to find any present justification for it. Justice Holmes wrote: "It is revolting to have no better reason for a rule of law than that so it was laid down in the time of Henry IV. It is still more revolting if the grounds upon which it was laid down have vanished long since, and the rule simply persists from blind imitation of the past" (Holmes, The Path of the Law, 10 Harv. L. Rev. 457, 469). This statement is an apt characterization of the marital exemption; it lacks a rational basis, and therefore violates the equal protection clauses of both the Federal and State Constitutions.

B. The Exemption for Females

Under the Penal Law only males can be convicted of rape in the first degree. . . . Insofar as the rape statute applies to acts of "sexual intercourse," which, as defined in the Penal Law (see Penal Law, § 130.00) can only occur between a male and a female, it is true that a female cannot physically rape a female and that therefore there is no denial of equal protection when punishing only males for forcibly engaging in sexual intercourse with females. The equal protection issue, however, stems from the fact that the statute applies to males who forcibly rape females but does not apply to females who forcibly rape males.

Rape statutes historically applied only to conduct by males against females, largely because the purpose behind the proscriptions was to protect the chastity of women and thus their property value to their fathers or husbands. New York's rape statute has always protected only females, and has thus applied only to males. Presently New York is one of only 10 jurisdictions that does not have a gender-neutral statute for forcible rape.

A statute which treats males and females differently violates equal protection unless the classification is substantially related to the achievement of an important governmental objective. This test applies whether the statute discriminates against males or against females. The People bear the burden of showing both the existence of an important objective and the substantial relationship between the discrimination in the statute and that objective. This burden is not met in the present case, and therefore the gender exemption also renders the statute unconstitutional. . . .

To meet their burden of showing that a gender-based law is substantially related to an important governmental objective the People must set forth an " 'exceedingly persuasive justification' " for the classification, which requires, among other things, a showing that the gender-based law serves the governmental objective better than would a gender-neutral law. The fact that the act of a female forcibly raping a male may be a difficult or rare occurrence does not mean that the gender exemption satisfies the constitutional test. A gender-neutral law would indisputably better serve, even if only marginally, the objective of deterring and punishing forcible sexual assaults. The only persons "benefited" by the gender exemption are females who forcibly rape males. As the Supreme Court has stated, "[a] gender-based classification which, as compared to a gender-neutral one, generates additional benefits only for those it has no reason to prefer cannot survive equal protection scrutiny."

Accordingly, we find that section 130.35 of the Penal Law violates equal protection because it exempts females from criminal liability for forcible rape.

V

Having found that the statutes for rape in the first degree and sodomy in the first degree are unconstitutionally underinclusive, the remaining issue is the appropriate remedy for these equal protection violations. When a statute is constitutionally defective because of underinclusion, a court may either strike the statute, and thus make it applicable to nobody, or extend the coverage of the statute to those formerly excluded. Accordingly, the unconstitutionality of one part of a criminal statute does not necessarily render the entire statute void.

This court's task is to discern what course the Legislature would have chosen to follow if it had foreseen our conclusions as to underinclusiveness.

The question then is whether the Legislature would prefer to have statutes which cover forcible rape and sodomy, with no exemption for married men who rape or sodomize their wives and no exception made for females who rape males, or instead to have no statutes proscribing forcible rape and sodomy. . . . Statutes prohibiting such behavior are of the utmost importance, and to declare such statutes a nullity would have a disastrous effect on the public interest and safety. The inevitable conclusion is that the Legislature would prefer to eliminate the exemptions and thereby preserve the statutes. Accordingly we choose the remedy of striking the marital exemption from sections 130.35 and 130.50 of the Penal Law and the gender exemption from section 130.35 of the Penal Law, so that it is now the law of this State that any person who engages in sexual intercourse or deviate sexual intercourse with any other person by forcible compulsion is guilty of either rape in the first degree or sodomy in the first degree. Because the statutes under which the defendant was convicted are not being struck down, his conviction is affirmed. . . .

In her 2000 article on the *Legal History of Marital Rape*, Professor Jill Hasday notes:[38]

> A majority of states still retain some form of the common law regime: They criminalize a narrower range of offenses if committed within marriage, subject the marital rape they do recognize to less serious sanctions, and/or create special procedural hurdles for marital rape prosecutions. . . . Virtually every state legislature has revisited the marital rape exemption over the last twenty-five years, but most have chosen to preserve the exemption in some substantial manifestation. With rare exception, moreover, courts have not invalidated state laws protecting marital rape. Political protest and legislative action, rather than any clear judicial statement of constitutional norms, has driven the partial and uneven modification of the common law rule.

How should the law treat spousal rape?

---

38. Jill Elaine Hasday, *Contest and Consent: A Legal History of Marital Rape*, 88 Cal. L. Rev. 1373, 1375-1376 (2000).

2. Acquaintance Rape

Criminal statutes on their face rarely distinguish stranger from acquaintance rape. Nonetheless, researchers indicate that acquaintance rape regularly receives a more critical reception at almost every stage of the criminal justice process. Consider again, for example, the results of the jury study by Kalven and Zeisel, as summarized by Professor Susan Estrich, in the introductory materials to this chapter. As you read the materials in this Section, think about how the criminal law should treat acquaintance rape.

Consider the following account:

> "Well, I guess I just thought you wanted it," Andy said. "I guess I just thought you were the kind of person that, whatever, that it would be okay."
>
> "What kind of person deserves to be raped?" Ellen demanded. "What do you mean?"
>
> "Well, you have sex with a lot of people," Andy replied. "And I just thought you wanted it."
>
> "Didn't you hear me say no?" Ellen said. "Didn't you understand?"
>
> "Yeah, I heard you," Andy said. "I kind of knew, but I just sort of wanted to do it anyway."[39]

In the following excerpt, Professor Samuel Pillsbury argues that there is a "nonrecognition" problem for acquaintance rape.[40]

> In the last generation we developed a new legal and moral appreciation of the wrongs of sexual coercion, even between acquaintances. Yet we experience great difficulty in identifying particular instances of forced sex. Episodes of sexual coercion between acquaintances tend to be categorized as "bad sex" or "bad romance" rather than serious criminal wrongs. There exists a troubling and persistent gap between our formal understanding of sexual wrongdoing and actual recognition of such wrongs when they occur. Our intellectual and emotional understandings of rape and romance are at odds. . . .
>
> In many cases no one (including the victim) labels what happened a crime. When it comes to sexual assaults between acquaintances, we often do not recognize the wrong.
>
> Nonrecognition comes in many forms. Men who use force to obtain sexual gratification from social partners may admit violating the rules of romance, but heatedly deny any criminal wrongdoing. Meanwhile female victims often blame themselves for provoking the man's conduct or putting themselves in a vulnerable position. And they often deny the extent of the wrong done to them. Similarly third parties asked to judge the incident go through a variety of psychological and forensic maneuvers to avoid labeling what occurred in a quasi-romantic setting as criminal.
>
> What links these forms of nonrecognition is the assumption that ordinary sexual interaction — romance — is fundamentally distinct from rape. . . . Confronted with an incident in which the man does not use dramatic force and in which the overall pattern of interaction is consistent with that of courtship, many read an incident of forced sex between social acquaintances as bad romance rather than rape. Because the incident does not fit the emotional construct of rape, it does not trigger the horror that we expect rape incidents to inspire. Without this emotional reaction,

---

39. Lisa Gerson, *Rape at Harvard*, Boston Magazine, 104, 153 (Aug. 1999) (reporting the victim's account of a conversation with her assailant, a fellow student and acquaintance at Harvard, subsequent to the sexual assault), cited in Samuel H. Pillsbury, *Crimes Against the Heart: Recognizing the Wrongs of Forced Sex*, 35 Loy. L. Rev. 845 (2002).

40. Samuel H. Pillsbury, *supra* note 39 at 845, 846-849 (footnotes omitted).

the person presumes that what happened—however unfortunate—cannot be classified as a serious criminal wrong.

Has Professor Pillsbury accurately characterized societal reaction to acquaintance rapes? If so, what measures could be taken to change society's perceptions? If not, where does his analysis err?

In response to discrimination against victims who knew their assailants, some jurisdictions have enacted statutes on consent like the Minnesota statute that follows:

Minnesota Statute Annotated § 609.341 Subd. 4(a) (2001)

(a) "Consent" means words or overt actions by a person indicating a freely given present agreement to perform a particular sexual act with the actor. Consent does not mean the existence of a prior or current social relationship between the actor and the complainant or that the complainant failed to resist a particular sexual act.

H. THE CURRENT STATUS OF RAPE LAW AND REFORM EFFORTS

Professor Joshua Dressler suggests the following about the status of rape law and its reform:

> Until not very long ago, American rape law unmitigatedly and universally represented what Susan Estrich aptly described as "boys' rules." Indeed, rape law has been male-oriented at least since Biblical times. One does not have to accept the view that rape law was devised for the misogynistic purpose of "embodying and ensuring male control over women's sexuality," to agree with the assertion that the common law approach to the offense—a crime which by definition deals with male conduct in relation to females—was male-centered. After all, the law of rape developed during a time when women played no role in legal affairs, even as to offenses that affected them intimately.
>
> Boys' rules have certainly not been eradicated everywhere and in every case, but feminists can take legitimate pride in the fact that rape law has undergone significant reform in just the past decade or two, largely as a result of their efforts. The thesis of my comments here is that although additional legal reform is in order, the time may also be right for us to concern ourselves at least a little with the possibility that rape reform *could* go (or perhaps *is* going) down some other paths that fair-minded persons will later regret. Just a few decades ago, rape law was so irrational and insensitive to the legitimate interests of women that there was really no need to strike a balance: virtually any reform effort was likely to result in improvement. But, we are past that extreme stage. It is worthwhile now, I think, to pause for a moment, take stock of the reforms that have been implemented and the ones that remain to be realized, and make sure that our efforts to provide justice to rape victims do not result in unfairness to those who might be accused of this heinous offense. . . . [41]

Review here Professor Dressler's criticism of the *M.T.S.* case. Has rape reform proceeded too far?

---

41. Joshua Dressler, *Where We Have Been, and Where We Might Be Going: Some Cautionary Reflections on Rape Law Reform*, 46 Clev. St. L. Rev. 410, 410, 421-423, 426-428 (1998).

Contrast Professor Stephen Schulhofer's assessment, from his 1998 book, of the status of rape law:

> Despite three decades of supposedly dramatic change in cultural attitudes and legal standards, criminal law still fails to guarantee a woman's right to determine for herself when she will become sexually intimate with another person. . . .
>
> Criminal law easily creates false impressions in this respect. Resistance requirements supposedly have been restricted or abolished. But when a woman says "no," clearly and insistently, the man can still roll on top of her, remove her clothes, and penetrate her, all without committing rape. The obstacles in these cases are not conflicting versions of the truth, credibility questions, and the notorious difficulties of sorting out the facts when "he said . . . she said. . . . " The man can simply admit to the facts, more or less with impunity. His conduct, even today, remains perfectly legal, because he has not used what the law calls force, that is, physical power *in addition* to the force that is intrinsic to intercourse.
>
> The upshot is that resistance requirements remain in effect even where the law says they have been abolished. The woman's right to bodily integrity and her right to control her sexual choices just do not exist — until she begins to scream or fight back physically.

The Myth of Radical Change

> These large gaps in American law will seem surprising to anyone whose impressions are formed by recent media coverage of the antirape movement and its supposedly far-reaching success in achieving legal change. Opponents of rape reform have managed to convince a wide audience that the standards of permissible conduct are now dictated by "hypersensitive" young women and by "radical" feminists committed to a highly restrictive, Victorian conception of sexual propriety. . . .
>
> The reality is far different. The claim that legal rules, campus behavior codes, and company policies enshrine radically overprotective, puritanical rules of conduct is a myth. It is a particularly unfortunate myth because it obscures the serious risks women continue to face and blocks informed discussion of reforms that are still urgently needed.
>
> What have recent reforms accomplished? When a woman says "no" insistently and attempts any degree of physical struggle, courts today, far more than in the past are likely to see the assailant's conduct as rape. When a man's language carries a threat of bodily injury, the woman's failure to resist no longer precludes a conviction.
>
> Yet once we move beyond situations of potentially severe physical violence, the limited reach of recent reforms becomes apparent. . . .
>
> Existing criminal law resolves the dilemmas of sexual autonomy by making almost no effort to control abuses that are not physically violent. This "solution" indirectly places an imprimatur of social permission on virtually all pressures and inducements that can be considered nonviolent. It leaves women unprotected against forms of pressure that any society should consider morally improper and legally intolerable. What may be even worse, the existing approach distorts social conceptions of legitimate behavior and raises the threshold for the kind of physical violence that the law is willing to recognize as "abnormal" force. As became starkly clear for the Illinois woman who was accosted while bike riding, current standards are so strict that they shelter many truly intimidating and physically dangerous abuses that the law in theory claims to forbid.[42] . . .

---

42. Schulhofer, *supra* note 19 (referring to People v. Warren, *supra*, in Section D.2.a).

We live in a time of changing sexual mores, and we are likely to for some time
to come. In such times the law can bind us to the past or help push us into the
future. . . . It may be impossible — and unwise — to try to use the criminal law to
articulate any of our ideal visions of male-female relationships. But recognition of
the limits of the criminal sanction need not be taken to justify the status quo. As for
choosing between reinforcing the old and the new in a world of changing norms,
it is not necessarily more legitimate or neutral to choose the old. There are lines to
be drawn short of the ideal. The challenge we face in thinking about rape is to use
the legitimatizing power of law to reinforce what is best, not what is worst, in our
changing sexual mores.[43] . . .

Professor Andrew Taslitz argues for reforms outside the formal doctrinal definition of rape. He focuses on rape trials and reforms needed in the approach to the
trial of rape cases.[44] He suggests that reformers need to focus on how jurors process
testimony and how that testimony is presented. He argues that human beings use
stories to interpret and evaluate the world around us. "Many of these stories," he
writes, "tend to channel the political and economic power that our society most
values to men and to privilege male perceptions of reality." He labels these "patriarchal stories." Using these, jurors may discredit the testimony of female victims.
He notes that compounding the problem posed by patriarchal stories, the court
process fosters an "adversarial" and "competitive" use of language that he says
"muzzles" the victim. He laments that "[r]ape law reform, despite some modest
successes, has largely failed. But this has been so because the reformers did not
appreciate the storied, linguistic nature of the problem."

Ultimately, Professor Taslitz proposes reforms to ethical and evidentiary rules
to enhance jurors' abilities to credit rape victims' accounts at trial.

Reform efforts outside formal doctrine also include public education campaigns. Consider the poster on page 643. In the spring of 2000, it appeared in
bus stops around the City of San Francisco.[45]

---

43. Susan Estrich, *Real Rape* 101 (1987).
44. Quotations in this paragraph are from Andrew E. Taslitz, Rape and the Culture of the
Courtroom 7-11 (1999).
45. Reprinted by permission. Copyright 2000, The Department on the Status of Women, San
Francisco, CA.

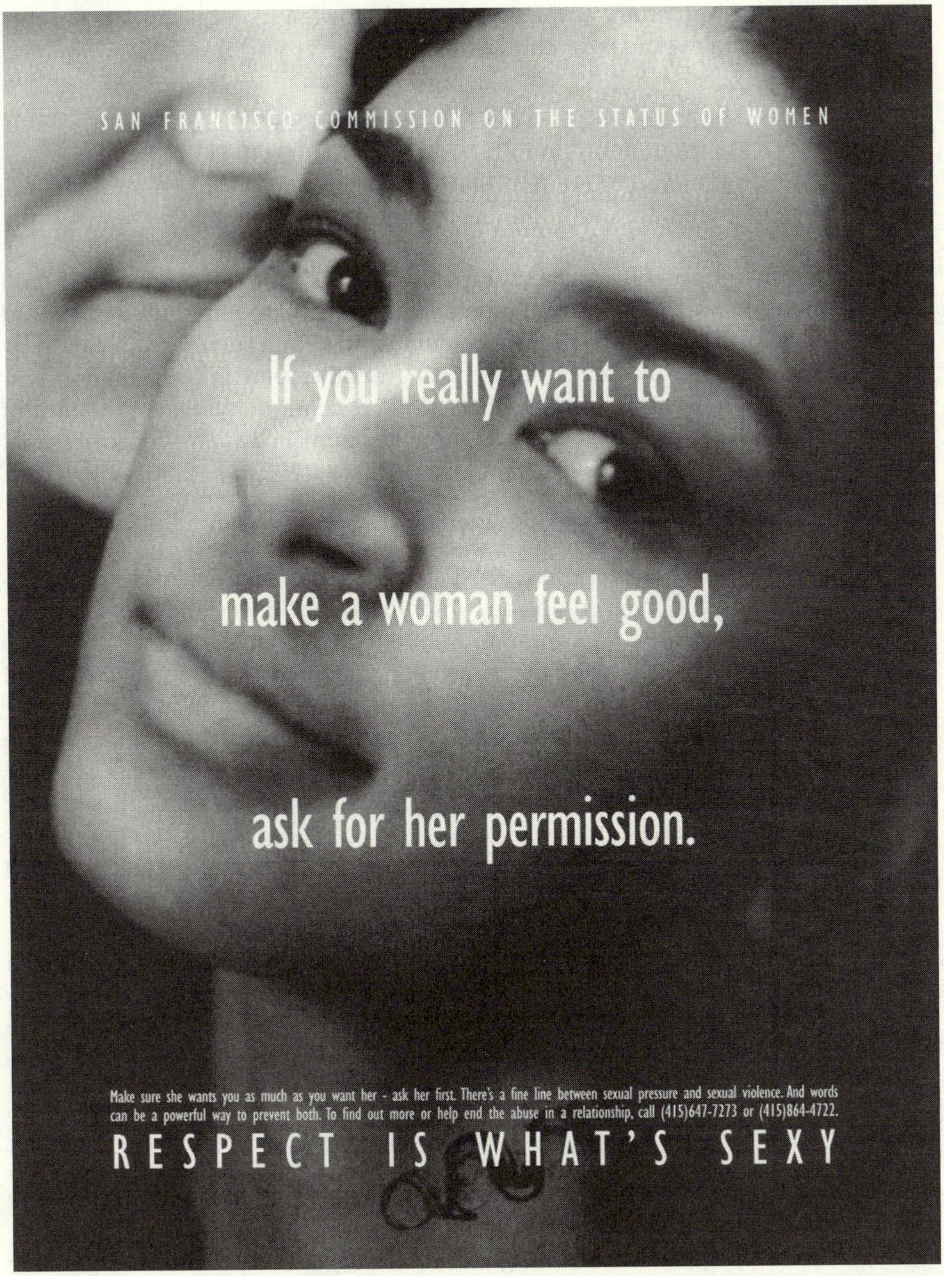
SAN FRANCISCO COMMISSION ON THE STATUS OF WOMEN
If you really want to
make a woman feel good,
ask for her permission.
Make sure she wants you as much as you want her - ask her first. There's a fine line between sexual pressure and sexual violence. And words can be a powerful way to prevent both. To find out more or help end the abuse in a relationship, call (415)647-7273 or (415)864-4722.
RESPECT IS WHAT'S SEXY

In concluding our study of the evolution of rape law, contrast the approaches proposed by the following two scholars:

Donald A. Dripps, BEYOND RAPE: AN ESSAY ON THE DIFFERENCE BETWEEN THE PRESENCE OF FORCE AND THE ABSENCE OF CONSENT

92 Colum. L. Rev. 1780, 1796-1797, 1807-1808 (1992)

[F]or all the efforts of reformers, rape law is still a mess. Legislators should give up on the common-law formulation and anything based upon it, and instead distinguish two quite distinct offenses calculated to obtain sexual gratification by culpable means. First, the purpose of causing another person to engage in sexual acts should enhance the penalty for assault. Second, nonviolent disregard of another's refusal to engage in sexual acts should be punished as an offense of sexual expropriation. . . .

I. SEXUALLY MOTIVATED ASSAULT

(1) For purposes of this section, "sexual act" means any act of coitus, fellatio, cunnilingus, buggery, or any insertion of an object into the vagina or anus.

(2) Whoever purposely or knowingly gives another person cause to fear physical injury, or purposely or knowingly inflicts physical injury on another person, or purposely or knowingly overpowers another's physical resistance, for the purpose of causing any person to engage in a sexual act, is guilty of Sexually Motivated Assault. Sexually Motivated Assault is subject to the same sentence as aggravated assault.

(3) Whoever purposely or knowingly gives another person reasonable cause to fear death, injury from a deadly weapon, dismemberment or disfigurement, or who purposely or knowingly injures another with a deadly weapon, dismembers, or disfigures another person, for the purpose of causing any person to engage in a sexual act with any other person, commits Aggravated Sexually Motivated Assault. Aggravated Sexually Motivated Assault is subject to the sentence previously applicable to rape.

II. SEXUAL EXPROPRIATION

(1) For purpose of this section, "sexual act" has the same meaning as for the purposes of Sexually Motivated Assault.

(2) Whoever purposely or knowingly commits any sexual act with or upon any person

A. known by the actor to have expressed the refusal to engage in that act, without subsequently expressly revoking that refusal; or

B. believed by the actor to have refrained from expressing refusal because the actor has committed Sexually Motivated Assault or Aggravated Sexually Motivated Assault; or

C. known by the actor to be unconscious, physically helpless, mentally incompetent, or otherwise unable to express the refusal to engage in that act, commits Sexual Expropriation. Sexual Expropriation is punishable by a maximum prison sentence of one year and one day.

(3) In any prosecution under section (2)(C), it shall be a defense that an actor who had previously engaged in sexual acts with the victim reasonably believed that the victim would not have refused to engage in the sexual act committed, had the victim been capable of expressing refusal.

Professor Schulhofer advocates adoption of the following approach to sexual offenses, based on sexual autonomy:

§ 201   *Sexual Assault*

(a) An actor is guilty of sexual assault, a felony of the second degree, if he uses physical force to compel another person to submit to an act of sexual penetration.

(b) An actor is guilty of sexual assault, a felony of the second degree, if he commits an act of sexual penetration with another person when he knows that the victim is less than thirteen years old.

(c) An actor is guilty of aggravated sexual assault, a felony of the first degree, if he violates subsection (a) of this section while using a weapon or if he violates subsection (a) of this section and causes serious bodily harm to the victim.

§ 202   *Sexual Abuse*

(a) An actor is guilty of sexual abuse, a felony of the third degree, if he commits an act of sexual penetration with another person, when he knows that he does not have the consent of the other person.

(b) Consent, for purposes of this section, means that at the time of the act of sexual penetration there are actual words or conduct indicating affirmative, freely given permission to the act of sexual penetration.

(c) Consent is not freely given, for purposes of this section, whenever:

(1) the victim is physically helpless, mentally defective, or mentally incapacitated; or

(2) the victim is at least thirteen years old but less than sixteen years old and the actor is at least four years older than the victim; or

(3) the victim is at least sixteen years old but less than eighteen years old and the actor is a parent, foster parent, guardian, or other person with supervisory or disciplinary authority over the victim; or

(4) the victim is on probation or parole, or is detained in a hospital, prison, or other custodial institution, and the actor has supervisory or disciplinary authority over the victim; or

(5) the actor obtains the victim's consent by threatening to:

(i) inflict bodily injury on a person other than the victim or commit any other criminal offense; or

(ii) accuse anyone of a criminal offense; or

(iii) expose any secret tending to subject any person to hatred, contempt, or ridicule, or to impair the credit or business repute of any person; or

(iv) take or withhold action as an official or cause an official to take or withhold action; or

(v) violate any other right of the victim or inflict any other harm that would not benefit the actor; or

(6) the actor is engaged in providing professional treatment, assessment, or counseling of a mental or emotional illness, symptom, or condition of the victim

over a period concurrent with or substantially contemporaneous with the time when the act of sexual penetration occurs; or

(7) the actor obtains the victim's consent by representing that the act of sexual penetration is for purposes of medical treatment; or

(8) the actor obtains the victim's consent by leading the victim to believe that he is a person with whom the victim has been sexually intimate, or by representing that the victim is in danger of physical injury or illness.

§ 203   *Culpability*

(a) Recklessness. Whenever knowledge of a fact is required to convict an actor of violating any provision of section 201 or 202, the requirement of knowledge can be met by proof that, at the time of his conduct, the actor was consciously aware of a substantial and unjustifiable risk that the fact in question existed.

(b) Criminal Negligence. If the actor was not consciously aware of such a risk, he can nonetheless be convicted of violating the provision in question, provided that the prosecution proves that his failure to appreciate that risk involved a gross deviation from the standard of care that a reasonable person would observe in the actor's situation. If an actor is convicted of violating Article 201 on the basis of criminal negligence, the offense shall be graded as a felony of the third degree. If an actor is convicted of violating Article 202 on the basis of criminal negligence, the offense shall be graded as a felony of the fourth degree.[46]

How do these proposals differ?[47] On what assumptions are they based? How should the criminal law define its prohibition against rape?

I. STATUTORY RAPE

1. Historical and Contemporary Justifications

The common law did not penalize consensual sexual intercourse with a minor as a form of rape,[48] but the English Parliament enacted a statute creating the crime of "statutory rape."[49] Where lack of consent was a critical element of common law rape, the minor's consent or lack thereof was and is irrelevant to an offense of statutory rape. Statutory rape laws have been in use for centuries, during which both the laws and their purposes have evolved. Examination of those purposes reveals a range of rationales, many of which continue to cause controversy.

Whose interests do these statutes protect? The interests of minors? Their parents? Or society? Preventing the loss of chastity in young women provided an early motivation for laws criminalizing sexual intercourse with minors. Indeed, for many years, young women who had lost their chastity also lost the protection afforded by the law of statutory rape. Chastity was viewed as precious in part because its loss adversely affected a father's financial interests.

---

46. *Supra* note 19 at 283-284.

47. For an extensive evaluation of a number of proposals to redefine the crime of rape, *see* David P. Bryden, *Redefining Rape*, 3 Buff. Crim. L. Rev. 317 (2000).

48. Wayne R. LaFave, *Criminal Law* 777 (3d ed. 2000).

49. *Id.*

Under customary dowry practices, a non-virgin was considered less desirable for marriage, and therefore less likely to bring financial reward to her father upon marriage. Indeed, if she failed to marry, a daughter represented a lifelong financial burden to her father. From this perspective, statutory rape laws were an outgrowth of biblical precepts, by which virginity was so highly prized that a man who took a girl's virginity without her father's permission was considered to have committed a theft against the father. The father could demand compensation either in the form of payment, or by forcing the rapist to marry the victim.[50]

Loss of chastity also raised fears about the immoral influence of an unchaste young woman on other members of society. The Missouri Supreme Court in a 1923 statutory rape case expressed this view:

> The purpose of the lawmakers . . . is manifest. Experience has shown that girls under the age of 16, as the statute now reads, are not always able to resist temptation. They lack the discretion and firmness that comes with maturer years. Fathers and mothers know that this is true of boys as well. . . . A lecherous woman is a social menace; she is more dangerous than T.N.T.
>
> This wretched girl was young in years but old in sin and shame. A number of callow youths, of otherwise blameless lives so far as this record shows, fell under her seductive influence. They flocked about her, if her story is to be believed, like moths about the flame of a lighted candle and probably with the same result. The girl was a common prostitute as the record shows. The boys were immature and doubtless more sinned against than sinning.[51]

Chastity was important, then, to father and society, and the Missouri Supreme Court thought young women could not be trusted to guard it on their own. Young women were thus seen simultaneously as both innocent and a potential menace. Over time, the view of women's chastity as a commodity, of value to the patriarch of the family, and the view of young women as corrupting influences triggered substantial criticism. In more recent decades, this criticism along with changing social attitudes have generally discredited these views as legitimate motivations for statutory rape laws.

More recent discussions shift the focus from the goals of preserving chastity and virtue to pragmatic concerns with pregnancy. In *Michael M.*, a 17-year-old male challenged a California statutory rape law as a violation of equal protection because it protected only females and penalized only males. The California Supreme Court upheld the statute, emphasizing that it was "supported not by mere social convention but by the immutable physiological fact that it is the female exclusively who can become pregnant."[52] The United States Supreme Court affirmed the California Supreme Court. Justice Rehnquist explained that

> teenage pregnancies, which have increased dramatically over the last two decades, have significant social, medical, and economic consequences for both the mother and her child, and the State. Of particular concern to the State is that approximately half of all teenage pregnancies end in abortion.
>
> And of those children who are born, their illegitimacy makes them likely candidates to become wards of the State. We need not be medical doctors to discern that young men and young women are not similarly situated with respect to the

---

50. Michelle Oberman, *Girls in the Master's House: Of Protection, Patriarchy and the Potential for Using the Master's Tools to Reconfigure Statutory Rape Law*, 50 DePaul L. Rev. 799, 802 (2001).

51. State v. Snow, 252 S.W. 629, 632 (1923).

52. Michael M. v. Superior Ct., 25 Cal. 3d 608, 611 (1979).

problems and the risks of sexual intercourse. Only women may become pregnant, and they suffer disproportionately the profound physical, emotional, and psychological consequences of sexual activity. The statute at issue here protects women from sexual intercourse at an age when those consequences are particularly severe.

Because virtually all of the significant harmful and inescapably identifiable consequences of teenage pregnancy fall on the young female, a legislature acts well within its authority when it elects to punish only the participant who, by nature, suffers few of the consequences of his conduct. It is hardly unreasonable for a legislature acting to protect minor females to exclude them from punishment. Moreover, the risk of pregnancy itself constitutes a substantial deterrence to young females. No similar natural sanctions deter males. A criminal sanction imposed solely on males thus serves to roughly "equalize" the deterrents on the sexes.[53]

Beyond pregnancy, sexual activity may result in emotional, psychological, and physical harm to minors, such as transmission of HIV and other diseases. The following case study description gives a vivid sense of some of these potential harms.

Case 6

When this subject was 11, a 16-year-old baby-sitter pulled off his pajamas and sat on him putting his penis in her vagina. He did not understand what was happening but remembers feeling terrified, confused, and ashamed. He had no previous sexual experience, had never ejaculated, and did not ejaculate during the intercourse. Subsequently, he did not masturbate and avoided any direct sexual contact. At 19, he met his wife. There was no premarital genital petting or any attempt at intercourse. On their wedding night he was impotent and did not allow her to touch him. He was seen with his wife for sex therapy, the complaint being his aversion to sexual activity and an unconsummated marriage due to primary impotence. It is worth noting that he had been in psychotherapy for 2 years prior to his marriage but had shared his sexual history with neither his therapist nor his wife.[54]

Are the dangers of sexual activity the same for teenagers as they are for pre-adolescent children? Some commentators argue that consensual adolescent sexuality is not necessarily harmful and that current statutory rape provisions are too restrictive as applied to adolescents. They argue that sexual activity offers benefits at the same time that it poses problems for adolescents.

Heidi Kitrosser, MEANINGFUL CONSENT: TOWARD A NEW GENERATION OF STATUTORY RAPE LAWS

4 Va. J. Soc. Poly. & L. 287, 322-326 (1997)

POSITIVE ASPECTS OF ADOLESCENT SEXUALITY

Sexual activity in adolescence is extremely common. In the United States, about sixty percent of unmarried eighteen-year-olds are sexually active, a figure consistent across many Western nations, although there is variation within groups. Aside from the frequency of adolescent sex, the literature on adolescent sexuality suggests that adolescent sex can play a positive role in young people's lives, both

---

53. Michael M. v. Superior Court, 450 U.S. 464 (1981).
54. Philip M. Sarrel & William H. Masters, *Sexual Molestation of Men by Women*, 11 Archives of Sexual Behavior 91 (1982).

through the nature of the sexual experience itself, and through the potential for the experience to serve as a growth tool, preparing an adolescent to deal with future relationships. . . .

Researchers also note that sexual experimentation "is one way in today's society for young people to gain a sense of independence from parents, to begin the process of growing up and taking on adult roles."

Indeed, even though many teenagers, particularly girls, find their first coital experience unrewarding, "many teenagers find subsequent sexual intercourse to be a positive experience. . . . "

PROBLEMS IN ADOLESCENT SEXUALITY

While [confronting sexual feelings in adolescence] can contribute to successful sexual development, their unsuccessful resolution can affect and be affected by experiences in the sexual domain. Adolescents can use sex indiscriminately in an attempt to bolster popularity and self-esteem, a strategy that is not always successful. . . . Sex can be used to gain power over others, or can become the inappropriate focus of identity formation, for example the person who feels they are defined by their level of sexual attractiveness. Selverstone suggests that sexual involvement is one of the ways we learn to feel lovable, but that inappropriate involvement and sexual risk-taking can be counterproductive in the quest toward self-definition and personal integration.[55]

Within this framework of enhanced vulnerability, it is notable that many of the destructive aspects of adolescent sexuality, particular those related to coercive sexual norms, reflect the same framework of male aggressiveness and female passivity that permeates notions of heterosexual sex generally. For example, girls are less likely to envision sex as something for their own pleasure, and more likely to think of sex as something that they are supposed to "give" to boys. Boys, in turn, often feel that it is their role to pressure girls into having sex.

As to the latter, one study found, for example, that:

Many boys who might not consider rape or physical force were not averse to strong persuasion in order to get their own way sexually. A variety of techniques such as shaming, teasing, trickery, and perseverance were considered appropriate. . . . In all, over two-thirds of the teenage boys interviewed said they would try to convince a reluctant female partner to have sex. They appeared to regard their partner's reticence as a weak barrier to intercourse, one which it was part of the male role to overcome.[56]

Research further indicates that the psychology of teenage girls in our society is such that they are often particularly vulnerable to such pressures due to limited self-esteem and the correlative assumption that their opinions and feelings are not worth expressing. . . .

Aside from diminished self-esteem and a desire to be perceived as "feminine," the reaction to the physical process of becoming a woman also contributes to girls' insecurity. Most girls view the physical changes of adolescence — the complete alteration of the body's shape — not as an empowering experience, but as a loss of control. As they reach puberty, girls become objects of male desire, and the experience of seeing and valuing (or devaluing) themselves through the eyes of others is a traumatic one.

55. Robert Selverstone, *Adolescent Sexuality: Developing Self-Esteem and Mastering Developmental Tasks*, 18 SIECUS Rep. 1 (1989).
56. Susan Moore & Doreen Rosenthal, *Sexuality in Adolescence* 179-180 (1993).

Thus, one of the most insidious aspects of girls' psycho-social development is that they become less certain of their physical boundaries and less able to declare their own limits, at precisely the time at which they begin to explore their own sexuality. The implications of this convergence of bodily maturity and moral dispossession are particularly disturbing because male sexual initiative remains a societal norm.

Hence, while sexuality in adolescence is an extremely common phenomenon, and is not necessarily unhealthy or coercive, it is underscored by the same sexist norms of male aggressiveness and female passivity that make . . . heterosexual sex problematic in general. Furthermore, these norms occur within a framework of particular vulnerability due to the difficult period of adolescence. While this framework of vulnerability makes both boys and girls vulnerable sexually, a sexist social context clearly heightens this vulnerability in the case of females, again reflective of broader social norms.

An additional problem is the incidence of violence in adolescent dating relationships. Studies have revealed that roughly 10 percent of high school students report the occurrence of violence in dating relationships.

Statutory rape laws also give prosecutors an alternative means for prosecuting a forcible rape against a minor. In *Michael M.*, which was prosecuted as a statutory rape case, for example,

> The evidence adduced at a preliminary hearing showed that at approximately midnight on June 3, 1978, petitioner [a 17-1/2 year-old male] and two friends approached Sharon, a 16-1/2-year-old female, and her sister as they waited at a bus stop. Petitioner and Sharon, who had already been drinking, moved away from the others and began to kiss. After being struck in the face for rebuffing petitioner's initial advances, Sharon submitted to sexual intercourse with petitioner. (Michael M., 450 U.S. 464, at 466-467.)

Some have estimated that half of all rapes are committed against adolescents. Earlier in this chapter we discussed the problems prosecutors encounter obtaining convictions in forcible rape cases. Think back on those materials and assess why the prosecutor may have chosen to prosecute in *Michael M.* for statutory rape rather than forcible rape.

QUESTIONS

1. If you were a state legislator, would you favor or oppose penalizing consensual sexual intercourse involving minors? Should sexual activity other than intercourse be penalized? Are such laws sexist attempts to secure male control over female sexuality? Do they treat females as incapable of making choices about sex? Or are they simply a logical response to existing "sexist" patterns of male and female behavior?

2. If you favor such laws, on which rationale(s) would you rely? How does the choice of rationale affect your answers to the following questions:

(a) What age limits should the statute set?
(b) Should sex between adolescents close in age be exempted? If so, what age span should the exemption use?

(c) Should the statute recognize both males and females as potential perpetrators? As potential victims? Should it include homosexual as well as heterosexual activity?

3. Can the legislative purpose behind a statute change over time? In interpreting a statute, should a court focus on the intent of the legislature that enacted the statute? Or the reasons the current legislature would give for enacting the statute if it came before them today? What significance should attach to the fact that a statute was originally enacted for a sexist reason?

4. Should the criminal law penalize video depictions of sexual activity by those who appear to be minors but are in fact of legal age? What are the arguments for and against such a criminal prohibition?

2. Non-Mental Elements

PROBLEMS

9.7 Apply the statutes that appear below to the following factual scenarios. Assume that both parties are willing participants in sexual intercourse.

Roy is a 30-year-old high school math teacher who recently went through a difficult divorce. He has been tutoring Doris, a 15-year-old female student in one of his classes. Doris develops a crush on Roy and begins buying him gifts and sending him flowers. One evening, Roy invites Doris to his house and the two have sexual intercourse.

(a) What if Doris is 16?
(b) What if the teacher is female and the student male?
(c) What if the teacher and student are both male? Both female?
(d) Assume Doris engaged in sexual intercourse on prior occasions with males other than Roy. Would this affect Roy's liability?
(e) What if, rather than being her teacher, Roy is Doris's stepfather?

9.8 Arthur is an 18-year-old high school senior. Julie, his girl friend, is 15 and a high school freshman. Arthur invites Julie to his senior prom and Julie accepts. Without informing Julie, Arthur reserves a hotel room for the night of the dance. After the dance, Arthur and Julie go to the hotel room and have intercourse.

(a) What if Arthur is 17 and Julie 15?
(b) What if Arthur is 16 and Julie 15?

Idaho Code § 16101 (2001) *Rape Defined*

Rape is defined as the penetration, however slight, of the oral, anal, or vaginal opening with the perpetrator's penis accomplished with a female under the following circumstances:

1. Where the female is under the age of eighteen (18) years.

Alabama Code § 13A-6-62 (2001)   *Rape; second degree*

(a) A person commits the crime of rape in the second degree if:
(1) Being 16 years old or older, he or she engages in sexual intercourse with a member of the opposite sex less than 16 and more than 12 years old; provided, however, the actor is at least two years older than the member of the opposite sex.

Georgia Code Annotated § 16-6-3 (2001)   *Statutory rape*

(a) A person commits the offense of statutory rape when he or she engages in sexual intercourse with any person under the age of 16 years and not his or her spouse, provided that no conviction shall be had for this offense on the unsupported testimony of the victim.

(b) A person convicted of the offense of statutory rape shall be punished by imprisonment for not less than one nor more than 20 years; provided, however, that if the person so convicted is 21 years of age or older, such person shall be punished by imprisonment for not less than ten nor more than 20 years; provided, further, that if the victim is 14 or 15 years of age and the person so convicted is no more than three years older than the victim, such person shall be guilty of a misdemeanor.

Louisiaua Statutes Annotated § 80 (2002)

A. Felony carnal knowledge of a juvenile is committed when:
(1) A person who is nineteen years of age or older has sexual intercourse, with consent, with a person who is twelve years of age or older but less than seventeen years of age, when the victim is not the spouse of the offender; or
(2) A person who is seventeen years of age or older has sexual intercourse, with consent, with a person who is twelve years of age or older but less than fifteen years of age, when the victim is not the spouse of the offender; or . . .
B. As used in this Section, "sexual intercourse" means anal, oral, or vaginal sexual intercourse.
C. Lack of knowledge of the juvenile's age shall not be a defense. Emission is not necessary, and penetration, however slight, is sufficient to complete the crime.
D. Whoever commits the crime of felony carnal knowledge of a juvenile shall be fined not more than five thousand dollars, or imprisoned, with or without hard labor, for not more than ten years, or both. . . .

Arizona Revised Statute § 13-1405 (2001)   *Sexual conduct with a minor; classification*

A. A person commits sexual conduct with a minor by intentionally or knowingly engaging in sexual intercourse or oral sexual contact with any person who is under eighteen years of age.
B. Sexual conduct with a minor who is under fifteen years of age is a class 2 felony. . . . Sexual conduct with a minor who is at least fifteen years of age is a class 6 felony. Sexual conduct with a minor who is at least fifteen years of age is a class 2 felony if the person is the minor's parent, stepparent, adoptive parent, legal guardian or foster parent and the convicted person is not eligible for suspension of sentence, probation, pardon or release from confinement . . . until the sentence imposed has been served or commuted.

Note that the Idaho statute is gender-specific, recognizing only male perpetrators and female victims. Such statutes were once common, but a new generation of gender-neutral laws has largely replaced gender-specific statutes. Modern statutes controlling sexual activity with minors often give names other than "statutory rape" to the crimes they create and vary in the scope of conduct they prohibit. Some seem to contemplate only traditional intercourse, while others reach a broader range of sexual activity. These laws often use age span provisions excluding from criminal sanction or lessening punishment for sexual activity between people fairly close in age. What underlying purpose do these age span exemptions reflect? Another common feature is the recognition of certain status categories, such as parent or teacher, as an aggravating element.

3. Mental State

PROBLEMS

Apply the statutes and cases that appear below to the following factual scenarios. Assume that both parties are willing participants in sexual intercourse.

9.9 A friend introduced Raymond, a 20-year-old man, to Erica, who was 13 at the time. The two subsequently talked occasionally by telephone. One evening, Raymond, apparently wishing to call for a ride home, approached Erica's house at about nine o'clock. Erica opened her bedroom window, through which Raymond entered. Raymond later stated that "she just told me to get a ladder and climb up to her window." The two talked and later engaged in sexual intercourse. Raymond left at about 4:30 a.m. the following morning. Nine months later, Erica gave birth to a baby, of which Raymond is the biological father. Raymond wishes to introduce into evidence testimony that Erica and her friends told him that she was 16 years old and that he believed them. Should the trial judge admit this testimony?

9.10 Same facts as in 9.8 above, except assume that Raymond is mentally disabled. His I.Q. is 52. His school guidance counselor describes him as a mildly retarded person who reads at a third-grade level, does arithmetic on a fifth-grade level, and interacts with others socially at school at the level of someone 11 or 12 years of age. Should the trial judge admit the testimony about Erica and her friends telling Raymond that Erica was 16 years old and his belief in their representations?

Ohio Revised Code Annotated § 2907.04 (2001) *Unlawful sexual conduct with minor*

(A) No person who is eighteen years of age or older shall engage in sexual conduct with another, who is not the spouse of the offender, when the offender knows the other person is thirteen years of age or older but less than sixteen years of age, or the offender is reckless in that regard.

(B) Whoever violates this section is guilty of unlawful sexual conduct with a minor.

(1) Except as otherwise provided in divisions (B)(2), (3), and (4) of this section, unlawful sexual conduct with a minor is a felony of the fourth degree.

(2) Except as otherwise provided in division (B)(4) of this section, if the offender is less than four years older than the other person, unlawful sexual conduct with a minor is a misdemeanor of the first degree. . . .

Model Penal Code § 213.6 (1985)   *Mistake as to Age*

Whenever in this Article the criminality of conduct depends on a child's being below the age of 10, it is no defense that the actor did not know the child's age, or reasonably believed the child to be older than 10. When criminality depends on the child's being below a critical age other than 10, it is a defense for the actor to prove by a preponderance of the evidence that he reasonably believed the child to be above the critical age.

Florida Statute § 794.021 (2001)   *Ignorance or belief as to victim's age no defense.*

When, in this chapter, the criminality of conduct depends upon the victim's being below a certain specified age, ignorance of the age is no defense. Neither shall misrepresentation of age by such person nor a bona fide belief that such person is over the specified age be a defense.

Louisiana Statute Annotated § 80 (2002)

C. Lack of knowledge of the juvenile's age shall not be a defense. . . .

Arizona Revised Statute § 13-1405 (2001)   *Sexual conduct with a minor*

A. A person commits sexual conduct with a minor by intentionally or knowingly engaging in sexual intercourse or oral sexual contact with any person who is under eighteen years of age.

QUESTIONS

1. Jurisdictions vary in their treatment of mental state regarding age in statutory rape. What approach is reflected in each of the above statutes?
2. In what context earlier in the course have you encountered the position exemplified in Model Penal Code § 213.6?

Though some criminal codes explicitly address mental state concerning age, many are silent on the issue, leaving courts to grapple with that issue, as in the following opinions.

STATE *v.* ELTON

Supreme Court of Utah 657 P.2d 1261 (1982)

PER CURIAM. The defendant, 19, had sexual intercourse with a 14-year-old female, not his wife, and was found guilty by a jury of violating U.C.A., 1953,

76-5-401.[1] The offense is a third-degree felony, punishable by up to five years in prison. The trial court spared defendant the prison term, conditioned on a probationary completion of a half-way house program.

Defendant urges three points on appeal to the effect that (1) the offense charged requires a specific criminal intent, (2) his mistake in appraising the girl's age constitutes a defense to the charge, and (3) failure to allow evidence as to defendant's "belief" or "mistake" as to the girl's age, together with failure to instruct thereon, was error.

Defendant concedes that Utah courts, as elsewhere, traditionally have considered and approved sanctions for offenses like that charged here, connoting a "strict liability" that is implicit in the offense itself, whether those words are included in the legislation defining the offense or not. Such offenses have been considered to be punishable without the necessity of pleading or proving specific intent. Since they are *malum prohibitum* crimes, criminal responsibility attaches whenever the prohibited act is fully accomplished.

The defendant's whole thesis is to the effect that it would be ludicrous if the legislature intended that one be guilty of a felony if the sex act occurred shortly before a girl's sixteenth birthday, but guilty only of a misdemeanor if it happened a few minutes after that magic date. Irrespective of such hypothetics, defendant contends that he should be excused from criminal liability if he "believed" or was "mistaken" as to the girl's age.

Courts generally have not gone along with any of defendant's concepts as to what the law *should be*, leaving that determination to the legislature. Courts have taken the position that a statute calling for the protection of young women below a specific age is necessary and contributive to the common welfare. In rare instances, where one may not have intended to do violence because of belief or mistake, the law wisely has provided a mitigating process. This mitigating and ameliorating process has been employed in this very case in the sentencing phase, where the trial court placed the defendant on probation rather than impose a prison term.

The defendant cites but one case supporting his contention that his own subjective belief that the girl was 16 or over, should constitute a defense to the statutory charge.[2] This case has been rejected in numerous other jurisdictions. We agree in such rejection and quote with approval language found in the following two well-reasoned opinions apropos to the questions raised here:

> The arbitrary age of consent in these cases has been established by our legislature as a matter of public policy for the obvious protection of young and immature females. We cannot properly make exceptions. Therefore, in a prosecution for alleged statutory rape a defendant's knowledge of the age of the girl involved is immaterial and his reasonable belief that she is over the age of eighteen years is no defense.[3]

Petitioner claims that his honest belief that the prosecutrix of the statutory rape charge was over 16 years of age should constitute a defense, of constitutional dimensions, to statutory rape. The effect of *mens rea* and mistake on state criminal law has generally been left to the discretion of the states. The Supreme Court has never held that an honest mistake as to the age of the prosecutrix is a constitutional defense to statutory rape, and nothing in the Court's recent decisions clarifying the scope of procreative privacy suggests that a state may no longer place the risk of

---

[1] "A person commits unlawful sexual intercourse if that person has sexual intercourse with a person, not that person's spouse, who is under sixteen years of age."

[2] People v. Hernandez, 61 Cal.2d 529 (1964).

[3] State v. Fulks, 83 S.D. 433, 436 (1968).

mistake as to the prosecutrix's age on the person engaging in sexual intercourse with a partner who may be young enough to fall within the protection of the statute. Petitioner's argument is without merit.

Affirmed.

<hr>

STATE *v.* ELTON

Utah Supreme Court 680 P.2d 727 (1984)

STEWART, Justice. We have previously issued a *per curiam* opinion in this case, now published at 657 P.2d 1261. . . . We later withdrew that opinion for the purpose of rehearing the case and addressing more fully an issue of first impression. Upon reconsideration, we vacate our previous opinion and set aside the trial court's judgment of conviction and remand.

Defendant was convicted of the crime of unlawful sexual intercourse, a third degree felony, under U.C.A., 1953, § 76-5-401, which provided:[1]

(1) A person commits unlawful sexual intercourse if that person has sexual intercourse with a person, not that person's spouse, who is under sixteen years of age.

(2) Unlawful sexual intercourse is a felony of the third degree except when at the time of intercourse the actor is no more than three years older than the victim, in which case it is a class B misdemeanor. Evidence that the actor was not more than three years older than the victim at the time of the intercourse shall be raised by the defendant.

On September 16, 1981, defendant engaged in sexual intercourse with a girl, not his wife, who was fourteen years of age. Defendant was nineteen years of age at the time and therefore more than three years older than the girl. Defendant testified that the girl told him she was eighteen years of age and that he believed her representation. The girl testified that she participated in the act voluntarily, but that she told the defendant that she was fifteen years old. Although the trial court allowed testimony showing that the defendant knew the girl's age, the trial court excluded any further testimony by the defendant concerning the reasonableness of his belief as to the girl's age and instructed the jury that mistake as to the girl's age was no defense to the charge.

On this appeal, defendant argues that the trial court erred in (1) excluding the proffered evidence substantiating the basis of the defendant's alleged belief that the girl was over the age of sixteen years and (2) rejecting the defendant's requested jury instruction that a reasonable mistake as to the girl's age constituted a defense to the crime as charged. We note that even if the requested instruction had been given and the jury had found in accordance therewith, the defendant still would have been guilty of fornication under Utah law. U.C.A., 1953, § 76-7-104.

I.

The Utah Criminal Code follows the common law in establishing the basic proposition that a person cannot be found guilty of a criminal offense unless he harbors a requisite criminal state of mind or unless the prohibited act is based on strict liability. At the time in question, § 76-2-101 stated:

<hr>

[1] The section has since been amended. 1983 Utah Laws ch. 88, § 16.

No person is guilty of an offense unless his conduct is prohibited by law and:

    (1) He acts intentionally, knowingly, recklessly or with criminal negligence with respect to each element of the offense as the definition of the offense requires; or

    (2) His acts constitute an offense involving strict liability.[2]

Thus, for an act to constitute a crime, the act must be prohibited and the defendant must be shown to have possessed a culpable or criminal state of mind, a *mens rea*, "with respect to each element of the offense," unless the offense involves a strict liability offense. An established first principle of the criminal law, with few exceptions, is that the doing of a wrongful act without the requisite culpable mental state does not constitute a crime. Nor does the harboring of a criminal mental state, not translated into a prohibited act, constitute a crime.

Under the Utah Criminal Code, a crime may be a strict liability crime only if the statute specifically states it to be such.[3] At the time in dispute, § 76-2-102 stated:

> Every offense not involving strict liability shall require a culpable mental state, and when the definition of the offense does not specify a culpable mental state, intent, knowledge, or recklessness shall suffice to establish criminal responsibility. *An offense shall involve strict liability only when a statute defining the offense clearly indicates a legislative purpose to impose strict liability for the conduct by use of the phrase "strict liability" or other terms of similar import.* [Emphasis added.][4]

The unlawful sexual intercourse statute, § 76-5-401, *supra*, does not clearly indicate "a legislative purpose to impose strict liability" as required by § 76-2-102 to establish a strict liability offense. It does not even impliedly indicate a legislative purpose to impose strict liability. Thus, a crime of unlawful sexual intercourse, a crime different from the crime of fornication, cannot be proved unless the state proves the requisite criminal state of mind as to each element of the offense. §76-2-101(1).

The elements of the degree of unlawful sexual intercourse charged here are: (1) an act of sexual intercourse, (2) with a person, not the defendant's spouse, (3) who is under sixteen years of age. The punishment is enhanced if the defendant is more than three years older than the other person. § 76-5-401(2). In proving unlawful sexual intercourse, therefore, the state must prove a culpable mental state by showing that the defendant "act[ed] intentionally, knowingly, recklessly or with criminal negligence," § 76-2-101(1), as those terms are defined in § 76-2-103.

Clearly, the requisite culpable mental state as to the first and second elements of the offense is established by showing that defendant intentionally engaged in sexual intercourse with a female not his wife. However, since the crime of unlawful sexual intercourse is not a strict liability offense, the critical issue is what mental state must exist as to the victim's age.[5] On its face, the unlawful sexual intercourse

---

[2] The section has since been amended. 1983 Utah Laws ch. 90, § 1; ch. 98, § 1.

[3] Strict criminal liability is clearly an exception to long-established principles of criminal liability. Under Utah law, strict liability exists only when the statute defining the offense expressly so states. Generally, strict criminal liability is employed only in certain business or economic regulations. The United States Supreme Court discussed the subject of strict liability in *Morissette v. United States*, 342 U.S. 246, 96 L. Ed. 288, 72 S. Ct. 240 (1952), in which a defendant's conviction was overturned because no *mens rea* was shown and the crime was not a regulatory offense.

[4] This section has since been amended. 1983 Utah Laws, ch. 90, §2.

[5] We shall refer to the girl in this case as the "victim" where helpful and for ease of reference, although arguably this is a so-called "victimless" crime. Indeed, both the girl and the defendant could

statute does not require intent as to all elements of the crime. The *mens rea* necessary for the third element of the crime requires a consideration of the purposes of the statute. No doubt one purpose of the statute is to deter persons from engaging in intercourse with young, immature persons and to avoid the consequent risk of pregnancies because those subject to the prohibitions of the statute, both males and females, are not likely to be fully knowledgeable in any realistic way about the personal and social consequences of an out-of-wedlock pregnancy. The statute seeks to establish barriers around, and provide a measure of protection to, younger, more impressionable, and perhaps more persuadable persons in order to prevent them from engaging in sexual intercourse out of wedlock.

To accomplish those purposes and still remain true to long-established fundamental principles of the criminal law, which have been incorporated in the Utah Criminal Code, we hold that as to the third element of the crime, there must be proof of a culpable mental state which establishes that the defendant was at least criminally negligent as to the age of the partner. That is, the prosecution must prove that the defendant either was aware of the fact that the partner was underage or that the defendant ought to have been aware of a substantial and unjustifiable risk that his partner was underage. § 76-2-103(4). The test as to the latter part of the standard is an objective, reasonable person test.

Furthermore, § 76-2-304 provides that unless otherwise provided, ignorance or mistake of fact which disproves the culpable mental state is a defense to the crime charged but does not relieve a person from being prosecuted for a lesser included offense. There is no inconsistency in requiring a *mens rea* of criminal negligence as to age and an affirmative defense of mistake of fact as to age. The *mens rea* requirement may be based on objective criteria, while the ignorance or mistake of fact defense bears upon the subjective state of mind of the defendant.[6]

II.

We recognize that a number of courts have held that a defendant is strictly liable with respect to the age of a victim and that mistake of age is not a defense to the crime charged here. Many courts have argued that the crime is a strict liability offense because the age of the girl is not an element of the offense; therefore, no *mens rea* is required as to that. . . .   In such jurisdictions, the state would not have to prove that a defendant had knowledge of the partner's age or was criminally negligent in failing to ascertain it, and a defendant's reasonable mistake as to the victim's age would be irrelevant.

Other jurisdictions strive to satisfy the *mens rea* requirement and still disallow the defense of mistake of age by hypothesizing the necessary *mens rea* in the intention to have intercourse with a nonspouse, without requiring any *mens rea* as to the partner's age. That is, the defendant's intent to do one unlawful act is deemed to suffice for the commission of another, unintended act. R. Perkins, *Criminal Law* 819 (2d ed. 1969). Thus, where the law makes intercourse with any nonspouse illegal, irrespective of age (as under the Utah fornication statute, § 76-7-104), the theory is that since the defendant intended to commit *an* illegal act that constitutes

---

have been charged with violating § 76-5-401. The act prohibited is not rape but a consensual act on the part of both parties. However that may be, the policy of law is to prevent persons from engaging in intercourse outside of marriage.

[6] In a similar case, the California court held that a defendant is entitled to introduce evidence of mistake of age. People v. Hernandez, 61 Cal. 2d 529 (1964).

fornication at least, the unlawful intention or *mens rea* necessary for that crime is transferable to the charge of unlawful sexual intercourse.

Under that theory, the prosecution is not required to prove the *mens rea* as to the element of age, and the defendant's evidence of mistake is not recognized on the ground that because the defendant had a criminal intent to commit a crime, even though the intended crime is not the one with which he is charged. That is, the act of intercourse would be criminal under the unlawful sexual intercourse statute even if the defendant acted reasonably in attempting to ascertain the age of the victim and even if the victim actively misled the defendant. Thus, the *mens rea* of a lesser crime (fornication) is held to satisfy the *mens rea* required for a more serious crime (unlawful sexual intercourse or statutory rape). Other courts impose strict liability by not requiring a *mens rea* as to the age of the victim.

However unrealistic the position may be in a particular case, the criminal law presumes that one knows the criminal law. Paradoxically, if one does know the elements of the unlawful intercourse law and takes every possible precaution to avoid violation of that law, he may still be guilty of violating that law on the doctrine of transferred intent, i.e., that the criminal intent to commit one wrong may be used to convict one of another criminal act, or on the doctrine of strict liability. That is at odds with the belief that in a free society one should be held responsible for criminal activity only if he is culpable by virtue of a criminal or wrongful intent to do the wrongful act.

Both theories flout the constitutional principle that one should be responsible to ascertain and understand the criminal law and should be held accountable only for those acts of criminal conduct for which he or she is mentally culpable in the criminal sense. It is not consonant with our principles of criminal liability when dealing with *malum in se* crimes to hold a person responsible for a crime he did not intend to commit and indeed may even have taken every precaution to avoid committing, even though he intended to commit a lesser crime. To hold one liable for a greater crime which he actually sought to avoid committing on the ground that he committed a lesser crime turns the doctrine of lesser included offenses on its head and raises fundamental questions which may have constitutional implications.

In addition, it is fundamentally unfair to allow the victim in such a crime — who necessarily has also violated the law — to mislead the defendant as to an element of the crime and then place the blame for the mistake on the defendant rather than the person who created the deceit and entrapped the defendant into committing a crime he or she attempted to avoid. Finally, the theory that the age of the victim is not an element of the offense is plainly wrong. Surely no one would contend that if a prosecutor failed to prove the age of the girl, a conviction for unlawful intercourse could stand.

III.

The prosecution argued at trial and the trial court held that defendant's mental state with respect to the girl's age was irrelevant. That is, the trial court held that no *mens rea* was required for the third element of the crime. In denying the defendant the opportunity to present evidence as to mistake of age, the trial court stated, "I think . . . just intentionally knowing that you are having intercourse with a given individual, who it turns out is within the age restrictions that would cause this matter to be a felony." Thus, the intent to engage in sexual intercourse, with knowledge that the girl was not his spouse, was held sufficient to satisfy the *mens rea* requirement for all elements. In other words, the prosecution was only required to prove the elements of the crime of fornication, *see* § 76-7-104, of the more serious crime of unlawful sexual intercourse, a third degree felony. Thus, although the prosecution presented evidence that the defendant knew the girl was under sixteen, the defendant was not allowed to rebut that evidence.

Because defendant's mental state with respect to the age of the girl was considered irrelevant, his proffered defense based on a reasonable mistake as to her age was disallowed. The exclusion of the defendant's evidence does not comport with the provisions of the Utah Criminal Code.

The defense of mistake of fact is established by § 76-2-304:

> (1) Unless otherwise provided, ignorance or mistake of fact which disproves the culpable mental state is a defense to any prosecution for that crime. . . .
> (3) Although an actor's ignorance or mistake of fact or law may constitute a defense to the offense charged, he may nevertheless be convicted of a lesser included offense of which he would be guilty if the fact or law were as he believed.

Under subsection (1), if a defendant acts under a reasonable mistake of fact as to the victim's age, that mistake is a defense to the crime of unlawful sexual intercourse. Under subsection (3), such a defendant is still guilty of a lesser included offense of fornication. In other words, a defendant may rebut the prosecution's evidence that the defendant had knowledge or should have had knowledge of the victim's age by proving that he or she was misled by the partner's affirmatively misrepresenting his or her age. Of course, a misrepresentation is not an absolute defense. If the trier of fact were to conclude that the defendant had not relied on the misrepresentation, the defendant could still be convicted of the crime charged. Clearly the physical appearance of the victim may be persuasive against a defendant. The physical appearance of a very young girl would, at least in some cases, negate any affirmative misrepresentation she might make. But a defendant's showing that he acted reasonably under all the circumstances to avoid transgressing the statute in question may rebut the prosecution's charge that defendant acted with criminal negligence.

IV.

This construction of the statutes does not subvert the objectives of the law.[8] We certainly do not question the proposition that young people should be protected from sexual exploitation by older, more experienced persons until they reach the legal age of consent and can more maturely comprehend and appreciate the consequences of their sexual acts. However, where a younger participant intentionally misrepresents his or her age, so that the older participant reasonably relies on the misrepresentations as to the partner's age, the "victim" and society's interests generally are still protected by the statute prohibiting fornication. Not to require the prosecution to prove a *mens rea* as to the element of age and to deny the defense of mistake of fact would subject an honestly misled party, whether adult or fellow teenager, to criminal liability brought about by a sophisticated youth who seeks to abuse the criminal law for his or her own sensual indulgences or for even more

---

[8] We recognize that our decision in this case may have only limited significance, as the Legislature has amended the Utah Criminal Code in 1983 to disallow mistake of fact as to age as a defense to the crime of unlawful sexual intercourse: "It is not a defense to the crime of unlawful sexual intercourse, . . . that the actor mistakenly believed the victim to be sixteen years of age or older at the time of the alleged offense or was unaware of the victim's true age." U.C.A., 1953, § 76-2-304.5(2). That provision, however, is not applied retroactively to the facts of this case. . . .

insidious purposes, such as blackmail or an attempt to avoid community or familial condemnation by denying that he or she enticed another to participate in the sexual act. The unlawful sexual intercourse statute was not aimed at defendants such as these, nor should it place such weapons in the hands of those who would deny their own responsibilities. The denial of evidence of mistake of fact in such cases would subject the defendant to a liability out of proportion with his or her culpability.

Reversed and remanded for proceedings consistent with this opinion.

As Justice Stewart mentions in the second *Elton* opinion, the Utah legislature enacted the following statute in 1983:

Utah Code Annotated § 76-3-304.5 (2) (2001)   *Mistake as to victim's age not a defense*

(2) It is not a defense to the crime of unlawful sexual activity with a minor, . . . that the actor mistakenly believed the victim to be 16 years of age or older at the time of the alleged offense or was unaware of the victim's true age.

This statute was enacted after the first but prior to the second *Elton* opinion. With which opinion is the statute consistent? Why do you think the legislature passed this statute? In *State v. Martinez*, 14 P.3d 114 (2000), the Utah Court of Appeals held that an amended version of this Utah provision imposes strict liability for sex offenses involving victims under the age of 16, but that "no such provision precludes a mistake of fact defense when the alleged victim is a minor of sixteen or seventeen."

CHAPTER TEN

ATTEMPT AND SOLICITATION

A. INTRODUCTION

Modern criminal codes regularly treat an attempt to commit a crime as a separate offense. Attempt is an example of a category of crimes known as *anticipatory* offenses, as are solicitation and conspiracy. Each is anticipatory in the sense of looking forward to the commission of some other crime, often referred to as the "target offense." An attempt to commit a murder, for example, anticipates the target offense of murder. Conspiracy to commit bank robbery anticipates the crime of bank robbery. The adjective "inchoate" — meaning something in an initial or early stage, only partially developed — is also used to describe such offenses.

This chapter begins by examining the conduct required for attempt. Legislatures as well as courts vary greatly in regard to the conduct required. Some allow early steps in a course of conduct aimed at committing an offense to trigger attempt liability. Others require that a person be dangerously close to accomplishing the target offense. Still others take positions between these two extremes.

We then turn to mental state. Legislatures typically require purpose or intent as the mental state for attempt. We saw in Chapter 5, Mental States, that the word "intent" has been given a variety of meanings by courts and legislatures. In the context of attempt, "intent" is generally used as a synonym for "purpose." Following mental state, we address the question of whether a person can cancel liability for attempt by abandoning a course of conduct prior to committing the target offense. Finally, we deal with the problem of impossibility, whether or not a person will be held legally responsible for trying to commit a crime that it is not possible for her to commit.

We addressed in Chapter 4 the tension that may arise between incapacitation on the one hand and retribution and deterrence on the other in relation to the conduct requirement. A person typically must act on evil intentions in order to be sufficiently blameworthy to deserve criminal punishment. Conduct also serves the practical function of providing concrete circumstantial evidence of an actor's culpable mental state. The conduct requirement gives deterrence a chance to work. It is between formation of a purpose to commit a crime and action based on that purpose when the threat underlying deterrence in theory does its work.

But waiting until someone acts on evil intentions reduces and may even eliminate the opportunity for police to intervene and incapacitate a dangerous person. Anticipatory offenses such as attempt and conspiracy respond to the desire to incapacitate an actor before she has committed the target offense. But can we be sure an anticipatory offender really is harboring an evil purpose if she has not yet acted on it? And how do we know she would not have been deterred by the threat of punishment for the target offense if she is arrested and not allowed to choose whether or not to commit the target offense? This tension pitting incapacitation against retribution and deterrence underlies all anticipatory offenses. As you read the statutes and cases in this chapter, see how legislatures and courts have weighed concerns about blame, deterrence, and incapacitation.

How should attempts be punished? Consider the facts described in the following newspaper story.

Man Convicted For Shooting Arrow Into Ex-Lover's Head[1]

A man was convicted late Thursday of shooting an arrow into his former roommate's head with a crossbow. Doctors said it was a miracle that Arthur Ekvall, 30, survived the June 8 attack without brain or spinal cord damage. Jesse Solis, 24, Ekvall's roommate, was found guilty by a state jury of attempted murder and car theft. He could be sentenced to life in prison. Fired from a crossbow at point-blank range, the arrow entered the base of Ekvall's skull as he slept, passed through his head and lodged with the tip barely protruding just above his left eyebrow. Prosecutors contended that Solis tried to kill his former lover because Ekvall wanted to break off their relationship. Sentencing is set for Nov. 20.

The crossbow shooter certainly seems blameworthy. His conduct also suggests future dangerousness, which could warrant punishment on various utilitarian grounds. The victim, for example, might be particularly interested in specifically deterring and incapacitating the shooter. Should the shooter's punishment be discounted because the victim miraculously did not die? If so, on what ground? How do the purposes of punishment you studied in Chapter 2 bear on setting the punishment for attempt?

As the statutes below reflect, jurisdictions vary in punishing attempt. Which statute do you think reflects the preferable view?

Montana Code Annotated § 45-4-103 (2001)   *Attempt*

(3) A person convicted of the offense of attempt shall be punished not to exceed the maximum provided for the offense attempted.

Minnesota Statutes § 609.17   *Attempts*

4. Whoever attempts to commit a crime may be sentenced as follows:
(1) If the maximum sentence provided for the crime is life imprisonment, to not more than 20 years; or
(2) For any other attempt, to not more than one-half of the maximum imprisonment or fine or both provided for the crime attempted, but such maximum in any case shall not be less than imprisonment for 90 days or a fine of $100.

---

1. Orlando Sentinel Tribune, Oct. 24, 1992, Copyright 1992, at A13.

Model Penal Code § 5.05

(1) *Grading.* Except as otherwise provided in this Section, attempt, solicitation and conspiracy are crimes of the same grade and degree as the most serious offense that is attempted or solicited or is an object of the conspiracy. An attempt, solicitation or conspiracy to commit a [capital crime or a] felony of the first degree is a felony of the second degree.

B. CONDUCT

In Chapter 4 you encountered the general proposition that criminal law does not punish evil intentions alone. Rather, some form of conduct is typically required. In reading the materials in this Section, determine whether anticipatory offenses are consistent with this proposition.

PROBLEMS

10.1 Gwen is a radical environmentalist who decides to assassinate Albert, the president of Oilco, an oil and gas exploration company. Oilco has obtained permission to drill for oil and gas in an area recognized until recently as wilderness protected from such drilling. To enact her plan, Gwen first hacks into Oilco's computer and learns Albert's home address. She then follows Albert for several days to determine when and on what route he drives to and from work each day. Gwen scouts the route for a good place for an ambush. Albert lives in a rural area about an hour outside the city in which Oilco has its headquarters. Gwen chooses a wooded spot about a mile from Albert's house for the assassination and constructs a shelter of tree limbs so she cannot be seen from the road. She buys a high-powered deer-hunting rifle and ammunition from a local gun dealer using a false name and identification papers. On the day she has chosen for the shooting, Gwen dons camouflage hunting clothes and takes up her position in the woods with the hunting rifle. About half an hour later, Albert drives by Gwen's location. Gwen takes aim and fires. Assume that the police have legally wiretapped Gwen's telephone, have recorded statements by Gwen to other radical environmentalists about her plan to kill Albert, and have placed her under surveillance. Under the statutes and cases below, at what point could the police have arrested Gwen for attempted murder? Would it make a difference if Gwen shot her rifle at Albert during deer-hunting season?

10.2. Carl Davis and Alberdina Lourie decide to hire a hit man to kill Alberdina's husband so that Davis and Lourie can collect $60,000 in insurance money and cohabit. Davis, acting on behalf of himself and Alberdina, arrange to have one Leverton obtain "the services of an ex-convict to murder" the victim. Instead of "procuring the services

of an ex-convict . . . [Leverton] disclosed the plot to [Police Officer
Dill,] . . . who agreed to pose as an ex-convict. . . . Several meetings
were had between [Davis], Leverton, and Dill, defendant stating that
he and Alberdina were in love and desired Edmon Lourie killed. . . .
Defendant outlined his plan, offering Dill the sum of six hundred dollars, with the further agreement that Alberdina, who was to be with
her husband at the time of the contemplated assault, would wear
diamonds of the value of three thousand dollars. . . . [D]efendant
arranged for Dill to go to Chicago to kill . . . [the victim] there, defendant making and giving Dill a map or drawing showing where Lourie
could be found, as well as two photographs of him. . . . [The victim,
however, unexpectedly indicated that he would arrive home early
from Chicago. Dill was notified of the early arrival.] Defendant paid
Dill six hundred dollars, advising him that Alberdina would persuade . . . [the victim] to accompany her to a place of amusement and
that she planned to leave their home at eight o'clock P.M. on February 13, 1926. It was further planned that Alberdina was to carry the
diamonds on her person, and that Dill was to shoot . . . [the victim]
either as they left their home or as they returned, and that Alberdina was to be mussed up and the diamonds taken from her, so that
it might appear the result of a robbery. Alberdina was to appear to
faint, giving Dill time to make his escape. However, on the night of
February 13, 1926, Dill, accompanied by three other police officers,
proceeded about eight o'clock P.M. to the home of . . . [the victim]
as arranged. [The victim] . . . and Alberdina Lourie were there found
dressed and ready to leave, with the diamonds on her person. As Dill
and the officers entered the room, she turned her face to the wall as
planned."[2]

Assume that Davis and Alberdina Lourie would be liable for acts
performed by Dill at Davis and Alberdina Lourie's direction. Did
Davis and Lourie attempt to murder Lourie's husband under the
statutes and cases below?

UNITED STATES v. HENG AWKAK ROMAN   356 F. Supp. 434, 437 (S.D.N.Y. 1973)

"There is no comprehensive statutory definition of attempt in federal
law."

Montana Code Annotated § 45-4-103 (2001)   *Attempt*

(1) A person commits the offense of attempt when, with the purpose to commit
a specific offense, he does any act toward the commission of such offense.

Wisconsin Statutes § 939.32 (2000)

(3) An attempt to commit a crime requires that the actor have an intent to perform
acts and attain a result which, if accomplished, would constitute such crime and

---

2. Based on and quotations from State v. Davis, 319 Mo. 1222 (1928).

that the actor does acts toward the commission of the crime which demonstrate unequivocally, under all the circumstances, that the actor formed that intent and would commit the crime except for the intervention of another person or some other extraneous factor.

Model Penal Code § 5.01 *Criminal Attempt*

(1) *Definition of Attempt.* A person is guilty of an attempt to commit a crime if . . . he:

(a) purposely engages in conduct that would constitute the crime if the attendant circumstances were as he believes them to be; or

(b) when causing a particular result is an element of the crime, does or omits to do anything with the purpose of causing or with the belief that it will cause such result without further conduct on his part; or

(c) purposely does or omits to do anything that, under the circumstances as he believes them to be, is an act or omission constituting a substantial step in a course of conduct planned to culminate in his commission of the crime.

(2) *Conduct Which May Be Held Substantial Step Under Subsection (1)(c).* Conduct shall not be held to constitute a substantial step under Subsection (1)(c) of this Section unless it is strongly corroborative of the actor's criminal purpose. Without negativing the sufficiency of other conduct, the following, if strongly corroborative of the actor's criminal purpose, shall not be held insufficient as a matter of law:

(a) lying in wait, searching for or following the contemplated victim of the crime;

(b) enticing or seeking to entice the contemplated victim of the crime to go to the place contemplated for its commission;

(c) reconnoitering the place contemplated for the commission of the crime;

(d) unlawful entry of a structure, vehicle or enclosure in which it is contemplated that the crime will be committed;

(e) possession of materials to be employed in the commission of the crime, that are specially designed for such unlawful use or that can serve no lawful purpose of the actor under the circumstances;

(f) possession, collection or fabrication of materials to be employed in the commission of the crime, at or near the place contemplated for its commission, if such possession, collection or fabrication serves no lawful purpose of the actor under the circumstances;

(g) soliciting an innocent agent to engage in conduct constituting an element of the crime.

KANSAS *v.* GOBIN
216 Kan. 278 (1975)

FROMME, J. . . . . The Kansas Criminal Code defines an attempt as follows:

"An attempt is any overt act toward the perpetration of a crime done by a person who intends to commit such crime but fails in the perpetration thereof or is prevented or intercepted in executing such crime." . . .

Next let us consider the type of an overt act necessary to support an attempt to commit any crime. The essential elements to establish an attempt have been repeatedly set forth in our cases ... where it is said:

"[the Kansas attempt statute] contains three essential elements (1) the intent to commit the crime, (2) an overt act toward the perpetration of the crime, and (3) a failure to consummate it...."

The comment of the committee on pattern jury instructions covering attempts is:

"A problem inherent in the law of attempts concerns the point when criminal liability attaches for the overt act. On the one hand mere acts of preparation are insufficient while, on the other, if the accused has performed the final act necessary for the completion of the crime, he could be prosecuted for the crime intended and not for an attempt. The overt act lies somewhere between these two extremes and each case must depend upon its own particular facts...."

It becomes apparent from reading the ... cases that no definite rule as to what constitutes an overt act for the purposes of an attempt can or should be laid down. Each case must depend largely on its particular facts and the inferences which the jury may reasonably draw therefrom. The problem should be approached with a desire to accomplish substantial justice.

QUESTIONS

1. The *Gobin* court states that "no definite rule as to what constitutes an overt act for the purposes of an attempt can or should be laid down." Is the court's position consistent with the language of the Kansas Criminal Code?

2. If the legislature and the court don't define the conduct required for an attempt, who will determine what conduct warrants an attempt conviction?

3. What does the adjective "overt" mean in the Kansas attempt statute? What, if anything, does it add to the statute's requirements for an attempt conviction?

4. If a defendant *succeeds* in completing the target offense, won't she have satisfied any conduct requirement for attempt? Should completion of the target offense eliminate attempt liability? Does completion of the target offense eliminate attempt liability under the Kansas attempt statute?

PEOPLE *v.* RIZZO
246 N.Y. 334 (1927)

CRANE, J. The police of the city of New York did excellent work in this case by preventing the commission of a serious crime. It is a great satisfaction to realize that we have such wide-awake guardians of our peace. Whether or not the steps which the defendant had taken up to the time of his arrest amounted to the commission of a crime, as defined by our law, is, however, another matter. He has been convicted of an attempt to commit the crime of robbery in the first degree and sentenced to State's prison. There is no doubt that he had the intention to commit robbery if he got the chance. An examination, however, of the facts is necessary to determine whether his acts were in preparation to commit the crime if the opportunity offered, or constituted a crime in itself, known to our law as an attempt to commit robbery in the first degree. Charles Rizzo, the defendant, appellant, with three others, Anthony J. Dorio, Thomas Milo and John Thomasello, on January 14th planned to rob one Charles Rao of a payroll valued at about $1,200 which he was to carry from the bank for the United Lathing Company. These defendants, two of whom had firearms, started out in an automobile, looking for Rao or the man who had the payroll on that day. Rizzo claimed to be able to identify the man and was to point him out to the others who were to do the actual holding up. The four rode about in their car looking for Rao. They went to the bank from which he was supposed to get the money and to various buildings being constructed by the United Lathing Company. At last they came to One Hundred and Eightieth street and Morris Park avenue. By this time they were watched and followed by two police officers. As Rizzo jumped out of the car and ran into the building all four were arrested. The defendant was taken out from the building in which he was hiding. Neither Rao nor a man named Previti, who was also supposed to carry a payroll, were at the place at the time of the arrest. The defendants had not found or seen the man they intended to rob; no person with a payroll was at any of the places where they had stopped and no one had been pointed out or identified by Rizzo. The four men intended to rob the payroll man, whoever he was; they were looking for him, but they had not seen or discovered him up to the time they were arrested.

Does this constitute the crime of an attempt to commit robbery in the first degree? The Penal Law, section 2, prescribes, "An act, done with intent to commit a crime, and tending but failing to effect its commission, is 'an attempt to commit that crime.'" The word "tending" is very indefinite. It is perfectly evident that there will arise differences of opinion as to whether an act in a given case is one tending to commit a crime. "Tending" means to exert activity in a particular direction. Any act in preparation to commit a crime may be said to have a tendency towards its accomplishment. The procuring of the automobile, searching the streets looking for the desired victim, were in reality acts tending toward the commission of the proposed crime. The law, however, has recognized that many acts in the way of preparation are too remote to constitute the crime of attempt. The line has been drawn between those acts which are remote and those which are proximate and near to the consummation. The law must be practical, and, therefore, considers those acts only as tending to the commission of the crime which are so near to its accomplishment that in all reasonable probability the crime itself would have been committed but for timely interference. The cases which have been before the courts express this idea in different language, but the idea remains the same. The act or acts must come or advance very near to the accomplishment of the intended crime. In *People v. Mills* it was said: "Felonious intent alone is not enough, but there must be an overt act shown in order to establish even an attempt. An overt act is one done to carry out the intention, and it must be such as would naturally effect that result, unless prevented by some extraneous cause." In *Hyde v. U.S.* it was stated that the act amounts to an attempt when it is so near to the result that the danger of success is very great. "There must be dangerous proximity to success." Halsbury in his "Laws of England" says: "An act, in order to be a criminal attempt, must be immediately, and not remotely, connected with and directly tending to the commission of an offence." *Commonwealth v. Peaslee* refers to the acts constituting an attempt as coming very near to the accomplishment of the crime.

The method of committing or attempting crime varies in each case so that the difficulty, if any, is not with this rule of law regarding an attempt, which is well understood, but with its application to the facts. As I have said before, minds differ over proximity and the nearness of the approach.

How shall we apply this rule of immediate nearness to this case? The defendants were looking for the payroll man to rob him of his money. This is the charge in the indictment. Robbery is defined in section 2120 of the Penal Law as "the unlawful taking of personal property, from the person or in the presence of another, against his will, by means of force, or violence, or fear of injury, immediate or future, to his person;" and it is made robbery in the first degree by section 2124 when committed by a person aided by accomplices actually present. To constitute the crime of robbery the money must have been taken from Rao by means of force or violence, or through fear. The crime of attempt to commit robbery was committed if these defendants did an act tending to the commission of this robbery. Did the acts above described come dangerously near to the taking of Rao's property? Did the acts come so near the commission of robbery that there was reasonable likelihood of its accomplishment but for the interference? Rao was not found; the defendants were still looking for him; no attempt to rob him could be made, at least until he came in sight; he was not in the building at One Hundred and Eightieth street and Morris Park avenue. There was no man there with the payroll for the United Lathing Company whom these defendants could rob. Apparently no money had been drawn from the bank for the payroll by anybody at the time of the arrest. In a word, these defendants had planned to commit a crime and were looking around the city for an opportunity to commit it, but the opportunity fortunately never came. Men would not be guilty of an attempt at burglary if they had planned to break into a building and were arrested while they were hunting about the streets for the building not knowing where it was. Neither would a man be guilty of an attempt to commit murder if he armed himself and started out to find the person whom he had planned to kill but could not find him. So here these defendants were not guilty of an attempt to commit robbery in the first degree when they had not found or reached the presence of the person they intended to rob.

For these reasons, the judgment of conviction of this defendant, appellant, must be reversed and a new trial granted.

A very strange situation has arisen in this case. I called attention to the four defendants who were convicted of this crime of an attempt to commit robbery in the first degree. They were all tried together upon the same evidence, and jointly convicted, and all sentenced to State's prison for varying terms. Rizzo was the only one of the four to appeal to the Appellate Division and to this court. His conviction was affirmed by the Appellate Division by a divided court, two of the justices dissenting, and we have now held that he was not guilty of the crime charged. If he were not guilty, neither were the other three. As the others, however, did not appeal, there is no remedy for them through the court; their judgments stand, and they must serve their sentences. This of course is a situation which must in all fairness be met in some way. Two of these men were guilty of the crime of carrying weapons, pistols, contrary to law, for which they could be convicted. Two of them, John Thomasello and Thomas Milo, had also been previously convicted, which may have had something to do with their neglect to appeal. However, the law would fail in its function and its purpose if it permitted these three men whoever or whatever they are to serve a sentence for a crime which the courts subsequently found and declared had not been committed. We, therefore, suggest to the district attorney of Bronx county that he bring the cases of these three men to the attention of the Governor to be dealt with as to him seems proper in the light of this opinion.

The judgment of the Appellate Division and that of the County Court should be reversed and a new trial ordered.

Judgment accordingly.

QUESTIONS

1. Which branch of government defines the conduct required for attempt in New York? The legislature? The New York courts?

2. What role did statutory text and legislative intent play in Justice Crane's analysis? What statutory arguments might the prosecutor have made in support of the government's position that Rizzo's conduct was sufficient for attempt liability? Is Justice Crane's analysis consistent with the language of the New York attempt statute?

3. What test does *Rizzo* use for the conduct element of an attempt? What are the advantages and disadvantages of this test?

4. Justice Crane states that Rizzo's three co-defendants were not guilty of attempt despite their convictions. Why, then, does he conclude that despite this fact, "they must serve their sentences"? Should the court take steps to free them? Should the prosecutor?

UNITED STATES *v.* JACKSON
560 F.2d 112 (2d Cir. 1977)

BRYAN, J.

Robert Jackson, William Scott, and Martin Allen appeal from judgments of conviction entered on November 23, 1976 in the United States District Court for the Eastern District of New York after a trial before Chief Judge Jacob Mishler without a jury.

Count one of the indictment alleged that between June 11 and June 21, 1976 the appellants conspired to commit an armed robbery of the Manufacturers Hanover Trust branch located at 210 Flushing Avenue, Brooklyn, New York, in violation of 18 U.S.C. § 371. Counts two and three each charged appellants with an attempted robbery of the branch on June 14 and on June 21, 1976, respectively, in violation of 18 U.S.C. §§ 2113(a) and 2. Count four charged them with possession of two unregistered sawed-off shotguns on June 21, 1976, in violation of 26 U.S.C. § 5861(d) and 18 U.S.C. § 2.

After a suppression hearing on July 23, 1976 and a one-day trial on August 30, 1976, Chief Judge Mishler filed a memorandum of decision finding each defendant guilty on all four counts.[1]

Appellants' principal contention is that the court below erred in finding them guilty on counts two and three. While they concede that the evidence supported the conspiracy convictions on count one, they assert that, as a matter of law, their conduct never crossed the elusive line which separates "mere preparation" from "attempt."...

---

[1] Jackson was sentenced to imprisonment for two years on count one, and was given a suspended sentence with concurrent three-year terms of probation, to commence at the end of the prison sentence, on each of the other counts. Scott was sentenced to imprisonment for five years on count one, and to seven years imprisonment on each of the remaining three counts, all sentences to run concurrently. Allen received a five-year term of imprisonment on count one, and terms of ten years on each of the remaining three counts, all sentences to run concurrently.

I.

The Government's evidence at trial consisted largely of the testimony of Vanessa Hodges, an unindicted co-conspirator, and of various FBI agents who surveilled the Manufacturers Hanover branch on June 21, 1976. Since the facts are of critical importance in any attempt case, *United States v. Stallworth*, [543 F.2d 1038 (2d Cir. 1970)], at 1039, we shall review the Government's proof in considerable detail.[2]

On June 11, 1976, Vanessa Hodges was introduced to appellant Martin Allen by Pia Longhorne, another unindicted co-conspirator. Hodges wanted to meet someone who would help her carry out a plan to rob the Manufacturers Hanover branch located at 210 Flushing Avenue in Brooklyn, and she invited Allen to join her. Hodges proposed that the bank be robbed the next Monday, June 14th, at about 7:30 A.M. She hoped that they could enter with the bank manager at that time, grab the weekend deposits, and leave. Allen agreed to rob the bank with Hodges, and told her he had access to a car, two sawed-off shotguns, and a .38 caliber revolver.

The following Monday, June 14, Allen arrived at Longhorne's house about 7:30 A.M. in a car driven by appellant Robert Jackson. A suitcase in the back seat of the car contained a sawed-off shotgun, shells, materials intended as masks, and handcuffs to bind the bank manager. While Allen picked up Hodges at Longhorne's, Jackson filled the car with gas. The trio then left for the bank.

When they arrived, it was almost 8:00 A.M. It was thus too late to effect the first step of the plan, viz., entering the bank as the manager opened the door. They rode around for a while longer, and then went to a restaurant to get something to eat and discuss their next move. After eating, the trio drove back to the bank. Allen and Hodges left the car and walked over to the bank. They peered in and saw the bulky weekend deposits, but decided it was too risky to rob the bank without an extra man.

Consequently, Jackson, Hodges, and Allen drove to Coney Island in search of another accomplice. In front of a housing project on 33rd Street they found appellant William Scott, who promptly joined the team. Allen added to the arsenal another sawed-off shotgun obtained from one of the buildings in the project, and the group drove back to the bank.

When they arrived again, Allen entered the bank to check the location of any surveillance cameras, while Jackson placed a piece of cardboard with a false license number over the authentic license plate of the car.[3] Allen reported back that a single surveillance camera was over the entrance door. After further discussion, Scott left the car and entered the bank. He came back and informed the group that the tellers were separating the weekend deposits and that a number of patrons were now in the bank. Hodges then suggested that they drop the plans for the robbery that day, and reschedule it for the following Monday, June 21. Accordingly, they left the vicinity of the bank and returned to Coney Island where, before splitting up, they purchased a pair of stockings for Hodges to wear over her head as a disguise and pairs of gloves for Hodges, Scott, and Allen to don before entering the bank.

Hodges was arrested on Friday, June 18, 1976 on an unrelated bank robbery charge, and immediately began cooperating with the Government. After relating

---

[2] None of the appellants took the stand or offered any other evidence.

[3] Hodges' testimony indicates that, in order to avert suspicion, Jackson would first lift the trunk or hood of the car as though he were working under it before covering or uncovering the genuine license plates.

the events of June 14, she told FBI agents that a robbery of the Manufacturers branch at 210 Flushing Avenue was now scheduled for the following Monday, June 21. The three black male robbers, according to Hodges, would be heavily armed with hand and shoulder weapons and expected to use a brown four-door sedan equipped with a cardboard license plate as the getaway car. She told the agents that Jackson, who would drive the car, was light-skinned with a moustache and a cut on his lip, and she described Allen as short, dark-skinned with facial hair, and Scott as 5 feet 9 inches, slim build, with an afro hair style and some sort of defect in his right eye.

At the request of the agents, Hodges called Allen on Saturday, June 19, and asked if he were still planning to do the job. He said that he was ready. On Sunday she called him again. This time Allen said that he was not going to rob the bank that Monday because he had learned that Hodges had been arrested and he feared that federal agents might be watching. Hodges nevertheless advised the agents that she thought the robbery might still take place as planned with the three men proceeding without her.

At about 7:00 A.M. on Monday, June 21, 1976, some ten FBI agents took various surveilling positions in the area of the bank. At about 7:39 A.M. the agents observed a brown four-door Lincoln, with a New York license plate on the front and a cardboard facsimile of a license plate on the rear, moving in an easterly direction on Flushing Avenue past the bank, which was located on the southeast corner of Flushing and Washington Avenues. The front seat of the Lincoln was occupied by a black male driver and a black male passenger with mutton-chop sideburns. The Lincoln circled the block and came to a stop at a fire hydrant situated at the side of the bank facing Washington Avenue, a short distance south of the corner of Flushing and Washington.

A third black male, who appeared to have an eye deformity, got out of the passenger side rear door of the Lincoln, walked to the corner of Flushing and Washington, and stood on the sidewalk in the vicinity of the bank's entrance. He then walked south on Washington Avenue, only to return a short time later with a container of coffee in his hand. He stood again on the corner of Washington and Flushing in front of the bank, drinking the coffee and looking around, before returning to the parked Lincoln.

The Lincoln pulled out, made a left turn onto Flushing, and proceeded in a westerly direction for one block to Waverly Avenue. It stopped, made a U-turn, and parked on the south side of Flushing between Waverly and Washington — a spot on the same side of the street as the bank entrance but separated from it by Washington Avenue. After remaining parked in this position for approximately five minutes, it pulled out and cruised east on Flushing past the bank again. The Lincoln then made a right onto Grand Avenue, the third street east of the bank, and headed south. It stopped halfway down the block, midway between Flushing and Park Avenues, and remained there for several minutes. During this time Jackson was seen working in the front of the car, which had its hood up.

The Lincoln was next sighted several minutes later in the same position it had previously occupied on the south side of Flushing Avenue between Waverly and Washington. The front license plate was now missing. The vehicle remained parked there for close to thirty minutes. Finally, it began moving east on Flushing Avenue once more, in the direction of the bank.

At some point near the bank as they passed down Flushing Avenue, the appellants detected the presence of the surveillance agents. The Lincoln accelerated down

Flushing Avenue and turned south on Grand Avenue again. It was overtaken by FBI agents who ordered the appellants out of the car and arrested them. The agents then observed a black and red plaid suitcase in the rear of the car. The zipper of the suitcase was partially open and exposed two loaded sawed-off shotguns,[4] a toy nickelplated revolver, a pair of handcuffs, and masks. A New York license plate was seen lying on the front floor of the car. All of these items were seized.

In his memorandum of decision, Chief Judge Mishler concluded that the evidence against Jackson, Scott, and Allen was "overwhelming" on counts one and four. In contrast, he characterized the question of whether the defendants had attempted a bank robbery as charged in counts two and three or were merely engaged in preparations as "a close one." After canvassing the authorities on what this court one month later called a "perplexing problem," Chief Judge Mishler applied the following two-tiered inquiry. . . .

First, the defendant must have been acting with the kind of culpability otherwise required for the commission of the crime which he is charged with attempting. . . .

Second, the defendant must have engaged in conduct which constitutes a substantial step toward commission of the crime. A substantial step must be conduct strongly corroborative of the firmness of the defendant's criminal intent.

He concluded that on June 14 and again on June 21, the defendants took substantial steps, strongly corroborative of the firmness of their criminal intent, toward commission of the crime of bank robbery and found the defendants guilty on each of the two attempt counts. These appeals followed.

II.

"There is no comprehensive statutory definition of attempt in federal law." *United States v. Heng Awkak Roman.* Fed. R. Crim. P. 31(c), however, provides in pertinent part that a defendant may be found guilty of "an attempt to commit either the offense charged or an offense necessarily included therein if the attempt is an offense." 18 U.S.C. § 2113(a)[5] specifically makes attempted bank robbery an offense.

Appellant Scott argues that the very wording of 18 U.S.C. § 2113(a) precludes a finding that the actions charged in counts two and three reached the level of attempts. Relying on *United States v. Baker*, 129 F. Supp. 684 (S.D. Cal. 1955), he contends that since the statute only mentions attempted taking and not attempted force, violence, or intimidation, it clearly contemplates that actual use of force, violence, or intimidation must precede an attempted taking in order to make out the offense of attempted bank robbery.

---

[4] One of the shotguns proved to be inoperative.

[5] The subsection provides:

> Whoever, by force and violence, or by intimidation, takes, or attempts to take, from the person or presence of another any property or money or any other thing of value belonging to, or in the care, custody, control, management, or possession of, any bank, credit union, or any savings and loan association; or
>
> Whoever enters or attempts to enter any bank, credit union, or any savings and loan association, or any building used in whole or in part as a bank, credit union, or as a savings and loan association, with intent to commit in such bank, credit union, or in such savings and loan association, or building, or part thereof, so used, any felony affecting such bank or such savings and loan association and in violation of any statute of the United States, or any larceny—
>
> Shall be fined not more than $5,000 or imprisoned not more than twenty years, or both.

The *Stallworth* court faced a similar statutory construction argument which also relied heavily on *United States v. Baker, supra*. In response to the assertion that the defendants in that case could not be convicted of attempted bank robbery because they neither entered the bank nor brandished weapons, Chief Judge Kaufman stated:

> We reject this wooden logic. Attempt is a subtle concept that requires a rational and logically sound definition, one that enables society to punish malefactors who have unequivocally set out upon a criminal course without requiring law enforcement officers to delay until innocent bystanders are imperiled.

Chief Judge Kaufman, writing for the court [in *Stallworth*], selected the two-tiered inquiry of *United States v. Mandujano*, "properly derived from the writings of many distinguished jurists," as stating the proper test for determining whether the foregoing conduct constituted an attempt. He observed that this analysis "conforms closely to the sensible definition of an attempt proffered by the American Law Institute's Model Penal Code."

The draftsmen of the Model Penal Code recognized the difficulty of arriving at a general standard for distinguishing acts of preparation from acts constituting an attempt. They found general agreement that when an actor committed the "last proximate act," i.e., when he had done all that he believed necessary to effect a particular result which is an element of the offense, he committed an attempt. They also concluded, however, that while the last proximate act is *sufficient* to constitute an attempt, it is not *necessary* to such a finding. The problem then was to devise a standard more inclusive than one requiring the last proximate act before attempt liability would attach, but less inclusive than one which would make every act done with the intent to commit a crime criminal. . . .

The draftsmen considered and rejected the following approaches to distinguishing preparation from attempt, later summarized in *Mandujano*:

> (a) The physical proximity doctrine — the overt act required for an attempt must be proximate to the completed crime, or directly tending toward the completion of the crime, or must amount to the commencement of the consummation.
>
> (b) The dangerous proximity doctrine — a test given impetus by Mr. Justice Holmes whereby the greater the gravity and probability of the offense, and the nearer the act to the crime, the stronger is the case for calling the act an attempt.
>
> (c) The indispensable element test — a variation of the proximity tests which emphasizes any indispensable aspect of the criminal endeavor over which the actor has not yet acquired control.
>
> (d) The probable desistance test — the conduct constitutes an attempt if, in the ordinary and natural course of events, without interruption from an outside source, it will result in the crime intended.
>
> (e) The abnormal step approach — an attempt is a step toward crime which goes beyond the point where the normal citizen would think better of his conduct and desist.
>
> (f) The res ipsa loquitur or unequivocality test — an attempt is committed when the actor's conduct manifests an intent to commit a crime.

The formulation upon which the draftsmen ultimately agreed required, in addition to criminal purpose, that an act be a substantial step in a course of conduct designed to accomplish a criminal result, and that it be strongly corroborative of criminal purpose in order for it to constitute such a substantial step. The following differences between this test and previous approaches to the preparation-attempt problem were noted:

> First, this formulation shifts the emphasis from what remains to be done — the chief concern of the proximity tests — to what the actor has already done. The fact that further major steps must be taken before the crime can be completed does not preclude a finding that the steps already undertaken are substantial. It is expected, in the normal case, that this approach will broaden the scope of attempt liability.
>
> Second, although it is intended that the requirement of a substantial step will result in the imposition of attempt liability only in those instances in which some firmness of criminal purpose is shown, no finding is required as to whether the actor would probably have desisted prior to completing the crime. Potentially the probable desistance test could reach very early steps toward crime — depending upon how one assesses the probabilities of desistance — but since in practice this test follows closely the proximity approaches, rejection of probable desistance will not narrow the scope of attempt liability.
>
> Finally, the requirement of proving a substantial step generally will prove less of a hurdle for the prosecution than the res ipsa loquitur approach, which requires that the actor's conduct must itself manifest the criminal purpose. The difference will be illustrated in connection with the present section's requirement of corroboration. Here it should be noted that, in the present formulation, the two purposes to be served by the res ipsa loquitur test are, to a large extent, treated separately. Firmness of criminal purpose is intended to be shown by requiring a substantial step, while problems of proof are dealt with by the requirement of corroboration (although, under the reasoning previously expressed, the latter will also tend to establish firmness of purpose). Model Penal Code § 5.01, Comment at 47 (Tent. Draft No. 10, 1960).

The draftsmen concluded that, in addition to assuring firmness of criminal design, the requirement of a substantial step would preclude attempt liability, with its accompanying harsh penalties, for relatively remote preparatory acts. At the same time, however, by not requiring a "last proximate act" or one of its various analogues it would permit the apprehension of dangerous persons at an earlier stage than the other approaches without immunizing them from attempt liability. . . .

In the case at bar, Chief Judge Mishler anticipated the precise analysis which this Court adopted in the strikingly similar *Stallworth* case. He then found that on June 14 the appellants, already agreed upon a robbery plan, drove to the bank with loaded weapons. In order to carry the heavy weekend deposit sacks, they recruited another person. Cardboard was placed over the license, and the bank was entered and reconnoitered. Only then was the plan dropped for the moment and rescheduled for the following Monday. On that day, June 21, the defendants performed essentially the same acts. Since the cameras had already been located there was no need to enter the bank again, and since the appellants had arrived at the bank earlier, conditions were more favorable to their initial robbery plan than they had been on June 14. He concluded that on both occasions these men were seriously dedicated to the commission of a crime, had passed beyond the stage of preparation, and would have assaulted the bank had they not been dissuaded by certain external factors, viz., the breaking up of the weekend deposits and crowd of patrons in the bank on the afternoon of June 14 and the detection of the FBI surveillance on June 21.

We cannot say that these conclusions which Chief Judge Mishler reached as the trier of fact as to what the evidence before him established were erroneous. As in *Stallworth*, the criminal intent of the appellants was beyond dispute. The question remaining then is the substantiality of the steps taken on the dates in question, and how strongly this corroborates the firmness of their obvious criminal intent. This is a matter of degree. See Model Penal Code § 5.01, Comments at 47 (Tent. Draft No. 10, 1960).

On two separate occasions, appellants reconnoitered the place contemplated for the commission of the crime and possessed the paraphernalia to be employed in the commission of the crime — loaded sawed-off shotguns, extra shells, a toy revolver, handcuffs, and masks — which was specially designed for such unlawful use and which could serve no lawful purpose under the circumstances. Under the Model Penal Code formulation, *supra* at 4816-18, approved by the *Stallworth* court, either type of conduct, standing alone, was sufficient as a matter of law to constitute a "substantial step" if it strongly corroborated their criminal purpose. Here both types of conduct coincided on both June 14 and June 21, along with numerous other elements strongly corroborative of the firmness of appellants' criminal intent. The steps taken toward a successful bank robbery thus were not "insubstantial" as a matter of law, and Chief Judge Mishler found them "substantial" as a matter of fact. We are unwilling to substitute our assessment of the evidence for his, and thus affirm the convictions for attempted bank robbery on counts two and three.

The judgments of conviction are affirmed.

QUESTIONS

1. Judge Bryan in Section II first raises Scott's argument based on "the very wording of 18 U.S.C. § 2113(a)." What was Scott's argument? If you were the prosecutor, how would you respond to this argument? If you were the judge, how would you rule on this argument?

2. At what point did Jackson and his confederates become liable for attempt under the Model Penal Code? What about under the other approaches mentioned in the *Jackson* case as having been considered and rejected by those who drafted the MPC attempt provision? What about under the other cases and statutes in this section?

PROBLEM

10.3 Many states have modeled attempt statutes on the Model Penal Code sections discussed in *Jackson*. Some of those states, though, have altered its provisions. How have the following three statutes modified the Model Penal Code's treatment of the conduct element in attempt? What is the significance of these modifications?

Arizona Revised Statutes § 13-1001

A. A person commits attempt if, acting with the kind of culpability otherwise required for commission of an offense, such person:

1. Intentionally engages in conduct which would constitute an offense if the attendant circumstances were as such person believes them to be; or

2. Intentionally does or omits to do anything which, under the circumstances as such person believes them to be, is any step in a course of conduct planned to culminate in commission of an offense; . . .

Tennessee Code Annotated § 39-12-101

(b) Conduct does not constitute a substantial step . . . unless the person's entire course of action is corroborative of the intent to commit the offense.

Kentucky Revised Statutes § 506.010

(2) Conduct shall not be held to constitute a substantial step . . . unless it is an act or omission which leaves no reasonable doubt as to the defendant's intention to commit the crime which he is charged with attempting.

Modern readers often find the *McQuirter* case, which follows, troubling. The case raises important issues about the intersection of the criminal law of attempt and attitudes about race. As you read the case, think about how the 1953 Alabama law of attempt, reflected in *McQuirter*, might be reformulated to address these issues.

McQUIRTER *v.* STATE

36 Ala. App. 707 (1953)

PRICE, J. Appellant, a Negro man, was found guilty of an attempt to commit an assault with intent to rape, under an indictment charging an assault with intent to rape. The jury assessed a fine of $500.

About 8:00 o'clock on the night of June 29, 1951, Mrs. Ted Allen, a white woman, with her two children and a neighbor's little girl, were drinking Coca-Cola at the "Tiny Diner" in Atmore. When they started in the direction of Mrs. Allen's home she noticed appellant sitting in the cab of a parked truck. As she passed the truck appellant said something unintelligible, opened the truck door and placed his foot on the running board.

Mrs. Allen testified appellant followed her down the street and when she reached Suell Lufkin's house she stopped. As she turned into the Lufkin house appellant was within two or three feet of her. She waited ten minutes for appellant to pass. When she proceeded on her way, appellant came toward her from behind a telephone pole. She told the children to run to Mr. Simmons' house and tell him to come and meet her. When appellant saw Mr. Simmons he turned and went back down the street to the intersection and leaned on a stop sign just across the street from Mrs. Allen's home. Mrs. Allen watched him at the sign from Mr. Simmons' porch for about thirty minutes, after which time he came back down the street and appellant went on home.

Mrs. Allen's testimony was corroborated by that of her young daughter. The daughter testified the appellant was within six feet of her mother as she approached the Lufkin house, and this witness said there was a while when she didn't see appellant at the intersection.

Mr. Lewis Simmons testified when the little girls ran up on his porch and said a Negro was after them, witness walked up the sidewalk to meet Mrs. Allen and saw appellant. Appellant went on down the street and stopped in front of Mrs. Allen's home and waited there approximately thirty minutes.

Mr. Clarence Bryars, a policeman in Atmore, testified that appellant stated after his arrest that he came to Atmore with the intention of getting him a white woman that night.

Mr. W. E. Strickland, Chief of Police of Atmore, testified that appellant stated in the Atmore jail he didn't know what was the matter with him; that he was drinking a little; that he and his partner had been to Pensacola; that his partner went to the "Front" to see a colored woman; that he didn't have any money and he sat in the truck and made up his mind he was going to get the first woman that came by and that this was the first woman that came by. He said he got out of the truck, came around the gas tank and watched the lady and when she started off he started off behind her; that he was going to carry her in the cotton patch and if she hollered he was going to kill her. He testified appellant made the same statement in the Brewton jail.

Mr. Norvelle Seals, Chief Deputy Sheriff, corroborated Mr. Strickland's testimony as to the statement by appellant at the Brewton jail.

Appellant, as a witness in his own behalf, testified he and Bill Page, another Negro, carried a load of junk-iron from Monroeville to Pensacola; on their way back to Monroeville they stopped in Atmore. They parked the truck near the "Tiny Diner" and rode to the "Front," the colored section, in a cab. Appellant came back to the truck around 8:00 o'clock and sat in the truck cab for about thirty minutes. He decided to go back to the "Front" to look for Bill Page. As he started up the street he saw prosecutrix and her children. He turned around and waited until he decided they had gone, then he walked up the street toward the "Front." When he reached the intersection at the telegraph pole he decided he didn't want to go to the "Front" and sat around there a few minutes, then went on to the "Front" and stayed about 25 or 30 minutes, and came back to the truck.

He denied that he followed Mrs. Allen or made any gesture toward molesting her or the children. He denied making the statements testified to by the officers.

He testified he had never been arrested before and introduced testimony by two residents of Monroeville as to his good reputation for peace and quiet and for truth and veracity.

Appellant insists the trial court erred in refusing the general affirmative charge and in denying the motion for a new trial on the ground the verdict was contrary to the evidence.

" 'An attempt to commit an assault with intent to rape,'... means an attempt to rape which has not proceeded far enough to amount to an assault." Under the authorities in this state, to justify a conviction for an attempt to commit an assault with intent to rape the jury must be satisfied beyond a reasonable doubt that defendant intended to have sexual intercourse with prosecutrix against her will, by force or by putting her in fear.

Intent is a question to be determined by the jury from the facts and circumstances adduced on the trial, and if there is evidence from which it may be inferred that at the time of the attempt defendant intended to gratify his lustful desires against the resistance of the female a jury question is presented. In determining the question of intention the jury may consider social conditions and customs founded upon racial differences, such as that the prosecutrix was a white woman and defendant was a Negro man.

After considering the evidence in this case we are of the opinion it was sufficient to warrant the submission of the question of defendant's guilt to the jury, and was ample to sustain the judgment of conviction.

Defense counsel contends in brief that the testimony of the officers as to defendant's declarations of intent was inadmissible because no attempt or overt act toward carrying that intent into effect had been proven.

Defendant's grounds of objection to this evidence were that it was "irrelevant, incompetent and immaterial." Proper predicates were laid for the introduction of each of said statements. In the absence of a ground of objection calling the court's attention to the fact that the corpus delicti has not been sufficiently proven to authorize admission of a confession such question cannot be reviewed here.

Moreover, if any facts are proven from which the jury may reasonably infer that the crime has been committed proof of the confession is rendered admissible.

We find no reversible error in the record and the judgment of the trial court is affirmed.

Affirmed.

QUESTIONS

1. What conduct was required in *McQuirter* for an attempt conviction? What mental state was required? On what evidence of mental state did the prosecution rely?

2. What role do you think the state of race relations in Alabama in 1953 may have played in the *McQuirter* case? What significance did the court attach to McQuirter's race and Mrs. Allen's race? Would a court today attach the same significance? What about a modern jury?

3. An attempt to assault someone with intent to commit rape is a serious crime. Why was the defendant punished with only a fine?

C. MENTAL STATE

PROBLEM

10.4 Look back at the crossbow incident described at the beginning of this chapter. According to the article, a disgruntled lover shot an arrow into the victim's head but missed his brain and caused only minor injury. With what crimes might the shooter be charged? What mental state did he have with respect to his conduct? What mental state did he have with regard to the death of the victim? At trial, the shooter's lawyer argued that his client accidentally fired the crossbow.[3] If the jury decided that the firing of the crossbow was in fact accidental, would the shooter be liable for attempted homicide?

---

3. *Man Convicted For Shooting Arrow Into Ex-Lover's Head*, Orlando Sentinel Tribune, Oct. 24, 1992, at A13.

Kansas Statutes Annotated § 21-3301 (2000)

(a) An attempt is any overt act toward the perpetration of a crime done by a person who intends to commit such crime but fails in the perpetration thereof or is prevented or intercepted in executing such crime.

Wisconsin Statutes § 939.32 (2000)

(3) An attempt to commit a crime requires that the actor have an intent to perform acts and attain a result which, if accomplished, would constitute such crime and that the actor does acts toward the commission of the crime which demonstrate unequivocally, under all the circumstances, that the actor formed that intent and would commit the crime except for the intervention of another person or some other extraneous factor.

Model Penal Code 5.01   *Criminal Attempt*

(1) **Definition of Attempt.** A person is guilty of an attempt to commit a crime if, acting with the kind of culpability otherwise required for commission of the crime, he:

(a) purposely engages in conduct that would constitute the crime if the attendant circumstances were as he believes them to be; or

(b) when causing a particular result is an element of the crime, does or omits to do anything with the purpose of causing or with the belief that it will cause such result without further conduct on his part; or

(c) purposely does or omits to do anything that, under the circumstances as he believes them to be, is an act or omission constituting a substantial step in a course of conduct planned to culminate in his commission of the crime.

SOUTH DAKOTA *v.* LYERLA

424 N.W.2d 908 (1988)

KONENKAMP, J. A jury convicted Gerald K. Lyerla (Lyerla) of second degree murder and two counts of attempted second degree murder. We affirm the second degree murder conviction, but reverse the convictions for attempted second degree murder.

On the night of January 18, 1986, while driving east on Interstate 90 in Haakon County, Lyerla fired three shots with his .357 magnum pistol at a pickup truck carrying three teenage girls. One was killed, the other two were injured. Only one bullet entered the pickup cab, the one that killed seventeen-year-old Tammy Jensen. Another bullet was recovered from the engine block; the third was never found. Lyerla fled the scene, but was later apprehended. He was charged in the alternative with first degree murder or second degree murder for the death of Tammy Jensen and two counts each of attempted first degree murder and alternatively two counts of attempted second degree murder of the two surviving girls.

Before the shooting, the teenagers and Lyerla were traveling in the same direction. The vehicles passed each other a few times. At one point when Lyerla tried to pass the girls, their truck accelerated so that he could not overtake them. Lyerla decided to leave the interstate. When he exited, the Jensen pickup pulled to the side of the road near the entry ramp. Lyerla loaded his pistol, reentered the interstate and passed the Jensen pickup. When the girls attempted to pass him, he fired at the passenger side of their truck.

At his trial, Lyerla told the jury that the teenagers were harassing him to such an extent that he feared for his life and fired the shots to disable their pickup. The two girls gave a different rendition of the events leading up to the shooting, but the prosecutor conceded in closing argument that Tammy Jensen was "trying to play games" with Lyerla by not letting him pass. Both Lyerla's version and that of the girls had a number of discrepancies. We view these inconsistencies to have been resolved by the jury's verdicts.

ATTEMPTED SECOND DEGREE MURDER

Lyerla argues that it is a legal impossibility to attempt to commit murder in the second degree and his two convictions for this offense should be reversed. Lyerla did not object to the court's instructions on attempted second degree murder.[4] Ordinarily we will not consider questions on allegedly erroneous instructions unless the defendant made a timely objection to them.

Criminal offenses are created only by statute. SDCL 22-1-8. If attempted second degree murder is not a crime in South Dakota, then a defendant's failure to object cannot establish that crime. Jurisdictional defects are not waived by failure to object. . . . To attempt second degree murder one must intend to have a criminally reckless state of mind, i.e. perpetrating an imminently dangerous act while evincing a depraved mind, regardless of human life, but without a design to kill any particular person.

---

[4] In various instructions the trial court framed the elements of attempted second degree murder:
Instruction No. 15
The essential elements of murder in the second degree . . . are:

1. That the defendant at the time and place alleged in the Indictment inflicted an injury or injuries upon Tammy Jensen from which the said Tammy Jensen died.
2. That the defendant did so by perpetrating an act imminently dangerous to others and evincing a depraved mind, regardless of human life, although without any premeditated design to effect the death of any particular individual.
3. That the killing was not justifiable homicide or excusable homicide.

Instruction No. 20
The essential elements of the offense of attempting to commit crime as charged, each of which the state must prove beyond a reasonable doubt, are:

1. That the defendant has the *specific intent to commit the crime of* murder in the first degree as charged in counts III and V or *murder in the second degree* as charged in counts IV and VI; and
2. That at the time and place alleged in the Indictment he did a direct act in the execution of such specific intent and toward the execution of the crime; and
3. That he failed or was prevented or was intercepted in the perpetration of the crime.
4. That the conduct alleged in the Indictment as an attempt to commit a crime was without justification or without excusable cause.

Instruction No. 37
In the crimes of murder in the second degree and attempted murder in the second degree, *a criminal intent must exist at the time the act or acts are committed or attempted.*
To constitute criminal intent it is not necessary that one intends to violate the law. Where one intentionally does that which the law says is a crime, he is acting with criminal intent, even though he may not actually know that this conduct is unlawful. The intent with which an act is done is shown by the circumstances attending the act, the manner in which it is done, the means used, and the sound mind and discretion of the person committing the act. (Emphasis added.)

Whether there can be such a crime as attempted second degree murder has never been determined in South Dakota. Interpreting a similar statute the Minnesota Supreme Court ruled in *State v. Dahlstrom*:

> We do not conceive of any practical basis upon which the jury could have found defendant guilty of attempted murder in the third degree. Philosophically, it might be possible to attempt to perpetrate an act imminently dangerous to others and evincing a depraved mind regardless of human life within the meaning of the phrase as used in 609.195, defining murder in the third degree. . . . But we cannot conceive of a factual situation which could make such conduct attempted murder in the third degree where the actor did not intend the death of anyone and where no death occurred.

Unlike the *Dahlstrom* case, a death occurred here, but the jury obviously decided that Lyerla did not intend the death of the deceased since he was found guilty of the lesser count of second degree murder. Nor did he intend to kill the other two girls as the verdicts for attempted second degree murder confirm.

Other courts have likewise found attempted reckless homicide a logical impossibility. In *People v. Perez*, [a New York case] it was stated:

> However, murder in the second degree under PL 125.25 subdivision 2, involves no intent but instead requires a culpable mental state of recklessness. One may not intentionally attempt to cause the death of another by a reckless act.

The Colorado Supreme Court [in *People v. Hernandez*] held:

> An attempt to commit criminal negligent homicide thus requires proof that the defendant intended to perpetrate an unintended killing—a logical impossibility. The words "attempt" and "negligence" are at war with one another; they are internally inconsistent and cannot sensibly co-exist.

[Wisconsin courts have also] held under a statute similar to our own that the crime of attempted second degree murder does not exist. We agree with the reasoning of these courts. Stating the rule most succinctly:

> To commit murder, one need not intend to take life; but to be guilty of an attempt to murder, he must so intend. It is not sufficient that his act, had it proved fatal, would have been murder. [citing *Merritt v. Commonwealth*, a Virginia case].

. . . Defendant's convictions for attempted second degree murder are reversed. In all other respects, the judgment of the trial court is affirmed.

SABERS, J. dissenting.

I dissent from the majority opinion on "attempted second degree murder.". . . I agree that "to attempt second degree murder one must intend to have a criminally reckless state of mind, i.e. perpetrating an imminently dangerous act while evincing a depraved mind, regardless of human life, but without a design to kill any particular person." However, the majority also cites the Minnesota Supreme Court case of *State v. Dahlstrom*, in part as follows:

> "... But we cannot conceive of a factual situation which could make such conduct attempted murder in the third degree where the actor did not intend the death of anyone and where no death occurred."

That concept is not that difficult:

For example, knowing he is a bad shot, A attempts to shoot B's eyelashes off from fifty feet away

— if A misses and kills B, it constitutes second-degree murder under South
   Dakota law;
— if A misses and wounds B, it constitutes attempted second-degree murder
   under South Dakota law;
— if A misses all together, it may constitute attempted second-degree murder
   under South Dakota law.

I agree with the majority that the jury obviously decided that Lyerla did not
intend the death of the deceased since he was found guilty of the lesser count of
second-degree murder. Nor did he intend to kill the other two girls as the verdicts
for attempted second-degree murder confirm. However, had his acts resulted in
their deaths, either directly as in the case of Tammy Jensen, or indirectly, through a
resulting car accident, he would have been guilty of second-degree murder. Since
deaths did not result he was guilty of attempted second-degree murder under
South Dakota law.

SDCL 22-4-1 provides:

"Any person who attempts to commit a crime and in the attempt does any act
toward the commission of the crime, but fails or is prevented or intercepted in
the perpetration thereof, is punishable where no provision is made by law for the
punishment of such attempt[.]"

SDCL 22-16-7 provides:

"Homicide is murder in the second degree when perpetrated by any act imminently dangerous to others and evincing a depraved mind, regardless of human
life, although without any premeditated design to effect the death of any particular
individual."

This statute deals with "homicide" which is named "murder in the second
degree." Neither statute contains an element of specific intent. SDCL 22-16-7 simply
requires an act. The act required must be dangerous to others (or stupid) under
South Dakota law. If one attempts a "dangerous" or "stupid" act it is sufficient. The
only "intent" or "attempt" necessary is a voluntary as opposed to a non-volitional
or forced act. In this case, Lyerla clearly attempted the dangerous and stupid act of
pulling the trigger and shooting the gun at or near the people or the car in which
they were riding. This is sufficient for attempted second-degree murder under
South Dakota law. SDCL 22-16-7 and SDCL 22-4-1.

The cases from other jurisdictions cited by Lyerla have a common flaw. In each
case the attempt statute contains an element of specific intent while the standard
of culpability otherwise required for the commission of the underlying offense is
something less than specific intent. In this respect, Instruction No. 20 (as set forth
in footnote 4 of the majority opinion) was more favorable to Lyerla than the law
required in that paragraph 1 implies that specific intent might also be required for
second-degree murder.

The majority opinion cites *People v. Perez* and *People v. Hernandez* for the proposition that one cannot intentionally attempt to cause the death of another by a reckless
act and for the proposition that the perpetration of an unintended killing is a logical impossibility. Further, these cases are cited to support the proposition that the
words "attempt" and "negligence" are at war with one another; that they are internally inconsistent and cannot sensibly co-exist. These cases place emphasis on the

word "intentional" contrary to the South Dakota statute on attempt. As previously indicated, the "intent" or "attempt" required under the South Dakota statute is simply to voluntarily act as opposed to an involuntary or forced action. In other words, an attempt to pull the trigger and shoot the gun is enough. This type of "attempt" and the "dangerous" or "stupid" act are not at war with one another; they are internally consistent and can sensibly co-exist.

Much of the confusion in this matter results from the use of the word murder, which implies an intent to take life. What we are really dealing with under South Dakota law is homicide, named second-degree murder. To intentionally pull the trigger and shoot a gun in this dangerous manner was not homicide because neither Gropper girl died, but it was attempted homicide, also known as attempted second-degree murder. Accordingly, attempted second-degree murder is a crime in South Dakota, and Lyerla's convictions for attempted second-degree murder should be affirmed.

QUESTIONS

1. Justice Konenkamp notes that "[c]riminal offenses are created only by statute." Does he refer to the South Dakota attempt statute in his analysis? Does the language of that statute support his position?

2. Which position is better reasoned, the majority or the dissent? Do the purposes of punishment support the majority or the dissent?

3. What are the consequences in terms of the scope of attempt liability of adopting the dissent's position?

MONTANA v. HEMBD

197 Mont. 438 (1982)

SHEEHY, J. John Hembd was charged by information in the District Court of the Thirteenth Judicial District, Yellowstone County, with the crime of negligent arson under section 45-6-102(1)(a), MCA. A jury found him guilty of "attempted misdemeanor negligent arson" and he appeals.

In the early evening of February 13, 1981, Hembd, who had been sitting in the lobby of the Billings Sheraton Hotel for two hours, was asked to leave by the hotel's security guard. Hotel employees watched Hembd after he left. They soon observed him in front of a hotel fire exit, with his back to certain doors that lead into the building. As he started to walk away, the employees entered the area in which he had been standing and discovered a styrofoam donut wrapper burning on top of a heater next to the wall. After extinguishing the flame the two employees seized Hembd who was a short distance away. Hembd allegedly stated, "You didn't see anything. You can't prove anything. You guys are crazy." Hembd admitted at trial that he was drunk at the time of the incident but denied setting the fire.

Hembd was charged with the crime of arson pursuant to section 45-6-102(1)(a), MCA. The jury was instructed on four alternate forms of verdict: felony negligent arson, "attempted felony negligent arson," misdemeanor negligent arson, and "attempted misdemeanor negligent arson." Hembd was found guilty of "attempted misdemeanor negligent arson."

This appeal raises two issues: (1) Is "attempted misdemeanor (or felony) negligent arson" a crime?; and (2) If Hembd was convicted of a nonexistent crime, did the purported conviction impliedly acquit him of misdemeanor or felony negligent arson?

We find that attempted misdemeanor negligent arson and attempted felony negligent arson are nonexistent crimes. Furthermore, we find that the jury's verdict, notwithstanding the fact that it convicted Hembd of a nonexistent crime, constituted an implied acquittal of the crimes of misdemeanor negligent arson and felony negligent arson, and therefore Hembd may not be retried for these offenses.

Hembd contends that there is no such crime as "attempted misdemeanor negligent arson." The State concedes this point in the following passage quoted from its brief:

"Attempt is defined by section 45-5-103, MCA, as follows:

"'1) A person commits the offense of attempt when with the purpose to commit a specific offense, he does any act toward the commission of such offense.'

"The crime of misdemeanor negligent arson occurs when a person 'purposely or knowingly starts a fire or causes an explosion . . . and thereby negligently' places property in danger of destruction, section 45-6-102, MCA. It is in combining these definitions that the problem becomes clear. It is possible to purposely attempt to start a fire. The crime of negligent arson, however, requires purposely or knowingly starting a fire and negligently placing property in danger. To purposely attempt to be negligent is a contradiction in terms. The trial court ruled that attempt modifies only the act of 'purposely or knowingly starting a fire.' That ruling ignores the definition of attempt. Attempt requires 'purpose to commit a specific offense' and, standing by itself, purposely starting a fire is not a punishable offense. The second requirement, negligently placing property in danger, is necessary to complete the crime of negligent arson. It is impossible to show one purposely was negligent."

Attempted negligent arson, be it misdemeanor or felony, is a nonexistent crime.

The judgment is reversed and remanded with instructions to dismiss the action.

QUESTIONS

1. What are the elements of negligent arson under Montana law? Why do you think Hembd was not convicted of negligent arson? Lack of proof of a non-mental element? Lack of proof of a mental element? What mental state do you think Hembd had toward each of the non-mental elements of negligent arson?

2. Should Hembd have been convicted of attempt? Of some other crime? Was he blameworthy? Dangerous?

3. Is it ever possible to attempt a negligent crime? A reckless crime? Is it possible to attempt manslaughter? Negligent homicide? Reckless driving?

4. Is it possible to attempt felony murder?

Mental State Regarding a Circumstance

We have seen that purpose as to a required result is typically needed for an attempt conviction even if a lower mental state as to that result suffices for conviction of the target offense. So the law of attempt effectively raises lower mental states regarding results in a target offense to the level of purpose. Should mental states regarding circumstance elements be treated similarly? Imagine, for example, a statute that punished the sale of any illegal drug "within 1,000 feet of a school" and that strict liability attaches to the element of "within 1,000 feet of a school." What mental state toward this circumstance element should be required for an attempt to sell an illegal drug within 1,000 feet of a school?

Comment to Model Penal Code § 5.01

The general principle is ... that the actor must affirmatively desire to engage in the conduct or to cause the result that will constitute the principal offense. . . . The requirement of purpose extends to the conduct of the actor and to the results that his conduct causes, but his purpose need not encompass all of the circumstances included in the formal definition of the substantive offense. As to them, it is sufficient that he acts with the culpability that is required for commission of the completed crime.

Several illustrations may serve to clarify the point. Assume, for example, a statute that provides that sexual intercourse with a female under a prescribed age is an offense, and that a mistake as to age will not afford a defense no matter how reasonable its foundation. The policy of the substantive offense as to age, therefore, is one of strict liability, and if the actor has sexual intercourse with a female, he is guilty or not, depending upon her age and irrespective of his views as to her age. Suppose, however, that he is arrested before he engages in the proscribed conduct, and that the charge is an attempt to commit the offense. Should he then be entitled to rely on a mistake as to age as a defense? Or should the policy of the substantive crime on this issue carry over to the attempt as well? Or, assume a statute that makes it a federal offense to murder an FBI agent and treats the agent's status as a member of the FBI as a jurisdictional ingredient, with no culpability required in respect to that element. The question again is whether the policy of the substantive crime should control the same issue when it arises on a charge of attempt, or whether there is a special policy that the law of attempt should embrace to change the result on this point.

Under the formulation . . . [in the Model Penal Code], the proffered defense would not succeed in either case. In the statutory rape example, the actor must have a purpose to engage in sexual intercourse with a female in order to be charged with the attempt, and must engage in a substantial step in a course of conduct planned to culminate in his commission of that act. With respect to the age of the victim, however, it is sufficient if he acts "with the kind of culpability otherwise required for the commission of the crime," which in the case supposed is none at all. Since, therefore, mistake as to age is irrelevant with respect to the substantive offense, it is likewise irrelevant with respect to the attempt. The same result would obtain in the murder illustration. The actor must, in the case supposed, engage in a substantial step in a course of conduct planned to culminate in the death of his victim. But with respect to his awareness of the status of his victim as an FBI agent, a mistake would not be relevant since the policy of the substantive offense controls on such matters and that policy is one of strict liability.

The judgment is thus that if the defendant manifests a purpose to engage in the type of conduct or to cause the type of result that is forbidden by the criminal law, he has sufficiently exhibited his dangerousness to justify the imposition of criminal sanctions, so long as he otherwise acts with the kind of culpability that is sufficient for the completed offense. The objective is to select out those elements of the completed crime that, if the defendant desires to bring them about, indicate with clarity that he poses the type of danger to society that the substantive offense is designed to prevent.

This objective is well served by the Code's approach...of allowing the policy of the substantive offense to control with respect to circumstance elements.

QUESTION

Why does the MPC raise the mental state for attempt to purpose in regard to conduct and result, but not circumstance?

D. ABANDONMENT

PROBLEMS

10.5 Maria and Tim plan to rob Sam, who owns a camera shop. Maria visits Sam's store, pretending to be a customer, and locates the wire for a surveillance camera that monitors Sam's store. On her way out, she surreptitiously cuts the wire. Maria and Tim buy disguises and purchase a toy gun that looks real. Tim joins Maria at the coffee shop next door to the camera shop. In the coffee shop's restrooms, they both change into their disguises. Maria hides the toy gun in her handbag. Just as Maria and Tim exit the coffee shop, Tim notices a police officer enter Sam's shop. Maria and Tim decide it's too risky to try the robbery that afternoon. Each goes home. That evening Maria calls Tim and tells him that she's decided it's too dangerous to rob the shop and backs out of the robbery. Did Maria attempt a robbery under any of the provisions you encountered earlier in this chapter? If so, did Maria abandon the robbery? If so, will it extinguish Maria's attempt liability?

10.6 Assume the same facts as in Problem 10.5 above, except that as Maria and Tim leave the coffee shop, instead of observing a police officer, they see Tim's friend, Harry. Harry reminds Tim of Tim's dream to go to law school. Tim realizes that the robbery is a foolish idea and tells Maria that he will not commit the robbery. Did Tim attempt a robbery under any of the provisions you encountered earlier in this chapter? If so, did Tim abandon the robbery? If so, will it extinguish Tim's attempt liability?

PEOPLE v. STAPLES
6 Cal. App. 3d 61 (1970)

REPPY, J. Defendant was charged in an information with attempted burglary (Pen. Code, §§ 664, 459). Trial by jury was waived, and the matter submitted on the testimony contained in the transcript of the preliminary hearing together with exhibits. Defendant was found guilty. . . .

I. The Facts

In October 1967, while his wife was away on a trip, defendant, a mathematician, under an assumed name, rented an office on the second floor of a building in Hollywood which was over the mezzanine of a bank. Directly below the mezzanine was the vault of the bank. Defendant was aware of the layout of the building, specifically of the relation of the office he rented to the bank vault. Defendant paid rent for the period from October 23 to November 23. The landlord had 10 days before commencement of the rental period within which to finish some interior repairs and painting. During this prerental period defendant brought into the office certain equipment. This included drilling tools, two acetylene gas tanks, a blow torch, a blanket, and a linoleum rug. The landlord observed these items when he came in from time to time to see how the repair work was progressing. Defendant learned from a custodian that no one was in the building on Saturdays. On Saturday, October 14, defendant drilled two groups of holes into the floor of the office above the mezzanine room. He stopped drilling before the holes went through the floor. He came back to the office several times thinking he might slowly drill down, covering the holes with the linoleum rug.[1] At some point in time he installed a hasp lock on a closet, and planned to, or did, place his tools in it. However, he left the closet keys on the premises. Around the end of November, apparently after November 23, the landlord notified the police and turned the tools and equipment over to them. Defendant did not pay any more rent. It is not clear when he last entered the office, but it could have been after November 23, and even after the landlord had removed the equipment. On February 22, 1968, the police arrested defendant. After receiving advice as to his constitutional rights, defendant voluntarily made an oral statement which he reduced to writing.

Among other things which defendant wrote down were these:

> "Saturday, the 14th . . . I drilled some small holes in the floor of the room. Because of tiredness, fear, and the implications of what I was doing, I stopped and went to sleep.
>
> "At this point I think my motives began to change. The actual [sic] commencement of my plan made me begin to realize that even if I were to succeed a fugitive life of living off of stolen money would not give the enjoyment of the life of a mathematician however humble a job I might have.
>
> "I still had not given up my plan however. I felt I had made a certain investment of time, money, effort and a certain pschological [sic] commitment to the concept.
>
> "I came back several times thinking I might store the tools in the closet and slowly drill down (covering the hole with a rug of linoleum square. As time went on (after two weeks or so). My wife came back and my life as bank robber seemed more and more absurd."

II. Discussion of Defendant's Contentions

Defendant's position in this appeal is that, as a matter of law, there was insufficient evidence upon which to convict him of a criminal attempt under Penal Code section 664. Defendant claims that his actions were all preparatory in nature and never reached a stage of advancement in relation to the substantive crime which he concededly intended to commit (burglary of the bank vault) so that criminal responsibility might attach. . . .

---

[1] This is defendant's characterization of what occurred after his initial drilling session. (See partial text of confession, post.)

The required specific intent was clearly established in the instant case. Defendant admitted in his written confession that he rented the office fully intending to burglarize the bank, that he brought in tools and equipment to accomplish this purpose, and that he began drilling into the floor with the intent of making an entry into the bank.

The question of whether defendant's conduct went beyond "mere preparation" raises some provocative problems. The briefs and the oral argument of counsel in this case point up a degree of ambiguity and uncertainty that permeates the law of attempts in this state. Each side has cited us to a different so-called "test" to determine whether this defendant's conduct went beyond the preparatory stage. Predictably each respective test in the eyes of its proponents yielded an opposite result. . . .

None of the above statements of the law applicable to this category of attempts provide a litmus-like test, and perhaps no such test is achievable. Such precision is not required in this case, however. There was definitely substantial evidence entitling the trial judge to find that defendant's acts had gone beyond the preparation stage. . . .

The instant case provides an out-of-the-ordinary factual situation. . . . Here, there was no direct proof of any actual interception. But it was clearly inferable by the trial judge that defendant became aware that the landlord had resumed control over the office and had turned defendant's equipment and tools over to the police. This was the equivalent of interception.

The inference of this nonvoluntary character of defendant's abandonment was a proper one for the trial judge to draw. However, it would seem that the character of the abandonment in situations of this type, whether it be voluntary (prompted by pangs of conscience or a change of heart) or nonvoluntary (established by inference in the instant case), is not controlling. The relevant factor is the determination of whether the acts of the perpetrator have reached such a stage of advancement that they can be classified as an attempt. Once that attempt is found there can be no exculpatory abandonment. "One of the purposes of the criminal law is to protect society from those who intend to injure it. When it is established that the defendant intended to commit a specific crime and that in carrying out this intention he committed an act that caused harm[5] or sufficient danger of harm, it is immaterial that for some collateral reason he could not complete the intended crime."

The order is affirmed.

Model Penal Code § 5.01

(4) *Renunciation of Criminal Purpose.* When the actor's conduct would otherwise constitute an attempt under Subsection (1)(b) or (1)(c) of this Section, it is an affirmative defense that he abandoned his effort to commit the crime or otherwise prevented its commission, under circumstances manifesting a complete and voluntary renunciation of his criminal purpose. The establishment of such defense does not, however, affect the liability of an accomplice who did not join in such abandonment or prevention.

Within the meaning of this Article, renunciation of criminal purpose is not voluntary if it is motivated, in whole or in part, by circumstances, not present or apparent at

---

[5] In the instant case defendant's drilling was done without permission and did cause property damage.

the inception of the actor's course of conduct, that increase the probability of detection or apprehension or that make more difficult the accomplishment of the criminal purpose. Renunciation is not complete if it is motivated by a decision to postpone the criminal conduct until a more advantageous time or to transfer the criminal effort to another but similar objective or victim.

QUESTIONS

The *Staples* court states that "Once . . . attempt is found there can be no exculpatory abandonment." The Model Penal Code, by contrast, recognizes abandonment as a defense. Which is the better view? Why?

E. IMPOSSIBILITY

Should the fact that the target offense is "impossible" to commit exonerate? Commentators identify at least three variations of impossibility: (1) factual, (2) legal, and (3) inherent impossibility. Courts sometimes classify situations under legal impossibility that scholars explain would be better described as involving the principle of legality.[4] We consider below each variation of impossibility as well as the relationship of legality to impossibility.

1. Factual Impossibility

Factual impossibility occurs "when extraneous circumstances unknown to the actor or beyond the actor's control prevent consummation of the intended crime."[5] Simply put, factual impossibility is not a defense to attempt.

PROBLEM

10.7 Silvia has long coveted Dorothy's electronic organizer. Silvia observes Dorothy slip the organizer into her right-hand coat pocket before lunch. After lunch, Silvia maneuvers herself next to Dorothy's right side while Dorothy is absorbed watching a television trivia game. Silvia slips her hand into Dorothy's right-hand pocket, but the pocket is empty. Unbeknownst to Silvia, Dorothy's pocket has a hole in it and the organizer had fallen out during lunch. Is Silvia guilty of attempted theft?

---

4. Joshua Dressler, *Understanding Criminal Law* 400 (3d ed. 2001).
5. United States v. Berrigan, 482 F.2d 171, 188 (3d Cir. 1973).

2. Legal Impossibility

Of the categories of impossibility, legal impossibility may present the greatest conceptual challenge. Historically, legal impossibility provided a defense to attempt. A fundamental difficulty in legal impossibility stems from the failure of courts to distinguish between two different types of situations.[6]

The first situation that courts sometimes label "legal impossibility" occurs when a person commits or attempts to commit what s/he believes is a crime but in reality it does not qualify as a crime under the law[7] or "when the law does not proscribe the goal that the defendant sought to achieve."[8] Consider the following hypothetical:

Jenny grew up in a country where most of the population lacked enough to eat. It was a crime to keep animals that were not raised for consumption. No one, therefore, had cats or dogs as pets. Jenny's family recently immigrated to this country. She discovers a stray dog in her neighborhood and brings it home. She feeds and cares for it, and keeps it as a pet. Jenny mistakenly believes that the law here is the same as in her country of birth. She believes that she is violating the law.

Jenny has committed no crime. Some courts might term this a case of legal impossibility. The modern approach is to call the result in this case a function of the principle of legality. Legality prevents prosecution and conviction in these circumstances. Keeping pets was not a crime when Jenny befriended the stray dog.

The second type of situation that courts have treated under legal impossibility involves errors by the defendant regarding some legal aspect of the situation that makes completion of the crime impossible. As Professor Joshua Dressler explains, this type of impossibility "exists if the actor's goal is illegal, but commission of the offense is impossible due to a *factual* mistake (and not simply a misunderstanding of the law) regarding the legal status of some attendant circumstance that constitutes an element of the charged offense."[9] Consider the facts below from the *Jaffe* case,[10] one of the most famous cases cited on legal impossibility:

> Defendant having . . . repeatedly received goods stolen from a dry goods firm by one of its employees, suggested to the employee that a certain specified kind of cloth be taken, he was told by the employee that that particular kind of cloth was not kept on his floor, and he then said that he would take a roll of certain Italian cloth. The employee then stole a roll of the Italian cloth and carried it away, but left it in another store where he could subsequently get it for delivery to the defendant. Before it was actually delivered to the defendant the employers discovered that the employee had been stealing from them and they accused him of the thefts. The employee then confessed his guilt and told them of the piece of cloth that had been stolen for the defendant, but had not actually been delivered to him. The roll of cloth so stolen was then taken by another employee of the firm and it was arranged at the police headquarters that the employee who had taken the cloth should deliver it to the defendant, which he did, and the defendant paid the employee about one-half value thereof.

---

6. Dressler, *supra* note 4.

7. Berrigan, 482 F.2d at 186 (citing G. Williams, *Criminal Law, The General Part* 633 (2d ed. 1961) & J. Hall, *General Principles of Criminal Law* 586 (2d ed. 1960).

8. Dressler, *supra* note 4 (citing P. Robbins, *Attempting the Impossible: The Emerging Consensus*, 23 Harv. J. on Legis. 377, at 389).

9. Dressler, *supra* note 4, at 402.

10. People v. Jaffe, 185 N.Y. 497, 502 (1906) (facts from the dissenting opinion by J. Chase).

Under a traditional approach to legal impossibility, Jaffe's goal — to receive stolen property — was illegal, but the commission of the offense was impossible due to a factual mistake regarding the legal status of some attendant circumstance: Jaffe was mistaken that the property was stolen because, in fact, it had been returned to the owner (through the second employee) and was being used with the owner's permission in the "sting" and therefore had lost its legal quality of being stolen property. The New York Court of Appeals majority in *Jaffe* reversed Jaffe's conviction for attempt to receive stolen property.

The modern trend is to treat situations like Jaffe's as a form of factual impossibility and subject to the same rule — it is not a defense to an attempt prosecution. In the words of the National Commission on Reform of Criminal Laws: "Factual or legal impossibility of committing a crime is not a defense if the crime could have been committed had the attendant circumstances been as the actor believed them to be."[11] Under the modern approach, in the *Jaffe* case, because Jaffe believed he was receiving stolen property, Jaffe would have been guilty of receiving stolen property had the circumstances been as he believed them to be.

In reading the *Dlugash* case that follows, determine whether the New York court takes a modern or more traditional approach to impossibility:

PEOPLE *v.* DLUGASH
41 N.Y.2d 725 (1977)

JASON, J. The criminal law is of ancient origin, but criminal liability for attempt to commit a crime is comparatively recent. . . . The ultimate issue is whether an individual's intentions and actions, though failing to achieve a manifest and malevolent criminal purpose, constitute a danger to organized society of sufficient magnitude to warrant the imposition of criminal sanctions. . . . Phrased somewhat differently, the concern centers on whether an individual should be liable for an attempt to commit a crime when, unknown to him, it was impossible to successfully complete the crime attempted. For years, serious studies have been made on the subject in an effort to resolve the continuing controversy when, if at all, the impossibility of successfully completing the criminal act should preclude liability for even making the futile attempt. The 1967 revision of the Penal Law approached the impossibility defense to the inchoate crime of attempt in a novel fashion. The statute provides that, if a person engages in conduct which would otherwise constitute an attempt to commit a crime, "it is no defense to a prosecution for such attempt that the crime charged to have been attempted was, under the attendant circumstances, factually or legally impossible of commission, if such crime could have been committed had the attendant circumstances been as such person believed them to be." (Penal Law, § 110.10.) This appeal presents to us, for the first time, a case involving the application of the modern statute. We hold that, under the proof presented by the People at trial, defendant Melvin Dlugash may be held for attempted murder, though the target of the attempt may have already been slain, by the hand of another, when Dlugash made his felonious attempt.

On December 22, 1973, Michael Geller, 25 years old, was found shot to death in the bedroom of his Brooklyn apartment. The body, which had literally been riddled by bullets, was found lying face up on the floor. An autopsy revealed that the victim

---

11. Berrigan, 482 F.2d 171 at 186 (citing § 1001(1)).

had been shot in the face and head no less than seven times. Powder burns on the face indicated that the shots had been fired from within one foot of the victim. Four small caliber bullets were recovered from the victim's skull. The victim had also been critically wounded in the chest. One heavy caliber bullet passed through the left lung, penetrated the heart chamber, pierced the left ventricle of the heart upon entrance and again upon exit, and lodged in the victim's torso. A second bullet entered the left lung and passed through to the chest, but without reaching the heart area. Although the second bullet was damaged beyond identification, the bullet tracks indicated that these wounds were also inflicted by a bullet of heavy caliber. A tenth bullet, of unknown caliber, passed through the thumb of the victim's left hand. The autopsy report listed the cause of death as "[multiple] bullet wounds of head and chest with brain injury and massive bilateral hemothorax with penetration of [the] heart." Subsequent ballistics examination established that the four bullets recovered from the victim's head were .25 caliber bullets and that the heart-piercing bullet was of .38 caliber. . . .

Defendant stated that, on the night of December 21, 1973, he, [Joe] Bush and Geller had been out drinking. Bush had been staying at Geller's apartment and, during the course of the evening, Geller several times demanded that Bush pay $100 towards the rent on the apartment. According to defendant, Bush rejected these demands, telling Geller that "you better shut up or you're going to get a bullet." All three returned to Geller's apartment at approximately midnight, took seats in the bedroom, and continued to drink until sometime between 3:00 and 3:30 in the morning. When Geller again pressed his demand for rent money, Bush drew his .38 caliber pistol, aimed it at Geller and fired three times. Geller fell to the floor. After the passage of a few minutes, perhaps two, perhaps as much as five, defendant walked over to the fallen Geller, drew his .25 caliber pistol, and fired approximately five shots in the victim's head and face. Defendant contended that, by the time he fired the shots, "it looked like Mike Geller was already dead." After the shots were fired, defendant and Bush walked to the apartment of a female acquaintance. Bush removed his shirt, wrapped the two guns and a knife in it, and left the apartment, telling Dlugash that he intended to dispose of the weapons. Bush returned 10 or 15 minutes later and stated that he had thrown the weapons down a sewer two or three blocks away.

For proof of defendant's culpability, the prosecution relied upon defendant's own admissions as related by the detective and the prosecutor. From the physicians, the prosecution sought to establish that Geller was still alive at the time defendant shot at him. Both physicians testified that each of the two chest wounds, for which defendant alleged Bush to be responsible, would have caused death without prompt medical attention. However, the victim would have remained alive until such time as his chest cavity became fully filled with blood. Depending on the circumstances, it might take 5 to 10 minutes for the chest cavity to fill. Neither prosecution witness could state, with medical certainty, that the victim was still alive when, perhaps five minutes after the initial chest wounds were inflicted, the defendant fired at the victim's head.

The defense produced but a single witness, the former Chief Medical Examiner of New York City. This expert stated that, in his view, Geller might have died of the chest wounds "very rapidly" since, in addition to the bleeding, a large bullet going through a lung and the heart would have other adverse medical effects. "Those wounds can be almost immediately or rapidly fatal or they may be delayed in there, in the time it would take for death to occur. But I would say that wounds like that which are described here as having gone through the lungs and the heart would be fatal wounds and in most cases they're rapidly fatal.". . .

The jury found the defendant guilty of murder. The defendant then moved to set the verdict aside. He submitted an affidavit in which he contended that he "was absolutely, unequivocally and positively certain that Michael Geller was dead before [he] shot him." Further, the defendant averred that he was in fear for his life when he shot Geller. "This fear stemmed from the fact that Joseph Bush, the admitted killer of Geller, was holding a gun on me and telling me, in no uncertain terms, that if I didn't shoot the dead body I, too, would be killed." This motion was denied.[1]

On appeal, the Appellate Division reversed the judgment of conviction on the law and dismissed the indictment. . . .

Preliminarily, we state our agreement with the Appellate Division that the evidence did not establish, beyond a reasonable doubt, that Geller was alive at the time defendant fired into his body. To sustain a homicide conviction, it must be established, beyond a reasonable doubt, that the defendant caused the death of another person. The People were required to establish that the shots fired by defendant Dlugash were a sufficiently direct cause of Geller's death. While the defendant admitted firing five shots at the victim approximately two to five minutes after Bush had fired three times, all three medical expert witnesses testified that they could not, with any degree of medical certainty, state whether the victim had been alive at the time the latter shots were fired by the defendant. Thus, the People failed to prove beyond a reasonable doubt that the victim had been alive at the time he was shot by the defendant. Whatever else it may be, it is not murder to shoot a dead body. Man dies but once. . . .

[W]e must now decide whether, under the evidence presented, the defendant may be held for attempted murder, though someone else perhaps succeeded in killing the victim.

The concept that there could be criminal liability for an attempt, even if ultimately unsuccessful, to commit a crime is comparatively recent. The modern concept of attempt has been said to date from *Rex v Scofield* (Cald 397), decided in 1784. . . . The Revised Penal Law now provides that a person is guilty of an attempt to commit a crime when, with intent to commit a crime, he engages in conduct which tends to effect the commission of such crime. The most intriguing attempt cases are those where the attempt to commit a crime was unsuccessful due to mistakes of fact or law on the part of the would-be criminal. A general rule developed in most American jurisdictions that legal impossibility is a good defense but factual impossibility is not. Thus, for example, it was held that defendants who shot at a stuffed deer did not attempt to take a deer out of season, even though they believed the dummy to be a live animal. The court stated that there was no criminal attempt because it was no crime to "take" a stuffed deer, and it is no crime to attempt to do that which is legal. On the other hand, factual impossibility was no defense. For example, a man was held liable for attempted murder when he shot into the room in which his target usually slept and, fortuitously, the target was sleeping elsewhere in the house that night. Although one bullet struck the target's customary pillow, attainment of the criminal objective was factually impossible. . . .

---

[1] It should be noted that Joe Bush pleaded guilty to a charge of manslaughter in the first degree. . . .

As can be seen from even this abbreviated discussion, the distinction between "factual" and "legal" impossibility was a nice one indeed and the courts tended to place a greater value on legal form than on any substantive danger the defendant's actions posed for society. The approach of the draftsmen of the Model Penal Code was to eliminate the defense of impossibility in virtually all situations. Under the code provision, to constitute an attempt, it is still necessary that the result intended or desired by the actor constitute a crime. However, the code suggested a fundamental change to shift the locus of analysis to the actor's mental frame of reference and away from undue dependence upon external considerations. The basic premise of the code provision is that what was in the actor's own mind should be the standard for determining his dangerousness to society and, hence, his liability for attempted criminal conduct. In the belief that neither of the two branches of the traditional impossibility arguments detracts from the offender's moral culpability, the Legislature substantially carried the code's treatment of impossibility into the 1967 revision of the Penal Law. Thus, a person is guilty of an attempt when, with intent to commit a crime, he engages in conduct which tends to effect the commission of such crime. (Penal Law, § 110.00.) It is no defense that, under the attendant circumstances, the crime was factually or legally impossible of commission, "if such crime could have been committed had the attendant circumstances been as such person believed them to be." (Penal Law, § 110.10.) Thus, if defendant believed the victim to be alive at the time of the shooting, it is no defense to the charge of attempted murder that the victim may have been dead.

Turning to the facts of the case before us, we believe that there is sufficient evidence in the record from which the jury could conclude that the defendant believed Geller to be alive at the time defendant fired shots into Geller's head. Defendant admitted firing five shots at a most vital part of the victim's anatomy from virtually point blank range. Although defendant contended that the victim had already been grievously wounded by another, from the defendant's admitted actions, the jury could conclude that the defendant's purpose and intention was to administer the coup de grace. . . . Indeed, not only did defendant not come forward with his story immediately, but when the police arrived at his house, he related a false version designed to conceal his and Bush's complicity in the murder. All of these facts indicate a consciousness of guilt which defendant would not have had if he had truly believed that Geller was dead when he shot him. . . . In this case, there is ample other evidence to contradict the defendant's assertion that he believed Geller dead. There were five bullet wounds inflicted with stunning accuracy in a vital part of the victim's anatomy. The medical testimony indicated that Geller may have been alive at the time defendant fired at him. The defendant voluntarily left the jurisdiction immediately after the crime with his coperpetrator. Defendant did not report the crime to the police when left on his own by Bush. Instead, he attempted to conceal his and Bush's involvement with the homicide. In addition, the other portions of defendant's admissions make his contended belief that Geller was dead extremely improbable. Defendant, without a word of instruction from Bush, voluntarily got up from his seat after the passage of just a few minutes and fired five times point blank into the victim's face, snuffing out any remaining chance of life that Geller possessed. Certainly, this alone indicates a callous indifference to the taking of a human life. His admissions are barren of any claim of duress and reflect, instead, an unstinting cooperation in efforts to dispose of vital incriminating evidence. Indeed, defendant maintained a false version of the occurrence until such time as the police informed him that they had evidence that he lately possessed a gun of the same caliber as one of the weapons involved in the shooting. From all of this, the jury was certainly warranted in concluding that the defendant acted in the belief that Geller was yet alive when shot by defendant.

The jury convicted the defendant of murder. Necessarily, they found that defendant intended to kill a live human being. Subsumed within this finding is the conclusion that defendant acted in the belief that Geller was alive. Thus, there is no need for additional fact findings by a jury. Although it was not established beyond a reasonable doubt that Geller was, in fact, alive, such is no defense to attempted murder since a murder would have been committed "had the attendant circumstances been as [defendant] believed them to be." (Penal Law, § 110.10.) The jury necessarily found that defendant believed Geller to be alive when defendant shot at him. . . .

3. Inherent Impossibility

A third category of impossibility involves cases in which the means chosen by the actor are manifestly unlikely to achieve the ends sought.[12] Consider the following hypothetical:

Maggie believes that United States trade with Country Z is contributing to the deplorable labor conditions in Country Z. She convinces herself that she must end the trade between the United States and Country Z. Maggie learns that the chairperson of the board of the corporation that promotes the deplorable labor practices in Country Z will be arriving on a flight today. She decides she must take drastic action and kill the chairperson. To effectuate her plan, Maggie travels to the airport and positions herself on the frontage road next to the landing strip awaiting the arrival of the plane from Country Z carrying the chairperson. At the closest point, the plane will be 200 feet from Maggie during its landing. When the plane descends, Maggie takes out her five-inch sling shot, made from two small sticks, and shoots rubberbands as fast and as hard as she can at the plane. Maggie believes that if a rubberband makes contact with the plane, it will cause the plane to lose momentum and fall from the sky and crash. The plane lands safely. Should Maggie be liable for attempted murder?

Cases involving "inherent impossibility" rarely reach the stage of an appellate opinion.[13] Consequently, "it is difficult to generalize about the existing state of the law concerning inherent impossibility."[14] At least one state, Minnesota, recognizes inherent impossibility in its body of statutes as grounds for exoneration, as follows:[15]

Minnesota Statute Annotated § 609.17 (2003)

Subdivision 1. Whoever, with intent to commit a crime, does an act which is a substantial step toward, and more than preparation for, the commission of the crime is guilty of an attempt to commit that crime. . . .

---

12. Joshua Dressler, *Understanding Criminal Law* 399 (3d ed. 2001).
13. Wayne LaFave, *Criminal Law* 603-605 (4th ed. 2003).
14. *Id.* at 604.
15. Minn. Stat. Ann. § 609.17(2). Cited in Joshua Dressler, *Understanding Criminal Law* 399 (3d ed. 2001).

Subd. 2. An act may be an attempt notwithstanding the circumstances under which it was performed or the means employed to commit the crime or the act itself were such that the commission of the crime was not possible, unless such impossibility would have been clearly evident to a person of normal understanding.

Apply the Minnesota Statute above to the following problem:

PROBLEM[16]

10.8 Officer Dennis responded to a possible suicide. When he entered the apartment, the defendant, Haines,

> was lying face down in a pool of blood. Dennis attempted to revive Haines and noticed that Haines' wrists were slashed and bleeding. When Haines heard the paramedics arriving, he stood up, ran toward Dennis, and screamed that he should be left to die because he had AIDS. Dennis told Haines they were there to help him, but he continued yelling and stated he wanted to... "give it to him." Haines told Dennis that he would "use his wounds" and began jerking his arms at Dennis, causing blood to spray into Dennis' mouth and eyes. .... Haines repeatedly yelled that he had AIDS, that he could not deal with it and that he was going to make Dennis deal with it. Haines also struggled with emergency medical technicians... threatening to infect them with AIDS and began spitting at them. When Dennis grabbed Haines, Haines scratched, bit, and spit at him. At one point, Haines grabbed a blood-soaked wig and struck Dennis in the face with it. This caused blood again to splatter onto Dennis' eyes, mouth, and skin. When Dennis finally handcuffed Haines, Dennis was covered with blood. He also had scrapes and scratches on his arms and a cut on his finger that was bleeding.

In the *Haines* case, the defendant was charged with the attempted murder of Officer Dennis under the Indiana attempt statute, which reads as follows:

Indiana Code Annotated § 35-41-5-1

(a) A person attempts to commit a crime when, acting with the culpability required for commission of the crime, he engages in conduct that constitutes a substantial step toward the commission of the crime.

(b) It is no defense, that, because of a misapprehension of the circumstances, it would have been impossible for the accused person to commit the crime charged.

How would your analysis under the Indiana statute differ from your analysis under the Minnesota statute?

---

16. Quotation from and Problem based on State v. Haines, 545 N.E.2d 834 (Ind. Ct. App. 1989), cited in Dressler, *supra* note 12 at 399 n. 143.

QUESTIONS

1. Why might appellate opinions in inherent impossibility cases be rare?
2. Should courts recognize inherent impossibility as a means of exoneration?

4. The Model Penal Code Approach to Impossibility

As the *Dlugash* case suggests, the Model Penal Code represents the modern approach to impossibility.

Model Penal Code § 5.01 *Criminal Attempt*

(1) *Definition of Attempt.* A person is guilty of an attempt to commit a crime if, acting with the kind of culpability otherwise required for commission of the crime, he:

(a) purposely engages in conduct that would constitute the crime if the attendant circumstances were as he believes them to be. . . .

The Model Penal Code drafters explained the approach as follows:

"Subsection (1) is also designed to reject the defense of impossibility, which has sometimes been successful in attempt prosecutions. It does so . . . by providing that the defendant's conduct should be measured according to the circumstances as he believes them to be, rather than the circumstances as they may have existed in fact."[17]

How would the MPC treat each of the examples in the impossibility Section of this chapter?

To accommodate situations like Maggie's, above, the Code provides in § 5.05(2):

If the particular conduct charged to constitute a criminal attempt, solicitation or conspiracy is so inherently unlikely to result or culminate in the commission of a crime that neither such conduct nor the actor presents a public danger warranting the grading of such offense under this Section, the Court shall exercise its power . . . to enter judgment and impose sentence for a crime of lower grade or degree or, in extreme cases, may dismiss the prosecution.

5. Synthesis and Review Problem on Impossibility

PROBLEM[18]

10.9 Deputy William Liczbinski conducted an undercover investigation of Internet crimes. As instructed, he logged onto a "chat room" with the name "Bekka." The defendant, Chris Thousand, a 23-year-old male, contacted Bekka. Bekka represented herself as a 14-year-old

---

17. Model Penal Code Commentaries, Part 1, at 307.
18. Quotations from and based on People v. Thousand, 465 Mich. 149 (2001).

female. The defendant sent Bekka an Internet photograph of his face. During their chats, the defendant

> made repeated lewd invitations to Bekka to engage in various sexual acts, despite various indications of her young age.
>
> During one of his online conversations with Bekka, after asking her whether anyone was "around there," watching her, defendant indicated that he was sending her a picture of himself. Within seconds, Liczbinski received over the Internet a photograph of male genitalia. Defendant [then] . . . described in a graphic manner the type of sexual acts he wished to perform with her. Defendant invited Bekka to come see him at his house for the purpose of engaging in sexual activity. Bekka replied that she wanted to do so, and defendant cautioned her that they had to be careful, because he could "go to jail." Defendant asked whether Bekka looked "over sixteen," so that if his roommates were home he could lie.

The defendant and Bekka arranged to meet at a restaurant. Defendant arrived at the restaurant in the clothes and car that he had described to Bekka. In his car, he had brought white teddy bears that Bekka had requested as a present from the defendant.

The defendant was arrested and charged, inter alia, with "attempted distribution of obscene material to a minor." The defense contended that because "the existence of a child victim was an element," the evidence was insufficient to support the charge; that is, it was legally impossible for the defendant to have committed the offense. How should the court have ruled?

F. SOLICITATION

Solicitation is an anticipatory crime. Historically, it required an effort by one person to persuade another person to commit a felony. In modern times, solicitation may also embrace misdemeanors as possible target crimes. Some of the most notorious examples of solicitation involve individuals who hire or persuade others to commit murder.

A successful solicitor will also usually qualify as an accomplice. Punishment is then available under accomplice liability theories. The challenging cases involve the unsuccessful solicitor.[19] This situation occurs, for example, when the solicitee declines the solicitor's invitation, and the target offense is neither attempted nor consummated. Under these circumstances, there is no attempt, no conspiracy, and no target offense. Without solicitation, the solicitor's conduct would generally be beyond the reach of the law. Although solicitation has unique features, many of the arguments supporting and opposing its inclusion in criminal codes are the same as those for and against other anticipatory offenses.

In this Section, we turn first to the conduct element of solicitation and then to the two mental states of the crime of solicitation. Following our study of the basic

19. Working Papers from the National Commission on the Reform of Criminal Law, Vol. 1, pp. 368-369 (1970).

elements of the offense, we consider the defense of renunciation. We then analyze the nuanced problem of the innocent agent, which involves soliciting a person who may lack the mental state required to commit the target crime. Finally, we offer a brief but challenging synthesis Problem.

1. Conduct

PROBLEMS

10.10 Stan knows that Leila has long held a grudge against Raymond. Stan hates Raymond but has kept his hatred a secret. One day, Stan notices that Raymond has left his heart medication in the coffee room of the offices where all three work. Raymond has made quite clear that he must take his heart medication three times a day or he will die. Stan casually mentions his observation to Leila, hoping secretly that she will hide the medication. Leila runs off to the break room and hides Raymond's medication. Raymond dies from a heart attack caused by the failure to consume his heart medication. Is Stan liable for solicitation under the statutes that follow?

10.11 Allie decides to rob the corner liquor store. Because she knows that the proprietor has a gun under the cashier's counter, she asks Ben to help her with the robbery. She tells Ben to stand as a lookout outside the store in case Allie has to use force to subdue the proprietor. Is Allie liable for solicitation under the statutes below?

10.12 Steve is disgruntled with his neighbor, Kay, and asks Leo to burn her house. Leo spurns Steve's request. Is Steve guilty of solicitation?[20]

10.13 While in jail awaiting trial on charges of molesting his stepdaughter, the defendant, James Cotton, discussed with other inmates "his desire to persuade his stepdaughter not to testify against him. . . . [Subsequently], defendant addressed a letter . . . to his wife [requesting] . . . that she assist him in defending against the pending charges by persuading his stepdaughter not to testify at his trial. . . . [The defendant] also urged his wife to influence [the stepdaughter to leave the state] or give her money to leave the state so that she would be unavailable to testify. After writing this letter, he gave it to [his cellmate] and asked him to obtain a stamp for it so that it could [be] mailed later. Unknown to defendant, [the cellmate] removed the letter from the envelope, replaced it with a blank sheet of paper, and returned the sealed envelope to him. [The cellmate] gave the original letter written by defendant to law enforcement authorities, and it is undisputed that defendant's original letter . . . was never in fact mailed nor received by defendant's wife."

Defendant composed a second letter superseding his prior letter. This letter indicated that defendant "[w]as arranging to be released

---

20. Adapted from State v. Hampton, 186 S.E. 251 (1936).

on bond" and that "his wife should try to talk the stepdaughter out of testifying or talk her into testifying favorably for defendant. Defendant also said in the letter that his wife should 'warn' his stepdaughter that if she did testify for the state 'it won't be nice...and she'll make...[the] news,' and that, if the stepdaughter was not available to testify, the prosecutor would have to drop the charges against defendant." The second letter was in the defendant's possession at the time he was rearrested, some 24 hours after his release on bail. This second letter also was never mailed. Did the defendant criminally solicit another "to engage in conduct constituting a felony — to-wit: Bribery or Intimidation of a Witness"?[21]

Official Code of Georgia § 16-4-7   *Criminal Solicitation*

(a) A person commits the offense of criminal solicitation when, with intent that another person engage in conduct constituting a felony, he solicits, requests, commands, importunes, or otherwise attempts to cause the other person to engage in such conduct.

Oregon Revised Statutes § 161.435

(1) A person commits the crime of solicitation if with the intent of causing another to engage in specific conduct constituting a crime punishable as a felony or as a Class A misdemeanor or an attempt to commit such felony or Class A misdemeanor the person commands or solicits such other person to engage in that conduct.

Virginia Code Annotated § 18.2-29

Any person who commands, entreats, or otherwise attempts to persuade another person to commit a felony other than murder, shall be guilty of a...felony. . . .

Wyoming Statutes Annotated § 6-1-302

(a) A person is guilty of solicitation to commit a felony if, with intent that a felony be committed, he commands, encourages or facilitates the commission of that crime under circumstances strongly corroborative of the intention that the crime be committed but the solicited crime is not attempted or committed.

Kansas Statutes Annotated Criminal Solicitation § 21-3303

(a) Criminal solicitation is commanding, encouraging or requesting another person to commit a felony, attempt to commit a felony or aid and abet in the commission or attempted commission of a felony for the purpose of promoting or facilitating the felony.

(b) It is immaterial under subsection (a) that the actor fails to communicate with the person solicited to commit a felony if the person's conduct was designed to effect a communication.

---

21. Based on and quotations from State v. Cotton, 790 P.2d 1050 (1990).

PROBLEM

10.14 List the conduct elements of each of the statutes above. Compare the conduct required for solicitation with the conduct required for attempt. Which allows earlier intervention by police? Which theories of punishment support early intervention? Which support delaying intervention?

Consider the comments on solicitation in the Working Papers of the National Commission on the Reform of Federal Law:

> [T]he purposes of providing punishment of solicitation and attempt are similar: permitting law enforcement intervention, dealing with persons who have indicated their dangerousness, and avoiding inequality of treatment when some fortuity has prevented the intended criminal result. . . . [I]t may be said that the requirement of action by an independent third party raises the possibility that he will be deterred by the penalty prescribed for the commission of the offense. Moreover, despite the earnestness of the solicitation, the actor is merely engaging in talk which may never be taken seriously. The remoteness from completion of the offense is therefore different from that for an attempt.[22]

What issues involving conduct do Problems 10.10 through 10.13 above raise? Consider also the risks discussed below regarding the crime of solicitation:

> [E]ven for persons trained in the art of speech, words do not always perfectly express what is in a man's mind. Thus in cold print or even through misplaced emphasis, a rhetorical question may appear to be a solicitation. The erroneous omission of a word could turn an innocent statement into a criminal one (for example, "You shoot the [Emperor] *versus* "Should you shoot the [Emperor]?"[23]

How should these risks be addressed by legislators?

Consider the following case on the conduct element required for solicitation.

PEOPLE *v.* QUENTIN

District Court of New York, 58 Misc. 2d 601; 296 N.Y.S.2d 443; 1968 N.Y. Misc. (1968)

OPINION: The defendants, Robert Quentin and John Garcia, have been charged . . . [with] criminal solicitation in the third degree in violation of section 100.00 of the Penal Law. The defendants move for leave to withdraw their not guilty pleas and interpose a demurrer to the information on the ground that it does not state facts sufficient to constitute a crime.

The brochure in question . . . is worthy of note. The inside front cover concisely describes the philosophy of the defendants. In part it reads:

---

22. Working Papers, *supra* note 19, at 370.
23. *Id.* at 372 (the example is a modified version of the one provided in the Working Papers).

"America is carnivorous. She eats the world for dessert. Behind slick pictures of pretty-suburban-middle-church-going-family lie hamburgers seasoned with napalm, race crimes too brutal to recall, cultures plundered, and triviality elevated into a way of life. . . . The rich are rich because they are thieves and the poor because they are victims, and the future will condemn those who accept the present as reality. Break down the family, church, nation, city, economy. . . . Subversiveness saves us . . . our professors are spies; let us close the schools and flow into the streets. . . . Grow hair long and become too freaky to fit into the machine culture. What's needed is a generation of people who are freaky, crazy, irrational, sexy, angry, irreligious, childish and mad: people who burn draft cards, burn high school and college degrees: people who say: 'To hell with your goals.'; people who lure the youth with music, pot and acid: people who re-define reality, who re-define the normal; . . . . Burn their house down, and you will be free."

This is followed by a paragraph entitled "How to make a fire bomb," and a recipe for Tryptamine, a psychedelic agent. The recipe ends with the statements: "This last (Tetrahydrofurane) is a very powerful reducing agent; wear safety glasses, add very cautiously, and perform this step with ventilation, away from flames (H_2 is evolved). The yield is about 40 grams of DMT, in tetrahydrofurane solution. This cannot be drunk or injected, but may be smoked by sprinkling on mint or cannabis leaves and letting the solution evaporate. It's evaporated when it starts smelling like DMT instead of tetrahydrofurane.". . .

Count three . . . alleges . . . criminal solicitation in the third degree. It charges that the defendants violated the section in that they attempted to cause persons to whom a brochure was distributed to possess a chemical compound known as DET and DMT which violates section 229 (429) of the Mental Hygiene Law. The brochure on one of its pages gives a formula for making a fire bomb. Below that is also a formula for making both DET and DMT. On the page with the formula is no other solicitation, request or advocacy concerning the drugs. The formula taken alone appears to be such as would be found in a chemistry book or encyclopedia. It is clear that section 100.00 was intended to cover a situation where a particular person importunes another specified individual to do a specific act which constitutes a crime. The purpose was to hold the solicitor criminally responsible even if the one solicited fails to commit the act. It does not appear that section 100.00 was designed to cover a situation where the defendant makes a general solicitation (however reprehensible) to a large indefinable group to commit a crime.

The defendants' motion is granted and all counts of the information are dismissed with leave to the District Attorney to file a new information.

QUESTIONS

1. Had the court ruled that the brochure constituted a solicitation, what implications would that have had?

2. If it is a crime to solicit one person to commit a crime, why isn't it a crime simultaneously to solicit hundreds of people to commit a crime?

In the crime of solicitation, speech is often the only form of conduct. Consequently, it sometimes raises First Amendment free speech issues. The *Davis* case that follows provides an example.

STATE *v.* DAVIS
Supreme Court of Georgia 272 S.E.2d, 721 (1980)

BOWLES, J. . . . Defendant was charged with the offense of criminal solicitation in that he did "solicit, and request M. I. Lawson to engage in conduct constituting a felony, to wit: violation of the Georgia Controlled Substances Act, in that the accused did solicit, and request the said M. I. Lawson to sell marijuana.". . .

Defendant Davis was indicted for criminal solicitation under Code Ann. § 26-1007. Upon motion of the defendant, the trial court dismissed the indictment finding the statute unconstitutionally vague in its description of prohibited activity and unconstitutionally overbroad in that it embraced speech protected under the First Amendment as well as speech which may properly be punished.

Code Ann. § 26-1007 states, in pertinent part: "A person commits criminal solicitation when, with intent that another person engage in conduct constituting a felony he solicits, requests, commands, importunes or otherwise attempts to cause such other person to engage in such conduct." This is the first time this court has been called upon to interpret this statute since its enactment in 1978. We are dealing here with the allegation of facial unconstitutionality.

1. We begin with the proposition that a solemn act of the legislature is presumed to be constitutional. It is the duty of our legislators to support the Constitution of the United States just as it is our duty. In enacting this statute, we can presume that the legislature intended to enact a constitutional law and not one which violates the proscriptions of the First Amendment. "[A]ll statutes are presumed to be enacted by the legislature with full knowledge of the existing condition of the law and with reference to it; . . . they are to be construed in connection and in harmony with the existing law; and . . . their meaning and effect will be determined in connection, not only with the common law and the Constitution, but also with reference to other statutes and the decisions of the courts." *Buice v. Dixon*, [223 Ga. 645 (1967)] at 647.

All speech is not ultimately protected under the First Amendment. . . . However, even speech which advocates law violation is protected "except where such advocacy is directed to inciting or producing imminent lawless action and is likely to incite or produce such action." *Brandenburg v. Ohio*, 395 U.S. 444, 447 (89 SC 1827, 23 LE2d 430) (1969). The test is generally known as the "clear and present danger" test. "The question in every case is whether the words used are used in such circumstances and of such a nature as to create a clear and present danger that they will bring about the substantive evils that Congress has a right to prevent." *Schenck v. United States*, 249 U.S. 47, 52 (39 SC 247, 63 LE 470) (1919).

It is clear that the commission of a felony is a substantive evil which our legislature has a right to prevent. We construe Code Ann. § 26-1007 as prohibiting only such language as creates a clear and present danger of a felony being committed and is therefore not overbroad as encompassing protected speech.

2. The only language in Code Ann. § 26-1007 which could conceivably be described as vague is that language which states; "or otherwise attempts to cause such other person to engage in such conduct." The words "solicits, requests, commands" and "importunes" are all clearly understandable so that any person seeking to avoid violation of the law could do so.

"To withstand constitutional attack, a statute or ordinance which prohibits speech 'must be carefully drawn or be authoritatively construed to punish only unprotected speech and not be susceptible of application to protected expression.' *Gooding v. Wilson*, 405 U.S. 518, 522 (92 SC 1103, 31 LE2d 408) (1972)." *City of Macon v. Smith*, [244 Ga. 157 (1979)] at 158. Absent a narrowing construction, this relatively broad language ("or otherwise attempts to cause") might be susceptible of constitutional attack. However, we construe this language in conformity with the First Amendment and thereby give it a narrowing construction. Under the rule of "ejusdem generis" we will not construe these questionable words in their broadest sense but will limit them by the words immediately preceding them. In other words, only a relatively overt statement or request intended to bring about action on the part of another person will bring a defendant within the statute. Furthermore, in light of our holding in division one that the statute only embraces language which creates a clear and present danger that a felony will be committed, the phrase "or otherwise attempts to cause such other person to engage in such conduct" is construed as meaning "or otherwise creates a clear and present danger of such other person perpetrating a felony."

3. The word "felony" is not unconstitutionally vague. Our criminal code defines which crimes are felonies and which are not. Code Ann. § 26-401 (e). If a police officer overhears a solicitation for another to steal a television, absent further knowledge on his part, he has probable cause to arrest the solicitor. The fact that the television is worth less than $ 200 and therefore its theft would constitute a misdemeanor is a question of fact.

4. We have held only that the statute in question is not unconstitutional on its face. We have not decided whether or not it is unconstitutional as applied to defendant Davis. Whether or not Mr. Davis' statement or question constituted protected speech or did not create a clear and present danger of a felony being committed remains for determination by the trial court.

Judgment reversed.

QUESTIONS

1. Should the trial court on remand find the speech involved in *Davis* constitutionally protected and exempt from prosecution?

2. If the Supreme Court had ruled that the state had violated the First Amendment, what implications would that have had for solicitation as a crime?

2. Mental State

PROBLEMS

10.15 Sarah's family just moved to a new state. She is 18 and in her senior year of high school. Over the two weeks since her arrival, she has learned that all the "cool" girls belong to a group called the "thievers." Initiation requires that you persuade a younger student to steal from a teacher's wallet or purse. Sarah is desperate to join the group but reluctant to get into trouble. Finally, Sarah approaches an eleventh-grade student, Rhonda, who has secret hopes of joining the "thievers" next year. Sarah says: "Hey, Rhonda, can you get me a quarter out of Teacher Stodge's purse?" Sarah is hoping that Rhonda will get cold feet and produce a quarter from some legitimate source and claim it's from Teacher Stodge's purse. Is Sarah liable for criminal solicitation under the statutes that follow? Assume that petty theft is a possible target offense under these solicitation statutes.

10.16 Danny, Sarah's twin brother, has learned that to be part of the popular boys' clique, you must engage in "sideshows." The kids explain that this means driving wildly and recklessly on public streets at odd hours of the morning. Danny cannot believe kids would do something so foolish. He arrives at the prescribed location at 3:00 a.m. to see if these boys are serious. Hilton and Rodney, also potential new recruits, arrive shortly thereafter. Jeff, the leader of the boys' clique, arrives and briefly demonstrates a "sideshow." Danny, still refusing to believe that people would act so foolishly, sarcastically says: "Hilton and Rodney, you go right ahead. Don't let me stop you." Just as Hilton and Rodney are engaging in the "sideshow," they are arrested for violating a felony statute against such conduct. Is Danny liable for criminal solicitation under the statutes that follow?

Tennessee Code Annotated § 39-12-102   *Solicitation*

(a) Whoever, by means of oral, written or electronic communication, directly or through another, intentionally commands, requests or hires another to commit a criminal offense, or attempts to command, request or hire another to commit a criminal offense, with the intent that the criminal offense be committed, is guilty of solicitation.

General Laws of Rhode Island § 11-1-9 (2002)   *Soliciting another to commit a crime*

Every person who solicits another to commit or join in the commission of a felony under the laws of this state shall be [guilty of solicitation]. . . .

Kansas Statutes Annotated § 21-3303 (2001)   *Criminal Solicitation*

(a) Criminal solicitation is commanding, encouraging or requesting another person to commit a felony, attempt to commit a felony or aid and abet in the commission or attempted commission of a felony for the purpose of promoting or facilitating the felony.

(b) It is immaterial under subsection (a) that the actor fails to communicate with the person solicited to commit a felony if the person's conduct was designed to effect a communication.

How do the descriptions of the required mental states in these statutes differ? Which is clearest? What types of risks or issues does explicit treatment of the mental state avoid?

3. Renunciation

Solicitation's status as an anticipatory crime raises the possibility of acquittal based on renunciation. Following the Model Penal Code approach, Pennsylvania, for example, provides for renunciation of solicitation in its code:

18 Pennsylvania Consolidated Statutes Annotated § 902   *Criminal Solicitation*

. . .

(b) Renunciation. — It is a defense that the actor, after soliciting another person to commit a crime, persuaded him not to do so or otherwise prevented the commission of the crime, under circumstances manifesting a complete and voluntary renunciation of his criminal intent.

PROBLEM

10.17 Does the above renunciation provision exonerate Jeremy in the following situation?

Jeremy asks Horace to steal some DVD players that were being delivered to the local electronics store. Jeremy looks out his bedroom window at the time that the delivery truck arrives. Just then, he spots an armed guard inside the store. Jeremy signals frantically to Horace to desist. Horace sees Jeremy and instead of stealing the DVD players, Horace goes out for a café latte and a movie.

---

4. Innocent Agents

Interesting issues arise when a solicitor employs an innocent agent to carry out the criminal conduct. Consider the *Bush* case below:

STATE *v.* BUSH

Supreme Court of Montana 195 Mont. 475, 36 P. 2d 849 (1981)

HASWELL, J. Edward G. Bush appeals from his conviction and five-year sentence for the offense of solicitation to possess dangerous drugs. . . .

Edward Bush in September of 1980 went to Carmen's Lounge in Kalispell, Montana, where he met Kathleen Kohse, who was a bartender at the lounge. Bush told Kohse that he was a filmmaker who photographed animals, and that he had a job for someone as a film courier. Bush apparently actively recruited Kathleen Kohse for the job, as Kohse testified he came to the lounge several times and discussed it. Kohse also received several phone calls and a letter with application forms from a woman in California who was purportedly Bush's secretary.

Kohse was informed in October that she was hired for the position of film courier, and she then resigned from her job at Carmen's. She was told to send the application forms even though she was already hired because the company needed them for their files. Bush's secretary told Kohse there was a ticket to Los Angeles waiting for her at the Kalispell Airport.

Kohse used the ticket, flew to Los Angeles and met Bush at the Los Angeles Airport. She was then told by Bush that she was not going to be a film courier but rather a photographer. Bush knew that Kohse had no previous photography experience, and he spent several hours showing her how to operate the cameras she was given to use. She was told she was to go to Lima, Peru, to take pictures at the zoo and to learn how to be a photographer. Bush gave her three cameras, an aluminum camera case and $ 1,200. Part of the money was used to buy her ticket to Peru.

In Lima, Kohse met a person named Dan who took her to the zoo, left her there and took the camera case. She took pictures at the zoo for four hours although Dan had told her he would return in one hour. After staying in Lima for four days she was told to return to the States.

When she arrived in Los Angeles and went through customs she was arrested for possession of cocaine which was hidden in a compartment in the lining of the camera case. Kohse testified she had not placed the cocaine there, had no knowledge of it being there and did not see anyone put it there. After her arrest she had no contact with Bush or his associates.

Bush was charged with solicitation of Kohse to possess dangerous drugs, or in the alternative solicitation to possess dangerous drugs with intent to sell, and he was convicted of the former.

Appellant raises the following issue. . . .

Whether in Montana the crime of solicitation is complete even though the person solicited is unaware of the solicitor's actions and efforts. . . .

Appellant's . . . contention is that the crime of solicitation is not complete unless the person solicited is aware of the solicitor's criminal purpose and scheme. Since Kohse was unaware that she was to do anything but work for a movie company and since she was unaware of the drugs, appellant maintains she was not solicited.

At common law the use of an innocent agent to accomplish a crime was considered an attempt but not a solicitation. See Perkins on Criminal Law (2d Ed. 1969), 587-588. The common law has been affirmatively changed in some jurisdictions by statutes which provide that it is no defense to a charge of solicitation that the solicitee is unaware of the criminal nature of the conduct solicited or of the defendant's purpose. The theory behind the change is that one is no less guilty of a crime because he employs an innocent agent.

The Montana statute is not explicit in this regard. The language "facilitates the commission of that offense" does not imply that the person solicited must be aware of the criminal purpose. As above noted, the Montana legislature has changed the common law, as is its prerogative, and has not required that the solicitee be aware of the criminal purpose of the solicitor or of the criminal nature of the conduct solicited. To do so would defeat the purpose of the statute, which is to protect the citizens of this state from victimization and from exposure to inducements to commit or join in the commission of crime. The gravamen of the offense of solicitation is the intent of the solicitor and not the knowledge of the victim.

Affirm.

QUESTIONS

1. Should use of an innocent agent bar a prosecution for solicitation? When the solicitor employs an innocent agent, has she requested that the solicitee commit a crime? Or just part of a crime?

2. Should the law treat the acts of the solicitee as if they were the acts of the solicitor and hold the solicitor liable for the target crime, rather than solicitation?

PROBLEM

10.18 Howard decides to play a joke on Dennis. Unbeknownst to Dennis, Howard has a new sports car, which he previously loaned to Carol. Howard says that he will pay Dennis to steal the sports car in question from Carol so that Howard can drive it. Dennis agrees and takes the car from where it is parked in Carol's driveway. Assume that theft in this jurisdiction is defined as taking or removing something of value belonging to another with the intent to permanently or temporarily deprive the owner of it. Is Howard liable for solicitation?

G. SYNTHESIS AND REVIEW

PROBLEMS

10.19 Jerome is the leader of a group of anarchists who need money to fund a planned trip to Europe to demonstrate at an upcoming meeting of an organization devoted to developing world trade. Jerome decides to steal a famous painting from an art museum in a nearby city to fund the trip. Jerome confides his plan, which includes breaking into the museum in the middle of the night after disarming the alarm system, to his fellow anarchists and asks for their assistance. The other anarchists are happy to use the proceeds of the theft to travel but are unwilling to participate in the theft because any kind of organized, concerted action is against their principles. Jerome tells them he will steal the painting on his own. He visits the museum several times in order to be sure of its layout and to plan his getaway route. He obtains a number of false identification documents, including a driver's license with a false name and address. On the day before the planned theft, Jerome rents a van to use in the crime using the false name and the false identification documents. On the evening before the planned theft, Jerome is reviewing a map of the museum and his getaway route when he hears a knock at the door. He answers the door and finds police officers, who arrest him for attempted theft. It turns out that one of Jerome's fellow anarchists was in fact an undercover agent who tape-recorded Jerome's statements about his plan to steal the painting. Is Jerome liable for attempted theft?

10.20 You are the law clerk to a judge before whom a criminal case is being tried. The defendant in the case, Jake, is charged with an *attempt* to violate the following statute:

> It is a felony punishable by up to 10 years imprisonment knowingly to sell crack cocaine within 1,000 feet of any school.

Assume that the defendant's conduct was *not* sufficient to warrant conviction of this target offense but *was* sufficient to qualify for an attempt to violate the statute. The defendant admits the conduct but argues that he is not liable for attempt due to his alleged lack of knowledge that he was within 1,000 feet of a school. The school in question was a preschool serving children of families with working parents and located in a light industrial building in a primarily commercial area. Jake is arrested by an undercover police officer in front of the building in which the preschool is located. Jake testifies at trial and admits engaging in conduct that would qualify as an attempt and that he was at the time within 1,000 feet of the preschool, but he testifies that he was mistaken about whether the building in question contained a school. He believed the building and the surrounding area were strictly commercial. The judge is preparing the jury instructions for the attempt charge and wants to know the culpability required regarding the element of "within 1,000 feet of any school." What is the required culpability regarding this element?

Reconsider the possibility of removing liability for a completed anticipatory crime through what we have called abandonment or renunciation. In the following excerpt, Professor Evan Lee questions the current scope of these doctrines.

EVAN TSEN LEE, CANCELLING CRIME
30 Conn. L. Rev. 117-118, 125-126 (1997)

May one cancel liability for crimes already committed? In jurisdictions following the Model Penal Code ("MPC") on attempt, conspiracy, and solicitation, the answer is yes. The MPC provides a defense if the actor abandons the attempt, thwarts the conspiracy, or dissuades the person solicited under circumstances manifesting the actor's complete and voluntary renunciation of criminal purpose. The theory is not that the actor's desistance has left her short of liability for the attempt, conspiracy, or solicitation. The actor's renunciation relieves her of liability previously incurred.

The rather surprising proposition that one can erase existing criminal liability prompts [the following] question. . . . [I]f the MPC permits one to erase liability for attempts, conspiracies, and solicitations, why not for other crimes? Of course, no one should be able to reverse liability for a crime that necessarily entails a grave harm, such as a homicide or rape, because the harm cannot be undone. Harm is not an element of inchoate offenses. An attempted murder might involve harm, such as fright to the intended victim, but it might not, such as where the would-be killer breaks off the attempt before the intended victim learns of the plan. A conspiracy is nothing more than an agreement to commit an offense; it might culminate in the target offense, or it might die on the vine. The same is true of solicitation, which amounts to an attempted conspiracy. And yet there are many MPC offenses materially similar to attempts, conspiracies, and solicitations. A burglary requires only an unprivileged entry coupled with the purpose to commit a felony. No damage need be done to the structure, no person need be home, no underlying felony need be attempted. The burglary might result in no harm whatsoever. A larceny requires only the taking of property with the purpose of stealing. The item could be replaced undamaged without the victim ever learning of the taking. There are several other MPC offenses even more closely analogous to attempts and conspiracies than burglary and larceny. If the defense of renunciation is made available to attempt, conspiracy, and solicitation prosecutions, then why not for these analogous offenses?...

The MPC burglary provision makes no mention of renunciation. But because MPC burglaries are a subspecies of MPC interruption-type attempts, it should not surprise us that the fact of renunciation has an identical moral impact on burglary and attempt liability. Consider the following hypotheticals:

1. A walks up to a sidewalk vendor with the intent to steal an item. While the vendor is occupied with a customer, A reaches toward the item. At the last moment, he has a complete change of heart and walks away;

2. B walks calmly into Bloomingdale's through an open door just after closing time with the intent to shoplift an item. Two steps into the store, he has a complete change of heart and calmly walks out undetected; or

3. C intends to kill D while his back is turned. C raises his gun and aims it. At the last moment, he has a complete change of heart and walks away.

4. E intends to kill F, whom he knows to be sleeping in the upstairs bedroom. E calmly walks into F's house through an unlocked back door and starts up the staircase. He then has a complete change of heart and calmly walks back out undetected.

In jurisdictions following the MPC on renunciation, A and C are not guilty of attempted theft and attempted murder, respectively. In jurisdictions following the MPC on burglary, B and E are guilty of burglary. This combination of results is untenable. A and B are in identical moral situations, as are C and E.

QUESTIONS

1. Should the law allow abandonment or renunciation to cancel liability for anticipatory offenses in light of the disparity demonstrated by Professor Lee's examples? If so, why? If not, why not?

2. If the law should allow such cancellation, should it be available to cancel liability for crimes like burglary and larceny? If so, to what other crimes should it extend? If not, why not?

CHAPTER ELEVEN

COMPLICITY

A. INTRODUCTION

We typically think of someone committing a crime by doing an act proscribed by a criminal statute. The bank robber takes money from a bank teller. The drug dealer sells heroin. The hired killer shoots a victim. But what about those who do not personally engage in the conduct proscribed by the statute, but assist or encourage those who do? Someone may serve as a lookout and drive the getaway car for the bank robber. Another may carry a gun to provide protection for the drug dealer. And someone pays the hired killer and chooses the victim. None of these people engaged in the conduct prohibited by the robbery, drug sale, or homicide statutes. How should the criminal law deal with them?

The criminal law's answer is the doctrine of complicity, also known as accomplice liability. Under that doctrine, those who assist or encourage another to commit a crime may be held liable for that crime even though they did not themselves perform the act specified in the statute defining the crime. This is sometimes known as "derivative" liability because the accomplice's liability derives from that of the person who engages in the prohibited conduct, known as the principal or the primary actor. To understand complicity, then, it is important to realize that complicity is not an independent crime, but a way of sharing in the liability for a crime. As accomplices, the lookout and getaway car driver, the bodyguard, and the person hiring the killer may all become fully liable for the crimes committed by those they assist or encourage. Like the crimes that are the ultimate source of liability, complicity has both conduct and mental state requirements.

Imposing liability on accomplices comports with the purposes of punishment. Accomplices are typically blameworthy and so deserving of punishment from a retributive perspective. Without accomplices, crime can be harder for the principal to commit; so it seems logical to deter, incapacitate, and rehabilitate those who aid and encourage crime.

The common law developed a complex system for classifying various types of participation in crime. It recognized principals in the first and second degrees and accessories before and after the fact. Someone who committed a robbery by taking money from the person or the presence of another person by threat of force was a principal in the first degree. A person who accompanied the robber to the scene of the crime to act as a lookout and help carry away the robbery proceeds was a principal in the second degree. One who, prior to the robbery and in return for a share of the proceeds, loaned the robber a gun to use in the robbery was an accessory before the fact. Someone who, after the robbery, provided the robber with a place to hide the robbery proceeds was an accessory after the fact. The significance of these classifications usually related to punishment and procedural issues.

Most jurisdictions have adopted a simpler system of categorization and terminology. As explained by the California Supreme Court:

> The major purpose and effect of this abrogation of the common law distinction between parties to crime apparently has been to alleviate certain procedural difficulties. For instance, at common law an accessory before the fact was punishable where the incitement occurred while the principals were punishable where the offense occurred; one could not be convicted as an accessory if charged as a principal and vice versa; an accessory could not be tried before the principal had been found guilty.[1]

Many jurisdictions still treat accessory after the fact as a separate crime with a lesser punishment. But the categories of accessory before the fact and principal in the second degree have largely disappeared. Those who would have fallen under the categories of accessory before the fact and principal in the second degree today are often referred to simply as accomplices and are treated as principals in the sense that they become liable for the same offense as the principal and are exposed to the same potential punishment.

Under this simplified approach to complicity terminology, determine how we should classify each of the participants in the following Problems. Is the participant a principal, an accomplice, or an accessory after the fact? Assume that "theft" is defined as taking the property of another with the intent to permanently deprive the other of that property.

PROBLEMS

11.1 You decide to steal the answer key to this year's law school exams. Your study partner learns of your plans and provides you with a crowbar to pry open the vault in which the answers are stored. Both of you use the answers to prepare for the exam.

11.2 You decide to steal the answers to this year's law school exams. Your study partner learns of your plans and whispers "go for it" in your ear as you set off for the vault in which the answers are stored, break into the vault, and take the answers.

11.3 After you've stolen the answers and returned home, you tell your study partner what you've done. You then ask her to hide the answers in a safe place and she does so.

---

1. People v. Beeman, 35 Cal. 3d 547, 554 n.2 (1984).

In the following Sections of this chapter we explore the conduct and mental state elements of complicity. We then conclude with the Model Penal Code approach to complicity and four special issues relating to accomplice liability.

B. CONDUCT

PROBLEM

11.4 Modern statutes use an assortment of terms to describe acts that fulfill the conduct element for accomplice liability. Compare the conduct terminology found in the South Dakota and District of Columbia statutes that follow.

South Dakota Codified Laws § 22-3-3 (2003) *Aiding, abetting or advising — Accountability as principal*

Any person who, with the intent to promote or facilitate the commission of a crime, aids, abets or advises another person in planning or committing the crime, is legally accountable, as a principal to the crime.

District of Columbia Code § 22-1805 (2001) *Persons advising, inciting, or conniving at criminal offense to be charged as principals.*

[I]n prosecutions for any criminal offense all persons advising, inciting, or conniving at the offense, or aiding or abetting the principal offender, shall be charged as principals and not as accessories. . . .

Does the District of Columbia Code cover acts the South Dakota statute does not cover? Does South Dakota include acts that the District of Columbia Code does not cover?

1. Presence

Someone's presence at the scene of a crime can raise challenging issues in the context of complicity. Does presence signify participation in a crime? Does absence demonstrate lack of participation?

Under the Nevada statute, below, what role does presence play in determining criminal liability? What role should it play? What about absence? Is presence alone enough to fulfill the conduct requirement for accomplice liability? Does presence help prove acts that would fulfill the conduct requirement for accomplice liability?

Nevada Revised Statute Annotated § 195.020 (LEXIS 2001) *Principals*

Every person concerned in the commission of a felony, gross misdemeanor or misdemeanor, whether he directly commits the act constituting the offense, or aids or abets in its commission, and whether present or absent; and every person who, directly or indirectly, counsels, encourages, hires, commands, induces or otherwise procures another to commit a felony, gross misdemeanor or misdemeanor is a principal, and shall be proceeded against and punished as such.

STATE *v.* V.T.

Court of Appeals of Utah 5 P.3d 1234 (2000)

ORME, J. V.T. appeals the juvenile court's adjudication that by his continued presence during the crime, he was an accomplice to theft, a class A misdemeanor, in violation of Utah Code Ann. § 76-6-404 (1999). We reverse.

BACKGROUND

On June 12, 1998, V.T. and two friends, "Moose" and Joey, went to a relative's apartment to avoid being picked up by police for curfew violations. The boys ended up spending the entire night at the apartment.

The next morning, the relative briefly left to run an errand, while the boys remained in her apartment. She returned about fifteen minutes later to find the boys gone, the door to her apartment wide open, and two of her guns missing. She immediately went in search of the group and found them hanging out together near her apartment complex. She confronted the boys about the theft of her guns and demanded that they return them to her. When they failed to do so, she reported the theft to the police.[1]

Two days after the theft of her guns, she discovered that her camcorder, which had been in the apartment when the boys visited, was also missing, and she immediately reported its theft to the police. The police found the camcorder at a local pawn shop, where it had been pawned on the same day the guns were stolen.

Still inside the camcorder was a videotape featuring footage of V.T., Moose, and Joey. The tape included a segment where Moose telephoned a friend, in V.T.'s presence, and discussed pawning the stolen camcorder. V.T. never spoke or gestured during any of this footage.[2]

V.T. was eventually picked up by the police, while riding in a car with Moose. V.T. was charged with two counts of theft of a firearm; one count of theft, relating to the camcorder; and, for having initially given the police a phony name, one count of giving false information to a peace officer, a violation of Utah Code Ann. § 76-8-507 (1999). . . .

V.T. was tried under an accomplice theory on the three theft charges. The court found that V.T. had committed class A misdemeanor theft of the camcorder and had provided false information to a peace officer. The juvenile court summarized the basis for its adjudication concerning the camcorder theft as follows:

> I am going to find him guilty and I think the additional information that I have here that brings me peace of mind is that he was present a second time, he was shown on the camcorder when the camcorder was being handled at a time when he could've

---

[1] A few days after confronting the boys about her stolen guns, one of the boys returned one of the guns to her and she found the butt of the other gun on her porch.

[2] The videotape was shown at trial, but was never admitted into evidence and is therefore not part of the record on appeal. As a result, we have not seen any of the footage of V.T. Both parties, however, are in agreement as to what the videotape shows—a silent V.T., being filmed by Joey, during which time Moose talks to another person on the phone about selling the stolen camcorder to a pawn shop.

distanced himself from the activity. Not only do I have him there once with the group . . . on the second incident . . . there is no gap on him being there when [the camcorder] is being handled and talked about and used in the confines of a room with a group of friends and those who were involved in this illegal activity.

V.T. appeals his adjudication concerning the theft of the camcorder.

ISSUE AND STANDARD OF REVIEW

The sole issue presented by V.T. is whether there was sufficient evidence to support the adjudication that he was an accomplice in the theft of the camcorder. When reviewing a juvenile court's decision for sufficiency of the evidence, we must consider all the facts, and all reasonable inferences which may be drawn therefrom, in a light most favorable to the juvenile court's determination, reversing only when it is "against the clear weight of the evidence, or if the appellate court otherwise reaches a definite and firm conviction that a mistake has been made."

ANALYSIS

Utah's accomplice liability statute, Utah Code Ann. § 76-2- 202 (1999), provides:

Every person, acting with the mental state required for the commission of an offense who directly commits the offense, who solicits, requests, commands, encourages, or intentionally aids another person to engage in conduct which constitutes an offense shall be criminally liable as a party for such conduct.

. . . The State argues that V.T.'s continued presence during the theft and subsequent phone conversation about selling the camcorder, coupled with his friendship with the other two boys, is enough evidence to support the inference that he had "encouraged" the other two in committing the theft and that he is therefore an accomplice to the crime. *Black's Law Dictionary* defines encourage as: "to instigate; to incite to action; to embolden; to help." *Black's Law Dictionary* 547 (7th ed. 1999). The plain meaning of the word confirms that to encourage others to take criminal action requires some form of active behavior, or at least verbalization, by a defendant. Passive behavior, such as mere presence — even continuous presence — absent evidence that the defendant affirmatively did something to instigate, incite, embolden, or help others in committing a crime is not enough to qualify as "encouragement" as that term is commonly used.

The case law in Utah is consistent with this definition: " 'Mere presence, or even prior knowledge, does not make one an accomplice' " to a crime absent evidence showing — beyond a reasonable doubt — that defendant "advis[ed], instigat[ed], encourage[d], or assist[ed] in perpetuation of the crime." . . .

[S]omething more than a defendant's passive presence during the planning and commission of a crime is required to constitute "encouragement" so as to impose accomplice liability in Utah. There must be evidence showing that the defendant engaged in some active behavior, or at least speech or other expression, that served to assist or encourage the primary perpetrators in committing the crime.

The juvenile court's conclusion that V.T. was an accomplice to the camcorder theft was not supported by the evidence in this case. No evidence whatsoever was produced indicating V.T. had encouraged — much less that he solicited, requested, commanded or intentionally aided — the other two boys in the theft of the camcorder.[7]

---

[7] We would, of course, conclude otherwise had the evidence shown, for example, that V.T. had suggested to his two friends that they go rob the apartment, that he had pointed out where the camcorder

Instead, the evidence, read in the light most favorable to the juvenile court's decision, shows only that V.T. was present with the other two youths, albeit at multiple times: when the camcorder was stolen; when they were confronted about the theft of the guns; and when the plan to pawn the camcorder was being discussed by Moose. . . . [T]here is no indication in the record that V.T. had instigated, incited to action, emboldened, helped, or advised the other two boys in planning or committing the theft. The circumstantial evidence presented in this case, which only shows V.T.'s continuous presence during the events surrounding the theft, is sufficient for finding only that V.T. was a witness — not an accomplice — to the theft of the camcorder. And knowledge of a theft, without more, does not make one an accomplice.

The juvenile court's conclusion of accomplice liability was heavily influenced by the videotape footage of V.T., who at the time of the filming was necessarily in the presence of the camcorder, after it had been stolen. In fact, the court found that even though there was not enough evidence presented to find that V.T. was an accomplice in the theft of the guns, which were stolen at the same time and from the same apartment as the camcorder, the videotape footage was enough to find that V.T. was an accomplice to the camcorder theft. The juvenile court's heavy reliance on this footage shows that it made its conclusion of accomplice liability based not on any evidence that V.T. had encouraged the others to steal the camcorder, as required by section 76-2-202, but instead on the sole fact that V.T. allowed himself to remain in the company of Joey, Moose, and the stolen camcorder before, during, and immediately after the theft. As explained above, this "guilt by association" theory is not a basis on which accomplice liability can be premised under Utah law. . . .

[W]e reverse. . . .

QUESTIONS

1. On what resources did the court rely in its efforts to understand the accomplice liability statute?

2. Mere presence is generally not enough to satisfy the conduct element for accomplice liability. What if, in addition to his presence, V.T. had suggested, while Moose was on the phone discussing the pawning of the video camera, that they use the proceeds from the pawning of it to buy new jackets? What if V.T.'s companions discussed taking the video camera with V.T. present and V.T. had given them a thumbs up sign?

3. "What if the item stolen from the apartment had not been a small camcorder but instead was a 500 pound television console?"[2] How do you think the court would have ruled?

4. Are criminals likely to commit a crime in the presence of someone who is not involved in the criminal scheme? What inference might one draw from the fact that Joey and Moose allowed V.T. to witness their crimes?

5. The appellate court in the *V.T.* case states that "No evidence whatsoever was produced indicating that V.T. had encouraged — much less that he solicited, requested, commanded or intentionally aided — the other two boys in the theft of the camcorder." Is this assessment accurate?

---

was kept, that he had helped carry the stolen goods out, or that he helped select the pawn shop at which to sell the camcorder.

2. State v. V.T., 5 P.3d 1234, 1238 n.8 (2000).

6. The facts in this case were determined by a judge rather than a jury. Should an appellate court give greater deference to a judge's factual findings than those of a jury? Should an appellate court give them less deference? Or should the factual findings of a judge and jury be treated the same on appeal?

WILCOX *v.* JEFFREY

King's Bench Division 1 All Eng. Rep. 464 (1951)

[A]t a court of summary jurisdiction . . . the appellant, Herbert William Wilcox, owner and managing editor of a monthly magazine entitled "Jazz Illustrated," was charged with aiding and abetting one Coleman Hawkins, a citizen of the United States, in contravening art. 1(4) of the Aliens Order, 1920, by failing to comply with a condition attached to a grant of leave to land in the United Kingdom, namely, that Hawkins should take no employment paid or unpaid during his stay, contrary to art. 18(4) of the Order. It was proved or admitted that on Dec. 11, 1949, Hawkins arrived at a London airport and was met by, among others, the appellant. The appellant was present when an immigration officer interviewed two other persons who had previously applied for permission for Hawkins to perform at a concert in London, but had been told by the Ministry of Labour that their application had been refused. At that interview it was stated that Hawkins would attend the concert and would be "spotlighted" and introduced to the audience, but would not perform. The appellant said he was not connected with the persons responsible for organising the concert and that he had only gone to the airport to report Hawkins' arrival for his magazine. The immigration officer gave permission to Hawkins to remain for three days in this country, making it a condition that he should not take any paid or unpaid employment. The appellant was aware that such a condition had been imposed. Later the same day the appellant attended the concert, paying for admission. Hawkins was seated in a box, but after being "spotlighted" he went on the stage and played the saxophone. A description of the performance by Hawkins with several pages of photographs was later published in the appellant's magazine. The magistrate was of the opinion that the appellant aided and abetted the contravention of the Order by Hawkins and imposed a fine of £25 and £21 costs.

Lord Goddard, C.J. . . . . Under the Aliens Order, art. 1(1), it is provided that

" . . . an alien coming . . . by sea to a place in the United Kingdom — (a) shall not land in the United Kingdom without the leave of an immigration officer. . . . "

It is provided by art 1(4) that

"An immigration officer, in accordance with general or special directions of the Secretary of State, may, by general order or notice or otherwise, attach such conditions as he may think fit to the grant of leave to land, and the Secretary of State may at any time vary such conditions in such manner as he thinks fit, and the alien shall comply with the conditions so attached or varied. . . ."

If the alien fails to comply, he is to be in the same position as if he has landed without permission, *i.e.*, he commits an offence.

The case is concerned with the visit of a celebrated professor of the saxophone, a gentleman by the name of Hawkins who was a citizen of the United States. He came here at the invitation of two gentlemen of the name of Curtis and Hughes, connected with a jazz club which enlivens the neighbourhood of Willesden. They, apparently, had applied for permission for Mr. Hawkins to land and it was refused, but, nevertheless, this professor of the saxophone arrived with four French musicians. When they came to the airport, among the people who were there to greet them was the appellant. He had not arranged their visit, but he knew they were coming and he was there to report the arrival of these important musicians for his magazine. So, evidently, he was regarding the visit of Mr. Hawkins as a matter which would be of interest to himself and the magazine which he was editing and selling for profit. Messrs. Curtis and Hughes arranged a concert at the Princes Theatre, London. The appellant attended that concert as a spectator. He paid for his ticket. Mr. Hawkins went on the stage and delighted the audience by playing the saxophone. The appellant did not get up and protest in the name of the musicians of England that Mr. Hawkins ought not to be here competing with them and taking the bread out of their mouths or the wind out of their instruments. It is not found that he actually applauded, but he was there having paid to go in, and, no doubt, enjoying the performance, and then, lo and behold, out comes his magazine with a most laudatory description, fully illustrated, of this concert. On those facts the magistrate has found that he aided and abetted. . . .

The appellant paid to go to the concert and he went there because he wanted to report it. He must, therefore, be held to have been present, taking part, concurring, or encouraging, whichever word you like to use for expressing this conception. It was an illegal act on the part of Hawkins to play the saxophone or any other instrument at this concert. The appellant clearly knew that it was an unlawful act for him to play. He had gone there to hear him, and his presence and his payment to go there was an encouragement. He went there to make use of the performance, because he went there, as the magistrate finds and was justified in finding, to get "copy" for his newspaper. It might have been entirely different, as I say, if he had gone there and protested, saying: "The musicians' union do not like you foreigners coming here and playing and you ought to get off the stage." If he had booed, it might have been some evidence that he was not aiding and abetting. If he had gone as a member of a *claque* to try to drown the noise of the saxophone, he might very likely be found not guilty of aiding and abetting. In this case it seems clear that he was there, not only to approve and encourage what was done, but to take advantage of it by getting "copy" for his paper. In those circumstances there was evidence on which the magistrate could find that the appellant aided and abetted, and for these reasons I am of opinion that the appeal fails.

Appeal dismissed with costs.

QUESTIONS

1. What did Wilcox do to become an accomplice to a crime? What was the crime? Who was the principal?

2. What if Wilcox had not met Mr. Hawkins at the airport? What if Wilcox had not attended the performance? In either case, would he then have been shielded from accomplice liability?

3. What if Wilcox succeeded at trial in proving that Mr. Hawkins would have played regardless of anything Wilcox did or did not do. Would that affect Wilcox's liability as an accomplice?

4. What if Mr. Hawkins had no idea that Wilcox was at the airport or attended the concert? Should that affect Wilcox's liability for the crime?

The following passage from a famous complicity case makes an important point about accomplice liability:

> The assistance given, however, need not contribute to the criminal result in the sense that but for it the result would not have ensued. It is quite sufficient if it facilitated a result that would have transpired without it. It is quite enough if the aid merely renders it easier for the principal actor to accomplish the end intended by him and the aider and abettor, though in all human probability the end would have been attained without it.

State ex rel. Attorney General v. Tally, 102 Ala. 25, 69 (1893).

In short, accomplice liability does not require "but for" causation between the accomplice's act and the acts of the principal.

PROBLEM

11.5 Based on the facts described below, should the defendant be convicted of burglary and theft? Assume burglary is defined as entering a building with the intent to steal.

> Stapleton was approached by two individuals who were attempting to sell certain stolen television sets. Stapleton [arranged for the sale of the sets to the defendant.] [T]he defendant stated that he would take all the color television sets that Stapleton could provide.
>
> On August 12, 1969, Stapleton and another stole three television sets from Mid-Continent Appliance Distributors, Inc. Stapleton then called the defendant and told him that he had three color television sets to sell. Later that same day, the defendant purchased the three sets.
>
> On the evening of August 12, 1969, the defendant supplied Stapleton with an old truck to be used in obtaining further TV sets. The defendant also promised to supply Stapleton with legal assistance and bail if he were apprehended. On that same evening, the truck had a flat tire and the defendant instructed Stapleton to leave it at a gas station. The next day, August 13, 1969, the defendant delivered to Stapleton a rented U-Haul truck, instructing Stapleton to abandon it if he were caught. On August 14, Stapleton stole four additional television sets and sold them to the defendant. On August 15, using another U-Haul truck which defendant had rented that day, Stapleton and others stole television sets from one store in Boulder, Colorado, and were apprehended while attempting to steal sets from another store.
>
> After the defendant was informed of Stapleton's arrest, he reported to the police that the U-Haul truck had been stolen. At trial, the defendant admitted that he intentionally filed a false theft report after learning of Stapleton's arrest.[3]

---

3. Quoted from State v. Lamirato, 180 Colo. 250 (1972).

2. Omissions

PROBLEM

11.6 Dale is the night watchman at a warehouse used by a computer retailer
to store its computers prior to shipping them around the country.
Terry approaches Dale and offers him $500 to refrain from interfering
with or reporting Terry's breaking into the warehouse and stealing
some computers. Dale agrees; Terry pays Dale $500 and steals the
computers. Dale does nothing to stop Terry and does not report the
theft. Does Dale have any criminal liability? If so, for what crimes?

Should an omission be sufficient to fulfill the conduct requirement for accomplice liability? The following case involves the parental duty to protect a child from abuse.

STATE *v.* WALDEN
Supreme Court of North Carolina 306 N.C. 466 (1982)

MITCHELL, Justice. The principal question presented is whether a mother may be found guilty of assault on a theory of aiding and abetting solely on the basis that she was present when her child was assaulted but failed to take reasonable steps to prevent the assault. We answer this question in the affirmative and reverse the opinion of the Court of Appeals which held to the contrary and ordered a new trial.

On 28 April 1980, defendant was indicted under G.S. 14-32 as follows:

THE JURORS FOR THE STATE UPON THEIR OATH PRESENT that on or about the 9th day of December, 1979, in Wake County Aleen Estes Walden [did] unlawfully and wilfully and feloniously assault Lamont Walden, age one year, with a certain deadly weapon, to wit: a leather belt with a metal buckle, inflicting serious bodiyly [sic] injuries, not resulting in death, upon the said Lamont Walden. . . .

Lamont Walden is defendant's son. Defendant was convicted by a jury and sentenced to 5-10 years imprisonment.

The State offered evidence at trial tending to show that Mr. Jasper Billy Davis heard a child crying in the apartment next to his on Saturday evening, 8 December 1979. On Sunday morning, 9 December 1979, at approximately 10:00 A.M., Davis heard a small child screaming and hollering and heard a popping sound coming from the same apartment next door. The sound of the child screaming and hollering and the popping sound lasted for approximately one to one and one-half hours. Davis made a complaint to the Raleigh Police Department requesting that they investigate the noise that he was hearing.

Officer D. A. Weingarten of the Raleigh Police Department testified that he went to Davis' apartment on 9 December 1979. After speaking with Davis, the officer knocked on the door of the apartment next to the Davis apartment. A Miss

Devine opened the door and allowed the officer to enter the apartment, where he stayed for a few minutes before leaving to obtain a search warrant. Officer Weingarten returned a short time later with a warrant to search the apartment in question. Upon entering the apartment, the officer saw Devine, the defendant Aleen Estes Walden and George Hoskins. The officer also saw five small children in a corner of the apartment and noticed cuts and bruises on the bodies of the children. One of the children the officer observed at this time was Lamont Walden, a small child in diapers. The officer observed red marks on the chest of Lamont Walden as well as a swollen lip, bruises on his legs and back and other bruises, scarring and cuts.

At trial three of these small children, Roderick Walden, ten years old, Stephen Walden, eight years old, and Derrick Walden, seven years old, testified that "Bishop" George Hoskins hit their brother Lamont Walden with a belt repeatedly over an extended period of time on Sunday, 9 December 1979. Each child testified that the defendant, their mother, was in the room with Hoskins and the baby (Lamont) at the time this beating occurred. Lamont Walden was crying and bleeding as a result of the beating Hoskins gave him. The children testified further that the defendant looked on the entire time the beating took place but did not say anything or do anything to stop the "Bishop" from beating Lamont or to otherwise deter such conduct.

Mrs. Annette McCullers, who is employed by Social Services of Wake County, testified that she observed the five children including Lamont on 9 December 1979. . . . McCullers talked with Lamont's brothers at this time, and each of them told her that Lamont had been beaten by "Bishop" George Hoskins. . . .

The defendant offered evidence in the form of testimony of her father, Mr. Meredith Estes, tending to show that James Walden, the father of the Walden children, had whipped the children in the past when living with them. Estes testified that the defendant had never mistreated the children. He further testified that the children had told him that it was their father who beat them on the occasion in question, but that they had later changed their story and stated that George Hoskins beat them and also beat Lamont.

The defendant testified that she was living in an apartment with Miss Devine on 8 December 1979. Three of the defendant's sons had gone to the store with Devine and Hoskins. The defendant's two youngest children were with her. There was a knock on the door and the children's father entered. The father immediately began hitting Lamont Walden with a belt. The defendant tried to stop him but could not do so. The defendant testified that she was struck by the children's father on this occasion and received injuries to her face.

Based on the preceding evidence, the defendant was convicted of assault with a deadly weapon inflicting serious injury in violation of G.S. 14-32(b). During the trial, the State proceeded on the theory that the defendant aided and abetted George Hoskins in the commission of the assault on her child and was, therefore, guilty as a principal to the offense charged.

The defendant assigned as error the action of the trial court in denying her motion to dismiss and allowing the case against her for the felonious assault charge to go to the jury, when all of the evidence tended to show that the defendant did not perform any affirmative act of commission to encourage the perpetrator and did not herself administer the beating to her child. In support of this assignment, the defendant contends, among other things, that the trial court erred in instructing the jury as follows:

It is the duty of a parent to protect their children and to do whatever may be reasonably necessary for their care and their safety. A parent has a duty to protect their children and cannot stand passively by and refuse to do so when it is reasonably within their power to protect their children. A parent is bound to provide such reasonable care as necessary, under the circumstances facing them at that particular time. However, a parent is not required to do the impossible or the unreasonable in caring for their children.

Now a person is not guilty of a crime merely because she is present at the scene. To be guilty she must aid or actively encourage the person committing the crime, or in some way communicate to this person her intention to assist in its commission; *or that she is present with the reasonable opportunity and duty to prevent the crime and fails to take reasonable steps to do so.*

So I charge that if you find from the evidence beyond a reasonable doubt, that on or about December 9th, 1979, Bishop Hoskins committed assault with a deadly weapon inflicting serious injury on Lamont Walden, that is that Bishop Hoskins intentionally hit Lamont Walden with a belt and that the belt was a deadly weapon, thereby inflicting serious injury upon Lamont Walden; and that the defendant was present at the time the crime was committed and did nothing and that in so doing the defendant knowingly advised, instigated, encouraged or aided Bishop Hoskins to commit that crime; *or that she was present with the reasonable opportunity and duty to prevent the crime and failed to take reasonable steps to do so*; it would be your duty to return a verdict of guilty of assault with a deadly weapon, inflicting serious injury. (Emphases added.)

The defendant contends that the quoted instructions of the trial court are erroneous in that they permitted the jury to convict her for failing to interfere with or attempt to prevent the commission of a felony. She argues that the law of this State does not allow a conviction in any case for aiding and abetting the commission of a crime absent some affirmative act of commission by the defendant assisting or encouraging the commission of the crime or indicating the defendant's approval and willingness to assist. We do not agree. . . .

The mere presence of a person at the scene of a crime at the time of its commission does not make him a principal in the second degree; and this is so even though he makes no effort to prevent the crime, or even though he may silently approve of the crime, or even though he may secretly intend to assist the perpetrator in the commission of the crime in case his aid becomes necessary to its consummation. *State v. Birchfield*, 235 N.C. 410, 413 (1952). However, this general rule allows some exceptions. Where the common law has imposed affirmative duties upon persons standing in certain personal relationships to others, such as the duty of parents to care for their small children, one may be guilty of criminal conduct by failure to act or, stated otherwise, by an act of omission. Individuals also have been found criminally liable for failing to perform affirmative duties required by statute. . . .

[W]e believe that to require a parent as a matter of law to take affirmative action to prevent harm to his or her child or be held criminally liable imposes a reasonable duty upon the parent. Further, we believe this duty is and has always been inherent in the duty of parents to provide for the safety and welfare of their children, which duty has long been recognized by the common law and by statute. This is not to say that parents have the legal duty to place themselves in danger of death or great bodily harm in coming to the aid of their children. To require such, would require every parent to exhibit courage and heroism which, although commendable in the extreme, cannot realistically be expected or required of all people. But parents do have the duty to take every step reasonably possible under the circumstances of a given situation to prevent harm to their children.

In some cases, depending upon the size and vitality of the parties involved, it might be reasonable to expect a parent to physically intervene and restrain the person attempting to injure the child. In other circumstances, it will be reasonable for a parent to go for help or to merely verbally protest an attack upon the child. What is reasonable in any given case will be a question for the jury after proper instructions from the trial court.

We think that the rule we announce today is compelled by our statutes and prior cases establishing the duty of parents to provide for the safety and welfare of their children. Further, we find our holding today to be consistent with our prior cases regarding the law of aiding and abetting. It remains the law that one may not be found to be an aider and abettor, and thus guilty as a principal, solely because he is present when a crime is committed. It will still be necessary, in order to have that effect, that it be shown that the defendant said or did something showing his consent to the criminal purpose and contribution to its execution. But we hold that the failure of a parent who is present to take all steps reasonably possible to protect the parent's child from an attack by another person constitutes an act of omission by the parent showing the parent's consent and contribution to the crime being committed. *Cf. State v. Haywood*, 295 N.C. 709 (1978) (When a bystander is a friend of the perpetrator and knows his presence will be regarded as encouragement, presence alone may be regarded as aiding and abetting.)

Thus, we hold that the trial court properly allowed the jury in the present case to consider a verdict of guilty of assault with a deadly weapon inflicting serious injury, upon a theory of aiding and abetting, solely on the ground that the defendant was present when her child was brutally beaten by Hoskins but failed to take all steps reasonable to prevent the attack or otherwise protect the child from injury. Further, the jury having found that the defendant committed an act of omission constituting consent to and encouragement of the commission of the crime charged, the defendant would properly be found to have aided and abetted the principal. A person who so aids or abets another in the commission of a crime is equally guilty with that other person as a principal. Therefore, we find no error in the trial court's instructions, the verdict or the judgment on the charge of assault with a deadly weapon inflicting serious injury. . . .

Reversed and remanded.

QUESTIONS

1. What was the defendant's conduct in the *Walden* case?

2. Would it have made any difference if the child's father had inflicted the injuries? Would the arguments for holding the mother as an accomplice be stronger or weaker?

3. Should it change the result if the jury believed that the defendant had tried to stop the assault but was herself assaulted? Why might a mother not intervene in violence against her children?

4. If you had been a juror in the *Walden* case, would you have voted for conviction or acquittal?

5. The *Walden* court states that "[a] person who so aids and abets another in the commission of a crime is equally guilty with that other person...." Did Aleen Walden's blameworthiness equal that of George Hoskins? Was she as dangerous as George Hoskins?

6. Would it be preferable to treat Walden as a principal for the crime of child neglect? Or is it preferable to treat her as an accomplice to assault? If Hoskins had killed one of the children, should she have been held liable for homicide?

7. The court refers to Walden's "act of omission." Is this phrase self-contradictory?

8. Is a belt a "deadly weapon"? What interpretation arguments could you make as the prosecutor for an affirmartive answer to this question? What interpretation arguments could you make as defense counsel for a negative answer?

9. The *Walden* court holds that "the failure of a parent who is present to take all steps reasonably possible to protect the parent's child from an attack by another person" shows "the parent's consent ... to the crime." Do you agree that failure to protect a child shows consent to harming the child?

The following excerpt is from a speech by Professor Sarah Buel, a former assistant district attorney and head of a domestic violence unit. Professor Buel was herself a victim of domestic violence and a foster parent.[4]

> Probably the person that taught me most about the connection between domestic violence and child abuse was a foster child named Christopher, who came to me when he was three years old. When he first came to me he had two broken ribs and he had cigarette burns on the bottoms of his feet. And he stayed for about three months and then his father, who was the acknowledged perpetrator, said he was real sorry, and it would never happen again.
>
> And so the court allowed Christopher to go home, and within a few weeks I got a call, Christopher was in the hospital again. He had new cigarette burns on the bottoms of his feet and the palms of his hands and all of his ribs were broken. Those of you who know about early childhood development know how resilient a child's ribs are. It's very hard to break them so it must have been a tremendous amount of force. So Christopher came home with me, and his mother was allowed to have visitation, as again his father acknowledged he was the one who had abused him.
>
> But I was so righteous with her, because she was staying with the man who had done this to her child. What was wrong with this woman? She would come in, I would sort of notice that there were bruises on her, I didn't really let it register. My focus, my obsession, was with Christopher and keeping him safe. . . . And after a few months Christopher's father went back into court, and [said] he was real, real sorry, and it was never, never going to happen again. And the court allowed Christopher to go home with him.
>
> The following August we buried Christopher, and we buried his mother right next to him. And as hard as it is for me to think and talk about Christopher even now, it is ten times harder, a hundred times harder for me to think about his mother. Because I did everything humanly possible to save Christopher. I went to every hearing, I went to every possible meeting, I called and wrote the mayor,

---

4. *Violence Against Women: How to Improve the Legal Services' Response*, Nov. 18, 1991 (cited in Defending Our Lives, Study and Resource Guide 13, 19).

the governor, the president, but I did nothing for his mother. Because I was so busy judging her, and so busy being righteous, and she could not have presented herself more clearly as a battered woman if she had a megaphone and a neon sign.

We learned at the murder trial that DSS [Department of Social Services], in writing, had told Christopher's mother that she needed to stay with his father if she ever wanted her child back.

3. The Model Penal Code Approach to Conduct for Complicity

Model Penal Code § 2.06 (1985) *Liability for Conduct of Another; Complicity*

(1) A person is guilty of an offense if it is committed by his own conduct or by the conduct of another person for which he is legally accountable, or both.

(2) A person is legally accountable for the conduct of another person when: . . .

(c) he is an accomplice of such other person in the commission of an offense.

(3) A person is an accomplice of another person in the commission of an offense if:

(a) with the purpose of promoting or facilitating the commission of the offense, he

(i) solicits the other person to commit it, or

(ii) aids or agrees or attempts to aid such other person in planning or committing it, or

(iii) having a legal duty to prevent the commission of the offense, fails to make proper effort so to do; or

(b) his conduct is expressly declared by law to establish his complicity.

QUESTIONS

1. What conduct is necessary under the MPC to establish complicity?

2. Would the results in the *V.T.* and *Walden* cases have been different under the MPC? If so, why? If not, why not?

PROBLEM

11.7 Imagine that you want an outline for this course made by student *A* and you learn that student *B* is planning to steal that outline from student *A*'s locker. Student *A*'s locker is high up on a wall, and student *B* is quite short. You leave a rope attached to a hook in the ceiling above student *A*'s locker to facilitate *B*'s crime. Student *B* arrives in the locker room and cannot reach the rope. She obtains a step ladder and, without using the rope, steals the outline. Under the MPC, would you be guilty of theft of the outline? Does it matter whether you communicated with student *B* about the theft?

C. MENTAL STATES

What mental states do the following statutes require for accomplice liability? Which statute is clearer?

Utah Code Annotated § 76-2-202 (2001)   *Criminal responsibility for direct commission of offense or for conduct of another*

Every person, acting with the mental state required for the commission of an offense who directly commits the offense, who solicits, requests, commands, encourages, or intentionally aids another person to engage in conduct which constitutes an offense shall be criminally liable as a party for such conduct.

Kansas Statutes Annotated § 21-3205 (2000)   *Liability for crimes of another*

(1) A person is criminally responsible for a crime committed by another if such person intentionally aids, abets, advises, hires, counsels or procures the other to commit the crime.

PEOPLE *v.* BEEMAN
California Supreme Court 35 Cal. 3d 547 (1984)

REYNOSO, J. — Timothy Mark Beeman appeals from a judgment of conviction of robbery, burglary, false imprisonment, destruction of telephone equipment and assault with intent to commit a felony (Pen. Code, §§ 211, 459, 236, 591, 221). Appellant was not present during commission of the offenses. His conviction rested on the theory that he aided and abetted his acquaintances James Gray and Michael Burk.

The primary issue before us is whether the standard California Jury Instructions (CALJIC Nos. 3.00 and 3.01) adequately inform the jury of the criminal intent required to convict a defendant as an aider and abettor of the crime.

We hold that instruction No. 3.01 is erroneous. Sound law, embodied in a long line of California decisions, requires proof that an aider and abettor rendered aid with an intent or purpose of either committing, or of encouraging or facilitating commission of, the target offense. It was, therefore, error for the trial court to refuse the modified instruction requested by appellant. Our examination of the record convinces us that the error in this case was prejudicial and we therefore reverse appellant's convictions.

James Gray and Michael Burk drove from Oakland to Redding for the purpose of robbing appellant's sister-in-law, Mrs. Marjorie Beeman, of valuable jewelry, including a 3.5 carat diamond ring. They telephoned the residence to determine that she was home. Soon thereafter Burk knocked at the door of the victim's house, presented himself as a poll taker, and asked to be let in. When Mrs. Beeman asked for identification, he forced her into the hallway and entered. Gray, disguised in a ski mask, followed. The two subdued the victim, placed tape over her mouth and eyes and tied her to a bathroom fixture. Then they ransacked the house, taking numerous pieces of jewelry and a set of silverware. The jewelry included a 3.5 carat, heart-shaped diamond ring and a blue sapphire ring. The total value of these two rings was over $100,000. In the course of the robbery, telephone wires inside the house were cut.

Appellant was arrested six days later in Emeryville. He had in his possession several of the less valuable of the stolen rings. He supplied the police with information that led to the arrests of Burk and Gray. With Gray's cooperation appellant assisted police in recovering most of the stolen property.

Burk, Gray and appellant were jointly charged. After the trial court severed the trials, Burk and Gray pled guilty to robbery. At appellant's trial they testified that he had been extensively involved in planning the crime.

Burk testified that he had known appellant for two and one-half years. He had lived in appellant's apartment several times. Appellant had talked to him about rich relatives in Redding and had described a diamond ring worth $50,000. According to Burk the feasibility of robbing appellant's relatives was first mentioned two and one-half months before the incident occurred. About one week before the robbery, the discussions became more specific. Appellant gave Burk the address and discussed the ruse of posing as a poll taker. It was decided that Gray and Burk would go to Redding because appellant wanted nothing to do with the actual robbery and because he feared being recognized. On the night before the offense appellant drew a floor plan of the victim's house and told Burk where the diamond ring was likely to be found. Appellant agreed to sell the jewelry for 20 percent of the proceeds.

After the robbery was completed, Burk telephoned appellant to report success. Appellant said that he would call the friend who might buy the jewelry. Burk and Gray drove to appellant's house and showed him the "loot." Appellant was angry that the others had taken so much jewelry, and demanded that his cut be increased from 20 percent to one-third.

Gray's testimony painted a similar picture. Gray also had known appellant for approximately two years prior to the incident. Gray said Burk had initially approached him about the robbery, supplied the victim's address, and described the diamond ring. Appellant had at some time described the layout of the house to Gray and Burk and had described to them the cars driven by various members of the victim's family. Gray and Burk, but not appellant, had discussed how to divide the proceeds. Both Gray and Burk owed money to appellant. In addition, Burk owed Gray $3,200.

According to Gray appellant had been present at a discussion three days before the robbery when it was mentioned that appellant could not go because his 6 foot 5 inch, 310-pound frame could be too easily recognized. Two days before the offense, however, appellant told Gray that he wanted nothing to do with the robbery of his relatives. On the day preceding the incident appellant and Gray spoke on the telephone. At that time appellant repeated he wanted nothing to do with the robbery, but confirmed that he had told Burk that he would not say anything if the others went ahead.

Gray confirmed that appellant was upset when he saw that his friends had gone through with the robbery and had taken all of the victim's jewelry. He was angered further when he discovered that Burk might easily be recognized because he had not disguised himself. Appellant then asked them to give him all of the stolen goods. Instead Burk and Gray gave appellant only a watch and some rings which they believed he could sell. Gray and Burk then traveled to San Jose where they sold the silverware for $900. Burk used this money to flee to Los Angeles. Sometime later appellant asked for Gray's cooperation in recovering and returning the property to the victim. On several occasions when Burk called them for more money, appellant stalled and avoided questions about the sale of the jewelry.

Appellant Beeman's testimony contradicted that of Burk and Gray as to nearly every material element of his own involvement. Appellant testified that he did not participate in the robbery or its planning. He confirmed that Burk had lived with him on several occasions, and that he had told Burk about Mrs. Beeman's jewelry, the valuable diamond ring, and the Beeman ranch, in the course of day-to-day conversations. He claimed that he had sketched a floor plan of the house some nine months prior to the robbery, only for the purpose of comparing it with the layout of a house belonging to another brother. He at first denied and then admitted describing the Beeman family cars, but insisted this never occurred in the context of planning a robbery.

Appellant stated that Burk first suggested that robbing Mrs. Beeman would be easy some five months before the incident. At that time, and on the five or six subsequent occasions when Burk raised the subject, appellant told Burk that his friends could do what they wanted but that he wanted no part of such a scheme.

Beeman admitted Burk had told him of the poll taker ruse within a week before the robbery, and that Burk told him they had bought a cap gun and handcuffs. He further admitted that he had allowed Burk to take some old clothes left at the apartment by a former roommate. At that time Beeman told Burk: "If you're going to do a robbery, you can't look like a bum." Nevertheless, appellant explained that he did not know Burk was then planning to commit this robbery. Further, although he knew there was a possibility Burk and Gray would try to rob Mrs. Beeman, appellant thought it very unlikely they would go through with it. He judged Burk capable of committing the crime but knew he had no car and no money to get to Redding. Appellant did not think Gray would cooperate.

Appellant agreed that he had talked with Gray on the phone two days before the robbery, and said he had then repeated he did not want to be involved. He claimed that Burk called him on the way back from Redding because he feared appellant would report him to the police, but knew appellant would want to protect Gray, who was his closer friend.

Appellant claimed he told the others to come to his house after the robbery and offered to sell the jewelry in order to buy time in which to figure out a way to collect and return the property. He took the most valuable piece to make sure it was not sold. Since Burk had a key to his apartment, appellant gave the diamond ring and a bracelet to a friend, Martinez, for safekeeping.[1] After Burk fled to Los Angeles, appellant showed some of the jewelry to mutual acquaintances in order to lull Burk into believing he was attempting to sell it. During this time Burk called him on the phone several times asking for money and, when appellant told him of plans to return the property, threatened to have him killed.

When confronted with his prior statement to the police that he had given one of the rings to someone in exchange for a $50 loan, appellant admitted making the statement but denied that it was true. He also claimed that his statement on direct examination that "his [Burk's] face was seen. He didn't wear a mask. Didn't do anything he was supposed to do. . . ." referred only to the reason Gray had given for wanting to return the victim's property.

---

[1] Martinez corroborated that appellant had given him a diamond ring and other jewelry belonging to appellant's family for this purpose.

Appellant requested that the jury be instructed in accord with *People v. Yarber* (1979) 90 Cal.App.3d 895 that aiding and abetting liability requires proof of intent to aid. The request was denied.

After three hours of deliberation, the jury submitted two written questions to the court: "We would like to hear again how one is determined to be an accessory and by what actions can he absolve himself"; and "Does inaction mean the party is guilty?" The jury was reinstructed in accord with the standard instructions, CALJIC Nos. 3.00 and 3.01. The court denied appellant's renewed request that the instructions be modified as suggested in *Yarber*, explaining that giving another, slightly different instruction at this point would further compli- cate matters. The jury returned its verdicts of guilty on all counts two hours later.

I

Penal Code section 31 provides in pertinent part: "All persons concerned in the commission of a crime, . . . whether they directly commit the act constituting the offense, or aid and abet in its commission, or, not being present, have advised and encouraged its commission, . . . are principals in any crime so committed." Thus, those persons who at common law would have been termed accessories before the fact and principals in the second degree as well as those who actually perpetrate the offense, are to be prosecuted, tried and punished as principals in California. (See Pen. Code, § 971.) The term "aider and abettor" is now often used to refer to principals other than the perpetrator, whether or not they are present at the commission of the offense.

CALJIC No. 3.00 defines principals to a crime to include "Those who, with knowledge of the unlawful purpose of the one who does directly and actively commit or attempt to commit the crime, aid and abet in its commission . . . , or . . . Those who, whether present or not at the commission or attempted com- mission of the crime, advise and encourage its commission. . . ." CALJIC No. 3.01 defines aiding and abetting as follows: "A person aids and abets the commission of a crime if, with knowledge of the unlawful purpose of the perpetrator of the crime, he aids, promotes, encourages or instigates by act or advice the commission of such crime."

Prior to 1974 CALJIC No. 3.01 read: "A person aids and abets the commission of a crime if he knowingly and with criminal intent aids, promotes, encourages or instigates by act or advice, or by act and advice, the commission of such crime."

Appellant asserts that the current instructions, in particular CALJIC No. 3.01, substitute an element of knowledge of the perpetrator's intent for the element of criminal intent of the accomplice, in contravention of common law principles and California case law. He argues that the instruction given permitted the jury to con- vict him of the same offenses as the perpetrators without finding that he harbored either the same criminal intent as they, or the specific intent to assist them, thus depriving him of his constitutional rights to due process and equal protection of the law. Appellant further urges that the error requires reversal because it removed a material issue from the jury and on this record it is impossible to conclude that the jury necessarily resolved the same factual question that would have been presented by the missing instruction.

The People argue that the standard instruction properly reflects California law, which requires no more than that the aider and abettor have knowledge of the perpetrator's criminal purpose and do a voluntary act which in fact aids the

perpetrator. The People further contend that defendants are adequately protected
from conviction for acts committed under duress or which inadvertently aid a
perpetrator by the limitation of the liability of an aider and abettor to those acts
knowingly aided and their natural and reasonable consequences. Finally, the People argue that the modification proposed by *Yarber, supra,* is unnecessary because
proof of intentional aiding in most cases can be inferred from aid with knowledge of the perpetrator's purpose. Thus, respondent argues, it is doubtful that the
requested modification would bring about different results in the vast majority of
cases.

II

There is no question that an aider and abettor must have criminal intent in
order to be convicted of a criminal offense. Decisions of this court dating back to
1898 hold that "the word 'abet' includes knowledge of the wrongful purpose of the
perpetrator and counsel and encouragement in the crime" and that it is therefore
error to instruct a jury that one may be found guilty as a principal if one aided *or*
abetted. The act of encouraging or counseling itself implies a purpose or goal of
furthering the encouraged result. "An aider and abettor's fundamental purpose,
motive and intent is to aid and assist the perpetrator in the latter's commission of
the crime."

The essential conflict in current appellate opinions is between those cases which
state that an aider and abettor must have an intent or purpose to commit or assist
in the commission of the criminal offenses , and those finding it sufficient that the
aider and abettor engage in the required acts with knowledge of the perpetrator's
criminal purpose.[3] . . .

[W]e conclude that the weight of authority and sound law require proof that
an aider and abettor act with knowledge of the criminal purpose of the perpetrator
and with an intent or purpose either of committing, or of encouraging or facilitating
commission of, the offense.

When the definition of the offense includes the intent to do some act or achieve
some consequence beyond the *actus reus* of the crime, the aider and abettor must
share the specific intent of the perpetrator. By "share" we mean neither that the
aider and abettor must be prepared to commit the offense by his or her own act
should the perpetrator fail to do so, nor that the aider and abettor must seek to share
the fruits of the crime. Rather, an aider and abettor will "share" the perpetrator's
specific intent when he or she knows the full extent of the perpetrator's criminal
purpose and gives aid or encouragement with the intent or purpose of facilitating
the perpetrator's commission of the crime The liability of an aider and abettor
extends also to the natural and reasonable consequences of the acts he knowingly
and intentionally aids and encourages.

CALJIC No. 3.01 inadequately defines aiding and abetting because it fails to
insure that an aider and abettor will be found to have the required mental state
with regard to his or her own act. While the instruction does include the word
"abet," which encompasses the intent required by law, the word is arcane and its
full import unlikely to be recognized by modern jurors. Moreover, even if jurors
were made aware that "abet" means to encourage or facilitate, and implicitly to
harbor an intent to further the crime encouraged, the instruction does not *require*

---

[3] Some cases which take the latter viewpoint intimate that the aider and abettor must also know
that his acts will probably facilitate the perpetrator's commission of the offense

them to find that intent because it defines an aider and abettor as one who "aids, promotes, encourages *or* instigates" (italics added). Thus, as one appellate court recently recognized, the instruction would "technically allow a conviction if the defendant knowing of the perpetrator's unlawful purpose, negligently or accidentally aided the commission of the crime." *People v. Patrick* (1981) 126 Cal. App. 3d 952, 967, fn. 10. . . .

The convictions are reversed.

QUESTIONS

1. What mental state(s) does *Beeman* require regarding assistance in order to be liable as an accomplice? Where in Penal Code § 31 did the court find these mental states?

2. What mental state does *Beeman* require regarding the underlying crime? Where in Penal Code § 31 did the court find this mental state?

3. Do you agree with the court's decision in *Beeman*? With its interpretation of Penal Code § 31?

4. Burk, Gray, and Beeman provided different versions of Beeman's role. As a juror, how would you have evaluated the credibility of each of these witnesses? What facts support the credibility of each witness? What factors undermine the credibility of each? Which version do you find most credible?

PROBLEM

11.8 Assume that Beeman knew that Burk and Gray were going to rob the victim and that he provided the map, clothing, and information about the victim and her home. Assume further that Beeman was not in favor of the robbery. Would Beeman have been liable under the following statutes?

Tennessee Code Annotated § 39-11-402 (2004) *Criminal responsibility for conduct of another.*

A person is criminally responsible for an offense committed by the conduct of another if:

(1) Acting with the culpability required for the offense, the person causes or aids an innocent or irresponsible person to engage in conduct prohibited by the definition of the offense;

(2) Acting with intent to promote or assist the commission of the offense, or to benefit in the proceeds or results of the offense, the person solicits, directs, aids, or attempts to aid another person to commit the offense; or

(3) Having a duty imposed by law or voluntarily undertaken to prevent commission of the offense and acting with intent to benefit in the proceeds or results of the offense, or to promote or assist its commission, the person fails to make a reasonable effort to prevent commission of the offense.

Tennessee Code Annotated § 39-11-403 (2004)   *Criminal responsibility for facilitation of felony.*

(a) A person is criminally responsible for the facilitation of a felony if, knowing that another intends to commit a specific felony, but without the intent required for criminal responsibility under § 39-11-402(2), the person knowingly furnishes substantial assistance in the commission of the felony.

(b) The facilitation of the commission of a felony is an offense of the class next below the felony facilitated by the person so charged.

Connecticut General Statute § 53a-8 (2001)   *Criminal liability for acts of another*

(a) A person, acting with the mental state required for commission of an offense, who solicits, requests, commands, importunes or intentionally aids another person to engage in conduct which constitutes an offense shall be criminally liable for such conduct and may be prosecuted and punished as if he were the principal offender.

(b) A person who sells, delivers or provides any firearm . . . to another person to engage in conduct which constitutes an offense knowing or under circumstances in which he should know that such other person intends to use such firearm in such conduct shall be criminally liable for such conduct and shall be prosecuted and punished as if he were the principal offender.

We saw in Chapter 5, Mental States, that the word "intent" has been given many meanings in the criminal law. In some contexts, it is used as a synonym for purpose. In other contexts, it is used to convey knowledge. In the context of accomplice liability, debate has often focused on whether the law should require purpose or knowledge regarding the principal's crime for accomplice liability to attach. Judge Learned Hand expressed the prevailing view in favor of purpose in his often cited opinion in the *Peoni* case:

> [After reviewing a series of definitions of "accomplice liability," Judge Hand wrote:] [A]ll these definitions . . . demand that he in some sort associate himself with the venture, that he participate in it as in something that he wishes to bring about, that he seek by his action to make it succeed. All the words used — even the most colorless, "abet" — carry an implication of purposive attitude towards it.

United States v. Peoni, 100 F.2d 401, 402 (2d Cir. 1938).

The *Backun* decision, published two years later, by contrast staked out the minority view and lauded the virtues of knowledge as the required mental state for complicity:

> Guilt as an accessory depends, not on "having a stake" in the outcome of crime, . . . but on aiding and assisting the perpetrators; and those who make a profit by furnishing to criminals, whether by sale or otherwise, the means to carry on their nefarious undertakings, aid them just as truly as if they were actual partners with them, having a stake in the fruits of their enterprise. To say that the sale of goods is a normally lawful transaction is beside the point. The seller may not ignore the purpose for which the purchase is made if he is advised of that purpose, or wash his hands of the aid that he has given the perpetrator of a felony by the plea that he has merely made a sale of merchandise. One who sells a gun to another knowing that he is buying it to commit a murder, would hardly escape conviction as an accessory to the murder by showing that he received full price for the gun; and no difference in principle can be drawn between such a case and any other case of

a seller who knows that the purchaser intends to use the goods which he is purchasing in the commission of a felony. In any such case, not only does the act of the seller assist in the commission of the felony, but his will assents to its commission, since he could refuse to give assistance by refusing to make the sale.

Backun v. United States, 112 F.2d 635, 637 (4th Cir. 1940).

How should the criminal law treat the seller in the following cartoon?[5]

"This is the perfect choice for whatever you're perpetrating."

1. Liability for Crimes of Recklessness and Negligence

Given the mental states required for accomplice liability, can one aid and abet a crime of recklessness or negligence?

WASHINGTON *v.* HOPKINS

Washington Supreme Court 147 Wash. 198 (1928)

PARKER, J. — The defendant, Mrs. Hopkins, was by information filed in the superior court for King county jointly, with one John Doe, charged with the crime of manslaughter. The information charges, in substance, that John Doe, his true name

---

being unknown, by his wilful, reckless and unlawful driving of an automobile on a public highway in King county, caused the death of Lois Ames. Mrs. Hopkins was, by the concluding language of the information, charged with aiding and abetting John Doe in the death of Lois Ames, as follows:

"And she, said Christine Hopkins, being then and there present, and being then and there the owner of said Studebaker automobile and a passenger therein and knowing said John Doe to be intoxicated, wilfully and unlawfully entrusted the operation of said automobile to said John Doe and permitted him to drive the same upon said highway and did then and there wilfully, unlawfully and feloniously aid, encourage, assist, advise, counsel and abet him, the said John Doe, in said unlawful acts as hereinbefore set forth and in the said unlawful operation of said Studebaker automobile aforesaid."

Trial in the superior court sitting with a jury resulted in a verdict of guilty and a judgment thereon being rendered against Mrs. Hopkins, from which she has appealed to this court.

The principal question here presented is as to the sufficiency of the evidence to sustain the verdict and judgment. That question was presented to the trial court by appropriate timely motions which were overruled, and is here presented by appropriate assignments of error. At the time in question, Mrs. Hopkins was proprietor of, and lived at, a small hotel situated in the southerly portion of the main business district of Seattle. She was then, and had been for about three years, the owner of an enclosed Studebaker automobile which she was accustomed and well qualified to drive. Shortly before ten o'clock of the night in question, her friend "Jimmie Burns," as she called him, came to the hotel to see her. They then agreed to take an automobile ride northerly to a so-called "chicken dinner" resort beyond the city limits on the Bothell Highway. It was agreed that they would go in her automobile and that he would drive. Accordingly they proceeded northerly through the city some six or seven miles to a point very near and just inside the northerly city limits.

There is no direct evidence as to what occurred during this portion of their journey, nor is there any direct evidence as to the condition of either of them as to being intoxicated up to that time, other than she admitted to the police officers that she had taken two or three drinks of whiskey earlier in the evening. According to the evidence of a witness, who was driving north on the highway, just before reaching the city limits, the Hopkins' car passed close to the left of the car the witness was driving, going in the same direction. The witness noticed this particularly, because the car passed dangerously close and turned quickly to the right in front of the car of the witness, requiring some care on the part of the witness to avoid a collision at that time. The witness' car was going about twenty miles per hour; the Hopkins' car probably about twenty-five miles per hour. According to this witness and some other witnesses, the Hopkins' car was, upon and after passing that car, driven in a very erratic and apparently reckless manner. It proceeded in this manner so that, in going approximately a distance of two or three blocks farther, it, for the most part, proceeded on its left, the west, side of the somewhat wide pavement, its speed continuing at from twenty-five to thirty miles per hour.

While so proceeding for a distance of about two blocks to a short distance north of the city limits, it came in collision with the Ames car which was then being driven south on its right, the west, side of the pavement. When the driver of the Ames' car saw the approach of the Hopkins' car on its wrong side of the pavement, he checked his speed, which had previously been about twenty-five miles per hour, and finally seeing that he would have a head-on collision with the Hopkins' car, as it was proceeding on his side of the pavement, and there being a bank on that side preventing his turning off the pavement, to avoid the impending collision, if possible, he turned his car east to his left. The driver of the Hopkins' car, an instant later, turned his car east to its right, and struck the right side of the Ames' car back of the front wheel, forcing the Ames' car to the east side of the pavement and in some manner causing Mrs. Ames and her daughter Lois Ames to fall from their car to the pavement and come to rest partly under the Hopkins' car which was a much heavier car than the Ames' car. From the injuries so received Lois Ames died a few hours later.

There is practically no room for controversy over the facts we have thus far summarized. We think they leave no room for seriously arguing that they are not sufficient to warrant the jury in believing beyond a reasonable doubt that John Doe (Jimmie Burns), the driver of the Hopkins' car, was guilty of such reckless and unlawful acts on his part causing the death of Lois Ames as to make him guilty of manslaughter. This, of course, is but a part of our problem here.

We now notice facts, as the jury were warranted in believing them to exist, touching more particularly on Mrs. Hopkins' relation to the reckless and unlawful acts of Jimmie Burns resulting in the death of Lois Ames. Jimmie Burns, as Mrs. Hopkins called the driver of her car, disappeared from the scene of the collision very soon after its occurrence, while others present were intent on and busily engaged in extricating Mrs. Ames and Lois Ames from the wreck. He has not been seen since then, hence the trial of Mrs. Hopkins alone. Mrs. Hopkins had been acquainted with Jimmie Burns some two or three months only. She did not know what his business or vocation was, or where he lived, only that he had come to her hotel occasionally. . . .

Mrs. Hopkins sat in her car for some time immediately following the collision. One witness testified to talking to her there as follows:

"I informed her that she had been in a very bad wreck and had probably killed my little girl. Q. What did she say then? A. Well, she said — for a minute she didn't say anything, and then she said, 'I told him that he could not drive.' "

The jury could well believe from the evidence that Mrs. Hopkins was considerably under the influence of intoxicating liquor, though she apparently knew what she was doing and was conscious of her surroundings. That was apparently about an hour after she had the drinks of whiskey, as admitted by her.

As to the intoxication of the driver of Mrs. Hopkins' car, we have the testimony of a witness as to what he saw very soon after the collision, as follows:

"Q. Now, may I ask if, before you left, you saw any one else standing there? A. There was a man standing alongside of the car there. Q. Which car did you see him standing alongside? A. The Studebaker. Q. Which side was he standing on? A. He was standing on the right hand side of that car. Q. Did you have an opportunity to ascertain whether he was intoxicated or not? A. Yes, he was. Q. What was his posture or position? A. Just standing leaning against the car like that (indicating). Q. Did he render any assistance while you were lifting the car? A. None. Q. Did Mrs. Hopkins? A. None. Q. While you were there did Mrs. Hopkins get out of the Studebaker? A. Yes, she did after I came back, after I called the ambulance. Q. Where did she go to when she got out? A. In another lady's car; Mrs. Atkinson's car. Q. You say then you had some conversation with her? A. Yes. Q. Relate just exactly what was said. A. I went over to the car and I asked her what became of the driver, and she said she didn't know. I asked her who he was. She said 'Jimmie Burns.' I said, 'Where did he go to?' She said 'I don't know.' "

This witness judged of the man's intoxication by his actions and the strong smell of liquor on his breath. No witness actually saw a man sitting as a driver or otherwise in the Hopkins' car. While the identity of the drunk man leaning against the Hopkins' car as the driver of that car is not testified to directly, we have the additional circumstance of his sudden disappearance in the darkness and confusion.

We think, under all the circumstances shown, that the jury might well conclude that the intoxicated man leaning against Mrs. Hopkins' car, while she was sitting therein, very soon after the collision, was the driver of that car; that his intoxicated condition was such that he was unfit to drive a car; that it was not of sudden acquiring; that in time it extended back at least over the period of the approximately one half hour elapsing from the time that Mrs. Hopkins placed her car in his charge upon leaving her hotel; and that his intoxication was, or should have been, known to Mrs. Hopkins had she used due care in deciding whether or not she would entrust the driving of her car to him. Our opinion is that the evidence is sufficient to sustain the verdict and judgment.

It is contended in behalf of Mrs. Hopkins that the information does not state facts constituting the crime of manslaughter as against her. This, as we understand her counsel, is rested upon the theory that manslaughter is a crime of such nature as to preclude the possibility of there being an accessory before the fact to such crime. There does seem to be language of that purport in the decisions of this court in *State v. Robinson* 12 Wash. 349 and *State v. McFadden* 48 Wash. 259 However, Judge Hadley, speaking for the court in the latter case, said:

"It is argued that such facts can in no event amount to other than a charge that appellant was an accessory before the fact, whereas the authorities hold that there cannot be such an accessory to the crime of manslaughter. This court so held in *State v. Robinson*. Our statute, Bal. Code, § 6782, however, abolishes all distinctions between an accessory before the fact and a principal, and provides that 'all persons concerned in the commission of an offense, whether they directly counsel the act constituting the offense, or counsel, aid and abet in its commission, though not present, shall hereafter be indicted, tried, and punished as principals.' Under the said statute appellant may be, and is, charged here as a principal and not as an accessory." . . .

"Every person concerned in the commission of a felony, gross misdemeanor or misdemeanor, whether he directly commits the act constituting the offense, or aids or abets in its commission, and whether present or absent; and every person who directly or indirectly counsels, encourages, hires, commands, induces or otherwise procures another to commit a felony, gross misdemeanor or misdemeanor, is a principal, and shall be proceeded against and punished as such. The fact that the person aided, abetted, counseled, encouraged, hired, commanded, induced or procured, could not or did not entertain a criminal intent, shall not be a defense to any person aiding, abetting, counseling, encouraging, hiring, commanding, inducing or procuring him."

It is now the settled law in this state that intent to cause the death of another is not an element in the crime of manslaughter[.] This plainly does not mean that intent to do an unlawful or grossly negligent act resulting in the unintentional death of another, is not an element of the crime of manslaughter. We think these are elements in the crime of manslaughter. So it seems to us that Mrs. Hopkins was by this information charged with negligence, in a criminal sense, in the placing of her car in the charge of John Doe, as driver, while he was intoxicated, she then knowing him to be intoxicated, and in then permitting him to drive it in the reckless, unlawful manner that resulted in the death of Lois Ames. So we conclude that the information sufficiently charged her, in contemplation of our law, as principal, though somewhat in form charging her as an accessory before the fact. . . .

The judgment is affirmed.

FRENCH, J. (dissenting) — In the case of *State v. Robinson* 12 Wash. 349, a prosecution under the aiding and abetting statute, this court laid down the rule:

"We think that § 1319 [Code Proc.] contains but the usual provisions in force in all, or nearly all, of the states, and we have been cited to no case, nor have we found one in which a conviction for manslaughter has been sustained under circumstances similar to those disclosed by the record here. *The offense of manslaughter from its legal character excludes the possibility* of an accessory before the fact as an element in its composition."

. . . The doctrine announced in the above cases is that the killing of a human being in order to constitute manslaughter must be involuntary and unintentional. I am unable to understand how a person can be aided and abetted in the doing of an unintentional and involuntary act by another person who has no intent.

QUESTIONS

1. Did Mrs. Hopkins' conduct satisfy the requirements for accessorial liability? If so, what was that conduct?

2. What mental state do you think Mrs. Hopkins had with respect to the death of Lois Ames? With respect to entrusting her car to Jimmie Burns?

3. Could Mrs. Hopkins be charged as a principal or primary actor? Recall that as a principal Mrs. Hopkins' conduct would have had to cause the death. Would the prosecution encounter any problems proving that Mrs. Hopkins caused the death?

2. The Model Penal Code Approach to Mental States in Complicity

Model Penal Code § 2.06 (1985) *Liability for Conduct of Another; Complicity*

(3) A person is an accomplice of another person in the commission of the offense if:

(a) with the purpose of promoting or facilitating the commission of the offense, he

(i) solicits such other person to commit it, or

(ii) aids or agrees or attempts to aid such other person in planning or committing it, or

(iii) having a legal duty to prevent the commission of the offense, fails to make proper effort so to do; or

(b) his conduct is expressly declared by law to establish his complicity.

(4) When causing a particular result is an element of an offense, an accomplice in the conduct causing such result is an accomplice in the commission of that offense if he acts with the kind of culpability, if any, with respect to that result that is sufficient for the commission of the offense.

QUESTIONS

1. What mental states does the MPC require for complicity?
2. How would each of the following cases be resolved under the MPC?
   (a) *V.T.*
   (b) *Walden*
   (c) *Beeman*
   (d) *Hopkins*

PEOPLE *v.* FLAYHART

Court of Appeals of New York, 72 N.Y.2d 737 (1988)

Titone, J. Defendants Richard and Beatrice Flayhart, who are husband and wife, were charged with reckless manslaughter and criminally negligent homicide on the theory that, acting together and with the requisite culpable mental states, they engaged in conduct that brought about the death of Richard's brother, Terry Flayhart. Terry, who lived with defendants during the last period of his life, was mentally retarded and afflicted with a number of ailments, including cerebral palsy and epilepsy. The People's case against defendants was based on the premise that Terry, who weighed approximately 75 pounds just before his death, had died of neglect while he was living in defendants' home and was totally dependent upon their care.

The medical evidence introduced at defendants' trial showed that Terry had died of malnutrition and inflammation of the lungs, with pneumonia as a complicating factor. There was also evidence that the lung inflammation was the result of Terry's having aspirated food from his stomach which had been ingested some six hours earlier. The other evidence against defendants consisted primarily of their own statements to Sheriff's deputies regarding their care of Terry, some background information relating to Terry's history, proof of a $122,000 trust fund that had been established to pay for Terry's care and proof that Terry had not seen his regular doctor during the last two years of his life.

At the close of the evidence, the trial court submitted the charged counts to the jury, along with an instruction on accomplice liability under Penal Law § 20.00. The jury found defendants guilty of criminally negligent homicide, and each defendant was sentenced to a term of imprisonment. The judgments of conviction were affirmed by the Appellate Division. This appeal, taken by permission of a Judge of this court, ensued.

Defendants' primary contention on their appeals to this court is that the convictions cannot be sustained because it is logically impossible to "aid and abet" criminally negligent homicide, an unintentional crime. Specifically, they contend that the crime of which they were convicted is nonexistent because one cannot "intentionally aid" another to "fail to perceive a substantial and unjustifiable risk" of death, the requisite mental state for criminally negligent homicide.

However, Penal Law § 20.00 imposes accessorial liability on an accomplice not for aiding or encouraging another to reach a particular mental state, but rather for intentionally aiding another to engage in *conduct* which constitutes the charged offense while himself "acting with the mental culpability required for the commission" of that offense. Thus, defendants were convicted because the jury found that each of them, while "[failing] to perceive a substantial and unjustifiable risk" of death, intentionally aided the other to engage in certain conduct, such as failure to provide food and medical care, which ultimately brought about Terry Flayhart's death. There is no logical or conceptual difficulty with such convictions.

QUESTIONS

1. What mental states does the *Flayhart* court find are required for complicity?
2. What theories of punishment support this finding?
3. Is an accomplice liability theory necessary to find the defendants liable for the victim's death in *Flayhart*?

What is the relationship between attempt and complicity? Can one be an accessory to an attempt? Can one attempt to be an accessory? Consider the following provision from the attempt section of the MPC:

Model Penal Code § 5.01 (1985) *Criminal Attempt*

(3) *Conduct Designed to Aid Another in Commission of a Crime.* A person who engages in conduct designed to aid another to commit a crime that would establish his complicity under Section 2.06 if the crime were committed by such other person, is guilty of an attempt to commit the crime, although the crime is not committed or attempted by such other person.

PROBLEM

11.9 Cory stumbles upon Michelle's diary. From the diary Cory learns that Michelle plans to rob the local video store. Cory detests the video store owner and is delighted that Michelle plans to rob the store. Michelle has not yet acted on her plan. Unbeknownst to Michelle, Cory reconnoiters the video store and draws a map of the surveillance cameras. Cory leaves the map, a disguise, and burglary tools on Michelle's back porch on the evening Michelle plans to commit the robbery. Michelle

> notices the package on the back porch, looks inside and sees the map,
> the disguise, and the tools. Just then, the police arrive. Someone else,
> it turns out, had also stumbled on Michelle's diary and warned the
> police of Michelle's plan. The police discover the package left by Cory
> and arrest Cory. Could a prosecutor in a jurisdiction that follows the
> MPC charge Cory with a crime? Could they charge Michelle with a
> crime?

3. Abandonment and Other Limiting Principles

The common law provided a number of limitations on complicity liability, and
so does the Model Penal Code. The MPC provides:

Model Penal Code § 2.06 (1985)   *Liability for Conduct of Another; Complicity*

... (6) Unless otherwise provided by the Code or by the law defining the
offense, a person is not an accomplice in an offense committed by another
person if:

(a) he is a victim of that offense; or

(b) the offense is so defined that his conduct is inevitably incident to its
commission; or

(c) he terminates his complicity prior to the commission of the offense
and

(i) wholly deprives it of effectiveness in the commission of the offense; or

(ii) gives timely warning to the law enforcement authorities or
otherwise makes proper effort to prevent the commission of the
offense.

Model Penal Code Commentators include as examples of the victim exclusion both a parent who pays ransom to the kidnapper of her child and a business
person who yields to extortion by a racketeer.[6] With respect to conduct that
is inevitably incident to a crime, the Commentators give as examples the purchaser in an unlawful sale and the previously unmarried party to a bigamous
marriage.[7]

PROBLEM

11.10 In the *Beeman* case, Beeman testified that "[t]wo days before the
offense" he "told Gray that he wanted nothing to do with the robbery of his relatives." Review Beeman's testimony. If accepted as
true, would MPC § 2.06 (6) absolve Beeman of liability?

---

6. Model Penal Code Commentaries § 2.06, art. 2, 323-324 (1985).
7. *Id.*

D. SPECIAL ISSUES

1. Conviction of the Principal

Indiana Code § 35-41-2-4 (2002)   *Aiding, inducing, or causing an offense*

A person who knowingly or intentionally aids, induces, or causes another person to commit an offense commits that offense, even if the other person:
   (1) Has not been prosecuted for the offense;
   (2) Has not been convicted of the offense; or
   (3) Has been acquitted of the offense.

Kansas Statute Annotated § 21-3205 (2001)   *Liability for crimes of another*

(1) A person is criminally responsible for a crime committed by another if such person intentionally aids, abets, advises, hires, counsels or procures the other to commit the crime. . . .

(3) A person liable under this section may be charged with and convicted of the crime although the person alleged to have directly committed the act constituting the crime lacked criminal or legal capacity or has not been convicted or has been acquitted or has been convicted of some other degree of the crime or of some other crime based on the same act.

PROBLEM

11.11   Alan and Rob meet in a bar one night while watching World Cup soccer matches on television. Both are fans of the Brazilian team playing Germany in the final match. While they are watching, boisterous fans of the German team enter the bar and begin loudly insulting Alan, who replies in kind. One of the fans of the German team invites Alan to step into an alleyway outside to settle their differences. Before Alan heads outside, Rob slips Alan a set of brass knuckles and says "beat the [expletive deleted] out of that jerk." Outside, Alan severely beats the fan of the German team. Assume both that self-defense is unavailable for Alan because he could have walked away from the challenge and that brass knuckles are a deadly weapon. Is Rob liable for assault with a deadly weapon under the following scenarios?

   (a) Alan is a British citizen working at the British Embassy and therefore has diplomatic immunity and cannot be prosecuted.
   (b) Alan is an American citizen but is a fugitive from justice at the time Rob is prosecuted.
   (c) Alan was an American citizen but died in a high-speed chase when police attempted to arrest him.

> **(d)** Alan suffers from a mental disease. This disease did not render him insane at the time of the offense but makes it impossible for him to understand the charge against him and to assist his lawyer in his defense. Therefore, he is incompetent to be tried.
> **(e)** Alan suffered from a mental disease that rendered him insane at the time of the offense.

2. Other Crimes Committed by the Principal

17-A Maine Revised Statute § 57 (2001)   *Criminal liability for conduct of another; accomplices*

3. A person is an accomplice of another person in the commission of a crime if:
  A. With the intent of promoting or facilitating the commission of the crime, he solicits such other person to commit the crime, or aids or agrees to aid or attempts to aid such other person in planning or committing the crime. A person is an accomplice under this subsection to any crime the commission of which was a reasonably foreseeable consequence of his conduct. . . .

Kansas Statute Annotated § 21-3205 (2001)   *Liability for crimes of another*

(1) A person is criminally responsible for a crime committed by another if such person intentionally aids, abets, advises, hires, counsels or procures the other to commit the crime.

(2) A person liable under subsection (1) hereof is also liable for any other crime committed in pursuance of the intended crime if reasonably foreseeable by such person as a probable consequence of committing or attempting to commit the crime intended.

Model Penal Code § 2.06 (1985)   *Liability for Conduct of Another; Complicity*

(3) A person is an accomplice of another person in the commission of the offense if:
  (a) with the purpose of promoting or facilitating the commission of the offense, he
    (i) solicits such other person to commit it, or
    (ii) aids or agrees or attempts to aid such other person in planning or committing it, or
    (iii) having a legal duty to prevent the commission of the offense, fails to make proper effort so to do; or
  (b) his conduct is expressly declared by law to establish his complicity.
(4) When causing a particular result is an element of an offense, an accomplice in the conduct causing such result is an accomplice in the commission of that offense if he acts with the kind of culpability, if any, with respect to that result that is sufficient for the commission of the offense.

PROBLEMS

11.12 Samantha and Jared plan a burglary of Larry's home to steal his valuable stamp collection, which was mentioned in a recent newspaper article. Samantha shows Jared a pistol she is carrying in case of trouble. How would the following scenarios be resolved under the Kansas and Maine statutes, as well as the MPC provision given above?

(a) When Samantha and Jared arrive at Larry's house, his fierce dog is blocking the entrance to the backyard. Samantha and Jared had surveilled the house on several prior occasions and knew that the dog was sometimes left in the backyard. Samantha shoots the dog with her pistol. Samantha is later convicted under a statute that reads as follows:

Any person who exhibits cruelty to animals in the form of physical assault causing injury or death is guilty of the crime of cruelty to animals.

Is Jared also liable for a cruelty-to-animals offense?

(b) When Samantha and Jared enter the house, they split up to search for the stamp collection. During his search, Jared finds $1,000 in cash hidden in a shoe box in Larry's bedroom closet. Jared puts the cash in his jacket pocket and does not tell Samantha about it. He then rejoins Samantha, who has found and taken the stamp collection. Jared is later arrested and convicted of theft of the $1,000 he took from Larry's closet. Is Samantha also liable for theft of the $1,000?

(c) What if Jared in (b) had found a stash of cocaine rather than cash and that Jared was later convicted of felony possession of cocaine. Is Samantha also liable for felony possession of cocaine?

(d) Assume in this part that when Samantha and Jared split up to search Larry's house, Samantha unexpectedly finds Larry and several friends playing cards in Larry's basement recreation room. One person there is Vince, an old enemy of Samantha's. Samantha ties and gags each of them. She then shoots and injures Vince. Samantha is later convicted of assault based on her shooting of Vince. Is Jared liable for assault based on Samantha's shooting of Vince?

11.13 Will and Virginia decide to rob a bank. Virginia enters the bank and using a threatening note, obtains money from a teller. Will drives Virginia to and from the bank and acts as a lookout while Virginia is in the bank. They agree that no one is to be injured during the robbery and Virginia does not carry a weapon during the robbery. The victim teller, however, suffers from a heart condition and dies of a heart attack as a result of the robbery. Assume Virginia is liable for felony murder. As her accomplice, is Will liable for felony murder as well?

3. Innocent Instrumentality

Reconsider a hypothetical you read in Chapter 5 about the political extremist who sends a letter containing anthrax to a government office and the mail carrier who delivers the letter. The terrorist's purpose is to infect and kill a legislator whom the terrorist has targeted because of the legislator's support for a particular policy. The mail carrier, by contrast, does not know the letter is contaminated. His only purpose is to deliver the mail. The legislator opens the letter, becomes infected, and dies.

This hypothetical provides an example of what is known as "innocent instrumentality." Who should be held liable here for the homicide of the legislator? Who should the law recognize as the principal actor? Here the mailman has no liability because he lacks the mental state required for attempted homicide — that is, the purpose to cause a death. But if no crime was committed by the mailman, how can the terrorist be held as an accomplice? Remember that an accomplice shares in the principal's liability. What if the person who would typically be cast as the principal is blameless? To resolve this problem, the law can treat the terrorist as the primary actor. He becomes liable for attempted murder having used the mailman as his innocent instrument.

4. The Feigning Accomplice and the Feigning Principal

Contrast the innocent instrumentality example with the following:

Richard believes that Josh has stolen Richard's watch. Josh denies the theft but does brag about having committed certain burglaries. Richard continues to believe that Josh is responsible for the missing watch. In the hopes of having the police catch Josh in the act of burglary, Richard agrees to help Josh steal some liquor. After store hours, Richard boosts Josh into the liquor store window. As soon as Josh is inside, Richard telephones the police and asks them to come to the liquor store. Before the police arrive, Josh hands several bottles of alcohol out the window to Richard. When the police arrive, they ask Richard how Josh got into the store. Richard acknowledges helping Josh enter. The police arrest Richard and Josh for theft. Richard moves the court to dismiss the theft charges. What should the court do?

This Problem, based substantially on the facts of *Wilson v. People*, 103 Colo. 441 (1939), illustrates the "feigning accomplice" Problem. To decide what action the court should take, consider whether Richard possessed the mental state(s) required for accomplice liability. Reconsider the Utah statute that describes two mental states required for accomplice liability: (1) a mental state regarding the underlying crime and (2) a mental state regarding the assistance. Does Richard possess both of these?[8]

The reverse issue, that of the "feigning principal," also arises in the case reports. Imagine that instead of Richard boosting Josh into the store, Josh boosts Richard inside. How might this change the court's analysis? If the liability of the accomplice derives from the liability of the primary actor, could a court properly convict Josh here?[9]

---

8. *See* Joshua Dressler, *Understanding Criminal Law* 472-474 (3d ed. 2001).
9. *Id.* at 483-484.

E. SYNTHESIS AND REVIEW

PROBLEMS

11.14 A newspaper reported the following story.[10] The Brazilian government is prosecuting Kube-i and Darrell Posey for violation of a criminal statute making it illegal for foreigners (i.e., non-Brazilian citizens) to interfere in Brazil's domestic affairs. Kube-i is a member of the Kaiapo Indian tribe, which inhabits the Amazon River Basin in Brazil. Kube-i *is* a citizen of Brazil and is the son of the chief of the Kaiapo tribe. Darrell Posey is an American anthropologist who has worked for the past 11 years among the Kaiapo and *is not* a citizen of Brazil. Posey has been active in recent years along with Kaiapo leaders in protesting the Brazilian government's destruction of the Amazon forest, pollution of the Amazon River and its tributaries, and general disregard of Indian rights. The criminal charge against Kube-i and Posey is based on a trip made by Kube-i and Posey to Washington D.C. to meet with officers of the World Bank, which is considering approval of a $500 million loan to Brazil for a hydroelectric project entailing construction of two vast new dams in the Amazon basin that would flood Kaiapo lands. The complaints of Kube-i and Posey have apparently delayed and complicated the loan approval, thus interfering in the eyes of the Brazilian prosecuting authorities with Brazil's domestic affairs. Assume that the activities of Kube-i and Posey constitute "interfering with domestic affairs" for the purpose of the statute under which they have been charged. Lawyers have argued that the charging of a Brazilian citizen, Kube-i, with a crime limited by definition to persons who are not citizens of Brazil is a "legal anomaly."[11] How might one explain the supposed anomaly? In what other situations in our course have we encountered a similar apparent anomaly?

11.15 You are a lawyer working at a law firm in a large city. Your firm represents a shelter for runaway teenagers as a pro bono client. One day you are called by a doctor who provides free medical services on a volunteer basis for the teenagers at the shelter. The doctor tells you that a 15-year-old girl who has been staying at the shelter in recent weeks recently confided in the doctor that she has been engaging in prostitution to earn money for food and clothes. The doctor has tried to talk the girl out of engaging in prostitution but without success. Since the girl appears to be determined to continue to engage in

---

10. Based on Marlise Simons, *Brazil Accuses Scholar of Aiding Indian Protest*, N.Y. Times, Aug. 14, 1988, at 14; Marlise Simons, *Dams vs. Indians: The Battle Calls for War Paint*, N.Y. Times, Oct. 14, 1988, at 4.

11. *Id.* n.10. *Dams vs. Indians: The Battle Calls for War Paint*, at 4.

prostitution, the doctor wants at least to provide her with protection against pregnancy. She is considering prescribing contraceptives for the girl, but is concerned that she may encounter legal problems for doing so. What is the doctor's potential criminal liability if she prescribes the contraceptives?

CHAPTER TWELVE

CONSPIRACY

A. INTRODUCTION

In this chapter, we turn to the crime of conspiracy. Like the crimes of solicitation and attempt, it is a form of anticipatory crime allowing the police to intervene and incapacitate criminals prior to the commission of the target offense. Unlike the crimes of attempt and solicitation, however, if the police are unable to intervene and prevent commission of the target crime, the prosecution in many jurisdictions can convict a defendant for both conspiracy and the target offense. Thus the penalty for conspiracy may be imposed as an addition to rather than a substitute for punishment for the target offense. Co-conspirators in some jurisdictions may also be vicariously liable for crimes committed by other conspirators. In this way, conspiracy is similar to accomplice liability.

Prosecutors make frequent use of conspiracy because it offers several evidentiary and procedural advantages. Charging a particular act as an overt act in furtherance of a conspiracy opens the door to its admission at trial even if the rules of evidence might otherwise exclude it. Also, out-of-court statements made by any co-conspirators during and in furtherance of a conspiracy are admissible at trial against other co-conspirators despite the fact that these statements are hearsay and otherwise would be barred by the evidentiary rule against hearsay. A conspiracy charge also helps justify the joint trial of co-conspirators, resulting in a number of potential strategic disadvantages for defendants such as the risks of guilt by association and use of inconsistent defense strategies. A conspiracy charge gives prosecutors greater flexibility in choosing the place for trial. A conspiracy may be prosecuted either where the agreement was formed or in any place where an act in furtherance of the conspiracy took place.

Legislatures and courts also grant prosecutors and police additional leeway in the investigative techniques they may use against conspiracies. A recent federal case dealing with the use of wiretaps captures this idea:

> Like the Hydra of Greek mythology, the conspiracy may survive the destruction of its parts unless the conspiracy is completely destroyed. For even if some or many conspirators are imprisoned, others may remain at large, free to recruit others eager to break the law and to pursue the conspiracy's illegal ends. Reflecting this concern,

we have "consistently upheld findings of necessity where traditional investigative techniques lead only to apprehension and prosecution of the main conspirators, but not to apprehension and prosecution of . . . other satellite conspirators." Because the government has a duty to extirpate conspiracy beyond its duty to prevent the mere commission of specific substantive offenses, we conclude that the government is entitled to more leeway in its investigative methods when it pursues a conspiracy.

Just as the punishment should fit the crime, so too the rigor of the government's investigation should fit the threat posed to society by criminals' illicit and coordinated plans. The principle we announce here — that government has considerable latitude to wiretap suspected members of a criminal conspiracy (particularly when the conspirators are bent on the government's destruction) — reflects a larger principle of proportionality embodied in the wiretapping statute: The more grave the threat posed to our society, the greater the government's leeway in pursuing it.[1]

The crime of conspiracy is the focal point of considerable controversy. The classic justification offered for conspiracy is that by joining forces criminals pose increased danger to society. Such a combination is thought both to increase the likelihood of success and decrease the likelihood of repentance and desistance. As the quotation above suggests, a conspiracy once started may live on despite the repentance of any particular conspirator.

Critics complain that the crime of conspiracy is vague and that its conduct requirement is too minimal to assure both danger and blame. Some claim that it is now unnecessary given the reach of modern attempt statutes and other anticipatory offenses. Others argue that the advantages it gives to police and prosecutors are simply unfair.

Our study of the elements of conspiracy begins with conduct. As the statutes below reflect, statutory conspiracy formulations routinely require some form of agreement to commit another crime. These statutes also reveal that jurisdictions vary on whether conspiracy requires any additional conduct beyond agreement. We then examine the mental states that the government must prove to obtain a conspiracy conviction. The remainder of the chapter deals with an assortment of issues, such as the scope of conspiracy and whether and how a co-conspirator may terminate his association with a conspiracy.

PROBLEM

12.1 What are the elements the government must prove to obtain a conspiracy conviction under the following statutes? What features do these statutes share? How do they differ?

Illinois Compiled Statutes § 720 ILCS 5/8-2   *Conspiracy*

(a) Elements of the offense. A person commits conspiracy when, with intent that an offense be committed, he agrees with another to the commission of that offense.

---

1. United States v. McGuire, 307 F.3d 1192, 1198 (9th Cir. 2002).

No person may be convicted of conspiracy to commit an offense unless an act in furtherance of such agreement is alleged and proved to have been committed by him or by a co-conspirator.

Model Penal Code § 5.03   *Criminal Conspiracy*

(1) Definition of Conspiracy. A person is guilty of conspiracy with another person or persons to commit a crime if with the purpose of promoting or facilitating its commission he:

> (a) agrees with such other person or persons that they or one or more of them will engage in conduct that constitutes such crime or an attempt or solicitation to commit such crime; or
>
> (b) agrees to aid such other person or persons in the planning or commission of such crime or of an attempt or solicitation to commit such crime. . . .

(5) Overt Act. No person may be convicted of conspiracy to commit a crime, other than a felony of the first or second degree, unless an overt act in pursuance of such conspiracy is alleged and proved to have been done by him or by a person with whom he conspired.

Ohio Revised Code § 2923.01   *Conspiracy*

(A) No person, with purpose to commit or to promote or facilitate the commission of [certain enumerated crimes] . . . shall do either of the following:

> (1) With another person or persons, plan or aid in planning the commission of any of the specified offenses;
>
> (2) Agree with another person or persons that one or more of them will engage in conduct that facilitates the commission of any of the specified offenses.

(B) No person shall be convicted of conspiracy unless a substantial overt act in furtherance of the conspiracy is alleged and proved to have been done by the accused or a person with whom the accused conspired, subsequent to the accused's entrance into the conspiracy. For purposes of this section, an overt act is substantial when it is of a character that manifests a purpose on the part of the actor that the object of the conspiracy should be completed.

North Dakota Code § 12.1-06-04   *Criminal conspiracy*

1. A person commits conspiracy if he agrees with one or more persons to engage in or cause conduct which, in fact, constitutes an offense or offenses, and any one or more of such persons does an overt act to effect an objective of the conspiracy. The agreement need not be explicit but may be implicit in the fact of collaboration or existence of other circumstances.

B. CONDUCT

It is sometimes said that the "essence" of conspiracy, a word derived from a Latin verb meaning "to breathe together," is agreement. This seems simple enough. But what does it mean to agree to commit a crime? Need the agreement be explicit?

Or will an implicit agreement suffice? As one might expect, agreements to commit crimes, unlike commercial contracts, are not typically committed to writing and usually are kept secret. How then do prosecutors prove and judges and juries decide whether such an agreement existed? Such questions are not easily answered.

1. Agreement

PROBLEMS

12.2 You are defense counsel representing Shawn, a young man charged with first-degree murder. Your conversations with Shawn and the discovery provided by the prosecutor reveal the following. On the evening in question, Shawn was driving in his car with two friends, Terry and James. Terry, who was seated in the passenger's seat, recognized the driver of a nearby pickup truck as Marcus, a man with whom Terry had been feuding for the past several months over a woman each had dated. Terry told Shawn to follow the truck. Shawn did so. Shawn was aware of the feud between Terry and Marcus and also knew that Terry was usually armed. After several minutes of pursuit, the truck turned into an alley and Shawn pulled his car in behind the truck. Marcus stepped out of the truck and started walking toward Shawn's car. Terry in the meantime had rolled down the passenger's window in Shawn's car. Terry pulled a 9 millimeter pistol out of his pocket, leaned out the window, and fired several shots at Marcus, striking him several times and killing him. Shawn then drove away from the scene of the shooting with both Terry and James still in the car. James, who was seated in the back seat throughout the incident, has agreed to testify for the prosecution.

The prosecution offers to dismiss the first-degree murder charge in return for Shawn's guilty plea to a charge of conspiracy to commit murder. Is Shawn liable for conspiracy under the facts given? How would you advise him regarding the plea offer?

12.3 (a) Anna is married to Tim. Her brother, Frank, lives with them. Anna has two young children by her prior marriage to Lee. Anna divorced Lee several years ago, and Lee was awarded primary physical custody of the children. Anna has visitation rights on alternate weekends. Custody and visitation have been ongoing sources of tension and conflict between Lee and Anna. Anna wants to see the children more often and is trying through her lawyer to obtain joint custody. Lee did not want a divorce from Anna and has been resisting her desire for greater access to the children. On several occasions, Lee has offered Anna greater access in return for having sexual relations with him. Frank is close to Anna's children. He also knows of the attempts Lee has made to use access to the children to pressure Anna to have sexual relations with him. One evening after Anna and Lee argue on the phone about an upcoming visit with the children, Anna is visibly upset. She, Frank, and Tim are sitting in the kitchen of their house when Frank says "I have an idea about how to take care of Lee." When Tim asks what his idea is, Frank says "Anna should call Lee on the phone, tell him that she has gotten separated from Tim, and that she wants Lee to come over. Then Anna should leave the house. When Lee gets here, I'll kill him." Neither Anna nor Tim says anything in response to Frank's proposal. Is either Anna or Tim liable for conspiracy?

(b) Would Anna or Tim's liability change given the following additional facts? If so, which do you find significant? About ten days after Frank described his idea, Anna and Tim go away on an overnight camping trip. While they are away, Lee goes to their house, where Frank kills him. When Anna and Tim return, they help Frank place Lee's body in a 55-gallon steel drum and hide it in a ravine in a remote area. Police later determine that on the day before Anna and Tim left on their camping trip, someone made a phone call from their house to Lee's house. The police cannot determine who the caller was.

12.4 Members of two rival gangs, the Sharks and the Jets, attend a high school dance. At the dance, Tony, a member of the Jets, dances with Maria, the sister of the leader of the Sharks. The Sharks take offense and make insulting comments toward various Jets, who respond in kind. The confrontation quickly escalates, and several members of the Jets draw knives and assault a number of Sharks, causing serious injuries. On these facts, can the Jets who attacked the Sharks be convicted of conspiracy to commit aggravated assault?

MARTINEZ v. WYOMING
Supreme Court of Wyoming 943 P.2d 1178 (1997)

MACY, J. Appellant Ben Martinez appeals from the judgment and sentence which the trial court entered after a jury found that he was guilty of conspiring to deliver a controlled substance and attempting to deliver a controlled substance. . . .

At 5:00 A.M. on September 1, 1995, a confidential informant for the Division of Criminal Investigation (DCI) contacted Martinez, seeking to buy morphine. The informant was wearing a wire and was under surveillance at that time. Due to the early hour, Martinez told the informant that he would contact her between 8:30 and 9:00 A.M. and that he could get her five to ten vials of morphine for $200 each. When Martinez telephoned the informant at her home later that morning, DCI agents tape recorded the conversation.

After being again fitted with a wire monitor and being given $1,000 in recorded buy money, the informant drove to Martinez's home. Martinez got into the informant's vehicle, and they left to go meet Martinez's source. While they were en route, Martinez asked the informant to pull into a grocery store parking lot so that he could call his source to make sure that he was still at the agreed upon meeting place. When Martinez returned to the car, he told the informant that his source was "jittery" but that he thought he could still get five vials of morphine. The informant drove a short distance further before Martinez had her stop at a convenience store so that he could make another telephone call to his source. When Martinez returned to the car, he acted "jittery" and told the informant that he had to meet his source alone. He left in the informant's car with the buy money and returned approximately twenty minutes later. At that time, he told the informant that DCI agents had followed him and that he had decided not to go to his source's house. He went inside the convenience store where he again called his source. While Martinez was talking on the telephone, DCI agents entered the store and arrested him. . . .

A jury found that Martinez was guilty of conspiring to deliver a controlled substance . . . . The trial court sentenced him to serve . . . not less than four years nor more than eight years for the conspiracy conviction . . . .

SUFFICIENCY OF THE EVIDENCE

Martinez contends that the evidence which was produced at the trial was not sufficient to prove all the elements which were necessary to convict him of conspiring to deliver a controlled substance. . . .

W.S. 35-7-1042 provides in part:

> Any person who attempts or conspires to commit any offense under this article within the state of Wyoming . . . shall be punished by imprisonment or fine or both which may not exceed the maximum punishment prescribed for the offense the commission of which was the object of the attempt or conspiracy. . . .

For a conspiracy-to-deliver-a-controlled-substance conviction to be sustained, the evidence must show beyond a reasonable doubt that the parties to the conspiracy voluntarily agreed to commit an offense under the Wyoming Controlled Substances Act of 1971. The existence of an agreement may be established in whole or in part by circumstantial evidence, and it is not necessary to demonstrate that the conspirators performed an overt act to complete the agreement's objective.

In *Smith v. State*, 902 P.2d 1271 (Wyo. 1995), we considered what type of agreement was necessary for a conspiracy to exist.

> "One might suppose that the agreement necessary for conspiracy is essentially like the agreement or 'meeting of the minds' which is critical to a contract, but this is not the case. Although there continues to exist some uncertainty as to the precise meaning of the word in the context of conspiracy, it is clear that the definition in this setting is somewhat more lax than elsewhere. A mere tacit understanding will suffice, and there need not be any written statement or even a speaking of words which expressly communicates agreement. . . .
>
> "Because most conspiracies are clandestine in nature, the prosecution is seldom able to present direct evidence of the agreement. Courts have been sympathetic to this problem, and it is thus well established that the prosecution may 'rely on inferences drawn from the course of conduct of the alleged conspirators.'"

902 P.2d at 1281-82 (quoting Wayne R. LaFave & Austin W. Scott, Jr., Criminal Law at 460-61 (1972)).

The informant in this case testified that Martinez agreed to procure five to ten vials of morphine for her but that he had to get it from his source. She also explained in detail how Martinez called his source at different times while they were on their way to the source's house. Additionally, the jury heard a recording which had been made of the discussions that occurred between the informant and Martinez throughout the course of this transaction. The recording allowed the jury to hear Martinez making a deal with the informant to get morphine for her from another source. The deal specified the price for, as well as the amount of, morphine which was available. Furthermore, Martinez told DCI agents that he was on his way to get the morphine but that he changed his mind when he discovered he was being followed. He also informed them that he had received the buy money from the informant.

This evidence demonstrated that Martinez was planning to purchase morphine from his source and to deliver it to the informant. We hold, after reviewing the evidence in the light most favorable to the State, that the jury had sufficient evidence before it to conclude beyond a reasonable doubt that Martinez had an agreement with another person to violate the controlled substances act. . . .

Affirmed.

QUESTIONS

1. With whom did Martinez agree? The informant? His source? Both?
2. Was the agreement in the *Martinez* case explicit or implicit? What evidence did the prosecution offer to prove the agreement?
3. How does the agreement needed for a conspiracy differ from the agreement needed for a contract?
4. Should it make any difference if one of the parties to the agreement on which a conspiracy charge is based is an informant working for the police? Can someone working for the government to foil a conspiracy's objective be considered a party to that conspiracy?

Bilateral or Unilateral Agreement?

What if two people discuss the possibility of committing a crime, but only one of the two sincerely commits herself to the criminal venture? The other person, perhaps a police officer or an informant working for the police, merely pretends to go along. Does this fall within the meaning of the word "agrees"? In answering this question, should any weight be given to the fact that answering it in the affirmative gives the police greater power to interdict and incapacitate dangerous individuals?

13 Vermont Statutes Annotated § 1404   *Conspiracy*

(a) A person is guilty of conspiracy if, with the purpose that an offense . . . be committed, that person agrees with one or more persons to commit or cause the commission of that offense, and at least two of the co-conspirators are persons who are neither law enforcement officials acting in official capacity nor persons acting in cooperation with a law enforcement official.

PROBLEM

12.5 James approached Matthew in a bar one night and asked if he was interested in making some money. James proposed that together they rob an elderly man who kept money and valuables at his home.

> Matthew told James he was interested but did so only to learn the details of James' plan so he could report him to the police. James then confided to Matthew the details of his plan for the robbery, which was to take place the following night. Immediately after they parted company, Matthew called the police and told them of James' plan. Following police instructions, Matthew met James the following evening and proceeded to the elderly gentleman's home. As they approached the home, James was arrested and charged with conspiracy to commit burglary and robbery. Is James liable for conspiracy?

WASHINGTON *v.* PACHECO

Supreme Court of Washington (En Banc) 125 Wash. 2d 150 (1994)

JOHNSON, J. The Defendant, Herbert Pacheco, appeals his convictions for conspiracy to commit first degree murder and conspiracy to deliver a controlled substance. He contends he did not commit conspiracy within the meaning of RCW 9A.28.040 because no genuine agreement existed between him and his sole coconspirator, an undercover police agent. We hold RCW 9A.28.040 and RCW 69.50.407 require an actual agreement between two coconspirators, and, therefore, reverse his convictions for conspiracy to commit murder in the first degree and conspiracy to deliver a controlled substance.

FACTS

Herbert Pacheco met Thomas Dillon in 1985, when Pacheco worked about 2 months for Dillon's private investigation firm. Pacheco bragged to Dillon about his involvement in illegal activities, including enforcement, collecting debts, procuring weapons, providing protection, and performing "hits."

In 1989, Dillon learned that Pacheco was a Clark County deputy sheriff. Dillon contacted the FBI and volunteered to inform on Pacheco. The FBI began an investigation of Pacheco. The Clark County Sheriff's office joined, and later directed the investigation.

The investigation involved the recording of conversations, face-to-face and over the telephone, between Dillon and Pacheco. During these conversations Dillon asked Pacheco to perform various jobs, including collections and information checks on individuals.

On March 26, 1990, according to a plan designed by the sheriff's office and the FBI, Dillon called Pacheco and told him he would like to meet to discuss a possible deal. Dillon and Pacheco met at a restaurant. Dillon said he had ties to the "Mafia" and offered Pacheco $ 500 in exchange for protection during a cocaine deal. Dillon told Pacheco that a buyer (an undercover FBI agent) would arrive shortly, and Pacheco was to protect Dillon during the transaction. Pacheco agreed. The undercover agent arrived and the purported drug transaction took place. Afterward, Dillon paid Pacheco $ 500.

The same scenario was replayed at a second purported drug transaction on April 2, 1990. Dillon again paid Pacheco $ 500. Later that night Dillon called Pacheco and pretended he had been shortchanged $ 40,000 in that afternoon's drug transaction. Dillon said he had been given $ 10,000 by his superiors to take care of the situation. Dillon agreed to meet Pacheco at a convenience store. At the store, Pacheco offered to kill the drug buyer for $10,000. Pacheco indicated if he had to kill anyone else, it would cost more. Pacheco proposed he go get his gun while Dillon located the drug buyer at his motel.

Dillon and Pacheco met at a lounge near the motel. They decided Pacheco would go to the lobby of the motel, call the buyer and convince him to come down to the lobby where Pacheco would then shoot him. Pacheco went to the lobby with a loaded gun, but he did not call the buyer's room. As Pacheco left the lobby, sheriff's deputies arrested him. Pacheco contended he was collecting evidence to build a case against Dillon and he thought he was following police procedures.

Pacheco was charged with conspiracy to commit first degree murder, attempted first degree murder, two counts of unlawful delivery of a controlled substance, two counts of conspiracy to deliver a controlled substance, and official misconduct. The official misconduct charge was dismissed. The jury found Pacheco not guilty of attempted first degree murder, but convicted him on all other counts.

The Court of Appeals affirmed the convictions. We accepted review of the conspiracy convictions, limited to the issue of whether a conspiracy exists when the sole coconspirator is an undercover agent.

ANALYSIS

The Defendant contends he did not commit conspiracy within the meaning of RCW 9A.28.040 because his sole coconspirator was an undercover police agent who never "agreed" to commit the crime of murder in the first degree.

The Defendant argues the statute retains the common law, bilateral approach to conspiracy, which requires an actual agreement to commit a crime between the defendant and at least one other. Therefore, a government agent feigning agreement with the defendant does not constitute a conspiracy under the common law approach because no genuine agreement is reached. The Defendant asserts Washington is among those states whose statutes are patterned after the Model Penal Code but have been interpreted as adopting only a limited form of the code's unilateral approach, and retaining the requirement of a bilateral underlying agreement.

The State contends RCW 9A.28.040 follows the code's purely unilateral approach. Under the code, actual agreement is not required as long as the defendant believes another is agreeing to commit the criminal act. Therefore, a purported agreement between a government agent and a defendant would satisfy the code's unilateral conspiratorial agreement approach.

Adopted in 1975, as a part of the overhaul of the criminal code § RCW 9A.28.040 provides in part:

> (1) A person is guilty of criminal conspiracy when, with intent that conduct constituting a crime be performed, he agrees with one or more persons to engage in or cause the performance of such conduct, and any one of them takes a substantial step in pursuance of such agreement.
>
> (2) It shall not be a defense to criminal conspiracy that the person or persons with whom the accused is alleged to have conspired:
>
>> (a) Has not been prosecuted or convicted; or
>> (b) Has been convicted of a different offense; or
>> (c) Is not amenable to justice; or
>> (d) Has been acquitted; or
>> (e) Lacked the capacity to commit an offense.

In construing a statute, our primary objective is to carry out the intent of the Legislature. When a term is not defined in a statute, the court may look to common law or a dictionary for the definition. As a general rule, we presume the Legislature intended undefined words to mean what they did at common law.

Subsection (1) of RCW 9A.28.040 expressly requires an agreement, but does not define the term. Black's Law Dictionary defines *agreement* as, "[a] meeting of two or more minds; a coming together in opinion or determination; the coming together in accord of two minds on a given proposition." Similarly, *agreement* is defined in Webster's as "1 a: the act of agreeing or coming to a mutual agreement . . . b: oneness of opinion. . .". *Webster's Third New International Dictionary* 43 (1986). The dictionary definitions thus support the Defendant's argument.

Likewise, the common law definition of the agreement required for a conspiracy is defined not in unilateral terms but rather as a confederation or combination of minds. A conspiratorial agreement necessarily requires more than one to agree because it is impossible to conspire with oneself. We conclude that by requiring an agreement, the Legislature intended to retain the requirement of a genuine or bilateral agreement.

Subsection (2) provides the conspiratorial agreement may still be found even though the coconspirator cannot be convicted. In this sense, the statute incorporates a limited form of the code's unilateral conspiracy in that it is no longer necessary that agreement be proved against both conspirators. Thus, under subsection (2)'s unilateral approach, the failure to convict an accused's sole coconspirator will not prevent proof of the conspiratorial agreement against the accused. However, this does not indicate the Legislature intended to abandon the traditional requirement of two criminal participants reaching an underlying agreement.

Our case law supports this interpretation of RCW 9A.28.040. In *State v. Valladares*, two codefendants were charged with conspiracy to deliver cocaine. In a joint trial, one defendant was acquitted and the other, Valladares, was found guilty.

On appeal, the court held acquittal of Valladares' only alleged coconspirator mandated reversal of Valladares' conviction because the two outcomes were logically inconsistent. The inconsistent verdicts to the charge of conspiracy in the same trial nullified the possibility that the two coconspirators reached an agreement, a necessary element of the conspiracy. We said:

> RCW 9A.28.040(2)(d) provides that it shall not be a defense to a charge of criminal conspiracy that the person with whom the accused is alleged to have conspired has been acquitted. In this regard, the Washington Legislature appears to have adopted a unilateral approach to conspiracy by focusing on the culpability of the individual actor. At the same time, however, RCW 9A.28.040(1) makes an *agreement* with one or more persons a necessary element of the crime of conspiracy.

Valladares thus makes clear the Legislature adopted the unilateral approach to the limited extent set out in RCW 9A.28.040(2). However, the element of the "requisite corrupt agreement," or the bilateral agreement, is still necessary as set out in RCW 9A.28.040(1). Indeed, the essence of a conspiracy is the agreement to commit a crime. We will not presume the Legislature intended to overturn this long-established legal principle unless that intention is made very clear.

Additionally, the unilateral approach fails to carry out the primary purpose of the statute. The primary reason for making conspiracy a separate offense from the substantive crime is the increased danger to society posed by group criminal activity. However, the increased danger is nonexistent when a person "conspires" with a government agent who pretends agreement. In the feigned conspiracy there is no increased chance the criminal enterprise will succeed, no continuing criminal enterprise, no educating in criminal practices, and no greater difficulty of detection.

Indeed, it is questionable whether the unilateral conspiracy punishes criminal activity or merely criminal intentions. The "agreement" in a unilateral conspiracy is a legal fiction, a technical way of transforming nonconspiratorial conduct into a prohibited conspiracy. When one party merely pretends to agree, the other party, whatever he or she may believe about the pretender, is in fact not conspiring with anyone. Although the deluded party has the requisite criminal intent, there has been no criminal act.

The federal courts agree. In *Sears v. United States*, 343 F.2d 139, 142 (5th Cir. 1965), the Court of Appeals established the rule that "as it takes two to conspire, there can be no indictable conspiracy with a government informer who secretly intends to frustrate the conspiracy." Every federal court which has since considered the issue has adopted this approach.

Another concern with the unilateral approach is its potential for abuse. In a unilateral conspiracy, the State not only plays an active role in creating the offense, but also becomes the chief witness in proving the crime at trial. We agree with the Ninth Circuit this has the potential to put the State in the improper position of manufacturing crime. At the same time, such reaching is unnecessary because the punishable conduct in a unilateral conspiracy will almost always satisfy the elements of either solicitation or attempt. The State will still be able to thwart the activity and punish the defendant who attempts agreement with an undercover police officer. . . .

In sum, the State has not persuaded us the Legislature intended to abandon the traditional requirement of an actual agreement. We hold RCW 9A.28.040 and RCW 69.50.407 require the defendant to reach a genuine agreement with at least one other coconspirator. The Defendant's convictions for conspiracy to commit murder in the first degree and conspiracy to deliver a controlled substance are reversed.

DURHAM, J. (dissenting) — The jury found that Herbert Pacheco, an aspiring hit man, planned a murder for money. Moreover, he took a substantial step toward that objective. Yet the majority overturns his conviction for conspiracy to commit murder solely because he conspired with a government agent rather than with another hit man. The Washington conspiracy statute does not require a co-conspirator to be a nongovernment actor. In fact, the statute explicitly envisages so-called unilateral conspiracies, as the majority admits. Because neither our case law, the statute, nor the rationale of conspiracy crimes compel the result arrived at by the majority, I dissent.

We accepted review solely to determine whether Washington's conspiracy statute countenances unilateral conspiracies. Yet the majority fails to provide even a cursory analysis of the essential differences between the bilateral and unilateral approaches to conspiracy. The bilateral approach asks whether there is an agreement between two or more persons to commit a criminal act. Its focus is on the content of the agreement and whether there is a shared understanding between the conspirators. The unilateral approach is not concerned with the content of the agreement or whether there is a meeting of minds. Its sole concern is whether the agreement, shared or not, objectively manifests the criminal intent of at least one of the conspirators. The majority does not even mention this crucial difference, and instead merely assumes that all conspiracies must be bilateral. In other words, the majority assumes precisely what it is supposed to prove; it begs the question.

The result is a tangle of inaccuracies. First, the majority repeatedly contends that our decision in *State v. Valladares* either adopted or supports the bilateral theory of conspiracies. That is not true. In fact, *Valladares* explicitly reserved the question. ("We need not decide here what result might have been reached had" the defendant been charged with conspiring with two government agents.) *Valladares* decided only that, in a joint trial of co-conspirators, the jury verdict is inconsistent if one defendant is convicted of conspiracy while "his alleged coconspirator has been found not to have entered into any alleged agreement and no conspiracy with an unnamed coconspirator has been alleged." *Valladares* is about jury verdict consistency. The closest *Valladares* comes to commenting on the conspiracy statute itself is to note that "the Washington Legislature appears to have adopted a unilateral approach to conspiracy by focusing on the culpability of the individual actor."

Next, the majority portrays the unilateral approach to conspiracy as an outdated relic from a bygone era. The Model Penal Code endorses unilateral conspiracies, the majority admits, but "every federal court, which has since considered the issue" has adopted the bilateral approach. The majority neglects to mention that all the federal courts adopting bilateral conspiracy are construing a different statute, one whose language requires bilateral conspiracies. See 18 U.S.C. § 371 ("If two or more persons conspire . . . to commit any offense against the United States"). In contrast, the Model Penal Code defines conspiracy "in terms of one person's agreeing with another, rather than in terms of an agreement among or between two or more people."

The code embodies a significant change in emphasis. In its view, the major basis of conspiratorial liability is not the group nature of the activity but the firm purpose of an individual to commit a crime which is objectively manifested in conspiring. See Model Penal Code § 5.03(1) cmt. at 104-05 (Tentative Draft No. 10, 1960). The Washington conspiracy statute tracks the Model Penal Code's language rather than the "two or more persons" language of the general federal conspiracy statute. In any event, far from being antiquated or obsolete, the "movement toward a unilateral theory of the crime is the modern trend in conspiracy law."

A comparison of the revised Washington conspiracy statute with its predecessor is far more revealing of legislative intent than the majority's simplistic and premature resort to dictionary definitions.[2] The predecessor statute used the phrase "whenever two or more persons shall conspire," which parallels the federal conspiracy statute and clearly requires bilateral conspiracy. Former RCW 9.22.010 (repealed in 1975). The revised statute, in contrast, tracks the definitional language of the Model Penal Code, which adopts unilateral conspiracy.[3]

---

[2] The majority relies on a vague definition from Black's Law Dictionary of "agreement" as "[a] meeting of two or more minds" . . . that is equally applicable to conspiracies and contracts. Not only does this ignore the far more relevant question of the actual changes in the sequence of statutes, it also disregards the crucial differences between a conspiracy and a contract. 2 Wayne R. LaFave & Austin W. Scott, Jr., *Substantive Criminal Law* § 6.4, at 71 (1986) ("One might suppose that the agreement necessary for conspiracy is essentially like the agreement or 'meeting of the minds' which is critical to a contract, but this is not the case.").

[3] As the code's commentary states, the new definition "departs from the traditional view of conspiracy as an entirely bilateral or multilateral relationship, the view inherent in the standard formulation cast in terms of 'two or more persons' agreeing or combining to commit a crime. Attention is directed instead to each individual's culpability by framing the definition in terms of the conduct which suffices

Under a unilateral formulation, the crime of conspiracy is committed when a person agrees to proceed in a prohibited manner; under a bilateral formulation, the crime of conspiracy is committed when two or more persons agree to proceed in such manner. The contrast between the prior and the present statute is clear, precise, and determinative.

Next, the majority constructs a straw man by claiming that the primary purpose of conspiracy is "the increased danger to society posed by group criminal activity." Preventing group criminal activity is the rationale behind bilateral conspiracy, but that rationale was decisively rejected by the Model Penal Code. At best, controlling group criminal activity is only one rationale for conspiracy statutes.

A bilateral theory of conspiracy and the rigid standard of mutuality that it demands . . . are inconsistent with the recognition of an independent rationale for conspiracy law based on a conspirator's firm expectation of committing a crime.

The majority compounds its own confusion by contending that unilateral conspiracies are factually impossible and therefore presumptively invalid. ("When one party merely pretends to agree, the other party, whatever he or she may believe about the pretender, is in fact not conspiring with anyone."). This argument amounts to the truism that it is factually impossible to have a "meeting of minds" on the commission of a future crime if one of the minds is a government agent who does not intend to commit the criminal act. However, a "meeting of minds" is not a prerequisite of unilateral conspiracy. In any event, factual impossibility is not a recognized defense. See 2 Wayne R. LaFave & Austin W. Scott, Jr., Substantive Criminal Law § 6.3(2), at 42 (1986). The majority does nothing more than restate the discredited assumption that all conspiracies must be bilateral because conspiracy statutes attempt to target only group criminal activity.

Finally, I share the majority's concern about the potential for abuse of unilateral conspiracy. However, the majority fails to take into consideration the effect of the entrapment defense. The potential for abuse is further restricted by the statute itself, which requires not only an agreement to engage in criminal conduct but also "a substantial step in pursuance of such agreement." RCW 9A.28.040(1). In the end, the majority succeeds only in providing a superfluous protection to criminal defendants at the price of hamstringing government attempts to nip criminal acts in the bud.

After the *Pacheco* case, the Washington Legislature amended its conspiracy statute as follows:

Revised Code of Washington § 9A.28.040 (2003)   *Criminal conspiracy*

(1) A person is guilty of criminal conspiracy when, with intent that conduct constituting a crime be performed, he or she agrees with one or more persons to engage in or cause the performance of such conduct, and any one of them takes a substantial step in pursuance of such agreement.

(2) It shall not be a defense to criminal conspiracy that the person or persons with whom the accused is alleged to have conspired:

(a) Has not been prosecuted or convicted; or

(b) Has been convicted of a different offense; or

---

to establish the liability of any given actor, rather than the conduct of a group of which he is charged to be a part." Model Penal Code § 5.03(1) cmt. at 104-05 (Tentative Draft No. 10, 1960).

(c) Is not amenable to justice; or
(d) Has been acquitted; or
(e) Lacked the capacity to commit an offense; or
(f) Is a law enforcement officer or other government agent who did not intend that a crime be committed.

QUESTIONS

1. Which is the better approach to conspiracy, requiring unilateral agreement or bilateral agreement?

2. Which approach is more compatible with the word "agree," the unilateral approach or the bilateral approach? Should legislatures use a word other than "agree" if they wish to penalize conduct such as Pacheco's?

3. Is it possible for someone to be criminally liable for an attempt to conspire?

2. Overt Act

What does each of the following conspiracy statutes require in terms of conduct? How does each differ from the statutes that appear in Problem 12.1 in terms of conduct?

New Mexico Statutes Annotated § 30-28-2   *Conspiracy*

A. Conspiracy consists of knowingly combining with another for the purpose of committing a felony within or without this state.

Utah Code Annotated § 76-4-201   *Conspiracy—Elements*

For purposes of this part a person is guilty of conspiracy when he, intending that conduct constituting a crime be performed, agrees with one or more persons to engage in or cause the performance of the conduct and any one of them commits an overt act in pursuance of the conspiracy, except where the offense is a capital felony, a felony against the person, arson, burglary, or robbery, the overt act is not required for the commission of conspiracy.

Maine Criminal Code § 151   *Conspiracy*

1. A person is guilty of conspiracy if, with the intent that conduct be performed that in fact would constitute a crime or crimes, the actor agrees with one or more others to engage in or cause the performance of such conduct. . . .

4. A person may not be convicted of conspiracy to commit a crime unless it is alleged and proved that the actor or one with whom the actor conspired, took a substantial step toward commission of the crime. A substantial step is any conduct which, under the circumstances in which it occurs, is strongly corroborative of the firmness of the actor's intent to complete commission of the crime; provided that speech alone may not constitute a substantial step.

STATE *v.* DENT

Supreme Court of Washington (En Banc) 123 Wash. 2d 467, 869 P.2d 392 (1994)

BRACHTENBACH, J. Defendants Dent and Balcinde were charged with conspiracy to commit first degree murder. Both defendants were convicted at a joint trial. [Both defendants raised the issue of] how the jury should be instructed as to the meaning of the "substantial step" element of a conspiracy . . . .

Roland C. Dent and Carlos A. Balcinde were charged with conspiring to murder Dent's former girlfriend, Ann Powell. In late 1989 and early 1990, while on parole from an earlier conviction, Dent had a relationship with Powell. On February 22, 1990, Dent's parole was revoked based on an accusation made by Powell to Dent's parole officer that Dent had assaulted her. Following Powell's accusation, Dent was initially incarcerated in the King County Jail. Balcinde was also in the King County Jail at that time. It was during this time, when the codefendants were both in the King County Jail, that the conspiracy is alleged to have been formed. On February 23, 1990, Dent was transferred to the Shelton Corrections Center.

After his transfer, Dent contacted his then girlfriend, Joyful Tryon, to seek her help in communicating with Balcinde to advance the murder plan. Through numerous phone calls and letters, he asked her to (1) forward letters from Dent to Balcinde using a different or false return address; (2) give her handgun to Balcinde upon his release, after removing the serial number and reporting it stolen; (3) set aside $300 to $400 to pay Balcinde; (4) pick Balcinde up from the King County Jail upon his release; (5) show Balcinde a videotape from which he could identify Powell; and (6) show Balcinde where Powell was then residing. In one telephone conversation, Tryon asked what the gun was for, and Dent told her that "it was gonna [*sic*] be used for Ann [Powell]." During the time between Dent's transfer to the Shelton facility and Balcinde's release, Tryon and her sons also received phone calls from Balcinde.

During the time Tryon was receiving communications from codefendants, her sons became concerned that Dent was trying to involve her in some type of illegal activity. After they persuaded her to tell them what was being planned, they went to the police. After meeting with the police, Tryon agreed to cooperate with the police. With Tryon's cooperation, the investigating officers recorded a call from Dent to Tryon on March 15, 1990, pursuant to an order authorizing intercept. During the conversation, Tryon asked Dent if it was necessary to go through with "[p]utting [Powell] in the ground." Defendant Dent answered "I cannot allow the [Parole] Board to have the argument that there's someone who's afraid of me, someone who thinks I'm a threat to. As far as they're concerned, I should never get out of prison under those conditions."

The police also had Tryon write a letter to Balcinde telling him that she would pick him up on March 19, 1990, when he was scheduled to be released. A deputy posing as Tryon was sent to meet Balcinde, and, pursuant to a second order authorizing intercept, the conversation between the deputy and Balcinde was recorded. In response to questions asked by the deputy, Balcinde stated that he was "going to do what you write me before," that Tryon was supposed to pay him $300, and that he was supposed to view a picture or videotape relating to a person named Ann. In addition, Balcinde asked the deputy posing as Tryon whether she had been in contact with "RC."[1] Following this conversation, Balcinde entered the

---

[1] Defendant Dent's full name is Roland C. Dent.

deputy's car and was placed under arrest as he reached for the money offered by the deputy. . . .

Prior to the giving of the jury instructions, codefendants objected to the jury instruction defining the "substantial step" element of a conspiracy. The court rejected the instruction proposed by both defendants which defined "substantial step" as "more than mere preparation". . . .

The jury found both defendants guilty of conspiracy to commit first degree murder. Dent appealed his conviction. . . . The first issue presented on review is whether the trial court properly refused to give defendant's proposed instruction which provided that the "substantial step" element of a conspiracy requires "more than mere preparation". An individual commits conspiracy when

> with intent that conduct constituting a crime be performed, he [or she] agrees with one or more persons to engage in or cause the performance of such conduct, and any one of them takes a *substantial step* in pursuance of such agreement. (Italics ours.)

The trial court instructed the jury that a "substantial step" is "conduct which strongly indicates a criminal purpose." Defendants' proposed instruction . . . defines the "substantial step" element of an *attempt* as "conduct which strongly indicates a criminal purpose and which is more than mere preparation."

The first difference between the two crimes is in the language describing the type of "substantial step" that is required for each. RCW 9A.28.020(1) provides:

> A person is guilty of an attempt to commit crime if, with intent to commit a specific crime, he does *any act which is a substantial step toward the commission of that crime.* (Italics ours.)

In contrast, RCW 9A.28.040(1) provides:

> A person is guilty of criminal conspiracy when, with intent that conduct constituting a crime be performed, he agrees with one or more persons to engage in or cause the performance of such conduct, and any one of them takes a *substantial step in pursuance of such agreement.* (Italics ours.)

The focus or end toward which a "substantial step" must be taken is described differently in each statute.

Additional differences between the two crimes can be found in the nature of the conduct sought to be prohibited and in the significance of the "substantial step" requirement (or overt act requirement in other jurisdictions), in each context, for determining whether the prohibited conduct has occurred. "In the case of attempt the act must go beyond preparation because the attempt is deemed a punishable segment of the crime intended." A "substantial step" is required in the attempt context to prevent the imposition of punishment based on intent alone.

The purpose of the "substantial step" or overt act requirement is different in the conspiracy context. A conspiracy has been defined as "a partnership in criminal purposes. The gist of the crime is the confederation or combination of minds." The purpose of the "substantial step" requirement is, therefore, to "manifest 'that the conspiracy is at work,' and is neither a project still resting solely in the minds of the conspirators nor a fully completed operation no longer in existence."

The different purposes underlying the act requirements of the two offenses are well recognized.

> [C]onspiracy focuses on the additional dangers inherent in group activity. In theory, once an individual reaches an agreement with one or more persons to

perform an unlawful act, it becomes more likely that the individual will feel a greater commitment to carry out his original intent, providing a heightened group danger.

As an inchoate crime, conspiracy allows law-enforcement officials to intervene at a stage far earlier than attempt does. To obtain an attempt conviction, the prosecutor must prove that the actor performed an act beyond mere preparation. . . . To obtain a conspiracy conviction, however, the prosecutor need only prove that the conspirators agreed to undertake a criminal scheme or, at most, that they took an overt step in pursuance of the conspiracy. *Even an insignificant act may suffice.* (Italics ours.)

Robbins, *Double Inchoate Crimes*, 26 Harv. J. on Legis. 1, 27-29 (1989). *See* 2 W. LaFave & A. Scott, *Substantive Criminal Law* § 6.5, at 95 (2d ed. 1986) (explaining that "[i]f the agreement has been established but the object has not been attained, virtually any act will satisfy the overt act requirement" of a conspiracy). Similarly, in distinguishing the crime of conspiracy from the crime of attempt, one court has explained that the essence of a conspiracy is the agreement to commit a crime. If an overt act is committed in furtherance of the conspiracy then, regardless of the act's importance to the overall scheme, there is no need to prove that the conspirators made a serious effort to carry out their agreement.

Other courts have implicitly recognized the distinction between the act requirements of the two crimes in discussing the type of acts which will support a conspiracy conviction. In Missouri, for an act to qualify as an overt act in furtherance of a conspiracy "there is no requirement that such act be a physical one or be a substantial step in the commission of the target offense." *State v. Madwell*, 846 S.W.2d 208, 209 (Mo. Ct. App. 1993). For example, "[a] telephone conversation or even mere silence can be an overt act." *State v. Ray*, 768 S.W.2d 119, 121 (Mo. Ct. App. 1988). Other courts have held that telephone conversations and meetings during which planning is done are overt acts. *United States v. Lewis*, 676 F.2d 508, 511 (11th Cir.) (holding that a telephone call to arrange a meeting to plan the conspiracy was a sufficient overt act); *United States v. Civella*, 648 F.2d 1167, 1174 (8th Cir.) (holding that "[t]elephone conversations and meetings in which plans and arrangements are made in furtherance of the conspiracy are overt acts"); *United States v. Marable*, 574 F.2d 224, 230 (5th Cir. 1978) (holding that the overt act requirement was met where the defendant, through phone conversations and meetings, participated in discussing and arranging the conspiracy). An attempt to collect compensation under the agreement might also serve as the necessary overt act for a conspiracy.

We agree that the conspiracy statute requires a lesser act than does the attempt statute. We are particularly persuaded by the fact that RCW 9A.28.040 requires only an act that is a "substantial step in pursuance of [the] agreement" as opposed to a "substantial step toward the commission of [the] crime." We hold that preparatory conduct which furthers the ability of the conspirators to carry out the agreement can be "a substantial step in pursuance of [the] agreement." Therefore, we hold that the trial court properly refused to instruct the jury that the "substantial step" element of a conspiracy requires more than mere preparation. . . . Defendants' convictions are affirmed.

QUESTIONS

1. Should the law require an act beyond an agreement for the crime of conspiracy? If so, what type of act should the law require?

2. If Joyful Tryon had not become an informant and instead had gone along with Dent's plan and performed the acts described in the third paragraph of the *Dent* opinion, when would she have committed a substantial step in pursuance of the conspiracy? In other words, when could the police have arrested Dent, Balcinde, and Tryon for the crime of conspiracy?

3. Does a substantial step under the Washington conspiracy statute as interpreted in *Dent* differ from a substantial step under the Maine conspiracy statute? Does it differ from a substantial overt act under the Ohio statute in Problem 12.1?

4. Is there a difference between an overt act and a substantial step?

5. Should what constitutes a substantial step for purposes of a conspiracy differ from what constitutes a substantial step for purposes of an attempt?

6. The *Dent* court states that "attempt is deemed a punishable segment of the crime intended." Do you agree with this description? Is conspiracy not "a punishable segment of the crime intended"?

PROBLEM

12.6 Jules and Robert are baseball fans sitting in the back row of the bleachers at a baseball stadium. They learn that a homerun ball from a World Series game is being temporarily stored in a locker at the stadium. Two men claim ownership of the ball and are litigating their dispute. Experts estimate that the ball is worth $1 million. Jules is a locksmith. He proposes to Robert, who has actually seen the storage locker, that the two of them break into the locker and steal the ball. Jules assures Robert that Jules can pick the lock without any damage to the lock. Robert agrees and sketches a picture of the front of the storage locker to show Jules what the outside of the lock looks like. Unbeknownst to Jules and Robert, a police officer is working undercover posing as a hotdog vendor so she can scout the ballpark for possible terrorist activity. She overhears the conversation, sees Robert's sketch, and arrests Jules and Robert for conspiracy to commit grand theft. Should Jules and Robert be held liable under the statutes that appear in Problem 12.1?

C. MENTAL STATES

Wyoming Statutes § 6-1-303   *Conspiracy*

(a) A person is guilty of conspiracy to commit a crime if he agrees with one (1) or more persons that they or one (1) or more of them will commit a crime and one (1) or more of them does an overt act to effect the objective of the agreement.

Tennessee Code § 39-12-103   *Criminal conspiracy*

(a) The offense of conspiracy is committed if two (2) or more people, each having the culpable mental state required for the offense which is the object of the conspiracy and each acting for the purpose of promoting or facilitating commission of an offense, agree that one (1) or more of them will engage in conduct which constitutes such offense.

(b) If a person guilty of conspiracy, as defined in subsection (a), knows that another with whom the person conspires to commit an offense has conspired with one (1) or more other people to commit the same offense, the person is guilty of conspiring with such other person or persons, whether or not their identity is known, to commit such offense.

Model Penal Code § 5.03   *Criminal Conspiracy*

(1) **Definition of Conspiracy.** A person is guilty of conspiracy with another person or persons to commit a crime if with the purpose of promoting or facilitating its commission he:

(a) agrees with such other person or persons that they or one or more of them will engage in conduct that constitutes such crime or an attempt or solicitation to commit such crime; or

(b) agrees to aid such other person or persons in the planning or commission of such crime or of an attempt or solicitation to commit such crime.

PEOPLE *v.* LAURIA
251 Cal. App. 2d 471 (1967)

FLEMING, J. In an investigation of call-girl activity the police focused their attention on three prostitutes actively plying their trade on call, each of whom was using Lauria's telephone answering service, presumably for business purposes.

On January 8, 1965, Stella Weeks, a policewoman, signed up for telephone service with Lauria's answering service. Mrs. Weeks, in the course of her conversation with Lauria's office manager, hinted broadly that she was a prostitute concerned with the secrecy of her activities and their concealment from the police. She was assured that the operation of the service was discreet and "about as safe as you can get." It was arranged that Mrs. Weeks need not leave her address with the answering service, but could pick up her calls and pay her bills in person.

On February 11, Mrs. Weeks talked to Lauria on the telephone and told him her business was modelling and she had been referred to the answering service by Terry, one of the three prostitutes under investigation. She complained that because of the operation of the service she had lost two valuable customers, referred to as tricks. Lauria defended his service and said that her friends had probably lied to her about having left calls for her. But he did not respond to Mrs. Weeks' hints that she needed customers in order to make money, other than to invite her to his house for a personal visit in order to get better acquainted. In the course of his talk he said "his business was taking messages.". . .

On April 1 Lauria and the three prostitutes were arrested. Lauria complained to the police that this attention was undeserved, stating that Hollywood Call Board had 60 to 70 prostitutes on its board while his own service had only 9 or 10, that he kept separate records for known or suspected prostitutes for the convenience of himself and the police. When asked if his records were available to police who might come to the office to investigate call girls, Lauria replied that they were whenever the police had a specific name. However, his service didn't "arbitrarily tell the police about prostitutes on our board. As long as they pay their bills we tolerate them." In a subsequent voluntary appearance before the grand jury Lauria testified he had always cooperated with the police. But he admitted he knew some of his customers were prostitutes, and he knew Terry was a prostitute because he had personally used her services, and he knew she was paying for 500 calls a month.

Lauria and the three prostitutes were indicted for conspiracy to commit prostitution, and nine overt acts were specified. Subsequently the trial court set aside the indictment as having been brought without reasonable or probable cause. The People have appealed, claiming that a sufficient showing of an unlawful agreement to further prostitution was made.

To establish agreement, the People need show no more than a tacit, mutual understanding between coconspirators to accomplish an unlawful act. Here the People attempted to establish a conspiracy by showing that Lauria, well aware that his codefendants were prostitutes who received business calls from customers through his telephone answering service, continued to furnish them with such service. This approach attempts to equate knowledge of another's criminal activity with conspiracy to further such criminal activity, and poses the question of the criminal responsibility of a furnisher of goods or services who knows his product is being used to assist the operation of an illegal business. Under what circumstances does a supplier become a part of a conspiracy to further an illegal enterprise by furnishing goods or services which he knows are to be used by the buyer for criminal purposes?

The two leading cases on this point face in opposite directions. In *United States v. Falcone*, the sellers of large quantities of sugar, yeast, and cans were absolved from participation in a moonshining conspiracy among distillers who bought from them, while in *Direct Sales Co. v. United States*, a wholesaler of drugs was convicted of conspiracy to violate the federal narcotic laws by selling drugs in quantity to a codefendant physician who was supplying them to addicts. The distinction between these two cases appears primarily based on the proposition that distributors of such dangerous products as drugs are required to exercise greater discrimination in the conduct of their business than are distributors of innocuous substances like sugar and yeast.

In the earlier case, *Falcone*, the sellers' knowledge of the illegal use of the goods was insufficient by itself to make the sellers participants in a conspiracy with the distillers who bought from them. Such knowledge fell short of proof of a conspiracy, and evidence on the volume of sales was too vague to support a jury finding that respondents knew of the conspiracy from the size of the sales alone.

In the later case of *Direct Sales*, the conviction of a drug wholesaler for conspiracy to violate federal narcotic laws was affirmed on a showing that it had actively promoted the sale of morphine sulphate in quantity and had sold codefendant physician, who practiced in a small town in South Carolina, more than 300 times his normal requirements of the drug, even though it had been repeatedly warned of the dangers of unrestricted sales of the drug. The court contrasted the restricted goods involved in *Direct Sales* with the articles of free commerce involved in *Falcone*: "All articles of commerce may be put to illegal ends," said the court. "But all do not have inherently the same susceptibility to harmful and illegal use. . . . This difference is important for two purposes. One is for making certain that the seller knows the buyer's intended illegal use. The other is to show that by the sale he intends to further, promote, and cooperate in it. This intent, when given effect by overt act, is the gist of conspiracy. While it is not identical with mere knowledge that another proposes unlawful action it is not unrelated to such knowledge. . . . The step from knowledge to intent and agreement may be taken. There is more than suspicion, more than knowledge, acquiescence, carelessness, indifference, lack of concern. There is informed and interested cooperation, stimulation, instigation. And there is also a 'stake in the venture' which, even if it may not be essential, is not irrelevant to the question of conspiracy."

While *Falcone* and *Direct Sales* may not be entirely consistent with each other in their full implications, they do provide us with a framework for the criminal liability of a supplier of lawful goods or services put to unlawful use. Both the element of knowledge of the illegal use of the goods or services and the element of intent to further that use must be present in order to make the supplier a participant in a criminal conspiracy.

Proof of knowledge is ordinarily a question of fact and requires no extended discussion in the present case. The knowledge of the supplier was sufficiently established when Lauria admitted he knew some of his customers were prostitutes and admitted he knew that Terry, an active subscriber to his service, was a prostitute. In the face of these admissions he could scarcely claim to have relied on the normal assumption an operator of a business or service is entitled to make, that his customers are behaving themselves in the eyes of the law. Because Lauria knew in fact that some of his customers were prostitutes, it is a legitimate inference he knew they were subscribing to his answering service for illegal business purposes and were using his service to make assignations for prostitution. On this record we think the prosecution is entitled to claim positive knowledge by Lauria of the use of his service to facilitate the business of prostitution.

The more perplexing issue in the case is the sufficiency of proof of intent to further the criminal enterprise. The element of intent may be proved either by direct evidence, or by evidence of circumstances from which an intent to further a criminal enterprise by supplying lawful goods or services may be inferred. Direct evidence of participation, such as advice from the supplier of legal goods or services to the user of those goods or services on their use for illegal purposes, . . . provides the simplest case. When the intent to further and promote the criminal enterprise comes from the lips of the supplier himself, ambiguities of inference from circumstance need not trouble us. But in cases where direct proof of complicity is lacking, intent to further the conspiracy must be derived from the sale itself and its surrounding circumstances in order to establish the supplier's express or tacit agreement to join the conspiracy.

In the case at bench the prosecution argues that since Lauria knew his customers were using his service for illegal purposes but nevertheless continued to furnish it to them, he must have intended to assist them in carrying out their illegal activities. Thus through a union of knowledge and intent he became a participant in a criminal conspiracy. Essentially, the People argue that knowledge alone of the continuing use of his telephone facilities for criminal purposes provided a sufficient basis from which his intent to participate in those criminal activities could be inferred.

In examining precedents in this field we find that sometimes, but not always, the criminal intent of the supplier may be inferred from his knowledge of the unlawful use made of the product he supplies. Some consideration of characteristic patterns may be helpful.

1. Intent may be inferred from knowledge, when the purveyor of legal goods for illegal use has acquired a stake in the venture. For example, in *Regina v. Thomas*, a prosecution for living off the earnings of prostitution, the evidence showed that the accused . . . rented a room at a grossly inflated rent to a prostitute for the purpose of carrying on her trade, a jury could find he was living on the earnings of prostitution.

In the present case, no proof was offered of inflated charges for the telephone answering services furnished the codefendants.

2. Intent may be inferred from knowledge, when no legitimate use for the goods or services exists. The leading California case is *People v. McLaughlin*, in which the court upheld a conviction of the suppliers of horse-racing information by wire for conspiracy to promote bookmaking, when it had been established that wire-service information had no other use than to supply information needed by bookmakers to conduct illegal gambling operations. . . .

Other services of a comparable nature come to mind: the manufacturer of crooked dice and marked cards who sells his product to gambling casinos; the tipster who furnishes information on the movement of law enforcement officers to known lawbreakers. In such cases the supplier must necessarily have an intent to further the illegal enterprise since there is no known honest use for his goods.

However, there is nothing in the furnishing of telephone answering service which would necessarily imply assistance in the performance of illegal activities. Nor is any inference to be derived from the use of an answering service by women, either in any particular volume of calls, or outside normal working hours. Night-club entertainers, registered nurses, faith healers, public stenographers, photographic models, and free lance substitute employees, provide examples of women in legitimate occupations whose employment might cause them to receive a volume of telephone calls at irregular hours.

3. Intent may be inferred from knowledge, when the volume of business with the buyer is grossly disproportionate to any legitimate demand, or when sales for illegal use amount to a high proportion of the seller's total business. In such cases an intent to participate in the illegal enterprise may be inferred from the quantity of the business done. For example, in *Direct Sales*, supra, the sale of narcotics to a rural physician in quantities 300 times greater than he would have normal use for provided potent evidence of an intent to further the illegal activity. . . .

No evidence of any unusual volume of business with prostitutes was presented by the prosecution against Lauria.

Inflated charges, the sale of goods with no legitimate use, sales in inflated amounts, each may provide a fact of sufficient moment from which the intent of the seller to participate in the criminal enterprise may be inferred. In such instances participation by the supplier of legal goods to the illegal enterprise may be inferred because in one way or another the supplier has acquired a special interest in the operation of the illegal enterprise. His intent to participate in the crime of which he has knowledge may be inferred from the existence of his special interest.

Yet there are cases in which it cannot reasonably be said that the supplier has a stake in the venture or has acquired a special interest in the enterprise, but in which he has been held liable as a participant on the basis of knowledge alone. Some suggestion of this appears in *Direct Sales*, supra, where both the knowledge of the illegal use of the drugs and the intent of the supplier to aid that use were inferred. . . . It seems apparent from these cases that a supplier who furnishes equipment which he knows will be used to commit a serious crime may be deemed from that knowledge alone to have intended to produce the result. Such proof may justify an inference that the furnisher intended to aid the execution of the crime and that he thereby became a participant. For instance, we think the operator of a telephone answering service with positive knowledge that his service was being used to facilitate the extortion of ransom, the distribution of heroin, or the passing of counterfeit money who continued to furnish the service with knowledge of its use, might be chargeable on knowledge alone with participation in a scheme to extort money, to distribute narcotics, or to pass counterfeit money. The same result would follow the seller of gasoline who knew the buyer was using his product to make Molotov cocktails for terroristic use.

Logically, the same reasoning could be extended to crimes of every description. Yet we do not believe an inference of intent drawn from knowledge of criminal use properly applies to the less serious crimes classified as misdemeanors. The duty to take positive action to dissociate oneself from activities helpful to violations of the criminal law is far stronger and more compelling for felonies than it is for misdemeanors or petty offenses. In this respect, as in others, the distinction between felonies and misdemeanors, between more serious and less serious crime, retains continuing vitality. . . . We believe the distinction between the obligations arising from knowledge of a felony and those arising from knowledge of a misdemeanor continues to reflect basic human feelings about the duties owed by individuals to society. . . .

With respect to misdemeanors, we conclude that positive knowledge of the supplier that his products or services are being used for criminal purposes does not, without more, establish an intent of the supplier to participate in the misdemeanors. With respect to felonies, we do not decide the converse, viz., that in all cases of felony knowledge of criminal use alone may justify an inference of the supplier's intent to participate in the crime. The implications of *Falcone* make the matter uncertain with respect to those felonies which are merely prohibited wrongs. But decision on this point is not compelled, and we leave the matter open.

From this analysis of precedent we deduce the following rule: the intent of a supplier who knows of the criminal use to which his supplies are put to participate in the criminal activity connected with the use of his supplies may be established by (1) direct evidence that he intends to participate, or (2) through an inference that he intends to participate based on, (a) his special interest in the activity, or (b) the aggravated nature of the crime itself.

When we review Lauria's activities in the light of this analysis, we find no proof that Lauria took any direct action to further, encourage, or direct the call-girl activities of his codefendants and we find an absence of circumstance from which his special interest in their activities could be inferred. Neither excessive charges for standardized services, nor the furnishing of services without a legitimate use, nor an unusual quantity of business with call girls, are present. The offense which he is charged with furthering is a misdemeanor, a category of crime which has never been made a required subject of positive disclosure to public authority. Under these circumstances, although proof of Lauria's knowledge of the criminal activities of his patrons was sufficient to charge him with that fact, there was insufficient evidence that he intended to further their criminal activities, and hence insufficient proof of his participation in a criminal conspiracy with his codefendants to further prostitution.

In absolving Lauria of complicity in a criminal conspiracy we do not wish to imply that the public authorities are without remedies to combat modern manifestations of the world's oldest profession. . . . The furnishing of telephone answering service in aid of prostitution could be made a crime. (Cf. Pen. Code, § 316, which makes it a misdemeanor to let an apartment with knowledge of its use for prostitution.) Other solutions will doubtless occur to vigilant public authorities if the problem of call-girl activity needs further suppression.

The order is affirmed.

QUESTIONS

1. Should knowingly furnishing goods that will be used in criminal activity be sufficient for conspiracy?

2. Should the assurances by Lauria's office manager that the service was "about as safe as you can get" coupled with Lauria's knowledge of what the women who used his service were doing be enough to show Lauria's intent?

3. Is the distinction drawn in the *Lauria* case, based on the severity of the target crime, an appropriate one? Is it based on retribution? Utility? Both?

PROBLEM

12.7   Leo and Michael both enjoy working on and racing their cars. One day they agree that on the following Saturday night they will race each other on a stretch of highway outside town. They tell several of their friends, and when the evening arrives a crowd of several dozen people gathers to see the race. Leo and Michael arrive at the scene of the race and are revving the engines of their cars at the starting line when a police cruiser pulls up. Both Leo and Michael are arrested for conspiracy to commit the crime of reckless driving. Are they liable? Assume that the race took place and that Leo's car spun out of control and killed a bystander while Leo was trying to pass Michael. Could Leo and Michael be convicted of conspiracy to commit manslaughter?

Mental State Regarding a Circumstance

PROBLEM

12.8   Max is a part-time gun dealer who sells primarily at weekend gun shows. One weekend he is approached by Sid, who wants to buy a number of powerful handguns. Max doesn't typically carry the particular handgun Sid wants because it is more expensive and powerful than the sort of weapon buyers at weekend shows want to purchase. Sid is tall and husky and looks considerably older than his 17 years of age. Max tells Sid that he can introduce him to someone who can sell him the weapons if Sid is willing to pay Max a fee for doing so. Sid agrees to this arrangement. Max then contacts Adam, another gun dealer who maintains a supply of the handguns Sid is interested in, and proposes to introduce him to Sid if Adam will give Max a 10 percent commission for arranging the sale. Adam agrees to this arrangement. Max then calls Sid and meets with him to set up a time and place for the sale and to collect a down payment on the weapons. Prior to the actual culmination of the sale, the police arrest both Max and Adam for conspiracy to violate a state law that makes it a felony to sell a handgun to anyone under the age of 18. This state law makes clear that strict liability applies to its age element. Is Max liable for the charged conspiracy? Is Adam liable for the charged conspiracy?

In the *Feola* case, below, the United States charged Feola with conspiracy under the following statute:

18 United States Code § 371

If two or more persons conspire either to commit any offense against the United States, or to defraud the United States, or any agency thereof in any manner or for any purpose, and one or more of such persons do any act to effect the object of the conspiracy, each shall be fined not more than $10,000 or imprisoned not more than five years, or both.

The object of the charged conspiracy in *Feola* was assault on a federal officer in violation of:

18 United States Code § 111   *Assaulting, resisting, or impeding certain officers or employees*

Whoever forcibly assaults, resists, opposes, impedes, intimidates, or interferes with any person designated in section 1114 of this title while engaged in or on account of the performance of his official duties, shall be fined not more than $ 5,000 or imprisoned not more than three years, or both.

Whoever, in the commission of any such acts uses a deadly or dangerous weapon, shall be fined not more than $ 10,000 or imprisoned not more than ten years, or both.

Among the persons "designated in section 1114" of 18 United States Code is "any officer or employee . . . of the Bureau of Narcotics and Dangerous Drugs."

UNITED STATES *v.* FEOLA
420 U.S. 671 (1975)

BLACKMUN, J. This case presents the issue whether knowledge that the intended victim is a federal officer is a requisite for the crime of conspiracy, under 18 U.S.C. § 371, to commit an offense violative of 18 U.S.C. § 111, that is, an assault upon a federal officer while engaged in the performance of his official duties.

Respondent Feola and three others . . . were indicted for violations of §§ 371 and 111. A jury found all four defendants guilty of both charges. . . . [T]he United States Court of Appeals for the Second Circuit . . . affirmed the judgment of conviction on the substantive charges, but reversed the conspiracy convictions. Because of a conflict among the Federal Circuits on the scienter issue with respect to a conspiracy charge, we granted the Government's petition for a *writ of certiorari* in Feola's case.

I

The facts reveal a classic narcotics "rip-off." . . . [T]he evidence shows that Feola and his confederates arranged for a sale of heroin to buyers who turned out to be undercover agents for the Bureau of Narcotics and Dangerous Drugs. The group planned to palm off on the purchasers, for a substantial sum, a form of sugar in place of heroin and, should that ruse fail, simply to surprise their unwitting buyers and relieve them of the cash they had brought along for payment. The plan failed when one agent, his suspicions being aroused, drew his revolver in time to counter an assault upon another agent from the rear. . . . Feola and his associates found themselves charged, to their undoubted surprise, with conspiring to assault, and with assaulting, federal officers.

At the trial, the District Court, without objection from the defense, charged the jurors that, in order to find any of the defendants guilty on either the conspiracy count or the substantive one, they were not required to conclude that the defendants were aware that their quarry were federal officers.

The Court of Appeals reversed the conspiracy convictions on a ground not advanced by any of the defendants. Although it approved the trial court's instructions to the jury on the substantive charge of assaulting a federal officer, it nonetheless concluded that the failure to charge that knowledge of the victim's official identity must be proved in order to convict on the conspiracy charge amounted to plain error. The court perceived itself bound by a line of cases, commencing with Judge Learned Hand's opinion in *United States v. Crimmins*, all holding that scienter of a factual element that confers federal jurisdiction, while unnecessary for conviction of the substantive offense, is required in order to sustain a conviction for conspiracy to commit the substantive offense. . . .

II

The Government's plea is for symmetry. It urges that since criminal liability for the offense described in 18 U.S.C. § 111 does not depend on whether the assailant harbored the specific intent to assault a federal officer, no greater scienter requirement can be engrafted upon the conspiracy offense, which is merely an agreement to commit the act proscribed by § 111. Consideration of the Government's contention requires us preliminarily to pass upon its premise, the proposition that responsibility for assault upon a federal officer does not depend upon whether the assailant was aware of the official identity of his victim at the time he acted.

That the "federal officer" requirement is anything other than jurisdictional[9] is not seriously urged upon us; indeed, both Feola and the Court of Appeals concede that scienter is not a necessary element of the substantive offense under § 111. . . .

. . . This interpretation poses no risk of unfairness to defendants. It is no snare for the unsuspecting. Although the perpetrator of a narcotics "rip-off," such as the one involved here, may be surprised to find that his intended victim is a federal officer in civilian apparel, he nonetheless knows from the very outset that his planned course of conduct is wrongful. The situation is not one where legitimate conduct becomes unlawful solely because of the identity of the individual or agency affected. In a case of this kind the offender takes his victim as he finds him. The concept of criminal intent does not extend so far as to require that the actor understand not only the nature of his act but also its consequence for the choice of a judicial forum. . . .

We hold, therefore, that in order to incur criminal liability under § 111 an actor must entertain merely the criminal intent to do the acts therein specified. We now consider whether the rule should be different where persons conspire to commit those acts.

III

Our decisions establish that in order to sustain a judgment of conviction on a charge of conspiracy to violate a federal statute, the Government must prove at least the degree of criminal intent necessary for the substantive offense itself. . . . Respondent Feola urges upon us the proposition that the Government must show a degree of criminal intent in the conspiracy count greater than is necessary to convict for the substantive offense; he urges that even though it is not necessary to show that he was aware of the official identity of his assaulted victims in order to find him guilty of assaulting federal officers, in violation of 18 U.S.C. § 111, the Government nonetheless must show that he was aware that his intended victims were undercover agents, if it is successfully to prosecute him for conspiring to assault federal agents. And the Court of Appeals held that the trial court's failure to charge the jury to this effect constituted plain error.

The general conspiracy statute, 18 U.S.C. § 371, offers no textual support for the proposition that to be guilty of conspiracy a defendant in effect must have known that his conduct violated federal law. The statute makes it unlawful simply to "conspire . . . to commit any offense against the United States." A natural reading of these words would be that since one can violate a criminal statute simply by engaging in the forbidden conduct, a conspiracy to commit that offense is nothing more than an agreement to engage in the prohibited conduct. Then where, as here, the substantive statute does not require that an assailant know the official status of

---

[9] We are content to state the issue this way despite its potential to mislead. Labeling a requirement "jurisdictional" does not necessarily mean, of course, that the requirement is not an element of the offense Congress intended to describe and to punish. Indeed, a requirement is sufficient to confer jurisdiction on the federal courts for what otherwise are state crimes precisely because it implicates factors that are an appropriate subject for federal concern. With respect to the present case, for example, a mere general policy of deterring assaults would probably prove to be an undesirable or insufficient basis for federal jurisdiction; but where Congress seeks to protect the integrity of federal functions and the safety of federal officers, the interest is sufficient to warrant federal involvement. The significance of labeling a statutory requirement as "jurisdictional" is not that the requirement is viewed as outside the scope of the evil Congress intended to forestall, but merely that the existence of the fact that confers federal jurisdiction need not be one in the mind of the actor at the time he perpetrates the act made criminal by the federal statute. The question, then, is not whether the requirement is jurisdictional, but whether it is jurisdictional only.

his victim, there is nothing on the face of the conspiracy statute that would seem to require that those agreeing to the assault have a greater degree of knowledge. . . .

With no support on the face of the general conspiracy statute . . . respondent relies solely on the line of cases commencing with *United States v. Crimmins*, for the principle that the Government must prove "antifederal" intent in order to establish liability under § 371. In *Crimmins*, the defendant had been found guilty of conspiring to receive stolen bonds that had been transported in interstate commerce. Upon review, the Court of Appeals pointed out that the evidence failed to establish that *Crimmins* actually knew the stolen bonds had moved into the State. Accepting for the sake of argument the assumption that such knowledge was not necessary to sustain a conviction on the substantive offense, Judge Learned Hand nevertheless concluded that to permit conspiratorial liability where the conspirators were ignorant of the federal implications of their acts would be to enlarge their agreement beyond its terms as they understood them. He capsulized the distinction in what has become well known as his "traffic light" analogy:

> While one may, for instance, be guilty of running past a traffic light of whose existence one is ignorant, one cannot be guilty of conspiring to run past such a light, for one cannot agree to run past a light unless one supposes that there is a light to run past.

Judge Hand's attractive, but perhaps seductive, analogy has received a mixed reception in the Courts of Appeals. The Second Circuit, of course, has followed it; others have rejected it. It appears that most have avoided it by the simple expedient of inferring the requisite knowledge from the scope of the conspiratorial venture. We conclude that the analogy, though effective prose, is, as applied to the facts before us, bad law.[24] . . .

One may run a traffic light "of whose existence one is ignorant," but assaulting another "of whose existence one is ignorant," probably would require unearthly intervention. Thus, the traffic light analogy, even if it were a correct statement of the law, is inapt, for the conduct proscribed by the substantive offense, here assault, is not of the type outlawed without regard to the intent of the actor to accomplish the result that is made criminal. If the analogy has any vitality at all, it is to conduct of the latter variety; that, however, is a question we save for another day. We hold here only that where a substantive offense embodies only a requirement of *mens rea* as to each of its elements, the general federal conspiracy statute requires no more. . . .

QUESTIONS

1. Feola made no objection to the trial court's conspiracy instruction. Nor did he raise the issue on appeal. Why, then, did the Court of Appeals reverse Feola's conviction based on the conspiracy instruction? Should appellate courts consider questions not raised by a party?

2. What mental state should the crime of conspiracy require regarding an attendant circumstance? What language would you add to the statutes in Problem 12.1

---

[24] The Government rather effectively exposes the fallacy of the *Crimmins* traffic light analogy by recasting it in terms of a jurisdictional element. The suggested example is a traffic light on an Indian reservation. Surely, one may conspire with others to disobey the light but be ignorant of the fact that it is on the reservation. As applied to a jurisdictional element of this kind the formulation makes little sense.

to implement your answer to the previous question? Should there be symmetry between the mental states required for conspiracy and the mental states required for the target offense of the conspiracy, as the government argued before the Supreme Court in *Feola*?

3. On which theory of statutory interpretation does Justice Blackmun rely in his *Feola* opinion?

4. How would the *Feola* case be resolved under the MPC statute that appears in Problem 12.1?

D. SCOPE: THE PINKERTON DOCTRINE, ASSOCIATION OF PARTIES, AND DURATION

1. The Pinkerton Doctrine

Model Penal Code § 5.03 *Criminal Conspiracy*

(2) **Scope of Conspiratorial Relationship.** If a person guilty of conspiracy, as defined by Subsection (1) of this Section, knows that a person with whom he conspires to commit a crime has conspired with another person or persons to commit the same crime, he is guilty of conspiring with such other person or persons, whether or not he knows their identity, to commit such crime.

Code of Alabama § 13A-4-3 *Criminal conspiracy; generally*

(b) If a person knows or should know that one with whom he agrees has in turn agreed or will agree with another to effect the same criminal objective, he shall be deemed to have agreed with such other person, whether or not he knows the other's identity.

PINKERTON *v.* UNITED STATES
328 U.S. 640 (1946)

DOUGLAS, J. [Daniel and Walter [Pinkerton], who were brothers living near each other, were charged in several counts with substantive offenses, and then a conspiracy count was added naming those offenses as overt acts. The proof showed that Walter alone committed the substantive crimes. There was none to establish that Daniel participated in them, aided and abetted Walter in committing them, or knew that he had done so. Daniel in fact was in the penitentiary, under sentence for other crimes, when some of Walter's crimes were done.

There was evidence, however, to show that over several years Daniel and Walter had confederated to commit similar crimes concerned with unlawful possession, transportation, and dealing in whiskey, in fraud of the federal revenues.][2]

[2. These two paragraphs were relocated from the dissent to the majority opinion to enhance comprehensibility. — EDS.]

[Although t]here is . . . no evidence to show that Daniel participated directly in the commission of the substantive offenses[5] . . . there was evidence to show that these substantive offenses were in fact committed by Walter in furtherance of the unlawful agreement or conspiracy existing between the brothers. The question was submitted to the jury on the theory that each petitioner could be found guilty of the substantive offenses, if it was found at the time those offenses were committed petitioners were parties to an unlawful conspiracy and the substantive offenses charged were in fact committed in furtherance of it.[6] . . . [The jury convicted Walter on nine of the substantive counts and on the conspiracy count. It found Daniel guilty on six of the substantive counts and the conspiracy count.]

It is contended that there was insufficient evidence to implicate Daniel in the conspiracy. But we think there was enough evidence for submission of the issue to the jury. . . .

We have here a continuous conspiracy. There is here no evidence of the affirmative action on the part of Daniel which is necessary to establish his withdrawal from it. *Hyde v. United States*, 225 U.S. 347, 369. As stated in that case, "Having joined in an unlawful scheme, having constituted agents for its performance, scheme and agency to be continuous until full fruition be secured, until he does some act to disavow or defeat the purpose he is in no situation to claim the delay of the law. As the offense has not been terminated or accomplished he is still offending. And we think, consciously offending, offending as certainly, as we have said, as at the first moment of his confederation, and consciously through every moment of its existence." And so long as the partnership in crime continues, the partners act for each other in carrying it forward. It is settled that "an overt act of one partner may be the act of all without any new agreement specifically directed to that act." Motive or intent may be proved by the acts or declarations of some of the conspirators in furtherance of the common objective. A scheme to use the mails to defraud, which is joined in by more than one person, is a conspiracy. Yet all members are responsible, though only one did the mailing. The governing principle is the same when the substantive offense is committed by one of the conspirators in furtherance of the unlawful project. The criminal intent to do the act is established by the formation of the conspiracy. Each conspirator instigated the commission of the crime. The unlawful agreement contemplated precisely what was done. It was formed for the purpose. The act done was in execution of the enterprise. The rule which holds responsible one who counsels, procures, or commands another to commit a crime is founded on the same principle. That principle is recognized in the law of

---

[5] This question does not arise as to Walter. He was the direct actor in some of the substantive offenses on which his conviction rests. So the general sentence and fine are supportable under any one of those.

[6] The trial court charged: ". . . after you gentlemen have considered all the evidence in this case, if you are satisfied from the evidence beyond a reasonable doubt that at the time these particular substantive offenses were committed, that is, the offenses charged in the first ten counts of this indictment if you are satisfied from the evidence beyond a reasonable doubt that the two defendants were in an unlawful conspiracy, as I have heretofore defined unlawful conspiracy to you, then you would have a right, if you found that to be true to your satisfaction beyond a reasonable doubt, to convict each of these defendants on all these substantive counts, provided the acts referred to in the substantive counts were acts in furtherance of the unlawful conspiracy or object of the unlawful conspiracy, which you have found from the evidence existed." Daniel was not indicted as an aider or abettor (*see* Criminal Code, § 332, 18 U.S.C. 550), nor was his case submitted to the jury on that theory.

conspiracy when the overt act of one partner in crime is attributable to all. An overt act is an essential ingredient of the crime of conspiracy under § 37 of the Criminal Code, 18 U.S.C. § 88. If that can be supplied by the act of one conspirator, we fail to see why the same or other acts in furtherance of the conspiracy are likewise not attributable to the others for the purpose of holding them responsible for the substantive offense.

A different case would arise if the substantive offense committed by one of the conspirators was not in fact done in furtherance of the conspiracy, did not fall within the scope of the unlawful project, or was merely a part of the ramifications of the plan which could not be reasonably foreseen as a necessary or natural consequence of the unlawful agreement. But as we read this record, that is not this case.

Affirmed.

RUTLEDGE, J. (dissenting in part) The judgment concerning Daniel Pinkerton should be reversed. In my opinion it is without precedent here and is a dangerous precedent to establish. . . .

I think this ruling violates both the letter and the spirit of what Congress did when it separately defined the three classes of crime, namely, (1) completed substantive offenses;[1] (2) aiding, abetting or counseling another to commit them;[2] and (3) conspiracy to commit them.[3] Not only does this ignore the distinctions Congress has prescribed shall be observed. It either convicts one man for another's crime or punishes the man convicted twice for the same offense.

The three types of offense are not identical. Nor are their differences merely verbal. The gist of conspiracy is the agreement; that of aiding, abetting or counseling is in consciously advising or assisting another to commit particular offenses, and thus becoming a party to them; that of substantive crime, going a step beyond mere aiding, abetting, counseling to completion of the offense. . . .

The Court's theory seems to be that Daniel and Walter became general partners in crime by virtue of their agreement and because of that agreement without more on his part Daniel became criminally responsible as a principal for everything Walter did thereafter in the nature of a criminal offense of the general sort the agreement contemplated, so long as there was not clear evidence that Daniel had withdrawn from or revoked the agreement. Whether or not his commitment to the penitentiary had that effect, the result is a vicarious criminal responsibility as broad as, or broader than, the vicarious civil liability of a partner for acts done by a copartner in the course of the firm's business.

Such analogies from private commercial law and the law of torts are dangerous, in my judgment, for transfer to the criminal field. Guilt there with us remains personal, not vicarious, for the more serious offenses. It should be kept so. The effect of Daniel's conviction in this case, to repeat, is either to attribute to him

---

[1] These of course comprehend the vast variety of offenses prescribed by federal law, conspiracies for accomplishing which may be charged under the catchall conspiracy statute, note 3.

[2] "Whoever directly commits any act constituting an offense defined in any law of the United States, or aids, abets, counsels, commands, induces, or procures its commission, is a principal." 18 U.S.C. § 550.

[3] "If two or more persons conspire either to commit any offense against the United States, or to defraud the United States in any manner or for any purpose, and one or more of such parties do any act to effect the object of the conspiracy, each of the parties to such conspiracy shall be fined not more than $ 10,000, or imprisoned not more than two years, or both." 18 U.S.C. § 88.

Walter's guilt or to punish him twice for the same offense, namely, agreeing with Walter to engage in crime. Without the agreement Daniel was guilty of no crime on this record. With it and no more, so far as his own conduct is concerned, he was guilty of two. . . .

QUESTIONS

1. What are the criteria of the *Pinkerton* doctrine as explained in the majority opinion?
2. How does the doctrine affect the scope of liability of a conspirator?
3. To what doctrine in complicity is the *Pinkerton* doctrine similar?

2. Association of Parties to a Conspiracy

UNITED STATES *v.* McDERMOTT
245 F.3d 133 (2d Cir. 2001)

OAKES, Senior Circuit Judge. Defendant James J. McDermott appeals from a judgment entered against him in the United States District Court for the Southern District of New York following a jury trial . . . convicting him of conspiracy to commit insider trading in violation of 18 U.S.C. § 371 and of insider trading in violation of 15 U.S.C. §§ 78j(b) and 78ff and of 17 C.F.R. § 240.10b-5. On appeal, McDermott contends . . . that the evidence was insufficient as a matter of law to support his convictions. . . . We agree that there is insufficient evidence to support the conspiracy count, although sufficient evidence exists to support McDermott's conviction on the substantive offenses. . . .

The present prosecution arose out of a triangulated love affair involving the president of a prominent investment bank, a pornographic film star and a New Jersey businessman.

Until May 1999, McDermott was the president, CEO and Chairman of Keefe Bruyette & Woods ("KBW"), an investment bank headquartered in New York City that specializes in mergers and acquisitions in the banking industry. Around 1996, McDermott began having an extramarital affair with Kathryn Gannon. Gannon was an adult film star and an alleged prostitute who performed using the stage name "Marylin Star." During the course of their affair, McDermott made numerous stock recommendations to Gannon. Unbeknownst to McDermott, Gannon was simultaneously having an affair with Anthony Pomponio and passing these recommendations to him. Although neither Gannon nor Pomponio had extensive training or expertise in securities trading, together they earned around $170,000 in profits during the period relevant to this case.

The government indicted McDermott, Gannon and Pomponio for conspiracy to commit insider trading and for insider trading on the theory that McDermott's recommendations to Gannon were based on non-public, material information. McDermott and Pomponio were tried together, but Gannon was not present.

The evidence at trial concerned primarily the relationship between McDermott and Gannon and the trading activities of Gannon and Pomponio. The Government built its case against McDermott almost entirely on circumstantial evidence linking records of telephone conversations between McDermott and Gannon with records of Gannon's and Pomponio's trading activities. Telephone records revealed that McDermott and Gannon engaged in approximately 800 telephone calls during the charged period, including up to 29 calls in one day. Trading records revealed correlations between the telephone calls and stock trades. In addition to these records, the sensational highlight of the government's evidence . . . consisted of audiotape recordings of Pomponio's SEC deposition. These tapes undermined Pomponio's defense and credibility, as they recorded him poorly telling lies, evading questions and affecting incredulous reactions.[4] McDermott was sentenced to eight months' imprisonment, to be followed by a two-year term of supervised release, a $25,000 fine and $600 in special assessments.

Legal Sufficiency

McDermott challenges the sufficiency of the evidence to establish his convictions both for a single conspiracy to commit insider trading and for the related substantive offenses.

"A defendant challenging the sufficiency of the evidence bears a heavy burden[.]" When reviewing sufficiency challenges, "we 'view the evidence in the light most favorable to the government, drawing all inferences in the government's favor'[.]" An appellant must demonstrate that "no 'rational trier of fact could have found the essential elements of the crime charged beyond a reasonable doubt.'" We apply these principles equally to direct and to circumstantial evidence. Finally, we note that the task of choosing among competing, permissible inferences is for the fact-finder, not for the reviewing court.

Measured against this high standard, we find that the evidence was insufficient as a matter of law on the conspiracy count, but sufficient to establish McDermott's conviction for the substantive offenses.

A. The Conspiracy Count

"[I]n order to prove a single conspiracy, the government must show that each alleged member agreed to participate in what he knew to be a collective venture directed toward a common goal. The coconspirators need not have agreed on the details of the conspiracy, so long as they agreed on the essential nature of the plan." We have frequently noted that the "essence of conspiracy is the agreement and not the commission of the substantive offense." Additionally, it is a long-standing principle of this Court's law of conspiracy that "[n]obody is liable in conspiracy

---

[4] The following is an excerpt from Pomponio's SEC audiotape testimony at the moment when the SEC lawyer confronted Pomponio with evidence that he and Gannon had purchased the same stocks within a short period of one another:

Q: Our records reflect that Ms. Gannon purchased her stock at 8:59 a.m. on August 26, 1997.
A: That's the same day you're saying?
Q: The same day, a half-hour before you did.
A: You're kidding? I'm serious. You really have that?
Q: Yes.
A: I can't believe that. I mean I believe you, I'm not saying I don't believe you but that is sheer coincidence. That's the kind of stuff that I don't like. That is sheer coincidence.

except for the fair import of the concerted purpose or agreement as he understands it; if later comers change that, he is not liable for the change; his liability is limited to the common purposes while he remains in it."

Despite this well-settled law, the government here asks us to redefine a conspiracy by its purpose, rather than by the agreement of its members to that purpose. The government argues that from the perspective of Gannon and Pomponio, albeit not from McDermott's perspective, there was a unitary purpose to commit insider trading based on information furnished by McDermott. According to the government, therefore, McDermott was part of the conspiracy even though he did not agree to pass information to both Gannon and Pomponio.

United States v. Carpenter forecloses the government's argument. In *Carpenter*, we reversed the conspiracy conviction of defendant Winans, a Wall Street Journal reporter who participated in a scheme with his friends Felis and Brant to misappropriate insider information and to use it for personal gain. Felis then passed the insider information to Spratt, who was not part of the original agreement. We reversed Winans's conspiracy conviction to the extent that it involved Spratt's trades. Because Winans's original trading agreement with Felis and Brant was narrowly limited to specific persons not including Spratt, about whom Winans had no knowledge, we found that by passing the information to Spratt, Felis had "'used the information obtained from Winans beyond the scope of the original agreement.'"

In *Carpenter*, we left open three hypothetical avenues of liability against Winans. First, we emphasized that Winans "might have been liable for the Spratt trades had the scope of the trading agreement been broader, to include trading by or for persons other than the small group of conspirators herein." Second, we noted that Winans might have been liable for the Spratt trades had the trades been "'part of the ramifications of the plan which could . . . be reasonably forseen [sic] as a necessary or natural consequence of the unlawful agreement.'" Third, we suggested that Winans might have been liable had he "at least known of the Felis-Spratt relationship."

Because none of these avenues of liability is applicable to this case, we find that McDermott is not liable for the trades made by Pomponio. There is no record evidence suggesting that McDermott's agreement with Gannon encompassed a broader scope than the two of them. McDermott and Gannon were having an affair, and it is not obvious that it was or should have been within McDermott's frame of reference that Gannon would share stock information with others similarly situated, or even that there existed others similarly situated. We decline to hold as a matter of law that a cheating heart must foresee a cheating heart. Indeed, the only evidence that McDermott did foresee or should have foreseen Gannon passing information to Pomponio consisted of evidence suggesting that Gannon was a prostitute—evidence that the district court explicitly prohibited. Moreover, the proof at trial established that McDermott had no knowledge of Pomponio's existence.

Accordingly, we hold that, as a matter of law, no rational jury could find McDermott guilty beyond a reasonable doubt of a single conspiracy with Pomponio to commit insider trading. The government has failed to show the most basic element of a single conspiracy, namely, an agreement to pass insider information to Gannon and possibly to another person, even if unknown. We therefore reverse the judgment of conviction on that count.

QUESTIONS

1. Should conpiracy liability for Z be limited to Z's awareness of the other participants in the conspiracy? Or should the law treat Z as assuming the risk that a co-conspirator will involve another party, with whom Z may then be found to have conspired?

2. McDermott did not apparently know about Pomponio, but Pomponio presumably knew about McDermott. From whose perspective should the scope of the conspiracy be measured? McDermott's? Gannon's? Pomponio's?

3. Even if McDermott did not know and should not have known of Gannon's intimate relationship with Pomponio, why isn't it reasonably foreseeable that Gannon might pass along stock tips to another person, such as a friend or family member?

4. Was it fair for the government to try McDermott and Pomponio together when the two had never met? What strategic advantages might there be for the prosecution in having such a joint trial?

3. Duration of a Conspiracy

UNITED STATES *v.* JIMENEZ RECIO

537 U.S. 270 (2003)

BREYER, J. We here consider the validity of a Ninth Circuit rule that a conspiracy ends automatically when the object of the conspiracy becomes impossible to achieve—when, for example, the Government frustrates a drug conspiracy's objective by seizing the drugs that its members have agreed to distribute. In our view, conspiracy law does not contain any such "automatic termination" rule.

In *United States v. Cruz*, the Ninth Circuit . . . wrote that a conspiracy terminates when "'there is affirmative evidence of abandonment, withdrawal, disavowal *or defeat of the object of the conspiracy*'" (emphasis added). It considered the conviction of an individual who, the Government had charged, joined a conspiracy (to distribute drugs) after the Government had seized the drugs in question. The Circuit found that the Government's seizure of the drugs guaranteed the "defeat" of the conspiracy's objective, namely, drug distribution. The Circuit held that the conspiracy had terminated with that "defeat," *i.e.*, when the Government seized the drugs. Hence the individual, who had joined the conspiracy after that point, could not be convicted as a conspiracy member.

In this case the lower courts applied the *Cruz* rule to similar facts: On November 18, 1997, police stopped a truck in Nevada. They found, and seized, a large stash of illegal drugs. With the help of the truck's two drivers, they set up a sting. The Government took the truck to the drivers' destination, a mall in Idaho. The drivers paged a contact and described the truck's location. The contact said that he would call someone to get the truck. And three hours later, the two defendants, Francisco Jimenez Recio and Adrian Lopez-Meza, appeared in a car. Jimenez Recio drove away in the truck; Lopez-Meza drove the car away in a similar direction. Police stopped both vehicles and arrested both men.

A federal grand jury indicted Jimenez Recio, Lopez-Meza, and the two original truck drivers, charging them with having conspired, together and with others, to possess and to distribute unlawful drugs. A jury convicted all four. But the trial judge then decided that the jury instructions had been erroneous in respect to Jimenez Recio and Lopez-Meza. The judge noted that the Ninth Circuit, in *Cruz* had held that the Government could not prosecute drug conspiracy defendants unless they had joined the conspiracy before the Government seized the drugs. That holding, as applied here, meant that the jury could not convict Jimenez Recio and Lopez-Meza unless the jury believed they had joined the conspiracy before the Nevada police stopped the truck and seized the drugs. The judge ordered a new trial where the jury would be instructed to that effect. The new jury convicted the two men once again.

Jimenez Recio and Lopez-Meza appealed. They pointed out that, given *Cruz* the jury had to find that they had joined the conspiracy before the Nevada stop, and they claimed that the evidence was insufficient at both trials to warrant any such jury finding. The Ninth Circuit panel, by a vote of 2 to 1, agreed. . . . The Government sought certiorari. It noted that the Ninth Circuit's holding in this case was premised upon the legal rule enunciated in *Cruz*. And it asked us to decide the rule's validity, *i.e.*, to decide whether "a conspiracy ends as a matter of law when the government frustrates its objective." We agreed to consider that question.

In *Cruz*, the Ninth Circuit held that a conspiracy continues " 'until there is affirmative evidence of abandonment, withdrawal, disavowal or defeat of the object of the conspiracy.' " The critical portion of this statement is the last segment, that a conspiracy ends once there has been "defeat of [its] object." The Circuit's holdings make clear that the phrase means that the conspiracy ends through "defeat" when the Government intervenes, making the conspiracy's goals impossible to achieve, even if the conspirators do not know that the Government has intervened and are totally unaware that the conspiracy is bound to fail. In our view, this statement of the law is incorrect. A conspiracy does not automatically terminate simply because the Government, unbeknownst to some of the conspirators, has "defeat[ed]" the conspiracy's "object."

Two basic considerations convince us that this is the proper view of the law. First, the Ninth Circuit's rule is inconsistent with our own understanding of basic conspiracy law. The Court has repeatedly said that the essence of a conspiracy is "an agreement to commit an unlawful act." That agreement is "a distinct evil," which "may exist and be punished whether or not the substantive crime ensues." The conspiracy poses a "threat to the public" over and above the threat of the commission of the relevant substantive crime — both because the "[c]ombination in crime makes more likely the commission of [other] crimes" and because it "decreases the probability that the individuals involved will depart from their path of criminality." Where police have frustrated a conspiracy's specific objective but conspirators (unaware of that fact) have neither abandoned the conspiracy nor withdrawn, these special conspiracy-related dangers remain. So too remains the essence of the conspiracy — the agreement to commit the crime. That being so, the Government's defeat of the conspiracy's objective will not necessarily and automatically terminate the conspiracy.

Second, the view we endorse today is the view of almost all courts and commentators but for the Ninth Circuit. No other Federal Court of Appeals has adopted the Ninth Circuit's rule. Three have explicitly rejected it. . . . [T]he American Law

Institute's Model Penal Code § 5.03 would find that a conspiracy "terminates when the crime or crimes that are its object are committed" or when the relevant "agreement . . . is abandoned." It would not find "impossibility" a basis for termination.

The *Cruz* majority argued that the more traditional termination rule threatened "endless" potential liability. To illustrate the point, the majority posited a sting in which police instructed an arrested conspirator to go through the "telephone directory . . . [and] call all of his acquaintances" to come and help him, with the Government obtaining convictions of those who did so. The problem with this example, however, is that, even though it is not necessarily an example of entrapment itself, it draws its persuasive force from the fact that it bears certain resemblances to entrapment. The law independently forbids convictions that rest upon entrapment. And the example fails to explain why a different branch of the law, conspiracy law, should be modified to forbid entrapment-like behavior that falls outside the bounds of current entrapment law. At the same time, the *Cruz* rule would reach well beyond arguable police misbehavior, potentially threatening the use of properly run law enforcement sting operations. . . . We conclude that the Ninth Circuit's conspiracy-termination law holding set forth in *Cruz* is erroneous in the manner discussed. We reverse the present judgment insofar as it relies upon that holding.

QUESTIONS

1. When should a conspiracy that fails to achieve its objective be treated as ending? When the objective of the conspiracy becomes impossible to achieve (e.g., when the government seizes drugs the conspiracy aims to distribute)? Or when the agreement underlying the conspiracy is abandoned? What are the arguments for and against each termination point?

2. When should a conspiracy that achieves its objective be treated as ending? When the target crime is committed? Or should the criminal law recognize that an agreement to commit a crime is likely to include an explicit or implicit agreement to conceal aspects of the crime extending well beyond the time of the crime's commission (e.g., to conceal the identity of the criminals, the means used to commit the crime, or even commission of the crime itself)? What are the arguments for and against recognizing such a concealment phase to conspiracies?

E. THE CORRUPT MOTIVE DOCTRINE AND THE TARGET OF THE CONSPIRACY

Consider the following scenario.[3]

Nancy and Terry are newly elected city council members. In the six months since the election, the council has voted to re-landscape downtown parks. The council appoints Nancy and Terry to administer the project. Nancy and Terry have

---

3. The corrupt motive doctrine is also sometimes known as the *Powell* doctrine, based on People v. Powell, 63 N.Y. 88 (1875). *See* MPC Commentaries § 5.03 p. 415 (1985). The scenario above involving Nancy and Terry focuses on a variation of the *Powell* facts.

both seen the work of Helen, a well-respected landscape architect in a neighboring community. They decide to award the contract to Helen without advertising for bids. A local law makes it a misdemeanor for an official to award a municipal contract without seeking bids. It reads:

It is a misdemeanor for any city official to fail to advertise for bids before awarding a government contract.

Another landscape architect learns of the award and the failure to advertise for bids and reports Nancy and Terry to the local police. Nancy and Terry did not know of the local law that required them to advertise for bids. Can Nancy and Terry be prosecuted for conspiracy to violate the misdemeanor law of failing to seek bids?

Under the principles that we've studied, Nancy and Terry engaged in the requisite conduct — they agreed to perform the act prohibited by the statute by awarding the contract without seeking bids. They presumably possessed whatever mental state the statute might require — as they intended not to advertise for bids. This classic example of ignorance of the law should not exonerate them if either Nancy or Terry were charged individually for violating the misdemeanor. Under a conspiracy theory, however, the corrupt motive doctrine may save them from conviction. The corrupt motive doctrine can operate as an exception to the general maxim "ignorance of the law is no defense." Pursuant to this doctrine, if the conspirators, acting in good faith, lack a "corrupt" or "wrongful" rationale for their acts, they are not guilty. According to Professor Wayne LaFave, "many jurisdictions utilize the *malum in se-malum prohibitum* distinction here and thus recognize a claim of good faith only if the criminal objective of the conspiracy was not inherently wrong."[4] Thus, courts will generally find the doctrine unavailable for conspiracy to commit traditional common law crimes such as murder, arson, and assault, but may permit exoneration for conspiracy to commit the type of offense with which Nancy and Terry are charged.

Under modern recodifications following the MPC approach, codes usually limit conspiracy liability to those in which the object is a crime. Under the traditional approach to conspiracies, however, courts upheld conspiracy liability when the conspiracy sought " 'to accomplish some purpose, not in itself criminal or unlawful, by criminal or unlawful means.' "[5]

Wharton's Rule

Another limitation on conspiracy liability is known as Wharton's Rule. It prevents prosecution for conspiracy " 'when the crime is of such a nature as to necessarily require the participation of two persons for its commission.' "[6] For example, assume that the crime of dueling requires the participation of two persons. Under such circumstances, even if Joe and Linda agree to duel against one another, and otherwise fulfill the jurisdiction's requirements for conspiracy, application of the Wharton Rule would prevent a successful conspiracy prosecution against them. According to Wharton, "the author whose name . . . [the Rule] bears, . . . conspiracy

---

4. Wayne LaFave, *Criminal Law* 585 (3d ed. 2000).
5. *Id.* at 587, quoting Commonwealth v. Hunt, 45 Mass. 111 (1842).
6. Ianelli v. United States, 420 U.S. 770 , 773 at n.5 (1975) (quoting 1 R. Anderson, *Wharton's Criminal Law and Procedure* § 89, p.191 (1957)).

'assumes . . . a crime of such a nature that it is aggravated by a plurality of agents.' "[7] Since dueling here already requires two people, dueling would not be a crime aggravated by having two people agree to duel. In 1975, the United States Supreme Court noted that "[t]he [Wharton] Rule ha[d] been applied by numerous courts, state and federal alike."[8]

In which of the following problems could the Wharton Rule prevent successful prosecution for conspiracy?

PROBLEMS

12.9 Claire agrees to sell narcotics to John, and they commit a sufficient overt act to satisfy the applicable conspiracy statute. Can the prosecutor charge Claire with conspiracy to sell narcotics to John?

12.10 Travis and Hope agree to marry each other and then proceed to get married. Travis, however, is already married to Pam. Can the prosecution charge Travis with conspiracy to commit bigamy?

12.11 Yolanda and Nevil agree to and commit robbery. Can the prosecution charge Yolanda with conspiracy to commit robbery?

Consider, however, a variation on the two-person conspiracy hypotheticals involved in the above Problems. Claire agrees with Sally, John, and Fritz that Claire will sell narcotics to John. Claire then sells the narcotics to John pursuant to this agreement. Should Wharton's Rule prevent a conspiracy charge here? This situation illustrates the " 'third-party exception,' which renders Wharton's Rule inapplicable when the conspiracy involves the cooperation of a greater number of persons than is required for the commission of the substantive offense."[9] "The rationale supporting this exception appears to be that the legislature would not have intended to preclude punishment for a combination of greater dimension than that required to commit the substantive offense."[10]

QUESTIONS

1. Is Wharton's Rule an anachronism? Should it continue to apply today? Who should decide this question? Legislators? Or judges?

2. What arguments can you make for eliminating the third-party exception? What arguments can you make in favor of the exception?

---

7. MPC Commentaries § 5.04, p. 482 (1985) (citing 2 F. Wharton, *Criminal Law* § 1604 (12th ed. 1932)).
8. *Ianelli*, 420 U.S. at 774.
9. *Id.* at 775.
10. *Id.* at 784.

F. ABANDONMENT

PROBLEMS

12.12 Timothy and Karen live in a dilapidated house. Extensive termite damage is causing the walls to decay and collapse. They decide to burn the house down to obtain the insurance proceeds and build a new house. Karen retrieves the lighter they use for the BBQ. Timothy goes to the garage to get a can of gasoline to pour around the perimeter of the building in order to accelerate the fire. When Timothy picks up the can, though, he realizes the can is empty. When he goes back into the house, Karen says: "Maybe this is a sign that we shouldn't be doing this." Timothy dismisses her suggestion and drives to the local gas station to fill the gas can. Karen, concerned that Timothy will try to burn down the house, uses the garden hose to thoroughly soak the foundation of the house. She believes that saturating the foundation will prevent the house from burning. Then she leaves the house to walk the dog. While Karen and Timothy are gone, lightning strikes the house, setting a fire that burns the house to the ground. Are Timothy and Karen liable for conspiracy to commit arson under the MPC, Tennessee, or Georgia statutes that appear below? Assume that arson is defined as intentionally burning a building used for habitation.

12.13 Bill and Bob are driving in Bill's car one night when they notice a young woman alone and heading to her car in a remote corner of the parking lot. They quickly decide to rob the woman and use the money to go drinking at a local bar. Bill turns into the parking lot and pulls his car up next to the woman. Bob rolls down his window and, pretending to be lost, attempts to engage her in conversation. The woman is suspicious, though, and runs to her car. Bob yells "Let's get her!" Bill steps on the gas and pulls his car in front of the woman's car, attempting to prevent her escape. She then begins flashing her car's lights and honking its horn in an effort to draw attention to her plight. Bill abruptly pulls away and speeds out of the parking lot. Can Bill and Bob avoid liability for conspiracy by asserting they abandoned their conspiracy to rob the young woman?

(a) What if, after the woman runs to her car, instead of yelling "Let's get her!", Bob tells Bill he thinks it is not such a good idea to rob the woman, but Bill nonetheless continues with the plan and in fact robs the woman of her purse. Can Bob use an abandonment defense to a conspiracy charge?

(b) What if, after the woman runs to her car, Bill tells Bob he thinks it is not such a good idea to rob the woman, then turns the car around and leaves the parking lot. Can Bill use an abandonment defense to a conspiracy charge?

Model Penal Code § 5.03 *Criminal Conspiracy*

(6) **Renunciation of Criminal Purpose.** It is an affirmative defense that the actor, after conspiring to commit a crime, thwarted the success of the conspiracy, under circumstances manifesting a complete and voluntary renunciation of his criminal purpose.

Tennessee Code Annotated § 39-12-103 *Criminal conspiracy*

(e) (2) Abandonment of a conspiracy is presumed if neither the person nor anyone with whom the person conspired does any overt act in pursuance of the conspiracy during the applicable period of limitation.

(3) If an individual abandons the agreement, the conspiracy is terminated as to that person only if and when the person advises those with whom the person conspired of the abandonment, or the person informs law enforcement authorities of the existence of the conspiracy and of the person's participation therein.

Official Code of Georgia § 16-4-9 *Withdrawal by coconspirator from agreement to commit crime*

A coconspirator may be relieved from the effects of [the Georgia conspiracy statute] if he can show that before the overt act occurred he withdrew his agreement to commit a crime.

G. SYNTHESIS AND REVIEW

PROBLEMS

12.14 Professor Phillip Johnson has argued that conspiracy is an "unnecessary crime" given the reach of modern attempt statutes.[11] Based on your study of these two anticipatory crimes, does the crime of conspiracy serve any function not served by the law of attempt?

12.15 If someone succeeds in committing the target offense, she cannot typically also be punished for an attempt to commit that offense although she will often have met all the requirements for an attempt. In other words, attempt liability evaporates upon completion of the target offense, a phenomenon traditionally described as the attempt *merging* with the completed offense. The same is not true of conspiracy. One who conspires to rob a bank and succeeds in robbing the bank may receive separate, cumulative punishments for both the bank robbery and the conspiracy. In traditional terminology, the crime of conspiracy does not merge with the completed target offense. When a defendant succeeds in committing the target offense, should separate punishment for anticipatory offenses be

---

11. Phillip E. Johnson, *The Unnecessary Crime of Conspiracy*, 61 Cal. L. Rev. 1137 (1973).

imposed? Why? Does it make sense to distinguish between attempt and conspiracy in answering these questions?

12.16 Should anticipatory offenses be combined? In other words, should we allow an anticipatory offense to be the target crime for another anticipatory offense? Consider the following possibilities:

(a) a conspiracy to attempt a crime?

(b) a conspiracy to solicit another to commit a crime?

(c) an attempt to conspire to commit a crime?

(d) a solicitation to conspire to commit a crime?

CHAPTER THIRTEEN

THEFT

A. INTRODUCTION

Many crimes, such as homicide and rape, focus on physical harm or the risk of physical harm. But criminal law is also concerned with protecting property. The subject of this chapter, the law of theft, is one example.

This chapter starts with the study of four of the traditional theft offenses: larceny, larceny by trick, embezzlement, and false pretenses. We look at them through the lenses of jury instructions, cases, and Problems. Following our examination of the components of these offenses, an excerpt on the historical development of theft discusses why the distinctions among these types of theft arose. From there, we consider the fundamental and challenging issue of what types of property can be the subject of theft laws. Finally, we examine the Model Penal Code's consolidation of many previously distinct theft offenses into a single statutory scheme.

B. LARCENY

California Jury Instructions, Criminal (6th ed.) No. 14.02 *Theft by Larceny—Defined (Penal Code § 487) [brackets omitted]*

Defendant is accused of having committed the crime of grand theft, a violation of section 487 of the Penal Code.

Every person who steals, takes, carries, leads, or drives away the personal property of another with the specific intent to deprive the owner permanently of his property is guilty of the crime of theft by larceny. To constitute a "carrying away," the property need not be actually removed from the place or premises where it was kept, nor need it be retained by the perpetrator.

In order to prove this crime, each of the following elements must be proved:

(1) A person took personal property of some value belonging to another;

(2) When the person took the property she had the specific intent to deprive the alleged victim permanently of his property; and

(3) The person carried the property away by obtaining physical possession and control for some period of time and by some movement of the property.

"The elements of theft by larceny are well settled: the offense is committed by every person who (1) takes possession (2) of personal property (3) owned or possessed by another, (4) by means of trespass and (5) with intent to steal the property, and (6) carries the property away."[1] "Trespass" here means without permission or consent.

PROBLEMS

Apply the jury instruction and the standard from the *Davis* case, above, to the following Problems.

13.1 Rob heads out to remove the snow from the sidewalk in front of his home, only to discover that his snowblower is out of gasoline. Is Rob guilty of larceny in the following scenarios?

    (a) Rob notices that the garage of his neighbor, Penelope, is open. He enters and takes her snowblower to clear his path. He intends to clear his path quickly and return the blower in less than an hour.

    (b) Rob notices that the garage of his neighbor, Penelope, is open. He enters and siphons some of the gasoline from her snowblower into his. When he siphons the gas, he makes a mental note to replace the gas that afternoon.

13.2 Terrance steals Jill's notebook computer, intending to sell it on eBay. On his way home from Jill's, Terrance stops at the grocery store. While Terrance is in the store, Hailey steals the computer from Terrance's car. Terrance discovers the computer missing and calls authorities, who discover the computer at Hailey's home. Can the prosecutor charge Hailey with larceny?

13.3 Sarah admires Bruce's new credit-card-size electronic organizer. Sarah asks to try it. Bruce hands it to her. Sarah takes off running with it and disappears into a waiting car. Can the prosecutor charge Sarah with larceny?

13.4 Delilah thinks that Samson's attachment to his long hair is silly. One evening while he sleeps, Delilah cuts off Samson's ponytail. When Samson awakes, he is furious and calls the authorities, requesting that Delilah be charged with larceny. Should the prosecutor charge Delilah with larceny in the fact patterns below?

    (a) Delilah takes Samson's ponytail and auctions it in the local market for a substantial sum of money. She keeps the money.

    (b) Delilah auctions the ponytail as in (a) but gives the money to Samson.

    (c) Delilah leaves the ponytail on the pillow next to Samson.

---

1. People v. Davis, 19 Cal. 4th 301 (1998).

1. Conduct

STATE *v.* CARSWELL

296 N.C. 101, 249 S.E.2d 427 (1978)

Upon a proper bill of indictment defendant was tried and convicted of felonious breaking and entering and felonious larceny. Respective consecutive sentences of ten and five years were imposed. He appealed both convictions to the Court of Appeals but they reversed as to the larceny conviction only and we allowed discretionary review thereon.

The State's evidence tended to show the following:

On the morning of 18 April 1976, Donald Ray Morgan was at the Day's Inn Motel where he was employed as a security guard. With him was Richard Strickland, a helper, and Mrs. Strickland, Richard's mother, who had brought her son some food. The motel was not in use at that time as it was still under construction. Upon inspection of the premises that morning, Mr. Morgan discovered that five or six rooms had been broken into during the night. In one of these, Room 158, the window air conditioner had been pried away from the base on which it rested in the bottom of the window, but it had not been removed.

Mr. Morgan asked Mrs. Strickland to stay at the motel while he called to report the incident to the Sheriff's Department. While he was gone, a pickup truck pulled into the motel with three people in it, one of them being the defendant. They wanted to get into the motel building and claimed that they were sent there by their boss. They left after Mrs. Strickland would not let them in.

Instead of relocking the doors that had been broken into, Mr. Morgan stayed at the motel and guarded the rooms from a point on the balcony of the second level some fifty to seventy-five feet away. Around 10:30 P.M. that night, the defendant and another man walked onto the premises of Day's Inn Motel from some nearby woods and entered Room 158. Through the window running across the entire front of the room, Mr. Morgan saw the two men take the air conditioner off its stand in the window and put it on the floor. The unit was moved approximately four to six inches toward the door.

After setting the air conditioner on the floor, the men left Room 158. Mr. Morgan stopped them as they appeared to be entering another room. The guard sent Mrs. Strickland, who again had come to the motel that night with food for her son, to the nearby Holiday Inn to call the Sheriff's Department.

Later that night, a pickup truck was seen driving up and down a road adjacent to the Day's Inn Motel. Mrs. Strickland testified that it was the same truck she had seen the defendant in that morning at the motel. . . .

COPELAND, J. The Court of Appeals held that the movement of the air conditioner in this case was an insufficient taking and asportation to constitute a case of larceny against the defendant. Because we believe that there was enough evidence to send the larceny charge to the jury, we reverse the Court of Appeals. . . .

[T]he evidence [here] is considered in the light most favorable to the State, and the State is given the benefit of all reasonable inferences.

Larceny has been defined as "a wrongful taking and carrying away of the personal property of another without his consent, . . . with intent to deprive the owner of his property and to appropriate it to the taker's use fraudulently." "A bare removal from the place in which he found the goods, though the thief does not quite make off with them, is a sufficient asportation, or carrying away." 4 W. Blackstone, Commentaries 231.

In *State v. Green*, 81 N.C. 560 (1879), the defendant unlocked his employer's safe and completely removed a drawer containing money. He was stopped before any of the money was taken from the drawer. This Court found these actions sufficient to constitute asportation of the money, and we upheld the larceny conviction.

The movement of the air conditioner in this case off its window base and four to six inches toward the door clearly is "a bare removal from the place in which the thief found [it]." The Court of Appeals apparently agreed; however, it correctly recognized that there is a taking element in larceny in addition to the asportation requirement. The Court of Appeals stated that "here the problem with the State's case is that the evidence of asportation does not also constitute sufficient evidence of taking."

This Court has defined "taking" in this context as the "severance of the goods from the possession of the owner." Thus, the accused must not only move the goods, but he must also have them in his possession, or under his control, even if only for an instant. This defendant picked the air conditioner up from its stand and laid it on the floor. This act was sufficient to put the object briefly under the control of the defendant, severed from the owner's possession.

In rare and somewhat comical situations, it is possible to have an asportation of an object without taking it, or gaining possession of it.

"In a very famous case a rascal walking by a store lifted an overcoat from a dummy and endeavored to walk away with it. He soon discovered that the overcoat was secured by a chain and he did not succeed in breaking the chain. This was held not to be larceny because the rascal did not at any time have possession of the garment. He thought he did until he reached the end of the chain, but he was mistaken." R. Perkins, Criminal Law 222 (1957).

The air conditioner in question was not permanently connected to the premises of Day's Inn Motel at the time of the crime. It had previously been pried up from its base; therefore, when defendant and his companion moved it, they had possession of it for that moment. Thus, there was sufficient evidence to take the larceny charge to the jury.

The defendant's and the Court of Appeals' reliance on *State v. Jones*, 65 N.C. 395 (1871), is misplaced. In that case, the defendant merely turned a large barrel of turpentine, that was standing on its head, over on its side. This Court held that shifting the position of an object without moving it from where it was found is insufficient asportation to support a larceny conviction. The facts of this case show that there was an actual removal of the air conditioner from its base in the window to a point on the floor four to six inches toward the door. Thus, *Jones* is not controlling.

For the reasons stated above, the decision of the Court of Appeals is reversed, and the larceny judgment reinstated. . . .

QUESTIONS

1. Why might courts have traditionally required both asportation and taking for a theft by larceny?

2. Should the "rascal" who "lifted the overcoat from a dummy" be guilty of a crime?

UNITED STATES *v.* MAFNAS

701 F.2d 83 (9th Cir. 1983)

PER CURIAM. Appellant (Mafnas) was convicted in the U.S. District Court of Guam of stealing money from two federally insured banks in violation of 18 U.S.C. § 2113(b) which makes it a crime to "... take ... with intent to steal ... any money belonging to ... any bank. ... "

Mafnas was employed by the Guam Armored Car Service (Service), which was hired by the Bank of Hawaii and the Bank of America to deliver bags of money. On three occasions Mafnas opened the bags and removed money. As a result he was convicted of three counts of stealing money from the banks.

This Circuit has held that § 2113(b) applies only to common law larceny which requires a trespassory taking. Mafnas argues his taking was embezzlement rather than larceny as he had lawful possession of the bags, with the consent of the banks, when he took the money.

This problem arose centuries ago, and common law has evolved to handle it. The law distinguishes between possession and custody.

> Ordinarily, ... if a person receives property for a limited or temporary purpose, he is only acquiring custody. Thus, if a person receives property from the owner with instructions to deliver it to the owner's house, he is only acquiring custody; therefore, his subsequent decision to keep the property for himself would constitute larceny.

3 Wharton's Criminal Law, at 353.

The District Court concluded that Mafnas was given temporary custody only, to deliver the money bags to their various destinations. The later decision to take the money was larceny, because it was beyond the consent of the owner, who retained constructive possession until the custodian's task was completed. This rationale was used in *United States v. Pruitt*, 446 F.2d 513, 515 (6th Cir. 1971). There, Pruitt was employed by a bank as a messenger. He devised a plan with another person to stage a fake robbery and split the money which Pruitt was delivering for the bank. The Sixth Circuit found that Pruitt had mere custody for the purpose of delivering the money, and that his wrongful conversion constituted larceny.

Mafnas distinguishes *Pruitt*, because the common law sometimes differentiates between employees, who generally obtain custody only, and others (agents), who acquire possession. Although not spelled out, Mafnas essentially claims that he was a bailee, and that the contract between the banks and Service resulted in Service having lawful possession, and not mere custody over the bags.

The common law also found an answer to this situation. A bailee who "breaks bulk" commits larceny. Under this doctrine, the bailee-carrier was given possession of a bale, but not its contents. Therefore, when the bailee pilfered the entire bale, he was not guilty of larceny; but when he broke open the bale and took a portion or all of the contents, he was guilty of larceny because his taking was trespassory and it was from the constructive possession of another. 3 Wharton's Criminal Law 353-54.

Either way, Mafnas has committed the common law crime of larceny, replete with Trespassory taking.

Mafnas also cannot profit from an argument that any theft on his part was from Service and not from the banks. Case law is clear that since what was taken was property belonging to the banks, it was property or money "in the care, custody, control, management, or possession of any bank" within the meaning of 18 U.S.C. § 2113(b), notwithstanding the fact that it may have been in the possession of an armored car service serving as a bailee for hire.

Therefore, his conviction is AFFIRMED.

QUESTIONS

1. Based on the Court's opinion, how is possession distinguished from custody?

2. Should what Mafnas did be a crime or subject only to civil penalties?

PROBLEM

13.5 John plays in a band that is in need of several guitar amps and other electronic equipment. One day he drives to a town about 50 miles from the one in which he lives. There he uses a false identity and phony driver's license to rent the needed equipment from a music store. The time period specified in the rental agreement is three days. At the end of the three days, John keeps the equipment to use in his band. Is John liable for larceny?

---

2. Mental State

PEOPLE *v.* DAVIS
19 Cal. 4th 301 (1998)

Mosk, J. We granted review to determine what crime is committed in the following circumstances: the defendant enters a store and picks up an item of merchandise displayed for sale, intending to claim that he owns it and to "return" it for cash or credit; he carries the item to a sales counter and asks the clerk for a "refund"; without the defendant's knowledge his conduct has been observed by a store security agent, who instructs the clerk to give him credit for the item; the clerk gives the defendant a credit voucher, and the agent detains him as he leaves the counter with the voucher; he is charged with theft of the item. In the case at bar the Court of Appeal held the defendant is guilty of theft by trespassory larceny. We agree, and therefore affirm the judgment of the Court of Appeal.

FACTS

Defendant entered a Mervyn's department store carrying a Mervyn's shopping bag. As he entered he was placed under camera surveillance by store security agent Carol German. While German both watched and filmed, defendant went to the men's department and took a shirt displayed for sale from its hanger; he then carried the shirt through the shoe department and into the women's department on the other side of the store. There he placed the shirt on a sales counter and told cashier Heather Smith that he had "bought it for his father" but it didn't fit and he wanted to "return" it. Smith asked him if he had the receipt, but he said he did not because "it was a gift." Smith informed him that if the value of a returned item is more than $20 and there is no receipt, the store policy is not to make a cash refund but to issue a Mervyn's credit voucher. At that point Smith was interrupted by a telephone call from German; German asked her if defendant was trying to "return" the shirt, and directed her to issue a credit voucher. Smith prepared the voucher and asked defendant to sign it; he did so, but used a false name. German detained him as he walked away from the counter with the voucher. Upon being questioned in the store security office, defendant gave a second false name and three different dates of birth; he also told German that he needed money to buy football cleats, asked her if they could "work something out," and offered to pay for the shirt.

Count 1 of the information charged defendant with the crime of petty theft with a prior theft-related conviction, a felony-misdemeanor alleging that defendant did "steal, take and carry away the personal property" of Mervyn's in violation of Penal Code section 484, subdivision (a).[1] In a motion for judgment of acquittal filed after the People presented their case, defendant argued that on the facts shown he could be convicted of no more than an *attempt* to commit petty theft, and therefore sought dismissal of the petty theft charge. The court denied the motion.

The only theories of theft submitted to the jury in the instructions were theft by larceny and theft by trick and device. The jury found defendant guilty of petty theft as charged in the information. Defendant waived further jury trial, and the court found the allegation of a prior conviction to be true. The court denied defendant's motion to treat the petty theft as a misdemeanor and sentenced him to state prison.

The Court of Appeal deemed defendant's primary contention to be that the evidence was insufficient to support his conviction of petty theft on either theory submitted to the jury. The court held defendant could properly have been convicted of theft by larceny; the court therefore declined to reach the alternate theory of theft by trick and device, and affirmed the judgment. We granted review.

When the formerly distinct offenses of larceny, embezzlement, and obtaining property by false pretenses were consolidated in 1927 into the single crime of "theft" defined by Penal Code section 484, most of the procedural distinctions between those offenses were abolished. But their substantive distinctions were not: "The elements of the several types of theft included within section 484 have not been changed, however, and a judgment of conviction of theft, based on a general verdict of guilty, can be sustained only if the evidence discloses the elements of one of the consolidated offenses."

(1) The elements of theft by larceny are well settled: the offense is committed by every person who (1) takes possession (2) of personal property (3) owned or possessed by another, (4) by means of trespass and (5) with intent to steal the property, and (6) carries the property away. The act of taking personal property from the possession of another is always a trespass[2] unless the owner consents

---

[1] Insofar as it defines theft by larceny, Penal Code section 484, subdivision (a), provides simply that "Every person who shall feloniously steal, take, carry, lead, or drive away the personal property of another . . . is guilty of theft." The statute is declaratory of the common law. . . .

[2] This is not traditional trespass onto real property, of course, but trespass *de bonis asportatis* or trespass "for goods carried away." ([Perkins & Boyce, *Criminal Law* (3d ed. 1982),] at p. 304.)

to the taking freely and unconditionally[3] or the taker has a legal right to take the property. The intent to steal or *animus furandi* is the intent, without a good faith claim of right, to permanently deprive the owner of possession. And if the taking has begun, the slightest movement of the property constitutes a carrying away or asportation.

To begin with, the question is not whether Mervyn's consented to Smith's issuance of the voucher after defendant asked to "return" the shirt; rather, the question is whether Mervyn's consented to defendant's taking the shirt in the first instance. As the Court of Appeal correctly reasoned, a self-service store like Mervyn's impliedly consents to a customer's picking up and handling an item displayed for sale and carrying it from the display area to a sales counter with the intent of purchasing it; the store manifestly does not consent, however, to a customer's removing an item from a shelf or hanger if the customer's intent in taking possession of the item is to steal it.

Although we have found no California case addressing the precise question, a recent decision of the Ohio Court of Appeals is relevant. In *State v. Higgs* the defendant entered a Sears, Roebuck store and was observed on camera by store security agents as he removed a paper bag from his pocket, took a toy airplane from the merchandise display, and put it in the bag. He then carried the bag to a cashier and told her that the airplane had been a gift to his son but he was "returning" it because his son was too young for the toy. A security agent telephoned the cashier and instructed her to proceed with the transaction; the cashier gave the defendant a cash refund, and the security agents detained him. He was convicted of theft by larceny.

On appeal, the defendant contended inter alia that although the indictment charged theft of the toy airplane, the evidence showed the crime was, instead, theft of the cash refund by means of false pretenses; that the store, acting through its agents, consented to the refund and thereby vitiated an element of the crime; and that in any event the store also consented to customers' carrying merchandise around the store without first paying for it.

> Rejecting those claims and affirming the conviction, the appellate court reasoned: "The fact that a retail store permits customers to carry merchandise from one area of the store to another does not imply consent to conceal the merchandise in a bag and return the same for a cash refund. This act, not the act of taking the refund, constituted the criminal offense for which appellant was charged. . . . The fact that Sears consented to permitting a refund for the toy airplane was not relevant to the disposition of this case. The item unlawfully taken was the airplane, not the money. The record reveals neither Sears nor its authorized agents consented to the taking of that airplane."

In these circumstances the issue of consent — and therefore trespass — depends on the issue of intent to steal. We turn to that issue.

As noted earlier, the general rule is that the intent to steal required for conviction of larceny is an intent to deprive the owner *permanently* of possession of the property. For example, we have said it would not be larceny for a youth to take and hide another's bicycle to "get even" for being teased if he intends to return it the following day. But the general rule is not inflexible: "The word 'permanently,' as used here is not to be taken literally." Our research discloses three relevant categories of cases

---

[3] When the consent is procured by fraud it is invalid and the resulting offense is commonly called larceny by trick and device.

holding that the requisite intent to steal may be found even though the defendant's primary purpose in taking the property is not to deprive the owner permanently of possession: i.e., (1) when the defendant intends to "sell" the property back to its owner, (2) when the defendant intends to claim a reward for "finding" the property, and (3) when, as here, the defendant intends to return the property to its owner for a "refund." There is thus ample authority for the *result* reached in the case at bar; the difficulty is in finding a rationale for so holding that is consistent with basic principles of the law of larceny. The cases in these three categories offer a variety of such rationales, some more relevant or more persuasive than others. We review them seriatim.[4]

A. THE "SALE" CASES

The classic case of the first category is *Regina v. Hall* (1848) 169 Eng. Rep. 291. The defendant, an employee of a man named Atkin who made candles from tallow, took a quantity of tallow owned by Atkin and put it on Atkin's own scales, claiming it belonged to a butcher who was offering to sell it to Atkin. The jury were instructed that if they found the defendant took Atkin's property with the intent to sell it back to him as if it belonged to another and appropriate the proceeds, he was guilty of larceny. The jury so found, and the conviction was upheld on further review.

The defendant contended that his assertion of temporary ownership of the property for a particular purpose was not enough to constitute the required intent to permanently deprive. The justices expressed two rationales for holding to the contrary. First, one justice stressed that the deprivation would in fact have been permanent unless the owner had agreed to the condition imposed by the defendant, i.e., to "buy" the property. Baron Parke reasoned, "The intention was that the goods should never revert to the owner as his own property except by sale. They were therefore severed from the owner completely unless he chose to buy back what was in truth his own property."

The second rationale was that the defendant's claim of the right to sell the property was an assertion of a *right of ownership* and therefore evidence of an intent to permanently deprive: Chief Justice Denman reasoned, "The only question attempted to be raised here is as to the *animus furandi*, the intent to deprive the owner of his property. What better proof can there be of such intent, than the assertion of such a right of ownership by the prisoner as to entitle him to sell it." . . .

Perkins offers yet another rationale for the rule that a defendant who takes property for the purpose of "selling" it back to its owner has the requisite intent to permanently deprive: by so doing the defendant creates a *substantial risk of permanent loss*, because if the owner does not buy back his property the defendant will have a powerful incentive to keep it in order to conceal the theft. As Perkins

---

[4] Other categories of cases of temporary taking amounting to larceny have also been recognized. Thus the commentators agree there is an intent to steal when the *nature* of the property is such that even a temporary taking will deprive the owner of its primary economic value, e.g., when the property is dated material or perishable in nature or good for only seasonal use. (E.g., Perkins, *supra*, at p. 327 [taking cut flowers from a florist without consent, with intent to return them in a week]; Model Pen. Code & Commentaries, com. 6 to § 223.2, p. 175 [taking a neighbor's lawn mower without consent for the summer, with intent to return it in the fall].) Another such category is composed of cases in which the defendant takes property with intent to use it temporarily and then to *abandon* it in circumstances making it unlikely the owner will recover it. (E.g., *State v. Davis* (1875) 38 N.J.L. 176, 178 [horse and carriage abandoned on a public road "after many miles and hours of reckless driving"]; *State v. Ward* (1886) 19 Nev. 297 [10 P. 133, 135-136] [two horses abandoned on open road miles from ranch where taken]; *State v. Langis* (1968) 251 Or. 130 [444 P.2d 959, 960] [automobile taken with intent to leave it in city 70 miles away].)

explains, "in the type of case suggested there is also a very considerable risk that [the owner] will not get back the property at all. If, for example, he should decide that his supply was ample and decline to pay the price, the trespasser would take away the property in order to conceal his own wrongdoing." (Perkins, *supra*, at p. 329.) As will appear, we find this rationale persuasive.

B. THE "REWARD" CASES

The cases in the second category hold that a defendant who takes property for the purpose of claiming a reward for "finding" it has the requisite intent to permanently deprive. Again the courts invoke differing rationales for this holding. One line of these cases is exemplified by *Commonwealth v. Mason* (1870) 105 Mass. 163. The defendant took possession of a horse that had strayed onto his property, with the intent to conceal it until the owner offered a reward and then to return it and claim the reward, or until the owner was induced to sell it to him for less than its worth. The court affirmed a conviction of larceny on the theory that the requisite felonious intent was shown because the defendant intended to deprive the owner of "a portion of the value of the property." The court did not explain this theory further, but later cases suggested that the "portion of the value" in question was the right to claim a reward — ordinarily less than the property's full value-for its return. . . .

Another line of cases in this category also noted the taker's intent to appropriate "part of the value" of the property, but went on to emphasize a different rationale, i.e., that the taker had made the return of property *contingent* on the offer of a satisfactory reward, and if the contingency did not materialize the taker would keep the property. . . .

The same rationale has been invoked when the defendant sought not a reward but a ransom. Thus in *State v. Hauptmann* (1935) 115 N.J.L. 412 [180 A. 809], the defendant kidnapped the infant son of Charles Lindbergh. The child was wearing a sleeping suit when he was abducted. In preliminary negotiations with Condon, Lindbergh's representative, the defendant agreed to send Condon the sleeping suit as evidence that Condon was dealing with "the right party"; the negotiations continued, the defendant sent the sleeping suit to Condon, and Condon there-upon accepted the defendant's ransom terms. The child was later found dead. The defendant was convicted of murder and of larceny of the sleeping suit, and the New Jersey high court affirmed.

On appeal, the defendant contended inter alia that there was no larceny because his intent was not to keep the sleeping suit permanently but to return it in order to advance the ransom negotiations. The court's rationale for rejecting the claim was the same as that of the "reward" cases discussed above: "the intent to return should be unconditional; and, where there is an element of coercion or of reward, as a condition of return, larceny is inferable." The court acknowledged that the sleeping suit "was surrendered without payment; but, on the other hand, it was an initial and probably essential step in the intended extortion of money, and it seems preposterous to suppose that it would ever have been surrendered except as a result of the first conversation between Condon and the holder of the suit, and as a guaranty that there was no mistake as to the 'right party.' It was well within the province of the jury to infer that, if Condon had refused to go on with the preliminaries, *the sleeping suit would never have been delivered*. In that situation, the larceny was established." . . .

Finally, Perkins again proposes the rationale of a substantial risk of permanent loss. He reasons that a taking with intent to hold for reward creates such a risk because "the intent will result in a permanent loss to the owner if he fails to offer or give a reward for the return of the property." Indeed, even the offer or payment of a reward may not eliminate the risk because the defendant still has an incentive to keep the property rather than expose himself to detection by returning it.

C. The "Refund" Cases

The third category comprises a substantial number of recent cases from our sister states affirming larceny convictions on facts identical or closely similar to those of the case at bar: in each, the defendant took an item of merchandise from a store display, carried it to a sales counter, claimed to own it, and asked for a "refund" of cash or credit. Although the cases are thus factually in point, the reasoning of their opinions is, ironically, of less assistance than the "sale" or "reward" cases in our search for a satisfactory rationale on the issue of the intent to permanently deprive. . . .

. . . Several of the rationales articulated in the "sale" and "reward" cases, however, are also applicable to the "refund" cases. On close analysis, moreover, the relevant rationales may be reduced to a single line of reasoning that rests on both a principled and a practical basis.

First, as a matter of principle, a claim of the right to "return" an item taken from a store display is no less an assertion of a *right of ownership* than the claim of a right to "sell" stolen property back to its owner. And an intent to return such an item to the store only if the store pays a satisfactory "refund" is no less *conditional* than an intent to return stolen property to its owner only if the owner pays a satisfactory "reward." Just as in the latter case, it can be said in the former that "the purpose to return was founded wholly on the contingency that a [refund] would be offered, and unless the contingency happened the conversion was complete." It follows that a defendant who takes an item from a store display with the intent to claim its ownership and restore it only on condition that the store pay him a "refund" must be deemed to intend to permanently deprive the store of the item within the meaning of the law of larceny.

Second, as a practical matter, the risk that such a taking will be permanent is not a mere theoretical possibility; rather, by taking an item from a store display with the intent to demand a refund a defendant creates a substantial risk of permanent loss. This is so because if the defendant's attempt to obtain a refund for the item fails for any reason, he has a powerful incentive to keep the item in order to avoid drawing attention to the theft. A person who has taken an item from a store display and has claimed the right to "return" it at a sales counter, but has been rebuffed because, for example, he has no receipt, will not be inclined to run the risk of confirming the suspicions of the sales clerk or store security personnel by *putting the item back* in the display. Instead, just as in the case of a failed attempt to "sell" property back to its owner, "the trespasser would take away the property in order to conceal his own wrongdoing."

Applying the foregoing reasoning to the facts of the case at bar, we conclude that defendant's intent to claim ownership of the shirt and to return it to Mervyn's only on condition that the store pay him a "refund" constitutes an intent to permanently deprive Mervyn's of the shirt within the meaning of the law of larceny, and hence an intent to "feloniously steal" that property within the meaning of Penal Code section 484, subdivision (a) (fn. 1, *ante*). Because Mervyn's cannot be deemed to have consented to defendant's taking possession of the shirt with the intent to steal it, defendant's conduct also constituted a trespassory taking within the meaning of the law of larceny. It follows that the evidence supports the final two elements of the offense of theft by larceny, and the Court of Appeal was correct to affirm the judgment of conviction.

PROBLEM

13.6 The November 3, 2002, New York Times reported that after being caught by security guards outside the Saks Fifth Avenue department store with merchandise from the store worth $3,000 dollars for which she had not paid, Winona Ryder told the guards that she "had taken the items only because a director had told her to research a role in a forthcoming film."[2] Assume Ms. Ryder is charged with larceny. If true, would Ms. Ryder's explanation affect her liability?

As the *Davis* case illustrates, traditional larceny required an intent to permanently deprive the possessor or the owner of the property. Consider the following Problems. Does the appropriate actor have the intent to permanently deprive?

PROBLEMS

13.7 On a hot summer day, George gets ready to set up his snap-together backyard pool. He discovers, much to his dismay, that the filter is faulty. He knows that Wan has the same pool set and is away for a few weeks. George hops the fence between their yards and disconnects Wan's pool filter. When Wan returns, George tells Wan that George has borrowed Wan's filter and will return it at the end of the summer. Does George have the mental state required for larceny?

13.8 During property class, when Carol steps out during a break to hand in her moot court brief, Janette removes Carol's notebook computer from the classroom and hides it. When Carol returns, Janette offers to return Carol's computer if Carol pays Janette a finder's fee of $50. Does Janette have the mental state required for larceny?

How would you describe the mental state of the relevant actor in each of these Problems? Reconsider footnote 4 in the *Davis* opinion. Does the analysis of that footnote affect your description?

---

2. Rick Lyman, *"For the Ryder Trial, a Hollywood Script,"* New York Times, Nov. 3, 2002, section 9 at 1.

Claim of Right

In the following Problem does Chantal have an intent to permanently deprive the owner of the property?

PROBLEM

13.9 Chantal lends Paul her 10 and 20 pound free weights for a weekend workout. The next day, she sees Paul in the park working out. She notices that he often leaves the weights unattended. Chantal feels that Paul is too careless with her property. She decides to retrieve the weights and take them back home where they will be safe. Paul, whose workout included a one-half mile run between two sets of free weights at opposite sides of the park, returns from the other side of the park to discover the weights missing. He calls the police to report the theft. When the police arrive, he explains that he was using two sets of weights, Chantal's, of which he is still in possession, and his own, which are now missing. The police track Paul's weights to Chantal's house. Could the police prove Chantal guilty of larceny?

Courts have often recognized the situation above, in which the actor presents a claim of right to the specific property s/he takes, as exonerating the actor from a charge of larceny. If we parse the actor's mental state carefully, we would likely conclude that she lacks the intent to permanently deprive the owner of the property as she believes she is the owner of the property. Although Chantal's belief that she owns the weights must be held in good faith, it need not be reasonable. The mental state in larceny associated with ownership of the property is a subjective one. In traditional common law parlance, larceny is a specific intent crime. Chantal lacks that required intent. Similar claims of right also arise when the accused is mistaken about whether s/he has permission to take the items or about whether the items have an owner.[3]

C. LARCENY BY TRICK

California Jury Instruction, Criminal (6th ed.) No. 14.05   *Theft by Trick and Device — Defined . . . (Penal Code § 487) [brackets omitted]*

In order to prove this crime, each of the following elements must be proved:
 1) A person obtained possession of personal property of some value belonging to the alleged victim;
 2) That person obtained possession by making [a] false promise which [he] had no intention of performing, or by means of other fraud, artifice, trick, or device;

---

3. *See* Wayne LaFave, *Criminal Law* 811 (3d ed. 2000).

3) In surrendering possession of the property, the alleged victim did not intend to transfer the ownership; and

4) The person who obtained possession did so with the specific intent to deprive the alleged victim permanently of [his] property.

QUESTIONS

1. How do larceny and larceny by trick differ?

2. Review Problems 13.1 through 13.4, which appear at the outset of this Chapter. Do any of those Problems present an example of larceny by trick?

PROBLEMS

13.10 Jethro approaches Karen, the manager of the local grocery store, and asks if he can buy one of the store's shopping carts. Jethro claims that he is a homeless individual with no place to store and no means of transporting his belongings. Karen believes Jethro's claims and offers to sell Jethro a cart for $25, the wholesale cost of the cart. Jethro promises to return later that afternoon with $25 worth of recyclables, which he will trade in for cash at the recycling center in the store's parking lot and then pay Karen the $25 for the cart. Jethro takes the cart and does not return to pay Karen. In fact, at the time that Jethro approached Karen, Jethro was not a homeless person. He planned to use the cart for an art project but did not believe that Karen would sell it to him for that purpose and certainly not at the wholesale price. Is Jethro guilty of the crime of larceny by trick under the jury instruction above?

13.11 Same facts as 13.10 except that Jethro asked to borrow the cart for one week and promised to return to pay Karen $5 for the use of the cart. Karen had agreed to the $5 fee for use of the cart for one week. Is Jethro guilty of the crime of larceny by trick under the jury instruction above?

D. EMBEZZLEMENT

California Jury Instructions, Criminal (6th ed.) No. 14.07   *Theft by Embezzlement — Defined (Penal Code § 487) [brackets omitted]*

Defendant is accused of having committed the crime of grand theft, a violation of section 487 of the Penal Code.

Every person to whom property has been entrusted who fraudulently appropriates that property to her own use or purpose, is guilty of the crime of theft by embezzlement.

In order to prove this crime, each of the following elements must be proved:

(1) A relation of trust and confidence existed between two persons;

(2) Pursuant to that relationship one of those persons accepted property entrusted to her by the other person; and

(3) With the specific intent to deprive the other person of his property, the person appropriated or converted it to her own use or purpose.

QUESTIONS

1. How do larceny and larceny by trick differ from embezzlement?
2. Reconsider the *Mafnas* decision. Would Mafnas' crime be better character-ized as embezzlement or larceny?

STATE *v.* ARCHIE

Court of Appeals of New Mexico 123 N.M. 503 (1997)

Bosson, Judge.

Defendant appeals his conviction for embezzlement after a trial to the court without a jury. Defendant was on probation, confined by the conditions of his pro-bation to stay within 150 feet of his telephone. As part of his probation, Defendant agreed to wear an electronic monitoring device (EMD) around his ankle which would communicate electronically with a computer connected to his telephone and thereby verify his presence as long as he continued to wear the EMD. Contrary to the conditions of probation, Defendant removed the EMD, damaging it, and threw it into a field. The value of the EMD was placed at over $ 250 and under $ 2500, thereby making this a fourth degree felony. On appeal, Defendant does not dispute that he violated his probation or that he may have committed the lesser crime of criminal damage to property. Defendant contends that his actions do not constitute the specific crime of embezzlement. We analyze Defendant's actions in light of the specific statutory elements of embezzlement and affirm.

DISCUSSION

The embezzlement statute, NMSA 1978, Section 30-16-8 (Cum. Supp. 1996), states: "Embezzlement consists of the embezzling or converting to his own use of anything of value, with which he has been entrusted, with fraudulent intent to deprive the owner thereof." The Uniform Jury Instruction 14-1641, further defines the elements of embezzlement:

For you to find the defendant guilty of embezzlement . . . , the state must prove to your satisfaction beyond a reasonable doubt each of the following elements of the crime:

1. The defendant was entrusted with _____ . . . ;

2. The defendant converted this _____ (property or money) to the defen-dant's own use. "Converting something to one's own use" means keeping another's property rather than returning it, or using another's property for one's own pur-pose [rather than] [even though the property is eventually used] for the purpose authorized by the owner;

3. At the time the defendant converted _____ (property or money), the defendant fraudulently intended to deprive the owner of the owner's property. "Fraudulently intended" means intended to deceive or cheat; . . .

Defendant first argues that there was no showing of a traditional fiduciary relationship, without which he maintains an embezzlement conviction cannot stand. We disagree. Our earlier case of *State v. Moss*, 83 N.M. 42, 44, 487 P.2d 1347, 1349 (Ct. App. 1971), stands for the proposition that a specific or technical fiduciary relationship is not necessary to sustain an embezzlement conviction under New Mexico law. While some jurisdictions may require a special fiduciary relationship, such as employment or agency, as an element of the crime, New Mexico does not.

Defendant maintains there was no such evidence because Defendant, a convicted felon, was not holding the EMD under any assumption of trust or confidence on his part. We disagree. "Entrustment" occurs when property is committed or surrendered to another with a certain confidence regarding the care, use, or disposal of that property. As *Moss* states, the usual and ordinary meaning of "entrustment" is applicable unless an expression of legislative intent requires otherwise. In determining what is required by the element of entrustment, we are guided by legislative intent in enacting the embezzlement statute.

The crime of embezzlement did not exist at common law. Larceny, a common law crime, required that the thief take property from the victim's possession and that there be a "trespass in the taking." [2 Wayne R. LaFave & Austin W. Scott, Jr., *Substantive Criminal Law* (1986)] § 8.1(a), at 328. When the defendant is in lawful possession of the owner's property, which the defendant then fraudulently converts to his or her own use, the defendant cannot be convicted of larceny because there is no trespassory taking.

Statutes establishing embezzlement as an offense were passed to eliminate this loophole in the common law. We construe the term "entrusted" in New Mexico's embezzlement statute in accordance with this objective and in a manner to accomplish the legislative intent.

It is clear from the evidence that when the State turned over the EMD to Defendant, the State was relying on Defendant to act in a manner consistent with, and not adverse to, the State's interests with respect to the EMD. Defendant was after all on probation; he was free from incarceration on the strength of just such assurances that he would do what he was told and live up to his promises. Defendant even signed a written agreement with his probation officer by which he created these assurances with respect to his continued care and possession of the EMD. The agreement states:

Emd Wearer's Agreement

1. I, Andre Archie, understand that the electronic monitoring device (EMD) and all of its accessories are the property of the Adult Probation Parole Division of the Corrections Department with the State of New Mexico.

2. I accept full responsibility for the care of and return of the electronic monitoring device.

3. I understand that it is my responsibility to immediately notify the Adult Probation Parole Office if the monitor is damaged in any way or if the bracelet is purposely/accidentally removed from my leg.

4. I understand that if any part of the electronic monitoring device is damaged or lost while it is in my possession, I will be charged with Embezzlement, Theft, or Criminal Damage. The cost of the device is $ 1,950.00.

In addition, although Defendant argues that the transfer of possession was only for the State's benefit, Defendant received the benefit of being placed on probation, rather than being incarcerated. Therefore, assuming that Defendant is correct in arguing that he must receive a benefit, we are satisfied from the record that there was an entrustment of property sufficient to meet the requirements of the statute.

Defendant argues there was no evidence that he "converted" the EMD "to his own use"; instead, he disposed of the EMD or abandoned it but did not put it to "use" within the meaning of the statute. Again, we do not agree. When a person having possession of another's property treats the property as his own, whether he uses it, sells it, or discards it, he is using the property for his own purpose. Because Defendant threw away the EMD in an effort to end the State's ability to monitor his movements, there was evidence in this case that Defendant was using the EMD for his own purpose.

According to Professor LaFave, the gravamen of conversion is interfering with the rights of the owner, either to the property itself or to the benefit from the manner in which the property was supposed to have been used. LaFave, *supra*, § 8.6(b), at 369. The details of the interference are less important than the interference itself. Professor LaFave describes the manner of the interference in broad terms: "using it up, selling it, pledging it, giving it away, delivering it to one not entitled to it, inflicting serious damage to it, claiming it against the owner . . . each of these acts seriously interferes with the owner's rights and so constitutes a conversion" within the meaning of embezzlement. The statutory reference that the wrongdoer's conversion must be "to his own use" is more a reference to a "use" other than that authorized by the owner; or as LaFave states: "These words are not to be taken literally, however, for it is not a requirement for a conversion that the converter gain a personal benefit from his dealing with the property."

Defendant also claims there was no evidence of the kind of specific fraudulent intent that is necessary to support a conviction for embezzlement. Defendant protests that the district court had to infer intent, since it had not been specifically shown by the State. We do not see this as a basis for reversal. Defendant threw away the EMD after removing it, contrary to his promises in the EMD Wearer's Agreement. This gives rise to a reasonable inference that Defendant fraudulently intended to deprive the State of its property and the intended use thereof. Defendant knew that the EMD belonged to the State and not to him. Defendant also knew that he was not free to dispose of the EMD by throwing it away. Intent involves a defendant's state of mind and is seldom, if ever, susceptible to direct proof. Therefore, intent may be proved by circumstantial evidence. Under the circumstances of this case, it was reasonable for the fact finder to infer that Defendant threw away the State's property with the specific fraudulent intent "to deprive the owner thereof." Fraudulent intent is defined as an intent "to deceive or cheat." UJI 14-1641. In light of Defendant's surreptitious actions, the evidence supports a reasonable inference to that effect. . . .

CONCLUSION

The conviction is affirmed.

QUESTIONS

1. What does conversion mean in the context of embezzlement?
2. Historically, why might some jurisdictions have required a fiduciary relationship for the crime of embezzlement?

E. THEFT BY FALSE PRETENSES

California Jury Instructions, Criminal (6th ed.) No. 14.10   *Theft by False Pretense — Defined and Elements (Penal Code § 487) [brackets omitted]*

Defendant is accused of having committed the crime of grand theft, a violation of section 487 of the Penal Code. Every person who knowingly and designedly by any false or fraudulent representation or pretense, defrauds another person of money, labor, real or personal property, is guilty of the crime of theft by false pretense.

In order to prove this crime, each of the following elements must be proved:

(1) A person made or caused to be made to the alleged victim by word or conduct, either (a) a promise without intent to perform it, or (b) a false pretense or representation of an existing or past fact known to the person to be false or made recklessly and without information which would justify a reasonable belief in its truth;

(2) The person made the pretense, representation or promise with the specific intent to defraud;

(3) The pretense, representation or promise was believed and relied upon by the alleged victim and was material in inducing her to part with her money or property even though the false pretense, representation or promise was not the sole cause; and

(4) The theft was accomplished in that the alleged victim parted with her money or property intending to transfer ownership thereof.

QUESTIONS

1. How does theft by false pretenses differ from larceny and larceny by trick?
2. How does it differ from embezzlement?

PROBLEMS

13.12 Dan, who was perennially short of cash, noticed that his colleague, Jessie, liked to wear jewels. One day, Dan bought a ring for $10 with a stone that the street seller said was cubic zirconium. Dan intended to trick Jessie into believing that the stone was a genuine diamond. Dan showed the ring to Jessie and claimed it held a genuine one-half carat diamond. Dan offered to sell Jessie the ring for $500. Jessie agreed and gave Dan $500 in cash. When Jessie had the ring appraised, it turned out that the stone in the ring was indeed a genuine one-half carat diamond. Is Dan guilty of the crime of false pretenses?

13.13 Fred works as a private message courier in the port area of New York. He sees tourists from nations around the world arrive every day. Many seem eager to spend their money and buy something to commemorate their New York experience. One day, he prints out a series of fancy and official-looking certificates on his home computer. Each certificate states that the bearer has duly paid $50 and is now a 1/1,000,000 percent owner of the Brooklyn Bridge. Fred sets up a small booth near the docking area for ships. When tourists stop, Fred claims that he works for the Manhattan Transportation Department and that he raises money for the city by selling interests in Manhattan public works. With each certificate, Fred supplies a small metal replica of the bridge, worth about $10. Has he committed theft in the circumstances described below?

(a) Nellie purchases a certificate and pays Fred the $50. Fred is very convincing, and she believes him. She asks Fred whether she will receive any distributions on her ownership interest from the tolls paid by those crossing the bridge. Fred assures her that, if she leaves her address, she will receive distributions.

(b) Ruby purchases a certificate and pays Fred the $50. Ruby is skeptical that Fred can sell ownership shares in the Brooklyn Bridge but thinks the certificate is a great souvenir.

(c) Jeff purchases a certificate and pays Fred the $50. Jeff is an undercover NYPD police officer. He is assigned to the fraud unit and was alerted by Nellie to Fred's entrepreneurial activities. Jeff knows that Fred doesn't work for the city and wants evidence to prove that Fred's enterprise is a scam.

People v. Marsh, 58 Cal. 2d 732 (1962), excerpted below, addresses the mental state required by the crime of false pretenses.

PEOPLE *v.* MARSH
58 Cal. 2d 732 (1962)

OPINION:

Defendants Marsh, Crane and Bateson were charged with attempted grand theft. . . . They were convicted. . . .

The trial was a protracted one. The prosecution produced substantial evidence that defendants, none of whom possessed a medical license, worked together to obtain money from the sick and the neurotic on the false representation that the electric machines they possessed could cure almost any ailment. Most of the vital evidence was secured by undercover agents of the Food and Drug Administration, and is in the form of tape recordings of conversations between the defendants and the agents. This evidence, because of its nature, is uncontradicted. The prosecution evidence is overwhelming that such representations were made, that they were false, and that money was obtained from various persons based on such representations. . . . The amount secured from users of the machines varied between $ 175 to $ 2,000. It was usually exacted in the form of a "donation" to defendants' nonprofit organization for the "loan" of the machines. The evidence also shows that the $ 175 machine was identical in design with a device used commonly by radio and TV repairmen that retails for $ 49.95. . . .

In each instance, obtaining money by false representations is the form of theft relied on by the prosecution, and the case was submitted to the jury on that theory. Under section 484 of the Penal Code an essential element of that offense is that defendant had the specific intent to defraud. Under this section, even if the defendants made false representations but made them in the bona fide belief, based upon reasonable grounds, that they were true, no offense was committed. In other words, a conviction of theft based on false representations cannot be sustained if the false representations were made in the actual and reasonable belief that they were true. The burden of proof on this issue is on the prosecution. It follows, as a matter of course, that a defendant is entitled, in such a case, to introduce proper evidence that tends to establish that he did not, in fact, possess the intent required by the code section. Such evidence may be introduced either to controvert the evidence produced by the prosecution, or to establish affirmatively the lack of the required criminal intent. It is elementary that if the prosecution can introduce evidence of a required specific intent, the defendant must be given the equal privilege of showing the lack of such intent.

In the instant case . . . the making of the false representations, and the obtaining of money by the defendants was proved by overwhelming evidence. The defendants' defense was twofold: (1) That the representations were true in that the machines possessed the curative powers represented, and (2) that even if the representations made were false they were believed by defendants to be true; that they were based upon certain reports received from certain doctors and scientists; that reliance on such reports was reasonable. The first defense was clearly refuted by the prosecution. The evidence demonstrates that the representations were false. The main point involved on these appeals relates to the second defense — good faith reliance. In this connection, defendants properly produced some 15 witnesses who testified that the machines in question had in fact cured them of various ailments. The defendants were also permitted to testify that they relied on various reports of named scientists and doctors. But defendants were consistently prohibited from introducing into evidence the contents of the reports and conversations had with the doctors and scientists about the curative powers of the machines. In offering such evidence, defendants' counsel clearly stated to the trial court that he was not offering this evidence in the form of conversations, reports and letters to prove that the machines could cure, but was offering it solely to show the information the defendants relied upon in forming their belief that the machines could cure. While the trial court did permit defendants to testify that they had conversations with and had received communications from doctors and others commenting on the effectiveness of the machines, the trial court consistently excluded . . . the introduction of the contents of these conversations and communications. . . .

Ultimately in *Marsh*, the court ruled that the contents of the conversations and communications were admissible under an exception to the general rule excluding hearsay statements, those statements made outside of court that are offered to prove that something is true. If jurors found that the defendants in the *Marsh* case actually believed that Marsh and his colleagues thought the machines had curative powers, how should the jurors vote on the charge of theft by false pretenses?

PROBLEMS

What type of theft is involved in the following Problems?

13.14 Erin and Mathilda are college roommates. One morning, Erin tells Matilda that Erin is stopping at the bank on the way to class and asks Mathilda if she needs anything dropped off. Matilda, who is always running late, asks Erin to take Matilda's ATM card and withdraw $100 from Matilda's account for her. Erin, who is desperately short of money, realizes that this is an opportunity to pay off some loans. Erin takes the ATM card, intending to keep it and withdraw an extra $250 to pay off Erin's loans. When Erin and Mathilda return to the apartment that evening, Erin claims to have lost the ATM card after retrieving Mathilda's requested $100. In fact, Erin has hidden the ATM card and has kept the $250 that she withdrew, in addition to the $100 that she brought back for Mathilda.

13.15 Yolanda places an ad in the local paper to sell her car. Yolanda then receives a call and arranges to meet with Fallon, who is interested in the car. When they meet:

(a) Fallon asks to test-drive the car. Yolanda gives Fallon the keys. Fallon drives off into the sunset with the car, never to return.

(b) After Fallon test-drives the car, she returns and indicates that she would like to purchase it. Fallon gives Mathilda a false cashier's check for the full amount of the purchase price. Mathilda takes the check and signs over the pink slip that transfers ownership of the car to Fallon.

PEOPLE *v.* CAGE

Supreme Court of Michigan 410 Mich. 401 (1981)

Per Curiam

The issue presented is whether the crime of false pretenses, MCL 750.218; MSA 28.415,[1] may be predicated upon the misrepresentation of a present intent to do a future act. We conclude that it may not.

---

[1] "Any person who, with intent to defraud or cheat, shall designedly, by color of any false token or writing or by any false or bogus check or other written, printed or engraved instrument, by spurious coin or metal in the similitude of coin, or by any other false pretense, cause any person to grant, convey, assign, demise, lease or mortgage any land or interest in land, or obtain the signature of any person to any written instrument, the making whereof would be punishable as forgery, or obtain from any person any money or personal property or the use of any instrument, facility or article or other valuable thing or service, or by means of any false weights or measures obtain a larger amount of quantity of property than was bargained for, or by means of any false weights or measures sell or dispose of a less amount of

The defendant in the instant case pled guilty in Washtenaw Circuit Court to the charge of obtaining property having a value over $ 100 by false pretenses. During his plea, he admitted that he went to a Lincoln-Mercury dealer in Ypsilanti and obtained possession of a used car by telling a salesman that he would buy the car if he liked it after test driving it and having it "checked out" at a local service station. The defendant admitted that he had no such intention and made the statements in order to get possession of the car so that he could convert it to his own use.

On appeal, the defendant challenged the factual sufficiency of his plea, one of the grounds being that his misrepresentations related solely to future events or facts and not, as required for conviction of false pretenses under Michigan law, to past or present facts or circumstances.

The Court of Appeals affirmed defendant's conviction, holding in relevant part:

"While it might appear that defendant's misrepresentations were of a future fact, in reality what he misrepresented was his present intention which was clearly fraudulent. While there does not appear to be any Michigan case clearly on point we quote from a Texas court in *Kinder v State*, 477 SW2d 584, 586 (Tex Crim App, 1971), wherein the court stated:

"'The rule is that false promises or representations as to future happenings by which a person is induced to part with his property may form the basis of the offense of theft by false pretense so long as the proof shows that such promises are false *ab initio*.'

"We find the foregoing rule enunciated by the Texas court to be sound and hereby adopt it. Defendant's contention is therefore without merit." *People v Cage*, 90 Mich App 497, 499; 282 NW2d 368 (1979).

The defendant has applied for leave to appeal to this Court.

We hold that the adoption of a rule construing false pretenses to incorporate misrepresentation of present mental state is at odds with Michigan law. The crime of false pretenses in Michigan, as in other jurisdictions, was created by statute. It is universally held, except where the statute specifically provides otherwise, that the pretense relied on to establish the offense must be a misrepresentation as to a present or existing fact, or a past fact or event, and may not be as to some event to take place in the future. Although it is quite possible to view a false statement of intention, such as a promise which the promisor intends not to keep, as a misrepresentation of existing mental state, the great weight of authority holds that a false promise will not suffice for false pretenses, however fraudulent it may be.

A minority of jurisdictions do recognize a false promise or intention as a false pretense and there does appear to be a modern trend in this direction.[5] . . .

Our review of Michigan precedent leaves us convinced that this jurisdiction early aligned itself with the majority rule that false statements of promise or intention may not form the basis for a conviction of false pretenses. . . .

Although there may be valid arguments supporting an amendment of the false pretenses statute to incorporate misrepresentation of present mental state within

---

quantity of property than was bargained for, if such land or interest in land, money, personal property, use of such instrument, facility or article, valuable thing, service, larger amount obtained or less amount disposed of, shall be of the value of $ 100.00 or less, shall be guilty of a misdemeanor; and if such land, interest in land, money, personal property, use of such instrument, facility or article, valuable thing, service, larger amount obtained or less amount disposed of shall be of the value of more than $ 100.00, such person shall be guilty of a felony, punishable by imprisonment in the state prison not more than 10 years or by a fine of not more than $ 5,000.00."

[5] LaFave & Scott, [*Criminal Law*] . . . , p 658.

the meaning of the crime of false pretenses, we are convinced that it should be done by legislative enactment.

In lieu of granting leave to appeal, pursuant to GCR 1963, 853.2(4), we reverse the defendant's conviction and remand the case to the Washtenaw Circuit Court for further proceedings.

QUESTIONS

1. Why did the traditional approach limit conviction under a false pretenses theory to misrepresentations of past or existing facts rather than false statements of promise or intention?

2. What advantages did the traditional approach offer? What disadvantages?

PROBLEM

13.16 (a) Priscilla attended a garage sale at which she found a used mountain bicycle for sale for $40. When she looked in her wallet, she realized that she didn't have enough cash with her to purchase the bike. Priscilla offered to pay the owners $20 now and to ride the bike home and bring back the remaining $20. Priscilla had every intention of returning promptly with the remaining $20. The owners agreed. After Priscilla rode off on the bike, she forgot about the remaining $20. Three days later, when she finally remembered that she owed the money to the owners, she was too embarrassed to go back to pay them. She kept the bike but never paid the remaining $20. Is Priscilla guilty of theft by false pretenses?

(b) Same as (a) above except, at the time that Priscilla offered to bring the remaining $20, she had already decided that she would not return with the balance of the money. She believed that $20 for a used mountain bike was an appropriate price. Is Priscilla guilty of false pretenses under the *Cage* approach?

PEOPLE v. LORENZO

Superior Court of California 64 Cal. App. 3d Supp. 43 (1976)

Opinion by COLE, Acting P. J. Defendant appeals from his conviction of theft, in violation of Penal Code section 484, subdivision (a).

Defendant was observed by the manager of a Von's market to switch price tags from one kind of glove to another kind of glove and also to switch price tags placed on chickens. The manager of the store stood five or six feet behind defendant as the latter went through the check-out counter. Defendant paid for a number of chickens, a pair of gloves and other merchandise. Defendant had no conversation with the check-out clerk. Defendant then wheeled the shopping cart into the parking lot where he was arrested by the manager. Among the merchandise in the cart was a pair of gloves which bore a price tag lower than their regular and correct price. Testimony also established that two of the chickens in the cart had price tags on them which were for less amounts than should have been the case. Two other chickens handled by defendant but left by him in the store, and not taken to the check-out counter bore loose price tags that should have been on the two chickens in question which defendant "purchased."

In other words, the evidence convincingly showed (although defendant denied it to be the case) that defendant switched price tags so as to buy merchandise for less than its correct price.

On this state of facts the question is whether defendant committed the offense for which he was convicted. The jury was instructed solely on the offense of theft by false pretenses. "[Obtaining] property by false pretenses is the fraudulent or deceitful acquisition of both title and possession" of the property." It is clear that had defendant not been observed by the store manager he would have succeeded in acquiring title and possession.[1]

"To support a conviction of theft for obtaining property by false pretenses, it must be shown that the defendant made a false pretense or representation with intent to defraud the owner of his property, and that the owner was in fact defrauded. . . . The false pretense or representation must have materially influenced the owner to part with his property. . . . " In other words, as in any other case of fraud, the injured party must have been induced to part with his property in reliance on the false representation.

It is apparent to us that the crime of theft by false pretenses was not committed here. The victim of the crime was alleged to be Von's market. The manager of the market at all times was aware that defendant had switched the price labels and merely allowed defendant apparently to consummate his scheme in order to be able to arrest him in the parking lot. The manager at no time relied upon defendant's conduct. Since the manager is the agent of the victim-market owner and his knowledge is that of the victim (Civ. Code, § 2332) we cannot hold on these facts that theft by false pretenses was established.

The People argue, nevertheless, that another species of theft, larceny by trick, was established. Aside from the fact that the jury was never instructed on this theory, a considerable obstacle in the way of our adopting it, that crime is not established either for the same reason — lack of reliance. While our attention has not been called to any cases dealing with the element of reliance in the case of theft committed in the guise of larceny by trick, it is apparent that reliance is as much an element of this kind of theft as it is in the case of theft committed by the use of false pretenses. The only difference between larceny by trick and false pretenses is that in the latter both title and possession to the property in question is

---

[1] State v. Hauck is the only case called to our attention which deals with the anomalous nature of a theft committed by a patron of a self-service store who switches price tag labels. An article *Changing of Price Tags by Patron in Self-Service Store as Criminal Offense*, 60 A.L.R.3d 1293, confirms that the *Hauck* case is the only one to discuss the subject. Since, in Nebraska, there was no statutory crime of attempted theft and, unlike California (Pen. Code, § 664), no statutory general criminal attempt statute, the Nebraska Supreme Court was forced to reverse a conviction where the evidence showed that the victim store personnel did not rely on defendant's attempted price tag switch.

As will be seen, we have a similar lack of reliance here.

acquired by fraudulent means, whereas larceny by trick consists of the fraudulent acquisition of possession only and not title. It is basic law that reliance on a false representation is an element of fraud; since fraudulent means are required in order for larceny by trick to be committed, a lack of such reliance must be equally fatal to the commission of that offense.

We are of the view, however, that the evidence amply establishes defendant's attempt to commit theft. Reliance is not an element of that offense. The successful consummation of the offense was prevented only by the manager's alertness. But for the manager's observations defendant would have carried the actual theft to its completion. Accordingly, pursuant to the authority vested in us by Penal Code section 1181, subdivision 6, we hold that the verdict and judgment must be modified to show that defendant is guilty of attempted theft only and not theft. Since we do not know what punishment the trial court would assess in light of this reduced offense it will be necessary for us to remand the matter to the trial court for resentencing. . . .

QUESTIONS

1. Should actual deception of the intended victim be required for a theft offense? Or should the offense depend on the wrongful intention of the actor?

2. Why doesn't attempt require the same reliance as the completed crime?

Model Penal Code § 223.1

Comment

Development of Traditional Theft Offenses. Distinctions among larceny, embezzlement, obtaining by false pretenses, extortion, and the other closely related theft offenses are explicable in terms of a long history of expansion of the role of the criminal law in protecting property. That history begins with a concern for crimes of violence — in the present context, the taking of property by force from the possession of another, i.e., robbery. The criminal law then expanded, . . . to cover all taking of another's property from his possession without his consent, even though no force was used. This misconduct was punished as larceny. The law then expanded once more, through some famous judicial manipulation of the concept of possession, to embrace misappropriation by a person who with the consent of the owner already had physical control over the property, as in the case of servants and even bailees in certain particularly defined situations.

At this point in the chronology of the law of theft, about the end of the 18th century, a combination of circumstances caused the initiative in the further development of the criminal law to pass from the courts to the legislature. . . . Perhaps the most direct influence of all was a revulsion against capital punishment, which was the penalty for all theft offenses except petty larceny during much of the 18th century. The severity of this penalty not only made the judges reluctant to enlarge felonious larceny but also may account for the host of artificial limitations that they engrafted on the offense, e.g., the exclusion of growing crops, fixtures, deeds, and dogs.

Under legislative initiative, then, the law of theft continued to expand. The earliest statutes dealt with embezzlement by such narrowly defined groups as bank clerks. Subsequent laws extended coverage to agents, attorneys, bailees, fiduciaries, public officers, partners, mortgagors in possession, etc., until at last a few American legislatures enacted fraudulent-conversion statutes penalizing misappropriation by anyone who received or had in his possession or control the property of another or property which someone else "is entitled to receive and have." Indeed, some modern embezzlement statutes go so far as to penalize breach of faith without regard to whether anything is misappropriated. Thus, the fiduciary who makes forbidden investments, the official who deposits public funds in an unauthorized depository, the financial advisor who betrays his client into paying more for a property than the market value, may be designated an embezzler. Although this kind of coverage is relatively new for Anglo-American penal law, certain foreign codes have long recognized criminal "breach of trust" as a distinct entity.

The fraud aspects of theft, never regarded with such abhorrence as larceny, begin with the common-law misdemeanor of cheat. This offense required use of false weights or similar "tokens," thus limiting criminal deception to certain special techniques conceived as directed against the public generally. . . . A mere lie for the purpose of deceiving another in a business transaction did not become criminal until the Statute of 30 Geo. 2, ch. 24 (1757), created the misdemeanor of obtaining property by false pretenses. Even this statute was not at first believed to make mere misrepresentation criminal. Instead, it was thought to require some more elaborate swindling stratagem, such as French law to this day requires. Eventually it was settled in Anglo-American law that false representations of "fact," if "material," would suffice. Today's battleground is over such matters as misrepresentation of "opinion," "law," or "value," as well as "misleading omissions" and "false promises."

F. PROPERTY

In recent decades, substantial attention has focused on the types of property that can be the subject of theft. The cases that follow address this issue.

LUND v. COMMONWEALTH
2171 Va. 688 (1977)

I'anson, C.J. Defendant, Charles Walter Lund, was charged in an indictment with the theft of keys, computer cards, computer print-outs and using "without authority computer operation time and services of Computer Center Personnel at Virginia Polytechnic Institute and State University [V.P.I. or University] with intent to defraud, such property and services having a value of one hundred dollars or more." Code §§ 18.1-100 and 18.1-118 were referred to in the indictment as the applicable statutes. Defendant pleaded not guilty and waived trial by jury. He was found guilty of grand larceny and sentenced to two years in the State penitentiary. The sentence was suspended, and defendant was placed on probation for five years.

Defendant was a graduate student in statistics and a candidate for a Ph.D. degree at V.P.I. The preparation of his dissertation on the subject assigned to him by his faculty advisor required the use of computer operation time and services of the computer center personnel at the University. His faculty advisor neglected to arrange for defendant's use of the computer, but defendant used it without obtaining the proper authorization.

The computer used by the defendant was leased on an annual basis by V.P.I. from the IBM Corporation. The rental was paid by V.P.I. which allocates the cost of the computer center to various departments within the University by charging it to the budget of that department. This is a bookkeeping entry, and no money actually changes hands. The departments are allocated "computer credits [in dollars] back for their use [on] a proportional basis of their [budgetary] allotments." Each department manager receives a monthly statement showing the allotments used and the running balance in each account of his department.

An account is established when a duly authorized administrator or "department head" fills out a form allocating funds to a department of the University and an individual. When such form is received, the computer center assigns an account number to this allocation and provides a key to a locked post office box which is also numbered to the authorized individual and department. The account number and the post office box number are the access code which must be provided with each request before the computer will process a "deck of cards" prepared by the user and delivered to computer center personnel. The computer print-outs are usually returned to the locked post office box. When the product is too large for the box, a "check" is placed in the box, and it is used to receive the print-outs at the "computer center main window."

Defendant came under surveillance on October 12, 1974, because of complaints from various departments that unauthorized charges were being made to one or more of their accounts. When confronted by the University's investigator, defendant initially denied that he had used the computer service, but later admitted that he had. He gave to the investigator seven keys for boxes assigned to other persons. One of these keys was secreted in his sock. He told the investigating officer he had been given the keys by another student. A large number of computer cards and print-outs were taken from defendant's apartment.

The director of the computer center testified that the unauthorized sum spent out of the accounts associated with the seven post office box keys, amounted to $5,065. He estimated that on the basis of the computer cards and print-outs obtained from the defendant, as much as $26,384.16 in unauthorized computer time had been used by the defendant. He said, however, that the value of the cards and print-outs obtained from the defendant was "whatever scrap paper is worth."

Defendant testified that he used the computer without specific authority. He stated that he knew he was a large computer user, but, because he was doing work on his doctoral dissertation, he did not consider this use excessive or that "he was doing anything wrong."

Four faculty members testified in defendant's behalf. They all agreed that computer time "probably would have been" or "would have been" assigned to defendant if properly requested. Dr. Hinkleman, who replaced defendant's first advisor, testified that the computer time was essential for the defendant to carry out his assignment. He assumed that a sufficient number of computer hours had been arranged by Lund's prior faculty advisor.

The head of the statistics department, at the time of the trial, agreed with the testimony of the faculty members that Lund would have been assigned computer time if properly requested. He also testified that the committee, which recommended the awarding of degrees, was aware of the charges pending against defendant when he was awarded his doctorate by the University.

The defendant contends that his conviction of grand larceny of the keys, computer cards, and computer print-outs cannot be upheld under the provisions of Code § 18.1-100 because (1) there was no evidence that the articles were stolen, or that they had a value of $100 or more, and (2) computer time and services are not the subject of larceny under the provisions of Code §§ 18.1-100 or 18.1-118.

Code § 18.1-100 (now § 18.2-95) provides as follows:

"Any person who: (1) Commits larceny from the person of another of money or other thing of value of five dollars or more, or

(2) Commits simple larceny not from the person of another of goods and chattels of the value of one hundred dollars or more, shall be deemed guilty of grand larceny . . . ."

Section 18.1-118 (now § 18.2-178) provides as follows:

"If any person obtain, by any false pretense or token, from any person, with intent to defraud, money or other property which may be the subject of larceny, he shall be deemed guilty of larceny thereof; . . . ."

The Commonwealth concedes that the defendant could not be convicted of grand larceny of the keys and computer cards because there was no evidence that those articles were stolen and that they had a market value of $100 or more. The Commonwealth argues, however, that the evidence shows the defendant violated the provisions of § 18.1-118 when he obtained by false pretense or token, with intent to defraud, the computer print-outs which had a value of over $5,000.

Under the provisions of Code § 18.1-118, for one to be guilty of the crime of larceny by false pretense, he must make a false representation of an existing fact with knowledge of its falsity and, on that basis, obtain from another person money or other property which may be the subject of larceny, with the intent to defraud.

At common law, larceny is the taking and carrying away of the goods and chattels of another with intent to deprive the owner of the possession thereof permanently. Code § 18.1-100 defines grand larceny as a taking from the person of another money or other thing of value of five dollars or more, or the taking not from the person of another goods and chattels of the value of $100 or more. The phrase "goods and chattels" cannot be interpreted to include computer time and services in light of the often repeated mandate that criminal statutes must be strictly construed.

At common law, labor or services could not be the subject of the crime of false pretense because neither time nor services may be taken and carried away. It has been generally held that, in the absence of a clearly expressed legislative intent, labor or services could not be the subject of the statutory crime of false pretense. Some jurisdictions have amended their criminal codes specifically to make it a crime to obtain labor or services by means of false pretense. We have no such provision in our statutes.

Furthermore, the unauthorized use of the computer is not the subject of larceny. Nowhere in Code § 18.1-100 or § 18.1-118 do we find the word "use." The language of the statutes connotes more than just the unauthorized use of the property of another. It refers to a taking and carrying away of a certain concrete article of personal property. . . .

We hold that labor and services and the unauthorized use of the University's computer cannot be construed to be subjects of larceny under the provisions of Code §§ 18.1-100 and 18.1-118.

The Commonwealth argues that even though the computer print-outs had no market value, their value can be determined by the cost of the labor and services that produced them. We do not agree.

The cost of producing the print-outs is not the proper criterion of value for the purpose here. Where there is no market value of an article that has been stolen, the better rule is that its actual value should be proved. . . .

Here the evidence shows that the print-outs had no ascertainable monetary value to the University or the computer center. Indeed, the director of the computer center stated that the print-outs had no more value than scrap paper. Nor is there any evidence of their value to the defendant, and value to him could only be based on pure speculation and surmise. Hence, the evidence was insufficient to convict the defendant of grand larceny under either Code § 18.1-100 or § 18.1-118.

For the reasons stated, the judgment of the trial court is reversed, and the indictment is quashed.

QUESTIONS

1. What factors do you believe influenced the court to rule as it did?
2. Why do you suppose Lund waived his right to be tried by a jury?

UNITED STATES *v.* FARRAJ

142 F. Supp. 2d 484 (2001)

MARRERO, J.

In summer of 2000, Said Farraj was a paralegal with the law firm of Orrick, Harrington & Sutcliffe LLP ("Orrick"). At the time, Orrick represented plaintiffs in a class action tobacco case: Falise v. American Tobacco Co., ("Falise"). In preparation for the Falise trial, the attorneys and paralegals at Orrick created a trial plan (the "Trial Plan"), "exceeding 400 pages and including, among other things, trial strategy, deposition excerpts and summaries, and references to anticipated trial exhibits." Only Orrick employees assigned to Falise were permitted access to the Trial Plan. The Indictment does not reveal whether Said was included among such employees.

The Government charges that Said, using the moniker "FlyGuyNYt," e-mailed an 80-page excerpt of the Trial Plan to the Falise defendants' attorneys and offered to sell them the entire Plan. An FBI agent posing as one of the Falise defendants' attorneys negotiated with Said via e-mail and ultimately agreed to purchase the Trial Plan for $2 million. On July 21, 2000, Yeazid, Said's brother, met with a second undercover FBI agent at a McDonald's restaurant in lower Manhattan to receive payment. Yeazid was arrested then and gave a statement to the FBI implicating his brother.

The Government charges in count two that by e-mailing the Trial Plan excerpt across state lines, Said violated 18 U.S.C. § 2314, which provides, in relevant part, that "whoever transports, transmits, or transfers in interstate or foreign commerce any goods, wares, merchandise, securities, or money, of the value of $5,000 or more, knowing the same to have been stolen, converted, or taken by fraud . . . shall be fined under this title or imprisoned. . . . " Said moves to dismiss, arguing that § 2314 applies only to the physical asportation of tangible goods or currency, not to "information" stored and transmitted electronically, such as the Trial Plan excerpt e-mailed here. Neither the Supreme Court nor the Second Circuit has addressed this question directly, and this appears to be an issue of first impression in this District.

Interpretation of a criminal statute may be the judicial equivalent of juggling on a high wire. It demands a delicate balancing act, requiring the courts to walk a very fine line, hazards inherent in all directions. Read the law too broadly, and the court may overstep its bounds, treading on legislative prerogatives, and by judicial fiat extending the criminal law to conduct the lawmakers did not intend to proscribe, thereby infringing on the rights of individuals not meant to be prosecuted. Construing the law too narrowly, on the other hand, runs an equally grave risk. It could undermine the will of the legislators, allowing a potentially guilty offender to go free, and depriving the public of a measure of law enforcement and protection the statute contemplated. Either way, one misstep may plunge into misfortune, both violating the Constitution and offending common sense.

To manage these challenges, and somewhat complicate matters, the court's path is guided by competing doctrinal guidance. On the one hand is the long-standing stricture expressed by Chief Justice Marshall during the formative years of American constitutional jurisprudence:

> The rule that penal laws are to be construed strictly is perhaps not much less old than construction itself. It is founded on the tenderness of the laws for the rights of individuals; and on the plain principle that the power of punishment is vested in the legislative, not in the judicial department. It is the legislature, not the court, which is to define a crime, and ordain its punishment.

United States v. Wiltberger, 18 U.S. 76, 95, 5 L. Ed. 37 (1820).

Recognizing that the definition of federal crimes is solely a statutory function, the Supreme Court repeatedly has admonished that in assessing whether particular conduct is encompassed by criminal statutes the courts should be guided by a principle of narrow interpretation, demanding that Congress' intent be expressed in language that is clear and definite. When determining the reach of a federal criminal statute, a court "must pay close heed to language, legislative history, and purpose in order to strictly determine the scope of the conduct the enactment forbids." A criminal charge must be dismissed where the statute, as applied to the defendant's actions would not give "a person of ordinary intelligence fair notice that his contemplated conduct is forbidden."

At the same time, courts have been instructed to "free our minds from the notion that criminal statutes must be construed by some artificial and conventional rule."

This seemingly contrasting guidance, however, does not reflect a true dichotomy, but only an adaptation of the general rule to fit the contours of a particular case.

The Second Circuit has held that the phrase "goods, wares, or merchandise" is " 'a general and comprehensive designation of such personal property or chattels as are ordinarily a subject of commerce.' " *In re Vericker*, 446 F.2d 244, 248 (2d Cir. 1971) (Friendly, J.). Said, relying on *Vericker*, argues that the Second Circuit has at times determined that documents fall outside the scope of § 2314. At other times, however, the Second Circuit and other courts have held that documents may be considered "goods, wares, [or] merchandise" under § 2314. See, e.g., *United States v. Greenwald*, 479 F.2d 320 (6th Cir. 1973) (documents containing secret chemical formulae); *United States v. Bottone*, 365 F.2d 389 (2d Cir. 1966) (drug manufacturing processes); *United States v. Seagraves*, 265 F.2d 876 (geophysical maps); *United States v. Caparros*, 1987 U.S. Dist. LEXIS 2163, No. 85 Cr. 990, 1987 WL 8653 (S.D.N.Y. March 25, 1987) (secret business plans).

The FBI documents at issue in *Vericker* detailed the criminal activity of certain individuals. Judge Friendly reasoned that the FBI documents were not "goods, wares, [or] merchandise" within the meaning of the statute because the substance contained in the documents was not ordinarily the subject of commerce. The Trial Plan at issue here, however, as is true for trial plans generally, was the work product of a business relationship between client and attorney, and may thus be viewed as an ordinary subject of commerce, created for a commercial purpose and carrying inherent commercial value at least as to the persons directly interested in the matter.

Said argues that even if trial plans generally may be viewed as goods under § 2314, he is accused of transmitting an "intangible," an electronic form of the document, and therefore that it was not a good, but merely "information."

The text of § 2314 makes no distinction between tangible and intangible property, or between electronic and other manner of transfer across state lines. Indeed, in 1988, Congress amended § 2314 to include the term "transmits" to reflect its agreement with the Second Circuit and other courts which had held that § 2314 applied to money wire transfers, where the only interstate transportation took place electronically and where there was no transportation of any physical item. In *United States v. Gilboe*, the Second Circuit addressed the issue of electronic transfer for the first time and recognized that the manner in which funds were moved does not affect the ability to obtain tangible paper dollars or a bank check from the receiving account. . . . Indeed, we suspect that actual dollars rarely move between banks, particularly in international transactions. . . . The primary element of this offense, transportation, "does not require proof that any specific means of transporting were used."

The Second Circuit has also held that § 2314 was violated when the defendants stole documents containing some drug manufacturing process, copied and returned them, and then sent the copies abroad. The court noted that it did not matter that the item stolen was not the same as that transported. Rather, as observed by Judge Friendly, where the physical form of the stolen goods is secondary in every respect to the matter recorded in them, the transformation of the information in the stolen papers into a tangible object never possessed by the original owner should be deemed immaterial. It would offend common sense to hold that these defendants fall outside the statute simply because, in efforts to avoid detection, their confederates were at pains to restore the original papers to [the employer] and transport only copies or notes. . . .

Relying in part on the Second Circuit's decisions in *Gilboe* and *Bottone*, the court in *United States v. Riggs*, 739 F. Supp. 414 (N.D. Ill. 1990) held that the defendant violated § 2314 when he downloaded a text file containing propriety information onto a home computer, transferred it over a computer network to his co-defendant in another state, who then uploaded it onto a computer bulletin board. The court reasoned that just because the defendant stored the information on a computer, rather than printing it on paper, his acts were not removed from the purview of the statute:

> In the instant case, if the information in Bell South's E911 text file had been affixed to a floppy disk, or printed out on a computer printer, then [the defendant's] transfer of that information across state lines would clearly constitute the transfer of "goods, wares, or merchandise" within the meaning of § 2314. This court sees no reason to hold differently simply because [the defendant] stored the information inside a computer instead of printing it out on paper. In either case, the information is in a transferable, accessible, even salable form.

The court noted that "reading a tangibility requirement into the definition of "'goods, wares, or merchandise' might unduly restrict the scope of §2314, especially in this modern technological age," and recognized that although not tangible in a conventional sense, the stolen property was physically stored on a computer hard drive and could be viewed and printed out with the push of a button. "The accessibility of the information in readable form from a particular storage place also makes the information tangible, transferable, salable, and in this court's opinion, brings it within the definition of 'goods, wares, or merchandise' under § 2314."

The Supreme Court's decision in *Dowling*, 473 U.S. 207, 87 L. Ed. 2d 152, 105 S. Ct. 3127 (1986), relied on here by Said, was appropriately distinguished by the *Riggs* court. In *Dowling*, the Supreme Court held that where the victim holds only a copyright, distinct from the possessory interest of the owner of a simple good, and the only act charged involves an unauthorized infringement of that copyright, there is no violation of §2314. The *Dowling* Court remarked that §2314 contemplates "a physical identity between the items unlawfully obtained and those eventually transported." Said reads this statement to mean that the electronic transfer of a document falls without the statute.

The Tenth Circuit, relying on *Dowling*, has also taken the view that § 2314 requires the transfer of physical goods, wares, or merchandise. The defendant in *Brown* crossed state lines with stolen computer code stored on a computer disk. The district court dismissed the indictment, stating that the material contained in the notebooks and on the hard drive was "not the type of property which is contemplated within the language of the statute, goods, wares or merchandise." *Brown*, 925 F.2d at 1306-07. The Tenth Circuit affirmed the dismissal, observing that, "§ 2314 applies only to physical 'goods, wares or merchandise.' Purely intellectual property is not within this category. It can be represented physically, such as through writing on a page, but the underlying, intellectual property itself remains intangible." *Brown*, 925 F.2d at 1306-07. In this Court's view, the reasoning in *Brown* does not square with the Second Circuit's *Bottone* decision, and may be based on a misapplication of *Dowling*.

Lastly, Said turns to *United States v. Stafford*, 136 F.3d 1109 (7th Cir. 1998). In *Stafford*, the objects of the questioned transfers were "Comdata codes" — a sequence of numbers truckers use to acquire cash while on the road. The driver receives the code from his employer, writes them down on a "comcheck" and then cashes it like a check. The Seventh Circuit held that the codes were not "goods" but merely "information," and that therefore stealing them did not violate §2314. Importantly, the Seventh Circuit does not reveal how the codes were transferred (presumably they were communicated over the telephone), and the court specifically declined to address whether § 2314 would be implicated if the perpetrator had written down the codes on a piece of paper and transported them across state lines. Consequently, the reasoning in Stafford sheds little light on the statute's application to the conduct charged against Said.

Weighing the scant authority at hand, the Court is persuaded that the view most closely analogous to Second Circuit doctrine is that which holds that the transfer of electronic documents via the internet across state lines does fall within the purview of § 2314. The indictment is therefore upheld and the motion to dismiss count two is denied.

For the reasons set forth above, it is hereby

ORDERED that the defendants' pretrial motions to dismiss and for other relief are denied.

QUESTIONS

1. After reading the *Farraj* case, can you describe something that does not constitute property?

2. Reconsider Problem 13.4 involving Samson's ponytail. Does the analysis in *Farraj* affect your answer to that Problem?

3. In light of the court's decision in *Farraj* defining "property," if you access a Web site and view the contents on your screen, are you in possession of that information? If the Web site were password-protected and required a fee to obtain the password, would you have committed theft if you access the Web site without paying the fee?

4. *Lund* was decided in 1977. Do you think that the *Lund* court would reach a different conclusion today?

G. CONSOLIDATION OF THEFT OFFENSES

With the proliferation of variations in theft offenses, successful prosecution of theft became quite complex. Consider Professor Louis Schwartz's comments on the need for consolidation of theft crimes:[4]

> Penalizing thievish rascality by means of a variety of distinguishable offenses entailed a number of technical legal problems that led twentieth-century legislators to attempt to consolidate the historic array of theft offenses into a single comprehensive offense called theft or stealing. One of these problems was legislative, having to do with the propriety of prescribing different penalties for different forms of theft. More pressing was the prosecutor's problem of choosing the right offense to charge. From information provided by the police, [the prosecutor] might reasonably conclude that a case was larceny by trick, only to have that charge defeated by evidence that the culprit secured not merely possession but title; this would make the offense an obtaining by false pretenses rather than a larceny. If the prosecutor were foresighted enough, [the prosecutor] might have charged both offenses, leaving it to the jury to select the proper one. But the vagaries of juries and the subtlety of the distinction might result in conviction on the wrong count and acquittal on the other. Upon appeal, the conviction on the wrong count would be reversed, and reprosecution on the right count would be barred by constitutional prohibition against retrying an accused on a charge upon which he has once been acquitted.

As a result of problems in this arena, the drafters of the Model Penal Code consolidated the theft and related offenses into one set of crimes. Many jurisdictions have followed suit. Although the CALJIC instructions used in this chapter to define "larceny," "larceny by trick," "embezzlement," and "false pretenses" furnished distinct definitions of the four types of theft, a separate instruction (CALJIC 14.47) explains that:

> If you are satisfied beyond a reasonable doubt and unanimously agree that defendant committed the crime of theft, you should find the defendant guilty. You are not required to agree as to which particular form of theft the defendant committed.[5]

---

4. Louis B. Schwartz, *Theft*, 4 Encyclopedia of Crime and Justice 1551 (1983).
5. California Jury Instructions—Criminal 14.47 (2004).

Model Penal Code art. 223   *Theft and Related Offenses*

§ 223.0   *Definitions*

(1) "deprive" means: (a) to withhold property of another permanently or for so extended a period as to appropriate a major portion of its economic value, or with intent to restore only upon payment of reward or other compensation; or (b) to dispose of the property so as to make it unlikely that the owner will recover it. . . .

(4) "movable property" means property the location of which can be changed, including things growing on, affixed to, or found in land, and documents although the rights represented thereby have no physical location; "immovable property" is all other property.

(5) "obtain" means: (a) in relation to property, to bring about a transfer or pur-ported transfer of a legal interest in the property, whether to the obtainer or another; or (b) in relation to labor or service, to secure performance thereof.

(6) "property" means anything of value, including real estate, tangible and intan-gible personal property, contract rights, choses-in-action and other interests in or claims to wealth, admission or transportation tickets, captured or domestic animals, food and drink, electric or other power.

(7) "property of another" includes property in which any person other than the actor has an interest which the actor is not privileged to infringe, regardless of the fact that the actor also has an interest in the property and regardless of the fact that the other person might be precluded from civil recovery because the property was used in an unlawful transaction or was subject to forfeiture as contraband. Property in possession of the actor shall not be deemed property of another who has only a security interest therein, even if legal title is in the creditor pursuant to a conditional sales contract or other security agreement.

§ 223.1   *Consolidation of Theft Offenses; Grading; Provisions Applicable to Theft Generally*

(1) **Consolidation of Theft Offenses.** Conduct denominated theft in this Article constitutes a single offense. An accusation of theft may be supported by evidence that it was committed in any manner that would be theft under this Article, notwithstanding the specification of a different manner in the indictment or information, subject only to the power of the Court to ensure fair trial by granting a continuance or other appropriate relief where the conduct of the defense would be prejudiced by lack of fair notice or by surprise.

(2) **Grading of Theft Offenses**. . . .

(c) The amount involved in a theft shall be deemed to be the highest value, by any reasonable standard, of the property or services which the actor stole or attempted to steal. Amounts involved in thefts committed pursuant to one scheme or course of conduct, whether from the same person or several persons, may be aggregated in determining the grade of the offense.

(3) **Claim of Right**. It is an affirmative defense to prosecution for theft that the actor:

(a) was unaware that the property or service was that of another; or

(b) acted under an honest claim of right to the property or service involved or that he had a right to acquire or dispose of it as he did; or

(c) took property exposed for sale, intending to purchase and pay for it promptly, or reasonably believing that the owner, if present, would have consented.

(4) **Theft from Spouse.** It is no defense that theft was from the actor's spouse, except that misappropriation of household and personal effects, or other property normally accessible to both spouses, is theft only if it occurs after the parties have ceased living together.

§ 223.2 *Theft by Unlawful Taking or Disposition*

(1) **Movable Property**. A person is guilty of theft if he unlawfully takes, or exercises unlawful control over, movable property of another with purpose to deprive him thereof.

(2) **Immovable Property**. A person is guilty of theft if he unlawfully transfers immovable property of another or any interest therein with purpose to benefit himself or another not entitled thereto.

§ 223.3 *Theft by Deception*

A person is guilty of theft if he purposely obtains property of another by deception. A person deceives if he purposely:

(1) creates or reinforces a false impression, including false impressions as to law, value, intention or other state of mind; but deception as to a person's intention to perform a promise shall not be inferred from the fact alone that he did not subsequently perform the promise; or

(2) prevents another from acquiring information which would affect his judgment of a transaction; or

(3) fails to correct a false impression which the deceiver previously created or reinforced, or which the deceiver knows to be influencing another to whom he stands in a fiduciary or confidential relationship; or

(4) fails to disclose a known lien, adverse claim or other legal impediment to the enjoyment of property which he transfers or encumbers in consideration for the property obtained, whether such impediment is or is not valid, or is or is not a matter of official record.

The term "deceive" does not, however, include falsity as to matters having no pecuniary significance, or puffing by statements unlikely to deceive ordinary persons in the group addressed.

QUESTIONS

1. How does the MPC deal with the issues raised by the common law term "permanently deprive"?

2. What position does the MPC take on the traditional common law approach limiting theft to tangible property?

3. How would the MPC apply to Problems 13.1-13.15?

CHAPTER FOURTEEN

BOUNDARIES OF
THE CRIMINAL LAW

A. INTRODUCTION

How far should criminal law reach? This chapter focuses on whether certain categories of behavior should be exempt from criminal sanction and addressed instead through civil remedies, treatment, and moral suasion.

Criminal law evolves. Oliver Wendell Holmes explains that "[t]he felt necessities of the time, the prevalent moral and political theories, intuitions of public policy . . . [and] even the prejudices which judges share with their fellow-men" cause legal rules to change over time.[1] Parts of the criminal law have been stable for centuries. There has long been consensus, for example, that criminal law should apply to murder, assault, and theft. But many parts of the criminal law have changed over time, contracting in some areas and expanding in others.

A doctor providing a woman with the means for birth control[2] or a medical abortion,[3] for example, were criminal offenses in the first part of the twentieth century. As late as the 1960s, the Virginia Code made interracial marriage a felony.[4] Such criminal prohibitions are now seen as violations of the United States Constitution.[5] Monopolization of commerce was not a crime in the late 1800s, when John D. Rockefeller consolidated American oil refineries under his control. Trading securities on information not available to the public was not a crime in the

---

1. Oliver Wendell Holmes, Jr., *The Common Law* 1 (1881).
2. *See, e.g.,* Commonwealth v. Gardner, 300 Mass. 372 (1938) (affirming felony convictions of doctor, nurse, and two social workers for providing contraceptives to married women); Tileston v. Ullman, 129 Conn. 84 (1942) (declaratory judgment that state criminal statutes prohibit licensed physician from prescribing contraceptives to married women when pregnancy would endanger life or health); Andrea Tone, Devices and Desires: A History of Contraceptives in America (2001).
3. *See* Roe v. Wade, 410 U.S. 113, 117 n.1 (1973) (quoting Texas criminal statute imposing a penalty of "not less than two nor more than five years" for performing an abortion).
4. Loving v. Virginia, 388 U.S. 1, 4 (1967) ("Section 20-59, which defines the penalty for miscegenation, provides: 'Punishment for marriage. If any white person intermarry with a colored person, or any colored person intermarry with a white person, he shall be guilty of a felony and shall be punished by confinement in the penitentiary for not less than one nor more than five years.'")
5. Griswold v. Connecticut, 381 U.S. 479 (1965) (state statute forbidding use and distribution of contraceptives violates constitutional right to privacy); Loving v. Virginia, 388 U.S. 1 (1967) (Virginia miscegenation statute violates equal protection and due process); Roe v. Wade, 410 U.S. 113 (1973) (Texas abortion statute violates constitutional right to privacy).

early part of the twentieth century. Both are now federal criminal offenses. More recent expansions of the criminal law have dealt with cybercrime[6] and identity theft.[7]

Where should the criminal law now expand or contract? We will examine in this chapter four categories—environmental crime, fetal endangerment through the use of illegal drugs by pregnant women, sodomy, and prostitution. The application of criminal sanctions to each of these categories is currently cause for controversy. The first two topics deal with expansion of the criminal law, expansion that has already taken place in regard to environmental crime and potential expansion in the case of fetal endangerment. The last two topics deal with contraction— actual contraction in the case of sodomy and potential contraction in regard to prostitution.

In each of these categories, there is considerable debate about whether use of criminal sanctions is just or useful, raising questions about retributive blame, deterrence, incapacitation, and rehabilitation. Some common questions recur in the debates about many of these issues.

One question is whether use of criminal sanctions in each of these areas breeds disrespect for law and thereby undermines its ability to control the conduct of citizens. In the area of environmental crime, disrespect may flow from application of criminal sanctions to those who lack blameworthiness. In the areas of prostitution and sodomy, the means of enforcement used by the police to investigate intimate consensual behavior may bring disrespect. A second question is whether too much power is given to police and prosecutorial discretion in each of these categories. Are police and prosecutors likely to use that discretionary power wisely and fairly, or are they likely to use it in an arbitrary or discriminatory manner? A third question is how effective criminal sanctions are in shaping conduct in each of these areas. Would providing education, treatment, and social services be more effective, for example, in discouraging drug use by pregnant women and prostitution?

B. ENVIRONMENTAL CRIME

John C. Coffee, DOES "UNLAWFUL" MEAN "CRIMINAL"? REFLECTIONS ON THE DISAPPEARING TORT/CRIME DISTINCTION IN AMERICAN LAW

71 B.U. L. Rev. 193 (1991)

[T]he dominant development in substantive federal criminal law over the last decade has been the disappearance of any clearly definable line between civil and criminal law. . . . [T]his blurring of the border between tort and crime predictably will result in injustice, and ultimately will weaken the efficacy of the criminal law as an instrument of social control. . . . The criminal law is obeyed not simply because there is a legal threat underlying it, but because the public perceives its norms to be legitimate and deserving of compliance. Far more than tort law, the criminal law is a system for public communication of values. . . .

---

6. *See, e.g.,* the Computer Abuse and Fraud Act, 18 U.S.C. 1030 (1984).
7. *See, e.g.,* Wisconsin Statutes § 943.201(2) (1998); Kansas Statutes § 21-4018 (1998).

[T]he criminal sanction has been applied broadly, and sometimes thoughtlessly, to a broad range of essentially civil obligations, some of which were intended as inspirational standards and others which are inherently open-ended and evolving in character. . . . [T]here has also been a retreat from the traditional "method" of the criminal law, as the role of mens rea has been diminished and that of vicarious liability expanded. . . . [A] transition is evident in the characteristic "white collar" prosecution. Prosecutions increasingly tend to be less for violations of a statutory standard than for failures to comply with administrative regulations. Characteristically, these regulations resemble what an earlier era called "public welfare offenses," but with two differences: (1) substantial criminal sentences are authorized, and (2) the sheer volume of regulations that are now potentially enforceable through criminal prosecution means that the criminal sanction has penetrated much further into everyday life. . . .

Since the mid-1980s, American law has experienced a little noticed explosion in the use of public welfare offenses. By one estimate, there are over 300,000 federal regulations that may be enforced criminally. Over the . . . three years [prior to 1991], the federal government has prosecuted more than 400 cases involving environmental crimes, resulting in cumulative prison sentences of nearly 300 years. The total fines annually imposed in environmental crime cases rose from $ 3.6 million in 1987 to over $ 12 million in 1989. With the advent of sentencing guidelines, prison terms for environmental crime have become both more likely and longer, with the presumptive benchmark for a felony conviction now estimated at two years in prison. . . .

Obviously, environmental crime is important, and knowing violations — such as falsification of records or willful endangerment — are serious offenses that do not merit leniency. But, the typical environmental offense involves the mishandling of toxic substances, and recent decisions have reduced or eliminated the role of mens rea in these statutes. . . . As a result, the traditional public welfare offense has now been coupled with felony level penalties. . . .

Public concern about a newly perceived social problem — the environment, worker safety, child neglect, etc. — seems to trigger a recurring social response: namely, an almost reflexive resort to criminal prosecution, either through the enactment of new legislation or the use of old standby theories that have great elasticity. Increasingly, criminal liability may be imposed based only on negligence or even on a strict liability basis. The premise appears to be that if a problem is important enough, the partial elimination of mens rea and the use of vicarious responsibility are justified. No doubt, the criminal sanction does provide additional deterrence, but what are the costs of resorting to strict liability and vicarious responsibility as instruments of social control? . . .

If the disposal of toxic wastes, securities fraud, the filling-in of wetlands, the failure to conduct aircraft maintenance, and the causing of workplace injuries become crimes that can be regularly indicted on the basis of negligence or less, society as a whole may be made safer, but a substantial population of the American workforce (both at white collar and blue collar levels) becomes potentially entangled with the criminal law. Today, most individuals can plan their affairs so as to avoid any realistic risk of coming within a zone where criminal sanctions might apply to their conduct. Few individuals have reason to fear prosecution for murder, robbery, rape, extortion or any of the other traditional common law crimes. Even the more contemporary, white collar crimes — price fixing, bribery, insider trading, etc. — can be easily avoided by those who wish to minimize their risk of criminal liability.

At most, these statutes pose problems for individuals who wish to approach the line but who find that no bright line exists. In contrast, modern industrial society inevitably creates toxic wastes that must be disposed of by someone.

Similarly, workplace injuries are, to a degree, inevitable. As a result, some individuals must engage in legitimate professional activities that are regulated by criminal sanctions; to this extent, they become unavoidably "entangled" with the criminal law. That is, they cannot plan their affairs so as to be free from the risk that a retrospective evaluation of their conduct, often under the uncertain standard of negligence, will find that they fell short of the legally mandated standard. Ultimately, if the new trend toward greater use of public welfare offenses continues, it will mean a more pervasive use of the criminal sanction, a use that intrudes further into the mainstream of American life and into the everyday life of its citizens than has ever been attempted before.

Several replies are predictable to this claim that there is a social loss in defining the criminal law so that individuals cannot safely avoid its application. Liberals may claim that the traditionally limited use of the criminal sanction was class-biased and that a more pervasive use of it simply corrects that imbalance. Economists may argue that the affected individuals will only demand a "risk premium" in the labor market and, having received one, cannot later complain when the risk for which they were compensated arises. Others may conclude that the anxiety imposed on such employees, while regrettable, is necessary, because it is small in comparison to the lives saved, injuries averted, and other social benefits realized from generating greater deterrence. This may be true, but the cost/benefit calculus is a complex and indeterminate one that depends upon a comparison of marginal gain (in terms of injuries averted) in comparison to other law enforcement strategies (such as greater use of corporate liability or civil penalties) that have not yet been utilized fully. . . . In addition, there is a cost to civil libertarian values, because statutes that apply broadly can never be enforced evenly. Hence, some instances of "targeting" or selective prosecutions (based on whatever criteria influence the individual prosecutor) become predictable. These costs would be more tolerable if the conduct involved were inherently blameworthy, but negligence, like death and taxes, is inevitable.

Ultimately, much depends on how we define the purposes of the criminal law. If its purpose is simply to prevent crime, the costs of the broad use of the criminal sanction against corporate managers to deter pollution, negligence-caused injuries, or other social harms may be justified. But if we define the criminal law's purposes more broadly — for example, as to "liberate" society from fear, or to enable the realization of human potential — these broader goals may be seriously compromised by a pervasive use of the criminal sanction against individuals who cannot escape its potential threat.

QUESTIONS

1. If we are concerned about damage to the environment, should we not deploy our legal system's heaviest weapons — criminal sanctions — to halt the damage? Doesn't a prison sentence create a more powerful disincentive against causing or risking environmental harm than the monetary sanctions typically available through the civil justice system? What are the advantages and disadvantages of criminal sanctions? What are the advantages and disadvantages of civil sanctions?

Which are more likely to be imposed? Which are more costly? On balance, which are more likely to be effective?

2. Are Professor Coffee's concerns based on retributive justice? On utilitarian grounds? He states that negligence and the creation of toxic wastes are inevitable. If true, how does this support his arguments?

3. If environmental standards are open-ended and evolving, what issues does that raise for the imposition of criminal sanctions?

4. Professor Coffee seems concerned that extending use of the criminal sanction to those who cause environmental damage will undermine public perception of the criminal justice system's norms as "legitimate and deserving of compliance." But he also describes "an almost reflexive resort to criminal prosecution" on the part of society in responding to a new social problem such as damage to the environment. If society is inclined to resort to criminal sanctions to punish those who damage the environment, is the actual imposition of such sanctions likely to be viewed by society as illegitimate?

5. Which branches of the government are involved in defining environmental crimes? Which of those branches wields the greatest power in defining those crimes?

UNITED STATES v. HANOUSEK
176 F.3d 1116 (9th Cir. 1999)

THOMPSON, J. Edward Hanousek, Jr., appeals his conviction and sentence for negligently discharging a harmful quantity of oil into a navigable water of the United States, in violation of the Clean Water Act. . . .

Hanousek was employed by the Pacific & Arctic Railway and Navigation Company (Pacific & Arctic) as roadmaster of the White Pass & Yukon Railroad, which runs between Skagway, Alaska, and Whitehorse, Yukon Territory, Canada. As roadmaster, Hanousek was responsible under his contract "for every detail of the safe and efficient maintenance and construction of track, structures and marine facilities of the entire railroad . . . and [was to] assume similar duties with special projects."

One of the special projects under Hanousek's supervision was a rock-quarrying project at a site alongside the railroad referred to as "6-mile," located on an embankment 200 feet above the Skagway River. The project was designed to realign a sharp curve in the railroad and to obtain armor rock for a ship dock in Skagway. The project involved blasting rock outcroppings alongside the railroad, working the fractured rock toward railroad cars, and loading the rock onto railroad cars with a backhoe. Pacific & Arctic hired Hunz & Hunz, a contracting company, to provide the equipment and labor for the project.

At 6-mile, a high-pressure petroleum products pipeline owned by Pacific & Arctic's sister company, Pacific & Arctic Pipeline, Inc., runs parallel to the railroad at or above ground level, within a few feet of the tracks. To protect the pipeline during the project, a work platform of sand and gravel was constructed on which the backhoe operated to load rocks over the pipeline and into railroad cars. The location of the work platform changed as the location of the work progressed along the railroad tracks. In addition, when work initially began in April 1994, Hunz & Hunz covered an approximately 300-foot section of the pipeline with railroad ties, sand, and ballast material to protect the pipeline, as was customary. After Hanousek took over responsibility for the project in May 1994, no further sections of the pipeline along the 1000-foot work site were protected, with the exception of the movable backhoe work platform.

On the evening of October 1, 1994, Shane Thoe, a Hunz & Hunz backhoe operator, used the backhoe on the work platform to load a train with rocks. After the train departed, Thoe noticed that some fallen rocks had caught the plow of the train as it departed and were located just off the tracks in the vicinity of the unprotected pipeline. At this location, the site had been graded to finish grade and the pipeline was covered with a few inches of soil. Thoe moved the backhoe off the work platform and drove it down alongside the tracks between 50 to 100 yards from the work platform. While using the backhoe bucket to sweep the rocks from the tracks, Thoe struck the pipeline causing a rupture. The pipeline was carrying heating oil, and an estimated 1,000 to 5,000 gallons of oil were discharged over the course of many days into the adjacent Skagway River, a navigable water of the United States. . . .

After a twenty-day trial, the jury convicted Hanousek of negligently discharging a harmful quantity of oil into a navigable water of the United States, but acquitted him on [a] charge of conspiring to provide false information. The district court imposed a sentence of six months of imprisonment, six months in a halfway house and six months of supervised release, as well as a fine of $ 5,000. This appeal followed.

A. Negligence Jury Instruction

Hanousek contends the district court erred by failing to instruct the jury that . . . the government had to prove that Hanousek acted with criminal negligence, as opposed to ordinary negligence, in discharging a harmful quantity of oil into the Skagway River. In his proposed jury instruction, Hanousek defined criminal negligence as "a gross deviation from the standard of care that a reasonable person would observe in the situation." *See* American Law Institute, Model Penal Code § 2.02(2)(d) (1985). Over Hanousek's objection, the district court instructed the jury that the government was required to prove only that Hanousek acted negligently, which the district court defined as "the failure to use reasonable care."

Whether the jury instruction provided by the district court misstated an element of 33 U.S.C. § 1319(c)(1)(A) presents a question of statutory interpretation, which we review de novo.

Statutory interpretation begins with the plain language of the statute. If the language of the statute is clear, we need look no further than that language in determining the statute's meaning. "Particular phrases must be construed in light of the overall purpose and structure of the whole statutory scheme." "When we look to the plain language of a statute in order to interpret its meaning, we do more than view words or sub-sections in isolation. We derive meaning from context, and this requires reading the relevant statutory provisions as a whole."

Codified sections 1319(c)(1)(A) & 1321(b)(3) of the Clean Water Act work in tandem to criminalize the conduct of which Hanousek was convicted. § 1319(c)(1)(A) provides that any person who negligently violates 33 U.S.C. § 1321(b)(3) shall be punished by fine or imprisonment, or both.[8] Section 1321(b)(3) proscribes the actual discharge of oil in harmful quantities into navigable waters of the United States,

---

8. 33 U.S.C. § 1319(c)(1)(A) provides that first-time negligent violators shall be punished by a fine of not less than $ 2,500 nor more than $ 25,000 per day of violation, or by imprisonment for not more than one year, or by both. The same statute provides that second-time negligent violators shall be punished by a fine of not more than $ 50,000 per day of violation, or by imprisonment of not more than two years, or both.

adjoining shorelines or waters of a contiguous zone, as well as other specified activity.

Neither section defines the term "negligently," nor is that term defined elsewhere in the CWA. In this circumstance, we "start with the assumption that the legislative purpose is expressed by the ordinary meaning of the words used." The ordinary meaning of "negligently" is a failure to use such care as a reasonably prudent and careful person would use under similar circumstances. *See Black's Law Dictionary* 1032 (6th ed. 1990); *The Random House College Dictionary* 891 (Rev. ed. 1980).

If Congress intended to prescribe a heightened negligence standard, it could have done so explicitly, as it did in 33 U.S.C. § 1321(b)(7)(D). This section of the CWA provides for increased civil penalties "in any case in which a violation of [33 U.S.C. § 1321(b)(3)] was the result of gross negligence or willful misconduct." 33 U.S.C. § 1321(b)(7)(D). This is significant. "Where Congress includes particular language in one section of a statute but omits it in another section of the same Act, it is generally presumed that Congress acts intentionally and purposely in the disparate inclusion or exclusion."

Hanousek argues that Congress could not have intended to distinguish "negligently" in 33 U.S.C. § 1319(c)(1)(A) from "gross negligence" in 33 U.S.C. § 1321(b)(7)(D) because the phrase "gross negligence" was only recently added to the statute in 1990. We reject this argument because Congress is presumed to have known of its former legislation and to have passed new laws in view of the provisions of the legislation already enacted.

We conclude from the plain language of 33 U.S.C. § 1319(c)(1)(A) that Congress intended that a person who acts with ordinary negligence in violating 33 U.S.C. § 1321(b)(3) may be subject to criminal penalties.[9] We next consider Hanousek's argument that, by imposing an ordinary negligence standard for a criminal violation, section 1319(c)(1)(A) violates the due process clause of the Constitution.

B. Due Process

We review de novo whether a statute violates a defendant's right to due process.

The criminal provisions of the CWA constitute public welfare legislation. *See* [*United States v.*] *Weitzenhoff*, 35 F.3d [1275] at 1286 [(9th Cir. 1996)] ("The criminal provisions of the CWA are clearly designed to protect the public at large from the potentially dire consequences of water pollution and as such fall within the category of public welfare legislation."). Public welfare legislation is designed to protect the public from potentially harmful or injurious items and may render criminal "a type of conduct that a reasonable person should know is subject to stringent public regulation and may seriously threaten the community's health or safety."

It is well established that a public welfare statute may subject a person to criminal liability for his or her ordinary negligence without violating due process. . . . In light of our holding in *Weitzenhoff* that the criminal provisions of the CWA constitute public welfare legislation, and the fact that a public welfare statute may impose criminal penalties for ordinary negligent conduct without offending due process, we conclude that section 1319(c)(1)(A) does not violate due process by permitting criminal penalties for ordinary negligent conduct.

---

9. In light of our conclusion that 33 U.S.C. § 1319(c)(1)(A) unambiguously permits criminal penalties for ordinary negligence, the rule of lenity has no application.

C. Vicarious Liability Jury Instruction

Hanousek next contends that the district court erred by failing to instruct the jury that he could not be found vicariously liable for the negligence of Shane Thoe, the Hunz & Hunz backhoe operator.

We review de novo whether a district court's instructions adequately cover a defense theory. We will affirm a district court's refusal to give an otherwise proper theory-of-defense instruction if the instructions actually given, in their entirety, adequately cover the defense theory.

The first of Hanousek's proposed instructions dealing with vicarious liability reads as follows:

> You are instructed that Defendant Edward Hanousek is not responsible for and cannot be held criminally liable for any negligent acts or omissions by Shane Thoe or other Hunz & Hunz personnel.

Hanousek also requested a more general instruction that "a person is responsible under the criminal law only for acts he performs or causes to be performed on behalf of a corporation."

The district court rejected Hanousek's proposed instructions without explanation. However, the district court did instruct the jury as follows:

> In order for the defendant Ed Hanousek to be found guilty of negligent discharge of oil, the government must prove the following elements beyond a reasonable doubt:
>
> 1. The particular defendant caused the discharge of oil;
> 2. The discharge of oil was into a navigable waterway of the United States;
> 3. The amount of oil was of a quantity that may be harmful; and
> 4. The discharge was caused by the negligence of the particular defendant.

We conclude that the district court's instructions adequately explained to the jury that Hanousek could be convicted only on the basis of his own negligent conduct and not on the basis of the negligence of others working at 6-mile. Accordingly, the district court's failure to provide Hanousek's proposed instructions on vicarious liability does not constitute reversible error.

In a related argument, Hanousek argues that the district court erred by allowing the government to strike "foul blows" during closing argument by inviting the jury to convict Hanousek on a theory of vicarious liability. We disagree. In the course of closing argument, the prosecutor stated, "[w]hen Shane Thoe hit that unprotected pipeline and that oil fired out of that pipeline, sprayed up into the air, and got into that Skagway River, these two defendants are guilty of negligent discharging [oil] into the Skagway River." The prosecutor also told the jury that "the buck stops" with Hanousek and M. Paul Taylor, an officer of both Arctic & Pacific and Arctic & Pacific Pipeline, Inc. When read in context, the prosecutor was appropriately arguing to the jury that Hanousek and Taylor failed to adequately protect the pipeline and that both should be held responsible for their negligent conduct. . . .

E. Sufficiency of the Evidence

Although Hanousek did not list sufficiency of the evidence as one of the issues in his briefs, he nevertheless included in his opening and reply briefs an extensive discussion of the evidence and argued that the evidence was insufficient to support his conviction. The government responded to this argument in its brief, and both sides at oral argument argued the issue of whether the evidence was sufficient to support Hanousek's conviction. Because the issue has been presented in this way by the parties, and fully argued, we consider it.

We review the evidence in the light most favorable to the government to determine whether any rational trier of fact could have found the essential elements of the crime beyond a reasonable doubt.

The government presented evidence at trial that Hanousek was responsible for the rock-quarrying project at 6-mile; that the project involved the use of heavy equipment and machinery along the 1000-foot work site; that Hanousek directed the daily activities of Hunz & Hunz employees and equipment; and that it was customary to protect the pipeline with railroad ties and fill when using heavy equipment in the vicinity of the pipeline. The government also presented evidence that when work initially began in April, 1994, Hunz & Hunz covered an approximately 300-foot section of the pipeline with railroad ties, sand, and ballast material to protect the pipeline; that after Hanousek took over responsibility for the project in May, 1994, no further sections of the pipeline along the work site were protected; and that the section of the pipeline where the rupture occurred was not protected with railroad ties, sand or ballast. Finally, the government presented evidence that although the rock quarrying work had been completed in the location of the rupture, rocks would sometimes fall off the loaded railroad cars as they proceeded through the completed sections of the work site; that no policy prohibited the use of backhoes off the work platform for other activities; that a backhoe operator ruptured the unprotected pipeline while using a backhoe to remove a rock from the railroad tracks; and that a harmful quantity of oil was discharged into the Skagway River.

The totality of this evidence is sufficient to support Hanousek's conviction for negligently discharging a harmful quantity of oil into a navigable water of the United States, in violation of 33 U.S.C. § § 1319(c)(1)(A) & 1321(b)(3).

F. SENTENCING

Based on an offense level of 12 and a criminal history category of I, the district court sentenced Hanousek to 6 months in prison, 6 months in a halfway house, and 6 months of supervised release.

1. UPWARD ADJUSTMENT FOR SUPERVISORY ROLE

Hanousek contends that the district court erred by making a two-point upward adjustment under United States Sentencing Guidelines § 3B1.1(c) based on his role as a supervisor in a criminal activity. We disagree.

Pursuant to U.S.S.G. § 3B1.1, the district court may make an upward adjustment if the defendant supervised one or more participants. A participant is "a person who is criminally responsible for the commission of the offense, but need not have been convicted." Here, the district court did not clearly err by finding that Hanousek was a supervisor because, although the backhoe operator was not prosecuted, he was nonetheless a participant in the criminal activity, and Hanousek supervised the project at 6-mile.

Affirmed.

Following the Ninth Circuit's affirmance of his conviction, Hanousek sought review in the Supreme Court through a petition for a writ of certiorari. The Court refused to review the case by denying his petition. Justices Thomas and O'Connor dissented from that denial.

HANOUSEK v. UNITED STATES
528 U.S. 1102 (2000)

Petition for writ of certiorari to the United States Court of Appeals for the Ninth Circuit denied.

Justice THOMAS, with whom Justice O'CONNOR joins, dissenting [from denial of Hanousek's petition for certiorari]. . . . In rejecting the due process claim, the Court of Appeals reasoned, in part, that the criminal provisions of the CWA are "public welfare legislation" because the CWA "is designed to protect the public from potentially harmful or injurious items" and criminalizes " 'a type of conduct that a reasonable person should know is subject to stringent public regulation and may seriously threaten the community's health or safety.' " Whether the CWA is appropriately characterized as a public welfare statute is an issue on which the Courts of Appeals are divided.

Whatever the merits of petitioner's underlying due process claim, I think that it is erroneous to rely, even in small part, on the notion that the CWA is a public welfare statute. We have said that "to determine as a threshold matter whether a particular statute defines a public welfare offense, a court must have in view some category of dangerous and deleterious devices that will be assumed to alert an individual that he stands in 'responsible relation to a public danger.' " Although provisions of the CWA regulate certain dangerous substances, this case illustrates that the CWA also imposes criminal liability for persons using standard equipment to engage in a broad range of ordinary industrial and commercial activities. This fact strongly militates against concluding that the public welfare doctrine applies. As we have said, "even dangerous items can, in some cases, be so commonplace and generally available" that we would not consider regulation of them to fall within the public welfare doctrine. I think we should be hesitant to expose countless numbers of construction workers and contractors to heightened criminal liability for using ordinary devices to engage in normal industrial operations.

We have also distinguished those criminal statutes within the doctrine of "public welfare offenses" from those outside it by considering the severity of the penalty imposed. We have said, with respect to public welfare offenses, that: "penalties commonly are relatively small, and conviction does no grave damage to an offender's reputation." The CWA provides that any person who "negligently" violates the Act may be imprisoned for up to one year. A second negligent violation of the Act may subject a person to imprisonment for up to two years. The CWA also contains a felony provision that provides that any person who "knowingly" violates § 1321(b)(3) "shall be punished by a fine of not less than $ 5,000 nor more than $ 50,000 per day of violation, or by imprisonment for not more than three years, or by both. If a conviction of a person is for a violation committed after a first conviction of such person under this paragraph, punishment shall be by a fine of not more than $ 100,000 per day of violation, or by imprisonment of not more than 6 years, or by both." The seriousness of these penalties counsels against concluding that the CWA can accurately be classified as a public welfare statute.

The Court of Appeals disregarded these factors, and relied instead on our previous statements that public welfare offenses regulate " 'conduct that a reasonable person should know is subject to stringent public regulation and may seriously threaten the community's health or safety.' " But we have never held that any statute can be described as creating a public welfare offense so long as the statute regulates conduct that is known to be subject to extensive regulation and that may involve a risk to the community. Indeed, such a suggestion would extend this narrow doctrine to virtually any criminal statute applicable to industrial activities. I presume that in today's heavily regulated society, any person engaged in industry is aware that his activities are the object of sweeping regulation and that an industrial accident could threaten health or safety. To the extent that any of our prior opinions have contributed to the Court of Appeals' overly broad interpretation of this doctrine, I would reconsider those cases. Because I believe the Courts of Appeals invoke this narrow doctrine too readily, I would grant certiorari to further delineate its limits.

QUESTIONS

1. How does the "negligence" definition Hanousek requested differ from the one actually given by the court? Does the language Hanousek requested differ from the MPC definition of "negligence"?

2. Professor Coffee says that in the area of regulatory crime "there has . . . been a retreat from the traditional 'method' of the criminal law, as the role of mens rea has been diminished and that of vicarious liability expanded." Does *Hanousek* support Professor Coffee's claims?

3. Do the theories of punishment we studied in Chapter 2 — retribution, deterrence, incapacitation, rehabilitation, and denunciation — support Hanousek's conviction and sentence? Is Hanousek's conviction and sentence likely to undermine public perception of the criminal justice system's norms as "legitimate and deserving of compliance"?

4. The *Hanousek* court states that *gross* negligence under § 1321(b)(7)(D) of the Clean Water Act may result in increased *civil* penalties and that *simple* negligence under § 1319(c)(1)(A) may result in *criminal* liability (emphasis added). Does it make sense to impose criminal liability for simple negligence and civil liability for gross negligence?

James V. Delong, OUT OF BOUNDS AND OUT OF CONTROL: REGULATORY ENFORCEMENT AT THE EPA

30-33 (2002)

[*United States v. Hanousek*] is an appalling case.

First, the oil spill was not a significant incident; 5,000 gallons (the high end of the court's range) is a little more than half the size of a retail service station tank. EPA takes the view that *any* petroleum spill is serious. EPA says, "One pint of oil released into the water can spread and cover one acre of water surface area and seriously damage an aquatic habitat." This may be true technically, but oil degrades rapidly and does little lasting harm. This is a good thing, because in 1997, 8,624 reported incidents of oil spills into U.S. waters resulted in the release of 942 million gallons of oil, and 54 of them involved releases of between 1,000 and 5,000 gallons of oil. Water ways and ocean beds are also subject to numerous natural releases, but no numerical estimates are available. Obviously, the oil spill into the Skagway River was regrettable, but hardly catastrophic. And P&A had already paid heavily for the cleanup and damages. On balance, the government reaction seems out of all proportion to fault or harm, especially because running a railroad and piping heating oil to Alaska are worthy enterprises and the people involved in them are fulfilling an important social function and contributing to the betterment of humanity.

Second, it is impossible to understand wherein Hanousek was negligent. The appellate court seemed to assume that he had taken no steps to prevent the use of the backhoe away from the area where the pipeline was not covered. But the existence of a policy against using the backhoe in uncovered areas is readily implied by the fact that the pipeline *was* covered where the backhoe was working. One cannot help but imagine that the government told the backhoe operator, "You will be at the trial — as a defendant, or as a witness against your superiors — take your pick," which could certainly have affected his memory on whether he had violated standing instructions. The appellate court also assumed that Hanousek was negligent for not ordering the pipeline covered over the entire 1,000-foot project area. But this is a dubious proposition. Covering and then uncovering the pipeline would require work with heavy machinery in constant proximity to the 1,000-foot-long work site. The risk of accidental rupture might well be higher from this activity than from covering the pipeline only in the immediate vicinity of the backhoe work. The appellate court shrugged off this issue on the ground that it had, presumably, been argued in front of the jury. But who would want to have his freedom depend on the ability of 12 lay jurors to decide on complex technical issues of pipeline safety practices?

There is a real doubt that *anyone* was negligent, even the backhoe operator when he tried to move the rocks. Rocks near a rail line create a situation that is dangerous to both trains and a pipeline. In June 2000, EPA fined the Union Pacific Railroad $800,000 for seven derailments that caused the discharge of chemicals, including diesel fuel from locomotive fuel tanks, into navigable waters. Two of the derailments were due to rocks on the track, and as part of the settlement the railroad agreed to a comprehensive project to mitigate the hazards of falling rock. In the *Hanousek* case, the operator might well have decided that the rocks presented a menace and needed to be moved immediately. Because his execution was poor does not mean that his decision was wrong. . . .

Finally, consider the sentencing. Federal guidelines say that the trial judge may add to the sentence if the defendant supervised one or more participants. The *Hanousek* trial judge noted that a participant is someone who is "criminally responsible for the commission of the offense," even if he was not prosecuted. The Ninth Circuit said that the backhoe operator was a participant even though he was not prosecuted, and Hanousek supervised the whole project. Ergo, the augmentation was proper.

This part of the opinion is particularly disturbing. According to the appellate court, Hanousek could be convicted only for *his own* negligence. There was no basis for concluding that the backhoe operator was negligent because this issue was not tried. But if the backhoe operator was not negligent, then how could he have been a "participant," as was required for the augmentation of Hanousek's sentence? This case is almost certainly not the type envisioned by the drafters of the sentencing guidelines, and to pile the augmentation for supervision on top of negligence was clearly unjust.

It is impossible to avoid the conclusion that something was going on in the *Hanousek* case that is not set forth in the case reports. The most likely possibility is that the government decided Hanousek had given them false statements, so they severely punished him. But these charges did not result in a conviction, so obviously the jury did not think the defendant guilty of them.

One is left with the overall impression of a vindictive government, irritated at its inability to prove charges of false statements or obstruction of justice, and satisfied to rely on the distortions and confusions of the public welfare doctrine to put someone in jail for conduct that does not appear particularly blameworthy. That the government's action was approved by the Ninth Circuit and its appeal rejected by the Supreme Court makes the whole episode even more unsavory.

David Stirling of the Pacific Legal Foundation points out the contradiction between the government's harsh treatment of Hanousek and its infinitely forgiving attitude toward its own employees. In May 2000, shortly after the Supreme Court refused to hear Hanousek's appeal, an employee of the U.S. Forest Service ignored unfavorable weather forecasts and lit what was intended to be a controlled burn in the Los Alamos National Forest. The fire blew out of control, burning 47,000 acres of forestland and causing hundreds of millions of dollars of damage. Interior Secretary Bruce Babbitt said that no criminal action would be taken because "You do not prosecute people for making mistakes." As Stirling notes, this may be how the government treats its own, but Edward Hanousek is in jail even though he was at home in bed when an employee of a subcontractor made a mistake. Further, the spill involved in the Hanousek case did trivial damage compared with the disaster in Los Alamos.*

Harsh law for the governed and infinite leniency for the governors puts a new twist on the meaning of "the rule of law."

QUESTIONS

1. The EPA claims one pint of oil can cover an acre of water and cause environmental damage. DeLong tells us that "oil degrades rapidly and does little lasting harm." How, then, does one determine what a "harmful" quantity of oil is for purposes of the Clean Water Act? Who makes that determination?

2. DeLong reports that there were 8,624 reported oil spills into United States waters in 1997, releasing 942 million gallons of oil. Do these facts support or undercut the use of criminal sanctions against someone such as Hanousek?

3. If the corporation that employed Hanousek "had already paid heavily for the cleanup and damages," why impose individual criminal liability on Hanousek? What are the relative advantages and disadvantages of corporate civil liability in the form of money damages as compared with individual criminal liability?

4. Was Hanousek serving an "important social function" and making a contribution "to the betterment of humanity" at the rock-quarrying project? If so, what bearing does that have on his culpability? What bearing should it have?

5. Can a policy against using the backhoe in areas where the pipeline is uncovered be "readily implied," as DeLong suggests? Would it be easy for the backhoe operator, Thoe, to lie about this without fear of contradiction? If Hanousek relied

---

* David Stirling, *Most Favored Error Designation*, Washington Times, May 28, 2000, at B1.

on implication to communicate that policy, can he be faulted for not making the policy explicit?

6. Is the activity at issue in the *Hanousek* case beyond the experience of lay jurors? Are the issues raised in the case beyond the ability of most jurors to resolve fairly and accurately? Would this be true for all "regulated activities"? If so, who should be the fact finder in public welfare offense cases?

7. Was the backhoe operator, Thoe, necessarily negligent? What arguments might be made to defend his conduct? DeLong says that there is no basis for concluding that Thoe was negligent because the issue was not tried. Is this true? If Thoe was not negligent, would Hanousek still be at fault?

8. Assume that Hanousek did give false statements to agents investigating the oil spill. Was it improper for prosecutors on that basis to single out Hanousek for prosecution?

C. FETAL ENDANGERMENT

There is substantial evidence that drug and alcohol abuse by pregnant women can cause significant harm to the children they bear and impose considerable costs on society. Should criminal law be used to punish and deter such dangerous conduct? Is the use of criminal sanctions likely to be effective in changing this behavior? Or should we rely instead on treatment and social services to address this problem? These questions are central to the materials in this section.

PREGNANCY AND DRUG USE TRENDS[10]

Drug abuse can occur at any stage in a woman's life. Of women who use illicit drugs, however, about half are in the childbearing age group of 15 to 44. In 1992/1993, NIDA [the National Institute on Drug Abuse] conducted a nationwide hospital survey to determine the extent of drug abuse among pregnant women in the United States. This National Pregnancy and Health Survey still provides the most recent national data available.

The survey found that of the 4 million women who gave birth during the period, 757,000 women drank alcohol products and 820,000 women smoked cigarettes during their pregnancies. There was a strong link among cigarette, alcohol, and illegal drug use. Thirty-two percent of those who reported use of one drug also smoked cigarettes and drank alcohol.

Survey results showed that 221,000 women used illegal drugs during their pregnancies that year, with marijuana and cocaine being the most prevalent: 119,000 women reported use of marijuana and 45,000 reported use of cocaine. The survey estimated that the number of babies born to these women was 222,000, a close parallel to the number of mothers. Generally, rates of any illegal drug use were higher in women who were not married, had less than 16 years of formal education, were not working, and relied on some public source of funding to pay for their hospital stay.

---

10. National Institute on Drug Abuse, InfoFacts at *http://www.drugabuse.gov/Infofax/ pregnancytrends.html* (accessed on 11/18/03).

Despite a generally decreasing trend in the use of drugs from 3 months before pregnancy and through the pregnancy, women did not discontinue drug use. However, findings from other NIDA research on women in treatment, for example, indicate that once women are successfully detoxified and enrolled in a treatment program, their motivator to stay drug free is their children.

The survey also pointed to issues of prevalence differences among ethnic groups. While the rates of illegal substance abuse were higher for African-Americans, the estimated number of white women using drugs during pregnancy was larger at 113,000 than the number of African-American women at 75,000, or Hispanic women at 28,000.

As for the legal drugs, estimates of alcohol use were also highest among white women at about 588,000, compared to 105,000 among African-American women, and 54,000 among Hispanic women. Whites had the highest rates of cigarette use as well: 632,000 compared with 132,000 for African Americans and 36,000 for Hispanics.

Rates of marijuana use were highest among those under 25 and rates of cocaine use were higher among those 25 and older.

Consider the information that follows on the potential effects of drug use during pregnancy on fetuses and young children.

Deficient growth patterns are among the most frequently cited problems occurring among substance-exposed newborns. As a group, average birth weight is significantly reduced in most studies. Although as the child grows older, average weight "catches up" to normal, low birth weight is a significant risk factor for developmental outcome as a child gets older.

Accompanying poor weight gain of the drug-exposed fetus is poor head growth, a reflection of poor intrauterine brain growth. Alcohol, cocaine, and heroin have been shown to be the three drugs most closely associated with poor brain growth. In general small head circumference at birth is a significant marker of risk for poor developmental outcome. In follow up of prenatally-exposed children, it has been shown that average head circumference does not reach the normal range until four to five years of age, and for some prenatally-exposed children, head size continues to be smaller throughout early childhood.[11]

A recently published study in Cleveland examined 218 cocaine-exposed infants for two years after birth and compared their development with that of a control group of 197 unexposed infants. All 415 infants were born in a major metropolitan hospital and were from a high-risk, low-socioeconomic status population.

Our study found significant cognitive deficits, with cocaine-exposed children twice as likely to have significant delay throughout the first 2 years of life. The 13.7% rate of mental retardation is 4.89 times higher than that expected in the population at large, and the percentage of children with mild or greater delays requiring intervention was 38%, almost double the rate of the high-risk noncocaine-but polydrug-exposed comparison group.[12]

---

11. Ira J. Chasnoff, et al., *Understanding the Drug-Exposed Child* 4-5 (1998).
12. Lynn T. Singer, et al., *Cognitive and Motor Outcomes of Cocaine-Exposed Infants*, Vol. 287, 15 JAMA 1952 (2002).

The same study found no differences between the two groups of infants in motor development.

Efforts to apply criminal sanctions to the use of illegal drugs by pregnant women have proceeded on two fronts. In legislatures, proponents of criminalization have introduced statutes specifically addressed to prenatal maternal drug use, such as those that appear in Problem 14.1 below. In the courts, prosecutors have attempted to bring women who use illegal drugs during pregnancy within the reach of statutes not specifically addressed to drug use during pregnancy, such as child abuse, drug delivery, and homicide laws. The *Luster* and *Whitner* cases that follow exemplify this second strategy.

The case for applying criminal sanctions to the use of illegal drugs during pregnancy relies heavily on a deterrence rationale. Proponents argue that the problem of drug use during pregnancy is widespread and that the potential harm to the fetus and costs to society are substantial. The implicit claim is that the threat of criminal sanctions will reduce drug use during pregnancy through deterrence as well as incapacitation and thus reduce both harm to fetuses and costs to society. Such thinking is subject to a number of challenges. Women on whom such sanctions would be imposed are often drug addicts and thus, it may be argued, unlikely to engage in the conscious cost/benefit calculation that deterrent theory assumes. Even if they do calculate, it seems unlikely they would respond to the threat of prosecution by simply stopping their drug use. Given the nature of addiction, a more realistic hope might be that fear of prosecution would motivate these women to seek treatment. But opponents of criminalizing fetal endangerment point out that treatment for pregnant drug addicts is very difficult to find. A more effective way to reduce drug use during pregnancy and its negative consequences, opponents argue, would be to put the money that would be spent on prosecuting and imprisoning these women into treatment programs.

Perhaps the most compelling argument against criminalization is a utilitarian claim that points to an unintended consequence of the use of criminal sanctions. If fetal endangerment through drug use is made criminal, then pregnant drug users are unlikely to seek out prenatal medical care for fear that the doctors and nurses from whom they receive that care may discover their drug use and report it to police. Opponents of criminal sanctions point out that the risk of harm to a fetus resulting from lack of prenatal medical care is greater than the risk of harm from drug use.

One can also make a retributive argument in support of applying criminal sanctions to pre-natal maternal drug use. Taking illegal drugs is widely viewed as blameworthy, as is creating risk of or causing harm to a fetus. Some women have given birth to a number of addicted babies. In light of the probability that these women, in particular, are clearly aware of the risks posed by their conduct, they are often seen as especially blameworthy. The fact of addiction, though, can be viewed as negating the voluntariness of a woman's choice to take the drug to which she is addicted, eliminating or attenuating her blameworthiness. If one sees a woman's failure to seek treatment as a source of blame, then lack of treatment options again can be seen as undermining the voluntariness of that failure and her blameworthiness.

Opponents of making fetal endangerment a crime argue that such criminalization violates the right to privacy, a woman's right to make certain reproductive choices without state intervention. The threat of criminal sanctions may discourage a woman addicted to drugs from exercising her right to choose to get pregnant. Accordingly, some see the criminalization of drug use during pregnancy as penalizing the choice to get pregnant. Advocates of criminal sanctions see what is being penalized not as the woman's choice to get pregnant, but rather her choice to use illegal drugs once she is pregnant. This choice, they argue, enjoys no protection at all, much less constitutional protection.

A critic of criminalization could raise a host of other arguments. One is based on discriminatory impact. Only women can be prosecuted for the crime of fetal endangerment as currently envisioned by its proponents, and the women prosecuted are likely to be both poor and from disadvantaged minority groups. Another is that criminalizing fetal endangerment for illegal drug use could be a first step on a "slippery slope" leading to criminalization of fetal endangerment for smoking, drinking, or even failure to follow a doctor's advice. More broadly, extending the protection of the criminal law to a fetus may utlimately lead to undermining the constitutional right to choose an abortion.[13]

PROBLEM

14.1 You are a state senator in a jurisdiction considering legislation that would make it a crime for a pregnant woman to use illegal drugs. A recent series of newspaper articles about babies born addicted to crack cocaine has drawn public interest to the issue. You are also a member of the senate committee that will make a recommendation about such legislation to the entire senate. Two bills that appear below are under consideration. In a few days, your committee will hold hearings on these bills and then meet to vote on them. Prepare a statement of the position you will take on the bills and your reasoning.

Conduct Injurious to a Newborn[14]

Any woman who is pregnant and without a prescription knowingly or intentionally uses a dangerous drug or a narcotic drug and at the conclusion of her pregnancy delivers a newborn child, and such child shows signs of narcotic or dangerous drug exposure or addiction, or the presence of a narcotic or dangerous drug in the child's blood or urine, commits the offense of conduct injurious to a newborn.

It shall not be a violation of this section if a woman knowingly or intentionally uses a narcotic or dangerous drug in the first twelve weeks of pregnancy and:

1. She has no knowledge that she is pregnant; or
2. Subsequently, within the first twelve weeks of pregnancy, undergoes medical treatment for substance abuse or treatment or rehabilitation in a program or facility approved by the Illinois

---

13. Much has been written in recent years on criminalizing fetal endangerment through prosecution of drug use. For a representative array of arguments from various viewpoints, *see Symposium: Criminal Liability for Fetal Endangerment*, Vol. 9, 1 Criminal Justice Ethics 11-51 (1990).

14. The text of this statute was considered by the Illinois legislature. Paul Logli, *Drugs in the Womb: The Newest Battlefield in the War on Drugs*, Vol. 9, 1 Criminal Justice Ethics 23, 27-28 (1990).

Department of Alcoholism and Substance Abuse, and thereafter discontinues any further use of drugs or narcotics as previously set forth.

Prenatal Child Neglect[15]

(A) As used in this section: . . .

(2) 'Drug exposed at birth' means exposed prenatally to a . . . controlled substance, as evidenced by at least one of the following:

(a) Symptoms of withdrawal from the . . . controlled substance at birth;

(b) Results of tests of the child's blood, urine, stool, hair, chromosomes, or other bodily fluids or components that indicate the presence of the . . . controlled substance in the child's body;

(c) Medical effects or developmental delays that are apparent during the first three months after the child's birth.

(3) 'Use,' as it relates to a controlled substance, means injecting, ingesting, inhaling, or otherwise introducing into the human body a . . . controlled substance.

(B) No woman shall knowingly use a . . . controlled substance at a time when she knows or reasonably should know that she is pregnant if the use of the . . . controlled substance results in the child with whom she is pregnant being drug-exposed at birth.

(C) Division (B) of this section does not apply to a woman if the woman was prescribed the . . . controlled substance by a [licensed] physician . . . and the woman used the controlled substance in a manner substantially consistent with the instructions of the prescribing physician, or of any [licensed] pharmacist . . . who provided instructions for the use of the medication.

STATE *v.* LUSTER

204 Ga. App. 156, 419 S.E.2d 32 (1992)

SOGNIER, C.J. Darla Michelle Luster was charged in a two count indictment with violating the Georgia Controlled Substances Act. Count One charged Luster with possessing cocaine between January 1, 1991 and March 3, 1991. Count Two charged that between January 1, 1991 and March 3, 1991, Luster "did unlawfully deliver and distribute . . . cocaine . . . to Tiffany Luster," Luster's daughter, who was born on March 3, 1991. The trial court granted Luster's motion to dismiss Count Two of the indictment, and . . . the State appeals from the dismissal of that count. . . .

The record reveals that on the dates alleged in the indictment, Luster was pregnant. On March 4, 1991, one day after Tiffany's birth, a sample of Tiffany's urine was taken and tested. The sample proved positive for cocaine metabolites

---

15. The text of this statute was considered by the Ohio legislature in 1992. State v. Gray, 62 Ohio St. 3d 514, 517 n.3 (1992). It was not enacted.

and, based on those test results, Luster was charged both with possession of cocaine, which is punishable by imprisonment for not less than two nor more than 15 years, and with delivering and distributing cocaine to Tiffany, which is punishable by imprisonment for not less than five nor more than 30 years.

The trial court granted Luster's motion to dismiss Count Two of the indictment on the basis that O.C.G.A. § 16-13-30 (b) was not intended to encompass the transmission of cocaine metabolites to a fetus that occurs when a pregnant woman ingests cocaine.[16] The State contends the trial court erred by granting Luster's motion because, contrary to the trial court's finding, Luster's conduct was within the contemplation of O.C.G.A. § 16-13-30 (b), which provides that "it is unlawful for any person to . . . deliver [or] distribute . . . any controlled substance." We do not agree, and we affirm the trial court's order dismissing Count Two of the indictment.

It is well established that "criminal statutes must be strictly construed against the state and liberally in favor of human liberty." Thus, "no [person] shall be held criminally responsible for conduct which he [or she] could not reasonably understand to be proscribed," and one of the purposes of the Criminal Code of Georgia is "[t]o give fair warning of the nature of the conduct forbidden and the sentence authorized upon conviction." We look, therefore, to the language of the statute under which Luster was charged to determine whether she reasonably should have known that she could be prosecuted for delivering or distributing cocaine to her fetus if she ingested the controlled substance while pregnant.

O.C.G.A. § 16-13-21 (7) provides that " '[d]eliver' or 'delivery' means the actual, constructive, or attempted transfer from one person to another of a controlled substance, whether or not there is an agency relationship." O.C.G.A. § 16-13-21 (11) provides that " '[d]istribute' means to deliver a controlled substance, other than by administering or dispensing it." Since only licensed practitioners or others not involved here may "administer" or "dispense" controlled drugs, see O.C.G.A. § 16-13-21 (23), the terms "deliver" and "distribute" as used in the statute are identical for all practical purposes.

O.C.G.A. § 16-13-21 (20) defines " '[p]erson' " as "an individual, corporation, government, or governmental subdivision or agency, business trust, estate, trust, partnership, or association, or any other legal entity." Under Georgia law, the word "person" in a criminal statute may not be construed to include a fetus unless the legislature has expressly included it, since at common law a fetus was not considered a person. Our legislature has indicated by specific language when it intends to include unborn children within the contemplation of a criminal statute. See, e.g., O.C.G.A. § 16-5-80 (feticide). Although it is true, as asserted by the State, that Tiffany eventually became a "living, breathing person" when she was born, at the time any transfer of cocaine metabolites could have taken place from Luster upon which an indictment could be based, Tiffany was not a "person" within the meaning of the statute. After she became a person for legal purposes, it was physically impossible for the transfer to have taken place.

"[I]t is an elementary rule of statutory construction that, absent clear evidence to the contrary, words should be assigned their ordinary, logical, and common meaning. Since the statutory definitions are not sufficiently enlightening, we must assign to the terms "deliver" and "distribute" their ordinary meanings. The only applicable definitions supplied by Webster's New International Dictionary (2nd

---

16. Cocaine introduced into the human body results in cocaine metabolites being formed in the body fluids.

ed.) for "deliver" are "[t]o give or transfer; to yield possession or control of; to part with (to); to make or hand over; to make delivery of." The same dictionary's only applicable definition of "distribute" is "to deal out." The "ordinary, logical, and common" meanings of these terms encompass only transfers that take place between one person and another person, outside the bodies of the persons involved. This interpretation is in accord with prior judicial construction, as reported cases of criminal prosecutions pursuant to O.C.G.A. § 16-13-30 (b) for "delivering" or "distributing" controlled substances have all involved the transfer of controlled substances to another person.

It is well established that statutes should be read according to the natural and most obvious import of the language, without resorting to subtle and forced constructions, for the purpose of either limiting or extending their operation and this principle is particularly compelling when interpreting criminal statutes. We conclude, therefore, that because the common, ordinary meaning of the plain and unambiguous language of the statute shows it does not apply to the facts sub judice, Luster could not reasonably have known that she would be prosecuted for "delivering" or "distributing" cocaine to her unborn child if she ingested cocaine while pregnant, and thus she did not receive the "fair warning" mandated by O.C.G.A. § 16-1-2 (2). " 'The unambiguous words of a criminal statute are not to be altered by judicial construction so as to punish one not otherwise within its reach.' " Accordingly, the trial court correctly refused to place upon the statute the strained construction urged by the State that would impermissibly have expanded its reach.

Even assuming, arguendo, however, that O.C.G.A. § 16-13-30 (b) is ambiguous and susceptible of interpretation, the cardinal rule of statutory construction is that "the courts shall look diligently for the intention of the General Assembly." O.C.G.A. § 1-3-1 (a). In our attempt to discern whether the legislature intended the inclusion of transmission of a controlled substance to a fetus by a pregnant woman in the terms used in O.C.G.A. § 16-13-30 (b), we are aided by the knowledge that in 1990 the legislature defeated two bills which would have amended the Georgia Controlled Substances Act to create a new crime of distributing a controlled substance to an unborn child, and that in 1991 H.B. 276 was passed, emphasizing the importance of providing drug treatment on a priority basis for pregnant women. The 1991 legislation followed recommendations of the Council on Maternal and Infant Health (a body created by statute to advise the General Assembly and other state agencies on issues pertaining to maternal and infant health) and the General Assembly's Joint Conference on Children of Cocaine and Substance Abuse (convened on November 1, 1990) that the State de-emphasize and declare a moratorium on legislation seeking to prosecute drug dependent pregnant women and instead approach addiction as a disease and develop and fund appropriate and adequate treatment facilities and services for that population.

" 'It is a well-established rule of construction that the meaning of one statute may be arrived at by a consideration of a subsequent act of the legislature on the same subject.' " By attempting initially to pass legislation creating the new crime of distributing controlled substances to unborn children, the legislature signaled unequivocally that it had not intended to include such activity in the "delivery" and "distribution" already prohibited under O.C.G.A. § 16-13-30 (b). Further, by enacting legislation treating addiction during pregnancy as a health problem, the legislature indicated its view that addiction during pregnancy is a disease and signaled its preference for treatment over prosecution, which preference is overwhelmingly in accord with the opinions of local and national medical experts.

Accordingly, given this evidence that the legislature did not intend to include transmission of controlled substances to fetuses in the conduct prohibited by O.C.G.A. § 16-13-30 (b), even assuming the statute is ambiguous we find no error in the trial court's dismissal of Count Two of the indictment.

Judgments affirmed.

QUESTIONS

1. Chief Justice Sognier writes in *Luster* that "the word 'person' in a criminal statute may not be construed to include a fetus unless the legislature has expressly included it, since at common law a fetus was not considered a person." Is this reasoning sound? Remember that the majority opinion in *Keeler* (Chapter 3 Section A) pointed out that the common law of homicide did not consider a fetus a "human being." That historical fact played a major role in Justice Mosk's conclusion in *Keeler* that the California homicide statute, which was based on common law, did not apply to the killing of a fetus. Is the common law's attitude toward a fetus relevant in determining the legislative intent behind a drug delivery statute not based on common law? In *Commonwealth v. Welch*, 864 S.W.2d 280 (1993), the Kentucky Supreme Court held that the Kentucky child abuse statute did not apply to drug use during pregnancy. While conceding that the common law did not consider a fetus a "person" for homicide purposes, the *Welch* court stated that "the common law offers no similar line of demarcation for criminal child abuse, because, of course, it was not a common law crime in the first place. Thus we must look elsewhere to determine the meaning of 'person' under the criminal child abuse statutes." *Id.* at 282.

2. Chief Justice Sognier states that "Luster could not reasonably have known that she would be prosecuted for 'delivering' or 'distributing' cocaine to her unborn child." Would she have been more or less surprised than Khaliq was when he was prosecuted for selling glue-sniffing kits (Chapter 3 Section A)? How would the *Khaliq* court have handled Luster's notice claim?

3. The *Luster* opinion notes that the state legislature viewed drug use during pregnancy as a disease rather than a crime and accordingly adopted a treatment rather than a punitive approach. Which is the fairer characterization of drug use by pregnant women? What do you see as the advantages and disadvantages of the treatment approach? Will addicted women be more or less likely to seek treatment if they do not fear criminal punishment for using drugs while pregnant?

WHITNER *v.* STATE

South Carolina Supreme Court 328 S.C. 1 (1997)

TOAL, J. This case concerns the scope of the child abuse and endangerment statute in the South Carolina Children's Code (the Code), S.C. Code Ann. § 20-7-50 (1985). We hold the word "child" as used in that statute includes viable fetuses.

On April 20, 1992, Cornelia Whitner (Whitner) pled guilty to criminal child neglect, S.C. Code Ann. § 20-7-50 (1985), for causing her baby to be born with cocaine metabolites in its system by reason of Whitner's ingestion of crack cocaine during the third trimester of her pregnancy. The circuit court judge sentenced Whitner to eight years in prison. Whitner did not appeal her conviction.

Thereafter, Whitner filed a petition for Post Conviction Relief (PCR), pleading the circuit court's lack of subject matter jurisdiction to accept her guilty plea as well as ineffective assistance of counsel. Her claim of ineffective assistance of counsel was based upon her lawyer's failure to advise her the statute under which she was being prosecuted might not apply to prenatal drug use. The petition was granted on both grounds. The State appeals.

A. SUBJECT MATTER JURISDICTION

The State first argues the PCR court erred in finding the sentencing circuit court lacked subject matter jurisdiction to accept Whitner's guilty plea. We agree.

Under South Carolina law, a circuit court lacks subject matter jurisdiction to accept a guilty plea to a nonexistent offense. For the sentencing court to have had subject matter jurisdiction to accept Whitner's plea, criminal child neglect under section 20-7-50 would have to include an expectant mother's use of crack cocaine after the fetus is viable. All other issues are ancillary to this jurisdictional issue.

S.C. Code Ann. § 20-7-50 (1985) provides:

> Any person having the legal custody of any *child* or helpless person, who shall, without lawful excuse, refuse or neglect to provide, as defined in § 20-7-490, the proper care and attention for such *child* or helpless person, so that the life, health or comfort of such *child* or helpless person is endangered or is likely to be endangered, shall be guilty of a misdemeanor and shall be punished within the discretion of the circuit court (emphasis added).

The State contends this section encompasses maternal acts endangering or likely to endanger the life, comfort, or health of a *viable fetus.*

Under the Children's Code, "child" means a "person under the age of eighteen." The question for this Court, therefore, is whether a viable fetus is a "person" for purposes of the Children's Code.

In interpreting a statute, this Court's primary function is to ascertain the intent of the legislature. Of course, where a statute is complete, plain, and unambiguous, legislative intent must be determined from the language of the statute itself. We should consider, however, not merely the language of the particular clause being construed, but the word and its meaning in conjunction with the purpose of the whole statute and the policy of the law. Finally, there is a basic presumption that the legislature has knowledge of previous legislation as well as of judicial decisions construing that legislation when later statutes are enacted concerning related subjects.

South Carolina law has long recognized that viable fetuses are persons holding certain legal rights and privileges. In 1960, this Court decided *Hall v. Murphy*, 236 S.C. 257, 113 S.E.2d 790 (1960). That case concerned the application of South Carolina's wrongful death statute to an infant who died four hours after her birth as a result of injuries sustained prenatally during viability. The Appellants argued that a viable fetus was not a person within the purview of the wrongful death statute, because, inter alia, a fetus is thought to have no separate being apart from the mother.

We found such a reason for exclusion from recovery "unsound, illogical and unjust," and concluded there was "no medical or other basis" for the "assumed identity" of mother and viable unborn child. In light of that conclusion, this Court unanimously held: "We have no difficulty in concluding that a fetus having reached that period of prenatal maturity where it is capable of independent life apart from its mother is a person."

Four years later, in *Fowler v. Woodward*, 244 S.C. 608, 138 S.E.2d 42 (1964), we interpreted *Hall* as supporting a finding that a viable fetus injured while still in the womb need not be born alive for another to maintain an action for the wrongful death of the fetus.

> Since a viable child is a *person before separation from the body of its mother* and since prenatal injuries tortiously inflicted on such a child are actionable, it is apparent that the complaint alleges such an "act, neglect or default" by the defendant, to the injury of the child. . . .
>
> *Once the concept of the unborn, viable child as a person* is accepted, we have no difficulty in holding that a cause of action for tortious injury to such a child arises immediately upon the infliction of the injury.

Id. at 613, 138 S.E.2d at 44 (emphasis added). *Fowler* makes particularly clear that *Hall* rested on the concept of the viable fetus as a person vested with legal rights.

More recently, we held the word "person" as used in a *criminal* statute includes viable fetuses. *State v. Horne*, 282 S.C. 444, 319 S.E.2d 703 (1984), concerned South Carolina's murder statute, S.C. Code Ann. § 16-3-10 (1976). The defendant in that case stabbed his wife, who was nine months' pregnant, in the neck, arms, and abdomen. Although doctors performed an emergency caesarean section to deliver the child, the child died while still in the womb. The defendant was convicted of voluntary manslaughter and appealed his conviction on the ground South Carolina did not recognize the crime of feticide.

This Court disagreed. In a unanimous decision, we held it would be "grossly inconsistent . . . to construe a viable fetus as a 'person' for the purposes of imposing civil liability while refusing to give it a similar classification in the criminal context." Accordingly, the Court recognized the crime of feticide with respect to viable fetuses.

Similarly, we do not see any rational basis for finding a viable fetus is not a "person" in the present context. Indeed, it would be absurd to recognize the viable fetus as a person for purposes of homicide laws and wrongful death statutes but not for purposes of statutes proscribing child abuse. Our holding in *Hall* that a viable fetus is a person rested primarily on the plain meaning of the word "person" in light of existing medical knowledge concerning fetal development. We do not believe that the plain and ordinary meaning of the word "person" has changed in any way that would now deny viable fetuses status as persons.

The policies enunciated in the Children's Code also support our plain meaning reading of "person." S.C. Code Ann. § 20-7-20(C) (1985), which describes South Carolina's policy concerning children, expressly states: "It shall be the policy of this State to concentrate on the *prevention of children's problems* as the most important strategy which can be planned and implemented on behalf of children and their families." (emphasis added). The abuse or neglect of a child at any time during childhood can exact a profound toll on the child herself as well as on society as a whole. However, the consequences of abuse or neglect which takes place after birth often pale in comparison to those resulting from abuse suffered by the viable fetus before birth. This policy of prevention supports a reading of the word "person" to include viable fetuses. Furthermore, the scope of the Children's Code is quite broad. It applies "to *all* children who have need of services." S.C. Code Ann. § 20-7-20(B) (1985) (emphasis added). When coupled with the comprehensive remedial purposes of the Code, this language supports the inference that the legislature intended to include viable fetuses within the scope of the Code's protection.

Whitner advances several arguments against an interpretation of "person" as used in the Children's Code to include viable fetuses. We shall address each of Whitner's major arguments in turn.

Whitner's first argument concerns the number of bills introduced in the South Carolina General Assembly in the past five years addressing substance abuse by pregnant women. Some of these bills would have criminalized substance abuse by pregnant women;[3] others would have addressed the issue through mandatory reporting, treatment, or intervention by social service agencies.[4] Whitner suggests that the introduction of several bills touching the specific issue at hand evinces a belief by legislators that prior legislation had not addressed the issue. Whitner argues the introduction of the bills proves that section 20-7-50 was not intended to encompass abuse or neglect of a viable fetus.

We disagree with Whitner's conclusion about the significance of the proposed legislation. Generally, the legislature's subsequent acts "cast no light on the intent of the legislature which enacted the statute being construed." Rather, this Court will look first to the *language* of the statute to discern legislative intent, because the language itself is the best guide to legislative intent. Additionally, our existing case law strongly supports our conclusion about the meaning of the statute's language.

Whitner also argues an interpretation of the statute that includes viable fetuses would lead to absurd results obviously not intended by the legislature. Specifically, she claims if we interpret "child" to include viable fetuses, every action by a pregnant woman that endangers or is likely to endanger a fetus, whether otherwise legal or illegal, would constitute unlawful neglect under the statute. For example, a woman might be prosecuted under section 20-7-50 for smoking or drinking during pregnancy. Whitner asserts these "absurd" results could not have been intended by the legislature and, therefore, the statute should not be construed to include viable fetuses.

We disagree for a number of reasons. First, the same arguments against the statute can be made whether or not the child has been born. After the birth of a child, a parent can be prosecuted under section 20-7-50 for an action that is likely to endanger the child without regard to whether the action is illegal in itself. For example, a parent who drinks excessively could, under certain circumstances, be guilty of child neglect or endangerment even though the underlying act — consuming alcoholic beverages — is itself legal. Obviously, the legislature did not think it "absurd" to allow prosecution of parents for such otherwise legal acts when the acts actually or potentially endanger the "life, health or comfort" of the parents' born children. We see no reason such a result should be rendered absurd by the mere fact the child at issue is a viable fetus.

[3] *See, e.g.*, S. 4032 (1993) (proposing making it a crime for a pregnant woman to ingest a controlled substance); H. 4486 (1994) (proposing amendment to section 20-7-50 to apply to actions of pregnant women).

[4] *See* S. 1495 (1989-1990), reintroduced as S. 75 (1990-1991) (requiring drug testing of newborns and to include within civil definition of neglect any newborn testing positive for controlled substance); S. 1470 (1989-1990), reintroduced as S. 79 (1991) (mandating reporting to DSS pregnant woman believed to have used controlled substance; providing for education and drug treatment); H. 3858 (1990-1991) (requiring reporting of pregnant woman believed to be using controlled substance and expanding civil definition of "abused child" to include newborn testing positive for illegal drugs); S. 986 (1991) (mandating drug testing on newborn infants, requiring reporting such infants as abused under civil abuse laws, and requiring reversible sterilization or implantation of birth control until mother completes drug treatment program); S. 155 (1992-1994) (permitting testing newborns for controlled substances and reporting such test results to DSS for limited purposes); S. 1256 (1992), reintroduced as S. 150 (1992-1993) (permitting referral to DHEC of families with children prenatally exposed to drugs and giving pregnant women priority in drug treatment programs).

Moreover, we need not address this potential parade of horribles advanced by Whitner. In this case, which is the only case we are called upon to decide here, certain facts are clear. Whitner admits to having ingested crack cocaine during the third trimester of her pregnancy, which caused her child to be born with cocaine in its system. Although the precise effects of maternal crack use during pregnancy are somewhat unclear, it is well documented and within the realm of public knowledge that such use can cause serious harm to the viable unborn child. There can be no question here Whitner endangered the life, health, and comfort of her child. We need not decide any cases other than the one before us. . . .

[T]he dissent implies that we have ignored the rule of lenity requiring us to resolve any ambiguities in a criminal statute in favor of the defendant. The dissent argues that "at most, the majority only suggests that the term 'child' as used in § 20-7-50 is ambiguous," and that the ambiguity "is created not by reference to our decisions under the Children's Code or by reference to the statutory language and applicable rules of statutory construction, but by reliance on decisions in two different fields of the law, civil wrongful death and common law feticide."

Plainly, the dissent misunderstands our opinion. First, we do not believe the statute is ambiguous and, therefore, the rule of lenity does not apply. Furthermore, our interpretation of the statute is based primarily on the plain meaning of the word "person" as contained in the statute. We need not go beyond that language. However, because our prior decisions in *Murphy*, *Fowler*, and *Horne* support our reading of the statute, we have discussed the rationale underlying those holdings. We conclude that both statutory language and case law compel the conclusion we reach. We see no ambiguity. . . .

B. Ineffective Assistance of Counsel

The State next argues the PCR court erred in holding Whitner received ineffective assistance of counsel. We agree.

To prove ineffective assistance of counsel, a PCR applicant must show (1) deficient performance by her attorney and (2) prejudice resulting therefrom. To prove prejudice when challenging a guilty plea, the applicant must show that but for counsel's deficient performance, the applicant would not have pled guilty. In this case, the basis for the ineffective assistance claim was the failure of Whitner's counsel to inform her section 20-7-50 did not apply to prenatal drug use. Whitner contends she would not have pled guilty if her lawyer had given her such advice.

Given our holding that section 20-7-50 is applicable to an expectant mother's illegal drug use after the fetus is viable, we cannot say Whitner's lawyer's failure to advise her of the statute's *inapplicability* constituted deficient performance. In fact, both the unambiguous language of the statute and this Court's prior case law justify counsel's belief the child neglect statute applied to Whitner's actions. Therefore, the PCR court erred in ruling Whitner received ineffective assistance of counsel.

C. Constitutional Issues
1. Fair Notice/Vagueness

Whitner argues that section 20-7-50 does not give her fair notice that her behavior is proscribed. We disagree.

The statute forbids any person having legal custody of a child from refusing or neglecting to provide proper care and attention to the child so that the life, health, or comfort of the child is endangered or is likely to be endangered. As we have found above, the plain meaning of "child" as used in this statute includes a viable fetus. Furthermore, it is common knowledge that use of cocaine during pregnancy can harm the viable unborn child. Given these facts, we do not see how Whitner can claim she lacked fair notice that her behavior constituted child endangerment as proscribed in section 20-7-50. Whitner had all the notice the Constitution requires.

2. Right to Privacy

Whitner argues that prosecuting her for using crack cocaine after her fetus attains viability unconstitutionally burdens her right of privacy, or, more specifically, her right to carry her pregnancy to term. We disagree. . . .

[W]e do not think any fundamental right of Whitner's — or any right at all, for that matter — is implicated under the present scenario. It strains belief for Whitner to argue that using crack cocaine during pregnancy is encompassed within the constitutionally recognized right of privacy. Use of crack cocaine is illegal, period. No one here argues that laws criminalizing the use of crack cocaine are themselves unconstitutional. If the State wishes to impose additional criminal penalties on pregnant women who engage in this already illegal conduct because of the effect the conduct has on the viable fetus, it may do so. We do not see how the fact of pregnancy elevates the use of crack cocaine to the lofty status of a fundamental right. . . .

For the foregoing reasons, the decision of the PCR Court is reversed.

FINNEY, C.J. I respectfully dissent, and would affirm the grant of postconviction relief to respondent Whitner.

The issue before the Court is whether a fetus is a "child" within the meaning of S.C. Code Ann. § 20-7-50 (1985). . . . Since this is a penal statute, it is strictly construed against the State and in favor of respondent. . . .

[I]t is apparent from a reading of the entire statute that the word child in § 20-7-50 means a child in being and not a fetus. A plain reading of the entire child neglect statute demonstrates the intent to criminalize only acts directed at children, and not those which may harm fetuses. First, § 20-7-50 does not impose criminal liability on every person who neglects a child, but only on a person having legal custody of that child. The statutory requirement of legal custody is evidence of intent to extend the statute's reach only to children, because the concept of legal custody is simply inapplicable to a fetus. Second, § 20-7-50 refers to S.C. Code Ann. § 20-7-490 for the definition of neglect. Section 20-7-490 defines a neglected child as one harmed or threatened with harm, and further defines harm. The vast majority of acts which constitute statutory harm under § 20-7-490 are acts which can only be directed against a child, and not towards a fetus.[2] The reliance upon § 20-7-490 in § 20-7-50 is further evidence that the term child as used in the child neglect statute does not encompass a fetus. Read in context, and in light of the statutory purpose of protecting persons of tender years, it is clear that "child" as used in § 20-7-50 means a child in being.

At most, the majority only suggests that the term "child" as used in § 20-7-50 is ambiguous. This suggestion of ambiguity is created not by reference to our decisions under the Children's Code or by reference to the statutory language and applicable rules of statutory construction, but by reliance on decisions in two different fields of the law, civil wrongful death and common law feticide. Here, we

---

[2] Examples include condoning delinquency, using excessive corporal punishment, committing sexual offenses against the child, and depriving her of adequate food, clothing, shelter or education.

deal with the Children's Code, and the meaning of language used in a criminal statute under that Code. We have already indicated that a child within the meaning of § 20-7-90(A) (1985), which criminalizes non-support, must be one already born. *State v. Montgomery*, 246 S.C. 545, 144 S.E.2d 797 (1965) (indictment for violation of predecessor of § 20-7-90(A) fatally defective for failing to identify the child by description or date of birth). Even if these wrongful death, common law, and Children's Code decisions are sufficient to render the term child in § 20-7-50 ambiguous, it is axiomatic that the ambiguity must be resolved in respondent's favor.

I would affirm.

Moore, A.J. I concur with the dissent in this case but write separately to express my concerns with today's decision.

In my view, the repeated failure of the legislature to pass proposed bills addressing the problem of drug use during pregnancy is evidence the child abuse and neglect statute is not intended to apply in this instance. This Court should not invade what is clearly the sole province of the legislative branch. At the very least, the legislature's failed attempts to enact a statute regulating a pregnant woman's conduct indicate the complexity of this issue. While the majority opinion is perhaps an argument for what the law should be, it is for the General Assembly, and not this Court, to make that determination by means of a clearly drawn statute. With today's decision, the majority not only ignores legislative intent but embarks on a course of judicial activism rejected by every other court to address the issue.

As discussed in the Chief Justice's dissent, we are bound by the rules of statutory construction to strictly construe a criminal statute in favor of the defendant and resolve any ambiguity in her favor. I cannot accept the majority's assertion that the child abuse and neglect statute unambiguously includes a "viable fetus." If that is the case, then why is the majority compelled to go to such great lengths to ascertain that a "viable fetus" is a "child?" . . .

In construing this statute to include conduct not contemplated by the legislature, the majority has rendered the statute vague and set for itself the task of determining what conduct is unlawful. Is a pregnant woman's failure to obtain prenatal care unlawful? Failure to quit smoking or drinking? Although the majority dismisses this issue as not before it, the impact of today's decision is to render a pregnant woman potentially criminally liable for myriad acts which the legislature has not seen fit to criminalize. To ignore this "down-the-road" consequence in a case of this import is unrealistic. The majority insists that parents may already be held liable for drinking after a child is born. This is untrue, however, without some further act on the part of the parent. A parent who drinks and then hits her child or fails to come home may be guilty of criminal neglect. The mere fact of drinking, however, does not constitute neglect of a child in being.

The majority attempts to support an overinclusive construction of the child abuse and neglect statute by citing other legal protections extended equally to a viable fetus and a child in being. The only law, however, that specifically regulates the conduct of a mother toward her unborn child is our abortion statute under which a viable fetus is in fact treated differently from a child in being.[1]

---

[1] A woman may have a legal abortion of a viable fetus if necessary to preserve her health, S.C. Code Ann. § 44-41-20(c) (1985), while, of course, she may not justify the death of a child in being on this ground.

The majority argues for equal treatment of viable fetuses and children, yet its construction of the statute results in even greater inequities. If the statute applies only when a fetus is "viable," a pregnant woman can use cocaine for the first twenty-four weeks[2] of her pregnancy, the most dangerous period for the fetus, and be immune from prosecution under the statute so long as she quits drug use before the fetus becomes viable. Further, a pregnant woman now faces up to ten years in prison for ingesting drugs during pregnancy but can have an illegal abortion and receive only a two-year sentence for killing her viable fetus.[3]

Because I disagree with the conclusion § 20-7-50 includes a viable fetus, I would affirm the grant of post-conviction relief.

QUESTIONS

1. On which theories of interpretation does Justice Toal rely in his opinion? How would *Whitner* be resolved using a solely textualist approach? How would it be resolved using dynamic statutory interpretation?

2. In *Keeler* (Chapter 3 Section A), the California Supreme Court held that a fetus is not a "human being" for purposes of the California murder statute. How do you think Justice Mosk, who wrote the majority opinion in *Keeler*, and Justice Burke, who dissented in *Keeler*, would each decide the question of whether a fetus is a "child" under the child abuse statute at issue in *Whitner*?

3. Does it make sense for a court to rely on its prior interpretation of language used in a *civil* statute in construing the same language in a *criminal* statute?

4. Justice Toal in *Whitner* takes the position that in discerning legislative intent, "the legislature's subsequent acts 'cast no light on the intent of the legislature which enacted the statute being construed.'" Look closely at the footnotes describing the various bills rejected by the South Carolina legislature. What inferences about legislative intent might be drawn from the failure to enact these? Note that one was an effort to amend the child abuse statute under which Whitner was convicted. Chief Justice Sognier in *Luster* adopts a very different attitude toward the use of a legislature's "subsequent acts." Which approach makes more sense?

5. In his privacy analysis, Justice Toal suggests that the issue is whether or not a woman has a fundamental right to use crack cocaine during pregnancy. How else might the privacy issue be framed?

6. Should the issue of making fetal endangerment a crime be resolved in the courts through interpretation of existing statutes dealing with child abuse, drug delivery, and homicide? Or should it be resolved by the legislature? If the legislature decides to criminalize fetal endangerment, is it preferable to do so by expanding an existing statute, such as one on child abuse, through amendment or by creating a new statute specifically aimed at fetal endangerment?

The United States Supreme Court in *Ferguson v. Charleston*, 532 U.S. 67 (2001), recently addressed the constitutionality of South Carolina state hospital employees collaborating with prosecuting authorities to gather evidence of drug use by pregnant women receiving medical care at the hospital. The program, which was structured by Charleston's solicitor, identified pregnant women who were

---

[2] Viability is presumed to occur no sooner than the twenty-fourth week of pregnancy. S.C. Code Ann. § 44-41-10(1) (1985).

[3] S.C. Code Ann. § 44-41-80(b) (1985).

suspected of drug use based on a set of nine criteria, such as "no prenatal care," "preterm labor of no obvious cause," and "previously known drug or alcohol abuse." The hospital employees took urine samples from the suspects and ran a drug-screening test on each, maintaining chain of custody so that the test results could be introduced as evidence at a criminal trial. If a test was positive, the woman was offered education and substance abuse treatment and threatened with criminal prosecution if she refused or failed to complete the treatment. The Fourth Circuit found that such testing was valid under the Fourth Amendment regardless of whether the women had consented, concluding that it fell under a "special needs" exception to the Fourth Amendment's requirements of probable cause and a warrant. The Supreme Court reversed, finding that the drug tests were searches that violated the Fourth Amendment because of "the pervasive involvement of law enforcement with the development and application" of the drug-testing policy. *Id.* at 85. "The stark and unique fact that characterizes this case is that [the drug-testing policy] was designed to obtain evidence of criminal conduct by the tested patients that would be turned over to the police and that could be admissible in subsequent criminal prosecutions." *Id.* at 86. The Supreme Court did not bar drug testing of expectant mothers in *Ferguson*; it simply required probable cause and a warrant or consent or exigent circumstances to do it.

Do investigative methods such as those used in *Ferguson* degrade law enforcement? The Court in *Ferguson* noted that "[t]he reasonable expectation of privacy enjoyed by the typical patient undergoing diagnostic tests in a hospital is that the results of those tests will not be shared with nonmedical personnel." *Id.* at 78. Is violation of this expectation of privacy by police recruiting hospital personnel to gather information for criminal prosecution likely to result in public disrespect for the criminal justice system? Or will the public view it as a justifiable means for punishing and preventing criminal conduct?

D. SODOMY

The word "sodomy" derives from the biblical city of Sodom, whose inhabitants "indulged in sexual immorality and pursued unnatural lust"[17] and were punished with "sulfur and fire" rained down from heaven.[18] The Bible provides little detail of the sexual practices that brought about Sodom's demise, and some modern sodomy laws are equally vague, such as North Carolina General Statute § 14-177, captioned the "Crime against nature":

> If any person shall commit the crime against nature, with mankind or beast, he shall be punished as a Class I felon.

In 1960, all 50 states had sodomy statutes. Some statutes forbade only anal intercourse. Others included oral sex as well. The gay and lesbian civil rights movement brought about the repeal of many of these statutes. Courts also found some invalid on state constitutional grounds.[19] In 1986, the United States Supreme Court in *Bowers v. Hardwick* rejected a constitutional challenge on privacy grounds to

---

17. Jude 1:7.
18. Genesis 19:24.
19. Katharine B. Silbaugh, *Sex Offenses: Consensual*, in 4 Encyclopedia of Crime and Justice 1470 (2d ed. 2002).

a Georgia sodomy statute.[20] At that time, 24 states and the District of Columbia retained criminal prohibitions on sodomy.

In 2003, the United States Supreme Court in *Lawrence v. Texas*, the principal case in this Section, reexamined the constitutionality of a sodomy law, this time a Texas statute criminalizing only conduct between members of the same sex. By the time of the *Lawrence* case, only 13 states retained sodomy laws. Four banned only sodomy between members of the same sex, as did the following Texas statute at issue in *Lawrence*.

Texas Penal Code 21.06   *Homosexual Conduct*

(a) A person commits an offense if he engages in deviate sexual intercourse with another individual of the same sex;

(b) An offense under this section is a Class C misdemeanor.

Texas Penal Code 21.01   *Definitions*

In this chapter:
(1) "Deviate sexual intercourse" means:
(A) any contact between any part of the genitals of one person and the mouth or anus of another person; or
(B) the penetration of the genitals or the anus of another person with an object.

The other nine states' statutes covered both homosexual and heterosexual conduct.

Police and prosecutors infrequently enforced either type of sodomy statute for a variety of reasons, such as the difficulty of detecting and proving private consensual sexual behavior. The difference in scope between statutes focused on homosexual conduct and those encompassing heterosexual sodomy was of little practical import since the occasional application of the broader statutes was almost exclusively to homosexual conduct.

In *Lawrence*, the Court, in a broad ruling, found both types of statutes unconstitutional and explicitly disavowed its earlier decision in *Bowers*. Commentators have labeled the case a "constitutional watershed."[21] "In one judicial decision from the nation's highest court, gays and lesbians had gone from outsiders in the law and criminals in 13 states to possessing the same basic right to liberty and equality as heterosexuals."[22] Counsel for John Lawrence hailed the decision as "historic and transformative"[23] for gay and lesbian rights. Critics have conceded the significance of the case but have derided it as, among other things, "a frontal assault on democratic rule."[24] Both those who praise and those who condemn *Lawrence* view the case as a first step toward expansion of gay and lesbian rights in areas such as

---

20. In Powell v. State, 270 Ga. 327 (1998), the Georgia Supreme Court later invalidated Georgia's sodomy statute as a violation of the Georgia Constitution's protection of privacy.

21. Linda Greenhouse, *In a Momentous Term, Justices Remake the Law, and the Court*, New York Times, July 1, 2003, at A1.

22. David G. Savage, *In Rulings, Echoes of 1992*, ABA J. 21, 22 (Aug. 2003).

23. Linda Greenhouse, *The Supreme Court: Homosexual Rights; Justices, 6-3, Legalize Gay Sexual Conduct in Sweeping Reversal of Court's '86 Ruling*, New York Times, June 26, 2003 A1 (quoting Ruth Harlow, legal director of the Lambda Legal Defense and Education Fund).

24. Vernadette Ramirez Broyles, *Homosexual Agenda Has Ally in Court*, Atlanta Journal-Constitution, July 9, 2003, 13A.

marriage, adoption, child custody, and employment. As you read the case, think about whether in resolving such a case the Court should take into consideration the larger legal and social implications of its ruling in areas outside the criminal law or should focus solely on the merits of the particular case before it.

LAWRENCE *v.* TEXAS

539 U.S. 558 (2003)

Justice KENNEDY delivered the opinion of the Court.

Liberty protects the person from unwarranted government intrusions into a dwelling or other private places. In our tradition the State is not omnipresent in the home. And there are other spheres of our lives and existence, outside the home, where the State should not be a dominant presence. Freedom extends beyond spatial bounds. Liberty presumes an autonomy of self that includes freedom of thought, belief, expression, and certain intimate conduct. The instant case involves liberty of the person both in its spatial and more transcendent dimensions.

I

The question before the Court is the validity of a Texas statute making it a crime for two persons of the same sex to engage in certain intimate sexual conduct.

In Houston, Texas, officers of the Harris County Police Department were dispatched to a private residence in response to a reported weapons disturbance. They entered an apartment where one of the petitioners, John Geddes Lawrence, resided. The right of the police to enter does not seem to have been questioned. The officers observed Lawrence and another man, Tyron Garner, engaging in a sexual act. The two petitioners were arrested, held in custody over night, and charged and convicted before a Justice of the Peace.

The complaints described their crime as "deviate sexual intercourse, namely anal sex, with a member of the same sex (man)." The applicable state law is Tex. Penal Code Ann. § 21.06(a) (2003). It provides: "A person commits an offense if he engages in deviate sexual intercourse with another individual of the same sex." The statute defines "deviate sexual intercourse" as follows:

"(A) any contact between any part of the genitals of one person and the mouth or anus of another person; or

(B) the penetration of the genitals or the anus of another person with an object."

The petitioners exercised their right to a trial *de novo* in Harris County Criminal Court. They challenged the statute as a violation of the Equal Protection Clause of the Fourteenth Amendment and of a like provision of the Texas Constitution. Those contentions were rejected. The petitioners, having entered a plea of *nolo contendere*, were each fined $ 200 and assessed court costs of $ 141.25.

The Court of Appeals for the Texas Fourteenth District considered the petitioners' federal constitutional arguments under both the Equal Protection and Due Process Clauses of the Fourteenth Amendment. After hearing the case en banc the court, in a divided opinion, rejected the constitutional arguments and affirmed the convictions. The majority opinion indicates that the Court of Appeals considered our decision in *Bowers v. Hardwick*, 478 U.S. 186 (1986), to be controlling on the federal due process aspect of the case. *Bowers* then being authoritative, this was proper.

We granted certiorari to consider three questions:

"1. Whether Petitioners' criminal convictions under the Texas "Homosexual Conduct" law — which criminalizes sexual intimacy by same-sex couples, but not identical behavior by different-sex couples — violate the Fourteenth Amendment guarantee of equal protection of laws?

2. Whether Petitioners' criminal convictions for adult consensual sexual intimacy in the home violate their vital interests in liberty and privacy protected by the Due Process Clause of the Fourteenth Amendment?

3. Whether *Bowers v. Hardwick*, 478 U.S. 186 (1986), should be overruled?"

The petitioners were adults at the time of the alleged offense. Their conduct was in private and consensual.

II

We conclude the case should be resolved by determining whether the petitioners were free as adults to engage in the private conduct in the exercise of their liberty under the Due Process Clause of the Fourteenth Amendment to the Constitution. For this inquiry we deem it necessary to reconsider the Court's holding in *Bowers*.

There are broad statements of the substantive reach of liberty under the Due Process Clause in earlier cases . . . but the most pertinent beginning point is our decision in *Griswold v. Connecticut*, 381 U.S. 479 (1965).

In *Griswold* the Court invalidated a state law prohibiting the use of drugs or devices of contraception and counseling or aiding and abetting the use of contraceptives. The Court described the protected interest as a right to privacy and placed emphasis on the marriage relation and the protected space of the marital bedroom.

After *Griswold* it was established that the right to make certain decisions regarding sexual conduct extends beyond the marital relationship. In *Eisenstadt v. Baird*, 405 U.S. 438 (1972), the Court invalidated a law prohibiting the distribution of contraceptives to unmarried persons. The case was decided under the Equal Protection Clause but with respect to unmarried persons, the Court went on to state the fundamental proposition that the law impaired the exercise of their personal rights. It quoted from the statement of the Court of Appeals finding the law to be in conflict with fundamental human rights, and it followed with this statement of its own:

> "It is true that in *Griswold* the right of privacy in question inhered in the marital relationship. . . . If the right of privacy means anything, it is the right of the individual, married or single, to be free from unwarranted governmental intrusion into matters so fundamentally affecting a person as the decision whether to bear or beget a child."

The opinions in *Griswold* and *Eisenstadt* were part of the background for the decision in *Roe v. Wade*, 410 U.S. 113 (1973). As is well known, the case involved a challenge to the Texas law prohibiting abortions, but the laws of other States were affected as well. Although the Court held the woman's rights were not absolute, her right to elect an abortion did have real and substantial protection as an exercise of her liberty under the Due Process Clause. The Court cited cases that protect spatial freedom and cases that go well beyond it. *Roe* recognized the right of a woman to make certain fundamental decisions affecting her destiny and confirmed once more that the protection of liberty under the Due Process Clause has a substantive dimension of fundamental significance in defining the rights of the person.

In *Carey v. Population Services Int'l*, 431 U.S. 678 (1977), the Court confronted a New York law forbidding sale or distribution of contraceptive devices to persons under 16 years of age. Although there was no single opinion for the Court, the law was invalidated. Both *Eisenstadt* and *Carey*, as well as the holding and rationale in *Roe*, confirmed that the reasoning of Griswold could not be confined to the protection of rights of married adults. This was the state of the law with respect to some of the most relevant cases when the Court considered *Bowers v. Hardwick*.

The facts in *Bowers* had some similarities to the instant case. A police officer, whose right to enter seems not to have been in question, observed Hardwick, in his own bedroom, engaging in intimate sexual conduct with another adult male. The conduct was in violation of a Georgia statute making it a criminal offense to engage in sodomy. One difference between the two cases is that the Georgia statute prohibited the conduct whether or not the participants were of the same sex, while the Texas statute, as we have seen, applies only to participants of the same sex. Hardwick was not prosecuted, but he brought an action in federal court to declare the state statute invalid. He alleged he was a practicing homosexual and that the criminal prohibition violated rights guaranteed to him by the Constitution. The Court, in an opinion by Justice White, sustained the Georgia law. Chief Justice Burger and Justice Powell joined the opinion of the Court and filed separate, concurring opinions. Four Justices dissented.

The Court began its substantive discussion in *Bowers* as follows: "The issue presented is whether the Federal Constitution confers a fundamental right upon homosexuals to engage in sodomy and hence invalidates the laws of the many States that still make such conduct illegal and have done so for a very long time." That statement, we now conclude, discloses the Court's own failure to appreciate the extent of the liberty at stake. To say that the issue in *Bowers* was simply the right to engage in certain sexual conduct demeans the claim the individual put forward, just as it would demean a married couple were it to be said marriage is simply about the right to have sexual intercourse. The laws involved in *Bowers* and here are, to be sure, statutes that purport to do no more than prohibit a particular sexual act. Their penalties and purposes, though, have more far-reaching consequences, touching upon the most private human conduct, sexual behavior, and in the most private of places, the home. The statutes do seek to control a personal relationship that, whether or not entitled to formal recognition in the law, is within the liberty of persons to choose without being punished as criminals.

This, as a general rule, should counsel against attempts by the State, or a court, to define the meaning of the relationship or to set its boundaries absent injury to a person or abuse of an institution the law protects. It suffices for us to acknowledge that adults may choose to enter upon this relationship in the confines of their homes and their own private lives and still retain their dignity as free persons. When sexuality finds overt expression in intimate conduct with another person, the conduct can be but one element in a personal bond that is more enduring. The liberty protected by the Constitution allows homosexual persons the right to make this choice.

Having misapprehended the claim of liberty there presented to it, and thus stating the claim to be whether there is a fundamental right to engage in consensual sodomy, the *Bowers* Court said: "Proscriptions against that conduct have ancient roots." In academic writings, and in many of the scholarly amicus briefs filed to assist the Court in this case, there are fundamental criticisms of the historical premises relied upon by the majority and concurring opinions in *Bowers*. We need not enter this debate in the attempt to reach a definitive historical judgment, but the following considerations counsel against adopting the definitive conclusions upon which *Bowers* placed such reliance.

At the outset it should be noted that there is no longstanding history in this country of laws directed at homosexual conduct as a distinct matter. Beginning in colonial times there were prohibitions of sodomy derived from the English criminal laws passed in the first instance by the Reformation Parliament of 1533. The English prohibition was understood to include relations between men and women as well as relations between men and men. Nineteenth-century commentators similarly read American sodomy, buggery, and crime-against-nature statutes as criminalizing certain relations between men and women and between men and men. The absence of legal prohibitions focusing on homosexual conduct may be explained in part by noting that according to some scholars the concept of the homosexual as a distinct category of person did not emerge until the late 19th century. Thus early American sodomy laws were not directed at homosexuals as such but instead sought to prohibit nonprocreative sexual activity more generally. This does not suggest approval of homosexual conduct. It does tend to show that this particular form of conduct was not thought of as a separate category from like conduct between heterosexual persons.

Laws prohibiting sodomy do not seem to have been enforced against consenting adults acting in private. A substantial number of sodomy prosecutions and convictions for which there are surviving records were for predatory acts against those who could not or did not consent, as in the case of a minor or the victim of an assault. As to these, one purpose for the prohibitions was to ensure there would be no lack of coverage if a predator committed a sexual assault that did not constitute rape as defined by the criminal law. Thus the model sodomy indictments presented in a 19th-century treatise, addressed the predatory acts of an adult man against a minor girl or minor boy. Instead of targeting relations between consenting adults in private, 19th-century sodomy prosecutions typically involved relations between men and minor girls or minor boys, relations between adults involving force, relations between adults implicating disparity in status, or relations between men and animals.

To the extent that there were any prosecutions for the acts in question, 19th-century evidence rules imposed a burden that would make a conviction more difficult to obtain even taking into account the problems always inherent in prosecuting consensual acts committed in private. Under then-prevailing standards, a man could not be convicted of sodomy based upon testimony of a consenting partner, because the partner was considered an accomplice. A partner's testimony, however, was admissible if he or she had not consented to the act or was a minor, and therefore incapable of consent. The rule may explain in part the infrequency of these prosecutions. In all events that infrequency makes it difficult to say that society approved of a rigorous and systematic punishment of the consensual acts committed in private and by adults. The longstanding criminal prohibition of homosexual sodomy upon which the *Bowers* decision placed such reliance is as consistent with a general condemnation of nonprocreative sex as it is with an established tradition of prosecuting acts because of their homosexual character.

The policy of punishing consenting adults for private acts was not much discussed in the early legal literature. We can infer that one reason for this was the very private nature of the conduct. Despite the absence of prosecutions, there may have been periods in which there was public criticism of homosexuals as such and an insistence that the criminal laws be enforced to discourage their practices. But far from possessing "ancient roots," American laws targeting same-sex couples did not develop until the last third of the 20th century. The reported decisions concerning the prosecution of consensual, homosexual sodomy between adults for the years 1880-1995 are not always clear in the details, but a significant number involved conduct in a public place.

It was not until the 1970's that any State singled out same-sex relations for criminal prosecution, and only nine States have done so. Post *Bowers* even some of these States did not adhere to the policy of suppressing homosexual conduct. Over the course of the last decades, States with same-sex prohibitions have moved toward abolishing them.

In summary, the historical grounds relied upon in *Bowers* are more complex than the majority opinion and the concurring opinion by Chief Justice Burger indicate. Their historical premises are not without doubt and, at the very least, are overstated.

It must be acknowledged, of course, that the Court in *Bowers* was making the broader point that for centuries there have been powerful voices to condemn homosexual conduct as immoral. The condemnation has been shaped by religious beliefs, conceptions of right and acceptable behavior, and respect for the traditional family. For many persons these are not trivial concerns but profound and deep convictions accepted as ethical and moral principles to which they aspire and which thus determine the course of their lives. These considerations do not answer the question before us, however. The issue is whether the majority may use the power of the State to enforce these views on the whole society through operation of the criminal law. "Our obligation is to define the liberty of all, not to mandate our own moral code."

Chief Justice Burger joined the opinion for the Court in *Bowers* and further explained his views as follows: "Decisions of individuals relating to homosexual conduct have been subject to state intervention throughout the history of Western civilization. Condemnation of those practices is firmly rooted in Judeo-Christian moral and ethical standards." As with Justice White's assumptions about history, scholarship casts some doubt on the sweeping nature of the statement by Chief Justice Burger as it pertains to private homosexual conduct between consenting adults. In all events we think that our laws and traditions in the past half-century are of most relevance here. These references show an emerging awareness that liberty gives substantial protection to adult persons in deciding how to conduct their private lives in matters pertaining to sex. "History and tradition are the starting point but not in all cases the ending point of the substantive due process inquiry."

This emerging recognition should have been apparent when *Bowers* was decided. In 1955 the American Law Institute promulgated the Model Penal Code and made clear that it did not recommend or provide for "criminal penalties for consensual sexual relations conducted in private." It justified its decision on three grounds: (1) The prohibitions undermined respect for the law by penalizing conduct many people engaged in; (2) the statutes regulated private conduct not harmful to others; and (3) the laws were arbitrarily enforced and thus invited the danger of blackmail. In 1961 Illinois changed its laws to conform to the Model Penal Code. Other States soon followed.

In *Bowers* the Court referred to the fact that before 1961 all 50 States had outlawed sodomy, and that at the time of the Court's decision 24 States and the District of Columbia had sodomy laws. Justice Powell pointed out that these prohibitions often were being ignored, however. Georgia, for instance, had not sought to enforce its law for decades.

The sweeping references by Chief Justice Burger to the history of Western civilization and to Judeo-Christian moral and ethical standards did not take account of other authorities pointing in an opposite direction. A committee advising the British Parliament recommended in 1957 repeal of laws punishing homosexual conduct. The Wolfenden Report: Report of the Committee on Homosexual Offenses and Prostitution (1963). Parliament enacted the substance of those recommendations 10 years later.

Of even more importance, almost five years before *Bowers* was decided the European Court of Human Rights considered a case with parallels to *Bowers* and to today's case. An adult male resident in Northern Ireland alleged he was a practicing homosexual who desired to engage in consensual homosexual conduct. The laws of Northern Ireland forbade him that right. He alleged that he had been questioned, his home had been searched, and he feared criminal prosecution. The court held that the laws proscribing the conduct were invalid under the European Convention on Human Rights. *Dudgeon v. United Kingdom*, 45 Eur. Ct. H. R. (1981) P52. Authoritative in all countries that are members of the Council of Europe (21 nations then, 45 nations now), the decision is at odds with the premise in *Bowers* that the claim put forward was insubstantial in our Western civilization.

In our own constitutional system the deficiencies in *Bowers* became even more apparent in the years following its announcement. The 25 States with laws prohibiting the relevant conduct referenced in the *Bowers* decision are reduced now to 13, of which 4 enforce their laws only against homosexual conduct. In those States where sodomy is still proscribed, whether for same-sex or heterosexual conduct, there is a pattern of nonenforcement with respect to consenting adults acting in private. The State of Texas admitted in 1994 that as of that date it had not prosecuted anyone under those circumstances.

Two principal cases decided after *Bowers* cast its holding into even more doubt. In *Planned Parenthood of Southeastern Pa. v. Casey*, 505 U.S. 833, (1992), the Court reaffirmed the substantive force of the liberty protected by the Due Process Clause. The *Casey* decision again confirmed that our laws and tradition afford constitutional protection to personal decisions relating to marriage, procreation, contraception, family relationships, child rearing, and education. In explaining the respect the Constitution demands for the autonomy of the person in making these choices, we stated as follows:

> These matters, involving the most intimate and personal choices a person may make in a lifetime, choices central to personal dignity and autonomy, are central to the liberty protected by the Fourteenth Amendment. At the heart of liberty is the right to define one's own concept of existence, of meaning, of the universe, and of the mystery of human life. Beliefs about these matters could not define the attributes of personhood were they formed under compulsion of the State.

Persons in a homosexual relationship may seek autonomy for these purposes, just as heterosexual persons do. The decision in *Bowers* would deny them this right.

The second post *Bowers* case of principal relevance is *Romer v. Evans*, 517 U.S. 620, (1996). There the Court struck down class-based legislation directed at homosexuals as a violation of the Equal Protection Clause. *Romer* invalidated an amendment to Colorado's constitution which named as a solitary class persons who were homosexuals, lesbians, or bisexual either by "orientation, conduct, practices or relationships," (internal quotation marks omitted), and deprived them of protection under state antidiscrimination laws. We concluded that the provision was "born of animosity toward the class of persons affected" and further that it had no rational relation to a legitimate governmental purpose.

As an alternative argument in this case, counsel for the petitioners and some amici contend that *Romer* provides the basis for declaring the Texas statute invalid under the Equal Protection Clause. That is a tenable argument, but we conclude the instant case requires us to address whether *Bowers* itself has continuing validity. Were we to hold the statute invalid under the Equal Protection Clause some might question whether a prohibition would be valid if drawn differently, say, to prohibit the conduct both between same-sex and different-sex participants.

Equality of treatment and the due process right to demand respect for conduct protected by the substantive guarantee of liberty are linked in important respects, and a decision on the latter point advances both interests. If protected conduct is made criminal and the law which does so remains unexamined for its substantive validity, its stigma might remain even if it were not enforceable as drawn for equal protection reasons. When homosexual conduct is made criminal by the law of the State, that declaration in and of itself is an invitation to subject homosexual persons to discrimination both in the public and in the private spheres. The central holding of *Bowers* has been brought in question by this case, and it should be addressed. Its continuance as precedent demeans the lives of homosexual persons.

The stigma this criminal statute imposes, moreover, is not trivial. The offense, to be sure, is but a class C misdemeanor, a minor offense in the Texas legal system. Still, it remains a criminal offense with all that imports for the dignity of the persons charged. The petitioners will bear on their record the history of their criminal convictions. Just this Term we rejected various challenges to state laws requiring the registration of sex offenders. We are advised that if Texas convicted an adult for private, consensual homosexual conduct under the statute here in question the convicted person would come within the registration laws of a least four States were he or she to be subject to their jurisdiction. This underscores the consequential nature of the punishment and the state-sponsored condemnation attendant to the criminal prohibition. Furthermore, the Texas criminal conviction carries with it the other collateral consequences always following a conviction, such as notations on job application forms, to mention but one example.

The foundations of *Bowers* have sustained serious erosion from our recent decisions in *Casey* and *Romer*. When our precedent has been thus weakened, criticism from other sources is of greater significance. In the United States criticism of *Bowers* has been substantial and continuing, disapproving of its reasoning in all respects, not just as to its historical assumptions. The courts of five different States have declined to follow it in interpreting provisions in their own state constitutions parallel to the Due Process Clause of the Fourteenth Amendment, see *Jegley v. Picado*, 349 Ark. 600 (2002); *Powell v. State*, 270 Ga. 327 (1998); *Gryczan v. State*, 283 Mont. 433 (1997); *Campbell v. Sundquist*, 926 S.W.2d 250 (Tenn App.1996); *Commonwealth v. Wasson*, 842 S.W.2d 487 (Ky. 1992).

To the extent *Bowers* relied on values we share with a wider civilization, it should be noted that the reasoning and holding in *Bowers* have been rejected elsewhere. The European Court of Human Rights has followed not *Bowers* but its own decision in *Dudgeon v. United Kingdom*. Other nations, too, have taken action consistent with an affirmation of the protected right of homosexual adults to engage in intimate, consensual conduct. The right the petitioners seek in this case has been accepted as an integral part of human freedom in many other countries. There has been no showing that in this country the governmental interest in circumscribing personal choice is somehow more legitimate or urgent.

The doctrine of stare decisis is essential to the respect accorded to the judgments of the Court and to the stability of the law. It is not, however, an inexorable command. In *Casey* we noted that when a Court is asked to overrule a precedent recognizing a constitutional liberty interest, individual or societal reliance on the existence of that liberty cautions with particular strength against reversing course. The holding in *Bowers*, however, has not induced detrimental reliance comparable to some instances where recognized individual rights are involved. Indeed, there has been no individual or societal reliance on *Bowers* of the sort that could counsel against overturning its holding once there are compelling reasons to do so. *Bowers* itself causes uncertainty, for the precedents before and after its issuance contradict its central holding.

The rationale of *Bowers* does not withstand careful analysis. In his dissenting opinion in *Bowers* Justice Stevens came to these conclusions:

> Our prior cases make two propositions abundantly clear. First, the fact that the governing majority in a State has traditionally viewed a particular practice as immoral is not a sufficient reason for upholding a law prohibiting the practice; neither history nor tradition could save a law prohibiting miscegenation from constitutional attack. Second, individual decisions by married persons, concerning the intimacies of their physical relationship, even when not intended to produce offspring, are a form of "liberty" protected by the Due Process Clause of the Fourteenth Amendment. Moreover, this protection extends to intimate choices by unmarried as well as married persons.

Justice Stevens' analysis, in our view, should have been controlling in *Bowers* and should control here.

Bowers was not correct when it was decided, and it is not correct today. It ought not to remain binding precedent. *Bowers v. Hardwick* should be and now is overruled.

The present case does not involve minors. It does not involve persons who might be injured or coerced or who are situated in relationships where consent might not easily be refused. It does not involve public conduct or prostitution. It does not involve whether the government must give formal recognition to any relationship that homosexual persons seek to enter. The case does involve two adults who, with full and mutual consent from each other, engaged in sexual practices common to a homosexual lifestyle. The petitioners are entitled to respect for their private lives. The State cannot demean their existence or control their destiny by making their private sexual conduct a crime. Their right to liberty under the Due Process Clause gives them the full right to engage in their conduct without intervention of the government. "It is a promise of the Constitution that there is a realm of personal liberty which the government may not enter." The Texas statute furthers no legitimate state interest which can justify its intrusion into the personal and private life of the individual.

Had those who drew and ratified the Due Process Clauses of the Fifth Amendment or the Fourteenth Amendment known the components of liberty in its manifold possibilities, they might have been more specific. They did not presume to have this insight. They knew times can blind us to certain truths and later generations can see that laws once thought necessary and proper in fact serve only to oppress. As the Constitution endures, persons in every generation can invoke its principles in their own search for greater freedom.

The judgment of the Court of Appeals for the Texas Fourteenth District is reversed, and the case is remanded for further proceedings not inconsistent with this opinion.

Justice O'CONNOR, concurring in the judgment.

The Court today overrules *Bowers v. Hardwick*. I joined *Bowers* and do not join the Court in overruling it. Nevertheless, I agree with the Court that Texas' statute banning same-sex sodomy is unconstitutional. Rather than relying on the substantive component of the Fourteenth Amendment's Due Process Clause, as the Court does, I base my conclusion on the Fourteenth Amendment's Equal Protection Clause. . . .

The statute at issue here makes sodomy a crime only if a person "engages in deviate sexual intercourse with another individual of the same sex." Sodomy between opposite-sex partners, however, is not a crime in Texas. That is, Texas treats the same conduct differently based solely on the participants. Those harmed by this law are people who have a same-sex sexual orientation and thus are more likely to engage in behavior prohibited by § 21.06. . . .

This case raises a different issue than *Bowers*: whether, under the Equal Protection Clause, moral disapproval is a legitimate state interest to justify by itself a statute that bans homosexual sodomy, but not heterosexual sodomy. It is not. Moral disapproval of this group, like a bare desire to harm the group, is an interest that is insufficient to satisfy rational basis review under the Equal Protection Clause. Indeed, we have never held that moral disapproval, without any other asserted state interest, is a sufficient rationale under the Equal Protection Clause to justify a law that discriminates among groups of persons. . . .

That this law as applied to private, consensual conduct is unconstitutional under the Equal Protection Clause does not mean that other laws distinguishing between heterosexuals and homosexuals would similarly fail under rational basis review. Texas cannot assert any legitimate state interest here, such as national security or preserving the traditional institution of marriage. Unlike the moral disapproval of same-sex relations — the asserted state interest in this case — other reasons exist to promote the institution of marriage beyond mere moral disapproval of an excluded group.

Justice SCALIA, with whom The Chief Justice and Justice THOMAS join, dissenting.

"Liberty finds no refuge in a jurisprudence of doubt." *Planned Parenthood of Southeastern Pa. v. Casey*, 505 U.S. 83 (1992). That was the Court's sententious response, barely more than a decade ago, to those seeking to overrule *Roe v. Wade*, 410 U.S. 113 (1973). The Court's response today, to those who have engaged in a 17-year crusade to overrule *Bowers v. Hardwick*, is very different. The need for stability and certainty presents no barrier.

. . . [N]owhere does the Court's opinion declare that homosexual sodomy is a "fundamental right" under the Due Process Clause; nor does it subject the Texas law to the standard of review that would be appropriate (strict scrutiny) if homosexual sodomy were a "fundamental right." Thus, while overruling the outcome of *Bowers*, the Court leaves strangely untouched its central legal conclusion: "Respondent would have us announce . . . a fundamental right to engage in homosexual sodomy. This we are quite unwilling to do." Instead the Court simply describes petitioners' conduct as "an exercise of their liberty" — which it undoubtedly is — and proceeds to apply an unheard-of form of rational-basis review that will have far-reaching implications beyond this case. . . .

Our opinions applying the doctrine known as "substantive due process" hold that the Due Process Clause prohibits States from infringing fundamental liberty interests, unless the infringement is narrowly tailored to serve a compelling state interest. We have held repeatedly, in cases the Court today does not overrule, that only fundamental rights qualify for this so-called "heightened scrutiny" protection — that is, rights which are " 'deeply rooted in this Nation's history and tradition.' " . . .

Bowers held, first, that criminal prohibitions of homosexual sodomy are not subject to heightened scrutiny because they do not implicate a "fundamental right" under the Due Process Clause. Noting that "proscriptions against that conduct have ancient roots," that "sodomy was a criminal offense at common law and was forbidden by the laws of the original 13 States when they ratified the Bill of Rights," and that many States had retained their bans on sodomy, *Bowers* concluded that a right to engage in homosexual sodomy was not " 'deeply rooted in this Nation's history and tradition.' "

The Court today does not overrule this holding. Not once does it describe homosexual sodomy as a "fundamental right" or a "fundamental liberty interest," nor does it subject the Texas statute to strict scrutiny. Instead, having failed to establish that the right to homosexual sodomy is " 'deeply rooted in this Nation's history and tradition,' " the Court concludes that the application of Texas's statute to petitioners' conduct fails the rational-basis test, and overrules *Bowers'* holding to the contrary. "The Texas statute furthers no legitimate state interest which can justify its intrusion into the personal and private life of the individual." . . .

In any event, an "emerging awareness" is by definition not "deeply rooted in this Nation's history and traditions," as we have said "fundamental right" status requires. Constitutional entitlements do not spring into existence because some States choose to lessen or eliminate criminal sanctions on certain behavior. Much less do they spring into existence, as the Court seems to believe, because foreign nations decriminalize conduct. The *Bowers* majority opinion never relied on "values we share with a wider civilization," but rather rejected the claimed right to sodomy on the ground that such a right was not " 'deeply rooted in this Nation's history and tradition,' " *Bowers'* rational-basis holding is likewise devoid of any reliance on the views of a "wider civilization." The Court's discussion of these foreign views (ignoring, of course, the many countries that have retained criminal prohibitions on sodomy) is therefore meaningless dicta. Dangerous dicta, however, since "this Court . . . should not impose foreign moods, fads, or fashions on Americans."

IV

I turn now to the ground on which the Court squarely rests its holding: the contention that there is no rational basis for the law here under attack. This proposition is so out of accord with our jurisprudence — indeed, with the jurisprudence of *any* society we know — that it requires little discussion.

The Texas statute undeniably seeks to further the belief of its citizens that certain forms of sexual behavior are "immoral and unacceptable," — the same interest furthered by criminal laws against fornication, bigamy, adultery, adult incest, bestiality, and obscenity. *Bowers* held that this was a legitimate state interest. The Court today reaches the opposite conclusion. The Texas statute, it says, "furthers no legit-imate state interest which can justify its intrusion into the personal and private life of the individual." The Court embraces instead Justice Stevens' declaration in his *Bowers* dissent, that "the fact that the governing majority in a State has traditionally viewed a particular practice as immoral is not a sufficient reason for upholding a law prohibiting the practice." This effectively decrees the end of all morals leg-islation. If, as the Court asserts, the promotion of majoritarian sexual morality is not even a legitimate state interest, none of the above-mentioned laws can survive rational-basis review. . . .

Today's opinion is the product of a Court, which is the product of a law-profession culture, that has largely signed on to the so-called homosexual agenda, by which I mean the agenda promoted by some homosexual activists directed at eliminating the moral opprobrium that has traditionally attached to homosexual conduct. I noted in an earlier opinion the fact that the American Association of Law Schools (to which any reputable law school must seek to belong) excludes from membership any school that refuses to ban from its job-interview facilities a law firm (no matter how small) that does not wish to hire as a prospective partner a person who openly engages in homosexual conduct.

One of the most revealing statements in today's opinion is the Court's grim warning that the criminalization of homosexual conduct is "an invitation to sub-ject homosexual persons to discrimination both in the public and in the private spheres." It is clear from this that the Court has taken sides in the culture war, departing from its role of assuring, as neutral observer, that the democratic rules of engagement are observed. Many Americans do not want persons who openly engage in homosexual conduct as partners in their business, as scoutmasters for their children, as teachers in their children's schools, or as boarders in their home. They view this as protecting themselves and their families from a lifestyle that they believe to be immoral and destructive. The Court views it as "discrimination" which it is the function of our judgments to deter. So imbued is the Court with the law profession's anti-anti-homosexual culture, that it is seemingly unaware that the attitudes of that culture are not obviously "mainstream"; that in most States what the Court calls "discrimination" against those who engage in homosexual acts is perfectly legal; that proposals to ban such "discrimination" under Title VII have repeatedly been rejected by Congress; that in some cases such "discrimination" is mandated by federal statute, see 10 U.S.C. § 654(b)(1) (mandating discharge from the armed forces of any service member who engages in or intends to engage in homosexual acts); and that in some cases such "discrimination" is a constitutional right, *Boy Scouts of America v. Dale*, 530 U.S. 640 (2000).

Let me be clear that I have nothing against homosexuals, or any other group, promoting their agenda through normal democratic means. Social perceptions of sexual and other morality change over time, and every group has the right to per-suade its fellow citizens that its view of such matters is the best. That homosexuals have achieved some success in that enterprise is attested to by the fact that Texas is one of the few remaining States that criminalize private, consensual homosexual acts. But persuading one's fellow citizens is one thing, and imposing one's views in absence of democratic majority will is something else. I would no more require a State to criminalize homosexual acts — or, for that matter, display any moral dis-approbation of them — than I would forbid it to do so. What Texas has chosen to do is well within the range of traditional democratic action, and its hand should not be stayed through the invention of a brand-new "constitutional right" by a Court that is impatient of democratic change. It is indeed true that "later generations can see that laws once thought necessary and proper in fact serve only to oppress," and when that happens, later generations can repeal those laws. But it is the premise of our system that those judgments are to be made by the people, and not imposed by a governing caste that knows best.

QUESTIONS

1. Justice Kennedy notes that sodomy laws have largely been unenforced by police and prosecutors. One might argue that having such statutes on the books allows legislators and society to give verbal expression to their view that sodomy is immoral while not enforcing those statutes means that the liberty of those who wish to engage in sodomy is not infringed by actual prosecutions. Is this a desirable resolution of the debate over whether or not to make sodomy a crime?

2. Do you think the statute at issue in *Lawrence* had any impact on how people acted in Texas? In other words, is it likely that anyone in Texas who wanted to engage in sodomy refrained from doing so because of the Texas statute? Similarly, will the Supreme Court's decision in *Lawrence* affect behavior in Texas? Is it likely that the number of people engaging in sodomy in Texas will increase as a result of *Lawrence*? If the answers to these questions are all no — that neither a criminal sodomy statute nor a court's invalidation of that statute can be expected to have much impact on private sexual conduct, is *Lawrence* nonetheless a significant case?

3. One critic of *Lawrence* writes that "the court imposed the will of six unelected, unaccountable lawyers over the will of the majority of citizens of 13 states."[25] Should legislators or judges resolve the question of whether sodomy should be a crime? Should that decision be made at the federal, state, or county level of government? Does it make any difference that homosexual rights are currently controversial and an area in which society's values appear to be changing?

4. Justice Stone once wrote that "prejudice against discrete and insular minorities . . . which tends seriously to curtail the operation of those political processes ordinarily relied upon to protect minorities . . . may call for a correspondingly more searching judicial inquiry" into the constitutionality of legislation.[26] Was the Court in *Lawrence* defending the rights of a "discrete and insular" minority against oppression by the majority? Or was the Court imposing a majoritarian view of gay and lesbian rights on a minority?

5. What do sodomy laws aim to achieve? Protecting the moral well-being of potential violators? Protecting the moral well-being of society? Protecting members of society from physical harm?

6. Justice Scalia criticizes the majority for overruling *Bowers*, a precedent not even two decades old. Should the age of a prior decision have any impact on a court's inclination to overrule it? Does widespread opposition to that precedent strengthen or weaken the case for overturning it?

7. How should the constitutional issue in *Lawrence* be framed? In other words, what question does the case present for the Court to answer? In *Bowers*, the Court

---

25. Vernadette Ramirez Broyles, *Homosexual Agenda Has Ally in Court*, Atlanta Journal-Constitution, July 9, 2003, 13A.

26. United States v. Carolene Products Co., 304 U.S. 144, 153 n.4 (1938).

said: "[R]espondent would have us announce . . . a fundamental right to engage in homosexual sodomy. This we are quite unwilling to do." 478 U.S. 186, 191. Did the *Lawrence* Court, in rejecting *Bowers*, announce a fundamental right to engage in homosexual sodomy? How does Justice Kennedy frame the issue? What about Justice Scalia? If you were arguing the *Lawrence* case for the state of Texas, how would you characterize the issue for the Court to resolve? What if you were arguing for John Lawrence?

8. Both gay rights advocates and their conservative opponents agree that *Lawrence* lays the groundwork for legal recognition of gay marriages. Richard Lessner, of the conservative Family Research Council, stated that "[w]e find ourselves strangely in agreement with the gay rights people" on the question of whether *Lawrence* paves the way for legalizing gay marriages. "We think they brought this case to provide a foundation for same-sex marriage, and now they have it."[27] Should potential civil implications in areas such as family law influence the Supreme Court in deciding a criminal case?

9. The word "desuetude," meaning lack of use or obsolescence through disuse,[28] is sometimes employed to describe the idea that a long period of disregard of a particular law renders the law invalid. Should courts apply such a policy to criminal statutes that have been disregarded for a long time?

E. PROSTITUTION

PROBLEM

14.2[29] A large city, which is both a national business center and tourist destination, has experienced a dramatic increase in prostitution. It has spent a great deal of money in recent years enforcing its prostitution laws, but to no apparent avail. The number of prostitutes and their visibility in the city have only increased, raising concerns about sexually transmitted diseases, violence against prostitutes and their customers, the use of minors in prostitution, and deterioration in the image of the city as an attractive place to live, work, and visit. Police practice has been to focus enforcement efforts on arresting and charging prostitutes but not their customers, many of whom are visitors to the city. The typical penalty for prostitution is a fine. Several new city council members pledged during recent campaigns to take a fresh look at how to deal with prostitution. You are the attorney for the city. The city council asks you to: (1) suggest a list of possible responses to prostitution; and (2) review the relative advantages and disadvantages of each alternative. Among the responses that council

---

27. David G. Savage, *supra* note 22.
28. Black's Law Dictionary 458 (8th ed. 2004).
29. This Problem was inspired by a similar problem in Foote & Levy, *Criminal Law Cases and Materials*, 889 (1981).

members have indicated they wish you to consider are increasing the frequency and severity of punishing the typically male customers of the prostitutes and creating a district within the city in which the criminal laws regarding prostitution would not be enforced. Assume the state in which your city is located has enacted the following statutes:

Prostitution

A person is guilty of prostitution when such person engages or agrees or offers to engage in sexual conduct with another person in return for a fee. Prostitution is a class B misdemeanor punishable by a fine of up to $1,000 and/or a maximum of three months' incarceration.

Patronizing a Prostitute

A person is guilty of patronizing a prostitute when:

(1) Pursuant to a prior understanding, he pays a fee to another person as compensation for such person or a third person having engaged in sexual conduct with him; or

(2) He pays or agrees to pay a fee to another person pursuant to an understanding that in return therefor such person or a third person will engage in sexual conduct with him; or

(3) He solicits or requests another person to engage in sexual conduct with him in return for a fee.

Patronizing a prostitute is a class B misdemeanor punishable by a fine of up to $1,000 and/or a maximum of three months' incarceration.

Sylvia A. Law, COMMERCIAL SEX: BEYOND DECRIMINALIZATION

73 S. Cal. L. Rev. 523, 526-530 (2000)

The exchange of sexual services for money is the only form of consensual adult sexual activity that is systematically subject to criminal sanctions in the United States at the end of the twentieth century. The United States is unique among the nations of Western Europe and the British Commonwealth in imposing and enforcing criminal sanctions on people who offer sexual services for money.

The U.S. devotes substantial public resources to applying criminal sanctions to people who offer sex for money. Enforcement of laws prohibiting commercial sex typically targets the person who offers sex for money, rather than those who promote such work or profit from it, or those who offer money for sex. More particularly, the criminal law is enforced against street walkers, the poorest of the women who offer sex for money. In 1996, 99,000 people were arrested in the United States on prostitution and prostitution-related charges, and in 1994, 12,243 people were arrested in New York state alone. In 1985, police in the nation's sixteen largest cities made as many arrests for prostitution as for all violent crimes combined. And police in Boston, Cleveland and Houston arrested twice as many people for prostitution as they did for all homicides, rapes, robberies and assaults combined — and perpetrators evaded arrest for ninety percent of these violent crimes. In nearly all prostitution prosecutions arrest occurs when a male undercover officer seeks out women he thinks are willing to offer sex for money. He either waits for them to offer to engage in sex in exchange for money, or, more often, solicits the prostitute himself.

John Decker estimated that in 1974 between 230,000 and 350,000 U.S. women provided sex in exchange for money on a full-time basis, and far more did so on a part-time or occasional basis. Others estimate that as many as 1,300,000 U.S. women do so. An extensive study that used a variety of outreach methods to identify off-street commercial sex workers in Los Angeles found that 4,020 women in 1991 were involved in such work in that city.

Another way to approach the question of the prevalence of relations that the parties regard as prostitution is by asking the customers. A 1992 survey reported that 8.6% of men aged eighteen to fifty-nine had ever paid for sex, but in the twelve months of the study only 0.4% responded that they had done so. Decker speculates that in the 1960s and 1970s the number of young men who paid for sex declined, as social mores became more tolerant of extramarital sexuality, but that the number of older men seeking commercial sex may have increased during these decades. In the mid-1990s, Lisa E. Sanchez did the most extensive research on commercial sex workers in a mid-size city since Decker's study in the 1970s. Sanchez found dramatic increases in commercial sex during the period 1989 to 1996. During a similar period, 1986 to 1995, Department of Justice data show that the number of arrests for prostitution dropped by eighteen percent, primarily because local police departments decided that arresting prostitutes served little useful purpose. Justice Department figures show an increase in prostitution arrests from 1994 to 1996. In short, even though it is impossible to obtain precise data, explicitly commercial sexual relations and prosecutions for prostitution are common.

Tracy M. Clements summarizes a common way of conceptualizing the diversity of the experience of women who work in commercial sex:

> A somewhat static class system, mirroring the economic and racial stratification of the larger society, divides prostitutes into several categories. Streetwalkers — those who openly solicit on the street — represent the lowest, most marginalized class of prostitutes. They are most likely to be controlled by pimps, and to be subjected to violence in their work.
>
> Although streetwalkers are the most visible and familiar, they comprise only ten to twenty percent of all prostitutes. However, streetwalkers account for eighty-five to ninety percent of all prostitution arrests. This disparity in arrests has added significance when coupled with the fact that poor women and women of color are over represented among streetwalkers. Thus, fifty-five percent of all women arrested for prostitution, and eighty-five percent of those sentenced to jail, are women of color.[30]

The largest group of prostitutes, high-class "call girls" or "escorts," falls at the other end of the social and economic spectrum. These women often come from more privileged backgrounds. They typically have a higher level of education, exercise a larger degree of control over their lives, and earn substantially more for their services than do streetwalkers.

Between these two classes lies a group of women who work in various off-street settings, including massage parlors, brothels, hotels and bars. While these women

---

30. Tracy M. Clements, *Prostitution and the American Health Care System: Denying Access to a Group of Women in Need*, 11 Berkeley Women's L.J. 49, 52-53 (1996).

earn more and are less visible than streetwalkers, they work with less discretion and realize fewer profits than do call girls and escorts.

Virtually all of the purchasers of commercial sex are men. Significant numbers of men provide commercial sex to other men. Men are rarely prosecuted for prostitution. . . .

Every state in the United States defines the actions of a person who offers or provides sex for money as a crime. Every state also makes it a crime to knowingly, with the expectation of monetary or material gain, encourage or compel a person to sell sex for money. Every state also makes it a crime to receive "something of value, not for legal consideration, knowing that it was earned through an act of prostitution." Most states also impose criminal sanctions on the owners of property where commercial sex takes place, and on people who reside in such places. In a few states, the status of being a prostitute is a crime. Some states make it a crime to buy sex.

Melissa Farley & Howard Barkan, PROSTITUTION, VIOLENCE, AND POSTTRAUMATIC STRESS DISORDER

Vol. 27, 3 Women & Health 37, 39, 40-42, 44-47 (1998)

We interviewed respondents from several regions in San Francisco where street prostitution occurs. . . .

RESULTS

GENDER, RACE, AND AGE

Of the 136 people who were working as prostitutes we approached, 4% refused to participate in this research. Several of those who refused were in the process of being hired by a customer; two appeared to be pressured by pimps into refusing.

Seventy-five percent of the 130 interviewees recruited for this study were women, 13% were men, and 12% were transgendered. Thirty-nine percent were White European American, 33% were African American, 18% were Latina, 6% were Asian or Pacific Islander, and 5% described themselves as of mixed race or left the question blank.

Mean age was 30.9 yr. . . . Median age was 30.0 yr. . . . Ages ranged from 14 to 61 yr.

CHILDHOOD VIOLENCE

Fifty-seven percent reported a history of childhood sexual abuse, by an average of 3 perpetrators. Forty-nine percent of those who responded reported that as children, they had been hit or beaten by a caregiver until they had bruises or were injured in some way.

VIOLENCE IN PROSTITUTION

Eighty-two percent of these respondents reported having been physically assaulted since entering prostitution. Of those who had been physically assaulted, 55% had been assaulted by customers. Eighty-eight percent had been physically threatened while in prostitution, and 83% had been physically threatened with a weapon. Eight percent reported physical attacks by pimps and customers, which had resulted in serious injury (for example, gunshot wounds, knife wounds, injuries from attempted escapes).

Sixty-eight percent of these respondents reported having been raped since entering prostitution. Forty-eight percent had been raped more than five times. Forty-six percent of those who reported rapes stated that they had been raped by customers. Forty-nine percent reported that pornography was made of them in prostitution; and 32% had been upset by an attempt to make them do what customers had seen in pornography.

We examined the relation of gender to level of violence experienced in prostitution. The 3 gender groups differed in incidence of physical assault and in incidence of rape. Among those working as prostitutes, women and the transgendered were more likely than men to experience physical assaults in prostitution. Women and the transgendered were more likely than men to be raped in prostitution.

We did not find differences in likelihood of physical assaults and rapes on the basis of race.

Homelessness

Eighty-four percent of these interviewees reported current or past homelessness.

Physical Health

Fifty percent of these respondents stated that they had a physical health problem. Fourteen percent reported arthritis or nonspecific joint pain; 12% reported cardiovascular symptoms; 11% reported liver disorders; 10% reported reproductive system symptoms; 9% reported respiratory symptoms; 9% reported neurological symptoms, such as numbness or seizures. Eight percent reported HIV infection. Seventeen percent of these respondents stated that they would choose immediate admission to a hospital for an acute emotional problem or drug addiction or both. Five percent reported that they were currently suicidal.

A drug abuse problem was reported by 75% of these respondents and an alcohol abuse problem by 27%. Duration of the drug or alcohol problem ranged from 3 mo to 30 yr.

Posttraumatic Stress Disorder[31]

We summed respondents' ratings across the 17 items of the PTSD Checklist (PCL), generating a measure of PTSD symptom severity. . . . Sixty-eight percent of our respondents met criteria for a PTSD diagnosis. Seventy-six percent met criteria for partial PTSD. . . .

Discussion

We investigated history of violence and its association with the symptoms and diagnosis of PTSD among our 130 respondents, who were working as prostitutes on the streets of San Francisco.

The 57% prevalence of a history of childhood sexual abuse reported by these respondents is lower than that reported for those working in prostitution in other

---

31. The authors explain that "[t]he diagnosis of posttraumatic stress disorder (PTSD) describes symptoms which result from trauma. In the language of the American Psychiatric Association (1994), PTSD can result when people have experienced 'extreme traumatic stressors involving direct personal experience of an event that involves actual or threatened death or serious injury; or other threat to one's personal integrity; or witnessing an event that involves death, injury, or a threat to the physical integrity of another person; or learning about unexpected or violent death, serious harm, or threat of death or injury experienced by a family member or other close associate.' "

research. It is likely that, in the midst of ongoing trauma, reviewing childhood abuse was probably too painful. Several respondents commented that they did not want to think about their past when responding to the questions about childhood.

Many seemed profoundly uncertain as to just what "abuse" is. When asked why she answered "no" to the question regarding childhood sexual abuse, one woman whose history was known to one of the interviewers said: "Because there was no force, and, besides, I didn't even know what it was then — I didn't know it was sex." A number of respondents reported having been recruited into prostitution at the age of 12 or 13, but also denied having been molested as children.

All participants either filled out the questionnaires themselves or were assisted by interviewers who read the questions and recorded subjects' responses. Intoxication from alcohol or crack cocaine may have contributed to some interviewees' inability or unwillingness to delve into past trauma. As noted in Results, 75% of our respondents reported having a drug abuse problem, while 27% reported having an alcohol abuse problem. However, previous research with addicts has noted their high degree of accuracy in reporting life events.

Whether drug abuse tends to precede prostitution, or whether drugs were used after entering prostitution to numb the pain of working as a prostitute is unclear. Clinical experience suggests that drug and alcohol abuse may begin in latency or adolescence as a form of self-medication after incest or childhood sexual assault.

Pervasive violence was evident in the current lives of these people, with 82% reporting physical assault since entering prostitution and 68% reporting rape in prostitution. Female and transgendered people experienced significantly more violence (physical assault and rape) than did men. To be female, or to be perceived as female, was to be more intensely targeted for violence.

Sixty-eight percent of our respondents met criteria for a diagnosis of PTSD, with 76% qualifying for partial PTSD. These figures may be compared to those of help-seeking battered women, where PTSD incidence varies from 43% when self-rating scales are used to 84% with use of clinical interviews.

Our 130 interviewees' overall mean PCL score of 54.9 (an index of PTSD severity) may be compared to means of several other samples on the same measure: 50.6 for 123 PTSD treatment-seeking Vietnam veterans; 34.8 for 1006 Persian Gulf war veterans; and in a random sample of women in an HMO, 30.6 for 25 women who reported a history of physical abuse in childhood; 36.8 for 27 women who reported a history of physical and sexual abuse in childhood; and 24.4 for 26 controls in the same study. . . .

When prostitution has been discussed in the health literature, there has been a tendency to focus almost exclusively on STD, especially HIV. In a literature review, Vanwesenbeeck (1994) commented: "Researchers seem to identify more easily with clients than with prostitutes. . . . " Although HIV has certainly created a public health crisis, we propose that the violence which is described here, and the psychological distress resulting from the violence must also be considered a public health crisis. Any intervention attempting to reduce HIV risk behavior among people working as prostitutes must also address physical violence and psychological trauma.

Eighty-eight percent of this group of prostituted people expressed a desire to leave prostitution, with 84% reporting current or past homelessness. Homelessness is connected with prostitution in that survival may involve the exchange of sexual assault for a place to stay, and food. Our interviewees said that they needed . . . services . . . : housing, education, viable employment, substance abuse treatment, and participation in the design of treatment interventions for their communities.

Trauma research has been criticized for its failure to attend to social attitudes and behaviors which cause trauma (Allen, 1996). One of Vanwesenbeeck's (1994) respondents described prostitution as "volunteer slavery," clearly articulating both the *appearance* of "choice" *and* the overwhelming coercion behind that "choice." The extreme violence suffered by these respondents suggests that we cannot view prostitution as a neutral activity or simply as a vocational choice. Instead, prostitution must be understood as sexual violence against women. We must focus our attention on changing a social system that makes prostitution possible.

PROBLEM

14.3 A recent article in the New York Times reported the widespread use of sex slaves in cities throughout the United States.[32] Many are in their early teens or even younger and are brought into the United States against their will from other countries through extensive underground criminal networks. They earn no money and are often threatened with beatings or death if they try to escape. Kevin Bales, president of "Free the Slaves," an anti-slavery organization, estimates "that there are 30,000 to 50,000 sex slaves in captivity in the United States at any given time."[33] Does the existence of such sex slavery strengthen or weaken the rationale for making prostitution a crime? If prostitution were not a crime, would it be easier for police to enforce minimum age restrictions on prostitution? Would it be easier for police to control violence against prostitutes?

PEOPLE v. JAMES

98 Misc. 2d 755, 415 N.Y.S.2d 342 (1979)

GARTENSTEIN, J. The on-again off-again debate over prostitution and its impact on the criminal justice system returns for reconsideration in the light of a new statute and response thereto by the office of the District Attorney.

Prior to September 1, 1978, the moral sanction of society with regard to sex offenders as expressed in the Penal Law was discriminatory. A woman engaged in prostitution was guilty of a class B misdemeanor (Penal Law, § 230.00) while her male patron was guilty only of a violation (§ 230.03). Under the amended statute, the patron or so-called "John" is now also guilty of a class B misdemeanor. Because prostitution has traditionally been a blight upon important commercial and tourist areas, a problem unique to New York County, the People have steadfastly refused to plea bargain, insisting instead on a plea to the top charge. The one notable

---

32. Peter Landesman, *The Girls Next Door*, New York Times Magazine, Jan. 25, 2004, at 30.
33. *Id.* at 32.

exception to this policy, the first-offender prostitute, was traditionally offered an adjournment in contemplation of dismissal in the hope that her experience would have the beneficial effect of deterring her from further similar acts.

With the advent of the new statute raising the level of culpability of the patron, the District Attorney matched his policy of insisting on a plea to the charge by the prostitute with similar insistence as to the "John." As a corollary, a determination was made not to offer adjournments in contemplation of dismissal to the first-offender patron. This in turn in the name of equality of enforcement against each sex, triggered a reversal of the traditional policy of adjournments in contemplation of dismissal for first-offender prostitutes. Thus, escalated enforcement against the "John" to avoid discriminatory enforcement against the prostitute has now resulted in escalated prosecution of the prostitute in a manner impacting more harshly upon her than upon the patron. This result is occasioned by the fact that a prostitute who is no longer offered a second chance via an adjournment in contemplation of dismissal has infinitely more to lose by being sent out on the streets to earn her fine by selling her body again than the patron who is usually more affluent, often a substantial businessman away from home who can pay his fine and forget about the experience.

In the separate dockets before us, each defendant is a young woman charged with prostitution who has been arrested for the first time. Audrey James is 21 years old presently attending the American Business Institute majoring in business administration. She was the recipient of a basic educational opportunity grant and is an active member of the institute's student liaison group dealing with student problems. Laverne McCray is 23 years old, attending business school and resides with her parents in Queens County. She has returned to school in an effort to better herself after some years away from any academic pursuits. Each defendant has moved for dismissal in the interests of justice pursuant to CPL 170.30 and 170.40. These motions have been vigorously opposed by the District Attorney who argues that this relief is being sought in an effort to overrule the People's determination not to adjourn in contemplation of dismissal.

Under CPL 170.40 and 210.40 (subd 1) a court may dismiss an accusatory instrument where: "[Such] dismissal is required as a matter of judicial discretion by the existence of some *compelling* factor, consideration or circumstance *clearly* demonstrating that conviction or prosecution of the defendant upon such accusatory instrument or count would constitute or result in injustice." (emphasis supplied.). . . .

[The Appellate Division has listed] those factors which a court must consider in deciding a motion under this section. These are: (a) The nature of the crime; (b) Available evidence of guilt; (c) Prior record of defendant; (d) Punishment already suffered; (e) Purpose and effect of further punishment; (f) Prejudice resulting to defendant by passage of time; (g) Impact on public interest of dismissal. . . .

(a) The nature of the crime: Prostitution is a victimless crime in which two equal contracting parties negotiate for the performance of an act proscribed by law, usually performed in private by consenting adults. The failure of law enforcement officials to stem its tide is now being recognized to an extent where the latest thinking supports the establishment of specially zoned areas in which same would be permitted. Experience with its proliferation may be compared to prohibition, involving an act prohibited by law which morality of the marketplace failed to recognize as particularly heinous and concerning which the almost universal disregard of its illegality ultimately resulted in repeal to the jubilation of millions

and relief of law enforcement personnel. An object lesson that morality cannot
be legislated might properly be coupled with a realization that the real victim of
prostitution is the prostitute herself and the real criminal, her pimp, who keeps her
virtually enslaved by threats of cutting her up and by fostering ignorance of the
fact that she can make it in life without him. Our system of law enforcement has as
yet found no effective way of bringing these pimps to justice. Might it not be more
productive to focus society's efforts on the parasite rather than the host?

(b) *Available evidence of guilt:*   No comment is made on this factor; we
presume arguendo a provable case.

(c) *Prior record of defendant:*   Neither defendant has ever been arrested or
convicted of this or any other crime.

(d) *Punishment already suffered:*   Each of these defendants has been arrested
and spent at least some time incarcerated awaiting arraignment. The court considers this enough punishment . . . . We feel it in order, however, to comment that in
assessing punishment already suffered by each defendant, we refuse to pontificate
that she lacks sensitivity sufficient to perceive that this act with which she is charged
is self-destructive and degrading to her. To refuse each defendant the dignity of
recognizing that the act itself — or rather, the need to resort to it — is punishment
in a measure no court could exact, is to strip away her humanity and categorize
her with legally fungible goods. We have yet to reach that state of sophistication in
which we might be capable of this.

(e) *Purpose and effect of further punishment:*   Traditionally, prostitution has
been punished by assessment of a fine with alternative jail time for nonpayment.
If a prostitute is beholden to a pimp, his supplying funds to this fine will further obligate her to him by the rules of the jungle in which they function. If she
works alone, the net effect of this punishment is to send her back to the streets
to earn these funds by again selling her body. In recognizing this fact, we simply
give effect to the very same reasoning utilized by the District Attorney in adjourn-
ing first arrest prostitution cases in contemplation of dismissal prior to the new
statute. We fail to comprehend the District Attorney's argument that in drawing
the line precisely where he himself had previously chosen to draw it, we are abusing
our discretion. Understandably a line must be drawn somewhere. This reasoning,
like all arguments, can be applied reductio ad absurdum to every arrest to support a contention that we should not send a prostitute out for the 50th time to
pay the fine for her 49th arrest. That line has traditionally been drawn at the first
offense. We see no reason to depart from it. The concept of one permissible mistake is built into almost every phase of the criminal law. That we are disappointed
more often than not should be no deterrent to efforts to save the single individual
before us.

(f) *Prejudice to defendant by passage of time:*   This factor is irrelevant in this
context and not considered here.

(g) *Impact on public interest of dismissal:*   Whatever function one assigns to
our system of justice on a philosophical basis, there can be no argument that protection of the public interest ranks among society's priorities. In dollar-for-dollar terms
"[the] criminal justice system in New York City is big business. It costs over a billion

dollars a year to run; over $879 million for police; $120 million for corrections; $114 million for courts and judges; $37 million for District Attorneys; $19 million for probation; and $19 million for legal aid." Presumably, an expenditure of taxpayer dollars of such magnitude should generate the maximum in dollar-for-dollar efficiency. Nevertheless, "Among the areas where less use of valuable criminal justice resources seems clearly indicated are the arrest and prosecution of petty gamblers and prostitutes. These two areas of criminal prosecution are plainly anachronistic in today's social climate. Both account for a substantial volume of the arrests which presently utilize significant police resources (particularly in New York County) without any perceptible benefits." (Discussion Paper No. 5.) In statistical terms, "Prosecuting gambling and prostitution cases costs the city another $9 million per year. Those anachronisms of modern penology, revolving-door criminal prosecution of streetwalkers and bookmakers, which are concededly ineffective, run up a substantial annual cost to the city taxpayers while helping to clog the court system. The study reveals that it costs between $239.31 and $898.28 to process a prostitution arrest through the Criminal Court and between $239.31 and $789.21 to process a gambling case. The average cost for processing a prostitution case through the courts is $505.11; for processing a gambling case it is $625.78. Applying weighted time-cost study figures to the city-wide dispositions of weighted 1977 Criminal Court cases produces these total cost figures:

Prostitution (14,098)	$7,121,040
Gambling (2,842)	1,778,466
	$8,899,506

. . . [C]ompared to the average cost of a prostitution case of $505.11, the average kidnapping case costs $464.37; the average robbery $470.49. At a time of public outcry about the inability of our system of justice to deal effectively with violent crime, we are still wasting valuable court time and taxpayer funds on a victimless crime, the existence of which as a fact of human nature was recognized without particular disapproval as far back as Genesis 38:15. This in face of the fact that, "The Criminal Court of the City of New York staggers under an enormous caseload. Virtually every arrest made in the city must pass through the Criminal Court's doors — 235,761 case filings during 1977. An average of almost 650 cases a day, Sundays and holidays included."

We conclude that the public interest is not served by intransigence on an issue whose irrelevance to the real problem of violent crime is recognized almost universally. "A court must intervene boldly when unfairness . . . surfaces in a particular case. The purpose of CPL 210.40 [and 170.40] is to interpose the court between the prosecution and the accused in an appropriate case. . . . An independent judiciary must never fear the risk of retribution or the dismay of traditionalists when it makes a decision or issues an opinion that it believes is right." Ultimately an application in the interests of justice represents an appeal to one Judge's individual conscience. We cannot find it within ourselves to reject our own moral belief that ultimate protection of society is best achieved where at all possible by total rehabilitation of the one human being standing before us whose very presence calls out that he or she is human, unique and worth at least some effort — and faith — on our part.

Motions granted. Proceedings dismissed in the interests of justice.

QUESTIONS

1. How should criminal law treat the "patrons" or "johns" who pay prostitutes for sex? Should the treatment of patrons be equal to the criminal law's treatment of prostitutes? Or should one receive harsher punishment than the other? Should only those who pay for rather than sell sex be deemed criminals? In answering this question, refer back to Problem 2.7 about the punishment of drug sellers and drug buyers in Section C of Chapter 2.

2. If the criminal law should treat patrons and prostitutes equally, how should that be accomplished? By eliminating criminal punishment for each? Or by punishing both equally? What sorts of punishment would have equal impact on patrons and prostitutes? Incarceration? Fines? Shaming penalties such as those discussed in Chapter 2?

3. Is prostitution a "victimless" crime? Who might be seen as the victim?

4. Are the patron and the prostitute "two equal contracting parties," as described by Judge Gartenstein?

5. Is it proper for a judge based on her "individual conscience" and "moral belief" to dismiss a case the district attorney has chosen to prosecute and that falls under a statute the legislature has enacted?

Sylvia A. Law, COMMERCIAL SEX: BEYOND DECRIMINALIZATION

73 S. Cal. L. Rev. 523, 532-535, 540-542 (2000)

In the past quarter century, feminists have been the most influential voices in debates about commercial sex. Feminist analysis and action have had a dramatic impact on common cultural understandings, the law and social life. Two issues are central to feminist theory and action: work and sexuality. The legal and social treatment of the exchange of sex for money lies squarely at the intersection of core feminist concerns with work and sexuality. Feminists are divided on factual questions about the situation of women who trade sex for money, and on matters of vision and principle. Despite these disagreements, all feminists agree on three points. First, they condemn the current legal policy enforcing criminal sanctions against women who offer sex in exchange for money. Second, they agree that authentic consent is the sine qua non of legitimate sex, whether in commercial or non-commercial form. Third, all feminists recognize that commercial sex workers are subject to economic coercion and are often victims of violence, and that too little is done to address these problems. . . .

Still there are substantial disagreements among feminists. As a matter of principle, some feminists see commercial sex as inconsistent with a vision of a just society and inherently damaging to women, while others see commercial sex as a legitimate choice for some women in some circumstances. Feminists also disagree about facts. "We know very little about the reality of the lives of prostitutes. Whether prostitutes are more often sexual slaves than liberated women is not just a matter of perception, but depends on the facts of their daily existence." In the absence of hard data, people rely on personal stories that carry divergent messages. The experience of people who trade sex for money is diverse and highly contested.

For example, feminists who believe that commercial sex is never a legitimate choice assert that "fourteen is the average age of a woman's entry into prostitution."

The evidence offered does not support this claim; most women begin such work as adults. Some feminists look at these "facts" and conclude that no woman could ever authentically consent to engage in commercial sex, unless coerced by male supremacy or desperate economic need. Others, while recognizing the compelling necessity for better economic opportunities for women, and more effective protection against violence, assert that commercial sex is sometimes an authentic choice. COYOTE, "the most visible organization in the contemporary campaign for prostitutes' rights," asserts that "most women who work as prostitutes have made a conscious decision to do so, having looked at a number of work alternatives. . . . Only 15 percent of prostitutes are coerced by third parties." . . .

[Some feminists] see the freedom to explore sexuality and to recognize women as sexual agents as a central tenant and energizing, organizing principle of the women's liberation movement of the late twentieth century. Personal, communal and political efforts to understand and affirm women's sexuality have transformed understandings of homosexuality and heterosexuality. Since the 1970s, feminists, and millions of women who do not self-identify as feminists, have explored whether to seek traditional female values of commitment, monogamy, and marriage, or to try a traditional male norm of sexuality that embraces adventure, anonymity, diversity and a separation of sex from commitment; never before have women been so uppity or the meaning of gender been so challenged. . . .

Thus feminists agree that it does not make sense to define the women who sell sex as criminals; there is an urgent need to provide more effective remedies to protect women who sell sex from violence, rape and coercion; and authentic consent is key. Nonetheless there are real differences among feminists. Some favor vigorous prosecution of customers and other people who share the earnings of commercial sex workers while others oppose such laws. The dispute is empirical. What strategies are most likely to be effective in protecting women from violence and coercion? . . . More fundamentally, feminists disagree about whether a woman can ever authentically consent to commercial sex, and whether it would exist in a just society.

Martha Chamallas, CONSENT, EQUALITY, AND THE LEGAL CONTROL OF SEXUAL CONDUCT
61 S. Cal. L. Rev. 777, 827-829 (1988)

Prostitution remains a difficult issue in the law of sex for three reasons.

First, we know very little about the reality of the lives of prostitutes. Whether prostitutes are more often sexual slaves than liberated women is not just a matter of perception, but depends on the facts of their daily existence. If prostitutes are routinely beaten up, forced to give up most of their earnings to pimps, and likely to die young, it would be incorrect to categorize prostitution as a truly voluntary or consensual activity. However, this depressing portrait of the prostitute still competes with a far more favorable image. The competing image is that of a sexually uninhibited woman who has made a rational decision to sell sexual services, given her restricted options for other high paying work. Until we are able to discount the latter image as unrepresentative, there will be disagreement as to whether prostitution represents economic coercion or economic bargaining.

Second, the economic coercion present in prostitution appears to be of a different sort than that found in the paradigm sexual harassment case. Prostitutes are often subject to varying types of economic pressure. For example, pimps and other "protectors" may force prostitutes to pay them off from their earnings. This kind of economic exploitation is on an individual level and is readily accepted as coercion, primarily because we assume that pimps stand ready to back up their demand with physical force. But when the focus is directly on the sexual encounter between the customer and the prostitute herself, there likely exists no such individualized coercion. Instead, the economic pressure inherent in the transaction derives from social forces, rather than from any choice put to the prostitute by her individual customers. It is the prostitute's social predicament rather than the actions of the particular customer that may be characterized as coercive. Pressure at such a macro level is far less likely to be viewed as coercion in our individualistic legal system. Particularly in sexual matters, the law tends to regard an act as voluntary so long as it is not constrained by the will of another identifiable individual.

Third, it is difficult to classify a sexual encounter as coerced when the party who initiates the encounter is also the party subjected to economic pressure. In the search for a refurbished concept of consent that takes into account the needs and desires of women, it is risky to ignore the fact that it is the woman herself who proposed the encounter. Ordinarily we presume that persons who initiate sexual encounters consent to those transactions. Until we have a clearer definition of what constitutes exploitation in sexual encounters, it is difficult to override such presumption in any but the most extreme cases.

For these three reasons, prostitution is a particularly difficult problem for feminists trying to create an egalitarian model of sexual conduct; it poses the basic question of whether sex traded for money must always be viewed as exploitation.

F. SYNTHESIS AND REVIEW

1. Should the criminal law enforce morality? This question is the focal point of a classic debate. Some argue that "[s]ociety cannot ignore the morality of the individual any more than it can his loyalty; it flourishes on both and without either it dies."[34] From this viewpoint, the majority should be able to use the criminal law "to set parameters for the moral climate in which they wish to live."[35] Others take the position that society may use the criminal sanction to restrict individual conduct only "to prevent harm to others. His own good, either physical or moral, is not a sufficient warrant."[36] With which position do you agree? Do you resolve the question on grounds of principle or for pragmatic reasons? What constitutes "harm" to others? Physical harm? Offense to one's moral sensibilities? Harm to one's "moral environment?" Undermining social institutions such as marriage?

2. If criminal law may be used to enforce morality, what limits, if any, should be placed on such use of criminal law? Is it appropriate for criminal law to punish any of the following if engaged in privately by consenting adults?

(a) fornication
(b) polygamy

---

34. Patrick Devlin, *The Enforcement of Morals* 22 (1965).
35. Cal Thomas, *Rewriting of Constitution Opens Door to Depravity*, Baltimore Sun, July 2, 2003, at 13A.
36. John Stuart Mill, *On Liberty* 15 (1859).

(c) incest

(d) sadomasochistic sex

3. Justice Scalia noted in a portion of his *Lawrence* dissent not included in the earlier excerpt that execution was at one time imposed for violating the ban on sodomy. John Lawrence, in contrast, received a $200 fine. If criminal law may be used to enforce morality, what punishments are appropriate?

MODEL PENAL CODE EXCERPTS*

ARTICLE 1. PRELIMINARY

Section 1.02. *Purposes; Principles of Construction.*

(1) The general purposes of the provisions governing the definition of offenses are:

(a) to forbid and prevent conduct that unjustifiably and inexcusably inflicts or threatens substantial harm to individual or public interests;

(b) to subject to public control persons whose conduct indicates that they are disposed to commit crimes;

(c) to safeguard conduct that is without fault from condemnation as criminal;

(d) to give fair warning of the nature of the conduct declared to constitute an offense;

(e) to differentiate on reasonable grounds between serious and minor offenses.

(2) The general purposes of the provisions governing the sentencing and treatment of offenders are:

(a) to prevent the commission of offenses;

(b) to promote the correction and rehabilitation of offenders;

(c) to safeguard offenders against excessive, disproportionate or arbitrary punishment;

(d) to give fair warning of the nature of the sentences that may be imposed on conviction of an offense;

(e) to differentiate among offenders with a view to a just individualization in their treatment;

(f) to define, coordinate and harmonize the powers, duties and functions of the courts and of administrative officers and agencies responsible for dealing with offenders;

(g) to advance the use of generally accepted scientific methods and knowledge in the sentencing and treatment of offenders;

(h) to integrate responsibility for the administration of the correctional system in a State Department of Correction [or other single department or agency].

(3) The provisions of the Code shall be construed according to the fair import of their terms but when the language is susceptible of differing constructions it shall be interpreted to further the general purposes stated in this Section and the special purposes of the particular provision involved. The discretionary powers conferred by the Code shall be exercised in accordance with the criteria stated in the Code and, insofar as such criteria are not decisive, to further the general purposes stated in this Section. . . .

Section 1.07. *Method of Prosecution When Conduct Constitutes More Than One Offense.*

(1) *Prosecution for Multiple Offenses; Limitation on Convictions.* When the same conduct of a defendant may establish the commission of more than one offense, the defendant may be prosecuted for each such offense. He may not, however, be convicted of more than one offense if:

(a) one offense is included in the other, as defined in Subsection (4) of this Section; or

(b) one offense consists only of a conspiracy or other form of preparation to commit the other; or

(c) inconsistent findings of fact are required to establish the commission of the offenses; or

(d) the offenses differ only in that one is defined to prohibit a designated kind of conduct generally and the other to prohibit a specific instance of such conduct; or

(e) the offense is defined as a continuing course of conduct and the defendant's course of conduct was uninterrupted, unless the law provides that specific periods of such conduct constitute separate offenses. . . .

Section 1.12. *Proof Beyond a Reasonable Doubt; Affirmative Defenses; Burden of Proving Fact When Not an Element of an Offense; Presumptions.*

(1) No person may be convicted of an offense unless each element of such offense is proved beyond a reasonable doubt. In the absence of such proof, the innocence of the defendant is assumed. . . .

(5) When the Code establishes a presumption with respect to any fact that is an element of an offense, it has the following consequences:

(a) when there is evidence of the facts that give rise to the presumption, the issue of the existence of the presumed fact must be submitted to the jury, unless the Court is satisfied that the evidence as a whole clearly negatives the presumed fact; and

(b) when the issue of the existence of the presumed fact is submitted to the jury, the Court shall charge that while the presumed fact must, on all the evidence, be proved beyond a reasonable doubt, the law declares that the jury may regard the facts giving rise to the presumption as sufficient evidence of the presumed fact. . . .

Section 1.13.   *General Definitions.*

In this Code, unless a different meaning plainly is required:

(1) "statute" includes the Constitution and a local law or ordinance of a political subdivision of the State;

(2) "act" or "action" means a bodily movement whether voluntary or involuntary;

(3) "voluntary" has the meaning specified in Section 2.01;

(4) "omission" means a failure to act;

(5) "conduct" means an action or omission and its accompanying state of mind, or, where relevant, a series of acts and omissions;

(6) "actor" includes, where relevant, a person guilty of an omission;

(7) "acted" includes, where relevant, "omitted to act";

(8) "person," "he" and "actor" include any natural person and, where relevant, a corporation or an unincorporated association;

(9) "element of an offense" means (i) such conduct or (ii) such attendant circumstances or (iii) such a result of conduct as

(a) is included in the description of the forbidden conduct in the definition of the offense; or

(b) establishes the required kind of culpability; or

(c) negatives an excuse or justification for such conduct; or

(d) negatives a defense under the statute of limitations; or

(e) establishes jurisdiction or venue;

(10) "material element of an offense" means an element that does not relate exclusively to the statute of limitations, jurisdiction, venue, or to any other matter similarly unconnected with (i) the harm or evil, incident to conduct, sought to be prevented by the law defining the offense, or (ii) the existence of a justification or excuse for such conduct;

(11) "purposely" has the meaning specified in Section 2.02 and equivalent terms such as "with purpose," "designed" or "with design" have the same meaning;

(12) "intentionally" or "with intent" means purposely;

(13) "knowingly" has the meaning specified in Section 2.02 and equivalent terms such as "knowing" or "with knowledge" have the same meaning;

(14) "recklessly" has the meaning specified in Section 2.02 and equivalent terms such as "recklessness" or "with recklessness" have the same meaning;

(15) "negligently" has the meaning specified in Section 2.02 and equivalent terms such as "negligence" or "with negligence" have the same meaning;

(16) "reasonably believes" or "reasonable belief" designates a belief that the actor is not reckless or negligent in holding.

ARTICLE 2. GENERAL PRINCIPLES OF LIABILITY

Section 2.01.   *Requirement of Voluntary Act; Omission as Basis of Liability; Possession as an Act.*

(1) A person is not guilty of an offense unless his liability is based on conduct that includes a voluntary act or the omission to perform an act of which he is physically capable.

(2) The following are not voluntary acts within the meaning of this Section:

(a) a reflex or convulsion;

(b) a bodily movement during unconsciousness or sleep;

(c) conduct during hypnosis or resulting from hypnotic suggestion;

(d) a bodily movement that otherwise is not a product of the effort or determination of the actor, either conscious or habitual.

(3) Liability for the commission of an offense may not be based on an omission unaccompanied by action unless:

(a) the omission is expressly made sufficient by the law defining the offense; or

(b) a duty to perform the omitted act is otherwise imposed by law.

(4) Possession is an act, within the meaning of this Section, if the possessor knowingly procured or received the thing possessed or was aware of his control thereof for a sufficient period to have been able to terminate his possession.

Section 2.02. *General Requirements of Culpability.*

(1) *Minimum Requirements of Culpability.* Except as provided in Section 2.05, a person is not guilty of an offense unless he acted purposely, knowingly, recklessly or negligently, as the law may require, with respect to each material element of the offense.

(2) *Kinds of Culpability Defined.*

(a) *Purposely.*

A person acts purposely with respect to a material element of an offense when:

(i) if the element involves the nature of his conduct or a result thereof, it is his conscious object to engage in conduct of that nature or to cause such a result; and

(ii) if the element involves the attendant circumstances, he is aware of the existence of such circumstances or he believes or hopes that they exist.

(b) *Knowingly.*

A person acts knowingly with respect to a material element of an offense when:

(i) if the element involves the nature of his conduct or the attendant circumstances, he is aware that his conduct is of that nature or that such circumstances exist; and

(ii) if the element involves a result of his conduct, he is aware that it is practically certain that his conduct will cause such a result.

(c) *Recklessly.*

A person acts recklessly with respect to a material element of an offense when he consciously disregards a substantial and unjustifiable risk that the material element exists or will result from his conduct. The risk must be of such a nature and degree that, considering the nature and purpose of the actor's conduct and the circumstances known to him, its disregard involves a gross deviation from the standard of conduct that a law-abiding person would observe in the actor's situation.

(d) *Negligently.*

A person acts negligently with respect to a material element of an offense when he should be aware of a substantial and unjustifiable risk that the material element exists or will result from his conduct. The risk must be of such a nature and degree that the actor's failure to perceive it, considering the nature and purpose of his conduct and the circumstances known to him, involves a gross deviation from the standard of care that a reasonable person would observe in the actor's situation.

(3) *Culpability Required Unless Otherwise Provided.* When the culpability sufficient to establish a material element of an offense is not prescribed by law, such element is established if a person acts purposely, knowingly or recklessly with respect thereto.

(4) *Prescribed Culpability Requirement Applies to All Material Elements.* When the law defining an offense prescribes the kind of culpability that is sufficient for the commission of an offense, without distinguishing among the material elements thereof, such provision shall apply to all the material elements of the offense, unless a contrary purpose plainly appears.

(5) *Substitutes for Negligence, Recklessness and Knowledge.* When the law provides that negligence suffices to establish an element of an offense, such element also is established if a person acts purposely, knowingly or recklessly. When recklessness suffices to establish an element, such element also is established if a person acts purposely or knowingly. When acting knowingly suffices to establish an element, such element also is established if a person acts purposely.

(6) *Requirement of Purpose Satisfied if Purpose Is Conditional.* When a particular purpose is an element of an offense, the element is established although such purpose is conditional, unless the condition negatives the harm or evil sought to be prevented by the law defining the offense.

(7) *Requirement of Knowledge Satisfied by Knowledge of High Probability.* When knowledge of the existence of a particular fact is an element of an offense, such knowledge is established if a person is aware of a high probability of its existence, unless he actually believes that it does not exist.

(8) *Requirement of Wilfulness Satisfied by Acting Knowingly.* A requirement that an offense be committed wilfully is satisfied if a person acts knowingly with respect to the material elements of the offense, unless a purpose to impose further requirements appears.

(9) *Culpability as to Illegality of Conduct.* Neither knowledge nor recklessness or negligence as to whether conduct constitutes an offense or as to the existence, meaning or application of the law determining the elements of an offense is an element of such offense, unless the definition of the offense or the Code so provides.

(10) *Culpability as Determinant of Grade of Offense.* When the grade or degree of an offense depends on whether the offense is committed purposely, knowingly, recklessly or negligently, its grade or degree shall be the lowest for which the determinative kind of culpability is established with respect to any material element of the offense.

Section 2.03.   *Causal Relationship Between Conduct and Result; Divergence Between Result Designed or Contemplated and Actual Result or Between Probable and Actual Result.*

(1) Conduct is the cause of a result when:

(a) it is an antecedent but for which the result in question would not have occurred; and

(b) the relationship between the conduct and result satisfies any additional causal requirements imposed by the Code or by the law defining the offense.

(2) When purposely or knowingly causing a particular result is an element of an offense, the element is not established if the actual result is not within the purpose or the contemplation of the actor unless:

(a) the actual result differs from that designed or contemplated, as the case may be, only in the respect that a different person or different property is injured or affected or that the injury or harm designed or contemplated would have been more serious or more extensive than that caused; or

(b) the actual result involves the same kind of injury or harm as that designed or contemplated and is not too remote or accidental in its occurrence to have a [just] bearing on the actor's liability or on the gravity of his offense.

(3) When recklessly or negligently causing a particular result is an element of an offense, the element is not established if the actual result is not within the risk of which the actor is aware or, in the case of negligence, of which he should be aware unless:

(a) the actual result differs from the probable result only in the respect that a different person or different property is injured or affected or that the probable injury or harm would have been more serious or more extensive than that caused; or

(b) the actual result involves the same kind of injury or harm as the probable result and is not too remote or accidental in its occurrence to have a [just] bearing on the actor's liability or on the gravity of his offense.

(4) When causing a particular result is a material element of an offense for which absolute liability is imposed by law, the element is not established unless the actual result is a probable consequence of the actor's conduct.

Section 2.04.   *Ignorance or Mistake.*

(1) Ignorance or mistake as to a matter of fact or law is a defense if:

(a) the ignorance or mistake negatives the purpose, knowledge, belief, recklessness or negligence required to establish a material element of the offense; or

(b) the law provides that the state of mind established by such ignorance or mistake constitutes a defense.

(2) Although ignorance or mistake would otherwise afford a defense to the offense charged, the defense is not available if the defendant would be guilty of another offense had the situation been as he supposed. In such case, however, the ignorance or mistake of the defendant shall reduce the grade and degree of the offense of which he may be convicted to those of the offense of which he would be guilty had the situation been as he supposed.

(3) A belief that conduct does not legally constitute an offense is a defense to a prosecution for that offense based upon such conduct when:

(a) the statute or other enactment defining the offense is not known to the actor and has not been published or otherwise reasonably made available prior to the conduct alleged; or

(b) he acts in reasonable reliance upon an official statement of the law, afterward determined to be invalid or erroneous, contained in (i) a statute or other enactment; (ii) a judicial decision, opinion or judgment; (iii) an administrative order or grant of permission; or (iv) an official interpretation of the public officer or body charged by law with responsibility for the interpretation, administration or enforcement of the law defining the offense.

(4) The defendant must prove a defense arising under Subsection (3) of this Section by a preponderance of evidence.

Section 2.05.   *When Culpability Requirements Are Inapplicable to Violations and to Offenses Defined by Other Statutes; Effect of Absolute Liability in Reducing Grade of Offense to Violation.*

(1) The requirements of culpability prescribed by Sections 2.01 and 2.02 do not apply to:

(a) offenses that constitute violations, unless the requirement involved is included in the definition of the offense or the Court determines that its application is consistent with effective enforcement of the law defining the offense; or

(b) offenses defined by statutes other than the Code, insofar as a legislative purpose to impose absolute liability for such offenses or with respect to any material element thereof plainly appears.

(2) Notwithstanding any other provision of existing law and unless a subsequent statute otherwise provides:

(a) when absolute liability is imposed with respect to any material element of an offense defined by a statute other than the Code and a conviction is based upon such liability, the offense constitutes a violation; and

(b) although absolute liability is imposed by law with respect to one or more of the material elements of an offense defined by a statute other than the Code, the culpable commission of the offense may be charged and proved, in which event negligence with respect to such elements constitutes sufficient culpability and the classification of the offense and the sentence that may be imposed therefor upon conviction are determined by Section 1.04 and Article 6 of the Code.

Section 2.06.   *Liability for Conduct of Another; Complicity.*

(1) A person is guilty of an offense if it is committed by his own conduct or by the conduct of another person for which he is legally accountable, or both.

(2) A person is legally accountable for the conduct of another person when:

(a) acting with the kind of culpability that is sufficient for the commission of the offense, he causes an innocent or irresponsible person to engage in such conduct; or

(b) he is made accountable for the conduct of such other person by the Code or by the law defining the offense; or

(c) he is an accomplice of such other person in the commission of the offense.

(3) A person is an accomplice of another person in the commission of an offense if:

(a) with the purpose of promoting or facilitating the commission of the offense, he

(i)   solicits such other person to commit it, or

(ii) aids or agrees or attempts to aid such other person in planning or committing it, or

(iii) having a legal duty to prevent the commission of the offense, fails to make proper effort so to do; or

(b) his conduct is expressly declared by law to establish his complicity.

(4) When causing a particular result is an element of an offense, an accomplice in the conduct causing such result is an accomplice in the commission of that offense

if he acts with the kind of culpability, if any, with respect to that result that is sufficient for the commission of the offense.

(5) A person who is legally incapable of committing a particular offense himself may be guilty thereof if it is committed by the conduct of another person for which he is legally accountable, unless such liability is inconsistent with the purpose of the provision establishing his incapacity.

(6) Unless otherwise provided by the Code or by the law defining the offense, a person is not an accomplice in an offense committed by another person if:

(a) he is a victim of that offense; or

(b) the offense is so defined that his conduct is inevitably incident to its commission; or

(c) he terminates his complicity prior to the commission of the offense and

(i) wholly deprives it of effectiveness in the commission of the offense; or

(ii) gives timely warning to the law enforcement authorities or otherwise makes proper effort to prevent the commission of the offense.

(7) An accomplice may be convicted on proof of the commission of the offense and of his complicity therein, though the person claimed to have committed the offense has not been prosecuted or convicted or has been convicted of a different offense or degree of offense or has an immunity to prosecution or conviction or has been acquitted.

Section 2.07.   *Liability of Corporations, Unincorporated Associations and Persons Acting, or Under a Duty to Act, in Their Behalf.*

(1) A corporation may be convicted of the commission of an offense if:

(a) the offense is a violation or the offense is defined by a statute other than the Code in which a legislative purpose to impose liability on corporations plainly appears and the conduct is performed by an agent of the corporation acting in behalf of the corporation within the scope of his office or employment, except that if the law defining the offense designates the agents for whose conduct the corporation is accountable or the circumstances under which it is accountable, such provisions shall apply; or

(b) the offense consists of an omission to discharge a specific duty of affirmative performance imposed on corporations by law; or

(c) the commission of the offense was authorized, requested, commanded, performed or recklessly tolerated by the board of directors or by a high managerial agent acting in behalf of the corporation within the scope of his office or employment.

(2) When absolute liability is imposed for the commission of an offense, a legislative purpose to impose liability on a corporation shall be assumed, unless the contrary plainly appears.

(3) An unincorporated association may be convicted of the commission of an offense if:

(a) the offense is defined by a statute other than the Code that expressly provides for the liability of such an association and the conduct is performed by an agent of the association acting in behalf of the association within the scope of his office or employment, except that if the law defining the offense designates the agents for whose conduct the association is accountable or the circumstances under which it is accountable, such provisions shall apply; or

(b) the offense consists of an omission to discharge a specific duty of affirmative performance imposed on associations by law.

(4) As used in this Section:

(a) "corporation" does not include an entity organized as or by a governmental agency for the execution of a governmental program;

(b) "agent" means any director, officer, servant, employee or other person authorized to act in behalf of the corporation or association and, in the case of an unincorporated association, a member of such association;

(c) "high managerial agent" means an officer of a corporation or an unincorporated association, or, in the case of a partnership, a partner, or any other agent of a corporation or association having duties of such responsibility that his conduct may fairly be assumed to represent the policy of the corporation or association.

(5) In any prosecution of a corporation or an unincorporated association for the commission of an offense included within the terms of Subsection (1)(a) or Subsection (3)(a) of this Section, other than an offense for which absolute liability has been imposed, it shall be a defense if the defendant proves by a preponderance of evidence that the high managerial agent having supervisory responsibility over the subject matter of the offense employed due diligence to prevent its commission. This paragraph shall not apply if it is plainly inconsistent with the legislative purpose in defining the particular offense.

(6) (a) A person is legally accountable for any conduct he performs or causes to be performed in the name of the corporation or an unincorporated association or in its behalf to the same extent as if it were performed in his own name or behalf.

(b) Whenever a duty to act is imposed by law upon a corporation or an unincorporated association, any agent of the corporation or association having primary responsibility for the discharge of the duty is legally accountable for a reckless omission to perform the required act to the same extent as if the duty were imposed by law directly upon himself.

(c) When a person is convicted of an offense by reason of his legal accountability for the conduct of a corporation or an unincorporated association, he is subject to the sentence authorized by law when a natural person is convicted of an offense of the grade and the degree involved.

Section 2.08.   *Intoxication.*

(1) Except as provided in Subsection (4) of this Section, intoxication of the actor is not a defense unless it negatives an element of the offense.

(2) When recklessness establishes an element of the offense, if the actor, due to self-induced intoxication, is unaware of a risk of which he would have been aware had he been sober, such unawareness is immaterial.

(3) Intoxication does not, in itself, constitute mental disease within the meaning of Section 4.01.

(4) Intoxication that (a) is not self-induced or (b) is pathological is an affirmative defense if by reason of such intoxication the actor at the time of his conduct lacks substantial capacity either to appreciate its criminality [wrongfulness] or to conform his conduct to the requirements of law.

(5) *Definitions.* In this Section unless a different meaning plainly is required:

(a) "intoxication" means a disturbance of mental or physical capacities resulting from the introduction of substances into the body;

(b) "self-induced intoxication" means intoxication caused by substances that the actor knowingly introduces into his body, the tendency of which to cause intoxication he knows or ought to know, unless he introduces them pursuant to medical advice or under such circumstances as would afford a defense to a charge of crime;

(c) "Pathological intoxication" means intoxication grossly excessive in degree, given the amount of the intoxicant, to which the actor does not know he is susceptible.

Section 2.09.   *Duress.*

(1) It is an affirmative defense that the actor engaged in the conduct charged to constitute an offense because he was coerced to do so by the use of, or a threat to use, unlawful force against his person or the person of another, that a person of reasonable firmness in his situation would have been unable to resist.

(2) The defense provided by this Section is unavailable if the actor recklessly placed himself in a situation in which it was probable that he would be subjected to duress. The defense is also unavailable if he was negligent in placing himself in such a situation, whenever negligence suffices to establish culpability for the offense charged.

(3) It is not a defense that a woman acted on the command of her husband, unless she acted under such coercion as would establish a defense under this Section. [The presumption that a woman acting in the presence of her husband is coerced is abolished.]

(4) When the conduct of the actor would otherwise be justifiable under Section 3.02, this Section does not preclude such defense.

Section 2.11.   *Consent.*

(1) *In General.* The consent of the victim to conduct charged to constitute an offense or to the result thereof is a defense if such consent negatives an element of the offense or precludes the infliction of the harm or evil sought to be prevented by the law defining the offense.

(2) *Consent to Bodily Injury.* When conduct is charged to constitute an offense because it causes or threatens bodily injury, consent to such conduct or to the infliction of such injury is a defense if:

(a) the bodily injury consented to or threatened by the conduct consented to is not serious; or

(b) the conduct and the injury are reasonably foreseeable hazards of joint participation in a lawful athletic contest or competitive sport or other concerted activity not forbidden by law; or

(c) the consent establishes a justification for the conduct under Article 3 of the Code.

(3) *Ineffective Consent.* Unless otherwise provided by the Code or by the law defining the offense, assent does not constitute consent if:

(a) it is given by a person who is legally incompetent to authorize the conduct charged to constitute the offense; or

(b) it is given by a person who by reason of youth, mental disease or defect or intoxication is manifestly unable or known by the actor to be unable to make a reasonable judgment as to the nature or harmfulness of the conduct charged to constitute the offense; or

(c) it is given by a person whose improvident consent is sought to be prevented by the law defining the offense; or

(d) it is induced by force, duress or deception of a kind sought to be prevented by the law defining the offense.

Section 2.12.   *De Minimis Infractions.*

The Court shall dismiss a prosecution if, having regard to the nature of the conduct charged to constitute an offense and the nature of the attendant circumstances, it finds that the defendant's conduct:

(1) was within a customary license or tolerance, neither expressly negatived by the person whose interest was infringed nor inconsistent with the purpose of the law defining the offense; or

(2) did not actually cause or threaten the harm or evil sought to be prevented by the law defining the offense or did so only to an extent too trivial to warrant the condemnation of conviction;

or

(3) presents such other extenuations that it cannot reasonably be regarded as envisaged by the legislature in forbidding the offense.

The Court shall not dismiss a prosecution under Subsection (3) of this Section without filing a written statement of its reasons.

Section 2.13.   *Entrapment.*

(1) A public law enforcement official or a person acting in cooperation with such an official perpetrates an entrapment if for the purpose of obtaining evidence of the commission of an offense, he induces or encourages another person to engage in conduct constituting such offense by either:

(a) making knowingly false representations designed to induce the belief that such conduct is not prohibited; or

(b) employing methods of persuasion or inducement that create a substantial risk that such an offense will be committed by persons other than those who are ready to commit it.

(2) Except as provided in Subsection (3) of this Section, a person prosecuted for an offense shall be acquitted if he proves by a preponderance of evidence that his conduct occurred in response to an entrapment. The issue of entrapment shall be tried by the Court in the absence of the jury.

(3) The defense afforded by this Section is unavailable when causing or threatening bodily injury is an element of the offense charged and the prosecution is based on conduct causing or threatening such injury to a person other than the person perpetrating the entrapment.

ARTICLE 3. GENERAL PRINCIPLES OF JUSTIFICATION

Section 3.01. *Justification an Affirmative Defense; Civil Remedies Unaffected.*

(1) In any prosecution based on conduct that is justifiable under this Article, justification is an affirmative defense.

(2) The fact that conduct is justifiable under this Article does not abolish or impair any remedy for such conduct that is available in any civil action.

Section 3.02. *Justification Generally: Choice of Evils.*

(1) Conduct that the actor believes to be necessary to avoid a harm or evil to himself or to another is justifiable, provided that:

(a) the harm or evil sought to be avoided by such conduct is greater than that sought to be prevented by the law defining the offense charged; and

(b) neither the Code nor other law defining the offense provides exceptions or defenses dealing with the specific situation involved; and

(c) a legislative purpose to exclude the justification claimed does not otherwise plainly appear.

(2) When the actor was reckless or negligent in bringing about the situation requiring a choice of harms or evils or in appraising the necessity for his conduct, the justification afforded by this Section is unavailable in a prosecution for any offense for which recklessness or negligence, as the case may be, suffices to establish culpability.

Section 3.03. *Execution of Public Duty.*

(1) Except as provided in Subsection (2) of this Section, conduct is justifiable when it is required or authorized by:

(a) the law defining the duties or functions of a public officer or the assistance to be rendered to such officer in the performance of his duties; or

(b) the law governing the execution of legal process; or

(c) the judgment or order of a competent court or tribunal; or

(d) the law governing the armed services or the lawful conduct of war; or

(e) any other provision of law imposing a public duty.

(2) The other sections of this Article apply to:

(a) the use of force upon or toward the person of another for any of the purposes dealt with in such sections; and

(b) the use of deadly force for any purpose, unless the use of such force is otherwise expressly authorized by law or occurs in the lawful conduct of war.

(3) The justification afforded by Subsection (1) of this Section applies:

(a) when the actor believes his conduct to be required or authorized by the judgment or direction of a competent court or tribunal or in the lawful execution of legal process, notwithstanding lack of jurisdiction of the court or defect in the legal process; and

(b) when the actor believes his conduct to be required or authorized to assist a public officer in the performance of his duties, notwithstanding that the officer exceeded his legal authority.

Section 3.04.   *Use of Force in Self-Protection.*

(1) *Use of Force Justifiable for Protection of the Person.* Subject to the provisions of this Section and of Section 3.09, the use of force upon or toward another person is justifiable when the actor believes that such force is immediately necessary for the purpose of protecting himself against the use of unlawful force by such other person on the present occasion.

(2) *Limitations on Justifying Necessity for Use of Force.*

(a) The use of force is not justifiable under this Section:

(i) to resist an arrest that the actor knows is being made by a peace officer, although the arrest is unlawful; or

(ii) to resist force used by the occupier or possessor of property or by another person on his behalf, where the actor knows that the person using the force is doing so under a claim of right to protect the property, except that this limitation shall not apply if:

(A) the actor is a public officer acting in the performance of his duties or a person lawfully assisting him therein or a person making or assisting in a lawful arrest; or

(B) the actor has been unlawfully dispossessed of the property and is making a re-entry or recaption justified by Section 3.06; or

(C) the actor believes that such force is necessary to protect himself against death or serious bodily injury.

(b) The use of deadly force is not justifiable under this Section unless the actor believes that such force is necessary to protect himself against death, serious bodily injury, kidnapping or sexual intercourse compelled by force or threat; nor is it justifiable if:

(i) the actor, with the purpose of causing death or serious bodily injury, provoked the use of force against himself in the same encounter; or

(ii) the actor knows that he can avoid the necessity of using such force with complete safety by retreating or by surrendering possession of a thing to a person asserting a claim of right thereto or by complying with a demand that he abstain from any action that he has no duty to take, except that:

(A) the actor is not obliged to retreat from his dwelling or place of work, unless he was the initial aggressor or is assailed in his place of work by another person whose place of work the actor knows it to be; and

(B) a public officer justified in using force in the performance of his duties or a person justified in using force in his assistance or a person justified in using force in making an arrest or preventing an escape is not obliged to desist from efforts to perform such duty, effect such arrest or prevent such escape because of resistance or threatened resistance by or on behalf of the person against whom such action is directed.

(c) Except as required by paragraphs (a) and (b) of this Subsection, a person employing protective force may estimate the necessity thereof under the circumstances as he believes them to be when the force is used, without retreating, surrendering possession, doing any other act that he has no legal duty to do or abstaining from any lawful action.

(3) *Use of Confinement as Protective Force.* The justification afforded by this Section extends to the use of confinement as protective force only if the actor takes

all reasonable measures to terminate the confinement as soon as he knows that he safely can, unless the person confined has been arrested on a charge of crime.

Section 3.05.   *Use of Force for the Protection of Other Persons.*

(1) Subject to the provisions of this Section and of Section 3.09, the use of force upon or toward the person of another is justifiable to protect a third person when:

(a) the actor would be justified under Section 3.04 in using such force to protect himself against the injury he believes to be threatened to the person whom he seeks to protect; and

(b) under the circumstances as the actor believes them to be, the person whom he seeks to protect would be justified in using such protective force; and

(c) the actor believes that his intervention is necessary for the protection of such other person.

(2) Notwithstanding Subsection (1) of this Section:

(a) when the actor would be obliged under Section 3.04 to retreat, to surrender the possession of a thing or to comply with a demand before using force in self-protection, he is not obliged to do so before using force for the protection of another person, unless he knows that he can thereby secure the complete safety of such other person; and

(b) when the person whom the actor seeks to protect would be obliged under Section 3.04 to retreat, to surrender the possession of a thing or to comply with a demand if he knew that he could obtain complete safety by so doing, the actor is obliged to try to cause him to do so before using force in his protection if the actor knows that he can obtain complete safety in that way; and

(c) neither the actor nor the person whom he seeks to protect is obliged to retreat when in the other's dwelling or place of work to any greater extent than in his own.

Section 3.06.   *Use of Force for Protection of Property.*

(1) *Use of Force Justifiable for Protection of Property.* Subject to the provisions of this Section and of Section 3.09, the use of force upon or toward the person of another is justifiable when the actor believes that such force is immediately necessary:

(a) to prevent or terminate an unlawful entry or other trespass upon land or a trespass against or the unlawful carrying away of tangible, movable property, provided that such land or movable property is, or is believed by the actor to be, in his possession or in the possession of another person for whose protection he acts; or

(b) to effect an entry or re-entry upon land or to retake tangible movable property, provided that the actor believes that he or the person by whose authority he acts or a person from whom he or such other person derives title was unlawfully dispossessed of such land or movable property and is entitled to possession, and provided, further, that:

(i) the force is used immediately or on fresh pursuit after such dispossession; or

(ii) the actor believes that the person against whom he uses force has no claim of right to the possession of the property and, in the case of land, the circumstances, as the actor believes them to be, are of such urgency that it would be an exceptional hardship to postpone the entry or re-entry until a court order is obtained.

(2) *Meaning of Possession.* For the purposes of Subsection (1) of this Section:

(a) a person who has parted with the custody of property to another who refuses to restore it to him is no longer in possession, unless the property is movable and was and still is located on land in his possession;

(b) a person who has been dispossessed of land does not regain possession thereof merely by setting foot thereon;

(c) a person who has a license to use or occupy real property is deemed to be in possession thereof except against the licensor acting under claim of right.

(3) *Limitations on Justifiable Use of Force.*

(a) *Request to Desist.* The use of force is justifiable under this Section only if the actor first requests the person against whom such force is used to desist from his interference with the property, unless the actor believes that:

(i) such request would be useless; or

(ii) it would be dangerous to himself or another person to make the request; or

(iii) substantial harm will be done to the physical condition of the property that is sought to be protected before the request can effectively be made.

(b) *Exclusion of Trespasser.* The use of force to prevent or terminate a trespass is not justifiable under this Section if the actor knows that the exclusion of the trespasser will expose him to substantial danger of serious bodily injury.

(c) *Resistance of Lawful Re-entry or Recaption.* The use of force to prevent an entry or re-entry upon land or the recaption of movable property is not justifiable under this Section, although the actor believes that such re-entry or recaption is unlawful, if:

(i) the re-entry or recaption is made by or on behalf of a person who was actually dispossessed of the property; and

(ii) it is otherwise justifiable under Subsection (1)(b) of this Section.

(d) *Use of Deadly Force.* The use of deadly force is not justifiable under this Section unless the actor believes that:

(i) the person against whom the force is used is attempting to dispossess him of his dwelling otherwise than under a claim of right to its possession; or

(ii) the person against whom the force is used is attempting to commit or consummate arson, burglary, robbery or other felonious theft or property destruction and either:

(A) has employed or threatened deadly force against or in the presence of the actor; or

(B) the use of force other than deadly force to prevent the commission or the consummation of the crime would expose the actor or another in his presence to substantial danger of serious bodily injury.

(4) *Use of Confinement as Protective Force.* The justification afforded by this Section extends to the use of confinement as protective force only if the actor takes all reasonable measures to terminate the confinement as soon as he knows that he can do so with safety to the property, unless the person confined has been arrested on a charge of crime.

(5) *Use of Device to Protect Property.* The justification afforded by this Section extends to the use of a device for the purpose of protecting property only if:

(a) the device is not designed to cause or known to create a substantial risk of causing death or serious bodily injury; and

(b) the use of the particular device to protect the property from entry or trespass is reasonable under the circumstances, as the actor believes them to be; and

(c) the device is one customarily used for such a purpose or reasonable care is taken to make known to probable intruders the fact that it is used.

(6) *Use of Force to Pass Wrongful Obstructor.* The use of force to pass a person whom the actor believes to be purposely or knowingly and unjustifiably obstructing the actor from going to a place to which he may lawfully go is justifiable, provided that:

(a) the actor believes that the person against whom he uses force has no claim of right to obstruct the actor; and

(b) the actor is not being obstructed from entry or movement on land that he knows to be in the possession or custody of the person obstructing him, or in the possession or custody of another person by whose authority the obstructor acts, unless the circumstances, as the actor believes them to be, are of such urgency that it would not be reasonable to postpone the entry or movement on such land until a court order is obtained; and

(c) the force used is not greater than would be justifiable if the person obstructing the actor were using force against him to prevent his passage.

Section 3.07.   *Use of Force in Law Enforcement.*

(1) *Use of Force Justifiable to Effect an Arrest.* Subject to the provisions of this Section and of Section 3.09, the use of force upon or toward the person of another is justifiable when the actor is making or assisting in making an arrest and the actor believes that such force is immediately necessary to effect a lawful arrest.

(2) *Limitations on the Use of Force.*

(a) The use of force is not justifiable under this Section unless:

(i) the actor makes known the purpose of the arrest or believes that it is otherwise known by or cannot reasonably be made known to the person to be arrested; and

(ii) when the arrest is made under a warrant, the warrant is valid or believed by the actor to be valid.

(b) The use of deadly force is not justifiable under this Section unless:

(i) the arrest is for a felony; and

(ii) the person effecting the arrest is authorized to act as a peace officer or is assisting a person whom he believes to be authorized to act as a peace officer; and

(iii) the actor believes that the force employed creates no substantial risk of injury to innocent persons; and

(iv) the actor believes that:

(A) the crime for which the arrest is made involved conduct including the use or threatened use of deadly force; or

(B) there is a substantial risk that the person to be arrested will cause death or serious bodily injury if his apprehension is delayed.

(3) *Use of Force to Prevent Escape from Custody.* The use of force to prevent the escape of an arrested person from custody is justifiable when the force could justifiably have been employed to effect the arrest under which the person is in custody, except

that a guard or other person authorized to act as a peace officer is justified in using any force, including deadly force, that he believes to be immediately necessary to prevent the escape of a person from a jail, prison, or other institution for the detention of persons charged with or convicted of a crime.

(4) *Use of Force by Private Person Assisting an Unlawful Arrest.*

(a) A private person who is summoned by a peace officer to assist in effecting an unlawful arrest, is justified in using any force that he would be justified in using if the arrest were lawful, provided that he does not believe the arrest is unlawful.

(b) A private person who assists another private person in effecting an unlawful arrest, or who, not being summoned, assists a peace officer in effecting an unlawful arrest, is justified in using any force that he would be justified in using if the arrest were lawful, provided that (i) he believes the arrest is lawful, and (ii) the arrest would be lawful if the facts were as he believes them to be.

(5) *Use of Force to Prevent Suicide or the Commission of a Crime.*

(a) The use of force upon or toward the person of another is justifiable when the actor believes that such force is immediately necessary to prevent such other person from committing suicide, inflicting serious bodily injury upon himself, committing or consummating the commission of a crime involving or threatening bodily injury, damage to or loss of property or a breach of the peace, except that:

(i) any limitations imposed by the other provisions of this Article on the justifiable use of force in self-protection, for the protection of others, the protection of property, the effectuation of an arrest or the prevention of an escape from custody shall apply notwithstanding the criminality of the conduct against which such force is used; and

(ii) the use of deadly force is not in any event justifiable under this Subsection unless:

(A) the actor believes that there is a substantial risk that the person whom he seeks to prevent from committing a crime will cause death or serious bodily injury to another unless the commission or the consummation of the crime is prevented and that the use of such force presents no substantial risk of injury to innocent persons; or

(B) the actor believes that the use of such force is necessary to suppress a riot or mutiny after the rioters or mutineers have been ordered to disperse and warned, in any particular manner that the law may require, that such force will be used if they do not obey.

(b) The justification afforded by this Subsection extends to the use of confinement as preventive force only if the actor takes all reasonable measures to terminate the confinement as soon as he knows that he safely can, unless the person confined has been arrested on a charge of crime. . . .

Section 3.09.   *Mistake of Law as to Unlawfulness of Force or Legality of Arrest; Reckless or Negligent Use of Otherwise Justifiable Force; Reckless or Negligent Injury or Risk of Injury to Innocent Persons.*

(1) The justification afforded by Sections 3.04 to 3.07, inclusive, is unavailable when:

(a) the actor's belief in the unlawfulness of the force or conduct against which he employs protective force or his belief in the lawfulness of an arrest that he endeavors to effect by force is erroneous; and

(b) his error is due to ignorance or mistake as to the provisions of the Code, any other provision of the criminal law or the law governing the legality of an arrest or search.

(2) When the actor believes that the use of force upon or toward the person of another is necessary for any of the purposes for which such belief would establish a justification under Sections 3.03 to 3.08 but the actor is reckless or negligent in having such belief or in acquiring or failing to acquire any knowledge or belief that is material to the justifiability of his use of force, the justification afforded by those Sections is unavailable in a prosecution for an offense for which recklessness or negligence, as the case may be, suffices to establish culpability.

(3) When the actor is justified under Sections 3.03 to 3.08 in using force upon or toward the person of another but he recklessly or negligently injures or creates a risk of injury to innocent persons, the justification afforded by those Sections is unavailable in a prosecution for such recklessness or negligence towards innocent persons. . . .

Section 3.11.   *Definitions.*

In this Article, unless a different meaning plainly is required:

(1) "unlawful force" means force, including confinement, that is employed without the consent of the person against whom it is directed and the employment of which constitutes an offense or actionable tort or would constitute such offense or tort except for a defense (such as the absence of intent, negligence, or mental capacity; duress; youth; or diplomatic status) not amounting to a privilege to use the force. Assent constitutes consent, within the meaning of this Section, whether or not it otherwise is legally effective, except assent to the infliction of death or serious bodily injury.

(2) "deadly force" means force that the actor uses with the purpose of causing or that he knows to create a substantial risk of causing death or serious bodily injury. Purposely firing a firearm in the direction of another person or at a vehicle in which another person is believed to be constitutes deadly force. A threat to cause death or serious bodily injury, by the production of a weapon or otherwise, so long as the actor's purpose is limited to creating an apprehension that he will use deadly force if necessary, does not constitute deadly force.

(3) "dwelling" means any building or structure, though movable or temporary, or a portion thereof, that is for the time being the actor's home or place of lodging.

ARTICLE 4. RESPONSIBILITY

Section 4.01.   *Mental Disease or Defect Excluding Responsibility.*

(1) A person is not responsible for criminal conduct if at the time of such conduct as a result of mental disease or defect he lacks substantial capacity either to appreciate the criminality [wrongfulness] of his conduct or to conform his conduct to the requirements of law.

(2) As used in this Article, the terms "mental disease or defect" do not include an abnormality manifested only by repeated criminal or otherwise antisocial conduct.

Section 4.02.   *Evidence of Mental Disease or Defect Admissible When Relevant to Element of the Offense[; Mental Disease or Defect Impairing Capacity as Ground for Mitigation of Punishment in Capital Cases].*

(1) Evidence that the defendant suffered from a mental disease or defect is admissible whenever it is relevant to prove that the defendant did or did not have a state of mind that is an element of the offense.

[(2) Whenever the jury or the Court is authorized to determine or to recommend whether or not the defendant shall be sentenced to death or imprisonment upon conviction, evidence that the capacity of the defendant to appreciate the criminality [wrongfulness] of his conduct or to conform his conduct to the requirements of law was impaired as a result of mental disease or defect is admissible in favor of sentence of imprisonment.]

Section 4.03.   *Mental Disease or Defect Excluding Responsibility Is Affirmative Defense; Requirement of Notice; Form of Verdict and Judgment When Finding of Irresponsibility Is Made.*

(1) Mental disease or defect excluding responsibility is an affirmative defense.

(2) Evidence of mental disease or defect excluding responsibility is not admissible unless the defendant, at the time of entering his plea of not guilty or within ten days thereafter or at such later time as the Court may for good cause permit, files a written notice of his purpose to rely on such defense.

(3) When the defendant is acquitted on the ground of mental disease or defect excluding responsibility, the verdict and the judgment shall so state.

Section 4.04.   *Mental Disease or Defect Excluding Fitness to Proceed.*

No person who as a result of mental disease or defect lacks capacity to understand the proceedings against him or to assist in his own defense shall be tried, convicted or sentenced for the commission of an offense so long as such incapacity endures.

Section 4.05.   *Psychiatric Examination of Defendant with Respect to Mental Disease or Defect.*

(1) Whenever the defendant has filed a notice of intention to rely on the defense of mental disease or defect excluding responsibility, or there is reason to doubt his fitness to proceed, or reason to believe that mental disease or defect of the defendant will otherwise become an issue in the cause, the Court shall appoint at least one qualified psychiatrist or shall request the Superintendent of the _____ Hospital to designate at least one qualified psychiatrist, which designation may be or include himself, to examine and report upon the mental condition of the defendant. The Court may order the defendant to be committed to a hospital or other suitable facility for the purpose of the examination for a period of not exceeding sixty days or such longer period as the Court determines to be necessary for the purpose and may direct that a qualified psychiatrist retained by the defendant be permitted to witness and participate in the examination. . . .

Section 4.08. *Legal Effect of Acquittal on the Ground of Mental Disease or Defect Excluding Responsibility; Commitment; Release or Discharge.*

(1) When a defendant is acquitted on the ground of mental disease or defect excluding responsibility, the Court shall order him to be committed to the custody of the Commissioner of Mental Hygiene [Public Health] to be placed in an appropriate institution for custody, care and treatment.

(2) If the Commissioner of Mental Hygiene [Public Health] is of the view that a person committed to his custody, pursuant to Subsection (1) of this Section, may be discharged or released on condition without danger to himself or to others, he shall make application for the discharge or release of such person in a report to the Court by which such person was committed and shall transmit a copy of such application and report to the prosecuting attorney of the county [parish] from which the defendant was committed. The Court shall thereupon appoint at least two qualified psychiatrists to examine such person and to report within sixty days, or such longer period as the Court determines to be necessary for the purpose, their opinion as to his mental condition. To facilitate such examination and the proceedings thereon, the Court may cause such person to be confined in any institution located near the place where the Court sits, which may hereafter be designated by the Commissioner of Mental Hygiene [Public Health] as suitable for the temporary detention of irresponsible persons.

(3) If the Court is satisfied by the report filed pursuant to Subsection (2) of this Section and such testimony of the reporting psychiatrists as the Court deems necessary that the committed person may be discharged or released on condition without danger to himself or others, the Court shall order his discharge or his release on such conditions as the Court determines to be necessary. If the Court is not so satisfied, it shall promptly order a hearing to determine whether such person may safely be discharged or released. Any such hearing shall be deemed a civil proceeding and the burden shall be upon the committed person to prove that he may safely be discharged or released. According to the determination of the Court upon the hearing, the committed person shall thereupon be discharged or released on such conditions as the Court determines to be necessary, or shall be recommitted to the custody of the Commissioner of Mental Hygiene [Public Health], subject to discharge or release only in accordance with the procedure prescribed above for a first hearing.

(4) If, within [five] years after the conditional release of a committed person, the Court shall determine, after hearing evidence, that the conditions of release have not been fulfilled and that for the safety of such person or for the safety of others his conditional release should be revoked, the Court shall forthwith order him to be recommitted to the Commissioner of Mental Hygiene [Public Health], subject to discharge or release only in accordance with the procedure prescribed above for a first hearing.

(5) A committed person may make application for his discharge or release to the Court by which he was committed, and the procedure to be followed upon such application shall be the same as that prescribed above in the case of an application by the Commissioner of Mental Hygiene [Public Health]. However, no such application by a committed person need be considered until he has been confined for a period of not less than [six months] from the date of the order of commitment, and if the determination of the Court be adverse to the application, such person shall not be permitted to file a further application until [one year] has elapsed from the date of any preceding hearing on an application for his release or discharge.

Section 4.10.   *Immaturity Excluding Criminal Conviction; Transfer of Proceedings to Juvenile Court.*

(1) A person shall not be tried for or convicted of an offense if:

(a) at the time of the conduct charged to constitute the offense he was less than sixteen years of age[, in which case the Juvenile Court shall have exclusive jurisdiction*]; or

(b) at the time of the conduct charged to constitute the offense he was sixteen or seventeen years of age, unless:

(i) the Juvenile Court has no jurisdiction over him, or

(ii) the Juvenile Court has entered an order waiving jurisdiction and consenting to the institution of criminal proceedings against him.

(2) No court shall have jurisdiction to try or convict a person of an offense if criminal proceedings against him are barred by Subsection (1) of this Section. When it appears that a person charged with the commission of an offense may be of such an age that criminal proceedings may be barred under Subsection (1) of this Section, the Court shall hold a hearing thereon, and the burden shall be on the prosecution to establish to the satisfaction of the Court that the criminal proceeding is not barred upon such grounds. If the Court determines that the proceeding is barred, custody of the person charged shall be surrendered to the Juvenile Court, and the case, including all papers and processes relating thereto, shall be transferred.

ARTICLE 5. INCHOATE CRIMES

Section 5.01.   *Criminal Attempt.*

(1) *Definition of Attempt.* A person is guilty of an attempt to commit a crime if, acting with the kind of culpability otherwise required for commission of the crime, he:

(a) purposely engages in conduct that would constitute the crime if the attendant circumstances were as he believes them to be; or

(b) when causing a particular result is an element of the crime, does or omits to do anything with the purpose of causing or with the belief that it will cause such result without further conduct on his part; or

(c) purposely does or omits to do anything that, under the circumstances as he believes them to be, is an act or omission constituting a substantial step in a course of conduct planned to culminate in his commission of the crime.

(2) *Conduct That May Be Held Substantial Step Under Subsection (1)(c).* Conduct shall not be held to constitute a substantial step under Subsection (1)(c) of this Section unless it is strongly corroborative of the actor's criminal purpose. Without negativing the sufficiency of other conduct, the following, if strongly corroborative of the actor's criminal purpose, shall not be held insufficient as a matter of law:

(a) lying in wait, searching for or following the contemplated victim of the crime;

(b) enticing or seeking to entice the contemplated victim of the crime to go to the place contemplated for its commission;

(c) reconnoitering the place contemplated for the commission of the crime;

---

* The bracketed words are unnecessary if the Juvenile Court Act so provides or is amended accordingly.

(d) unlawful entry of a structure, vehicle or enclosure in which it is contemplated that the crime will be committed;

(e) possession of materials to be employed in the commission of the crime, that are specially designed for such unlawful use or that can serve no lawful purpose of the actor under the circumstances;

(f) possession, collection or fabrication of materials to be employed in the commission of the crime, at or near the place contemplated for its commission, if such possession, collection or fabrication serves no lawful purpose of the actor under the circumstances;

(g) soliciting an innocent agent to engage in conduct constituting an element of the crime.

(3) *Conduct Designed to Aid Another in Commission of a Crime.* A person who engages in conduct designed to aid another to commit a crime that would establish his complicity under Section 2.06 if the crime were committed by such other person, is guilty of an attempt to commit the crime, although the crime is not committed or attempted by such other person.

(4) *Renunciation of Criminal Purpose.* When the actor's conduct would otherwise constitute an attempt under Subsection (1)(b) or (1)(c) of this Section, it is an affirmative defense that he abandoned his effort to commit the crime or otherwise prevented its commission, under circumstances manifesting a complete and voluntary renunciation of his criminal purpose. The establishment of such defense does not, however, affect the liability of an accomplice who did not join in such abandonment or prevention.

Within the meaning of this Article, renunciation of criminal purpose is not voluntary if it is motivated, in whole or in part, by circumstances, not present or apparent at the inception of the actor's course of conduct, that increase the probability of detection or apprehension or that make more difficult the accomplishment of the criminal purpose. Renunciation is not complete if it is motivated by a decision to postpone the criminal conduct until a more advantageous time or to transfer the criminal effort to another but similar objective or victim.

Section 5.02.   *Criminal Solicitation.*

(1) *Definition of Solicitation.* A person is guilty of solicitation to commit a crime if with the purpose of promoting or facilitating its commission he commands, encourages or requests another person to engage in specific conduct that would constitute such crime or an attempt to commit such crime or would establish his complicity in its commission or attempted commission.

(2) *Uncommunicated Solicitation.* It is immaterial under Subsection (1) of this Section that the actor fails to communicate with the person he solicits to commit a crime if his conduct was designed to effect such communication.

(3) *Renunciation of Criminal Purpose.* It is an affirmative defense that the actor, after soliciting another person to commit a crime, persuaded him not to do so or otherwise prevented the commission of the crime, under circumstances manifesting a complete and voluntary renunciation of his criminal purpose.

Section 5.03.   *Criminal Conspiracy.*

(1) *Definition of Conspiracy.* A person is guilty of conspiracy with another person or persons to commit a crime if with the purpose of promoting or facilitating its commission he:

(a) agrees with such other person or persons that they or one or more of them will engage in conduct that constitutes such crime or an attempt or solicitation to commit such crime; or

(b) agrees to aid such other person or persons in the planning or commission of such crime or of an attempt or solicitation to commit such crime.

(2) *Scope of Conspiratorial Relationship.* If a person guilty of conspiracy, as defined by Subsection (1) of this Section, knows that a person with whom he conspires to commit a crime has conspired with another person or persons to commit the same crime, he is guilty of conspiring with such other person or persons, whether or not he knows their identity, to commit such crime.

(3) *Conspiracy with Multiple Criminal Objectives.* If a person conspires to commit a number of crimes, he is guilty of only one conspiracy so long as such multiple crimes are the object of the same agreement or continuous conspiratorial relationship.

(4) *Joinder and Venue in Conspiracy Prosecutions.*

(a) Subject to the provisions of paragraph (b) of this Subsection, two or more persons charged with criminal conspiracy may be prosecuted jointly if:

(i) they are charged with conspiring with one another; or

(ii) the conspiracies alleged, whether they have the same or different parties, are so related that they constitute different aspects of a scheme of organized criminal conduct.

(b) In any joint prosecution under paragraph (a) of this Subsection:

(i) no defendant shall be charged with a conspiracy in any county [parish or district] other than one in which he entered into such conspiracy or in which an overt act pursuant to such conspiracy was done by him or by a person with whom he conspired; and

(ii) neither the liability of any defendant nor the admissibility against him of evidence of acts or declarations of another shall be enlarged by such joinder; and

(iii) the Court shall order a severance or take a special verdict as to any defendant who so requests, if it deems it necessary or appropriate to promote the fair determination of his guilt or innocence, and shall take any other proper measures to protect the fairness of the trial.

(5) *Overt Act.* No person may be convicted of conspiracy to commit a crime, other than a felony of the first or second degree, unless an overt act in pursuance of such conspiracy is alleged and proved to have been done by him or by a person with whom he conspired.

(6) *Renunciation of Criminal Purpose.* It is an affirmative defense that the actor, after conspiring to commit a crime, thwarted the success of the conspiracy, under circumstances manifesting a complete and voluntary renunciation of his criminal purpose.

(7) *Duration of Conspiracy.* For purposes of Section 1.06(4):

(a) conspiracy is a continuing course of conduct that terminates when the crime or crimes that are its object are committed or the agreement that they be committed is abandoned by the defendant and by those with whom he conspired; and

(b) such abandonment is presumed if neither the defendant nor anyone with whom he conspired does any overt act in pursuance of the conspiracy during the applicable period of limitation; and

(c) if an individual abandons the agreement, the conspiracy is terminated as to him only if and when he advises those with whom he conspired of his abandonment or he informs the law enforcement authorities of the existence of the conspiracy and of his participation therein.

Section 5.04. *Incapacity, Irresponsibility or Immunity of Party to Solicitation or Conspiracy.*

(1) Except as provided in Subsection (2) of this Section, it is immaterial to the liability of a person who solicits or conspires with another to commit a crime that:

(a) he or the person whom he solicits or with whom he conspires does not occupy a particular position or have a particular characteristic that is an element of such crime, if he believes that one of them does; or

(b) the person whom he solicits or with whom he conspires is irresponsible or has an immunity to prosecution or conviction for the commission of the crime.

(2) It is a defense to a charge of solicitation or conspiracy to commit a crime that if the criminal object were achieved, the actor would not be guilty of a crime under the law defining the offense or as an accomplice under Section 2.06(5) or 2.06(6)(a) or (6)(b).

Section 5.05. *Grading of Criminal Attempt, Solicitation and Conspiracy; Mitigation in Cases of Lesser Danger; Multiple Convictions Barred.*

(1) *Grading.* Except as otherwise provided in this Section, attempt, solicitation and conspiracy are crimes of the same grade and degree as the most serious offense that is attempted or solicited or is an object of the conspiracy. An attempt, solicitation or conspiracy to commit a [capital crime or a] felony of the first degree is a felony of the second degree.

(2) *Mitigation.* If the particular conduct charged to constitute a criminal attempt, solicitation or conspiracy is so inherently unlikely to result or culminate in the commission of a crime that neither such conduct nor the actor presents a public danger warranting the grading of such offense under this Section, the Court shall exercise its power under Section 6.12 to enter judgment and impose sentence for a crime of lower grade or degree or, in extreme cases, may dismiss the prosecution.

(3) *Multiple Convictions.* A person may not be convicted of more than one offense defined by this Article for conduct designed to commit or to culminate in the commission of the same crime.

Section 5.06. *Possessing Instruments of Crime; Weapons.*

(1) *Criminal Instruments Generally.* A person commits a misdemeanor if he possesses any instrument of crime with purpose to employ it criminally. "Instrument of crime" means:

(a) anything specially made or specially adapted for criminal use; or

(b) anything commonly used for criminal purposes and possessed by the actor under circumstances that do not negative unlawful purpose.

(2) *Presumption of Criminal Purpose from Possession of Weapon.* If a person possesses a firearm or other weapon on or about his person, in a vehicle occupied by him, or otherwise readily available for use, it is presumed that he had the purpose to employ it criminally, unless:

(a) the weapon is possessed in the actor's home or place of business;

(b) the actor is licensed or otherwise authorized by law to possess such weapon; or

(c) the weapon is of a type commonly used in lawful sport.

"Weapon" means anything readily capable of lethal use and possessed under circumstances not manifestly appropriate for lawful uses it may have; the term includes a firearm that is not loaded or lacks a clip or other component to render it immediately operable, and components that can readily be assembled into a weapon.

(3) *Presumptions as to Possession of Criminal Instruments in Automobiles.* If a weapon or other instrument of crime is found in an automobile, it is presumed to be in the possession of the occupant if there is but one. If there is more than one occupant, it is presumed to be in the possession of all, except under the following circumstances:

(a) it is found upon the person of one of the occupants;

(b) the automobile is not a stolen one and the weapon or instrument is found out of view in a glove compartment, car trunk, or other enclosed customary depository, in which case it is presumed to be in the possession of the occupant or occupants who own or have authority to operate the automobile;

(c) in the case of a taxicab, a weapon or instrument found in the passengers' portion of the vehicle is presumed to be in the possession of all the passengers, if there are any, and, if not, in the possession of the driver.

Section 5.07.   *Prohibited Offensive Weapons.*

A person commits a misdemeanor if, except as authorized by law, he makes, repairs, sells, or otherwise deals in, uses, or possesses any offensive weapon. "Offensive weapon" means any bomb, machine gun, sawed-off shotgun, firearm specially made or specially adapted for concealment or silent discharge, any blackjack, sandbag, metal knuckles, dagger, or other implement for the infliction of serious bodily injury that serves no common lawful purpose. It is a defense under this Section for the defendant to prove by a preponderance of evidence that he possessed or dealt with the weapon solely as a curio or in a dramatic performance, or that he possessed it briefly in consequence of having found it or taken it from an aggressor, or under circumstances similarly negativing any purpose or likelihood that the weapon would be used unlawfully. The presumptions provided in Section 5.06(3) are applicable to prosecutions under this Section.

ARTICLE 210. CRIMINAL HOMICIDE

Section 210.0.   *Definitions.*

In Articles 210-213, unless a different meaning plainly is required:

(1) "human being" means a person who has been born and is alive;

(2) "bodily injury" means physical pain, illness or any impairment of physical condition;

(3) "serious bodily injury" means bodily injury which creates a substantial risk of death or which causes serious, permanent disfigurement, or protracted loss or impairment of the function of any bodily member or organ;

(4) "deadly weapon" means any firearm or other weapon, device, instrument, material or substance, whether animate or inanimate, which in the manner it is used

or is intended to be used is known to be capable of producing death or serious bodily injury.

Section 210.1.   *Criminal Homicide.*

(1) A person is guilty of criminal homicide if he purposely, knowingly, recklessly or negligently causes the death of another human being.

(2) Criminal homicide is murder, manslaughter or negligent homicide.

Section 210.2.   *Murder.*

(1) Except as provided in Section 210.3(l)(b), criminal homicide constitutes murder when:

(a) it is committed purposely or knowingly; or

(b) it is committed recklessly under circumstances manifesting extreme indifference to the value of human life. Such recklessness and indifference are presumed if the actor is engaged or is an accomplice in the commission of, or an attempt to commit, or flight after committing or attempting to commit robbery, rape or deviate sexual intercourse by force or threat of force, arson, burglary, kidnapping or felonious escape.

(2) Murder is a felony of the first degree [but a person convicted of murder may be sentenced to death, as provided in Section 210.6].

Section 210.3.   *Manslaughter.*

(1) Criminal homicide constitutes manslaughter when:

(a) it is committed recklessly; or

(b) a homicide which would otherwise be murder is committed under the influence of extreme mental or emotional disturbance for which there is reasonable explanation or excuse. The reasonableness of such explanation or excuse shall be determined from the viewpoint of a person in the actor's situation under the circumstances as he believes them to be.

(2) Manslaughter is a felony of the second degree.

Section 210.4.   *Negligent Homicide.*

(1) Criminal homicide constitutes negligent homicide when it is committed negligently.

(2) Negligent homicide is a felony of the third degree.

Section 210.5.   *Causing or Aiding Suicide.*

(1) *Causing Suicide as Criminal Homicide.* A person may be convicted of criminal homicide for causing another to commit suicide only if he purposely causes such suicide by force, duress or deception.

(2) *Aiding or Soliciting Suicide as an Independent Offense.* A person who purposely aids or solicits another to commit suicide is guilty of a felony of the second degree if his conduct causes such suicide or an attempted suicide, and otherwise of a misdemeanor.

[Section 210.6. *Sentence of Death for Murder; Further Proceedings to Determine Sentence.*

(1) *Death Sentence Excluded.* When a defendant is found guilty of murder, the Court shall impose sentence for a felony of the first degree if it is satisfied that:

(a) none of the aggravating circumstances enumerated in Subsection (3) of this Section was established by the evidence at the trial or will be established if further proceedings are initiated under Subsection (2) of this Section; or

(b) substantial mitigating circumstances, established by the evidence at the trial, call for leniency; or

(c) the defendant, with the consent of the prosecuting attorney and the approval of the Court, pleaded guilty to murder as a felony of the first degree; or

(d) the defendant was under 18 years of age at the time of the commission of the crime; or

(e) the defendant's physical or mental condition calls for leniency; or

(f) although the evidence suffices to sustain the verdict, it does not foreclose all doubt respecting the defendant's guilt.

(2) *Determination by Court or by Court and Jury.* Unless the Court imposes sentence under Subsection (1) of this Section, it shall conduct a separate proceeding to determine whether the defendant should be sentenced for a felony of the first degree or sentenced to death. The proceeding shall be conducted before the Court alone if the defendant was convicted by a Court sitting without a jury or upon his plea of guilty or if the prosecuting attorney and the defendant waive a jury with respect to sentence. In other cases it shall be conducted before the Court sitting with the jury which determined the defendant's guilt or, if the Court for good cause shown discharges that jury, with a new jury empanelled for the purpose.

In the proceeding, evidence may be presented as to any matter that the Court deems relevant to sentence, including but not limited to the nature and circumstances of the crime, the defendant's character, background, history, mental and physical condition and any of the aggravating or mitigating circumstances enumerated in Subsections (3) and (4) of this Section. Any such evidence, not legally privileged, which the Court deems to have probative force, may be received, regardless of its admissibility under the exclusionary rules of evidence, provided that the defendant's counsel is accorded a fair opportunity to rebut such evidence. The prosecuting attorney and the defendant or his counsel shall be permitted to present argument for or against sentence of death.

The determination whether sentence of death shall be imposed shall be in the discretion of the Court, except that when the proceeding is conducted before the Court sitting with a jury, the Court shall not impose sentence of death unless it submits to the jury the issue whether the defendant should be sentenced to death or to imprisonment and the jury returns a verdict that the sentence should be death. If the jury is unable to reach a unanimous verdict, the Court shall dismiss the jury and impose sentence for a felony of the first degree.

The Court, in exercising its discretion as to sentence, and the jury, in determining upon its verdict, shall take into account the aggravating and mitigating circumstances enumerated in Subsections (3) and (4) and any other facts that it deems relevant, but it shall not impose or recommend sentence of death unless it finds one of the aggravating circumstances enumerated in Subsection (3) and further finds that there are no mitigating circumstances sufficiently substantial to call for leniency. When the issue is submitted to the jury, the Court shall so instruct and also shall inform the jury of the nature of the sentence of imprisonment that may be imposed, including its implication with respect to possible release upon parole, if the jury verdict is against sentence of death.

Alternative formulation of Subsection (2):

(2) *Determination by Court.* Unless the Court imposes sentence under Subsection (1) of this Section, it shall conduct a separate proceeding to determine whether the defendant should be sentenced for a felony of the first degree or sentenced to death. In the proceeding, the Court, in accordance with Section 7.07, shall consider the report of the pre-sentence investigation and, if a psychiatric examination has been ordered, the report of such examination. In addition, evidence may be presented as to any matter that the Court deems relevant to sentence, including but not limited to the nature and circumstances of the crime, the defendant's character, background, history, mental and physical condition and any of the aggravating or mitigating circumstances enumerated in Subsections (3) and (4) of this Section. Any such evidence, not legally privileged, which the Court deems to have probative force, may be received, regardless of its admissibility under the exculsionary rules of evidence, provided that the defendant's counsel is accorded a fair opportunity to rebut such evidence. The prosecuting attorney and the defendant or his counsel shall he permitted to present argument for or against sentence of death.

The determination whether sentence of death shall be imposed shall be in the discretion of the Court. In exercising such discretion, the Court shall take into account the aggravating and mitigating circumstances enumerated in Subsections (3) and (4) and any other facts that it deems relevant but shall not impose sentence of death unless it finds one of the aggravating circumstances enumerated in Subsection (3) and further finds that there are no mitigating circumstances sufficiently substantial to call for leniency.

(3) *Aggravating Circumstances.*

(a) The murder was committed by a convict under sentence of imprisonment.

(b) The defendant was previously convicted of another murder or of a felony involving the use or threat of violence to the person.

(c) At the time the murder was committed the defendant also committed another murder.

(d) The defendant knowingly created a great risk of death to many persons.

(e) The murder was committed while the defendant was engaged or was an accomplice in the commission of, or an attempt to commit, or flight after committing or attempting to commit robbery, rape or deviate sexual intercourse by force or threat of force, arson, burglary or kidnapping.

(f) The murder was committed for the purpose of avoiding or preventing a lawful arrest or effecting an escape from lawful custody.

(g) The murder was committed for pecuniary gain.

(h) The murder was especially heinous, atrocious or cruel, manifesting exceptional depravity.

(4) *Mitigating Circumstances.*

(a) The defendant has no significant history of prior criminal activity.

(b) The murder was committed while the defendant was under the influence of extreme mental or emotional disturbance.

(c) The victim was a participant in the defendant's homicidal conduct or consented to the homicidal act.

(d) The murder was committed under circumstances which the defendant believed to provide a moral justification or extenuation for his conduct.

(e) The defendant was an accomplice in a murder committed by another person and his participation in the homicidal act was relatively minor.

(f) The defendant acted under duress or under the domination of another person.

(g) At the time of the murder, the capacity of the defendant to appreciate the criminality [wrongfulness] of his conduct or to conform his conduct to the requirements of law was impaired as a result of mental disease or defect or intoxication.

(h) The youth of the defendant at the time of the crime.]

ARTICLE 211. ASSAULT; RECKLESS ENDANGERING; THREATS

Section 211.0. *Definitions.*

In this Article, the definitions given in Section 210.0 apply unless a different meaning plainly is required.

Section 211.1. *Assault.*

(1) *Simple Assault.* A person is guilty of assault if he:

(a) attempts to cause or purposely, knowingly or recklessly causes bodily injury to another; or

(b) negligently causes bodily injury to another with a deadly weapon; or

(c) attempts by physical menace to put another in fear of imminent serious bodily injury.

Simple assault is a misdemeanor unless committed in a fight or scuffle entered into by mutual consent, in which case it is a petty misdemeanor.

(2) *Aggravated Assault.* A person is guilty of aggravated assault if he:

(a) attempts to cause serious bodily injury to another, or causes such injury purposely, knowingly or recklessly under circumstances manifesting extreme indifference to the value of human life; or

(b) attempts to cause or purposely or knowingly causes bodily injury to another with a deadly weapon.

Aggravated assault under paragraph (a) is a felony of the second degree; aggravated assault under paragraph (b) is a felony of the third degree.

Section 211.2. *Recklessly Endangering Another Person.*

A person commits a misdemeanor if he recklessly engages in conduct which places or may place another person in danger of death or serious bodily injury. Recklessness and danger shall be presumed where a person knowingly points a firearm at or in the direction of another, whether or not the actor believed the firearm to be loaded.

Section 211.3.   *Terroristic Threats.*

A person is guilty of a felony of the third degree if he threatens to commit any crime of violence with purpose to terrorize another or to cause evacuation of a building, place of assembly, or facility of public transportation, or otherwise to cause serious public inconvenience, or in reckless disregard of the risk of causing such terror or inconvenience.

ARTICLE 212. KIDNAPPING AND RELATED OFFENSES; COERCION

Section 212.0.   *Definitions.*

In this Article, the definitions given in Section 210.0 apply unless a different meaning plainly is required.

Section 212.1.   *Kidnapping.*

A person is guilty of kidnapping if he unlawfully removes another from his place of residence or business, or a substantial distance from the vicinity where he is found, or if he unlawfully confines another for a substantial period in a place of isolation, with any of the following purposes:

(a) to hold for ransom or reward, or as a shield or hostage; or

(b) to facilitate commission of any felony or flight thereafter; or

(c) to inflict bodily injury on or to terrorize the victim or another; or

(d) to interfere with the performance of any governmental or political function.

Kidnapping is a felony of the first degree unless the actor voluntarily releases the victim alive and in a safe place prior to trial, in which case it is a felony of the second degree. A removal or confinement is unlawful within the meaning of this Section if it is accomplished by force, threat or deception, or, in the case of a person who is under the age of 14 or incompetent, if it is accomplished without the consent of a parent, guardian or other person responsible for general supervision of his welfare.

Section 212.2.   *Felonious Restraint.*

A person commits a felony of the third degree if he knowingly:

(a) restrains another unlawfully in circumstances exposing him to risk of serious bodily injury; or

(b) holds another in a condition of involuntary servitude.

Section 212.3.   *False Imprisonment.*

A person commits a misdemeanor if he knowingly restrains another unlawfully so as to interfere substantially with his liberty.

Section 212.5.   *Criminal Coercion.*

(1) *Offense Defined.* A person is guilty of criminal coercion if, with purpose unlawfully to restrict another's freedom of action to his detriment, he threatens to:

(a) commit any criminal offense; or

(b) accuse anyone of a criminal offense; or

(c) expose any secret tending to subject any person to hatred, contempt or ridicule, or to impair his credit or business repute; or

(d) take or withhold action as an official, or cause an official to take or withhold action.

It is an affirmative defense to prosecution based on paragraphs (b), (c) or (d) that the actor believed the accusation or secret to be true or the proposed official action justified and that his purpose was limited to compelling the other to behave in a way reasonably related to the circumstances which were the subject of the accusation, exposure or proposed official action, as by desisting from further misbehavior, making good a wrong done, refraining from taking any action or responsibility for which the actor believes the other disqualified.

(2) *Grading.* Criminal coercion is a misdemeanor unless the threat is to commit a felony or the actor's purpose is felonious, in which cases the offense is a felony of the third degree.

ARTICLE 213. SEXUAL OFFENSES

Section 213.0.   *Definitions.*

In this Article, unless a different meaning plainly is required:

(1) the definitions given in Section 210.0 apply;

(2) "Sexual intercourse" includes intercourse per os or per anum, with some penetration however slight; emission is not required;

(3) "Deviate sexual intercourse" means sexual intercourse per os or per anum between human beings who are not husband and wife, and any form of sexual intercourse with an animal.

Section 213.1.   *Rape and Related Offenses.*

(1) *Rape.* A male who has sexual intercourse with a female not his wife is guilty of rape if:

(a) he compels her to submit by force or by threat of imminent death, serious bodily injury, extreme pain or kidnapping, to be inflicted on anyone; or

(b) he has substantially impaired her power to appraise or control her conduct by administering or employing without her knowledge drugs, intoxicants or other means for the purpose of preventing resistance; or

(c) the female is unconscious; or

(d) the female is less than 10 years old.

Rape is a felony of the second degree unless (i) in the course thereof the actor inflicts serious bodily injury upon anyone, or (ii) the victim was not a voluntary social companion of the actor upon the occasion of the crime and had not previously permitted him sexual liberties, in which cases the offense is a felony of the first degree.

(2) *Gross Sexual Imposition.* A male who has sexual intercourse with a female not his wife commits a felony of the third degree if:

(a) he compels her to submit by any threat that would prevent resistance by a woman of ordinary resolution; or

(b) he knows that she suffers from a mental disease or defect which renders her incapable of appraising the nature of her conduct; or

(c) he knows that she is unaware that a sexual act is being committed upon her or that she submits because she mistakenly supposes that he is her husband.

Section 213.2.   *Deviate Sexual Intercourse by Force or Imposition.*

(1) *By Force or Its Equivalent.* A person who engages in deviate sexual intercourse with another person, or who causes another to engage in deviate sexual intercourse, commits a felony of the second degree if:

(a) he compels the other person to participate by force or by threat of imminent death, serious bodily injury, extreme pain or kidnapping, to be inflicted on anyone; or

(b) he has substantially impaired the other person's power to appraise or control his conduct, by administering or employing without the knowledge of the other person drugs, intoxicants or other means for the purpose of preventing resistance; or

(c) the other person is unconscious; or

(d) the other person is less than 10 years old.

(2) *By Other Imposition.* A person who engages in deviate sexual intercourse with another person, or who causes another to engage in deviate sexual intercourse, commits a felony of the third degree if:

(a) he compels the other person to participate by any threat that would prevent resistance by a person of ordinary resolution; or

(b) he knows that the other person suffers from a mental disease or defect which renders him incapable of appraising the nature of his conduct; or

(c) he knows that the other person submits because he is unaware that a sexual act is being committed upon him.

Section 213.3.   *Corruption of Minors and Seduction.*

(1) *Offense Defined.* A male who has sexual intercourse with a female not his wife, or any person who engages in deviate sexual intercourse or causes another to engage in deviate sexual intercourse, is guilty of an offense if:

(a) the other person is less than [16] years old and the actor is at least [four] years older than the other person; or

(b) the other person is less than 21 years old and the actor is his guardian or otherwise responsible for general supervision of his welfare; or

(c) the other person is in custody of law or detained in a hospital or other institution and the actor has supervisory or disciplinary authority over him; or

(d) the other person is a female who is induced to participate by a promise of marriage which the actor does not mean to perform.

(2) *Grading.* An offense under paragraph (a) of Subsection (1) is a felony of the third degree. Otherwise an offense under this section is a misdemeanor.

Section 213.4.   *Sexual Assault.*

A person who has sexual contact with another not his spouse, or causes such other to have sexual conduct with him, is guilty of sexual assault, a misdemeanor, if:

(1) he knows that the contact is offensive to the other person; or

(2) he knows that the other person suffers from a mental disease or defect which renders him or her incapable of appraising the nature of his or her conduct; or

(3) he knows that the other person is unaware that a sexual act is being committed; or

(4) the other person is less than 10 years old; or

(5) he has substantially impaired the other person's power to appraise or control his or her conduct, by administering or employing without the other's knowledge drugs, intoxicants or other means for the purpose of preventing resistance; or

(6) the other person is less than [16] years old and the actor is at least [four] years older than the other person; or

(7) the other person is less than 21 years old and the actor is his guardian or otherwise responsible for general supervision of his welfare; or

(8) the other person is in custody of law or detained in a hospital or other institution and the actor has supervisory or disciplinary authority over him.

Sexual contact is any touching of the sexual or other intimate parts of the person for the purpose of arousing or gratifying sexual desire.

Section 213.5.   *Indecent Exposure.*

A person commits a misdemeanor if, for the purpose of arousing or gratifying sexual desire of himself or of any person other than his spouse, he exposes his genitals under circumstances in which he knows his conduct is likely to cause affront or alarm.

Section 213.6.   *Provisions Generally Applicable to Article 213.*

(1) *Mistake as to Age.* Whenever in this Article the criminality of conduct depends on a child's being below the age of 10, it is no defense that the actor did not know the child's age, or reasonably believed the child to be older than 10. When criminality depends on the child's being below a critical age other than 10, it is a defense for the actor to prove by a preponderance of the evidence that he reasonably believed the child to be above the critical age.

(2) *Spouse Relationships.* Whenever in this Article the definition of an offense excludes conduct with a spouse, the exclusion shall be deemed to extend to persons living as man and wife, regardless of the legal status of their relationship. The exclusion shall be inoperative as respects spouses living apart under a decree of judicial separation. Where the definition of an offense excludes conduct with a spouse or conduct by a woman, this shall not preclude conviction of a spouse or woman as accomplice in a sexual act which he or she causes another person, not within the exclusion, to perform.

(3) *Sexually Promiscuous Complainants.* It is a defense to prosecution under Section 213.3 and paragraphs (6), (7) and (8) of Section 213.4 for the actor to prove by a preponderance of the evidence that the alleged victim had, prior to the time of the offense charged, engaged promiscuously in sexual relations with others.

(4) *Prompt Complaint.* No prosecution may be instituted or maintained under this Article unless the alleged offense was brought to the notice of public authority within [3] months of its occurrence or, where the alleged victim was less than [16] years old or otherwise incompetent to make complaint, within [3] months after a parent, guardian or other competent person specially interested in the victim learns of the offense.

(5) *Testimony of Complainants.* No person shall be convicted of any felony under this Article upon the uncorroborated testimony of the alleged victim. Corroboration may be circumstantial. In any prosecution before a jury for an offense under this Article, the jury shall be instructed to evaluate the testimony of a victim or complaining witness with special care in view of the emotional involvement of the witness and the difficulty of determining the truth with respect to alleged sexual activities carried out in private.

ARTICLE 220. ARSON, CRIMINAL MISCHIEF, AND OTHER PROPERTY DESTRUCTION

Section 220.1.   *Arson and Related Offenses.*

(1) *Arson.* A person is guilty of arson, a felony of the second degree, if he starts a fire or causes an explosion with the purpose of:
  (a) destroying a building or occupied structure of another;
  (b) destroying or damaging any property, whether his own or another's, to collect insurance for such loss. It shall be an affirmative defense to prosecution under this paragraph that the actor's conduct did not recklessly endanger any building or occupied structure of another or place any other person in danger of death or bodily injury.

(2) *Reckless Burning or Exploding.* A person commits a felony of the third degree if he purposely starts a fire or causes an explosion, whether on his own property or another's, and thereby recklessly:
  (a) places another person in danger of death or bodily injury;
  (b) places a building or occupied structure of another in danger of damage or destruction.

(3) *Failure to Control or Report Dangerous Fire.* A person who knows that a fire is endangering life or a substantial amount of property of another and fails to take reasonable measures to put out or control the fire, when he can do so without substantial risk to himself, or to give a prompt fire alarm, commits a misdemeanor if:
  (a) he knows that he is under an official, contractual, or other legal duty to prevent or combat the fire; or
  (b) the fire was started, albeit lawfully, by him or with his assent, or on property in his custody or control.

(4) *Definitions.* "Occupied structure" means any structure, vehicle or place adapted for overnight accommodation of persons, or for carrying on business therein, whether or not a person is actually present. Property is that of another, for the purposes of this section, if anyone other than the actor has a possessory or proprietary interest therein. If a building or structure is divided into separately occupied units, any unit not occupied by the actor is an occupied structure of another.

Section 220.2.   *Causing or Risking Catastrophe.*

(1) *Causing Catastrophe.* A person who causes a catastrophe by explosion, fire, flood, avalanche, collapse of building, release of poison gas, radioactive material or other harmful or destructive force or substance, or by any other means of causing potentially widespread injury or damage, commits a felony of the second degree if

he does so purposely or knowingly, or a felony of the third degree if he does so recklessly.

(2) *Risking Catastrophe.* A person is guilty of a misdemeanor if he recklessly creates a risk of catastrophe in the employment of fire, explosives or other dangerous means listed in Subsection (1).

(3) *Failure to Prevent Catastrophe.* A person who knowingly or recklessly fails to take reasonable measures to prevent or mitigate a catastrophe commits a misdemeanor if:

   (a) he knows that he is under an official, contractual or other legal duty to take such measures; or

   (b) he did or assented to the act causing or threatening the catastrophe.

Section 220.3.   *Criminal Mischief.*

(1) *Offense Defined.* A person is guilty of criminal mischief if he:

   (a) damages tangible property of another purposely, recklessly, or by negligence in the employment of fire, explosives, or other dangerous means listed in Section 220.2(1); or

   (b) purposely or recklessly tampers with tangible property of another so as to endanger person or property; or

   (c) purposely or recklessly causes another to suffer pecuniary loss by deception or threat.

(2) *Grading.* Criminal mischief is a felony of the third degree if the actor purposely causes pecuniary loss in excess of $5,000, or a substantial interruption or impairment of public communication, transportation, supply of water, gas or power, or other public service. It is a misdemeanor if the actor purposely causes pecuniary loss in excess of $100, or a petty misdemeanor if he purposely or recklessly causes pecuniary loss in excess of $25. Otherwise criminal mischief is a violation.

ARTICLE 221. BURGLARY AND OTHER CRIMINAL INTRUSION

Section 221.0.   *Definitions.*

In this Article, unless a different meaning plainly is required:

(1) "occupied structure" means any structure, vehicle or place adapted for overnight accommodation of persons, or for carrying on business therein, whether or not a person is actually present.

(2) "night" means the period between thirty minutes past sunset and thirty minutes before sunrise.

Section 221.1.   *Burglary.*

(1) *Burglary Defined.* A person is guilty of burglary if he enters a building or occupied structure, or separately secured or occupied portion thereof, with purpose to commit a crime therein, unless the premises are at the time open to the public or the actor is licensed or privileged to enter. It is an affirmative defense to prosecution for burglary that the building or structure was abandoned.

(2) *Grading.* Burglary is a felony of the second degree if it is perpetrated in the dwelling of another at night, or if, in the course of committing the offense, the actor:

(a) purposely, knowingly or recklessly inflicts or attempts to inflict bodily injury on anyone; or

(b) is armed with explosives or a deadly weapon.

Otherwise, burglary is a felony of the third degree. An act shall be deemed "in the course of committing" an offense if it occurs in an attempt to commit the offense or in flight after the attempt or commission.

(3) *Multiple Convictions.* A person may not be convicted both for burglary and for the offense which it was his purpose to commit after the burglarious entry or for an attempt to commit that offense, unless the additional offense constitutes a felony of the first or second degree.

Section 221.2.   *Criminal Trespass.*

(1) *Buildings and Occupied Structures.* A person commits an offense if, knowing that he is not licensed or privileged to do so, he enters or surreptitiously remains in any building or occupied structure, or separately secured or occupied portion thereof. An offense under this Subsection is a misdemeanor if it is committed in a dwelling at night. Otherwise it is a petty misdemeanor.

(2) *Defiant Trespasser.* A person commits an offense if, knowing that he is not licensed or privileged to do so, he enters or remains in any place as to which notice against trespass is given by:

(a) actual communication to the actor; or

(b) posting in a manner prescribed by law or reasonably likely to come to the attention of intruders; or

(c) fencing or other enclosure manifestly designed to exclude intruders.

An offense under this Subsection constitutes a petty misdemeanor if the offender defies an order to leave personally communicated to him by the owner of the premises or other authorized person. Otherwise it is a violation.

(3) *Defenses.* It is an affirmative defense to prosecution under this Section that:

(a) a building or occupied structure involved in an offense under Subsection (1) was abandoned; or

(b) the premises were at the time open to members of the public and the actor complied with all lawful conditions imposed on access to or remaining in the premises; or

(c) the actor reasonably believed that the owner of the premises, or other person empowered to license access thereto, would have licensed him to enter or remain.

ARTICLE 222. ROBBERY

Section 222.1.   *Robbery.*

(1) *Robbery Defined.* A person is guilty of robbery if, in the course of committing a theft, he:

(a) inflicts serious bodily injury upon another; or

(b) threatens another with or purposely puts him in fear of immediate serious bodily injury; or

(c) commits or threatens immediately to commit any felony of the first or second degree.

An act shall be deemed "in the course of committing a theft" if it occurs in an attempt to commit theft or in flight after the attempt or commission.

(2) *Grading.* Robbery is a felony of the second degree, except that it is a felony of the first degree if in the course of committing the theft the actor attempts to kill anyone, or purposely inflicts or attempts to inflict serious bodily injury.

ARTICLE 223. THEFT AND RELATED OFFENSES

Section 223.0. *Definitions.*

In this Article, unless a different meaning plainly is required:

(1) "deprive" means: (a) to withhold property of another permanently or for so extended a period as to appropriate a major portion of its economic value, or with intent to restore only upon payment of reward or other compensation; or (b) to dispose of the property so as to make it unlikely that the owner will recover it.

(2) "financial institution" means a bank, insurance company, credit union, building and loan association, investment trust or other organization held out to the public as a place of deposit of funds or medium of savings or collective investment.

(3) "government" means the United States, any State, county, municipality, or other political unit, or any department, agency or subdivision of any of the foregoing, or any corporation or other association carrying out the functions of government.

(4) "movable property" means property the location of which can be changed, including things growing on, affixed to, or found in land, and documents although the rights represented thereby have no physical location; "immovable property" is all other property.

(5) "obtain" means: (a) in relation to property, to bring about a transfer or purported transfer of a legal interest in the property, whether to the obtainer or another; or (b) in relation to labor or service, to secure performance thereof.

(6) "property" means anything of value, including real estate, tangible and intangible personal property, contract rights, choses-in-action and other interests in or claims to wealth, admission or transportation tickets, captured or domestic animals, food and drink, electric or other power.

(7) "property of another" includes property in which any person other than the actor has an interest which the actor is not privileged to infringe, regardless of the fact that the actor also has an interest in the property and regardless of the fact that the other person might be precluded from civil recovery because the property was used in an unlawful transaction or was subject to forfeiture as contraband. Property in possession of the actor shall not be deemed property of another who has only a security interest therein, even if legal title is in the creditor pursuant to a conditional sales contract or other security agreement.

Section 223.1. *Consolidation of Theft Offenses; Grading; Provisions Applicable to Theft Generally.*

(1) *Consolidation of Theft Offenses.* Conduct denominated theft in this Article constitutes a single offense. An accusation of theft may be supported by evidence that it was committed in any manner that would be theft under this Article, notwithstanding the specification of a different manner in the indictment or information, subject only to the power of the Court to ensure fair trial by granting a continuance or other

appropriate relief where the conduct of the defense would be prejudiced by lack of fair notice or by surprise.

(2) *Grading of Theft Offenses.*

(a) Theft constitutes a felony of the third degree if the amount involved exceeds $500, or if the property stolen is a firearm, automobile, airplane, motorcycle, motorboat, or other motor-propelled vehicle, or in the case of theft by receiving stolen property, if the receiver is in the business of buying or selling stolen property.

(b) Theft not within the preceding paragraph constitutes a misdemeanor, except that if the property was not taken from the person or by threat, or in breach of a fiduciary obligation, and the actor proves by a preponderance of the evidence that the amount involved was less than $50, the offense constitutes a petty misdemeanor.

(c) The amount involved in a theft shall be deemed to be the highest value, by any reasonable standard, of the property or services which the actor stole or attempted to steal. Amounts involved in thefts committed pursuant to one scheme or course of conduct, whether from the same person or several persons, may be aggregated in determining the grade of the offense.

(3) *Claim of Right.* It is an affirmative defense to prosecution for theft that the actor:

(a) was unaware that the property or service was that of another; or

(b) acted under an honest claim of right to the property or service involved or that he had a right to acquire or dispose of it as he did; or

(c) took property exposed for sale, intending to purchase and pay for it promptly, or reasonably believing that the owner, if present, would have consented.

(4) *Theft from Spouse.* It is no defense that theft was from the actor's spouse, except that misappropriation of household and personal effects, or other property normally accessible to both spouses, is theft only if it occurs after the parties have ceased living together.

Section 223.2.   *Theft by Unlawful Taking or Disposition.*

(1) *Movable Property.* A person is guilty of theft if he unlawfully takes, or exercises unlawful control over, movable property of another with purpose to deprive him thereof.

(2) *Immovable Property.* A person is guilty of theft if he unlawfully transfers immovable property of another or any interest therein with purpose to benefit himself or another not entitled thereto.

Section 223.3.   *Theft by Deception.*

A person is guilty of theft if he purposely obtains property of another by deception. A person deceives if he purposely:

(1) creates or reinforces a false impression, including false impressions as to law, value, intention or other state of mind; but deception as to a person's intention to perform a promise shall not be inferred from the fact alone that he did not subsequently perform the promise; or

(2) prevents another from acquiring information which would affect his judgment of a transaction; or

(3) fails to correct a false impression which the deceiver previously created or reinforced, or which the deceiver knows to be influencing another to whom he stands in a fiduciary or confidential relationship; or

(4) fails to disclose a known lien, adverse claim or other legal impediment to the enjoyment of property which he transfers or encumbers in consideration for the property obtained, whether such impediment is or is not valid, or is or is not a matter of official record.

The term "deceive" does not, however, include falsity as to matters having no pecuniary significance, or puffing by statements unlikely to deceive ordinary persons in the group addressed.

Section 223.4.   *Theft by Extortion.*

A person is guilty of theft if he purposely obtains property of another by threatening to:

(1) inflict bodily injury on anyone or commit any other criminal offense; or

(2) accuse anyone of a criminal offense; or

(3) expose any secret tending to subject any person to hatred, contempt or ridicule, or to impair his credit or business repute;

(4) take or withhold action as an official, or cause an official to take or withhold action; or

(5) bring about or continue a strike, boycott or other collective unofficial action, if the property is not demanded or received for the benefit of the group in whose interest the actor purports to act; or

(6) testify or provide information or withhold testimony or information with respect to another's legal claim or defense; or

(7) inflict any other harm which would not benefit the actor.

It is an affirmative defense to prosecution based on paragraphs (2), (3) or (4) that the property obtained by threat of accusation, exposure, lawsuit or other invocation of official action was honestly claimed as restitution or indemnification for harm done in the circumstances to which such accusation, exposure, lawsuit or other official action relates, or as compensation for property or lawful services.

Section 223.5.   *Theft of Property Lost, Mislaid, or Delivered by Mistake.*

A person who comes into control of property of another that he knows to have been lost, mislaid, or delivered under a mistake as to the nature or amount of the property or the identity of the recipient is guilty of theft if, with purpose to deprive the owner thereof, he fails to take reasonable measures to restore the property to a person entitled to have it.

Section 223.6.   *Receiving Stolen Property.*

(1) *Receiving.* A person is guilty of theft if he purposely receives, retains, or disposes of movable property of another knowing that it has been stolen, or believing that it has probably been stolen, unless the property is received, retained, or disposed with purpose to restore it to the owner. "Receiving" means acquiring possession, control or title, or lending on the security of the property.

(2) *Presumption of Knowledge.* The requisite knowledge or belief is presumed in the case of a dealer who:

(a) is found in possession or control of property stolen from two or more persons on separate occasions; or

(b) has received stolen property in another transaction within the year preceding the transaction charged; or

(c) being a dealer in property of the sort received, acquires it for a consideration which he knows is far below its reasonable value.

"Dealer" means a person in the business of buying or selling goods including a pawnbroker.

ARTICLE 230. OFFENSES AGAINST THE FAMILY

Section 230.1.   *Bigamy and Polygamy.*

(1) *Bigamy.* A married person is guilty of bigamy, a misdemeanor, if he contracts or purports to contract another marriage, unless at the time of the subsequent marriage:

(a) the actor believes that the prior spouse is dead; or

(b) the actor and the prior spouse have been living apart for five consecutive years throughout which the prior spouse was not known by the actor to be alive; or

(c) a Court has entered a judgment purporting to terminate or annul any prior disqualifying marriage, and the actor does not know that judgment to be invalid; or

(d) the actor reasonably believes that he is legally eligible to remarry.

(2) *Polygamy.* A person is guilty of polygamy, a felony of the third degree, if he marries or cohabits with more than one spouse at a time in purported exercise of the right of plural marriage. The offense is a continuing one until all cohabitation and claim of marriage with more than one spouse terminates. This section does not apply to parties to a polygamous marriage, lawful in the country of which they are residents or nationals, while they are in transit through or temporarily visiting this State.

(3) *Other Party to Bigamous or Polygamous Marriage.* A person is guilty of bigamy or polygamy, as the case may be, if he contracts or purports to contract marriage with another knowing that the other is thereby committing bigamy or polygamy.

STATUTORY INTERPRETATION

PROBLEMS

A 2.1 Alvin was recently arrested and charged under the following criminal statute, which appears in the section of the Criminal Code entitled "Driving Offenses":

(a) No one shall operate a motor vehicle, aircraft, watercraft, or other means of conveyance on a public thoroughfare while under the influence of alcohol.

(b) For purposes of section (a), a person is under the influence of alcohol if that person's blood alcohol concentration is 0.10 percent or more by weight.

(c) Any person who violates this prohibition may be punished by imposition of a fine up to $2,500 and/or a jail term up to six months. The sentence imposed may include participation in a court-approved driver improvement program. If a child under the age of 14 is a passenger in the motor vehicle, aircraft, watercraft, or other means of motorized conveyance at the time of a violation of section (a), a minimum mandatory sentence of 30 days in jail shall be imposed.

At the time of his arrest, Alvin was riding his bicycle down the middle of a city street, weaving back and forth across the double yellow line in the middle of the street. The police officer who stopped Alvin smelled alcohol on Alvin's breath and person. Alvin then failed a field sobriety test conducted by the officer.

Sixty years ago, the state legislature enacted the statute Alvin is charged under to replace a statute that read:

(a) It shall be unlawful for any person who is under the influence of alcohol to drive any vehicle on a public thoroughfare.

(b) A vehicle is any device in, upon, or by which any person or property may be transported upon a public thoroughfare. A bicycle or a ridden animal shall be deemed a vehicle.

When the statute Alvin is charged under became law, this old statute was repealed.

Assume that Alvin's blood alcohol concentration was sufficient to qualify Alvin as being under the influence of alcohol and that the street on which he was riding qualifies as a public thoroughfare under the statute. Alvin's lawyer makes a motion before the trial judge to dismiss the charge against Alvin. The trial judge decides to hold a hearing on whether or not to grant the motion. What arguments can be made for and against dismissal?

A 2.2 Consider the following facts:

On the evening of July 23, 1998, Trooper John McAuliffe of the Washington State Patrol (WSP) was on routine patrol in King County. He was in uniform. He was driving a green 1997 Ford Crown Victoria that bore no official decals or other markings to identify it as a state patrol vehicle. The car was equipped with black push bars on the front bumper, which are used to push disabled vehicles to the side of the road. The car was also equipped with several antennas and an exterior spotlight mounted on the driver's door post. The car had numerous emergency lights, visible only when activated: white strobe lights in the parking light area, wig-wag headlights that alternate from left to right and from high to low beam, a red and blue flashing light mounted on the passenger's side of the front dashboard, red strobe lights in the rear parking lights, blue flashing strobe lights in the rear window dash, and an arrow indicator that flashes amber to signal vehicles approaching from the rear to move to the right or left. The car was also equipped with a three-tone siren. The car's license number was 865 WSP; "865" is Trooper McAuliffe's badge number and "WSP" signifies that the car is owned by the Washington State Patrol.

While traveling westbound on Route 520 in that car on July 23, 1998, the trooper saw a pickup truck repeatedly changing lanes, tailgating the cars in front of it and, in McAuliffe's opinion, driving recklessly. Argueta was later identified as driving the pickup. Trooper McAuliffe turned his lights on and off to get other drivers to move out of his way. He did not keep the lights on continuously so Argueta would not become aware of his presence before he was close enough to initiate a traffic stop. Argueta began to drive over the speed limit and continued to change lanes, so Trooper McAuliffe activated the emergency lights and siren continuously. With McAuliffe in pursuit with lights flashing and siren sounding, Arguetta exited Route 520 onto northbound 148th Street. He made a sharp turn into the parking area of a business park, turned into an alley, ran a stop sign, and ended up back on northbound 148th Street. While they were in the parking area, Trooper McAuliffe got close enough to the pickup to read its license plate. While they traveled through the alley, there were no cars separating the pickup and the trooper. Argueta, with Trooper McAuliffe still in pursuit, traveled north a few blocks on 148th Street and then turned right onto a cross street. Then he turned into another parking lot and came to a stop in a parking stall. Trooper McAuliffe's lights and siren were activated continuously from the time he was on Route 520 until Argueta stopped in the parking stall. After he stopped, Argueta got out of the car and raised his hands. Trooper McAuliffe took him into custody.[1]

Mr. Argueta is charged under the following statute.

> Any driver of a motor vehicle who wilfully fails or refuses to immediately bring his vehicle to a stop and who drives his vehicle in a manner indicating a wanton or wilful disregard for the lives or property of others while attempting to elude a pursuing police vehicle, after being given a visual or audible signal to bring the vehicle to a stop, shall be guilty of a class C felony. The signal given by the police officer may be by hand, voice, emergency light, or siren. The officer giving such a signal shall be in uniform and his vehicle shall be appropriately marked showing it to be an official police vehicle.

Assume the prosecution proves the facts related above beyond reasonable doubt at trial. Is Argueta liable under the statute? What are the arguments for and against liability?

McBOYLE v. UNITED STATES

43 F.2d 273 (10th Cir. 1930)

PHILLIPS, Circuit Judge. William W. McBoyle was convicted and sentenced for an alleged violation of the National Motor Vehicle Theft Act, 18 USCA § 408. The indictment charged that on October 10, 1926, McBoyle caused to be transported in interstate commerce from Ottawa, Ill., to Guymon, Okl., one Waco airplane, motor No. 6124, serial No. 256, which was the property of the United States Aircraft Corporation and which had theretofore been stolen; and that McBoyle then and there knew it had been stolen.

The evidence of the government established the following facts: During the year 1926, McBoyle operated a commercial airport at Galena, Ill. On July 2, 1926, McBoyle hired A. J. Lacey as an aviator for a period of six months. In October, 1926, McBoyle induced Lacey to go to the field of the Aircraft Corporation at Ottawa, Ill., and steal such Waco airplane from the Aircraft Corporation. Lacey went to Ottawa, stole the airplane, and flew it to Galena, arriving there October 6th. McBoyle inquired of Lacey if any one knew the latter had taken the airplane at Ottawa. Lacey replied in the negative. Thereupon, McBoyle changed the serial number to No. 249, and painted it over in order to conceal the alteration. McBoyle and Lacey serviced the airplane and supplied it with gas and oil. McBoyle gave Lacey $150 for expense money and instructed Lacey to fly the airplane to Amarillo, Tex., and there lease an airport for them to operate during the winter months.

---

1. Washington v. Argueta, 107 Wash. App. 532, 534-535, 27 P.3d 242, 243-244 (2001).

McBoyle arranged with Lacey to communicate with him en route by telegraphic code under the name of Pat Sullivan. Lacey left McBoyle's airport at Galena, Ill., on October 6th and flew the airplane to Guymon, Okl., stopping en route at St. Joseph, Mo., and Garden City, Kan. At Guymon, they communicated with each other by telegraph and McBoyle instructed Lacey to sell or store the stolen airplane and come back to Galena. Thereupon, Lacey returned to Galena. McBoyle then gave Lacey $250 for expenses and instructed Lacey to take an airplane of the same kind and make belonging to McBoyle back to Guymon and substitute it for the stolen airplane. The purpose was to deceive the officers when they found the Waco plane at Guymon. Lacey started back to Guymon with the second airplane but crashed near Inman, Kan. Thereupon, Lacey returned to Galena and continued to work for McBoyle until the following December.

McBoyle denied all of the facts incriminating him except the sending and receiving of the telegrams. He testified that the telegrams did not refer to the airplane but to liquor which Lacey was supposed to have had in his possession in the airplane.

The primary question is whether an airplane comes within the purview of the National Motor Vehicle Theft Act. This act defines the term "motor vehicle," as follows:

> "The term 'motor vehicle' when used in this section shall include an automobile, automobile truck, automobile wagon, motor cycle, or any other self-propelled vehicle not designed for running on rails."

Counsel for McBoyle contend that the word "vehicle" includes only conveyances that travel on the ground; that an airplane is not a vehicle but a ship; and that, under the doctrine of ejusdem generis, the phrase "any other self-propelled vehicle" cannot be construed to include an airplane.

The Century Dictionary gives the derivation of the word "vehicle" as follows: "F. Vehicule, L. Vehiculum," meaning a "conveyance, carriage, *ship*." It defines the word as "Any receptacle, or means of transport, in which something is carried or conveyed, or *travels*." (Italics ours.)

It will be noted that the Latin word "vehiculum" means a ship as well as a carriage.

Webster defines the word "vehicle" as follows:

> "(1) That in or on which any person or thing is or may be carried, esp. on land, as a coach, wagon, car, bicycle, etc.; a means of conveyance.
> "(2) That which is used as the instrument of conveyance or communication."

Corpus Juris defines a motor vehicle, as follows:

> "A 'motor vehicle' is a vehicle operated by a power developed within itself and used for the purpose of carrying passengers or materials; and as the term is used in the different statutes regulating such vehicles, it is generally defined as including all vehicles propelled by any power other than muscular power, except traction engines, road rollers, and such motor vehicles as run only upon rails or tracks."

Both the derivation and the definition of the word "vehicle" indicate that it is sufficiently broad to include any means or device by which persons or things are carried or transported, and it is not limited to instrumentalities used for traveling on land, although the latter may be the limited or special meaning of the word. We do not think it would be inaccurate to say that a ship or vessel is a vehicle of commerce.

An airplane is self-propelled, by means of a gasoline motor. It is designed to carry passengers and freight from place to place. It runs partly on the ground but principally in the air. It furnishes a rapid means for transportation of persons and comparatively light articles of freight and express. It therefore serves the same general purpose as an automobile, automobile truck, or motorcycle. It is of the same general kind or class as the motor vehicles specifically enumerated in the statutory definition and, therefore, construing an airplane to come within the general term, "any other self-propelled vehicle," does not offend against the maxim of ejusdem generis.

Furthermore, some meaning must be ascribed to the general phrase "any other self-propelled vehicle," which Congress wrote into the act. It specifically enumerated all of the known self-propelled vehicles designed for running on land. It used the word "automobile," a generic term, which includes all self-propelled motor vehicles that travel on land and are used for the transportation of passengers, except those designed for running on rails.

We conclude that the phrase, "any other self-propelled vehicle," includes an airplane, a motorboat, and any other like means of conveyance or transportation which is self-propelled, and is of the same general class as an automobile and a motorcycle. . . .

The judgment is therefore affirmed.

COTTERAL, Circuit Judge (dissenting). I feel bound to dissent on the ground that the National Motor Vehicle Theft Act should not be construed as relating to the transportation of airplanes.

A prevailing rule is that a penal statute is to be construed strictly against an offender and it must state clearly the persons and acts denounced.

It would have been a simple matter in enacting the statute to insert, as descriptive words, airplanes, aircraft, or flying machines. If they had been in the legislative mind, the language would not have been expressed in such uncertainty as "any other self-propelled vehicle not designed for running on rails." The omission to definitely mention airplanes requires a construction that they were not included. Furthermore, by excepting vehicles running on rails, the meaning of the act is clarified. These words indicate it was meant to be confined to vehicles that run, but not on rails, and it did not extend to those that fly. Is it not an unreasonable view that airplanes fall within the description of self-propelled vehicles that do not run on rails? The question is its own answer.

The rule of ejusdem generis has special application to this statute. General words following a particular designation are usually presumed to be restricted so as to include only things or persons of the same kind, class, or nature, unless there is a clear manifestation of a contrary purpose. The general description in this statute refers to vehicles of the same general class as those enumerated. We may assume an airplane is a vehicle, in being a means of transportation. And it has its own motive power. But is an airplane classified generally with "an automobile, automobile truck, automobile wagon, or motor cycle?" Are airplanes regarded as other types of automobiles and the like? A moment's reflection demonstrates the contrary.

Counsel for appellant have referred us to the debates in Congress when the act was pending as persuasive of an interpretation in his favor. The proceedings are not permissible aids, apart from the journals or committee reports. But they may be referred to as showing the history of the period. The discussions of the proposed measure are enlightening in this case from a historic standpoint, in showing that the theft of automobiles was so prevalent over the land as to call for punitive restraint, but airplanes were never even mentioned.

It is familiar knowledge that the theft of automobiles had then become a public menace, but that airplanes had been rarely stolen if at all, and it is a most uncommon thing even at this date. The prevailing mischief sought to be corrected is an aid in the construction of a statute.

I am constrained to hold that airplanes were not meant by the act to be embraced in the designation of motor vehicles, and that the indictment charged no offense against the defendant.

McBOYLE v. UNITED STATES
283 U.S. 25 (1931)

Mr. Justice HOLMES delivered the opinion of the Court. . . .

The question is the meaning of the word "vehicle" in the phrase "any other self-propelled vehicle not designed for running on rails." No doubt etymologically it is possible to use the word to signify a conveyance working on land, water or air, and sometimes legislation extends the use in that direction, e.g., land and air, water being separately provided for, in the Tariff Act. But in everyday speech "vehicle" calls up the picture of a thing moving on land. Thus in Rev. St. § 4 intended, the Government suggests, rather to enlarge than to restrict the definition, vehicle includes every contrivance capable of being used "as a means of transportation on land." And this is repeated, expressly excluding aircraft, in the Tariff Act. So here, the phrase under discussion calls up the popular picture. For after including automobile truck, automobile wagon and motor cycle, the words "any other self-propelled vehicle not designed for running on rails" still indicate that a vehicle in the popular sense, that is a vehicle running on land is the theme. It is a vehicle that runs, not something, not commonly called a vehicle, that flies. Airplanes were well known in 1919 when this statute was passed, but it is admitted that they were not mentioned in the reports or in the debates in Congress. It is impossible to read words that so carefully enumerate the different forms of motor vehicles and have no reference of any kind to aircraft, as including airplanes under a term that usage more and more precisely confines to a different class. The counsel for the petitioner have shown that the phraseology of the statute as to motor vehicles follows that of earlier statutes of Connecticut, Delaware, Ohio, Michigan and Missouri, not to mention the late Regulations of Traffic for the District of Columbia, none of which can be supposed to leave the earth.

Although it is not likely that a criminal will carefully consider the text of the law before he murders or steals, it is reasonable that a fair warning should be given to the world in language that the common world will understand, of what the law intends to do if a certain line is passed. To make the warning fair, so far as possible the line should be clear. When a rule of conduct is laid down in words that evoke in the common mind only the picture of vehicles moving on land, the statute should not be extended to aircraft simply because it may seem to us that a similar policy applies, or upon the speculation that if the legislature had thought of it, very likely broader words would have been used.

Judgment reversed.

QUESTIONS

1. What theories of interpretation are reflected in the various opinions in the *McBoyle* case? On what resources does each opinion draw to interpret the word "vehicle"? What rules of interpretation does each opinion use?

2. Both the majority and the dissent in the court of appeals rely on the *ejusdem generis* rule. How do they arrive at opposite conclusions about what that rule dictates in the *McBoyle* case? Justice Cotteral, writing in dissent, describes the *ejusdem generis* rule as follows:

> General words following a particular designation are usually presumed to be restricted so as to include only things or persons of the same kind, class, or nature, unless there is a clear manifestation of a contrary purpose.

How should the "kind," "class," and "nature" of the things particularly designated in the National Motor Vehicle Theft Act be described? As vehicles? As land vehicles?

3. In interpreting the text of a statute, is it appropriate to look at the derivation of the words chosen by the legislature? Does a word's derivation show its present meaning? Or does it show what a word used to mean?

4. Justice Holmes focuses on "common language," what a word would "evoke in the common mind." In interpreting the text of a statute, is it preferable to look at what the words of the statute mean in "everyday speech," as Justice Holmes suggests, or to look at the dictionary definition of the word? Might these differ? How would one prove to a court what a word evokes in the common mind? How would one disprove another party's claim about what a word evokes in the common mind? If there are competing claims about what a word evokes, how would the judge resolve them? What does Justice Holmes use to support his claim about what the word "vehicle" evokes in the common mind?

5. What role should dictionaries play in statutory interpretation? Do dictionaries necessarily or typically reflect common usage? Does it depend on the age of the dictionary? On the lexicographer's attitude toward accepting new meanings of words? Are legislators likely to consult a dictionary when writing a statute? Are potential violators of the statute likely to consult a dictionary?

STATE v. PETERS

263 Wis. 2d 475, 665 N.W.2d 171 (2003)

Diane S. SYKES, J. This case is before the court on certification from the court of appeals on a question of first-impression regarding the scope of Wisconsin's identity theft statute, Wis. Stat. § 943.201 (1999-2000). Specifically, the question is whether a defendant who misappropriates another's identity and uses it during an arrest and in subsequent bail proceedings to obtain lower bail has done so "to obtain credit, money, goods, services or anything else of value" within the meaning of the identity theft statute. We answer this question yes.

"Bail" is statutorily defined as "monetary conditions of release." Wis. Stat. § 969.001(1). "Monetary" means "of or relating to money." *Webster's Third New International Dictionary* 1457-58 (1998). Bail can consist of cash or an unsecured appearance bond or both. In either case, it operates as a form of credit, securing the defendant's return to court. Accordingly, a defendant who misappropriates another's identity and uses it during an arrest and in bail proceedings to obtain lower bail has stolen that identity to obtain credit or money, or both, within the meaning of the identity theft statute.

I. Facts and Procedural History

On September 30, 2001, the loss prevention staff at a Racine Shopko store attempted to detain Pamela Lynn Peters and her son after the two had shoplifted a videogame system. During the confrontation, Peters produced a box-cutter and attempted to escape with other stolen goods. Upon arrest, Peters falsely identified herself to police as Patricia A. Panzer, d/o/b November 25, 1955, of N898 Elmore Drive, Campbellsport, Wisconsin. Patricia Panzer is the ex-wife of Peters' husband.

The State charged Peters, under the falsely assumed name of Patricia A. Panzer, with armed robbery and retail theft. Peters made her initial appearance in Racine County Circuit Court on October 1, 2001. During the initial appearance, Peters continued to falsely represent herself as Patricia Panzer. The State asked for a $20,000 cash bail. Based on Peters' falsely assumed identity, Peters' attorney argued that a $1,000 cash bail was appropriate, citing Panzer's stable Campbellsport address, lack of a criminal record, lack of any history of failed court appearances, and valid driver's license.

The court commissioner set bail as follows: "What I'm going to do, it's going to be a combination cash and signature bond. Again, I'm going to knock down the cash portion somewhat, but maybe not as much as your client would like. The total bond is going to be $20,000. $10,000 cash, $10,000 signature bond."

The next day, on October 2, 2001, the circuit court, the Honorable Wayne J. Marik, held an evidentiary hearing at the State's request and made findings of fact concerning Peters' actual identity. The circuit court found that the defendant was not Patricia A. Panzer but in fact was Pamela Lynn Peters, d/o/b November 15, 1964, of 715 Main Street, Lomira, Wisconsin. . . .

The court amended the case caption to reflect Peters' true identity, and then revisited the issue of bail. The State informed the court that, unlike Panzer, Peters had a record of criminal arrests including multiple counts of theft, resisting arrest, contributing to the delinquency of a child, possession of drug paraphernalia, possession of cocaine, and criminal damage to property. Furthermore, unlike Panzer, Peters had eight outstanding warrants for her arrest. After considering the new information, the circuit court concluded that there was "a very strong inference in the court's mind that the defendant was trying to establish an identity that could be verified pursuant to which she may be released and then able to flee." Having concluded that Peters was a substantial flight risk, in part because of the falsely assumed identity and previously unknown outstanding warrants, the court increased Peters' bail to $30,000 cash.

The State amended the complaint to reflect Peters' correct identifying information and added a charge of obstructing an officer. The State later filed a second amended complaint adding the charge that is at issue on this appeal, violation of the identity theft statute. The identity theft statute makes it a crime to intentionally misappropriate another's identity "to obtain credit, money, goods, services or anything else of value" without the other's consent.

The second amended complaint alleged that Peters told police she had lied about her true identity "because she had warrants outstanding in other jurisdictions." The complaint alleged that Peters had misappropriated Panzer's identity to obtain something of value, to wit "(1) not being taken into custody on warrants from other jurisdictions and (2) to obtain a lesser bond at the initial appearance in this matter."

Peters moved to dismiss the identity theft charge. She claimed that the complaint failed to allege one of the elements of the crime required by statute, specifically, that she had misappropriated another's identity to obtain "credit, money, goods, services or anything else of value." Peters argued that the doctrine of *ejusdem generis* as applied to the catch-all statutory phrase "anything else of value" required dismissal of the charge because bail was not like the other itemized things of value in the statute, i.e., credit, money, goods, or services. The doctrine of *ejusdem generis* is a "canon of construction that when a general word or phrase follows a list of specific persons or things, the general word or phrase will be interpreted to include only persons or things of the same type as those listed."

The circuit court granted Peters' motion and dismissed the charge. Applying *ejusdem generis*, the circuit court concluded that the phrase "anything else of value" . . . was limited to "something that is in a category of credit, money, goods, services, or having those types of characteristics having measurable value and worth in a commercial sense in the marketplace," and that "[o]btaining a more favorable bond in a criminal case does not in the court's opinion fall within that category."

The State appealed the dismissal of the identity theft charge. We accepted the court of appeals' certification of the case and now reverse.

II. STANDARD OF REVIEW AND PRINCIPLES OF INTERPRETATION

This case presents a question regarding the scope and interpretation of the identity theft statute. Questions of statutory interpretation are reviewed de novo.

If the language of a statute is clear on its face, we need not look any further than the statutory text to determine the statute's meaning. "When a statute unambiguously expresses the intent of the legislature, we apply that meaning without resorting to extrinsic sources" of legislative intent. Statutory language is given its common, ordinary and accepted meaning. Rules of statutory construction are inapplicable if the language of the statute has a plain and reasonable meaning on its face.

III. DISCUSSION

Wisconsin's identity theft statute, entitled "Misappropriation of personal identifying information or personal identification documents," provides as follows:

> Whoever intentionally uses or attempts to use any personal identifying information or personal identification document of an individual *to obtain credit, money, goods, services or anything else of value* without the authorization or consent of the individual and by representing that he or she is the individual or is acting with the authorization or consent of the individual is guilty of a Class D felony. Wis. Stat. § 943.210(2) (emphasis added).

. . . We disagree with the circuit court's restrictive reading of the identity theft statute. There is nothing in [the statute] that explicitly limits its application to identity thefts that are carried out to obtain something that has "commercial value" or "market value." Neither does the statute implicitly contain such a limitation.

The identity theft statute prohibits misappropriation of another's identity "to obtain credit, money, goods, services or anything else of value." Here, Peters is alleged to have misappropriated Panzer's identity to obtain a lower bail.

" 'Bail' means monetary conditions of release." Wis. Stat. § 939.001. "Monetary" means "of or relating to money." *Webster's, supra,* at 1457-58. Bail can also include an unsecured appearance or "signature" bond, in addition to or in lieu of cash. Wis. Stat. § 969.02(1) (misdemeanor bail) and § 969.03(1) (felony bail). The term "bond" as used in this context means "a writing . . . by which a person binds himself to pay a certain sum . . . ; also: the amount of money so guaranteed — often used with *give* <each must give [bond] for his appearance before the court>." *Webster's, supra,* at 250. Bail therefore represents either cash or the promise of cash, that is, an unsecured grant of credit. In either case, bail operates as a form of credit (secured or unsecured) for the defendant's return to court. As used in this context, bail as a form of "credit" is "the balance in a person's favor in an account."

Accordingly, a misappropriated identity that is used to obtain a lower bail obtains: 1) a reduced cash bail; 2) a signature bond with a lower money forfeiture; or 3) both. Therefore, because bail is statutorily defined as "monetary conditions of release," and can be expressed as either cash or a bond, or both, one who misappropriates another's identity and uses it to obtain lower bail in a criminal case has done so to obtain credit or money within the meaning of the identity theft statute.

True, bail does not have "commercial value" or "market value" in the sense that it is not bought, sold, or traded in the marketplace. But it plainly does have monetary value, is expressed in terms of cash or a bond, and operates as a form of credit. The circuit court's imposition of a requirement of measurable commercial or market value unduly restricted the statute's application contrary to its terms.

The circuit court arrived at this interpretation of the identity theft statute by applying the *ejusdem generis* canon of construction to the catch-all phrase "or anything else of value." We have concluded, however, that bail constitutes credit, money, or both, within the meaning of the identity theft statute, because bail is statutorily defined as "monetary conditions of release," takes the form of cash, a bond or a combination of the two, and operates as a form of credit.

Accordingly, this case does not require us to determine the precise meaning or scope of the phrase "or anything else of value" in the identity theft statute. It is enough to note that the addition of the phrase "or anything else of value" to the itemized list of "credit, money, goods [or] services" does not *narrow* the meaning of "credit, money, goods [or] services." There is no purpose for the presence of the phrase "or anything else of value" except to expand the list of potential qualifying "things of value." But we do not need to determine the precise meaning or scope of the phrase "or anything else of value" or attempt to delineate the outer limits of the identity theft statute in order to decide this case. Because bail can be cash, a bond, or both, and operates as a form of credit, the misappropriation of another's identity to obtain lower bail meets the statute's requirement that the perpetrator misappropriate an identity to obtain credit or money. . . .

Resort to the doctrine of *ejusdem generis* to determine the scope of the statutory phrase "or anything else of value" was unnecessary here. A person who misappropriates another's identity to obtain a lower bail has misappropriated that identity to obtain credit or money within the meaning of the identity theft statute. Accordingly, we reverse the circuit court's order dismissing the identity theft charge, and remand for reinstatement of the charge and further proceedings consistent with the opinion.

The order of the Racine County Circuit Court is reversed and the cause remanded for further proceedings consistent with this opinion.

Shirley S. ABRAHAMSON, Chief Justice (concurring).

I agree with the majority that a defendant who misappropriates another's identity and uses it during an arrest and subsequent proceedings to obtain lower bail does so in violation of Wis. Stat. § 943.201.

I

I write separately to reflect yet again on this court's approach to statutory interpretation. The majority opinion invokes the plain meaning rule in this case, explaining that it will not look beyond the statutory text to determine a statute's meaning if the language is clear on its face.[2] It then announces that "canons of construction . . . are inapplicable when a statute is clear" and uses this "rule" as a bar to applying the ejusdem generis canon of construction in the present case.

How strange. First, the plain meaning rule is itself a canon of construction.[6] Second, many of the other interpretive techniques employed by the majority opinion to construe Wis. Stat. § 943.201 are also canons of construction. For example, the maxim that statutory language is given its common, ordinary and accepted meaning is a canon of construction.[7] So is the rule that courts may refer to a recognized dictionary to determine the common meaning of terms,[8] and the rule that a statutory definition declaring what a term means is binding upon the court.[9] The majority opinion openly invokes all of these canons of construction despite concluding that the language is plain on its face. It offers no reason why the plain meaning rule permits the use of these canons, but not use of the canon of ejusdem generis.

The majority opinion creates a false division between the plain meaning rule and canons of construction. Proponents of the plain meaning rule reject the use of "extrinsic aids" to construction such as legislative history, history of the enactment process, committee reports, and legislative debates, when the language of a statute is "clear and unambiguous." The plain meaning rule's advocates do not, however, reject the use of "intrinsic aids" that assist in discerning whether the language of a statute is plain on its face, such as other statutes, statutory definitions, and dictionaries.

---

[2] Needless to say, "clarity and ambiguity are in the eyes of the beholder."

[6] See Karl N. Llewellyn, Remarks on the Theory of Appellate Decision and the Rules or Canons About How Statutes Are To Be Construed, 3 Vand. L. Rev. 395, 403 (1950) ("If language is plain and unambiguous it must be given effect" is canon of construction); David L. Shapiro, Continuity and Change in Statutory Interpretation, 67 N.Y.U. L. Rev. 921, 927-934 (1992) (describing inclusio unius, ejusdem generis, and the plain meaning rule as linguistic canons of interpretation); see also Conn. Nat'l Bank v. Germain, 503 U.S. 249, 254, 112 S. Ct. 1146, 117 L. Ed. 2d 391 (1992) ("When the words of a statute are unambiguous, then, this first canon [of interpretation] is also the last: 'judicial inquiry is complete.' "); CBS Inc. v. PrimeTime 24 Joint Venture, 245 F.3d 1217, 1225 n. 6 (11th Cir. 2001) (the plain meaning rule "is the largest caliber canon of them all").

[7] Perrin v. United States, 444 U.S. 37, 43, 100 S. Ct. 311, 62 L. Ed. 2d 199 (1979) ("A fundamental canon of statutory construction is that, unless otherwise defined, words will be interpreted as taking their ordinary, contemporary, common meaning.").

[8] JVC Co. of America v. United States, 234 F.3d 1348, 1352 (Fed. Cir. 2000) ("A court may rely upon its own understanding of the terms used, lexicographic and scientific authorities, dictionaries, and other reliable information" to determine the common meaning of a term.)

[9] Norman J. Singer, Statutes and Statutory Construction § 47:07, at 227-28 (6th ed. 2000) (citing Nat'l City Lines, Inc. v. LLC Corp., 687 F.2d 1122, 1133 (8th Cir. 1982)).

"Intrinsic aids" to construction, including rules of grammar and generalizations about customary habits in the use of language, are essential to any application of the plain meaning rule. "Even when a judge claims not to be construing a statute, he [or she] can not help using what he [or she] has learned about customary language usage and common understanding associated with the relevant text." The rules that words should be given their plain and ordinary meaning and that courts may resort to a dictionary to ascertain the meaning of words are simply generalizations about customary habits in the use of language that are part and parcel of the process of interpreting the meaning of a statute's text.

One benefit of applying canons of construction, rather than considering legislative history, is that their application does not require resort to extrinsic material. Instead, the canons of construction focus on the text actually approved by Congress and made a part of our country's laws. As the Supreme Court [recently confirmed] where the meaning of a statute is discernible in light of canons of construction, we should not resort to legislative history or other extrinsic evidence. Canons of construction are essentially tools which help us to determine whether the meaning of a statutory provision is sufficiently plain, in light of the text of the statute as a whole, to avoid the need to consider extrinsic evidence of Congress' intent.

Similarly, ejusdem generis is simply a generalization about the use of words. Ejusdem generis is Latin for "of the same kind," and means that when general words follow specific words in a statutory enumeration, the general words are construed to embrace objects similar in nature to those objects enumerated by the preceding specific words. For example, ejusdem generis might suggest that the phrase "any other games" in a statute encompassing "baseball, basketball, football, and any other games" would be limited to team sports (like soccer) and not include "games" like chess or video games. An enumeration followed by a "catch all" phrase is a common drafting technique that saves a legislature from having to spell out every contingency in advance.

Ejusdem generis is not always an appropriate canon of construction, even when a statute includes a list of specific words followed by general words in an enumeration. The applicability of this canon must be resolved as part of a court's effort to determine the meaning of a statute's text. The canon is an "intrinsic aid" that is germane to a textualist approach to statutory interpretation; that is, it is both compatible with and necessary to the plain meaning rule, just like the other canons the majority opinion relies on in the present case.

The vast majority of cases coming to this court involve the interpretation of some writing, be it a statute, a constitution, a contract, or some other document. The consistency and coherence of our approach to interpretation is therefore vital. Litigants, lawyers, legislators, judges, and the citizens of Wisconsin deserve to know and understand how we approach interpretation.

As I have stated, proper statutory interpretation requires that a court take a comprehensive view toward discerning legislative intent that begins with consideration of the language of a statute and then looks to all relevant evidence of legislative intent including its scope, history, context, subject matter and purpose.

II

Finally, while on the topic of rules, let me turn to another rule. The majority opinion violates a basic rule of appellate decision making: courts are not to reach out and decide issues unnecessary to the case at hand. The majority opinion correctly concludes that a person is guilty of identity theft under Wis. Stat. § 943.201 when he or she misappropriates another's identity to obtain lower bail because bail falls within the statutory words "to obtain credit or money." It is thus not necessary to the present case to reach out and further state in what amounts to dicta that the phrase "or anything else of value" in § 943.201 is unduly restricted if it is interpreted to include only items with measurable commercial or market value.[21] As I have written before, there is a growing tendency for this court to reach out and decide issues that are not squarely presented. This tendency is, I believe, detrimental to the development of Wisconsin law.

Similarly here, we reject the narrow reading of the identity theft statute adopted by the circuit court. We conclude that the circuit court improperly restricted the scope of the identity theft statute to preclude its application to the facts present in this case. Resort to the doctrine of ejusdem generis to determine the scope of the statutory phrase "or anything else of value" was unnecessary here.

For the foregoing reasons, I write separately.

William A. Bablitch, J. (concurring).

"That depends on what the meaning of the word 'is' is." William Jefferson Clinton

I write only to emphasize that canons of statutory construction, such as the "plain meaning" rule, are tools, not rules. They are all designed to reach one fundamental goal: discerning legislative intent. Ignoring relevant evidence on legislative intent in the name of "plain meaning" will necessarily at times lead to an interpretation that is completely contrary to what the legislature intended.

Language is inherently ambiguous — perhaps not as ambiguous as the quotation above would have us believe, but the quote makes a point: plain meaning is frequently in the eye of the beholder. What is plain to one may be ambiguous to another. If good evidence as to legislative intent is present, why not use it? Accordingly, I join Chief Justice Abrahamson's concurrence.

QUESTIONS

1. Was it likely the Wisconsin legislature thought about a criminal defendant obtaining bail through use of a false identity when it wrote the Wisconsin identity theft statute? If not, should that make any difference in whether or not a Wisconsin court interprets the statute as applying to such conduct?

2. In explaining the *ejusdem generis* canon, Chief Justice Abrahamson states that legislative use of a "catch all" phrase "saves the legislature from having to spell out every contingency in advance." Shouldn't the legislature be required to spell out every contingency in advance in order to give clear notice to potential violators? Why? Why not?

3. Justice Sykes says that "Rules of statutory construction are inapplicable if the language of the statute has a plain and reasonable meaning on its face." Do you think she means what she says? Or do you think she means that when the text of a statute is clear, no extrinsic aids should be used to determine legislative intent?

---

[21] We disagree with the circuit court's restrictive reading of the identity theft statute. There is nothing in Wis. Stat. § 943.201 that explicitly limits its application to identity thefts that are carried out to obtain something that has "commercial value" or "market value." Neither does the statute implicitly contain such a limitation.

Should one adopt a textualist approach in interpreting what Justice Sykes wrote? Or an intentionalist approach?

4. What do the words "intrinsic" and "extrinsic" mean in referring to aids to interpretation? What intrinsic and extrinsic aids have you encountered in the criminal law course besides those mentioned by Chief Justice Abrahamson? Chief Justice Abrahamson states that a benefit of use of canons of construction is that "their application does not require resort to extrinsic material." Is this true? Are all canons, then, intrinsic?

5. The prosecution charged Ms. Peters with having misappropriated Ms. Panzer's identity to obtain two different things of value: "(1) not being taken into custody on warrants from other jurisdictions and (2) to obtain a lesser bond at the initial appearance in this matter." The Supreme Court addressed only the question of whether the second of these, obtaining a lesser bond, fell within the identity theft statute. Is "not being taken into custody on warrants from other jurisdictions" a thing of value for purposes of the identity theft statute? Should the court have addressed this question?

STATE v. COURCHESNE
262 Conn. 537, 816 A.2d 562 (2003)

BORDEN, J. Under our statutory scheme, a defendant becomes eligible for the death penalty if he is convicted of a capital felony for the "murder of two or more persons at the same time or in the course of a single transaction. . . . " One of the aggravating factors that permits the imposition of the death penalty is that "the defendant committed the offense in an especially heinous, cruel or depraved manner. . . . " Although in *State v. Breton* we had been asked to decide whether it was necessary for the state, in order to seek the death penalty based on that factor, to prove that the defendant had killed "both . . . of the victims in an especially cruel manner," rather than just one of the victims, we ultimately did not have to answer that question because the evidence was sufficient to show that he had done so with respect to both victims. The present case, however, requires us to decide that question.

Thus, the sole issue of this appeal is whether, when the defendant has been convicted of a capital felony for the murder of two persons in the course of a single transaction . . . the state, in order to establish the aggravating factor defined by § 53a-46 (i)(4), must prove that the defendant murdered both victims in an especially heinous, cruel or depraved manner.[3] We conclude that proof that the defendant committed at least one of the murders in the specified aggravated manner is sufficient. Accordingly, we reverse the ruling of the trial court to the contrary. . . .

[The facts of the case were described by the court as follows.]

. . . In the late evening hours of December 15, 1998, [Courchesne] stabbed Demetris Rodgers to death. At the time she was stabbed, she was pregnant with Antonia Rodgers. Although Demetris Rodgers was dead on arrival at the hospital,

---

[3] Pursuant to General Statutes § 52-265a and Practice Book §§ 83-1 and 61-6(c), the Chief Justice granted the state's request to appeal from the interlocutory ruling of the trial court that, in order for the death penalty to be imposed, the state must prove that both murders were committed in the aggravated manner.

the physicians at the hospital performed an emergency cesarean section and delivered Antonia Rodgers, who lived for forty-two days before dying from global anoxic encephalopathy, or deprivation of oxygen to the brain. . . .

[In the paragraphs that follow, a majority of the justices decide that the plain meaning rule, though used by the court for many years, should be abandoned as a tool of statutory interpretation.]

III

We take this opportunity to clarify the approach of this court to the process of statutory interpretation. For at least a century, this court has relied on sources beyond the specific text of the statute at issue to determine the meaning of the language as intended by the legislature. For that same period of time, however, this court often has eschewed resort to those sources when the meaning of the text appeared to be plain and unambiguous.

In 1994, however, we noted a dichotomy in our case law regarding whether resort to extratextual sources was appropriate even in those instances where the text's meaning appeared to be plain and unambiguous. In *Frillici v. Westport*, we stated: "It is true that, in construing statutes, we have often relied upon the canon of statutory construction that we need not, and indeed ought not, look beyond the statutory language to other interpretive aids unless the statute's language is not absolutely clear and unambiguous. That maxim requires some slight but plausible degree of linguistic ambiguity as a kind of analytical threshold that must be surmounted before a court may resort to aids to the determination of the meaning of the language as applied to the facts of the case. It is also true, however, that we have often eschewed such an analytical threshold, and have stated that, in interpreting statutes, we look at all the available evidence, such as the statutory language, the legislative history, the circumstances surrounding its enactment, the purpose and policy of the statute, and its relationship to existing legislation and common law principles. This analytical model posits that the legislative process is purposive, and that the meaning of legislative language (indeed, of any particular use of our language) is best understood by viewing not only the language at issue, but by its context and by the purpose or purposes behind its use."

Since then, we have not been consistent in our formulation of the appropriate method of interpreting statutory language. At times, we have adhered to the formulation that requires identification of some degree of ambiguity in that language before consulting any sources of its meaning beyond the statutory text. We refer herein to that formulation as the "plain meaning rule," which we discuss in further detail later in this opinion. At other times, we have . . . adhered to a more encompassing formulation that does not require passing any threshold of ambiguity as a precondition of consulting extratextual sources of the meaning of legislative language.

A

We now make explicit that our approach to the process of statutory interpretation is governed by the . . . formulation [set forth in *Bender v. Bender*, 258 Conn. 733, 785 A.2d 197 (2001),] as further explicated herein. The first two sentences of that formulation set forth the fundamental task of the court in engaging in the process of statutory interpretation, namely, engaging in a "reasoned search for the intention of the legislature," which we further defined as a reasoned search for "the meaning of the statutory language as applied to the facts of [the] case, including the question of whether the language actually does apply."[21] The rest of the formulation sets forth the range of sources that we will examine in order to determine that meaning. That formulation admonishes the court to consider all relevant sources of meaning of the language at issue — namely, the words of the statute, its legislative history and the circumstances surrounding its enactment, the legislative policy it was designed to implement, and its relationship to existing legislation and to common-law principles governing the same general subject matter. We also now make explicit that we ordinarily will consider all of those sources beyond the language itself, without first having to cross any threshold of ambiguity of the language.

We emphasize, moreover, that the language of the statute is the most important factor to be considered, for three very fundamental reasons. First, the language of the statute is what the legislature enacted and the governor signed. It is, therefore, the law. Second, the process of interpretation is, in essence, the search for the meaning *of that language* as applied to the facts of the case, including the question of whether it does apply to those facts. Third, all language has limits, in the sense that we are not free to attribute to legislative language a meaning that it simply will not bear in the usage of the English language.

Therefore — and we make this explicit as well — we always *begin* the process of interpretation with a searching examination of that language, attempting to determine the range of plausible meanings that it may have in the context in which it appears and, if possible, narrowing that range down to those that appear most plausible. Thus, the statutory language is always the starting point of the interpretive inquiry. A significant point of the *Bender* formulation, however, is that we do not end the process with the language.

The reason for this . . . is that "the legislative process is purposive, and . . . the meaning of legislative language (indeed, of any particular use of our language) is best understood by viewing not only the language at issue, but by its context and by the purpose or purposes behind its use."

Thus, the purpose or purposes of the legislation, and the context of that legislative language, which includes the other sources noted in *Bender* are directly relevant to its meaning as applied to the facts of the case before us.

Indeed, in our view, the concept of the context of statutory language should be broadly understood. That is, the context of statutory language necessarily includes the other language used in the statute or statutory scheme at issue, the language used in other relevant statutes, the general subject matter of the legislation at issue, the history or genealogy of the statute, as well as the other, extratextual sources identified by the *Bender* formulation. All of these sources, textual as well as contextual, are to be considered, along with the purpose or purposes of the legislation, in determining the meaning of the language of the statute as applied to the facts of the case.

B

This brings us to a discussion of what is commonly known as the "plain meaning rule." Although we have used many different formulations of the plain meaning

---

[21] We need not enter a semiotic debate with the dissent about whether a group such as a legislature can have an "intent," as opposed to a "purpose," in enacting legislation. Both this court and courts throughout the nation have long employed the language of "legislative intent," both within and outside the confines of the plain meaning rule, without any apparent confusion about what it means. . . .

rule, all of them have in common the fundamental premise, stated generally, that, where the statutory language is plain and unambiguous, the court must stop its interpretive process with that language; there is in such a case no room for interpretation; and, therefore, in such a case, the court must not go beyond that language.

It is useful to note that both the plain meaning rule and the *Bender* formulation have, as a general matter, their starting points in common: both begin by acknowledging that the task of the court is to ascertain the intent of the legislature in using the language that it chose to use, so as to determine its meaning in the context of the case. Where these approaches differ, however, is on how to go about that task.

Unlike the *Bender* formulation, under the plain meaning rule, there are certain cases in which that task must, as a matter of law, end with the statutory language. Thus, it is necessary to state precisely what the plain meaning rule means.

The plain meaning rule means that in a certain category of cases — namely, those in which the court first determines that the language at issue is plain and unambiguous — the court is *precluded as a matter of law* from going beyond the text of that language to consider any extratextual evidence of the meaning of that language, no matter how persuasive that evidence might be. Indeed, the rule even precludes reference to that evidence where that evidence, if consulted, would *support or confirm* that plain meaning. Furthermore, inherent in the plain meaning rule is the admonition that the courts are to seek the objective meaning of the language used by the legislature "not in what [the legislature] meant to say, but in [the meaning of] what it did say."[25] Another inherent part of the plain meaning rule is the exception that the plain and unambiguous meaning is *not* to be applied if it would produce an unworkable or absurd result.[26]

Thus, the plain meaning rule, at least as most commonly articulated in our jurisprudence, may be restated as follows: If the language of the statute is plain and unambiguous, and if the result yielded by that plain and unambiguous meaning is not absurd or unworkable, the court must not *interpret* the language (i.e., there is no room for construction); instead, the court's sole task is to apply that language literally to the facts of the case, and it is precluded as a matter of law from consulting any extratextual sources regarding the meaning of the language at issue. Furthermore, in deciding whether the language is plain and unambiguous, the court is confined to what may be regarded as the objective meaning of the language used by the legislature, and may not inquire into what the legislature may have intended the language to mean — that is, it may not inquire into the purpose or purposes for which the legislature used the language. Finally, the plain meaning rule sets forth a set of thresholds of ambiguity or uncertainty, and the court must surmount each of those thresholds in order to consult additional sources of meaning of the language

---

[25] There are, however, directly contradictory statements about this method of approach in our jurisprudence. In Doe v. Institute of Living, Inc., 175 Conn. 49, 57, 392 A.2d 491 (1978), for example, we stated: "Legislative intent is to be found *not in what the legislature meant to say, but in the meaning of what it did say.*" (Emphasis added.) In that same case, however, we also stated: "Indeed, [t]he particular inquiry is *not what is the abstract force of the words or what they may comprehend, but in what sense were they intended to be understood* or what understanding do they convey as used in the particular act." (Emphasis added; internal quotation marks omitted.) Id.

[26] Although we have not confronted it in our jurisprudence, another commonly recognized exception to the plain meaning rule is that the rule will not be applied where resort to the legislative history discloses a drafting error in the statutory language as enacted. This exception demonstrates a fundamental flaw in the dissent's methodology. If the court is precluded from examining legislative history where the statute appears unambiguous, it will not discover such a drafting error.

of the statute. Thus, whatever may lie beyond any of those thresholds may in any given case be barred from consideration by the court, irrespective of its ultimate usefulness in ascertaining the meaning of the statutory language at issue.

We now make explicit what is implicit in what we have already said: in performing the process of statutory interpretation, we do not follow the plain meaning rule in whatever formulation it may appear. We disagree with the plain meaning rule as a useful rubric for the process of statutory interpretation for several reasons.

First, the rule is fundamentally inconsistent with the purposive and contextual nature of legislative language. Legislative language *is* purposive and contextual, and its meaning simply cannot be divorced from the purpose or purposes for which it was used and from its context. Put another way, it *does* matter, in determining that meaning, what purpose or purposes the legislature had in employing the language; it *does* matter what meaning the legislature intended the language to have.

Second, the plain meaning rule is inherently self-contradictory. It is a misnomer to say, as the plain meaning rule says, that, if the language is plain and unambiguous, there is no room for interpretation, because application of the statutory language to the facts of the case *is interpretation* of that language. In such a case, the task of interpretation may be a simple matter, but that does not mean that no interpretation is required.

The plain meaning rule is inherently self-contradictory in another way. That part of the rule that excepts from its application cases in which the plain language would yield an absurd or unworkable result is implicitly, but necessarily, premised on the process of going beyond the text of the statute to the legislature's intent in writing that text. This is because the only plausible reason for that part of the rule is that the legislature could not have intended for its language to have a meaning that yielded such a result. Indeed, we have explicitly acknowledged as much. Thus, application of this aspect of the plain meaning rule requires an implicit inquiry into the legislature's intent or purpose, beyond the bare text, thus, in effect, permitting the court to *rule out* the plain meaning of the language because that meaning would produce an absurd or unworkable result. We see no persuasive reason for a rule of law that prohibits a court from similarly going beyond the bare text of the statute to *rule in* a *different* meaning that other sources of meaning might suggest in any given case. Yet such a prohibition is precisely what the plain meaning rule accomplishes.

Third, application of the plain meaning rule necessarily requires the court to engage in a threshold determination of whether the language is ambiguous. This requirement, in turn, has led this court into a number of declarations that are, in our view, intellectually and linguistically dubious, and risk leaving the court open to the criticism of being result-oriented in interpreting statutes.[28] Thus, for example, we have stated that statutory language does not become ambiguous "merely because the parties contend for different meanings." Yet, if parties contend for different meanings, and each meaning is plausible, that is essentially what "ambiguity" ordinarily means in such a context in our language. See Webster's Third

---

[28] As Justice Stevens of the United States Supreme Court aptly stated: "Justice Aharon Barak of the Supreme Court of Israel . . . has perceptively noted that the 'minimalist' judge 'who holds that the purpose of the statute may be learned only from its language' has more discretion than the judge 'who will seek guidance from every reliable source.' Judicial Discretion 62 (Y. Kaufmann transl. 1989). A method of statutory interpretation that is deliberately uninformed, and hence unconstrained, may produce a result that is consistent with a court's own views of how things should be, but it may also defeat the very purpose for which a provision was enacted." Circuit City Stores, Inc. v. Adams, 532 U.S. 105, 133, 121 S. Ct. 1302, 149 L. Ed. 2d 234 (2001) (Stevens, J., dissenting).

New International Dictionary, and Merriam-Webster's Collegiate Dictionary (10th Ed.), for the various meanings of "ambiguity" and "ambiguous" in this context. For example, in Merriam Webster's Collegiate Dictionary, the most apt definition of "ambiguous" for this context is: "[C]apable of being understood in two or more possible senses or ways." We also have stated that, although the statutory language is clear on its face, it contains a "latent ambiguity" that is disclosed by its application to the facts of the case, or by reference to its legislative history and purpose. Statutory language, however, always requires some application to the facts of the case. Therefore, the notion of such a "latent ambiguity" as a predicate to resort to extratextual sources simply does not make sense. Moreover, we have stated that the plain meaning principle does not apply where the statutory language, although clear and unambiguous, is not *absolutely* clear and unambiguous. . . . " The line of demarcation between clear and unambiguous language, on one hand, and *absolutely* clear and unambiguous language, on the other hand, however, eludes us. We have stated further that the court may go beyond the literal language of the statute when "a common sense interpretation leads to an ambiguous . . . result. . . . " It is similarly difficult to make sense of the notion of otherwise clear language becoming ambiguous because it leads to an "ambiguous . . . result. . . . " Indeed, within the very same case: (1) we have stated that the language of the statute is clear and unambiguous and, therefore, "is not subject to construction"; and (2) nonetheless, "we *construe[d]*" the statute so as to avoid a particular result that one of the parties had pointed out would otherwise come within that plain language. (Emphasis added.) Thus, in that case, in applying the plain meaning rule, we directly violated it. We see little value in a rule of law that has led this court into such dubious distinctions.

We emphasize here that we do not contend that any of this court's applications of the plain meaning rule in the past, or that any current adherence to it, involves such result-oriented decision-making. Our point, drawing from Justice Stevens' remarks, is, rather, twofold: (1) attempting to follow the rule necessarily has led to dubious analytical methods and distinctions, which in turn may give the appearance of such result-oriented decision-making; and (2) the more evidence that a court consults about the meaning of legislative language, the more constrained it will be in arriving at a conclusion about that meaning.

Eschewing the plain meaning rule does not mean, however, that we will not in any given case follow what may be regarded as the plain meaning of the language.[30] Indeed, in most cases, that meaning will, once the extratextual sources of meaning contained in the *Bender* formulation *are* considered, prove to be the legislatively intended meaning of the language.

There are cases, however, in which the extratextual sources will indicate a different meaning strongly enough to lead the court to conclude that the legislature intended the language to have that different meaning. Importantly, and consistent with our admonition that the statutory language is the most important factor in this analysis, in applying the *Bender* formulation, we necessarily employ a kind of sliding scale: the more strongly the bare text of the language suggests a particular

---

[30] It is important in this connection to define what we mean in this context by the phrase, "what may be regarded as the plain meaning of the language." By that phrase we mean the meaning that is so strongly indicated or suggested by the language as applied to the facts of the case, without consideration, however, of its purpose or the other, extratextual sources of meaning contained in the *Bender* formulation, that, when the language is read as so applied, it appears to be *the* meaning and appears to preclude any other likely meaning. . . .

meaning, the more persuasive the extratextual sources will have to be in order for us to conclude that the legislature intended a different meaning.[31] Such a sliding scale, however, is easier to state than to apply. In any given case, it necessarily will come down to a judgmental weighing of all of the evidence bearing on the question.

The point of the *Bender* formulation, however, is that it requires the court, in *all* cases, to consider *all* of the relevant evidence bearing on the meaning of the language at issue. Thus, *Bender's* underlying premise is that, the more such evidence the court considers, the more likely it is that the court will arrive at a proper conclusion regarding that meaning.

Moreover, despite the fact that, as we noted at the outset of this discussion, no other jurisdiction specifically has adopted the particular formulation for statutory interpretation that we now adopt, there is really nothing startlingly new about its core, namely, the idea that the court may look for the meaning of otherwise clear statutory language beyond its literal meaning, even when that meaning would not yield an absurd or unworkable result. . . .

Before concluding this discussion, we respond to several of the main points of the dissent. The dissent takes issue with both the appropriateness and the reliability of ascertaining the purpose or purposes of the statute under consideration in determining its meaning. This point demonstrates a fundamental difference between our view and the dissent's view of the nature of legislation. We think that legislation is inherently purposive and that, therefore, it is not only appropriate, but necessary to consider the purpose or purposes of legislation in order to determine its meaning. Furthermore, the experience of this court demonstrates no particular difficulty in reliably ascertaining such purposes, based not on our own personal preferences but on both textual and extratextual sources. . . .

The dissent also suggests that judges, by employing a purposive approach to statutory interpretation rather than the plain meaning rule, will substitute our own notions of wise and intelligent policy for the policy of the legislature. We agree that this may happen; any court *may* be intellectually dishonest in performing *any* judicial task, whether it be interpreting a statute or adjudicating a dispute involving only the common law. We suggest, however, that the risk of intellectual dishonesty is just as great, or as minimal, in employing the plain meaning rule as in employing the method of interpretation that we articulate. If a court is determined to be intellectually dishonest and reach the result that it *wants* the statute to mandate, rather than the result that an honest and objective appraisal of its meaning would yield, it will find a way to do so under any articulated rubric of statutory interpretation. Furthermore, by insisting that *all* evidence of meaning be considered and explained before the court arrives at the meaning of a statute, we think that the risk of intellectual dishonesty in performing that task will be minimized. Indeed, resort to and explanation of extratextual sources may provide a certain transparency to the court's analytical and interpretive process that could be lacking under the employment of the plain meaning rule. In sum, we have confidence in the ability of this court to ascertain, explain and apply the purpose or purposes of a statute in an intellectually honest manner.

The dissent also contends that the plain meaning rule is based on the constitutional doctrine of the separation of powers. Our only response to this assertion is that there is simply no basis for it. In our view, contrary to that of the dissent,

---

[31] Alaska has adopted a similar sliding scale approach. See Wold v. Progressive Preferred Ins. Co., 52 P.3d 155, 161 (Alaska 2002).

there is nothing in either the federal or the Connecticut constitutional doctrine of the separation of powers that compels *any* particular method or rubric of statutory interpretation, that precludes a court from employing a purposive and contextual method of interpreting statutes, or that compels the judiciary to employ the plain meaning rule, in performing its judicial task of interpreting the meaning of legislative language. Simply put, the task of the legislative branch is to draft and enact statutes, and the task of the judicial branch is to interpret and apply them in the context of specific cases. The constitution says nothing about what type of language the legislature must employ in performing its tasks, and nothing about what method or methods the judiciary must employ in ascertaining the meaning of that language.[32] . . .

The ruling of the trial court requiring the state to prove that both murders were committed in the aggravated manner is reversed and the case is remanded for further proceedings according to law.

ZARELLA, J., with whom SULLIVAN, C.J., joins, dissenting. . . .

I . . . strongly disagree with the majority's approach to statutory interpretation and its abandonment of the plain meaning rule. . . . The majority's method of statutory interpretation is radical, its central premise is misguided, and its application is likely to lead to an unpredictable and unconstrained statutory interpretation jurisprudence. . . .

The plain meaning rule encourages both judicial restraint and predictability in interpretation. Indeed, a court's disregard of the plain meaning of a legislature's enactments amounts to little more than judicial lawmaking. Such judicial lawmaking constitutes an arrogation of the legislature's constitutional responsibility to enact laws.

Moreover, the majority's abandonment of the plain meaning rule and its adoption of the alternative purposive approach to statutory interpretation pays little heed to this fundamental principle of the separation of powers. In applying the majority's approach, a judge will ask himself for what purpose was the statute enacted. In answering this question, a judge likely will ask what purpose a wise and intelligent lawmaker would have attached to the statute. The judge then will ask himself what he, who, after all, also is wise and intelligent, believes the law's purpose is. In so doing, the judge will assume the role of law giver and substitute judicially ascribed notions of the statute's purpose for the plain meaning of the text that the legislature has chosen. See *id.* This is precisely what the majority transparently has done in the present case. Indeed, each step in the majority's analysis begins with a statement such as, "[w]e can conceive of no rationale for the legislature" to have enacted a statute that differs in interpretation from that proposed by the majority.

---

[32] In this connection, we also reject the dissent's suggestion that, by employing the plain meaning rule, we will give the legislature an incentive to write clear statutes and, presumably, therefore, also give it a disincentive to write poorly drafted statutes. We do not regard it as appropriate for the judiciary, by creating incentives or disincentives, to instruct the legislature on how to write statutes, any more than it would be appropriate for the legislature, directly or indirectly, to instruct the judiciary on how to write opinions. We presume that the legislature, within the constraints of time and other resources, does the best it can in attempting to capture in legislative language what it is attempting to accomplish by its legislation. No legislature, or legislative drafter, has the ability to foresee all of the questions that may arise under the language that it employs. Our task is to do the best we can in interpreting its language, within the context of specific factual situations presented by specific cases and within the limits of that language, so as to make sense of the statute before us and so as to carry out the legislature's purpose or purposes in enacting that statute.

Conversely, the incentive for legislators to write clear statutes and for interest groups to prevail in getting their views enacted into law takes on a diminished importance if it is made known to them that this court will not limit itself to the plain meaning of the law but, rather, will decide cases on the basis of the unenacted purposes behind a law. By contrast, the plain meaning rule encourages legislators to "fulfill their constitutional responsibility to legislate by disabusing them of the expectation that the courts will do it for them."

For the foregoing reasons, I respectfully dissent.

The *Courchesne* case was decided on March 11, 2003. On June 26, 2003, the Connecticut legislature passed the following statute, effective October 1, 2003.

Connecticut General Statutes Annotated, P.A. No. 03-154   *An Act Concerning Statutory Interpretation*

The meaning of a statute shall, in the first instance, be ascertained from the text of the statute itself and its relationship to other statutes. If, after examining such text and considering such relationship, the meaning of such text is plain and unambiguous and does not yield absurd or unworkable results, extratextual evidence of the meaning of the statute shall not be considered.

QUESTIONS

1. What are the advantages and disadvantages of the plain meaning rule?

2. What are the advantages and disadvantages of the "sliding scale" approach to statutory interpretation described in *Courchesne*? The *Courchesne* majority opinion states that the premise of the sliding scale approach is that "[t]he more evidence the court considers, the more likely it is that the court will arrive at a proper conclusion regarding that meaning." Is this true? Is the public likely to have access to such information? What about the police?

3. Justice Borden writes for the majority in *Courchesne*:

We do not regard it as appropriate for the judiciary, by creating incentives or disincentives, to instruct the legislature on how to write statutes, any more than it would be appropriate for the legislature, directly or indirectly, to instruct the judiciary on how to write opinions.

Should the legislature instruct the judiciary on how to interpret the statutes the legislature writes? Or should judges choose the methods and rules they use when interpreting a statute?

4. Lon Fulller has written that it is not "possible to interpret a word in a statute without knowing the aim of the statute."[2] Would Justice Scalia agree with Professor Fuller? Do you agree with Professor Fuller?

------

[2] L. Fuller, *Positivism and Fidelity to Law—A Reply to Professor Hart*, 71 Harv. L. Rev. 630, 664 (1958).

PEOPLE VERSUS KNOLLER AND NOEL

On January 26, 2001, Diane Whipple, a 33-year-old college lacrosse coach, died from wounds inflicted by at least one, and perhaps two, Presa Canario dogs, named Bane and Hera. The dog(s) had attacked her just outside the door of her apartment inside her San Francisco apartment building. Diane Whipple's neighbors, Marjorie Knoller and Robert Noel, owned the dogs.

A grand jury indicted Ms. Knoller for second-degree murder (California Penal Code § 187) (Count 1), involuntary manslaughter (California Penal Code § 192(b)) (Count 2), and negligent ownership of a mischievous animal that causes the death of a human being (California Penal Code § 399) (Count 3), and Mr. Noel for the latter two offenses. The defendants were tried before a jury, which found them guilty on all charges.

The defense filed a motion for a new trial. Judge Warren granted the motion on the second-degree murder charge.

Below you will find excerpts of the June 17, 2002, transcript of the proceedings in which Judge Warren announced his grant of the defense motion for a new trial for Ms. Knoller on the second-degree murder charge.

As you read the material below, think about the mental state requirements in California for second-degree murder and involuntary manslaughter. Consider whether, in your view, based on the summary given by Judge Warren, the prosecution proved its case against Ms. Knoller on the second-degree murder, as compared with the involuntary manslaughter, charge beyond a reasonable doubt. Marshal the best arguments you can for the prosecution and for the defense.

In addition, consider the evidence, as presented by Judge Warren, with respect to the charges against Mr. Noel. Note Judge Warren's comments regarding Mr. Noel's culpability. Would the evidence have supported a conviction of Mr. Noel on a second-degree murder charge?

---

1. Based on materials provided by Professor Lois Weithorn. The line and page numbers of the excerpted transcript, which follows, do not necessarily correspond to the line numbers and pages in the original transcript.

SUPERIOR COURT OF CALIFORNIA

COUNTY OF SAN FRANCISCO

HONORABLE JAMES L. WARREN, JUDGE

DEPARTMENT NO. 26

THE PEOPLE OF THE STATE OF   )
)
          CALIFORNIA, Plaintiff,   )   S.C. No. 181813-01
)   C. No. 1977360
               -vs-   )   S.C. No. 181813-02
)   C. No. 1977361
MARJORIE KNOLLER and ROBERT NOEL,   )
)   Page 5565-5612
                    Defendants.   )
_____   )

REPORTER'S TRANSCRIPT OF PROCEEDINGS

Held on Monday, June 17, 2002

APPEARANCES:

For the People: TERENCE HALLINAN
                          DISTRICT ATTORNEY
                          JAMES HAMMER, A.D.A.
                          KIMBERLY GUILFOYLE
                          NEWSOM, A.D.A.

For Defendant Knoller: DONALD HORGAN, ESQ.
                          DYLAN SHAEFFER, ESQ.

For Defendant Noel: BRUCE HOTCHKISS, ESQ.

Official Court Reporters: Christina T. Paxton, C.S.R.
                          Certificate No. 1558

1   THE COURT:

                          * * * *

2   The key here is implied malice, what constitutes implied

3   malice. It is my responsibility as the trial judge to review

4   all of the evidence in the case. . . .

                          * * * *

5   . . . The evidence in this case established the following.

6   The defendants became the owners, as the jury has found, of

7   two Presa Canario dogs which they picked up from Hayfork,

8   California. The dogs had originally been obtained by two

9   members of the prison gang Aryan Brotherhood who were in

1 Pelican Bay State Prison. There was substantial evidence
2 tending to indicate that the purpose of getting these dogs
3 was to have big, massive, dangerous fighting dogs that could
4 be used to be sold for the benefit of the Aryan Brotherhood.
5 There is no question that the defendants knew that this was
6 the case and that this was indeed the plan of the Aryan
7 Brotherhood.
8   When the defendants first saw the dogs, -- it was in
9 Hayfork -- they were being transferred to the defendants'
10 care. The woman who was in charge of the dogs at that time
11 told the defendants that these dogs were rather dangerous,
12 that they had not been personalized and that they had to
13 be very, very careful about what these dogs could do. She
14 indicated that the dogs had already killed chickens, sheep.
15 And when I say "dogs," the Court points out that there was a
16 large number of Presa Canarios up there. Interestingly, the
17 Court did not find any evidence in any of this that Bane, the
18 male dog who everybody concedes was involved in the death of
19 Diane Whipple, had done any of the killing of the animals at
20 the Hayfork farm. Hera is a different story.
21   The dogs were examined by a veterinarian. The veterina-
22 rian said that he found these dogs extremely dangerous, that
23 he wrote a letter, the first time he had ever written a letter
24 along this nature in his life stating that to take these
25 dogs into the city was essentially foolish, there was no
26 question but that these dogs would eventually cause trouble,
27 they were huge, they were not well-mannered, they were not
28 trained and to take dogs of this massive size into a city
29 environment was not a good thing to do. The defendants did
30 it anyway. They brought the dogs down. The dogs had some
31 medical problems requiring that they get veterinary care
32 but ultimately, the dogs ended up in the Noel and Knoller
33 apartment on Pacific Avenue.

1   From the very beginning, we have encounters. We talked at

2   the trial about good dog witnesses, bad dog witnesses. The

3   bad dog witnesses were people that came and testified, some

4   34 of them as to things they had witnessed with these animals

5   that they considered to be dangerous: lunging, growling,

6   teeth baring, snarling, and in one case it was with Mr. Noel

7   almost severing a finger. The Court is quick to point out

8   that that was not because the dog was aggressive against

9   Mr. Noel. The dog got involved in a fight on the beach. Who

10   started it is irrelevant to the Court's consideration. All

11   the Court knows is that the hand of Mr. Noel was put into

12   the middle of this fight and he ended up with four fingers

13   instead of five, not literally but very close to it. The

14   point of that is that the dogs could clearly do some pretty

15   bad stuff.

16   I am not going to go through -- and I have here all

17   of the bad dog witnesses. The Court for all practical

18   purposes is discounting the good dog witnesses in this case

19   incidentally. The fact that there are 20 some odd witnesses

20   who came and said these dogs were nice, they sat in my

21   restaurant, they came to my house, they walked down the

22   street, they never did anything is fine. In fact, I suspect

23   if you really looked around, you could probably find 2,000

24   witnesses who could say the same thing. That is not the

25   point. If all we had were bad dog witnesses, those dogs

26   should have been put down the very first day they arrived in

27   San Francisco. You would expect nothing but an overwhelming

28   large number of so-called good dog witnesses in a case like

29   this. What we are talking about is who the bad dog witnesses

30   were and what they said.

31   There are two encounters that I want to talk about

32   particularly. One of them is the encounter of TMO, little

33   Mr. -- just a moment, let me get the full name. O'Connell,

1   I believe it is. Well, my notes -- T-M-O is the initials of

2   John O'Connell's six-year-old son, TMO.

3   Here is what we have. The dogs are being walked. Mr.

4   O'Connell is taking his six-year-old son to school. They

5   are going down a public street. Mr. Noel has Bane on a leash,

6   Bane lunges at the boy, comes within anywhere from 12 to 6

7   inches of the boy's face and the testimony is using his great

8   might, referring to Mr. Noel, was able to pull the dog back.

9   The dog never came in contact with TMO'S face but that's

10 where the teeth were going. The question becomes this. Had

11 the dog hit TMO'S face, what would have happened and what is

12 the reasonable inference that could be drawn from that?

13   The second that I wish to go to -- just a moment, please.

14 I simply have too many of them here. The pregnant lady.

15   MR. HAMMER: Jill Davis.

16   THE COURT: Right. Ms. Davis was the pregnant lady

17 right down at the bottom of the page. This is a pregnant

18 lady, eight months pregnant. She is in the lobby of the

19 building. The dog jumps up and once again we have the dog on

20 its hind legs. Mr. Noel with his substantial size -- and this

21 testimony was elicited by counsel by the defense, not by the

22 People -- and with his substantial size was able to restrain

23 the dog and pull it back and as a result, there was not a

24 contact of teeth or claws and flesh either of Ms. Davis or

25 her unborn child. And later on, the child was in a stroller

26 and passed the dogs and there wasn't anything that happened.

27 We don't really [know] what the reason for that is.

28   We can go through any one of a number of additional

29 witnesses. Derek Brown had three particular encounters. The

30 dogs were lunging and barking and were up on their hind

31 legs going berserk. Violetta Pristel -- that's Mr. Browns

32 wife -- saw the dogs barking, up on their hind legs. Jason

33 Edelman, the dog jumped up on his chest, he put the dog off,

1   there were not bites however. He also testified that the

2   dog jumped an elderly woman in January. That was the only

3   testimony to that effect, there was nothing corroborating

4   it so the Court gives that particular testimony very little

5   weight.

6   Jane Lu, the mail person, I don't think anybody who was

7   in court could miss the testimony of Ms. Lu. There were a few

8   words in there but most of the testimony consisted of screams

9   and efforts to recreate the sounds the dogs were making. Skip

10 Cooley pointed out that the dogs, while they were docile most

11 of the time, which is typical, at times lunged at him when

12 he was coming out of the elevator -- lunged at him, lunged at

13 his wife.

14   Abraham Taylor saw Hera break free from Ms. Knoller

15 and the dog charged him and the dog he was walking. Mario

16 Montepeque or Montepeque was the dog trainer. He said that

17 he would be more than happy to help the defendants deal with

18 their dogs. Mr. Noel said he's going to be breeding these

19 dogs. Henry Putek said that Bane charged out of the apartment

20 right at him, he froze and the dogs charged up to him and

21 stopped, the dogs didn't do anything after that.

22   Mary Willard testified the dogs bolted for something on

23 the other side of the street and literally pulled Mr. Noel

24 off the ground and dragged him, Mr. Noel's might was not

25 entirely sufficient to control Bane when Bane really got

26 going. Ron Bosia testified that Hera attacked a dog in the

27 park with no particular warning and it took five minutes for

28 the dog handler to get Hera to release the dog that she had

29 latched on to.

30   Kelly Harris testified to Marjorie that this dog has been

31 abused and will kill -- I am sorry -- Marjorie said "This dog

32 has been abused and will kill your dogs." Diana Curtiss

33 has testified that Hera tried to attack her dog, there was

1 lunging, there was growling, there was snarling, there was

2 showing of teeth, there was pulling forward. Mr. Noel at

3 one point was trying to hold Bane back in an incident here

4 yelling "Whoa, boy," holding on to the dog with both hands

5 as he was pulling Mr. Noel across the park. Marjorie could

6 not control the dog. The testimony was she didn't walk them,

7 quote, they walked her.

8   David Moser testified about an incident coming out of

9 the elevator when, according to his testimony, Hera bit him

10 on his buttocks. The reaction was that didn't happen, he

11 simply bumped his rear end against the side of the elevator,

12 but when Hera allegedly bit him on the buttocks, Mr.

13 Noel's response was "Um, interesting" and that was the end

14 of that.

15   Stephen West was there with his dog Bacas. There was more

16 testimony there about Hera biting other dogs, this was not a

17 personal attack, this was a dog attack. And Ms. Aimee West,

18 Stephen West's wife, testified to very much the same thing.

19 Lynn Gaines, who was a dog walker, was with several dogs

20 walking down -- just walking and Bane was trying to get at

21 the dog she was walking. Buster in particular was the dog I

22 think that caused Bane to be most unhappy. Bane was snarling,

23 growling, pulling at the leash. Again, Ms. Gaines told Mr.

24 Noel that he ought to muzzle Bane and Mr. Noel's response

25 was he called her a bitch.

26   Neil Bardack testified that he saw Ms. Knoller getting

27 dragged and knocked down and pulled off of her feet. John

28 Watanabe, another postal carrier, gave us testimony about

29 trying to use his mail cart as a shield to block the dogs

30 from attacking him. The testimony was filled with evidence

31 of that nature.

32   During the -- I am sorry. Then onto the nature of the

33 dogs, themselves. We have the books that were found in the

1 defendant's apartment, in their house: Manstopper, Dogs

2 About Kill, Attacking Animals, Presa Canarios, Dog-of-War.

3 The epithets were legion and consistent.

4   When we had closing argument on the motion, I asked

5 counsel Mr. Riordan, who is not here today, what would

6 have happened hypothetically if the defendants had both

7 dogs, they were still alive and they took them for a walk

8 today, the dogs had already killed Diane Whipple, that's

9 an established fact, and while walking today, the dogs

10 jumped and killed somebody else. This was in response to

11 Mr. Riordan's argument that essentially, -- and I call it

12 the one-free-death-argument -- you cannot have notice of the

13 fact that a dog, whether it's a dog or Presa Canario breed

14 or some other, is likely to kill unless the dog has already

15 done so. The best Mr. Riordan said is well, it would be

16 a much more difficult case. The question I should have

17 asked him is what would have happened had Mr. Noel's might

18 not sufficiently pulled back Bane when he was jumping at

19 TMO. If TMO had been hit by that dog's face, this court

20 has no doubt that there would have been serious bodily

21 injury, if not death. If the dog, in fact, hit Ms. Davis

22 and bit her, the Court has no doubt that there would have

23 been serious bodily injury, if not death, but is that an

24 observation that I am making based upon what happened on

25 January 26th, 2001? Here is where we are really getting into

26 trouble.

27   The law requires that there be a subjective understanding

28 on the part of the person that on the day in question -- and I

29 do not read that as being January 26th, 2001 because by this

30 time, with all of the information that had come out dealing

31 with the dogs, the defendants were fully on notice that they

32 had a couple of wild, uncontrollable and dangerous dogs that

33 were likely going to do something bad.

1   Is the "something bad" death? That is the ultimate
2   question in the case. There is no question but that the
3   something bad was going to be that somebody was going to
4   be badly hurt. I defy either defendant to stand up and tell
5   me they had no idea that those dogs were going to hurt
6   somebody one day. But can they stand up and say that they
7   knew subjectively -- not objectively and that's an important
8   distinction -- that these dogs were going to stand up and
9   kill somebody?
10   Look at what happened in the hallway on January 26th. In
11   fact, we will never know what happened in the hallway. The
12   only witness that testified to what happened there is the
13   witness Knoller. With very few exceptions, the Court -- Ms.
14   Knoller, I did not believe you. I did not believe a lot of
15   what you said as to what happened. I believe a lot of things
16   that happened in the hallway did happen somewhat along the
17   lines that you said but there is more there and frankly, we
18   are never going to know. Nobody is ever going to know what
19   happened, why after all of these circumstances that we had in
20   a confined place where there had been lots of confined places
21   before, the lobby of the building but not the hallway, the
22   dog all of a sudden went and attacked a defenseless woman
23   trying to get her groceries into her apartment.
24   . . .

* * * *

25   I believe unfortunately, Mr. Noel, Ms. Knoller, that you
26   are the most despised couple in the City. I don't believe
27   anybody likes you.
28   "It's the victim's fault." "She did it to herself."
29   "Sarcastic Characterizations." "Whipple must have known she
30   was asking for trouble by using pheromones around malicious
31   dogs." . . . "Whipple had ample opportunity to go into her
32   apartment but she didn't, she could have just slammed the

1 door.". . . . "What's the big deal? You know, it was just an
2 accident and nobody's fault."
3 . . .

* * * *

4   "Whipple was acting macho." I don't know how one acts
5 macho with a bag of lettuce in her hands.
6   "No responsibility for the attack." Ms. Knoller getting
7 on Good Morning America saying "I wouldn't say that I was
8 unable to control the dogs, I wouldn't say it was an attack."
9 . . .

* * * *

10   Which brings us to the decision that this court has to
11 make in this case. I want to draw everybody's attention to
12 the case of State of Kansas versus Sabine Davidson, a second
13 degree murder case involving a dog. That's it. In the United
14 States of America, that's pretty much it. It's very close
15 to what's going on here except in that case, the dogs were
16 actually trained to attack. In the case that we have in front
17 of us, there really is no evidence that these dogs were
18 trained to attack by the defendants or by anybody who had
19 them before. They were not taken care of properly and did
20 not demonstrate any meaningful socialization although they
21 became very close to the defendants in this case.
22   Particularly important here are things such as this
23 defendant in the case in People versus Davidson laughing
24 when she found out that somebody got attacked by her dogs,
25 arguing she didn't know what the dogs could do. It's pretty
26 close but it's in Kansas. The other cases we have all have
27 to do with involuntary manslaughter.
28   The Court's decision in this case is as follows. I am
29 guided by a variety of principles. One of them is that
30 public emotion, public outcry, feeling, passion, sympathy
31 do not play a role in the application of the law. The other

1   is that I am required to review all of the evidence and

2   determine independently rather than as a jury what the

3   evidence showed. I have laid out most of the evidence as it

4   harms the defendants in this case. Their conduct from the

5   time that they got the dogs to the time -- to the weeks after

6   Diane Whipple's death was despicable.

7   There was one time on the stand, Ms. Knoller, when I truly

8   believed what you said. You broke down in the middle of a

9   totally scripted answer and you actually, instead of crying,

10 you actually got mad and you said you had no idea that this

11 dog could do what he did and pounded the table. I believed

12 you. That was the only time, but I did believe you.

13   The California Legislature, which is the governing body

14 in this case, has said that the owner of a dangerous dog that

15 kills is guilty of a violation of 399 of the Penal Code. If a

16 person acts with criminal negligence and a death occurs, the

17 person is guilty of involuntary manslaughter. A person is

18 guilty of second degree murder if that person subjectively

19 knows, based on everything, that the conduct that he or she

20 is about to engage in has a high probability of death to

21 another human being.

22   What we have in this case as it relates to Ms. Knoller is

23 the decision to take the dog outside, into the hallway, up to

24 the roof, go to the bathroom, bring it back down and put it in

25 the apartment. There was no question but that taking the dog

26 out into the hallway by that very act exposed other people in

27 the apartment, whether they are residents there or guests,

28 invitees to what might happen with the dog. When you take

29 everything as a totality, the question is whether or not as

30 a subjective matter and as a matter of law Ms. Knoller knew

31 that there was a high probability that day, or on the day

32 before or on the day after, -- I reject totally the argument

33 of the defendants that she had to know when she walked out

1   the door -- she was going to kill somebody that morning. The

2   Court finds that the evidence does not support it.

3   This does not in any way -- in any way excuse or change or

4   otherwise affect the horror of what happened. This does not

5   minimize the loss that happened in this case, this does not

6   minimize or excuse the despicable conduct of the defendants.

7   I don't believe that there is anybody in San Francisco who

8   would rather not see Ms. Knoller go to prison for second

9   degree murder. I received letters suggesting that the death

10 penalty is appropriate in this case. The Court has no choice,

11 however, taking the Legislature's scheme, the evidence that

12 was received, as despicable as it is, but to determine not

13 that she is acquitted of second degree murder but to find

14 that on the state of the evidence, I cannot say as a matter

15 of law that she subjectively knew on January 26th that her

16 conduct was such that a human being was likely to die.

17   The Court also notes a great troubling feature of this

18 case that Mr. Noel was never charged as Ms. Knoller was.

19 In the Court's view, given the evidence, Mr. Noel is more

20 culpable than she. Mr. Noel personally knew that she could

21 not control those dogs. He could not control those dogs. Mr.

22 Noel was substantially haughtier than she was. In brushing

23 off all of the incidents that happened out in the street, Mr.

24 Noel knew as a theological certainty that that dog, which

25 had recently been operated on, was taking medication that

26 had given it diarrhea, was going to go out into the hallway

27 or out into the street possibly, at the hands of Ms. Knoller.

28 He knew that he couldn't take of her and he left her there to

29 do that.

30   To argue that he is not responsible because he wasn't

31 there is to argue that by setting a bomb off in a locker and

32 then getting on an airplane and going to New York City, you

33 are not responsible for the damages caused by the bomb. And

1 yet Mr. Noel was not charged. Equality of sentencing and the

2 equal administration of justice is an important feature in

3 any criminal court. That played a role as well.

4   As far as the involuntary manslaughter charges and as

5 far as the ownership of a mischievous dog that kills, the

6 evidence is overwhelming. Taking into account all of the

7 [. . . assignments] of error, they are supported utterly and

8 without question by the jury's verdict in this case.

9   The motion for a new trial as to second degree murder as

10 to Marjorie Knoller is granted. The motion for new trial as

11 to involuntary manslaughter and owner of a mischievous dog

12 as to Ms. Knoller and Mr. Noel is denied.

* * * *

LEGAL ETHICS

A. CONFIDENTIALITY

PROBLEMS

A 4.1 Alex is a twenty-two-year-old indigent man with a history of heroin addiction and other drug use who is charged with possession of $30,000 worth of stolen Treasury checks. Alex's family is well off financially. His father is a successful real estate developer, and his mother is a well-known fashion designer. Alex's parents hire you to represent Alex and pay you a $10,000 retainer as an advance against your hourly fees. The information you can glean from the charging documents and a brief conversation with one of the arresting police officers indicates that Alex and two of his friends broke into a postal delivery truck by throwing a rock through the window and then grabbed several sacks of mail. In the sacks were a significant number of United States Treasury checks to be delivered to recipients of federal benefits. Alex tried to sell the stolen checks for cash to buy heroin. Unfortunately for Alex, the person to whom he chose to sell the checks was an undercover police officer. Once arrested, Alex asserted his right to remain silent and made no statement to the police.

    (a) You meet with Alex in a private interview room at the local jail. Only the two of you are present when you ask him "What happened?" He then tells you that he stole the Treasury checks from the postal truck and tried to sell them for money to buy drugs. Must you reveal Alex's admission to the police? May you reveal Alex's admission to the police?

    (b) Immediately after leaving your interview with Alex, you meet with his parents at your office. His father asks "What did Alex tell you?" Must you reveal Alex's admission to his parents? May you reveal Alex's admission to his parents?

(c) Alex makes his initial appearance in court on the possession charge, and you inform the court that you will be representing Alex. The judge releases Alex on a $20,000 bond while the charges are pending with a restriction that he not travel outside the county in which he is being prosecuted. You set a date with Alex to meet at your office in two weeks to discuss how to proceed in the case. When the date for your meeting with Alex arrives, he does not appear. You call his phone number and find it has been disconnected. A few days later, Alex calls and leaves a message on your voicemail with a return phone number. You recognize the area code as that of a major metropolitan area outside your state. When you call the number, an operator answers by giving you the name of the hotel and then connects you with Alex. Alex tells you that, with money his parents gave him, he has bought an airline ticket to Europe and is leaving in a few days because he cannot endure going to jail. Must you reveal Alex's admission of his intent to flee to the police? Must you reveal his location? May you reveal either of these?

A 4.2 Diane is a criminal defense lawyer who represents Jake, one of several defendants charged with an armed bank robbery. Jake and his co-defendants have been held without bail pending trial. During a jailhouse conference with Jake, Diane tells him that his chances for acquittal appear slim because, in addition to the testimony of the bank teller whom Jake robbed, Jake's girlfriend, Viola, has agreed to cooperate with the prosecution and testify against him. Viola was present in Jake's apartment when he and his accomplices planned the robbery. Jake tells Diane not to worry about his girlfriend's testimony because she "will be taken care of" prior to trial. When Diane asks Jake what he means, he smiles and tells her that he has friends who will make sure that Viola never takes the stand at his trial. Must Diane reveal to the police what Jake told her? May Diane reveal to the police what Jake told her? May Diane seek advice from other partners in her law firm about how she should respond to Jake's statement? May she seek advice from a lawyer outside her law firm who specializes in legal ethics issues?

A 4.3 Ken is a corporate lawyer at a major metropolitan law firm. His firm represents Biotech, a corporation making its first public offering of stock. Ken has performed for Biotech all the legal work necessary for the public offering, including an assessment of the disclosures he concludes Biotech needs to make about its financial liabilities in order to conform with applicable securities fraud laws. Biotech's president agrees to reveal some of the items but refuses to reveal several others because it would be "financial suicide." Biotech then goes ahead with the public offering without disclosing the contested items. Must Ken reveal to government securities regulators that Biotech has failed to disclose material financial liabilities? May Ken reveal this information? If so, when should he make the revelation? Does it make any difference if Ken might be charged criminally or sued civilly as an accomplice to Biotech's securities fraud? Does it make any difference whether Ken is an associate at the firm or a partner?

Georgia Rules of Professional Conduct (2004)

Rule 1.6 *Confidentiality of Information.*

(a) A lawyer shall maintain in confidence all information gained in the professional relationship with a client, including information which the client has requested to be held inviolate or the disclosure of which would be embarrassing or would likely be detrimental to the client, unless the client consents after consultation, except for disclosures that are impliedly authorized in order to carry out the representation, or are required by these rules or other law, or by order of the Court.

(b)(1) A lawyer may reveal information covered by paragraph (a) which the lawyer reasonably believes necessary:

(i) to avoid or prevent harm or substantial financial loss to another as a result of client criminal conduct or third party criminal conduct clearly in violation of the law;

(ii) to prevent serious injury or death not otherwise covered by subparagraph (i) above;

(iii) to establish a claim or defense on behalf of the lawyer in a controversy between the lawyer and the client, to establish a defense to a criminal charge or civil claim against the lawyer based upon conduct in which the client was involved, or to respond to allegations in any proceeding concerning the lawyer's representation of the client.

(2) In a situation described in Subsection (1), if the client has acted at the time the lawyer learns of the threat of harm or loss to a victim, use or disclosure is permissible only if the harm or loss has not yet occurred.

(3) Before using or disclosing information pursuant to Subsection (1), if feasible, the lawyer must make a good faith effort to persuade the client either not to act or, if the client has already acted, to warn the victim.

(c) The lawyer may, where the law does not otherwise require, reveal information to which the duty of confidentiality does not apply under paragraph (b) without being subjected to disciplinary proceedings.

(d) The lawyer shall reveal information under paragraph (b) as the applicable law requires.

(e) The duty of confidentiality shall continue after the client-lawyer relationship has terminated.

The maximum penalty for a violation of this Rule is disbarment.

Comment

[1] The lawyer is part of a judicial system charged with upholding the law. One of the lawyer's functions is to advise clients so that they avoid any violation of the law in the proper exercise of their rights.

[2] The observance of the ethical obligation of a lawyer to hold inviolate confidential information of the client not only facilitates the full development of facts essential to proper representation of the client but also encourages people to seek early legal assistance.

[3] Almost without exception, clients come to lawyers in order to determine what their rights are and what is, in the maze of laws and regulations, deemed to be legal and correct. The common law recognizes that the client's confidences must be protected from disclosure. Based upon experience, lawyers know that almost all clients follow the advice given, and the law is upheld.

[4] A fundamental principle in the client-lawyer relationship is that the lawyer maintain confidentiality of information relating to the representation. The client is thereby encouraged to communicate fully and frankly with the lawyer even as to embarrassing or legally damaging subject matter.

[5] . . . Rule 1.6: Confidentiality of Information applies not merely to matters communicated in confidence by the client but also to all information relating to the representation, whatever its source. A lawyer may not disclose such information except as authorized or required by the Rules of Professional Conduct or other law. The requirement of maintaining confidentiality of information relating to representation applies to government lawyers who may disagree with the client's policy goals.

Authorized Disclosure

[6] A lawyer is impliedly authorized to make disclosures about a client when appropriate in carrying out the representation, except to the extent that the client's instructions or special circumstances limit that authority. In litigation, for example, a lawyer may disclose information by admitting a fact that cannot properly be disputed, or in negotiation by making a disclosure that facilitates a satisfactory conclusion.

[7] Lawyers in a firm may, in the course of the firm's practice, disclose to each other information relating to a client of the firm, unless the client has instructed that particular information be confined to specified lawyers.

Disclosure Adverse to Client

[8] The confidentiality rule is subject to limited exceptions. In becoming privy to information about a client, a lawyer may foresee that the client intends serious harm to another person. The public is better protected if full and open communication by the client is encouraged than if it is inhibited.

[9] Several situations must be distinguished. First, the lawyer may not knowingly assist a client in conduct that is criminal or fraudulent. Similarly, a lawyer has a duty . . . not to use false evidence.

[10] Second, the lawyer may have been innocently involved in past conduct by the client that was criminal or fraudulent. In such a situation the lawyer has not violated Rule 1.2(d): Scope of Representation, because to "knowingly assist" criminal or fraudulent conduct requires knowing that the conduct is of that character.

[11] Third, the lawyer may learn that a client intends prospective conduct that is criminal and likely to result in death or substantial bodily harm. As stated in paragraph (b)(1), the lawyer has professional discretion to reveal information in order to prevent such consequences. The lawyer may make a disclosure in order to prevent death or serious bodily injury which the lawyer reasonably believes will occur. It is very difficult for a lawyer to "know" when such a heinous purpose will actually be carried out, for the client may have a change of mind.

[12] The lawyer's exercise of discretion requires consideration of such factors as the nature of the lawyer's relationship with the client and with those who might be injured by the client, the lawyer's own involvement in the transaction and factors that may extenuate the conduct in question. Where practical, the lawyer should seek to persuade the client to take suitable action. In any case, a disclosure adverse to the client's interest should be no greater than the lawyer reasonably believes necessary to the purpose. A

lawyer's decision not to take preventive action permitted by paragraph (b)(1) does not violate this Rule.

Withdrawal

[13] If the lawyer's services will be used by the client in materially furthering a course of criminal or fraudulent conduct, the lawyer must withdraw. . . .

[14] After withdrawal the lawyer is required to refrain from making disclosure of the client's confidences, except as otherwise provided in Rule 1.6: Confidentiality of Information. Neither this rule nor Rule 1.8(b): Conflict of Interest nor Rule 1.16(d): Declining or Terminating Representation prevents the lawyer from giving notice of the fact of withdrawal, and the lawyer may also withdraw or disaffirm any opinion, document, affirmation, or the like.

[15] Where the client is an organization, the lawyer may be in doubt whether contemplated conduct will actually be carried out by the organization. Where necessary to guide conduct in connection with this Rule, the lawyer may make inquiry within the organization. . . .

Dispute Concerning a Lawyer's Conduct

[16] Where a legal claim or disciplinary charge alleges complicity of the lawyer in a client's conduct or other misconduct of the lawyer involving representation of the client, the lawyer may respond to the extent the lawyer reasonably believes necessary to establish a defense. The same is true with respect to a claim involving the conduct or representation of a former client. The lawyer's right to respond arises when an assertion of such complicity has been made. Paragraph (b)(1)(iii) does not require the lawyer to await the commencement of an action or proceeding that charges such complicity, so that the defense may be established by responding directly to a third party who has made such an assertion. The right to defend, of course, applies where a proceeding has been commenced. Where practicable and not prejudicial to the lawyer's ability to establish the defense, the lawyer should advise the client of the third party's assertion and request that the client respond appropriately. In any event, disclosure should be no greater than the lawyer reasonably believes is necessary to vindicate innocence, the disclosure should be made in a manner which limits access to the information to the tribunal or other persons having a need to know it, and appropriate protective orders or other arrangements should be sought by the lawyer to the fullest extent practicable.

[17] If the lawyer is charged with wrongdoing in which the client's conduct is implicated, the rule of confidentiality should not prevent the lawyer from defending against the charge. Such a charge can arise in a civil, criminal or professional disciplinary proceeding, and can be based on a wrong allegedly committed by the lawyer against the client, or on a wrong alleged by a third person; for example, a person claiming to have been defrauded by the lawyer and client acting together. A lawyer entitled to a fee is permitted by paragraph (b)(1)(iii) to prove the services rendered in an action to collect it. This aspect of the rule expresses the principle that the beneficiary of a fiduciary relationship may not exploit it to the detriment of the fiduciary. As stated above, the lawyer must make every effort practicable to avoid unnecessary disclosure of information relating to a representation, to limit disclosure to those having the need to know it, and to obtain protective orders or make other arrangements minimizing the risk of disclosure. . . .

Connecticut Rules of Professional Conduct (2004)

Rule 1.6   *Confidentiality of Information*

(a) A lawyer shall not reveal information relating to representation of a client unless the client consents after consultation, except for disclosures that are impliedly authorized in order to carry out the representation, and except as stated in subsections (a), (b), (c), and (d).

(b) A lawyer shall reveal such information to the extent the lawyer reasonably believes necessary to prevent the client from committing a criminal act that the lawyer believes is likely to result in death or substantial bodily harm.

(c) A lawyer may reveal such information to the extent the lawyer reasonably believes necessary to:

(1) Prevent the client from committing a criminal act that the lawyer believes is likely to result in substantial injury to the financial interest or property of another;

(2) Rectify the consequence of a client's criminal or fraudulent act in the commission of which the lawyer's services had been used.

(d) A lawyer may reveal such information to establish a claim or defense on behalf of the lawyer in a controversy between the lawyer and the client, to establish a defense to a criminal charge or civil claim against the lawyer based upon conduct in which the client was involved, or to respond to allegations in any proceeding concerning the lawyer's representation of the client.

COMMENTARY

. . . Subsection (b) requires a lawyer to reveal confidences when reasonably necessary to prevent a client from committing a criminal act that is likely to cause death or serious injury to the person of another. In determining whether disclosure of confidences is required, the lawyer should consider the proximity and likelihood of the client's committing the criminal act, and the nature of the lawyer's relationship with the client. Where practical, the lawyer should seek to persuade the client to take suitable action. Disclosure adverse to the client should be no greater than the lawyer reasonably believes necessary to the purpose.

Subsection (c)(1) permits a lawyer to reveal a client's intent to commit a criminal act that is likely to cause substantial injury to the financial interests or property of another. The lawyer's exercise of discretion requires consideration of factors discussed above, and the magnitude of the effect of the act on the prospective victim, if within the lawyer's knowledge. Disclosure adverse to the client should be no greater than the lawyer reasonably believes necessary to the purpose, and, if practical, should follow an attempt by the lawyer to persuade the client to follow a lawful course. A lawyer's decision not to take preventive action under subsection (c) does not violate this Rule. . . .

In the following opinion, Judge Fletcher quotes from ABA Model Rule 1.6. The rules you just read, both of which are based on the ABA's Model Rule 1.6, differ from the version quoted by Judge Fletcher. How do the Georgia and Connecticut rules differ from the version quoted by Judge Fletcher? How do they differ from each other?

McCLURE *v.* THOMPSON

323 F.3d 1233 (9th Cir. 2003)

W. FLETCHER, J. Oregon state prisoner Robert A. McClure appeals the district court's denial of his 28 U.S.C. § 2254 habeas corpus petition challenging his jury trial conviction for three aggravated murders. McClure's original defense attorney,

Christopher Mecca, placed an anonymous telephone call to law enforcement officials directing them to the locations of the bodies of two children whom McClure was ultimately convicted of killing. The district court rejected McClure's arguments that the disclosure constituted ineffective assistance of counsel, holding there was no breach of the duty of confidentiality. . . . We affirm.

I. BACKGROUND

A. OFFENSE, ARREST AND CONVICTION

On Tuesday, April 24, 1984, the body of Carol Jones was found in her home in Grants Pass, Oregon. She had been struck numerous times on the head, arms and hands with a blunt object. A gun cabinet in the home had been forced open and a .44 caliber revolver was missing. Two of Jones' children—Michael, age 14, and Tanya, age 10—were also missing. The fingerprints of Robert McClure, a friend of Jones, were found in the blood in the home, and on Saturday, April 28, McClure was arrested in connection with the death of Carol Jones and the disappearance of the children.

That same day, McClure's mother contacted attorney Christopher Mecca and asked him to represent her son. As discussed in more detail below, sometime in the next three days, under circumstances described differently by McClure and Mecca, McClure revealed to Mecca the separate remote locations where the children could be found. On Tuesday, May 1, Mecca, armed with a map produced during his conversations with McClure, arranged for his secretary to place an anonymous phone call to a sheriff's department telephone number belonging to a law enforcement officer with whom Mecca had met earlier.

Later that day and the following day, sheriff's deputies located the children's bodies, which were in locations more than 60 miles apart. The children had each died from a single gunshot wound to the head. Mecca then withdrew from representation. On May 3, McClure was indicted for the murders of Carol Jones and her children. At trial, the prosecution produced extensive evidence that stemmed from the discovery of the children's bodies and introduced testimony regarding the anonymous phone call. McClure was found guilty of all three murders and was sentenced to three consecutive life sentences with 30-year minimums. On direct appeal, his conviction was affirmed without opinion.

B. DISCLOSURE OF THE CHILDREN'S WHEREABOUTS

The parties agree that Mecca and McClure met at the jail and spoke on the telephone on a number of occasions between April 28 and May 1. However, the substance of the conversations between McClure and Mecca [is] the subject of significant dispute.

Mecca recorded his account in notes that he wrote immediately after the children's bodies were discovered. Mecca also gave deposition testimony for McClure's state post conviction proceeding, submitted an affidavit prior to McClure's federal habeas proceeding, and gave testimony at the federal district court evidentiary hearing in the habeas proceeding.

In his notes, Mecca wrote that McClure had initially claimed that he was "being framed" for the murder, but that he was nervous about his fingerprints being in the house. He had asked Mecca to help him remove some other potential evidence, which Mecca declined to do. According to the notes, on the Sunday night after McClure's Saturday arrest, Mecca received a "frantic phone call" from McClure's sister, who was convinced that McClure had murdered Jones, but had reason to believe that the children were alive and perhaps "tied up or bound someplace." In response, Mecca set up a meeting with McClure, his sister and his mother at the jail, at which McClure's sister "directly confronted McClure and begged him to divulge information about the whereabouts of the kids." McClure and his sister discussed how McClure sometimes did "crazy things" when he was using drugs, but McClure strongly maintained his innocence as to Carol Jones' murder and the children's disappearance.

According to his notes, when Mecca next spoke with McClure on Monday, McClure was less adamant in his denial. Mecca described how, when they met on Monday afternoon, McClure began to tell him of his "sexual hallucinations and fantasies" involving young girls and about "other situations that happened in the past involving things he would do while under the influence of drugs." "It was at that time," Mecca wrote, "when I realized in my own mind that he had committed the crime and the problem regarding the children intensified." Mecca wrote that he "was extremely agitated over the fact that these children might still be alive."

After a Monday night visit to the crime scene, Mecca returned to the jail to speak with McClure again, at which time he "peeled off most of the outer layers of McClure and realized that there was no doubt in my mind that he had killed Carol Jones." McClure told Mecca he wanted to see a psychiatrist, then launched into "bizarre ramblings." "Each time as I would try to leave," Mecca recalled in his notes, "McClure would spew out other information, bits about the children, and he would do it in the form of a fantasy." Mecca wrote that he "wanted to learn from him what happened to those children." He told McClure "that we all have hiding places, that we all know when we go hiking or driving or something, we all remember certain back roads and remote places," and that McClure "related to me one place where a body might be" and then "described where the other body would be located." Mecca wrote that he "wasn't going to push him for anything more," but "when I tried to leave, he said, and he said it tentatively, 'would you like me to draw you a map and just give you an idea?' and I said 'Yes' and he did." Mecca recorded that "at that time, I felt in my own mind the children were dead, but, of course, I wasn't sure."

Very late on Monday evening, McClure telephoned Mecca at home and said, "I know who did it." Mecca recorded in his notes that the next morning he went to meet with McClure, and asked him about this statement. McClure told Mecca that "Satan killed Carol." When Mecca asked, "What about the kids?" McClure replied, "Jesus saved the kids." Mecca wrote in his notes that this statement "hit me so abruptly, I immediately assumed that if Jesus saved the kids, that the kids are alive." Mecca wrote that he "kind of felt that McClure was talking about a sexual thing, but, in any event, I wasn't sure." Mecca's notes indicate that on Monday, before McClure made the "Jesus saved the kids" comment, and again on Tuesday, immediately after the meeting at which he made that comment, Mecca had conversations with fellow lawyers, seeking advice regarding "the dilemma that he faced." After the second of these conversations, which took place Tuesday morning, Mecca arranged for a noon meeting with the undersheriff and the prosecutor. At the meeting, he "mentioned to them that I may have information which would be of interest to the State" and attempted to negotiate a plea. When the prosecutor responded that there would be no deal, Mecca recorded in his notes, "I had made up my mind then that I had to do the correct thing. The only option I had, as far as I was concerned, was to disclose the whereabouts of the body." (Recall that by the time Mecca wrote these notes, he had learned that the children were dead.) A law enforcement official testified in a federal court deposition that, after both the state bar association and the attorney general "recommended that it would be unwise for Mr. Mecca to provide us information," Mecca "indicated that, even though there might be sanctions, that he still was wanting to provide information that he had regarding the children." Mecca stated that when he spoke with McClure's sister and mother, they were adamant that he do whatever he could to locate the children, and that "they were still under the impression that one or both of the children were alive, or at least there was a chance they were alive."

Mecca then returned to the jail Tuesday afternoon and, according to his notes, "advised McClure that if there was any possibility that these children were alive, we were obligated to disclose that information in order to prevent, if possible, the occurrence of what could be the elevation of an assault to a murder, for instance. I further indicated that if he really requested psychiatric help, to help him deal with his problem, that this perhaps was the first step." "In any event," Mecca recorded in his notes, "he consented." "I arranged to have the information released anonymously to the Sheriff's Department with directions to the bodies." He noted that there was "no provable way to connect" McClure to the information, "but I think it's rather obvious from those in the know, who the information came from."

In the deposition conducted in conjunction with McClure's state habeas proceeding, Mecca gave a similar account of the events surrounding disclosure of the locations of the children. He emphasized that "it all happened relatively quickly" and that there was a public "hysteria about these kids, whether the kids were dead, whether the kids were alive." Mecca reiterated that much of the later conversations with McClure consisted of hypotheticals and fantasies—"like he was playing a game with me"—but that it was clear that McClure wanted to tell him where the children were. Mecca stated in his deposition that "the condition of the children was never discussed," but that the insistence by McClure's mother and sister that McClure wouldn't hurt the children put him "in this mode of thinking these kids might be alive someplace."

Mecca testified in his deposition that he thought that if the children were alive, it might relieve McClure of additional murder charges, but that the children were his main concern. When asked if he was "primarily concerned with the children's welfare or . . . with Mr. McClure's welfare" at the time he disclosed the location of the bodies, Mecca replied, "At that point I was concerned with the children's welfare." When asked if he explained to McClure that "if they were in fact dead, that revealing the location of the bodies would lead to evidence which could implicate Mr. McClure in their murders," Mecca answered: "No. I don't think I had the presence of mind to sit down and analyze every single detail and go over with him, 'Geez, you know, if they are really dead, why don't you tell me.'" However, he testified, "McClure knew I thought there was a chance those kids were alive."

Mecca testified in the deposition that the plan to place the anonymous telephone call was his, but that McClure knew that he planned to do it, and that, in his late-night call, McClure had made clear that he "absolutely" "wanted to disclose where those kids were." When asked, "Did he give you permission to reveal this information?" Mecca responded, "Oh, yes."

In a 1999 affidavit submitted in conjunction with McClure's federal habeas proceeding, Mecca gave an additional statement regarding McClure's consent: "Mr. McClure did not orally or expressly consent to the disclosure. I inferred consent from the circumstances, specifically, the fact that Mr. McClure called me at home on several occasions with the request that I see him at the jail, and the fact that he drew a map of the location of the bodies of the victim in his own handwriting and gave me the map."

In addition to reviewing Mecca's notes, his state-court deposition testimony, and his federal-court affidavit, the federal district court heard testimony from Mecca at an evidentiary hearing. In this testimony, Mecca emphasized that he generally takes a low-keyed approach to questioning his clients. He also emphasized that McClure was "fully engaged in his defense" and "was running the show." Every time they met or conversed, he said, it was at McClure's request. He said that he and McClure "discussed at various times various methods of what I was going to do with this information." Mecca testified that McClure never expressly said that he consented to the disclosure, and that Mecca never asked for such consent. He confirmed his earlier testimony that he inferred consent, and added for the first time that this inference was based on McClure's nodding, saying "okay," and otherwise manifesting assent. He said this was what he had meant when he had written in his notes that McClure consented. Mecca also reiterated that he never told McClure of the legal risks involved in disclosing the children's locations.

Mecca testified that after the Monday conversation with McClure, "the conclusion I came to was that, without telling me, he told me he had killed three people." But he stated that he did not confirm that conclusion by directly asking McClure if it was the case. Instead, he said, he emphasized to McClure that if there was a chance the children were alive, they needed to save them, and in response McClure "never said they were dead." After the "Jesus saved the kids" comment on Tuesday, Mecca testified, "I allowed myself to believe that these kids might somehow be alive." When asked on cross examination whether, at the time he decided to make the anonymous call, he thought there was "a strong possibility the kids still may be alive," Mecca responded that he "felt that it was a possibility. I wouldn't say a strong possibility." One of the reasons he felt this possibility existed, he said, was that his "client had not indicated anything differently." He testified that the possibility of saving his client from additional murder charges "was something that was going through his mind" during his decisionmaking. He noted that the weather at that time of year was "warm" and "pleasant," and that if the children had been left in the woods it was possible that the weather would not have contributed to their death.

McClure disagreed with Mecca's account of the events leading up to the anonymous call. In testimony in both the state and federal district court proceedings, he repeatedly insisted that he did not give Mecca permission to disclose any information and that he was reassured that everything he told Mecca would remain confidential. He said Mecca pressured him into disclosing information by setting up the meeting with his sister and mother, and then disseminated that information to his detriment without his knowledge or consent. McClure testified that Mecca never asked him directly if the children were alive or dead, but that the hypothetical conversations that they had were about where Mecca might find dead "bodies," not live "children." He said his disclosure of those locations was his way of admitting to having killed them. He testified that Mecca never told him that he intended to make an anonymous telephone call.

II. STANDARD OF REVIEW

The district court's decision to deny a 28 U.S.C. § 2254 habeas petition is reviewed de novo. Findings of fact made by the district court are reviewed for clear error. This clearly erroneous standard is significantly deferential, requiring a "definite and firm conviction that a mistake has been committed" before reversal is warranted. This deference stems from the fact that findings of fact are made on the basis of evidentiary hearings and usually involve credibility determinations. These credibility determinations are also given special deference and are likewise reviewed for clear error. . . .

III. Discussion

McClure's single claim is that habeas relief is appropriate because he received ineffective assistance of counsel under the Sixth Amendment. He asserts three independent grounds on which ineffectiveness could be found. The first two are based on alleged breaches of Mecca's professional duty to maintain client confidentiality. McClure argues that this duty was breached both by a failure to obtain informed consent prior to the disclosure of confidential information, and by a failure to inquire thoroughly before concluding that disclosure was necessary to prevent the deaths of the children. . . .

The overarching standard for a claim of ineffective assistance of counsel is set out in *Strickland v. Washington*, 466 U.S. 668 (1984), in which the Supreme Court emphasized that a successful claim must establish both (1) deficient performance, such that "counsel was not functioning as the 'counsel' guaranteed the defendant by the Sixth Amendment," and (2) prejudice resulting from that deficiency. The Court in *Strickland* noted that the Sixth Amendment "relies on the legal profession's maintenance of standards sufficient to justify the law's presumption that counsel will fulfill the role in the adversary process that the Amendment envisions," and that "the proper measure of attorney performance" is "reasonableness under prevailing professional norms." The Court specified a limited number of "basic duties" that are essential components of reasonable performance by criminal defense counsel, including "a duty of loyalty" and "a duty to avoid conflicts of interest," but held that this list was not exhaustive and that every case will involve an inquiry into "whether counsel's assistance was reasonable considering all the circumstances." "Prevailing norms of practice as reflected in American Bar Association standards and the like are guides to determining what is reasonable, but they are only guides."

The Court has yet to "define with greater precision the weight to be given to recognized canons of ethics, the standards established by the state in statutes or professional codes, and the Sixth Amendment" in defining the proper scope of and limits on attorney conduct for *Strickland* purposes. It has, however, suggested that when "virtually all of those sources speak with one voice" as to what constitutes reasonable attorney performance, departure from ethical canons and ABA guidelines "makes out a deprivation of the Sixth Amendment right to counsel."

We examine each of McClure's three assertions of deficient performance in turn.[2]

A. The Duty of Confidentiality

McClure contends that Mecca's disclosure of McClure's confidential statements about the location of the children violated McClure's Sixth Amendment right to effective assistance of counsel. ABA Model Rule of Professional Conduct 1.6 sets forth a widely recognized duty of confidentiality: "A lawyer shall not reveal information relating to representation of a client." Our legal system is premised on the strict adherence to this principle of confidentiality, and "the Supreme Court has

---

[2] Because we ultimately hold that Mecca's performance was not constitutionally deficient, we do not reach the question of prejudice.

long held attorneys to stringent standards of loyalty and fairness with respect to their clients." There are few professional relationships "involving a higher trust and confidence than that of attorney and client," and "few more anxiously guarded by the law, or governed by sterner principles of morality and justice."

As critical as this confidential relationship is to our system of justice, the duty to refrain from disclosing information relating to the representation of a client is nonetheless not absolute. The ABA Model Rule provides a list of well-established exceptions to the general principle of confidentiality, two of which are pertinent to the present case. First, a lawyer may reveal confidential information if "the client consents after consultation." Second, "a lawyer may reveal such information to the extent the lawyer reasonably believes necessary to prevent the client from committing a criminal act that the lawyer believes is likely to result in imminent death or substantial bodily harm." The relevant provisions of the Oregon Code of Professional Responsibility echo both the general principle of confidentiality and these particular exceptions.[3]

The parties, apparently agreeing that these consistently recognized ethical standards provide important guidance as to whether Mecca's counsel was deficient under the first prong of *Strickland*, focus much of their dispute on the reasonableness of Mecca's actions in light of these exceptions to the general principle of confidentiality. We agree that this approach is proper. The duty of an attorney to keep his or her client's confidences in all but a handful of carefully defined circumstances is so deeply ingrained in our legal system and so uniformly acknowledged as a critical component of reasonable representation by counsel that departure from this rule "makes out a deprivation of the Sixth Amendment right to counsel." With this uncontested premise as our starting point, we examine whether the circumstances surrounding Mecca's revelation of a confidential client communication excused his disclosure, such that his performance could have been found by the state court and the district court to be constitutionally adequate. Specifically, we look to see if Mecca's client "consented after consultation" or if Mecca "reasonably believed the revelation was necessary to prevent the client from committing a criminal act that Mecca believed was likely to result in imminent death or substantial bodily harm." We conclude that the first of these exceptions does not apply to justify Mecca's behavior, but that the second does.

1. Consent After Consultation

McClure argues that Mecca rendered constitutionally ineffective assistance because he breached his duty of confidentiality by not obtaining McClure's informed consent before disclosure. The professional standard that allows disclosure of confidential communications when "the client consents after consultation" has two distinct parts: consent by the client, and consultation by the counsel. Our required deference to both the state court's factual findings and the district court's credibility determination leads us to hold that the first of these elements was met. However, despite this deference, we hold that the second element was not met.

---

[3] A lawyer may reveal:

    (1) Confidences or secrets with the consent of the client or clients affected, but only after full disclosure to the client or clients.

    * * *

    (3) The intention of the lawyer's client to commit a crime and the information necessary to prevent the crime.

Oregon Code Prof. Resp. D.R. 4-101.

a. Consent

The state court made the following finding: "Trial counsel received petitioner's permission to anonymously disclose the whereabouts of the children to the authorities." [The federal statute governing habeas corpus review by federal courts of criminal convictions in state courts] demands that this finding of consent be presumed correct and accepted as true unless McClure rebuts the presumption with clear and convincing evidence to the contrary. The district court, whose credibility determinations are given great weight, and whose findings of fact are reviewed only for clear error, explicitly accepted that finding, and stated that it did "not find credible petitioner's assertion that he did not consent to the disclosure of the information contained in the map." It found that McClure "voluntarily drew the map and gave it to Mecca," and that, even in the absence of the words "I consent," Mecca could infer consent from the circumstances and from McClure's conduct. It stated that it found Mecca's testimony "entirely credible and corroborated by his contemporaneous notes which state specifically that petitioner consented to the disclosure."

There is evidence in the record to cast doubt on these consent findings—indeed, enough evidence that if we were sitting as trier of fact, we might find that McClure did not give consent. McClure repeatedly denied that he consented, and certainly would have had good reason not to consent. The state court determination that McClure had consented was made before Mecca clarified that the consent was implied and not express. Moreover, it was based on Mecca's unconditional affirmative response, in his state-court deposition, to the question of whether permission to reveal the information was granted. Only later, in the federal habeas proceeding, did it come to light that Mecca had merely inferred McClure's consent.

Further, Mecca's account of the circumstances from which he inferred McClure's consent changed over the years. His initial account stated that he inferred consent from the fact that McClure called him at home, drew the map, and gave it to him. It is a significant leap to infer McClure's consent to disclose the map to law enforcement authorities from the fact that McClure gave the map to Mecca. Virtually all clients provide information to their attorneys, but they do so assuming that the attorneys will not breach their duty of confidentiality. Further, Mecca's behavior at the time of the disclosure suggested that he thought he lacked the kind of informed consent that would give him the legal authority to act.

However, the findings reached by the state and district courts are not so "implausible"—particularly in light of the district court's credibility determinations—that they produce a definite and firm conviction that a mistake has been committed. The district court believed Mecca's account at the evidentiary hearing, disbelieved McClure's, and found the discrepancies in Mecca's testimony to be "minor." Because there are two permissible views of the evidence, the factfinder's choice between them cannot be clearly erroneous. We therefore hold that McClure gave his consent to the disclosure.

b. Consultation

However, the mere fact of consent is not sufficient to excuse what would otherwise be a breach of the duty of confidentiality. Consent must also be informed. That is, the client can provide valid consent only if there has been appropriate "consultation" with his or her attorney. Mecca's consultation with McClure regarding his consent to disclosure was addressed in the state court and district court findings. Both courts found that Mecca did not advise McClure about the potential harmful consequences of disclosure. The state court found that "before petitioner authorized trial counsel to reveal the childrens' [sic] locations to authorities, trial counsel did not advise petitioner that if authorities located the children, he could be further implicated in the criminal activity and the evidence against him would be stronger." The district court found that "Mecca admits that he did not advise petitioner of all potential adverse consequences."

Emphasizing that McClure was "fully engaged" in his defense and that he was told that the obligation to disclose the children's location arose only if the children were alive, the district court held that "under the circumstances, Mecca's failure to advise petitioner of all possible adverse consequences was not unreasonable." We believe this holding is inconsistent with the consultation requirement because it does not attach sufficient importance to the role that an attorney's advice plays in the attorney-client relationship. It is not enough, as the district court suggests, that McClure "did not dissuade Mecca from his intentions" to share the map with authorities. The onus is not on the client to perceive the legal risks himself and then to dissuade his attorney from a particular course of action. The district court's statement that Mecca was relieved of his duty to counsel his client because "common sense dictated that petitioner understood the consequences of his actions" fails to acknowledge the seriousness of those consequences and the importance of good counsel regarding them.

Even in cases in which the negative ramifications seem obvious—for example, when criminal defendants opt for self-representation—we require that a criminal defendant's decision be made on the basis of legal guidance and with full cautionary explanation. We disagree with the district court's conclusion that this case was so exceptional that the attorney's basic consultation duties did not apply. It is precisely because the stakes were so high that Mecca had an obligation to consult carefully with his client. In the absence of some other exception to the duty of confidentiality, his failure to obtain informed consent would demonstrate constitutionally deficient performance under the Sixth Amendment.

2. Prevention of Further Criminal Acts

The State contends that, even if Mecca did not have informed consent, his revelation of client confidences did not amount to ineffective assistance of counsel because he reasonably believed that disclosing the location of the children was necessary in order to prevent further criminal acts. That is, Mecca reasonably believed that revealing the children's locations could have prevented the escalation of kidnapping to murder. This is not a traditional "prevention of further criminal acts" case, because all of the affirmative criminal acts performed by McClure had been completed at the time Mecca made his disclosure. Mecca was thus acting to prevent an earlier criminal act from being transformed by the passage of time into a more serious criminal offense.

Nonetheless, we believe that where an attorney's or a client's omission to act could result in "imminent death or substantial bodily harm" constituting a separate and more severe crime from the one already committed, the exception to the duty of confidentiality may be triggered.

This exception, however, requires that an attorney reveal confidences only to the extent that he "reasonably believes necessary to prevent" those criminal acts and imminent harms. In assessing the effectiveness of McClure's counsel in light of this standard, the first step is to determine what a constitutionally effective counsel should be required to do before making a disclosure. That is, we must determine what basis the attorney had for believing that the precondition to disclosure was present, and how much investigation he or she must have undertaken before it was "reasonable" to "believe it necessary" to make the disclosure to prevent the harm. The second step is to apply that standard to the facts surrounding Mecca's decision to disclose.

There is remarkably little case law addressing the first analytical step. Citing cases dealing with a separate confidentiality exception allowing attorneys to reveal intended perjury on the part of their clients, McClure argues that a lawyer must have a "firm factual basis" before adopting a belief of impending criminal conduct. However, we are not persuaded that the perjury cases provide the proper standard.

McClure is correct that our inquiry must acknowledge the importance of the confidential attorney-client relationship and the gravity of the harm that results from an unwarranted breach of that duty. However, the standard applied in the professional responsibility code asks only if the attorney *"reasonably* believes" disclosure is necessary to prevent the crime. Further, the *Strickland* standard likewise focuses on "whether counsel's assistance was *reasonable* considering all the circumstances." Accordingly, we hold that the guiding rule for purposes of the exception for preventing criminal acts is objective reasonableness in light of the surrounding circumstances.

Reasonableness of belief may be strongly connected to adequacy of investigation or sufficiency of inquiry in the face of uncertainty. Significantly, as indicated above, *Strickland* explicitly imposes a duty on counsel "to make reasonable investigations or to make a reasonable decision that makes particular investigations unnecessary." In any ineffectiveness of counsel case, "a particular decision not to investigate must be directly assessed for reasonableness in all the circumstances, applying a heavy measure of deference to counsel's judgments." Thus, in determining whether Mecca's disclosure of confidential client information constituted ineffective assistance of counsel, we must examine whether Mecca "reasonably believed" that the precondition for disclosure existed and whether, in coming to that belief, Mecca conducted a reasonable investigation and inquiry.

The parties vigorously debate both the reasonableness of Mecca's belief that the children were alive and the reasonableness of his level of investigation and inquiry on that point. McClure argues that any conclusion that Mecca had a reasonable belief is unsupported because Mecca himself indicated that he harbored doubts as to the children's state, and yet failed to inquire further. He points to evidence in the record that Mecca, at least at some stages of his representation of McClure, did not believe the children were alive—or that he, at the least, suspected that they were dead. It is indisputable that this evidence exists, and that most of this evidence is contained in statements by Mecca himself, whom the district court found "highly credible." Mecca's notes state that, after McClure drew the map, Mecca "felt in my own mind that the children were dead, but, of course, I wasn't sure." He testified in the district court evidentiary hearing that the conclusion he came to was that, "without telling me, McClure had told me he had killed three people." And he stated in this same testimony that, at the time he had his secretary place the anonymous call, he thought there was a "possibility," but not a "strong possibility," that the children were alive.

McClure argues that the statement Mecca says abruptly changed his mind about the status of the children—McClure's comment that "Jesus saved the kids"— was so vague and ambiguous that it was not a sufficient basis for a "reasonable belief" that disclosure was necessary. Despite Mecca's acknowledgment that this comment led him only to "assume" that McClure was saying the children were alive, Mecca never directly asked a question that could have confirmed or refuted that assumption. Mecca repeatedly testified that he never squarely asked about the condition of the children or whether McClure had killed them. Accordingly, McClure argues, any finding that Mecca believed the children were alive is not sufficient to establish effective assistance of counsel, because Mecca's failure to engage in a reasonable level of investigation and inquiry rendered that belief unreasonable.

Given the implicit factual findings of the state court, and the explicit factual findings of the district court, which are at least plausible in light of the record viewed in its entirety, we disagree. The ultimate question of the reasonableness of Mecca's belief is a question of law, which we review de novo. In answering that question, however, we look to the facts and circumstances of the case, and as to these facts, we give great deference to the findings of the state court and the district court.

The district court made a number of specific findings regarding the factual basis for Mecca's belief that the children were alive. It found that only McClure knew the true facts and that he deliberately withheld them, leading Mecca to believe the children were alive. It found that McClure controlled the flow of information, and that when Mecca informed McClure that he had an obligation to disclose the children's whereabouts if there were a chance they were alive, McClure did not tell him they were dead. It specifically rejected McClure's assertion that Mecca in fact believed that the children were dead or that he lacked information that they were alive, noting that at the time there was no evidence, other than their disappearance and the passage of time, that they had been injured or killed.

The district court also made specific factual findings regarding the nature of Mecca's investigation and inquiry. It found that "Mecca attempted to discern whether the children were alive" and "that Mecca investigated to the best of his ability under extremely difficult circumstances." McClure argues that these findings are clearly erroneous, and that "arguments that Mr. McClure was manipulative and difficult are essentially irrelevant to the lawyer's obligations." But *Strickland* holds otherwise. The *Strickland* Court emphasized that "the reasonableness of counsel's actions may be determined or substantially influenced by the defendant's own statements or actions." More specifically, it held that "what investigation decisions are reasonable depends critically" on the "information supplied by the defendant."

This is a close case, even after we give the required deference to the state and district courts. The choices made by McClure's counsel give us significant pause, and, were we deciding this case as an original matter, we might decide it differently. But we take as true the district court's specific factual findings as to what transpired—including what McClure said and did, and what actions Mecca took and why he took them—and we conclude that Mecca made the disclosure "reasonably believing it was necessary to prevent the client from committing a criminal act that Mecca believed was likely to result in imminent death or substantial bodily harm." Mecca therefore did not violate the duty of confidentiality in a manner that rendered his assistance constitutionally ineffective. . . .

CONCLUSION

For the foregoing reasons, we conclude that McClure did not receive constitutionally ineffective assistance of counsel. Accordingly, the district court's denial of McClure's petition for writ of habeas corpus is affirmed.

FERGUSON, Circuit Judge, dissenting:

. . . I too sympathize with Mecca for being concerned with the welfare of the children, as do the majority, the District Court and the state court. It would scarcely be wrong to criticize him for, as the District Court stated, being "a human being." However, because at the time of the disclosure Mecca was playing a critical and unique role as McClure's defense attorney, I cannot sanction his behavior. It seems that the time has come for Mecca to take responsibility for the choice he made to breach his client's confidence and for a court, *this court*, to recognize that whether or not Mecca did the "right" thing does not diminish the fact that his doing so constituted an abdication of his professional duties and rendered his performance as McClure's defense attorney deficient under the Sixth Amendment. Mecca's concern for the children is certainly understandable and laudable, however, it does not negate the infirmity of McClure's conviction. Therefore, I must dissent.

QUESTIONS

1. Judge Fletcher describes the duty of confidentiality as "deeply ingrained in our legal system" and as "a critical component of reasonable representation by counsel." Why is lawyer-client confidentiality viewed as so important? What are the advantages of confidentiality? What are its disadvantages?

2. Judge Ferguson, in dissent, indicates that even if McClure's lawyer "did the 'right' thing," it would nonetheless constitute "an abdication of his professional duties." In other words, it seems that the legal ethics rules, in Judge Ferguson's view, prevent a lawyer from doing "the 'right' thing." How can doing the right thing be unethical? Judge Ferguson also describes McClure's lawyer's concern for the children who might have been found alive as "understandable and laudable." How can doing something based on a motive that is "understandable and laudable" violate a lawyer's ethical obligations?

3. Was the crime that triggered disclosure a past crime? A future crime? Why is the characterization of McClure's crime as past or present significant?

4. Should the future crime exception to the lawyer's ethical duty of confidentiality be limited to cases in which there is risk of death or substantial bodily injury? Should it be limited to cases in which such death or substantial bodily injury is imminent? Should lawyer disclosure of a client's future crime be mandatory (i.e., the lawyer *must* reveal) or discretionary (i.e., the lawyer *may* reveal)?

5. Should confidential client information disclosed by a lawyer to prevent a future crime be admissible against the lawyer's client in a criminal or civil case against the client? What about evidence that is discovered as a result of that disclosure? Should it make any difference if the lawyer who made the disclosure represents the client in the case in which the opposing side seeks to admit the lawyer's disclosure or evidence discovered as a result of the disclosure?

6. Client consent to disclosure is a well-recognized exception to the duty of confidentiality. Should explicit client consent be required to trigger this exception? Or should implied consent be sufficient?

7. As Judge Fletcher points out, client consent to disclosure of confidential information must be informed. If you had been in Mecca's position, what would you have told McClure about the potential risks and rewards of disclosure? Should there be any exceptions to the requirement that the consent be informed?

8. McClure's habeas corpus petition was based on a claim that his constitutional rights were violated. What is the relationship between legal ethics rules,

which are normally determined by state authorities and subject to variation from state to state, and the United States Constitution? If the United States Constitution trumps conflicting state laws, including legal ethics rules, why is it that Judge Fletcher uses legal ethics rules to determine whether McClure's lawyer's conduct violated McClure's constitutional rights?

9. Judge Fletcher states that on appeal a district court's determinations regarding the credibility of a witness "are given great weight." Why is this so?

B. REPRESENTING A GUILTY CLIENT

JOHNS v. SMYTH
176 F. Supp. 949 (1959)

HOFFMAN, J. Petitioner is a state prisoner serving a life sentence for the murder of one Melvin Childress in accordance with a final judgment of the Circuit Court of the City of Richmond, Virginia, entered on December 17, 1942. Petitioner and Childress were inmates at the State Penitentiary when the killing took place on October 7, 1942. While there is no transcript of the evidence available from the state court, as no court reporter was present, the petitioner's signed statement given on the day following the crime is to the effect that he killed Childress with a knife in the cell of the latter, when Childress took hold of the petitioner and suggested an unnatural sexual act. An investigation by prison authorities points to other motives for the killing but, for the purpose of this proceeding by way of habeas corpus, we are not particularly concerned with the details of the crime.

On some date following the return of an indictment on October 14, 1942, the state court assigned counsel to represent petitioner. The record reveals that the court-appointed attorney had been practicing for a period of approximately fifteen years at the time of petitioner's trial. There is nothing in this proceeding which would reflect that the trial judge or prosecutor were negligent in the performance of their duties with respect to the appointment of court-assigned counsel and the ensuing trial. . . .

While the petition alleges several points for consideration, it is only necessary to determine whether petitioner had a fair trial by reason of the actions of court-appointed counsel. All too often the incompetency of counsel is assigned in vague allegations which are invariably without merit. It is on the basis of the testimony now given by court-assigned counsel that this court has arrived at the conclusion that petitioner's constitutional rights have been invaded.

One of the cardinal principles confronting every attorney in the representation of a client is the requirement of complete loyalty and service in good faith to the best of his ability. In a criminal case the client is entitled to a fair trial, but not a perfect one. These are fundamental requirements of due process under the Fourteenth Amendment. The same principles are applicable in Sixth Amendment cases (not pertinent herein) and suggest that an attorney should have no conflict of interest and that he must devote his full and faithful efforts toward the defense of his client.

With this in mind, let us examine the facts to determine (1) whether the representation afforded petitioner at his murder trial was so totally lacking that it cannot be said that he had a fair trial in the usual sense of the word, and (2) whether the court-appointed attorney was so prejudiced and convinced of his client's guilt of *first degree murder* that he was unable to, and did not, give his client the "undivided allegiance and faithful, devoted service" which the Supreme Court has held to be the right of the accused under the Constitution, and (3) whether the attorney's interest in his client was so diverted by his personal beliefs that there existed a conflict in interest between his duty to his client and his conscience.

The importance of the attorney's undivided allegiance and faithful service to one accused of crime, irrespective of the attorney's personal opinion as to the guilt of his client, lies in Canon 5 of the American Bar Association Canon of Ethics, in effect during 1942, where it is said:

> It is the right of the lawyer to undertake the defense of a person accused of crime, regardless of his personal opinion as to the guilt of the accused; otherwise innocent persons, victims only of suspicious circumstances, might be denied proper defense. Having undertaken such defense, the lawyer is bound, by all fair and honorable means, to present every defense that the law of the land permits, to the end that no person may be deprived of life or liberty, but by due process of law.

The difficulty lies, of course, in ascertaining whether the attorney has been guilty of an error of judgment, such as an election with respect to trial tactics, or has otherwise been actuated by his conscience or belief that his client should be convicted in any event. All too frequently courts are called upon to review actions of defense counsel which are, at the most, errors of judgment, not properly reviewable on habeas corpus unless the trial is a farce and a mockery of justice which requires the court to intervene. But when defense counsel, in a truly adverse proceeding, admits that his conscience would not permit him to adopt certain customary trial procedures, this extends beyond the realm of judgment and strongly suggests an invasion of constitutional rights.

Little need be said of the trial. The accused did not testify. No proposed instructions were submitted to the trial judge in behalf of the defendant, although under the law of Virginia it was possible for the defendant to have been convicted of involuntary manslaughter and received a sentence of only five years. The defense attorney agreed with the prosecutor that the case would be submitted to the jury without argument of counsel. The instructions given by the court were generally acceptable in covering the categories of first and second degree murder, but failed to mention the possibility of a manslaughter verdict.

Standing alone these complaints would have no merit as they may properly be considered as trial tactics. However, when we look at the motivating force which prompted these decisions of trial counsel, it is apparent that "tactics" gave way to "conscience." In explanation of the agreement not to argue the case before the jury, the court-appointed attorney said:

> I think an argument to the jury would have made me appear ridiculous in the light of evidence that was offered.
>
> I had enough confidence in the judgment of the jury to know that they could have drawn an inference, and I would have been a hypocrite and falsifier if I had gone before the jury and argued in the light of what Johns told me that that statement was accurate.
>
> Well, sir, I did not and I wouldn't be dishonest enough to do it in the light of Mr. Johns' statement to me. You can say what the law is and what the record discloses, but if I asked a client, an accused on defense, to explain some such statement as this

and he gives me the explanation that Johns gave me, I consider it dishonest. You can talk about legal duty to client all you wish, but I consider it dishonest for me to get up before a jury and try to argue that the statement that came out from the Commonwealth was true when Johns had told me that it wasn't. The explanation that he gave me was very vague.

Immediately thereafter, the following occurred:

Q. That you could not conscientiously argue to the jury that he should be acquitted? A. I definitely could not.

Q. Regardless of what the law is or what your duty to a client is? A. You can talk about law and you can talk about my duty to clients, I felt it was my—that I couldn't conscientiously stand up there and argue that point in the light of what Johns had told me.

The attorney was then asked whether he ever considered requesting permission to withdraw from the case. He replied in the negative.

No attorney should "frame" a factual defense in any case, civil or criminal, and it is not intimated by this opinion that the attorney should plant the seeds of falsehood in the mind of his client. In the instant case, however, the evidence adduced by the prosecution suggested some provocation for the act through the summary of the statement given by the defendant on the day following the killing. When the defendant was interviewed by his court-appointed attorney, the attorney stated that he had reason to doubt the accuracy of the defendant's statement. It was at this time that the attorney's conscience actuated his future conduct which continued throughout the trial. If this was the evidence presented by the prosecution, the defendant was entitled to the faithful and devoted services of his attorney uninhibited by the dictating conscience. The defendant could not be compelled to testify against himself, and if the prosecution saw fit to use the defendant's statement in aid of the prosecution, the attorney was duty bound to exert his best efforts in aid of his client. The failure to argue the case before the jury, while ordinarily only a trial tactic not subject to review, manifestly enters the field of incompetency when the reason assigned is the attorney's conscience. It is as improper as though the attorney had told the jury that his client had uttered a falsehood in making the statement. The right to an attorney embraces effective representation throughout all stages of the trial, and where the representation is of such low caliber as to amount to no representation, the guarantee of due process has been violated.

The entire trial in the state court had the earmarks of an ex parte proceeding. If petitioner had been without the services of an attorney, but had remained mute, it is unlikely that he would have been worse off. The state argues that the defendant may have received a death sentence. Admitting this to be true, it affords no excuse for lack of effective representation.

Holding that the petitioner was not accorded a "fair trial" in the true sense of the word, because of the motivating forces which dictated the actions and decisions of his court-appointed counsel, we turn to the legal problem which has given this court grave concern. It is a general rule of law that a federal court cannot order the release of a state prisoner, grounded upon the lack of effective counsel in the state court proceeding, unless the incompetence and ineffectiveness of the attorney is so obvious that it becomes the duty of the trial judge or prosecutor (both state officers) to intervene and protect the rights of the accused. With this general statement, this court is in accord.

As indicated, there is nothing apparent in this case which would require the trial judge or prosecutor to intervene. But the state of facts here presented indicates that the general rule should not be considered as inflexible. In *Massey v. Moore*, the Supreme Court indicated that, on the question of the mental condition of the accused at the time of trial, the presence or absence of affirmative misconduct on the part of the state at the trial was irrelevant.

If it be necessary to engraft an exception on the general rule, it would appear that one is appropriate here, for indeed it would be a dark day in the history of our judicial system if a conviction is permitted to stand where an attorney, furnished to an indigent defendant, candidly admits that his conscience prevented him from effectively representing his client according to the customary standards prescribed by attorneys and the courts.

Counsel for petitioner will prepare an appropriate order granting the writ of habeas corpus and remanding petitioner to the proper authorities of the State of Virginia for further proceedings on the charge of murder. Should the respondent elect to appeal from the order of this court, the effectiveness of the order shall be stayed pending appeal, provided that the appeal is promptly noted and perfected.

QUESTIONS

1. Judge Hoffman states that a criminal defense lawyer must faithfully serve "one accused of crime, irrespective of the attorney's personal opinion as to the guilt of his client." Why is a criminal defense lawyer, having undertaken representation, obligated to represent a guilty client as if he were innocent? What are the advantages and disadvantages of having lawyers represent guilty clients in criminal cases? How would you answer this last question from the point of view of the criminal defendant? From the lawyer's point of view? From society's point of view?

2. Johns's lawyer apparently did not attempt to withdraw from representing Johns. Should he have done so? Why? Is it ethically permissible for a lawyer to do so? Should it be ethically permissible for him to do so? Why?

3. Johns's lawyer was concerned that he would have been "a hypocrite and falsifier" if he argued to the jury that Johns's statement to the police was accurate. If the statement was in fact false, would his lawyer have had to argue that it was accurate in his closing argument in order to rely on provocation? Does this depend on who bears the burden of proof regarding provocation in Virginia?

4. What is the basis of Johns's constitutional law claim? How do his lawyer's ethical obligations affect Johns's constitutional law claim?

5. Might Johns's lawyer have decided against relying on provocation based on strategic rather than personal moral grounds? Why? What disadvantages might reliance on provocation have had for Johns? If Johns's lawyer had made the decision to refrain from relying on provocation for strategic rather than personal moral grounds, would his conduct have been unethical? Would Johns's constitutional rights have been violated?

6. Would Johns have a viable provocation claim under the cases you read in Section 3 of Chapter 6? Judge Hoffman notes that evidence of the statement Johns made to the police regarding provocation was "adduced by the prosecution." Why would the prosecution introduce a statement that might support a claim of provocation?

C. PERJURY

PROBLEM

A 4.4 Donald is charged with the first-degree murder of Vince. Donald was having an affair with Vince's wife, Adrian, and the prosecution's theory is that Donald killed Vince to free Adrian to marry Donald. Police had to search for several days before finding Donald hiding in a friend's hunting cabin. The friend who owns the cabin told police that Donald told him that he planned to kill Vince so he could "be with Adrian." When the police arrested Donald, he asserted his right to remain silent and made no statement. Donald's fingerprints were later found on the gun used to kill Vince. Police suspect Adrian of helping Donald plan the killing, but they do not have enough evidence to charge her.

Lisa is a private attorney who represents Donald in the murder case. Donald admits to Lisa that he was having an affair with Adrian, but during Lisa's first interview of Donald and for a few months thereafter, Donald maintains that he did not kill Vince and claims that someone framed him. As the trial draws near, though, and Lisa reviews the evidence with Donald, he finally admits to her that he did kill Vince, but he claims he did so in self-defense when Vince found him with Adrian and tried to kill him with the gun Donald used to kill Vince.

(a) Consider the following scenarios. Assume that each takes places a few days before trial.

(1) Donald's self-defense claim is corroborated by Adrian and by Vince's sister, who happened to be with Vince when he came home and found Adrian and Donald together.
(2) Donald's self-defense claim is corroborated only by Adrian.
(3) Donald's self-defense claim is uncorroborated by any other witness.
(4) Donald's self-defense claim is contradicted by Adrian, who says that Vince had not discovered their affair.
(5) Same as (4), but when confronted with Adrian's testimony contradicting his claim, Donald says "If I don't say he attacked me, I'm dead."
(6) Same as (4), but when confronted with Adrian's testimony contradicting his self-defense claim, Donald admits Vince never attacked him. Donald nonetheless says he wants to take the stand and testify that he acted in self-defense.

What *may* Lisa do under each scenario if Donald wants to testify that he acted in self-defense? What *must* Lisa do under each scenario if Donald wants to testify that he acted in self-defense?

(b) Would it make a difference if Lisa learned that Donald's self-defense claim was false *after* he testified? What if Donald surprised

Lisa with his self-defense claim by offering it for the first time during her direct examination of him?

(c) What if Donald did not testify, but Adrian offered to testify on Donald's behalf that Donald acted in self-defense when Vince found Donald and Adrian together?

ARIZONA RULES OF PROFESSIONAL CONDUCT
ER 3.3 *Candor Toward the Tribunal*

(a) A lawyer shall not knowingly: . . .

(3) offer evidence that the lawyer knows to be false. If a lawyer, the lawyer's client, or a witness called by the lawyer, has offered material evidence and the lawyer comes to know of its falsity, the lawyer shall take reasonable remedial measures, including, if necessary, disclosure to the tribunal. A lawyer may refuse to offer evidence, other than the testimony of a defendant in a criminal matter, that the lawyer reasonably believes is false.

(b) A lawyer who represents a client in an adjudicative proceeding and who knows that a person intends to engage, is engaging or has engaged in criminal or fraudulent conduct related to the proceeding shall take reasonable remedial measures, including, if necessary, disclosure to the tribunal.

(c) The duties stated in paragraphs (a) and (b) continue to the conclusion of the proceeding, and apply even if compliance requires disclosure of information otherwise protected by Rule 1.6.

Comment

[1] . . .

[2] This Rule sets forth the special duties of lawyers as officers of the court to avoid conduct that undermines the integrity of the adjudicative process. A lawyer acting as an advocate in an adjudicative proceeding has an obligation to present the client's case with persuasive force. Performance of that duty while maintaining confidences of the client, however, is qualified by the advocate's duty of candor to the tribunal. Consequently, although a lawyer in an adversary proceeding is not required to present an impartial exposition of the law or to vouch for the evidence submitted in a cause, the lawyer must not mislead the tribunal by false statements of law or fact or evidence that the lawyer knows to be false. . . .

Offering Evidence

[5] Paragraph (a)(3) requires that the lawyer refuse to offer evidence that the lawyer knows to be false, regardless of the client's wishes. This duty is premised on the lawyer's obligation as an officer of the court to prevent the trier of fact from being misled by false evidence. A lawyer does not violate this Rule if the lawyer offers the evidence for the purpose of establishing its falsity.

[6] If a lawyer knows that the client intends to testify falsely or wants the lawyer to introduce false evidence, the lawyer should seek to persuade the client that the evidence should not be offered. If the persuasion is ineffective and the lawyer continues to represent the client, the lawyer must refuse to offer the false evidence. If only a portion of a witness's testimony will be false, the lawyer may call the witness to testify but may not elicit or otherwise permit the witness to present the testimony that the lawyer knows is false.

[7] The duties stated in paragraphs (a) and (b) apply to all lawyers, including defense counsel in criminal cases. In some jurisdictions, however, courts have required counsel to present the accused as a witness or to give a narrative statement if the accused so desires, even if counsel knows that the testimony or statement will be false. Counsel first must attempt to persuade the accused to testify truthfully or not at all. If the client persists, counsel must proceed in a manner consistent with the accused's constitutional rights. The obligation of the advocate under the Rules of Professional Conduct is subordinate to such constitutional requirements.

[8] The prohibition against offering false evidence only applies if the lawyer knows that the evidence is false. A lawyer's reasonable belief that evidence is false does not preclude its presentation to the trier of fact. A lawyer's knowledge that evidence is false, however, can be inferred from the circumstances. Thus, although a lawyer should resolve doubts about the veracity of testimony or other evidence in favor of the client, the lawyer cannot ignore an obvious falsehood.

[9] Although paragraph (a)(3) only prohibits a lawyer from offering evidence the lawyer knows to be false, it permits the lawyer to refuse to offer testimony or other proof that the lawyer reasonably believes is false. Offering such proof may reflect adversely on the lawyer's ability to discriminate in the quality of evidence and thus impair the lawyer's effectiveness as an advocate. Because of the special protections historically provided criminal defendants, however, this Rule does not permit a lawyer to refuse to offer the testimony of such a client where the lawyer reasonably believes but does not know that the testimony will be false. Unless the lawyer knows the testimony will be false, the lawyer must honor the client's decision to testify.

Remedial Measures

[10] Having offered material evidence in the belief that it was true, a lawyer may subsequently come to know that the evidence is false. Or, a lawyer may be surprised when the lawyer's client or another witness called by the lawyer offers testimony the lawyer knows to be false, either during the lawyer's direct examination or in response to cross-examination by the opposing lawyer. In such situations or if the lawyer knows of the falsity of testimony elicited from the client during a deposition, the lawyer must take reasonable remedial measures. In such situations, the advocate's proper course is to remonstrate with the client confidentially, advise the client of the lawyer's duty of candor to the tribunal and seek the client's cooperation with respect to the withdrawal or correction of the false statements or evidence. If that fails, the advocate must take further remedial action. If withdrawal from the representation is not permitted or will not undo the effect of the false evidence, the advocate must make such disclosure to the tribunal as is reasonably necessary to remedy the situation, even if doing so requires the lawyer to reveal information that otherwise would be protected by Rule 1.6. It is for the tribunal then to determine what should be done—making a statement about the matter to the trier of fact, ordering a mistrial or perhaps nothing.

[11] The disclosure of a client's false testimony can result in grave consequences to the client, including not only a sense of betrayal but also loss of the case and perhaps a prosecution for perjury. But the alternative is that the lawyer cooperate in deceiving the court, thereby subverting the truth-finding process which the adversary system is designed to implement. Furthermore, unless it is clearly understood that the lawyer will act upon the duty to disclose the existence of false evidence, the client can simply reject the lawyer's advice to reveal the false evidence and insist that the lawyer keep silent. Thus the client could in effect coerce the lawyer into being a party to fraud on the court.

Preserving Integrity of Adjudicative Process

[12] Lawyers have a special obligation to protect a tribunal against criminal or fraudulent conduct that undermines the integrity of the adjudicative process, such as bribing, intimidating or otherwise unlawfully communicating with a witness, juror,

court official or other participant in the proceeding, unlawfully destroying or conceal-ing documents or other evidence or failing to disclose information to the tribunal when required by law to do so. Thus, paragraph (b) requires a lawyer to take reasonable remedial measures, including disclosure if necessary, whenever the lawyer knows that a person, including the lawyer's client, intends to engage, is engaging or has engaged in criminal or fraudulent conduct related to the proceeding.

Duration of Obligation

[13] A practical time limit on the obligation to rectify false evidence or false state-ments of law and fact has to be established. The conclusion of the proceeding is a reasonably definite point for the termination of the obligation. A proceeding has con-cluded within the meaning of this Rule when a final judgment in the proceeding has been affirmed on appeal or the time for review has passed. . . .

Withdrawal

[15] Normally, a lawyer's compliance with the duty of candor imposed by this Rule does not require that the lawyer withdraw from the representation of a client whose interests will be or have been adversely affected by the lawyer's disclosure. The lawyer may, however, be required by Rule 1.16(a) to seek permission of the tribunal to withdraw if the lawyer's compliance with this Rule's duty of candor results in such an extreme deterioration of the client-lawyer relationship that the lawyer can no longer compe-tently represent the client. . . . In connection with a request for permission to withdraw that is premised on a client's misconduct, a lawyer may reveal information relating to the representation only to the extent reasonably necessary to comply with this Rule or as otherwise permitted by ER 1.6.

Brian Slipakoff & Roshini Thayaparan, CURRENT DEVELOPMENT 2001-2002: THE CRIMINAL DEFENSE ATTORNEY FACING PROSPECTIVE CLIENT PERJURY

15 Geo. J. Legal Ethics, 935, 935, 948-953 (2002)

INTRODUCTION

The American Bar Association (ABA) *Model Rules of Professional Conduct (Model Rules)* create an obligation for lawyers to disclose to the tribunal when perjured testi-mony has been or may be introduced. The problems of identifying such perjury and the obligations that arise from Model Rule 3.3 are varied and complex. Client per-jury puts the criminal defense attorney in an unenviable position. It creates a tension between the duty of zealous advocacy and the duty of candor toward the court.

Dean Monroe Freedman famously presents this problem in terms of the "perjury trilemma." Dean Freedman notes that lawyers face three obligations in performance. The first two stem from the important, almost sacred, attorney-client relationship. First, there is the duty to investigate a client's case. As Dean Freedman argues, "in order to give clients the effective assistance of counsel to which they are entitled, lawyers are required to seek out all relevant facts." Second, there is the obligation of zealous client advocacy. These are potentially at odds with the third duty, the obligation of lawyers to the court. Lawyers are officers of the court and hold certain responsibilities as such. They have specific requirements imposed upon them in such a capacity that cannot be forsaken. . . .

IV. Remedies Available to a Defense Lawyer . . .

A. Client Persuasion

All courts and commentators agree that a lawyer in this situation ought to attempt to dissuade the client from committing perjury at trial. This involves informing the client of suspicions that the client may be considering perjury, a discussion of attorney duties to the court, and a reminder of the consequences of perjury. In most situations where the attorney suspects that her client is preparing to lie, the lawyer acts in the client's best interests in counseling the client not to do so, irrespective of whether the client's testimony is actually true. This principle is prominent in *Nix* [*v. Whiteside*, 475 U.S. 157 (1986)] where the defendant planned to claim that he saw "something metallic" to bolster his self-defense claim. As counsel in that case pointed out, the defendant could have made out his self-defense claim without the additional fabrication; the lie actually harmed the defendant's chances of acquittal because no weapon was found on the scene. Where a client, such as the defendant in *Nix*, insists on lying because he believes it will benefit him to do so, the attorney should, before going any further, warn the defendant that a falsehood or embellishment will, if exposed, only make him seem more guilty to the trier of fact. Thus, in such circumstances, it is both beneficial to the defendant and ethical for the attorney to satisfy the duty of candor. In those cases, the attorney, in attempting to persuade the client not to lie, can couch her advice to get across to the defendant that he is much better off not fabricating details. Such details are often extraneous, uncorroborable, or contradictory to the defendant's case.

The persuasion solution is appealing because it "involves neither the presentation of the perjured testimony nor disclosure of client confidences." However, it is not effective if the client persists in perjuring himself at trial despite his attorney's best efforts to dissuade him. The lawyer then remains in the same dilemma as when she began. Courts and commentators may agree on persuasion as a first step, but if that fails, there is great diversity in proposed solutions.

B. Disclosure to the Tribunal

One obvious solution to the problem, given the text of Model Rule 3.3, is disclosure of the prospective perjury to the tribunal. This approach follows the premise that the attorney has a duty as an officer of the court to disclose imminent perjury to the tribunal, putting the responsibility of inquiry and reprimand in the hands of the judge. The major benefit of direct disclosure is its "involvement of the judge as a neutral arbiter in testing whether or not defense counsels' conclusion that the defendant does in fact intend to give perjured testimony is justified, and if so, what to do about it." Direct disclosure requires the judge, rather than the client's attorney, to question the client in any necessary manner. The clearest defense of this approach comes from Judge Marvin Frankel, who values the search for truth as the paramount objective in a criminal trial.

There are several critiques to this response. First, although lawyers have duties as officers of the court to report such potential misconduct, they also have a duty to their client. Disclosure of intended perjury may cause irreparable harm to the client-attorney relationship. Second, there is a constitutional question— a lawyer cannot waive rights for her client. The client has the constitutional right to testify on his own behalf. Further, the issue here is *prospective* client perjury. The client has not actually committed a crime in the mere contemplation of perjury. . . .

C. The Do Nothing Approach

At the opposite extreme from full disclosure to the tribunal, a lawyer may choose to do nothing about potential client perjury. Under this approach, the lawyer would treat perjured testimony as any other evidence in her client's case. The main proponent of this tactic is Dean Freedman.[1] He argues that this is the only constitutional solution to the perjury trilemma. . . .

If the lawyer takes any action to treat this testimony differently from other evidence, it is clear that there will be adverse consequences for the client. The justification for this approach is that it puts the client's constitutional rights at the forefront of the lawyer's work. This is especially important given that in this situation, the client has only, at most, threatened to commit perjury. No actual crime has been committed.

The major criticism of this approach is that, although there is a clear right to effective counsel, there is no right to commit perjury. The Court in *Nix* held that "whatever the scope of a constitutional right to testify, it is elementary that such a right does not extend to testifying falsely." Freedman counters this by arguing that this is not lawyer-sanctioned perjury as long as the lawyer "uses her knowledge of the perjury to make ongoing, good faith efforts to dissuade the client from committing it, and the lawyer then proceeds with the perjury only under the compulsion of her systemic role." . . .

D. Refusal to Call the Client to the Stand

A lawyer might be tempted to refrain from presenting potentially perjurious testimony by refusing to call the client to the stand. The primary argument in support of this position is that "an attorney has an ethical obligation not to participate in the presentation of perjured testimony and the defendant has no right to commit perjury." The lawyer thus prevents her client from presenting perjured testimony to the tribunal and can still otherwise advocate for the client's cause.

The major criticism of such an approach is that the courts have clearly established a client's constitutional right to testify. . . .

E. The Narrative Approach

A fifth approach to the problem of potential client perjury has been termed the narrative approach. The narrative approach allows the lawyer to put the client on the stand and allow him to tell his story in a free narrative manner. While this occurs, the lawyer does not engage in the testimony; she asks no questions of the client and presents no corroborating evidence. The client is allowed to present his testimony to the court without help from the attorney. In closing argument, the attorney does not and cannot rely on any of the client's false testimony.

The justification for this approach is that it leaves the lawyer's hands clean of any wrongdoing. The client exercises his constitutional right to testify, and yet, the lawyer is not actively presenting perjury to the court. The main proponent of this

---

1. Dean Freedman has recently described the approach he endorses as follows: "If the lawyer learns that the client is contemplating perjury, she should make continuing, good faith efforts to dissuade the client from that course. . . . In the relatively small number of cases in which the client who has contemplated perjury rejects the lawyer's advice and decides to proceed to trial, to take the stand, and to give false testimony, the lawyer should go forward in the ordinary way. That is, the lawyer should examine the client in a normal professional manner and should argue the client's testimony to the jury in summation to the extent that sound tactics justify doing so." Monroe H. Freedman & Abbe Smith, *Understanding Lawyers' Ethics*, 164 (2d ed. 2002).

approach is Dean Norman Lefstein. Dean Lefstein justifies this approach in several ways. First, he argues, "use of the narrative approach mitigates the harsh effect that will occur if defense counsel incorrectly concludes that the client is planning to lie." This ensures that the constitutional right to testify is not accidentally infringed in a lawyer's effort to comply with ethical standards. Further, this approach tempers the duty of counsel not to offer perjured testimony, because the lawyer has limited involvement with the presentation of the perjured testimony and she is not offering the lies to the tribunal directly. Finally, "if a client is advised that the narrative approach will have to be used, there is a good chance that the client will decide not to testify. On the other hand, if the client chooses to testify and makes a narrative statement, the attorney-client relationship will likely be preserved." Several courts have allowed this approach.

This solution is also subject to several criticisms. Despite the fact that the client can still testify, the use of the narrative approach still infringes on attorney-client responsibilities. Attorneys have an obligation to represent their clients to the utmost. The lack of questioning indicates a failure of the lawyer to question her client or aid him in providing testimony and may limit the effectiveness of such representation. Moreover, the narrative approach has been critiqued on the basis that the perjury is still obvious to the court and trier of fact. Dean Lefstein himself has noted:

> If disclosure of a defendant's intent to commit perjury will not violate the Sixth Amendment, permitting defendant to tell his or her story in a narrative fashion will not do so either. Admittedly, this latter procedure implicitly informs the court that counsel believes that defendant is testifying falsely, but this is obviously no more prejudicial to the defendant (and arguably less) than expressly telling a judge that a client plans to commit perjury.

F. WITHDRAWAL

The withdrawal method takes seriously the commitment that the lawyer makes to zealous advocacy. Under this approach, because the lawyer cannot in good faith present his client's case *in toto*, she asks the court for permission to withdraw from the representation relationship. . . .

An important critique of this method is that it does not solve the problem; it just passes along the ethical dilemma to another attorney. If a lawyer withdraws based on her "knowledge" of perjury, the replacement lawyer is then left in the same situation. Further, it has been criticized for being no more than an "'ostrich-like approach' which does little to resolve the problem."

G. SEPARATE HEARING

A less frequently discussed approach to the client perjury problem is to conduct a separate hearing on the issue of the potential perjury. Where the defendant's attorney believes that she knows of the defendant's intention to commit perjury, "the attorney should request a recess, and the court should conduct an *ex parte, in camera* hearing before a judge other than the trial judge, so that the confidences of the client are revealed only to a disinterested jurist."

The benefit of such a scheme is that the approach allows the lawyer to have judicial support in her decision to disclose potential perjury with minimum prejudice to her client. This keeps the judge in the prosecution case neutral. At least one appellate court has held that "once defense counsel had informed the court of the merits of his client's case and the fact that his client intended to commit perjury, the proceedings should have been certified to another judge. The failure to do so has deprived the appellant of due process."

QUESTIONS

1. Which of the approaches to the problem of client perjury do you think strikes the best balance between the competing obligations of a criminal defense lawyer?

2. Model Rule 3.3 states that "[a] lawyer shall not knowingly . . . offer evidence that the lawyer knows to be false." How certain does the lawyer need to be in order to know that his client will commit perjury? What if the lawyer is aware of a substantial risk that the client will commit perjury? What if the lawyer merely suspects that the client will commit perjury? Is it appropriate for a lawyer to consciously avoid knowledge that his client will commit perjury in order to avoid the obligations imposed by Model Rule 3.3? If a lawyer does consciously avoid knowledge of client perjury, should she be treated as having such knowledge?

D. THE DECISION TO PROSECUTE

PROBLEMS

A 4.5 Paul and Sharon are the parents of a 10-month-old infant boy named Jarod. Jarod's pediatrician reports to the County Department of Social Services that she suspects that Jarod has been the victim of child abuse. An investigation reveals evidence of repeated instances of abuse and that one of his parents is most likely the abuser. Neither Paul nor Sharon cooperates with the police. Immediately after the pediatrician's report, Paul hires a lawyer to represent Sharon and him, and the lawyer advises both Paul and Sharon not to speak with the police. Most of the evidence gathered without the parents' cooperation points to Paul as the abuser. Among other things, neighbors overheard Paul make violent threats toward both Jarod and Sharon. Also, Paul was charged seven years ago with abusing one of his children from a prior marriage. That charge was dismissed when Paul agreed to undergo counseling. The evidence in the present case does not exclude the possibility that Sharon might be the abuser, but the police and social workers assigned to the case believe that she is not the abuser but rather is herself the victim of spousal abuse by Paul. The prosecutor concludes that there is enough evidence to establish probable cause against Paul, but not enough evidence to convict him unless Sharon cooperates and testifies against him. Though the prosecutor believes that Sharon did not abuse Jarod, the prosecutor is considering charging her along with Paul in order to use the charge as leverage to obtain her cooperation and testimony in prosecuting Paul. Should the prosecutor charge Sharon with child abuse? Should she threaten to charge Sharon with child abuse?

A 4.6 Here again are the facts from Problem 2.4 in Chapter 2:

> Monica was a member in the 1970s of a radical group called the People's Liberation Army (PLA), which was bitterly opposed to the United States war in Vietnam. Monica helped plan the bombing of a police car in retaliation for police killing several PLA members in a shootout at a PLA hideout. She did not actually plant the bomb, but assisted those who did by obtaining materials for the bomb and acting as a lookout when the bomb was placed under a police car. The police discovered the bomb before it exploded and no one was injured. Shortly thereafter, Monica disappeared and remained a fugitive for over 25 years. Recently she was arrested and prosecuted for her part in the attempted bombing. In the past 25 years, Monica changed her name, married, and had three children. She remained a committed social activist, became involved in local politics and community theater, and did charity work such as reading to blind people and serving meals at a local soup kitchen. She engaged in no criminal conduct during the past 25 years.

> Assume that Monica has not been tried or convicted. You are the prosecutor and, after considerable deliberation, you decide that on balance the purposes of punishment will not be served by prosecuting Monica. However, you believe that Monica was a witness to criminal activities by other members of the PLA, including a murder, and that her former comrades do deserve to be punished for their past crimes. Should you prosecute Monica solely for the purpose of forcing her to testify against her former comrades?

A 4.7 Cliff is a postal worker who was recently caught stealing a credit card from the mail he processes at a large postal distribution center. You are a prosecutor investigating a series of thefts of large numbers of treasury checks from the same postal facility that employed Cliff. These treasury checks have turned up in the Philippines, where they were exchanged for heroin that was brought back into the United States. When Cliff is interviewed about his credit card theft, he admits his crime and also provides postal investigators with useful information about Norm, another postal worker who is responsible for the check thefts you are investigating. Surveillance of Norm confirms what Cliff told the investigators. Ordinarily, your office would decline to prosecute a postal employee such as Cliff for a single credit card theft since it is a first offense. Cliff was candid with investigators and accepted responsibility for the theft, and he agreed not to contest the loss of his postal job and pension benefits. But Cliff also agrees to cooperate and testify against Norm. You are concerned that failure to prosecute Cliff will make him a less credible witness at trial. Norm has a capable lawyer who will focus on the "deal" Cliff struck with the government in exchange for his testimony. Cliff's theft offense carries a potential maximum five-year sentence. You are sure the defense lawyer will ask the jury in her closing argument: "Who wouldn't lie to avoid being prosecuted and sent to jail for five years? Cliff, an admitted criminal, is giving the prosecutor the testimony she needs and in return they just let Cliff walk. Can you in good conscience convict someone on that kind of testimony?" Should you prosecute Cliff in order to make him a more credible witness and to try to defuse this potential line of attack on his credibility?

A 4.8 Johnny is a 25-year-old drug addict who has been arrested for a series of three bank robberies over the past few months. He obtained a total of $10,000 in the three robberies. No person was physically injured in the robberies, but Johnny threatened and frightened a number of people, and one bank teller has quit her job because of the psychological trauma of the robbery. Each robbery carries a maximum sentence of 20 years in prison. Johnny does not have a serious prior record, and he confessed to all three crimes at the time of his arrest. You are the prosecutor on the case. You have sufficient evidence to prove beyond a reasonable doubt that Johnny committed all three robberies. After conferring with colleagues in your office, you determine that a single ten-year sentence along with mandatory drug treatment is appropriate for the three crimes. For how many of the bank robberies should you charge Johnny? One robbery charge alone will expose him to a 20-year sentence, more than enough for you to seek and obtain a 10-year sentence. By charging him with all three robberies, you would expose Johnny to a potential 60-year sentence.

ARIZONA RULES OF PROFESSIONAL CONDUCT
ER 3.8 *Special Responsibilities of a Prosecutor*

The prosecutor in a criminal case shall:

(a) refrain from prosecuting a charge that the prosecutor knows is not supported by probable cause; . . .

American Bar Association Standards Relating to the Administration of Criminal Justice (1974)

Standard 3.9 *Discretion in the charging decision*

(a) It is unprofessional conduct for a prosecutor to institute or cause to be instituted criminal charges when he knows that the charges are not supported by probable cause.

(b) The prosecutor is not obliged to present all charges which the evidence might support. The prosecutor may in some circumstances and for good cause consistent with the public interest decline to prosecute, notwithstanding that evidence may exist which would support a conviction. Illustrative of the factors which the prosecutor may properly consider in exercising his discretion are:

(i)   the prosecutor's reasonable doubt that the accused is in fact guilty;

(ii) the extent of the harm caused by the offense;

(iii) the disproportion of the authorized punishment in relation to the particular offense or the offender;

(iv) possible improper motives of a complainant;

(v)   reluctance of the victim to testify;

(vi) cooperation of the accused in the apprehension or conviction of others;

(vii) availability and likelihood of prosecution by another jurisdiction.

(c) In making the decision to prosecute, the prosecutor should give no weight to the personal or political advantages or disadvantages which might be involved or to a desire to enhance his record of convictions.

(d) In cases which involve a serious threat to the community, the prosecutor should not be deterred from prosecution by the fact that in his jurisdiction juries have tended to acquit persons accused of the particular kind of criminal act in question.

(e) The prosecutor should not bring or seek charges greater in number or degree than he can reasonably support with evidence at trial.

H. Richard Uviller, THE VIRTUOUS PROSECUTOR IN QUEST OF AN ETHICAL STANDARD: GUIDANCE FROM THE ABA

71 Mich. L. Rev. 1145, 1145, 1155-1159 (1973)

Among his other endeavors, the public prosecutor strives to maintain an upright stance in the stained halls of criminal justice. He correctly senses that the people demand more of him than diligent, workmanlike performance of his public chores. Virtue is the cherished ingredient in his role: the honorable exercise of the considerable discretionary power with which our legal system has endowed his office. Daily, the ethical fibre of the prosecutor is tested—and through him, in large measure, the rectitude of the system of justice.

Discerning and articulating the elusive strains of ethical imperatives there-fore seems a worthy task. And, accordingly, a special project of the American Bar Association (ABA) not long ago formulated a number of canons, while a few commentators have contributed observations underscoring the importance of the ethical exercise of discretion by the powerful public prosecutor. But there is little danger that one more submission will overcrowd the field. . . .

II. PREJUDGING CREDIBILITY

Our system of justice provides for a fact finder. A rather elaborate process has been devised to enhance the accuracy of that divining mechanism. Although far from infallible, it is still believed by many to be the best design yet conceived. And the prime function of that official fact finder, be it judge or jury, is to determine credibility. To what extent should the prosecutor, in the performance of his proper role, assume a supervening truth-detecting responsibility?

As with any good lawyer anticipating trial, the prosecutor should seek to learn the stories of as many witnesses as he can find. And when presented with inexact, incomplete, or conflicting accounts, as is commonly the case, I do not suppose he can be censured for encouraging witnesses to try to improve their memories and get their stories "straight." But, as every trial lawyer knows, obtaining a coherent account of a set of events is a long way from forming a personal judgment of the truth of the matter reported. Some defense counsel I know studiously avoid taking that large and difficult step to private judgment. They correctly feel no obligation to judge credibility. And they may feel their enthusiasm for their task would be dampened by a private assessment of the case. Assuming that, as an advocate, the prosecutor experiences a similar disinclination, is he impelled by the ethical commands of his special role to seek a personal evaluation of the truth?

While ABA standard 3.9(a) condemns in its strongest terms the prosecutor who institutes or causes to be instituted criminal charges when he knows them to be unsupported by "probable cause," paragraph (b)(i) of the same standard suggests that the prosecutor may decline to prosecute a case when he himself entertains a "reasonable doubt that the accused is in fact guilty."

The matter is somewhat complicated by paragraph (e), which injects, subcutaneously, a third standard of certitude in the charging decision. On its surface, paragraph (e) instructs the prosecutor not to "bring or seek" charges greater in number or degree than he can "reasonably support with evidence at the trial." The term "reasonably support" may occasion some mystification, which the commentary seeks to explain. The paragraph, we are informed, is addressed exclusively to permissible multiplicity and gravity of charges at the point of accusation, providing the prosecutor's ethical escape from an imputation of harassment or the untoward acquisition of leverage for future plea negotiation. In this context, the commentary paraphrases the provision: "hence, he [the prosecutor] may charge in accordance with what he then believes he can establish as a prima facie case." With this enlightenment, the rather awkwardly expressed phrase "can reasonably support with evidence at trial" may be read: "can reasonably expect that at the time of trial—despite evaporation, suppression, or other misfortune—he will be able to support with legally sufficient evidence."

The standard of probable cause does not require exacting judgment from the prosecutor, for it does not entail great certainty concerning the underlying truth of the matter; "probable cause" may be predicated on hearsay, and, indeed, does not even import a substantial likelihood of guilt. Like probable cause, the prima facie standard takes little account of credibility questions, but it is a significantly more demanding criterion, satisfied only by (1) "legal" (i.e., admissible) evidence (2) sufficiently complete to establish every element of the crime in question, credence aside. So the standard countenances accusation on no greater certitude than the belief warranting arrest (probable cause), but the prosecutor should not "overcharge," that is, he should not accuse of more than he reasonably anticipates he will be able to support with legally sufficient evidence. Read together, then, the trio of provisions sounds like this: The prosecutor must abjure prosecution without probable cause, should refuse to charge without a durable prima facie case, and may decline to proceed if the evidence fails to satisfy him beyond a reasonable doubt.

The interesting part of the standard is the suggestion that if the prosecutor, imagining himself in the seat of a juror, would not vote for a verdict of guilty, he may decline to present the matter to the system's designated fact finder. I have heard prosecutors, as a matter of personal conscience, take this notion as an ethical imperative. "I never try a defendant," so runs the credo, "unless I am personally convinced of his guilt beyond a reasonable doubt." Or, for some: "beyond any doubt." Realistically, the prosecutor figures that, inflamed by the brutal facts of the crime or for some other reason, the jury may overlook the basis for the doubt which nags his own judgment. And he could not sleep at night having contributed to the conviction of a man who might just possibly be innocent. Of course, in reaching this extrajudicial judgment, the prosecutor will allow himself to consider relevant items which might be excluded from trial evidence. Nor would his refusal to prosecute the case necessarily mean he would decline to recommend the acceptance of a guilty plea, for the confession which normally accompanies the plea may remove the prosecutor's doubt.

Yet withal, the prosecutor's conscientious stand represents a notable modification of our system of determining truth and adjudicating guilt. At the least it creates a new subtrial, informal and often ex parte, interposed between the determinations of the accusing and judging authorities.

Can there be any objection to the prosecutor's transformation of the standard's "may" into a personal "must"? A defendant, of course, can only benefit from this additional safety procedure, and its adoption may move the prosecutor to more diligent and painstaking pretrial investigation, including an open-minded search for persuasive defense evidence. This latter effort comports nicely with the familiar injunction duly intoned by standard 1.1(c): "The duty of the prosecutor is to seek justice, not merely to convict." From these features it may appear that the standards should have placed this burden of internal persuasion on the prosecutor in every case. I think not.

A concrete, commonplace example may illustrate the operation of the precept and flesh out our appraisal of its wisdom. Practitioners know too well a sticky item: the one-eye-witness-identification case. For instance, an elderly white person is suddenly grabbed from behind in a dimly lit vestibule by a black youth who shows a knife and takes the victim's wallet. The entire incident occupies thirty seconds. Some days later, the victim spots the defendant in the neighborhood and has him arrested by the nearest policeman. Although the prosecutor presses him hard, the victim swears he has picked the right man. There is nothing unusual about the defendant's appearance, the victim never saw him before the crime, and he admits he does not know many [blacks] personally, but his certainty cannot be shaken. He insists that in those few moments of terror his attacker's face was "indelibly engraved on his memory." The defendant may have an alibi: his mother will testify that at the time of the crime he was at home watching television with her (not evidence readily credited). And that is the entire case.

Many prosecutors, I think, would concede that as jurors they would hesitate to vote "guilty" on this evidence. His sincerity unmistakable, the victim might well be correct in his identification of the defendant; perhaps it is more likely than not that the defendant is the perpetrator. And juries regularly convict in such cases. But since he knows the fallibility of identification under such circumstances, the basis for reasonable doubt is clear to the prosecutor.

Should the ethical prosecutor refuse to put this sort of evidence before the jury, withhold from the regular fact-finding process the opportunity to decide the issue? Indeed, should the conscientious prosecutor set himself the arduous task of deciding whether in this instance the complainant is right? If it is his duty to do so, how does he rationally reach a conclusion? For this purpose, are his mental processes superior to the jurors' or the judge's? Or may he—should he—abstain from prejudging the case and simply pass the responsibility to those who cannot escape it?

Let us take the problem in a somewhat different, equally common form. The defendant, let us assume, is charged with the illegal possession of a quantity of narcotics. There is little doubt of his guilt; indeed, he is ready to plead guilty. However, he claims that the drug was obtained by an illegal search of his automobile and should therefore be suppressed. The police officer insists that he retrieved the bag of drugs after the defendant abandoned it by throwing it from the window of the vehicle at the officer's approach. Now, the prosecutor knows that some drug carriers do try to divest themselves of the contraband when approached by police, but he also knows that many police seek to escape the strictures of the exclusionary rule by reciting an abandonment to cover an illegal search and seizure. Despite his general suspicion, however, the prosecutor has no reason to believe that the case in question is based on false testimony. Moreover, he has every reason to believe that on the ultimate issue of the defendant's guilt, justice will be done. What is his ethical course?

I confess I have no clear release from the prosecutor's predicament. I recognize as laudable the taking of one more precaution to avert the horror of convicting an innocent person. Yet, on balance, I do not believe the prosecutor must—or should—decide to proceed only in those cases where he, as a fact finder, would resolve the issue for the prosecution.

Where the prosecutor, from all he knows of the case, believes that there is a substantial likelihood that the defendant is innocent of the charge, he should, of course, not prosecute. Similarly, if he has good reason to believe that a witness is lying about a material fact, he should not put the witness on the stand, and if his case falls without the witness' testimony he should dismiss it regardless of whether inadmissible evidence persuades him of the culpability of the defendant. Short of these grounds for declining prosecution on the merits, I deem the ethical obligations of the prosecutor satisfied if he makes known to the court, or the defense, discovered adverse evidence and defects of credibility in witnesses.

Thus, when the issue stands in equipoise in his own mind, when he is honestly unable to judge where the truth of the matter lies, I see no flaw in the conduct of the prosecutor who fairly lays the matter before the judge or jury. He need not vouch for his cause implicitly, as he may not explicitly. Nor should he lose sleep over his reliance upon the device that the system has constructed for the task of truth-seeking, inexact though he knows it to be. Although the prosecutor's discretionary powers may be important, and his detached and honorable presence vital, he is not, after all, the sole repository of justice. Thus, I do not believe that the system is served by canons which overplay the prosecutor's "quasi-judicial" role. He is, let us remember, an advocate as well as a minister of public justice, and the due discharge of his many obligations of fair and detached judgment should not inhibit his participation in what is, for better or worse, essentially a dialectic process. In our well-guided efforts to imbue the system with flexibility and personal qualities of sympathy, we need not sacrifice the values which may yet inhere in the design of controlled contention.

QUESTIONS

1. Professor Uviller tells us that ABA standard 3.9(e) instructs that a prosecutor may not "bring or seek" charges greater in number or degree than he can "reasonably support with evidence at trial." Why might a prosecutor be tempted to bring charges greater than she can reasonably support with evidence?

2. How do the following differ: (a) probable cause; (b) a prima facie case; and (c) proof beyond a reasonable doubt? With which of these should the prosecutor be concerned?

3. Why might a prosecutor who would decline to prosecute a case nonetheless be willing to accept a guilty plea in the case? Does a guilty plea necessarily resolve the question of guilt?

4. Professor Uviller writes that ABA standard 3.9(b)(i) "suggests that the prosecutor may decline to prosecute a case when he himself entertains a 'reasonable doubt that the accused is in fact guilty.'" He then states that if "may" is transformed to "must" in this standard, "[a] defendant . . . can only benefit from this

additional safety procedure. . . . " The use of DNA evidence in recent years has revealed a shockingly high percentage of innocent persons who have been convicted of crime. Does this fact warrant giving defendants "an additional safety procedure" by making it mandatory for prosecutors to decline to prosecute if they entertain reasonable doubt about guilt?

Bennett L. Gershman, A MORAL STANDARD FOR THE PROSECUTOR'S EXERCISE OF THE CHARGING DISCRETION

20 Fordham Urb. L.J. 513, 513-516, 517-519, 521-525, 527-529 (1993)

I. INTRODUCTION

The prosecutor's decision to institute criminal charges is the broadest and least regulated power in American criminal law. The judicial deference shown to prosecutors generally is most noticeable with respect to the charging function. Limited constitutional and statutory constraints on charging are manifested in the presumption of prosecutorial good faith, and are reflected in the courts' acknowledgment that they lack the knowledge and expertise to supervise the prosecutor's exercise of discretion. The Separation of Powers doctrine merely reinforces this policy of judicial noninterference. To the extent that sufficient evidence exists, and no improper motivation is shown, the charging decision is virtually immune from legal attack.

This is not to say that the prosecutor's discretion is unbounded. Various legal,[3] political,[4] experiential,[5] and ethical considerations[6] inform and guide the charging decision. Still, no subject in criminal law is as elusive as that of prosecutorial discretion in the charging process. . . .

Through [the following hypothetical cases] we can examine the circumstances that might lead an ethical prosecutor to institute or decline to institute criminal charges when she believes that the defendant is probably guilty, that prosecution of this particular crime would be consistent with the public interest, and that legally sufficient and admissible proof exists to convince a jury beyond a reasonable doubt of the defendant's guilt. They provide the setting in which a moral standard is proposed to guide the prosecutor's discretion. . . .

A. A ROBBERY CASE

Steven, a white, thirty-five-year-old accountant, was returning home from work on January 21st. He entered his apartment building at 5:30 P.M. and waited in the lobby for the elevator. The lobby is illuminated by recessed lighting in the ceiling, but visibility is not as clear as it would be in daylight. As Steven waited, a male darted up to him from somewhere in the lobby, put a sharp-looking object to

---

[3] Legal considerations include an evaluation of the strength of the case, the credibility of complainants and witnesses, the existence and admissibility of corroborating proof, and the nature and strength of the defense.

[4] Political considerations include an assessment of the harm caused by the offense, the availability of investigative and litigation resources, the existence of non-criminal alternatives, and an alertness to relevant social and community concerns.

[5] Experiential considerations include the prosecutor's background, training, experience, intuition, judgment, and common sense.

[6] Ethical considerations involve a sensitive appreciation that in the context of the above factors, the ends of justice would be served by criminal prosecution, and that neither personal, political, discriminatory, nor retaliatory motives have influenced the charging decision.

Steven's midsection, and demanded Steven's wallet. Steven quickly fumbled for his wallet and gave it to him. The male fled out the front door of the building. There were no witnesses.

Entering his apartment, Steven immediately dialed 911 to report the crime. The police arrived in about twenty minutes and took a statement. Steven, clearly unsettled by the experience, described his assailant as a black male, dark complexion, about six feet tall, stocky build, and wearing a green jacket and dungarees. He reported that the event took less than a minute, but that he believed he could identify the person if he saw him again.

Three days later, the police called Steven and asked him to come to the police station to look at photographs. There, Steven was asked to look through a large folder filled with several hundred "mug-shots," and to advise the police if he recognized the person who robbed him. The photographs were chosen based on Steven's description, and constituted a fair sample of persons with relatively similar appearances. After examining the photographs for more than an hour, Steven chose two pictures, and after looking carefully at the two for about five minutes, selected the picture of the person whom he recognized as the person who robbed him.

The man Steven identified, Fred, was located by the police and asked to come to the police station. After he arrived, Fred was placed in a line-up with five other males of similar appearance. Steven viewed the line-up carefully and positively identified Fred as the perpetrator. Fred was arrested on a charge of robbery in the first degree. A search of Fred's apartment yielded no tangible proof linking Fred to Steven's robbery. Fred, a thirty-two-year-old African American, has a record of two previous arrests within the past five years for narcotics possession offenses. One charge was dismissed and Fred pleaded guilty to the other and received a sentence of six months. Fred matched the general description that Steven had given the police with the exception of a noticeable scar on his forehead, which Steven never mentioned. At his arraignment, Fred pleaded not guilty, and was remanded to the county jail since he was unable to post the $ 5,000 bail. Fred's public defender has informed the prosecutor that Fred claims he had nothing to do with the robbery, was in a different part of the city at the time, but has no alibi witness to support this claim. Fred refuses to plead guilty to second degree robbery, which the prosecutor's office routinely offers.

Prior to deciding what charges to institute, the prosecutor interviewed Steven.[8] Steven is intelligent and articulate. He is emphatic that he has identified the right person. If a jury believes Steven's testimony, Fred will be found guilty. However, the prosecutor knows that the case has weaknesses, i.e., Steven's limited opportunity to observe his assailant, his failure to recall the scar, the lack of any corroborating evidence, Steven's initial selection of two photographs from the array, and the cross-racial nature of the identification. Moreover, the prosecutor is aware that eyewitness

---

[8] Each of these hypotheticals allows the prosecutor some lead time between the defendant's arrest by the police and the prosecutor's charging decision, thereby enabling the prosecutor to evaluate the case with greater care. In busy prosecutors' offices, particularly in urban areas, the huge volume of cases may require more expeditious case processing and impose substantial time constraints on the thoroughness of the investigation and evaluation. These pressures are not incompatible with responsible and nonmechanical decision-making. For example, the most experienced prosecutors could be assigned to the earliest stages of the decision-making process, or in the unit that determines whether felony charges will be sought. Similarly, policies could be adopted that require more extensive investigation in cases that traditionally have presented difficult factual or legal choices. The hypothetical cases in this Essay represent prototypes of the kinds of situations that might require more extensive investigation before instituting formal charges.

identifications historically have resulted in innocent persons being wrongfully convicted. Nevertheless, on the basis of Steven's convincing testimony, the prosecutor knows from experience that a jury could very likely convict. The prosecutor is preparing the case for charging purposes. Should the prosecutor charge Fred with robbery? What degree of moral confidence should guide the prosecutor's decision? . . .

C. A MURDER CASE

Ella had been married to Don for six years. They had one child, Tina, who is five years old. During virtually the entire period of the marriage, Don physically abused Ella. Don often drank excessively, and it was on these occasions that he would become most brutal. Ella summoned the police on several of these occasions when Don was out of control and the beatings were most violent, the last time being one week earlier. Ella went to the hospital on these occasions. Police and medical records confirm these facts, and describe Ella's injuries. Nevertheless, Ella was in love with Don, and because of their longstanding relationship, and for the sake of their child, she never initiated criminal charges against him, did not seek court orders of protection, and never left the household. Following the periods of abuse, Don would cry and ask Ella for forgiveness. Ella always forgave him.

Until the evening of June 5th. That evening, Don, drinking heavily and in a rage, punched Tina in her head for spilling her milk. Don had never before struck Tina so viciously. When Ella screamed at him and sought to intervene, Don beat her repeatedly on her head and body with a broom handle. Don shouted that if Ella ever questioned his authority again, he would kill her. Ella, in terror, locked herself and Tina in the bathroom. Don left the apartment. He returned two hours later, undressed, and went to bed. Ella, under emotional shock and confusion, went into the kitchen and obtained a knife. She walked into the bedroom and stabbed Don, killing him. Ella immediately called the police and told them what happened. They arrested her on a charge of murder.

Ella's lawyer has informed the prosecutor of his client's version of the events, part of which Tina has confirmed, and has asked the prosecutor to review the report of Dr. Wall, a highly respected clinical psychologist who has treated battered women, has written in scholarly journals about forensic issues concerning the "Battered Women's Syndrome," and has testified as an expert witness in many criminal and civil proceedings involving this issue. Dr. Wall's lengthy report details the relationship between Ella and Don and provides considerable factual data for his conclusion that under the circumstances, on the night of the killing, Ella was in a state of shock, was afraid for her life and that of her child, and believed that she and her child were in danger of being killed by Don. Dr. Wall concluded that Ella's belief under the circumstances was reasonable.

The prosecutor, from background and experience, is sensitive to issues of domestic violence. The prosecutor does not doubt that Ella believed that the only way to protect her life and that of her child was to take her husband's life. The prosecutor has no reason to dispute Dr. Wall's conclusions that Ella was a battered victim who felt she had no other recourse than to kill her husband. The prosecutor knows from experience, however, that juries tend to reject the battered spouse syndrome as a defense to murder, and would probably find her guilty. Ella would then be subject to a mandatory sentence of fifteen years to life imprisonment. Should the prosecutor charge the defendant with murder? What degree of moral confidence should guide the prosecutor's decision?

III. The Decision-Making Process

These cases share several common characteristics. Each involves a serious felony; each involves a violent crime that commands the highest priority in a prosecutor's office and consequently does not realistically raise concerns over allocating scarce resources. Moreover, there is legally sufficient admissible evidence to charge each of these defendants with robbery . . . and murder, respectively, and to convince a jury of each defendant's guilt. Further, these cases are within the prosecutor's jurisdiction and cannot be referred to a different prosecutorial or correctional agency.

Analysis of these cases rests on the same body of assumptions. First, the prosecutor in each of these cases is acting responsibly with a view toward seeking justice for the victim, the accused, and society. Second, the prosecutor does not want to prosecute an innocent person, and does not want to see a guilty person go free. Third, the prosecutor is concerned that an acquittal can have a negative effect on her reputation, or engender public cynicism about the weaknesses of the criminal justice system. Despite this, the prosecutor would not let embarrassment or public criticism over a possible acquittal prevent an otherwise valid prosecution. . . .

Would it be proper for the prosecutor to bring criminal charges in the expectation that the defendant probably would later accept a favorable plea offer to a reduced charge? It is improper for prosecutors to use overcharging as a leverage device to more readily obtain guilty pleas or to provide a trial jury a broader range of charges that might more readily produce a compromise verdict. However, proving such improper prosecutorial motivation is virtually impossible. Moreover, this option is tactically unwise as well as unethical. Since the prosecutor cannot control the defendant's decision-making, the prosecutor cannot ensure that the defendant inevitably will accept a plea offer. The prosecutor may be forced to fully litigate a charge that arguably should not have been brought in the first place, and that may result in a wrongful conviction.

Finally, is it proper for a prosecutor to bring charges in a close case in the expectation that if the case ultimately goes to trial, a jury will be entrusted to determine the truth, thereby absolving the prosecutor from the moral responsibility of convicting an innocent person? The central theme of this Essay goes to precisely this question. To what extent should the prosecutor allow the jury system to resolve close questions of guilt rather than grappling with those questions independently? One of the major flaws in this option is the assumption that juries always do the right thing and do not make mistakes. To the extent that juries are politically motivated, succumb to inflammatory appeals, or rely on ambiguous or uncertain proof, they can convict innocent persons. Although the adjudicatory process attempts to minimize the risk of jury error, its procedural protections come into play only after the prosecutor has made the independent judgment that criminal prosecution is appropriate. Under my thesis, rather than pass this responsibility to the jury, then, the prosecutor functions almost literally as a gatekeeper of justice with the obligation to prevent an injustice before the system, if left to its own devices, miscarries.

IV. A Moral Standard for Decision-Making

Once it is agreed that a prosecutor cannot avoid the charging decision by recourse to the kinds of options noted above, it is necessary to examine how a responsible prosecutor should approach the charging decisions presented in each of the hypothetical cases. I am not suggesting that there is one correct decision. My objective is less to suggest any particular charging result than it is to provoke inquiry into the degree of moral confidence that a prosecutor should have before bringing criminal charges. My thesis is that the prosecutor should engage in a moral struggle over charging decisions, and should not mechanically initiate charges. First, the prosecutor should apply all of the legal, political, experiential, and ethical factors noted above.[17] After considering these factors, and before making the ultimate decision to charge, the prosecutor should then assure herself that she is morally certain that the defendant is both factually and legally guilty, and that criminal punishment is morally just. This standard of moral certainty governs the resolution of the ... hypotheticals: it applies to charging decisions involving the reliability of a witness ... and the applicability of a defense.[18]

Why a standard of moral certainty? Such a standard fits the reality that the prosecutor is the gatekeeper of justice. It requires the prosecutor to engage in a rigorous moral dialogue in the context of factual, political, experiential, and ethical considerations. It also requires the prosecutor to make and give effect to the kinds of bedrock value judgments that underlie our system of justice—that the objective of convicting guilty persons is outweighed by the objective of ensuring that innocent persons are not punished.[19] Under this precept, society bears the cost of the prosecutor's moral uncertainty, rather than the defendant. Finally, the prosecutor who acknowledges moral uncertainty about a defendant's guilt but decides nonetheless to bring charges, violates the prosecutor's special obligation to seek justice, and tacitly invites the system to miscarry.

A. The Robbery Case

The robbery case presents the question of the degree of moral confidence that the prosecutor must have in a witness's reliability. The overriding challenge for the prosecutor in such cases is to make an assessment of the degree of reliability of the witness's identification, so that the prosecutor can feel morally certain that Fred is guilty and that punishing him would be proper. Thus, the prosecutor is not required to decide, nor usually able to decide, whether the complaining witness is telling the truth. The prosecutor in such cases does not doubt the victim's sincerity, i.e., that he honestly believes that he has accurately identified his assailant. The critical question for the prosecutor is not whether Steven is positive but whether he is right.

Several factors undermine the prosecutor's moral certainty of Fred's guilt. There is no corroborative proof that might confirm the accuracy of Steven's identification. No property was recovered that might link Fred to the crime. Fred gave no

---

[17] See supra notes 3-6.

[18] The term "moral certainty" is used in criminal cases based solely on circumstantial evidence. In such cases, the term is intended to convey to the jury the high level of confidence that the jury must have to convict. People v. Barnes, 406 N.E.2d 1071 (N.Y. 1980). My use of the term in this Essay requires that same degree of confidence on the part of the prosecutor in bringing charges. It requires the prosecutor to engage in a process of rigorous intellectual and emotional scrutiny and to act only if that scrutiny yields a conclusion that is so personally compelling that the prosecutor would not hesitate to act on that decision in vital matters affecting the prosecutor's own life. In short, only if the prosecutor would herself convict on that charge should the prosecutor institute that charge.

[19] In re Winship, 397 U.S. 358, 372 (1970) (there exists "a fundamental value determination of our society that it is far worse to convict an innocent man than to let a guilty man go free.") (Harlan, J., concurring).

false alibi, and made no other statements that might have implied a consciousness of guilt.[20] Fred has no significant criminal history, e.g., a background involving robbery or other crimes of violence.[21] Steven's description of Fred omits any detailed, distinctive, or unique attributes—i.e., a scar, hair style, or tone of voice—that might enhance the prosecutor's confidence in Steven's identification. Although Steven seems to be an intelligent and perceptive person, the amount of time he had to observe his assailant was not considerable—less than a minute—and under less than ideal viewing conditions. Moreover, the prosecutor knows from experience that although stress may heighten one's powers of observation, it also can interfere with a person's perception and memory. Moreover, Steven's identification of the defendant's photograph came after he narrowed a large sample to two persons. This selection process could demonstrate either that Steven was being extraordinarily careful in making his selection, or unduly tentative and uncertain as to which of those two persons actually robbed him. Steven is positive that he has picked out the right person, but the prosecutor also knows from experience and training that there is little correspondence between an eyewitness's assurance and the accuracy of that identification.

There is also the issue of race. The prosecutor cannot avoid the question of whether, and to what extent, the race of the victim and the defendant might influence the accuracy of an identification. The prosecutor knows that cross-racial identifications present special problems that might undermine accuracy. The prosecutor also is aware of the inherent difficulties faced by a defense lawyer in raising this subject before a jury.[25] Finally, from training and experience, the prosecutor is acutely aware of the inherent dangers of eyewitness identifications, i.e., the disproportionate impact such identifications can have upon juries, and the numerous studies and case reports that have documented miscarriages of justice based on erroneous eyewitness identifications.

What standard should the prosecutor use in deciding whether to charge Fred with robbery? Before pressing ahead with criminal charges, a responsible prosecutor should be morally certain that the defendant is guilty and that criminal punishment is appropriate. Under the above analysis, the prosecutor has no basis other than her own experience and intuition to trust Steven's identification. Should the prosecutor charge Fred based on a visceral feeling that Steven is correct? If the prosecutor is unable to articulate a factual doubt as to Fred's guilt, ethical codes would allow the prosecutor to bring charges. However, the inability of the prosecutor to articulate a doubt is neither surprising nor dispositive. The complainant has stated quite firmly that "That's the man!" Such an assertion would probably be sufficient to convince many prosecutors that charges are appropriate.

Fred should not be charged with robbery. Fred may in fact be guilty, and the prosecutor may believe that he probably is guilty, but for all of the reasons outlined above, the prosecutor cannot be morally certain that he is guilty. The prosecutor

---

[20] There exists the possibility that the prosecutor might ask Fred to submit to a polygraph examination as a means of determining his truthfulness. Based on my knowledge and experience, most prosecutors do not use such tests in these circumstances because the tests do not have sufficient reliability and therefore do not add to the decision-making process.

[21] Although this factor may have no independent evidentiary value, it might justifiably influence a prosecutor's evaluation of the case by enhancing the prosecutor's moral confidence of Steven's accuracy.

[25] The lawyer may be perceived as bringing up a racial stereotype—i.e., that all persons of a particular race look alike. This suggestion may offend certain jurors.

will try to explain to Steven the grounds for her decision. Steven, the victim of a particularly heinous crime, will probably be outraged by the decision. Crime victims, the prosecutor will be told with biting sarcasm, have no rights, and through this decision are being further victimized by an insensitive and overly technical criminal justice system. Steven's reaction is perfectly understandable, and there is no satisfactory response. The prosecutor will try to explain that she is required to serve different, and conflicting, constituencies. Steven, Fred, and society are actual constituencies. Values such as justice and the presumption of innocence are abstract constituencies. The prosecutor will try to explain that these latter values transcend individual and societal harm, and involve a sensitive appreciation of the uses of power. That Steven may not be convinced merely underscores the difficulty and complexity of the decision, and why the prosecutor's task, as I have noted, "is more exacting than that of any other public official." . . .

C. The Murder Case

The murder case presents the prosecutor with [another] type of charging problem. Unlike the robbery . . . [case], the murder case presents no dispute about the facts. The prosecutor knows what happened but is required to resolve a legal problem: whether these facts establish a defense. The prosecutor faces a legal challenge to the traditional approach to legal justification, or self-defense. Traditionally, the defense of justification could be sustained only if the defendant reasonably believed that it was necessary to protect herself or another person from the imminent use of deadly force. How could Fred imminently use deadly force if he was asleep? Why did Ella not leave the apartment? These are predictable questions from a judge or a jury. Even if the prosecutor concludes to a moral certainty that Ella killed her husband based on her honest belief that the killing was necessary to protect her life and that of her child, is the prosecutor nonetheless required to charge Ella with murder?

Most prosecutors, I believe, would conclude that Ella's justification defense—even if honestly asserted—could not legally be sustained because the element of imminency of danger is lacking. However, a prosecutor with experience in domestic violence complaints, who has studied the legal and scholarly literature surrounding the phenomenon of spousal battering, who believes Ella's story and does not dispute Dr. Wall's conclusions, would find it morally difficult to charge Ella with murder. Should the prosecutor institute such a charge if she is morally certain that Ella honestly believed that in order to protect herself and her child she needed to kill her husband, that such claim is supported by considerable social and psychological literature, but if she also knows that Ella would not be able to sustain the defense?

A more likely scenario might be that the prosecutor is morally uncertain of the scope of the justification defense as it relates to Ella's case. The prosecutor may be convinced that Ella honestly believed that her life was being imminently threatened by her husband, but that she acted unreasonably because she had other reasonable alternatives to killing her husband. The prosecutor undoubtedly could locate an expert witness to support that view. Based on her intuition and experience, the prosecutor strongly believes that a jury would find Ella guilty of murder, and that a judge would be required under the law to impose a substantial mandatory sentence. However, the prosecutor also knows that thousands of battered women throughout the country are incarcerated in prison under substantial sentences for crimes similar to Ella's, whose claims of justification either were not raised at trial, or were rejected by the jury.[36]

Under either scenario, Ella should not be charged with murder. The prosecutor knows that the reasonableness of Ella's belief that she was exposed to imminent danger will be the critical issue in her ability to raise that defense. The prosecutor is aware that her unreasonableness would as a matter of law prevent her from successfully raising this defense. However, even if Ella was unreasonable, the honesty of her belief under the circumstances of her abuse makes the prosecutor morally uncertain whether justice would be served by charging Ella with murder and subjecting her to substantial mandatory imprisonment. Under these circumstances, the prosecutor should look to other charging options. The prosecutor could choose between bringing no charges, or charging Ella with a lesser degree of homicide based on her honest but unreasonable belief that killing her husband was necessary to protect herself and her child. The prosecutor's choice would depend on her assessment of Ella's conduct, the harm Ella caused and the amount of punishment Ella should receive, the impact of prosecution on the incidence of domestic violence, and the impact of prosecution on the public's perception of the prosecutor's commitment and fairness in domestic violence cases. . . .

QUESTION

How does Professor Gershman's view of how prosecutors should decide which cases to prosecute differ from Professor Uviller's? On what issues do they agree? Which view would you adopt if you were a prosecutor? Why?

E. PROSECUTORIAL DISCLOSURE OF EXCULPATORY INFORMATION

PROBLEM

A 4.9 The government indicts a defendant on an armed robbery charge arising from a violent mugging. The prosecution's case is based

---

[36] A prosecutor who seeks to avoid making a difficult decision might believe that she could present this case to a grand jury, advise the grand jury of the justification defense, and allow the grand jury to take whatever action the grand jury believes is appropriate. As noted above, however, this option is unrealistic, for it does not relieve the prosecutor of the charging decision; it only disguises the actual source of decision-making authority. The grand jury will indict only if that is the prosecutor's recommendation. The prosecutor might also be tempted to institute murder charges, believing that she could induce any rational defendant to plead guilty to a reduced charge of manslaughter under a very favorable sentence promise. This option assumes that the defendant will plead guilty, and that the judge will impose the desired sentence. These assumptions are mere speculation. Moreover, even if these assumptions are correct, the prosecutor is engaging in unethical behavior when she uses her charging power not because it is the morally correct charge, but as a leverage device to compel a defendant to plead guilty. Finally, a prosecutor could simply avoid making the difficult moral decision and bring murder charges against Ella, recognizing that if plea negotiations fail to produce a settlement, a jury will decide the case on the merits. If the prosecutor is morally uncertain that Ella is guilty of murder, then allowing a jury to convict her of murder would violate the prosecutor's duty to prevent a miscarriage of justice.

entirely on the testimony of the victim, who identified the defendant from police photographs of persons with a record of similar
violent crime. With only the victim's testimony to rely on, the prosecutor is unsure of her ability to obtain a conviction at trial. She
offers the defendant a guilty plea limiting his sentencing exposure
to five years, a significant concession in light of the defendant's substantial prior record and the fact that the charged offense carries a
maximum penalty of fifteen years' incarceration. As trial nears, the
victim's confidence in the identification appears to wane. The robbery took place at night. He was frightened and saw his assailant
for a matter of seconds. The victim refuses to talk to the defense,
but confides to the prosecutor his fear of a mistake in the photo
identification. He is now unsure if the man he picked from the
police photographs is the man who robbed him. On the eve of trial,
the defendant responds to the prosecutor's plea offer. He indicates
that he is willing to plead guilty if the prosecutor will limit the
sentence to one year. Is the prosecutor free to accept a guilty plea
without disclosing the victim's statement of uncertainty about the
identification?[2]

ARIZONA RULES OF PROFESSIONAL CONDUCT
ER 3.8   *Special Responsibilities of a Prosecutor*

The prosecutor in a criminal case shall: . . .

(d) make timely disclosure to the defense of all evidence or information
known to the prosecutor that tends to negate the guilt of the accused or mitigates the offense, and, in connection with sentencing, disclose to the defense
and to the tribunal all unprivileged mitigating information known to the prosecutor, except when the prosecutor is relieved of this responsibility by a protective
order of the tribunal; . . .

Comment

[1] A prosecutor has the responsibility of a minister of justice and not simply that
of an advocate. This responsibility carries with it specific obligations to see that the
defendant is accorded procedural justice and that guilt is decided upon the basis of
sufficient evidence. Precisely how far the prosecutor is required to go in this direction is
a matter of debate and varies in different jurisdictions. . . . Applicable law may require
other measures by the prosecutor and knowing disregard of those obligations or a
systematic abuse of prosecutorial discretion could constitute a violation of ER 8.4.

---

2. This hypothetical is from Kevin C. McMunigal, *Disclosure and Accuracy in the Guilty Plea Process,*
40 Hastings L.J. 957, 957 (1989).

American College Of Trial Lawyers,[6] PROPOSAL: PROPOSED CODIFICATION OF DISCLOSURE OF FAVORABLE INFORMATION UNDER FEDERAL RULES OF CRIMINAL PROCEDURE 11 AND 16

41 Am. Crim. L. Rev. 93, 94-99 (2004)

BACKGROUND AND SUMMARY

In the 1963 landmark decision of *Brady v. Maryland*, 373 U.S. 83 (1963), the Supreme Court held that prosecutors have a constitutional duty to turn over "evidence favorable to an accused . . . where the evidence is material either to guilt or to punishment." Four decades later, Federal Rules of Criminal Procedure 11 and 16, which govern federal plea negotiations and criminal discovery, respectively, still do not address this duty, let alone require the government to timely disclose to the defendant favorable information that is material to either guilt or sentencing.

With neither a clear definition of favorable evidence nor a disclosure timetable, prosecutors have interpreted the constitutional discovery obligation inconsistently, and too often disclosed favorable information on the eve of, during, or after trial— or not at all. Timely disclosure of favorable information can greatly impact the plea decision, trial strategy, presentation of evidence and sentencing.

Since approximately ninety percent of federal criminal cases are resolved through pleas of guilty, the timely disclosure of information favorable to punishment is particularly important to fair and open plea negotiations, and to the honest and consistent implementation of the United States Sentencing Guidelines. Information that tends to diminish either the degree of the defendant's culpability or their Offense Level under the Guidelines can significantly affect a defendant's punishment. Nonetheless, prosecutors have recently sought to require defendants to enter into knowing and voluntary plea agreements when they have not received information favorable to punishment. Worse, these defendants have often been required to waive their constitutional right to exculpatory material, without even knowing what favorable evidence may exist. This practice threatens to deprive defendants and courts of information critical to a fair and honest sentencing process. . . .

I. *BRADY v. MARYLAND* BACKGROUND

A prosecution that withholds evidence on demand of an accused which, if made available, would tend to exculpate him or reduce the penalty helps shape a trial that bears heavily on the defendant.
Justice William O. Douglas

A. *BRADY v. MARYLAND*

Brady v. Maryland represents the first time the Supreme Court created a bright-line constitutional duty on the part of prosecutors to turn over "evidence favorable to an accused . . . where the evidence is material either to guilt or to punishment." In *Brady*, the defendant had been convicted of first-degree murder and sentenced to death. Although he had admitted to participating in the crime, Brady maintained that he should be spared the death penalty because his accomplice had

---

6. The principal draftsman of this report was Robert W. Tarun (Chicago, IL). He was assisted by a subcommittee of the Federal Criminal Procedure Committee of the American College of Trial Lawyers consisting of Locke T. Clifford (Greensboro, NC), William F. Manifesto (Pittsburgh, PA), and Jordan Green (Phoenix, AZ).

done the actual killing. In an attempt to prove this, Brady's lawyer requested that the prosecution show him several statements made by Brady's accomplice. Despite this request, the prosecution never provided the attorney with a statement in which Brady's accomplice admitted to committing the actual homicide. The government's behavior prompted Justice Douglas to comment:

> Society wins not only when the guilty are convicted but when criminal trials are fair; our system of the administration of justice suffers when any accused is treated unfairly. . . . A prosecution that withholds evidence on demand of an accused which, if made available, would tend to exculpate him or reduce the penalty helps shape a trial that bears heavily on the defendant. That casts the prosecutor in the role of an architect of a proceeding that does not comport with standards of justice. . . .

The Court held that "the suppression by the prosecution of evidence favorable to an accused upon request violates due process where the evidence is material either to guilt or to punishment, irrespective of the good faith or bad faith of the prosecution."

B. *Brady* Evolution

Since *Brady*, five major Supreme Court cases have construed the prosecutor's obligation to disclose evidence favorable to an individual criminally accused. In *Giglio v. United States*, 405 U.S. 150 (1972), the Court applied *Brady*'s mandate to impeachment evidence, as well as classically exculpatory evidence. Giglio had been convicted of passing forged money orders, and, while his appeal was pending, his attorney learned that the government had failed to disclose a promise of immunity made to its key witness. Chief Justice Burger ordered a new trial as a result of the prosecution's misconduct, stating that "when the reliability of a given witness may well be determinative of guilt or innocence, nondisclosure of evidence affecting credibility falls within" the rule of *Brady*.

In *United States v. Agurs*, 427 U.S. 97 (1976), the Court reviewed for *Brady* violations the second-degree murder conviction of a defendant for whom self-defense was the sole argument presented. The defendant had not requested, and the government had not disclosed, evidence that the victim possessed a criminal record that included prior convictions for assault and possession of deadly weapons. The Court found that a prosecutor's constitutional duty to disclose favorable evidence was not limited to situations in which the defendant had specifically requested the evidence. Noting that "the prudent prosecutor will resolve doubtful questions in favor of disclosure," Justice Stevens observed:

> There are situations in which evidence is obviously of such substantial value to the defense that elementary fairness requires it to be disclosed even without a specific request. For though the attorney for the sovereign must prosecute the accused with earnestness and vigor, he must always be faithful to his client's overriding interest that "justice shall be done." He is the "servant of the law, the twofold aim of which is that guilt shall not escape or innocence suffer." This description of the prosecutor's duty illuminates the standard of materiality that governs his obligation to disclose exculpatory evidence.

The Court concluded that undisclosed evidence should be deemed material, and therefore violative *of Brady*'s dictates, if it "created a reasonable doubt that did not otherwise exist." It nonetheless upheld the conviction because the trial judge remained convinced of the defendant's guilt notwithstanding the newly discovered evidence.

In *United States v. Bagley*, 473 U.S. 667 (1985), the Supreme Court revisited the issue of "materiality" and held that undisclosed evidence is "material" for purposes of a *Brady* violation where "there is a reasonable probability that, had the evidence been disclosed to the defense, the result of the proceeding would have been different." Bagley, charged with violations of federal narcotics and firearms statutes, filed a motion requesting "any deals, promises or inducements made to witnesses in exchange for their testimony." In response, the government provided affidavits from two government witnesses who asserted that their statements had been given without any threats, rewards, or promises of reward. Following his conviction, Bagley filed a Freedom of Information Act request with the Bureau of Alcohol, Tobacco and Firearms and learned that the agency had entered into contracts with the two witnesses, under which the government had promised to pay them money for their cooperation. Finding that the prosecutor's response had misleadingly induced defense counsel into believing the witnesses could not be impeached on the basis of bias, the Court remanded the case to the trial court to decide whether there was a "reasonable probability" that the result would have been different if the evidence had been disclosed to the defense.

A decade later, in *Kyles v. Whitley*, 514 U.S. 419 (1995), the Court explained that the materiality standard does not require a defendant to demonstrate that disclosure of the suppressed material would have ultimately resulted in his acquittal. Instead, the standard requires a defendant to show that suppression of the relevant evidence caused him to receive a trial which did not "result[] in a verdict worthy of confidence." In *Kyles*, the defendant faced first-degree murder charges for allegedly shooting an elderly woman in a grocery store parking lot. When his counsel filed a lengthy *Brady* motion requesting "any exculpatory or impeachment evidence," the government responded that there was "no exculpatory evidence of any nature." In fact, however, the prosecution knew of no fewer than seven key pieces of exculpatory evidence, including substantial evidence affirmatively inculpating its star witness. After analyzing the prosecution's failure to disclose this evidence, the Court reversed the defendant's conviction and death sentence, finding that "fairness [could not] be stretched to the point of calling this a fair trial." The *Kyles* Court held that the "prosecutor has a duty to learn of any favorable evidence known to the others acting on the government's behalf in the case, including the police."

In *Strickler v. Greene*, 527 U.S. 263 (1999), the Supreme Court reviewed a prosecutor's failure, in a capital murder case, to disclose exculpatory materials in police files consisting of detective notes about a key witness and a letter written by the witness. Justice Stevens clarified that "there are three components of a true *Brady* violation: The evidence at issue must be favorable to the accused, either because it is exculpatory, or because it is impeaching; that evidence must have been suppressed by the State, either willfully or inadvertently; and prejudice must have ensued." Finding that no prejudice had ensued from the non-disclosure, the Court declined to reverse the defendant's conviction.

QUESTIONS

1. What differences do you see between Model Rule 3.8(d) and the *Brady* rule as interpreted by the Supreme Court?

2. The Comment to Model Rule 3.8 says that the prosecutor has "the responsibility of a minister of justice and not simply that of an advocate." Justice Stevens in *United States v. Agurs* writes that the prosecutor "must always be faithful to his client's overriding interest that 'justice shall be done.' He is the 'servant of the law . . . .'" What do you think it means for the prosecutor to be a "minister of justice" and a "servant of the law"? How do a prosecutor's role and obligations differ from the role and obligations of defense counsel in a criminal case?

3. Should prosecutorial disclosure of exculpatory information be limited to evidence that is material? What does it mean for evidence to be material? Or should prosecutors be required to disclose all exculpatory evidence to a defendant?

4. What are the advantages of requiring prosecutors to disclose exculpatory information in a case that goes to trial? Are there disadvantages to imposing such a duty on prosecutors?

UNITED STATES *v.* RUIZ

536 U.S. 622 (2002)

BREYER, J. In this case we primarily consider whether the Fifth and Sixth Amendments require federal prosecutors, before entering into a binding plea agreement with a criminal defendant, to disclose "impeachment information relating to any informants or other witnesses." We hold that the Constitution does not require that disclosure.

I

After immigration agents found 30 kilograms of marijuana in Angela Ruiz's luggage, federal prosecutors offered her what is known in the Southern District of California as a "fast track" plea bargain. That bargain—standard in that district—asks a defendant to waive indictment, trial, and an appeal. In return, the Government agrees to recommend to the sentencing judge a two-level departure downward from the otherwise applicable United States Sentencing Guidelines sentence. In Ruiz's case, a two-level departure downward would have shortened the ordinary Guidelines-specified 18-to-24-month sentencing range by 6 months, to 12-to-18 months.

The prosecutors' proposed plea agreement contains a set of detailed terms. Among other things, it specifies that "any [known] information establishing the factual innocence of the defendant" "has been turned over to the defendant," and it acknowledges the Government's "continuing duty to provide such information." At the same time it requires that the defendant "waiv[e] the right" to receive "impeachment information relating to any informants or other witnesses" as well as the right to receive information supporting any affirmative defense the defendant raises if the case goes to trial. Because Ruiz would not agree to this last-mentioned waiver, the prosecutors withdrew their bargaining offer. The Government then indicted Ruiz for unlawful drug possession. And despite the absence of any agreement, Ruiz ultimately pleaded guilty.

At sentencing, Ruiz asked the judge to grant her the same two-level downward departure that the Government would have recommended had she accepted the "fast track" agreement. The Government opposed her request, and the District Court denied it, imposing a standard Guideline sentence instead.

. . . Ruiz appealed her sentence to the United States Court of Appeals for the Ninth Circuit. The Ninth Circuit vacated the District Court's sentencing determination. The Ninth Circuit pointed out that the Constitution requires prosecutors to make certain impeachment information available to a defendant before trial. It decided that this obligation entitles defendants to receive that same information before they enter into a plea agreement. The Ninth Circuit also decided that the Constitution prohibits defendants from waiving their right to that information. And it held that the prosecutors' standard "fast track" plea agreement was unlawful because it insisted upon that waiver. The Ninth Circuit remanded the case so that the District Court could decide any related factual disputes and determine an appropriate remedy.

The Government sought certiorari. It stressed what it considered serious adverse practical implications of the Ninth Circuit's constitutional holding. And it added that the holding is unique among courts of appeals. We granted the Government's petition. . . .

III

The constitutional question concerns a federal criminal defendant's waiver of the right to receive from prosecutors exculpatory impeachment material—a right that the Constitution provides as part of its basic "fair trial" guarantee.

When a defendant pleads guilty he or she, of course, forgoes not only a fair trial, but also other accompanying constitutional guarantees. Given the seriousness of the matter, the Constitution insists, among other things, that the defendant enter a guilty plea that is "voluntary" and that the defendant must make related waivers "knowing[ly], intelligent[ly], [and] with sufficient awareness of the relevant circumstances and likely consequences."

In this case, the Ninth Circuit in effect held that a guilty plea is not "voluntary" (and that the defendant could not, by pleading guilty, waive her right to a fair trial) unless the prosecutors first made the same disclosure of material impeachment information that the prosecutors would have had to make had the defendant insisted upon a trial. We must decide whether the Constitution requires that preguilty plea disclosure of impeachment information. We conclude that it does not.

First, impeachment information is special in relation to the fairness of a trial, not in respect to whether a plea is voluntary ("knowing," "intelligent," and "sufficient[ly] aware"). Of course, the more information the defendant has, the more aware he is of the likely consequences of a plea, waiver, or decision, and the wiser that decision will likely be. But the Constitution does not require the prosecutor to share all useful information with the defendant. And the law ordinarily considers a waiver knowing, intelligent, and sufficiently aware if the defendant fully understands the nature of the right and how it would likely apply in general in the circumstances—even though the defendant may not know the specific detailed consequences of invoking it. A defendant, for example, may waive his right to remain silent, his right to a jury trial, or his right to counsel even if the defendant does not know the specific questions the authorities intend to ask, who will likely serve on the jury, or the particular lawyer the State might otherwise provide.

It is particularly difficult to characterize impeachment information as critical information of which the defendant must always be aware prior to pleading guilty given the random way in which such information may, or may not, help a particular defendant. The degree of help that impeachment information can provide will depend upon the defendant's own independent knowledge of the prosecution's potential case—a matter that the Constitution does not require prosecutors to disclose.

Second, we have found no legal authority embodied either in this Court's past cases or in cases from other circuits that provides significant support for the Ninth Circuit's decision. To the contrary, this Court has found that the Constitution, in respect to a defendant's awareness of relevant circumstances, does not require complete knowledge of the relevant circumstances, but permits a court to accept a guilty plea, with its accompanying waiver of various constitutional rights, despite various forms of misapprehension under which a defendant might labor. It is difficult to distinguish, in terms of importance, (1) a defendant's ignorance of grounds for impeachment of potential witnesses at a possible future trial from (2) the varying forms of ignorance at issue in these cases.

Third, due process considerations . . . argue against the existence of the "right" that the Ninth Circuit found here. This Court has said that due process considerations include not only (1) the nature of the private interest at stake, but also (2) the value of the additional safeguard, and (3) the adverse impact of the requirement upon the Government's interests. Here, as we have just pointed out, the added value of the Ninth Circuit's "right" to a defendant is often limited, for it depends upon the defendant's independent awareness of the details of the Government's case. And in any case, as the proposed plea agreement at issue here specifies, the Government will provide "any information establishing the factual innocence of the defendant" regardless. That fact, along with other guilty-plea safeguards, diminishes the force of Ruiz's concern that, in the absence of impeachment information, innocent individuals, accused of crimes, will plead guilty.

At the same time, a constitutional obligation to provide impeachment information during plea bargaining, prior to entry of a guilty plea, could seriously interfere with the Government's interest in securing those guilty pleas that are factually justified, desired by defendants, and help to secure the efficient administration of justice. The Ninth Circuit's rule risks premature disclosure of Government witness information, which, the Government tells us, could "disrupt ongoing investigations" and expose prospective witnesses to serious harm. And the careful tailoring that characterizes most legal Government witness disclosure requirements suggests recognition by both Congress and the Federal Rules Committees that such concerns are valid.

Consequently, the Ninth Circuit's requirement could force the Government to abandon its "general practice" of not "disclos[ing] to a defendant pleading guilty information that would reveal the identities of cooperating informants, undercover investigators, or other prospective witnesses." It could require the Government to devote substantially more resources to trial preparation prior to plea bargaining, thereby depriving the plea-bargaining process of its main resource-saving advantages. Or it could lead the Government instead to abandon its heavy reliance upon plea bargaining in a vast number—90% or more—of federal criminal cases. We cannot say that the Constitution's due process requirement demands so radical a change in the criminal justice process in order to achieve so comparatively small a constitutional benefit.

These considerations, taken together, lead us to conclude that the Constitution does not require the Government to disclose material impeachment evidence prior to entering a plea agreement with a criminal defendant.

In addition, we note that the "fast track" plea agreement requires a defendant to waive her right to receive information the Government has regarding any "affirmative defense" she raises at trial. We do not believe the Constitution here requires provision of this information to the defendant prior to plea bargaining—for most (though not all) of the reasons previously stated. That is to say, in the context of this agreement, the need for this information is more closely related to the fairness of a trial than to the voluntariness of the plea; the value in terms of the defendant's added awareness of relevant circumstances is ordinarily limited; yet the added burden imposed upon the Government by requiring its provision well in advance of trial (often before trial preparation begins) can be serious, thereby significantly interfering with the administration of the plea-bargaining process.

For these reasons the judgment of the Court of Appeals for the Ninth Circuit is Reversed.

Justice THOMAS, concurring in the judgment.

I agree with the Court that the Constitution does not require the Government to disclose either affirmative defense information or impeachment information relating to informants or other witnesses before entering into a binding plea agreement with a criminal defendant. The Court, however, suggests that the constitutional analysis turns in some part on the "degree of help" such information would provide to the defendant at the plea stage, a distinction that is neither necessary nor accurate. To the extent that the Court is implicitly drawing a line based on a flawed characterization about the usefulness of certain types of information, I can only concur in the judgment. The principle supporting *Brady* was "avoidance of an unfair trial to the accused." That concern is not implicated at the plea stage regardless.

QUESTIONS

1. What are the disadvantages of requiring prosecutors to disclose exculpatory information in a case in which the defendant pleads guilty? Are there advantages to imposing such a duty on prosecutors?

2. How would mandatory disclosure of exculpatory impeachment information that qualified as material under the Supreme Court's *Brady* line of cases impact the parties to a guilty plea negotiation? Would the prosecutor be likely to dismiss the case? Or would the prosecutor offer a steeper discount in exchange for the guilty plea? Would the defendant reject any plea offers and insist on going to trial?

3. Does Model Rule 3.8(d) require prosecutors to disclose exculpatory information prior to a guilty plea? Does it depend on whether or not the information establishes factual innocence, relates to impeachment of a government witness, or bears on an affirmative defense?

4. Is the prosecution constitutionally required to provide any exculpatory information prior to a guilty plea? What about information establishing the factual innocence of the defendant? Did *Ruiz* resolve this question?

5. Ruiz's lawyers apparently expressed concern that "in the absence of impeachment information, innocent individuals, accused of crimes, will plead guilty." Should we be concerned about innocent individuals pleading guilty to crimes? Would requiring disclosure of exculpatory impeachment information help address this concern? What about requiring disclosure of exculpatory information bearing on affirmative defenses? What about information "establishing the factual

innocence of the defendant"? Why did the prosecution under its "fast track" plea agreement agree to provide this last category of information but not the first two?

6. Justice Breyer stated that "the Constitution does not require the prosecutor to share all useful information with the defendant." In particular, he noted that the Constitution does not require prosecutors to disclose "the prosecution's potential case." Why doesn't the Constitution require prosecutors to disclose information that demonstrates the defendant's guilt? Are prosecutors nonetheless likely to disclose inculpatory information during plea negotiations? Why?

MATERIALS ON FEDERAL SENTENCING DISPARITIES BETWEEN CRACK AND POWDER COCAINE*

One of the most controversial issues in the federal criminal justice system involves the disparities in sentences between crack cocaine and powder cocaine offenses. In reading the materials that follow, imagine that you are the Chair of the Congressional Committee whose task is to determine whether the disparities should be eliminated.

REPORT TO CONGRESS: COCAINE AND FEDERAL SENTENCING POLICY
United States Sentencing Commission iv, v (2002)

[In the mid-1980s,] Congress responded to a national sense of urgency surrounding drugs generally and crack cocaine specifically by enacting the Anti-Drug Abuse Act of 1986 [hereinafter the 1986 Act]. The 1986 Act created the basic framework of statutory mandatory minimum penalties currently applicable to federal drug trafficking offenses generally. . . .

In considering the mandatory minimum penalties for cocaine offenses, Congress differentiated between powder cocaine and crack cocaine and, concluding that crack cocaine was more dangerous, established significantly higher penalties for crack cocaine offenses. The 1986 Act implemented this differential by requiring 100 times less crack cocaine than powder cocaine to trigger five and ten-year mandatory minimum penalties. As a result of the 1986 Act, 21 U.S.C. § 841 (b)(1) provides the following penalties for a first-time cocaine trafficking offense:

5 grams or more of crack cocaine

or   = five-year mandatory minimum penalty

500 grams or more of powder cocaine

---

* On January 12, 2005, just as this book was entering its final publication stages, the United States Supreme Court decided United States v. Booker, 2005 U.S. LEXIS 628. In *Booker*, the court held, inter alia, that the Federal Sentencing Guidelines are "effectively advisory" rather than mandatory. As a result, the Federal Sentencing Act "requires a sentencing court to consider Guidelines ranges, but it permits the court to tailor the sentence in light of other statutory concerns as well . . ." Consider how this change may affect the issues raised in this Appendix.

50 grams or more of crack cocaine
or

= ten-year mandatory minimum
penalty

5,000 grams or more of powder cocaine

The Commission responded to the 1986 Act by incorporating the statutory 100-to-1 drug quantity ratio into the sentencing guidelines and extrapolating upward and downward to effectively set sentencing guideline penalty ranges for all drug quantities. Because of the statutory and guideline differentiation between crack cocaine and powder cocaine, the sentencing guideline range based solely on drug quantity is three to over six times longer for crack cocaine offenders than powder cocaine offenders with equivalent drug quantities, depending on the exact quantity of drug involved. In great part because of the difference in quantity-based penalties, in 2000 the average sentence for a crack cocaine offense was 44 months longer than the average sentence for a powder cocaine offense, 118 months compared to 74 months.

UNITED STATES OF AMERICA v. BUCKNER

United States Court of Appeals for the Eighth Circuit 894 F.2d 975 (1990)

SNEED, Senior Circuit Judge:
Reginald S. Buckner was convicted of possession with intent to distribute 53 grams of cocaine base[1] or "crack" in violation of 21 U.S.C. §§ 841(a)(1) and 841(b)(1)(A)(iii) and was sentenced under the United States Sentencing Guidelines to 250 months in federal prison. He appeals his sentence, claiming that the "100 to 1 ratio" of cocaine to cocaine base in the Guidelines, *see* Section 2D1.1(a)(3), violates the due process clause of the Fifth Amendment and the cruel and unusual punishment clause of the Eighth Amendment. We affirm. . . .

On March 1, 1989, the district court applied the United States Sentencing Guidelines in sentencing Buckner. The quantity of drugs found at Buckner's residence led to a base offense level of 32. The Guidelines direct that a person with a criminal history such as Buckner's who committed a level 32 offense be sentenced to federal prison for 210 to 262 months. A prison sentence of 250 months, followed by five years of supervised release during which Buckner must perform 395 hours of community service, was imposed. . . .

Buckner contends that the "100 to 1 ratio" of cocaine to cocaine base in the Sentencing Guidelines is arbitrary and irrational and therefore offends principles of substantive due process. He points to a statement in the commentary to the Guidelines which notes that "the ratios in the Drug Equivalency Tables do not necessarily reflect dosages based on pharmacological equivalents." Commentary, § 2D1.1, *United States Sentencing Commission Guidelines Manual*, at 2.41. He argues

---

[1] Cocaine base or "crack" "is any form of cocaine with [a] hydroxyl radical" in the chemical compound. In lay terms, "crack" is a form of cocaine that can be inhaled, goes rapidly to the brain, and for which very small dosage units are sufficient for initial uses. *See "Crack" Cocaine: Hearing Before the Permanent Subcomm. on Investigations of the Senate Comm. on Governmental Affairs*, 99th Cong., 2d Sess. 20 (1986) (statement of Robert Byck, M.D., Prof. of Psychiatry and Pharmacology, Yale University School of Medicine) [hereinafter " *Crack" Cocaine: Hearing*].

that, because there is no difference between cocaine and cocaine base,[5] there is no rational basis for distinguishing between the penalties for cocaine and cocaine base. In his Eighth Amendment challenge, Buckner insists that his 250 month prison sentence is so grossly disproportionate to an offense of possessing 53 grams of cocaine base as to constitute cruel and unusual punishment.

II. . . .

A. Due Process Challenge

[T]he sole question before us in deciding Buckner's substantive due process challenge is whether the decision by Congress to apply a "100 to 1 ratio" is constitutional.

We review acts of Congress with considerable deference. . . . Appellate courts should not and do not try "to determine whether [the statute] was the correct judgment or whether it best accomplishes Congressional objectives; rather, [courts] determine [only] whether Congress' judgment was rational." *United States v. Holmes*, 838 F.2d 1175, 1178 (11th Cir. 1988), *cert. denied*, 486 U.S. 1058, 108 S. Ct. 2829, 100 L. Ed. 2d 930 (1989).

We do not believe that requiring more severe penalties for crimes involving cocaine base than for those involving cocaine was either arbitrary or irrational. Members of Congress considered cocaine base to be more dangerous to society than cocaine because of crack's potency, its highly addictive nature, its affordability, and its increasing prevalence.[9] Senator D'Amato addressed specifically the reasoning underlying the "100 to 1 ratio":

> Because crack is so potent, drug dealers need to carry much smaller quantities of crack than of cocaine powder. By treating 1,000 grams of feebase [sic] cocaine no more seriously than 1,000 grams of cocaine powder, which is far less powerful than freebase, current law provides a loophole that actually encourages drug dealers to sell the more deadly and addictive substance, and lets them sell thousands of doses without facing the maximum penalty possible.

132 Cong. Rec. S8092 (daily ed. June 20, 1986).

---

[5] He asserts that cocaine can easily be turned into cocaine base simply by cooking it in baking soda. He also alleges that, when injected into the blood stream, the rush and addictive quality of cocaine is just as powerful as that of cocaine base.

[9] *See, e.g., "Crack" Cocaine: Hearing* (statement of Sen. Roth, Chair of Subcomm.) ("a frightening and dangerous new twist in the drug abuse problem [is] the growing availability and use of a cheap, highly addictive, and deadly form of cocaine known on the streets as 'crack'"); *id.* at 4 (statement of Sen. Nunn) ("crack cocaine [is] an unprecedented peril to the health and well-being of our Nation"); *id.* at 7 (statement of Sen. Chiles) ("the carnage that [crack] is going to leave in its path is something I don't know if this country can literally survive"); 132 Cong. Rec. S8091 (daily ed. June 20, 1986) (statement of Sen. D'Amato) (citation omitted) ("'crack represent[s] a quantum leap in the addictive properties of cocaine'"); 132 Cong. Rec. S14282 (daily ed. Sept. 30, 1986) (statement of Sen. Kennedy) ("A new, cheaper—and far more dangerous—form of cocaine, called 'crack' or 'rock,' is easier to transport and use"); 132 Cong. Rec. S14293 (daily ed. Sept. 30, 1986) (statement of Sen. Bumpers) ("The recent introduction of 'crack' cocaine, an even more potent and dangerous substance [than cocaine,] has allowed [the] percentage [of children using drugs in the U.S.] to spiral upward").

Several drug abuse experts testified before Congress as to the comparative dangers of cocaine base and cocaine. *See, e.g., "Crack" Cocaine: Hearing.* . . . In explaining the difference between crack and cocaine, Dr. Robert Byck, M.D., Prof. of Psychiatry and Pharmacology, Yale University School of Medicine, stated:

> If you heat [cocaine base] to about the temperature of boiling water, it goes off into a vapor. [Then you can] inhale it into your lungs, and you can take a lot [in]. [By contrast, with cocaine,] you can pack your nose only so far. . . . As long as you keep breathing [the crack] vapor, you can get more dosage into yourself. That is the reason why crack . . . is so dangerous. There is an unlimited amount that can go in.

. . . We conclude that the "100 to 1 ratio" of cocaine to cocaine base in the Sentencing Guidelines is rationally related to Congress's objective of protecting the public welfare. Consequently, we reject Buckner's substantive due process challenge. . . .

AFFIRMED.

REPORT TO CONGRESS: COCAINE AND FEDERAL SENTENCING POLICY

United States Sentencing Commission 9-10 (2002)

[T]he legislative history does suggest that Congress concluded that crack cocaine was more dangerous than powder cocaine and therefore warranted higher penalties based on five important beliefs:

- Crack cocaine was extremely addictive. The addictive nature of crack cocaine was stressed not only in comparison to powder cocaine, but also in absolute terms.[30]

- The correlation between crack cocaine use and distribution and the commission of other serious and violent crimes was greater than that with other drugs. Floor statements focused on psycho-pharmacologically driven, economically compulsive, as well as systemic crime (although members did not typically use these terms).[31]

The speed of the material going to the brain is very rapid. . . . You get an intense change in the mood of the individual, which initially is extremely pleasant, and someone wants to repeat it. But because it has gone in so fast, the level drops down quickly, and . . . somebody feels terrible. . . . So you take some more.

. . . You realize that this is going to get you a bit edgy, so you take alcohol along with it. Multidrug abuse is very common. . . . Taking heroin . . . along with crack is fairly common.

So here we have a substance that is tailor-made to addict people. What do we graft on to it? We graft on, first of all, this gigantic import industry of many billions of dollars. Second, our own American marketing methods. . . . What we have here is the fast food solution . . . already prepared, . . . ready to go, and . . . in a little package. Here suddenly, we have cocaine available in a little package, in unit dosage, available at a price that kids can pay initially.

Id. at 20.

[30] 132 CONG. REC. 22,667 (daily ed. Sept. 10, 1986) (statement of Rep. James Traficant) ("Crack is reported by many medical experts to be the most addictive narcotic drug known to man."); 132 CONG. REC. 22,993 (daily ed. Sept. 11, 1986) (statement of Rep. LaFalce) ("Crack is thought to be even more highly addictive than other forms of cocaine or heroin."); 132 CONG. REC. 31,329 (daily ed. Oct. 15, 1986) (statement of Sen. Chiles) ("[I]f you try it once, chances are that you will be hooked. If you use it up to three times, we know that you will become hooked, and it is the strongest addiction that we have found.").

[31] 132 CONG. REC. 22,667 (daily ed. Sept. 10, 1986) (statement of Rep. James Traficant) ("The widespread use of crack in New York City is said by many law enforcement officials in that city to have caused a rise in violent crimes last year."); 132 CONG. REC. 31,329-30 (daily ed. Oct. 15, 1986) (statement of Sen. Chiles):

We find again once people are hooked, all they can think about is staying high, that euphoria which they get, but there is a corresponding down that is just as deep in its trough as the high is at the crest of the wave. And so we find that people, when they are addicted will go out and steal, rob, lie, cheat, take money from any savings, take refrigerators out of their houses, anything they can get their hands on to maintain that habit. That, of course, has caused crime to go up at a tremendously increased rate in our cities and in our States—the crimes of burglary, robbery, assault, purse snatching, mugging, those crimes where people are trying to feed that habit. Our local police and our sheriffs have found themselves unable to cope with the crime. . . .

- Physiological effects of crack cocaine were considered especially perilous, resulting in death to some users and causing devastating effects on children prenatally exposed to the drug.[32]
- Young people were particularly prone to using and/or being involved in trafficking crack cocaine.[33]
- Crack cocaine's purity and potency, low cost per dose, and the ease with which it was manufactured, transported, disposed of, and administered, were all leading to its widespread use.[34]

SPECIAL REPORT TO THE CONGRESS: COCAINE AND FEDERAL SENTENCING POLICY

United States Sentencing Commission, Executive Summary iv-xiv (Feb. 1995)

In the Omnibus Violent Crime Control and Law Enforcement Act of 1994, Congress directed the United States Sentencing Commission to study federal sentencing policy as it relates to possession and distribution of all forms of cocaine. Specifically, Congress directed the Sentencing Commission to report on the current federal structure of differing penalties for powder cocaine and crack cocaine offenses and to provide recommendations for retention or modification of these differences.

The Commission balanced conflicting policy goals in developing its recommendations concerning powder and crack cocaine sentencing. In reviewing the evidence, the Commission found that, under some criteria, crack offenses deserve lengthier punishment than powder offenses, but on other criteria differential treatment could not be justified. The recommendations reflect our weighing of these competing considerations to yield a cautious and balanced judgment of the best federal sentencing policy for cocaine offenders. The major conclusions can be summarized as follows:

1. Drugs are a serious problem, and crack and powder cocaine are dangerous drugs.
2. While some aspects of crack cocaine use and distribution suggest that a higher penalty for crack offenses compared to powder cocaine offenses is appropriate, the present 100-to-1 quantity ratio is too great.
3. Among other problems, the 100-to-1 quantity ratio creates anomalous results by potentially punishing low-level (retail) crack dealers far more severely

---

[32] 132 CONG. REC. 27,176 (daily ed. Sept. 30, 1986) (statement of Sen. Gary Hart) ("then along came crack-cocaine — and the high was available to all. So too, however, were the lows: The raging paranoia, the addiction rooted deep in the brain's chemical structure, and worst, the senseless deaths.")

[33] 132 CONG. REC. 26,447 (daily ed. Sept. 26, 1986) (statement of Sen. Chiles) ("[Crack] can turn promising young people into robbers and thieves, stealing anything they can to get the money to feed their habit."); 132 CONG. REC. 27, 187 (daily ed. Sept. 30, 1986) (statement of Sen. Leahy) ("Crack is available to the young, and it will be in the schools this fall. I have heard stories of children as young as nine who are already crack users. The sellers also use these children as lookouts and as workers in houses that manufacture crack."); 132 CONG. REC. 944 (daily ed. Mar. 21, 1986) (statement of Rep. Rangel) ("What is most frightening about crack is that it has made cocaine widely available and affordable for abuse among our youth").

[34] 132 CONG. REC. 22,993 (daily ed. Sept. 11, 1986) (statement of Rep. LaFalce) ("While a gram of cocaine sells for at least $100, two small pieces of crack, or enough to get three people high can be purchased in almost any American city for about $10."); 132 CONG. REC. daily ed. Sept. 26, 1986) (statement of Sen. Chiles) ("[Crack] can be bought for the price of a cassette tape, and make people into slaves.").

than their high-level (wholesale) suppliers of the powder cocaine that served as the product for conversion into crack. . . .

6. The quantity and form of cocaine involved in an offense are two factors for determining appropriate punishment, but in a given case other characteristics of the offense and the offender can be equally or more important. The guidelines should be refined to address better those harms that prompted Congress to establish the 100-to-1 quantity ratio.

The Commission's recommendations are twofold:

1. That the Commission establish methods within the guidelines structure to deal with the crimes of possession and distribution of both crack cocaine and powder cocaine; such Commission action to take place by the normal 1995-1996 amendment cycle.

2. That, in light of the Commission's guideline amendments, Congress revisit the 100-to-1 quantity ratio as well as the penalty structure for simple possession that provides a mandatory five-year penalty for simple possession of crack cocaine but a statutory maximum penalty of one year for simple possession of any other drug. . . .

4. Despite the unprecedented level of public attention focused on crack cocaine, a substantial gap continues to exist between the anecdotal experiences that often prompt a call for action and empirical knowledge upon which to base sound policy. Three factors account for this gap. First, although powder cocaine and crack cocaine are two forms of the same drug that are consumed in different ways, much of the data collected on cocaine and its effects does not distinguish between its different forms. Second, because drug users constitute a primary source of information, conclusions are difficult to draw with any degree of confidence.

Third, as crack cocaine has only been on the market a relatively short period of time, research that might more fully address outstanding concerns has not yet occurred. Accordingly, given the current information gap, policymakers must draw conclusions cautiously.

FINDINGS [CHAPTER REFERENCES OMITTED]

The extant research and empirical data support the following findings:

- *Pharmacology*: Cocaine is a naturally occurring substance, derived from the leaves of the erythroxylon plant, that has two prominent actions: 1) it is a potent anesthetic; and 2) it is a powerful stimulant.

- *Forms of Cocaine*: Powder cocaine and crack cocaine are two forms of the same drug, containing the same active ingredient—the cocaine alkaloid. Powder cocaine (cocaine hydrochloride), the most commonly used form of cocaine, is produced by reacting coca paste, derived from leaves of the coca plant, with hydrochloric acid. Crack cocaine, in turn, is made from powder cocaine in a simple process that requires baking soda, water, and a stove or microwave. Approximately ten percent of the drug is lost during the conversion process; hence, one gram of powder cocaine will yield .89 grams of crack cocaine. Less frequently consumed forms of cocaine include coca leaves, coca paste, and freebase cocaine.

- *Routes of Administration*: Cocaine in any form—paste, powder, freebase, or crack—produces the same physiological and psychotropic effects. The onset, intensity, and duration of effects, however, differ according to the route of the drug's administration which, in turn, is dictated in part by the form of cocaine. Powder cocaine can be snorted, injected, or ingested; crack cocaine can only be smoked.

- *Time to Maximum Effect*: Reactions to cocaine use differ; the faster cocaine reaches the brain, the greater the intensity of the psychotropic effects. Research shows that maximum psychotropic effects can be realized as quickly as one minute after smoking crack cocaine; these effects dissipate after approximately 30 minutes. Some four minutes or more are required to achieve maximum effects after injecting powder cocaine, with the effects lasting for a similar 30 minutes. Powder cocaine that is snorted, on the other hand, takes up to 20 minutes or more to reach maximum psychotropic effect, but the "high" lasts as much as 60 minutes — twice as long as injecting or smoking.

- *Physiological and Psychotropic Effects*: Cocaine use produces alertness and heightens energy, increases the user's heart rate, elevates blood pressure, and produces symptoms similar to hypertension. Additionally, cocaine acts on the pleasure centers of the brain, causing a sense of euphoria, decreased anxiety and social inhibitions, and heightened sexuality. Increased doses of cocaine, together with the most rapid drug administration routes (*i.e.*, smoking or injecting), produce euphoric experiences that create vivid, long-term psychological memories that, in turn, form the basis for subsequent craving for the drug.

- *Addiction*: Neither powder cocaine nor crack cocaine are physiologically addictive; however, both are psychologically addictive. Moreover, psychological dependence usually is as devastating as physiological addiction. The greater the intensity of cocaine's psychotropic effects and the shorter their duration, the greater the likelihood cocaine use will lead to dependence and abuse. As discussed above, the route of administration determines the intensity and duration of these effects. For a given quantity of cocaine, smoking crack cocaine or injecting powder cocaine produces the most intense physiological and psychotropic effects. However, the ease of smoking, compared to the greater difficulty and unpleasantness involved in injecting any substance, suggests that smoking is more tempting for the first time user and more appealing for the repeat user than is injection. This observation is borne out by the limited available data, which suggest that almost three times more people smoke cocaine than inject it.

- *Usage Trends*: Determining patterns and trends of powder and crack cocaine use is difficult. Usage data suggest that casual use of cocaine has diminished while heavy use of cocaine has remained constant. Data on current cocaine usage from the National Household Survey on Drug Abuse show that 75 percent of users snort powder cocaine, 28 percent smoke crack, and 10 percent of cocaine users inject powder cocaine.[6]

- *Importation*: Crack cocaine is not cultivated or imported independently of powder cocaine. Rather, cocaine is cultivated, processed, imported, and distributed almost exclusively in the powder form at the higher levels of the drug distribution chain. Some of this powder cocaine is later processed into crack cocaine at the wholesale and retail levels. Wholesale distributors generally smuggle large quantities of powder cocaine into the United

---

[6] The sum of the percentages exceeds 100 percent because some respondents report multiple routes of administration.

States from Colombia, Mexico, and the Caribbean nations through Arizona, southern California, southern Florida, and Texas. The powder cocaine is channeled to what Drug Enforcement Administration (DEA) refers to as "source" cities — Houston, Los Angeles, Miami, and New York City — for distribution throughout the country.

- *Evolution of the Crack Market*: The types of organizations dominating crack cocaine distribution have undergone an evolution, at least in big city markets like Los Angeles and New York City. In the early days of crack cocaine sales (1984-1985), freelance distributors operated in a growing, non-competitive market. By 1986, well-organized gangs used violence to consolidate individual dealers and eliminate uncooperative distributors, and, together with small-group distributors, took control of the crack cocaine market. This is a pattern typical of the introduction of new illicit drugs. However, today, researchers and law enforcement officials believe the market is again dominated by a "cottage industry" of small-group and freelance distributors, a deviation from the "normal" pattern. Because these smaller volume distributors now are competing in a market that no longer is expanding, this may indicate that a higher level of violence will continue to be associated with crack cocaine distribution.

- *Forums for Distribution*: Powder and crack cocaine are distributed at the retail level by similar means, primarily in urban and suburban dwellings and on innercity street corners. Street-corner or open air sales typically involve small retail quantities sold to walk-up or drive-up buyers. This distribution forum particularly is prone to violence, as security of street-corner transactions often is maintained by lookouts or enforcers who carry firearms. A second cocaine distribution system involves "beepermen" who exchange drugs with a user after having been contacted by telephone or beeper. Crack houses and shooting houses for powder cocaine provide a third forum for distribution and involve the use of a fixed location from which drugs are sold to visiting consumers.

- *Marketability*: Crack cocaine's ease of manufacture and relatively low cost-per-dose have made it more readily marketable than powder cocaine to large numbers of lower income people. For example, crack can be packaged efficiently and marketed in single-dosage units weighing 0.1 to 0.5 gram and priced from $5 to $20. In contrast, powder cocaine generally is sold by the gram (*i.e.*, five to ten doses) for between $65 and $100 per gram.

- *Cost/Dosage Comparisons*: Five hundred grams of powder cocaine (the quantity necessary to trigger the five-year mandatory minimum penalty) generally produces 2,500 to 5,000 doses. In contrast, five grams of crack cocaine (the five-year mandatory minimum penalty amount) produces 10 to 50 doses. According to DEA estimates, 500 grams of powder cocaine costs between $32,500 and $50,000. In contrast, five grams of crack cocaine costs between $225 and $750.

- *Role of Juveniles and Women*: Research indicates that both powder cocaine and crack cocaine distributors are young, but those distributing crack are younger. For example, in New York City, 38 percent of offenders arrested for distributing crack cocaine were under 21 years of age, compared to 29 percent for powder cocaine. Older crack cocaine dealers tend to use juveniles in visible roles such as lookouts, steerers, and drug runners in the belief that juveniles are more likely to escape detection and prosecution. The DEA suggests that women also have greater roles in crack cocaine distribution relative to distribution of other drugs. As with juveniles, women are used in more visible roles (such as, making straw purchases of firearms and renting residences to use as crack stash houses) because of the perceived decreased likelihood of detection and prosecution perception.

- *Violence*: Crack cocaine is associated with systemic crime — crime related to its marketing and distribution — to a greater degree than powder cocaine. Researchers and law enforcement officials report that much of the violence associated with crack cocaine stems from attempts by competing factions to consolidate control of drug distribution in urban areas. Some portion of the distribution of powder cocaine, and the majority of the distribution of crack cocaine, is done on street-corners or in open-air markets, crack houses, or powder shooting galleries between anonymous buyers and sellers. These distribution environments, by their very nature, are highly susceptible to conflict and intense competition. As a result, individuals operating in these surroundings are prone to be involved in, as well as victimized by, increased levels of violence. Consistent with its distribution forums, crack offenders are more likely to carry weapons than individuals trafficking in other drugs (27.9% of crack offenders possess dangerous weapons compared to 15.1% of powder cocaine offenders) and are more likely to have more extensive criminal records (10.4% of crack cocaine defendants have the highest criminal history category compared to 4.8% for powder cocaine defendants).

Many cocaine users, both crack and powder, sell drugs to raise money to support their drug habits. There is little empirical evidence, though, to suggest that either crack or powder cocaine users commit large numbers of violent acts to raise money to buy drugs. However, some research reports a significant percentage of petty property offenses and trading sex for drugs associated with crack cocaine use. Furthermore, one study reports that 98 percent of crack users sell drugs to help support their habits. The Commission finds no research to suggest, however, that powder cocaine users are any less likely to commit crimes to support their habits. Studies report that neither powder nor crack cocaine excite or agitate users to commit criminal acts and that the stereotype of a drug-crazed addict committing heinous crimes is not true for either form of cocaine.

- *HIV/STD Transmission*: Crack cocaine smokers and powder cocaine injectors exhibit more high-HIV-risk behavior than powder cocaine snorters, but for different reasons. Intravenous powder cocaine use presents a higher risk of HIV infection than heroin and other IV-injected drugs because of the relatively shortlived euphoria of cocaine (*i.e.*, cocaine injectors are likely to reinject more frequently to sustain the high, thereby presenting a greater risk of acquiring the HIV virus through contaminated needles). Research also shows that, compared to powder cocaine injectors, crack smokers exhibit more high-risk sexual behaviors, including multiple sexual partners, sex without condoms, and sexual activity during or following drug use. Given such behaviors, crack cocaine users also are more likely to contract other sexually transmitted diseases like syphilis and gonorrhea. Additionally, sex-for-drugs — while not unique to crack cocaine — thrives in venues like crack houses. Consequently, the rates of HIV infection are nearly equal between crack smokers and powder cocaine injectors.

- *Effects on Fetus*: Cocaine use by pregnant women can produce detrimental effects on the fetus that include premature delivery, brain lesions, and mal-formed limbs. In general, however, reliable information comparing babies born to mothers using crack versus those born to mothers using powder is not available, because medical tests cannot distinguish between the presence of crack as opposed to powder in mother or newborn child. Unless the mother self-reported crack cocaine use, blood tests would simply reveal the presence of cocaine. Nevertheless, because crack cocaine produces more intense "highs" and quicker "lows" than powder cocaine, crack users are more likely to use increased quantities of the drug or to engage in binging. Such practices by pregnant women expose their babies to greater quantities of the drug and, thus, greater potential for harm. Furthermore, babies exposed to crack may experience greater problems because crack smokers achieve a higher concentration of the drug in their bloodstreams than do cocaine snorters. While data are sketchy at best, one researcher estimates that 7.5 percent to 17 percent of all pregnant women use illicit drugs during their pregnancy, resulting in 100,000 to 740,000 drug-exposed babies each year. The estimate of cocaine exposed babies ranges from 30,000 to 160,000.
- *"Boarder Babies" and Maternal Neglect*: The Commission's research reveals virtually no studies that address concerns related specifically to crack cocaine use and maternal neglect, teenage pregnancy, and the phenomenon of "boarder babies." That these societal problems exist seems quite clear, but research has focused on the association of these problems to substance abuse in general as opposed to their association with powder or crack cocaine. Furthermore, that these phenomena coincide with a rise in crack cocaine use leads many to believe that the two are related. Research necessary to support or refute that relationship has not been done.

Many states consider the birth of drug-exposed infants to be evidence of maternal neglect. Several states have enacted laws that allow child abuse charges to be brought against any woman with illegal drugs in her bloodstream who gives birth to a child. Other states simply remove drug-exposed babies from their mothers, making them wards of the state. Some states have tried these methods and rejected them in favor of mandatory treatment programs in which mothers must enter treatment or lose their children.

- *State Distinctions*: Thirty-six states do not distinguish between powder cocaine and crack cocaine in their statutory penalty structures. No state has elected to follow, in its entirety, the federal penalty scheme for powder and crack cocaine offenses and none provides a differential between powder and crack cocaine that approaches the federal system's 100-to-1 quantity ratio at the five- and ten-year mandatory minimum levels.[7]
- *Prosecutorial Discretion*: Federal cocaine prosecutions vary widely by district. For example, four defendants were sentenced for trafficking in less than 50 grams of crack cocaine in the Central District of California (which includes Los Angeles) in 1993. By comparison, 111 defendants were sentenced for the same offense during the same period in Washington, D.C. In 1993, the Southern District of West Virginia sentenced 113 offenders for trafficking in any amount of crack cocaine; the Eastern District of New York — which

---

[7] North Dakota provides a 100-to-1 distinction between powder and crack cocaine but limits it to the five-year mandatory minimum amounts.

includes Brooklyn—sentenced 24. During the same period, the Southern District of West Virginia sentenced 41 offenders for trafficking in powder cocaine compared to Eastern New York's 175.[8]

- *Demographic/Offender Information*: The data show that federal crack cocaine offenders, on average, are younger than federal powder cocaine offenders, have somewhat less education, and have more extensive prior criminal records. Crack cocaine defendants also are more likely to possess a weapon.
- *Race*: Blacks accounted for 88.3 percent of federal crack cocaine distribution convictions in 1993, Hispanics 7.1 percent, Whites 4.1 percent, and others 0.5 percent. The racial breakdown for powder cocaine distribution offenses sentenced in 1993 shows 32.0 percent White, 27.4 percent Black, 39.3 percent Hispanic, and 1.3 percent other. On the other hand, the 1991 Household Survey shows that 52 percent of those reporting crack use in the past year, as opposed to distribution, were White, 38 percent were Black, and 10 percent Hispanic; 75 percent of those reporting powder use in the past year were White, 15 percent were Black, and 10 percent Hispanic.[9]

Based on this limited information, the Sentencing Commission identifies the following concerns:

1) *Racial Disparity*: Federal sentencing data leads to the inescapable conclusion that Blacks comprise the largest percentage of those affected by the penalties associated with crack cocaine. This does not mean, however, that the penalties are racially motivated. Clearly the penalties (both statutory and guideline-based) apply equally to similar defendants regardless of race. Many individual criminal statutes, when enforced, produce a pool of defendants who are not representative of the racial make-up of criminal law violators generally or of society. However, as all appellate courts have found, there is no evidence that Congress or the Sentencing Commission acted with any discriminatory intent in setting different statutory and guideline penalties for different forms of cocaine.

Nevertheless, the high percentage of Blacks convicted of crack cocaine offenses is a matter of great concern to the Sentencing Commission. Penalties clearly must be racially neutral on their face and by design. The Sentencing Commission is committed to these goals. When one form of a drug can be rather easily converted to another form of the same drug and when that second form is punished at a quantity ratio 100 times greater than the original form, it would appear reasonable to require the existence of sufficient policy bases to support such a sentencing scheme regardless of racial impact. Moreover, when such an enhanced ratio for a particular form of a drug has a disproportionate effect on one segment of the population, it is particularly important that sufficient policy bases exist in support of the enhanced ratio.

---

[8] The Commission does not mean to suggest that any apparent disparities are unwarranted. As a general matter, the Commission has not analyzed various factors that might explain these and other differences, including the strength of the state and local law enforcement efforts directed at the crack cocaine trade, the relative punishment available through state statutes, differing needs and problems facing each district, and resource allocation issues.

[9] The National Household Survey potentially underrepresents lower-income populations and overrepresents middle or upper-income populations or those who reside in households.

Further, it is instructive that — although appellate courts have not found the 100-to-1 quantity ratio constitutionally deficient — some have commented upon the problematic nature of the sentencing scheme from a policy standpoint and further indicated that the resolution of such questions is better left to those with the proper authority and institutional capacity.

2) *Quantifying Harm*: Some argue that a sentencing system must punish different forms of the same drug equally. The Sentencing Commission disagrees. If a particular form of a drug results in greater harms than a different form of that drug, then logically a harsher penalty for the more harmful drug can be justified. In assessing the relative harms posed by the two forms, the aim is to arrive at a penalty differential that approximates the increased dangers posed by the more harmful drug. . . .

3) *Level Within the Drug Chain*: The substantial difference in the ratio between crack and powder cocaine punishes the retail dealer of crack far more severely than the powder cocaine supplier who may have sold the powder cocaine from which multiple street dealers made crack. This issue, however, cannot be viewed in the abstract, because concerns over street violence and other harms affect the determination of an appropriate quantity ratio. Nevertheless, five grams of crack cocaine — the quantity that triggers a five-year mandatory minimum penalty — appears to be much more a retail quantity than 500 grams of powder cocaine — the quantity of powder cocaine necessary to trigger the five-year mandatory penalty. Consequently, retail-level crack cocaine dealers are being punished like wholesaler- and importer-level powder cocaine dealers.

For example, under the 100-to-1 quantity ratio, a wholesaler convicted of moving five kilograms of powder cocaine may receive a lesser sentence than a distributor who buys one of the five kilograms but is caught after having converted the powder into crack cocaine. This anomalous result highlights the fact that individuals higher in the cocaine distribution chain can be punished less severely than certain lower-level traffickers because of the intervening change in the form of cocaine, *i.e.*, the change to crack.

4) *Societal Concerns*: Congress and the public are troubled by the apparent relationship between crack and societal problems, particularly in American cities. The Sentencing Commission shares these concerns.

Many Americans do not feel safe walking the streets, driving in their automobiles, or even sitting in their homes for fear of stray bullets from drive-by shootings or disputes between rival drug traffickers. The medical community sees increased incidence of gunshot victims, infants born exposed to drugs, boarder babies, HIV/AIDS and other sexually transmitted diseases, and increasingly younger victims and perpetrators of violent crime. The use of women and youth to facilitate the drug trade seems higher at this point in the country's history than ever before, with no clear answer as to why this may be true.

There has been significant growth in the rate of drug-exposed infants in this country, with nine percent or 350,000 babies each year exposed to drugs in the womb. Certainly, the rate of cocaine-exposed babies continues to rise. And while medical science cannot distinguish between the two forms of cocaine, certain factors put crack-exposed babies at greater peril; because the highs and lows associated with drug use are quicker when using crack cocaine, crack users are more likely to use increased quantities of the drug or engage in binging, exposing the infant to greater quantities of the drug and, thus, to more harm.

With the growth in drug-exposed babies has come an increase in maternal neglect and the phenomenon of boarder babies. In general, studies have not focused on a particular drug type when studying these issues, instead looking broadly at the question of substance abuse. The problem of substance abuse among women and its effect on children raises serious policy concerns.

As Americans have watched these devastating changes to their everyday lives, they also have witnessed the proliferation of crack cocaine sale and use. While there is some indication that crack use is declining, it is difficult to ignore the potential association between these phenomena.

In summary, while it is true that powder cocaine and crack cocaine pharmacologically are the same drug and equally true that neither form of cocaine is physiologically addictive, important distinctions between the two may warrant higher penalties for crack than powder. For example, factors in the route of administration (*i.e.*, smoking versus snorting) and attributes of the crack cocaine market make crack different from powder from a policy perspective. These factors generally include: 1) a greater risk for psychological addiction due to the rapid high and concomitant rapid low resulting from inhalation of crack; 2) because powder cocaine can be converted easily into smaller doses of crack that can be sold more cheaply and in potent quantities, crack is more readily available to a larger segment of the population, particularly women, children, and the economically disadvantaged; 3) the apparently higher correlation between crack and violence than between powder and violence; and 4) the increased use of young people in the distribution of crack.

Even so, given its review of the subject, the Sentencing Commission cannot support the current penalty scheme. The factors that suggest a difference between the two forms of cocaine do not approach the level of a 100-to-1 quantity ratio. Research and public policy may support somewhat higher penalties for crack versus powder cocaine, but a 100-to-1 quantity ratio cannot be recommended.

Notwithstanding the Sentencing Commission's broad examination of these issues, much more research is needed into the distinctions between powder and crack cocaine. To the extent practicable, medical and social science research, as well as law enforcement arrest data, must distinguish between the two forms of cocaine. The present failure to distinguish between crack and powder in data on arrests, cocaine-exposed babies, maternal neglect and substance abuse, and violence associated with drug use and distribution continuously frustrated the Commission's study.

RECOMMENDATIONS: . . .

Rather than propose a specific statutory change in the current 100-to-1 quantity ratio, the Sentencing Commission recommends that the guidelines system be revised to further the purposes of sentencing and to address congressional concerns. . . .

"On May 1, 1995, by a four-to-three vote, the Commission submitted to Congress an amendment to the sentencing guidelines that, among other things, would have equalized the guideline penalties for powder cocaine and crack cocaine offenses based solely on drug quantity."[1]

MAJORITY AND MINORITY OPINIONS ON CRACK AND POWDER COCAINE

United States Sentencing Commission (1995) www.ussc.gov/JUDCONF/JCPART2.HTM
(accessed October 11, 2004)

STATEMENT OF THE COMMISSION MAJORITY IN SUPPORT OF RECOMMENDED
CHANGES IN COCAINE AND FEDERAL SENTENCING POLICY

I.

On February 28, 1995, a unanimous Sentencing Commission issued a special report to the Congress on cocaine and federal sentencing policy recommending that the current sentencing scheme for cocaine offenses be changed. The report was issued in response to both a specific congressional directive contained in the Violent Crime Control and Law Enforcement Act of 1994 and general criticism received by the Commission of current cocaine sentencing policy. Congressional and public concern over current policy stem primarily from the fact that those convicted of crack cocaine distribution, most of whom are minorities, are punished much more severely than those convicted of powder cocaine distribution without sufficient justification.

In its report, the Commission strongly affirmed that not only are crack cocaine and powder cocaine very dangerous drugs, but crack cocaine is associated with greater harms than powder cocaine. Of greatest concern to the Commission was the seemingly random, predatory violence (particularly the drive-by shootings), as well as the use of juveniles, that seems to accompany the distribution of crack cocaine. The Commission concluded, however, that the current sentencing scheme which calculates sentences for all crack cocaine offenders using a 100-to-1 quantity ratio and provides for sentences several times longer on average than for similar powder distributors is unfair and mistargeted. Under the 100-to-1 quantity ratio, an offender must distribute 100 times as much powder cocaine as a similar crack offender to receive the same base sentence. Thus all crack cocaine offenders, whether violent or non-violent, receive the especially severe sentences.

The Commission indicated in its report that it would seek to develop a method by which the discrete and substantial harms, such as use of firearms, associated with some crack cocaine offenses could be addressed and accounted for through targeted guideline enhancements. These enhancements would adjust the base sentences and consequently would result in more severe punishment for those defendants responsible for the added harms. After adding these enhancements, the Commission would determine if other differences between crack and powder cocaine were sufficient to justify different penalties based solely on the form of the drug.

In examining crack cocaine's distinct harms detailed in the report, it is clear that many in fact are already accounted for in the current guidelines. For instance, the report recognized that federal crack cocaine offenders generally have more

---

[1] Report to Congress: Cocaine and Federal Sentencing Policy v (2002).

extensive criminal records and thus pose a greater danger to society. The current guidelines already properly provide for enhanced penalties for those with greater criminal histories as well as very severe sentences for career offenders and armed career criminals.

However, the Commission determined that other harms were not adequately addressed. For example, crack offenders who use a firearm in the course of the drug offense only receive approximately a 25 percent increase in their sentence under the current guidelines. Through its normal amendment process, the Commission has adopted a number of amendments to the guidelines that specifically address weapons and other aggravating factors associated with some crack cocaine offenses. These amendments provide for considerably higher sentences for the use of a firearm during a drug offense, the involvement of assault and other prohibited weapons, the involvement of criminal street gangs in drug offenses, drive-by shootings, and the use of juveniles in the commission of offenses. Together with existing guidelines, substantially higher sentences will result for offenders who are responsible for the predatory harms associated with crack cocaine trafficking through enhancements for the following aggravating factors:

1. enhanced penalties if death or serious bodily injury results from the use of the drug (2D1.1(a));
2. substantially enhanced penalties for possession and use of a dangerous weapon in the course of a drug crime (2D1.1(b)(1));
3. enhanced penalties for possession of prohibited assault or other National Firearms Act weapons in a drug crime (2D1.1(b)(2));
4. enhanced penalties if a victim was murdered in the course of a drug crime (2D1.1.(d));
5. enhanced penalties if the drug crime involved either a juvenile or a pregnant woman or occurred in a protected location (2D1.2, 3B1.4) . . .

[Remaining factors omitted.]

. . . In historical context, these sentences are substantially longer than typical sentences imposed on cocaine offenders before implementation of the guidelines. Moreover, we have no evidence that the sentences for powder cocaine are too low or that equalizing the quantity ratio between powder and crack cocaine will result in crack cocaine sentences that are too low.

Importantly, equalizing the quantity ratio between crack and powder cocaine will not result in equal sentences for crack cocaine and powder cocaine offenders who differ in relevant ways. Commission analysis shows that, under the amended guidelines, crack offenders will receive sentences that are, on average, generally at least twice as long as powder cocaine offenders involved with the same amount of drug. These longer sentences are due primarily to the fact that crack offenders are more likely to receive the aggravating adjustments provided under the guidelines. Table 1 shows the average guideline sentence for powder and crack cocaine offenders at each base offense level. At base offense level 18, for example, corresponding to drug amounts of 100-200 grams, powder cocaine offenders receive average sentences of 28.6 months, while crack cocaine offenders receive average sentences of 53.6 months. As this example indicates, the guideline enhancements work to lengthen sentences for the worst offenders. By the same token, offenders whose crime involves no aggravating characteristics receive appropriately shorter sentences. As noted in Table 1, the lengthier sentences for crack compared to powder offenders are consistent at all base offense levels. This, we feel, comports with the fairness concept Congress had in mind when the guidelines scheme was adopted.

II.

. . . [S]ix inescapable facts lead the Commission to conclude that the base sentence for crack and powder cocaine should be the same. First, the Commission's guidelines provide for severe punishment for those trafficking in powder cocaine. There have been few if any complaints about the leniency of these guidelines. Second, powder and crack cocaine have the same active ingredient — the cocaine alkaloid — and both produce the same type of physiological and psychological effects. Third, while smoking crack cocaine can lead to addiction in a greater number of cases than can snorting powder, injecting powder cocaine is as dangerous as or more dangerous than smoking crack. In light of the fact that crack cocaine can be easily produced from powder cocaine, the form of cocaine is simply not a reasonable proxy for dangerousness associated with use. Fourth, any quantity ratio greater than equivalency will lead to the unfair result that more sophisticated, higher-level powder distributors will be sentenced relatively less severely than some of the retailers they supply. Fifth, the present system results in obvious punishment inequities by providing the same penalty for 500 grams of powder (1/2 kilo) — yielding between 1,000 and 5,000 doses and costing up to $75,000 — as for five grams of crack cocaine — yielding between 10 and 50 doses and costing up to $750. And sixth, any quantity ratio higher than equivalency will impact almost entirely on minority defendants.

We are aware that a host of social maladies have been attributed to the emergence of crack cocaine, such as urban decay or parental neglect among user groups. After careful consideration, the Commission majority concluded that increased penalties are not an appropriate response to many of these social problems. We were unable to establish that these social problems result from the drug itself rather than from the disadvantaged social and economic environment in which the drug often is used. We note that these problems are not unique to crack cocaine, but are associated to some extent with abuse of any drug or alcohol. Nor does the fact that crack is typically sold in small amounts, which may make it more readily available among lower-income groups, justify increased punishment compared to a form of the drug that is more commonly sold in amounts available only to the affluent. The Commission does not believe that longer punishment can be justified solely because a particular form of a drug is more likely to be used by a disadvantaged population. . . .

III.

When the Commission began studying cocaine sentencing policy, it found that the picture of crack painted by the media bore little resemblance to the reality portrayed by scientific research on the subject. What the Commission learned was that there really is not much of a distinction, at least pharmacologically, between powder and crack cocaine, and that wherever crack is distributed, inevitably powder cocaine is somewhere nearby. After all, crack cocaine is actually powder cocaine converted through a very simple process. Experience suggests that most drug distributors traffic in multiple drugs, and that crack cocaine distributions frequently involve powder as well. To target crack cocaine for dramatically higher penalties ignores the reality of these polydrug distributions and the risks associated with the other drugs present in a "crack cocaine" distribution. On the other hand, the

Commission has learned that the purveyors of crack cocaine have found a way to get the drug to the people on the lowest rungs of the economic ladder in our country and into the hands of children, because the drug is cheap and easy to use.

Commissioners voting in the majority were particularly struck by the words of police officers involved in fighting the drug "war" on a daily basis in the streets of our cities. They could see no reason to make a distinction between powder and crack cocaine — their words in effect were "they (the drugs) are all bad" and should all be prosecuted severely; however, the greater penalties in their view should go to offenders who traffic in larger quantities of powder cocaine as opposed to crack. This should come as no surprise: the basic theory in drug enforcement is to prosecute and seek punishment at the highest levels for offenders dealing in the greatest quantities.

The Commission has some sympathy for the concept that through sentencing the Government should try to protect those who have the least ability to protect themselves. But it is not clear that this protection is accomplished by punishing economically disadvantaged people more severely than their affluent counterparts for the same conduct. People who deal drugs should be punished severely. That is precisely what the sentencing guidelines do.

IV.

With respect to the Commission's recommendation regarding an appropriate cocaine sentencing policy, the record must be clear. While the Commission's recommendation to eliminate the distinction between powder and crack cocaine trafficking offenses flows from a 4-3 vote among commissioners, the Commission was not divided in its belief that the 100-to-1 quantity ratio is inappropriate. The Commission is united in unambiguously opposing the present ratio and recommending a dramatic reduction. In fact, the Commission consideration of an appropriate ratio generally revolved around a ratio between 1-to-1 and 5-to-1.

For those commissioners who voted with the majority, the issue was one of basic fairness and a deep conviction that Government must treat each citizen fairly. It is bad enough when individuals are unfair to one another, or when we punish each other too harshly, but when the Government is perceived as not being fair or punishes one segment of society more harshly than another for the same basic conduct, serious distrust results of the criminal justice system and the Government as a whole.

The Commission recognizes that cocaine is a tragic problem in this country. But it is as tragic in the boardrooms, offices, and suburbs of America as it is in the innercities. Because people in the upper echelons of society do not live in the troubled neighborhoods, they are not subject to the same enforcement or penalties as the poorer people in society.

In the course of our study, we were faced with clear evidence that crack cocaine penalties are imposed largely on African-Americans. Almost 90 percent of federal crack offenders are Black. This disproportionate impact creates a perception of unfairness and raises allegations of racial bias. Everyone concerned with the legitimacy of the criminal justice system — and with the willingness of all citizens to accept its judgments as fair and final — must be troubled by allegations of unfairness, particularly racial discrimination. Perceptions and allegations cannot be the basis for policy, however.

As a fundamental principle, the Commission is committed to criminal penalties that are racially neutral on their face and by design. Our conclusion, like that of courts that have considered the matter, is that there is no evidence that racial bias or animus motivated the current penalty differential. Furthermore, we believe that fairness is a matter of individuals — treating similarly persons who are similar in sentencing-relevant ways. It is not a matter of statistical group averages or percentages. If more persons of one group behave in ways that justify harsher treatment, then the Commission believes it is fair to treat those individuals more harshly, even if it results in a higher percentage of one group going to prison for longer periods of time.

At the same time, the Commission believes that our evaluation of the fairness of current penalties must go beyond ensuring that the rules are racially neutral. When a sentencing policy has a severe disproportionate impact on a minority group, it is important that sufficient bases exist for the policy. The law should not draw distinctions that single out some offenders for harsher punishment unless these distinctions are clearly related to a legitimate policy goal. For the reasons described above, we do not believe that a sufficient policy basis for the current penalty differential exists.

Congress was correct when it enacted the Sentencing Reform Act. It intended to create a sentencing guideline system that guarded against basic unfairness in criminal punishment. That basic intent is no less true with respect to the question of sentencing for cocaine offenses — that is, similar defendants convicted of similar offenses must be treated similarly. . . .

VIEW OF COMMISSIONER TACHA JOINED BY COMMISSIONERS GOLDSMITH AND CARNES, DISSENTING, IN PART, FROM AMENDMENT FIVE AND RELATED LEGISLATIVE RECOMMENDATION

We respectfully dissent and write separately to express our dismay that this question has been publicly framed by some as a racial issue. In our view, the sentencing issue turns on trying to craft a race-neutral sentencing policy that appropriately accounts for the societal harms associated with a particular crime. We deplore the socioeconomic factors associated with crack cocaine (as opposed to powder) that lead to different marketing patterns, different street-level dosages and prices, and the exploitation of vulnerable populations. We cannot, however, ignore the harms that are peculiarly associated with crack. The market, the dosages, the prices, and the means of distribution are elements of the drug's harm, and they cannot be discounted by simply saying that crack and powder cocaine are the same substance pharmacologically.

We joined in the Commission's Special Report to Congress: Cocaine and Federal Sentencing Policy, in which the Commission concluded, "the 100-to-1 quantity ratio that presently drives sentencing policy for cocaine trafficking offenses should be re-examined and revised." U.S. Sentencing Commission, Special Report to Congress: Cocaine and Federal Sentencing Policy 197 (Feb. 1995) [hereinafter Special Report]. We write separately on Amendment Five and the proposed legislation to equalize statutory mandatory minimum penalties for crack and powder cocaine offenses, however, because we cannot endorse the proposed one-to-one quantity ratio for distribution offenses. The reasons for retaining differential penalties for crack and powder cocaine distribution offenses, . . . do not apply to possession offenses. Thus, we fully endorse equalization of sentences for crack and powder cocaine possession offenses. Sentencing crack distribution offenses identically to powder cocaine distribution offenses fails to account for the increased harms associated with crack. Moreover, adjusting crack distribution sentences downward to parallel powder cocaine sentences provides for penalties that are, in our opinion, often too low.

In the Special Report, the Commission concluded that an inference can be drawn that "crack cocaine poses greater harms to society than does powder cocaine." Special Report, *supra* . . . , at 195. At that time, the Commission stated that it may be possible to develop specific guideline enhancements to account for some or all of the increased harms associated with crack. *Id.* at 198-200. The Commission also indicated, however, that "[i]f guideline enhancements cannot sufficiently account for harms associated with crack, the guidelines can provide an increased ratio through the base offense level." *Id.* at xv.

The Commission has now completed its self-appointed task of developing guideline enhancements. While the Commission has proposed new enhancements that take into account the use of a firearm and a defendant's use of a juvenile in the offense, in addition to bodily injury departure language, the Commission has been unable to account fully for the increased harmfulness of crack through guideline enhancements. Thus, consistent with the Special Report, a differential quantity ratio is required.

In the Special Report, the Commission identified several dangers associated to a greater degree with crack than with powder cocaine. Most importantly, the Commission found that, based upon common route of administration, crack is more addictive than powder cocaine. Because smoking crack produces more intense physiological and psychotropic effects than snorting powder cocaine, the Commission found that the crack user is more vulnerable to binging and dependency than persons who snort powder cocaine. Moreover, although powder cocaine, if injected, is equally as addictive as crack, injection of powder cocaine does not pose the same danger to society as does crack. Indeed, over three times as many people smoke crack than inject powder cocaine. This statistic confirms the common sense observation that a substance that can be smoked will always be inherently more appealing, particularly to first time users, than one which must be injected through a vein with a hypodermic needle. [References omitted.]

Addictiveness, however, is but one of the harms associated to a greater degree with crack than with powder cocaine. Another significant danger of crack is that, because of its ease of manufacture and relatively low cost-per-dose, crack is more readily marketable than powder cocaine to a greater segment of the population. *Id.* at viii. That crack can be administered easily and sold cheaply has made it particularly appealing and accessible to the most vulnerable members of our society — *i.e.*, the poor and the young. *Id.* at 195. Indeed, 12- to 17-year-olds choose crack over powder cocaine more than any other age group. *Id.* at 187. Additionally, more criminal activity, including violent crime, is associated with crack than with powder cocaine. *Id.* at viii. Crack is also accountable for more emergency room visits than powder cocaine, *Id.* at 184. Although our Special Report also found, based upon very limited data, that "most cocaine-related deaths result from injection of powder," *id.*, this factor alone does not convince us that crack is less dangerous to society than powder cocaine. In comparing the relative harms of these two substances, we have considered a variety of factors, some of which may offset one another. In our view, the higher death rate associated with powder cocaine is one of the factors that justifies bringing crack and powder penalties more in line with each other. In other respects, however, the higher death rate from powder is outweighed by the multitude of increased harms occasioned by crack. and evidence suggests a high correlation between crack and a host of social harms including parental neglect, child and domestic abuse, and high risk sexual behaviors.

The Commission was unable to account for all of these harms through guideline enhancements. Indeed, the proposed enhancements only address, to a limited extent, the systemic crime associated with crack. Thus, a one-to-one quantity ratio allows crack distributors to go virtually unpunished for the addictiveness, ease of use, marketability, and physical and social harms associated to a greater degree with crack than with powder cocaine. The majority asserts that under a one-to-one ratio, "crack offenders will receive sentences that are, on average, generally at least twice as long as powder cocaine offenders involved with the same amount of drug." Statement of Commission Majority in Support of Recommended Changes in Cocaine and Federal Sentencing Policy 3 (May 1, 1995) [hereinafter Commission Majority]. This difference reflects the fact that crack defendants are more likely to have extensive criminal histories and are more likely to use weapons than powder cocaine defendants. The difference does not, however, reflect the fact that crack offenders sell a substance that is far more dangerous than powder cocaine. We cannot support this result. Interestingly, in the Special Report, the Commission indicated that crack's addictiveness and ease of use alone could support heightened penalties for crack distributors. . . .

The majority's rationale for a one-to-one quantity ratio appears to be that fairness dictates identical treatment of crack and powder cocaine defendants because crack and powder cocaine are pharmacologically the same drug. See Commission Majority, supra note 15, at 4-5. This is not the end of the inquiry, however. Penalties for drug offenses are not solely based on pharmacology. Instead, penalties are fashioned to account for the amount of societal harm attributable to a particular drug or form of drug. Indeed, providing varying penalties for different forms of the same drug based upon relative harmfulness is not unprecedented in the guidelines. See, e.g., U.S.S.G. 2D1.1(c) (assigning base offense levels for Methamphetamine, as compared to "Ice" [a different form of Methamphetamine] at a ten-to-one quantity ratio). We note that Methamphetamine bears a five-to-one ratio to powder cocaine and that "Ice" has a ten-to-one ratio to Methamphetamine, or a fifty-to-one ratio to powder. Thus, if a one-to-one ratio between powder and crack is adopted, crack will be punished at a ratio of fifty times less than "Ice."

Sentencing policy is not an exact science. It can only reflect our best judgment as to the appropriate sentences for particular criminal acts, taking into consideration the harms resulting from those acts and the related societal interests in deterrence and prevention. Regrettably, statistical evidence demonstrates that sentencing policy based on thoughtful, appropriate, and race-neutral factors may result in differing impacts on defendants according to race, socioeconomic group, and geographic area. These disparities in impact, however, cannot divert attention from our objective judgments about the underlying criminal activity and the attendant societal interests. In sum, because, as the Commission unanimously concluded in the Special Report, crack poses a greater threat to society than does powder cocaine, and because a one-to-one quantity ratio provides insufficient punishment for crack distributors, we respectfully dissent.

VIEW OF COMMISSIONER GOLDSMITH DISSENTING, IN PART, FROM AMENDMENT
FIVE AND RELATED LEGISLATIVE RECOMMENDATION

I join in Commissioner Tacha's dissent, but write separately to underscore a few key points. . . .

I dissent from the majority position because the Commission's new enhancements do not account for all of the systemic harms uniquely associated with crack cocaine. For example, the evidence shows that, given common routes of administration, crack is potentially much more addictive than powder cocaine. *Id.* at 24-28. However, this aggravating danger cannot be integrated into the guidelines simply as a separate enhancement factor. Similarly, crack cocaine poses special risks to minors, *Id.* at 195 and to pregnant women. *Id.* at 189-90. More specifically, the immediate risk is to the fetus. These risks, however, exist even if a sale occurs to someone other than such vulnerable victims. Under most circumstances typical of the crack market, eventual usage by minors or pregnant women is readily foreseeable even if the immediate case (or the defendant's relevant conduct) does not involve such participants.

Since such systemic risks cannot be captured by guideline enhancements standing alone, we must find some other way to weigh these factors in determining punishment. . . .

In my view, a ratio range between four-to-one and ten-to-one would be most appropriate.

This failure occurs because the one-to-one ratio disregards important organizational and market factors that distinguish crack and powder cocaine. The presence of these factors often means that comparable quantities of powder and crack do not necessarily correlate with culpability. For example, given the way that crack is marketed, a person convicted of selling 100 grams may often be characterized as a mid-level dealer (*i.e.,* someone who provides the drug to street level retailers). By comparison, 100 grams of powder is rarely suggestive of a mid-level powder dealer. Rather, 100 grams of powder usually typifies a low-level retailer; 500 grams is more indicative of a mid-level dealer (*i.e.,* someone who supplies the street sales retailer). *See* Special Report, supra . . . , at 118-21 (emphasizing that Congress selected five-year mandatory minimum quantities, which include 500 grams for powder distributors, as representative of quantities associated with serious or mid-level traffickers). Thus, for punishment purposes, a defendant convicted of selling 500 grams of powder (*i.e.,* a mid-level dealer) is roughly comparable to a person guilty of selling 100 grams of crack (*i.e.,* also a mid-level dealer.)

This analysis suggests that a five-to-one quantity ratio between powder and crack more accurately reflects the realities of two distinct drug trades. If anything, Commission data suggests that mid-level powder cocaine distributors generally deal in quantities ranging between 2,000 and 3,500 grams. Moreover, the Drug Enforcement Administration assigns the same priority level to crack dealers distributing 50 grams and powder dealers distributing 1,000 grams. Therefore, a ratio of higher than five-to-one may appropriately reflect the market differences between crack and powder cocaine. A five-to-one quantity ratio is also consistent with the manner in which the law distinguishes between powder cocaine and heroin. Ordinarily, for example, 5 units of powder cocaine are punished as severely as one unit of heroin. *See* U.S.S.G. 2D1.1(c). Of course, further research may be required to arrive at an appropriate ratio between powder and crack cocaine, and I do not contend that five-to-one is necessarily the right outcome. Reasonable arguments can certainly support a ratio as high as ten- to-one. I merely suggest that, given the many distinct differences between powder and crack cocaine, a five-to-one ratio may be a good starting point for analysis.

Finally, I concur with Commissioner Tacha's concern that this issue has been unduly framed in racial terms by some constituency groups. No persuasive evidence exists that federal sentencing policy in this area is based on discriminatory considerations. Nor does the record demonstrate that African-American crack dealers are treated more severely than Caucasian crack dealers. On the contrary, our Special Report found that "[c]learly the penalties (both statutory and guideline-based) apply equally to similar defendants regardless of race." Special Report, *supra* . . . , at 156. The Special Report also found that the 100-to-1 quantity ratio affected a disproportionate number of African-American defendants. Special Report, *supra* . . . , at 156. However, this result reflects the reality of the crack trade, which has been dominated by African-American retailers who, in turn, have devastated many inner-city, economically disadvantaged African-American communities throughout the country. Furthermore, a federal law is not unconstitutionally discriminatory so long as it is applied equally to all persons who violate it. By analogy, the federal RICO statute was first applied to established organized crime groups dominated by persons of Sicilian descent. This application, however, reflected the reality of organized crime in America at that time rather than any improper discriminatory purpose. Moreover, RICO has since been applied to other violators across ethnic and racial lines. This same principle governs federal narcotics laws, which apply even-handedly to all violators.

For these reasons, I dissent from the majority's vote to reduce the quantity ratio between powder and crack cocaine to one-to-one. The Commission properly rejected the 100-to-1 ratio as too extreme. By suggesting that a one-to-one ratio is appropriate, however, the Commission proposes returning to the other extreme. I suggest a more appropriate course based on the policy and market differences between crack and powder cocaine rather than on a formula — misleading in its simplicity — that overlooks the realities of the drug trade.

Joseph E. Kennedy, DRUG WARS IN BLACK AND WHITE

66 L. & Contemp. Probs. 153-154 (2003) (footnotes omitted)

Over the past two decades, we have waged war on drugs. . . . [T]he primary casualties of that war have been African Americans and other individuals of color. The debate over the racial complexion of the war against drugs often devolves into a clash of fundamental assumptions that are difficult to either validate or refute. Do we wage the war against drugs in African-American communities because "that is where the drugs are?" Or do we find most illegal drug users and sellers in African-American communities because that is where we spend most of our time looking? Do we punish the sale of crack cocaine so severely because of the effects of the drug or because of the race of those using it most openly?

Critics of the racial disparities of the current effort often point to social science research revealing high illegal drug use among whites. They reason from this evidence that many whites must be engaged in the sales and distribution of illegal drugs given the plausible — and somewhat verified — assumption that people tend to purchase illegal drugs from members of their own race. By failing to go after white users and sellers as aggressively as African-American users and sellers, the system both creates racial disparities in justice and generates a stream of convictions that tautologically confirms the animating premise that illegal drug use is a predominantly "black problem."

There is, of course, a standard rejoinder. Law enforcement naturally and logically focuses on those communities where illegal drug use has created the most harmful and most visible effects. Selling crack openly in the streets or out of notorious "crack houses" should attract disproportionate attention. Perhaps the predominantly white students of college campuses use as much illegal drugs as denizens of inner city neighborhoods, but drug- related drive by shootings often take place in the inner city and not on college campuses. More generally, illegal drug use is seen as devastating African-American communities in a way that is not seen outside the inner city. People losing jobs, kids dropping out of school, parents neglecting or abandoning their children — all of these social costs are more readily seen in the inner city than in the more affluent white communities where illegal drug use seems to be relatively benign. Even more to the point, illegal drug use in the inner city is seen as crimogenic — the inner-city user of illegal drugs is thought to be more likely to steal or commit some other crime to finance his drug use.

It is difficult to break outside of this simplistic debate because the contemporary data about illegal activity and its consequences are difficult to collect in any way that is both comprehensive and independent. Excellent social science research has challenged some of the assumptions about the nature of drug addiction in the inner cities and its relationship to crime, but the relatively small scale of this research has been drowned out in the public debate by mind-numbing quantities of statistics generated by the criminal justice system, statistics that purport to validate enforcement decisions to focus on inner city communities of color. Ultimately, however, the criminal justice system is destined to find crime only where it looks for crime.

TABLE OF CASES

INDEX